Eighth Edition

Statistical Methods *for* Psychology

DAVID C. HOWELL
University of Vermont

WADSWORTH
CENGAGE Learning·

Australia • Brazil • Japan • Korea • Mexico • Singapore • Spain • United Kingdom • United States

WADSWORTH
CENGAGE Learning·

**Statistical Methods for Psychology,
Eighth Edition, International Edition**
David C. Howell

Senior Publishor: Linda Schreiber-Ganster

Acquisitions Sponsoring Editor: Timothy Matray

Assistant Editor: Paige Leeds

Editorial Assistant: Lauren K. Moody

Senior Media Editor: Mary Noel

Marketing Program Manager: Janay Pryor

Production Management, and Composition: PreMediaGlobal

Manufacturing Planner: Karen Hunt

Rights Acquisition Specialist: Don Schlotman

Cover Designer: Denise Davidson

Cover credit: © MrTwister/Shutterstock.com

Interior Credit: © Jens Ottoson/ Shutterstock.com

For product information and technology assistance, contact us at **Cengage Learning Customer & Sales Support, 1-800-354-9706.**

For permission to use material from this text or product, submit all requests online at **www.cengage.com/permissions.** Further permissions questions can be e-mailed to **permissionrequest@cengage.com.**

Library of Congress Control Number: 2011934926

International Edition:
ISBN-13: 978-1-111-84085-3
ISBN-10: 1-111-84085-7

Cengage Learning International Offices

Asia
www.cengageasia.com
tel: (65) 6410 1200

Australia/New Zealand
www.cengage.com.au
tel: (61) 3 9685 4111

Brazil
www.cengage.com.br
tel: (55) 11 3665 9900

India
www.cengage.co.in
tel: (91) 11 4364 1111

Latin America
www.cengage.com.mx
tel: (52) 55 1500 6000

UK/Europe/Middle East/Africa
www.cengage.co.uk
tel: (44) 0 1264 332 424

**Represented in Canada by
Nelson Education, Ltd.**
www.nelson.com
tel: (416) 752 9100 / (800) 668 0671

Cengage Learning is a leading provider of customized learning solutions with office locations around the globe, including Singapore, the United Kingdom, Australia, Mexico, Brazil, and Japan. Locate your local office at: **www.cengage.com/global**

For product information and free companion resources: **www.cengage.com/international**

Visit your local office: **www.cengage.com/global**

Printed in The United States of America
3 4 5 6 7 20 19 18 17 16

To Donna

Brief Contents

Contents

CHAPTER 7   Hypothesis Tests Applied to Means   177

CHAPTER 8   Power   229

CHAPTER 9   Correlation and Regression   251

CHAPTER 10   **Alternative Correlational Techniques   303**

CHAPTER 11   **Simple Analysis of Variance   325**

CHAPTER 12   **Multiple Comparisons Among Treatment Means   369**

CHAPTER 16   Analyses of Variance and Covariance as General Linear Models   573

CHAPTER 17   Meta-Analysis and Single-Case Designs   623

CHAPTER **18**   **Resampling and Nonparametric Approaches to Data   657**

Preface

This eighth edition of *Statistical Methods for Psychology*, like the previous editions, surveys statistical techniques commonly used in the behavioral and social sciences, especially psychology and education. Although it is designed for advanced undergraduates and graduate students, it does not assume that students have had either a previous course in statistics or a course in mathematics beyond high-school algebra. Those students who have had an introductory course will find that the early material provides a welcome review. The book is suitable for either a one-term or a full-year course, and I have used it successfully for both. Because I have found that students, and faculty, frequently refer back to the book from which they originally learned statistics when they have a statistical problem, I have included material that will make the book a useful reference for future use. The instructor who wishes to omit this material will have no difficulty doing so. I have cut back on that material, however, to include only what is likely to be useful. The idea of including every interesting idea had led to a book that was beginning to be daunting.

In some ways this edition represents a break from past editions. Over the years each edition has contained a reasonable amount of new material and the discussion has changed to reflect changes in theory and practice. This edition is no exception, except that some of the changes will be more extensive than usual. There are additional topics that I feel that students need to understand, and that could not be covered without removing some of the older material. However, thanks to the Internet the material will largely be moved rather than deleted. If you would prefer to see the older, more complete version of the chapter on multiple comparison tests or log-linear models, you can download the previous versions from my Web site.

The first edition of this book was written in 1973–1974 while I was on sabbatical at the University of Durham, England. At that time most statistics courses in psychology were aimed at experimental psychologists, and a large percentage of that work related to the analysis of variance. B. J. Winer's *Statistical Principles in Experimental Design*, 1962, 1971, dominated a large part of the statistical field and influenced how experiments were designed, run, and analyzed. My book followed much of that trend, and properly so. Since that time statistical analysis of data has seen considerable change. While the analysis of variance is still a dominant technique, followed closely by multiple regression, many other topics have worked their way onto the list. For example, measures of effect size are far more important than they were then, meta-analysis has grown from virtually nothing to an important way to summarize a field, and the treatment of missing data has changed significantly thanks to introduction of linear mixed models and methods of data imputation. We can no longer turn out students who are prepared to conduct high-quality research without including discussion of these issues.

But to include these and similar topics, something had to go if the text was to remain at a manageable size. In the past multiple comparison procedures, for example, were the subject of considerable attention with many competing approaches. But if you look at what people are actually doing in the literature, most of the competing approaches are more of interest to theoreticians than to practitioners. I think that it is far more useful to write about the treatment of missing data than to list all of the alternatives for making comparisons among means. This is particularly true now that it is easy to make that older material readily available for all who would like to read it.

My intention in writing this book was to explain the material at an intuitive level. This should not be taken to mean that the material is "watered down," but only that the emphasis is on conceptual understanding. The student who can successfully derive the sample distribution of t, for example, may not have any understanding of how that distribution is to be used. With respect to this example, my aim has been to concentrate on the meaning of a sampling distribution, and to show the role it plays in the general theory of hypothesis testing. In my opinion this approach allows students to gain a better understanding than would a more technical approach of the way a particular test works and of the interrelationships among tests.

Contrary to popular opinion, statistical methods are constantly evolving. This is in part because the behavioral sciences are branching into many new areas and in part because we are finding better ways of asking questions of our data. No book can possibly undertake to cover all of the material that needs to be covered, but it is critical to prepare students and professionals to take on that material when needed. For example, multilevel/hierarchical models are becoming much more common in the research literature. An understanding of these models requires specialized texts, but fundamental to even beginning to sort through that literature requires an understanding of fixed versus random variables and of nested designs. This book cannot undertake the former, deriving the necessary models, but it can, and does, address the latter by building a foundation under both fixed and random designs and nesting. I have tried to build similar foundations for other topics; for example, more modern graphical devices and resampling statistics, where I can do that without dragging the reader deeper into a swamp. In some ways my responsibility is to try to anticipate where we are going and give the reader a basis for moving in that direction.

Changes in the 8th edition

This eighth edition contains several new, or expanded, features that make the book more appealing to the student and more relevant to the actual process of methodology and data analysis:

- I have continued to respond to the issue faced by the American Psychological Association's committee on null hypothesis testing, and have included even more material on effect size and magnitude of effect. The coverage in this edition goes beyond the coverage in previous editions, and should serve as a thorough introduction to the material.
- In the seventh edition I included new material on graphical displays, including probability plots, kernel density plots, and residual plots. Each of these helps us to better

understand our data and to evaluate the reasonableness of the assumptions we make. I have extended the use of graphical displays in this edition.

- I have further developed the concept of resampling to illustrate what the more traditional approaches are attempting to do on the basis of underlying assumptions. There has been an accelerated change in the direction of resampling, and many computer solutions offer the user options such as "bootstrap," "simulate," and "resample," all of which rely on that approach.

- The coverage of Cochran-Mantel-Haenszel analysis of contingency tables is tied to the classic example of Simpson's Paradox as applied to the Berkeley graduate admissions data. This relates to the underlying motivation to lead students to think deeply about what their data mean.

- I have further modified Chapter 12 on multiple comparison techniques to narrow the wide range of tests that I previously discussed and to include coverage of Benjamini and Hochberg's False Discovery Rate. As we move our attention away from familywise error rates to the false discovery rate we increase the power of our analyses at relatively little cost in terms of Type I errors.

- A section in the chapter on repeated measures analysis of variance extends the discussion of mixed models. This approach allows for much better treatment of missing data and relaxes unreasonable assumptions about compound symmetry. This serves as an introduction to mixed models without attempting to take on a whole new field at once.

- Several previous editions contained a chapter on log-linear models. I have replaced this chapter with material on both meta-analysis and single subject designs. Meta-analyses have grown in importance in the behavioral sciences and underlie the emphasis on "evidence-based medicine." Given that a text can cover only a limited amount of material, I feel that an introduction to these two topics is more valuable that a chapter on log-linear models. However for those who miss the latter, that chapter is still available on the Web under the section on supplemental material.

- Each month a free computing environment named R, along with its commercial package S-PLUS, increases its influence over statistical analysis. I have no intention of trying to provide instruction in R on top of everything else, but I do make a large number of programs or selections of R code available on the book's Web site. This provides a starting point for those interested in using R and allows for interesting demonstrations of points made in the text.

- I have spent a substantial amount of time pulling together material for instructors and students, and placing it on Web pages on the Internet. Users can readily get at additional (and complex) examples, discussion of topics that aren't covered in the text, additional data, other sources on the Internet, demonstrations that would be suitable for class or for a lab, and so on. Many places in the book refer specifically to this material if the student wishes to pursue a topic further. All of this is easily available to anyone with an Internet connection. I continue to add to this material, and encourage people to use it and critique it. The address of the book's Web site is http://www.uvm.edu/~dhowell/methods8/, and an additional Web site with more extensive coverage is available at http://www.uvm.edu/~dhowell/StatPages/StatHomePage.html, (capitalization in this address is critical). I encourage users to explore both sites.

This edition shares with its predecessors two underlying themes that are more or less independent of the statistical hypothesis tests that are the main content of the book.

- The first theme is the importance of looking at the data before jumping in with a hypothesis test. With this in mind, I discuss, in detail, plotting data, looking for outliers, and checking assumptions. (Graphical displays are used extensively.) I try to do this with each data set as soon as I present it, even though the data set may be intended as an example of a sophisticated statistical technique.

- The second theme is the importance of the relationship between the statistical test to be employed and the theoretical questions being posed by the experiment. To emphasize this relationship, I use real examples in an attempt to make the student understand the purpose behind the experiment and the predictions made by the theory. For this reason I sometimes use one major example as the focus for an entire section, or even a whole chapter. For example, interesting data on the moon illusion from a well-known study by Kaufman and Rock (1962) are used in several forms of the *t* test (pages 191–213), and much of Chapter 12 is organized around an important study of morphine addiction by Siegel (1975). Each of these examples should have direct relevance for students. The increased emphasis on effect sizes in this edition helps to drive home that point that one must think carefully about one's data and research questions.

Although no one would be likely to call this book controversial, I have felt it important to express opinions on a number of controversial issues. After all, the controversies within statistics are part of what makes it an interesting discipline. For example, I have argued that the underlying measurement scale is not as important as some have suggested, and I have argued for a particular way of treating analyses of variance with unequal group sizes (unless there is a compelling reason to do otherwise). I do not expect every instructor to agree with me, and in fact I hope that some will not. This offers the opportunity to give students opposing views and help them to understand the issues. It seems to me that it is unfair and frustrating to the student to present several different multiple comparison procedures (which I do), and then to walk away and leave that student with no recommendation about which procedure is best for his or her problem. Though I have cut back on the number of procedures I discuss, I make every attempt to explain to the student what needs to be considered in choosing an approach.

An Instructor's Manual with worked out solutions to all problems is available from the publisher.

Acknowledgments

I would like to thank the following reviewers who read the manuscript and provided valuable feedback: Angus MacDonald, University of Minnesota; William Smith, California State University–Fullerton; Carl Scott, University of St. Thomas–Houston; Jamison Fargo, Utah State University; Susan Cashin, University of Wisconsin–Milwaukee; and Karl Wuensch, East Carolina University, who has provided valuable guidance over many editions. In earlier editions, I received helpful comments and suggestions from Kenneth J. Berry, Colorado State University; Tim Bockes, Nazareth College; Richard Lehman, Franklin and Marshall College; Tim Robinson, Virginia Tech; Paul R. Shirley, University of California–Irvine; Mathew Spackman, Brigham Young University; Mary Uley, Lindenwood University; and Christy Witt, Louisiana State University. Their influence is still evident in this edition.

For this edition I would like to thank Deborah A. Carroll, Southern Connecticut University; Paul Chang, Edith Cowen University; Ann Huffman, Northern Arizona University; Samuel Moulton, Harvard University; Therese Pigott, Loyola University Chicago; Lucy Troup, Colorado State University; and Meng-Jia Wu, Loyola University Chicago.

The publishing staff was exceptionally helpful throughout, and I would like to thank Jessica Egbert, Marketing Manager; Vernon Boes and Pamela Galbreath, Art Directors; Mary Noel, Media Editor; Kristin Ruscetta, Production Project Manager; Lauren Moody, Editorial Assistant; and Timothy Matray, Acquisition Editor.

David C. Howell
Professor Emeritus
University of Vermont
5/6/2011

About the Author

Courtesy David C. Howell

Professor Howell is Emeritus Professor at the University of Vermont. After gaining his Ph.D. from Tulane University in 1967, he was associated with the University of Vermont until retiring as chair of the Department of Psychology in 2002. He also spent two separate years as visiting professor at two universities in the United Kingdom.

Professor Howell is the author of several books and many journal articles and book chapters. He continues to write in his retirement and was most recently the co-editor, with Brian Everitt, of *The Encyclopedia of Statistics in Behavioral Sciences,* published by Wiley. He has recently authored a number of chapters in various books on research design and statistics.

Professor Howell now lives in Colorado where he enjoys the winter snow and is an avid skier and hiker.

Chapter 1

Basic Concepts

Objectives

To examine the kinds of problems presented in this book and the issues involved in selecting a statistical procedure.

Contents

STRESS IS SOMETHING that we are all forced to deal with throughout life. It arises in our daily interactions with those around us, in our interactions with the environment, in the face of an impending exam, and, for many students, in the realization that they are required to take a statistics course. Although most of us learn to respond and adapt to stress, the learning process is often slow and painful. This rather grim preamble may not sound like a great way to introduce a course on statistics, but it leads to a description of a practical research project, which in turn illustrates a number of important statistical concepts. I was involved in a very similar project a number of years ago, so this example is far from hypothetical.

A group of educators has put together a course designed to teach high-school students how to manage stress and the effect of stress management on self-esteem. They need an outside investigator, however, who can tell them how well the course is working and, in particular, whether students who have taken the course have higher self-esteem than do students who have not taken the course. For the moment we will assume that we are charged with the task of designing an evaluation of their program. The experiment that we design will not be complete, but it will illustrate some of the issues involved in designing and analyzing experiments and some of the statistical concepts with which you must be familiar.

1.1   Important Terms

Although the program in stress management was designed for high-school students, it clearly would be impossible to apply it to the population of all high-school students in the country. First, there are far too many such students. Moreover, it makes no sense to apply a program to everyone until we know whether it is a useful program. Instead of dealing with the entire population of high-school students, we will draw a sample of students from that population and apply the program to them. But we will not draw just any old sample. We **random sample** would like to draw a random sample, though I will say shortly that truly random samples are normally impractical if not impossible. To draw a random sample, we would follow a particular set of procedures to ensure that each and every element (student) in the population has an equal chance of being selected. (The common example to illustrate a random sample is to speak of putting names in a hat and drawing blindly. Although almost no one ever does exactly that, it is a nice illustration of what we have in mind.) Having drawn our **randomly assign** sample of students, we will randomly assign half the subjects to a group that will receive the stress-management program and half to a group that will not receive the program.

This description has already brought out several concepts that need further elaboration; **population** namely, a population, a sample, a random sample, and random assignment. A population is the entire collection of events (students' scores, people's incomes, rats' running speeds, etc.) in which you are interested. Thus, if you are interested in the self-esteem scores of all high-school students in the United States, then the collection of all high-school students' self-esteem scores would form a population—in this case, a population of many millions of elements. If, on the other hand, you were interested in the self-esteem scores of high-school seniors only in Fairfax, Vermont (a town of fewer than 4,000 inhabitants), the population would consist of only about 100 elements.

The point is that populations can be of any size. They can range from a relatively small set of numbers, which can be collected easily, to a large but finite set of numbers, which would be impractical to collect in their entirety. In fact they can be an infinite set of numbers, such as the set of all possible cartoon drawings that students could theoretically produce, which would be impossible to collect. Unfortunately for us, the populations we are interested in are usually very large. The practical consequence is that we seldom if ever measure entire **sample** populations. Instead, we are forced to draw only a sample of observations from that population and to use that sample to infer something about the characteristics of the population.

Assuming that the sample is truly random, we cannot only estimate certain characteristics of the population, but we can also have a very good idea of how accurate our estimates are. To the extent that the sample is not random, our estimates may or may not be meaningful, because the sample may or may not accurately reflect the entire population.

Randomness has at least two aspects that we need to consider. The first has to do with whether the sample is representative of the population to which it is intended to make inferences. This primarily involves random *sampling* from the population and leads to what **external validity** is called **external validity**. External validity refers to the question of whether the sample reflects the population. A sample drawn from a small town in Nebraska would not produce a valid estimate of the percentage of the population of the United States that is Hispanic— nor would a sample drawn solely from the American Southwest. On the other hand, a sample from a small town in Nebraska might give us a reasonable estimate of the reaction time of people to stimuli presented suddenly. Right here you see one of the problems with discussing random sampling. A nonrandom sample of subjects or participants may still be useful for us if we can convince ourselves and others that it closely resembles what we would obtain if we could take a truly random sample. On the other hand if our nonrandom sample is not representative of what we would obtain with a truly random sample, our ability to draw inferences is compromised and our results might be very misleading.

Before going on, let us clear up one point that tends to confuse many people. The problem is that one person's sample might be another person's population. For example, if I were to conduct a study on the effectiveness of this book as a teaching instrument, I might consider one class's scores on an examination as a sample, albeit a nonrandom one, of the population of scores of all students using, or potentially using, this book. The class instructor, on the other hand, is probably not terribly concerned about this book, but instead cares only about his or her own students. He or she would regard the same set of scores as a population. In turn, someone interested in the teaching of statistics might regard my population (everyone using my book) as a very nonrandom sample from a larger population (everyone using any textbook in statistics). Thus, the definition of a population depends on what you are interested in studying.

In our stress study it is highly unlikely that we would seriously consider drawing a truly random sample of U.S. high-school students and administering the stress-management program to them. It is simply impractical to do so. How then are we going to take advantage of statistical methods and procedures based on the assumption of random sampling? The only way that we can do this is to be careful to apply those methods and procedures only when we have faith that our results would generally represent the population of interest. If we cannot make this assumption, we need to redesign our study. The issue is not one of statistical refinement so much as it is one of common sense. To the extent that we think our sample is not representative of U.S. high-school students, we must limit our interpretation of the results. To the extent that the sample is representative of the population, our estimates have validity.

random assignment The second aspect of randomness concerns **random assignment**. Whereas random selection concerns the *source* of our data and is important for generalizing the results of our study to the whole population, random assignment of subjects (once selected) to treatment groups is fundamental to the integrity of our experiment. Here we are speaking about what **internal validity** is called **internal validity**. We want to ensure that the results we obtain are of the differences in the way we treat our groups, not a result of who we happen to place in those groups. If, for example, we put all of the timid students in our sample in one group and all of the assertive students in another group, it is very likely that our results are as much or more a function of group assignment than of the treatments we applied to those groups. Letting students self-select into groups runs similar risks and is generally a bad idea unless that is the nature of the phenomenon under study. In actual practice, random assignment is usually far more important than random sampling. In studies in medicine, random assignment can become extremely complex due to the nature of the study, and there are sometimes people whose job is simply to control this aspect of the experiment.

Having dealt with the selection of subjects and their assignment to treatment groups, it is time to consider how we treat each group and how we will characterize the data that will result. Because we want to study the ability of subjects to deal with stress and maintain high self-esteem under different kinds of treatments, and because the response to stress is a function of many variables, a critical aspect of planning the study involves selecting the variables to be studied. A **variable** is a property of an object or event that can take on different values. For example, hair color is a variable because it is a property of an object (hair) and can take on different values (brown, yellow, red, gray, etc.). With respect to our evaluation of the stress-management program, such things as the treatments we use, the student's self-confidence, social support, gender, degree of personal control, and treatment group are all relevant variables.

In statistics, we dichotomize the concept of a variable in terms of independent and dependent variables. In our example, group membership is an **independent variable**, because we control it. We decide what the treatments will be and who will receive each treatment. We decide that this group over here will receive the stress management treatment and that group over there will not. If we had been comparing males and females we clearly do not control a person's gender, but we do decide on the genders to study (hardly a difficult decision) and that we want to compare males versus females. On the other hand the data—such as the resulting self-esteem scores, scores on feelings of personal control, and so on—are the **dependent variables**. Basically, the study is about the independent variables, and the results of the study (the data) are the dependent variables. Independent variables may be either quantitative or qualitative and discrete or continuous, whereas dependent variables are generally, but certainly not always, quantitative and continuous, as we are about to define those terms.[1]

We make a distinction between **discrete variables**, such as gender or high-school class, which take on only a limited number of values, and **continuous variables**, such as age and self-esteem score, which can assume, at least in theory, any value between the lowest and highest points on the scale.[2] As you will see, this distinction plays an important role in the way we treat data.

Closely related to the distinction between discrete and continuous variables is the distinction between quantitative and categorical data. By **quantitative data** (sometimes called **measurement data**), we mean the results of any sort of measurement—for example, grades on a test, people's weights, scores on a scale of self-esteem, and so on. In all cases, some sort of instrument (in its broadest sense) has been used to measure something, and we are interested in "how much" of some property a particular object represents.

On the other hand, **categorical data** (also known as **frequency data** or **qualitative data**) are illustrated in such statements as, "There are 34 females and 26 males in our study" or "Fifteen people were classed as 'highly anxious,' 33 as 'neutral,' and 12 as 'low anxious.'" Here we are categorizing things, and our data consist of frequencies for each category (hence the name categorical data). Several hundred subjects might be involved in our study, but the results (data) would consist of only two or three numbers—the number of subjects falling in each anxiety category. In contrast, if instead of sorting people with

variable

independent variable

dependent variables

discrete variables

continuous variables

quantitative data

measurement data

categorical data

frequency data

qualitative data

---

[1] Many people have difficulty remembering which is the dependent variable and which is the independent variable. Notice that both "dependent" and "data" start with a "d."

[2] Actually, a continuous variable is one in which *any* value between the extremes of the scale (e.g., 32.485687. . .) is possible. In practice, however, we treat a variable as continuous whenever it can take on many different values, and we treat it as discrete whenever it can take on only a few different values.

respect to high, medium, and low anxiety, we had assigned them each a score based on some more-or-less continuous scale of anxiety, we would be dealing with measurement data, and the data would consist of scores for each subject on that variable. Note that in both situations the variable is labeled *anxiety*. As with most distinctions, the one between measurement and categorical data can be pushed too far. The distinction is useful, however, and the answer to the question of whether a variable is a measurement or a categorical one is almost always clear in practice.

1.2   Descriptive and Inferential Statistics

Returning to our intervention program for stress, once we have chosen the variables to be measured and schools have administered the program to the students, we are left with a collection of raw data—the scores. There are two primary divisions of the field of statistics that are concerned with the use we make of these data.

descriptive statistics

Whenever our purpose is merely to describe a set of data, we are employing descriptive statistics. For example, one of the first things we want to do with our data is to graph them, to calculate means (averages) and other measures, and to look for extreme scores or oddly shaped distributions of scores. These procedures are called descriptive statistics because they are primarily aimed at describing the data. The field of descriptive statistics was once looked down on as a rather uninteresting field populated primarily by those who drew distorted-looking graphs for such publications as *Time* magazine. Twenty-five years ago John Tukey developed what he called exploratory statistics, or exploratory data analysis (EDA). He showed the necessity of paying close attention to the data and examining them in detail before invoking more technically involved procedures. Some of Tukey's innovations have made their way into the mainstream of statistics and will be studied in subsequent chapters; some have not caught on as well. However, the emphasis that Tukey placed on the need to closely examine your data has been very influential, in part because of the high esteem in which Tukey was held as a statistician.

exploratory data analysis (EDA)

inferential statistics

After we have described our data in detail and are satisfied that we understand what the numbers have to say on a superficial level, we will be particularly interested in what is called inferential statistics. In fact, most of this book deals with inferential statistics. In designing our experiment on the effect of stress on self-esteem, we acknowledged that it was not possible to measure the entire population, and therefore we drew samples from that population. Our basic questions, however, deal with the population itself. We might want to ask, for example, about the average self-esteem score for an entire population of students who could have taken our program, even though all that we really have is the average score of a sample of students who actually went through the program.

parameter

statistic

A measure, such as the average self-esteem score, that refers to an entire population is called a parameter. That same measure, when it is calculated from a sample of data that we have collected, is called a statistic. Parameters are the *real* entities of interest, and the corresponding statistics are *guesses* at reality. Although most of what we do in this book deals with sample statistics (or guesses, if you prefer), keep in mind that the reality of interest is the corresponding population parameter. We want to *infer* something about the characteristics of the population (parameters) from what we know about the characteristics of the sample (statistics). In our hypothetical study we are particularly interested in knowing whether the average self-esteem score of a population of students who might be potentially enrolled in our program is higher, or lower, than the average self-esteem score of students who might not be enrolled. Again we are dealing with the area of inferential statistics, because we are inferring characteristics of populations from characteristics of samples.

1.3   Measurement Scales

The topic of measurement scales is one that some writers think is crucial and others think is irrelevant. Although I tend to side with the latter group, it is important that you have some familiarity with the general issue. (You do not have to agree with something to think that it is worth studying. After all, evangelists claim to know a great deal about sin, though they can hardly be said to advocate it.) Statistics as a subject is not merely a cut-and-dried set of facts but, rather, is a set of facts put together with a variety of interpretations and opinions.

Probably the foremost leader of those who see measurement scales as crucial to the choice of statistical procedures was S. S. Stevens.[3] Zumbo and Zimmerman (2000) have discussed measurement scales at considerable length and remind us that Stevens's system has to be seen in its historical context. In the 1940s and 1950s, Stevens was attempting to defend psychological research against those in the "hard sciences" who had a restricted view of scientific measurement. He was trying to make psychology "respectable." Stevens spent much of his very distinguished professional career developing measurement scales for the field of psychophysics and made important contributions. However, outside of that field there has been little effort in psychology to develop the kinds of scales that Stevens pursued, nor has there been much real interest. The criticisms that so threatened Stevens have largely evaporated, and with them much of the belief that measurement scales critically influence the statistical procedures that are appropriate. But the terms describing those measures continue to be important.

Nominal Scales

nominal scales

In a sense, nominal scales are not really scales at all; they do not scale items along any dimension, but rather label them. Variables such as gender and political-party affiliation are nominal variables. Categorical data are usually measured on a nominal scale, because we merely assign category labels (e.g., male or female; Republican, Democrat, or Independent) to observations. A numerical example is the set of numbers assigned to football players. Frequently, these numbers have no meaning other than as convenient labels to distinguish the players from one another. Letters or pictures of animals could just as easily be used.

Ordinal Scales

ordinal scale

The simplest true scale is an ordinal scale, which orders people, objects, or events along some continuum. An excellent example of such a scale is the ranks in the Navy. A commander is lower in prestige than a captain, who in turn is lower than a rear admiral. However, there is no reason to think that the *difference* in prestige between a commander and a captain is the same as that between a captain and a rear admiral. An example from psychology is the Holmes and Rahe (1967) scale of life stress. Using this scale, you count (sometimes with differential weightings) the number of changes (marriage, moving, new job, etc.) that have occurred during the past six months of a person's life. Someone who has a score of 20 is presumed to have experienced more stress than someone with a score of 15, and the latter in turn is presumed to have experienced more stress than someone with a score of 10. Thus, people are ordered, in terms of stress, by their number of recent life changes. This is an example of an ordinal scale because nothing is implied about the

---

[3] Chapter 1 in Stevens's *Handbook of Experimental Psychology* (1951) is an excellent reference for anyone wanting to examine the substantial mathematical issues underlying this position.

differences between points on the scale. We do not assume, for example, that the difference between 10 and 15 points represents the same difference in stress as the difference between 15 and 20 points. Distinctions of that sort must be left to interval scales.

Interval Scales

interval scale

With an interval scale, we have a measurement scale in which we can legitimately speak of differences between scale points. A common example is the Fahrenheit scale of temperature, where a 10-point difference has the same meaning anywhere along the scale. Thus, the difference in temperature between 10° F and 20° F is the same as the difference between 80° F and 90° F. Notice that this scale also satisfies the properties of the two preceding ones. What we do not have with an interval scale, however, is the ability to speak meaningfully about ratios. Thus, we cannot say, for example, that 40° F is half as hot as 80° F, or twice as hot as 20° F. We have to use ratio scales for that purpose. (In this regard, it is worth noting that when we perform perfectly legitimate conversions from one interval scale to another—for example, from the Fahrenheit to the Celsius scale of temperature—we do not even keep the same ratios. Thus, the ratio between 40° and 80° on a Fahrenheit scale is different from the ratio between 4.4° and 26.7° on a Celsius scale, although the temperatures are comparable. This highlights the arbitrary nature of ratios when dealing with interval scales.)

Ratio Scales

ratio scale

A ratio scale is one that has a *true* zero point. Notice that the zero point must be a true zero point and not an arbitrary one, such as 0° F or even 0° C. (A true zero point is the point corresponding to the absence of the thing being measured. Since 0° F and 0° C do not represent the absence of temperature or molecular motion, they are not true zero points.) Examples of ratio scales are the common physical ones of length, volume, time, and so on. With these scales, we have the properties of not only the preceding scales but we also can speak about ratios. We can say that in physical terms 10 seconds is twice as long as 5 seconds, that 100 lb is one-third as heavy as 300 lb, and so on.

You might think that the kind of scale with which we are working would be obvious. Unfortunately, especially with the kinds of measures we collect in the behavioral sciences, this is rarely the case. The type of scale you use often depends on your purpose in using it. Among adults of the same general build, weight is a ratio scale of how much they weigh, but probably at best an ordinal scale of physical fitness or health.

As an example of a form of measurement that has a scale that depends on its use, consider the temperature of a house. We generally speak of Fahrenheit temperature as an interval scale. We have just used it as an example of one, and there is no doubt that, to a physicist, the difference between 62° F and 64° F is exactly the same as the difference between 92° F and 94° F. If we are measuring temperature as an index of *comfort*, rather than as an index of molecular activity, however, the same numbers no longer form an interval scale. To a person sitting in a room at 62° F, a jump to 64° F would be distinctly noticeable (and welcome). The same cannot be said about the difference between room temperatures of 92° F and 94° F. This points up the important fact that *it is the underlying variable that we are measuring (e.g., comfort), not the numbers themselves, that is important in defining the scale.* As a scale of *comfort*, degrees Fahrenheit do not form an interval scale—they don't even form an ordinal scale because comfort would increase with temperature to a point and would then start to decrease.

The Role of Measurement Scales

I stated earlier that writers disagree about the importance assigned to measurement scales. Some authors have ignored the problem totally, whereas others have organized whole textbooks around the different scales. A reasonable view (in other words, *my* view) is that the central issue is the absolute necessity of separating in our minds the numbers we collect from the objects or events to which they refer. Such an argument was made for the example of room temperature, where the scale (interval or ordinal) depended on whether we were interested in measuring some physical attribute of temperature or its effect on people (i.e., comfort). A difference of 2° F is the same, *physically*, anywhere on the scale, but a difference of 2° F when a room is already warm may not *feel* as large as does a difference of 2° F when a room is relatively cool. In other words, we have an interval scale of the physical units but no more than an ordinal scale of comfort (again, up to a point).

Because statistical tests use numbers without considering the objects or events to which those numbers refer, we may carry out any of the standard mathematical operations (addition, multiplication, etc.) regardless of the nature of the underlying scale. An excellent, entertaining, and highly recommended paper on this point is one by Lord (1953), entitled "On the Statistical Treatment of Football Numbers," in which he argues that these numbers can be treated in any way you like because, "The numbers do not remember where they came from" (p. 751).

The problem arises when it is time to interpret the results of some form of statistical manipulation. At that point, we must ask whether the statistical results are related in any meaningful way to the objects or events in question. Here we are no longer dealing with a statistical issue but with a methodological one. No *statistical* procedure can tell us whether the fact that one group received higher scores than another on an anxiety questionnaire reveals anything about group differences in underlying anxiety levels. Moreover, to be satisfied because the questionnaire provides a ratio scale of anxiety *scores* (a score of 50 is twice as large as a score of 25) is to lose sight of the fact that we set out to measure anxiety, which may not increase in a consistent way with increases in scores. Our statistical tests can apply only to the numbers that we obtain, and the validity of statements about the objects or events that we think we are measuring hinges primarily on our knowledge of those objects or events, not on the measurement scale. We do our best to ensure that our measures relate as closely as possible to what we want to measure, but our results are ultimately only the numbers we obtain and our faith in the relationship between those numbers and the underlying objects or events.[4]

From the preceding discussion, the apparent conclusion—and the one accepted in this book—is that the underlying measurement scale is not crucial in our choice of statistical techniques. Obviously, a certain amount of common sense is required in interpreting the results of these statistical manipulations. Only a fool would conclude that a painting judged as excellent by one person and contemptible by another should be classified as mediocre.

1.4   Using Computers

When I wrote the first edition of this book thirty-five years ago most statistical analyses were done on desktop or hand calculators, and textbooks were written accordingly. Methods have changed, however, and most calculations are now done by computers.

This book deals with the increased availability of computers by incorporating them into the discussion. The level of computer involvement increases substantially as the book

---

[4] As Cohen (1965) has pointed out, "Thurstone once said that in psychology we measure men by their shadows. Indeed, in clinical psychology we often measure men by their shadows while they are dancing in a ballroom illuminated by the reflections of an old-fashioned revolving polyhedral mirror" (p. 102).

proceeds and as computations become more laborious. For the simpler procedures, the calculational formulae are important in defining the concept. For example, the formula for a standard deviation or a *t* test defines and makes meaningful what a standard deviation or a *t* test actually is. In those cases, hand calculation is emphasized even though examples of computer solutions are also given. Later in the book, when we discuss multiple regression or techniques for dealing with missing data, for example, the formulae become less informative. The formula for deriving regression coefficients with five predictor variables would not reasonably be expected to add to your understanding of the resulting statistics. In fact it would only confuse the issue. In those situations, we will rely almost exclusively on computer solutions.

But what statistical package will we use? At present, many statistical software packages are available to the typical researcher or student conducting statistical analyses. The most important large statistical packages, which will carry out nearly every analysis that you will need in conjunction with this book, are Minitab®, SAS®, and SPSS™, Stata®, and S-PLUS. These are highly reliable and relatively easy-to-use packages, and one or more of them is generally available in any college or university computer center. (But there are fights among the experts as to which package is best.) Many examples of SPSS printout will appear in this book. I originally used a variety of packages, but reviewers suggested limiting myself to one, and SPSS is by far the most common in the behavioral sciences. You can find excellent program files of SAS code at http://core.ecu.edu/psyc/wuenschk /sas/sas-programs.htm, and many of these are linked to this book's examples.

If you would like to download an inexpensive package that will do almost everything you will need, I recommend OpenStat. Just go to http://statpages.org/miller/openstat/. I find it a little fussy about reading data files, but otherwise it works well. You can open it and enter examples as you come to them, or you can see what happens when you modify my examples.

I must mention a programming environment called R, which is freely available public domain software. It is a program that I love (or love to hate, depending on how much I have forgotten since I last used it). R is very flexible, many texts are beginning to give the R code for some of their analyses, and it has hundreds of special purpose functions that people have written for it and made publicly available. R is becoming surprisingly popular in many different disciplines and I would expect that to continue. You can download R at http://www.r-project.org/. Throughout this book I will occasionally refer to Web pages that I have written that contain R code for carrying out important calculations, and they can easily be pasted into R. A Web page that will get you started on using R is available at www .uvm.edu/~dhowell/methods8/R-Programs/Using-R.html. Perhaps a better source for getting started is a paper by Arnholt (2007), although the main content deals with material that we will not see until later.

I should mention widely available spreadsheets such as Excel. These programs are capable of performing a number of statistical calculations, and they produce reasonably good graphics and are an excellent way of carrying out hand calculations. They force you to go about your calculations logically, while retaining all intermediate steps for later examination. In the past such programs were criticized for the accuracy of their results. Recent extensions that have been written for them have greatly increased the accuracy, so do not underestimate their worth. Programs like Excel also have the advantage that most people have one or more of them installed on their personal computers.

1.5   What You Should Know about this Edition

In some ways this edition represents a break from past editions. Over the years each edition has contained a reasonable amount of new material and the discussion has been altered to reflect changes in theory and practice. In this edition I intend to bring in a number of

additional topics that students need to understand, and I can't really do that without removing some of the older material. However, thanks to the Internet the material will largely be
moved rather than deleted. For example, if you would prefer to see the older, more complete version of the chapter on multiple comparison tests or the one on log-linear models,
you can download the previous version from my Web site. The same holds for other major
deletions.

The first edition of this book was written in 1973–1974, while I was on sabbatical
at the University of Durham, England. At that time most statistics courses in psychology
were aimed at experimental psychologists, and a large percentage of that work related to
the analysis of variance. B. J. Winer's *Statistical Principles in Experimental Design* (1962,
1971) dominated a large part of the field of psychological statistics and influenced how experiments were designed, run, and analyzed. My first edition followed much of that trend,
and properly so. Since that time statistical analysis of data has seen considerable change.
Although the analysis of variance is still a dominant technique, followed closely by multiple
regression, many other topics have worked their way onto the list. For example, measures of
effect size are far more important than they were then, meta-analysis has grown from virtually nothing to an important way to summarize a field, and the treatment of missing data
has changed significantly thanks to the introduction of linear mixed models and methods
of data imputation. We can no longer turn out students who are prepared to conduct high-
quality research without including discussion of these issues.

But to include these and similar topics, something has to go if the text is to remain
at a manageable size. In the past multiple comparison procedures, for example, were the
subject of considerable attention with many competing approaches. But if you look at what
people are actually doing in the literature, most of the competing approaches are more of
interest to theoreticians than to practitioners. I think that it is far more useful to write about
the treatment of missing data than to list all of the alternatives for making comparisons
among means. This is particularly true now that it is easy to make that older material readily available for all who would like to read it.

So what changes can you expect? The most important topics to be included, as of this
writing, include more extensive treatment of missing data, the use of linear mixed models
to handle repeated measures, greater emphasis on confidence intervals, and an introduction to meta-analysis and to single-subject designs, which are very important in clinical
interventions. I cannot cover all of this material to the depth that I would like, but at least I
can get you started and point you to relevant sources. In many cases I have additional material that I have created, and that material is available to you over the Internet. You can get
to it at either http://www.uvm.edu/~dhowell/methods8/ or http://www.uvm.edu/~dhowell
/StatPages/. At the former site you also have access to all data files, extended answers to
odd-numbered exercises, errors and corrections, and my own manuals on SPSS. That is the
site to which I refer when I mention "this book's Web site." Just follow the links that you
find there.

Perhaps the biggest change coming to the field of statistical methods goes under the
heading of "resampling." For the past 100 years we have solved statistical problems by
computing some test statistic and then saying "if the population from which I sampled
has certain characteristics, then I can fairly compare my statistic to the appropriate tabled
value." But what if the population doesn't have these characteristics? Well, just hope that
it does.

With the very high computational speed of even a standard laptop, we can avoid certain
of these assumptions about the population. We can work out what a statistic will look like
when drawing from almost any population. These resampling procedures are extremely
powerful and are beginning to play an important role. For the near future the traditional approaches will maintain their status, if only because they are what people have been taught

how to use. But that is changing. Whenever you see a check box on one of the screens of your software that says something like "simulate" or "bootstrap," that is another nail in the coffin of traditional methods.

To anticipate this change, this book will bring in resampling methods along with the usual approaches. These methods will *not* make your life harder, because they are easy to understand. All I want you to come away with is the underlying concepts. And I will even supply short programs that you can use to do the sampling yourself, though you can skip them if you choose. The new methods will help you to better understand what the older methods were all about.

Key Terms

Random sample (1.1)

Randomly assign (1.1)

Population (1.1)

Sample (1.1)

External validity (1.1)

Random assignment (1.1)

Internal validity (1.1)

Variable (1.1)

Independent variable (1.1)

Dependent variable (1.1)

Discrete variables (1.1)

Continuous variables (1.1)

Quantitative data (1.1)

Measurement data (1.1)

Categorical data (1.1)

Frequency data (1.1)

Qualitative data (1.1)

Descriptive statistics (1.2)

Exploratory data analysis (EDA) (1.2)

Inferential statistics (1.2)

Parameter (1.2)

Statistic (1.2)

Nominal scale (1.3)

Ordinal scale (1.3)

Interval scale (1.3)

Ratio scale (1.3)

Exercises

1.1   Under what conditions would the entire student body of your college or university be considered a population?

1.2   Why would choosing names from a local telephone book not produce a random sample of the residents of that city? Who would be underrepresented and who would be overrepresented?

1.3   If the student body of your college or university were considered a sample, as in Exercise 1.4, would this sample be random or nonrandom? Why?

1.4   Under what conditions would the entire student body of your college or university be considered a sample?

1.5   Give two examples of independent variables and two examples of dependent variables.

1.6   Give an example of a study in which we do not care about the actual numerical value of a population average, but want to know whether the average of one population is greater than the average of a different population.

1.7   Give three examples of continuous variables.

1.8   Write a sentence describing an experiment in terms of an independent and a dependent variable.

1.9   Give an example of a study in which we are interested in estimating the average score of a population.

1.10   Give three examples of discrete variables.

1.11   Give three examples of categorical data.

1.12   Give one example of each kind of measurement scale.

1.13   Give an example in which the thing we are studying could be either a measurement or a categorical variable.

1.14   Give three examples of measurement data.

1.15   Give an example of a variable that might be said to be measured on a ratio scale for some purposes and on an interval or ordinal scale for other purposes.

1.16   Do a Google search for a clear discussion of internal validity.

1.17   What does Exercise 1.18 say about speed used as an index of motivation?

1.18   We trained rats to run a straight-alley maze by providing positive reinforcement with food. On trial 12, a rat lay down and went to sleep halfway through the maze. What does this say about the measurement scale when speed is used as an index of learning?

1.19   Give two examples of studies in which our primary interest is in looking at differences among groups.

1.20   Give two examples of studies in which our primary interest is in looking at relationships between variables.

1.21   Do a Google search to find synonyms for what we have called an independent variable. (Always remember that Google is your friend when you don't fully understand what I have presented.)

Discussion Questions

1.22   The *Chicago Tribune* of July 21, 1995, reported on a study by a fourth-grade student named Beth Peres. In the process of collecting evidence in support of her campaign for a higher allowance, she polled her classmates on what they received for an allowance. She was surprised to discover that the 11 girls who responded reported an average allowance of $2.63 per week, whereas the 7 boys reported an average of $3.18, 21% more than for the girls. At the same time, boys had to do fewer chores to earn their allowance than did girls. The story had considerable national prominence and raised the question of whether the income disparity for adult women relative to adult men may actually have its start very early in life.

  a.   What are the dependent and independent variables in this study, and how are they measured?

  b.   What kind of a sample are we dealing with here?

  c.   How could the characteristics of the sample influence the results Beth obtained?

  d.   How might Beth go about "random sampling"? How would she go about "random assignment"?

  e.   If random assignment is not possible in this study, does that have negative implications for the validity of the study?

  f.   What are some of the variables that might influence the outcome of this study separate from any true population differences between boys' and girls' incomes?

  g.   Distinguish clearly between the descriptive and inferential statistical features of this example.

1.23   The *Journal of Public Health* published data on the relationship between smoking and health (see Landwehr & Watkins [1987]). They reported the cigarette consumption per adult for 21 mostly Western and developed countries, along with the coronary heart disease rate for each country. The data clearly show that coronary heart disease is highest in those countries with the highest cigarette consumption.

  a.   Why might the sampling in this study have been limited to Western and developed countries?

  b.   How would you characterize the two variables in terms of what we have labeled "scales of measurement"?

c. If our goal is to study the health effects of smoking, how do these data relate to that overall question?

d. What other variables might need to be considered in such a study?

e. It has been reported that tobacco companies are making a massive advertising effort in Asia. At present, only 7% of Chinese women smoke (compared with 61% of Chinese men). How would a health psychologist go about studying the health effects of likely changes in the incidence of smoking among Chinese women?

Chapter 2

Describing and
Exploring Data

Objectives

To show how data can be reduced to a more interpretable form by using graphical representation and measures of central tendency and dispersion.

Contents

A COLLECTION OF RAW DATA, taken by itself, is no more exciting or informative than junk mail before Election Day. Whether you have neatly arranged the data in rows on a data collection form or scribbled them on the back of an out-of-date announcement you tore from the bulletin board, a collection of numbers is still just a collection of numbers. To be interpretable, they first must be organized in some sort of logical order. The following actual experiment illustrates some of these steps.

How do human beings process information that is stored in their short-term memory? If I asked you to tell me whether the number "6" was included as one of a set of five digits that you just saw presented on a screen, do you use sequential processing to search your short-term memory of the screen and say "Nope, it wasn't the first digit; nope, it wasn't the second," and so on? Or do you use parallel processing to compare the digit "6" with your memory of all the previous digits at the same time? The latter approach would be faster and more efficient, but human beings don't always do things in the fastest and most efficient manner. How do you think that you do it? How do you search back through your memory and identify the person who just walked in as Jennifer? Do you compare her one at a time with all the women her age whom you have met, or do you make comparisons in parallel? (This second example uses long-term memory rather than short-term memory, but the questions are analogous.)

In 1966, Saul Sternberg ran a simple, famous, and important study that examined how people recall data from short-term memory. This study is still widely cited in research literature. He briefly presented a comparison set of one, three, or five digits on a screen in front of the subject. Shortly after each presentation he flashed a single test digit on the screen and required the subject to push one button (the positive button) if the test digit had been included in the comparison set or another button (the negative button) if the test digit had not been part of the comparison set. For example, the two stimuli might look like this:

Comparison	2	7	4	8	1
Test			5		

(Remember, the two sets of stimuli were presented sequentially, not simultaneously, so only one of those lines was visible at a time.) The numeral "5" was not part of the comparison set, and the subject should have responded by pressing the negative button. Sternberg measured the time, in hundredths of a second, that the subject took to respond. This process was repeated over many randomly organized trials. Because Sternberg was interested in how people process information, he was interested in how reaction times varied as a function of the number of digits in the comparison set and as a function of whether the test digit was a positive or negative instance for that set. (If you make comparisons sequentially, the time to make a decision should increase as the number of digits in the comparison set increases. If you make comparisons in parallel, the number of digits in the comparison set shouldn't matter.)

Although Sternberg's goal was to compare data for the different conditions, we can gain an immediate impression of our data by taking the full set of reaction times, regardless of the stimulus condition. The data in Table 2.1 were collected in an experiment similar to Sternberg's but with only one subject—myself. No correction of responses was allowed, so the data presented here come only from correct trials.

2.1 Plotting Data

As you can see, there are simply too many numbers in Table 2.1 for us to interpret them at a glance. One of the simplest methods to reorganize data to make them more intelligible is to plot them in some sort of graphical form. There are several

Table 2.1   Reaction time data from number identification experiment

Comparison Stimuli*	Reaction Times, in 100ths of a Second																
1Y	40	41	47	38	40	37	38	47	45	61	54	67	49	43	52	39	46
	47	45	43	39	49	50	44	53	46	64	51	40	41	44	48	50	42
	90	51	55	60	47	45	41	42	72	36	43	94	45	51	46	52	
1N	52	45	74	56	53	59	43	46	51	40	48	47	57	54	44	56	47
	62	44	53	48	50	58	52	57	66	49	59	56	71	76	54	71	104
	44	67	45	79	46	57	58	47	73	67	46	57	52	61	72	104	
3Y	73	83	55	59	51	65	61	64	63	86	42	65	62	62	51	62	72
	55	58	46	67	56	52	46	62	51	51	61	60	75	53	59	56	50
	43	58	67	52	56	80	53	72	62	59	47	62	53	52	46	60	
3N	73	47	63	63	56	66	72	58	60	69	74	51	49	69	51	60	52
	72	58	74	59	63	60	66	59	61	50	67	63	61	80	63	60	64
	64	57	59	58	59	60	62	63	67	78	61	52	51	56	95	54	
5Y	39	65	53	46	78	60	71	58	87	77	62	94	81	46	49	62	55
	59	88	56	77	67	79	54	83	75	67	60	65	62	62	62	60	58
	67	48	51	67	98	64	57	67	55	55	66	60	57	54	78	69	
5N	66	53	61	74	76	69	82	56	66	63	69	76	71	65	67	67	55
	65	58	64	65	81	69	69	63	68	70	80	68	63	74	61	85	125
	59	61	74	76	62	83	58	72	65	61	95	58	64	66	66	72	

© Cengage Learning 2013

*Y = Yes, test stimulus was included; N = No, it was not included 1, 3, and 5 refer to the number of digits in the comparison stimuli

common ways that data can be represented graphically. Some of these methods are frequency distributions, histograms, and stem-and-leaf displays, which we will discuss in turn. (I believe strongly in making plots as simple as possible so as not to confuse the message with unnecessary elements. However, if you want to see a remarkable example of how plotting data can reveal important information you would not otherwise see, the video at http://blog.ted.com/2007/06/hans_roslings_j_1.php is very impressive.)

Frequency Distributions

frequency distribution

As a first step, we can make a frequency distribution of the data as a way of organizing them in some sort of logical order. For our example, we would count the number of times that each possible reaction time occurred. For example, the subject responded in 50/100 of a second 5 times and in 51/100 of a second 12 times. On one occasion he became flustered and took 1.25 seconds (125/100 of a second) to respond. The frequency distribution for these data is presented in Table 2.2, which reports how often each reaction time occurred.

From the distribution shown in Table 2.2, we can see a wide distribution of reaction times, with times as low as 36/100 of a second and as high as 125/100 of a second. The data tend to cluster around about 60/100, with most of the scores between 40/100 and 90/100. This tendency was not apparent from the unorganized data shown in Table 2.1.

Table 2.2   Frequency distribution of reaction times

Reaction Time, in 100ths of a Second	Frequency	Reaction Time, in 100ths of a Second	Frequency
36	1	71	4
37	1	72	8
38	2	73	3
39	3	74	6
40	4	75	2
41	3	76	4
42	3	77	2
43	5	78	3
44	5	79	2
45	6	80	3
46	11	81	2
47	9	82	1
48	4	83	3
49	5	84	0
50	5	85	1
51	12	86	1
52	10	87	1
53	8	88	1
54	6	89	0
55	7	90	1
56	10	91	0
57	7	92	0
58	12	93	0
59	11	94	2
60	12	95	2
61	11	96	0
62	14	97	0
63	10	98	1
64	7	99	0
65	8	…	…
66	8	…	…
67	14	104	2
68	2	…	…
69	7	125	1
70	1		

2.2   Histograms

From the distribution given in Table 2.1 we could easily graph the data as shown in Figure 2.1. But when we are dealing with a variable, such as this one, that has many different values, each individual value often occurs with low frequency, and there is often substantial fluctuation of the frequencies in adjacent intervals. Notice, for example, that there are fourteen 67s, but only two 68s. In situations such as this, it makes more sense

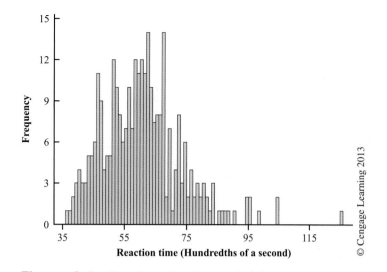

Figure 2.1   Plot of reaction times against frequency

histogram

to group adjacent values together into a **histogram**.[1] Our goal in doing so is to obscure some of the random "noise" that is not likely to be meaningful, but still preserve important trends in the data. We might, for example, group the data into blocks of 5/100 of a second, combining the frequencies for all outcomes between 35 and 39, between 40 and 44, and so on. An example of such a distribution is shown in Table 2.3.

real lower limit

real upper limit

In Table 2.3, I have reported the upper and lower boundaries of the intervals as whole integers, for the simple reason that it makes the table easier to read. However, you should realize that the true limits of the interval (known as the **real lower limit** and the **real upper limit**) are decimal values that fall halfway between the top of one interval and the bottom of the next. The real lower limit of an interval is the smallest value that would be classed as falling into the interval. Similarly, an interval's real upper limit is the largest value that would be classed as being in the interval. For example, had we recorded reaction times to the nearest thousandth of a second, rather than to the nearest hundredth, the interval 35–39 would include all values between 34.5 and 39.5 because values falling between those points

Table 2.3   Grouped frequency distribution

Interval	Midpoint	Frequency	Cumulative Frequency	Interval	Midpoint	Frequency	Cumulative Frequency
35–39	37	7	7	85–89	87	4	291
40–44	42	20	27	90–94	92	3	294
45–49	47	35	62	95–99	97	3	297
50–54	52	41	103	100–104	102	2	299
55–59	57	47	150	105–109	107	0	299
60–64	62	54	204	110–114	112	0	299
65–69	67	39	243	115–119	117	0	299
70–74	72	22	265	120–124	122	0	299
75–79	77	13	278	125–129	127	1	300
80–84	82	9	287				

© Cengage Learning 2013

---

[1] Different people seem to mean different things when they talk about a "histogram." Some use it for the distribution of the data regardless of whether or not categories have been combined (they would call Figure 2.1 a histogram), and others reserve it for the case where adjacent categories are combined. You can probably tell by now that I am not a stickler for such distinctions, and I will use "histogram" and "frequency distribution" more or less interchangeably.

would be rounded up or down into that interval. (People often become terribly worried about what we would do if a person had a score of exactly 39.50000000 and therefore sat right on the breakpoint between two intervals. Don't worry about it. First, it doesn't happen very often. Second, you can always flip a coin. Third, there are many more important things to worry about. Just make up an arbitrary rule of what you will do in those situations, and then stick to it. This is one of those non-issues that make people think the study of statistics is confusing, boring, or both. I prefer to round to an even integer. Thus 25.5000 rounds to 26, and 44.5000 rounds to 44.)

midpoints

The midpoints listed in Table 2.3 are the averages of the upper and lower limits and are presented for convenience. When we plot the data, we often plot the points as if they all fell at the midpoints of their respective intervals.

Table 2.3 also lists the frequencies that scores fell in each interval. For example, there were seven reaction times between 35/100 and 39/100 of a second. The distribution in Table 2.3 is shown as a histogram in Figure 2.2.

People often ask about the optimal number of intervals to use when grouping data. Keen (2010) gives at least six possible rules for determining the optimal number of intervals, but these rules are primarily intended for those writing software who need rules to handle the general case. If you are dealing with a particular set of data, you can pretty much ignore formal rules and fiddle with the settings until the result looks meaningful. Although there is no right answer to the question of intervals to use, somewhere around 10 or 12 intervals is usually reasonable. In this example I used 19 intervals because the numbers naturally broke that way and I had a lot of observations. In general, and when practical, it is best to use natural breaks in the number system (e.g., 0−9, 10−19, . . . or 100−119, 120−139) rather than break up the range into exactly 10 arbitrarily defined intervals. However, if another kind of limit makes the data more interpretable, then use those limits. Remember that you are trying to make the data meaningful—don't try to follow a rigid set of rules made up by someone who has never seen your problem.

Notice in Figure 2.2 that the reaction time data are generally centered on 50–70 hundredths of a second, that the distribution rises and falls fairly regularly, and that the distribution trails off to the right. We would expect such times to trail off to the right (referred to as being positively skewed) because there is some limit on how quickly the person

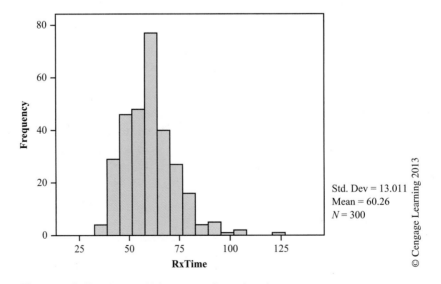

Std. Dev = 13.011
Mean = 60.26
$N = 300$

© Cengage Learning 2013

Figure 2.2   Grouped histogram of reaction times

Outliers

can respond, but really there is no limit on how slowly he can respond. Notice also the extreme value of 125 hundredths. This value is called an outlier because it is widely separated from the rest of the data. **Outliers** frequently represent errors in recording data, but in this particular case it was just a trial in which the subject couldn't decide which button to push.

2.3   Fitting Smoothed Lines to Data

Histograms such as the ones shown in Figures 2.1 and 2.2 can often be used to display data in a meaningful fashion, but they have their own problems. A number of people have pointed out that histograms, as common as they are, often fail as a clear description of data. This is especially true with smaller sample sizes where minor changes in the location or width of the interval can make a noticeable difference in the shape of the distribution. Wilkinson (1994) has written an excellent paper on this and related problems. Maindonald and Braun (2007) give the example shown in Figure 2.3 plotting the lengths of possums. The first collapses the data into bins with breakpoints at 72.5, 77.5, 82.5, ... The second uses breakpoints at 70, 75, 80, ... People who care about possums, and there are such people, might draw quite different conclusions from these two graphs depending on the breakpoints you use. The data are fairly symmetric in the histogram on the right, but have a noticeable tail to the left in the histogram on the left.

Figure 2.2 is actually a pretty fair representation of reaction times, but we often can do better by fitting a smoothed curve to the data—with or without the histogram itself. I will discuss two of many approaches to fitting curves, one of which superimposes a normal distribution (to be discussed more extensively in the next chapter) and the other uses what is known as a kernel density plot.

Fitting a Normal Curve

Although you have not yet read Chapter 3, you should be generally familiar with a normal curve. It is often referred to as a bell curve and is symmetrical around the center of the distribution, tapering off on both ends. The normal distribution has a specific definition, but we will put that off until the next chapter. For now it is sufficient to

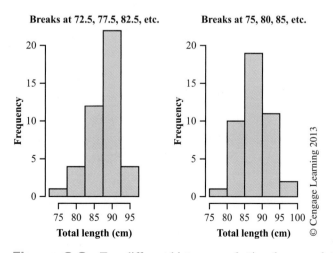

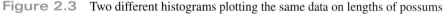

Figure 2.3   Two different histograms plotting the same data on lengths of possums

say that we will often assume that our data are normally distributed, and superimposing a normal distribution on the histogram will give us some idea how reasonable that assumption is.[2]

Figure 2.4, was produced by SPSS and you can see that although the data are roughly described by the normal distribution, the actual distribution is somewhat truncated on the left and has more than the expected number of observations on the extreme right. The normal curve is not a terrible fit, but we can do better. An alternative approach would be to create what is called a kernel density plot.

Kernel Density Plots

Kernel density plots

In Figure 2.4, we superimposed a theoretical distribution on the data. This distribution made use of only a few characteristics of the data, its mean and standard deviation, and did not make any effort to fit the curve to the actual shape of the distribution. To put that a little more precisely, we can superimpose the normal distribution by calculating only the mean and standard deviation (to be discussed later in this chapter) from the data. The individual data points and their distributions play no role in plotting that distribution. **Kernel density plots** do almost the opposite. They actually try to fit a smooth curve to the data while at the same time taking account of the fact that there is a lot of random noise in the observations that should not be allowed to distort the curve too much. Kernel density plots pay no attention to the mean and standard deviation of the observations.

The idea behind a kernel density plot is that each observation might have been slightly different. For example, on a trial where the respondent's reaction time was 80 hundredths of a second, the score might reasonably have been 79 or 82 instead. It is even conceivable that the score could have been 73 or 86, but it is not at all likely that the score would have been 20 or 100. In other words there is a distribution of alternative possibilities around any obtained value, and this is true for all obtained values. We will use this fact to produce an overall curve that usually fits the data quite well.

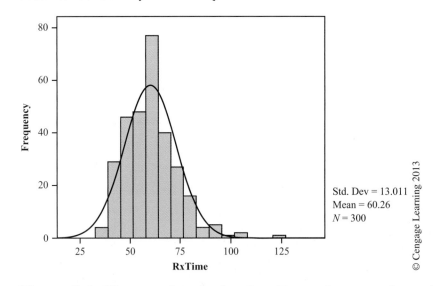

Figure 2.4   Histogram of reaction time data with normal curve superimposed

---

[2] This is not the best way of evaluating whether or not a distribution is normal, as we will see in the next chapter. However, it is a common way of proceeding.

Kernel estimates can be illustrated graphically by taking an example from Everitt & Hothorn (2006). They used a very simple set of data with the following values for the dependent variable (*X*).

| *X* | 0.0 | 1.0 | 1.1 | 1.5 | 1.9 | 2.8 | 2.9 | 3.5 |

If you plot these points along the *X* axis and superimpose small distributions representing alternative values that might have been obtained instead of the actual values you have, you obtain the distribution shown on the left in Figure 2.5. Everitt and Hothorn give these small distributions a technical name: "bumps." Notice that these bumps are normal distributions, but I could have specified some other shape if I thought that a normal distribution was inappropriate.

Now we will literally sum these bumps vertically. For example, suppose that we name each bump by the score over which it is centered. Above a value of 3.8 on the *X*-axis you have a small amount of bump_2.8, a little bit more of bump_2.9, and a good bit of bump_3.5. You can add the heights of these three bumps at *X* = 3.8 to get the kernel density of the overall curve at that position. You can do the same for every other value of *X*. If you do so you find the distribution plotted on the right in Figure 2.5. Above the bumps we have a squiggly distribution (to use another technical term) that represents our best guess of the distribution underlying the data that we began with.

Now we can go back to the reaction time data and superimpose the kernel density function on that histogram. (I am leaving off the bumps as there are too many of them to be legible.) This resulting plot is shown in Figure 2.6. Notice that this curve does a much better job of representing the data than did the superimposed normal distribution. In particular it fits the tails of the distribution quite well.

SPSS fits kernel density plots using syntax, and you can fit them using SAS and S-Plus (or its close cousin R). It is fairly easy to find examples for those programs on the Internet. As psychology expands into more areas, and particularly into the neurosciences and health sciences, techniques like kernel density plots are becoming more common. There are a number of technical aspects behind such plots, for example, the shape of the bumps and the bandwidth used to create them, but you now have the basic information that will allow you to understand and work with such plots. A Web page describing how to calculate kernel density plots in R and in SPSS is available at http://www.uvm.edu/~dhowell/methods8/Supplements/R-Programs/kernel-density/kernel-density.html and a program in R is available at the book's Web site at http://www.uvm.edu/~dhowell/methods8/Supplements/R-Programs/R-Programs.html.

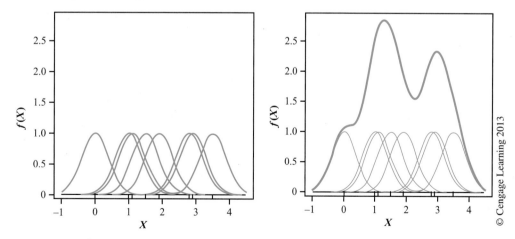

© Cengage Learning 2013

Figure 2.5   Illustration of the kernel density function for *X*

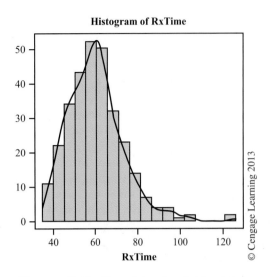

Histogram of RxTime

© Cengage Learning 2013

Figure 2.6   Kernel density plot for data on reaction time

2.4 Stem-and-Leaf Displays

stem-and-leaf display

exploratory data analysis (EDA)

Although histograms, frequency distributions, and kernel density functions are commonly used methods of presenting data, each has its drawbacks. Because histograms often portray observations that have been grouped into intervals, they frequently lose the actual numerical values of the individual scores in each interval. Frequency distributions, on the other hand, retain the values of the individual observations, but they can be difficult to use when they do not summarize the data sufficiently. An alternative approach that avoids both of these criticisms is the stem-and-leaf display.

John Tukey (1977), as part of his general approach to data analysis, known as exploratory data analysis (EDA), developed a variety of methods for displaying data in visually meaningful ways. One of the simplest of these methods is the stem-and-leaf display, which you will see presented by most major statistical software packages. I can't start with the reaction-time data here because that would require a slightly more sophisticated display due to the large number of observations. Instead, I'll use a hypothetical set of data in which we record the amount of time (in minutes per week) that each of 100 students spends playing electronic games. Some of the raw data are given in Figure 2.7. On the left side of the figure is a portion of the data (data from students who spend between 40 and 80 minutes per week playing games) and on the right is the complete stem-and-leaf display that results.

leading digits

most significant digits

stem

trailing digits

less significant digits

leaves

From the raw data in Figure 2.7, you can see that there are several scores in the 40s, another bunch in the 50s, two in the 60s, and some in the 70s. We refer to the tens' digits—here 4, 5, 6, and 7—as the leading digits (sometimes called the most significant digits) for these scores. These leading digits form the stem, or vertical axis, of our display. Within the set of 14 scores that were in the 40s, you can see that there was one 40, two 41s, one 42, two 43s, one 44, no 45s, three 46s, one 47, one 48, and two 49s. The units' digits 0, 1, 2, 3, and so on, are called the trailing (or less significant) digits. They form the leaves—the horizontal elements—of our display.[3]

---

[3] It is not always true that the tens' digits form the stem and the units' digits the leaves. For example, if the data ranged from 100 to 1,000, the hundreds' digits would form the stem, the tens' digits the leaves, and we would ignore the units' digits.

Raw Data	Stem	Leaf
.	0	0000000000000233566678
.	1	2223555579
.	2	33577
40 41 41 42 43	3	22278999
43 44 46 46 46	4	01123346667899
47 48 49 49	5	24557899
52 54 55 55 57	6	37
58 59 59	7	1556689
63 67	8	34779
71 75 75 76 76	9	466
78 79	10	23677
.	11	3479
.	12	2557899
.	13	89

© Cengage Learning 2013

Figure 2.7 Stem-and-leaf display of electronic game data

On the right side of Figure 2.7 you can see that next to the stem entry of 4 you have one 0, two 1s, a 2, two 3s, a 4, three 6s, a 7, an 8, and two 9s. These leaf values correspond to the units' digits in the raw data. Similarly, note how the leaves opposite the stem value of 5 correspond to the units' digits of all responses in the 50s. From the stem-and-leaf display you could completely regenerate the raw data that went into that display. For example, you can tell that 11 students spent zero minutes playing electronic games, one student spent two minutes, two students spent three minutes, and so on. Moreover, the shape of the display looks just like a sideways histogram, giving you all of the benefits of that method of graphing data as well.

One apparent drawback of this simple stem-and-leaf display is that for some data sets it will lead to a grouping that is too coarse for our purposes. In fact, that is why I needed to use hypothetical data for this introductory example. When I tried to use the reaction-time data, I found that the stem for 50 (i.e., 5) had 88 leaves opposite it, which was a little silly. Not to worry; Tukey was there before us and figured out a clever way around this problem.

If the problem is that we are trying to lump together everything between 50 and 59, perhaps what we should be doing is breaking that interval into smaller intervals. We could try using the intervals 50–54, 55–59, and so on. But then we couldn't just use 5 as the stem, because it would not distinguish between the two intervals. Tukey suggested using "5*" to represent 50–54, and "5." to represent 55–59. But that won't solve our problem here, because the categories still are too coarse. So Tukey suggested an alternative scheme where "5*" represents 50–51, "5t" represents 52–53, "5f" represents 54–55, "5s" represents 56–57, and "5." represents 58–59. (Notice that "Two" and "Three" both start with "t," "Four" and "Five" both start with an "f," and "Six" and "Seven" both start with an "s.") If we apply this scheme to the data on reaction times, we obtain the results shown in Figure 2.8. In deciding on the number of stems to use, the problem is similar to selecting the number of categories in a histogram. Again, you want to do something that makes sense and conveys information in a meaningful way. The one restriction is that the stems should be the same width. You would not let one stem be 50–54, and another 60–69.

Notice that in Figure 2.8 I did not list the extreme values as I did in the others. I used the word High in place of the stem and then inserted the actual values. I did this to highlight the presence of extreme values, as well as to conserve space.

Raw Data	Stem	Leaf
36 37 38 38 39 39 39 40	3s	67
40 40 40 41 41 41 42 42	3.	88999
42 43 43 43 43 43 44 44	4*	0000111
44 44 44 45 45 45 45 45	4t	22233333
45 46 46 46 46 46 46 46	4f	44444555555
46 46 46 46 47 47 47 47	4s	666666666667777777777
47 47 47 47 47 48 48 48	4.	888899999
48 49 49 49 49 49 50 50	5*	00000111111111111
50 50 50 51 51 51 51 51	5t	222222222233333333
51 51 51 51 51 51 51 52	5f	4444445555555
52 52 52 52 52 52 52 52	5s	66666666667777777
52 53 53 53 53 53 53 53	5.	8888888888889999999999999
53 54 54 54 54 54 54 55	6*	00000000000011111111111
55 55 55 55 55 55	6t	22222222222222233333333333
…	6f	444444455555555
	6s	6666666677777777777777
	6.	889999999
	7*	01111
	7t	22222222333
	7f	44444455
	7s	666677
	7.	88899
	8*	00011
	8t	2333
	8f	5
	8s	67
	8.	8
	9*	0
	9t	
	9f	4455
	9s	
	93	8
	High	104; 10; 125

© Cengage Learning 2013

Figure 2.8   Stem-and-leaf display for reaction time data

Stem-and-leaf displays can be particularly useful for comparing two different distributions. Such a comparison is accomplished by plotting the two distributions on opposite sides of the stem. Figure 2.9 shows the actual distribution of numerical grades of males and females in a course I taught on experimental methods that included a substantial statistics component. These are actual data. Notice the use of stems such as 6* (for 60–64) and 6. (for 65–69). In addition, notice the code at the bottom of the table that indicates how entries translate to raw scores. This particular code says that |4*|1 represents 41, not 4.1 or 410. Finally, notice that the figure nicely illustrates the difference in performance between the male students and the female students.

Male	Stem	Female
	3*	
6	3.	
	4*	1
	4.	
	5*	
	5.	
2	6*	03
6.	6.	568
32200	7*	0144
88888766666655	7.	555556666788899
4432221000	8*	0000011112222334444
7666666555	8.	556666666666667788888899
422	9*	000000000133
	9.	56
Code |4*|1 = 41		

© Cengage Learning 2013

Figure 2.9   Grades (in percent) for an actual course in experimental methods, plotted separately by gender

2.5 Describing Distributions

symmetric

The distributions of scores illustrated in Figures 2.1 and 2.2 were more or less regularly shaped distributions, rising to a maximum and then dropping away smoothly—although even those figures were not completely symmetric. However, not all distributions are peaked in the center and fall off evenly to the sides (see the stem-and-leaf display in Figure 2.6), and it is important to understand the terms used to describe different distributions. Consider the two distributions shown in Figure 2.10(a) and (b). These plots are of data that were computer generated to come from populations with specific shapes. These plots, and the other four in Figure 2.10, are based on samples of 1,000 observations, and the slight irregularities are just random variability. Both of the distributions in Figure 2.10(a) and (b) are called symmetric because they have the same shape on both sides of the center.

bimodal

unimodal
modality

The distribution shown in Figure 2.10(a) came from what we will later refer to as a normal distribution. The distribution in Figure 2.10(b) is referred to as bimodal, because it has two peaks. The term bimodal is used to refer to any distribution that has two predominant peaks, whether or not those peaks are of exactly the same height. If a distribution has only one major peak, it is called unimodal. The term used to refer to the number of major peaks in a distribution is modality.

negatively skewed
positively skewed
skewness

Next consider Figure 2.10(c) and (d). These two distributions obviously are not symmetric. The distribution in Figure 2.10(c) has a tail going out to the left, whereas that in Figure 2.10(d) has a tail going out to the right. We say that the former is negatively skewed and the latter positively skewed. (Hint: To help you remember which is which, notice that negatively skewed distributions point to the negative, or small, numbers, and that positively skewed distributions point to the positive end of the scale.) There are statistical measures of the degree of asymmetry, or skewness, but they are not commonly used in the behavioral sciences.

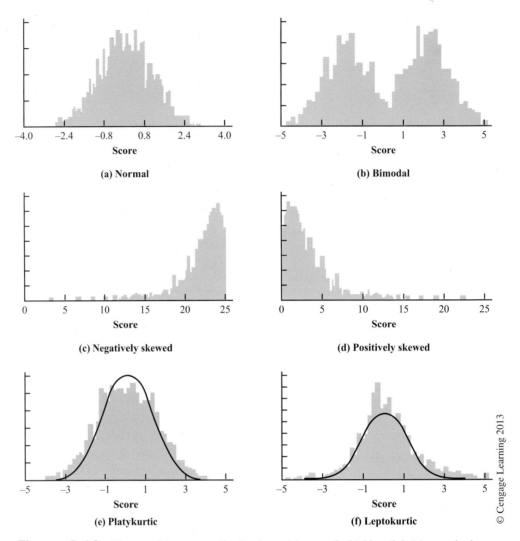

Figure 2.10 Shapes of frequency distributions: (a) normal, (b) bimodal, (c) negatively skewed, (d) positively skewed, (e) platykurtic, and (f) leptokurtic

An interesting real-life example of a positively skewed, and slightly bimodal, distribution is shown in Figure 2.11. These data were generated by Bradley (1963), who instructed subjects to press a button as quickly as possible whenever a small light came on. Most of the data points are smoothly distributed between roughly 7 and 17 hundredths of a second, but a small but noticeable cluster of points lies between 30 and 70 hundredths, trailing off to the right. This second cluster of points was obtained primarily from trials on which the subject missed the button on the first try. Their inclusion in the data significantly affects the distribution's shape. An experimenter who had such a collection of data might seriously consider treating times greater than some maximum separately, on the grounds that those times were more a reflection of the accuracy of a psychomotor response than a measure of the speed of that response. Even if we could somehow make that distribution look better, we would still have to question whether those missed responses belong in the data we analyze.

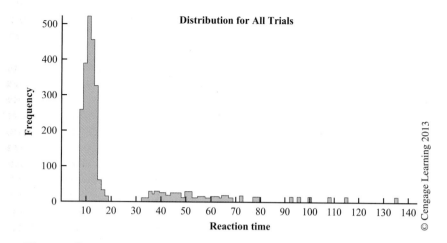

Figure 2.11   Frequency distribution of Bradley's reaction-time data

It is important to consider the difference between Bradley's data, shown in Figure 2.11, and the data that I generated, shown in Figures 2.1 and 2.2. Both distributions are positively skewed, but my data generally show longer reaction times without the second cluster of points. One difference was that I was making a decision on which button to press, whereas Bradley's subjects only had to press a single button whenever the light came on. Decisions take time. In addition, the program I was using to present stimuli recorded data from only correct responses, not from errors. There was no chance to correct and hence nothing equivalent to missing the button on the first try and having to press it again. I point this out to illustrate that differences in the way data are collected can have noticeable effects on the kinds of data we see.

kurtosis

The last characteristic of a distribution that we will examine is **kurtosis**. Kurtosis has a specific mathematical definition, but it basically refers to the relative concentration of scores in the center, the upper and lower ends (tails), and the shoulders (between the center and the tails) of a distribution. In Figure 2.10(e) and (f) I have superimposed a normal distribution on top of the plot of the data to make comparisons clear. A normal distribution (which will be described in detail in Chapter 3) is called **mesokurtic**. Its tails are neither too thin nor too thick, and there are neither too many nor too few scores concentrated in the center. If you start with a normal distribution and move scores from both the center and the tails into the shoulders, the curve becomes flatter and is called **platykurtic**. This is clearly seen in Figure 2.10(e), where the central portion of the distribution is much too flat. If, on the other hand, you moved scores from the shoulders into both the center and the tails, the curve becomes more peaked with thicker tails. Such a curve is called **leptokurtic**, and an example is Figure 2.10(f). Notice in this distribution that there are too many scores in the center and too many scores in the tails.[4]

mesokurtic

platykurtic

leptokurtic

It is important to recognize that quite large samples of data are needed before we can have a good idea about the shape of a distribution, especially its kurtosis. With sample sizes of around 30, the best we can reasonably expect to see is whether the data tend to pile up in the tails of the distribution or are markedly skewed in one direction or another.

---

[4] I would like to thank Karl Wuensch of East Carolina University for his helpful suggestions on understanding skewness and kurtosis. His ideas are reflected here, although I'm not sure that he would be satisfied by my statements on kurtosis. Except in the extreme, most people, including statisticians, are unlikely to be able to look at a distribution of sample data and tell whether it is platykurtic or leptokurtic without further calculations.

So far in our discussion almost no mention has been made of the numbers themselves. We have seen how data can be organized and presented in the form of distributions, and we have discussed a number of ways in which distributions can be characterized: symmetry or its lack (skewness), kurtosis, and modality. As useful as this information might be in certain situations, it is inadequate in others. We still do not know the average speed of a simple decision reaction time nor how alike or dissimilar are the reaction times for individual trials. To obtain this knowledge, we must reduce the data to a set of measures that carry the information we need. The questions to be asked refer to the location, or central tendency, and to the dispersion, or variability, of the distributions along the underlying scale. Measures of these characteristics are considered in Sections 2.8 and 2.9. But before going to those sections we need to set up a notational system that we can use in that discussion.

2.6 Notation

Any discussion of statistical techniques requires a notational system for expressing mathematical operations. You might be surprised to learn that no standard notational system has been adopted. Although many attempts to formulate a general policy have been made, the fact remains that no two textbooks use exactly the same notation.

The notational systems commonly used range from the very complex to the very simple. The more complex systems gain precision at the expense of easy intelligibility, whereas the simpler systems gain intelligibility at the expense of precision. Because the loss of precision is usually minor when compared with the gain in comprehension, in this book we will adopt an extremely simple system of notation.

Notation of Variables

The general rule is that an uppercase letter, often X or Y, will represent a variable as a whole. The letter and a subscript will then represent an individual value of that variable. Suppose for example that we have the following five scores on the length of time (in seconds) that third-grade children can hold their breath: [45, 42, 35, 23, 52]. This set of scores will be referred to as X. The first number of this set (45) can be referred to as X_1, the second (42) as X_2, and so on. When we want to refer to a single score without specifying which one, we will refer to X_i, where i can take on any value between 1 and 5. In practice, the use of subscripts is often a distraction, and they are generally omitted if no confusion will result.

Summation Notation

sigma (Σ)

One of the most common symbols in statistics is the uppercase Greek letter **sigma** (Σ), which is the standard notation for summation. It is readily translated as "add up, or sum, what follows." Thus, ΣX_i is read "sum the X_is." To be perfectly correct, the notation for summing all N values of X is $\sum_{i=1}^{N} X_i$, which translates to "sum all of the X_is from $i=1$ to $i=N$." In practice, we seldom need to specify what is to be done this precisely, and in most cases all subscripts are dropped and the notation for the sum of the X_i is simply ΣX.

Several extensions of the simple case of ΣX must be noted and thoroughly understood. One of these is ΣX^2, which is read as "sum the squared values of X" (i.e., $45^2 + 42^2 + 35^2 + 23^2 + 52^2 = 8,247$). Note that this is quite different from $(\Sigma X)^2$, which tells us to sum the Xs and then square the result. This would equal $(\Sigma X)^2 = (45 + 42 + 35 + 23 + 52)^2 = (197)^2 = 38,809$. The rule that always applies is to perform operations

Table 2.4 Illustration of operations involving summation notation

	Anxiety Score (X)	Tests Missed (Y)	X²	Y²	X – Y	XY
	10	3	100	9	7	30
	15	4	225	16	11	60
	12	1	144	1	11	12
	9	1	81	1	8	9
	10	3	100	9	7	30
Sum	56	12	650	36	44	141

$$\sum X = (10 + 15 + 12 + 9 + 10) = 56$$
$$\sum Y = (3 + 4 + 1 + 1 + 3) = 12$$
$$\sum X^2 = (10^2 + 15^2 + 12^2 + 9^2 + 10^2) = 650$$
$$\sum Y^2 = (3^2 + 4^2 + 1^2 + 1^2 + 3^2) = 36$$
$$\sum(XY) = (7 + 11 + 11 + 8 + 7) = 44$$
$$\sum XY = (10)(3) + (15)(4) + (12)(1) + (9)(1) + (10)(3) = 141$$
$$\sum(X)^2 = 56^2 = 3136$$
$$\sum(Y)^2 = 12^2 = 144$$
$$(\sum(X - Y))^2 = 44^2 = 1936$$
$$(\sum X)(\sum Y) = (56)(12) = 672$$

within parentheses before performing operations outside parentheses. Thus, for $(\sum X)^2$, we sum the values of X and then we square the result, as opposed to $\sum X^2$, for which we square the Xs before we sum.

Another common expression, when data are available on two variables (X and Y), is $\sum XY$, which means "sum the products of the corresponding values of X and Y." The use of these and other terms will be illustrated in the following example.

Imagine a simple experiment in which we record the anxiety scores (X) of five students and also record the number of days during the last semester that they missed a test because they were absent from school (Y). The data and simple summation operations on them are illustrated in Table 2.4. Some of these operations have been discussed already, and others will be discussed in the next few chapters.

Double Subscripts

A common notational device is to use two or more subscripts to specify exactly which value of X you have in mind. Suppose, for example, that we were given the data shown in Table 2.5. If we want to specify the entry in the ith row and jth column, we will denote this as X_{ij} Thus, the score on the third trial of Day 2 is $X_{2,3} = 13$. Some notational systems use $\sum_{i=1}^{2} \sum_{j=1}^{5} X_{ij}$, which translates as "sum the X_{ij}s where i takes on values 1 and 2 and j takes on all values from 1 to 5." You need to be aware of this system of notation because some other textbooks use it. In this book, however, the simpler, but less precise, $\sum X$ is used where possible, with $\sum X_{ij}$ used only when absolutely necessary, and $\sum \sum X_{ij}$ never appearing.

Table 2.5   Hypothetical data illustrating notation

		Trial					Total
		1	2	3	4	5	
Day	1	8	7	6	9	12	42
	2	10	11	13	15	14	63
	Total	18	18	19	24	26	105

© Cengage Learning 2013

You must thoroughly understand notation if you are to learn even the most elementary statistical techniques. You should study Table 2.4 until you fully understand all the procedures involved.

2.7 Measures of Central Tendency

We have seen how to display data in ways that allow us to begin to draw some conclusions about what the data have to say. Plotting data shows the general shape of the distribution and gives a visual sense of the general magnitude of the numbers involved. In this section you will see several statistics that can be used to represent the "center" of the distribution. These statistics are called **measures of central tendency**. In the next section we will go a step further and look at measures that deal with how the observations are dispersed around that central tendency, but first we must address how we identify the center of the distribution.

measures of central tendency

The phrase "measures of central tendency", or sometimes "**measures of location**," refers to the set of measures that reflect where on the scale the distribution is centered. These measures differ in how much use they make of the data, particularly of extreme values, but they are all trying to tell us something about where the center of the distribution lies. The three major measures of central tendency are the mode, which is based on only a few data points; the median, which ignores most of the data; and the mean, which is calculated from all of the data. We will discuss these in turn, beginning with the mode, which is the least used (and often the least useful) measure.

measures of location

The Mode

mode (Mo)

The **mode (Mo)** can be defined simply as the most common score, that is, the score obtained from the largest number of subjects. Thus, the mode is that value of X that corresponds to the highest point on the distribution. If two adjacent times occur with equal (and greatest) frequency, a common convention is to take an average of the two values and call that the mode. If, on the other hand, two nonadjacent reaction times occur with equal (or nearly equal) frequency, we say that the distribution is bimodal and would most likely report both modes. For example, the distribution of time spent playing electronic games is roughly bimodal (see Figure 2.7), with peaks at the intervals of 0–9 minutes and 40–49 minutes. (You might argue that it is trimodal, with another peak at 120+ minutes, but that is a catchall interval for "all other values," so it does not make much sense to think of it as a modal value.)

The Median

median (Mdn)

The **median (Mdn)** is the score that corresponds to the point at or below which 50% of the scores fall when the data are arranged in numerical order. By this definition, the median is also called the 50th percentile.[5] For example, consider the numbers (5, 8, 3, 7, 15). If the

---

[5] A specific percentile is defined as the point on a scale at or below which a specified percentage of scores fall.

numbers are arranged in numerical order (3, 5, 7, 8, 15), the middle score would be 7, and it would be called the median. Suppose, however, that there were an even number of scores, for example (5, 11, 3, 7, 15, 14). Rearranging, we get (3, 5, 7, 11, 14, 15), and no score has 50% of the values below it. That point actually falls between the 7 and the 11. In such a case the average (9) of the two middle scores (7 and 11) is commonly taken as the median.[6]

median location

A term that we will need shortly is the **median location**. The median location of N numbers is defined as follows:

$$\text{Median Location} = \frac{N + 1}{2}$$

Thus, for five numbers the median location = (5 + 1)/2 = 3, which simply means that the median is the third number in an ordered series. For 12 numbers, the median location = (12 + 1)/2 = 6.5; the median falls between, and is the average of, the sixth and seventh numbers.

For the data on reaction times in Table 2.2, the median location = (300 + 1)/2 = 150.5. When the data are arranged in order, the 150th time is 59 and the 151st time is 60; thus the median is (59 + 60)/2 = 59.5 hundredths of a second. You can calculate this for yourself from Table 2.2. For the electronic games data there are 100 scores, and the median location is 50.5. We can tell from the stem-and-leaf display in Figure 2.7 that the 50th score is 44 and the 51st score is 46. The median would be 45, which is the average of these two values.

The Mean

mean

The most common measure of central tendency, and one that really needs little explanation, is the **mean**, or what people generally have in mind when they use the word average. The mean ($\overline{X}$) is the sum of the scores divided by the number of scores and is usually designated $\overline{X}$ (read "X bar").[7] It is defined (using the summation notation given on page 30) as:

$$\overline{X} = \frac{\sum X}{N}$$

where $\sum X$ is the sum of all values of X, and N is the number of X values. As an illustration, the mean of the numbers 3, 5, 12, and 5 is

$$\frac{3 + 5 + 12 + 5}{4} = \frac{25}{4} = 6.25$$

For the reaction-time data in Table 2.2, the sum of the observations is 18,078. When we divide that number by $N = 300$, we get 18,078/300 = 60.26. Notice that this answer agrees well with the median, which we found to be 59.5. The mean and the median will be close whenever the distribution is nearly symmetric (as defined on page 27). It also agrees well with the modal interval (60–64).

---

[6] The definition of the median is another one of those things about which statisticians love to argue. The definition given here, in which the median is defined as a point on a distribution of numbers, is the one most critics prefer. It is also in line with the statement that the median is the 50th percentile. On the other hand, there are many who are perfectly happy to say that the median is either the middle number in an ordered series (if N is odd) or the average of the two middle numbers (if N is even). Reading these arguments is a bit like going to a faculty meeting when there is nothing terribly important on the agenda. The less important the issue, the more there is to say about it.

[7] The American Psychological Association would prefer the use of M for the mean instead of $\overline{X}$, but I have used $\overline{X}$ for so many years that it would offend my delicate sensibilities to give it up. The rest of the statistical world generally agrees with me on this, so we will use $\overline{X}$ throughout.

Relative Advantages and Disadvantages of the Mode, the Median, and the Mean

Only when the distribution is symmetric will the mean and the median be equal, and only when the distribution is symmetric and unimodal will all three measures be the same. In all other cases—including almost all situations with which we will deal—some measure of central tendency must be chosen. There are no good rules for selecting a measure of central tendency, but it is possible to make intelligent choices among the three measures.

The Mode

The mode is the most commonly occurring score. By definition, then, it is a score that actually occurred, whereas the mean and sometimes the median may be values that never appear in the data. The mode also has the obvious advantage of representing the largest number of people. Someone who is running a small store would do well to concentrate on the mode. If 80% of your customers want the giant economy family-size detergent and 20% want the teeny-weeny, single-person size, it wouldn't seem particularly wise to aim for some other measure of location and stock only the regular size.

The Median

The major advantage of the median, which it shares with the mode, is that it is unaffected by extreme scores. The medians of both (5, 8, 9, 15, 16) and (0, 8, 9, 15, 206) are 9. Many experimenters find this characteristic to be useful in studies in which extreme scores occasionally occur but have no particular significance. For example, the average trained rat can run down a short runway in approximately 1 to 2 seconds. Every once in a while this same rat will inexplicably stop halfway down, scratch himself, poke his nose at the photocells, and lie down to sleep. In that instance it is of no practical significance whether he takes 30 seconds or 10 minutes to get to the other end of the runway. It may even depend on when the experimenter gives up and pokes him with a pencil. If we ran a rat through three trials on a given day and his times were (1.2, 1.3, and 20 seconds), that would have the same meaning to us—in terms of what it tells us about the rat's knowledge of the task—as if his times were (1.2, 1.3, and 136.4 seconds). In both cases the median would be 1.3. Obviously, however, his daily mean would be quite different in the two cases (7.5 versus 46.3 seconds). This problem frequently induces experimenters to work with the median rather than the mean time per day.

The Mean

Of the three principal measures of central tendency, the mean is by far the most common. It would not be too much of an exaggeration to say that for many people statistics is nearly synonymous with the study of the mean.

As we have already seen, certain disadvantages are associated with the mean: It is influenced by extreme scores, its value may not actually exist in the data, and its interpretation in terms of the underlying variable being measured requires at least some faith in the interval properties of the data. You might be inclined to politely suggest that if the mean has all the disadvantages I have just ascribed to it, then maybe it should be quietly forgotten and allowed to slip into oblivion along with statistics like the "critical ratio," a statistical concept that hasn't been heard of for years. The mean, however, is made of sterner stuff.

The mean has several important advantages that far outweigh its disadvantages. Probably the most important of these from a historical point of view (though not necessarily from your point of view) is that the mean can be manipulated algebraically. In other words, we can use the mean in an equation and manipulate it through the normal rules of algebra, specifically because we can write an equation that defines the mean. Because you cannot write a standard equation for the mode or the median, you have no real way of manipulating those statistics using standard algebra. Whatever the mean's faults, this accounts in large part for its widespread application. The second important advantage of the mean is that it has several desirable properties with respect to its use as an estimate of the population mean. In particular, if we drew many samples from some population, the sample means that resulted would be more stable (less variable) estimates of the central tendency of that population than would the sample medians or modes. The fact that the sample mean is generally a better estimate of the population mean than is the mode or the median is a major reason that it is so widely used.

Trimmed means

Trimmed means

Trimmed means are means calculated on data for which we have discarded a certain percentage of the data at each end of the distribution. For example, if we have a set of 100 observations and want to calculate a 10% trimmed mean, we simply discard the highest 10 scores and the lowest 10 scores and take the mean of what remains. This is an old idea that is coming back into fashion, and perhaps its strongest advocate is Rand Wilcox (Wilcox, 2003, 2005).

There are several reasons for trimming a sample. As I mentioned in Chapter 1, and will come back to repeatedly throughout the book, a major goal of taking the mean of a sample is to estimate the mean of the population from which that sample was taken. If you want a good estimate, you want one that varies little from one sample to another. (To use a term we will define in later chapters, we want an estimate with a small standard error.) If we have a sample with a great deal of dispersion, meaning that it has a lot of high and low scores, our sample mean will not be a very good estimator of the population mean. By trimming extreme values from the sample our estimate of the population mean is a more stable estimate. That is often an advantage, though we want to be sure that we aren't throwing away useful information at the same time.

Another reason for trimming a sample is to control problems in skewness. If you have a very skewed distribution, those extreme values will pull the mean toward themselves and lead to a poorer estimate of the population mean. One reason to trim is to eliminate the influence of those extreme scores. But consider the data from Bradley (1963) on reaction times, shown in Figure 2.10. I agree that the long reaction times are probably the result of the respondent missing the key, and therefore do not relate to strict reaction time, and could legitimately be removed, but do we really want to throw away the same number of observations at the other end of the scale?

Wilcox has done a great deal of work on the problems of trimming, and I certainly respect his well-earned reputation. In addition I think that students need to know about trimmed means because they are being discussed in the current literature. But I don't think that I can go as far as Wilcox in promoting their use. However, I don't think that my reluctance should dissuade people from considering the issue seriously, and I recommend Wilcox's book (Wilcox, 2003).

2.8 Measures of Variability

In the previous section we considered several measures related to the center of a distribution. However, an average value for the distribution (whether it be the mode, the median, or the mean) fails to give the whole story. We need some additional measure (or measures) to indicate the degree to which individual observations are clustered about or, equivalently,

dispersion

deviate from that average value. The average may reflect the general location of most of the scores, or the scores may be distributed over a wide range of values, and the "average" may not be very representative of the full set of observations. Everyone has had experience with examinations on which all students received approximately the same grade and with those on which the scores ranged from excellent to dreadful. Measures referring to the differences between these two situations are what we have in mind when we speak of **dispersion**, or variability, around the median, the mode, or any other point. In general, we will refer specifically to dispersion around the mean.

An example to illustrate variability was recommended by Weaver (1999) and is based on something with which I'm sure you are all familiar—the standard growth chart for infants. Such a chart appears in Figure 2.12, in the bottom half of the chart, where you can see the normal range of girls' weights between birth and 36 months. The bold line labeled "50" through the center represents the mean weight at each age. The two lines on each side represent the limits within which we expect the middle half of the distribution to fall; the next two lines as you go each way from the center enclose the middle 80% and the middle 90% of children, respectively. From this figure it is easy to see the increase in dispersion as children increase in age. The weights of most newborns lie within 1 pound of the mean, whereas the weights of 3-year-olds are spread over about 5 pounds on each side of the mean. Obviously the mean is increasing too, though we are more concerned here with dispersion.

For our second illustration we will take some interesting data collected by Langlois and Roggman (1990) on the perceived attractiveness of faces. Think for a moment about some of the faces you consider attractive. Do they tend to have unusual features (e.g., prominent noses or unique-looking eyebrows), or are the features rather ordinary? Langlois and Roggman were interested in investigating what makes faces attractive. To that end, they presented students with computer-generated pictures of faces. Some of these pictures had been created by averaging together snapshots of four different people to create a composite. We will label these photographs Set 4. Other pictures (Set 32) were created by averaging across snapshots of 32 different people. As you might suspect, when you average across four people, there is still room for individuality in the composite. For example, some composites show thin faces, while others show round ones. However, averaging across 32 people usually gives results that are very "average." Noses are neither too long nor too short; ears don't stick out too far nor sit too close to the head; and so on. Students were asked to examine the resulting pictures and rate each one on a 5-point scale of attractiveness. The authors were primarily interested in determining whether the mean rating of the faces in Set 4 was less than the mean rating of the faces in Set 32. It was, suggesting that faces with distinctive characteristics are judged as less attractive than more ordinary faces. In this section, however, we are more interested in the degree of similarity in the ratings of faces. We suspect that composites of 32 faces would be more homogeneous, and thus would be rated more similarly, than would composites of four faces.

The data are shown in Table 2.6.[8] From the table you can see that Langlois and Roggman correctly predicted that Set 32 faces would be rated as more attractive than Set 4 faces. (The means were 3.26 and 2.64, respectively.) But notice also that the ratings for the composites

[8] These data are not the actual numbers that Langlois and Roggman collected, but they have been generated to have exactly the same mean and standard deviation as the original data. Langlois and Roggman used six composite photographs per set. I have used 20 photographs per set to make the data more applicable to my purposes in this chapter. The conclusions that you would draw from these data, however, are exactly the same as the conclusions you would draw from theirs.

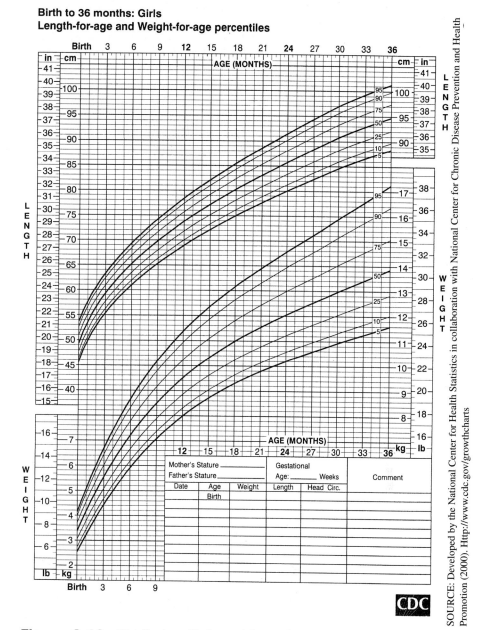

Birth to 36 months: Girls
Length-for-age and Weight-for-age percentiles

SOURCE: Developed by the National Center for Health Statistics in collaboration with National Center for Chronic Disease Prevention and Health Promotion (2000). Http://www.cdc.gov/growthcharts

Figure 2.12   Distribution of infant weight as a function of age

of 32 faces are considerably more homogeneous than the ratings of the composites of four faces. Figure 2.13 plots these sets of data as standard histograms.

Even though it is apparent from Figure 2.12 that there is greater variability in the rating of composites of four photographs than in the rating of composites of 32 photographs, some sort of measure is needed to reflect this difference in variability. A number of measures could be used, and they will be discussed in turn, starting with the simplest.

Table 2.6   Rated attractiveness of composite faces

Set 4		Set 32	
Picture	Composite of 4 faces	Picture	Composite of 32 Faces
1	1.20	21	3.13
2	1.82	22	3.17
3	1.93	23	3.19
4	2.04	24	3.19
5	2.30	25	3.20
6	2.33	26	3.20
7	2.34	27	3.22
8	2.47	28	3.23
9	2.51	29	3.25
10	2.55	30	3.26
11	2.64	31	3.27
12	2.76	32	3.29
13	2.77	33	3.29
14	2.90	34	3.30
15	2.91	35	3.31
16	3.20	36	3.31
17	3.22	37	3.34
18	3.39	38	3.34
19	3.59	39	3.36
20	4.02	40	3.38
Mean = 2.64		Mean = 3.26	

© Cengage Learning 2013

Range

range

The **range** is a measure of distance, namely the distance from the lowest to the highest score. For our data, the range for Set 4 is $(4.02 - 1.20) = 2.82$ units; for Set 32 it is $(3.38 - 3.13) = 0.25$ unit. The range is an exceedingly common measure and is illustrated in everyday life by such statements as "The price of red peppers fluctuates over a $3 range from $.99 to $3.99 per pound." The range suffers, however, from a total reliance on extreme values, or, if the values are unusually extreme, on outliers. As a result, the range may give a distorted picture of the variability.

Interquartile Range and other Range Statistics

interquartile range

first quartile

third quartile

second quartile

The interquartile range represents an attempt to circumvent the problem of the range's heavy dependence on extreme scores. An **interquartile range** is obtained by discarding the upper 25% and the lower 25% of the distribution and taking the range of what remains. The point that cuts off the lowest 25% of the distribution is called the **first quartile** and is usually denoted as $Q1$. Similarly, the point that cuts off the upper 25% of the distribution is called the **third quartile** and is denoted $Q3$. (The median is the **second quartile**, $Q2$.) The difference between the first and third quartiles $(Q3 - Q1)$ is the interquartile range. We can calculate the interquartile range for the data on attractiveness of faces by omitting the lowest five scores and the highest five scores and determining

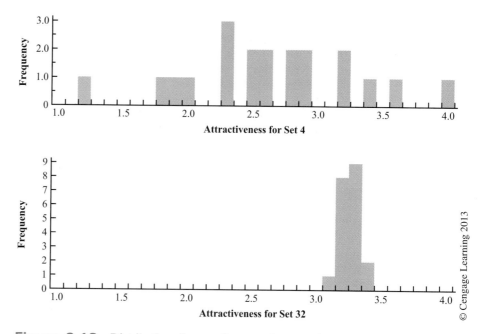

Figure 2.13   Distribution of scores for attractiveness of composite

the range of the remainder. In this case the interquartile range for Set 4 would be 0.58 and the interquartile range for Set 32 would be only 0.11. The interquartile range plays an important role in a useful graphical method known as a boxplot. This method is discussed in Section 2.10.

The interquartile range suffers from problems that are just the opposite of those found with the range. Specifically, the interquartile range discards too much of the data. If we want to know whether one set of photographs is judged more variable than another, it may not make much sense to toss out those scores that are most extreme and thus vary the most from the mean.

There is nothing sacred about eliminating the upper and lower 25% of the distribution before calculating the range. Actually, we could eliminate any percentage we wanted, as long as we could justify that number to ourselves and to others. What we really want to do is eliminate those scores that are likely to be errors or attributable to unusual events without eliminating the variability we seek to study.

In an earlier section we discussed the use of trimmed samples to generate trimmed means. Trimming can be a valuable approach to skewed distributions or distributions with large outliers. But when we use **trimmed samples** to estimate variability, we use a variation based on what is called a **Winsorized** sample. We create a 10% Winsorized sample, for example, by dropping the lowest 10% of the scores and replacing them by copies of the smallest score that remains, then dropping the highest 10% and replacing those by copies of the highest score that remains, and then computing the measure of variation on the modified data.

trimmed samples
Winsorized

The Average Deviation

At first glance it would seem that if we want to measure how scores are dispersed around the mean (i.e., deviate from the mean), the most logical thing to do would be to obtain all the deviations (i.e., $X_i - \overline{X}$) and average them. You might reasonably think that the more widely the scores are dispersed, the greater the deviations and therefore the greater the average of the deviations. However, common sense has led you astray here. If you calculate the deviations from the mean, some scores will be above the mean and have a positive deviation, whereas others will be below the mean and have negative deviations. In the end, the positive and negative deviations will balance each other out and the sum of the deviations will always be zero. This will not get us very far.

The Mean Absolute Deviation

mean absolute deviation (m.a.d)

If you think about the difficulty in trying to get something useful out of the average of the deviations, you might well suggest that we could solve the whole problem by taking the absolute values of the deviations. (The absolute value of a number is the value of that number with any minus signs removed. The absolute value is indicated by vertical bars around the number, e.g., $|-3| = 3$.) The suggestion to use absolute values makes sense because we want to know how much scores deviate from the mean without regard to whether they are above or below it. The measure suggested here is a perfectly legitimate one and even has a name: the mean absolute deviation (m.a.d.). The sum of the absolute deviations is divided by N (the number of scores) to yield an average (mean) deviation: m.a.d. For all its simplicity and intuitive appeal, the mean absolute deviation has not played an important role in statistical methods. Much more useful measures—the variance and the standard deviation—are normally used instead.

The Variance

standard deviation

sample variance (s^2)

population variance

The measures that we have discussed so far have much greater appeal to statisticians than to psychologists and their like. They are things that you need to know about, but the variance, and the standard deviation to follow, will take up most of our attention. The measure we will consider in this section, the sample variance (s^2), represents a different approach to the problem of the deviations themselves averaging to zero. (When we are referring to the population variance, rather than the sample variance, we use σ^2 [lowercase sigma squared] as the symbol.) In the case of the variance we take advantage of the fact that the square of a negative number is positive. Thus, we sum the squared deviations rather than the absolute deviations. Because we want an average, we next divide that sum by some function of N, the number of scores. Although you might reasonably expect that we would divide by N, we actually divide by $(N - 1)$. We use $(N - 1)$ as a divisor for the sample variance because, as we will see shortly, it leaves us with a sample variance that is a better estimate of the corresponding population variance. (The population variance is calculated by dividing the sum of the squared deviations, for each value in the population, by N rather than $[N - 1]$. However, we only rarely calculate a population variance; we almost always estimate it from a sample variance.)

If it is important to specify more precisely the variable to which s^2 refers, we can subscript it with a letter representing the variable. Thus, if we denote the data in Set 4 as X, the variance could be denoted as s_X^2. You could refer to $s_{Set\,4}^2$, but long subscripts are usually awkward. In general, we label variables with simple letters like X and Y.

For our example, we can calculate the sample variances of Set 4 and Set 32 as follows:[9]

Set 4 (X)

$$s_X^2 = \frac{\sum (X - \bar{X})^2}{N - 1}$$

$$= \frac{(1.20 - 2.64)^2 + (1.82 - 2.64)^2 + \cdots + (4.02 - 2.64)^2}{20 - 1}$$

$$= \frac{8.1569}{19} = 0.4293$$

Set 32 (Y)

$$s_Y^2 = \frac{\sum (Y - \bar{Y})^2}{N - 1}$$

$$= \frac{(3.13 - 3.26)^2 + (3.17 - 3.26)^2 + \cdots + (3.38 - 3.26)^2}{20 - 1}$$

$$= \frac{0.0903}{19} = 0.0048$$

From these calculations we see that the difference in variances reflects the differences we see in the distributions.

Although the variance is an exceptionally important concept and one of the most commonly used statistics, it does not have the direct intuitive interpretation we would like. Because it is based on squared deviations, the result is in squared units. Thus, Set 4 has a mean attractiveness rating of 2.64 and a variance of 0.4293 squared unit. But squared units are awkward things to talk about and have little meaning with respect to the data. Fortunately, the solution to this problem is simple: Take the square root of the variance.

The Standard Deviation

The standard deviation (s or σ) is defined as the positive square root of the variance and, for a sample, is symbolized as s (with a subscript identifying the variable if necessary) or, occasionally, as SD.[10] (The notation σ is used in reference to a population standard deviation.) The following formula defines the sample standard deviation:

$$s_X = \sqrt{\frac{\sum (X - \bar{X})^2}{N - 1}}$$

For our example,

$$s_X = \sqrt{s_X^2} = \sqrt{0.4293} = 0.6552$$

$$s_Y = \sqrt{s_Y^2} = \sqrt{0.0048} = 0.0689$$

---

[9] In these calculations and others throughout the book, my answers may differ slightly from those that you obtain for the same data. If so, the difference is most likely caused by rounding. If you repeat my calculations and arrive at a *similar, though different,* answer, that is sufficient.

[10] The American Psychological Association prefers to abbreviate the standard deviation as "SD," but everyone else uses "*s.*"

For convenience, I will round these answers to 0.66 and 0.07, respectively.

If you look at the formula for the standard deviation, you will see that, like the mean absolute deviation, it is basically a measure of the average of the deviations of each score from the mean. Granted, these deviations have been squared, summed, and so on, but at heart they are still deviations. And even though we have divided by $(N - 1)$ instead of N, we still have obtained something very much like a mean or an "average" of these deviations. Thus, we can say without too much distortion that attractiveness ratings for Set 4 deviated, on the average, 0.66 unit from the mean, whereas attractiveness ratings for Set 32 deviated, on the average, only 0.07 unit from the mean. This way of thinking about the standard deviation as a sort of average deviation goes a long way toward giving it meaning without doing serious injustice to the concept.

These results tell us two interesting things about attractiveness. If you were a subject in this experiment, the fact that computer averaging of many faces produces similar composites would be reflected in the fact that your ratings of Set 32 would not show much variability—all those images are judged to be essentially alike. Second, the fact that those ratings have a higher mean than the ratings of faces in Set 4 reveals that averaging over many faces produces composites that seem more attractive. Does this conform to your everyday experience? I, for one, would have expected that faces judged attractive would be those with distinctive features, but I would have been wrong. Go back and think again about those faces you class as attractive. Are they really distinctive? If so, do you have an additional hypothesis to explain the findings?

We can also look at the standard deviation in terms of how many scores fall no more than a standard deviation above or below the mean. For a wide variety of reasonably symmetric and mound-shaped distributions, we can say that approximately two-thirds of the observations lie within one standard deviation of the mean (for a normal distribution, which will be discussed in Chapter 3, it is almost exactly two-thirds). Although there certainly are exceptions, especially for badly skewed distributions, this rule is still useful. If I told you that for elementary school teachers the average salary is expected to be $39,259 with a standard deviation of $4,000, you probably would not be far off to conclude that about two-thirds of the people in these jobs will earn between $35,000 and $43,000. In addition, most (e.g., 95%) fall within two standard deviations of the mean. (But if you are really interested in salaries, the median would probably be a better measure than the mean.)

Computational Formulae for the Variance and the Standard Deviation

The previous expressions for the variance and the standard deviation, although perfectly correct, are incredibly unwieldy for any reasonable amount of data. They are also prone to rounding errors, because they usually involve squaring fractional deviations. They are excellent definitional formulae, but we will now consider a more practical set of calculational formulae. These formulae are algebraically equivalent to the ones we have seen, so they will give the same answers but with much less effort.

The definitional formula for the sample variance was given as

$$s_X^2 = \frac{\Sigma(X - \overline{X})^2}{N - 1}$$

A more practical computational formula is

$$s_X^2 = \frac{\Sigma X^2 - \dfrac{(\Sigma X)^2}{N}}{N - 1}$$

Similarly, for the sample standard deviation

$$s_X = \sqrt{\frac{\Sigma(X - \overline{X})^2}{N - 1}}$$

$$= \sqrt{\frac{\Sigma X^2 - \dfrac{(\Sigma X)^2}{N}}{N - 1}}$$

Recently, people whose opinions I respect have suggested that I should remove such formulae as these from the book because people rarely calculate variances by hand anymore. Although that is true, and I have only waved my hands at most formulae in my own courses, many people still believe it is important to be able to do the calculation. More important, perhaps, is the fact that we will see these formulae again in different disguises, and it helps to understand what is going on if you recognize them for what they are. However, I agree with those critics in the case of more complex formulae, and in those cases I have restructured recent editions of the text around definitional formulae.

Applying the computational formula for the sample variance for Set 4, we obtain

$$s_X^2 = \frac{\Sigma X^2 - \dfrac{(\Sigma X)^2}{N}}{N - 1}$$

$$= \frac{1.20^2 + 1.82^2 + \cdots + 4.02^2 - \dfrac{52.89^2}{20}}{19}$$

$$= \frac{148.0241 - \dfrac{52.89^2}{20}}{19} = 0.4293$$

Note that the answer we obtained here is exactly the same as the answer we obtained by the definitional formula. Note also, as pointed out earlier, that $\Sigma X^2 = 148.0241$ is quite different from $(\Sigma X)^2 = 52.89^2 = 279.35$ I leave the calculation of the variance for Set 32 to you.

You might be somewhat reassured to learn that the level of mathematics required for the previous calculations is about as much as you will need anywhere in this book—not because I am watering down the material, but because an understanding of most applied statistics does not require much in the way of advanced mathematics. (I told you that you learned it all in high school.)

The Influence of Extreme Values on the Variance and Standard Deviation

The variance and standard deviation are very sensitive to extreme scores. To put this differently, extreme scores play a disproportionate role in determining the variance. Consider a set of data that range from roughly 0 to 10, with a mean of 5. From the definitional formula for the variance, you will see that a score of 5 (the mean) contributes nothing to the variance, because the deviation score is 0. A score of 6 contributes $1/(N - 1)$ to s^2, because $(X - \overline{X})^2 = (6 - 5)^2 = 1$. A score of 10, however, contributes

25/(N − 1) units to s^2, because $(10 − 5)2 = 25$. Thus, although 6 and 10 deviate from the mean by 1 and 5 units, respectively, their relative contributions to the variance are 1 and 25. This is what we mean when we say that large deviations are disproportionately represented. You might keep this in mind the next time you use a measuring instrument that is "OK because it is unreliable only at the extremes." It is just those extremes that may have the greatest effect on the interpretation of the data. This is one of the major reasons why we do not particularly like to have skewed data.

The Coefficient of Variation

One of the most common things we do in statistics is to compare the means of two or more groups, or even two or more variables. Comparing the variability of those groups or variables, however, is also a legitimate and worthwhile activity. Suppose, for example, that we have two competing tests for assessing long-term memory.

One of the tests typically produces data with a mean of 15 and a standard deviation of 3.5. The second, quite different, test produces data with a mean of 75 and a standard deviation of 10.5. All other things being equal, which test is better for assessing long-term memory? We might be inclined to argue that the second test is better, in that we want a measure on which there is enough variability that we are able to study differences among people, and the second test has the larger standard deviation. However, keep in mind that the two tests also differ substantially in their means, and this difference must be considered.

If you think for a moment about the fact that the standard deviation is based on deviations from the mean, it seems logical that a value could more easily deviate substantially from a large mean than from a small one. For example, if you rate teaching effectiveness on a 7-point scale with a mean of 3, it would be impossible to have a deviation greater than 4. On the other hand, on a 70-point scale with a mean of 30, deviations of 10 or 20 would be common. Somehow we need to account for the greater opportunity for large deviations in the second case when we compare the variability of our two measures. In other words, when we look at the standard deviation, we must keep in mind the magnitude of the mean as well.

The simplest way to compare standard deviations on measures that have quite different means is simply to scale the standard deviation by the magnitude of the mean. That is what **coefficient of variation (CV)** we do with the **coefficient of variation (CV)**.[11] We will define that coefficient as simply the standard deviation divided by the mean:

$$\text{CV} = \frac{\text{Standard deviation}}{\text{Mean}} = \frac{s_X}{\overline{X}} \times 100$$

(We multiply by 100 to express the result as a percentage.) To return to our memory-task example, for the first measure, CV = (3.5/15) × 100 = 23.3. Here the standard deviation is approximately 23% of the mean. For the second measure, CV = (10.5/75) × 100 = 14. In this case the coefficient of variation for the second measure is about half as large as for the first. If I could be convinced that the larger coefficient of variation in the first measure was not attributable simply to sloppy measurement, I would be inclined to choose the first measure over the second.

To take a second example, Katz, Lautenschlager, Blackburn, and Harris (1990) asked students to answer a set of multiple-choice questions from the Scholastic Aptitude Test[12]

---

[11] I want to thank Andrew Gilpin (personal communication, 1990) for reminding me of the usefulness of the coefficient of variation. It is a meaningful statistic that is often overlooked.

[12] The test is now known simply as the SAT, or, more recently, the SAT-I.

(SAT). One group read the relevant passage and answered the questions. Another group answered the questions without having read the passage on which they were based—sort of like taking a multiple-choice test on Mongolian history without having taken the course. The data follow:

	Read Passage	Did Not Read Passage
Mean	69.6	46.6
SD	10.6	6.8
CV	15.2	14.6

The ratio of the two standard deviations is 10.6/6.8 = 1.56, meaning that the Read group had a standard deviation that was more than 50% larger than that of the Did Not Read group. On the other hand, the coefficients of variation are virtually the same for the two groups, suggesting that any difference in variability between the groups can be explained by the higher scores in the first group. (Incidentally, chance performance would have produced a mean of 20 with a standard deviation of 4. Even without reading the passage, students score well above chance levels just by intelligent guessing.)

In using the coefficient of variation, it is important to keep in mind the nature of the variable you are measuring. If its scale is arbitrary, you might not want to put too much faith in the coefficient. But perhaps you don't want to put too much faith in the variance either. This is a place where a little common sense is particularly useful.

Unbiased Estimators

I pointed out in Chapter 1 that we generally calculate measures such as the mean and variance to use as estimates of the corresponding values in the populations. Characteristics of samples are called statistics and are designated by Roman letters (e.g., $\overline{X}$). Characteristics of populations are called parameters and are designated by Greek letters. Thus, the population mean is symbolized by μ (mu). In general, then, we use statistics as estimates of parameters.

If the purpose of obtaining a statistic is to use it as an estimator of a parameter, then it should come as no surprise that our choice of a statistic (and even how we define it) is based partly on how well that statistic functions as an estimator of the parameter in question. Actually, the mean is usually preferred over other measures of central tendency because of its performance as an estimator of μ. The sample variance (s^2) is defined as it is, with ($N - 1$) in the denominator, specifically because of the advantages that accrue when s^2 is used to estimate the population variance (σ^2).

Statisticians define several different properties of estimators (sufficiency, efficiency, resistance, and bias). The first three are not particularly important to us in this book, so I will skip them. But the distinction between biased and **unbiased estimators** is important, and we generally (though not always) look for unbiased estimators.

unbiased estimators

Suppose we have a population for which we somehow know the mean (μ); for instance, the heights of all basketball players in the NBA. If we were to draw one sample from that population and calculate the sample mean ($\overline{X}_1$), we would expect $\overline{X}_1$ to be reasonably close to μ, particularly if N is large, because it is an estimator of μ. So if the average height in this population is 7.0' ($\mu = 7.0'$), we would expect a sample of, say, 10 players to have an average height of approximately 7.0 as well, although it probably would not be exactly equal to 7.0'. (We can write $\overline{X} \approx 7$, where the symbol $\approx$ means "approximately equal.") Now suppose we draw another sample and obtain its mean ($\overline{X}_2$). (The subscript is used to differentiate the means of successive samples. Thus, the mean of the 43rd sample, if we drew that many, would be denoted by $\overline{X}_{43}$.) This mean would probably also be reasonably close to μ, but again

expected value

we would not expect it to be exactly equal to μ or to $\overline{X}_1$. If we were to keep up this procedure and draw sample means ad infinitum, we would find that the average of the sample means would be precisely equal to μ. Thus, we say that the expected value (i.e., the long-range average of many, many samples) of the sample mean is equal to μ, the population mean that it is estimating. An estimator whose expected value equals the parameter to be estimated is called an unbiased estimator and that is a very important property for a statistic to possess. Both the sample mean and the sample variance are unbiased estimators of their corresponding parameters. (We use $N - 1$ as the denominator of the formula for the sample variance precisely because we want to generate an unbiased estimate.) By and large, unbiased estimators are like unbiased people—they are nicer to work with than biased ones.

The Sample Variance as an Estimator of The Population Variance

The sample variance offers an excellent example of what was said in the discussion of unbiasedness. You may recall that I earlier sneaked in the divisor of $N - 1$ instead of N for the calculation of the variance and standard deviation. Now is the time to explain why. (You may be perfectly willing to take the statement that we divide by $N - 1$ on faith, but I get a lot of questions about it, so I guess you will just have to read the explanation—or skip it.)

There are a number of ways to explain why sample variances require $N - 1$ as the denominator. Perhaps the simplest is phrased in terms of what has been said about the sample variance (s^2) as an unbiased estimate of the population variance (σ^2). Assume for the moment that we have an infinite number of samples (each containing N observations) from one population and that we know the population variance. Suppose further that we are foolish enough to calculate sample variances as

$$\frac{\Sigma(X - \overline{X})^2}{N}$$

(Note the denominator.) If we take the average of these sample variances, we find

$$\text{Average } \frac{\Sigma(X - \overline{X})^2}{N} = \mathrm{E}\left[\frac{\Sigma(X - \overline{X})^2}{N}\right] = \frac{(N - 1)\sigma^2}{N}$$

where E[ ] is read as "the expected value of (whatever is in brackets)." Thus the average value of $\Sigma(X - \overline{X})^2/N$ is not σ^2. It is a biased estimator.

degrees of freedom (*df*)

The foregoing discussion is very much like saying that we divide by $N - 1$ because it works. But why does it work? To explain this, we must first consider degrees of freedom (*df*). Assume that you have in front of you the three numbers 6, 8, and 10. Their mean is 8. You are now informed that you may change any of these numbers, as long as the mean is kept constant at 8. How many numbers are you free to vary? If you change all three of them in some haphazard fashion, the mean almost certainly will no longer equal 8. Only two of the numbers can be freely changed if the mean is to remain constant. For example, if you change the 6 to a 7 and the 10 to a 13, the remaining number is determined; it must be 4 if the mean is to be 8. If you had 50 numbers and were given the same instructions, you would be free to vary only 49 of them; the 50th would be determined.

Now let us go back to the formulae for the population and sample variances and see why we lost one degree of freedom in calculating the sample variances.

$$\sigma^2 = \frac{\Sigma(X - \mu)^2}{N} \qquad s^2 = \frac{\Sigma(X - \overline{X})^2}{N - 1}$$

In the case of σ^2, μ is known and does not have to be estimated from the data. Thus, no *df* are lost and the denominator is *N*. In the case of s^2, however, μ is not known and must be estimated from the sample mean ($\overline{X}$). Once you have estimated μ from $\overline{X}$, you have fixed it for purposes of estimating variability. Thus, you lose that degree of freedom that we discussed, and you have only $N - 1$ *df* left ($N - 1$ scores free to vary). We lose this one degree of freedom whenever we estimate a mean. It follows that the denominator (the number of scores on which our estimate is based) should reflect this restriction. It represents the number of independent pieces of data.

2.9 Boxplots: Graphical Representations of Dispersions and Extreme Scores

boxplot

box-and-whisker plot

Earlier you saw how stem-and-leaf displays represent data in several meaningful ways at the same time. Such displays combine data into something very much like a histogram, while retaining the individual values of the observations. In addition to the stem-and-leaf display, John Tukey has developed other ways of looking at data, one of which gives greater prominence to the dispersion of the data. This method is known as a **boxplot**, or, sometimes, **box-and-whisker plot**.

The data and the accompanying stem-and-leaf display in Table 2.7 were taken from normal- and low-birthweight infants participating in a study of infant development at the University of Vermont and represent preliminary data on the length of hospitalization of 38 normal-birthweight infants. Data on three infants are missing for this particular variable and are represented by an asterisk (*). (Asterisks are included to emphasize that we should not just ignore missing data.) Because the data vary from 1 to 10, with two exceptions, all the leaves are zero. The zeros really just fill in space to produce a histogram-like distribution. Examination of the data as plotted in the stem-and-leaf display reveals that the distribution is positively skewed with a median stay of 3 days. Near the bottom of the stem you will see the entry HI and the values 20 and 33. These are extreme values, or outliers, and are set off in this way to highlight their existence. Whether they are large enough to make us suspicious is one of the questions a boxplot is designed to address. The last line of the stem-and-leaf display indicates the number of missing observations.

Tukey originally defined boxplots in terms of special measures that he devised. Most people now draw boxplots using more traditional measures, and I am adopting that approach in this edition.

We earlier defined the median location of a set of *N* scores as $(N + 1)/2$. When the median location is a whole number, as it will be when *N* is odd, then the median is simply the value that occupies that location in an ordered arrangement of data. When the median location is a fractional number (i.e., when *N* is even), the median is the average of the two values on each side of that location. For the data in Table 2.6 the median location is $(38 + 1)/2 = 19.5$, and the median is 3. To construct a boxplot, we are also going to take the first and third quartiles, defined earlier. The easiest way to do this is to define the **quartile location**, which is defined as

quartile location

$$\text{Quartile location} = \frac{\text{Median location} + 1}{2}$$

If the median location is a fractional value, the fraction should be dropped from the numerator when you compute the quartile location. The quartile location is to the quartiles

Table 2.7 Data and stem-and-leaf display on length of hospitalization for full-term newborn infants (in days)

Data			Stem-and-Leaf	
2	1	7	1	000
1	33	2	2	000000000
2	3	4	3	00000000000
3	*	4	4	0000000
3	3	10	5	00
9	2	5	6	0
4	3	3	7	0
20	6	2	8	
4	5	2	9	0
1	*	*	10	0
3	3	4	HI	20, 33
2	3	4	Missing = 3	
3	2	3		
2	4			

© Cengage Learning 2013

inner fences

adjacent values

what the median location is to the median. It tells us where, in an ordered series, the quartile values[13] are to be found. For the data on hospital stay, the quartile location is $(19 + 1)/2 = 10$. Thus, the quartiles are going to be the tenth scores from the bottom and from the top. These values are 2 and 4, respectively. For data sets without tied scores, or for large samples, the quartiles will bracket the middle 50% of the scores.

To complete the concepts required for understanding boxplots, we need to consider three more terms: the interquartile range, **inner fences**, and **adjacent values**. As we saw earlier, the interquartile range is simply the range between the first and third quartiles. For our data, the interquartile range $4 - 2 = 2$. An inner fence is defined by Tukey as a point that falls 1.5 times the interquartile range below or above the appropriate quartile. Because the interquartile range is 2 for our data, the inner fence is $2 \times 1.5 = 3$ points farther out than the quartiles. Because our quartiles are the values 2 and 4, the inner fences will be at $2 - 3 = -1$ and $4 + 3 = 7$. Adjacent values are those actual values in the data that are no more extreme (no farther from the median) than the inner fences. Because the smallest value we have is 1, that is the closest value to the lower inner fence and is the lower adjacent value. The upper inner fence is 7, and because we have a 7 in our data, that will be the higher adjacent value. The calculations for all the terms we have just defined are shown in Table 2.8.

Inner fences and adjacent values can cause some confusion. Think of a herd of cows scattered around a field. (I spent most of my life in Vermont, so cows seem like a natural example.) The fence around the field represents the inner fence of the boxplot. The cows closest to but still inside the fence are the adjacent values. Don't worry about the cows that have escaped outside the fence and are wandering around on the road. They are not involved in the calculations at this point. (They will be the outliers.)

Now we are ready to draw the boxplot. First, we draw and label a scale that covers the whole range of the obtained values. This has been done at the bottom of Table 2.7. We then draw a rectangular box from Q_1 to Q_3, with a vertical line representing the

---

[13] Tukey referred to the quartiles in this situation as "hinges," but little is lost by thinking of them as the quartiles.

Table 2.8   Calculation and boxplots for data from Table 2.7

Median location $= (N + 1)/2 = (38 + 1)/2 = 19.5$
Median $= 3$
Quartile location $= $ (median location† $+ 1)/2 = (19 + 1)/2 = 10$
$Q_1 = $ 10th lowest score $= 2$
$Q_3 = $ 10th highest score $= 4$
Interquartile range $= 4 - 2 = 2$
Interquartile range $* 1.5 = 2*1.5 = 3$
Lower inner fence $= Q_1 - 1.5$(interquartile range) $= 2 - 3 = -1$
Upper inner fence $= Q_3 + 1.5$(interquartile range) $= 4 + 3 = 7$
Lower adjacent value $= $ smallest value $\geq$ lower fence $= 1$
Upper adjacent value $= $ largest value $\leq$ upper fence $= 7$

0	5	10	15	20	25	30	35

†Drop any fractional values.

© Cengage Learning 2013

whiskers

location of the median. Next we draw lines (**whiskers**) from the quartiles out to the adjacent values. Finally, we plot the locations of all points that are more extreme than the adjacent values.

From Table 2.8 we can see several important things. First, the central portion of the distribution is reasonably symmetric. This is indicated by the fact that the median lies in the center of the box and was apparent from the stem-and-leaf display. We can also see that the distribution is positively skewed, because the whisker on the right is substantially longer than the one on the left. This also was apparent from the stem-and-leaf display, although not so clearly. Finally, we see that we have four outliers; an outlier is defined here as any value more extreme than the whiskers (and therefore more extreme than the adjacent values). The stem-and-leaf display did not show the position of the outliers nearly as graphically as does the boxplot.

Outliers deserve special attention. An outlier could represent an error in measurement, in data recording, or in data entry, or it could represent a legitimate value that just happens to be extreme. For example, our data represent length of hospitalization, and a full-term infant might have been born with a physical defect that required extended hospitalization. Because these are actual data, it was possible to go back to hospital records and look more closely at the four extreme cases. On examination, it turned out that the two most extreme scores were attributable to errors in data entry and were readily correctable. The other two extreme scores were caused by physical problems of the infants. Here a decision was required by the project director as to whether the problems were sufficiently severe to cause the infants to be dropped from the study (both were retained as subjects). The two corrected values were 3 and 5 instead of 33 and 20, respectively, and a new boxplot for the corrected data is shown in Figure 2.14. This boxplot is identical to the one shown in Table 2.8 except for the spacing and the two largest values. (You should verify for yourself that the corrected data set would indeed yield this boxplot.)

Boxplots are extremely useful tools for examining data with respect to dispersion. I find them particularly useful for screening data for errors and for highlighting potential problems before subsequent analyses are carried out. Boxplots are presented often in the remainder of this book as visual guides to the data.

Figure 2.14 Boxplot for corrected data from Table 2.7
© Cengage Learning 2013

A word of warning: Different statistical computer programs may vary in the ways they define the various elements in boxplots. (See Frigge, Hoaglin, and Iglewicz [1989] for an extensive discussion of this issue.) You may find two different programs that produce slightly different boxplots for the same set of data. They may even identify different outliers. However, boxplots are normally used as informal heuristic devices, and subtle differences in definition are rarely, if ever, a problem. I mention the potential discrepancies here simply to explain why analyses that you do on the data in this book may come up with slightly different results if you use different computer programs. (Simple coding to create boxplots in R can be found on the Web site as Boxplots.R.)

The real usefulness of boxplots comes when we want to compare several groups. We will use the example with which we started this chapter, where we have recorded the reaction times of response to the question of whether a specific digit was presented in a previous slide, as a function of the number of stimuli on that slide. The boxplot in Figure 2.15, produced by SPSS, shows the reaction times for those cases in which the stimulus was actually present, broken down by the number of stimuli in the original. The outliers are indicated by their identification number, which here is the same as the number of the trial on which the stimulus was presented. The most obvious conclusion from this figure is that as the number of stimuli in the original increases, reaction times also increase, as does the dispersion. We can also see that the distributions are reasonably symmetric (the boxes are roughly centered on the medians, and there are a few outliers, all of which are long reaction times).

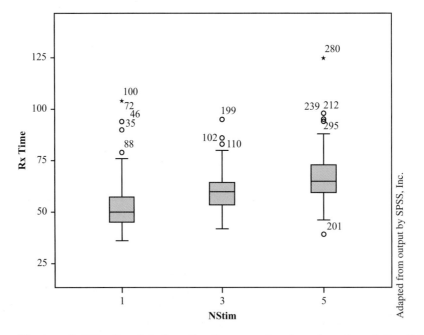

Figure 2.15 Boxplot of reaction times as a function of number of stimuli in the original set of stimuli

Report: RxTime

NStim	N	Mean	Median	Std. Deviation	Variance
1	100	53.27	50.00	13.356	178.381
3	100	60.65	60.00	9.408	88.153
5	100	66.86	65.00	12.282	150.849
Total	300	60.26	59.50	13.011	169.277

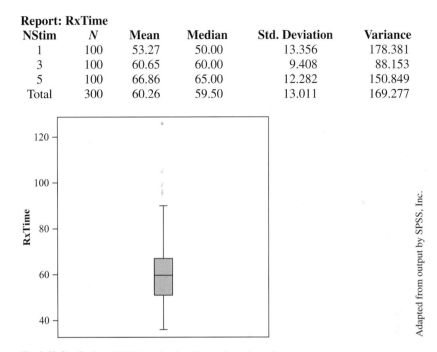

Adapted from output by SPSS, Inc.

Exhibit 2.1   SPSS analysis of reaction-time data

2.10   Obtaining Measures of Dispersion Using SPSS

We can also use SPSS to calculate measures of central tendency and dispersion, as shown in Exhibit 2.1, which is based on our data from the reaction-time experiment. I used the Analyze/Compare Means/Means menu command because I wanted to obtain the descriptive statistics separately for each level of NStim (the number of stimuli presented). Notice that you also have these statistics across the three groups. The command Graphs/Interactive/Boxplot produced the boxplot shown below. Because you have already seen the boxplot broken down by NStim in Figure 2.13, I only present the combined data here. Note how well the extreme values stand out.

2.11   Percentiles, Quartiles, and Deciles

A distribution has many properties besides its location and dispersion. We saw one of these briefly when we considered boxplots, where we used quartiles, which are the values that divide the distribution into fourths. Thus, the first quartile cuts off the lowest 25%, the second quartile cuts off the lowest 50%, and the third quartile cuts off the lowest 75%. (Note that the second quartile is also the median.) These quartiles were shown clearly on the growth chart in Figure 2.10. If we want to examine finer gradations of the distribution, we can look at **deciles**, which divide the distribution into tenths, with the first decile cutting off the lowest 10%, the second decile cutting off the lowest 20%, and so on. Finally, most of you have had experience with **percentiles**, which are values that divide the distribution into hundredths. Thus, the 81st percentile is that point on the distribution below which 81% of the scores lie.

deciles

percentiles

quantiles
fractiles

Quartiles, deciles, and percentiles are the three most common examples of a general class of statistics known by the generic name of quantiles, or, sometimes, fractiles. We will not have much more to say about quantiles in this book, but they are usually covered extensively in more introductory texts (e.g., Howell, 2008a). They also play an important role in many of the techniques of exploratory data analysis advocated by Tukey.

2.12   The Effect of Linear Transformations on Data

linear
transformations

Frequently, we want to transform data in some way. For instance, we may want to convert feet into inches, inches into centimeters, degrees Fahrenheit into degrees Celsius, test grades based on 79 questions to grades based on a 100-point scale, four- to five-digit incomes into one- to two-digit incomes, and so on. Fortunately, all of these transformations fall within a set called linear transformations, in which we multiply each X by some constant (possibly 1) and add a constant (possibly 0): $X_{new} = bX_{old} + a$ where a and b are our constants. (Transformations that use exponents, logarithms, trigonometric functions, etc., are classed as nonlinear transformations.) An example of a linear transformation is the formula for converting degrees Celsius to degrees Fahrenheit:

$$F = 9/5(C) + 32$$

As long as we content ourselves with linear transformations, a set of simple rules defines the mean and variance of the observations on the new scale in terms of their means and variances on the old one:

1. Adding (or subtracting) a constant to (or from) a set of data adds (or subtracts) that same constant to (or from) the mean:

   For $X_{new} = X_{old} \pm a$: $\overline{X}_{new} = \overline{X}_{old} \pm a$.

2. Multiplying (or dividing) a set of data by a constant multiplies (or divides) the mean by the same constant:

   For $X_{new} = bX_{old}$: $\overline{X}_{new} = b\overline{X}_{old}$.

   For $X_{new} = X_{old}/b$: $\overline{X}_{new} = \overline{X}_{old}/b$.

3. Adding or subtracting a constant to (or from) a set of scores leaves the variance and standard deviation unchanged:

   For $X_{new} = X_{old} \pm a$: $s^2_{new} = s^2_{old}$.

4. Multiplying (or dividing) a set of scores by a constant multiplies (or divides) the variance by the square of the constant and the standard deviation by the constant:

   For $X_{new} = bX_{old}$: $s^2_{new} = b^2 s^2_{old}$ and $s_{new} = bs_{old}$.
   For $X_{new} = X_{old}/b$: $s^2_{new} = s^2_{old}/b^2$ and $s_{new} = s_{old}/b$.

The following example illustrates these rules. In each case, the constant used is 3.

Addition of a constant:

Old Data	$\overline{X}$	s^2	s	New Data	$\overline{X}$	s^2	s
4, 8, 12	8	16	4	7, 11, 15	11	16	4

Multiplication by a constant:

Old				New			
Data	$\overline{X}$	s^2	s	Data	$\overline{X}$	s^2	s
4, 8, 12	8	16	4	12, 24, 36	24	144	12

Centering

centering

It is becoming more and more common to see the word **centering** used in conjunction with data. The basic idea is very simple. You subtract the sample mean from all of the observations. This means that the new mean will be 0.00, but the standard deviation and variance will remain unaffected. We will see several examples of this, but I'll sneak a quick one in here. Suppose that we wrote an equation to predict sexual attractiveness from height. That equation would have what is called an intercept, which is the predicted attractiveness when height equals 0. But of course no one is 0 inches tall, so that is somewhat of a meaningless statistic. But if we centered heights by subtracting the mean height from our height data, the intercept, which is the value of attractiveness when height equals 0, would now represent the predicted attractiveness for someone whose height was at the mean, and that is a much more informative statistic. Centering is used in a number of situations, but this example comes close to illustrating the general goal.

Reflection as a Transformation

A very common and useful transformation concerns reversing the order of a scale. For example, assume that we asked subjects to indicate on a 5-point scale the degree to which they agree or disagree with each of several items. To prevent the subjects from simply checking the same point on the scale all the way down the page without thinking, we phrase half of our questions in the positive direction and half in the negative direction. Thus, given a 5-point scale where 5 represents "strongly agree" and 1 represents "strongly disagree," a 4 on "I hate movies" would be comparable to a 2 on "I love plays." If we want the scores to be comparable, we need to rescore the negative items (for example), converting a 5 to a 1, a **reflection** 4 to a 2, and so on. This procedure is called **reflection** and is quite simply accomplished by a linear transformation. We merely write $X_{new} = 6 - X_{old}$ The constant (6) is just the largest value on the scale plus 1. It should be evident that when we reflect a scale, we also reflect its mean but have no effect on its variance or standard deviation. This is true by Rule 3 in the preceding list.

Standardization

deviation scores

One common linear transformation often employed to rescale data involves subtracting the mean from each observation. Such transformed observations are called **deviation scores**, and the transformation itself includes centering because we are centering the mean at 0. Centering is most often used in regression, which is discussed later in the book. An even more common transformation involves creating deviation scores and then dividing the **standard scores** deviation scores by the standard deviation. Such scores are called **standard scores**, and **standardization** the process is referred to as **standardization**. Basically, standardized scores are simply transformed observations that are measured in standard deviation units. Thus, for example, a standardized score of 0.75 is a score that is 0.75 standard deviation above the mean; a standardized score of -0.43 is a score that is 0.43 standard deviation below the mean. I will

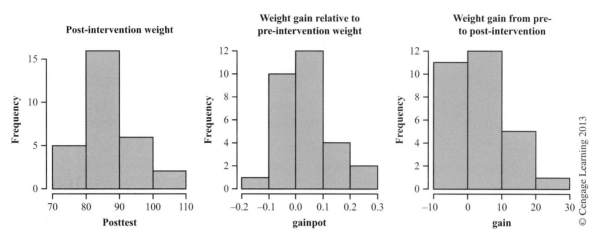

Figure 2.16 Alternative measures of the effect of a cognitive-behavior intervention on weight in anorexic girls

have much more to say about standardized scores when we consider the normal distribution in Chapter 3. I mention them here specifically to show that we can compute standardized scores regardless of whether or not we have a normal distribution (defined in Chapter 3). People often think of standardized scores as being normally distributed, but there is absolutely no requirement that they be. Standardization is a simple linear transformation of the raw data, and, as such, it does not alter the shape of the distribution.

Nonlinear Transformations

nonlinear transformations

Whereas linear transformations are usually used to convert the data to a more meaningful format—such as expressing them on a scale from 0 to 100, putting them in standardized form, and so on, **nonlinear transformations** are usually invoked to change the shape of a distribution. As we saw, linear transformations do not change the underlying shape of a distribution. Nonlinear transformations, on the other hand, can make a skewed distribution look more symmetric, or vice versa, and can reduce the effects of outliers.

Some nonlinear transformations are so common that we don't normally think of them as transformations. Everitt (in Hand, 1994) reported pre- and post-treatment weights for 29 girls receiving cognitive-behavior therapy for anorexia. One logical measure would be the person's weight after the intervention (Y). Another would be the weight gain from pre- to post-intervention, as measured by ($Y - X$). A third alternative would be to record the weight gain as a function of the original score. This would be ($Y - X$)/X. We might use this measure because we assume that how much a person's score increases is related to how underweight she was to begin with. Figure 2.16 portrays the histograms for these three measures based on the same data.

From Figure 2.16 you can see that the three alternative measures, the second two of which are nonlinear transformations of X and Y, appear to have quite different distributions. In this case the use of gain scores as a percentage of pretest weight seems to be more nearly normally distributed than the others. Later in this book you will see how to use other nonlinear transformations (e.g., square root or logarithmic transformations) to make the shape of the distribution more symmetrical. For example, in several places we will use Stress and a predictor of psychological Symptoms. But Symptoms are not very nicely distributed, so we will take the $\log_e$ of Symptoms and use LnSymptoms as our variable.

Key Terms

Frequency distribution (2.1)

Histogram (2.2)

Real lower limit (2.2)

Real upper limit (2.2)

Midpoints (2.2)

Outlier (2.2)

Kernel density plot (2.3)

Stem-and-leaf display (2.4)

Exploratory data analysis (EDA) (2.4)

Leading digits (2.4)

Most significant digits (2.4)

Stem (2.4)

Trailing digits (2.4)

Less significant digits (2.4)

Leaves (2.4)

Symmetric (2.5)

Bimodal (2.5)

Unimodal (2.5)

Modality (2.5)

Negatively skewed (2.5)

Positively skewed (2.5)

Skewness (2.5)

Kurtosis (2.5)

Mesokurtic (2.5)

Platykurtic (2.5)

Leptokurtic (2.5)

Sigma (Σ) (2.6)

Measures of central tendency (2.7)

Measures of location (2.7)

Mode (Mo) (2.7)

Median (Med) (2.7)

Median location (2.7)

Mean (2.7)

Trimmed mean (2.7)

Dispersion (2.8)

Range (2.8)

Interquartile range (2.8)

First quartile (2.8)

Second quartile (2.8)

Third quartile (2.8)

Trimmed samples (2.8)

Winsorized (2.8)

Mean absolute deviation (m.a.d.) (2.8)

Standard deviation (s) (2.8)

Sample variance (s^2) (2.8)

Population variance (σ^2) (2.8)

Coefficient of variation (CV) (2.8)

Unbiased estimator (2.8)

Expected value (2.8)

Degrees of freedom (*df*) (2.8)

Boxplots (2.9)

Box-and-whisker plots (2.9)

Quartile location (2.9)

Inner fence (2.9)

Adjacent values (2.9)

Whiskers (2.9)

Deciles (2.11)

Percentiles (2.11)

Quantiles (2.11)

Fractiles (2.11)

Linear transformations (2.12)

Centering (2.12)

Reflection (2.12)

Deviation scores (2.12)

Standard scores (2.12)

Standardization (2.12)

Nonlinear transformation (2.12)

Exercises

Many of the following exercises can be solved using either computer software or pencil and paper. The choice is up to you or your instructor. Any software package should be able to work these problems. Some of the exercises refer to a large data set named ADD.dat, which is available at www.uvm.edu/~dhowell/methods8/DataFiles/Add.dat. These data come from an actual research study (Howell and Huessy, 1985). The study is described in Appendix: Data Set on page (686).

2.1 Any of you who have listened to children tell stories will recognize that, unlike adults, they tend to recall stories as a sequence of actions rather than as an overall plot. Their descriptions of a movie are filled with the phrase "and then. . . ." An experimenter with supreme patience asked 50 children to tell her about a given movie. Among other variables, she counted the number of "and then . . ." statements, which is the dependent variable. The data follow:

18 15 22 19 18 17 18 20 17 12 16 16 17 21 23 18 20 21 20 20 15 18 17 19 20
23 22 10 17 19 19 21 20 18 18 24 11 19 31 16 17 15 19 20 18 18 40 18 19 16

a. Plot an ungrouped frequency distribution for these data.

b. What is the general shape of the distribution?

2.2 As part of the study described in Exercise 2.1, the experimenter obtained the same kind of data for 50 adults. The data follow:

10 12 5 8 13 10 12 8 7 11 11 10 9 9 11 15 12 17 14 10 9 8 15 16
10 14 7 16 9 1 4 11 12 7 9 10 3 11 14 8 12 5 10 9 7 11 14 10 15 9

  a. What can you tell just by looking at these numbers? Do children and adults seem to recall stories in the same way?

  b. Plot an ungrouped frequency distribution for these data using the same scale on the axes as you used for the children's data in Exercise 2.1.

  c. Overlay the frequency distribution from part (b) on the one from Exercise 2.1.

2.3 What difficulty would you encounter in making a stem-and-leaf display of the data in Exercise 2.1?

2.4 Create a histogram for the data in Exercise 2.1 using a reasonable number of intervals.

2.5 Use a back-to-back stem-and-leaf display (see Figure 2.5) to compare the data from Exercises 2.1 and 2.2.

2.6 The following stem-and-leaf displays show the individual grades referred to in Exercise 2.10 separately for males and females. From these results, what would you conclude about any differences between males and females?

Stem-and-leaf of Percent Sex = 1 (Male) N = 29 Leaf Unit = 0.010			Stem-and-leaf of Percent Sex = 2 (Female) N = 78 Leaf Unit = 0.010		
3	6	677	2	6	77
3	6		3	6	8
3	7		6	7	000
5	7	33	10	7	2233
7	7	45	15	7	45555
7	7		15	7	
10	7	999	22	7	8899999
12	8	01	34	8	011111111111
14	8	22	(8)	8	22222233
(4)	8	4455	36	8	445555555
11	8	6677	27	8	666777777
7	8	8	18	8	888889999
6	9		9	9	00001
6	9	23	4	9	333
4	9	4445	1	9	5

© Cengage Learning 2013

2.7 Create a bimodal set of data that represents some actual phenomenon and plot it.

2.8 Create a positively skewed set of data and plot it.

2.9 In Exercise 2.10, what would be the first and third quartiles (approximately) for males and females?

2.10 In my undergraduate research methods course, women generally do a bit better than men. One year I had the grades shown in the following boxplots. What might you conclude from these boxplots?

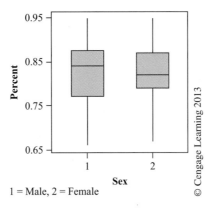

1 = Male, 2 = Female

2.11 What would you predict to be the shape of the distribution of the number of movies attended per month for the next 200 people you meet?

2.12 In a hypothetical experiment, researchers rated 10 Europeans and 10 North Americans on a 12-point scale of musicality. The data for the Europeans were [10 8 9 5 10 11 7 8 2 7]. Using X for this variable,

    a. what are X_3, X_5, and X_8?

    b. calculate $\sum X$.

    c. write the summation notation from part (b) in its most complex form.

2.13 Create a stem-and-leaf display for the ADDSC score in Appendix: Data Set.

2.14 Draw a histogram for the GPA data in Appendix: Data Set referred to at the beginning of these exercises. (These data can also be obtained at http://www.uvm.edu/~dhowell/methods8/DataFiles/Add.dat.)

2.15 The data for the North Americans in Exercise 2.17 were [9 9 5 3 8 4 6 6 5 2]. Using Y for this variable,

    a. what are Y_1 and Y_{10}?

    b. calculate $\sum Y$.

2.16 In Table 2.1 (page 17), the reaction-time data are broken down separately by the number of digits in the comparison stimulus. Create three stem-and-leaf displays, one for each set of data, and place them side-by-side. (Ignore the distinction between positive and negative instances.) What kinds of differences do you see among the reaction times under the three conditions?

2.17 Using the data from Exercise 2.15,

    a. calculate $\left(\sum Y\right)^2$ and $\sum Y^2$.

    b. calculate $\dfrac{\sum Y^2 - \dfrac{\left(\sum Y\right)^2}{N}}{N-1}$

    c. calculate the square root of the answer for part (b).

    d. what are the units of measurement for parts (b) and (c)?

2.18 Using the data from Exercise 2.12,

    a. calculate $\left(\sum X\right)^2$ and $\sum X^2$.

    b. calculate $\sum X/N$, where $N =$ the number of scores.

    c. what do you call what you calculated in part (b)?

2.19 Use the data from Exercises 2.12 and 2.15 to show that

    a. $\sum(X + Y) = \sum X + \sum Y$.

    b. $\sum XY \neq \sum X \sum Y$.

    c. $\sum CX = C\sum X$. (where C represents any arbitrary constant)

    d. $\sum X^2 \neq \left(\sum X\right)^2$.

2.20 Using the data from Exercises 2.12 and 2.15, record the two data sets side-by-side in columns, name the columns X and Y, and treat the data as paired.

    a. Calculate $\sum XY$.

    b. Calculate $\sum X \sum Y$.

    c. Calculate $\dfrac{\sum XY - \dfrac{\sum X \sum Y}{N}}{N - 1}$.

(You will come across these calculations again in Chapter 9.)

2.21 Sternberg ran his original study (the one that is replicated in Table 2.1) to investigate whether people process information simultaneously or sequentially. He reasoned that if they process information simultaneously, they would compare the test stimulus against all digits in the comparison stimulus at the same time, and the time to decide whether a digit was part of the comparison set would not depend on how many digits were in the comparison. If people process information sequentially, the time to come to a decision would increase with the number of digits in the comparison. Which hypothesis do you think the figures you drew in Exercise 2.16 support?

2.22 The following figure is adapted from a paper by Cohen, Kaplan, Cunnick, Manuck, and Rabin (1992), which examined the immune response of nonhuman primates raised in stable and unstable social groups. In each group, animals were classed as high or low in affiliation, measured by the amount of time they spent in close physical proximity to other animals. Higher scores on the immunity measure represent greater immunity to disease. How would you interpret these results?

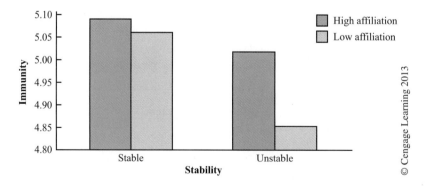

2.23 One frequent assumption in statistical analyses is that observations are independent of one another. (Knowing one response tells you nothing about the magnitude of another response.) How would you characterize the reaction-time data in Table 2.1, just based on what you know about how they were collected? (A lack of independence would not invalidate anything we have done with these data in this chapter.)

2.24 In addition to comparing the three distributions of reaction times, as in Exercise 2.23, how else could you use the data from Table 2.1 to investigate how people process information?

2.25 Rogers and Prentice-Dunn (1981) had subjects deliver shock to their fellow subjects as part of a biofeedback study. They recorded the amount of shock that the subjects delivered to white participants and black participants when the subjects had and had not been insulted by the experimenter. Their results are shown in the accompanying figure. Interpret these results.

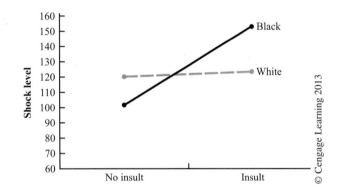

2.26 Make up a set of data for which the mean is greater than the median.

2.27 The following data represent the number of AIDS cases in the United States among people aged 13–29 for the years 1981 to 1990. This is the time when AIDS was first being widely recognized. Plot these data to show the trend over time. (The data are in thousands of cases and come from two different data sources.)

Year	Cases
1981–1982	196
1983	457
1984	960
1985	1685
1986	2815
1987	4385
1988	6383
1989	6780
1990	5483

© Cengage Learning 2013

(Before becoming complacent that the incidence of AIDS/HIV is now falling in the United States, you need to know that in 2006 the United Nations estimated that 39.5 million people were living with AIDS/HIV. Just a little editorial comment.)

2.28   The following data represent U.S. college enrollments by census categories as measured from 1976 to 2007. The data are in percentages. Plot the data in a form that represents the changing ethnic distribution of college students in the United States. (The data entries are in thousands.) From http://nces.ed.gov/fastfacts/display.asp?id=98.

Percentage distribution of students enrolled in degree-granting institutions, by race/ethnicity: Selected years, fall 1976 through fall 2007

Race/ethnicity	Year									
	1976	1980	1990	2000	2002	2003	2004	2005	2006	2007
White	82.6	81.4	77.6	68.3	67.1	66.7	66.1	65.7	65.2	64.4
Total minority	15.4	16.1	19.6	28.2	29.4	29.8	30.4	30.9	31.5	32.2
Black	9.4	9.2	9.0	11.3	11.9	12.2	12.5	12.7	12.8	13.1
Hispanic	3.5	3.9	5.7	9.5	10.0	10.1	10.5	10.8	11.1	11.4
Asian or Pacific Islander	1.8	2.4	4.1	6.4	6.5	6.4	6.4	6.5	6.6	6.7
American Indian/Alaskan Native	0.7	0.7	0.7	1.0	1.0	1.0	1.0	1.0	1.0	1.0
Nonresident alien	2.0	2.5	2.8	3.5	3.6	3.5	3.4	3.3	3.4	3.4

Plot the data over time to illustrate the changing composition of students in higher education.

2.29   The following data from http://www.bsos.umd.edu/socy/vanneman/socy441/trends/marrage .html show society changes of age at marriage over a 50-year period. What trends do you see in the data and what might have caused them?

Average age at first marriage

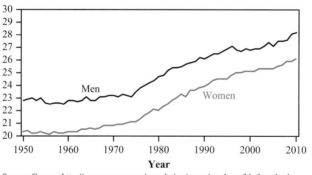

Source: Census: http://www.census.gov/population/www/socdemo/hh-fam.thml

2.30   More recent data on AIDS/HIV world-wide can be found at http://data.unaids.org/pub /EpiReport/2006/2006_EpiUpdate_en.pdf. How does the change in U.S. incidence rates compare to rates in the rest of the world?

2.31   Using the positively skewed set of data that you created in Exercise 2.8, does the mean fall above or below the median?

2.32   Given the following set of data, demonstrate that subtracting a constant (e.g., 5) from every score reduces all measures of central tendency by that constant:

[8, 7, 12, 14, 3 7].

2.33   A group of 15 rats running a straight-alley maze required the following number of trials to perform at a predetermined criterion level:

Trials required to reach criterion:	18	19	20	21	22	23	24
Number of rats (frequency):	1	0	4	3	3	3	1

Calculate the mean and median of the required number of trials for this group.

2.34 Make up a unimodal set of data for which the mean and median are equal but are different from the mode.

2.35 Given the following set of data, show that multiplying each score by a constant multiplies all measures of central tendency by that constant:

[8 3 5 5 6 2].

2.36 Calculate the range, variance, and standard deviation for the data in Exercise 2.1.

2.37 The accompanying output applies to the data on ADDSC and GPA described in Appendix: Data Set. The data can be downloaded as the Add.dat file at this book's Web site. How do these answers on measures of central tendency compare to what you would predict from the answers to Exercises 2.13 and 2.14?

Descriptive Statistics

	ADDSC	GPA	Valid N (listwise)
N	88	88	88
Minimum	26	1	
Maximum	85	4	
Mean	52.60	2.46	
Std.Deviation	12.42	.86	
Variance	154.311	.742	

© Cengage Learning 2013

Descriptive Statistics for ADDSC and GPA

2.38 Create a sample of 10 numbers that has a mean of 8.6. How does this illustrate the point we discussed about degrees of freedom?

2.39 Use SPSS to superimpose a normal distribution on top of the histogram in the previous exercise. (Hint: This is easily done from the pulldown menus in the graphics procedure.)

2.40 In one or two sentences, describe what the following graphic has to say about the grade point averages for the students in our sample.

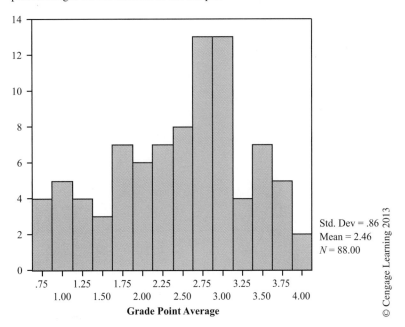

Std. Dev = .86
Mean = 2.46
N = 88.00

© Cengage Learning 2013

Histogram for grade point average

2.41   Calculate the range, variance, and standard deviation for the data in Exercise 2.2.

2.42   In Exercise 2.2, what percentage of the scores fall within plus or minus two standard deviations from the mean?

2.43   In Exercise 2.1, what percentage of the scores fall within plus or minus two standard deviations from the mean?

2.44   Compare the answers to Exercises 2.36 and 2.41. Is the standard deviation for children substantially greater than for adults?

2.45   Using the results demonstrated in Exercises 2.32 and 2.35, transform the following set of data to a new set that has a standard deviation of 1.00:

[5 8 3 8 6 9 9 7].

2.46   Go to Google and find an example of a study in which the coefficient of variation was reported.

2.47   Create a boxplot for the variable ADDSC in Appendix Data Set.

2.48   Create a boxplot for the data in Exercise 2.2.

2.49   For the data in Appendix Data Set, the GPA has a mean of 2.456 and a standard deviation of 0.8614. Compute the coefficient of variation as defined in this chapter.

2.50   Compute the coefficient of variation to compare the variability in usage of "and then ..." statements by children and adults in Exercises 2.1 and 2.2.

2.51   Compute the 10% trimmed mean for the data in Table 2.6—Set 32.

2.52   Under what conditions will a transformation alter the shape of a distribution?

2.53   Draw a boxplot to illustrate the difference between reaction times to positive and negative instances in reaction time for the data in Table 2.1. (These data can be found at this book's Web site as Tab2-1.dat.)

2.54   Compute the 10% Winsorized standard deviation for the data in Table 2.6—Set 32.

2.55   Do an Internet search using Google to find how to create a kernel density plot using SAS or S-Plus.

Chapter *3*

The Normal Distribution

Objectives

To develop the concept of the normal distribution and how we can judge the normality of a sample. This chapter also shows how the normal distribution can be used to draw inferences about observations.

Contents

normal
distribution

FROM WHAT HAS BEEN discussed in the preceding chapters, it is apparent that we are going to be very concerned with distributions—distributions of data, hypothetical distributions of populations, and sampling distributions. Of all the possible forms that distributions can take, the class known as the **normal distribution** is the most important for our purposes.

Before elaborating on the normal distribution, however, it is worth a short digression to explain just why we are so interested in distributions in general, not just the normal distribution. The important link between distributions and probabilities is the most critical factor. If we know something about the distribution of events (or of sample statistics), we know something about the probability that one of those events (or statistics) is likely to occur. To see the issue in its simplest form, take the lowly pie chart. (This is the only time you will see a pie chart in this book, because I find it very difficult to compare little slices of pie in different orientations to see which one is larger. There are much better ways to present data. However, the pie chart serves a useful purpose here.)

The pie chart shown in Figure 3.1 is taken from a report by the Joint United Nations Program on AIDS/HIV and was retrieved from http://data.unaids.org/pub /EpiReport/2006/2006_EpiUpdate_en.pdf in September 2007. The chart displays the source of AIDS/HIV infection for people in Eastern Europe and Central Asia; remarkably, it shows that in this region of the world the great majority of AIDS/HIV cases result from intravenous drug use. (This is not the case in Latin America, the United States, or South and Southeast Asia, where the corresponding percentage is approximately 20%, but we will focus on the data at hand.)

From Figure 3.1 you can see that 67% of people with HIV contracted it from injected drug use (IDU), 4% of the cases involved sexual contact between men (MSM), 5% of cases were among commercial sex workers (CSW), 6% of cases were among clients of commercial sex workers (CSW-cl), and 17% of cases were unclassified or from other sources. You can also see that the percentages of cases in each category are directly reflected in the percentage of the area of the pie that each wedge occupies. The area taken up by each segment is directly proportional to the percentage of individuals in that segment. Moreover, if we declare that the total area of the pie is 1.00 unit, then the area of each segment is equal to the proportion of observations falling in that segment.

It is easy to go from speaking about areas to speaking about probabilities. The concept of probability will be elaborated in Chapter 5, but even without a precise definition of probability we can make an important point about areas of a pie chart. For now, simply think of

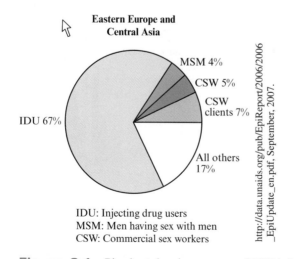

IDU: Injecting drug users
MSM: Men having sex with men
CSW: Commercial sex workers

http://data.unaids.org/pub/EpiReport/2006/2006 _EpiUpdate_en.pdf, September, 2007.

Figure 3.1   Pie chart showing sources of HIV infections in different populations

probability in its common everyday usage, referring to the likelihood that some event will occur. From this perspective it is logical to conclude that because 67% of those with HIV/AIDS contracted it from injected drug use, if we were to randomly draw the name of one person from a list of people with HIV/AIDS, then the probability is .67 that the individual would have contracted the disease from drug use. To put this in slightly different terms, if 67% of the area of the pie is allocated to IDU, then the probability that a person would fall in that segment is .67.

This pie chart also allows us to explore the addition of areas. It should be clear that if 5% are classed as CSW, 7% are classed as CSW-cl, and 4% are classed as MSM, then 5 + 7 + 4 = 16% contracted the disease from sexual activity. (In that part of the world the causes of HIV/AIDS are quite different from what we in the West have come to expect, and prevention programs would need to be modified accordingly.) In other words, we can find the percentage of individuals in one of several categories just by adding the percentages for each category. The same thing holds in terms of areas, in the sense that we can find the percentage of sexually related infections by adding the areas devoted to CSW, CSW-cl, and MSM. And finally, if we can find percentages by adding areas, we can also find probabilities by adding areas. Thus the probability of contracting HIV/AIDS as a result of sexual activity if you live in Eastern Europe or Central Asia is the probability of being in one of the three segments associated with that source, which we can get by summing the areas (or their associated probabilities).

bar chart

There are other ways to present data besides pie charts. Two of the simplest are a histogram (discussed in Chapter 2) and its closely related cousin, the **bar chart**. Figure 3.2 is a redrawing of Figure 3.1 in the form of a bar chart. Although this figure does not contain any new information, it has two advantages over the pie chart. First, it is easier to compare categories, because the only thing we need to look at is the height of the bar, rather than trying to compare the lengths of two different arcs in different orientations. The second advantage is that the bar chart is visually more like the common distributions we will deal with, in that the various levels or categories are spread out along the horizontal dimension, and the percentages (or frequencies) in each category are shown along the vertical dimension. (However, in a bar chart the values on the *X* axis can form a nominal scale, as they do here. This is not true in a histogram.) Here again you can see that the various areas of the

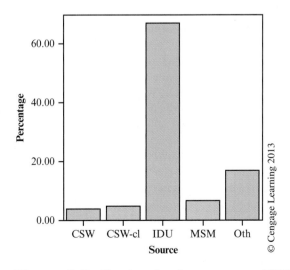

Figure 3.2 Bar chart showing percentage of HIV/AIDS cases attributed to different sources

distribution are related to probabilities. Further, you can see that we can meaningfully sum areas in exactly the same way that we did in the pie chart. When we move to more common distributions, particularly the normal distribution, the principles of areas, percentages, probabilities, and the addition of areas or probabilities carry over almost without change.

3.1 The Normal Distribution

Now we'll move closer to the normal distribution. I stated earlier that the normal distribution is one of the most important distributions we will encounter. There are several reasons for this:

1. Many of the dependent variables with which we deal are commonly assumed to be normally distributed in the population. That is to say, we frequently assume that if we were to obtain the whole population of observations, the resulting distribution would closely resemble the normal distribution.

2. If we can assume that a variable is at least approximately normally distributed, then the techniques that are discussed in this chapter allow us to make a number of inferences (either exact or approximate) about values of that variable.

3. The theoretical distribution of the hypothetical set of sample means obtained by drawing an infinite number of samples from a specified population can be shown to be approximately normal under a wide variety of conditions. Such a distribution is called the sampling distribution of the mean and is discussed and used extensively throughout the remainder of this book.

4. Most of the statistical procedures we will employ have, somewhere in their derivation, an assumption that the population of observations (or of measurement errors) is normally distributed.

To introduce the normal distribution, we will look at one additional data set that is approximately normal (and would be even closer to normal if we had more observations). The data we will look at were collected using the Achenbach Youth Self-Report form (Achenbach, 1991b), a frequently used measure of behavior problems that produces scores on a number of different dimensions. We will focus on the dimension of Total Behavior Problems, which represents the total number of behavior problems reported by the child (weighted by the severity of the problem). (Examples of Behavior Problem categories are "Argues," "Impulsive," "Shows off," and "Teases.") Figure 3.3 is a histogram of data from 289 junior high school students. A higher score represents more behavior problems. You can see that this distribution has a center very near 50 and is fairly symmetrically distributed on each side of that value, with the scores ranging between about 25 and 75. The standard deviation of this distribution is approximately 10. The distribution is not perfectly even—it has some bumps and valleys—but overall it is fairly smooth, rising in the center and falling off at the ends. (The actual mean and standard deviation for this particular sample are 49.1 and 10.56, respectively.)

One thing that you might note from this distribution is that if you add the frequencies of subjects falling in the intervals 52–54 and 54–56, you will find that 54 students obtained scores between 52 and 56. Because there are 289 observations in this sample, $54/289 = 19\%$ of the observations fell in this interval. This illustrates the comments made earlier on the addition of areas.

We can take this distribution and superimpose a normal distribution on top of it. This is frequently done to casually evaluate the normality of a sample although, as we will see, that is not the best way to judge normality. The smooth distribution superimposed on the

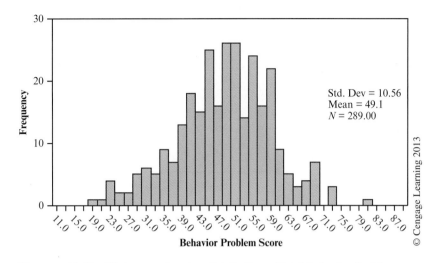

Figure 3.3   Histogram showing distribution of total Behavior Problem scores

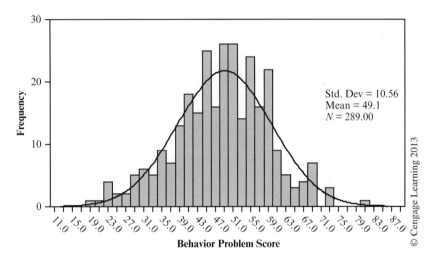

Figure 3.4   A characteristic normal distribution representing the distribution of Behavior Problem scores

abscissa
ordinate

raw data in Figure 3.4 is a characteristic normal distribution. It is a symmetric, unimodal distribution, frequently referred to as "bell shaped," and has limits of $\pm\infty$. The **abscissa**, or horizontal axis, represents different possible values of X, while the **ordinate**, or vertical axis, is referred to as the density and is related to (but not the same as) the frequency or probability of occurrence of X. The concept of density is discussed in further detail in the next chapter. (Although superimposing a normal distribution, as we have just done, helps in evaluating the shape of the distribution, there are better ways of judging whether sample data are normally distributed. We will discuss Q-Q plots later in this chapter, and you will see a relatively simple way of assessing normality.)

We often discuss the normal distribution by showing a generic kind of distribution with X on the abscissa and density on the ordinate. Such a distribution is shown in Figure 3.5.

The normal distribution has a long history. It was originally investigated by DeMoivre (1667–1754), who was interested in its use to describe the results of games of chance

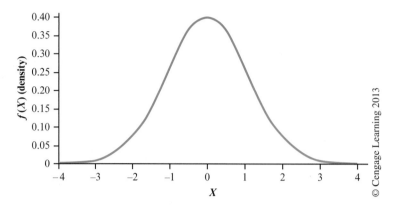

© Cengage Learning 2013

Figure 3.5   A characteristic normal distribution with values of *X* on the abscissa and density on the ordinate

(gambling). The distribution was defined precisely by Pierre-Simon Laplace (1749–1827) and put in its more usual form by Carl Friedrich Gauss (1777–1855), both of whom were interested in the distribution of errors in astronomical observations. In fact, the normal distribution is variously referred to as the Gaussian distribution and as the "normal law of error." Adolph Quetelet (1796–1874), a Belgian astronomer, was the first to apply the distribution to social and biological data. Apparently having nothing better to do with his time, he collected chest measurements of Scottish soldiers and heights of French soldiers. He found that both sets of measurements were approximately normally distributed. Quetelet interpreted the data to indicate that the mean of this distribution was the ideal at which nature was aiming, and observations to each side of the mean represented error (a deviation from nature's ideal). (For 5'8" males like myself, it is somehow comforting to think of all those bigger guys as nature's mistakes.) Although we no longer think of the mean as nature's ideal, this is a useful way to conceptualize variability around the mean. In fact, we still use the word *error* to refer to deviations from the mean. Francis Galton (1822–1911) carried Quetelet's ideas further and gave the normal distribution a central role in psychological theory, especially the theory of mental abilities. Some would insist that Galton was *too* successful in this endeavor, and we tend to assume that measures are normally distributed even when they are not. I won't argue the issue here.

Mathematically the normal distribution is defined as

$$f(X) = \frac{1}{\sigma\sqrt{2\pi}}(e)^{-(X-\mu)^2/2\sigma^2}$$

where π and e are constants ($\pi = 3.1416$ and $e = 2.7183$), and μ and σ are the mean and the standard deviation, respectively, of the distribution. If μ and σ are known, the ordinate, $f(X)$, for any value of X can be obtained simply by substituting the appropriate values for μ, σ, and X and solving the equation. This is not nearly as difficult as it looks, but in practice you are unlikely ever to have to make the calculations. The cumulative form of this distribution is tabled, and we can simply read the information we need from the table.

Those of you who have had a course in calculus may recognize that the area under the curve between any two values of X (say X_1 and X_2), and thus the probability that a randomly drawn score will fall within that interval, can be found by integrating the function over the range from X_1 to X_2. Those of you who have not had such a course can take comfort from the fact that tables in which this work has already been done for us are readily available or by use of which we can easily do the work ourselves. Such a table appears in Appendix z (page 714).

You might be excused at this point for wondering why anyone would want to table such a distribution in the first place. Just because a distribution is common (or at least commonly assumed), it doesn't automatically suggest a reason for having an appendix that tells all about it. The reason is quite simple. By using Appendix z, we can readily calculate the probability that a score drawn at random from the population will have a value lying between any two specified points (X_1 and X_2). Thus, by using the appropriate table, we can make probability statements in answer to a variety of questions. You will see examples of such questions in the rest of this chapter. This issue comes up when we want to ask if a child is importantly different from a population of normal children or if we want to ask if some outcome, such as a mean, is extreme. They will also appear in many other chapters throughout the book.

3.2 The Standard Normal Distribution

standard normal distribution

A problem arises when we try to table the normal distribution, because the distribution depends on the values of the mean and the standard deviation (μ and σ) of the distribution. To do the job right, we would have to make up a different table for every possible combination of the values of μ and σ, which certainly is not practical. The solution to this problem is to work with what is called the **standard normal distribution**, which has a mean of 0 and a standard deviation of 1. Such a distribution is often designated as $N(0,1)$, where N refers to the fact that it is normal, 0 is the value of μ, and 1 is the value of σ^2. ($N(\mu, \sigma^2)$ is the more general expression.) Given the standard normal distribution in the appendix and a set of rules for transforming any normal distribution to standard form and vice versa, we can use Appendix z to find the areas under any normal distribution.

Consider the distribution shown in Figure 3.6, with a mean of 50 and a standard deviation of 10 (variance of 100). It represents the distribution of *an entire population* of Total Behavior Problem scores from the Achenbach Youth Self-Report form, of which the data in Figures 3.3 and 3.4 are a sample. If we knew something about the areas under the curve in Figure 3.6, we could say something about the probability of various values of Behavior Problem scores and could identify, for example, those scores that are so high that they are obtained by only 5% or 10% of the population. You might wonder why we would want to

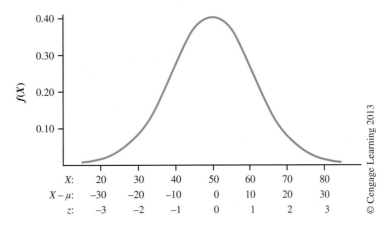

Figure 3.6 A normal distribution with various transformations on the abscissa

do this, but it is often important in diagnosis to separate extreme scores from more typical scores.

The only tables of the normal distribution that are readily available are those of the *standard* normal distribution. Therefore, before we can answer questions about the probability that an individual will get a score above some particular value, we must first transform the distribution in Figure 3.6 (or at least specific points along it) to a standard normal distribution. That is, we want to say that a score of X_i from a normal distribution with a mean of 50 and a variance of 100—often denoted $N(50,100)$—is comparable to a score of z_i from a distribution with a mean of 0 and a variance, and standard deviation, of 1—denoted $N(0,1)$. Then anything that is true of z_i is also true of X_i, and z and X are comparable variables. (Statisticians sometimes call z a **pivotal quantity** because its *distribution* does not depend on the values of μ and σ^2. The distribution will always be normal regardless of the values of the two parameters. The correlation coefficient, which we will see in Chapter 9, is not pivotal because its distribution takes on different shapes depending on the value of the population correlation.)

pivotal quantity

From Exercise 2.32 we know that subtracting a constant from each score in a set of scores reduces the mean of the set by that constant. Thus, if we subtract 50 (the mean) from all the values for X, the new mean will be $50 - 50 = 0$. In other words we have centered the distribution on 0. (More generally, the distribution of $(X - \mu)$ has a mean of 0 and the $(X - \mu)$ scores are called **deviation scores** because they measure deviations from the mean.) The effect of this transformation is shown in the second set of values for the abscissa in Figure 3.6. We are halfway there, because we now have the mean down to 0, although the standard deviation (σ) is still 10. We also know that if we multiply or divide all values of a variable by a constant (e.g., 10), we multiply or divide the standard deviation by that constant. Thus, if we divide all deviation scores by 10, the standard deviation will now be $10/10 = 1$, which is just what we wanted. We will call this transformed distribution z and define it, on the basis of what we have done, as

deviation scores

$$z = \frac{X - \mu}{\sigma}.$$

For our particular case, where $\mu = 50$ and $\sigma = 10$,

$$z = \frac{X - \mu}{\sigma} = \frac{X - 50}{10}.$$

The third set of values (labeled z) for the abscissa in Figure 3.6 shows the effect of this transformation. Note that aside from a linear transformation of the numerical values, the data have not been changed in any way. The distribution has the same shape and the observations continue to stand in the same relation to each other as they did before the transformation. It should not come as a great surprise that changing the unit of measurement does not change the shape of the distribution or the relative standing of observations. Whether we measure the quantity of alcohol that people consume per week in ounces or in milliliters really makes no difference in the relative standing of people. It just changes the numerical values on the abscissa. (The town drunk is still the town drunk, even if now his liquor is measured in milliliters.) It is important to realize exactly what converting X to z has accomplished. A score that used to be 60 is now 1. That is, a score that used to be one standard deviation (10 points) above the mean remains one standard deviation above the mean, but now is given a new value of 1. A score of 45, which was 0.5 standard deviation *below* the mean, now is given the value of -0.5, and so on. In other words, a z score represents the number of standard deviations that X_i is above or below the mean—a positive z score being above the mean and a negative z score being below the mean.

z scores

The equation for *z* is completely general. We can transform any distribution to a distribution of *z* **scores** simply by applying this equation. Keep in mind, however, the point that was just made. The *shape* of the distribution is unaffected by a linear transformation. That means that *if the distribution was not normal before it was transformed, it will not be normal afterward.* Some people believe that they can "normalize" (in the sense of producing a normal distribution) their data by transforming them to *z*. It just won't work.

You can see what happens when you draw random samples from a population that is normal by going to http://surfstat.anu.edu.au/surfstat-home/surfstat.html and clicking on "Hotlist for Java Applets." Just click on the histogram, and it will present another histogram that you can modify in various ways. By repeatedly clicking "start" without clearing, you can add cases to the sample. It is useful to see how the distribution approaches a normal distribution as the number of observations increases. (And how nonnormal a distribution with a small sample size can look.)

3.3 Using the Tables of the Standard Normal Distribution

As already mentioned, the standard normal distribution is extensively tabled. Such a table can be found in Appendix *z*, part of which is reproduced in Table 3.1.[1] To see how we can make use of this table, consider the normal distribution represented in Figure 3.7. This might represent the standardized distribution of the Behavior Problem scores as seen in Figure 3.6. Suppose we want to know how much of the area under the curve is above one standard deviation from the mean, if the total area under the curve is taken to be 1.00. (Remember that we care about areas because they translate directly to probabilities.) We already have seen that *z* scores represent standard deviations from the mean, and thus we know that we want to find the area above $z = 1$.

Only the positive half of the normal distribution is tabled. Because the distribution is symmetric, any information given about a positive value of *z* applies equally to the corresponding negative value of *z*. (The table in Appendix *z* also contains a column labeled "y." This is just the height [density] of the curve corresponding to that value of *z*. I have not included it here to save space and because it is rarely used.) From Table 3.1 (or Appendix *z*) we find the row corresponding to $z = 1.00$. Reading across that row, we can see that the area from the *mean to z* = 1 is 0.3413, the area in the *larger portion* is 0.8413, and the area in the *smaller portion* is 0.1587. If you visualize the distribution being divided into the segment below $z = 1$ (the unshaded part of Figure 3.7) and the segment above $z = 1$ (the shaded part), the meanings of the terms *larger portion* and *smaller portion* become obvious. Thus, the answer to our original question is 0.1587. Because we already have equated the terms *area* and *probability*, we now can say that if we sample a child at random from the population of children, and if Behavior Problem scores are normally distributed, then the probability that the child will score more than one standard deviation above the mean of the population (i.e., above 60) is .1587. Because the distribution is symmetric, we also know that the probability that a child will score more than one standard deviation *below* the mean of the population is also .1587.

Now suppose that we want the probability that the child will be more than one standard deviation (10 points) from the mean *in either direction*. This is a simple matter of the summation of areas. Because we know that the normal distribution is symmetric, then the area

---

[1] If you prefer electronic tables, many small Java programs are available on the Internet. One of my favorite programs for calculating *z* probabilities is at http://psych.colorado.edu/~mcclella/java/zcalc.html. An online video displaying properties of the normal distribution is available at http://huizen.dds.nl/~berrie/normal.html.

Table 3.1 The normal distribution (abbreviated version of Appendix *z*).

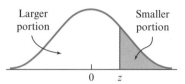

z	Mean to z	Larger Portion	Smaller Portion	z	Mean to z	Larger Portion	Smaller Portion
0.00	0.0000	0.5000	0.5000	0.45	0.1736	0.6736	0.3264
0.01	0.0040	0.5040	0.4960	0.46	0.1772	0.6772	0.3228
0.02	0.0080	0.5080	0.4920	0.47	0.1808	0.6808	0.3192
0.03	0.0120	0.5120	0.4880	0.48	0.1844	0.6844	0.3156
0.04	0.0160	0.5160	0.4840	0.49	0.1879	0.6879	0.3121
0.05	0.0199	0.5199	0.4801	0.50	0.1915	0.6915	0.3085
. . .	. . .	. . .	. . .	. . .	. . .	. . .	. . .
0.97	0.3340	0.8340	0.1660	1.42	0.4222	0.9222	0.0778
0.98	0.3365	0.8365	0.1635	1.43	0.4236	0.9236	0.0764
0.99	0.3389	0.8389	0.1611	1.44	0.4251	0.9251	0.0749
1.00	0.3413	0.8413	0.1587	1.45	0.4265	0.9265	0.0735
1.01	0.3438	0.8438	0.1562	1.46	0.4279	0.9279	0.0721
1.02	0.3461	0.8461	0.1539	1.47	0.4292	0.9292	0.0708
1.03	0.3485	0.8485	0.1515	1.48	0.4306	0.9306	0.0694
1.04	0.3508	0.8508	0.1492	1.49	0.4319	0.9319	0.0681
1.05	0.3531	0.8531	0.1469	1.50	0.4332	0.9332	0.0668
. . .	. . .	. . .	. . .	. . .	. . .	. . .	. . .
1.95	0.4744	0.9744	0.0256	2.40	0.4918	0.9918	0.0082
1.96	0.4750	0.9750	0.0250	2.41	0.4920	0.9920	0.0080
1.97	0.4756	0.9756	0.0244	2.42	0.4922	0.9922	0.0078
1.98	0.4761	0.9761	0.0239	2.43	0.4925	0.9925	0.0075
1.99	0.4767	0.9767	0.0233	2.44	0.4927	0.9927	0.0073
2.00	0.4772	0.9772	0.0228	2.45	0.4929	0.9929	0.0071
2.01	0.4778	0.9778	0.0222	2.46	0.4931	0.9931	0.0069
2.02	0.4783	0.9783	0.0217	2.47	0.4932	0.9932	0.0068
2.03	0.4788	0.9788	0.0212	2.48	0.4934	0.9934	0.0066
2.04	0.4793	0.9793	0.0207	2.49	0.4936	0.9936	0.0064
2.05	0.4798	0.9798	0.0202	2.50	0.4938	0.9938	0.0062

© Cengage Learning 2013

below $z = -1$ will be the same as the area above $z = +1$. This is why the table does not contain negative values of z—they are not needed. We already know that the areas in which we are interested are each 0.1587. Then the total area outside $z = \pm 1$ must be 0.1587 + 0.1587 = 0.3174. The converse is also true. If the area outside $z = \pm 1$ is 0.3174, then the area between $z = +1$ and $z = -1$ is equal to $1 - 0.3174 = 0.6826$. Thus, the probability that a child will score between 40 and 60 is .6826.

To extend this procedure, consider the situation in which we want to know the probability that a score will be between 30 and 40. A little arithmetic will show that this is simply the probability of falling between 1.0 standard deviation below the mean and 2.0 standard deviations below the mean. This situation is diagrammed in Figure 3.8. (*Hint:* It is always

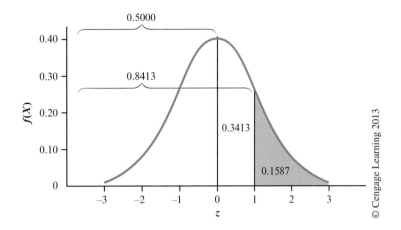

Figure 3.7   Illustrative areas under the normal distribution

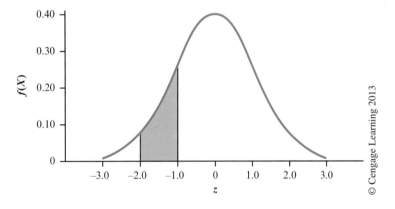

Figure 3.8   Area between 1.0 and 2.0 standard deviations below the mean

wise to draw simple diagrams such as Figure 3.8. They eliminate many errors and make clear the area(s) for which you are looking.)

From Appendix z we know that the area from the mean to $z = -2.0$ is 0.4772 and from the mean to $z = -1.0$ is 0.3413. The difference is these two areas must represent the area between $z = -2.0$ and $z = -1.0$. This area is $0.4772 - 0.3413 = 0.1359$. Thus, the probability that Behavior Problem scores drawn at random from a normally distributed population will be between 30 and 40 is .1359.

Discussing areas under the normal distribution as we have done in the last two paragraphs is the traditional way of presenting the normal distribution. However, you might legitimately ask why I would ever want to know the probability that someone would have a Total Behavior Problem score between 50 and 60. The simple answer is that I probably don't care. But, suppose that you took your child in for an evaluation because you were worried about his behavior. And suppose that your child had a score of 75. A little arithmetic will show that $z = (75 - 50)/10 = 2.5$, and from Appendix z we can see that only 0.62% of normal children score that high. If I were you I'd start worrying. Seventy-five really is a high score.

3.4   Setting Probable Limits on an Observation

For a final example, consider the situation where we want to identify limits within which we have some specified degree of confidence that a child sampled at random will fall. In other words we want to make a statement of the form, "If I draw a child at random from this population, 95% of the time her score will lie between _____ and _____." From Figure 3.9 you can see the limits we want—the limits that include 95% of the scores in the population.

If we are looking for the limits within which 95% of the scores fall, we also are looking for the limits beyond which the remaining 5% of the scores fall. To rule out this remaining 5%, we want to find that value of z that cuts off 2.5% at each end, or "tail," of the distribution. (We do not need to use symmetric limits, but we typically do because they usually make the most sense and produce the shortest interval.) From Appendix z we see that these values are $z = \pm 1.96$. Thus, we can say that 95% of the time a child's score sampled at random will fall between 1.96 standard deviations above the mean and 1.96 standard deviations below the mean.

Because we generally want to express our answers in terms of raw Behavior Problem scores, rather than z scores, we must do a little more work. To obtain the raw score limits, we simply work the formula for z backward, solving for X instead of z. Thus, if we want to state the limits encompassing 95% of the population, we want to find those scores that are 1.96 standard deviations above and below the mean of the population. This can be written as

$$z = \frac{X - \mu}{\sigma}$$

$$\pm 1.96 = \frac{X - \mu}{\sigma}$$

$$X - \mu = \pm 1.96\sigma$$

$$X = \mu \pm 1.96\sigma$$

where the values of X corresponding to $(\mu + 1.96\sigma)$ and $(\mu - 1.96\sigma)$ represent the limits we seek. For our example the limits will be

$$\text{Limits} = 50 \pm (1.96)(10) = 50 \pm 19.6 = 30.4 \text{ and } 69.6.$$

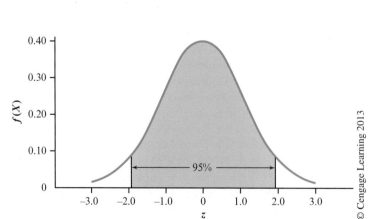

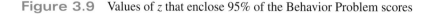

Figure 3.9   Values of z that enclose 95% of the Behavior Problem scores

So the probability is .95 that a child's score (*X*) chosen at random would be between 30.4 and 69.6. We may not be very interested in low scores, because they don't represent problems. But anyone with a score of 69.6 or higher is a problem to someone. Only 2.5% of children score at least that high.

What we have just discussed is closely related to, but not quite the same as, what we will later consider under the heading of confidence limits. The major difference is that here we knew the population mean and were trying to predict where a single observation (*X*) would fall. We will later call something like this a **prediction interval**. When we discuss confidence limits, we will have a sample mean (or some other statistic) and will want to set limits that have a probability of .95 of bracketing the population mean (or some other relevant parameter). You do not need to know anything at all about confidence limits at this point. I simply mention the issue to forestall any confusion in the future.

prediction interval

3.5 Assessing Whether Data Are Normally Distributed

There will be many occasions in this book where we will assume that data are normally distributed, but it is difficult to look at a distribution of sample data and assess the reasonableness of such an assumption. Statistics texts are filled with examples of distributions that look normal but aren't, and these are often followed by statements of how distorted the results of some procedure are because the data were nonnormal. As I said earlier, we can superimpose a true normal distribution on top of a histogram and have some idea of how well we are doing, but that is often a misleading approach. A far better approach is to use what are called **Q-Q plots (quantile-quantile plots)**.

Q-Q plots (quantile-quantile plots)

Q-Q plots

The idea behind quantile-quantile (Q-Q) plots is basically quite simple. Suppose that we have a sample of 100 observations that is perfectly normally distributed with mean = 0 and standard deviation = 1. (The mean and standard deviation could be any values, but 0 and 1 just make the discussion simpler.) With that distribution we can easily calculate what value would cut off, for example, the lowest 1% of the distribution. From Appendix *z* this would be a value of –2.33. We would also know that a cutoff of –2.054 cuts off the lowest 2%. We could make this calculation for every value of $0.00 < p < 1.00$, and we could name the results the *expected quantiles* of a normal distribution.

Now we go to the data we actually have. Because I have specified that they are perfectly normally distributed and that there are $n = 100$ observations, the lowest score will be the lowest 1% and it will be –2.33. Similarly the second lowest value would cut off 2% of the distribution and would be –2.054. We will call these the *obtained quantiles* because they were calculated directly from the data. For a perfectly normal distribution the two sets of quantiles should agree exactly. The value that forms the 15th percentile of the obtained distribution should be exactly that value that the normal distribution would have given the population mean and standard deviation.

But suppose that our sample data were not normally distributed. Then we might find that the score cutting off the lowest 1% of our sample was –2.8 instead of –2.33. The same could happen for other quantiles. Here the expected quantiles from a normal distribution and the obtained quantiles from our sample would not agree.

But how do we measure agreement? The easiest way is to plot the two sets of quantiles against each other, putting the expected quantiles on the *Y* axis and the obtained quantiles on the *X* axis. If the distribution is normal the plot should form a straight line running at a 45-degree angle. These plots are illustrated in Figure 3.10 for a set of data drawn from a normal distribution and a set drawn from a decidedly nonnormal distribution.

In Figure 3.10 you can see that for normal data the Q-Q plot shows that most of the points fall nicely on a straight line. They depart from the line a bit at each end, but that commonly happens unless you have very large sample sizes. For the nonnormal data, however, the plotted points depart drastically from a straight line. At the lower end where we would expect quantiles of around –1, the lowest obtained quantile was actually about –2. In other words the distribution was truncated on the left. At the upper right of the Q-Q plot where we obtained quantiles of around 2.0, the expected value was at least 3.0. In other words the obtained data did not depart enough from the mean at the lower end and departed too much from the mean at the upper end. A program to plot Q-Q plots in R is available at the book's Web site.

We have been looking at Achenbach's Total Behavior Problem scores and I have suggested that they are very normally distributed. Figure 3.11 presents a Q-Q plot for those scores. From this plot it is apparent that Behavior Problem scores are normally distributed, which is, in part, a function of the fact that Achenbach worked very hard to develop that scale and give it desirable properties.

However, let's look at the reaction-time data that began this book. In discussing Figure 2.4, I said that the data are roughly normally distributed though truncated on the

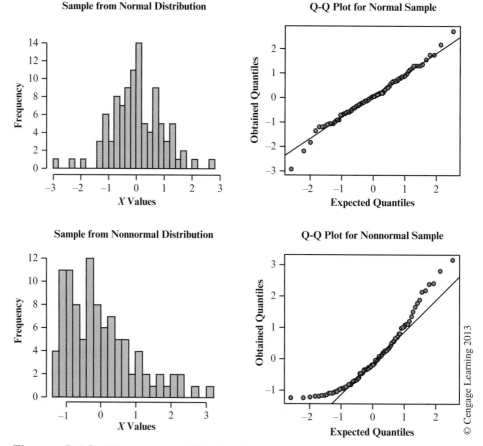

Figure 3.10 Histograms and Q-Q plots for normal and nonnormal data

left. And the figure did, indeed, pretty much show that. But Figure 3.12 shows the Q-Q plot for RxTime, and you can see that it is far from a straight line. I did this to illustrate that it is more difficult than you might think to look at a simple histogram, with or without a superimposed normal distribution, and decide whether or not a distribution is normal.

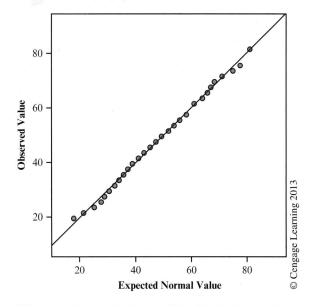

Figure 3.11   Q-Q plot of Total Behavior Problem scores

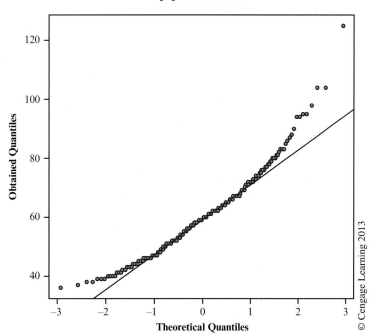

Figure 3.12   Q-Q plot of reaction time data

The Axes for a Q-Q Plot

In presenting the logic behind a Q-Q plot I spoke as if the variables in question were standardized, although I did mention that it was not a requirement. I did so because it was easier to send you to tables of normal distribution. However, you will often come across Q-Q plots where one or both axes are in different units, which is not a problem. The important consideration is the distribution of points within the plot and not the scale of either axis. In fact, different statistical packages not only use different scaling, but they also differ on which variable is plotted on which axis. If you see a plot that looks like a mirror image (vertically) of one of my plots that simply means they have plotted the observed values on the X axis instead of the expected ones.

The Kolmogorov-Smirnov Test

Kolmogorov-Smirnov test

The best-known statistical test for normality is the **Kolmogorov-Smirnov test**, which is available within SPSS under the nonparametric tests. Although you should know that the test exists, *most people do not recommend its use*. In the first place most small samples will pass the test even when they are decidedly nonnormal. On the other hand, when you have very large samples the test is very likely to reject the hypothesis of normality even though minor deviations from normality will not be a problem. D'Agostino and Stephens (1986) put it even more strongly when they wrote, "The Kolmogorov-Smirnov test is only a historical curiosity. It should never be used." I mention the test here only because you will come across references to it and SPSS will offer to calculate it for you. You should know its weaknesses.

3.6 Measures Related to *z*

We already have seen that the z formula given earlier can be used to convert a distribution with any mean and variance to a distribution with a mean of 0 and a standard deviation (and variance) of 1. We frequently refer to such transformed scores as **standard scores**. There are also other transformational scoring systems with particular properties, some of which people use every day without realizing what they are.

standard scores

A good example of such a scoring system is the common IQ. The raw scores from an IQ test are routinely transformed to a distribution with a mean of 100 and a standard deviation of 15 (or 16 in the case of the Binet). Knowing this, you can readily convert an individual's IQ (e.g., 120) to his or her position in terms of standard deviations above or below the mean (i.e., you can calculate the z score). Because IQ scores are more or less normally distributed, you can then convert z into a percentage measure by use of Appendix z. (In this example, a score of 120 has approximately 91% of the scores below it. This is known as the 91st **percentile**.)

percentile

Other common examples are standard diagnostic tests that are converted to a fixed mean and standard deviation. (Achenbach's test is an example.) The raw scores are transformed by the producer of the test and reported as coming from a distribution with a mean of 50 and a standard deviation of 10 (for example). Such a scoring system is easy to devise. We start by converting raw scores to z scores (using the obtained raw score mean and standard deviation). We then convert the z scores to the particular scoring system we have in mind. Thus

New score = New SD * (z) + New mean,

where z represents the z score corresponding to the individual's raw score. Scoring systems such as the one used on Achenbach's Youth Self-Report checklist, which have a mean set

T scores   at 50 and a standard deviation set at 10, are called **T scores** (the T is always capitalized). These tests are useful in psychological measurement because they have a common frame of reference. For example, people become used to seeing a cutoff score of 63 as identifying the highest 10% of the subjects.

Key Terms

Normal distribution (Introduction)	Pivotal quantity (3.2)	Kolmogorov-Smirnov test (3.5)
Bar chart (Introduction)	Deviation score (3.2)	Standard scores (3.6)
Abscissa (3.1)	z score (3.2)	Percentile (3.6)
Ordinate (3.1)	Prediction interval (3.4)	T scores (3.6)
Standard normal distribution (3.2)	Quantile-quantile (Q-Q) plots (3.5)	

Exercises

3.1 Assume that the following data represent a population with $\mu = 4$ and $\sigma = 1.63$: X = [1 2 2 3 3 3 4 4 4 4 5 5 5 6 6 7]

    a. Plot the distribution as given.

    b. Convert the distribution in part (a) to a distribution of $X - \mu$.

    c. Go the next step and convert the distribution in part (b) to a distribution of z.

3.2 Using the example from Exercise 3.3:

    a. What two values of X (the count) would encompass the middle 50% of the results?

    b. 75% of the counts would be less than ———.

    c. 95% of the counts would be between ——— and ———.

3.3 Suppose we want to study the errors found in the performance of a simple task. We ask a large number of judges to report the number of people seen entering a major department store in one morning. Some judges will miss some people, and some will count others twice, so we don't expect everyone to agree. Suppose we find that the mean number of shoppers reported is 975 with a standard deviation of 15. Assume that the distribution of counts is normal.

    a. What percentage of the counts will lie between 960 and 990?

    b. What percentage of the counts will lie below 975?

    c. What percentage of the counts will lie below 990?

3.4 Using the distribution in Exercise 3.1, calculate z scores for $X = 2.5$, 6.2, and 9. Interpret these results.

3.5 The person in charge of the project in Exercise 3.3 counted only 950 shoppers entering the store. Is this a reasonable answer if he was counting conscientiously? Why or why not?

3.6 We have sent out everyone in a large introductory course to check whether people use seat belts. Each student has been told to look at 100 cars and count the number of people wearing seat belts. The number found by any given student is considered that student's score. The mean score for the class is 44, with a standard deviation of 7.

    a. Diagram this distribution, assuming that the counts are normally distributed.

    b. A student who has done very little work all year has reported finding 62 seat belt users out of 100. Do we have reason to suspect that the student just made up a number rather than actually counting?

3.7 Under what conditions would the answers to parts (b) and (c) of Exercise 3.8 be equal?

3.8   A set of reading scores for fourth-grade children has a mean of 25 and a standard deviation of 5. A set of scores for ninth-grade children has a mean of 30 and a standard deviation of 10. Assume that the distributions are normal.

    a.   Draw a rough sketch of these data, putting both groups in the same figure.

    b.   What percentage of the fourth-graders score better than the average ninth-grader?

    c.   What percentage of the ninth-graders score worse than the average fourth-grader? (We will come back to the idea behind these calculations when we study power in Chapter 8.)

3.9   A dean must distribute salary raises to her faculty for the next year. She has decided that the mean raise is to be $2,000, the standard deviation of raises is to be $400, and the distribution is to be normal.

    a.   The most productive 10% of the faculty will have a raise equal to or greater than $_____.

    b.   The 5% of the faculty who have done nothing useful in years will receive no more than $_____ each.

3.10   A certain diagnostic test is indicative of problems only if a child scores in the lowest 10% of those taking the test (the 10th percentile). If the mean score is 150 with a standard deviation of 30, what would be the diagnostically meaningful cutoff?

3.11   A number of years ago a friend of mine produced a diagnostic test of language problems. A score on her scale is obtained simply by counting the number of language constructions (e.g., plural, negative, passive) that the child produces correctly in response to specific prompts from the person administering the test. The test had a mean of 48 and a standard deviation of 7. Parents had trouble understanding the meaning of a score on this scale, and my friend wanted to convert the scores to a mean of 80 and a standard deviation of 10 (to make them more like the kinds of grades parents are used to). How could she have gone about her task?

3.12   In Exercise 3.13 what score would be equal to or greater than 75% of the scores on the exam? (This score is the 75th percentile.)

3.13   In October 1981, the mean and the standard deviation on the Graduate Record Exam (GRE) for all people taking the exam were 489 and 126, respectively. What percentage of students would you expect to have a score of 600 or less? (This is called the percentile rank of 600.)

3.14   Unfortunately, the whole world is not built on the principle of a normal distribution. In the preceding example the real distribution is badly skewed because most children do not have language problems and therefore produce all or most constructions correctly.

    a.   Diagram how the distribution might look.

    b.   How would you go about finding the cutoff for the bottom 10% if the distribution is not normal?

3.15   For all seniors and non-enrolled college graduates taking the GRE in October 1981, the mean and the standard deviation were 507 and 118, respectively. How does this change the answers to Exercises 3.12 and 3.13?

3.16   Use a standard computer program such as SPSS, OpenStat, or R to generate 5 samples of normally distributed variables with 20 observations per variable. (For SPSS the syntax for the first sample would be **COMPUTE norm1 = RV.NORMAL(0,1)**. For R it would be **norm1 <- rnorm(20, 0, 1)**.)

    a.   Then create a Q-Q plot for each variable and notice the differences from one plot to the next. That will give you some idea of how closely even normally distributed data conform to the 45-degree line. How would you characterize the differences?

    b.   Repeat this exercise using $n = 50$.

3.17   What is the 75th percentile for GPA in Appendix Data Set? (This is the point below which 75% of the observations are expected to fall.)

3.18   What does the answer to Exercise 3.15 suggest about the importance of reference groups?

3.19 In Section 3.6, I said that T scores are designed to have a mean of 50 and a standard devia-
      tion of 10 and that the Achenbach Youth Self-Report measure produces T scores. The data
      in Figure 3.3 do not have a mean and standard deviation of exactly 50 and 10. Why do you
      suppose this is so?

3.20 Assuming that the Behavior Problem scores discussed in this chapter come from a popu-
      lation with a mean of 50 and a standard deviation of 10, what would be a diagnostically
      meaningful cutoff if you wanted to identify those children who score in the highest 2% of
      the population?

3.21 In Chapter 2, Figure 2.16, I plotted three histograms corresponding to three different depend-
      ent variables in Everitt's example of therapy for anorexia. Those data are available at www.
      uvm.edu/~dhowell/methods8/DataFiles/Fig2-16.dat. (The variable labels are in the first line of
      the file.) Prepare Q-Q plots corresponding to each of the plots in Figure 2.16. Do the conclu-
      sions you would draw from that figure agree with the conclusions that you would draw from
      the Q-Q plots? (Note: None of these three distributions would fail the Kolmogorov-Smirnov
      test for normality, though no test of normality is very good with small sample sizes.)

Discussion Questions

3.22 The data plotted below represent the distribution of salaries paid to full professors of
      Psychology with 7–11 years of service in 2008–2009, the last year that data are available.
      The data are available on the Web site at Ex3-24.dat, which also includes salaries for 24+
      years in rank. Although the data are obviously skewed to the right, what would you expect
      to happen if you treated these data as if they were normally distributed? What would happen
      if you converted salaries to log(salaries) (use your calculator to take logs of several values of
      X and see what happens)? What explanation could you hypothesize to account for the
      extreme values?

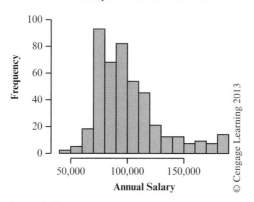

3.23 Recently in answer to a question that was sent to me I had to create a set of 16 scores that
      were more-or-less normally distributed with a mean of 16.3 and a standard deviation of 4.25.
      The approach taken in 3.18 could be used to produce data with a mean and standard deviation
      close to this, but I want them to be exactly right. How could I go about generating the data?

3.24 If you go back to the reaction-time data presented as a frequency distribution in Table 2.2
      and Figure 2.1, you will see that for the full set of scores they are not normally distributed.
      For these data the mean is 60.26 and the standard deviation is 13.01. By simple counting,
      you can calculate exactly what percentage of the sample lies above or below ± 1.0, 1.5, 2.0,
      2.5, and 3.0 standard deviations from the mean. You can also calculate, from tables of the
      normal distribution, what percentage of scores would lie above or below those cutoffs if the
      distribution were perfectly normal. Calculate these values and plot them against each other.
      (You have just created a partial Q-Q plot.) Using either this plot or a complete Q-Q plot
      describe what it tells you about how the data depart from a normal distribution. How would
      your answers change if the sample had been very much larger or very much smaller?

3.25   The data file named SAT.dat on the Web site contains data on SAT scores for all 50 states as well as the amount of money spent on education, and the percentage of students taking the SAT in that state. (The data are described in Appendix Data set.) Draw a histogram of the Combined SAT scores. Is this distribution normal? The variable adjcomb is the combined score adjusted for the percentage of students in that state who took the exam. What can you tell about this variable? How does its distribution differ from that for the unadjusted scores?

Chapter 4

Sampling Distributions and Hypothesis Testing

Objectives

To lay the groundwork for the procedures discussed in this book by examining the general theory of hypothesis testing and describing specific concepts as they apply to all hypothesis tests.

Contents

IN CHAPTER 2 we examined a number of different statistics and saw how they might be used to describe a set of data or to represent the frequency of the occurrence of some event. Although the description of the data is important and fundamental to any analysis, it is not sufficient to answer many of the most interesting problems we encounter. In a typical experiment, we might treat one group of people in a special way and wish to see whether their scores differ from the scores of people in general. Or we might offer a treatment to one group but not to a control group and wish to compare the means of the two groups on some variable. Descriptive statistics will not tell us, for example, whether the difference between a sample mean and a hypothetical population mean, or the difference between two obtained sample means, is small enough to be explained by chance alone or whether it represents a true difference that might be attributable to the effect of our experimental treatment(s).

Statisticians frequently use phrases such as "chance variability" or "sampling error" and assume that you know what they mean. Perhaps you do; however, if you do not, you are headed for confusion in the remainder of this book unless we spend a minute clarifying the meaning of these terms. We will begin with a simple example.

In Chapter 3 we considered the distribution of Total Behavior Problem scores from Achenbach's Youth Self-Report form. Total Behavior Problem scores are normally distributed in the population (i.e., the complete population of such scores is approximately normally distributed) with a population mean (μ) of 50 and a population standard deviation (σ) of 10. We know that different children show different levels of problem behaviors and therefore have different scores. We also know that if we took a sample of children, their sample mean would probably not equal exactly 50. One sample of children might have a mean of 49, while a second sample might have a mean of 52.3. The actual sample means would depend on the particular children who happened to be included in the sample. This expected variability from sample to sample is what is meant when we speak of "variability due to chance" or "error variance." The phrase refers to the fact that statistics (in this case, means) obtained from samples naturally vary from one sample to another.

sampling error

Along the same lines, the term **sampling error** often is used in this context as a synonym for variability due to chance. It indicates that the numerical value of a sample statistic probably will be in error (i.e., will deviate from the parameter it is estimating) as a result of the particular observations that happened to be included in the sample. In this context, "error" does not imply carelessness or mistakes. In the case of behavior problems, one random sample might just happen to include an unusually obnoxious child, whereas another sample might happen to include an unusual number of relatively well-behaved children.

4.1 Two Simple Examples Involving Course Evaluations and Rude Motorists

One example that we will investigate when we discuss correlation and regression looks at the relationship between how students evaluate a course and the grade they expect to receive in that course. Many faculty feel strongly about this topic, because even the best instructors turn to the semiannual course evaluation forms with some trepidation—perhaps with the same amount of trepidation that many students open their grade report form. Some faculty think that a course is good or bad independently of how well a student feels he or she will do in terms of a grade. Others feel that a student who seldom came to class and who will do poorly as a result will also unfairly rate the course as poor. Finally, there are those who argue that students who do well and experience success take something away from the course other than just a grade and that those students will generally rate the course highly. But the relationship between course ratings and student performance is an empirical question and, as such, can be answered by looking at relevant data. Suppose that in a random sample of 50 courses we find a general trend for students to rate a course they expect to do well in highly, and for students to rate a course where they expect to do poorly as low in overall quality. How do we tell whether this trend in our small data set is representative of a trend among students in general or just an odd result that would disappear if we ran the study over? (For your own interest, make your prediction of what kind of results we will find. We will return to this issue later.)

A second example comes from a study by Doob and Gross (1968), who investigated the influence of perceived social status. They found that if an old, beat-up (low-status) car failed to start when a traffic light turned green, 84% of the time the driver of the second car in line honked the horn. However, when the stopped car was an expensive, high-status car, only 50% of the time did the following driver honk. These results could be explained in one of two ways:

- The difference between 84% in one sample and 50% in a second sample is attributable to sampling error (random variability among samples); therefore, we cannot conclude that perceived social status influences horn-honking behavior.

- The difference between 84% and 50% is large and reliable. The difference is not attributable to sampling error; therefore, we conclude that people are less likely to honk at drivers of high-status cars.

Although the statistical calculations required to answer this question are different from those used to answer the one about course evaluations (because the first deals with relationships and the second deals with proportions), the underlying logic is fundamentally the same.

hypothesis testing

These examples of course evaluations and horn honking are two kinds of questions that fall under the heading of **hypothesis testing**. This chapter is intended to present the theory of hypothesis testing in as general a way as possible, without going into the specific techniques or properties of any particular test. I will focus largely on the situation involving differences instead of the situation involving relationships, but the logic is basically the same. (You will see additional material on examining relationships in Chapter 9.) I am very deliberately glossing over details of computation, because my purpose is to explore the concepts of hypothesis testing without involving anything but the simplest technical details.

We need to be explicit about what the problem is here. The reason for having hypothesis testing in the first place is that data are ambiguous. Suppose that we want to decide whether larger classes receive lower student ratings. We all know that some large classes are terrific, and others are really dreadful. Similarly, there are both good and bad small classes. So if we collect data on large classes, for example, the mean of several large classes will depend to some extent on which large courses just happen to be included in our sample. If we reran our data collection with a new random sample of large classes that mean would almost certainly be different. A similar situation applies for small classes. When we find a difference between the means of samples of large and small classes, we know that the difference would come out slightly differently if we collected new data. So a difference between the means is ambiguous. Is it greater than zero because large classes are worse than small ones, or because of the particular samples we happened to pick? Well, if the difference is quite large, it probably reflects differences between small and large classes. If it is quite small, it probably reflects just random noise. But how large is "large" and how small is "small?" That is the problem we are beginning to explore, and that is the subject of this chapter.

If we are going to look at either of the two examples laid out above, or at a third one to follow, we need to find some way of deciding whether we are looking at a small chance fluctuation between the horn-honking rates for low- and high-status cars or a difference that is sufficiently large for us to believe that people are much less likely to honk at those they consider higher in status. If the differences are small enough to attribute to chance variability, we may well not worry about them. On the other hand, it we can rule out chance as the source of the difference, we probably need to look further. This decision about chance is what we mean by hypothesis testing.

4.2 Sampling Distributions

In addition to course evaluations and horn honking, we will add a third example, to which we can all relate. It involves those annoying people who spend what seems an unreasonable amount of time vacating the parking space we are waiting for. Ruback and Juieng (1997) ran a simple study in which they divided drivers into two groups of 100 participants each—those who had someone waiting for their space and those who did not. They then recorded the amount of time it took the driver to leave the parking space. For those drivers who had no one waiting, it took an average of 32.15 seconds to leave the space. For those who did have someone waiting, it took an average of 39.03 seconds. For each of these groups the standard deviation of waiting times was 14.6 seconds. Notice that a driver took 6.88 seconds longer to leave a space when someone was waiting for it. (If you think about it, 6.88 seconds is a long time if you are the person doing the waiting.)

There are two possible explanations here. First, it is entirely possible that having someone waiting doesn't make any difference in how long it takes to leave a space, and that normally drivers who have no one waiting for them take, on average, the same length of time as drivers who do have someone waiting. In that case the difference that we found is just a result of the particular samples we happened to obtain. What we are saying here is that if we had whole populations of drivers in each of the two conditions, the populations means (μ_{nowait} and μ_{wait}) would be identical and any difference we find in our samples is sampling error. The alternative explanation is that the population means really are different and that people actually do take longer to leave a space when there is someone waiting for it. If the sample means had come out to be 32.15 and 32.18, you and I would probably side with the first explanation—or at least not be willing to reject it. If the means had come out to be 32.15 and 59.03, we would probably side with the second explanation—having someone waiting actually makes a difference. But the difference we found is somewhere in between, and we need to decide which explanation is more reasonable.

We want to answer the question "Is the obtained difference too great to be attributable to chance?" To do this we have to use what are called **sampling distributions**, which tell us specifically what degree of sample-to-sample variability we can expect by chance as a function of sampling error.

The most basic concept underlying all statistical tests is the sampling distribution of a statistic. It is fair to say that if we did not have sampling distributions, we would not have any statistical tests. Roughly speaking, sampling distributions tell us what values we might (or might not) expect to obtain for a particular statistic under a set of predefined conditions (e.g., what the sample differences between our two samples might be expected to be if the true means of the populations from which those samples came are equal). In addition, the standard deviation of that distribution of differences between sample means (known as the **standard error** of the distribution) reflects the variability that we would expect to find in the values of that statistic (differences between means) over repeated trials. Sampling distributions provide the opportunity to evaluate the likelihood (given the value of a sample statistic) that such predefined conditions actually exist.

Basically, the sampling distribution of a statistic can be thought of as the distribution of values obtained for that statistic over repeated sampling (i.e., running the experiment, or drawing samples, an unlimited number of times). Sampling distributions are almost always

sampling distributions

standard error

derived mathematically, but it is easier to understand what they represent if we consider how they could, in theory, be derived empirically with a simple sampling experiment.

We will take as an illustration the sampling distribution of the differences between means, because it relates directly to our example of waiting times in parking lots. The **sampling distribution of differences between means** is the distribution of differences between means of an infinite number of pairs of random samples drawn under certain specified conditions (e.g., under the condition that the true means of our populations are equal). Suppose we have two populations with known means and standard deviations. (Here we will suppose that the two population means are 35 and the population standard deviation is 15, though what the values are is not critical to the logic of our argument. In the general case we rarely know the population standard deviation, but for our example suppose that we do.) Further suppose that we draw a very large number (theoretically an infinite number) of pairs of random samples from these populations, with each sample consisting of 100 scores. For each sample we will calculate its sample mean and then the difference between the two means in that draw. When we finish drawing all the pairs of samples, we will plot the distribution of these differences. Such a distribution would be a sampling distribution of the difference between means. I wrote a nine line program in R (available at this book's Web site and named Sampling Distribution. R) to do the sampling I have described, drawing 10,000 pairs of samples of $n = 100$ from a population with a mean of 35 and a standard deviation of 15 and computing the difference between means for each pair. A histogram of this distribution is shown on the left of Figure 4.1 with a Q-Q plot on the right. I don't think that there is much doubt that this distribution is normally distributed. The center of this distribution is at 0.0, because we expect that, on average, differences between sample means will be 0.0. (The individual means themselves will be roughly 35.) We can see from this figure that differences between sample means of approximately −3 to +3, for example, are quite likely to occur when we sample from identical populations. We also can see that it is extremely unlikely that we would draw samples from these populations that differ by 10 or more. The fact that we know the kinds of values to expect for the difference of means of samples drawn from these populations is going to allow us to turn the question around and ask whether an obtained sample mean difference can be taken as evidence in favor of the hypothesis that we actually are sampling from identical populations—or populations with the same mean.

sampling distribution of differences between means

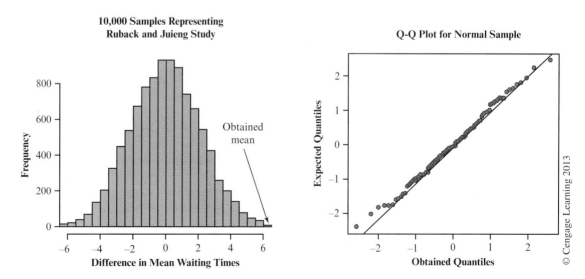

Figure 4.1   Distribution of difference between means, each based on 25 observations

Ruback and Juieng (1997) found a difference of 6.88 seconds in leaving times between the two conditions. It is quite clear from Figure 4.1 that this is very unlikely to have occurred if the true population means were equal. In fact, my little sampling study only found 6 cases out of 10,000 when the mean difference was more extreme than 6.88, for a probability of .0006. We are certainly justified in concluding that people wait longer to leave their space, for whatever reason, when someone is waiting for it.

4.3   Theory of Hypothesis Testing

Preamble

One of the major ongoing discussions in statistics in the behavioral sciences relates to hypothesis testing. The logic and theory of hypothesis testing has been debated for at least 75 years, but recently that debate has intensified considerably. The exchanges on this topic have not always been constructive (referring to your opponent's position as "bone-headedly misguided," "a perversion of the scientific method," or "ridiculous" usually does not win them to your cause), but some real and positive changes have come as a result. The changes are sufficiently important that much of this chapter, and major parts of the rest of the book, have been rewritten to accommodate them.

The arguments about the role of hypothesis testing concern several issues. First, and most fundamental, some people question whether hypothesis testing is a sensible procedure in the first place. I think that it is, and whether it is or isn't, the logic involved is related to so much of what we do, and is so central to what you will see in the experimental literature, that you have to understand it whether you approve of it or not. The second issue concerns the logic we will use for hypothesis testing. The dominant logic has been an amalgam of positions put forth by R. A. Fisher, and by Neyman and Pearson, dating from the 1920s and 1930s. (This amalgam is one about which both Fisher and Neyman and Pearson would express deep reservations, but it has grown to be employed by many, particularly in the behavioral sciences.) We will discuss that approach first, but follow it by more recent conceptualizations that lead to roughly the same point, but do so in what many feel is a more logical and rational process. Third, and perhaps most importantly, what do we need to consider *in addition* to traditional hypothesis testing? Running a statistical test and declaring a difference to be statistically significant at "$p \leq .05$" is no longer sufficient. A hypothesis test can only suggest whether a relationship is reliable or it is not, or that a difference between two groups is likely to be due to chance, or that it probably is not. In addition to running a hypothesis test, we need to tell our readers something about the difference itself, about confidence limits on that difference, and about the power of our test. This will involve a change in emphasis from earlier editions, and will affect how I describe results in the rest of the book. I think the basic conclusion is that simple hypothesis testing, no matter how you do it, is important, but it is not enough. If the debate has done nothing else, getting us to that point has been very important. You can see that we have a lot to cover, but once you understand the positions and the proposals, you will have a better grasp of the issues than most people in your field.

In the mid-1990s the American Psychological Association put together a task force to look at the general issue of hypothesis tests, and its report is available (Wilkinson, 1999; see also http://www.apa.org/science/leadership/bsa/statistical/tfsi-followup-report.pdf). Further discussion of this issue was included in an excellent paper by Nickerson (2000). These two documents do a very effective job of summarizing current thinking in the field. These recommendations have influenced the coverage of material in this book, and you will see more frequent references to confidence limits and effect size measures than you would have seen in previous editions.

The Traditional Approach to Hypothesis Testing

For the next several pages we will consider the traditional treatment of hypothesis testing. This is the treatment that you will find in almost any statistics text and is something that you need to fully understand. The concepts here are central to what we mean by hypothesis testing, no matter who is speaking about it.

We have just been discussing sampling distributions, which lie at the heart of the treatment of research data. We do not go around obtaining sampling distributions, either mathematically or empirically, simply because they are interesting to look at. We have important reasons for doing so. The usual reason is that we want to test some hypothesis. Let's go back to the sampling distribution of differences in mean times that it takes people to leave a parking space. We want to test the hypothesis that the obtained difference between sample means could reasonably have arisen had we drawn our samples from populations with the same mean. This is another way of saying that we want to know whether the mean departure time when someone is waiting is different from the mean departure time when there is no one waiting. One way we can test such a hypothesis is to have some idea of the probability of obtaining a difference in sample means as extreme as 6.88 seconds, for example, *if* we actually sampled observations from populations with the same mean. The answer to this question is precisely what a sampling distribution is designed to provide.

Suppose we obtained (constructed) the sampling distribution plotted in Figure 4.1. Suppose, for example, that our sample mean difference was only 2.88 instead of 6.88 and that we determined from our sampling distribution that the probability of a difference in means as great as 2.88 was .092. (How we determine this probability is not important here.) Our reasoning could then go as follows: "If we did in fact sample from populations with *the same mean*, the probability of obtaining a sample mean difference as high as 2.88 seconds is .092—that is not a terribly high probability, but it certainly isn't a low probability event. Because a sample mean difference at least as great as 2.88 is frequently obtained from populations with equal means, we have no reason to doubt that our two samples came from such populations."

In fact our sample mean difference was 6.88 seconds, and we calculated from the sampling distribution that the probability of a sample mean difference as large as 6.88, when the population means are equal, was only .0006. Our argument could then go like this: *If* we did obtain our samples from populations with *equal means*, the probability of obtaining a sample mean difference as large as 6.88 is only .0006—an unlikely event. Because a sample mean difference that large is unlikely to be obtained from such populations, we can reasonably conclude that these samples probably came from populations with different means. People take longer to leave when there is someone waiting for their parking space.

It is important to realize the steps in this example, because the logic is typical of most tests of hypotheses. The actual test consisted of several stages:

research hypothesis

1. We wanted to test the hypothesis, often called the **research hypothesis**, that people backing out of a parking space take longer when someone is waiting.

2. We obtained random samples of behaviors under the two conditions.

null hypothesis

3. We set up the hypothesis (called the **null hypothesis**, H_0) that the samples were in fact drawn from populations with the same means. This hypothesis states that leaving times do not depend on whether someone is waiting.

4. We then obtained the sampling distribution of the differences between means under the assumption that H_0 (the null hypothesis) is true (i.e., we obtained the sampling distribution of the differences between means when the population means are equal).

5. Given the sampling distribution, we calculated the probability of a mean difference *at least as large* as the one we actually obtained between the means of our two samples.

6. On the basis of that probability, we made a decision: either to reject or fail to reject H_0. Because H_0 states the means of the populations are equal, rejection of H_0 represents a belief that they are unequal, although the actual value of the difference in population means remains unspecified.

The preceding discussion is slightly oversimplified, but we can deal with those specifics when the time comes. The logic of the approach is representative of the logic of most, if not all, statistical tests.

1. Begin with a research hypothesis.
2. Set up the null hypothesis.
3. Construct the sampling distribution of the particular statistic on the assumption that H_0 is true.
4. Collect some data.
5. Compare the sample statistic to that distribution.
6. Reject or retain H_0, depending on the probability, under H_0, of a sample statistic as extreme as the one we have obtained.

The First Stumbling Block

I probably slipped something past you there, and you need to at least notice what. This is one of the very important issues that motivates the fight over hypothesis testing, and it is something that you need to understand even if you can't do much about it. What I imagine that you would like to know is "What is the probability that the null hypothesis (drivers don't take longer when people are waiting) is true *given* the data we obtained?" But that is not what I gave you, and it is not what I am going to give you in the future. I gave you the answer to a different question, which is "What is the probability that I would have obtained these data given that the null hypothesis is true?" I don't know how to give you an answer to the question you would like to answer—not because I am a terrible statistician, but because the answer is much too difficult in most situations and is often impossible. However, the answer that I did give you is still useful—and is used all the time. When the police ticket a driver for drunken driving because he can't drive in a straight line and can't speak coherently, they are saying that *if he were sober* he would not behave this way. Because he behaves this way we will conclude that he is not sober. This logic remains central to most approaches to hypothesis testing.

4.4 The Null Hypothesis

As we have seen, the concept of the null hypothesis plays a crucial role in the testing of hypotheses. People frequently are puzzled by the fact that we set up a hypothesis that is directly counter to what we hope to show. For example, if we hope to demonstrate the research hypothesis that college students do not come from a population with a mean self-confidence score of 100, we immediately set up the null hypothesis that they do. Or if we hope to demonstrate the validity of a research hypothesis that the means (μ_1 and μ_2) of the populations from which two samples are drawn are different, we state the null hypothesis that the population means are the same (or, equivalently, $\mu_1 - \mu_2 = 0$). (The term "null hypothesis" is most easily seen in this second example, in which it refers to the hypothesis that the difference between the two population means is zero, or null—some people call this the "nil null" but that complicates the issue too much and doesn't get us anywhere). We use the null hypothesis for several reasons. The philosophical argument, put forth by Fisher when he first introduced the concept, is that we can never prove something to be true, but we can prove something to be false. Observing 3,000 people with two arms does not prove the statement "Everyone has two arms." However, finding one person with one arm does disprove the original statement beyond any shadow of a doubt. Although one might argue with Fisher's basic position—and many people have—the null hypothesis retains its dominant place in statistics.

A second and more practical reason for employing the null hypothesis is that it provides us with the starting point for any statistical test. Consider the case in which you want to show that the mean self-confidence score of college students is greater than 100. Suppose further that you were granted the privilege of proving the truth of some hypothesis. What hypothesis are you going to test? Should you test the hypothesis that $\mu = 101$, or maybe the hypothesis that $\mu = 112$, or how about $\mu = 113$? The point is that in almost all research in the behavioral sciences we do not have a specific **alternative** (research) **hypothesis** in mind, and without one we cannot construct the sampling distribution we need. (This was one of the arguments raised against the original Neyman/Pearson approach, because they often spoke as if there were a specific alternative hypothesis to be tested, rather than just the diffuse negation of the null.) However, if we start off by assuming $H_0: \mu = 100$, we can immediately set about obtaining the sampling distribution for $\mu = 100$ and then, if our data are convincing, reject that hypothesis and conclude that the mean score of college students is greater than 100, which is what we wanted to show in the first place.

alternative

hypothesis

Statistical Conclusions

When the data differ markedly from what we would expect if the null hypothesis were true, we simply reject the null hypothesis and there is no particular disagreement about what our conclusions mean—we conclude that the null hypothesis is false. (This is not to suggest that we still don't need to tell our readers more about what we have found.) The interpretation is murkier and more problematic, however, when the data do not lead us to reject the null hypothesis. How are we to interpret a nonrejection? Shall we say that we have "proved" the null hypothesis to be true? Or shall we claim that we can "accept" the null, or that we shall "retain" it, or that we shall "withhold judgment"?

The problem of how to interpret a nonrejected null hypothesis has plagued students in statistics courses for over 75 years, and it will probably continue to do so (but see Section 4.10). The idea that if something is not false then it must be true is too deeply engrained in common sense to be dismissed lightly.

The one thing on which all statisticians agree is that we can never claim to have "proved" the null hypothesis. As I pointed out, the fact that the next 3,000 people we meet all have two arms certainly does not prove the null hypothesis that all people have two arms. In fact we know that many perfectly normal people have fewer than two arms. Failure to reject the null hypothesis often means that we have not collected enough data.

The issue is easier to understand if we use a concrete example. Wagner, Compas, and Howell (1988) conducted a study to evaluate the effectiveness of a program for teaching high school students to deal with stress. (This example began this book.) If this study found that students who participate in such a program had significantly fewer stress-related problems than did students in a control group who did not have the program, then we could, without much debate, conclude that the program was effective. However, if the groups did not differ at some predetermined level of statistical significance, what could we conclude?

We know we cannot conclude from a nonsignificant difference that we have proved that the mean of a population of scores of treatment subjects is the same as the mean of a population of scores of control subjects. The two treatments may in fact lead to subtle differences that we were not able to identify conclusively with our relatively small sample of observations.

Fisher's position was that a nonsignificant result is an inconclusive result. For Fisher, the choice was between rejecting a null hypothesis and suspending judgment. He would have argued that a failure to find a significant difference between conditions could result from the fact that the students who participated in the program handled stress only slightly better than did control subjects, or that they handled it only slightly less well, or that there was no difference between the groups. For Fisher, a failure to reject H_0 merely means that our data are insufficient to allow us to choose among these three alternatives; therefore, we must suspend judgment. You will see this position return shortly when we discuss a proposal by Jones and Tukey (2000).

A slightly different approach was taken by Neyman and Pearson (1933), who took a much more pragmatic view of the results of an experiment. Suppose that we were hired by a school board to evaluate a stress-management program. And suppose that our initial study produced a nonsignificant result. Fisher would just encourage us to withhold judgment. Neyman and Pearson would look at things differently. They would be concerned with the problem faced by the school board, who must decide whether to continue spending money on this stress-management program that we are providing for them. The school board would probably not be impressed if we told them that our study was inconclusive and then asked them to give us money to continue operating the program until we had sufficient data to state confidently whether or not the program was beneficial (or harmful). In the Neyman–Pearson position, one either rejects or accepts the null hypothesis. But when we say that we "accept" a null hypothesis, however, we do not mean that we take it to be proven as true. We simply mean that we will act as if it is true, at least until we have more adequate data. Whereas given a nonsignificant result, the ideal school board from Fisher's point of view would continue to support the program until we finally were able to make up our minds; the school board with a Neyman–Pearson perspective would conclude that the available evidence is not sufficient to defend continuing to fund the program, and they would cut off our funding.

This discussion of the Neyman–Pearson position has been much oversimplified, but it contains the central issue of their point of view. The debate between Fisher on the one hand and Neyman and Pearson on the other was a lively (and rarely civil) one, and present practice contains elements of both viewpoints. Most statisticians prefer to use phrases such as "retain the null hypothesis" and "fail to reject the null hypothesis" because these make clear the tentative nature of a nonrejection. These phrases have a certain Fisherian ring to them. On the other hand, the important emphasis on Type II errors (failing to reject a false null hypothesis), which we will discuss in Section 4.7, is clearly an essential feature of the Neyman–Pearson school. If you are going to choose between two alternatives (accept or reject), then you have to be concerned with the probability of falsely accepting as well as that of falsely rejecting the null hypothesis. Because Fisher would never accept a null hypothesis in the first place, he did not need to worry much about the probability of accepting a false one.[1] We will return to this whole question in Section 4.10, where we will consider an alternative approach, after we have developed several other points. First, however, we need to consider some basic information about hypothesis testing so as to have a vocabulary and an example with which to go further into hypothesis testing. This information is central to any discussion of hypothesis testing under any of the models that have been proposed.

---

[1] Excellent discussions of the differences between the theories of Fisher on the one hand, and Neyman and Pearson on the other can be found in Chapter Four of Gigerenzer, Swijtink, Porter, Daston, Beatty, & Krüger (1989); Lehman (1993); and Oakes (1990). The central issues involve the whole concept of probability, the idea of an infinite population or infinite resampling, and the choice of a critical value, among other things. The controversy is far from a simple one.

4.5 Test Statistics and Their Sampling Distributions

sample statistics

test statistics

We have been discussing the sampling distribution of the mean, but the discussion would have been essentially the same had we dealt instead with the median, the variance, the range, the correlation coefficient (as in our course evaluation example), proportions (as in our horn-honking example), or any other statistic you care to consider. (Technically the shapes of these distributions would be different, but I am deliberately ignoring such issues in this chapter.) The statistics just mentioned usually are referred to as **sample statistics** because they describe characteristics of samples. There is a whole different class of statistics called **test statistics**, which are associated with specific statistical procedures and that have their own sampling distributions. Test statistics are statistics such as t, F, and χ^2, which you may have run across in the past. (If you are not familiar with them, don't worry—we will consider them separately in later chapters.) This is not the place to go into a detailed explanation of any test statistics. I put this chapter where it is because I didn't want readers to think they were supposed to worry about technical issues. This chapter is the place, however, to point out that the sampling distributions for test statistics are obtained and used in essentially the same way as the sampling distribution of the mean.

As an illustration, consider the sampling distribution of the statistic t, which will be discussed in Chapter 7. For those who have never heard of the t test, it is sufficient to say that the t test is often used, among other things, to determine whether two samples were drawn from populations with the same means. Let μ_1 and μ_2 represent the means of the populations from which the two samples were drawn. The null hypothesis is the hypothesis that the two population means are equal, in other words, $H_0: \mu_1 = \mu_2$ (or $\mu_1 - \mu_2 = 0$). If we were extremely patient, we could empirically obtain the sampling distribution of t when H_0 is true by drawing an infinite number of pairs of samples, all from two identical populations, calculating t for each pair of samples (by methods to be discussed later), and plotting the resulting values of t. In that case H_0 must be true because we forced it to be true by drawing the samples from identical populations. The resulting distribution is the sampling distribution of t when H_0 is true. If we later had two samples that produced a particular value of t, we would test the null hypothesis by comparing our sample t to the sampling distribution of t. We would reject the null hypothesis if our obtained t did not look like the kinds of t values that the sampling distribution told us to expect when the null hypothesis is true.

I could rewrite the preceding paragraph, substituting χ^2, or F, or any other test statistic in place of t, with only minor changes dealing with how the statistic is calculated. Thus, you can see that all sampling distributions can be obtained in basically the same way (calculate and plot an infinite number of statistics by sampling from identical populations).

4.6 Making Decisions About the Null Hypothesis

In Section 4.2 we actually tested a null hypothesis when we considered the data on the time to leave a parking space. You should recall that we first drew pairs of samples from a population with a mean of 35 and a standard deviation of 15. (Don't worry about how we knew those were the parameters of the population—I made them up.) Then we calculated the differences between pairs of means in each of 10,000 replications and plotted those. Then we discovered that under those conditions a difference as large as the one that Ruback and Juieng found would happen only about 6 times out of 10,000 trials, for a probability of .0006. That is such an unlikely finding that we concluded our two means did not come from populations with the same mean.

decision-making

At this point we have to become involved in the **decision-making** aspects of hypothesis testing. We must decide whether an event with a probability of .0006 is sufficiently unlikely to cause us to reject H_0. Here we will fall back on arbitrary conventions that have been established over the years. The rationale for these conventions will become clearer as we go along, but for the time being keep in mind that they are merely conventions. One convention calls for rejecting H_0 if the probability under H_0 is less than or equal to .05 ($p \leq .05$), while another convention—one that is more conservative with respect to the probability of rejecting H_0—calls for rejecting H_0 whenever the probability under H_0 is less than or equal to .01. These values of .05 and .01 are often referred to as

rejection level

the **rejection level,** or the **significance level,** of the test. (When we say that a difference

significance level

is statistically significant at the .05 level, we mean that a difference that large would occur less than 5% of the time if the null were true.) Whenever the probability obtained under H_0 is less than or equal to our predetermined significance level, we will reject H_0. Another way of stating this is to say that any outcome whose probability under H_0 is less

rejection region

than or equal to the significance level falls in the **rejection region,** because such an outcome leads us to reject H_0.

For the purpose of setting a standard level of rejection for this book, we will use the .05 level of statistical significance, keeping in mind that some people would consider this level too lenient.[2] For our particular example we have obtained probabilities of $p = .0006$, and it is clearly less than .05. Because we have specified that we will reject H_0 if the probability of the data under H_0 is less than .05, we must conclude that we have reason to decide that the scores for the two conditions were drawn from populations with different means.

4.7 Type I and Type II Errors

Whenever we reach a decision with a statistical test, there is always a chance that our decision is the wrong one. Although this is true of almost all decisions, statistical or otherwise, the statistician has one point in her favor that other decision makers normally lack. She not only makes a decision by some rational process, but she can also specify the conditional probabilities of a decision being in error. In everyday life we make decisions with only subjective feelings about what is probably the right choice. The statistician, however, can state quite precisely the probability that she would make an erroneous rejection of H_0 if it were true. This ability to specify the probability of erroneously rejecting a true H_0 follows directly from the logic of hypothesis testing.

Consider the parking lot example, this time ignoring the difference in means that Ruback and Juieng found. The situation is diagrammed in Figure 4.2, in which the distribution is the distribution of differences in sample means when the null hypothesis is true, and the shaded portion represents the upper 5% of the distribution. The actual score that cuts off

critical value

the highest 5% is called the **critical value.** Critical values are those values of X (the variable) that describe the boundary or boundaries of the rejection region(s). For this particular example the critical value is 4.94.

[2] The particular view of hypothesis testing described here is the classical one that a null hypothesis is rejected if the probability of obtaining the data when the null hypothesis is true is less than the predefined significance level, and not rejected if that probability is greater than the significance level. Currently a substantial body of opinion holds that such cut-and-dried rules are inappropriate and that more attention should be paid to the probability value itself. In other words, the classical approach (using a .05 rejection level) would declare $p = .051$ and $p = .150$ to be (equally) "statistically nonsignificant" and $p = .048$ and $p = .0003$ to be (equally) "statistically significant." The alternative view would think of $p = .051$ as "nearly significant" and $p = .0003$ as "very significant." Although this view has much to recommend it, especially in light of current trends to move away from only reporting statistical significance of results, it will not be wholeheartedly adopted here. Most computer programs do print out exact probability levels, and those values, when interpreted judiciously, can be useful. The difficulty comes in defining what is meant by "interpreted judiciously."

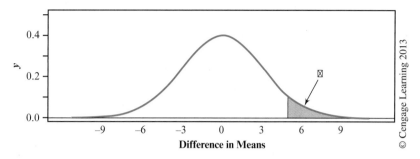

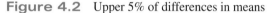

Figure 4.2   Upper 5% of differences in means

If we have a decision rule that says to reject H_0 whenever an outcome falls in the highest 5% of the distribution, we will reject H_0 whenever the difference in means falls in the shaded area; that is, whenever difference as high as the one we found has a probability of .05 or less of coming from the situation where the population means are equal. Yet by the very nature of our procedure, 5% of the differences in means when a waiting car has no effect on the time to leave will themselves fall in the shaded portion. Thus if we actually have a situation where the null hypothesis of no mean difference is true, we stand a 5% chance of any sample mean difference being in the shaded tail of the distribution, causing us erroneously to reject the null hypothesis. This kind of error (rejecting H_0 when in fact it

Type I error
α (alpha)

is true) is called a **Type I error**, and its conditional probability (the probability of rejecting the null hypothesis given that it is true) is designated as **α (alpha)**, the size of the rejection region. (Alpha was identified in Figure 4.2.) In the future, whenever we represent a probability by α, we will be referring to the probability of a Type I error.

Keep in mind the "conditional" nature of the probability of a Type I error. This means that you should be sure you understand that when we speak of a Type I error we mean the probability of rejecting H_0 *given that it is true*. We are not saying that we will reject H_0 on 5% of the hypotheses we test. We would hope to run experiments on important and meaningful variables and, therefore, to reject H_0 often. But when we speak of a Type I error, we are speaking only about rejecting H_0 in those situations in which the null hypothesis happens to be true.

You might feel that a 5% chance of making an error is too great a risk to take and suggest that we make our criterion much more stringent, by rejecting, for example, only the lowest 1% of the distribution. This procedure is perfectly legitimate, but realize that the more stringent you make your criterion, the more likely you are to make another kind of error—failing to reject H_0 when it is in fact false and H_1 is true. This type of error is called

Type II error
β (beta)

a **Type II error**, and its probability is symbolized by β **(beta)**.

The major difficulty in terms of Type II errors stems from the fact that if H_0 is false, we almost never know what the true distribution (the distribution under H_1) would look like for the population from which our data came. In other words, we never know exactly how false the null hypothesis is. We know only the distribution of scores under H_0. Put in the present context, we know the distribution of differences in means when having someone waiting for a parking space makes no difference in response time, but we don't know what the difference would be if waiting did make a difference. This situation is illustrated in Figure 4.3, in which the distribution labeled H_0 represents the distribution of mean differences when the null hypothesis is true, the distribution labeled H_1 represents our hypothetical distribution of differences when the null hypothesis is false, and the alternative hypothesis (H_1) is true. Remember that the distribution for H_1 is only hypothetical. We really do not know the location of that distribution, other than that it is higher (greater differences) than the distribution of H_0. (I have arbitrarily drawn that distribution so that its mean is 2 units above the mean under H_0.)

The darkly shaded portion in the top half of Figure 4.3 represents the rejection region. Any observation falling in that area (i.e., to the right of about 3.5) would lead to rejection of the null hypothesis. If the null hypothesis is true, we know that our observation will fall in this area 5% of the time. Thus, we will make a Type I error 5% of the time.

The cross-hatched portion in the bottom half of Figure 4.3 represents the probability (β) of a Type II error. This is the situation in which having someone waiting makes a difference in leaving time, but whose value is not sufficiently high to cause us to reject H_0.

In the particular situation illustrated in Figure 4.3, where I made up the mean and variance, we can in fact calculate β by using the normal distribution to calculate the probability of obtaining a score greater than 3.5 (the critical value) if $\mu = 35$ and $\sigma = 15$ for each condition. The actual calculation is not important for your understanding of β; because this chapter was designed specifically to avoid calculation, I will simply state that this probability (i.e., the area labeled β) is .76. Thus for this example, 76% of the occasions when waiting times (in the population) differ by 3.5 seconds (i.e., H_1 is actually true), we will make a Type II error by failing to reject H_0 when it is false.

From Figure 4.3 you can see that if we were to reduce the level of α (the probability of a Type I error) from .05 to .01 by moving the rejection region to the right, it would reduce the probability of Type I errors but would increase the probability of Type II errors. Setting α at .01 would mean that $\beta = .92$. Obviously there is room for debate over what level of significance to use. The decision rests primarily on your opinion concerning the relative importance of Type I and Type II errors for the kind of study you are conducting. If it were important to avoid Type I errors (such as falsely claiming that the average driver is rude),

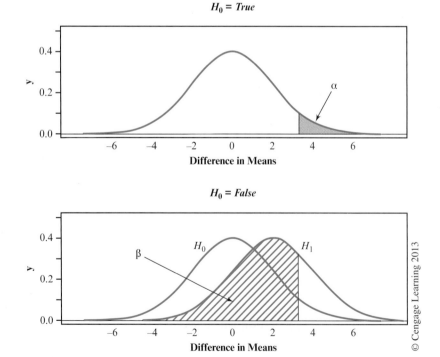

Figure 4.3 Distribution of mean differences under H_0 and H_1

Table 4.1   Possible outcomes of the decision-making process

Decision	True State of the World	
	H_0 True	H_0 False
Reject H_0	Type I error $p = \alpha$	Correct decision $p = 1 - \beta$ = Power
Don't reject H_0	Correct decision $p = 1 - \alpha$	Type II error $p = \beta$

then you would set a stringent (i.e., small) level of α. If, on the other hand, you want to avoid Type II errors (patting everyone on the head for being polite when actually they are not), you might set a fairly high level of α. (Setting $\alpha = .20$ in this example would reduce β to .46.) Unfortunately, in practice most people choose an arbitrary level of α, such as .05 or .01, and simply ignore β. In many cases this may be all you can do. (In fact you will probably use the alpha level that your instructor recommends.) In other cases, however, there is much more you can do, as you will see in Chapter 8.

I should stress again that Figure 4.3 is purely hypothetical. I was able to draw the figure only because I arbitrarily decided that the population means differed by 2 units, and the standard deviation of each population was 15. The answers would be different if I had chosen to draw it with a difference of 2.5 and/or a standard deviation of 10. In most everyday situations we do not know the mean and the variance of that distribution and can make only educated guesses, thus providing only crude estimates of β. In practice we can select a value of μ under H_1 that represents the minimum difference we would like to detect, because larger differences will have even smaller βs.

From this discussion of Type I and Type II errors we can summarize the decision-making process with a simple table. Table 4.1 presents the four possible outcomes of an experiment. The items in this table should be self-explanatory, but the one concept that we have not discussed is **power**. The power of a test is the probability of rejecting H_0 when it is actually false. Because the probability of failing to reject a false H_0 is β, then power must equal $1 - \beta$. Those who want to know more about power and its calculation will find power covered in Chapter 8.

power

4.8   One- and Two-Tailed Tests

The preceding discussion brings us to a consideration of one- and two-tailed tests. In our parking lot example we were concerned if people took longer when there was someone waiting, and we decided to reject H_0 only if a those drivers took longer. In fact, I chose that approach simply to make the example clearer. However, suppose our drivers left 16.88 seconds sooner when someone was waiting. Although this is an extremely unlikely event to observe if the null hypothesis is true, it would not fall in the rejection region, which consisted solely of long times. As a result we find ourselves in the position of not rejecting H_0 in the face of a piece of data that is very unlikely, but not in the direction expected.

The question then arises as to how we can protect ourselves against this type of situation (if protection is thought necessary). One answer is to specify before we run the experiment that we are going to reject a given percentage (say 5%) of the extreme outcomes, both those that are extremely high and those that are extremely low. But if we reject the lowest 5% and the highest 5%, then we would in fact reject H_0 a total of 10% of the time when it is actually true, that is, $\alpha = .10$. That is not going to work because we are rarely willing to work with α as high as .10 and prefer to see it set no higher than .05. The way to accomplish this is to reject the lowest 2.5% and the highest 2.5%, making a total of 5%.

one-tailed
directional, test

two-tailed
nondirectional,
test

The situation in which we reject H_0 for only the lowest (or only the highest) mean differences is referred to as a **one-tailed**, **or** **directional, test**. We make a prediction of the direction in which the individual will differ from the mean and our rejection region is located in only one tail of the distribution. When we reject extremes in both tails, we have what is called a **two-tailed**, **or** **nondirectional, test**. It is important to keep in mind that while we gain something with a two-tailed test (the ability to reject the null hypothesis for extreme scores in either direction), we also lose something. A score that would fall in the 5% rejection region of a one-tailed test may not fall in the rejection region of the corresponding two-tailed test, because now we reject only 2.5% in each tail.

In the parking example I chose a one-tailed test because it simplified the example. But that is not a rational way of making such a choice. In many situations we do not know which tail of the distribution is important (or both are), and we need to guard against extremes in either tail. The situation might arise when we are considering a campaign to persuade children not to start smoking. We might find that the campaign leads to a decrease in the incidence of smoking. Or, we might find that campaigns run by adults to persuade children not to smoke simply make smoking more attractive and exciting, leading to an increase in the number of children smoking. In either case we would want to reject H_0.

In general, two-tailed tests are far more common than one-tailed tests for several reasons. First, the investigator may have no idea what the data will look like and therefore has to be prepared for any eventuality. Although this situation is rare, it does occur in some exploratory work.

Another common reason for preferring two-tailed tests is that the investigators are reasonably sure the data will come out one way but want to cover themselves in the event they are wrong. This type of situation arises more often than you might think. (Carefully formed hypotheses have an annoying habit of being phrased in the wrong direction, for reasons that seem so obvious after the event.) The smoking example is a case in point, where there is some evidence that poorly contrived antismoking campaigns actually do more harm than good. A frequent question that arises when the data may come out the other way around is, "Why not plan to run a one-tailed test and then, if the data come out the other way, just change the test to a two-tailed test?" This kind of approach just won't work. If you start an experiment with the extreme 5% of the left-hand tail as your rejection region and then turn around and reject any outcome that happens to fall in the extreme 2.5% of the right-hand tail, you are working at the 7.5% level. In that situation you will reject 5% of the outcomes in one direction (assuming that the data fall in the desired tail), and you are willing also to reject 2.5% of the outcomes in the other direction (when the data are in the unexpected direction). There is no denying that 5% + 2.5% = 7.5%. To put it another way, would you be willing to flip a coin for an ice cream cone if I have chosen "heads" but also reserve the right to switch to "tails" after I see how the coin lands? Or would you think it fair of me to shout, "Two out of three!" when the coin toss comes up in your favor? You would object to both of these strategies, and you should. For the same reason, the choice between a one-tailed test and a two-tailed one is made before the data are collected. It is also one of the reasons that two-tailed tests are usually chosen.

A third reason for two-tailed tests concerns the case where we can't really define a one-tailed test. One example is the case when we have more than two groups. We will consider this situation at length when we discuss the analysis of variance. When we have more than two groups a one-tailed test is pretty much undefined, and we will actually have a multi-tailed test. And when we come to the chi-square test in Chapter 6, the way that the test statistic is defined precludes the idea of a one-tailed test unless we engage in additional steps, which I would not suggest.

Although the preceding discussion argues in favor of two-tailed tests, as will the discussion in Section 4.10, and although in this book we generally confine ourselves to such procedures, there are no hard-and-fast rules. The final decision depends on what you already know about the relative severity of different kinds of errors. It is important to keep in mind that with respect to a given tail of a distribution, the difference between a one-tailed test and a two-tailed test is that the latter just uses a different cutoff. A two-tailed test at $\alpha = .05$ is more liberal than a one-tailed test at $\alpha = .01$.

If you have a sound grasp of the logic of testing hypotheses by use of sampling distributions, the remainder of this course will be relatively simple. For any new statistic you encounter, you will need to ask only two basic questions:

- How and with which assumptions is the statistic calculated?
- What does the statistic's sampling distribution look like under H_0?

If you know the answers to these two questions, your test is accomplished by calculating the test statistic for the data at hand and comparing the statistic to the sampling distribution. Because the relevant sampling distributions are tabled in the appendices, all you really need to know is which test is appropriate for a particular situation and how to calculate its test statistic. (Of course there is way more to statistics than just hypothesis testing, so perhaps I'm doing a bit of overselling here. There is a great deal to understanding the field of statistics beyond how to calculate, and evaluate, a specific statistical test. Calculation is the easy part, especially with modern computer software.)

4.9   What Does it Mean to Reject the Null Hypothesis?

One of the common problems that even well-trained researchers have with the null hypothesis is the confusion over what rejection really means. I earlier mentioned the fact that we calculate the probability that we would obtain these particular data given that the null is true. We are not calculating the probability of the null being true given the data. I am repeating myself, but the issue bears repeating.

Suppose that we test a null hypothesis about the difference between two population means and reject it at $p = .045$. There is a temptation to say that such a result means that the probability of the null being true is .045. But that is *not* what this probability means. What we have shown is that *if the null hypothesis were true*, the probability of obtaining a difference between means as great as the difference we found is only .045. That is quite different from saying that the probability that the null is true is .045. What we are doing here is confusing the probability of the hypothesis given the data, and the probability of the data given the hypothesis. These are called **conditional probabilities,** and will be discussed in Chapter 5. The probability of .045 that we have here is the probability of the data given that H_0 is true [written $p(D \mid H_0)$]—the vertical line is read "given." It is not the probability that H_0 is true given the data [written $p(H_0 \mid D)$]. The best discussion of this issue that I have read is in an excellent paper by Nickerson (2000).

conditional probabilities

4.10   An Alternative View of Hypothesis Testing

What I have presented so far about hypothesis testing is the traditional approach. It is found in virtually every statistics text, and you need to be very familiar with it. However, there has recently been an interest in different ways of looking at hypothesis testing, and a new approach proposed by Jones and Tukey (2000) avoids some of the problems of the traditional approach.

We will begin with an example comparing two population means that is developed further in Chapter 7. Adams, Wright, and Lohr (1996) showed a group of homophobic heterosexual males and a group of nonhomophobic heterosexual males a videotape of sexually explicit erotic homosexual images and recorded the resulting level of sexual arousal in the participants. They were interested in seeing whether there was a difference in sexual arousal between the two categories of viewers. (Notice that I didn't say which group they expected to come out with the higher mean, just that there would be a difference.)

The traditional hypothesis testing approach would be to set up the null hypothesis that $\mu_h = \mu_n$, where μ_h is the population mean for homophobic males, and μ_n is the population mean for nonhomophobic males. The traditional alternative (two-tailed) hypothesis is that $\mu_n \neq \mu_v$. Many people have pointed out that the null hypothesis in such a situation is never going to be true. It is not reasonable to believe that if we had a population of all homophobic males their mean would be exactly equal to the mean of the population of all nonhomophobic males to an unlimited number of decimal places. Whatever the means are, they will certainly differ by at least some trivial amount.[3] So we know before we begin that the null hypothesis is false, and we might ask ourselves why we are testing the null in the first place. (Many people have asked that question.)

Jones and Tukey (2000) and Harris (2005) have argued that we really have three possible hypotheses or conclusions we could draw—Jones and Tukey speak primarily in terms of "conclusions." One is that $\mu_h < \mu_n$, another is that $\mu_h > \mu_n$, and the third is that $\mu_h = \mu_n$. This third hypothesis is the traditional null hypothesis, and we have just said that it is never going to be exactly true, so we can rule it out. These three hypotheses lead to three courses of action. If we test the first ($\mu_h < \mu_n$) and reject it, we conclude that homophobic males are more aroused than nonhomophobic males. If we test the second ($\mu_h > \mu_n$) and reject it, we conclude that homophobic males are less aroused than nonhomophobic males. If we cannot reject either of those hypotheses, we conclude that we have insufficient evidence to make a choice—the population means are almost certainly different, but we don't know which is the larger.

The difference between this approach and the traditional one may seem minor, but it is important. In the first place, when Lyle Jones and John Tukey tell us something, we should definitely listen. These are not two guys who just got out of graduate school; they are two very highly respected statisticians. (If there were a Nobel Prize in statistics, John Tukey would have won it.) In the second place, this approach acknowledges that the null is never strictly true, but that sometimes the data do not allow us to draw conclusions about which mean is larger. So instead of relying on fuzzy phrases like "fail to reject the null hypothesis" or "retain the null hypothesis," we simply do away with the whole idea of a null hypothesis and just conclude that "we can't decide whether μ_h is greater than μ_n, or is less than μ_n." In the third place, this looks as if we are running two one-tailed tests, but with an important difference. In a traditional one-tailed test, we must specify in advance which tail we are testing. If the result falls in the extreme of that tail, we reject the null and declare that $\mu_h < \mu_n$, for example. If the result does not fall in that tail we must not reject the null, no matter how extreme it is in the other tail. But that is not what Jones and Tukey are suggesting. They do not require you to specify the direction of the difference before you begin.

Jones and Tukey are suggesting that we do not specify a tail in advance, but that we collect our data and determine whether the result is extreme in either tail. If it is extreme in

---

[3] You may think that we are quibbling over differences in the third decimal place, but if you think about homophobia it is reasonable to expect that whatever the difference between the two groups, it is probably not going to be trivial. Similarly with the parking example. The world is filled with normal people who probably just get in their car and leave regardless of whether or not someone is waiting. But there are also the extremely polite people who hurry to get out of the way, and some jerky people who deliberately take extra time. I don't know which of the latter groups is larger, but I'm sure that there is nothing like a 50:50 split. The difference is going to be noticeable whichever way it comes out. I can't think of a good example, that isn't really trivial, where the null hypothesis would be very close to true.

the lower tail, we conclude that $\mu_h < \mu_n$. If it is extreme in the upper tail, we conclude that $\mu_h > \mu_n$. And if neither of those conditions apply, we declare that the data are insufficient to make a choice. (Notice that I didn't once use the word "reject" in the last few sentences. I said "conclude." The difference is subtle, but I think that it is important.)

But Jones and Tukey go a bit further and alter the significance level. First of all, we know that the probability that the null is true is .00. (In other words, $p(\mu_h = \mu_n = 0)$.) The difference may be small, but there is nonetheless a difference. We cannot make an error by not rejecting the null because saying that we don't have enough evidence is not the same as incorrectly rejecting a hypothesis. As Jones and Tukey (2000) wrote:

> With this formulation, a conclusion is in error only when it is 'a reversal,' when it asserts one direction while the (unknown) truth is in the other direction. Asserting that the direction is not yet established may constitute a wasted opportunity, but it is not an error. We want to control the rate of error, the reversal rate, while minimizing wasted opportunity, that is, while minimizing indefinite results. (p. 412)

So one of two things is true—either $\mu_h > \mu_n$ or $\mu_h < \mu_n$. If $\mu_h > \mu_n$ is actually true, meaning that homophobic males are more aroused by homosexual videos, then the only error we can make is to erroneously conclude the reverse—that $\mu_h < \mu_n$. And the probability of that error is, at most, .025 if we were to use the traditional two-tailed test with 2.5% of the area in each tail. If, on the other hand, $\mu_h < \mu_n$, the only error we can make is to conclude that $\mu_h > \mu_n$, the probability of which is also at most .025. Thus if we use the traditional cutoffs of a two-tailed test, the probability of a reversal error is at most .025. We don't have to add areas or probabilities here because only one of those errors is possible. Jones and Tukey go on to suggest that we could use the cutoffs corresponding to 5% in each tail (the traditional two-tailed test at $\alpha = .10$) and still have only a 5% chance of making a Type I error. Although this is true, I think you will find that many traditionally trained colleagues, including journal reviewers, will start getting a bit "squirrelly" at this point, and you might not want to push your luck.

I wouldn't be surprised if at this point students are throwing up their hands with one of two objections. First would be the claim that we are just "splitting hairs." My answer to that is "No, we're not." These issues have been hotly debated in the literature, with some people arguing that we abandon hypothesis testing altogether (Hunter, 1997). The Jones-Tukey formulations make sense of hypothesis testing and increase statistical power if you follow all of their suggestions. (I believe that they would prefer the phrase "drawing conclusions" to "hypothesis testing.") Second, students could very well be asking why I spent many pages laying out the traditional approach and then another page or two saying why it is all wrong. I tried to answer that at the beginning—the traditional approach is so engrained in what we do that you cannot possibly get by without understanding it. It will lie behind most of the studies you read, and your colleagues will expect that you understand it. The fact that there is an alternative, and better, approach does not release you from the need to understand the traditional approach. And unless you change α levels, as Jones and Tukey recommend, you will be doing almost the same things but coming to more sensible conclusions. My strong recommendation is that you consistently use two-tailed tests, probably at $\alpha = .05$, but keep in mind that the probability that you will come to an incorrect conclusion about the direction of the difference is really only .025 if you stick with $\alpha = .05$.

4.11   Effect Size

effect size

Earlier in the chapter I mentioned that there was a movement afoot to go beyond simple significance testing to report some measure of the size of an effect, often referred to as the **effect size**. In fact, some professional journals are already insisting on it. I will expand on this topic in detail as we go along, but it is worth noting here that I have already sneaked a measure of effect size past you, and I'll bet that nobody noticed. When writing about waiting for parking spaces to open up, I pointed out that Ruback and Juieng (1997) found a difference of 6.88 seconds, which is not trivial when you are the one doing the waiting. I could have gone a step further and pointed out that, because the standard deviation of waiting times was 14.6 seconds, we are seeing a difference of nearly half a standard deviation. Expressing the difference between waiting times in terms of the actual number of seconds or as being "nearly half a standard deviation" provides a measure of how large the effect was—and it is a very reputable measure. There is much more to be said about more formal effect size measures, but at least this gives you some idea of what we are talking about. I will expand on this idea repeatedly in the following chapters.

I should say one more thing on this topic. One of the difficulties in understanding the debates over hypothesis testing is that for years statisticians have been very sloppy in selecting their terminology. Thus, for example, in rejecting the null hypothesis it is very common for someone to report that they have found a "significant difference." Most readers could be excused for taking this to mean that the study has found an "important difference," but that is not at all what is meant. When statisticians and researchers say "significant," that is shorthand for "statistically significant." It merely means that the difference, even if trivial, is not likely to be due to chance. The recent emphasis on effect sizes is intended to go beyond statements about chance, and tell the reader something, though perhaps not much, about "importance." I will try in this book to insert the word "statistically" before "significant," when that is what I mean, but I can't promise to always remember.

4.12   A Final Worked Example

Let's take an example that differs from the first because it involves only a single score rather than a sample mean. For illustrative purposes we will go about our test by way of what we know about the formula for the standard normal distribution. Finger-tapping speed is actually a common measure used in neuropsychology. Studies have shown impaired performance on a finger-tapping task for populations with Alzheimer's disease, traumatic brain injury, and schizophrenia. We have widely available normative data from the Halstead Reitan Battery against which we can compare patients who have been sent to us. In general those norms are based on large populations, and for females the mean performance on normal patients is 47.8 with a standard deviation of 5.3. Suppose that we have a patient whose tapping speed is 35. Is this person far enough below normal that we would suspect some sort of neurological damage?

I will stick with the traditional approach to hypothesis testing in what follows, though you should be able to see the difference between this and the Jones and Tukey approach. We have two possible choices here: the individual is or is not impaired. If she is not impaired we know the mean and the standard deviation of the population from which her score was sampled: 47.8 and 5.3, respectively. If she is impaired we have no idea what the mean and standard deviation are for the population from which her score was sampled, nor do we even need to know. We don't even have to think of her as part of any particular population. To help us draw a reasonable conclusion about this person's status, we will set up the null hypothesis that this individual is not impaired, or more precisely that she was drawn from a population with a mean of 47.8; that is, $H_0 : \mu = 47.8$. We will identify H_1 with the hypothesis that the individual is impaired ($\mu \neq 47.8$). (Note that Jones and Tukey would [simultaneously] test $H_1 : \mu < 47.8$ and $H_2 : \mu > 47.8$, and would associate the null hypothesis with the conclusion that we don't have sufficient data to make a decision.)

For the traditional approach we now need to choose between a one-tailed and a two-tailed test. In this particular case we will choose a one-tailed test on the grounds that finger tapping more rapidly than normal has no diagnostic significance. Because we have chosen a one-tailed test, we have set up the alternative hypothesis as $H_1 : \mu < 47.8$.

Before we can apply our statistical procedures to the data at hand, we must make one additional decision. We have to decide on a level of significance for our test. In this case I have chosen to run the test at the 5% level instead of the 1% level, because I am using $\alpha = .05$ as a standard for this book and also because I am more worried about a Type II error than I am about a Type I error. If I make a Type I error and erroneously conclude that the individual is impaired, subsequent evidence is likely to disconfirm that conclusion. If I make a Type II error and do not identify her as impaired, I am making a more serious error.

Next we need to calculate the probability of a non-impaired individual obtaining a score as low as 35. We first calculate the z score corresponding to a raw score of 35. From Chapter 3 we know how to make such a calculation. Although the mean and standard deviation from a large normative sample are not true parameters (they are based on a sample), they will be close enough for what we need in this case. (When the normative samples are small, we will need an alternative approach, which is covered in Chapter 7.) We know from Chapter 3 that we can compute a z statistic that will tell us how far, in standard deviation units, a score of 35 is from a mean of 47.8. If such a score is very extreme, we would be inclined to think that our patient was suffering from some sort of disease. To do this we compute

$$z = \frac{X - \mu}{\sigma} = \frac{35 - 47.8}{5.3} = -2.42$$

The patient's score is -2.42 standard deviations below the mean of all unimpaired test takers. We then go to tables of z to calculate the probability that we would obtain a z value less than or equal to -2.42. From Appendix z we find that this probability is .0078. Because this probability is less than the 5% significance level we chose to work with, we will reject the null hypothesis on the grounds that it is too unlikely that we would obtain a score as low as 35 if we had sampled an observation from a population of unimpaired individuals. Instead, we will conclude that we have an observation from an individual who is impaired and needs treatment.

It is important to note that in rejecting the null hypothesis, we could have made a Type I error. We know that if we do sample unimpaired women, .78% of them will score this low. It is possible that our applicant was normal and just did poorly. All we are saying is that such an event is sufficiently unlikely that we will place our bets with the alternative hypothesis.

4.13 Back to Course Evaluations and Rude Motorists

We started this chapter with a discussion of the relationship between how students evaluate a course and the grade they expect to receive in that course. Our second example looked at the probability of motorists honking their horns at low- and high-status cars that did not move when a traffic light changed to green. As you will see in Chapter 9, the first example uses a correlation coefficient to represent the degree of relationship. The second example simply compares two proportions. Both examples can be dealt with using the techniques discussed in this chapter. In the first case, if there were no relationship between the grades and ratings, we would expect that the true correlation in the population of students is 0.00. We simply set up the null hypothesis that the population correlation is 0.00 and then ask about the probability that a sample of observations would produce a correlation as large as the one we obtained. In the second case, we set up the null hypothesis that there is no difference between the proportion of motorists in the population who honk at low- and high-status cars. Then we calculate the probability of obtaining a difference in sample proportions as large as the one we obtained (in our case .34) if the null hypothesis is true. This is very similar to what we did with the parking example except that this involves proportions instead of means. I do not expect you to run these tests now, but you should have a general sense of the way we will set up the problem when we do learn to run them.

Key Terms

Sampling error (Introduction)

Hypothesis testing (4.1)

Sampling distributions (4.2)

Standard error (4.2)

Sampling distribution of the mean (4.2)

Research hypothesis (4.3)

Null hypothesis (H_0) (4.3)

Alternative hypothesis (H_1) (4.4)

Sample statistics (4.5)

Test statistics (4.5)

Decision making (4.6)

Rejection level (significance level) (4.6)

Rejection region (4.6)

Critical value (4.7)

Type I error (4.7)

α (alpha) (4.7)

Type II error (4.7)

β (beta) (4.7)

Power (4.7)

One-tailed test (directional test) (4.8)

Two-tailed test (nondirectional test) (4.8)

Conditional probabilities (4.9)

Effect size (4.11)

Exercises

4.1   Suppose I told you that last night's NHL hockey game resulted in a score of 26–13. You would probably decide that I had misread the paper and was discussing something other than a hockey score. In effect, you have just tested and rejected a null hypothesis.

   a.   What was the null hypothesis?

   b.   Outline the hypothesis-testing procedure that you have just applied.

4.2   What would be a Type II error in Exercise 4.4?

4.3   What would be a Type I error in Exercise 4.4?

4.4   For the past year I have spent about $4.00 a day for lunch, give or take a quarter or so.

   a.   Draw a rough sketch of this distribution of daily expenditures.

   b.   If, without looking at the bill, I paid for my lunch with a $5 bill and received $.75 in change, should I worry that I was overcharged?

   c.   Explain the logic involved in your answer to part (b).

4.5   Using the example in Exercise 4.4, describe what we mean by the rejection region and the critical value.

4.6   Imagine that you have just invented a statistical test called the Mode Test to test whether the mode of a population is some value (e.g., 100). The statistic (M) is calculated as

$$M = \frac{\text{Sample mode}}{\text{Sample range}}.$$

Describe how you could obtain the sampling distribution of M. (Note: This is a purely fictitious statistic as far as I am aware.)

4.7   A recently admitted class of graduate students at a large state university has a mean Graduate Record Exam verbal score of 650 with a standard deviation of 50. (The scores are reasonably normally distributed.) One student, whose mother just happens to be on the board of trustees, was admitted with a GRE score of 490. Should the local newspaper editor, who loves scandals, write a scathing editorial about favoritism?

4.8   Why might I want to adopt a one-tailed test in Exercise 4.4, and which tail should I choose? What would happen if I chose the wrong tail?

4.9   Why might (or might not) the GRE scores be normally distributed for the restricted sample (admitted students) in Exercise 4.7?

4.10   Why is such a small standard deviation reasonable in Exercise 4.7?

4.11   In Exercise 4.6 what would we call M in the terminology of this chapter?

4.12   Define "sampling error."

4.13   In Exercise 4.7 what would be the alternative hypothesis (H_1)?

4.14   Describe a situation in daily life in which we routinely test hypotheses without realizing it.

4.15   What is the difference between a "distribution" and a "sampling distribution"?

4.16   In the example in Section 4.11 how would the test have differed if we had chosen to run a two-tailed test?

4.17   Give two examples of research hypotheses and state the corresponding null hypotheses.

4.18   How would decreasing α affect the probabilities given in Table 4.1?

4.19   Rerun the calculations in Exercise 4.20 for $\alpha = .01$.

4.20   For the distribution in Figure 4.3, I said that the probability of a Type II error (β) is .74. Show how this probability was obtained.

4.21   Describe the steps you would go through to flesh out the example given in this chapter about the course evaluations. In other words, how might you go about determining whether there truly is a relationship between grades and course evaluations?

4.22   Describe the steps you would go through to test the hypothesis that motorists are ruder to fellow drivers who drive low-status cars than to those who drive high-status cars.

Discussion Questions

4.23   In Chapter 1 we discussed a study of allowances for fourth-grade children. We considered that study again in the exercises for Chapter 2, where you generated data that might have been found in such a study.

    a.   Consider how you would go about testing the research hypothesis that boys receive more allowance than girls. What would be the null hypothesis?

    b.   Would you use a one- or a two-tailed test?

    c.   What results might lead you to reject the null hypothesis and what might lead you to retain it?

    d.   What single thing might you do to make this study more convincing?

4.24   What effect might the suggestion to experimenters that they report effect sizes have on the conclusions we draw from future research studies in Psychology?

4.25   Discuss the different ways that the traditional approach to hypothesis testing and the Jones and Tukey approach would address the question(s) inherent in the example of waiting times for a parking space.

4.26   Simon and Bruce (1991), in demonstrating resampling statistics, tested the null hypothesis that the mean price of liquor (in 1961) for the 16 "monopoly" states, where the state owned the liquor stores, was different from the mean price in the 26 "private" states, where liquor stores were privately owned. (The means were $4.35 and $4.84, respectively, giving you some hint at the effects of inflation.) For technical reasons several states don't conform to this scheme and could not be analyzed.

    a.   What is the null hypothesis that we are really testing?

    b.   What label would you apply to $4.35 and $4.84?

c.   If these are the only states that qualify for our consideration, why are we testing a null hypothesis in the first place?

d.   Can you think of a situation where it does make sense to test a null hypothesis here?

4.27   The rate of depression in women tends to be about twice that of men. A graduate student took a sample of 100 cases of depression from area psychologists and found that 61 of them were women. You can model what the data would look like over repeated samplings when the probability of a case being a woman by creating 1,000 samples of 100 cases each when $p(\text{woman}) = .50$. This is easily done using SPSS by first creating a file with 1,000 rows. (This is a nuisance to do, and you can best do it by downloading the file http://www.uvm. edu/~dhowell/methods8/DataFiles/Ex4-27.sav, which already has a file set up with 1,000 rows, though that is all that is in the file.) Then use the Transform/Compute menu to create numberwomen = RV.BINOM(100,.5). For each trial the entry for numberwomen is the number of people in that sample of 100 who were women.

a.   Does it seem likely that 61 women (out of 100 clients) would arise if $p = .50$?

b.   How would you test the hypothesis that 75% of depressed cases are women? An R program to do these calculations is available on the book's Web site.

Chapter 5

Basic Concepts of Probability

Objectives

To develop the concept of probability, present some basic rules for manipulating probabilities, outline the basic ideas behind Bayes' theorem, and introduce the binomial distribution and its role in hypothesis testing.

Contents

IN CHAPTER 3 we began to make use of the concept of probability. For example, we saw that about 19% of children have Behavior Problem scores between 52 and 56 and thus concluded that if we chose a child at random, the probability that he or she would score between 52 and 56 is .19. When we begin concentrating on inferential statistics in Chapter 6, we will rely heavily on statements of probability. There we will be making statements of the form, "If this hypothesis were correct, the probability is only .015 that we would have obtained a result as extreme as the one we actually obtained." If we are to rely on statements of probability, it is important to understand what we mean by probability and to understand a few basic rules for computing and manipulating probabilities. That is the purpose of this chapter.

The material covered in this chapter has been selected for two reasons. First, it is directly applicable to an understanding of the material presented in the remainder of the book. Second, it is intended to allow you to make simple calculations of probabilities that are likely to be useful to you. Material that does not satisfy either of these qualifications has been deliberately omitted. For example, we will not consider such things as the probability of drawing the queen of hearts, given that 14 cards, including the four of hearts, have already been drawn. Nor will we consider the probability that your desk light will burn out in the next 25 hours of use, given that it has already lasted 250 hours. The student who is interested in those topics is encouraged to take a course in probability theory to cover such material in depth.

5.1 Probability

analytic view

The concept of probability can be viewed in several different ways. There is not even general agreement as to what we mean by the word probability. The oldest and perhaps most common definition of a probability is called the **analytic view**. One of the examples that is often drawn into discussions of probability is that of one of my favorite candies, M&M's. M&M's are a good example because everyone is familiar with them, they are easy to use in class demonstrations because they don't get your hand all sticky, and you can eat them when you're done. The Mars Candy Company is so fond of having them used as an example that they keep lists of the percentage of colors in each bag—though they seem to keep moving the lists around, making it a challenge to find them on occasions. At present the data on the milk chocolate version is shown in Table 5.1.

Suppose that you have a bag of M&M's in front of you and you reach in and pull one out. Just to simplify what follows, assume that there are 100 M&M's in the bag, though that is not a requirement. What is the probability that you will pull out a blue M&M? You can probably answer this question without knowing anything more about

Table 5.1 Distribution of colors in an average bag of M&M's

Color	Percentage
Brown	13
Red	13
Yellow	14
Green	16
Orange	20
Blue	24
Total	**100**

© Cengage Learning 2013

probability. Because 24% of the M&M's are blue, and because you are sampling randomly, the probability of drawing a blue M&M is .24. This example illustrates one definition of probability:

> If an event can occur in A ways and can fail to occur in B ways, and if all possible ways are equally likely (e.g., each M&M in the bag has an equal chance of being drawn), then the probability of its occurrence is $A/(A + B)$, and the probability of its failing to occur is $B/(A + B)$.

Because there are 24 ways of drawing a blue M&M (one for each of the 24 blue M&M's in a bag of 100 M&M's) and 76 ways of drawing a different color, $A = 24$, $B = 76$, and $p(A) = 24/(24 + 76) = .24$.

frequentist view

An alternative view of probability is the frequentist view. Suppose that we keep drawing M&M's from the bag, noting the color on each draw. In conducting this sampling study we **sample with replacement**, meaning that each M&M is replaced before the next one is drawn. If we made a very large number of draws, we would find that (very nearly) 24% of the draws would result in a blue M&M. Thus we might define probability as the limit[1] of the relative frequency of occurrence of the desired event that we approach as the number of draws increases. (A program written in R can be found on the book's Web site that demonstrates how the probability approaches p as the sample size increases.)

sample with replacement

subjective probability

Yet a third concept of probability is advocated by a number of theorists. That is the concept of **subjective probability**. By this definition probability represents an individual's subjective belief in the likelihood of the occurrence of an event. For example, the statement, "I think that tomorrow will be a good day," is a subjective statement of degree of belief, which probably has very little to do with the long-range relative frequency of the occurrence of good days, and in fact may have no mathematical basis whatsoever. This is not to say that such a view of probability has no legitimate claim for our attention. Subjective probabilities play an extremely important role in human decision-making and govern all aspects of our behavior. Just think of the number of decisions you make based on subjective beliefs in the likelihood of certain outcomes. You order pasta for dinner because it is probably better than the mystery meat special; you plan to go skiing tomorrow because the weather forecaster says that there is an 80% chance of snow overnight; you bet your money on a horse because you think that the odds of its winning are better than the 6:1 odds the bookies are offering. We will shortly discuss what is called Bayes' theorem, which is essential to the use of subjective probabilities. Statistical decisions as we will make them have generally been stated with respect to frequentist or analytical approaches, although even so the interpretation of those probabilities has a strong subjective component. Recently there seems to have been a shift toward viewing probabilities more subjectively, and we will touch on this when we talk about confidence limits in later chapters. Although Bayesian statistics is a separate field, elements of it have been creeping into analysis in the behavioral sciences, which I think is a good thing.

Although the particular definition that you or I prefer may be important to each of us, any of the definitions will lead to essentially the same result in terms of hypothesis testing, the discussion of which runs through the rest of the book. (It should be said that those who favor subjective probabilities often disagree with the general hypothesis-testing orientation.) In actual fact most people use the different approaches interchangeably. When we say that the probability of losing at Russian roulette is 1/6, we are referring to the fact that one

---

[1] The word limit refers to the fact that as we sample more and more M&M's, the proportion of blue will get closer and closer to some value. After 100 draws, the proportion might be .23; after 1,000 draws it might be .242; after 10,000 draws it might be .2398, and so on. Notice that the answer is coming closer and closer to $p = .2400000. \ldots$ The value that is being approached is called the limit.

of the gun's six cylinders has a bullet in it. When we buy a particular car because *Consumer Reports* says it has a good repair record, we are responding to the fact that a high proportion of these cars have been relatively trouble-free. When we say that the probability of the Colorado Rockies winning the pennant is high, we are stating our subjective belief in the likelihood of that event (or perhaps engaging in wishful thinking). But when we reject some hypothesis because there is a very low probability that the actual data would have been obtained if the hypothesis had been true, it may not be important which view of probability we hold.

5.2 Basic Terminology and Rules

event

The basic bit of data for a probability theorist is called an **event**. The word *event* is a term that statisticians use to cover just about anything. An event can be the occurrence of a king when we deal from a deck of cards, a score of 36 on a scale of likeability, a classification of "female" for the next person appointed to the Supreme Court, or the mean of a sample. Whenever you speak of the probability of something, the "something" is called an event. When we are dealing with a process as simple as flipping a coin, the event is the outcome of that flip—either heads or tails. When we draw M&M's out of a bag, the possible events are the 6 possible colors. When we speak of a grade in a course, the possible events are the letters A, B, C, D, and F.

independent events

Two events are said to be **independent events** when the occurrence or nonoccurrence of one has no effect on the occurrence or nonoccurrence of the other. The voting behaviors of two randomly chosen subjects normally would be assumed to be independent, especially with a secret ballot, because how one person votes could not be expected to influence how the other will vote. However, the voting behaviors of two members of the same family probably would not be independent events, because those people share many of the same beliefs and attitudes. This would be true even if those two people were careful not to let the other see their ballot.

mutually exclusive

exhaustive

Two events are said to be **mutually exclusive** if the occurrence of one event precludes the occurrence of the other. For example, the standard college classes of First Year, Sophomore, Junior, and Senior are mutually exclusive because one person cannot be a member of more than one class. A set of events is said to be **exhaustive** if it includes all possible outcomes. Thus the four college classes in the previous example are exhaustive with respect to full-time undergraduates, who have to fall in one or another of those categories—if only to please the registrar's office. At the same time, they are not exhaustive with respect to total university enrollments, which include graduate students, medical students, nonmatriculated students, hangers-on, and so forth.

As you already know, or could deduce from our definitions of probability, probabilities range between 0.00 and 1.00. If some event has a probability of 1.00, then it must occur. (Very few things have a probability of 1.00, including the probability that I will be able to keep typing until I reach the end of this paragraph.) If some event has a probability of 0.00, it is certain not to occur. The closer the probability comes to either extreme, the more likely or unlikely is the occurrence of the event.

Basic Laws of Probability

Two important theorems are central to any discussion of probability. (If my use of the word *theorems* makes you nervous, substitute the word *rules*.) They are often referred to as the additive and multiplicative rules.

The Additive Rule

additive law
of probability

To illustrate the additive rule, we will use our M&M's example and consider all six colors. From Table 5.1 we know from the analytic definition of probability that p(blue) $= 24/100 = .24$, p(green) $= 16/100 = .16$, and *so on*. But what is the probability that I will draw a blue or green M&M instead of an M&M of some other color? Here we need the **additive law of probability**.

> Given a set of mutually exclusive events, the probability of the occurrence of one event or another is equal to the sum of their separate probabilities.

Thus, p(blue or green) $= p$(blue) $+ p$(green) $= .24 + .16 = .40$. Notice that we have imposed the restriction that the events must be mutually exclusive, meaning that the occurrence of one event precludes the occurrence of the other. If an M&M is blue, it can't be green. This requirement is important. About one-half of the population of this country are female, and about one-half of the population is taller than 5'6¾".[2] But the probability that a person chosen at random will be female or will be taller than 5'6¾" is obviously not $.50 + .50 = 1.00$. Here the two events are not mutually exclusive. However, the probability that a girl born in Vermont in 1987 was named Ashley or Sarah, the two most common girls' names of that year, equals p(Ashley) $+ p$(Sarah) $= .010 + .009 = .019$. Here the names are mutually exclusive because you can't have both Ashley and Sarah as your first name (unless your parents got carried away and combined the two with a hyphen—and even sensible parents tend to get carried away when they have a baby).

The Multiplicative Rule

multiplicative law
of probability

Let's continue with the M&M's where p(blue) $= .24$, p(green) $= .16$, and p(other) $= .60$. Suppose I draw two M&M's, replacing the first before drawing the second. What is the probability that I will draw a blue M&M on the first trial and a blue one on the second? Here we need to invoke the **multiplicative law of probability**.

> The probability of the joint occurrence of two or more independent events is the product of their individual probabilities.

Thus p(blue, blue) $= p$(blue) $\times p$(blue) $= .24 \times .24 = .0576$. Similarly, the probability of a blue M&M followed by a green one is p(blue, green) $= p$(blue) $\times p$(green) $= .24 \times .16 = .0384$. Notice that we have restricted ourselves to independent events, meaning the occurrence of one event can have no effect on the occurrence or nonoccurrence of the other. Because gender and height are not independent, it would be wrong to state that p(female $\leq 5'6¾"$) $= .50 \times .50 = .25$. However, it most likely would be correct to state that p(female, born in January) $= .50 \times 1/12 = .50 \times .083 = .042$, because I know of no data to suggest that gender is dependent on birth month. (If month and gender were related, my calculation would be wrong.)

In Chapter 6 we will use the multiplicative law to answer questions about the independence of two variables. An example from that chapter will help illustrate a specific use of this law. In a study to be discussed in Chapter 6, Unah and Borger (2001) wanted to test the hypotheses of whether or not a defendant in a trial received the death penalty was related to that defendant's race. They identified defendants as white or nonwhite. Testing their hypothesis involves, in part, calculating the probability that a defendant would be

---

[2] http://en.wikipedia.org/wiki/Human_height

nonwhite and would be given a death sentence. We need to calculate what this probability would be *if the two events (race and death sentence) are independent*, as would be the case if verdicts are race-blind. If we assume that these two events are independent, the multiplicative law tells us that p(nonwhite, death) = p(nonwhite) $\times$ p(death). In their study 34.4% of the defendants were nonwhite, so the probability that a defendant chosen at random would be nonwhite is .344. Similarly, 8% of the defendants received a death sentence, giving p(death) = .08. Therefore, if the two events are independent, p(nonwhite, death) = .344 $\times$ .08 = .028 = 2.8%. (In fact, 4% of defendants were nonwhite and received a death sentence, which is higher than we would expect if the ultimate decision on sentencing was independent of race. If this difference is reliable, what does this suggest to you about the sentencing in capital crimes?)

Finally we can take a simple example that illustrates both the additive and the multiplicative laws. What is the probability that over two trials (sampling with replacement) I will draw one blue M&M and one green one, ignoring the order in which they are drawn? First we use the multiplicative rule to calculate

$$p(\text{blue, green}) = .24 \times .16 = .0384$$

$$p(\text{green, blue}) = .16 \times .24 = .0384$$

Because these two outcomes satisfy our requirement (and because they are the only ones that do), we now need to know the probability that one or the other of these outcomes will occur. Here we apply the additive rule:

$$p(\text{blue, green}) + p(\text{green, blue}) = .0384 + .0384 = .0768$$

Thus the probability of obtaining one M&M of each of those colors over two draws is approximately .08—that is, it will occur a little less than one-tenth of the time.

Students sometimes get confused over the additive and multiplicative laws because they almost sound the same when you hear them quickly. One useful idea is to realize the difference between the situations in which the rules apply. In those situations in which you use the additive rule, you know that you are going to have one outcome. An M&M that you draw may be blue or green, but there is only going to be one of them. In the multiplicative case, we are speaking about at least two outcomes (e.g., the probability that we will get one blue M&M and one green one). For single outcomes we add probabilities; for multiple independent outcomes we multiply them.

Sampling with Replacement

Why do I keep referring to "sampling with replacement"? The answer goes back to the issue of independence. Consider the example with blue and green M&M's. We had 24 blue M&M's and 16 green ones in the bag of 100 M&M's. On the first trial the probability of a blue M&M is .24/100 = .24. If I put that M&M back before I draw again, there will still be a .24/.76 split, and the probability of a blue M&M on the next draw will still be 24/100 = .24. But if I did not replace the M&M, the probability of a blue M&M on Trial 2 would depend on the result of Trial 1. If I had drawn a blue one on Trial 1, there would be 23 blue ones and 76 of other colors remaining, and p(blue) = 23/99 = .2323. If I had drawn a green one on Trial 1, for Trial 2 p(blue) = 24/99 = .2424. So when I sample with replacement, p(blue) stays the same from trial to trial, whereas when I sample without replacement the probability keeps changing. To take an extreme example, if I sample without replacement, what is the probability of exactly 25 blue M&M's out of 60 draws? The answer, of course, is .00, because there are only 24 blue M&M's to begin with and it is impossible to draw 25 of them. Sampling with replacement, however, would produce a possible result, though the probability would be only .0011.

Joint and Conditional Probabilities

Two types of probabilities play an important role in discussions of probability: joint probabilities and conditional probabilities.

joint probability

A **joint probability** is defined simply as the probability of the co-occurrence of two or more events. For example, in Unah and Borger's (2001) study of racial bias in sentencing, the probability that a defendant would both be nonwhite and receive a death sentence is a joint probability, as is the probability that a defendant would both be white and receive a death sentence. Given two events, their joint probability is denoted as $p(A, B)$, just as we have used p(blue, green). If those two events are independent, then the probability of their joint occurrence can be found by using the multiplicative law, as we have just seen. If they are not independent, the probability of their joint occurrence is more complicated to compute and will differ from what it would be if the events were independent. We won't compute that probability here.

conditional probability

A **conditional probability** is the probability that one event will occur given that some other event has occurred. The probability that a person will contract AIDS given that he or she is an intravenous drug user is a conditional probability. The probability that an in-store advertising flier will be thrown in the trash, given that it contains a message asking that the reader not litter, is another example. A third example is a phrase that occurs repeatedly throughout this book: "If the null hypothesis is true, the probability of obtaining a result such as this is. . . ." Here I have substituted the word "if" for "given," but the meaning is the same. In this book you will see the word "conditional" used often. It can essentially be read as "if . . . is true then . . . " For example, "Group differences in the number of items recalled is conditional on the level of verbal processing when the word was presented."

With two events, A and B, the conditional probability of A given B is denoted by use of a vertical bar, as $p(A \mid B)$, for example, p(AIDS | drug user) or p(death | nonwhite).

We often assume, with some justification, that parenthood breeds responsibility. People who have spent years acting in careless and irrational ways somehow seem to turn into different people once they become parents, changing many of their old behavior patterns. (Just wait a few years.) Suppose that a radio station sampled 100 people, 20 of whom had children. They found that 30 of the people sampled used seat belts, and that 15 of those people had children. The results are shown in Table 5.2.

The information in Table 5.2 allows us to calculate the simple, joint, and conditional probabilities. The simple probability that a person sampled at random will use a seat belt is $30/100 = .30$. The joint probability that a person will have children and will wear a seat belt is $15/100 = .15$. The conditional probability of a person using a seat belt given that he or she has children is $15/20 = .75$. Do not confuse joint and conditional probabilities. As you can see, they are quite different. You might wonder why I didn't calculate the joint probability here by multiplying the appropriate simple probabilities. The use of the multiplicative law requires that parenthood and seat belt use be independent. In this example they are not, because the data show that whether people use seat belts depends very much

Table 5.2   The relationship between parenthood and seat belt use

Parenthood	Wear Seat belt	Do Not Wear Seat belt	Total
Children	15	5	20
No children	15	65	80
Total	30	70	100

© Cengage Learning 2013

on whether or not they have children. (If I had assumed independence, I would have predicted the joint probability to be .30 × .20 = .06, which is less than half the size of the actual obtained value.)

To take another example, the probability that you have been drinking alcoholic beverages and that you have an accident is a joint probability. This probability is not very high, because relatively few people are drinking at any one time and relatively few people have accidents. However, the probability that you have an accident given that you have been drinking, or, in reverse, the probability that you have been drinking given that you have an accident, are both much higher. At night the conditional probability of p(drinking | accident) approaches .50, because nearly half of all automobile accidents at night in the United States involve alcohol. I don't know the conditional probability of p(accident | drinking), but I do know that it is much higher than the **unconditional probability** of an accident, that is, p(accident).

unconditional probability

NOTE

Conditional probabilities, denoted as $p(X|Y)$, always refer to the probability that something will occur *given* that something else has happened. Whenever the word "conditional" is used in this book, it will be used in that way and you should look for what the condition is.

5.3   Discrete versus Continuous Variables

In Chapter 1 a distinction was made between discrete and continuous variables. As mathematicians view things, a discrete variable is one that can take on a countable number of different values, whereas a continuous variable is one that can take on an infinite number of different values. For example, the number of people attending a specific movie theater tonight is a discrete variable because we literally can count the number of people entering the theater, and there is no such thing as a fractional person. However, the distance between two people in a study of personal space is a continuous variable because the distance could be 2, or 2.8, or 2.8173754814 feet. Although the distinction given here is technically correct, common usage is somewhat different.

In practice when we speak of a discrete variable, we usually mean a variable that takes on one of a relatively small number of possible values (e.g., a five-point scale of socioeconomic status). A variable that can take on one of many possible values is generally treated as a continuous variable if the values represent at least an ordinal scale. Thus we usually treat an IQ score as a continuous variable, even though we recognize that IQ scores come in whole units and we will not find someone with an IQ of 105.317. In Chapter 3, I referred to the Achenbach Total Behavior Problem score as normally distributed, even though I know that it can only take on positive values that are integers, whereas a normal distribution can take on all values between $\pm\infty$. I treat it as continuous because it can take on many different values. I treat it as normal because it is close enough to normal that my results will be reasonably accurate.

The distinction between discrete and continuous variables is reintroduced here because the distributions of the two kinds of variables are treated somewhat differently in probability theory. With discrete variables we can speak of the probability of a specific outcome. With continuous variables, on the other hand, we need to speak of the probability of obtaining a value that falls within a specific interval.

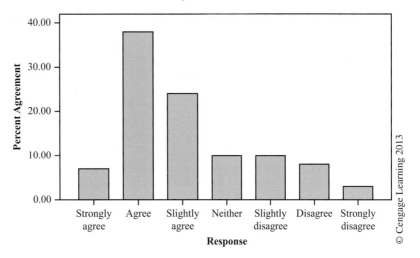

Figure 5.1   Distribution of Quality of Life

5.4   Probability Distributions for Discrete Variables

An interesting example of a discrete probability distribution is seen in Figure 5.1. The data plotted in this figure come from a Scottish Government survey of environmental attitudes, collected in 2009. They were interested in studying environmental issues, but in the process collected data on general life satisfaction using the Satisfaction With Life Scale (SWLS) by Edward Diener at the University of Illinois[3]. Figure 7.1 presents the distribution of responses for the question that asked respondents to rate the sentence "In most ways my life is close to ideal." The possible values of X (the rating) are presented on the abscissa or X axis, and the relative frequency (or proportion) of people choosing that response is plotted on the ordinate or Y axis. It is interesting to see how satisfied people are with their lives—I would not have expected such responses. Proportions translate directly to probabilities for the sample, and the probability that a person chosen at random will "Agree" that his or her life is close to ideal is .38. Adding together the three positive categories, as we did with the criminal data earlier, we have 69% of the sampled population at least in slight agreement that their life is close to ideal.

5.5   Probability Distributions for Continuous Variables

When we move from discrete to continuous probability distributions, things become more complicated. We dealt with a continuous distribution when we considered the normal distribution in Chapter 6. You may recall that in that chapter we labeled the ordinate of the distribution "density." We also spoke in terms of intervals rather than in terms of specific outcomes. Now we need to elaborate somewhat on those points.

---

[3] You can find out more about this scale at http://internal.psychology.illinois.edu/~ediener/SWLS.html
The particular study cited here can be found at http://www.scotland.gov.uk/Publications/2009/03/25155151/0.

Figure 5.2 shows the approximate distribution of the maternal age at first birth, from data supplied by the CDC (2003).[4] (Notice that this distribution is unimodal and slightly positively skewed. It is not the shape of a standard normal distribution.)

The mean is approximately 25 years, the standard deviation is approximately 5 years, and the distribution is slightly positively skewed. You will notice that in this figure the

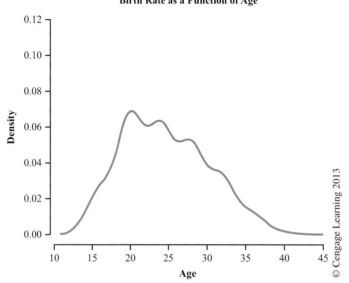

Figure 5.2   Age of mother at birth of first child

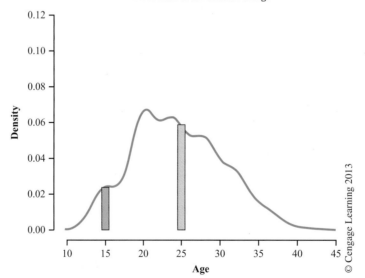

Figure 5.3   Probability of giving birth at ages 15 and 25 years

---

[4] http://www.cdc.gov/nchs/data/nvsr/nvsr52/nvsr52_10.pdf

Density

ordinate (*Y* axis) is labeled "density," whereas in Figure 5.1 it was labeled "relative frequency." **Density** is not synonymous with probability, and it is probably best thought of as merely the height of the curve at different values of *X*. At the same time, the fact that the curve is higher near 20 years than it is near 15 years tells us that children are more likely to be born when their mother is in her early twenties than when she is in her mid-teens. That is not a particular surprise. The reason for changing the label on the ordinate is that we now are dealing with a continuous distribution rather than a discrete one. If you think about it for a moment, you will realize that although the highest point of the curve is at 20 years, the probability that a mother picked at random will give birth at *exactly* 20 years (i.e., 20.00000000 years) is infinitely small—statisticians would argue that it is in fact 0. Similarly, the probability that the mother gave birth at 20.00001 years also is infinitely small. This suggests that it does not make any sense to speak of the probability of any *specific* outcome, although that is just what we did with discrete distributions. On the other hand, we know that many mothers give birth at *approximately* 20 years, and it does make considerable sense to speak of the probability of obtaining a score that falls within some specified *interval*. For example, we might be interested in the probability that an infant will be born when mom is between 24.5 and 25.5 years old. Such an interval is shown in Figure 5.3. If we arbitrarily define the total area under the curve to be 1.00, then the shaded area in Figure 5.3 between points 24.5 and 25.5 years will be equal to the probability that a mother will give birth at age 25. Those of you who have had calculus will probably recognize that if we knew the form of the equation that describes this distribution (i.e., if we knew the equation for the curve), we would simply need to integrate the function over the interval from 24.5 to 25.5. But you don't need calculus to solve this problem, because the distributions with which we will work are adequately approximated by other distributions that have already been tabled. In this book we will never integrate functions, but we will often refer to tables of distributions. You have already had experience with this procedure with regard to the normal distribution in Chapter 3.

We have just considered the area of Figure 5.3 between 24.5 and 25.5 years. However, the same things could be said for any interval. In Figure 5.3 you can also see the area that corresponds to the period that is half a year on either side of 15 years (denoted as the shaded area between 14.5 and 15.5 years). Although there is not enough information in this example for us to calculate actual probabilities, it should be clear by inspection of Figure 5.3 that the interval around 25 years has a higher probability (greater shaded area) than the area around 15 years.

A good way to get a feel for areas under a curve is to take a piece of transparent graph paper and lay it on top of the figure (or use a regular sheet of graph paper and hold the two up to a light). If you count the number of squares that fall within a specified interval and divide by the total number of squares under the whole curve, you will approximate the probability that a randomly drawn score will fall within that interval. It should be obvious that the smaller the size of the individual squares on the graph paper, the more accurate the approximation.

5.6 Permutations and Combinations

We will set continuous distributions aside until they are needed again in Chapter 7 and beyond. For now, we will concentrate on two discrete distributions (the binomial and the multinomial) that can be used to develop the chi-square test in Chapter 6. First we must consider the concepts of permutations and combinations, which are required for a discussion of those distributions.

combinatorics

The special branch of mathematics dealing with the number of ways in which objects can be put together (e.g., the number of different ways of forming a three-person committee with five people available) is known as **combinatorics**. Although not many instances in this book require a knowledge of combinatorics, there are enough of them to make it necessary to briefly define the concepts of permutations and combinations and to give formulae for their calculation.

Permutations

We will start with a simple example that is easily expanded into a more useful and relevant one. Assume that four people have entered a lottery for ice-cream cones. The names are placed in a hat and drawn. The person whose name is drawn first wins a double-scoop cone, the second wins a single-scoop cone, the third wins just the cone, and the fourth wins nothing. Assume that the people are named Abigail, Barbara, Cathy, and Donna, abbreviated A, B, C, and D. The following orders in which the names are drawn are all possible.

A B C D	B A C D	C A B D	D A B C
A B D C	B A D C	C A D B	D A C B
A C B D	B C A D	C B A D	D B A C
A C D B	B C D A	C B D A	D B C A
A D B C	B D A C	C D A B	D C A B
A D C B	B D C A	C D B A	D C B A

permutation

Each of these 24 orders presents a unique arrangement (called a **permutation**) of the four names taken four at a time. If we represent the number of permutations (arrangements) of N things taken r at a time as P_r^N, then

$$P_r^N = \frac{N!}{(N-r)!}$$

factorial

where the symbol $N!$ is read N **factorial** and represents the product of all integers from N to 1. [In other words, $N! = N(N-1)(N-2)(N-3)\cdots(1)$. By definition, $0! = 1$].

For our example of drawing four names for four entrants,

$$P_4^4 = \frac{4!}{(4-4)!} = \frac{4!}{0!} = \frac{4\cdot3\cdot2\cdot1}{1} = 24,$$

which agrees with the number of listed permutations.

Now, few people would get very excited about winning a cone without any ice cream in it, so let's eliminate that prize. Then out of the four people, only two will win on any drawing. The order in which those two winners are drawn is still important, however, because the first person whose name is drawn wins a larger cone. In this case, we have four names but are drawing only two out of the hat (because the other two are both losers). Thus, we want to know the number of permutations of four names taken two at a time, (P_2^4). We can easily write down these permutations and count them:

A	B	B	A	C	A	D	A
A	C	B	C	C	B	D	B
A	D	B	D	C	D	D	C

Or we can calculate the number of permutations directly:

$$P_2^4 = \frac{4!}{(4-2)!} = \frac{4\cdot3\cdot2\cdot1}{2} = 12.$$

Here there are 12 possible orderings of winners, and the ordering makes an important difference—it determines not only who wins, but also which winner receives the larger cone.

Now we will take a more useful example involving permutations. Suppose we are designing an experiment studying physical attractiveness judged from slides. We are concerned that the order of presentation of the slides is important. Given that we have six slides to present, in how many different ways can they be arranged? This again is a question of permutations, because the ordering of the slides is important. More specifically, we want to know the permutations of six slides taken six at a time. Or, suppose that we have six slides, but any given subject is going to see only three. Now how many orders can be used? This is a question about the permutations of six slides taken three at a time.

For the first problem, in which subjects are presented with all six slides, we have

$$P_6^6 = \frac{6!}{(6-6)!} = \frac{6!}{0!} = \frac{6 \cdot 5 \cdot 4 \cdot 3 \cdot 2 \cdot 1}{1} = 720$$

so there are 720 different ways of arranging six slides. If we want to present all possible arrangements to each participant, we are going to need 720 trials, or some multiple of that. That is a lot of trials. For the second problem, where we have six slides but show only three to any one subject, we have

$$P_3^6 = \frac{6!}{(6-3)!} = \frac{6!}{3!} = \frac{6 \cdot 5 \cdot 4 \cdot 3 \cdot 2 \cdot 1}{6} = 120.$$

If we want to present all possible arrangements to each subject, we need 120 trials, a result that may still be sufficiently large to lead us to modify further our design. This is one reason we often use random orderings rather than try to present all possible orderings[5].

Combinations

combinations

To return to the ice-cream lottery, suppose we now decide that we will award only single-dip cones to the two winners. We will still draw the names of two winners out of a hat, *but we will no longer care which of the two names was drawn first*—the result AB is for all practical purposes the same as the result BA because in each case Abigail and Barbara win a cone. When the order in which names are drawn is no longer important, we are no longer interested in permutations. Instead, we are now interested in what are called **combinations**. We want to know the number of possible combinations of winning names, without regard to the order in which they were drawn.

We can enumerate these combinations as

A	B	B	C
A	C	B	D
A	D	C	D

There are six of them. In other words, out of four people, we could compile six different sets of winners. (If you look back to the previous enumeration of permutations of winners, you will see that we have just combined outcomes containing the same names.)

---

[5] Later in the book we will come across what are often called "permutation tests." In practice these are really "randomization tests" because for many reasonable problems the possible number of permutations (and even the number of combinations) is absolutely huge, so we just draw random arrangements.

Normally, we do not want to enumerate all possible combinations just to find out how many of them there are. To calculate the number of combinations of N things taken r at a time C_r^N, we will define

$$C_r^N = \frac{N!}{r!(N-r)!}.$$

For our example,

$$C_2^4 = \frac{4!}{2!(4-2)!} = \frac{4 \cdot 3 \cdot 2 \cdot 1}{2 \cdot 1 \cdot 2 \cdot 1} = 6.$$

Let's return to the example involving slides to be presented to subjects. When we were dealing with permutations, we worried about the way in which each set of slides was arranged; that is, we worried about all possible orderings. Suppose we no longer care about the order of the slides within sets, but we need to know how many different sets of slides we could form if we had six slides but took only three at a time. This is a question of combinations.

For six slides taken three at a time, we have

$$C_3^6 = \frac{6!}{3!(6-3)!} = \frac{6 \cdot 5 \cdot \overset{2}{\cancel{4}} \cdot \overset{2}{\cancel{3}} \cdot \cancel{2} \cdot \cancel{1}}{\cancel{3} \cdot \cancel{2} \cdot \cancel{1} \cdot \cancel{3} \cdot \cancel{2} \cdot 1} = 20.$$

If we wanted every subject to get a different set of three slides but did not care about the order within a set, we would need 20 subjects.

Later in the book we will discuss procedures, called *permutation tests*, in which we imagine that the data we have are all the data we could collect, but we want to imagine what the sample means would likely be if the N scores fell into our two different experimental groups (of n_1 and n_2 scores) *purely at random*. To solve that problem we could calculate the number of different ways the observations could be assigned to groups, which is just the number of combinations of N things taken n_1 and n_2 at a time. (Please don't ask why it's called a permutation test if we are dealing with combinations—I haven't figured that out yet.) Knowing the number of different ways that data could have occurred at random, we will calculate the percentage of those outcomes that would have produced differences in means at least as extreme as the difference we found. That would be the probability of the data given H_0 : true, often written $p(D|H_0)$. I mention this only to give you an illustration of when we would want to know how to calculate permutations and combinations.

5.7 Bayes' Theorem

Bayes' theorem

We have one more basic element of probability theory to cover before we go on to use those basics in particular applications. **Bayes' theorem** is certainly not new (it was developed by Thomas Bayes and first read before the Royal Society in London in 1764—three years after Bayes' death), but each year we see more and more references to it in the behavioral sciences, and to Bayesian statistics, which is based on that theorem. You need to understand the theorem, even if you forget the calculational details. (You can always look up the details.)

Bayes' theorem is a theorem that tells us how to accumulate information to revise estimates of probabilities. By "accumulate information" I mean a process in which you continually revise a probability estimate as more information comes in. Suppose that I tell you that Fred was murdered and ask you for your personal (subjective) probability that Willard committed the crime. You think he is certainly capable of it and not a very nice person, so you say $p = .15$. Then I say that Willard was seen near the crime that night, and you raise your probability to .20. Then I say that Willard owns the right type of gun, and you might raise your probability to $p = .25$. Then I say that a fairly reliable witness says Willard was at a baseball game with him at the time, and you drop your probability to $p = .10$. And so on. This is a process of accumulating information to come up with a probability that some event occurred. For those interested in Bayesian statistics, probabilities are usually subjective or personal probabilities, meaning that they are a statement of personal belief, rather than having a frequentist or analytic basis as defined at the beginning of the chapter. Bayes' theorem will work perfectly well with any kind of probability, but it is most often seen with subjective probabilities.

Let's take a simple example that I have modified from Stefan Waner's Web site at http://people.hofstra.edu/Stefan_Waner/tutorialsf3/unit6_6.html. (That site has some other examples that may be helpful if you want them.) Psychologists have become quite interested in sports medicine, and this example is actually something that is relevant. In addition it fits perfectly with the work on decision making.

Let's assume that an unnamed bicyclist has just failed a test for banned steroids after finishing his race. (Waner used rugby instead of racing, but we all know that rugby guys are good guys and follow the rules, although we are beginning to have our doubts about cyclists.) Our cyclist argues that he is perfectly innocent and would never use performance-enhancing drugs. Our task is to determine a reasonable probability about the guilt or innocence of our cyclist. We do have a few facts that we can work with. First of all, the drug company that markets the test tells us that 95% of steroid users test positive. In other words, *if* you use drugs the probability of a positive result is .95. That sounds impressive. Drug companies like to look good, so they don't bother to point out that 10% of nonusers also test positive, but we coaxed it out of them. We also know one other thing, which is that past experience has shown that 10% of this racing team uses steroids (and the other 90% do not). We can put this information together in Table 5.3.

prior probability

One of the important pieces of information that we have is called the **prior probability**, which is the probability that the person is a drug user *before* we acquire any further information. This is shown in the table as $p(\text{user}) = .10$. What we want to determine is the **posterior probability**, which is our new probability *after* we have been given data (in this case the data that he failed the test). For a process in which we are continually accumulating information, this posterior probability will become the prior probability for the next step.

posterior probability

NOTE

Posterior probabilities at one level become prior probabilities for calculations at the next level as we keep refining our estimate. Sometimes we refine the estimate many times.

Table 5.3   Probabilities associated with steroid use

Knowns		p	Source of information
p(cyclist is user)	$p(U)$	.10	10% of team are users
p(cyclist not a user)	$p(NU)$	.90	90% of team are not
p(positive | user)	$p(P|U)$	.95	From drug company
p(positive | non-user)	$p(P|NU)$	.10	Also from drug company
p(user | positive test)	$p(U|P)$	?	Our goal

Bayes' theorem tells us that we can derive the posterior probability from the information we have above. We will let U (user) stand for the hypothesis that he did use steroids, NU (non-user) stand for the hypothesis that he is a non-user. We will let P stand for the new data, that the test was Positive. Then

$$p(U|P) = \frac{p(P|U) * p(U)}{p(P|U) * p(U) + p(P|NU) * p(NU)}$$

From the information in the above table we can calculate

$$p(U|P) = \frac{p(P|U) * p(U)}{p(P|U) * p(U) + p(P|NU) * p(NU)}$$

$$= \frac{(.95)(.10)}{(.95)(.10) + (.10)(.90)} = \frac{.095}{(.095 + .09)} = .513$$

Before we had the results of the drug test our subjective probability of his guilt was .10 because only 10% of the team used steroids. After the positive drug test our subjective probability increased, but perhaps not as much as you would have expected. The posterior probability is now .513.

As I said above, one of the powerful things about Bayes' theorem is that you can work with it iteratively. In other words you can now collect another piece of data (perhaps that he has a needle in his possession), take .513 as your new prior probability and include probabilities associated with the needle, and calculate a new posterior probability. In other words we can accumulate data and keep refining our estimate.

A second feature of Bayes' theorem is that it is useful even if some of our probabilities are just intelligent guesses. For example, if the drug company had refused to tell us how many nonusers tested positive and we took .20 as a tentative estimate, our resulting posterior probability would be .345, which, while lower than .513, is still a better estimate than our original estimate of .10.

A Second Example

There has been a lot of work in human decision-making that has been based on applications of Bayes' theorem. Much of it focuses on comparing what people *should* do or say in a situation, with what they *actually* do or say, for the purpose of characterizing how people really make decisions. A famous problem was posed to decision makers by Tversky and Kahneman (1980). This problem involved deciding which cab company was involved in an accident. We are told that there was an accident involving one of the two cab companies in the city (Green Cab and Blue Cab), but we are not told which one it was. We know that 85% of the cabs in that city are Green, and 15% are Blue. The prior probabilities then, based just on the percentage of Green and Blue cabs, are .85 and .15. If that was all you knew and you were told that someone was just run over by a cab, your best estimate would be that the probability of it being a Green cab is .85. Then a witness comes along who thinks that it was a Blue cab. You might think that was conclusive, but identifying colors at night is not a foolproof task, and the insurance company tested our informant and found that he was able to identify colors at night with only 80% accuracy. Thus if you show him a Blue cab, the probability that he will correctly say Blue is .80, and the probability that he will incorrectly say Green is .20. (Similarly if the cab is Green.) This information is sufficient to allow you to calculate the posterior probability that the cab was a Blue cab given that the witness said it was blue.

In the following formula let B stand for the event that it was a Blue cab, and let b stand for the event that the witness called it blue. Similarly for G and g.

$$p(B \mid b) = \frac{p(b \mid B)p(B)}{p(b \mid B)p(B) + p(b \mid G)p(G)}$$

$$= \frac{(.80)(.15)}{(.80)(.15) + (.20)(.85)}$$

$$= \frac{.12}{.121.17} = \frac{.12}{.29} = .414$$

Most of the participants in Tversky and Kahneman's experiment guessed that the probability that it was the blue cab was around .80, when in fact the correct answer is approximately half of that (.41). Thus Kahneman and Tversky concluded that judges place too much weight on the witness's testimony, and not enough weight on the prior probabilities.[6] Here is a situation where the discrepancy between what judges say and what they should say gives us clues to the strategies that judges use and where they go wrong. You would probably come to a similar conclusion if you asked people about our example of steroid use in cyclists.

A Generic Formula

The formulae given above were framed in terms of the specific example under discussion. It may be helpful to have a more generic formula that you can adapt to your own purposes. Suppose that we are asking about the probability that some hypothesis (H) is true, given certain data (D). For our examples H represented "the cyclist is a user" or "it was the Blue Cab company." The D represent "he tested positive" or "the witness reported that the cab was blue." The symbol $\overline{H}$ is read "not H" and stands for the case where the hypothesis is false. Then

$$p(H \mid D) = \frac{p(D \mid H)p(H)}{p(D \mid H)p(H) + p(D \mid \overline{H})p(\overline{H})}$$

Back to the Hypothesis Testing

In Chapter Four we discussed hypothesis testing and different approaches to it. Bayes' theorem has an important contribution to make to that discussion, although I am only going to touch on the issue here. (I want you to understand the nature of the argument, but it is not reasonable to expect you to go much beyond that.) Recall that I said in some ways a hypothesis test is not really designed to answer the question we would ideally like to answer. We want to collect some data and then ask about the probability that the null hypothesis is true given the data. But instead, our statistical procedures tell us the probability that we would obtain those data given that the null hypothesis (H_0) is true. In other words, we want $p(H_0|D)$ when what we really have is $p(D|H_0)$. Many people have pointed out that we could have the answer we seek if we simply apply Bayes' theorem.

The problem here is that we don't know most of the necessary probabilities. We could *estimate* those probabilities, but those would only be estimates. It is one thing to calculate the probability of a user testing positive, because we can collect a group of known users

---

[6] Daniel Kahneman was awarded the Nobel Prize in Economics in 2002 for his work on prospect theory, and everyone assumes that Amos Tversky would have shared that prize had the Nobel Prize committee not have a policy that prizes cannot be awarded posthumously. Their work has had an enormous influence on the psychology of decision behavior.

and see how many test positive. But it is quite a different thing to estimate the probability that the null hypothesis is true. Using the example of waiting times in parking lots, you and I might have quite different prior probability estimates that people leave a parking space at the same speed whether or not there is someone waiting. In addition, our statistical test is designed to give us $p(D|H_0)$, which is helpful. But where do we obtain $p(D|H_1)$ if we don't have a specific alternative hypothesis in mind (other than the negation of the null)? It was one thing to estimate it when we had something concrete like the percentage of nonusers who test positive, but considerably more difficult when the alternative is that people leave *more slowly* when someone is waiting if we don't know *how much* more slowly. The probabilities would be dramatically different if we were thinking in terms of "5 seconds more slowly" or "25 seconds more slowly." The fact that these probabilities we need are hard, or impossible, to come up with has stood in the way of developing this as a general approach to hypothesis testing—though many have tried. One approach is to choose a variety of reasonable estimates, and note how the results hold up under those different estimates. If most believable estimates lead to the same conclusion, that tells us something useful. What Bayesians actually do is to posit a *distribution* of possible values, called the "priors." Thus we might guess that the true prior probability is normally distributed with a mean of .25 and a standard deviation of .08. Alternatively we might use what is called a **noninformative prior** in which all possibilities are assigned equal prior probabilities.

noninformative prior

Bayesian statistics

There are a lot of people who are strong advocates of that approach, called **Bayesian statistics**, though its use is mostly restricted to situations where the null and alternative hypotheses are sharply defined, such as $H_0: \mu = 0$ and $H_1: \mu = 3$. But I have never seen clearly specified alternative hypotheses in the behavioral sciences. As time goes on the appeal of Bayesian statistics grows, and you will see one or two further instances of its influence in this book.

5.8   The Binomial Distribution

binomial distribution

We now have all the information on probabilities and combinations that we need for understanding one of the most common probability distributions—the **binomial distribution**. This distribution will be discussed briefly, and you will see how it can be used to test simple hypotheses. I don't think that I can write a chapter on probability without discussing the binomial distribution, but there are many students and instructors who would be more than happy if I did. There certainly are many applications for it (the sign test to be discussed shortly is one example), but I would easily forgive you for not wanting to memorize the necessary formulae—you can always look them up.

The binomial distribution deals with situations in which each of a number of independent trials results in one of two mutually exclusive outcomes. Such a trial is called a **Bernoulli trial** (after a famous mathematician of the same name). The most common example of a Bernoulli trial is flipping a coin, and the binomial distribution could be used to give us the probability of, for example, 3 heads out of 5 tosses of a coin. Because most people don't get turned on by the prospect of flipping coins, think of calculating the probability that 20 out of your 30 cancer patients will survive a diagnosis of myeloma by more than three years if the probability of survival for any one of them is .93[7].

Bernoulli trial

The binomial distribution is an example of a discrete, rather than a continuous, distribution, because one can flip coins and obtain 3 heads or 4 heads, but not, for example, 3.897 heads. Similarly one can have 21 survivors or 22 survivors, but not anything in between.

---

[7] In 1983 the median survival time for patients under 65 with myeloma was 2–3 years. Now the probability of survival for that group is reported as .93. It is much better to have myeloma now than it was about 30 years ago.

Mathematically, the binomial distribution is defined as

$$p(X) = C_X^N p^X q^{(N-X)} = \frac{N!}{X!(N-X)!} p^X q^{(N-X)}$$

where

$p(X) =$ The probability of X successes
$N =$ The number of trials
$p =$ The probability of a success on any one trial
$q = (1 - p) =$ The probability of a failure on any one trial
$C_X^N =$ The number of combinations of N things taken X at a time

That formula might make more sense if you break it into two parts. The second part $(p^X q^{N-X})$ is the probability for each possible ordering of X successes and N-X failures out of N trials. For example, the probability of SFSSFFF is one way to get 3 successes and 4 failures out of 7 trials. The first part $(N!/X!(N - X!))$ gives the number of different orderings that would also produce 3 successes and 4 failures—for example, SSSFFFF or FSFSFSF.

In the notation for combinations I have changed r to X because the symbol X is used to refer to data. Whether we call something r or X is arbitrary; the choice is made for convenience or intelligibility.

The words **success** and **failure** are used as arbitrary labels for the two alternative outcomes. If we are talking about cancer, the meaning is obvious. If we are talking about whether a driver will turn left or right at a fork, the designation is arbitrary. We will require that the trials be independent of one another, meaning that the result of $trial_i$ has no influence on $trial_j$.

To illustrate the binomial distribution we will take the classic example often referred to as perception without awareness, or that loaded phrase "subliminal perception."[8] A common example would be to flash *either* a letter or a number on a screen for a very short period (e.g., 3 msecs) and ask the respondent to report which it was. If we flash the two stimuli at equal rates, and if the respondent is purely guessing with no response bias, then the probability of being correct on any one trial is .50.

Suppose that we present the stimulus 10 times, and suppose that our respondent was correct 9 times and wrong 1 time. What is the probability of being correct 90% of the time (out of 10 trials) if the respondent really cannot see the stimulus and is just guessing?

The probability of being correct on any one trial is denoted p and equals .50, whereas the probability of being incorrect on any one trial is denoted q and also equals .50. Then we have

$$p(X) = \frac{N!}{X!(N-X)!} p^X q^{(N-X)}$$

$$p(9) = \frac{10!}{9!1!} (.50^9)(.50^1)$$

But $10! = 10 \cdot 9 \cdot 8 \cdots \cdot 2 \cdot 1 = 10 \cdot 9!$ so

$$p(9) = \frac{10 \cdot \cancel{9!}}{\cancel{9!}1!} (.50^9)(.50^1)$$

$$= 10(.001953)(.50) = .0098$$

---

[8] Philip Merikle wrote an excellent entry in Kazdin's *Encyclopedia of Psychology* (2000) covering subliminal perception and debunking some of the extraordinary claims that are sometimes made about it. That chapter is available at http://watarts.uwaterloo.ca/~pmerikle/papers/SubliminalPerception.html.

success
failure

Thus, the probability of making 9 correct choices out of 10 trials with $p = .50$ is remote, occurring approximately 1 time out of every 100 replications of this experiment. This would lead me to believe that even though the respondent does not perceive a particular stimulus, he is sufficiently aware to guess correctly at better than chance levels.

As a second example, the probability of 6 correct choices out of 10 trials is the probability of any one such outcome (p^6q^4) times the number of possible 6:4 outcomes (C_6^{10}). Thus,

$$p(6) = \frac{N!}{X!(N - X)!} p^X q^{(N-X)}$$

$$= \frac{10!}{6!4!} (.5)^6 (.5)^4$$

$$= \frac{10 \cdot 9 \cdot 8 \cdot 7 \cdot \cancel{6!}}{\cancel{6!}4 \cdot 3 \cdot 2 \cdot 1} (.5)^{10}$$

$$= \frac{5040}{24} (.00098)$$

$$= .2051$$

Here our respondent is not performing significantly better than chance.

Plotting Binomial Distributions

You will notice that the probability of six correct choices is greater than the probability of nine of them. This is what we would expect, because we are assuming that our judge is operating at random and would be right about as often as he is wrong. If we were to calculate the probabilities for each outcome between 0 and 10 correct out of 10, we would find the results shown in Table 5.4. Observe from this table that the sum of those probabilities is 1, reflecting the fact that all possible outcomes have been considered.

Now that we have calculated the probabilities of the individual outcomes, we can plot the distribution of the results, as has been done in Figure 5.4. (A very simple program in R to make similar plots can be found at the book's Web site.) Although this distribution

Table 5.4   Binomial distribution for $p = .50$, $N = 10$

Number Correct	Probability
0	.001
1	.010
2	.044
3	.117
4	.205
5	.246
6	.205
7	.117
8	.044
9	.010
10	.001
Sum	1.000

© Cengage Learning 2013

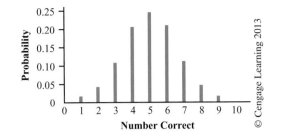

Figure 5.4   Binomial distribution for $N = 10$ and $p = .50$

resembles many of the distributions we have seen, it differs from them in two important ways. First, notice that the ordinate has been labeled "probability" instead of "frequency." This is because Figure 5.4 is not a frequency distribution at all, but rather is a probability distribution. This distinction is important. With frequency, or relative frequency, distributions, we were plotting the obtained outcomes of some experiment—that is, we were plotting real data. Here we are not plotting real data; instead, we are plotting the probability that some event or another will occur.

To reiterate a point made earlier, the fact that the ordinate (Y- axis) represents probabilities instead of densities (as in the normal distribution) reflects the fact that the binomial distribution deals with discrete rather than continuous outcomes. With a continuous distribution such as the normal distribution, the probability of any specified individual outcome is near 0. (The probability that you weigh 158.214567 pounds is vanishingly small.) With a discrete distribution, however, the data fall into one or another of relatively few categories, and probabilities for individual events can be obtained easily. In other words, with discrete distributions we deal with the probability of individual events, whereas with continuous distributions we deal with the probability of intervals of events.

The second way this distribution differs from many others we have discussed is that although it is a sampling distribution, it is obtained mathematically rather than empirically. The values on the abscissa represent statistics (the number of successes as obtained in a given experiment) rather than individual observations or events. We have already discussed sampling distributions in Chapter 4, and what we said there applies directly to what we will consider in this chapter.

The Mean and Variance of a Binomial Distribution

In Chapter 2 we saw that it is possible to describe a distribution in many ways—we can discuss its mean, its standard deviation, its skewness, and so on. From Figure 5.4 we can see that the distribution for the outcomes for our judge is symmetric. This will always be the case for $p = q = .50$, but not for other values of p and q. Furthermore, the mean and standard deviation of any binomial distribution are easily calculated. They are always:

Mean $= Np$
Variance $= Npq$
Standard deviation $= \sqrt{Npq}$

For example, Figure 5.4 shows the binomial distribution when $N = 10$ and $p = .50$. The mean of this distribution is $10(.5) = 5$ and the standard deviation is $\sqrt{10(.5)(.5)} = \sqrt{2.5} = 1.58$.

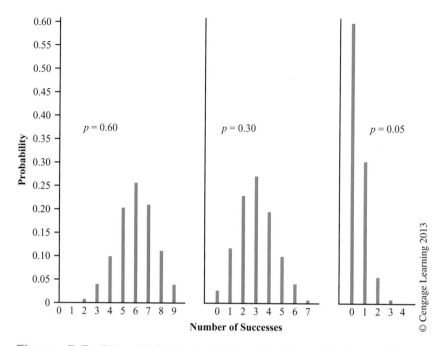

Figure 5.5   Binomial distribution for $N = 10$ and $p = .60, .30,$ and $.05$

We will see shortly that specifying the mean and standard deviation of any binomial distribution is exceptionally useful when it comes to testing hypotheses. First, however, it is necessary to point out two more considerations.

In the example of perception without awareness, we assumed that our judge was choosing at random ($p = q = .50$). Had we slowed down the stimulus so as to increase the person's accuracy of response on any one trial—the arithmetic would have been the same but the results would have been different. For purposes of illustration, three distributions obtained with different values of p are plotted in Figure 5.5.

For the distribution on the left of Figure 5.5, the stimulus is set at a speed that just barely allows the participant to respond at better than chance levels, with a probability of .60 of being correct on any given trial. The distribution in the middle represents the results expected from a judge who has a probability of only .30 of being correct on each trial. The distribution on the right represents the behavior of a judge with a nearly unerring ability to choose the *wrong* stimulus. On each trial, this judge had a probability of only .05 of being correct. From these three distributions, you can see that, for a given number of trials, as p and q depart more and more from .50, the distributions become more and more skewed although the mean and standard deviation are still Np and $\sqrt{Npq}$, respectively. Moreover, it is important to point out (although it is not shown in Figure 5.5, in which N is always 10) that as the number of trials increases, the distribution becomes more symmetric and approaches normal, regardless of the values of p and q. (You can easily demonstrate this for yourself by varying p and N in the R program referred to above.) As a rule of thumb, as long as both Np and Nq are greater than about 5, the distribution is close enough to normal that our estimates won't be far in error if we treat it as normal. Figure 5.6 shows the binomial distribution when $p = .70$ and there are 25 trials.

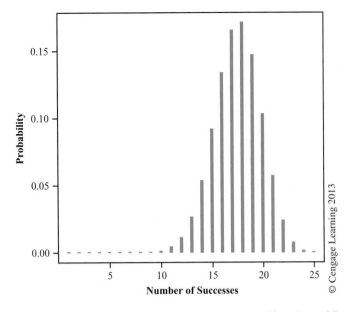

Figure 5.6   Binomial distribution with $p = .70$ and $n = 25$

5.9 Using the Binomial Distribution to Test Hypotheses

Many of the situations for which the binomial distribution is useful in testing hypotheses are handled equally well by the chi-square test, discussed in Chapter 6. For that reason, this discussion will be limited to those cases for which the binomial distribution is uniquely useful.

In the previous sections, we dealt with the situation in which a person was judging very brief stimuli, and we saw how to calculate the distribution of possible outcomes and their probabilities over $N = 10$ trials. Now suppose we turn the question around and ask whether the available data from a set of presentation trials can be taken as evidence that our judge really can identify presented characters at better than chance levels.

For example, suppose we had our judge view eight stimuli, and the judge has been correct on seven out of eight trials. Do these data indicate that she is operating at a better than chance level? Put another way, are we likely to have seven out of eight correct choices if the judge is really operating by blind guessing?

Following the procedure outlined in Chapter 4, we can begin by stating as our research hypothesis that the judge knows a digit when she sees it (at least that is presumably what we set out to demonstrate). In other words, the research hypothesis (H_1) is that her performance is at better than chance levels ($p > .50$). (We have chosen a one-tailed test merely to simplify the example; in general, we would prefer to use a two-tailed test.) The null hypothesis is that the judge's behavior does not differ from chance ($H_0: p = .50$). The sampling distribution of the number of correct choices out of eight trials, given that the null hypothesis is true, is provided by the binomial distribution with $p = .50$. Rather than calculate the probability of each of the possible number of correct choices (as we did in Figure 5.5, for example), all we need to do is calculate the probability of seven correct choices and the probability of eight correct choices, because we want to know the probability of our judge doing at least as well as she did if she were choosing randomly.

Letting N represent the number of trials (eight) and X represent the number of correct trials, the probability of seven correct trials out of eight is given by

$$p(X) = C_X^N p^X q^{(N-X)}$$
$$p(7) = C_7^8 p^7 q^1$$
$$= \frac{8!}{7!1!}(.5)^7(.5)^1 = 8(.0078)(.5) = 8(.0039) = .0312$$

Thus, the probability of making seven correct choices out of eight by chance is .0312. But we know that we test null hypotheses by asking questions of the form, "What is the probability of at least this many correct choices if H_0 is true?" In other words, we need to sum $p(7)$ and $p(8)$:

$$p(8) = C_8^8 p^8 q^0 = 1(.0039)(1) = .0039$$

Then

$$p(7) = .0312$$
$$+ p(8) = .0039$$
$$p(7 \text{ or } 8) = .0351$$

Here we see that the probability of at least seven correct choices is approximately .035. Earlier, we said that we will reject H_0 whenever the probability of a Type I error (α) is less than or equal to .05. Since we have just determined that the probability of making at least seven correct choices out of eight is only .035 if H_0 is true (i.e., if $p = .50$), we will reject H_0 and conclude that our judge is performing at better than chance levels. In other words, her performance is better than we would expect if she were just guessing.[9]

The Sign Test

sign test

Another example of the use of the binomial to test hypotheses is one of the simplest tests we have: the **sign test**. Although the sign test is very simple, it is also very useful in a variety of settings. Suppose we hypothesize that when people know each other they tend to be more accepting of individual differences. As a test of this hypothesis, we asked a group of first-year male students matriculating at a small college to rate 12 target subjects (also male) on physical appearance (higher scores represent greater attractiveness). At the end

Table 5.5 Median ratings of physical appearance at the beginning and end of the semester

Target	1	2	3	4	5	6	7	8	9	10	11	12
Beginning	12	21	10	8	14	18	25	7	16	13	20	15
End	15	22	16	14	17	16	24	8	19	14	28	18
Gain	3	1	6	6	3	−2	−1	1	3	1	8	3

© Cengage Learning 2013

---

[9] One problem with discrete distributions is that there is rarely a set of outcomes with a probability of exactly .05. In our particular example with 7 correct guesses you rejected the null because $p = .035$. If we had found 6 correct choices the probability would have been .133, and we would have failed to reject the null. There is no possible outcome with a tail area of exactly .05. So we are faced with the choice of a case where the critical value is either too conservative or too liberal. One proposal that has been seriously considered is to use what is called the "mid-p" value, which takes one half of the probability of the observed outcome, plus all of the probabilities of more extreme outcomes. For a discussion of this approach see Berger (2005).

of the first semester, when students have come to know one another, we again ask them to rate those same 12 targets. Assume we obtain the data in Table 5.5, where each entry is the median rating that person (target) received when judged by participants in the experiment on a 30-point scale.

The gain score in this table was computed by subtracting the score obtained at the beginning of the semester from the one obtained at the end of the semester. For example, the first target was rated 3 points higher at the end of the semester than at the beginning. Notice that in 10 of the 12 cases the score at the end of the semester was higher than at the beginning. In other words, the sign was positive. (The sign test gets its name from the fact that we look at the sign, but not the magnitude, of the difference.)

Consider the null hypothesis in this example. If familiarity does not affect ratings of physical appearance, we would not expect a systematic change in ratings (assuming that no other variables are involved). Ignoring tied scores, which we don't have anyway, we would expect that by chance about half the ratings would increase and half about the ratings would decrease over the course of the semester. Thus, under H_0, $p(\text{higher}) = p(\text{lower}) = .50$. The binomial can now be used to compute the probability of obtaining at least 10 out of 12 improvements if H_0 is true:

$$p(10) = \frac{12!}{10!2!}(.5)^{10}(.5)^2 = .0161$$

$$p(11) = \frac{12!}{11!1!}(.5)^{11}(.5)^1 = .0029$$

$$p(12) = \frac{12!}{12!0!}(.5)^{12}(.5)^0 = .0002$$

From these calculations we see that the probability of at least 10 improvements $= .0161 + .0029 + .0002 = .0192$ if the null hypothesis is true and ratings are unaffected by familiarity. Because this probability is less than our traditional cutoff of .05, we will reject H_0 and conclude that ratings of appearance have increased over the course of the semester. (Although variables other than familiarity could explain this difference, at the very least our test has shown that there is a significant difference to be explained.)

5.10 The Multinomial Distribution

multinomial distribution

The binomial distribution we have just examined is a special case of a more general distribution, the **multinomial distribution**. In binomial distributions, we deal with events that can have only one of two outcomes—a coin could land heads or tails, a wine could be judged as more expensive or less expensive, and so on. That is why it is called "binomial." In many situations, however, an event can have more than two possible outcomes—a roll of a die has six possible outcomes; a maze might present three choices (right, left, and center); political opinions could be classified as For, Maybe, Neutral, Against, Yuk. In these situations, we must invoke the more general multinomial distribution.

If we define the probability of each of k events (categories) as $p_1, p_2, \cdots, p_k$ and wish to calculate the probability of exactly X_1 outcomes of event$_1$, X_2 outcomes of event$_2$, ..., X_k outcomes of event$_k$, this probability is given by

$$p(X_1, X_2, \cdots, X_k) = \frac{N!}{X_1!X_2!\cdots X_k!} p_1^{X_1} p_2^{X_2} \cdots p_k^{X_k}$$

where N has the same meaning as in the binomial. Note that when $k = 2$ this is in fact the binomial distribution, where $p_2 = 1 - p_1$ and $X_2 = N - X_1$.

As a brief illustration, suppose we had a die with two black sides, three red sides, and one white side. If we roll this die, the probability of a black side coming up is 2/6 = .333, the probability of a red is 3/6 = .500, and the probability of a white is 1/6 = .167. If we roll the die 10 times, what is the probability of obtaining exactly four blacks, five reds, and one white? This probability is given as

$$p(4,5,1) = \frac{10!}{4!5!1!} (.333)^4 (.500)^5 (.167)^1$$

$$= 1260(.333)^4 (.500)^5 (.167)^1 = 1260(.000064)$$

$$= .081$$

At this point, this is all we will say about the multinomial. It will appear again in Chapter 6, when we discuss chi-square, and forms the basis for some of the other tests you are likely to run into in the future.

Key Terms

Analytic view (5.1)

Frequentist view (5.1)

Sample with replacement (5.1)

Subjective probability (5.1)

Event (5.2)

Independent events (5.2)

Mutually exclusive (5.2)

Exhaustive (5.2)

Additive law of probability (5.2)

Multiplicative law of probability (5.2)

Joint probability (5.2)

Conditional probability (5.2)

Unconditional probability (5.2)

Density (5.5)

Combinatorics (5.6)

Permutation (5.6)

Factorial (5.6)

Combinations (5.6)

Bayes' Theorem (5.7)

Prior probability (5.7)

Posterior probability (5.7)

Noninformative prior

Bayesian statistics (5.7)

Binomial distribution (5.8)

Bernoulli trial (5.8)

Success (5.8)

Failure (5.8)

Sign test (5.9)

Multinomial distribution (5.10)

Exercises

5.1   Give an example of an analytic, a relative-frequency, and a subjective view of probability.

5.2   Which parts of Exercise 5.3 deal with joint probabilities?

5.3   Assume the same situation as in 5.4, except that a total of only 10 tickets were sold and that there are two prizes.

    a.   Given that you don't win first prize, what is the probability that you will win second prize? (The first prize-winning ticket is not put back in the hopper.)

    b.   What is the probability that your brother will win first prize and you will win second prize?

    c.   What is the probability that you will win first prize and your brother will win second prize?

    d.   What is the probability that the two of you will win the first and second prizes?

5.4   Assume that you have bought a ticket for the local fire department lottery and that your brother has bought two tickets. You have just read that 1,000 tickets have been sold.

    a.   What is the probability that you will win the grand prize?

    b.   What is the probability that your brother will win?

    c.   What is the probability that you or your brother will win?

5.5   Which parts of Exercise 5.3 deal with conditional probabilities?

5.6   Suppose that we have a study of messages printed on supermarket fliers. We want to know if what people do with fliers is independent of the message that is on them. If the message has no effect on a shopper's behavior, the probability that a flier carrying a "do not litter" message would end up in the trash was .033. Suppose also that 4.5% of those messages actually ended up in the trash. What does this tell you about the effectiveness of messages?

5.7   Make up a simple example of a situation in which you are interested in conditional probabilities.

5.8   Make up a simple example of a situation in which you are interested in joint probabilities.

5.9   In Exercise 5.10, assume that both the mother and child are asleep from 8:00 P.M. to 7:00 A.M. What would the probability be now?

5.10   In some homes, a mother's behavior seems to be independent of her baby's, and vice versa. If the mother looks at her child a total of 2 hours each day, and the baby looks at the mother a total of 3 hours each day, and if they really do behave independently, what is the probability that they will look at each other at the same time?

5.11   Give an example of a common continuous distribution for which we have some real interest in the probability that an observation will fall within some specified interval.

5.12   A graduate-admissions committee has finally come to realize that it cannot make valid distinctions among the top applicants. This year, the committee rated all 300 applicants and randomly chose 10 from those in the top 20%. What is the probability that any particular applicant will be admitted (assuming you have no knowledge of her or his rating)?

5.13   Give two examples of discrete variables.

5.14   Give an example of a continuous variable that we routinely treat as if it were discrete.

5.15   With respect to Exercise 5.12,

   a.   What is the conditional probability that a person will be admitted given that she has the highest faculty rating among the 300 students?

   b.   What is the conditional probability given that she has the lowest rating?

5.16   Using the data for Appendix Data Set scores, compare the conditional probability of dropping out of school given an ADDSC score of at least 60, which you computed in Exercise 5.20, with the unconditional probability that a person will drop out of school regardless of his or her ADDSC score.

5.17   Using the file on the Web named Add.dat, described in Appendix Data Set,

   a.   What is the probability that a male will have an ADDSC score greater than 50 if the scores are normally distributed with a mean of 54.3 and a standard deviation of 12.9?

   b.   What percentage of the male sample actually exceeded 50?

5.18   Using the file on the Web named Add.dat, described in Appendix Data Set,

   a.   What is the probability that a person drawn at random will have an ADDSC score greater than 50 if the scores are normally distributed with a mean of 52.6 and a standard deviation of 12.4?

   b.   What percentage of the sample actually exceeded 50?

5.19   How might you use conditional probabilities to determine if an ADDSC cutoff score of 66 in Appendix Data is predictive of whether or not a person will drop out of school?

5.20   Using the data for Appendix Data Set, what is the empirical probability that a person will drop out of school given that he or she has an ADDSC score of at least 60? Here we do not need to assume normality.

5.21   In a five-choice task, subjects are asked to choose the stimulus that the experimenter has arbitrarily determined to be correct; the 10 subjects can only guess on the first trial. Plot the sampling distribution of the number of correct choices on trial 1.

5.22   People who sell cars are often accused of treating male and female customers differently. Make up a series of statements to illustrate simple, joint, and conditional probabilities with respect to such behavior. How might we begin to determine if those accusations are true?

5.23   Refer to Exercise 5.21. What is the minimum number of correct choices on a trial necessary for you to conclude that the subjects as a group are no longer performing at chance levels?

5.24   Refer to Exercise 5.21. What would you conclude if 6 of 10 subjects were correct on trial 2?

5.25   Assume you are a member of a local human rights organization. How might you use what you know about probability to examine discrimination in housing?

5.26   We are designing a study in which six external electrodes will be implanted in a rat's brain. The six-channel amplifier in our recording apparatus blew two channels when the research assistant took it home to run her stereo. How many different ways can we record from the brain? (It makes no difference what signal goes on which channel.)

5.27   Refer to Exercise 5.28. Assume we have just discovered that, because of time constraints, each subject can see only two of the four classes. The rest of the experiment will remain the same, however. Now how many subjects do we need? (Warning: Do not actually try to run an experiment like this unless you are sure you know how you will analyze the data.)

5.28   In a study of human cognition, we want to look at recall of different classes of words (nouns, verbs, adjectives, and adverbs). Each subject will see one of each. We are afraid that there may be a sequence effect, however, and want to have different subjects see the different classes in a different order. How many subjects will we need if we are to have one subject per order?

5.29   An ice-cream shop has six different flavors of ice cream, and you can order any combination of any number of them (but only one scoop of each flavor). How many different ice-cream cone combinations could they truthfully advertise? (We do not care if the Oreo Mint is above or below the Raspberry-Pistachio. Each cone must have at least one scoop of ice cream—an empty cone doesn't count.)

5.30   In a learning task, a subject is presented with five buttons. He must learn to press three specific buttons in a predetermined order. What chance does the subject have of pressing correctly on the first trial?

5.31   In a study of knowledge of current events, we give a 20-item true–false test to a class of college seniors. One of the not-so-alert students gets 11 answers right. Do we have any reason to believe that he has done anything other than guess?

5.32   Make up a simple experiment for which a sign test would be appropriate.

   a.   Create reasonable data and run the test.

   b.   Draw the appropriate conclusion.

5.33   This question is not an easy one, and requires putting together material in Chapters 3, 4, and 5. Suppose we make up a driving test that we have good reason to believe should be passed by 60% of all drivers. We administer it to 30 drivers, and 22 pass it. Is the result sufficiently large to cause us to reject H_0 $(p = .60)$? This problem is too unwieldy to be approached by solving the binomial for $X = 22, 23, \ldots, 30$. But you do know the mean and variance of the binomial, and something about its shape. With the aid of a diagram of what the distribution would look like, you should be able to solve the problem.

5.34   Earlier in this chapter I stated that the probability of drawing 25 blue M&M's out of 60 draws, with replacement, was .0011. Reproduce that result. (Warning, your calculator will be computing some very large numbers, which may lead to substantial rounding error. The value of .0011 is what my calculator produced.)

Discussion Questions

5.35   The "law of averages," or the "gambler's fallacy," is the oft-quoted belief that if random events have come out one way for a number of trials they are "due" to come out the other way on one of the next few trials. (For example, it is the [mistaken] belief that if a fair coin has come up heads on 18 out of the last 20 trials, it has a better than 50:50 chance of coming up tails on the next trial to balance things out.) The gambler's fallacy is just that, a fallacy—

coins have an even worse memory of their past performance than I do. Ann Watkins, in the spring 1995 edition of *Chance* magazine, reported a number of instances of people operating as if the "law of averages" were true. One of the examples that Watkins gave was a letter to Dear Abby in which the writer complained that she and her husband had just had their eighth child and eighth girl. She criticized fate and said that even her doctor had told her that the law of averages was in her favor 100 to 1. Watkins also cited another example in which the writer noted that fewer English than American men were fat, but the English must be fatter to keep the averages the same. And, finally, she quotes a really remarkable application of this (non-)law in reference to Marlon Brando: "Brando has had so many lovers, it would only be surprising if they were all of one gender; the law of averages alone would make him bisexual." (*Los Angeles Times*, September 18, 1994, "Book Reviews," p. 13) What is wrong with each of these examples? What underlying belief system would seem to lie behind such a law? How might you explain to the woman who wrote to Dear Abby that she really wasn't owed a boy to "make up" for all those girls?

5.36   What would happen to the answer to Exercise 5.38 if we were able to refine our test so that only 5% of women without breast cancer test positive? (In others words, we reduce the rate of false positives.)

5.37   Knowing that 80% of women with breast cancer have positive mammographies, the answer that you found in 5.38 is probably much lower than you expected. Why is it so low?

5.38   At age 40, 1% of women can be expected to have breast cancer. Of those women with breast cancer, 80% will have positive mammographies. In addition, 9.6% of women who do not have breast cancer will have a positive mammography. If a woman in this age group tests positive for breast cancer, what is the probability that she actually has it? Use Bayes' theorem to solve this problem. (Hint: Letting BC stand for "breast cancer," we have $p(BC) = .01$, $p(+|BC) = .80$, and $p(+|\overline{BC}) = .096$. You want to solve for $p(BC|+)$.)

Chapter 6

Categorical Data and Chi-Square

Objectives

To present the chi-square test as a procedure for testing hypotheses when the data are categorical, and to examine other measures that clarify the meaning of our results.

Contents

IN CHAPTER 1 a distinction was drawn between measurement data (sometimes called quantitative data) and categorical data (sometimes called frequency data). When we deal with measurement data, each observation represents a score along some continuum, and the most common statistics are the mean and the standard deviation. When we deal with categorical data, on the other hand, the data consist of the frequencies of observations that fall into each of two or more categories, and the data consist of counts of observations in each category (e.g., "How many people rate their mom as their best friend, and how many rate their dad as their best friend?").

In Chapter 5 we examined the use of the binomial distribution to test simple hypotheses. In those cases, we were limited to situations in which an individual event had one of only two possible outcomes, and we merely asked whether, over repeated trials, one outcome occurred (statistically) significantly more often than the other. We will shortly see how we can ask the same question using the chi-square test.

In this chapter we will expand the kinds of situations that we can evaluate. First we will deal with the case in which a single event can have two *or more* possible outcomes, and then we will deal with the case in which we have two independent variables to test null hypotheses concerning their independence. For both of these situations, the appropriate statistical test will be the chi-square (χ^2) test.

chi-square (χ^2)

The term **chi-square** (χ^2) has two distinct meanings in statistics, a fact that leads to some confusion. In one meaning, it is used to refer to a particular mathematical distribution that exists in and of itself without any necessary referent in the outside world. In the second meaning, it is used to refer to a statistical test that has a resulting test statistic that is distributed in approximately the same way as the χ^2 distribution. When you hear someone refer to chi-square, they usually have this second meaning in mind. (The test itself was developed by Karl Pearson (1900) and is often referred to as **Pearson's chi-square** to distinguish it from other tests that also produce a χ^2 statistic—for example, Friedman's test, discussed in Chapter 18, and the likelihood ratio tests discussed at the end of this chapter.) We will use the term in both ways, but the meaning should always be obvious.

Pearson's chi-square

6.1 The Chi-Square Distribution

chi-square (χ^2) distribution

The **chi-square (χ^2) distribution** is the distribution defined by

$$f(\chi^2) = \frac{1}{2^{\frac{k}{2}}\Gamma(k/2)}\chi^{2[(k/2)-1]}e^{\frac{-(\chi^2)}{2}}$$

This is a rather messy-looking function and most readers will be pleased to know that they will not have to work with it in any algebraic sense. We do need to consider some of its features, however, to understand what the distribution of χ^2 is all about. The first thing that should be mentioned is that the term $\Gamma(k/2)$ in the denominator, called a **gamma function** and is related to what we normally mean by *factorial*. In fact, when the argument of gamma ($k/2$) is an integer, then $\Gamma(k/2) = [(k/2) - 1]!$. We need gamma functions in part because arguments are not always integers. Mathematical statisticians have a lot to say about gamma, but we'll stop here.

gamma function

A second and more important feature of this equation is that the distribution has only one parameter (k). Everything else is either a constant (e) or else the value of χ^2 for which we want to find the ordinate $[f(\chi^2)]$. Whereas the normal distribution was a two-parameter function, with μ and σ as parameters, χ^2 is a one-parameter function with k as the only parameter. When we move from the mathematical to the statistical world, k will become our degrees of freedom. (We often signify the degrees of freedom by subscripting χ^2. Thus, χ^2_3 is read "chi-square with three degrees of freedom." Alternatively, some authors write it as $\chi^2(3)$.)

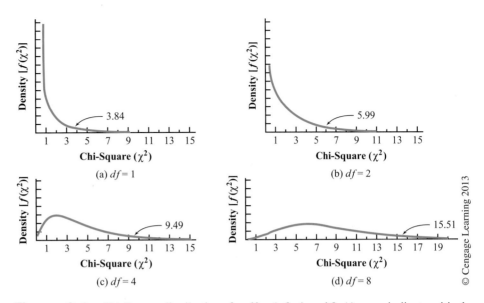

Figure 6.1   Chi-Square distributions for df = 1, 2, 4, and 8. (Arrows indicate critical values at alpha = .05.)

Figure 6.1 shows the plots for several different χ^2 distributions, each representing a different value of k. From this figure it is obvious that the distribution changes markedly with changes in k, and becoming more symmetric as k increases. It is also apparent that the mean and variance of each χ^2 distribution increase with increasing values of k and are directly related to k. It can be shown that in all cases

$$\text{Mean} = k$$
$$\text{Variance} = 2k$$

6.2 The Chi-Square Goodness-of-Fit Test—One-Way Classification

chi-square test

We now turn to what is commonly referred to as the **chi-square test**, which is based on the χ^2 distribution. We will first examine the test as it is applied to one-dimensional tables and then as applied to two-dimensional tables (contingency tables).

We will start with a simple but interesting example with only two categories and then move on to an example with more than two categories. Our first example comes from a paper on therapeutic touch that was published in the *Journal of the American Medical Association* (Rosa, Rosa, Sarner, and Barrett, 1998). (I should point out at the beginning that legitimate questions can be raised about my use of this first example, and I will discuss them shortly. However I have chosen to keep the example, while pointing out its shortcomings, because even the shortcomings are instructive.) One of the things that made this an interesting paper is that the second author, Emily Rosa, was only eleven years old at the time, and she was the principal experimenter.[1] To quote from the abstract, "Therapeutic Touch (TT) is a widely used

---

[1] An interesting feature of this paper is that Emily Rosa was an invited speaker at the "Ig Noble Prize" ceremony sponsored by the Annals of Irreproducible Results, located at MIT. This is a group of "whacky" scientists, to use a precise psychological term, who look for and recognize interesting research studies. Ig Nobel Prizes honor "achievements that cannot or should not be reproduced." Emily's invitation was meant as an honor, and true believers in therapeutic touch were less than kind to her. The society's web page is located at http://www.improb .com/ and I recommend going to it when you need a break from this chapter.

Table 6.1   Results of experiment on therapeutic touch

	Correct	Incorrect	Total
Observed	123	157	280
Expected	140	140	280

© Cengage Learning 2013

nursing practice rooted in mysticism but alleged to have a scientific basis. Practitioners of TT claim to treat many medical conditions by using their hands to manipulate a 'human energy field' perceptible above the patient's skin." Emily recruited practitioners of therapeutic touch, blindfolded them, and then placed her hand over one of their hands. If therapeutic touch is a real phenomenon, the principles behind it suggest that the participant should be able to identify which of their hands is below Emily's hand. Out of 280 trials (data were collapsed across judges), the participant was correct on 123 of them, which is an accuracy rate of 44%. By chance we would expect the participants to be correct 50% of the time, or 140 times.

Although we can tell by inspection that participants performed even worse than chance would predict, I have chosen this example in part because it raises an interesting question of the statistical significance of a test. We will return to that issue shortly. The first question that we want to answer is whether the data's departure from chance expectation is statistically significantly greater than we would expect if people's judgments are no better than random guesses. The data are shown in Table 6.1.

Even if participants were operating at chance levels, one category of response accuracy is likely to come out more frequently than the other. What we want is a **goodness-of-fit test** to ask whether the deviations from what would be expected by chance are large enough to lead us to conclude that responses weren't random.

The most common and important formula for χ^2 involves a comparison of observed and expected frequencies. The **observed frequencies**, as the name suggests, are the frequencies you actually observed in the data—the numbers in row two of the table above. The **expected frequencies** are the frequencies you would expect *if the null hypothesis were true*. The expected frequencies are shown in row 3 of Table 6.1. We will assume that participants' responses are independent of each other. (In this use of "independence" I mean that what the participant reports on trial k does not depend on what he or she reported on trial $k - 1$, though it does not mean that the two different categories of choice are equally likely, which is what we are about to test.)

Because we have two possibilities over 280 trials, we would expect, under the null hypothesis, that there would be 140 correct and 140 incorrect choices. We will denote the observed number of choices with the letter "O" and the expected number of choices with the letter "E." Then our formula for chi-square is

$$\chi^2 = \sum \frac{(O - E)^2}{E}$$

where summation is taken over both categories of response.

This formula makes intuitive sense. Start with the numerator. If the null hypothesis is true, the observed and expected frequencies (O and E) would be reasonably close together and the numerator would be small, even after it is squared. Moreover, how large the difference between O and E would be ought to depend on how large a number we expected. If we were talking about 140 correct choices, a difference of 5 choices would be a small difference. But if we had expected 10 correct choices, a difference of 5 would be substantial. To keep the squared size of the difference in perspective relative to the number of observations we expect, we divide the former by the latter. Finally, we sum over both possibilities to combine these relative differences.

goodness-of-fit test

observed frequencies

expected frequencies

The χ^2 statistic for these data using the observed and expected frequencies given in Table 6.1 follows.

$$\chi^2 = \sum \frac{(O - E)^2}{E} = \frac{(123 - 140)^2}{140} + \frac{(157 - 140)^2}{140}$$

$$= \frac{-17^2}{140} + \frac{17^2}{140} = 2(2.064) = 4.129$$

The Tabled Chi-Square Distribution

Now that we have obtained a value of χ^2, we must refer it to the χ^2 distribution to determine the probability of a value of χ^2 at least this extreme if the null hypothesis of a chance distribution were true. We can do this through the use of the standard tabled distribution of χ^2.

tabled distribu-tion of χ^2

The **tabled distribution of** χ^2, like that of most other statistics, differs in a very important way from the *tabled* standard normal distribution that we saw in Chapter 3 in that it depends on the **degrees of freedom**. In the case of a one-dimensional table, as we have

degrees of freedom

here, the degrees of freedom equal one less than the number of categories ($k - 1$). If we wish to reject H_0 at the .05 level, all that we really care about is whether or not our value of χ^2 is greater or less than the value of χ^2 that cuts off the upper 5% of the distribution. Thus, for our particular purposes, all we need to know is the 5% cutoff point for each *df*. Other people might want the 2.5% cutoff, 1% cutoff, and so on, but it is hard to imagine wanting the 17% cutoff, for example. Thus, tables of χ^2 such as the one given in Appendix χ^2 and reproduced in part in Table 6.2 supply only those values that might be of general interest.

Look for a moment at Table 6.2. Down the leftmost column you will find the degrees of freedom. In each of the other columns, you will find the critical values of χ^2 cutting off the percentage of the distribution labeled at the top of that column. Thus, for example, you will see that for 1 *df* a χ^2 of 3.84 cuts off the upper 5% of the distribution. (Note the boldfaced entry in Table 6.2.)

Returning to our example, we have found a value of $\chi^2 = 4.129$ on 1 *df*. We have already seen that, with 1 *df*, a χ^2 of 3.84 cuts off the upper 5% of the distribution. Because our obtained value (χ^2_{obt}) = 4.129 is greater than $\chi^2_{1.(05)} = 3.84$, we will reject the null hypothesis and conclude that the obtained frequencies differ significantly from those expected under the null hypothesis by more than could be attributed to chance. In this case participants performed *less* accurately than chance would have predicted.

Table 6.2   Upper percentage points of the χ^2 distribution

df	.995	.990	.975	.950	.900	.750	.500	.250	.100	.050	.025	.010	.005
1	0.00	0.00	0.00	0.00	0.02	0.10	0.45	1.32	2.71	**3.84**	5.02	6.63	7.88
2	0.01	0.02	0.05	0.10	0.21	0.58	1.39	2.77	4.61	5.99	7.38	9.21	10.60
3	0.07	0.11	0.22	0.35	0.58	1.21	2.37	4.11	6.25	7.82	9.35	11.35	12.84
4	0.21	0.30	0.48	0.71	1.06	1.92	3.36	5.39	7.78	9.49	11.14	13.28	14.86
5	0.41	0.55	0.83	1.15	1.61	2.67	4.35	6.63	9.24	11.07	12.83	15.09	16.75
6	0.68	0.87	1.24	1.64	2.20	3.45	5.35	7.84	10.64	12.59	14.45	16.81	18.55
7	0.99	1.24	1.69	2.17	2.83	4.25	6.35	9.04	12.02	14.07	16.01	18.48	20.28
8	1.34	1.65	2.18	2.73	3.49	5.07	7.34	10.22	13.36	15.51	17.54	20.09	21.96
9	1.73	2.09	2.70	3.33	4.17	5.90	8.34	11.39	14.68	16.92	19.02	21.66	23.59
...	...	...	...	...	...	...	...	...	...	...	...	...	...

As I suggested earlier, this result could raise a question about how we interpret a null hypothesis test. Whether we take the traditional view of hypothesis testing or the view put forth by Jones and Tukey (2000), we can conclude that the difference is greater than chance. If the pattern of responses had come out favoring the effectiveness of therapeutic touch, we would come to the conclusion that therapeutic touch is a real phenomenon. But these results were significant in the opposite direction, and it is difficult to argue that the effectiveness of touch has been supported because respondents were *wrong* more often than expected. Personally, I would conclude that we can reject the effectiveness of therapeutic touch. But there is an inconsistency here because if we had 157 correct responses I would say "See, the difference is significant!" but when there were 157 incorrect responses I say "Well, that's just bad luck and the difference really isn't significant." That makes me feel guilty because I am acting inconsistently. On the other hand, there is no credible theory that would predict participants being significantly wrong, so there is no real alternative explanation to support. People simply did not do as well as they should have if therapeutic touch works. (Sometimes life is like that!)

There is another problem with the chi-square distribution that we tend to ignore if we have a reasonable number of observations, partly because there is not much we can do about it. The problem is that the χ^2 distribution is continuous, but when we use the chi-square test discussed here, the possible values of chi-square that we can obtain are discrete, and especially so with small sample sizes. For example, if Emily Rosa had performed her experiment with only 10 observations, the only possible outcomes would be 10:0, 9:1, 8:2, etc. And half of these are just mirror images of the other half. As a result we are trying to fit a very discrete distribution with a continuous one, and the fit is not very good. In some situations there are ways around this, as we will see, but even those approaches do not completely solve the problem. We will return to this problem.

I began this example by admitting that there is a fundamental problem with it. One of the assumptions of the chi-square test is that observations are independent. Two readers have pointed out to me that the 280 observations came from 21 judges, and it is possible that what a judge reports on trial 15 may not be independent of what he or she reports on trial 14.[2] There is considerable evidence that humans are very bad at generating a sequence of responses that is random. I honestly can't decide whether that is a problem here or not. If respondents alternated left and right, they would drive the percentage of responses toward 50:50, which would work against the *experimental* hypothesis. In fact it is hard to see how a pattern of responses would work against the *null* hypothesis. However, the fact that I'm not smart enough to come up with a reason why the pattern would not be relevant is not a reason to say "well, I guess we can discard the problem of independence." That's why I left this example in the book—it highlights the fact that some research questions are not easily handled. We will see an alternative way to analyze these data that gets around this problem in Chapter 7.

An Example with More Than Two Categories

Many psychologists are particularly interested in how people make decisions, and they often present their subjects with simple games. A favorite example is called the Prisoner's Dilemma, and it consists of two prisoners (players) who are being interrogated separately. The optimal strategy in this situation is for each player to confess to the crime, but people often depart from optimal behavior. Psychologists use such a game to see how human behavior compares with optimal behavior. We are going to look at the presence or absence

---

[2] One person to raise this issue was Tim Rakow of the University of Essex in England. Unfortunately I no longer recall the name of the other reader, though I wish to thank him or her as well.

Table 6.3 Number of throws of each symbol in a playground game of rock/paper/scissors

Symbol	Rock	Paper	Scissors
Observed	30	21	24
Expected	(25)	(25)	(25)

© Cengage Learning 2013

of optimal behavior in a different type of game, the universal children's game of "rock /paper/scissors," often abbreviated as "RPS." In case your childhood was deprived of RPS, in this game each of two players "throws" a sign. A fist represents a rock, a flat hand represents paper, and two fingers represent scissors. Rocks break scissors, scissors cut paper, and paper covers rock. So if you throw a scissors and I throw a rock, I win because my rock will break your scissors. But if I had thrown a paper when you threw scissors, you'd win because scissors cut paper. Children can keep this up for an awfully long time. (Some adults take this game very seriously and you can get a flavor of what is involved by going to a fascinating article at http://www.danieldrezner.com/archives/002022.html. The topic is not as simple as you might think. There is even a World RPS Society with its own Web page.)

It seems obvious to a naive person like me that in rock/paper/scissors the optimal strategy is to be completely unpredictable and to throw each symbol equally often. Moreover, each throw should be independent of others so that your opponent can't predict your next throw. There are, however, other strategies, each with its own advocates. Aside from adults who go to championship RPS competitions, the most common players are children on the playground. Suppose that we observe a group of 75 children playing RPS and record the number of throws of each symbol on some arbitrarily selected trial. I have chosen to observe one response from each trial to avoid the question of independence that I was forced to face in the therapeutic touch example. The results of this hypothetical study are given in Table 6.3.

Although our players should throw each symbol equally often, our data suggest that they are throwing Rock more often than would be expected. However this may just be a random deviation due to chance. Even if you are deliberately randomizing your throws, one is likely to come out more frequently than others. (Moreover, people are notoriously poor at generating random sequences.) What we want is a goodness-of-fit test to ask whether the deviations from what would be expected by chance are large enough to lead us to conclude that the children's throws weren't random, and they were really throwing Rock at greater than chance levels.

The χ^2 statistic for these data using the observed and expected frequencies given in Table 6.3 follows. Notice that it is a simple extension of what we did when we had two categories.

$$\chi^2 = \Sigma \frac{(O - E)^2}{E}$$

$$= \frac{(30 - 25)^2}{25} + \frac{(21 - 25)^2}{25} + \frac{(24 - 25)^2}{25} = \frac{5^2 + 4^2 + 1^2}{25}$$

$$= 1.68$$

In this example we have three categories and thus 2 *df*. The critical value of χ^2 on 2 *df* = 5.99, and we have no reason to doubt that our players were equally likely to throw each symbol.

6.3 Two Classification Variables: Contingency Table Analysis

contingency
table

In the previous examples we considered the case in which data are categorized along only one dimension (classification variable). More often, however, data are categorized with respect to two (or more) variables, and we are interested in asking whether those variables are independent of one another. To reverse this, we often are interested in asking whether the distribution of one variable is *contingent* on or *conditional on* a second variable. (Statisticians often use the phrase "conditional on" instead of "contingent on," but they mean the same thing. I mention this because you will see the word "conditional" appearing often in this chapter and elsewhere.) In this situation we will construct a **contingency table** showing the distribution of one variable at each level of the other variable. A good example of such a test concerns the controversial question of whether or not there is racial bias in the assignment of death sentences. We have already seen one instance of this example.

There have been a number of studies over the years looking at whether the imposition of a death sentence is affected by the race of the defendant (and/or the race of the victim). You will see an extended example of such data in Exercise 6.1. Peterson (2001) reports data on a study by Unah and Borger (2001) examining the death penalty in North Carolina in 1993–1997. The data in Table 6.4 show the outcome of sentencing for white and nonwhite (mostly black and Hispanic) defendants when the victim was white. The expected frequencies are shown in parentheses.

Expected Frequencies for Contingency Tables

cell

marginal totals

row totals

column totals

The expected frequencies in a contingency table represent those frequencies that we would expect if the two variables forming the table (here, race and sentence) were independent. For a contingency table the expected frequency for a given row and column combination (called a **cell**) is obtained by multiplying together the totals for the row and column in which the cell is located and dividing by the total sample size (N). (These totals are known as **marginal totals**, because they sit at the margins of the table.) If E_{ij} is the expected frequency for the cell in row i and column j, R_i and C_j are the corresponding **row** and **column totals**, and N is the total number of observations, we have the following formula:

$$E_{ij} = \frac{R_i C_j}{N}$$

For our example

$$E_{11} = \frac{284 \times 66}{825} = 22.72$$

$$E_{12} = \frac{284 \times 759}{825} = 261.28$$

Table 6.4 Sentencing as a function of the race of the defendant—the victim was white

Defendant's Race	Death Sentence		Total
	Yes	No	
Nonwhite	33 (22.72)	251 (261.28)	284
White	33 (43.28)	508 (497.72)	541
Total	66	759	825

© Cengage Learning 2013

$$E_{21} = \frac{541 \times 66}{285} = 43.28$$

$$E_{22} = \frac{541 \times 759}{825} = 497.72$$

These are the values shown in parentheses in Table 6.4.

NOTE

This formula for the expected values is derived directly from the formula for the probability of the joint occurrence of two *independent* events given in Chapter 5 on probability. The probability of an observation falling in Row$_1$ is simply that row total divided by the total of all cells. This similarly occurs for the probability of an observation being in Column$_1$. If the observations are independent, we can multiply those two probabilities and then multiply the result by N to get the expected frequency.

Calculation of Chi-Square

Now that we have the observed and expected frequencies in each cell, the calculation of χ^2 is straightforward. We simply use the same formula that we have been using all along, although we sum our calculations over all cells in the table.

$$\chi^2 = \sum \frac{(O - E)^2}{E}$$

$$= \frac{(33 - 22.72)^2}{22.72} + \frac{(251 - 261.28)^2}{261.28} + \frac{(33 - 43.28)^2}{43.28} + \frac{(508 - 497.82)^2}{497.72}$$

$$= 7.71$$

Degrees of Freedom

Before we can compare our value of χ^2 to the value in Appendix χ^2, we must know the degrees of freedom. For the analysis of contingency tables, the degrees of freedom are given by

$$df = (R - 1)(C - 1)$$

where R and C = the number of rows and columns in the table.

For our example we have $R = 2$ and $C = 2$; therefore we have $(2 - 1)(2 - 1) = 1$ df. It may seem strange to have only 1 df when we have four cells, but once you know the row and column totals, you need to know only one cell frequency to determine the rest.[3]

Evaluation of χ^2

With 1 df the critical value of χ^2, as found in Appendix χ^2, is 3.84. Because our value of 7.71 exceeds the critical value, we will reject the null hypothesis that the variables are independent of each other. In this case we will conclude that whether a death sentence is

---

[3] This is where Pearson went wrong. He thought that the degrees of freedom would be RC-1 instead of $(R - 1)$ $(C - 1)$. He was more than a little angry when Fisher pointed out his error and then went on to prove himself right by using some of Pearson's son's own results.

imposed is related to the race of the defendant. When the victim was white, nonwhite defendants were more likely to receive the death penalty than white defendants.[4]

Another Example

A second example is offered in a study by Walsh et al. (2006) on the use of an antidepressant in the treatment of anorexia.

It has long been hypothesized that depression is one reason that girls who have been successfully treated for anorexia nervosa tend to relapse after treatment. (Even after returning to normal weight, 30% to 50% of patients are back in the hospital within one year.) A very common approach is to prescribe Prozac, or a related antidepressant drug, to newly recovered patients with the idea that the drug will reduce depression, which will in turn reduce relapse.

double blind study

Walsh et al. sampled 93 patients who had been successfully restored to an acceptable body mass. Forty nine of these patients were then prescribed Prozac for one year, while 44 of them were given a placebo. This was a **double blind study** in which neither the patient nor the study coordinators knew whether the drug or the placebo was being administered. The dependent variable was the number of patients in each group who successfully maintained their weight over one year. The data follow in Table 6.5 in the form of a contingency table. (Expected frequencies are shown in parentheses.)

This table is not encouraging. In the first place, just over 70% of the patients relapsed. The table also shows that not only did the Drug group not outperform the Placebo group— they actually underperformed that group (26.5% versus 31.5%). We still want to know if the underperformance is statistically significant or is simply a chance result. (It is conceivable that Prozac actually decreases a girl's ability to maintain weight, in which case it would actually be harmful to prescribe it to this population.)

As before, the expected frequencies are calculated as the product of the corresponding marginal totals divided by the grand total. For our example

$$E_{11} = \frac{49 \times 27}{93} = 14.226$$

$$E_{12} = \frac{49 \times 66}{93} = 34.774$$

$$E_{21} = \frac{44 \times 27}{93} = 12.774$$

$$E_{22} = \frac{44 \times 66}{93} = 31.226$$

Table 6.5   The relationship between Prozac and anorexia

Treatment	Outcome		Total
	Success	Relapse	
Drug	13 (14.226)	36 (34.774)	49
Placebo	14 (12.774)	30 (31.226)	44
Total	27	66	93

© Cengage Learning 2013

[4] If the victim was nonwhite there was no significant relationship between race and sentence, although that has been found in other data sets. The authors point out that when the victim was non-white the prosecutor was more likely to plea bargain, and the overall proportion of death sentences is much lower.

Then,

$$\chi^2 = \Sigma \frac{(O - E)^2}{E}$$

$$= \frac{(13 - 14.226)^2}{14.226} + \frac{(36 - 34.774)^2}{34.774} + \frac{(14 - 12.774)^2}{12.774} + \frac{(30 - 31.226)^2}{31.226}$$

$$= .315$$

In this example we again have a 2×2 table, giving us

$$df = (R - 1)(C - 1) = 1 \; df$$

Evaluation of χ^2

With 1 df the critical value of χ^2, as found in Appendix χ^2, is 3.84. Because our value of 0.315 falls below the critical value, we will not reject the null hypothesis that the variables are independent of each other. In this case we will conclude that we have no evidence to suggest that whether a girl does or does not relapse is dependent on whether she was provided with Prozac or a placebo. Notice that I have not said that we have proved that the two variables are independent, but only that we have not shown that they are related. However, given the fact that the difference actually favored the placebo and that the probability under the null was so large (the probability of chi-square $\geq 0.315 = .57$), we certainly would be justified in acting as if we have shown that Prozac did not have the desired effect.

2 × 2 Tables are Special Cases

There are some unique features of the treatment of 2×2 tables, and the example that we have been working with offers a good opportunity to explore them.

Correcting for continuity

Yates' correction for continuity

Many books advocate that for simple 2×2 tables such as Table 6.4 we should employ what is called **Yates' correction for continuity**, especially when the expected frequencies are small. (The correction merely involves reducing the absolute value of each numerator by 0.5 units before squaring.) There is an extensive literature on the pros and cons of Yates' correction, with firmly held views on both sides. However, the common availability of Fisher's Exact Test, to be discussed next, makes Yates' correction superfluous, though it appears in most computer printout and is occasionally the default option.

Fisher's Exact Test

Fisher introduced what is called Fisher's Exact Test in 1934 at a meeting of the Royal Statistical Society. (Good (1999) has reported that one of the speakers who followed Fisher referred to Fisher's presentation as "the braying of the Golden Ass." Statistical debates at that time were far from boring, and no doubt Fisher had something equally kind to say about that speaker.)

Without going into details, Fisher's proposal was to take all possible 2×2 tables that could be formed from the fixed set of marginal totals. He then determined the sum of the probabilities of those tables whose results were as extreme, or more so, than the table we obtained in our data. If this sum is less than α, we reject the null hypothesis that the two variables are independent, and conclude that there is a statistically significant relationship between the two variables that make up our contingency table. (This is classed as a **conditional test**

conditional test

because it is conditioned on the marginal totals actually obtained, instead of all possible marginal totals that could have arisen given the total sample size.) I will not present a formula for Fisher's Exact Test because it is almost always obtained using statistical software. (SPSS includes this statistic for all 2×2 tables, though, in general, the test is appropriate, with modification, to larger tables.) Notice that Fisher's Exact Test is not actually a chi-square test. It is often used in place of one. The advantage of this is that it does not rely on the assumptions behind chi-square because it is not based on the chi-square distribution.

Fisher's Exact Test has been controversial since the day he proposed it. One of the problems concerns the fact that it is a conditional test (conditional on the fixed marginals). Some have argued that if you repeated the experiment exactly you would likely find different marginal totals and have asked why those additional tables should not be included in the calculation. Making the test unconditional on the marginals would complicate the calculations, though not excessively given the speed of modern computers. This may sound like an easy debate to resolve, but if you read the extensive literature surrounding **fixed and random marginals**, you will find that it is not only a difficult debate to follow, but you will probably come away thoroughly confused. (An excellent discussion of some of the issues can be found in Agresti (2002), pages 95–96.)

fixed and random marginals

Fisher's Exact Test also leads to controversy because of the issue of one-tailed versus two-tailed tests and what outcomes would constitute a "more extreme" result in the opposite tail. Instead of going into how to determine what is a more extreme outcome, I will avoid that complication by simply telling you to decide in advance whether you want a one- or a two-tailed test (I strongly recommend two-tailed tests) and then report the values given by standard statistical software. Virtually all common statistical software prints out Fisher's Exact Test results along with Pearson's chi-square and related test statistics. Though the test does not produce a chi-square statistic, it does produce a p value. In our example the p value is extremely small (.007), just as it was for the standard chi-square test.

Fisher's Exact Test versus Pearson's Chi Square

We now have at least two statistical tests for 2×2 contingency tables and will soon have a third—which one should we use? Probably the most common solution is to go with Pearson's chi-square; perhaps because "that is what we have always done." In fact, in previous editions of this book I recommended against Fisher's Exact Test, primarily because of its conditional nature. However, in recent years there has been an important growth of interest in permutation and randomization tests, of which Fisher's Exact Test is an example. (This approach is discussed extensively in Chapter 18.) I am extremely impressed with the logic and simplicity of such tests, and have come to side with Fisher's Exact Test. In most cases the conclusion you draw will be the same for the two approaches, though this is not always the case. When we come to tables larger than 2×2, Fisher's approach does not apply without modification, and there we almost always use the Pearson Chi-Square. (But see Howell & Gordon, 1976 and an R program on the book's Web site.)

6.4   An Additional Example—A 4 × 2 Design

Sexual abuse is a serious problem in our society and it is important to understand the factors behind it. Jankowski, Leitenberg, Henning, and Coffey (2002) examined the relationship between childhood sexual abuse and later sexual abuse as an adult. They cross-tabulated the number of childhood abuse categories (in increasing order of severity) reported by 934 undergraduate women and their reports of adult sexual abuse. The results are shown in Table 6.6. The values in parentheses are the expected frequencies.

Table 6.6   Adult sexual abuse related to prior childhood sexual abuse

Number of Child Abuse Categories Checked	Abused as Adult		Total
	No	Yes	
0	512 (494.49)	54 (71.51)	566
1	227 (230.65)	37 (33.35)	264
2	59 (64.65)	15 (9.35)	74
3-4	18 (26.21)	12 (3.79)	30
Total	816	118	934

© Cengage Learning 2013

The calculation of chi-square for the data on sexual abuse follows.

$$\chi^2 = \sum \frac{(O - E)^2}{E}$$

$$= \frac{(512 - 494.19)^2}{494.19} + \frac{(54 - 71.51)^2}{71.51} \cdots \frac{(18 - 26.21)^2}{26.21} + \frac{(12 - 3.79)^2}{3.79}$$

$$= 29.63$$

The contingency table was a 4 × 2 table, so it has $(4-1) \times (2-1) = 3$ df. The critical value for χ^2 on 3 df is 7.82, so we can reject the null hypothesis and conclude that the level of adult sexual abuse is related to childhood sexual abuse. In fact adult abuse increases consistently as the severity of childhood abuse increases. We will come back to this idea shortly.[5]

Computer analyses

We will use Unah and Boger's data on criminal sentencing for this example because it illustrates Fisher's Exact Test as well as other tests. The first column of data (labeled Race) contains a W or an NW, depending on the race of the defendant. The second

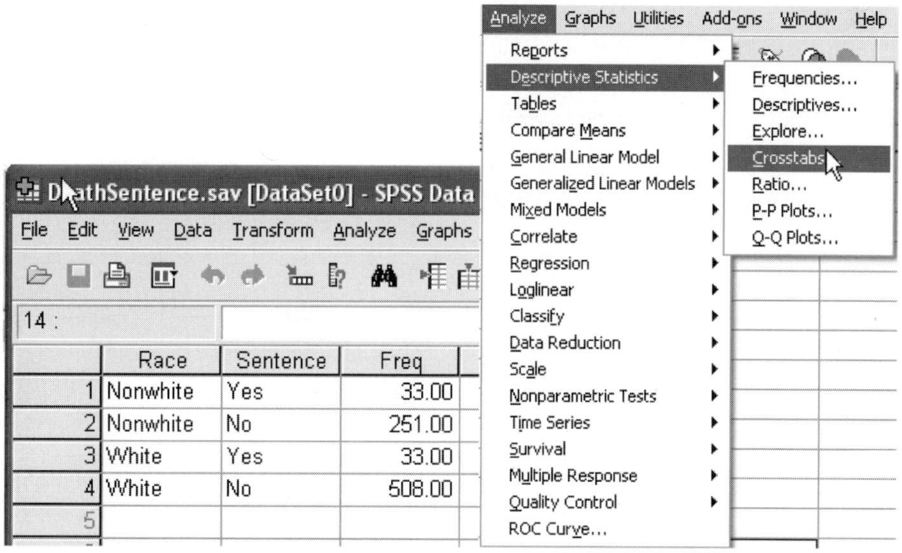

Exhibit 6.1a   SPSS Data file and dialogue box

---

[5] The most disturbing thing about these data is that nearly 40% of the women reported some level of abuse.

column (labeled Sentence) contains "Yes" or "No", depending on whether or not a death sentence was assigned. Finally, a third column contains the frequency associated with each cell. (We could use numerical codes for the first two columns if we preferred, so long as we are consistent.) In addition you need to specify that the column labeled Freq contains the cell frequencies. This is done by going to **Data/Weight cases** and entering Freq in the box labeled "Weight cases by." An image of the data file and the dialogue box for selecting the test are shown in Exhibit 6.1a, and the output follows in Exhibit 6.1b.

For some reason SPSS does not display the chi-square or related tests by default. You need to use the **Statistics** button to select that test and related statistics. But problems also arise when you look at the one-tailed test for Fisher's Exact Test. Suppose that I want to test the one-tailed hypothesis that non-whites receive the death sentence at a greater rate than whites. The one-tailed probability would be .005, which is what the printout gives. But suppose that instead I want to test the one-tailed probability that whites receive the death penalty at a higher rate. From the data you can clearly see that we cannot reject the null, but in fact the one-tailed probability that is printed out is also .005. My point is that you don't know what one-tailed hypothesis SPSS is testing, and I suggest not paying attention to that result in SPSS. (R, on the other hand, allows you to specify whether you want to test that the odds ratio in the hypothesis is greater than 1.00 or whether it is less than 1.00, and it gives two entirely different probabilities, as it should. An example using R to perform the test is available in the R files on the Web site for this book.)

Exhibit 6.1b contains several statistics we have not yet discussed. The Likelihood ratio test is one that we shall take up shortly, and is simply another approach to calculating chi-

Race * Death Crosstabulation
Count

		Death		Total
		Yes	No	
Race	NonWhite	33	251	284
	White	33	508	541
	Total	66	759	825

Chi-Square Tests

	Value	df	Asymp. Sig- (2-sided)	Exact Sig. (2-sided)	Exact Sig. (1-sided)
Pearson Chi Square	7.710[a]	1	.005		
Continuity Correction[b]	6.978	1	.008		
Likelihood Ratio	7.358	1	.007		
Fisher's Exact Test				.007	.005
Linear-by-Linear Association	7.701	1	.006		
McNemar Test				.000[c]	
N of Valid Cases	825				

[a] 0 cells (0%) have expected count less than 5. The minimum expected count is 22.72.
[b] Computed only for a 2 × 2 table.
[c] Binomal distribution used.

Exhibit 6.1b   SPSS output on death sentence data

Symmetric Measures

		Value	Asymp. Std. Error[a]	Approx. T[b]	Approx. Sig.
Nominal by Nominal	Phi	.097			.005
	Cramer's V	.097			.005
	Contingency Coefficient	.096			.005
Measure of Agreement	Kappa	.068	.026	2.777	.005
N of Valid Cases		825			

[a]Not assuming the null hypothesis.
[b]Using the asymptotic standard error assuming the null hypothesis.

Exhibit 6.1c   Measures of association for Unah & Boger's data

Risk Estimate

	Value	95% Confidence Interval	
		Lower	Upper
Odds Ratio for Race (NonWhite/White)	2.024	1.221	3.356
For cohort Death = Yes	1.905	1.202	3.019
For cohort Death = No	.941	.898	.987
N of Valid Cases	825		

Exhibit 6.1d   Risk estimates on death sentence data

square. I would suggest that you ignore the Continuity Correction. It is simply Yates's correction, and Fisher's test obviates the need for it. You can also ignore the measure of Linear by Linear association. It does not apply to this example, and we will see it again in Chapter 10. McNemar's test, to be discussed shortly, is also not relevant in this particular example.

The three statistics in Exhibit 6.1c (phi, Cramér's V, and the contingency coefficient) will also be discussed later in this chapter, as will the odds ratio shown in Exhibit 6.1d. Each of these statistics is an attempt at assessing the size of the effect.

Small Expected Frequencies

small expected frequency

One of the most important requirements for using the Pearson chi-square test, though not Fisher's test, concerns the size of the expected frequencies. We have already met this requirement briefly in discussing corrections for continuity. Before defining more precisely what we mean by *small*, we should examine why a small expected frequency causes so much trouble.

For a given sample size, there are often a limited number of different contingency tables that you could obtain and thus a limited number of different values of chi-square. If only a few different values of χ^2_{obt} are possible, then the χ^2 distribution, which is continuous, cannot provide a reasonable approximation to the distribution of our statistic, which is discrete. Those cases that result in only a few possible values of χ^2_{obt}, however, are the ones with small expected frequencies in one or more cells. (This is directly analogous to the fact that if you flip a fair coin three times, there are only four possible values for the number of heads, and the resulting sampling distribution certainly cannot be satisfactorily approximated by the normal distribution.)

We have seen that difficulties arise when we have small expected frequencies, but the question of how small is small remains. Those conventions that do exist are conflicting and have only minimal claims to preference over one another. Probably the most common is to require that all expected frequencies should be at least five. This is a conservative position and I don't feel overly guilty when I violate it. Bradley et al. (1979) ran a computer-based sampling study. They used tables ranging in size from 2×2 to 4×4 and found that for those applications likely to arise in practice, the actual percentage of Type I errors rarely exceeds .06, even for *total* sample sizes as small as 10, unless the row or column marginal totals are drastically skewed. Camilli and Hopkins (1979) demonstrated that even with quite small expected frequencies, the test produces few Type I errors in the 2×2 case as long as the total sample size is greater than or equal to eight; but they, and Overall (1980), point to the extremely low power to reject a false H_0 that such tests possess. With small sample sizes, power is more likely to be a problem than inflated Type I error rates.

One major advantage of Fisher's Exact Test is that it is not based on the χ^2 distribution, and is thus not affected by a lack of continuity. One of the strongest arguments for that test is that it applies well to cases with small expected frequencies.

Campbell (2007) did an extensive study of alternative treatments of 2×2 tables with small expected frequencies. He found that with an expected frequency of 1 in one cell, an adjusted chi-square statistic suggested by Egon Pearson as

$$\chi^2_{adj} = \frac{\chi^2 \times N}{N - 1}$$

was optimal. With all expected frequencies greater than 1, he recommended Fisher's Exact Test.

6.5   Chi-Square for Ordinal Data

Chi-square is an important statistic for the analysis of categorical data, but it can sometimes fall short of what we need. If you apply chi-square to a contingency table, and then rearrange one or more rows or columns and calculate chi-square again, you will arrive at exactly the same answer. That is as it should be, because chi-square does not take the ordering of the rows or columns into account.

But what do you do if the order of the rows and/or columns does make a difference? How can you take that ordinal information and make it part of your analysis? An interesting example of just such a situation was provided in a query that I received from Jennifer Mahon at the University of Leicester, in England.

Ms. Mahon collected data on a treatment for eating disorders. She was interested in how likely participants were to remain in treatment or drop out, and she wanted to examine this with respect to the number of traumatic events they had experienced in childhood. Her general hypothesis was that participants who had experienced more traumatic events during childhood would be more likely to drop out of treatment. Notice that her hypothesis treats the number of traumatic events as an ordered variable, which is something that chi-square ignores. There is a solution to this problem, but it is more appropriately covered after we have talked about correlations. I will come back to this problem in Chapter 10 and show you one approach. (You could probably skip now to Chapter 10, Section 10.4 and be able to follow the discussion.) I mention it here because it comes up most often when discussing χ^2 even though it is largely a correlational technique. In addition, anyone looking up such a technique would logically look at this chapter first. A discussion of the solution to this problem can also be found in the Supplements section of this book's Web site.

6.6 Summary of the Assumptions of Chi-Square

Because of the widespread misuse of chi-square still prevalent in the literature, it is important to pull together in one place the underlying assumptions of χ^2. For a thorough discussion of the misuse of χ^2, see the paper by Lewis and Burke (1949) and the subsequent rejoinders to that paper. These articles are not yet out of date, although it has been over 60 years since they were written. A somewhat more recent discussion of many of the issues raised by Lewis and Burke (1949) can be found in Delucchi (1983), but even that paper is more than 25 years old. (Some things in statistics change fairly rapidly, but other topics hang around forever.)

The Assumption of Independence

At the beginning of this chapter, we assumed that *observations* were independent of one another. The word *independence* has been used in two different ways in this chapter. A basic assumption of χ^2 deals with the independence of *observations* and is the assumption, for example, that one participant's choice among brands of coffee has no effect on another participant's choice. This is what we are referring to when we speak of an assumption of independence. We also spoke of the independence of *variables* when we discussed contingency tables. In this case, independence is what is being tested, whereas in the former use of the word it is an assumption. So we want the *observations* to be independent and we are testing the independence of *variables*.

As I pointed out earlier, my use of the example on therapeutic touch was challenged by readers who argued that the *observations* were not independent because they came from the same respondent. That is an excellent point, and it forced me to think about why I still use that example and why I think that I am right. Let's take a nice example from a paper by Sauerland, Lefering, Bayer-Sandow, and Neugebauer (2003) in the *Journal of the British Society for Surgery of the Hand*. (Perhaps you missed seeing that article in your evening reading.) The authors point out that certain diseases affect several parts of the hand at once, but a common practice is to measure (for example) three points on the hand of each of *n* patients. Here we really do have a problem, because if your first measurement is elevated, your second and third measurements probably are also. Looking at this a bit differently, it would be a serious loss if you spilled all of the measurements for 10 patients on the floor and then picked them up haphazardly. You would end up mixing the 3rd measurement for Sylvia with the 2nd measurement for Bob and perhaps the 2nd measurement for Walter. You would have lost the pairing of observations with patients and that is a serious loss.

But if you take the observations from the earlier therapeutic touch example and shake them up in a hat, you haven't lost anything of importance because it really doesn't matter if the 2nd observation had actually been the 22nd. In other words, the order of the observations is irrelevant to the study, whereas that is not the case for the Sauerland et al., example. As far as I am concerned, even if all of the observations came from one subject, the observations are independent. (I would have to think a lot harder about the case where you had 3 measurements from each of 85 children.)

At the risk of confusing things even further, suppose that I was interested in strategies for RPS. I made up a table showing how often Scissors was followed by Paper. How often it was followed by Rock, how often Rock was followed by Paper, and so on. I could still use a chi-square test because *under the null hypothesis* the order of observations is independent. That is what I am testing.

Inclusion of Nonoccurrences

Although the requirement that nonoccurrences be included has not yet been mentioned specifically, it is inherent in the derivation. It is probably best explained by an example. Suppose that out of 20 students from rural areas, 17 are in favor of having daylight savings time (DST) all year. Out of 20 students from urban areas, only 11 are in favor of DST on a permanent basis. We want to determine if significantly more rural students than urban students are in favor of DST. One *erroneous* method of testing this would be to set up the following data table on the number of students favoring DST:

	Rural	Urban	Total
Observed	17	11	28
Expected	14	14	28

nonoccurrences

We could then compute $\chi^2 = 1.29$ and fail to reject H_0. This data table, however, does not take into account the *negative* responses, which Lewis and Burke (1949) call **nonoccurrences**. In other words, it does not include the numbers of rural and urban students *opposed* to DST. However, the derivation of chi-square assumes that we have included both those opposed to DST and those in favor of it. So we need a table such as:

	Rural	Urban	Total
Yes	17	11	28
No	3	9	12
	20	20	40

Now $\chi^2 = 4.29$, which is significant at $\alpha = .05$, resulting in an entirely different interpretation of the results.

Perhaps a more dramatic way to see why we need to include nonoccurrences can be shown by assuming that 17 out of *2,000* rural students and 11 out of 20 urban students preferred DST. Consider how much different the interpretation of the two tables would be. Certainly our analysis must reflect the difference between the two data sets, which would not be the case if we failed to include nonoccurrences.

Failure to take the nonoccurrences into account not only invalidates the test, but also reduces the value of χ^2, leaving you less likely to reject H_0.

6.7 Dependent or Repeated Measures

The previous section stated that the standard chi-square test of a contingency table assumes that data are independent. We have discussed independence of observations at some length, and I argued that in cases where all of the data come from the same respondent independence is often not a problem. Here we need to come at the problem of independence differently to address a different kind of question. A good example was sent to me by Stacey Freedenthal at the University of Denver, though the data that I will use are fictitious and should not be taken to represent her results. Dr. Freedenthal was interested in studying help-seeking behavior in children. She took a class of 70 children and recorded the incidence of help-seeking before and after an intervention that was designed to increase students' help-seeking behavior. She measured help-seeking in the fall, introduced an intervention around Christmas time, and then measured help-seeking again, *for these same children*, in the spring.

Because we are measuring each child twice, we need to make sure that the dependence between measures does not influence our results. One way to do this is to focus on how each child *changed* over the course of the year. To do so it is necessary to identify the behavior separately for each child so that we know whether each specific child sought help in the fall and/or in the spring. We can then focus on the change and not on the multiple measurements per child. To see why independence is important, consider an extreme case. If exactly the same children who sought help in the fall also sought it in the spring, and none of the other children did, then the change in the percentage of help-seeking would be 0 and the standard error (over replications of the experiment) would also be 0. But if whether or not a child sought help in the spring was largely independent of whether he or she sought help in the fall, the difference in the two percentages might still be close to zero, but the standard error would be relatively large. In other words the standard error of change scores varies as a function of how dependent the scores are.

Suppose that we ran this experiment and obtained the following not-so-extreme data. Notice that Table 6.7 looks very much like a contingency table, but with a difference. This table basically shows how children *changed* or didn't change as a result of the intervention. Notice that two of the cells are shown in bold, and these are really the only cells that we care about. It is not surprising that some children would show a change in their behavior from fall to spring. And if the intervention had no effect (in other words if the null hypothesis is true) we would expect about as many to change from "Yes" to "No" as from "No" to "Yes." However, if the intervention was effective we would expect many more children to move from "No" to "Yes" than to move in the other direction. That is what we will test.

McNemar's test   The test that we will use is often called **McNemar's test** (McNemar, 1947) and reduces to a simple one-way goodness-of-fit chi-square where the data are those from the two off-diagonal cells and the expected frequencies are each half of the number of children changing. This is shown below.[6]

$$\chi^2 = \frac{\Sigma(O - E)^2}{E} = \frac{(4 - 8.0)^2}{8.0} + \frac{(12 - 8.0)^2}{8.0} = 4.00$$

This is a chi-square on 1 *df* and is significant because it exceeds the critical value of 3.84. There is reason to conclude that the intervention was successful.

Table 6.7   Help-seeking behavior in fall and spring

		Spring		
Fall		Yes	No	Total
	Yes	38	4	42
	No	12	18	30
	Total	50	22	72

© Cengage Learning 2013

Table 6.8   Results of experiment on help-seeking behavior in children

	No → Yes	Yes → No	Total
Observed	12	4	16
Expected	8.0	8.0	16

© Cengage Learning 2013

---

[6] This is exactly equivalent to the common *z* test on the difference in independent proportions where we are asking if a significantly greater proportion of people changed in one direction than in the other direction.

One Further Step

The question that Dr. Freedenthal asked was actually more complicated than the one that I just answered, because she also had a control group that did not receive the intervention but was evaluated at both times as well. She wanted to test whether the change in the intervention group was greater than the change in the control group. This actually turns out to be an easier test than you might suspect. The test is attributable to Marascuilo & Serlin (1979). The data are independent because we have different children in the two treatments and because those who change in one direction are different from those who change in the other direction. So all that we need to do is create a 2 × 2 contingency table with Treatment Condition on the columns and Increase vs. Decrease on the rows and enter data only from those children in each group who changed their behavior from fall to spring. The chi-square test on this contingency table tests the null hypothesis that there was an equal degree of change in the two groups. (A more extensive discussion of the whole issue of testing non-independent frequency data can be found at http://www.uvm.edu/~dhowell/StatPages /More_Stuff/Chi-square/Testing Dependent Proportions.pdf.)

6.8   One- and Two-Tailed Tests

People are often confused as to whether chi-square is a one- or a two-tailed test. This confusion results from the fact that there are different ways of defining what we mean by a one- or a two-tailed test. If we think of the sampling distribution of χ^2, we can argue that χ^2 is a one-tailed test because we reject H_0 only when our value of χ^2 lies in the extreme right tail of the distribution. On the other hand, if we think of the underlying data on which our obtained χ^2 is based, we could argue that we have a two-tailed test. If, for example, we were using chi-square to test the fairness of a coin, we would reject H_0 if it produced too many heads *or* if it produced too many tails, because either event would lead to a large value of χ^2.

The preceding discussion is not intended to start an argument over semantics (it does not really matter whether you think of the test as one-tailed or two); rather, it is intended to point out one of the weaknesses of the chi-square test, so that you can take this into account. The weakness is that the test, *as normally applied*, is nondirectional. To take a simple example, consider the situation in which you wish to show that increasing amounts of quinine added to an animal's food make it less appealing. You take 90 rats and offer them a choice of three bowls of food that differ in the amount of quinine that has been added. You then count the number of animals selecting each bowl of food. Suppose the data are

	Amount of Quinine	
Small	Medium	Large
39	30	21

The computed value of χ^2 is 5.4, which, on 2 *df*, is not significant at $p < .05$.

The important fact about the data is that any of the six possible configurations of the same frequencies (such as 21, 30, 39) would produce the same value of χ^2, and you receive no credit for the fact that the configuration you obtained is precisely the one that you predicted. Thus, you have made a *multi-tailed* test when in fact you have a specific prediction of the direction in which the totals will be ordered. I referred to this problem a few pages back when discussing a problem raised by Jennifer Mahon. A solution will be given in Chapter 10 (Section 10.4), where I discuss creating a correlational measure of the relationship between the two variables. I mention it here because this is where people would likely look for the answer.

6.9 Likelihood Ratio Tests

likelihood ratios

An alternative approach to analyzing categorical data is based on likelihood ratios. (The SPSS printout in Exhibit 6.1b included the likelihood ratio along with the standard Pearson chi-square.) For large sample sizes the two tests are equivalent, though for small sample sizes the standard Pearson chi-square is thought to be better approximated by the exact chi-square distribution than is the likelihood ratio chi-square (Agresti, 2002). Likelihood ratio tests are heavily used in log-linear models for analyzing contingency tables because of their additive properties. Such models are particularly important when we want to analyze multi-dimensional contingency tables. Such models are being used more and more, and you should be exposed to such methods, at least minimally.

Without going into detail, the general idea of a likelihood ratio can be described quite simply. Suppose we collect data and calculate the probability or likelihood of the data occurring given that the null hypothesis is true. We also calculate the likelihood that the data would occur under some alternative hypothesis (the hypothesis for which the data are most probable). If the data are much more likely for some alternative hypothesis than for H_0, we would be inclined to reject H_0. However, if the data are almost as likely under H_0 as they are for some other alternative, we would be inclined to retain H_0. Thus, the likelihood ratio (the ratio of these two likelihoods) forms a basis for evaluating the null hypothesis.

Using likelihood ratios, it is possible to devise tests, frequently referred to as "maximum likelihood χ^2," for analyzing both one-dimensional arrays and contingency tables. For the development of these tests, see Agresti (2002).

For the one-dimensional goodness-of-fit case,

$$\chi^2_{(C-1)} = 2 \sum O_i \ln \left(\frac{O_i}{E_i} \right)$$

where O_i and E_i are the observed and expected frequencies for each cell and "ln" denotes the natural logarithm (logarithm to the base e). This value of χ^2 can be evaluated using the standard table of χ^2 on $C - 1$ degrees of freedom.

For analyzing contingency tables, we can use essentially the same formula,

$$\chi^2_{(R-1)(C-1)} = 2 \sum O_{ij} \ln \left(\frac{O_{ij}}{E_{ij}} \right)$$

where O_{ij} and E_{ij} are the observed and expected frequencies in each cell. The expected frequencies are obtained just as they were for the standard Pearson chi-square test. This statistic is evaluated with respect to the χ^2 distribution on $(R - 1)(C - 1)$ degrees of freedom.

As an illustration of the use of the likelihood ratio test for contingency tables, consider the data found in the death-sentence study. The cell and marginal frequencies follow:

	Death Sentence		
Defendant's Race	Yes	No	Total
Nonwhite	33	251	284
White	33	508	541
Total	66	759	825

$$\chi^2 = 2 \sum O_{ij} \ln \left(\frac{O_{ij}}{E_{ij}} \right)$$

$$= 2 \left[33 \ln \left(\frac{33}{22.72} \right) + 251 \ln \left(\frac{251}{261.28} \right) + 33 \ln \left(\frac{33}{43.28} \right) + 508 \ln \left(\frac{508}{497.72} \right) \right]$$

$$= 2[33(.3733) + 251(-.0401) + 33(-0.2172) + 508(0.0204)]$$

$$= 2[3.6790] = 7.358$$

This answer agrees with the likelihood ratio statistic found in Exhibit 6.1b. It is a χ^2 on 1 df, and because it exceeds $\chi^2_{.05}(1) = 3.84$, it will lead to rejection of H_0.

6.10   Mantel-Haenszel Statistic

Mantel-Haenszel statistic

Cochran-Mantel-Haenszel

Simpson's paradox

We have been dealing with two-dimensional tables where the interpretation is relatively straightforward. But often we have a 2 × 2 table that is replicated over some other variable. There are many situations in which we wish to control for (often called "condition on") a third variable. We might look at the relationship between (X) stress (high/low) and (Y) mental status (normal/disturbed) when we have data collected across several different environments (Z). Or we might look at the relationship between the race of the defendant (X) and the severity of the sentence (Y) conditioned on the severity of the offense (Z)—see Exercise 6.1. The Mantel-Haenszel statistic (often referred to as the Cochran-Mantel-Haenszel statistic because of Cochran's (1954) early work on it) is designed to deal with just these situations. We will use a well-known example here involving a study of gender discrimination in graduate admissions at Berkeley in the early 1970s. This example will serve two purposes because it will also illustrate a phenomenon known as Simpson's paradox. This paradox was described by Simpson in the early 1950s, but was known to Yule nearly half a century earlier. (It should probably be called the Yule-Simpson paradox.) It refers to the situation in which the relationship between two variables, seen at individual levels of a third variable, reverses direction when you collapse over the third variable. The Mantel-Haenszel statistic is meaningful whenever you simply want to control the analysis of a 2 × 2 table for a third variable, but it is particularly interesting in the examination of the Yule-Simpson paradox.

In 1973 the University of California at Berkeley investigated gender discrimination in graduate admissions (Bickel, Hammel, and O'Connell, 1975). A superficial examination of admissions for that year revealed that approximately 45% of male applicants were admitted compared with only about 30% of female applicants. On the surface this would appear to be a clear case of gender discrimination. However, graduate admissions are made by departments, not by a university admissions office, and it is appropriate and necessary to look at admissions data at the departmental level. The data in Table 6.9 show the breakdown by gender in six large departments at Berkeley. (They are reflective of data from all 101 graduate departments.) For reasons that will become clear shortly, we will set aside for now the data from the largest department (Department A).

Looking at the bottom row of Table 6.9, which does not include Department A, you can see that 36.8% of males and 28.8% of females were admitted by the five departments. A chi-square test on the data produces $\chi^2 = 37.98$, which has a probability under H_0 that is 0.00 to the 9th decimal place. This seems to be convincing evidence that males are admitted at substantially higher rates than females. However, when we break the data down by departments, we see that in three of those departments women were admitted at a higher rate, and in the remaining two the differences in favor of men were quite small.

The Mantel-Haenszel statistic (Mantel and Haenszel (1959)) is designed to deal with the data from each department separately (i.e., we condition on departments). We then sum the results across departments. Although the statistic is not a sum of the chi-square statistics for each department separately, you might think of it as roughly that. It is more

Table 6.9   Admissions data for graduate departments at Berkeley (1973) (Percent admitted in parentheses)

Major	Males		Females	
	Admit	Reject	Admit	Reject
A	512 (62%)	313	89 (82%)	19
B	353 (63%)	207	17 (68%)	8
C	120 (37%)	205	202 (34%)	391
D	138 (33%)	279	131 (35%)	244
E	53 (28%)	138	94 (24%)	299
F	22 (6%)	351	24 (7%)	317
Total B-F	686	1,180	468	1,259
% of Total B-F	36.8%	63.2%	28.8%	71.2%

© Cengage Learning 2013

powerful than simply combining individual chi-squares and is less susceptible to the problem of small expected frequencies in the individual 2×2 tables (Cochran, 1954).

The computation of the Mantel-Haenszel statistic is based on the fact that for any 2×2 table, the entry in any one cell, given the marginal totals, determines the entry in every other cell. This means that we can create a statistic using only the data in cell$_{11}$ of the table for each department. There are several variations of the Mantel-Haenszel statistic, but the most common one is

$$M^2 = \frac{(|\Sigma O_{11k} - \Sigma E_{11k}| - \frac{1}{2})^2}{\Sigma n_{1+k}n_{2+k}n_{+1k}n_{+2k}/n_{++k}^2(n_{++k} - 1)}$$

where O_{11k} and E_{11k} are the observed and expected frequencies in the upper left cell of each of the k 2×2 tables and the entries in the denominator are the marginal totals and grand total of each of the k 2×2 tables. The denominator represents the variance of the numerator. The entry of $-\frac{1}{2}$ in the numerator is the same Yates's correction for continuity that I passed over earlier. These values are shown in the calculations that follow.

$$M^2 = \frac{(|\Sigma O_{11k} - \Sigma E_{11k}| - \frac{1}{2})^2}{\Sigma n_{1+k}n_{2+k}n_{+1k}n_{+2k}/n_{++k}^2(n_{++k} - 1)}$$

$$= \frac{(|686 - 681.93| - \frac{1}{2})^2}{132.603} = \frac{(4.07 - .5)^2}{132.603} = 0.096$$

This statistic can be evaluated as a chi-square on 1 df, and its probability under H_0 is .76. We certainly cannot reject the null hypothesis that admission is independent of gender, in direct contradiction to the result we found when we collapsed across departments.

Table 6.10   Observed and expected frequencies for Berkeley data

Department	O_{11}	E_{11}	Variance
A	512	531.43	21.913
B	353	354.19	5.563
C	120	114.00	47.809
D	138	141.63	44.284
E	53	48.08	24.210
F	22	24.03	10.737
Total B-F	686	681.93	132.603

© Cengage Learning 2013

In the calculation of the Mantel-Haenszel statistic I left out the data from Department A, and you are probably wondering why. The explanation is based on odds ratios, which I won't discuss until the next section. The short answer is that Department A had a different relationship between gender and admissions than did the other five departments, which were largely homogeneous in that respect. The Mantel-Haenszel statistic is based on the assumption that departments are homogeneous with respect to the pattern of admissions.

The obvious question following the result of our analysis of these data concerns why it should happen. How is it that there is a clear bias toward men in the aggregated data, but no such bias when we break the results down by department. If you calculate the percentage of applicants admitted by each department, you will find that Departments A, B, and D admit over 50% of their applicants, and those are also the departments to which males apply in large numbers. On the other hand, women predominate in applying to Departments C and E, which are among the departments that reject two-thirds of their applicants. In other words, women are admitted at a lower rate overall because they predominantly apply to departments with more selective admissions (for both males and females). This is obscured when you sum across departments.

6.11 Effect Sizes

The fact that a relationship is "statistically significant" doesn't tell us very much about whether it is of practical significance. The fact that two independent variables are not statistically independent does not necessarily mean that the lack of independence is important or worthy of our attention. In fact, if you allow the sample size to grow large enough, almost any two variables would likely show a statistically significant lack of independence.

What we need, then, are ways to go beyond a simple test of significance to present one or more statistics reflecting the size of the effect we are looking at. There are two different types of measures designed to represent the size of an effect. One type, called the **d-family** by Rosenthal (1994), is based on one or more measures of the *differences* between groups or levels of the independent variable. For example, as we will see shortly, the probability of receiving a death sentence is about 5 percentage points higher for defendants who are nonwhite. The other type of measure, called the **r-family**, represents some sort of correlation coefficient between the two independent variables. We will discuss correlation thoroughly in Chapter 9, but I will discuss these measures here because they are appropriate at this time. Measures in the *r*-family are often called **measures of association**.

d-family

r-family

measures of association

A Classic Example

An important study of the beneficial effects of small daily doses of aspirin on reducing heart attacks in men was reported in 1988. Over 22,000 physicians were administered aspirin or a placebo over a number of years, and the incidence of later heart attacks was recorded. The data follow in Table 6.11. Notice that this design is a **prospective study** because the treatments (aspirin vs. no aspirin) were applied and *then* future outcome was determined. This will become important shortly. Prospective studies are often called **cohort studies** (because we identify two or more cohorts of participants) or, especially in medicine, a **randomized clinical trial** because participants are randomized to conditions. On the other hand, a **retrospective study**, frequently called a **case-control design**, would select people who had, or had not, experienced a heart attack and then look backward in time to see whether they had been in the habit of taking aspirin in the past.

For these data $\chi^2 = 25.014$ on one degree of freedom, which is statistically significant at $\alpha = .05$, indicating that there is a relationship between whether or not one takes aspirin daily, and whether one later has a heart attack.

prospective study

cohort studies

randomized clinical trial

retrospective study

case-control design

Table 6.11   The effect of aspirin on the incidence of heart attacks

	Outcome		
	Heart Attack	No Heart Attack	
Aspirin	104	10,933	11,037
Placebo	189	10,845	11,034
	293	21,778	22,071

© Cengage Learning 2013

d-family: Risks and Odds

Two important concepts with categorical data, especially for 2×2 tables, are the concepts of risks and odds. These concepts are closely related, and often confused, but they are basically very simple.

For the aspirin data, 0.94% (104/11,037) of people in the aspirin group and 1.71% (189/11,034) of those in the control group suffered a heart attack during the course of the study. (Unless you are a middle-aged male worrying about your health, the numbers look rather small. But they are important.) These two statistics are commonly referred to as **risk** estimates because they describe the risk that someone with, or without, aspirin will suffer a heart attack. For example, I would expect 1.71% of men who do not take aspirin to suffer a heart attack over the same period of time as that used in this study. Risk measures offer a useful way of looking at the size of an effect.

risk

The **risk difference** is simply the difference between the two proportions. In our example, the difference is 1.71% − 0.94% = .77%. Thus there is about three-quarters of a percentage point difference between the two conditions. Put another way, the difference in risk between a male taking aspirin and one not taking aspirin is about three-quarters of one percent. This may not appear to be very large, but keep in mind that we are talking about heart attacks, which are serious events.

risk difference

One problem with a risk difference is that its magnitude depends on the overall level of risk. Heart attacks are quite low-risk events, so we would not expect a huge difference between the two conditions. (When we looked at the death-sentence data, the probability of being sentenced to death was 11.6% and 6.1% for a risk difference of 5 percentage points, which *appears* to be a much greater effect than the 0.75 percentage point difference in the aspirin study. Does that mean that the death sentence study found a larger effect size? Well, it depends—it certainly did with respect to risk difference.)

Another way to compare the risks is to form a **risk ratio**, also called **relative risk**, which is just the ratio of the two risks. For the heart attack data the risk ratio is

risk ratio

relative risk

$$RR = Risk_{\text{no aspirin}}/Risk_{\text{aspirin}} = 1.71\%/0.94\% = 1.819$$

Thus the risk of having a heart attack if you do not take aspirin is 1.8 times higher than if you do take aspirin. That strikes me as quite a difference. For the death-sentence study the risk ratio was 11.6%/6.1% = 1.90, which is virtually the same as the ratio we found with aspirin.

There is a third measure of effect size that we must consider, and that is the **odds ratio**. At first glance, odds and odds ratios look like risk and risk ratios, and they are often confused, even by people who know better. Recall that we defined the risk of a heart attack in the aspirin group as the number having a heart attack divided by the *total number of people in that group* (e.g., 104/11,037 = 0.0094 = .94%). The **odds** of having a heart attack for a member of the aspirin group is the number having a heart attack divided by the number *not having a heart attack* (e.g., 104/10,933 = 0.0095). The difference (though very slight here) comes in what we use as the denominator. Risk uses the total sample size and is thus

odds ratio

odds

the proportion of people in that condition who experience a heart attack. Odds uses as a denominator the number *not* having a heart attack, and is thus the ratio of the number having an attack versus the number not having an attack. Because in this example the denominators are so much alike, the results are almost indistinguishable. That is certainly not always the case. In Jankowski's study of sexual abuse, the risk of adult abuse if a woman was severely abused as a child is .40, whereas the odds are 0.67. (Don't think of the odds as a probability just because they look like one. Odds are not probabilities, as can be shown by taking the odds of *not* being abused, which are 1.50—the woman is 1.5 times more likely to not be abused than to be abused.)

Just as we can form a risk ratio by dividing the two risks, we can form an odds ratio by dividing the two odds. For the aspirin example the odds of heart attack given that you did not take aspirin were 189/10,845 = .017. The odds of a heart attack given that you did take aspirin were 104/10,933 = .010. The odds ratio is simply the ratio of these two odds and is

$$OR = \frac{Odds \mid NoAspirin}{Odds \mid Aspirin} = \frac{0.0174}{0.0095} = 1.83$$

Thus the odds of a heart attack without aspirin are 1.83 times higher than the odds of a heart attack with aspirin.[7]

Why do we have to complicate things by having both odds ratios and risk ratios, since they often look very much alike? That is a very good question, and it has some good answers. If you are going to do research in the behavioral sciences you need to understand both kinds of ratios. Risk is something that I think most of us have a feel for. When we say the risk of having a heart attack in the No Aspirin condition is .0171, we are saying that 1.7% of the participants in that condition had a heart attack, and that is pretty straightforward. Many people prefer risk ratios for just that reason. In fact, Sackett, Deeks, and Altman (1996) argued strongly for the risk ratio on just those grounds—they feel that odds ratios, while accurate, are misleading.[8] When we say that the odds of a heart attack in that condition are .0174, we are saying that the odds of having a heart attack are 1.7% of the odds of not having a heart attack. That may be a popular way of setting bets on race horses, but it leaves me dissatisfied. So why have an odds ratio in the first place?

The odds ratio has at least two things in its favor. In the first place, it can be calculated in situations in which a true risk ratio cannot be. In a retrospective study, where we find a group of people with heart attacks and of another group of people without heart attacks, and look back to see if they took aspirin, we can't really calculate *risk*. Risk is future oriented. If we give 1,000 people aspirin and withhold it from 1,000 others, we can look at these people ten years down the road and calculate the risk (and risk ratio) of heart attacks. But if we take 1,000 people with (and without) heart attacks and look backward, we can't really calculate risk because we have sampled heart attack patients at far greater than their normal rate in the population (50% of our sample has had a heart attack, but certainly 50% of the population does not suffer from heart attacks). But we can always calculate odds ratios. And, *when we are talking about low probability events*, such as having a heart attack, the odds ratio is usually a very good estimate of what the

---

[7] In computing an odds ratio there is no rule as to which odds go in the numerator and which in the denominator. It depends on convenience. Where reasonable I prefer to put the larger value in the numerator to make the ratio come out greater than 1.0, simply because I find it easier to talk about it that way. If we reversed them in this example we would find OR = 0.546, and conclude that your odds of having a heart attack in the aspirin condition are about half of what they are in the No Aspirin condition. That is simply the inverse of the original OR (0.546 = 1/1.83).

[8] An excellent discussion of why many people prefer risk ratios to odds ratios can be found at http://itre.cis.upenn .edu/~myl/languagelog/archives/004767.html

risk ratio would be.[9] (Sackett, Deeks, and Altman (1996), referred to above, agree that this is one case where an odds ratio is useful—and it is useful primarily because in this case it is so close to a relative risk.) The odds ratio is equally valid for prospective, retrospective, and cross-sectional sampling designs. That is important. However, when you do have a prospective study the risk ratio can be computed and actually comes closer to the way we normally think about risk.

A second important advantage of the odds ratio is that taking the natural log of the odds ratio [ln(OR)] gives us a statistic that is extremely useful in a variety of situations. Two of these are logistic regression and log-linear models. Logistic regression is discussed later in the book. I don't expect most people to be excited by the fact that a logarithmic transformation of the odds ratio has interesting statistical properties, but that is a very important point nonetheless.

Odds Ratios in 2 × *K* Tables

When we have a simple 2 × 2 table the calculation of the odds ratio (or the risk ratio) is straightforward. We simply take the ratio of the two odds (or risks). But when the table is a 2 × *k* table things are a bit more complicated because we have three or more sets of odds, and it is not clear what should form our ratio. Sometimes odds ratios here don't make much sense, but sometimes they do—especially when the levels of one variable form an ordered series. The data from Jankowski's study of sexual abuse offer a good illustration. These data are reproduced in Table 6.12.

Because this study was looking at how adult abuse is influenced by earlier childhood abuse, it makes sense to use the group who suffered no childhood abuse as the reference group. We can then take the odds ratio of each of the other groups against this one. For example, those who reported one category of childhood abuse have an odds ratio of 0.163/0.106 = 1.54. Thus the odds of being abused as an adult for someone from the Category 1 group are 1.54 times the odds for someone from the Category 0 group. For the other two groups the odds ratios relative to the Category 0 group are 2.40 and 6.29. (The corresponding risk ratios were 1.27, 2.13, and 4.20.) The effect of childhood sexual abuse becomes even clearer when we plot these results in Figure 6.2. The odds of being abused increase very noticeably with a more serious history of childhood sexual abuse. (If you prefer risk over odds, you can do exactly the same thing by taking ratios of risks.)

Table 6.12 Adult sexual abuse related to prior childhood sexual abuse

Number of Child Abuse Categories	Abused as Adult				
	No	Yes	Total	Risk	Odds
0	512	54	566	.095	.106
1	227	37	264	.140	.163
2	59	15	74	.203	.254
3-4	18	12	30	.400	.667
Total	816	118	934	.126	.145

© Cengage Learning 2013

[9] The odds ratio can be defined as $OR = RR\left(\dfrac{1 - p_2}{1 - p_2}\right)$, where OR = odds ratio, RR = relative risk, p_1 is the population proportion of heart attacks in one group, and p_2 is the population proportion of heart attacks in the other group. When those two proportions are close to 0, they nearly cancel each other and $OR \approx RR$.

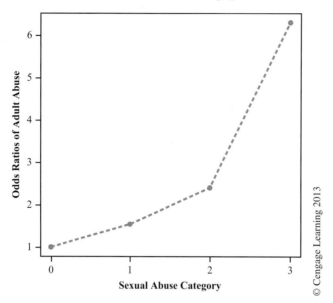

Figure 6.2   Odds ratios relative to the non-abused category

Odds Ratios in 2 × 2 × *K* Tables

Just as we can compute an odds ratio for a 2 × 2 table, so we can also compute an odds ratio when that same study is replicated over several strata such as departments. We will define the odds ratio for all strata together as

$$OR = \frac{\Sigma(n_{11k}n_{22k}/n_{..k})}{\Sigma(n_{12k}n_{21k}/n_{..k})}$$

For the Berkeley data we have

Department	Data		$n_{11k}n_{22k}/n_{..k}$	$n_{12k}n_{21k}/n_{..k}$
B	353	207	4.827	6.015
	17	8		
C	120	205	57.712	50.935
	202	391		
D	138	279	42.515	46.148
	131	244		
E	53	138	27.135	22.212
	94	299		
F	22	351	9.768	11.798
	24	317		
Sum			141.957	137.108

The two entries on the right for Department B are 353 × 8/585 = 4.827 and 207 × 17/585 = 6.015. The calculations for the remaining rows are computed in a similar manner. The overall odds ratio is just the ratio of the sums of those two columns. Thus

OR = 141.957 / 137.108 = 1.03.

The odds ratio tells us that the odds of being admitted if you are a male are 1.03 times the odds of being admitted if you are a female, which means that the odds are almost identical.

Underlying the Mantel-Haenszel statistic is the assumption that the odds ratios are comparable across all strata—in this case all departments. But Department A is clearly an outlier. In that department the odds ratio for men to women is 0.35, while all of the other odds ratios are near 1.0, ranging from 0.80 to 1.22. The inclusion of that department would violate one of the assumptions of the test. In this particular case, where we are checking for discrimination against women, it does not distort the final result to leave that department out. Department A actually admitted significantly more women than men. If it had been the other way around I would have serious qualms about looking only at the other five departments.

r-family Measures

The measures that we have discussed above are sometimes called *d*-family measures because they focus on comparing differences between conditions—either by calculating the difference directly or by using ratios of risks or odds. An older and more traditional set of measures sometimes called "measures of association" look at the correlation between two variables. Unfortunately we won't come to correlation until Chapter 9, but I would expect that you already know enough about correlation coefficients to understand what follows.

There are a great many measures of association, and I have no intention of discussing most of them. One of the nicest discussions of these can be found in Nie, Hull, Jenkins, Steinbrenner, and Bent (1970). It is such a classic that it is very likely to be available in your university library or through interlibrary loan.

Phi (ϕ) and Cramér's *V*

phi (ϕ)

In the case of 2×2 tables, a correlation coefficient that we will consider in Chapter 10 serves as a good measure of association. This coefficient is called **phi (ϕ)**, and it represents the correlation between two variables, each of which is a dichotomy (a dichotomy is a variable that takes on one of two distinct values). If we coded Aspirin as 1 for Yes and 2 for No, and coded Heart Attack as 1 for Yes and 2 for No, and then correlated the two variables (see Chapters 9 and 10), the result would be phi. (It doesn't even matter what two numbers we use as values for coding, so long as one condition always gets one value and the other always gets a different [but consistent] value.)

An easier way to calculate ϕ for these data is by the relation

$$\phi = \sqrt{\frac{\chi^2}{N}}$$

For the Aspirin data in Table 6.7, $\chi^2 = 25.014$ and $\phi = \sqrt{25.014/22,071} = .034$. That does not appear to be a very large correlation; but on the other hand we are speaking about a major, life-threatening event, and even a small correlation can be meaningful.

Phi applies only to 2×2 tables, but Cramér (1946) extended it to larger tables by defining

$$V = \sqrt{\frac{\chi^2}{N(k - 1)}}$$

Cramér's *V*

where N is the sample size and k is defined as the smaller of R and C. This is known as **Cramér's *V***. When $k = 2$ the two statistics are equivalent. For larger tables its interpretation is similar to that for ϕ. The problem with V is that it is hard to give a simple intuitive interpretation to it when there are more than two categories and they do not fall on an ordered dimension.

I am not happy with the *r*-family of measures simply because I don't think that they have a meaningful interpretation in most situations. It is one thing to use a *d*-family measure like the risk ratio and declare that the risk of having a heart attack if you don't take aspirin are 1.82 times higher than the risk of having a heart attack if you do take aspirin. Most people can understand what that statement means. But to use an *r*-family measure, such as phi, and say that the correlation between aspirin intake and heart attack is .034 doesn't seem to be telling them anything useful. (And squaring it and saying that aspirin usage accounts for 0.1% of the variance in heart attacks is even less helpful.) Although you will come across these coefficients in the literature, I would suggest that you stay away from the older *r*-family measures unless you really have a good reason to use them.

6.12   Measure of Agreement

We have one more measure that we should discuss. It is not really a measure of effect size, like the previous measures, but it is an important statistic for categorical data, especially when you want to ask about the agreement between judges.

Kappa (κ)—A Measure of Agreement

kappa (κ)

An important statistic that is not based on chi-square but that does use contingency tables is **kappa (κ)**, commonly known as Cohen's kappa (Cohen, 1960). This statistic measures interjudge agreement and is often used when we wish to examine the reliability of ratings.

Suppose we asked a judge with considerable clinical experience to interview 30 adolescents and classify them as exhibiting (1) no behavior problems, (2) internalizing behavior problems (e.g., withdrawn), and (3) externalizing behavior problems (e.g., acting out). Anyone reviewing our work would be concerned with the reliability of our measure—how do we know that this judge was doing any better than flipping a coin? As a check we ask a second judge to go through the same process and rate the same adolescents. We then set up a contingency table showing the agreements and disagreements between the two judges. Suppose the data are those shown in Table 6.13.

Ignore the values in parentheses for the moment. In this table, Judge I classified 16 adolescents as exhibiting no problems, as shown by the total in column 1. Of those 16, Judge II agreed that 15 had no problems, but also classed 1 of them as exhibiting internalizing problems and 0 as exhibiting externalizing problems. The entries on the diagonal (15, 3, 3) represent agreement between the two judges, whereas the off-diagonal entries represent disagreement.

percentage of agreement

A simple (but unwise) approach to these data is to calculate the **percentage of agreement**. For this statistic all we need to say is that out of 30 total cases, there were 21 cases (15 + 3 + 3) where the judges agreed. Then 21/30 = 0.70 = 70% agreement. This measure has problems, however. The majority of the adolescents in our sample exhibit no behavior

Table 6.13   Agreement data between two judges

Judge II	Judge I			Total
	No Problem	Internalizing	Externalizing	
No Problem	15 (10.67)	2	3	20
Internalizing	1	3 (1.20)	2	6
Externalizing	0	1	3 (1.07)	4
Total	16	6	8	30

problems, and both judges are (correctly) biased toward a classification of No Problem and away from the other classifications. The probability of No Problem for Judge I would be estimated as 16/30 = .53. The probability of No Problem for Judge II would be estimated as 20/30 = .67. If the two judges operated by pulling their diagnoses out of the air, the probability that they would both classify the same case as No Problem is .53 × .67 = .36, which for 30 judgments would mean that .36 × 30 = 10.67 agreements on No Problem alone, purely by chance.

Cohen (1960) proposed a chance-corrected measure of agreement known as kappa. To calculate kappa we first need to calculate the expected frequencies for each of the diagonal cells, assuming that judgments are independent. We calculate these the same way we calculate expected values for the standard chi-square test. For example, the expected frequency of both judges assigning a classification of No Problem, assuming that they are operating at random, is (20 × 16)/30 = 10.67. For Internalizing it is (6 × 6)/30 = 1.2, and for Externalizing it is (4 × 8)/30 = 1.07. These values are shown in parentheses in the table.

We will now define kappa as

$$\kappa = \frac{\sum f_O - \sum f_E}{N - \sum f_E}$$

where f_O represents the observed frequencies on the diagonal and f_E represents the expected frequencies on the diagonal. Thus

$$\sum f_O = 15 + 3 + 3 = 21$$

and

$$\sum f_E = 10.67 + 1.20 + 1.07 = 12.94.$$

Then

$$\kappa = \frac{21 - 12.94}{30 - 12.94} = \frac{8.06}{17.06} = .47$$

Notice that this coefficient is considerably lower than the 70% agreement figure that we calculated above. Instead of 70% agreement, we have 47% agreement after correcting for chance. Kappa is often referred to as a chance-corrected measure of agreement.

If you examine the formula for kappa, you can see the correction that is being applied. In the numerator we subtract, from the number of agreements, the number of agreements that we would expect merely by chance. In the denominator we reduce the total number of judgments by that same amount. We then form a ratio of the two chance-corrected values.

Cohen and others have developed statistical tests for the significance of kappa (see Fleiss, Nee, and Landis (1979)). However, its significance is rarely the issue. If kappa is low enough for us to even question its significance, the lack of agreement among our judges is a serious problem.

6.13 Writing up the Results

We will take as our example Jankowski's study of sexual abuse. If you were writing up these results, you would probably want to say something like the following:

> In an examination of the question of whether adult sexual abuse can be traced back to earlier childhood sexual abuse, 934 undergraduate women were asked to report on

the severity of any childhood sexual abuse and whether or not they had been abused as adults. Severity of abuse was taken as the number of categories of abuse to which the participants responded. The data revealed that the incidence of adult sexual abuse increased with the severity of childhood abuse. A chi-square test of the relationship between adult and childhood abuse produced $\chi^2_3 = 29.63$, which is statistically significant at $p < .05$. The relative risk ratio of being abused as an adult with only one category of childhood abuse, relative to the risk of abuse for the non-childhood abused group was 1.27. The risk ratio climbed to 2.13 and 4.2 as severity of childhood abuse increased. Sexual abuse as a child is a strong indicator of later sexual abuse as an adult.

Key Terms

Chi-square (χ^2) (Introduction)

Pearson's chi-square (Introduction)

Chi-square distribution (χ^2) (6.1)

Gamma function (6.1)

Chi-square test (6.2)

Goodness-of-fit test (6.2)

Observed frequencies (6.2)

Expected frequencies (6.2)

Tabled distribution of χ^2 (6.2)

Degrees of freedom (*df*) (6.2)

Contingency table (6.3)

Cell (6.3)

Marginal totals (6.3)

Row total (6.3)

Column total (6.3)

Double blind study (6.3)

Yates' correction for continuity (6.3)

Conditional test (6.3)

Fixed and Random margins (6.3)

Small expected frequency (6.4)

Nonoccurrences (6.6)

McNemar's Test (6.7)

Likelihood ratios (6.9)

Mantel-Haenszel test (6.10)

Cochran-Mantel-Haenszel (CMH) (6.10)

Simpson's Paradox (6.10)

d-family (6.11)

r-family (6.11)

Measures of association (6.11)

Prospective study (6.11)

Cohort study (6.11)

Randomized clinical trial (6.11)

Retrospective study (6.11)

Case-control design (6.11)

Risk (6.11)

Risk difference (6.11)

Risk ratio (6.11)

Relative risk (6.11)

Odds ratio (6.11)

Odds (6.11)

Phi (ϕ) (6.11)

Cramér's *V* (6.11)

Kappa (κ) (6.12)

Percentage of agreement (6.12)

Exercises

6.1   The chairperson of a psychology department suspects that some of her faculty are more popular with students than are others. There are three sections of introductory psychology, taught at 10:00 A.M., 11:00 A.M., and 12:00 P.M. by Professors Anderson, Klatsky, and Kamm. The number of students who enroll for each is

Professor Anderson	Professor Klatsky	Professor Kamm
32	25	10

State the null hypothesis, run the appropriate chi-square test, and interpret the results.

6.2   Thirty years after the Clark and Clark study, Hraba and Grant (1970) repeated the study referred to in Exercise 6.3. The studies, though similar, were not exactly equivalent, but the results were interesting. Hraba and Grant found that out of 89 African American children, 28 chose the white doll and 61 chose the black doll. Run the appropriate chi-square test on their data and interpret the results.

6.3 In a classic study by Clark and Clark (1939), African American children were shown black dolls and white dolls and were asked to select the one with which they wished to play. Out of 252 children, 169 chose the white doll and 83 chose the black doll. What can we conclude about the behavior of these children?

6.4 From the point of view of designing a valid experiment (as opposed to the arithmetic of calculation), there is an important difference between Exercise 6.1 and the examples used in this chapter. The data in Exercise 6.1 will not really answer the question the chairperson wants answered. What is the problem and how could the experiment be improved?

6.5 Combine the data from Exercises 6.2 and 6.3 into a two-way contingency table and run the appropriate test. How does the question that the two-way classification addresses differ from the questions addressed by Exercises 6.2 and 6.3?

6.6 In Exercise 6.10 children were classified as those who never showed ADD behavior and those who showed ADD behavior at least once in the second, fourth, or fifth grade. If we do not collapse across categories, we obtain the following data:

	Never	2nd	4th	2nd & 4th	5th	2nd & 5th	4th & 5th	2nd, 4th, & 5th
Remedial	22	2	1	3	2	4	3	4
Nonrem.	187	17	11	9	16	7	8	6

© Cengage Learning 2013

a. Run the chi-square test.

b. What would you conclude, ignoring the problem of small expected frequencies?

c. How comfortable do you feel with these small expected frequencies? If you are not comfortable, how might you handle the problem?

6.7 In discussing the correction for continuity, we referred to the idea of fixed marginals, meaning that a replication of the study would produce the same row and/or column totals. Give an example of a study in which

a. no marginal totals are fixed.

b. one set of marginal totals is fixed.

c. both sets of marginal totals (row and column) could reasonably be considered to be fixed. (This is a hard one.)

6.8 We know that smoking has a variety of ill effects on people; among other things, there is evidence that it affects fertility. Weinberg and Gladen (1986) examined the effects of smoking and the ease with which women become pregnant. They took 586 women who had planned pregnancies and asked how many menstrual cycles it had taken for them to become pregnant after discontinuing contraception. Weinberg and Gladen also sorted the women into smokers and non-smokers. The data follow.

	1 Cycle	2 Cycles	3+ Cycles	Total
Smokers	29	16	55	100
Non-smokers	198	107	181	486
Total	227	123	236	586

© Cengage Learning 2013

Does smoking affect the ease with which women become pregnant? (I do not recommend smoking as a birth control device, regardless of your answer.)

6.9 Use the data in Exercise 6.10 to demonstrate how chi-square varies as a function of sample size.

a. Double each cell entry and recompute chi-square.

b. What does your answer to (a) say about the role of the sample size in hypothesis testing?

6.10   Howell and Huessy (1981) used a rating scale to classify children in a second-grade class as showing or not showing behavior commonly associated with attention deficit disorder (ADD). They then classified these same children again when they later were in fourth and fifth grades. When the children reached the end of the ninth grade, the researchers examined school records and noted which children were enrolled in remedial English. In the following data, all children who were ever classified as exhibiting behavior associated with ADD have been combined into one group (labeled ADD):

	Remedial English	Nonremedial English	
Normal	22	187	209
ADD	19	74	93
	41	261	302

© Cengage Learning 2013

Does behavior during elementary school discriminate class assignment during high school?

6.11   In 2000 the State of Vermont legislature approved a bill authorizing civil unions between gay or lesbian partners. This was a very contentious debate with very serious issues raised by both sides. How the vote split along gender lines may tell us something important about the different ways that males and females looked at this issue. The data appear below. What would you conclude from these data?

	Vote		
	Yes	No	Total
Women	35	9	44
Men	60	41	101
Total	95	50	145

© Cengage Learning 2013

6.12   Use the likelihood ratio approach to analyze the data in Exercise 6.10.

6.13   In a study of eating disorders in adolescents, Gross (1985) asked each of her subjects whether they would prefer to gain weight, lose weight, or maintain their present weight. (Note: Only 12% of the girls in Gross's sample were actually more than 15% above their normative weight—a common cutoff for a label of "overweight.") When she broke down the data for girls by race (African-American versus white), she obtained the following results (other races have been omitted because of small sample sizes):

	Reducers	Maintainers	Gainers	Total
White	352	152	31	535
African American	47	28	24	99
	399	180	55	634

© Cengage Learning 2013

a.   What conclusions can you draw from these data?

b.   Ignoring race, what conclusion can you draw about adolescent girls' attitudes toward their own weight?

6.14   Stress has long been known to influence physical health. Visintainer, Volpicelli, and Seligman (1982) investigated the hypothesis that rats given 60 trials of inescapable shock would be less likely later to reject an implanted tumor than would rats who had received 60 trials of escapable shock or 60 no-shock trials. They obtained the following data:

	Inescapable Shock	Escapable Shock	No Shock	Total
Reject	8	19	18	45
No Reject	22	11	15	48
	30	30	33	93

© Cengage Learning 2013

What could Visintainer et al. conclude from the results?

6.15   Use the likelihood ratio approach to analyze the data in Exercise 6.6.

6.16   A more complete set of data on heart attacks and aspirin, from which Table 6.7 was taken, is shown below. Here we distinguish not just between Heart Attacks and No Heart Attacks, but also between Fatal and Nonfatal attacks.

© Cengage Learning 2013

| | Myocardial Infarction | | | |
	Fatal Attack	Nonfatal Attack	No Attack	Total
Placebo	18	171	10,845	11,034
Aspirin	5	99	10,933	11,037
Total	23	270	21,778	22,071

a.   Calculate both Pearson's chi-square and the likelihood ratio chi-square table. Interpret the results.

b.   Using only the data for the first two columns (those subjects with heart attacks), calculate both Pearson's chi-square and the likelihood ratio chi-square and interpret your results.

c.   Combine the Fatal and Nonfatal heart attack columns and compare the combined column against the No Attack column, using both Pearson's and likelihood ratio chi-squares. Interpret these results.

d.   Sum the Pearson chi-squares in (b) and (c) and then the likelihood ratio chi-squares in (b) and (c), and compare each of these results to the results in (a). What do they tell you about the partitioning of chi-square?

e.   What do these results tell you about the relationship between aspirin and heart attacks?

6.17   Suppose we asked a group of participants whether they liked Monday Night Football, then made them watch a game and asked them again. Our interest lies in whether watching a game changes people's opinions. Out of 80 participants, 20 changed their opinion from Favorable to Unfavorable, while 5 changed from Unfavorable to Favorable. (The others did not change.) Did watching the game have a systematic effect on opinion change? [This test on changes is the test suggested by McNemar (1969).]

a.   Run the test.

b.   Explain how this tests the null hypothesis.

c.   In this situation the test does not answer our question of whether watching football has a serious effect on opinion change. Why not?

6.18   It would be possible to calculate a one-way chi-square test on the data in row 2 of the table in Exercise 6.6. What hypothesis would you be testing if you did that? How would that hypothesis differ from the one you tested in Exercise 6.6?

6.19   The following SPSS output in Exhibit 6.2 represents that analysis of the data in Exercise 6.13.

a.   Verify the answer to Exercise 6.13a.

b.   Interpret the row and column percentages.

c.   What are the values labeled "Asymp. Sig."?

d.   Interpret the coefficients.

RACE*GOAL Crosstabulation

			Goal			
			Gain	Lose	Maintain	Total
RACE	African-Amer	Count	24	47	28	99
		Expected Count	8.6	62.3	28.1	99.0
		% within RACE	24.2%	47.5%	28.3%	100.0%
		% within GOAL	43.6%	11.8%	15.6%	15.6%
		% of Total	3.8%	7.4%	4.4%	15.6%
	White	Count	31	352	152	535
		Expected Count	46.43	336.7	151.9	535.0
		% within RACE	5.8%	65.8%	28.4%	100.0%
		% within GOAL	56.4%	88.2%	84.4%	84.4%
		% of Total	4.9%	55.5%	24.0%	84.4%
Total		Count	55	399	180	634
		Expected Count	55.03	99.0	180.0	634.0
		% within RACE	8.7%	62.9%	28.4%	100.0%
		% within GOAL	100.0%	100.0%	100.0%	100.0%
		% of Total	8.7%	62.9%	28.4%	100.0%

Chi-Square Tests

	Value	df	Asymp. Sig. (2-sided)
Pearson Chi-Square	37.229[a]	2	.000
Likelihood Ratio	29.104	2	.000
N of Valid Cases	634		

[a]0 cells (.0%) have expected count less than 5. The minimum expected count is 8.59.

Symmetric Measures

		Value	Approx. Sig.
Nominal by Nominal	Phi	.242	.000
	Cramer's V	.242	.000
	Contingency Coefficient	.236	.000
N of Valid Cases		634	

Exhibit 6-2

a.   Not assuming the null hypothesis.

b.   Using the asymptotic standard error assuming the null hypothesis.

6.20   Pugh (1983) conducted a study of how jurors make decisions in rape cases. He presented 358 people with a mock rape trial. In about half of those trials the *victim* was presented as being partly at fault, and in the other half of the trials she was presented as not at fault. The verdicts are shown in the following table. What conclusion would you draw?

Fault	Guilty	Not Guilty	Total
Little	153	24	177
Much	105	76	181
Total	258	100	358

© Cengage Learning 2013

6.21 Calculate and interpret Cramér's *V* and useful odds ratios for the results in Exercise 6.16.

6.22 Use SPSS or another statistical package to calculate Fisher's Exact Test for the data in Exercise 6.11. How does it compare to the probability associated with Pearson's chi-square?

6.23 Compute the odds ratio for Table 6.4. What does this ratio add to your understanding of the phenomenon being studied?

6.24 Compute the odds ratio for the data in Exercise 6.6. What does this value mean?

6.25 Dabbs and Morris (1990) examined archival data from military records to study the relationship between high testosterone levels and antisocial behavior in males. Out of 4,016 men in the Normal Testosterone group, 10.0% had a record of adult delinquency. Out of 446 men in the High Testosterone group, 22.6% had a record of adult delinquency. Is this relationship significant?

6.26 In a data set on this book's Web site named Mireault.dat and described in Appendix Data Set, Mireault and Bond (1992) collected data from college students on the effects of the death of a parent. Leaving the critical variables aside for a moment, let's look at the distribution of students. The data set contains information on the gender of the students and the college (within the university) in which they were enrolled.

    a. Use any statistical package to tabulate Gender against College.

    b. What is the chi-square test on the hypothesis that College enrollment is independent of Gender?

    c. Interpret the results.

6.27 In the study described in Exercise 6.25, 11.5% of the Normal Testosterone group and 17.9% of the High Testosterone group had a history of childhood delinquency.

    a. Is there a significant relationship between these two variables?

    b. Interpret this relationship.

    c. How does this result expand on what we already know from Exercise 6.25?

6.28 What is the odds ratio in Exercise 6.25? How would you interpret it?

6.29 Many school children receive instruction on child abuse around the "good touch-bad touch" model, with the hope that such a program will reduce sexual abuse. Gibson and Leitenberg (2000) collected data from 818 college students, and recorded whether they had ever received such training and whether they had subsequently been abused. Of the 500 students who had received training, 43 reported that they had subsequently been abused. Of the 318 who had not received training, 50 reported subsequent abuse.

    a. Do these data present a convincing case for the efficacy of the sexual abuse prevention program?

    b. What is the odds ratio for these data, and what does it tell you?

6.30 In a study examining the effects of individualized care of youths with severe emotional problems, Burchard and Schaefer (1990, personal communication) proposed to have caregivers rate the presence or absence of specific behaviors for each of 40 adolescents on a given day. To check for rater reliability, they asked two raters to rate each adolescent. The following hypothetical data represent reasonable results for the behavior of "extreme verbal abuse."

Rater B	Rater A		Total
	Presence	Absence	
Presence	12	2	14
Absence	1	25	26
	13	27	40

© Cengage Learning 2013

    a. What is the percentage of agreement for these raters?

    b. What is Cohen's kappa?

    c. Why is kappa noticeably less than the percentage of agreement?

    d. Modify the raw data, keeping N at 40, so that the two statistics move even farther apart. How did you do this?

6.31 When we look at the variables in Mireault's data, we will want to be sure that there are not systematic differences of which we are ignorant. For example, if we found that the gender of the parent who died was an important variable in explaining some outcome variable, we would not like to later discover that the gender of the parent who died was in some way related to the gender of the subject, and that the effects of the two variables were confounded.

    a. Run a chi-square test on these two variables.

    b. Interpret the results.

    c. What would it mean to our interpretation of the relationship between gender of the parent and some other variable (e.g., subject's level of depression) if the gender of the parent is itself related to the gender of the subject?

6.32 Hout, Duncan, and Sobel (1987) reported data on the relative sexual satisfaction of married couples. They asked each member of 91 married couples to rate the degree to which they agreed with "Sex is fun for me and my partner" on a four-point scale ranging from "never or occasionally" to "almost always." The data appear below:

Husband's Rating	Wife's Rating				Total
	Never	Fairly Often	Very Often	Almost Always	
Never	7	7	2	3	19
Fairly Often	2	8	3	7	20
Very Often	1	5	4	9	19
Almost Always	2	8	9	14	33
Total	12	28	18	33	91

© Cengage Learning 2013

    a. How would you go about analyzing these data? Remember that you want to know more than just whether or not the two ratings are independent. Presumably you would like to show that as one spouse's ratings go up, so do the other's, and vice versa.

    b. Use both Pearson's chi-square and the likelihood ratio chi-square.

    c. What does Cramér's V offer?

    d. What about odds ratios?

    e. What about Kappa?

    f. Finally, what if you combined the Never and Fairly Often categories and the Very Often and Almost Always categories? Would the results be clearer, and under what conditions might this make sense?

6.33 The Zuckerman et al. paper referred to in the previous question hypothesized that faculty were less accurate than students because they have a tendency to give negative responses to such questions. ("There must be a trick.") How would you design a study to test such a hypothesis?

6.34 Zuckerman, Hodgins, Zuckerman, and Rosenthal (1993) surveyed over 500 people and asked a number of questions on statistical issues. In one question a reviewer warned a researcher that she had a high probability of a Type I error because she had a small sample size. The researcher disagreed. Subjects were asked, "Was the researcher correct?" The proportions of respondents, partitioned among students, assistant professors, associate professors, and full professors, who sided with the researcher and the total number of respondents in each category were as follows:

	Students	Assistant Professors	Associate Professors	Full Professors
Proportion	.59	.34	.43	.51
Sample size	17	175	134	182

© Cengage Learning 2013

(Note: These data mean that 59% of the 17 students who responded sided with the researcher. When you calculate the actual obtained frequencies, round to the nearest whole person.)

a. Would you agree with the reviewer, or with the researcher? Why?

b. What is the error in logic of the person you disagreed with in (a)?

c. How would you set up this problem to be suitable for a chi-square test?

d. What do these data tell you about differences among groups of respondents?

6.35 In the previous question we were concerned with whether husbands and wives rate their degree of sexual fun congruently (i.e., to the same degree). But suppose that women have different cut points on an underlying scale of "fun." For example, maybe women's idea of Fairly Often or Almost Always is higher than men's. (Maybe men would rate "a couple of times a month" as "Very Often" while women would rate "a couple of times a month" as "Fairly Often.") How would this affect your conclusions? Would it represent an underlying incongruency between males and females?

6.36 In the text I calculated odds ratios for the data in Table 6.11. Do the same for relative risk.

6.37 Fidalgo (2005) presented data on the relationship between bullying in the work force (Yes/No) and gender (Male/Female) of the bully. He further broke the data down by job level. The data are given below.

		Bullying	
Gender	Job Category	No	Yes
Male	Manual	148	28
Female		98	22
Male	Clerical	68	13
Female		144	32
Male	Technician	121	18
Female		43	10
Male	Middle Manager	95	7
Female		38	7
Male	Manager/	29	2
Female	Executive	8	1

© Cengage Learning 2013

a. Do we have evidence that there is a relationship between bullying on the job and gender if we collapse across job categories?

b. What is the odds ratio for the analysis in part a?

c. When we condition on job category is there evidence of gender differences in bullying?

d. What is the odds ratio for the analysis in part c?

e. You probably do not have the software to extend the Mantel-Haenszel test to strata containing more than a 2×2 contingency table. However, using standard Pearson chi-square, examine the relationship between bullying and the Job Category separately by gender. Explain the results of this analysis.

6.38   The following data come from Ramsey and Shafer (1996) but were originally collected in conjunction with the trial of *McClesky v. Zant* in 1998. In that trial the defendant's lawyers tried to demonstrate that black defendants were more likely to receive the death penalty if the victim was white than if the victim was black. They were attempting to prove systematic discrimination in sentencing. The State of Georgia agreed with the basic fact, but argued that the crimes against whites tended to be more serious crimes than those committed against blacks, and thus the difference in sentencing was understandable. The data are shown below. Were the statisticians on the defendant's side correct in arguing that sentencing appeared discriminatory? Test this hypothesis using the Mantel-Haenszel procedure.

Seriousness	Race Victim	Death Penalty	
		Yes	No
1	White	2	60
	Black	1	181
2	White	2	15
	Black	1	21
3	White	6	7
	Black	2	9
4	White	9	3
	Black	2	4
5	White	9	0
	Black	4	3
6	White	17	0
	Black	4	0

© Cengage Learning 2013

Calculate the odds ratio of a death sentence with white versus black victims.

6.39   Appleton, French, and Vanderpump (1996) present data that would appear to show that smoking is good for you. They assessed smoking behavior in the early 1970s and then looked at survival data 20 years later. For simplicity they restricted their data to women who were current smokers or had never smoked. Out of 582 smokers, 139 (24%) had died. Out of 732 smokers, 230 (31%) had died. Obviously proportionally fewer smokers died than nonsmokers. But if we break the data down by age groups we have

Age	18–24		25–34		35–44		45–54		55–64		65–74		75+	
Smoker	S	NS	S	NS	S	NS	S	NS	S	NS	S	NS	S	NS
Dead	2	1	3	5	14	7	27	12	51	40	29	101	13	64
Alive	53	61	121	152	95	114	103	66	64	81	7	28	0	0

© Cengage Learning 2013

a.   Explain these results as an example of Simpson's paradox.
b.   Apply the Mantel-Haenszel test to these data.

6.40   The State of Maine collected data on seat belt use and highway fatalities in 1996. (Full data are available at http://maine.gov/dps/bhs/crash-data/stats/seatbelts.html)

Psychologists often study how to address self-injurious behavior, and the data shown below speak to the issue of whether seat belts prevent injury or death. (The variable "Occupants" counts occupants actually involved in highway accidents.)

	Not Belted	Belted
Occupants	6,307	65,245
Injured	2,323	8,138
Fatalities	62	35

© Cengage Learning 2013

Present these data in ways to show the effectiveness of seat belts in preventing death and injury.

Chapter 7

Hypothesis Tests Applied to Means

Objectives

To introduce the *t* test as a procedure for testing hypotheses with measurement data, and to show how it can be used with several different designs. To describe ways of estimating the magnitude of any differences that appear.

Contents

IN CHAPTERS 5 AND 6 we considered tests dealing with frequency (categorical) data. In those situations, the results of any experiment can usually be represented by a few subtotals—the frequency of occurrence of each category of response. In this and subsequent chapters, we will deal with a different type of data, which I have previously termed measurement or quantitative data.

In analyzing measurement data, our interest can focus either on differences between groups of subjects or on the relationship between two or more variables. The question of relationships between variables will be postponed until Chapters 9, 10, 15, and 16. This chapter is concerned with the question of differences, and the statistic we will be most interested in is the sample mean.

Low-birthweight (LBW) infants (who are often premature) are considered to be at risk for a variety of developmental difficulties. As part of an example we will return to later, Nurcombe et al. (1984) took 25 LBW infants in an experimental group and 31 LBW infants in a control group, provided training to the parents of those in the experimental group on how to recognize the needs of LBW infants, and, when these children were 2 years old, obtained a measure of cognitive ability for each infant. Suppose we found that the LBW infants in the experimental group had a mean score of 117.2, whereas those in the control group had a mean score of 106.7. Is the observed mean difference sufficient evidence for us to conclude that 2-year-old LBW children in the experimental group score higher, on average, than do 2-year-old LBW control children? We will answer this particular question later; I mention the problem here to illustrate the kind of question we will discuss in this chapter.

7.1   Sampling Distribution of the Mean

sampling distribution of the mean

central limit theorem

As you should recall from Chapter 4, the sampling distribution of any statistic is the distribution of values we would expect to obtain for that statistic if we drew an infinite number of samples from the population in question and calculated the statistic on each sample. Because we are concerned in this chapter with sample *means*, we need to know something about the **sampling distribution of the mean**. Fortunately, all the important information about the sampling distribution of the mean can be summed up in one very important theorem: the central limit theorem. The **central limit theorem** is a factual statement about the distribution of means. In an extended form it states:

> Given a population with mean μ and variance σ^2, the sampling distribution of the mean (the distribution of sample means) will have a mean equal to μ (i.e., $\mu_{\bar{X}} = \mu$), a variance ($\sigma_{\bar{X}}^2$) equal to σ^2/n, and a standard deviation ($\sigma_{\bar{X}}$) equal to $\sigma/\sqrt{n}$. The distribution will approach the normal distribution as n, the *sample size*, increases.[1]

This is one of the most important theorems in statistics. It tells us not only what the mean and variance of the sampling distribution of the mean must be for any given sample size, but it also states that as n increases, the shape of this sampling distribution approaches normal, *whatever* the shape of the parent population. The importance of these facts will become clear shortly.

The rate at which the sampling distribution of the mean approaches normal as n increases is a function of the shape of the parent population. If the population is itself normal, the sampling distribution of the mean will be normal regardless of n. If the population is

---

[1] The central limit theorem can be found stated in a variety of forms. The simplest form merely says that the sampling distribution of the mean approaches normal as n increases. The more extended form given here includes all the important information about the sampling distribution of the mean.

symmetric but nonnormal, the sampling distribution of the mean will be nearly normal even for small sample sizes, especially if the population is unimodal. If the population is markedly skewed, sample sizes of 30 or more may be required before the means closely approximate a normal distribution.

To illustrate the central limit theorem, suppose we have an infinitely large population of random numbers evenly distributed between 0 and 100. This population will have what is called a **uniform (rectangular) distribution**—every value between 0 and 100 will be equally likely. The distribution of 50,000 observations drawn from this population is shown in Figure 7.1. You can see that the distribution is flat, as would be expected. For uniform distributions the mean (μ) is known to be equal to one-half of the range (50), the standard deviation (σ) is known to be equal the range divided by the square root of 12, which is this case is 28.87, and the variance (σ^2) is thus 833.33.

Now suppose we drew 5,000 samples of size 5 ($n = 5$) from this population and plotted the resulting sample *means*. Such sampling can be easily accomplished with a simple computer program; the results of just such a procedure are presented in Figure 7.2a, with a normal distribution superimposed. (The first time I ran this example many years ago it took approximately 5 minutes to draw such samples on a mainframe computer. Today it took me 1.5 *seconds* on my laptop. Computer simulation is not a big deal.)[2]

It is apparent that the distribution of means, although not exactly normal, is at least peaked in the center and trails off toward the extremes. (In fact the superimposed normal distribution fits the data quite well.) The mean and standard deviation of this distribution are shown, and they are extremely close to $\mu = 50$ and $\sigma_{\bar{X}} = \sigma/\sqrt{n} = 28.87/\sqrt{5} = 12.91$. Any discrepancy between the actual values and those predicted by the central limit theorem is attributable to rounding error and to the fact that we did not draw an infinite number of samples.

uniform (rectangular) distribution

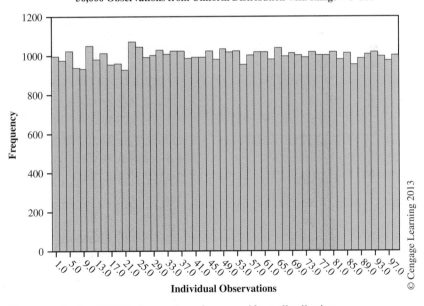

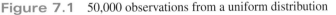

© Cengage Learning 2013

Figure 7.1   50,000 observations from a uniform distribution

---

[2] A simple program written for R that allows you to draw sampling distributions for samples of any size is available at this book's Web site and named SampDistMean.R.

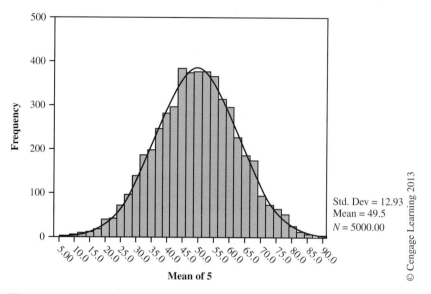

Figure 7.2a Sampling distribution of the mean when $n = 5$

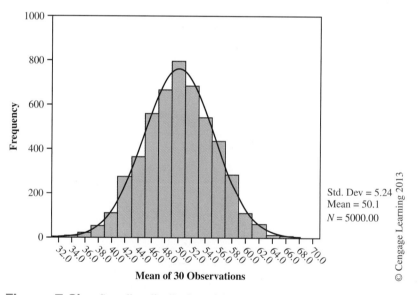

Figure 7.2b Sampling distribution of the mean when $n = 30$

Now suppose we repeated the entire procedure, only this time drawing 5,000 samples of 30 observations each. The results for these samples are plotted in Figure 7.2b. Here you see that just as the central limit theorem predicted, the distribution is approximately normal, the mean is again at $\mu = 50$, and the standard deviation has been reduced to approximately $28.87/\sqrt{30} = 5.27$.

You can get a better idea of the difference in the normality of the sampling distribution when $n = 5$ and $n = 30$ by looking at Figure 7.2c. This figure presents Q-Q plots for the two sampling distributions, and you can see that although the distribution for $n = 5$ is not very far from normal, the distribution with $n = 30$ is even closer to normal.

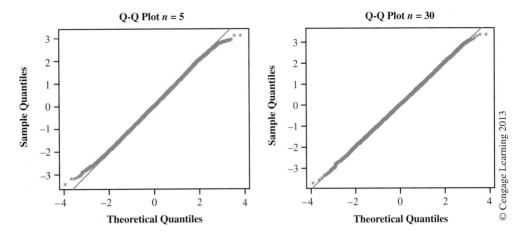

Figure 7.2c   Q-Q plots for sampling distributions with $n = 5$ and $n = 30$.

7.2 Testing Hypotheses About Means—σ Known

From the central limit theorem, we know all the important characteristics of the sampling distribution of the mean. (We know its shape, its mean, and its standard deviation.) On the basis of this information, we are in a position to begin testing hypotheses about means.

In most situations in which we test a hypothesis about a population mean, we don't have any knowledge about the variance of that population. (This is the main reason we have t tests, which are the main focus of this chapter.) However, in a limited number of situations we do know σ. A discussion of testing a hypothesis when σ is known provides a good transition from what we already know about the normal distribution to what we want to know about t tests.

We will start with an example based on an honors thesis by Williamson (2008), who was examining coping behavior in children of depressed parents. His study went much further than we will go, but it provides an illustration of a situation in which it makes sense to test a null hypothesis using the mean of a single sample.

Because there is evidence in the psychological literature that stress in a child's life may lead to subsequent behavior problems, Williamson expected that a sample of children of depressed parents would show an unusually high level of behavior problems. This suggests that if we use a behavioral checklist, such as the anxious/depressed subscale of Achenbach's Youth Self-Report Inventory (YSR), we would expect elevated scores from a sample of children whose parents suffer from depression. (This is a convenient example here because we know the actual population mean and standard deviation of YSR scores—they are 50 and 10.)

It does not seem likely that children would show reduced levels of depression, but to guard against that possibility we will test a two-tailed experimental hypothesis that the anxious/depressive scores among these children is different from similar scores from a normal sample. We can't test the experimental hypothesis directly, however. Instead we will test the null hypothesis (H_0) that the scores of stressed children came from a population of scores with the *same* mean as the population of scores of normal children, rejection of which would support the experimental hypothesis. More specifically, we want to decide between $H_0 : \mu = 50$ and $H_1 : \mu \neq 50$.

I have chosen the two-tailed alternative form of H_1 because I want to reject H_0 if $\mu > 50$ *or* if $\mu < 50$.

Because we know the mean and standard deviation of the population of Youth Self-Report scores, we can use the central limit theorem to obtain the sampling distribution when the null hypothesis is true. The central limit theorem states that if we obtain the sampling distribution of the mean from this population, it will have a mean of $\mu = 50$, a variance of **standard error** σ^2/n, and a standard deviation (usually referred to as the **standard error**[3]) of $\sigma/\sqrt{n}$.

Williamson (2008) had 166 children from homes in which at least one parent had a history of depression. These children all completed the Youth Self-Report, and the sample mean was 55.71 with a standard deviation of 7.35. We want to test the null hypothesis that these children come from a normal population with a mean of 50 and a standard deviation of 10.

We can create a test of our null hypothesis by beginning with the standard formula for z and then substitute the mean and standard error in place of a score and standard deviation.

$$z = \frac{X - \mu}{\sigma} \qquad \text{becomes} \qquad z = \frac{\overline{X} - \mu}{\sigma_{\overline{X}}}$$

which can also be written as

$$z = \frac{\overline{X} - \mu}{\dfrac{\sigma}{\sqrt{n}}}$$

Then

$$z = \frac{\overline{X} - \mu}{\dfrac{\sigma}{\sqrt{n}}} = \frac{55.71 - 50}{\dfrac{10}{\sqrt{166}}} = \frac{5.71}{0.776} = 7.36$$

We cannot use the table of the normal distribution simply because it does not go that high. The largest value of z in the table is 4.00. However even if our result had only been 4.00, it would have been significant with a probability less than .000 to three decimal places, so we can reject the null hypothesis in any event. (The exact probability for a two-tailed test would be .00000000000018, which is obviously a significant result.) So Williamson has every reason to believe that children in his study do not represent a random sample of scores from the anxious/depressed subscale of the YSR. (In the language of Jones and Tukey (2000) discussed earlier, we have evidence that the mean of stressed children is above that of other children.)

The test of one sample mean against a known population mean, which we have just performed, is based on the assumption that the sample means are normally distributed, or at least that the distribution is sufficiently normal that we will be only negligibly in error when we refer to the tables of the standard normal distribution. Many textbooks state that we assume we are sampling from a normal population (i.e., behavior problem scores themselves are normally distributed), but this is not strictly necessary in practical terms. What is most important is to assume that the sampling distribution of the mean (Figure 12.3) is nearly normal. This assumption can be satisfied in two ways: if either (1) the population from which we sample is normal or (2) the sample size is sufficiently large to produce at least approximate normality by way of the Central Limit Theorem. This is one of the great benefits of the Central Limit Theorem: It allows us to test hypotheses even if the parent population is not normal, provided only that N is sufficiently large.

---

[3] The standard deviation of any sampling distribution is normally referred to as the standard error of that distribution. Thus, the standard deviation of means is called the standard error of the mean (symbolized by $\sigma_{\overline{X}}$), whereas the standard deviation of differences between means, which will be discussed shortly, is called the standard error of differences between means and is symbolized by $\sigma_{\overline{X}_1 - \overline{X}_2}$.

> But Williamson also had the standard deviation of his sample. Why didn't we use that?
>
> The simple answer to this question is that we have something better. We have the *population* standard deviation. The YSR and its scoring system have been meticulously developed over the years, and we can have complete confidence that the standard deviation of scores of a whole population of normal children will be 10 or so close that the difference would not be meaningful. And we want to test that our sample came from a population of normal children. We will see in a moment that we usually do not have the population standard deviation and have to estimate it from the sample standard deviation, but when we do have it we should use it. For one thing, if these children really do score higher, I would expect that their sample standard deviation would underestimate σ. That is because the standard deviation of people who are biased toward one end of the distribution is very likely to be smaller than the standard deviation of scores that are more centrally placed.

7.3   Testing a Sample Mean When σ Is Unknown—The One-Sample t Test

The preceding example was chosen deliberately from among a fairly limited number of situations in which the population standard deviation (σ) is known. In the general case, we rarely know the value of σ and usually have to estimate it by way of the *sample* standard deviation (s). When we replace σ with s in the formula, however, the nature of the test changes. We can no longer declare the answer to be a z score and evaluate it using tables of z. Instead, we will denote the answer as t and evaluate it using tables of t, which are different from tables of z. The reasoning behind the switch from z to t is actually related to the sampling distribution of the sample variance.

The Sampling Distribution of s^2

Because the t test uses s^2 as an estimate of σ^2, it is important that we first look at the sampling distribution of s^2. This sampling distribution gives us some insight into the problems we are going to encounter. We saw in Chapter 2 that s^2 is an *unbiased* estimate of σ^2, meaning that with repeated sampling the average value of s^2 will equal σ^2. Although an unbiased estimator is a nice thing, it is not everything. The problem is that the shape of the sampling distribution of s^2 is positively skewed, especially for small samples. I drew 10,000 samples of $n = 5$ and $n = 30$ from a normally distributed population with $\mu = 5$ and $\sigma^2 = 50$. I calculated the variance for each sample, and have plotted those 10,000 variances in Figure 7.3. I have also used a Q-Q plot to look at normality. The mean of both distributions is almost exactly 50, reflecting the unbiased nature of s^2 as an estimate of σ^2. However, the distributions are very positively skewed, especially the one with small sample sizes. Because of the skewness of the distribution of the variance, an individual value of s^2 is more likely to underestimate σ^2 than to overestimate it, especially for small samples. Also because of this skewness, the resulting value of t is likely to be larger than the value of z that we would have obtained had σ been known and used.[4]

---

[4] You can demonstrate for yourself what happens as we vary the sample size by using an R program named SampDistVar.R on the book's Web site.

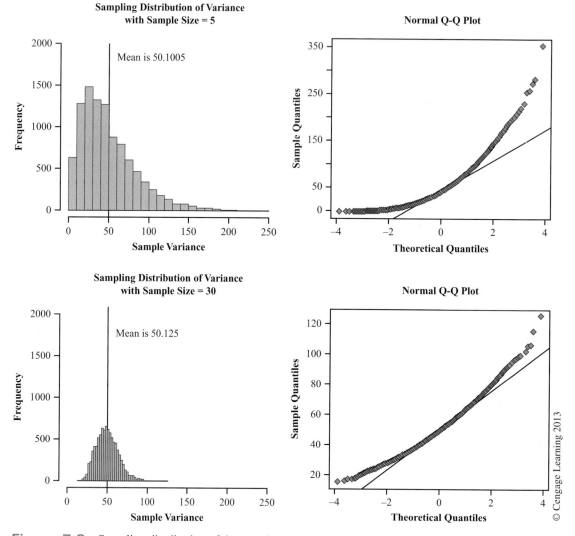

Figure 7.3 Sampling distribution of the sample variance for sample sizes of $n = 5$ and 30

The *t* Statistic

We are going to take the formula that we just developed for z,

$$z = \frac{\overline{X} - \mu}{\sigma_{\overline{X}}} = \frac{\overline{X} - \mu}{\dfrac{\sigma}{\sqrt{n}}} = \frac{\overline{X} - \mu}{\sqrt{\dfrac{\sigma^2}{n}}}$$

and substitute s for σ to give

$$t = \frac{\overline{X} - \mu}{s_{\overline{X}}} = \frac{\overline{X} - \mu}{\dfrac{s}{\sqrt{n}}} = \frac{\overline{X} - \mu}{\sqrt{\dfrac{s^2}{n}}}$$

Because we know that for any particular sample, s^2 is more likely than not to be smaller than the appropriate value of σ^2, we know that the denominator will more often be larger

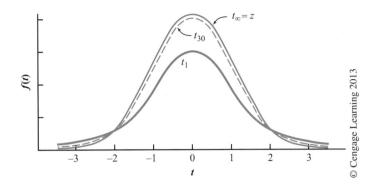

Figure 7.4 t distribution for 1, 30, and ∞ degrees of freedom along with its originator.

William S. Gosset
(1876–1937)

Student's t distribution

than it should be. This will mean that the t formula is more likely than not to produce a larger answer (in absolute terms) than we would have obtained if we had solved for z using the true but unknown value of σ^2 itself. (You can see this in Figure 7.3, where more than half of the observations fall to the left of σ^2.) As a result, it would not be fair to treat the answer as a z score and use the table of z. To do so would give us too many "significant" results—that is, we would make more than 5% Type I errors. (For example, when we were calculating z, we rejected H_0 at the .05 level of significance whenever z exceeded ± 1.96. If we create a situation in which H_0 is true, repeatedly draw samples of $n = 5$, and use s^2 in place of σ^2, we will obtain a value of ± 1.96 or greater more than 10% of the time. The $t_{.05}$ cutoff in this case is ± 2.776.)[5]

The solution to our problem was supplied in 1908 by William Gosset,[6] who worked for the Guinness Brewing Company, published under the pseudonym of Student, and wrote several extremely important papers in the early 1900s. Gosset showed that if the data are sampled from a normal distribution, using s^2 in place of σ^2 would lead to a particular sampling distribution, now generally known as **Student's t distribution**. As a result of Gosset's work, all we have to do is substitute s^2, denote the answer as t, and evaluate t with respect to its own distribution, much as we evaluated z with respect to the normal distribution.

The t distribution is tabled in Appendix t and examples of the actual distribution of t for various sample sizes are shown graphically in Figure 7.4.

As you can see from Figure 7.4, the distribution of t varies as a function of the degrees of freedom, which for the moment we will define as one less than the number of observations in the sample. As $n \Rightarrow \infty$, $p(s^2 < \sigma^2) \Rightarrow p(s^2 > \sigma^2)$. (The symbol $\Rightarrow$ is read "approaches.") Since the skewness of the sampling distribution of s^2 disappears as the number of degrees of freedom increases, the tendency for s to underestimate σ will also disappear. Thus, for an infinitely large number of degrees of freedom, t will be normally distributed and equivalent to z.

The test of one sample mean against a known population mean, which we have just performed, is based on the assumption that the sample was drawn from a normally distributed population. This assumption is required primarily because Gosset derived the t distribution

---

[5] A program that allows you to vary the sample size and see the difference in rejection rates using the t distribution and the normal distribution can be found at the book's Web site and is named Sampdistt.R. For example, using $n = 10$ will result in rejecting H_0 about 4.66% of the time using the tabled value of $t = \pm 2.262$, but 7.46% of the time using the standard z cutoff of ± 1.96.

[6] You would think that someone as important to statistics as William Sealy Gosset would at least get his named spelled correctly. But almost exactly half of the books I checked spelled it "Gossett." The people I most trust spell it with one "t". You can find an interesting biography of Gosset at http://en.wikipedia.org/wiki/William_Sealy_Gosset

assuming that the mean and variance are independent, which they are with a normal distribution. In practice, however, our t statistic can reasonably be compared to the t distribution whenever the sample size is sufficiently large to produce a nearly normal sampling distribution of the mean. Most people would suggest that an n of 25 or 30 is "sufficiently large" for most situations and for many situations it can be considerably smaller than that.

Degrees of Freedom

I have mentioned that the t distribution is a function of the degrees of freedom (df). For the one-sample case, $df = n - 1$; the one degree of freedom has been lost because we used the sample mean in calculating s^2. To be more precise, we obtained the variance (s^2) by calculating the deviations of the observations from their own mean ($X - \overline{X}$), rather than from the population mean ($X - \mu$). Because the sum of the deviations about the sample mean $\left[\sum(X - \overline{X})\right]$ is always zero, only $n - 1$ of the deviations are free to vary (the nth deviation is determined if the sum of the deviations is to be zero).

Psychomotor Abilities of Low-Birthweight Infants

An example drawn from an actual study of low-birthweight (LBW) infants will be useful at this point because that same general study can serve to illustrate both this particular t test and other t tests to be discussed later in the chapter. Nurcombe et al. (1984) reported on an intervention program for the mothers of LBW infants. These infants present special problems for their parents because they are (superficially) unresponsive and unpredictable, in addition to being at risk for physical and developmental problems. The intervention program was designed to make mothers more aware of their infants' signals and more responsive to their needs, with the expectation that this would decrease later developmental difficulties often encountered with LBW infants. The study included three groups of infants: an LBW experimental group, an LBW control group, and a normal-birthweight (NBW) group. Mothers of infants in the last two groups did not receive the intervention treatment.

One of the dependent variables used in this study was the Psychomotor Development Index (PDI) of the Bayley Scales of Infant Development. This scale was first administered to all infants in the study when they were 6 months old. Because we would not expect to see differences in psychomotor development between the two LBW groups as early as 6 months, it makes some sense to combine the data from the two groups and ask whether LBW infants in general are significantly different from the normative population mean of 100 usually found with this index.

The data for the LBW infants on the PDI are presented in Table 7.1. Included in this table are a stem-and-leaf display and a boxplot. These two displays are important for examining the general nature of the distribution of the data and for searching for the presence of outliers.

From the stem-and-leaf display, we can see that the data, although certainly not normally distributed, at least are not too badly skewed. In this case the lack of skewness is important, because it means that the sampling distribution of the mean will approach a normal distribution more quickly. They are, however, thick in the tails, which can be seen in the accompanying Q-Q plot. Given our sample size (56), it is reasonable to assume that the sampling distribution of the mean would be reasonably normal, although the Q-Q plot would give me pause if the sample size were small.[7] One interesting and unexpected finding that

---

[7] A simple resampling study (not shown) demonstrates that the sampling distribution of the mean for a population of this shape would be very close to normal. You can see a demonstration of this named BootstrapMeans.R at the book's Web site.

Table 7.1   Data and Plots for LBW infants on Psychomotor Development Index (PDI)

Raw Data			
96	120	112	100
125	96	86	124
89	104	116	89
127	89	89	124
102	104	120	102
112	92	92	102
120	124	83	116
108	96	108	96
92	108	108	95
120	86	92	100
104	100	120	120
89	92	102	98
92	98	100	108
89	117	112	126

Stem-and-Leaf Display	
Stem	Leaf
8*	3
8.	6 6 9 9 9 9 9 9
9*	2 2 2 2 2 2
9.	5 6 6 6 6 8 8
10*	0 0 0 0 2 2 2 2 4 4 4
10.	8 8 8 8 8
11*	2 2 2
11.	6 6 7
12*	0 0 0 0 0 0 4 4 4
12.	5 6 7

Mean = 104.125
S.D = 12.584
$N = 56$

Boxplot

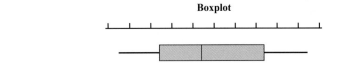

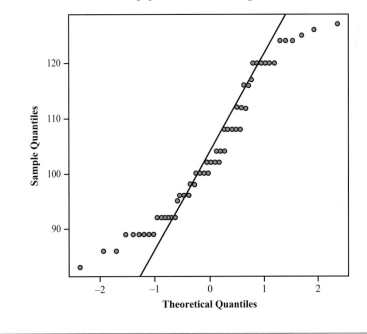

Q-Q Plot of Low-Birthweight Data

is apparent from the stem-and-leaf display is the prevalence of certain scores. For example, there are five scores of 108, but no other scores between 104 and 112. Similarly, there are six scores of 120, but no other scores between 117 and 124. Notice also that, with the exception of six scores of 89, there is a relative absence of odd numbers. A complete analysis of the data requires that we at least notice these oddities and try to track down their source. It would be worthwhile to examine the scoring process to see whether there is a reason why scores often tended to fall in bunches. It is probably an artifact of the way raw scores are converted to scale scores, but it is worth checking. (In fact, if you check the scoring manual, you will find that these peculiarities are to be expected.) The fact that Tukey's exploratory data analysis (EDA) procedures lead us to notice these peculiarities is one of the great virtues of these methods. Finally, from the boxplot we can see that there are no serious outliers we need to worry about, which makes our task noticeably easier.

From the data in Table 7.1, we can see that the mean PDI score for our LBW infants is 104.125. The norms for the PDI indicate that the population mean should be 100. Given the data, a reasonable first question concerns whether the mean of our LBW sample departs significantly from a population mean of 100. The t test is designed to answer this question.

From our formula for t and from the data, we have

$$t = \frac{\overline{X} - \mu}{s_{\overline{X}}} = \frac{\overline{X} - \mu}{\dfrac{s}{\sqrt{n}}}$$

$$= \frac{104.125 - 100}{\dfrac{12.584}{\sqrt{56}}} = \frac{4.125}{1.682}$$

$$= 2.45$$

This value will be a member of the t distribution on $56 - 1 = 55$ df if the null hypothesis is true—that is, if the data were sampled from a population with $\mu = 100$.

A t value of 2.45 in and of itself is not particularly meaningful unless we can evaluate it against the sampling distribution of t. For this purpose, the critical values of t are presented in Appendix t. In contrast to z, a different t distribution is defined for each possible number of degrees of freedom. Like the chi-square distribution, the tables of t differ in form from the table of the normal distribution (z) because instead of giving the area above and below each specific value of t, which would require too much space, the table instead gives those values of t that cut off particular critical areas—for example, the .05 and .01 levels of significance. Because we want to work at the two-tailed .05 level, we will want to know what value of t cuts off $5/2 = 2.5\%$ in each tail. These critical values are generally denoted $t_{\alpha/2}$ or, in this case, $t_{.025}$. From the table of the t distribution in Appendix t, an abbreviated version of which is shown in Table 7.2, we find that the critical value of $t_{.025}$ (rounding to 50 df for purposes of the table) $= 2.009$. (This is sometimes written as $t_{.025}(50) = 2.009$ to indicate the degrees of freedom.) Because the obtained value of t, written t_{obt}, is greater than $t_{.025}$, we will reject H_0 at $\alpha = .05$, two-tailed, that our sample came from a population of observations with $\mu = 100$. Instead, we will conclude that our sample of LBW children differed from the general population of children on the PDI. In fact, their mean was statistically significantly *above* the normative population mean. This points out the advantage of using two-tailed tests, because we would have expected this group to score below the normative mean. This might also suggest that we check our scoring procedures to make sure we are not systematically overscoring our subjects. In fact, however, a number of other studies using the PDI have reported similarly high means. (For an interesting nine-year follow-up of this study, see Achenbach, C. T. Howell, Aoki, and Rauh (1993).)

NOTE

Most of the tests that we will examine in this book only produce positive values of the test statistic—we saw that with the chi-square test and we will see it again with the F in the analysis of variance. But t can produce either positive or negative results, and we want to reject the null hypothesis whether our obtained t is too large or too small. This can lead to confusing notation for a two-tailed test. I represented the critical value for a two-tailed test as $t_{.025}(50) = 2.009$ above. In other words, 2.009 cuts off the upper 2.5% of the t distribution for 50 df and due to symmetry we know that -2.009 cuts off the lower 2.5%. But the other way that I could write it is to write $t_{.05}(50) = \pm 2.009$, meaning that –2.009 cuts of 2.5% and +2.009 cuts off 2.5% so that ± 2.009 cuts off $2.5 + 2.5 = 5\%$. Either way is correct. I try to be consistent, but I'm afraid that consistency is not my strong suit. I'll aim for $t_{.025}(df) = 2.009$, but sometimes I forget. Unless I specifically say otherwise, all tests in this book will be at $\alpha = .05$ (two-tailed), so it is the positive value of the two-tailed cutoff that I will report. (The other cutoff is just the negative value.)

Table 7.2   Percentage points of the t distribution

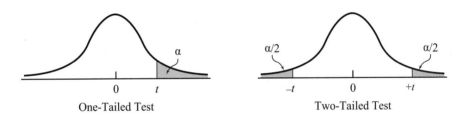

One-Tailed Test   Two-Tailed Test

				Level of Significance for One-Tailed Test				
	.25	.20	.15	.10	.05	.025	.01	.005	.0005
					Level of Significance for Two-Tailed Test				
df	.50	.40	.30	.20	.10	.05	.02	.01	.001
1	1.000	1.376	1.963	3.078	6.314	12.706	31.821	63.657	636.62
2	0.816	1.061	1.386	1.886	2.920	4.303	6.965	9.925	31.599
3	0.765	0.978	1.250	1.638	2.353	3.182	4.541	5.841	12.924
4	0.741	0.941	1.190	1.533	2.132	2.776	3.747	4.604	8.610
5	0.727	0.920	1.156	1.476	2.015	2.571	3.365	4.032	6.869
6	0.718	0.906	1.134	1.440	1.943	2.447	3.143	3.707	5.959
7	0.711	0.896	1.119	1.415	1.895	2.365	2.998	3.499	5.408
8	0.706	0.889	1.108	1.397	1.860	2.306	2.896	3.355	5.041
9	0.703	0.883	1.100	1.383	1.833	2.262	2.821	3.250	4.781
10	0.700	0.879	1.093	1.372	1.812	2.228	2.764	3.169	4.587
...	...	...	...	...	...	...	...	...	...
30	0.683	0.854	1.055	1.310	1.697	2.042	2.457	2.750	3.646
40	0.681	0.851	1.050	1.303	1.684	2.021	2.423	2.704	3.551
50	0.679	0.849	1.047	1.299	1.676	**2.009**	2.403	2.678	3.496
100	0.677	0.845	1.042	1.290	1.660	1.984	2.364	2.626	3.390
∞	0.674	0.842	1.036	1.282	1.645	1.960	2.326	2.576	3.291

Source: The entries in this table were computed by the author.

Things Are Changing

Contrary to what most people expect, statistical procedures do in fact change over time. This means that in a few years you will see things in professional papers that you never saw in your textbook. (I have made mention of this before and will again.) This is a good place to illustrate one of those movements because it shows you what is coming and it illustrates the issue of running a *t* test when the data are not normally distributed.

The biggest changes have come about due to the incredible speed of computer software. We can now carry out actual calculations when a few years ago we had to say "imagine that you could …" For example, in describing the *t* test we could say "Imagine that you had a normally distributed population. Imagine further that we drew a huge number of samples from that distribution, calculated *t* for each sample, and plotted the results. That would be the sampling distribution of *t*." Well, what if we don't have a normally distributed population, but instead had one with a nonnormal distribution like that in Table 7.1. Suppose that I had a huge population that was shaped exactly like the (nonnormal) distribution in Table 7.1. In other words it is higher in the shoulders than the normal distribution. We could create this population by duplicating each score in our sample a great many times, and, at the same time, adjusting this population mean so that it equals 100, the mean under the null hypothesis. (Remember that I have forced $\mu = 100$, so I have a distribution for which I know that the null hypothesis is true.) What I have really done instead is not to create that huge population, but to sample *with replacement* from the original data. This has exactly the same effect and is certainly much easier.

Now suppose that we draw a random sample of 56 observations from that population and compute the mean of that sample. Then we repeat this process 10,000 times. We can then ask what percentage of those means was greater than 104.125, the mean that we found in our original sample. If only a small percentage of our resampled means exceed 104.125, we can reject the null hypothesis because a mean of 104.125 would rarely occur if the population mean truly was 100. I actually went one step further by calculating the *t* statistic for each sample rather than just the mean for each sample. This doesn't really change anything, because if a sample mean is greater than 104.125, the corresponding *t* value will be greater than 2.4529. I did this so that I could plot both the resampled distribution of *t*, which does not depend on normality, and Student's theoretical sampling distribution of *t*, which does. The results are shown in Figure 7.5, where I have superimposed the theoretical sampling distribution of *t* for 55 *df* on top of the histogram of the *t* values that I obtained. Whether I calculate the probability of $t \geq \pm 2.4529$ or calculate the proportion of sample means that were more extreme than 104.125, the probability is .0146, meaning that we can reject the null hypothesis.

bootstrapping   What I have done in this example is normally referred to as **bootstrapping**. There are other ways of doing resampling, and we will see them as we go along, but for the bootstrap you sample with replacement from the obtained data, which has the effect of sampling from an infinite population of exactly the same shape as your sample. Bootstrapping is usually done to estimate the variability of some statistic over repeated sampling, but it can be used, as we have here, to test some hypothesis. I took the space to give this example because it is becoming common for statistical software to offer a checkbox option like "simulate," "bootstrap," "resample," or "randomize," all of which are doing something along the general lines of what I have done here. It is perfectly conceivable that 20 years from now we will think of Student's *t* test as "quaint."[8]

---

[8] There are other, and better, ways of using resampling in place of a standard *t* test, and I will come to those. For now I am simply trying to show that we have alternatives and to describe a way of going about solving the problem in a way that seems logical.

Distribution of Resampled Values

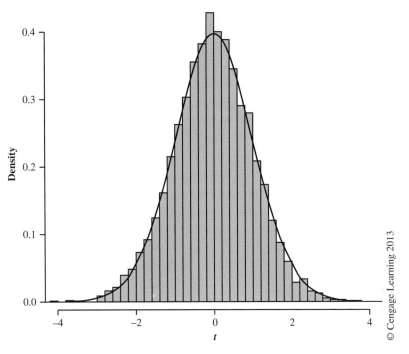

Figure 7.5   Empirical sampling distribution of t for low birth-weight example with theoretical t distribution superimposed

The Moon Illusion

It will be useful to consider a second example, this one taken from a classic paper by Kaufman and Rock (1962) on the moon illusion.[9] The moon illusion has fascinated psychologists for years, and refers to the fact that when we see the moon near the horizon, it appears to be considerably larger than when we see it high in the sky. Kaufman and Rock hypothesized that this illusion could be explained on the basis of the greater *apparent* distance of the moon when it is at the horizon. As part of a very complete series of experiments, the authors initially sought to estimate the moon illusion by asking subjects to adjust a variable "moon" that appeared to be on the horizon so as to match the size of a standard "moon" that appeared at its zenith, or vice versa. (In these measurements, they used not the actual moon but an artificial one created with special apparatus.) One of the first questions we might ask is whether this apparatus really produces a moon illusion—that is, whether a larger setting is required to match a horizon moon or a zenith moon. The following data for 10 subjects are taken from Kaufman and Rock's paper and present the ratio of the diameter of the variable and standard moons. A ratio of 1.00 would indicate no illusion, whereas a ratio other than 1.00 would represent an illusion. (For example, a ratio of 1.50 would mean that the horizon moon appeared to have a diameter 1.50 times the diameter of the zenith moon.) Evidence in support of an illusion would require that we reject $H_0: \mu = 1.00$ in favor of $H_0: \mu \neq 1.00$. (We have here a somewhat unusual situation where the null hypothesis posits a population mean other than 0. That does not create any problem as long as we enter the correct value for m in our formula.)

---

[9] A more recent paper on this topic by Lloyd Kaufman and his son James Kaufman was published in the January 2000 issue of the *Proceedings of the National Academy of Sciences.*

For these data, $n = 10$, $\overline{X} = 1.463$, and $s = 0.341$. A t test on $H_0: \mu = 1.00$ is given by

$$t = \frac{\overline{X} - \mu}{s_{\overline{X}}} = \frac{\overline{X} - \mu}{\dfrac{s}{\sqrt{n}}}$$

$$= \frac{1.463 - 1.000}{\dfrac{0.341}{\sqrt{10}}} = \frac{0.463}{0.108}$$

$$= 4.29$$

From Appendix t, with $10 - 1 = 9$ df for a two-tailed test at $\alpha = .05$, the critical value of $t_{.025}(9) = 2.262$. The obtained value of t was 4.29. Because $4.29 > 2.262$, we can reject H_0 at $\alpha = .05$ and conclude that the true mean ratio under these conditions is not equal to 1.00. In fact, it is greater than 1.00, which is what we would expect on the basis of our experience. (It is always comforting to see science confirm what we have all known since childhood, but in this case the results also indicate that Kaufman and Rock's experimental apparatus performed as it should.) For those who like technology, a probability calculator at http://www.danielsoper.com/statcalc/calc40.aspx gives the two-tailed probability as .001483.

Confidence Interval on μ

Confidence intervals are a useful way to convey the meaning of an experimental result that goes beyond the simple hypothesis test. The data on the moon illusion offer an excellent example of a case in which we are particularly interested in estimating the true value of μ—in this case, the true ratio of the perceived size of the horizon moon to the perceived size of the zenith moon. The sample mean ($\overline{X}$), as you already know, is an unbiased estimate of m. When we have one specific estimate of a parameter, we call this a **point estimate**. There are also interval estimates, which are attempts to set limits that have a high probability of encompassing the true (population) value of the mean [the mean (μ) of a whole population of observations]. What we want here are **confidence limits** on μ. These limits enclose what is called a **confidence interval**.[10] In Chapter 3, we saw how to set "probable limits" on an observation. A similar line of reasoning will apply here, where we attempt to set confidence limits on a parameter.

point estimate

confidence limits

confidence
interval

If we want to set limits that are likely to include μ given the data at hand, what we really want is to ask how large, or small, the true value of μ could be without causing us to reject H_0 if we ran a t test on the obtained sample mean. For example, when we tested the null hypothesis about the moon illusion that $\mu = 1.00$ we rejected that hypothesis. What if we tested the null hypothesis that $\mu = 0.93$? We would again reject that null. We can keep decreasing the value of μ to the point where we just barely do not reject H_0, and that is the smallest value of μ for which we would be likely to obtain our data at $p \geq .025$. Then we could start with larger values of μ (e.g., 2.2) and keep increasing μ until we again just barely fail to reject H_0. That is the largest value of μ for which we would expect to obtain the data at $p \geq .025$. Now any estimate of μ that fell between those lower and upper limits would lead us to retain the null hypothesis. Although we could do things this way, there is a shortcut that makes life easier. And it will come to the same answer.

---

[10] We often speak of "confidence limits" and "confidence interval" as if they were synonymous. The pretty much are, except that the limits are the end points of the interval. Don't be confused when you see them used interchangeably.

An easy way to see what we are doing is to start with the formula for t for the one-sample case:

$$t = \frac{\overline{X} - \mu}{s_{\overline{X}}} = \frac{\overline{X} - \mu}{\dfrac{s}{\sqrt{n}}}$$

From the moon illusion data we know $\overline{X} = 1.463$, $s = 0.341$, $n = 10$. We also know that the critical two-tailed value for t at $\alpha = .05$ is $t_{.025}(9) = 2.262$ [or $t_{.05}(9) = \pm 2.262$]. We will substitute these values in the formula for t, but this time we will solve for the μ associated with this value of t instead of the other way around.

$$t = \frac{\overline{X} - \mu}{\dfrac{s}{\sqrt{n}}} \qquad \pm 2.262 = \frac{1.463 - \mu}{\dfrac{0.341}{\sqrt{10}}} = \frac{1.463 - \mu}{0.108}$$

Rearranging to solve for μ, we have

$$\mu = \pm 2.262(0.108) + 1.463 = \pm 0.244 + 1.463$$

Using the $+0.244$ and -0.244 separately to obtain the upper and lower limits for μ, we have

$$\mu_{\text{upper}} = +0.244 + 1.463 = 1.707$$
$$\mu_{\text{lower}} = -0.244 + 1.463 = 1.219$$

and thus we can write the 95% confidence limits as 1.219 and 1.707 and the confidence interval as

$$CI_{.95} = 1.219 \leq \mu \leq 1.707$$

Testing a null hypothesis about any value of μ outside these limits would lead to rejection of H_0, while testing a null hypothesis about any value of μ inside those limits would not lead to rejection. The general expression is

$$CI_{1-\alpha} = \overline{X} \pm t_{\alpha/2}(s_{\overline{X}}) = \overline{X} \pm t_{\alpha/2}\frac{s}{\sqrt{n}}$$

We have a 95% confidence interval because we used the two-tailed critical value of t at $\alpha = .05$. For the 99% limits we would take $t_{.01/2} = t_{.005} = 3.250$. Then the 99% confidence interval is

$$CI_{.99} = \overline{X} \pm t_{.01/2}(s_{\overline{X}}) = 1.463 \pm 3.250(0.108) = 1.112 \leq \mu \leq 1.814$$

But What Is a Confidence Interval?

So what does it mean to say that the 95% confidence interval is $1.219 \leq \mu \leq 1.707$? For seven editions of each of two books I have worried and fussed about this question. It is very tempting to say that the probability is .95 that the interval 1.219 to 1.707 includes the true mean ratio for the moon illusion, and the probability is .99 that the interval 1.112 to 1.814 includes μ. However, most statisticians would object to the statement of a confidence limit expressed in this way. They would argue that *before the experiment is run and the calculations are made, an interval *of the form*

$$\overline{X} \pm t_{.025}(s_{\overline{X}})$$

has a probability of .95 of encompassing μ. However, μ is a fixed (though unknown) quantity, and once the data are in, the specific interval 1.219 to 1.707 either includes the value of μ ($p = 1.00$) or it does not ($p = .00$). This group would insist that we say "An interval constructed in the way that we have constructed this one has a probability of .95 of containing μ." That sounds almost the same, but not quite, and this group of people is quite adamant in their position. (Good (1999) has made the point that we place our confidence in the *method*, and not in the *interval*, and that statement makes a lot of sense. Put in slightly different form,

$$\overline{X} \pm t_{.025}(s_{\overline{X}})$$

is a random variable (it will vary from one experiment to the next), but the specific interval 1.219 to 1.707 is not a random variable and therefore does not have a probability associated with it.) On the other hand, Bayesian statisticians, who conceive of probability in terms of personal belief, are perfectly happy with saying that the probability is .95 that μ **credible interval**   lies between 1.219 and 1.707, although they name the interval the credible interval. In some ways the argument is very petty and looks like we are needlessly splitting hairs, but in other ways it reflects strongly held beliefs on the nature of probability. I have finally decided that for teaching purposes I'm going to go with the Bayesians.[11] Going with the traditionalists requires such convoluted sentences that you look like you are trying to confuse rather than clarify. They will probably take my statistics badge away, but they have to catch me first. For a good discussion of this issue I recommend Dracup (2005). See also Masson and Loftus (2003).

Note that neither the 95% nor the 99% confidence intervals that I computed include the value of 1.00, which represents no illusion. We already knew this for the 95% confidence interval because we had rejected that null hypothesis when we ran our t test at that significance level.

I should add another way of looking at the interpretation of confidence limits. The parameter μ is not a variable—it does not jump around from experiment to experiment. Rather, μ is a constant, and the interval is what varies from experiment to experiment. Thus, we can think of the parameter as a stake and the experimenter, in computing confidence limits, as tossing rings at it. Ninety-five percent of the time a ring of specified width will encircle the parameter; 5% of the time, it will miss. A confidence statement is a statement of the probability that the ring has been on target; it is not a statement of the probability that the target (parameter) landed in the ring.

A graphic demonstration of confidence limits is shown in Figure 7.6. To generate this figure, I drew 25 samples of $n = 4$ from a population with a mean (μ) of 5. For every sample, a 95% confidence limit on μ was calculated and plotted. For example, the limits produced from the first sample (the top horizontal line) were approximately 4.46 and 5.72, whereas those for the second sample were 4.83 and 5.80. Because in this case we know that the value of μ equals 5, I have drawn a vertical line at that point. Notice that the limits for samples 12 and 14 do not include $\mu = 5$. We would expect that 95% confidence limits would encompass μ 95 times out of 100. Therefore, two misses out of 25 seems reasonable. Notice also that the confidence intervals vary in width. This variability is due to the fact that the width of an interval is a function of the standard deviation of the sample, and some samples have larger standard deviations than others.

---

[11] Several highly respected statisticians phrase the confidence interval the way that I do, and they don't even blush when they do so.

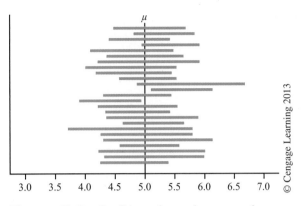

Figure 7.6   Confidence intervals computed on 25 samples from a population with $\mu = 5$.

Identifying Extreme Cases

In Chapter 3 we saw that we can use the properties of the normal distribution to identify extreme cases. For example, if we were working with the Achenbach Child Behavior Checklist we treat its mean (50) and standard deviation (10) as population parameters. We will identify children scoring more than 1.64 standard deviations above the mean as extreme. Then

$$z = \frac{X - \mu}{\sigma}$$

$$1.64 = \frac{X - 50}{10}$$

$$X = 1.64(10) + 50 = 64.4$$

Anyone scoring above 64.4 on the Behavior Problem Checklist is a candidate for treatment.

However, we could solve the problem this way only because Tom Achenbach's normative samples are so large that it is very reasonable to act as if $\mu = 50$ and $\sigma = 10$. We could do the same thing with something like the Beck Depression Inventory or the Wechsler IQ, whose norms are also based on huge samples. But there are many situations, especially in neuropsychology, where our normative sample is quite small. For example, the Auditory Verbal Learning test (Geffen, Moar, O'Hanlon, Clark, and Geffen (1990)) has norms based on 153 cases, but Gender and Age have an important influence on the scores (ages ranged from 16 to 86), and when you break the norms against those variables the modal sample size is 10. Taking the mean and standard deviation of 10 scores and treating them as population parameters seems a little silly. (Remember that the sampling distribution of the variance in small samples is badly positively skewed. We are likely to underestimate s and thus calculate an inappropriately large z.) Similarly, there has been a large increase in recent years with single case studies, and such studies take a very long time to build up norms with large samples. So what do we do instead?

Crawford and Howell (1998) addressed this problem and showed that we can substitute the t distribution for z. (See also Crawford, Garthwaite, and Howell (2009).) We take the mean $\overline{X}$ and standard deviation (s) of the small normative sample, and we treat the individual's score as a sample of $n = 1$. We then solve for t by

$$t = \frac{X_1 - \overline{X}}{s\sqrt{\dfrac{n + 1}{n}}}$$

This *t* is on *n–1 df*.

For example, suppose that we have a normative sample of 11 cases on a test of spatial memory, and that its mean ($\overline{X}$) = 45 and its standard deviation (*s*) = 9. We have a patient with a score of 31. Then

$$t = \frac{X_1 - \overline{X}}{s\sqrt{\dfrac{n+1}{n}}} = \frac{31 - 45}{9\sqrt{\dfrac{11+1}{11}}} = \frac{14}{9\sqrt{\dfrac{12}{11}}} = \frac{14}{9.4} = 1.49$$

If we will consider a case to be extreme if its score is less than 95% of the normative sample, we want a one-tailed test on $(n - 1) = 10$ *df*. The critical value of $t_{.05(10)} = 1.81$, so our case would not be considered extreme.

It is important to note that we are not asking if our case came from a population with a mean less than the mean of the normative sample. We have only one case, and do not think of it coming from some putative population. What would that population be? We are, instead, asking about the probability that we would have one score from the normative population that would be as extreme as ours.

A Final Example: We Aren't Done with Therapeutic Touch

In the last chapter we discussed an example involving therapeutic touch, and I commented that I felt on slightly shaky grounds testing the null hypothesis with chi-square because of a possible lack of independence. So in this chapter we will see a different way to go about testing the null hypothesis. This is closer to the way the study's authors analyzed their data.

The therapeutic touch experiment involved 28 testing sessions in which each respondent made 10 decisions about which hand the experimenter held her hand over. This means that the respondent could have been correct between 0 and 10 trials. For chance performance we would predict an average of 5 correct trials out of 10. The actual data in terms of trials correct are shown below, followed by the analysis both by hand and using R or S-PLUS.

Subject	1	2	3	4	5	6	7	8	9	10	11	12	13	14
Correct	1	2	3	3	3	3	3	3	3	3	4	4	4	4

Subject	15	16	17	18	19	20	21	22	23	24	25	26	27	28
Correct	4	5	5	5	5	5	5	5	6	6	7	7	7	8

Mean = 4.393
s = 1.663
n = 28

$$t = \frac{\overline{X} - \mu}{\dfrac{s}{\sqrt{n}}} = \frac{4.393 - 5.00}{\dfrac{1.663}{\sqrt{28}}} = \frac{-0.607}{0.314} = -1.93$$

Computer printout using R

data: number.correct

$t = -1.9318$, *df* = 27, *p*–value = 0.06395

alternative hypothesis: true mean is not equal to 5

95 percent confidence interval:

3.747978   5.037737

sample estimates:

mean of *x*

4.392857

Here is a case where if respondents were performing at chance we would expect 5 correct trials out of 10. So we test the null hypothesis that $\mu = 5$, against the alternative hypothesis that $\mu \neq 5$. In this example, $t = -1.93$, $df = 27$, and $p = .064$, so we will not reject the null hypothesis. We have no evidence that respondents are performing at other than chance levels. In fact they are performing (nonsignificantly) below chance.

Although the test of significance answered our basic question, it would be useful to compute confidence limits on μ. These limits can be calculated as

$$CI = X \pm t_{.025}s_{\overline{X}}$$

$$= 4.393 \pm 2.052(0.314)$$

$$= 4.393 \pm 0.644$$

$$= 3.750 < \mu < 5.038$$

As expected, the confidence limit includes $\mu = 5.00$.

Using SPSS to Run One-Sample *t* Tests

We often solve statistical problems using a program such as SPSS to compute t values. Exhibit 7.1 shows how SPSS can be used to obtain a one-sample t test and confidence limits for the moon illusion data. To compute t for the moon illusion example you simply choose **Analyze/Compare Means/One Sample t Test** from the pull-down menus and then specify the dependent variable in the resulting dialog box. Notice that the SPSS's result for the t test agrees, within rounding error, with the value we obtained by hand. Notice also that SPSS computes the exact probability of a Type I error (the ρ **level**), rather than comparing t to a tabled value. Thus, whereas we concluded that the probability of a Type I error was *less than* .05, SPSS reveals that the actual probability is .0020. Most computer programs operate in this way.

ρ **level**

But there is a difference between the confidence limits we calculated by hand and those that SPSS produced in the printout, though both are correct. When I calculated the confidence limits by hand I calculated limits based on the mean moon illusion estimate, which was 1.463. But SPSS is examining the difference between 1.463 and an illusion mean of 1.00 (no illusion), and its confidence limits are on this *difference*. In other words I calculated limits around 1.463, whereas SPSS calculated limits around (1.463 – 1.00 = 0.463). Therefore the SPSS limits are 1.00 less than my limits. Once you realize that the two procedures are calculating something slightly different, the difference in the result is explained.[12]

7.4 Hypothesis Tests Applied to Means—Two Matched Samples

In Section 7.3 we considered the situation in which we had one sample mean ($\overline{X}$) and wished to test to see whether it was reasonable to believe that such a sample mean would have occurred if we had been sampling from a population with some specified mean (often denoted μ_0). Another way of phrasing this is to say that we were testing to determine whether the mean of the population from which we sampled (call it μ_1) was equal to some particular value given by the null hypothesis (μ_0). In this section we will consider the case

---

[12] SPSS will give you the confidence limits that I calculated if you use **Analyze, Descriptive statistics/Explorer**.

□ *Untitled1 [DataSet0] - SPSS Data Editor				
File Edit View Data Transform	**Analyze** Graphs Utilities Add-ons Window Help			

Menu shown:

Reports ▶
Descriptive Statistics ▶
Tables ▶
Compare Means ▶   →   Means...
General Linear Model ▶   →   One-Sample T Test...
Generalized Linear Models ▶   →   Independent-Samples T Test...
Mixed Models ▶   →   Paired-Samples T Test...
Correlate ▶   →   One-Way ANOVA...
Regression ▶
Loglinear ▶
Classify ▶
Data Reduction ▶
Scale ▶
Nonparametric Tests ▶
Time Series ▶
Survival ▶
Multiple Response ▶
Quality Control ▶
ROC Curve...

15 :

	Ratio	var
1	1.73	
2	1.00	
3	6.00	
4	2.03	
5	1.40	
6	.95	
7	1.13	
8	1.41	
9	1.73	
10	1.63	
11		
12		
13		
14		

One-Sample Statistics

	N	Mean	Std. Deviation	Std. Error Mean
Ratio	10	1.4630	.34069	.10773

One-Sample Test

Test Value = 1

	t	df	Sig. (2-tailed)	Mean Difference	95% Confidence Interval of the Difference	
					Lower	Upper
Ratio	4.298	9	.002	.46300	.2193	.7067

SPSS Inc.

Exhibit 7.1   SPSS for one-sample *t*-test and confidence limits

matched samples

repeated measures

related samples

matched-sample *t* test

in which we have two **matched samples** (often called **repeated measures**, when the same subjects respond on two occasions, or **related samples**, correlated samples, paired samples, or dependent samples) and wish to perform a test on the difference between their two means. In this case we want what is often called the **matched-sample *t* test**.

Treatment of Anorexia

Everitt, in Hand et al., 1994, reported on family therapy as a treatment for anorexia. There were 17 girls in this experiment, and they were weighed before and after treatment. The weights of the girls can be found in Table 7.3. The row of difference scores was obtained by subtracting the Before score from the After score, so that a negative difference represents weight *loss*, and a positive difference represents a *gain*.

Table 7.3   Data from Everitt on Weight Gain

ID	1	2	3	4	5	6	7	8	9	10
Before	83.8	83.3	86.0	82.5	86.7	79.6	76.9	94.2	73.4	80.5
After	95.2	94.3	91.5	91.9	100.3	76.7	76.8	101.6	94.9	75.2
Diff	11.4	11.0	5.5	9.4	13.6	−2.9	−0.1	7.4	21.5	−5.3

ID	11	12	13	14	15	16	17	Mean	St. Dev
Before	81.6	82.1	77.6	83.5	89.9	86.0	87.3	83.23	5.02
After	77.8	95.5	90.7	92.5	93.8	91.7	98.0	90.49	8.48
Diff	−3.8	13.4	13.1	9.0	3.9	5.7	10.7	7.26	7.16

© Cengage Learning 2013

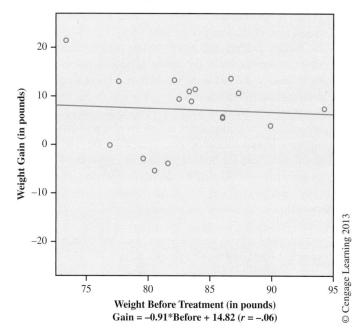

Weight Gain for Anorexia Data

Gain = −0.91*Before + 14.82 ($r = -.06$)

© Cengage Learning 2013

Figure 7.7   Relationship of weight before and after family therapy, for a group of 17 anorexic girls

One of the first things we should do, although it takes us away from *t* tests for a moment, is to plot the relationship between Before Treatment weight and weight gain, looking to see if there is, in fact, a relationship, and how linear that relationship is. Ideally we would like gain to be independent of initial weight. Such a plot is given in Figure 7.7. Notice that the relationship is basically linear, with a slope quite near 0.0. How much the girl weighed at the beginning of therapy did not seriously influence how much weight she gained or lost by the end of therapy. (We will discuss regression lines and slopes further in Chapter 9.)

The primary question we wish is ask is whether subjects gained weight as a result of the therapy sessions. We have an experimental problem here, because it is possible that weight gain resulted merely from the passage of time, and that therapy had nothing to do with it. However I know from other data in Everitt's experiment that a group that did not receive therapy did not gain weight over the same period of time, which strongly suggests that the simple passage of time was not an important variable. If you were to calculate the weight of these girls before and after therapy, the means would be 83.23 and 90.49 lbs, respectively, which translates to a gain of a little over 7 pounds. However, we still need to test to see whether this difference is likely to represent a true difference in population means or a chance difference. By this I mean that we need to test the null hypothesis that the mean *in the population* of Before scores is equal to the mean *in the population* of After scores. In other words, we are testing $H_0: \mu_A = \mu_B$.

Difference Scores

Although it would seem obvious to view the data as representing two samples of scores, one set obtained before the therapy program and one after, it is also possible, and very profitable, to transform the data into one set of scores—the set of differences between X_1 and

difference scores
gain scores

X_2 for each subject. These differences are called difference scores, or gain scores, and are shown in the third row of Table 7.1. They represent the degree of weight gain between one measurement session and the next—presumably as a result of our intervention. If in fact the therapy program had *no* effect (i.e., if H_0 is true), the average weight would not change from session to session. By chance some participants would happen to have a higher weight on X_2 than on X_1, and some would have a lower weight, but *on the average* there would be no important difference.

If we now think of our data as being the set of difference scores, the null hypothesis becomes the hypothesis that the mean of a population of difference scores (denoted μ_D) equals 0. Because it can be shown that $\mu_D = \mu_1 - \mu_2$, we can write $H_0: \mu_D = \mu_1 - \mu_2 = 0$. But now we can see that we are testing a hypothesis using *one* sample of data (the sample of difference scores), and we already know how to do that.

The *t* Statistic

We are now at precisely the same place we were in the previous section when we had a sample of data and a null hypothesis ($\mu = 0$). The only difference is that in this case the data are difference scores, and the mean and the standard deviation are based on the differences. Recall that t was defined as the difference between a sample mean and a population mean, divided by the standard error of the mean. Then we have

$$t = \frac{\overline{D} - 0}{s_{\overline{D}}} = \frac{\overline{D} - 0}{\dfrac{s_D}{\sqrt{n}}}$$

where $\overline{D}$ and s_D are the mean and the standard deviation of the difference scores and n is the number of difference scores (i.e., the number of *pairs,* not the number of raw scores). From Table 7.3 we see that the mean difference score was 7.26, and the standard deviation of the differences was 7.16. For our data

$$t = \frac{\overline{D} - 0}{s_{\overline{D}}} = \frac{\overline{D} - 0}{\dfrac{s_D}{\sqrt{n}}} = \frac{7.26 - 0}{\dfrac{7.16}{\sqrt{17}}} = \frac{7.26}{1.74} = 4.18$$

Degrees of Freedom

The degrees of freedom for the matched-sample case are exactly the same as they were for the one-sample case. Because we are working with the difference scores, n will be equal to the number of differences (or the number of *pairs* of observations, or the number of *independent* observations—all of which amount to the same thing). Because the variance of these difference scores (s_D^2) is used as an estimate of the variance of a population of difference scores (σ_D^2) and because this sample variance is obtained using the sample mean ($\overline{D}$), we will lose one *df* to the mean and have $n - 1$ *df*. In other words, *df* = number of *pairs* minus 1.

We have 17 difference scores in this example, so we will have 16 degrees of freedom. From Appendix *t*, we find that for a two-tailed test at the .05 level of significance, $t_{.025}(16) = 2.12$. Our obtained value of t (4.18) exceeds 2.12, so we will reject H_0 and conclude that the difference scores were not sampled from a population of difference scores where $\mu_D = 0$. In practical terms this means that the subjects weighed significantly more after the intervention program than before. Although we would like to think that this means the program was successful, keep in mind the possibility that this could just be normal growth. The fact remains, however, that for whatever reason, the weights were sufficiently higher on the second occasion to allow us to reject $H_0: \mu_D = \mu_1 - \mu_2 = 0$.[13]

Confidence Intervals

The fact that we have a significant difference between the group means all is well and good, but it would be even better to have a confidence interval on that difference. To obtain this we do essentially the same thing we did with the one sample case. We take the equation for *t*, insert the critical value of *t* for 16 *df*, and solve for μ.

$$t = \frac{D - \mu}{s_D/\sqrt{n}}$$

$$\pm 2.12 = \frac{7.26 - \mu}{7.16/\sqrt{17}} = \frac{7.26 - \mu}{1.74}$$

$$\mu = \pm 2.12 \times 1.74 + 7.26 = \pm 3.69 + 7.26$$

$$7.26 - 3.69 \leq \mu \leq 7.26 + 3.69$$

$$3.57 \leq \mu \leq 10.95$$

Here we can see that even at the low end girls gained about 3.5 pounds, which, given a mean pre-treatment weight of 83.23, is a 4% gain.

The Moon Illusion Revisited

As a second example, we will return to the work by Kaufman and Rock (1962) on the moon illusion. An important hypothesis about the source of the moon illusion was put forth by Holway and Boring (1940), who suggested that there is an illusion because when the

---

[13] On October 19, 2010 the *New York Times* carried a report of a study by Lock, Le Grange, Agras, Moye, Bryson, and Jo (2010) that compared family therapy as a treatment for anorexia (called the Maudsley method) against an alternative therapy. Those authors found, as did Everitt, that family therapy was significantly more successful with a low rate of remission.

Table 7. 4   Magnitude of the moon illusion when zenith moon is viewed with eyes level and with eyes elevated

Observer	Eyes Elevated	Eyes Level	Difference (D)
1	1.65	1.73	−0.08
2	1.00	1.06	−0.06
3	2.03	2.03	0.00
4	1.25	1.40	−0.15
5	1.05	0.95	0.10
6	1.02	1.13	−0.11
7	1.67	1.41	0.26
8	1.86	1.73	0.13
9	1.56	1.63	−0.07
10	1.73	1.56	0.17

$$\overline{D} = 0.019$$
$$s_D = 0.137$$
$$s_{\overline{D}} = 0.043$$

moon is on the horizon, the observer looks straight at it with eyes level, whereas when it is at its zenith, the observer has to elevate his eyes as well as his head. Holway and Boring proposed that this difference in the elevation of the eyes was the cause of the illusion. Kaufman and Rock thought differently. To test Holway and Boring's hypothesis, Kaufman and Rock devised an apparatus that allowed them to present two artificial moons (one at the horizon and one at the zenith) and to control whether the subjects elevated their eyes to see the zenith moon. In one case, the subject was forced to put his head in such a position to see the zenith moon with eyes level (i.e., lying down). In the other case, the subject was forced to see the zenith moon with eyes raised. (The horizon moon was always viewed with eyes level.) In both cases, the dependent variable was the ratio of the perceived size of the horizon moon to the perceived size of the zenith moon (a ratio of 1.00 would represent no illusion). If Holway and Boring were correct, there should have been a greater illusion (larger ratio) in the eyes-elevated condition than in the eyes-level condition, although the moon was always perceived to be in the same place, the zenith. The actual data for this experiment are given in Table 7.4.

In this example, we want to test the *null* hypothesis that the means are equal under the two viewing conditions. Because we are dealing with related observations (each subject served under both conditions), we will work with the difference scores and test $H_0: \mu_D = 0$. Using a two-tailed test at $\alpha = .05$, the alternative hypothesis is $H_1: \mu_D \neq 0$.

From the formula for a t test on related samples, we have

$$t = \frac{\overline{D} - 0}{s_{\overline{D}}} = \frac{\overline{D} - 0}{\dfrac{s_D}{\sqrt{n}}}$$

$$= \frac{0.019 - 0}{\dfrac{0.137}{\sqrt{10}}} = \frac{0.019}{0.043}$$

$$= 0.44$$

From Appendix t, we find that $t_{.025}(9) = 2.262$. Since $t_{obt} = 0.44$ is less than 2.262, we will fail to reject H_0 and will decide that we have no evidence to suggest that the illusion is affected by the elevation of the eyes.[14] (In fact, these data also include a second test of Holway and Boring's hypothesis because they would have predicted that there would not be an illusion if subjects viewed the zenith moon with eyes level. On the contrary, the data reveal a considerable illusion under this condition. A test of the significance of the illusion with eyes level can be obtained by the methods discussed in the previous section, and the illusion is in fact statistically significant.)

Effect Size

In Chapter 6 we looked at effect size measures as a way of understanding the magnitude of the effect that we see in an experiment—as opposed to simply the statistical significance. When we are looking at the difference between two related measures we can, and should, also compute effect sizes. In practice, many journals are insisting on effect size estimates or similar statistics rather than just being satisfied with a *t* test, or even a confidence interval on the difference. In the case of matched samples there is a slight complication as we will see shortly.

d-Family of Measures

There are a number of different effect sizes measures that are often recommended, and for a complete coverage of this topic I suggest the reference by Kline (2004). As I did in Chapter 6, I am going to distinguish between measures based on differences between groups (the *d*-family) and measures based on correlations between variables (the *r*-family). However, in this chapter, I am not going to discuss the *r*-family measures, partly because I find them less informative and partly because they are more easily and logically discussed in Chapter 11 when we come to the analysis of variance. An interesting paper on *d*-family versus *r*-family measures is McGrath and Meyer (2006).

There is considerable confusion in the naming of measures, and for clarification on that score I refer the reader to Kline (2004). Here I will use the most common approach, which Kline points out is not quite technically correct, and refer to my measure as **Cohen's *d***. Measures proposed by Hedges and by Glass are very similar, and are often named almost interchangeably. They all relate to dividing a difference in means by a standard deviation.

Cohen's *d*

The data on treatment of anorexia offer a good example of a situation in which it is relatively easy to report on the difference in ways that people will understand. All of us step onto a scale occasionally, and we have some general idea of what it means to gain or lose five or ten pounds. So for Everitt's data, we could simply report that the difference was significant ($t = 4.18$, $p < .05$), and that girls gained an average of 7.26 pounds. For girls who started out weighing, on average, 83 pounds, that is a substantial gain. In fact, it might make sense to convert pounds gained to a percentage, and say that the girls increased their weight by $7.26/83.23 = 9\%$.

An alternative measure would be to report the gain in standard deviation units. This idea goes back to Cohen, who originally formulated the problem in terms of a statistic (*d*), where

$$d = \frac{\mu_1 - \mu_2}{\sigma}$$

---

[14] In the language favored by Jones and Tukey (2000), there probably is a small difference between the two viewing conditions, but we don't have enough evidence to tell us the sign of the difference.

In this equation the numerator is the difference between two population means, and the denominator is the standard deviation of either population. In our case, we can modify that slightly to let the numerator be the mean gain ($\mu_{\text{After}} - \mu_{\text{Before}}$), and the denominator is the population standard deviation *of the pretreatment weights*. (Notice that we use the standard deviation of pre-treatment weights rather than the standard deviation of the difference scores, which is what we used to calculate *t* and confidence intervals. This is important.) To put our computations in terms of statistics, rather than parameters, we substitute sample means and standard deviations instead of population values. This leaves us with

$$\hat{d} = \frac{\overline{X}_1 - \overline{X}_2}{s_{X_1}} = \frac{90.49 - 83.23}{5.02} = \frac{7.26}{5.02} = 1.45$$

I have put a "hat" over the *d* to indicate that we are calculating an estimate of *d*, and I have put the standard deviation of the pretreatment scores in the denominator. Our estimate tells us that, on average, the girls involved in family therapy gained nearly one-and-a-half standard deviations of pretreatment weights over the course of therapy.

In this particular example I find it easier to deal with the mean weight gain, rather than *d*, simply because I know something meaningful about weight. However, if this experiment had measured the girls' self-esteem, rather than weight, I would not know what to think if you said that they gained 7.26 self-esteem points, because that scale means nothing to me. I would be impressed, however, if you said that they gained nearly one-and-a-half standard deviation units in self-esteem.

The issue is not quite as simple as I have made it out to be, because there are alternative ways of approaching the problem. One way would be to use the average of the pre- and post-score standard deviations, rather than just the standard deviation of the pre-scores. However, when we are measuring gain it makes sense to me to measure it in the metric of the original weights because we are asking where the girls ended up relative to where they began. You may come across other situations where you would think that it makes more sense to use the average standard deviation.

It would be perfectly possible to use the standard deviation of the difference scores in the denominator for *d*, but we would be measuring something else entirely. Kline (2004) discusses this approach and concludes that "If our natural reference for thinking about scores on (some) measure is their original standard deviation, it makes most sense to report standardized mean change (using that standard deviation)." However the important point here is to keep in mind that such decisions often depend on substantive considerations in the particular research field, and there is no one measure that is uniformly best. There are many concepts in statistics that are pretty much fixed. For example, you calculate the confidence limits on the mean of a single sample in only one way. But there are many cases where the researcher has considerable flexibility in how to represent something, and that representation should be based on whatever makes the most sense for that particular experiment. Whatever you do, it is important to tell your reader what standard deviation you used.

More About Matched Samples

In many, but certainly not all, situations in which we use the matched-sample *t* test, we will have two sets of data from the same subjects. For example, we might ask each of 20 people to rate their level of anxiety before and after donating blood. Or we might record ratings of level of disability made using two different scoring systems for each of 20 disabled individuals to see whether one scoring system leads to generally lower assessments than does the other. In both examples, we would have 20 sets of numbers, two numbers for each person, and would expect these two sets of numbers to be related (or, in the terminology we will later adopt, to be correlated). Consider the blood-donation example. People differ widely in level of anxiety. Some seem to be anxious all of the time no matter what happens, and others just take things as they come and do not worry about anything. Thus, there should be a relationship between an individual's anxiety level before donating blood and her anxiety level after donating blood. In other words, if we know what a person's anxiety score was before donation, we can make a reasonable guess what it was after donation. Similarly, some people are severely disabled whereas others are only mildly disabled. If we know that a particular person received a high assessment using one scoring system, it is likely that he also received a relatively high assessment using the other system. The relationship between data sets does not have to be perfect—it probably never will be. The fact that we can make better-than-chance predictions is sufficient to classify two sets of data as matched or related.

In the two preceding examples, I chose situations in which each person in the study contributed two scores. Although this is the most common way of obtaining related samples, it is not the only way. For example, a study of marital relationships might involve asking husbands and wives to rate their satisfaction with their marriage, with the goal of testing to see whether wives are, on average, more or less satisfied than husbands. (You will see an example of just such a study in the exercises for this chapter.) Here each individual would contribute only one score, but the couple *as a unit* would contribute a pair of scores. It is reasonable to assume that if the husband is very dissatisfied with the marriage, his wife is probably also dissatisfied, and vice versa, thus causing their scores to be related.

Many experimental designs involve related samples. They all have one thing in common, and that is the fact that knowing one member of a pair of scores tells you something—maybe not much, but something—about the other member. Whenever this is the case, we say that the samples are matched.

Missing Data

Ideally, with matched samples we have a score on each variable for each case or pair of cases. If a subject participates in the pretest, she also participates in the posttest. If one member of a couple provides data, so does the other member. When we are finished collecting data, we have a complete set of paired scores. Unfortunately, experiments do not usually work out as cleanly as we would like.

Suppose, for example, that we want to compare scores on a checklist of children's behavior problems completed by mothers and fathers, with the expectation that mothers are more sensitive to their children's problems than are fathers, and thus will produce higher scores. Most of the time both parents will complete the form. But there might be 10 cases where the mother sent in her form but the father did not, and 5 cases where we have a form from the father but not from the mother. The normal procedure in this situation is to eliminate the 15 pairs of parents where we do not have complete data, and then run a matched-sample *t* test on the data that remain. This is the way almost everyone would analyze the data. In the case of the matched sample *t* test there is an alternative; however, that allows us to use all of the data if we are willing to assume that data are missing at random and not systematically. (By this I mean that we have to assume that we are not more likely to be missing Dad's data when the child is reported by Mom to have very few problems, nor are we less likely to be missing Dad's data for a very behaviorally disordered child.)

Bhoj (1978) proposed an ingenious test in which you basically compute a matched-sample *t* for those cases where both scores are present, then compute an additional independent group *t* (to be discussed next) between the scores of mothers without fathers and fathers without mothers, and finally combine the two *t* statistics. This combined *t* can then be evaluated against special tables. These tables are available in Wilcox (1986), and approximations to critical values of this combined statistic are discussed briefly in Wilcox (1987a). This test is sufficiently awkward that you would not use it simply because you are missing two or three observations. But it can be extremely useful when many pieces of data are missing. For a more extensive discussion, see Wilcox (1987b).

Using Computer Software for *t* Tests on Matched Samples

The use of almost any computer software to analyze matched samples can involve nothing more than using a compute command to create a variable that is the difference between the two scores we are comparing. We then run a simple one-sample *t* test to test the null hypothesis that those difference scores came from a population with a mean of 0. Alternatively, most software, such as SPSS, allows you to specify that you want a *t* on two related samples, and then to specify the two variables that represent those samples. Because this is very similar to what we have already done, I will not repeat that here.

Writing up the Results of a Dependent *t* Test

Suppose that we wish to write up the results of Everitt's study of family therapy for anorexia. We would want to be sure to include the relevant sample statistics ($\overline{X}$, s^2, and N), as well as the test of statistical significance. But we would also want to include confidence limits on the mean weight gain following therapy, and our effect size estimate (d). We might write

> Everitt ran a study on the effect of family therapy on weight gain in girls suffering from anorexia. He collected weight data on 17 girls before therapy, provided family therapy to the girls and their families, and then collected data on the girls' weight at the end of therapy.
>
> The mean weight gain for the $N = 17$ girls was 7.26 pounds, with a standard deviation of 7.16. A two-tailed *t*-test on weight gain was statistically significant ($t(16) = 4.18$, $p < .05$), revealing that on average the girls did gain weight over the course of therapy. A 95% confidence interval on mean weight gain was 3.57—10.95, which is a notable weight gain even at the low end of the interval. Cohen's $d = 1.45$, indicating that the girls' weight gain was nearly 1.5 standard deviations relative to their original pre-test weights. It would appear that family therapy has made an important contribution to the treatment of anorexia in this experiment.

7.5 Hypothesis Tests Applied to Means—Two Independent Samples

One of the most common uses of the *t* test involves testing the difference between the means of two independent groups. We might wish to compare the mean number of trials needed to reach criterion on a simple visual discrimination task for two groups of rats—one raised under normal conditions and one raised under conditions of sensory deprivation. Or we might wish to compare the mean levels of retention of a group of college students asked to recall active declarative sentences and a group asked to recall passive negative sentences. Or we might place subjects in a situation in which another person needed help; we could compare the latency of helping behavior when subjects were tested alone and when different subjects were tested in groups. In these cases we assume that subjects are randomly assigned to groups, although this is not always possible (e.g., comparing genders).

In conducting any experiment with two independent groups, we would most likely find that the two sample means differed by some amount. The important question, however, is whether this difference is sufficiently large to justify the conclusion that the two samples were drawn from different populations. To put this in the terms preferred by Jones and Tukey (2000): Is the difference sufficiently large for us to identify the direction of the difference in population means? Before we consider a specific example, however, we will need to examine the sampling distribution of differences between means and the *t* test that results from it.

Distribution of Differences Between Means

sampling distribution of differences between means

When we are interested in testing for a difference between the mean of one population (μ_1) and the mean of a second population (μ_2), we will be testing a null hypothesis of the form $H_0: \mu_1 - \mu_2 = 0$ or, equivalently, $\mu_1 = \mu_2$. Because the test of this null hypothesis involves the difference between independent sample means, it is important that we digress for a moment and examine the **sampling distribution of differences between means**. Suppose that we have two populations labeled X_1 and X_2 with means μ_1 and μ_2 and variances σ_1^2 and σ_2^2. We now draw pairs of samples of size n_1 from population X_1 and of size n_2 from population X_2, and record the means and the difference between the means for each pair of samples. Because we are sampling independently from each population, the sample means will be independent. (Means are paired only in the trivial and presumably irrelevant sense of being drawn at the same time.) The results of an infinite number of replications of this procedure are presented schematically in Figure 7.8. In the lower portion of this figure, the first two columns represent the sampling distributions of X_1 and X_2, and the third column represents the sampling distribution of mean differences ($\overline{X}_1 - \overline{X}_2$). We are most interested in the third column because we are concerned with testing differences between means. The mean of this distribution can be shown to equal $\mu_1 - \mu_2$. The variance of this distribution of differences is given by what is commonly called the **variance sum law**, a limited form of which states

variance sum law

> The variance of a sum or difference of two *independent* variables is equal to the sum of their variances.[15]

We know from the central limit theorem that the variance of the distribution of $\overline{X}_1$ is σ_1^2/n_1 and the variance of the distribution of $\overline{X}_2$ is σ_2^2/n_2. Because the variables (sample means) are independent, the variance of the difference of these two variables is the sum of their variances. Thus

$$\sigma_{\overline{X}_1 - \overline{X}_2}^2 = \sigma_{\overline{X}_1}^2 + \sigma_{\overline{X}_2}^2 = \frac{\sigma_1^2}{n_1} + \frac{\sigma_2^2}{n_2}$$

Having found the mean and the variance of a set of differences between means, we know most of what we need to know. The general form of the sampling distribution of mean differences is presented in Figure 7.9.

The final point to be made about this distribution concerns its shape. An important theorem in statistics states that the sum or difference of two independent normally distributed

---

[15] The complete form of the law omits the restriction that the variables must be independent and states that the variance of their sum or difference is $\sigma_{X_1 \pm X_2}^2 = \sigma_1^2 + \sigma_2^2 \pm 2\rho\sigma_1\sigma_2$ where the notation $\pm$ is interpreted as plus when we are speaking of their sum and as minus when we are speaking of their difference. The term ρ (rho) in this equation is the correlation between the two variables (to be discussed in Chapter 9) and is equal to zero when the variables are independent. (The fact that $\rho \neq 0$ when the variables are not independent was what forced us to treat the related sample case separately.)

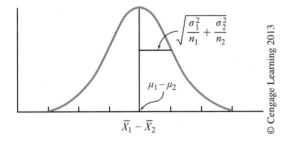

	X_1	X_2	
	$\overline{X}_{11}$	$\overline{X}_{21}$	$\overline{X}_{11} - \overline{X}_{21}$
	$\overline{X}_{12}$	$\overline{X}_{22}$	$\overline{X}_{12} - \overline{X}_{22}$
	$\overline{X}_{13}$	$\overline{X}_{23}$	$\overline{X}_{13} - \overline{X}_{23}$
	...	...	...
Mean	$\dfrac{\overline{X}_{1\infty}}{\mu_1}$	$\dfrac{\overline{X}_{2\infty}}{\mu_2}$	$\dfrac{\overline{X}_{1\infty} - \overline{X}_{2\infty}}{\mu_1 - \mu_2}$
Variance	$\dfrac{\sigma_1^2}{n_1}$	$\dfrac{\sigma_2^2}{n_2}$	$\dfrac{\sigma_1^2}{n_1} + \dfrac{\sigma_2^2}{n_2}$
S.D.	$\dfrac{\sigma_1}{\sqrt{n_1}}$	$\dfrac{\sigma_2}{\sqrt{n_2}}$	$\sqrt{\dfrac{\sigma_1^2}{n_1} + \dfrac{\sigma_2^2}{n_2}}$

© Cengage Learning 2013

Figure 7.8   Schematic set of means and mean differences when sampling from two populations

© Cengage Learning 2013

Figure 7.9   Sampling distribution of mean differences

variables is itself normally distributed. Because Figure 7.9 represents the difference between two sampling distributions of the mean, and because we know that the sampling distribution of means is at least approximately normal for reasonable sample sizes, the distribution in Figure 7.9 must itself be at least approximately normal.

The *t* Statistic

**standard error
of differences
between means**

Given the information we now have about the sampling distribution of mean differences, we can proceed to develop the appropriate test procedure. Assume for the moment that knowledge of the population variances (σ_i^2) is not a problem. We have earlier defined z as a statistic (a point on the distribution) minus the mean of the distribution, divided by the standard error of the distribution. Our statistic in the present case is $(\overline{X}_1 - \overline{X}_2)$, the observed difference between the sample means. The mean of the sampling distribution is $(\mu_1 - \mu_2)$, and, as we saw, the **standard error of differences between means**[16] is

---

[16] Remember that the standard deviation of any sampling distribution is called the standard error of that distribution.

$$\sigma_{\overline{X}_1 - \overline{X}_2} = \sqrt{\sigma_{\overline{X}_1}^2 + \sigma_{\overline{X}_2}^2} = \sqrt{\frac{\sigma_1^2}{n_1} + \frac{\sigma_2^2}{n_2}}$$

Thus we can write

$$z = \frac{(\overline{X}_1 - \overline{X}_2) - (\mu_1 - \mu_2)}{\sigma_{\overline{X}_1 - \overline{X}_2}}$$

$$= \frac{(\overline{X}_1 - \overline{X}_2) - (\mu_1 - \mu_2)}{\sqrt{\frac{\sigma_1^2}{n_1} + \frac{\sigma_2^2}{n_2}}}$$

The critical value for $\alpha = .05$ is $z = \pm 1.96$ (two-tailed), as it was for the one-sample tests discussed earlier.

The preceding formula is not particularly useful except for the purpose of showing the origin of the appropriate t test, because we rarely know the necessary population variances. (Such knowledge is so rare that it is not even worth imagining cases in which we would have it, although a few do exist.) We can circumvent this problem just as we did in the one-sample case, by using the sample variances as estimates of the population variances. This, for the same reasons discussed earlier for the one-sample t, means that the result will be distributed as t rather than z.

$$t = \frac{(\overline{X}_1 - \overline{X}_2) - (\mu_1 - \mu_2)}{s_{\overline{X}_1 - \overline{X}_2}}$$

$$= \frac{(\overline{X}_1 - \overline{X}_2) - (\mu_1 - \mu_2)}{\sqrt{\frac{s_1^2}{n_1} + \frac{s_2^2}{n_2}}}$$

Because the null hypothesis is generally the hypothesis that $\mu_1 - \mu_2 = 0$, we will drop that term from the equation and write

$$t = \frac{(\overline{X}_1 - \overline{X}_2)}{s_{\overline{X}_1 - \overline{X}_2}} = \frac{(\overline{X}_1 - \overline{X}_2)}{\sqrt{\frac{s_1^2}{n_1} + \frac{s_2^2}{n_2}}}$$

Pooling Variances

Although the equation for t that we have just developed is appropriate when the sample sizes are equal, it may require some modification when the sample sizes are unequal. This modification is designed to improve the estimate of the population variance, though there is some controversy whether it should be used. I will lay out the method of combining variances so as to account for differences in sample size, but later in the chapter I will come back and address the question of whether this is the best approach to take.

One of the assumptions required in the use of t for two independent samples is that $\sigma_1^2 = \sigma_2^2$ (i.e., the samples come from populations with equal variances, regardless of the truth or falsity of H_0). The assumption is required regardless of whether n_1 and n_2 are equal. Such an assumption is often reasonable. We frequently begin an experiment with two groups of subjects who are equivalent and then do something to one (or both) group(s) that will raise or lower the scores by an amount equal to the effect of the experimental treatment. In such a case, it often makes sense to assume that the variances will remain unaffected. (Recall that adding or subtracting a constant—here, the treatment effect—to or from a set of scores has no effect on its variance.) Because the population variances are assumed to be equal, this common variance can be represented by the symbol σ^2, without a subscript.

In our data we have two estimates of the common value of σ^2, namely s_1^2 and s_2^2. It seems appropriate to obtain some sort of an average of s_1^2 and s_2^2 on the grounds that this average should be a better estimate of σ^2 than either of the two separate estimates. We do not want to take the simple arithmetic mean, however, because doing so would give equal weight to the two estimates, even if one were based on considerably more observations. What we want is a **weighted average**, in which the sample variances are weighted by their degrees of freedom ($n_i - 1$). If we call this new estimate s_p^2 then

weighted average

$$s_p^2 = \frac{(n_1 - 1)s_1^2 + (n_2 - 1)s_2^2}{n_1 + n_2 - 2}$$

The numerator represents the sum of the variances, each weighted by their degrees of freedom, and the denominator represents the sum of the weights or, equivalently, the degrees of freedom for s_p^2.

pooled variance estimate

The weighted average of the two sample variances is usually referred to as a **pooled variance estimate**. Having defined the pooled estimate (s_p^2), we can now write

$$t = \frac{(\overline{X}_1 - \overline{X}_2)}{s_{\overline{X}_1 - \overline{X}_2}} = \frac{(\overline{X}_1 - \overline{X}_2)}{\sqrt{\dfrac{s_p^2}{n_1} + \dfrac{s_p^2}{n_2}}} = \frac{(\overline{X}_1 - \overline{X}_2)}{\sqrt{s_p^2\left(\dfrac{1}{n_1} + \dfrac{1}{n_2}\right)}}$$

Notice that both this formula for t and the one before it involve dividing the difference between the sample means by an estimate of the standard error of the difference between means. The only change concerns the way in which this standard error is estimated. When the sample sizes are equal, it makes absolutely no difference whether or not you pool variances; the answer will be the same. When the sample sizes are unequal, however, pooling can make quite a difference.

Degrees of Freedom

Two sample variances (s_1^2 and s_2^2) have gone into calculating t. Each of these variances is based on squared deviations about their corresponding sample means, and therefore each sample variance has $n_j - 1$ df. Across the two samples, therefore, we will have $(n_1 - 1) + (n_2 - 1) = (n_1 + n_2 - 2)$ df. Thus, the t for two independent samples will be based on $n_1 + n_2 - 2$ degrees of freedom.

Homophobia and Sexual Arousal

Adams, Wright, & Lohr (1996) were interested in some basic psychoanalytic theories that homophobia may be unconsciously related to the anxiety of being or becoming homosexual. They administered the Index of Homophobia to 64 heterosexual males, and classed them as homophobic or nonhomophobic on the basis of their score. They then exposed homophobic and nonhomophobic heterosexual men to videotapes of sexually explicit erotic stimuli portraying heterosexual and homosexual behavior, and recorded their level of sexual arousal. Adams et al. reasoned that if homophobia were unconsciously related to anxiety about ones own sexuality, homophobic individuals would show greater arousal to the homosexual videos than would nonhomophobic individuals.

In this example we will examine only the data from the homosexual video. (There were no group differences for the heterosexual and lesbian videos.) The data in Table 7.5 were

Table 7. 5   Data from Adams et al. on level of sexual arousal in homophobic and nonhomophobic heterosexual males

Homophobic						Nonhomophobic					
39.1	38.0	14.9	20.7	19.5	32.2	24.0	17.0	35.8	18.0	−1.7	11.1
11.0	20.7	26.4	35.7	26.4	28.8	10.1	16.1	−0.7	14.1	25.9	23.0
33.4	13.7	46.1	13.7	23.0	20.7	20.0	14.1	−1.7	19.0	20.0	30.9
19.5	11.4	24.1	17.2	38.0	10.3	30.9	22.0	6.2	27.9	14.1	33.8
35.7	41.5	18.4	36.8	54.1	11.4	26.9	5.2	13.1	19.0	−15.5	
8.7	23.0	14.3	5.3	6.3							
Mean		24.00				Mean		16.50			
Variance		148.87				Variance		139.16			
n		35				n		29			

created to have the same means and pooled variance as the data that Adams collected, so our conclusions will be the same as theirs.[17] The dependent variable is the degree of arousal at the end of the 4-minute video, with larger values indicating greater arousal.

Before we consider any statistical test, and ideally even before the data are collected, we must specify several features of the test. First we must specify the null and alternative hypotheses:

$$H_0 : \mu_1 = \mu_2$$

$$H_1 : \mu_1 \neq \mu_2$$

The alternative hypothesis is bidirectional (we will reject H_0 if $\mu_1 < \mu_2$ or if $\mu_1 > \mu_2$), and thus we will use a two-tailed test. For the sake of consistency with other examples in this book, we will let $\alpha = .05$. It is important to keep in mind, however, that there is nothing particularly sacred about any of these decisions. (Think about how Jones and Tukey (2000) would have written this paragraph. Where would they have differed from what is here, and why might their approach be clearer?)

Given the null hypothesis as stated, we can now calculate t:

$$t = \frac{\overline{X}_1 - \overline{X}_2}{s_{\overline{X}_1 - \overline{X}_2}} = \frac{\overline{X}_1 - \overline{X}_2}{\sqrt{\dfrac{s_p^2}{n_1} + \dfrac{s_p^2}{n_2}}} = \frac{\overline{X}_1 - \overline{X}_2}{\sqrt{s_p^2\left(\dfrac{1}{n_1} + \dfrac{1}{n_2}\right)}}$$

Because we are testing H_0, $\mu_1 - \mu_2 = 0$, the $\mu_1 - \mu_2$ term has been dropped from the equation. We can pool our sample variances because they are so similar that we do not have to worry about a lack of homogeneity of variance. Doing so we obtain

$$s_p^2 = \frac{(n_1 - 1)s_1^2 + (n_2 - 1)s_2^2}{n_1 + n_2 - 2}$$

$$= \frac{34(148.87) + 28(139.16)}{35 + 29 - 2} = 144.48$$

---

[17] I actually added 12 points to each mean, largely to avoid many negative scores, but it doesn't change the results or the calculations in the slightest.

Notice that the pooled variance is slightly closer in value to s_1^2 than to s_2^2 because of the greater weight given s_1^2 in the formula. Then

$$t = \frac{\overline{X}_1 - \overline{X}_2}{\sqrt{\dfrac{s_p^2}{n_1} + \dfrac{s_p^2}{n_2}}} = \frac{(24.00 - 16.50)}{\sqrt{\dfrac{144.48}{35} + \dfrac{144.48}{29}}} = \frac{7.50}{\sqrt{9.11}} = 2.48$$

For this example, we have $n_1 - 1 = 34$ *df* for the homophobic group and $n_2 - 1 = 28$ *df* for the nonhomophobic group, making a total of $n_1 - 1 + n_2 - 1 = 62$ *df*. From the sampling distribution of t in Appendix t, $t_{.025}(62) \cong 2.003$ (with linear interpolation). Because the value of t_{obt} far exceeds $t_{\alpha/2}$, we will reject H_0 (at $\alpha = .05$) and conclude that there is a difference between the means of the populations from which our observations were drawn. In other words, we will conclude (statistically) that $\mu_1 \neq \mu_2$ and (practically) that $\mu_1 > \mu_2$. In terms of the experimental variables, homophobic subjects show greater arousal to a homosexual video than do nonhomophobic subjects. (How would the conclusions of Jones and Tukey (2000) compare with the one given here?)

Confidence Limits on $\mu_1 - \mu_2$

In addition to testing a null hypothesis about population means (i.e., testing $H_0: \mu_1 - \mu_2 = 0$), and stating an effect size, which we will do shortly, it is useful to set confidence limits on the difference between μ_1 and μ_2. The logic for setting these confidence limits is exactly the same as it was for the one-sample case. The calculations are also exactly the same except that we use the *difference* between the means and the standard error of *differences* between means in place of the mean and the standard error of the mean. Thus for the 95% confidence limits on $\mu_1 - \mu_2$ we have

$$CI_{.95} = (\overline{X}_1 - \overline{X}_2) \pm t_{.025} s_{\overline{X}_1 - \overline{X}_2}$$

For the homophobia study we have

$$CI_{.95} = (\overline{X}_1 - \overline{X}_2) \pm t_{.025} s_{\overline{X}_1 - \overline{X}_2} = (24.00 - 16.5) \pm 2.00\sqrt{\dfrac{144.48}{35} + \dfrac{144.48}{29}}$$

$$= 7.50 \pm 2.00(3.018) = 7.5 \pm 6.04$$

$$1.46 \leq (\mu_1 - \mu_2) \leq 13.54$$

In the formal level of traditional statisticians, the probability is .95 that an interval computed as we computed this interval encloses the difference in arousal to homosexual videos between homophobic and nonhomophobic participants. A Bayesian would be happy to state that the probability is .95 that the true difference between population means falls in this interval. Although the interval is wide, it does not include 0. This is consistent with our rejection of the null hypothesis and allows us to state that homophobic individuals are, in fact, more sexually aroused by homosexual videos than are nonhomophobic individuals. However, I think that we would be remiss if we simply ignored the width of this interval. Although the difference between groups is statistically significant, there is still considerable uncertainty about how large the difference is. In addition, keep in mind that the dependent variable is the "degree of sexual arousal" on an arbitrary scale. Even if your confidence interval was quite narrow, it is difficult to know what to make of the result in absolute terms. To say that the groups differed by 7.5 units in arousal is not particularly informative. Is that a big difference or a little difference? We have no real way to know, because the units (mm of penile circumference) are not something that most of us have an intuitive feel for. But when we standardize the measure, as we will in the next section, it is often more informative.

Effect Size

The confidence interval just calculated has shown us that we still have considerable uncertainty about the difference in sexual arousal between groups, even though our statistically significant difference tells us that the homophobic group actually shows more arousal than the nonhomophobic group. Again we come to the issue of finding ways to present information to our readers that conveys the magnitude of the difference between our groups. We will use an effect size measure based on Cohen's d. It is very similar to the one that we used in the case of two matched samples, where we divide the difference between the means by a standard deviation. We will again call this statistic (d). In this case, however, our standard deviation will be the estimated standard deviation of either population. More specifically, we will pool the two variances and take the square root of the result, which will give us our best estimate of the standard deviation of the populations from which the numbers were drawn.[18] (If we had noticeably different variances, we would most likely use the standard deviation of one sample and note to the reader that this is what we had done.)

For our data on homophobia we have

$$\hat{d} = \frac{\overline{X}_1 - \overline{X}_2}{s_p} = \frac{24.00 - 16.50}{12.02} = 0.62$$

This result expresses the difference between the two groups in standard deviation units and tells us that the mean arousal for homophobic participants was nearly 2/3 of a standard deviation higher than the arousal of nonhomophobic participants. That strikes me as a big difference.

Confidence Limits on Effect Sizes

Just as we can set confidence limits on means and differences between means, so can we set them on effect sizes. However the arithmetic is considerably more difficult and deals with noncentral t distributions. (I present an approximation in Chapter 10, Section 10.1.) Software is available for the purpose of constructing exact confidence limits (Cumming and Finch, 2001), and I present a discussion of the issue in a supplementary document found at http://www.uvm.edu/~dhowell/methods8/Supplements/Confidence Intervals on Effect Size.pdf That document also provides helpful references that discuss not only the underlying methods but also the importance of reporting such limits. Using the software by Cumming and Finch (2001) we find that, for the study of homophobia, the confidence intervals on d are 0.1155 and 1.125, which is also rather wide. At the same time, even the lower limit on the confidence interval is meaningfully large. A short program to compute these intervals using R and the MBESS library are available on the book's Web site named KellyCI.R.

Some words of caution. In the example of homophobia, the units of measurement were largely arbitrary, and a 7.5 difference had no intrinsic meaning to us. Thus it made more sense to express it in terms of standard deviations because we have at least some understanding of what that means. However, there are many cases wherein the original units are meaningful, and in that case it may not make much sense to standardize the measure (i.e., report it in standard deviation units). We might prefer to specify the difference between means, or the ratio of means, or some similar statistic. The earlier example of the moon illusion is a case in point. There it is far more meaningful to speak of the horizon moon appearing approximately half-again as large as the zenith moon, and I see no advantage,

---

[18] Hedges (1982) was the one who first recommended stating this formula in terms of statistics with the pooled estimate of the standard deviation substituted for the population value. It is sometimes referred to as Hedges' **g**.

and some obfuscation, in converting to standardized units. The important goal is to give the reader an appreciation of the size of a difference, and you should choose that measure that best expresses this difference. In one case a standardized measure such as d is best, and in other cases other measures, such as the distance between the means, is better.

The second word of caution applies to effect sizes taken from the literature. It has been known for some time (Sterling, 1959; Lane and Dunlap, 1978; and Brand, Bradley, Best, and Stoica, 2008) that if we base our estimates of effect size solely on the published literature, we are likely to overestimate effect sizes. This occurs because there is a definite tendency to publish only statistically significant results, and thus those studies that did not have a significant effect are underrepresented in averaging effect sizes. (Rosenthal (1979) named this the "file drawer problem" because that is where the nonsignificant and nonpublished studies reside.) Lane and Dunlap (1978) ran a simple sampling study with the true effect size set at .25 and a difference between means of 4 points (standard deviation = 16). With sample sizes set at $n_1 = n_2 = 15$, they found an average difference between means of 13.21 when looking only at results that were statistically significant at $\alpha = .05$. In addition they found that the sample standard deviations were noticeably underestimated, which would result in a bias toward narrower confidence limits. We need to keep these findings in mind when looking at only published research studies.

Finally, I should note that the increase in interest in using trimmed means and Winsorized variances in testing hypotheses carries over to the issue of effect sizes. Algina, Keselman, and Penfield (2005) have recently pointed out that measures such as Cohen's d are often improved by use of these statistics. The same holds for confidence limits on the differences.

As you will see in the next chapter, Cohen laid out some very general guidelines for what he considered small, medium, and large effect sizes. He characterized $d = .20$ as an effect that is small, but probably meaningful, an effect size of $d = .50$ as a medium effect that most people would notice (such as a half of a standard deviation difference in IQ), and an effect size of $d = .80$ as large. We should not make too much of Cohen's levels, he certainly did not, but they are helpful as a rough guide.

Reporting Results

Reporting results for a t test on two independent samples is basically similar to reporting results for the case of dependent samples. In Adams's et al. study of homophobia, two groups of participants were involved—one group scoring high on a scale of homophobia, and the other scoring low. When presented with sexually explicit homosexual videos, the homophobic group actually showed a higher level of sexual arousal (the mean difference = 7.50 units). A t test of the difference between means produced a statistically significant result ($p < .05$), and Cohen's $d = .62$ showed that the two groups differed by nearly 2/3 of a standard deviation. However the confidence limits on the population mean difference were rather wide ($1.46 \leq \mu_1 - \mu_2 \leq 13.54$, suggesting that we do not have a tight handle on the size of our difference.

SPSS Analysis

The SPSS analysis of the Adams et al. (1996) data is given in Table 7.6. Notice that SPSS first provides what it calls Levene's test for equality of variances. We will discuss this test shortly, but it is simply a test on our assumption of homogeneity of variance. We do not come close to rejecting the null hypothesis that the variances are homogeneous ($p = .534$), so we don't have to worry about that here. We will assume equal variances, and for now we will focus on the next to bottom row of the table.

Table 7.6   SPSS analyses of Adams et al. (1996) data

Group Statistics

GROUP		N	Mean	Std. Deviation	Std. Error Mean
Arousal	Homophobic	35	24.0000	12.2013	2.0624
	Nonhomophobic	29	16.5034	11.7966	2.1906

Independent Samples Test

	Levene's Test for Equality of Variances		t-Test for Equality of Means						95% Confidence Interval of the Difference	
	F	Sig.	t	df	Sig. (2-tailed)	Mean Difference	Std. Error Difference	Lower	Upper
Equal variances assumed	.391	.534	2.484	62	.016	7.4966	3.0183	1.4630	13.5301
Equal variances not assumed			2.492	60.495	.015	7.4966	3.0087	1.4794	13.5138

Adapted from output by SPSS, Inc.

Next note that the *t* supplied by SPSS is the same as we calculated and that the probability associated with this value of *t* (.016) is less than $\alpha = .05$, leading to rejection of the null hypothesis. Note also that SPSS prints the difference between the means and the standard error of that difference, both of which we have seen in our own calculations. Finally, SPSS prints the 95% confidence interval on the difference between means, and it agrees with ours.

A Second Worked Example

Joshua Aronson has done extensive work on what he refers to as "stereotype threat," which refers to the fact that "members of stereotyped groups often feel extra pressure in situations where their behavior can confirm the negative reputation that their group lacks a valued ability" (Aronson, Lustina, Good, Keough, Steele, & Brown, 1998). This feeling of stereotype threat is then hypothesized to affect performance, generally by lowering it from what it would have been had the individual not felt threatened. Considerable work has been done with ethnic groups who are stereotypically reputed to do poorly in some area, but Aronson et al. went a step further to ask if stereotype threat could actually lower the performance of white males—a group that is not normally associated with stereotype threat.

Aronson et al. (1998) used two independent groups of college students who were known to excel in mathematics and for whom doing well in math was considered important. They assigned 11 students to a control group that was simply asked to complete a difficult mathematics exam. They assigned 12 students to a threat condition, in which they were told that Asian students typically did better than other students in math tests, and that the purpose of the exam was to help the experimenter to understand why this difference exists. Aronson reasoned that simply telling white students that Asians did better on math tests would arouse feelings of stereotype threat and diminish the students' performance.

The data in Table 7.7 have been constructed to have nearly the same means and standard deviations as Aronson's data. The dependent variable is the number of items correctly solved.

Table 7.7   Data from Aronson et al. (1998)

Control Subjects				Threat Subjects			
4	9	12	8	7	8	7	2
9	13	12	13	6	9	7	10
13	7	6		5	0	10	8
	Mean = 9.64				Mean = 6.58		
	st. dev. = 3.17				st. dev. = 3.03		
	$n_1 = 11$				$n_2 = 12$		

© Cengage Learning 2013

First we need to specify the null hypothesis, the significance level, and whether we will use a one- or a two-tailed test. We want to test the null hypothesis that the two conditions perform equally well on the test, so we have $H_0 : \mu_1 = \mu_2$. We will set alpha at $\alpha = .05$, in line with what we have been using. Finally, we will choose to use a two-tailed test because it is reasonably possible for either group to show superior math performance.

Next we need to calculate the pooled variance estimate.

$$s_p^2 = \frac{(n_1 - 1)s_1^2 + (n_2 - 1)s_2^2}{n_1 + n_2 - 2} = \frac{10(3.17^2) + 11(3.03^2)}{11 + 12 - 2}$$

$$= \frac{10(10.0489) + 11(9.1809)}{21} = \frac{201.4789}{21} = 9.5942$$

Finally, we can calculate t using the pooled variance estimate:

$$t = \frac{(\overline{X}_1 - \overline{X}_2)}{\sqrt{\dfrac{s_p^2}{n_1} + \dfrac{s_p^2}{n_2}}} = \frac{(9.64 - 6.58)}{\sqrt{\dfrac{9.5942}{11} + \dfrac{9.5942}{12}}} = \frac{3.06}{\sqrt{1.6717}} = \frac{3.06}{1.2929} = 2.37$$

For this example we have $n_1 + n_2 - 2 = 21$ degrees of freedom. From Appendix t we find $t_{.025} = 2.080$. Because $2.37 > 2.080$, we will reject H_0 and conclude that the two population means are not equal.

Writing up the Results

If you were writing up the results of this experiment, you might write something like the following:

An experiment testing the hypothesis that stereotype threat will disrupt the performance even of a group that is not usually thought of as having a negative stereotype with respect to performance on math tests was reported by Aronson et al. (1998). They asked two groups of participants to take a difficult math exam. These were white male college students who reported that they typically performed well in math and that good math performance was important to them. One group of students ($n = 11$) was simply given the math test and asked to do as well as they could. A second, randomly assigned group ($n = 12$) was informed that Asian males often outperformed white males, and that the test was intended to help explain the difference in performance. The test itself was the same for all participants. The results showed that the Control subjects answered a mean of 9.64 problems correctly, whereas the subjects in the Threat group completed only a mean of 6.58 problems. The standard deviations were 3.17 and 3.03, respectively. This represents an effect size (d) of .99, meaning that the two groups differed in terms of the number of items correctly completed by nearly one standard deviation.

Student's t test was used to compare the groups. The resulting t was 2.37, and was significant at $p < .05$, showing that stereotype threat significantly reduced the performance of those subjects to whom it was applied. The 95% confidence interval on the difference in means is $0.3712 \leq \mu_1 - \mu_2 \leq 5.7488$. This is quite a wide interval, but keep in mind that the two sample sizes were 11 and 12. An alternative way of comparing groups is to note that the Threat group answered 32% fewer items correctly than did the Control group.

7.6 Heterogeneity of Variance: the Behrens–Fisher Problem

homogeneity of variance

We have already seen that one of the assumptions underlying the t test for two independent samples is the assumption of **homogeneity of variance** ($\sigma_1^2 = \sigma_2^2 = \sigma^2$). To be more specific, we can say that *when* H_0 is true and *when* we have homogeneity of variance, then, pooling the variances, the ratio

$$t = \frac{(\overline{X}_1 - \overline{X}_2)}{\sqrt{\dfrac{s_p^2}{n_1} + \dfrac{s_p^2}{n_2}}}$$

is distributed as t on $n_1 + n_2 - 2 \ df$. If we can assume homogeneity of variance there is no difficulty, and the techniques discussed in this section are not needed. But what if we aren't too comfortable with the assumption of homogeneity of variance? If we have heterogeneous variances, however, this ratio is not, strictly speaking, distributed as t. This leaves us with a problem, but fortunately a solution (or a number of competing solutions) exists.

First of all, unless $\sigma_1^2 = \sigma_2^2 = \sigma^2$, it makes no sense to pool (average) variances, because the reason we were pooling variances in the first place was that we assumed them to be estimating the same quantity. For the case of **heterogeneous variances**, we will first dispense with pooling procedures and define

heterogeneous variances

$$t' = \frac{(\overline{X}_1 - \overline{X}_2)}{\sqrt{\dfrac{s_1^2}{n_1} + \dfrac{s_2^2}{n_2}}}$$

where s_1^2 and s_2^2 are taken to be heterogeneous variances. As noted above, the expression that I just denoted as t' is *not* necessarily distributed as t on $n_1 + n_2 - 2 \ df$. If we knew what the sampling distribution of t' actually looked like, there would be no problem. We would just evaluate t' against that sampling distribution. Fortunately, although there is no universal agreement, we know at least the approximate distribution of t'.

The Sampling Distribution of t'

Behrens–Fisher problem

One of the first attempts to find the exact sampling distribution of t' was begun by Behrens and extended by Fisher, and the general problem of heterogeneity of variance has come to be known as the **Behrens–Fisher problem**. Based on this work, the Behrens–Fisher distribution of t' was derived and tabled. However, because the table covers only a few degrees of freedom, and because almost no one (but me) has a copy of that table sitting on their bookshelf, it is not particularly useful except for historical interest. But don't give up.

Welch–Satterthwaite solution

An alternative solution was developed apparently independently by Welch (1938) and by Satterthwaite (1946). The **Welch–Satterthwaite solution** is particularly important because we will refer back to it when we discuss the analysis of variance. Using this method, t' is *df'*

viewed as a legitimate member of the *t* distribution, but for an unknown number of degrees of freedom. The problem then becomes one of solving for the appropriate *df*, denoted *df'*:

$$df' = \frac{\left(\frac{s_1^2}{n_1} + \frac{s_2^2}{n_2}\right)^2}{\frac{\left(\frac{s_1^2}{n_1}\right)^2}{n_1 - 1} + \frac{\left(\frac{s_2^2}{n_2}\right)^2}{n_2 - 1}}$$

The degrees of freedom (*df'*) are then taken to the nearest integer.[19] The advantage of this approach is that *df'* is bounded by the smaller of $n_1 - 1$ and $n_2 - 1$ at one extreme and $n_1 + n_2 - 2$ *df* at the other. More specifically, $Min(n_1 - 1, n_2 - 1) \leq df' \leq (n_1 + n_2 - 2)$.

In this book we will rely primarily on the Welch–Satterthwaite approximation. It has the distinct advantage of applying easily to problems that arise in the analysis of variance, and it is not noticeably more awkward than the other solutions.

Testing for Heterogeneity of Variance

How do we know whether we even have heterogeneity of variance to begin with? Because we obviously do not know σ_1^2 and σ_2^2 (if we did we would not be solving for *t*), we must in some way test their difference by using our two sample variances (s_1^2 and s_2^2).

A number of solutions have been put forth for testing for heterogeneity of variance. One of the simpler ones was advocated by Levene (1960), who suggested replacing each value of *X* either by its absolute deviation from the group mean—$d_{ij} = |X_{ij} - \overline{X}_j|$—or by its squared deviation—$d_{ij} = (X_{ij} - \overline{X}_j)^2$—where *i* and *j* represent the *i*th subject in the *j*th group. He then proposed running a standard two-sample *t* test on the d_{ij}s. This test makes intuitive sense, because if there is greater variability in one group, the absolute, or squared, values of the deviations will be greater. If *t* is significant, we would then declare the two groups to differ in their variances.[20] Alternative approaches have been proposed, see, for example, Brown and Forsythe (1974) and O'Brien (1981), but they are rarely implemented in standard software, and I will not elaborate on them here. Levene's statistic is the most often reported[21].

The procedures just described are suggested as replacements for the more traditional *F* test on variances, which is a ratio of the larger sample variance to the smaller. Although often reported by statistical software, this *F* has been shown by many studies to be severely affected by nonnormality of the data and should not be used.

The Robustness of *t* with Heterogeneous Variances

robust

I mentioned that the *t* test is what is described as **robust**, meaning that it is more or less unaffected by moderate departures from the underlying assumptions. For the *t* test for two independent samples, we have two major assumptions and one side condition that must

---

[19] Welch (1947) later suggested that it might be more accurate to write

$$df' = \left[\frac{\left(\frac{s_1^2}{n_1} + \frac{s_2^2}{n_2}\right)^2}{\frac{\left(\frac{s_1^2}{n_1}\right)^2}{n_1 + 1} + \frac{\left(\frac{s_2^2}{n_2}\right)^2}{n_2 + 1}}\right] - 2$$

although the difference is negligible.

[20] There is an obvious problem with this test. When we take the absolute value of the deviations, they are all going to be positive and their distribution will be very positively skewed. In spite of this problem, the test seems to work well.

[21] A good discussion of Levene's test can be found at http://www.ps.uci.edu/~markm/statistics/eda35a.pdf .

be considered. The two assumptions are those of normality of the sampling distribution of differences between means and homogeneity of variance. The side condition is the condition of equal sample sizes versus unequal sample sizes. Although we have just seen how the problem of heterogeneity of variance can be handled by special procedures, it is still relevant to ask what happens if we use the standard approach even with heterogeneous variances.

Many people have investigated the effects of violating, both independently and jointly, the underlying assumptions of t. The general conclusion to be drawn from these studies is that for equal sample sizes violating the assumption of homogeneity of variance produces very small effects—the nominal value of $\alpha = .05$ is most likely within ± 0.02 of the true value of α. By this we mean that if you set up a situation with unequal variances *but with H_0 true* and proceed to draw (and compute t on) a large number of pairs of samples, you will find that somewhere between 3% and 7% of the sample t values actually exceed $\pm t_{.025}$. This level of inaccuracy is not intolerable. The same kind of statement applies to violations of the assumption of normality, provided that the true populations are roughly the same shape or else both are symmetric. If the distributions are markedly skewed (especially in opposite directions), serious problems arise unless their variances are fairly equal.

With unequal sample sizes, however, the results are more difficult to interpret. I would suggest that whenever your sample sizes are more than trivially unequal you employ the Welch-Satterthwaite approach. You have little to lose and potentially much to gain.

Wilcox (1992) has argued persuasively for the use of trimmed samples for comparing group means with heavy-tailed distributions. (Interestingly, statisticians seem to have a fondness for trimmed samples, whereas psychologists and other behavioral science practitioners seem not to have heard of trimming.) Wilcox provides results showing dramatic increases in power when compared to more standard approaches. Alternative nonparametric approaches, including "resampling statistics" are discussed elsewhere in this book. These can be very powerful techniques that do not require unreasonable assumptions about the populations from which you have sampled. I suspect that resampling statistics and related procedures will be in the mainstream of statistical analysis in the not-too-distant future.

But Should We Test for Homogeneity of Variance?

At first glance this question might seem to have an obvious answer—of course we should. But then what? Hayes and Cai (2007) have suggested that such a test is unnecessary and may lead us astray. The traditional view has been that you run a test for homogeneity of variance. If variances are not homogeneous you pool the variance estimates, and if they are heterogeneous you use the separate variances without pooling them. But Hayes and Cai asked if it was effective to make the decision about pooled or separate variances based on the test of homogeneity. They asked what would happen if we always pooled the variances, or always kept them separate, or made that decision conditional on a test of homogeneity of variance. It turns out that we are probably better off always using separate variances. Our error rates stay closer to $\alpha = .05$ if we do that. So I have changed my usual advice to say that you are better off working with separate variances. You do lose a few degrees of freedom that way, but you will probably still come out ahead. We are going to come back to this problem in Chapter 12.

A Caution

When Welch, Satterthwaite, Behrens, and Fisher developed tests on means that are not dependent on homogeneous variances they may not have been doing us as much of a favor as we think. Venables (2000) pointed out that such a test "gives naive users a cozy feeling of protection that perhaps their test makes sense even if the variances happen to come out wildly different." His point is that we are often so satisfied with not having to worry about the fact that the variances are different that we often don't worry about the fact that variances are different. That sentence may sound circular, but we really *should* pay attention to unequal variances. It is quite possible that the variances are of more interest than the means in some experiments. For example, it is entirely possible that a study comparing family therapy with cognitive behavior therapy for treatment of anorexia could come out with similar means but quite different variances for the two conditions. In that situation perhaps we should focus on the thought that one therapy might be very effective for some people and very ineffective for others, leading to a high variance. Venables also points out that if one treatment produces a higher mean than another that may not be of much interest if it also has a high variance and is thus unreliable. Finally, Venables pointed out that whereas we are all happy and comfortable with the fact that we can now run a *t* test without worrying overly much about heterogeneity of variance, when we come to the analysis of variance in Chapter 11 we will not have such a correction and, as a result, we will happily go our way acting as if the lack of equality of variances is not a problem.

I am not trying to suggest that people ignore corrections for heterogeneity of variance. I think that they should be used. But I think that it is even more important to consider what those different variances are telling us. They may be the more important part of the story.

7.7   Hypothesis Testing Revisited

In Chapter 4 we spent time examining the process of hypothesis testing. I pointed out that the traditional approach involves setting up a null hypothesis, and then generating a statistic that tells us how likely we are to find the obtained results if, in fact, the null hypothesis is true. In other words we calculate the probability of the data given the null, and if that probability is very low, we reject the null.

In that chapter we also looked briefly at a proposal by Jones and Tukey (2000) in which they approached the problem slightly differently. Now that we have several examples, this is a good point to go back and look at their proposal. In discussing Adams et al.'s study of homophobia I suggested that you think about how Jones and Tukey would have approached the issue. I am not going to repeat the traditional approach because that is laid out in each of the examples of how to write up our results, but the study by Adams et al. (1996) makes a good example. I imagine that all of us would be willing to agree that the null hypothesis of equal population means in the two conditions is highly unlikely to be true. Even laying aside the argument about differences in the 10th decimal place, it just seems unlikely that people who differ appreciably in terms of their attitudes toward homosexuality would show exactly the same mean level of arousal to erotic videos. We may not know which group will show the greater arousal, but one population mean is certain to be larger than the other and, most likely, not trivially so. So we can rule out the null hypothesis (H_0: $\mu_H - \mu_N = 0$) as a viable possibility, which leaves us with three possible conclusions we could draw as a result of our test. The first is that $\mu_H < \mu_N$, the second is that $\mu_H > \mu_N$, and the third is that we do not have sufficient evidence to draw a conclusion.

Now let's look at the possibilities of error. It could actually be that $\mu_H < \mu_N$, but that we draw the opposite conclusion by deciding that the nonhomophobic participants are *more* aroused. This is what Jones and Tukey call a "reversal," and the probability of making this error if we use a *one-tailed* test at $\alpha = .05$ is .05. Alternatively, it could be that $\mu_H > \mu_N$ but we make the error of concluding that the nonhomophobic participants are less aroused. Again with a one-tailed test the probability of making this error is .05. It is not possible for us to make both of these errors because one of the hypotheses is true, so using a *one-tailed* test (in both directions) at $\alpha = .05$ gives us a 5% error rate. What they are really encouraging us to do is to always use a one-tailed test but *not* to worry about choosing a particular tail until after we see the results. It is that idea that is the biggest departure from traditional thinking. In our particular example the critical value for a one-tailed test on 62 *df* is approximately 1.68. Because our obtained value of *t* was 2.48, we will conclude that homophobic participants are more aroused, on average, than nonhomophobic participants. Notice that in writing this paragraph I have not used the phrase "Type I error," because that refers to rejecting a true null, and I have already said that the null can't possibly be true. In fact, notice that my conclusion did not contain the phrase "rejecting the hypothesis." Instead I referred to "drawing a conclusion." These are subtle differences, but I hope this example clarifies the position taken by Jones and Tukey.

Key Terms

Sampling distribution of the mean (7.1)

Central limit theorem (7.1)

Uniform (rectangular) distribution (7.1)

Standard error (7.2)

Student's *t* distribution (7.3)

Bootstrapping (7.3)

Point estimate (7.3)

Confidence limits (7.3)

Confidence interval (7.3)

Credible interval (7.3)

ρ level (7.3)

Matched samples (7.4)

Repeated measures (7.4)

Related samples (7.4)

Matched-sample *t* test (7.4)

Difference scores (7.4)

Gain scores (7.4)

Cohen's *d* (7.4)

Sampling distribution of differences between means (7.5)

Variance sum law (7.5)

Standard error of differences between means (7.5)

Weighted average (7.5)

Pooled variance estimate (7.5)

df' (7.6)

Homogeneity of variance (7.7)

Heterogeneous variances (7.7)

Behrens–Fisher problem (7.7)

Welch–Satterthwaite solution (7.7)

Robust (7.7)

Exercises

7.1   The following numbers represent 100 random numbers drawn from a rectangular population with a mean of 4.5 and a standard deviation of .2.7. Plot the distribution of these digits.

6	4	8	7	8	7	0	8	2	8	5	7
4	8	2	6	9	0	2	6	4	9	0	4
9	3	4	2	8	2	0	4	1	4	7	4
1	7	4	2	4	1	4	2	8	7	9	7
3	7	4	7	3	1	6	7	1	8	7	2
7	6	2	1	8	6	2	3	3	6	5	4
1	7	2	1	0	2	6	0	8	3	2	4
3	8	4	5	7	0	8	4	2	8	6	3
7	3	5	1								

7.2   In what way would the result in Exercise 7.4 differ if you had drawn more samples of size 5?

7.3   Compare the means and the standard deviations for the distribution of digits in Exercise 7.1 and the sampling distribution of the mean in Exercise 7.4.

a. What would the Central Limit Theorem lead you to expect in this situation?

b. Do the data correspond to what you would predict?

7.4   I drew 50 samples of 5 scores each from the same population that the data in Exercise 7.1 came from, and calculated the mean of each sample. The means are shown below. Plot the distribution of these means.

2.8	6.2	4.4	5.0	1.0	4.6	3.8	2.6	4.0	4.8
6.6	4.6	6.2	4.6	5.6	6.4	3.4	5.4	5.2	7.2
5.4	2.6	4.4	4.2	4.4	5.2	4.0	2.6	5.2	4.0
3.6	4.6	4.4	5.0	5.6	3.4	3.2	4.4	4.8	3.8
4.4	2.8	3.8	4.6	5.4	4.6	2.4	5.8	4.6	4.8

© Cengage Learning 2013

7.5.   In what way would the result in Exercise 7.4 differ if you had drawn 50 samples of size 15?

7.6   Compute 95% confidence limits on μ for the data in Exercise 7.10.

7.7.   Although I have argued against one-tailed tests from the traditional hypothesis testing view, why might a one-tailed test be appropriate for the question asked in the previous exercise?

7.8.   Kruger and Dunning (1999) published a paper called "Unskilled and unaware of it," in which they examined the hypothesis that people who perform badly on tasks are unaware of their general logical reasoning skills. Each student estimated at what percentile he or she scored on a test of logical reasoning. The eleven students who scored in the lowest quartile reported a mean estimate that placed them in the 68th percentile. Raw scores, in percentiles, with nearly the same mean and standard deviation as Kruger and Dunning found follow: [40 58 72 73 76 78 52 72 84 70 72] Is this an example of "all the children are above average?" In other words is their mean percentile ranking greater than an average ranking of 50?

7.9   The over- and underestimation of one's performance is partly a function of the fact that if you are near the bottom you have less room to underestimate your performance than to overestimate it. The reverse holds if you are near the top. Why doesn't that explanation account for the huge overestimation of the poor scorers?

7.10.   In the Kruger and Dunning study reported in the previous two exercises, the mean estimated percentile for the 11 students in the top quartile (their actual mean percentile = 86) was 70 with a standard deviation of 14.92, so they underestimated their abilities. Is this difference significant?

7.11   Everitt, in Hand et al., 1994, reported on several different therapies as treatments for anorexia. There were 29 girls in a cognitive-behavior therapy condition, and they were weighed before and after treatment. The weight gains of the girls, in pounds, are given below. The scores were obtained by subtracting the Before score from the After score, so that a negative difference represents weight *loss*, and a positive difference represents a *gain*.

1.7	0.7	−0.1	−0.7	−3.5	14.9	3.5	17.1	−7.6	1.6	11.7
6.1	1.1	−4.0	20.9	−9.1	2.1	−1.4	1.4	−0.3	−3.7	−0.8
2.4	12.6	1.9	3.9	0.1	15.4	−0.7			

a. What does the distribution of these values look like?

b. Did the girls in this group gain a statistically significant amount of weight?

c. Calculate 95% confidence limits on these results.

d. Compute an effect size measure for these results.

7.12   Compas and others (1994) were surprised to find that young children under stress actually report fewer symptoms of anxiety and depression than we would expect. But they also noticed that their scores on a Lie Scale (a measure of the tendency to give socially desirable answers) were higher than expected. The population mean for the Lie scale on the Children's Manifest Anxiety Scale (Reynolds and Richmond, 1978) is known to be 3.87. For a sample of 36 children under stress, Compas et al., found a sample mean of 4.39, with a standard deviation of 2.61.

    a. How would we test whether this group shows an increased tendency to give socially acceptable answers?

    b. What would the null hypothesis and research hypothesis be?

    c. What can you conclude from the data?

7.13 Katz, Lautenschlager, Blackburn, and Harris (1990) examined the performance of 28 students who answered multiple choice items on the SAT without having read the passages to which the items referred. The mean score (out of 100) was 46.6, with a standard deviation of 6.8. Random guessing would have been expected to result in 20 correct answers.

    a. Were these students responding at better-than-chance levels?

    b. If performance is statistically significantly better than chance, does it mean that the SAT test is not a valid predictor of future college performance?

7.14 Compute 95% confidence limits on the weight gain in Exercise 7.11.

7.15 Calculate the 95% confidence limits for μ for the data in Exercise 7.12. Are these limits consistent with your conclusion in Exercise 7.12?

7.16 In the study referred to in Exercise 7.19, what, if anything does your answer to that question tell us about whether couples are sexually compatible? What do we know from this analysis, and what don't we know?

7.17 Construct 95% confidence limits on the true mean difference between endorphin levels at the two times described in Exercise 7.18.

7.18 Hoaglin, Mosteller, and Tukey (1983) present data on blood levels of beta-endorphin as a function of stress. They took beta-endorphin levels for 19 patients 12 hours before surgery, and again 10 minutes before surgery. The data are presented below, in fmol/ml:

ID	1	2	3	4	5	6	7	8	9	10
12 hours	10.0	6.5	8.0	12.0	5.0	11.5	5.0	3.5	7.5	5.8
10 minutes	6.5	14.0	13.5	18.0	14.5	9.0	18.0	42.0	7.5	6.0

ID	11	12	13	14	15	16	17	18	19
12 hours	4.7	8.0	7.0	17.0	8.8	17.0	15.0	4.4	2.0
10 minutes	25.0	12.0	52.0	20.0	16.0	15.0	11.5	2.5	2.0

© Cengage Learning 2013

Based on these data, what effect does increased stress have on endorphin levels?

7.19 Hout, Duncan, and Sobel (1987) reported on the relative sexual satisfaction of married couples. They asked each member of 91 married couples to rate the degree to which they agreed with "Sex is fun for me and my partner" on a four-point scale ranging from 1, "never or occasionally", to 4, "almost always." The data appear below (I know it's a lot of data, but it's an interesting question):

Husband	1	1	1	1	1	1	1	1	1	1	1	1	1	1	1
Wife	1	1	1	1	1	1	1	2	2	2	2	2	2	2	3

Husband	1	1	1	1	2	2	2	2	2	2	2	2	2	2	2
Wife	3	4	4	4	1	1	2	2	2	2	2	2	2	2	3

Husband	2	2	2	2	2	2	2	2	2	3	3	3	3	3	3
Wife	3	3	4	4	4	4	4	4	4	1	2	2	2	2	2

| Husband | 3 | 3 | 3 | 3 | 3 | 3 | 3 | 3 | 3 | 3 | 3 | 3 | 3 | 4 | 4 | |
| Wife | 3 | 3 | 3 | 3 | 4 | 4 | 4 | 4 | 4 | 4 | 4 | 4 | 4 | 1 | 1 | |

| Husband | 4 | 4 | 4 | 4 | 4 | 4 | 4 | 4 | 4 | 4 | 4 | 4 | 4 | 4 | 4 | |
| Wife | 2 | 2 | 2 | 2 | 2 | 2 | 2 | 2 | 3 | 3 | 3 | 3 | 3 | 3 | 3 | |

| Husband | 4 | 4 | 4 | 4 | 4 | 4 | 4 | 4 | 4 | 4 | 4 | 4 | 4 | 4 | 4 | 4 |
| Wife | 3 | 3 | 4 | 4 | 4 | 4 | 4 | 4 | 4 | 4 | 4 | 4 | 4 | 4 | 4 | 4 |

© Cengage Learning 2013

Start out by running a match-sample *t* test on these data. Why is a matched-sample test appropriate?

7.20   Calculate an effect size for the data in Exercise 7.18.

7.21   Using any available software, create a scatterplot and calculate the correlation between husband's and wife's sexual satisfaction in Exercise 7.19. How does this amplify what we have learned from the analysis in Exercise 7.19. (I do not discuss scatterplots and correlation until Chapter 9, but a quick glance at Chapter 9 should suffice if you have difficulty. SPSS will easily do the calculation.)

7.22   Give an example of an experiment in which using related samples would be ill-advised because taking one measurement might influence another measurement.

7.23   Some would object that the data in Exercise 7.19 are clearly discrete, though ordinal, and that it is inappropriate to run a *t* test on them. Can you think what might be a counter argument? (This is not an easy question, and I really ask it mostly to make the point that there could be controversy here.)

7.24   Construct 95% confidence limits on the true mean difference between the Sexual Satisfaction scores in Exercise 7.19, and interpret them with respect to the data.

7.25   Sullivan and Bybee (1999) reported on an intervention program for women with abusive partners. The study involved a 10-week intervention program and a three-year follow-up, and used an experimental (intervention) and control group. At the end of the 10-week intervention period the mean quality-of-life score for the intervention group was 5.03 with a standard deviation of 1.01 and a sample size of 135. For the control group the mean was 4.61 with a standard deviation of 1.13 and a sample size of 130. Do these data indicate that the intervention was successful in terms of the quality-of-life measure?

7.26   Many mothers experience a sense of depression shortly after the birth of a child. Design a study to examine postpartum depression and, from material in this chapter, tell how you would estimate the mean increase in depression.

7.27   Another way to investigate the effectiveness of the intervention described in Exercise 7.25 would be to note that the mean quality-of-life score before the intervention was 4.47 with a standard deviation of 1.18. The quality-of-life score was 5.03 after the intervention with a standard deviation of 1.01. The sample size was 135 at each time. What do these data tell you about the effect of the intervention? (Note: You don't have the difference scores, but assume that the standard deviation of difference scores was 1.30.)

7.28   In Exercise 7.25 calculate a confidence interval for the difference in group means. Then calculate a *d*-family measure of effect size for that difference.

7.29   In the study referred to in Exercise 7.13, Katz et al. (1990) compared the performance on SAT items of a group of 17 students who were answering questions about a passage after having read the passage with the performance of a group of 28 students who had not seen the passage. The mean and standard deviation for the first group were 69.6 and 10.6, whereas for the second group they were 46.6 and 6.8.

   a.   What is the null hypothesis?
   b.   What is the alternative hypothesis?
   c.   Run the appropriate *t* test.
   d.   Interpret the results.

7.30 For the control condition of the experiment in Exercise 7.25 the beginning and 10-week means were 4.32 and 4.61 with standard deviations of 0.98 and 1.13, respectively. The sample size was 130. Using the data from this group and the intervention group, plot the change in pre- to post-test scores for the two groups and interpret what you see. (If you wish the information, the standard deviation of the difference was 1.25.)

7.31 In Exercise 7.25, data from Everitt showed that girls receiving cognitive behavior therapy gained weight over the course of the therapy. However, it is possible they just gained weight because they just got older. One way to control for this is to look at the amount of weight gained by the cognitive therapy group ($n = 29$) in contrast with the amount gained by girls in the Control group ($n = 26$) who received no therapy. The data on weight gain for the two groups is shown below.

Control		CognitiveTherapy	
−0.5	3.3	1.7	−9.1
−9.3	11.3	0.7	2.1
−5.4	0.0	−0.1	−1.4
12.3	−1.0	−0.7	1.4
−2.0	−10.6	−3.5	−0.3
−10.2	−4.6	14.9	−3.7
−12.2	−6.7	3.5	−0.8
11.6	2.8	17.1	2.4
−7.1	0.3	−7.6	12.6
6.2	1.8	1.6	1.9
−0.2	3.7	11.7	3.9
−9.2	15.9	6.1	0.1
8.3	−10.2	1.1	15.4
		−4.0	−0.7
		20.9	
Mean	**−0.45**		**3.01**
St Dev.	**7.99**		**7.31**
Variance	**63.82**		**53.41**

© Cengage Learning 2013

Run the appropriate test to compare the group means. What would you conclude?

7.32 Run the appropriate *t* test on the data in 7.19 assuming that the observations are independent. What would you conclude?

7.33 In Exercise 7.19 we saw pairs of observations on sexual satisfaction for husbands and wives. Suppose that those data had actually come from unrelated males and females, such that the data are no longer paired. What effect do you expect this to have on the analysis?

7.34 Calculate the confidence interval on $\mu_1 - \mu_2$ and d for the data in Exercise 7.31. If available, use the software mentioned earlier to calculate confidence limits on d.

7.35 Why isn't the difference between the results in 7.36 and 7.19 greater than it is?

7.36 Much has been made of the concept of experimenter bias, which refers to the fact that even the most conscientious experimenters tend to collect data that come out in the desired direction (they see what they want to see). Suppose we use students as experimenters. All the experimenters are told that subjects will be given caffeine before the experiment, but one-half of the experimenters are told that we expect caffeine to lead to good performance and one-half are told that we expect it to lead to poor performance. The dependent variable is the number of simple arithmetic problems the subjects can solve in 2 minutes. The data obtained are:

Expectation good: 19   15   22   13   18   15   20   25   22

Expectation poor: 14   18   17   12   21   21   24   14

What can you conclude?

7.37   The Thematic Apperception Test presents subjects with ambiguous pictures and asks them to tell a story about them. These stories can be scored in any number of ways. Werner, Stabenau, and Pollin (1970) asked mothers of 20 Normal and 20 Schizophrenic children to complete the TAT, and scored for the number of stories (out of 10) that exhibited a positive parent-child relationship. The data follow:

Normal	8	4	6	3	1	4	4	6	4	2
Schizophrenic	2	1	1	3	2	7	2	1	3	1
Normal	2	1	1	4	3	3	2	6	3	4
Schizophrenic	0	2	4	2	3	3	0	1	2	2

© Cengage Learning 2013

a.   What would you assume to be the experimental hypothesis behind this study?

b.   What would you conclude with respect to that hypothesis.

7.38   What is the role of random assignment in the Everitt's anorexia study referred to in Exercise 7.31, and under what conditions might we find it difficult to carry out random assignment?

7.39   In Exercise 7.37 a significant difference might lead someone to suggest that poor parent-child relationships are the cause of schizophrenia. Why might this be a troublesome conclusion?

7.40   In Exercise 7.37 why might it be smart to look at the variances of the two groups?

7.41   Calculate 95% confidence limits on $\mu_1 - \mu_2$ and d for the data in Exercise 7.36.

7.42   What does a comparison of Exercises 7.43 and 7.44 show you?

7.43   A second investigator repeated the experiment described in Exercise 7.44 and obtained the same results. However, she thought that it would be more appropriate to record the data in terms of minutes per problem (e.g., 4 problems in 10 minutes = 10/4 = 2.5 minutes/problem). Thus, her data were:

Innate ability:	2.50	2.00	1.25	3.33	1.43
Time-filling task:	0.91	1.67	1.11	1.43	1.11

Analyze and interpret these data with the appropriate t test.

7.44   An experimenter examining decision making asked 10 children to solve as many problems as they could in 10 minutes. One group (5 subjects) was told that this was a test of their innate problem-solving ability; a second group (5 subjects) was told that this was just a time-filling task. The data follow:

Innate ability:	4	5	8	3	7
Time-filling task:	11	6	9	7	9

Does the mean number of problems solved vary with the experimental condition?

7.45   I stated earlier that Levene's test consists of calculating the absolute (or squared) differences between individual observations and their group's mean, and then running a t test on those differences. By using any computer software it is simple to calculate those absolute and squared differences and then to run a t test on them. Calculate both and determine which approach SPSS is using in the example. (Hint, $F = t^2$ here, and the F value that SPSS actually calculated was 0.391148, to 6 decimal places.)

7.46   Present meaningful effect sizes estimate(s) for the two independent group data in Exercise 7.31.

7.47   It is commonly reported that women show more symptoms of anxiety and depression than men. Would the data from Mireault's study support this hypothesis?

7.48   Research on clinical samples (i.e., people referred for diagnosis or treatment) has suggested that children who experience the death of a parent may be at risk for developing depression or anxiety in adulthood. Mireault and Bond (1992) collected data on 140 college students who had experienced the death of a parent, 182 students from two-parent families, and

59 students from divorced families. The data are found in the file Mireault.dat and are described in Appendix: Computer Exercises.

    a. Use any statistical program to run *t* tests to compare the first two groups on the Depression, Anxiety, and Global Symptom Index *t* scores from the Brief Symptom Inventory (Derogatis, 1983).

    b. Are these three *t* tests independent of one another? [Hint: To do this problem you will have to ignore or delete those cases in Group 3 (the Divorced group). Your instructor or the appropriate manual will explain how to do this for the particular software that you are using.]

7.49 Present meaningful effect sizes estimate(s) for the matched pairs data in Exercise 7.25.

7.50 Now run separate *t* tests to compare Mireault's Group 1 versus Group 2, Group 1 versus Group 3, and Group 2 versus Group 3 on the Global Symptom Index. (This is not a good way to compare the three group means, but it is being done here because it leads to more appropriate analyses in Chapter 12.)

7.51 In Chapter 6 (Exercise 6.32) we examined data presented by Hout et al., on the sexual satisfaction of married couples. We did so by setting up a contingency table and computing χ^2 on that table. We looked at those data again in a different way in Exercise 7.19, where we ran a *t*-test comparing the means. Instead of asking subjects to rate their statement "Sex is fun for me and my partner" as "Never, Fairly Often, Very Often, or Almost Always," we converted their categorical responses to a four-point scale from 1 = "Never" to 4 = "Almost Always."

    a. How does the "scale of measurement" issue relate to this analysis?

    b. Even setting aside the fact that this exercise and Exercise 6.35 use different statistical tests, the two exercises are asking quite different questions of the data. What are those different questions?

    c. What might you do if 15 wives refused to answer the question, although their husbands did, and 8 husbands refused to answer the question when their wives did?

    d. How comfortable are you with the *t*-test analysis, and what might you do instead?

7.52 Write a short paragraph containing the information necessary to describe the results of the experiment discussed in Exercise 7.31. This should be an abbreviated version of what you would write in a research article.

Chapter 8

Power

Objectives

To introduce the concept of the power of a statistical test and to show how we can calculate the power of a variety of statistical procedures.

Contents

MOST APPLIED STATISTICAL WORK as it is actually carried out in analyzing experimental results is primarily concerned with minimizing (or at least controlling) the probability of a Type I error (α). When designing experiments, people tend to ignore the very important fact that there is a probability (β) of another kind of error, Type II errors. Whereas Type I errors deal with the problem of finding a difference that is not there, Type II errors concern the equally serious problem of not finding a difference that is there. When we consider the substantial cost in time and money that goes into a typical experiment, we could argue that it is remarkably short-sighted of experimenters not to recognize that they may, from the start, have only a small chance of finding the effect they are looking for, even if such an effect does exist in the population.[1]

There are very good historical reasons why investigators have tended to ignore Type II errors. Cohen placed the initial blame on the emphasis Fisher gave to the idea that the null hypothesis was either true or false, with little attention to H_1. Although the Neyman–Pearson approach does emphasize the importance of H_1, Fisher's views have been very influential. In addition, until recently, many textbooks avoided the problem altogether, and those books that did discuss power did so in ways that were not easily understood by the average reader. Cohen, however, discussed the problem clearly and lucidly in several publications.[2] Cohen (1988) presents a thorough and rigorous treatment of the material. In Welkowitz, Ewen, and Cohen (2000), an introductory book, the material is treated in a slightly simpler way through the use of an approximation technique. That approach is the one adopted in this chapter. Two extremely good papers that are accessible and provide useful methods are by Cohen (1992a, 1992b). You should have no difficulty with either of these sources, or, for that matter, with any of the many excellent papers Cohen published on a wide variety of topics not necessarily directly related to this particular one.

Speaking in terms of Type II errors is a rather negative way of approaching the problem, because it keeps reminding us that we might make a mistake. The more positive approach would be to speak in terms of **power**, which is defined as the probability of correctly rejecting a false H_0 when a particular alternative hypothesis is true. Thus, power $= 1 - \beta$. A more powerful experiment is one that has a better chance of rejecting a false H_0 than does a less-powerful experiment.

power

In this chapter we will generally take the approach of Welkowitz, Ewen, and Cohen (2000) and work with a method that gives a good approximation of the true power of a test. This approximation is an excellent one, especially in light of the fact that we do not really care whether the power is .85 or .83, but rather whether it is near .80 or nearer to .30. Certainly there is excellent software available for our use, and we will consider a particularly good program shortly, but the gain in precision is often illusory. By that I mean that the parameter estimates we make to carry out a power analysis are often sufficiently in error that the answer that comes from a piece of software may give an illusion of accuracy rather than greater precision. The method that I will use makes clear the concepts involved in power calculations, and if you wish more precise answers you can download very good, free, software. An excellent program named G*Power by Faul and Erdfelder is available on the Internet at http://www.psycho.uni-duesseldorf.de/abteilungen/aap/gpower3/, and there are both Macintosh and Windows programs at that site. In what follows I will show power calculations by hand, but then will show the results of using G*Power and the advantages that the program offers.

For expository purposes we will assume for the moment that we are interested in testing the difference between two sample means, although the approach will immediately generalize to testing other hypotheses.

---

[1] Recently journal editors have been more aggressive in asking for information on power, but I suspect that most power analyses are carried out after the experiment is completed just to satisfy the demands of editors and reviewers.

[2] A somewhat different approach is taken by Murphy and Myors (1998), who base all of their power calculations on the F distribution. The F distribution appears throughout this book, and virtually all of the statistics covered in this book can be transformed to a F. The Murphy and Myors approach is worth examining, and will give results very close to the results we find in this chapter.

8.1 The Basic Concept of Power

Before I explain the calculation of power estimates, we can examine the underlying concept by looking at power directly by using resampling. In the last chapter we considered a study by Aronson et al. (1998) on stereotype threat. Those authors showed that white male students to whom performance in mathematics was important performed more poorly when reminded that Asian students often perform better on math tests. This is an important finding, and it would not be unusual to try to replicate it. Suppose that we were planning to perform a replication, but wanted to use 20 students in each group—a control group and a threatened group. But before we spend the money and energy trying to replicate this study, we ought to have some idea of the probability of a successful replication. That is what power is all about.

To look at the calculation of power we need to have some idea what the mean and standard deviation of the populations of control and threatened respondents would be. Our best guess at those parameters would be the means and standard deviations that Aronson et al. found for their sample. They are not likely to be the exact parameters, but they are the best guess we have. So we will assume that the Control population would have a mean of 9.64 and a standard deviation of 3.17, and that the Threat population has a mean of 6.58 and a standard deviation of 3.03. We will also assume that the populations are normally distributed. As I said, we plan to use 20 participants in each group.

An easy way to model this is to draw 20 observations from a population of scores with mean and standard deviation equal to those of the Control condition. Similarly, we will draw 20 observations from a population with a mean and standard deviation equal to those of the experimental group. We will then calculate a t statistic for these data, store that away, and then repeat the process 9,999 times. This will give us 10,000 t values. We also know that with 38 df, the critical value of $t_a(38) = 2.024$, so we can ask how many of these 10,000 t values are significant (i.e., are greater than or equal to 2.024).

The result of just such a sampling study is presented in Figure 8.1, with the appropriate t distribution superimposed. Notice that although 86% of the results were greater than $t = 2.024$, 14% of them were less than the critical value. Therefore the power of this experiment, given the parameter estimates and sample size is .86, which is the percentage of outcomes exceeding the critical value. This is actually a reasonable level of power for most practical work.[3]

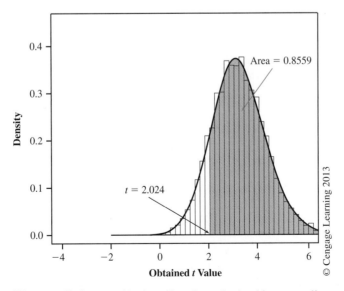

Figure 8.1   Distribution of t values obtained in resampling study

---

[3] A program to draw this figure is available at the Web site as ResampleForPower.R. You can vary parameters and sample sizes. That program also computes actual power, which in this case is .8601.

8.2 Factors Affecting the Power of a Test

Having looked at power from a heuristic perspective by actually drawing repeated samples, we will now look at it a bit more theoretically. As might be expected, power is a function of several variables. It is a function of (1) α, the probability of a Type I error, (2) the true alternative hypothesis (H_1), (3) the sample size, and (4) the particular test to be employed. With the exception of the relative power of independent versus matched samples, we will avoid this last relationship on the grounds that when the test assumptions are met, the majority of the procedures discussed in this book can be shown to be the uniformly most powerful tests of those available to answer the question at hand. It is important to keep in mind, however, that when the underlying assumptions of a test are violated, the nonparametric tests discussed in Chapter 18, and especially the resampling tests, are often more powerful.

A Short Review

First we need a quick review of the material covered in Chapter 4. Consider the two distributions in Figure 8.2. The distribution to the left (labeled H_0) represents the sampling distribution of the mean when the null hypothesis is true and $\mu = \mu_0$. The distribution on the right represents the sampling distribution of the mean that we would have if H_0 were false and the true population mean were equal to μ_1. The placement of this distribution depends entirely on what the value of μ_1 happens to be.

The heavily shaded right tail of the H_0 distribution represents α, the probability of a Type I error, assuming that we are using a one-tailed test (otherwise it represents $\alpha/2$). This area contains the sample means that would result in significant values of t. The second distribution (H_1) represents the sampling distribution of the mean when H_0 is false and the true mean is μ_1. It is readily apparent that even when H_0 is false, many of the sample means (and therefore the corresponding values of t) will nonetheless fall to the left of the critical value, causing us to fail to reject a false H_0, thus committing a Type II error. We saw this in the previous demonstration. The probability of this error is indicated by the lightly shaded area in Figure 8.2 and is labeled β. When H_0 is false and the test statistic falls to the right of the critical value, we will correctly reject a false H_0. The probability of doing this is what we mean by *power*, and it is shown in the unshaded area of the H_1 distribution. Figure 8.2 closely resembles Figure 8.1, although in that figure I did not superimpose the null distribution.

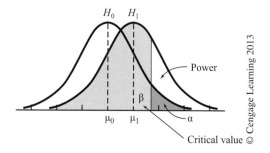

Figure 8.2   Sampling distribution of $\overline{X}$ under H_0 and H_1

Power as a Function of α

With the aid of Figure 8.2, it is easy to see why we say that power is a function of α. If we are willing to increase α, our cutoff point moves to the left, thus simultaneously decreasing β and increasing power, although with a corresponding rise in the probability of a Type I error.

Power as a Function of H_1

The fact that power is a function of the true alternative hypothesis [more precisely $(\mu_0 - \mu_1)$, the difference between μ_0 (the mean under H_0) and μ_1 (the mean under H_1)] is illustrated by comparing Figures 8.2 and 8.3. In Figure 8.3 the distance between μ_0 and μ_1 has been increased, and this has resulted in a substantial increase in power, though there is still sizable probability of a Type II error. This is not particularly surprising, because all that we are saying is that the chances of finding a difference depend on how large the difference actually is.

Power as a Function of n and σ^2

The relationship between power and sample size (and between power and σ^2) is only a little subtler. Because we are interested in means or differences between means, we are interested in the sampling distribution of the mean. We know that the variance of the sampling distribution of the mean decreases as either n increases or σ^2 decreases, because $\sigma_{\bar{X}}^2 = \sigma^2 / n$. Figure 8.4 illustrates what happens to the two sampling distributions (H_0 and H_1) as we increase n or decrease σ^2, relative to Figure 8.3. Figure 8.4 also shows that, as $\sigma_{\bar{X}}^2$ decreases, the overlap between the two distributions is reduced with a resulting increase in power. Notice that the two means (μ_0 and μ_1) remain unchanged from Figure 8.3.

If an experimenter concerns himself with the power of a test, then he is most likely interested in those variables governing power that are easy to manipulate. Because n is more easily manipulated than is either σ^2 or the difference $(\mu_0 - \mu_1)$, and since tampering

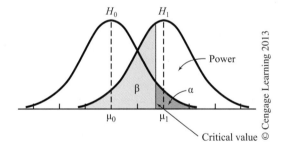

Figure 8.3   Effect on β of increasing $\mu_0 - \mu_1$

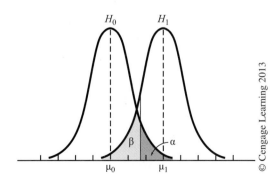

Figure 8.4   Effect on β of decrease in standard error of the mean

with α produces undesirable side effects in terms of increasing the probability of a Type I error, discussions of power are generally concerned with the effects of varying sample size, although McClelland (1997) has pointed out that simple changes in experimental design can also increase the power of an experiment.

8.3 Calculating Power the Traditional Way

As we saw in Figures 8.2 through 8.4, power depends on the degree of overlap between the sampling distributions under H_0 and H_1. Furthermore, this overlap is a function of both the distance between μ_0 and μ_1 and the standard error. One measure, then, of the degree to which H_0 is false would be the distance from μ_1 to μ_0 expressed in terms of the number of standard errors. The problem with this measure, however, is that it includes the sample size (in the computation of the standard error), when in fact we will usually wish to solve for the power associated with a given n or else for that value of n required for a given level of power. For this reason we will take as our distance measure, or **effect size (d)**

effect size (d)

$$d = \frac{\mu_1 - \mu_0}{\sigma}$$

ignoring the sign of d, and incorporating n later. Thus, d is a measure of the degree to which μ_1 and μ_0 differ in terms of the standard deviation of the parent population. (For the example we just looked at, $d = (9.64 - 6.58)/3.10 = .987$, which simply says that the means under H_1 differ by near one standard deviation. (I am using the pooled standard deviation here.) We see that d is estimated independently of n, simply by estimating μ_1, μ_0, and σ. In Chapter 7 we discussed effect size as the standardized difference between two means. This is the same measure here, though one of those means is the mean under the null hypothesis. I will point this out again when we come to comparing the means of two populations.

Estimating the Effect Size

The first task is to estimate d, because it will form the basis for future calculations. This can be done in three ways, ranging from most to least satisfactory:

1. *Prior research.* On the basis of past research, we can often get at least a rough approximation of d. Thus, we could look at sample means and variances from other studies and make an informed guess at the values we might expect for $\mu_1 - \mu_0$ and for σ. In practice, this task is not as difficult as it might seem, especially when you realize that a rough approximation is far better than no approximation at all.

2. *Personal assessment of how large a difference is important.* In many cases, an investigator is able to say, I am interested in detecting a difference of at least 10 points between μ_1 and μ_0. The investigator is essentially saying that differences less than this have no important or useful meaning, whereas greater differences do. (This is particularly common in biomedical research, where we are interesting in decreasing cholesterol, for example, by a certain amount, and have no interest in smaller changes. A similar situation arises when we want to compare drugs and are not interested in the new one unless it is better than the old one by some predetermined amount.) Here we are given the value of $\mu_1 - \mu_0$ directly, without needing to know the particular values of μ_1 and μ_0. All that remains is to estimate σ from other data. As an example, the investigator might say that she is interested in finding a procedure that will raise scores on the Graduate Record Exam by 40 points above normal. We already know that the standard deviation for this test is approximately 100. Thus $d = 40/100 = .40$. If our hypothetical experimenter says instead that she wants to raise scores by four-tenths of a standard deviation, she would be giving us d directly.

3. *Use of special conventions.* When we encounter a situation in which there is no way we can estimate the required parameters, we can fall back on a set of conventions proposed by Cohen (1988). Cohen more or less arbitrarily defined three levels of *d*:

Effect Size	*d*	Percentage of Overlap
Small	.20	.92
Medium	.50	.80
Large	.80	.69

Thus, *in a pinch*, the experimenter can simply decide whether she is after a small, medium, or large effect and set *d* accordingly. However, this solution should be chosen *only* when the other alternatives are not feasible. The right-hand column of the table is labeled Percentage of Overlap, and it records the degree to which the two distributions shown in Figure 8.2 overlap[4]. Thus, for example, when $d = 0.50$, 80% of the two distributions overlap (Cohen, 1988). This is yet another way of thinking about how big a difference a treatment produces.

Cohen chose a medium effect to be one that would be apparent to an intelligent viewer, a small effect as one that is real but difficult to detect visually, and a large effect as one that is the same distance above a medium effect as "small" is below it. Cohen (1969) originally developed these guidelines only for those who had no other way of estimating the effect size. But as time went on and he became discouraged by the failure of many researchers to conduct power analyses, presumably because they think them to be too difficult, he made greater use of these conventions (see Cohen, 1992a). However, Bruce Thompson, of Texas A&M, made an excellent point in this regard. He was speaking of expressing obtained differences in terms of *d*, in place of focusing on the probability value of a resulting test statistic. He wrote, "Finally, it must be emphasized that if we mindlessly invoke Cohen's rules of thumb, *contrary to his strong admonitions*, in place of the equally mindless consultation of *p* value cutoffs such as .05 and .01, we are merely electing to be thoughtless in a new metric (emphasis added)" (Thompson, 2000). The point applies to any use of arbitrary conventions for *d*, regardless of whether it is for purposes of calculating power or for purposes of impressing your readers with how large your difference is. Lenth (2001) has argued convincingly that the use of conventions such as Cohen's is dangerous. We need to concentrate on both the value of the numerator and the value of the denominator in *d*, and not just on their ratio. Lenth's argument is really an attempt at making the investigator more responsible for his or her decisions, and I suspect that Cohen would have wholeheartedly agreed.

It may strike you as peculiar that the investigator is being asked to define the difference she is looking for before the experiment is conducted. Most people would respond by saying, "I don't know how the experiment will come out. I just wonder whether there will be a difference." Although many experimenters speak in this way (and I am no virtuous exception), you should question the validity of this statement. Do we really not know, at least vaguely, what will happen in our experiments; if not, why are we running them? Although there is occasionally a legitimate "I-wonder-what-would-happen-if experiment," in general, "I do not know" translates to "I have not thought that far ahead."

Recombining the Effect Size and *n*

δ (delta)

We decided earlier to split the sample size from the effect size to make it easier to deal with *n* separately. We now need a method of combining the effect size with the sample size. We use the statistic δ (**delta**) $= d[f(n)]$[5] to represent this combination where the particular

---

[4] I want to thank James Grice and Paul Barrett for providing the corrected values of the percentage of overlap.
[5] About the only thing that will turn off a math-phobic student faster than reading "*f(n)*" is to have it followed in the next sentence with "*g(n)*." All it means is that *d* depends on *n* in some as yet unspecified way.

function of n [i.e., $f(n)$] will be defined differently for each individual test. The convenient thing about this system is that it will allow us to use the same table of δ for power calculations for all the statistical procedures to be considered.

8.4   Power Calculations for the One-Sample t

We will first examine power calculations for the one-sample t test. In the preceding section we saw that δ is based on d and some function of n. For the one-sample t, that function will be $\sqrt{n}$, and δ will then be defined as $\delta = d\sqrt{n}$. Given δ as defined here, we can immediately determine the power of our test from the table of power in Appendix Power.

Assume that a clinical psychologist wants to test the hypothesis that people who seek treatment for psychological problems have higher IQs than the general population. She wants to use the IQs of 25 randomly selected clients and is interested in using simple calculations to find the power of detecting a difference of 5 points between the mean of the general population and the mean of the population from which her clients are drawn. Thus, $\mu_1 = 105$, $\mu_0 = 100$, and $\sigma = 15$. We know that

$$d = \frac{105 - 100}{15} = 0.33$$

then

$$\delta = d\sqrt{n} = 0.33\sqrt{25} = 0.33(5)$$
$$= 1.65$$

Although the clinician expects the sample means to be above average, she plans to use a two-tailed test at $\alpha = .05$ to protect against unexpected events. From Appendix Power, for $\delta = 1.65$ with $\alpha = .05$ (two-tailed), power is between .36 and .40. By crude linear interpolation, we will say that power = .38. This means that, if H_0 is false and μ_1 is really 105, only 38% of the time can our clinician expect to find a "statistically significant" difference between her *sample* mean and that specified by H_0. (When we come to software called G*Power we will obtain a result of .359. You can see that these two approaches return pretty much the same result.) A probability of .38 is rather discouraging because it means that if the true mean really is 105, 62% of the time our clinician will make a Type II error.

Because our experimenter was intelligent enough to examine the question of power before she began her experiment, all is not lost. She still has the chance to make changes that will lead to an increase in power. She could, for example, set α at .10, thus increasing power to approximately .50, but this is probably unsatisfactory. (Reviewers, for example, generally hate to see α set at any value greater than .05.)

Estimating Required Sample Size

Alternatively, the investigator could increase her sample size, thereby increasing power. How large an n does she need? The answer depends on what level of power she desires. Suppose she wishes to set power at .80. From Appendix Power, for power = .80, and $\alpha = 0.05$, δ must equal 2.80. Thus, we have δ and d and can simply solve for n:

$$\delta = d\sqrt{n}$$
$$n = \left(\frac{\delta}{d}\right)^2 = \left(\frac{2.80}{0.33}\right)^2 = 8.48^2$$
$$= 71.91$$

Because clients generally come in whole lots, we will round off to 72. Thus, if the experimenter wants to have an 80% chance of rejecting H_0 when $d = 0.33$ (i.e., when $\mu_1 = 105$), she will have to use the IQs for 72 randomly selected clients. Although this may be more clients than she can test easily, the only alternatives is to settle for a lower level of power or recruit other clinical psychologists to contribute to her database.

You might wonder why we selected power $= .80$; with this degree of power, we still run a 20% chance of making a Type II error. The issue is a practical one. Suppose, for example, that we had wanted power $= .95$. A few simple calculations will show that this would require a sample of $n = 119$. For power $= .99$, you would need approximately 162 clients. These may well be unreasonable sample sizes for this particular experimental situation, or for the resources of the experimenter. Remember that increases in power are generally bought by increases in n and, at high levels of power, the cost can be very high. If you are taking data from data tapes supplied by the Bureau of the Census that is quite different from studying teenage college graduates. A value of power $= .80$ makes a Type II error four times as likely as a Type I error, which some would take as a reasonable reflection of their relative importance. I should also point out that Institutional Review Boards often balk at sample sizes that they consider excessive.

Noncentrality Parameters

noncentrality parameter

Our statistic δ is what most textbooks refer to as a **noncentrality parameter**. The concept is relatively simple, and well worth considering. (Some computer software will ask you to provide a noncentrality parameter.) First, we know that

$$t = \frac{\overline{X} - \mu}{s/\sqrt{n}}$$

is distributed around zero regardless of the truth or falsity of any null hypothesis, *as long as μ is the true mean* of the distribution from which the *X*s were sampled. If H_0 states that $\mu = \mu_0$ (some specific value of μ) *and if H_0 is true*, then

$$t = \frac{\overline{X} - \mu_0}{s/\sqrt{n}}$$

will also be distributed around zero. If H_0 is false and $\mu \neq \mu_0$, however, then

$$t = \frac{\overline{X} - \mu_0}{s/\sqrt{n}}$$

will not be distributed around zero because in subtracting μ_0, we have been subtracting the wrong population mean. In fact, the *t* distribution will be centered at the point

$$\delta = \frac{\mu_1 - \mu_0}{\sigma/\sqrt{n}}$$

This shift in the mean of the distribution from zero to δ is referred to as the *degree of noncentrality*, and δ is the noncentrality parameter, often denoted as *ncp*. (What is δ when $\mu_1 = \mu_0$?) The noncentrality parameter is just one way of expressing how wrong the null hypothesis is.

The question of power becomes the question of how likely we are to find a value of the noncentral (shifted) distribution that is greater than the critical value that *t* would have under H_0. In other words, even though larger-than-normal values of *t* are to be expected because H_0 is false, we will occasionally obtain small values by chance. The percentage of these values that happen to lie between $\pm t_{.025}$ is β, the probability of a Type II error. As we know, we can convert from β *to* power; power $= 1 - \beta$.

Cohen's contribution can be seen as splitting the noncentrality parameter (δ) into two parts—sample size and effect size. One part (d) depends solely on parameters of the populations, whereas the other depends on sample size. Thus, Cohen has separated parametric considerations (μ_0, μ_1, and σ), about which we can do relatively little, from sample characteristics (n), over which we have more control. Although this splitting produces no basic change in the underlying theory, it makes the concept easier to understand and use.

8.5 Power Calculations for Differences Between Two Independent Means

When we wish to test the difference between two independent means, the treatment of power is very similar to our treatment of the case that we used for only one mean. In Section 8.3 we obtained d by taking the difference between μ under H_1 and μ under H_0 and dividing by σ. In testing the difference between two independent means, we will do basically the same thing, although this time we will work with mean differences. Thus, we want the difference between the two population means ($\mu_1 - \mu_2$) under H_1 minus the difference ($\mu_1 - \mu_2$) under H_0, divided by σ. (Recall that we assume $\sigma_1^2 = \sigma_2^2 = \sigma^2$.) In most usual applications, however, ($\mu_1 - \mu_2$) under H_0 is zero, so we can drop that term from our formula. Thus,

$$d = \frac{(\mu_1 - \mu_2) - (0)}{\sigma} = \frac{\mu_1 - \mu_2}{\sigma}$$

where the numerator refers to the difference to be expected under H_1 and the denominator represents the standard deviation of the populations. You should recognize that this is the same d that we saw in Chapter 7 where it was also labeled Cohen's d, or sometimes Hedges' g. The only difference is that here it is expressed in terms of population means rather than sample means.

In the case of two samples, we must distinguish between experiments involving equal ns and those involving unequal ns. We will treat these two cases separately.

Equal Sample Sizes

Assume we wish to test the difference between two treatments and expect that either the difference in population means will be approximately 5 points or else are interested only in finding a difference of at least 5 points. Further assume that from past data we think that σ is approximately 10. Then

$$d = \frac{\mu_1 - \mu_2}{\sigma} = \frac{5}{10} = 0.50$$

Thus, we are expecting a difference of one-half of a standard deviation between the two means, what Cohen (1988) would call a moderate effect.

First we will investigate the power of an experiment with 25 observations in each of two groups. We will define the noncentrality parameter, δ, in the two-sample case as

$$\delta = d\sqrt{\frac{n}{2}}$$

where n = the number of cases *in any one sample* (there are $2n$ cases in all). Thus,

$$\delta = (0.50)\sqrt{\frac{25}{2}} = 0.50\sqrt{12.5} = 0.50(3.54)$$
$$= 1.77$$

From Appendix Power, by interpolation for $\delta = 1.77$ with a two-tailed test at $\alpha = .05$, power $= .43$. Thus, if our investigator actually runs this experiment with 25 subjects, and if her estimate of δ is correct, then she has a probability of .43 of actually rejecting H_0 if it is false to the extent she expects (and a probability of .57 of making a Type II error).

We next turn the question around and ask how many subjects would be needed for power $= .80$. From Appendix Power, this would require $\delta = 2.80$.

$$\delta = d\sqrt{\frac{n}{2}}$$

$$\frac{\delta}{d} = \sqrt{\frac{n}{2}}$$

$$\left(\frac{\delta}{d}\right)^2 = \frac{n}{2}$$

$$n = 2\left(\frac{\delta}{d}\right)^2$$

$$= 2\left(\frac{2.80}{0.50}\right)^2 = 2(5.6)^2$$

$$= 62.72$$

n refers to the number of subjects per sample, so for power $= .80$, we need 63 subjects per sample for a total of 126 subjects.

Unequal Sample Sizes

We just dealt with the case in which $n_1 = n_2 = n$. However, experiments often have two samples of different sizes. This obviously presents difficulties when we try to solve for δ, since we need one value for n. What value can we use?

With reasonably large and nearly equal samples, a conservative approximation can be obtained by letting n equal the smaller of n_1 and n_2. This is not satisfactory, however, if the sample sizes are small or if the two ns are quite different. For those cases we need a more exact solution.

One seemingly reasonable (but incorrect) procedure would be to set n equal to the arithmetic mean of n_1 and n_2. This method would weight the two samples equally, however, when in fact we know that the variance of means is proportional not to n, but to $1/n$. The measure that takes this relationship into account is not the arithmetic mean but the harmonic mean. The **harmonic mean** $(\overline{X}_h)$ of k numbers $(X_1, X_2, ..., X_k)$ is defined as

harmonic mean $(\overline{X}_h)$

$$\overline{X}_h = \frac{k}{\sum \dfrac{1}{X_i}}$$

Thus for two samples sizes (n_1 and n_2),

$$\overline{n}_h = \frac{2}{\dfrac{1}{n_1} + \dfrac{1}{n_2}} = \frac{2n_1 n_2}{n_1 + n_2}$$

We can then use $\overline{n}_h$ in our calculation of δ.

We looked at the work on stereotype threat by Aronson et al. (1998) at the beginning of this chapter. Here we will go back to that work but focus on direct calculation. What Aronson actually found, which is trivially different from the sample data I generated in

Chapter 7, were means of 9.58 and 6.55 for the Control and Threatened groups, respectively. Their pooled standard deviation was approximately 3.10. We will assume that Aronson's estimates of the population means and standard deviation are essentially correct. (They almost certainly suffer from some random error, but they are the best guesses that we have of those parameters.) This produces

$$d = \frac{\mu_1 - \mu_2}{\sigma} = \frac{9.58 - 6.55}{3.10} = \frac{3.03}{3.10} = 0.98$$

Perhaps I want to replicate this study in the research methods class, but I don't want to risk looking foolish and saying, "Well, it should have worked." My class has a lot of students, but only about 30 of them are males, and they are not evenly distributed across the lab sections. Because of the way that I have chosen to run the experiment, assume that I can expect that 18 males will be in the Control group and 12 in the Threat group. Then we will calculate the effective sample size (the sample size to be used in calculating δ) as

$$\bar{n}_h = \frac{2(18)(12)}{18 + 12} = \frac{432}{30} = 14.40$$

effective sample size

We see that the **effective sample size** is less than the arithmetic mean of the two individual sample sizes. In other words, this study has the same power as it would have had we run it with 14.4 subjects per group for a total of 28.8 subjects. Or, to state it differently, with unequal sample sizes it takes 30 subjects to have the same power 28.8 subjects would have in an experiment with equal sample sizes.

To continue,

$$\delta = d\sqrt{\frac{\bar{n}_h}{2}} = 0.98\sqrt{\frac{14.4}{2}} = 0.98\sqrt{7.2}$$
$$= 2.63$$

For δ = 2.63, power = .75 at α = .05 (two-tailed).

In this case the power is a bit too low to inspire confidence that the study will work out as a lab exercise is supposed to. I could take a chance and run the study, but it would be very awkward if the experiment failed.

An alternative would be to recruit some more students. I will use the 30 males in my course, but I can also find another 20 in another course who are willing to participate. At the risk of teaching bad experimental design to my students by combining two different classes (at least it gives me an excuse to mention that this could be a problem), I will add in those students and expect to get sample sizes of 28 and 22.

These sample sizes would yield $\bar{n}_h = 24.64$. Then

$$\delta = d\sqrt{\frac{\bar{n}_h}{2}} = 0.98\sqrt{\frac{24.64}{2}} = 0.98\sqrt{12.32}$$
$$= 3.44$$

From Appendix Power we find that power now equals approximately .93, which is sufficient for our purposes.

My sample sizes were unequal, but not seriously so. When we have quite unequal sample sizes, and they are unavoidable, the smaller group should be as large as possible relative to the larger group. You should never throw away subjects to make sample sizes equal. This is just throwing away power.[6]

---

[6] McClelland (1997) has provided a strong argument that when we have more than two groups and the independent variable is ordinal, power may be maximized by assigning disproportionately large numbers of subjects to the extreme levels of the independent variable.

8.6 Power Calculations for Matched-Sample *t*

When we want to test the difference between two matched samples, the problem becomes a bit more difficult and an additional parameter must be considered. For this reason, the analysis of power for this case is frequently impractical. However, the general solution to the problem illustrates an important principle of experimental design and thus justifies close examination.

With a matched-sample *t* test we define *d* as

$$d = \frac{\mu_1 - \mu_2}{\sigma_{X_1 - X_2}}$$

where $\mu_1 - \mu_2$ represents the expected difference in the means of the two populations of observations (the expected mean of the difference scores). The problem arises because $\sigma_{X_1 - X_2}$ is the standard deviation not of the populations of X_1 and X_2, but of difference scores drawn from these populations. Although we might be able to make an intelligent guess at σ_{X_1} or σ_{X_2}, we probably have no idea about $\sigma_{X_1 - X_2}$.

All is not lost, however; it is possible to calculate $\sigma_{X_1 - X_2}$ on the basis of a few assumptions. The variance sum law (discussed in Chapter 7, p. 207) gives the variance for a sum or difference of two variables. Specifically,

$$\sigma^2_{X_1 \pm X_2} = \sigma^2_{X_1} + \sigma^2_{X_2} \pm 2\rho\sigma_{X_1}\sigma_{X_2}$$

If we make the general assumption of homogeneity of variance $\sigma^2_{X_1} = \sigma^2_{X_2} = \sigma^2$, for the difference of two variables we have

$$\sigma^2_{X_1 - X_2} = 2\sigma^2 - 2\rho\sigma^2 = 2\sigma^2(1 - \rho)$$
$$\sigma_{X_1 - X_2} = \sigma\sqrt{2(1 - \rho)}$$

where ρ (rho) is the correlation in the population between X_1 and X_2 and can take on values between 1 and −1. It is positive for almost all situations in which we are likely to want a matched-sample *t*.

Assuming for the moment that we can estimate ρ, the rest of the procedure is the same as that for the one-sample *t*. We define

$$d = \frac{\mu_1 - \mu_2}{\sigma_{X_1 - X_2}}$$

and

$$\delta = d\sqrt{n}$$

We then estimate $\sigma_{X_1 - X_2}$ as $\sigma\sqrt{2(1 - \rho)}$, and refer the value of δ to the tables.

As an example, assume that I want to use the Aronson study of stereotype threat in class, but this time I want to run it as a matched-sample design. I have 30 male subjects available, and I can first administer the test without saying anything about Asian students typically performing better, and then I can readminister it in the next week's lab with the threatening instructions. (You might do well to consider how this study could be improved to minimize carryover effects and other contaminants.) Let's assume that we expect the scores to go down in the threatening condition, but because the test was previously given to these same people in the first week, the drop will be from 9.58 down to only 7.55. Assume that the standard deviation will stay the same at 3.10. To solve for the standard error of the difference between means we need the correlation between the two sets of exam scores, but here we are in luck. Aronson's math questions were taken from a practice exam for the Graduate Record Exam, and the correlation we seek is estimated simply by the test-retest reliability of that exam. We have a pretty good idea that the reliability of that exam will be somewhere around .92. Then

$$\sigma_{X_1-X_2} = \sigma\sqrt{2(1-\rho)} = 3.10\sqrt{2(1-.92)} = 3.1\sqrt{2(.08)}$$
$$= 1.24$$

$$d = \frac{\mu_1 - \mu_2}{\sigma_{X_1-X_2}} = \frac{9.58 - 7.55}{1.24} = 1.64$$

$$\delta = d\sqrt{n} = 1.64\sqrt{30} = 8.97$$

Power = .99

Notice that I have a smaller effect size than in my first lab exercise because I tried to be honest and estimate that the difference in means would be reduced because of the experimental procedures. However, my power is far greater than it was in my original example because of the added power of matched-sample designs.

Suppose, on the other hand, that we had used a less reliable test, for which $\rho = .40$. We will assume that σ remains unchanged and that we are expecting a 2.03-unit difference between the means. Then

$$\sigma_{X_1-X_2} = 3.10\sqrt{2(1-.40)} = 3.10\sqrt{2(.60)} = 3.10\sqrt{1.2} = 3.40$$

$$d = \frac{\mu_1 - \mu_2}{\sigma_{X_1-X_2}} = \frac{2.03}{3.40} = 0.60$$

$$\delta = 0.60\sqrt{30} = 3.29$$

Power = .91

We see that as ρ drops, so does power. (It is still substantial in this example, but much less than it was.) When $\rho = 0$, our two variables are not correlated and thus the matched-sample case has been reduced to very nearly the independent-sample case. The important point here is that for practical purposes the minimum power for the matched-sample case occurs when $\rho = 0$ and we have independent samples. Thus, for all situations in which we are even remotely likely to use matched samples (when we expect a positive correlation between X_1 and X_2), the matched-sample design is more powerful than the corresponding independent-groups design. This illustrates one of the main advantages of designs using matched samples, and was my primary reason for taking you through these calculations.

Remember that we are using an approximation procedure to calculate power. Essentially, we are assuming the sample sizes are sufficiently large that the t distribution is closely approximated by z. If this is not the case, then we have to take account of the fact that a matched-sample t has only one-half as many df as the corresponding independent-sample t, and the power of the two designs will not be quite equal when $\rho = 0$. This is not usually a serious problem.

8.7   Turning the Tables on Power

This is a good place to use power to make a different, and very important, point. We often run experiments, see that the result is significant at alpha = .05, and get quite excited. But there have been a number of people who have made the point that a "p" value isn't everything, and it doesn't tell us everything. These are some of the same people who keep reminding us that confidence limits are at least as informative as knowing that the difference is significant, and they tell as a great deal more. One of the best papers that I have read on this subject is Cumming (2008).

To illustrate Cumming's point, we'll go back to the study by Aronson et al. (1998) on stereotype threat. Suppose we change the mean of the Threat group to be 6.93 (instead of 6.58) and thus the mean difference has been reduced to 2.71 from 3.06. I left all of the other statistics untouched. If we now calculate t we find $t(21) = 2.092$. The critical value of t is $t_{21, .05} = 2.08$, so we can reject the null hypothesis at $\alpha = .05$. (The actual probability is .04875.) With this result, Aronson could conclude that he has found a significant effect of stereotype threat, and he would be correct. Moreover, his effect size measure is $d = .879$, indicating almost 9/10th of a standard deviation difference between the two conditions.

But now suppose that I come along and want to replicate his study. And suppose that I take his results as my best guess of the relevant parameters. That is not an unreasonable thing to do. But what will be the power of my experiment? A little calculation will show that power $= .520$. That means I have only about a 50/50 chance of obtaining a significant difference myself. That's not too impressive, but what conclusions should we draw from this. The first conclusion is that a p value is not a very good indicator of what will happen on the next experiment. The second conclusion would be that the confidence interval, which in this case is $.364 < \mu_1 - \mu_2 \leq 5.742$ is more informative and shows us that we don't have a very tight handle on the true size of the difference between conditions.

8.8   Power Considerations in More Complex Designs

In this chapter I have constrained the discussion largely to statistical procedures that we have already covered. But there are many designs that are more complex than the ones discussed here. In particular the one-way analysis of variance is an extension to the case of more than two independent groups, and the factorial analysis of variance is a similar extension to the case of more than one independent variable. In both of these situations we can apply reasonably simple extensions of the calculational procedures we used with the t test. I will discuss these calculations in the appropriate chapters, but in many cases you would be wise to use computer programs such as G*Power to make those calculations. The good thing is that we have now covered most of the theoretical issues behind power calculations, and indeed most of what will follow is just an extension of what we already know.

8.9   The Use of G*Power to Simplify Calculations

A program named G*Power has been available for a number of years, and they have recently come out with a new version.[7] The newer version is a bit more complicated to use, but it is excellent and worth the effort. I urge you to download it and try. I have to admit that it isn't always obvious how to proceed in G*Power—there are too many choices—but you can work things out if you take an example to which you already know the answer (at least approximately) and reproduce it with the program. (I'm the impatient type, so I just flail around trying different things until I get the right answer. Reading the help files would be a much more sensible way to go.) A help page created by the

---

[7] As of the time of this writing, the previous version was still available at their site, and you might wish to start with that because it has fewer choices, which I think makes it easier to use.

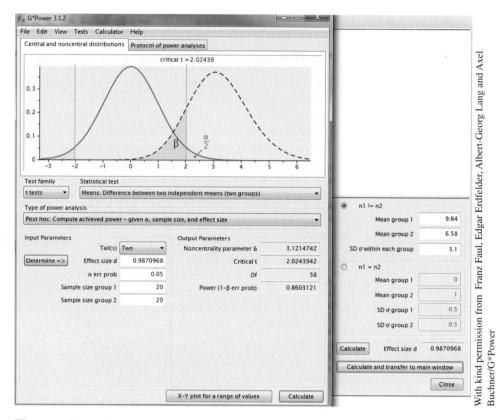

Figure 8.5   Main screen from G*Power (version 3.1.2)

authors of G*Power can be found at http://www.psycho.uni-duesseldorf.de/abteilungen /aap/gpower3/download-and-register/Dokumente/GPower3-BRM-Paper.pdf and offers an excellent discussion of its use.

To illustrate the use of the software I will reproduce the example from Section 8.4 using unequal sample sizes. Figure 8.5 shows the opening screen from G*Power, though yours may look slightly different when you first start. (I am using version 3.1.2.) For the moment ignore the plot at the top, which you probably won't have anyway, and go to the boxes where you can select a "Test Family" and a "Statistical test." Select "*t* tests" as the test family and "Means: Difference between two independent means (two groups)" as the statistical test. Below that select "Post hoc: Compute achieved power—given α, sample size, and effect size." If I had been writing this software I would not have used the phrase "Post hoc," because it is not necessarily reflective of what you are doing. (I discuss post hoc power in the next section. This choice will actually calculate the "a priori" power, which is the power you will have before the experiment if your estimates of means and standard deviation are correct and if you use the sample sizes you enter.)

Now you need to specify that you want a two-tailed test, you need to enter the alpha level you are working at (e.g., .05) and the sample sizes you plan to use. Next you need to add the estimated effect size (*d*). If you have computed it by hand, you just type it in. If not, you click on the button labeled "Determine ⇒" and a dialog box will open on the right. Just enter the expected means and standard deviation and click "calculate and transfer to main window." Finally, go back to the main window, enter the sample sizes, and click on the "Calculate" button. The distributions at the top will miraculously appear.

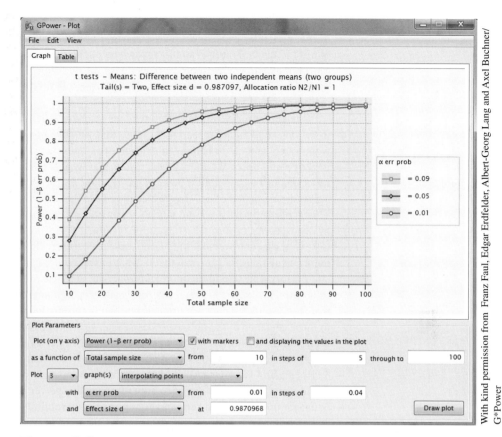

Figure 8.6   Power as a function of sample size and alpha.

These are analogous to Figure 8.2. You will also see that the program has calculated the noncentrality parameter (d), the critical value of t that you would need given the degrees of freedom available, and finally the power in our case is .860. This agrees with the result we found.

You can see how power increases with sample size and with the level of α by requesting an X-Y plot. I will let you work that out for yourself, but sample output is shown in Figure 8.6. From this figure it is clear that high levels of power require large effects or large samples. You could create your own plot showing how required sample size changes with changes in effect size, but I will leave that up to you.

8.10 Retrospective Power

priori power

In general the discussion above has focused on a **priori power**, which is the power that we would calculate before the experiment is conducted. It is based on reasonable estimates of means, variances, correlations, proportions, and so on that we believe represent the parameters for our population or populations. This is what we generally think of when we consider statistical power.

retrospective (or post hoc) power

In recent years there has been an increased interest in what is often called **retrospective (or post hoc) power**. For our purposes retrospective power will be defined as power that is calculated after an experiment has been completed, based on the results of that particular experiment. (That is why I objected to the use of the phrase "post hoc power" in the G*Power example—we were calculating power before the experiment was run.) For example, retrospective power asks the question "If the values of the population means and variances are equal to the values found in this experiment, what is the resulting power?"

One perfectly legitimate reason why we might calculate retrospective power is to help in the design of future research. Suppose that we have just completed an experiment and want to replicate it, perhaps with a different sample size and a demographically different pool of participants. We can take the results that we just obtained, treat them as an accurate reflection of the population means and standard deviations, and use those values to calculate the estimated effect size. We can then use that effect size to make power estimates. This is basically what we did when we considered replicating Aronson's study. This use of retrospective power, which is, in effect, the a priori power of our next experiment, is relatively noncontroversial. Many statistical packages, including SAS and SPSS, will make these calculations for you, and that is what I asked G*Power to do.

What is, and should be, more controversial is to use retrospective power calculations as an *explanation of the obtained results*. A common suggestion in the literature claims that if the study was not significant, but had high retrospective power, that result speaks to the acceptance of the null hypothesis. This view hinges on the argument that if you had high power, you would have been very likely to reject a false null, and thus nonsignificance indicates that the null is either true or nearly so. That sounds pretty convincing, but as Hoenig and Heisey (2001) point out, there is a false premise here. It is not possible to fail to reject the null and yet have high retrospective power. In fact, a result with p exactly equal to .05 will have a retrospective power of essentially .50,[8] and that retrospective power will decrease for $p > .05$. It is impossible to even create an example of a study that just barely failed to reject the null hypothesis at $\alpha = .05$ but that has power of .80. It can't happen!

The argument is sometimes made that retrospective power tells you more than you can learn from the obtained p value. This argument is a derivative of the one in the previous paragraph. However, it is easy to show that for a given effect size and sample size, there is a $1 : 1$ relationship between p and retrospective power. One can be derived from the other. Thus retrospective power offers no additional information in terms of explaining nonsignificant results.

As Hoenig and Heisey (2001) argue, rather than focus our energies on calculating retrospective power to try to learn more about what our results have to reveal, we are better off putting that effort into calculating confidence limits on the parameter(s) or the effect size(s). If, for example, we had a t test on two independent groups with t (48) $= 1.90, p = .063$, we would fail to reject the null hypothesis. When we calculate retrospective power we find it to be .46. When we calculate the 95% confidence interval on $\mu_1 - \mu_2$ we find $-1.10 \leq \mu_1 - \mu_2 \leq 39.1$. The confidence interval tells us more about what we are studying than does the fact that power is only .46. (Even had the difference been slightly greater, and thus significant, the confidence interval shows that we still do not have a very good idea of the magnitude of the difference between the population means.)

Retrospective power can be a useful tool when evaluating studies in the literature, as in a meta-analysis, or planning future work. But retrospective power is not a useful tool for explaining away our own nonsignificant results.

---

[8] We saw essentially this in Sections 8.1 and 8.5 where I calculated power for the replication of a modified version of Aronson et al.'s results.

8.11   Writing Up the Results of a Power Analysis

We usually don't say very much in a published study about the power of the experiment we just ran. Perhaps that is a holdover from the fact that we didn't even calculate power a relatively few years ago. It is helpful, however, to add a few sentences to your Methods section that describes the power of your experiment. For example, after describing the procedures you followed, you could say something like:

> Based on the work of Jones and others (list references) we estimated that our mean difference would be approximately 8 points, with a standard deviation within each of the groups of approximately 5. This would give us an estimated effect size (d) of 8/11 = .73. We were aiming for a power estimate of .80, and to reach that level of power with our estimated effect size, we used 30 participants in each of the two groups.

Key Terms

Power (Introduction)

Effect size (d) (8.3)

δ (delta) (8.3)

Noncentrality parameter (8.4)

Harmonic mean ($\overline{X}_h$) (8.5)

Effective sample size (8.5)

a priori power (8.10)

Retrospective power (8.10)

Post hoc power (8.10)

Exercises

8.1   A large body of literature on the effect of peer pressure has shown that the mean influence score for a scale of peer pressure is 520 with a standard deviation of 80. An investigator would like to show that a minor change in conditions will produce scores with a mean of only 500, and he plans to run a t test to compare his sample mean with a population mean of 520.

    a.   What is the effect size in question?

    b.   What is the value of δ if the size of his sample is 100?

    c.   What is the power of the test?

8.2   A second investigator thinks that she can show that a quite different manipulation can raise the mean influence score from 520 to 550.

    a.   What is the effect size in question?

    b.   What is the value of δ if the size of her sample is 100?

    c.   What is the power of the test?

8.3   In Exercise 8.1 what sample sizes would be needed to raise power to .70, .80, and .90?

8.4   Diagram the situation described in Exercise 8.1 along the lines of Figure 8.1.

8.5   Diagram the situation described in Exercise 8.2 along the lines of Figure 8.4.

8.6   We have just conducted a study comparing cognitive development of low- and normal-birthweight babies who have reached 1 year of age. Using a scale we devised, we found that the sample means of the two groups were 25 and 30, respectively, with a pooled standard deviation of 8. Assume that we wish to replicate this experiment with 20 subjects in each group. If we assume that the true means and standard deviations have been estimated exactly, what is the a priori probability that we will find a significant difference in our replication?

8.7   A physiological psychology laboratory has been studying avoidance behavior in rabbits for several years and has published numerous papers on the topic. It is clear from this research that the mean response latency for a particular task is 5.8 seconds with a standard deviation of 2 seconds (based on many hundreds of rabbits). Now the investigators wish to induce lesions in certain areas in the rabbits' amygdalae and then demonstrate poorer avoidance conditioning in these animals (i.e., show that the rabbits will repeat a punished response sooner). They expect latencies to decrease by about 1 second, and they plan to run a one-sample t test (of $\mu_0 = 5.8$).

   a. How many subjects do they need to have at least a 50 : 50 chance of success?

   b. How many subjects do they need to have at least an 80 : 20 chance of success?

8.8   Assume that a third investigator ran both conditions described in Exercises 8.4 and 8.5 and wanted to know the power of the combined experiment to find a difference between the two experimental manipulations.

   a. What is the effect size in question?

   b. What is the value of δ if the size of his sample is 50 for both groups?

   c. What is the power of the test?

8.9   A research assistant ran the experiment described in Exercise 8.10 without first carrying out any power calculations. He tried to run 20 subjects in each group, but he accidentally tipped over a rack of cages and had to void 5 subjects in the experimental group. What is the power of this experiment?

8.10   Suppose that the laboratory referred to in Exercise 8.7 decided not to run one group and compare it against $\mu_0 = 5.8$, but instead to run two groups (one with and one without lesions). They still expect the same degree of difference.

   a. How many subjects do they need (overall) if they are to have power = .60?

   b. How many subjects do they need (overall) if they are to have power = .90?

8.11   Run the t test on the original data in Exercise 8.6. What, if anything, does your answer to this question indicate about your answer to Exercise 8.6?

8.12   Make up a simple two-group example to demonstrate that for a total of 30 subjects, power increases as the sample sizes become more nearly equal.

8.13   Draw a diagram (analogous to Figure 8.2) to defend your answer to Exercise 8.10.

8.14   Two graduate students recently completed their dissertations. Each used a t test for two independent groups. One found a significant t using 10 subjects per group. The other found a significant t of the same magnitude using 45 subjects per group. Which result impresses you more?

8.15   A beleaguered PhD candidate has the impression that he must find significant results if he wants to defend his dissertation successfully. He wants to show a difference in social awareness, as measured by his own scale, between a normal group and a group of ex-delinquents. He has a problem, however. He has data to suggest that the normal group has a true mean of 38, and he has 50 of those subjects. He has access to 100 high school graduates who have been classed as delinquent in the past. Or, he has access to 25 high school dropouts who have a history of delinquency. He suspects that the high school graduates come from a population with a mean of approximately 35, whereas the dropout group comes from a population with a mean of approximately 30. He can use only one of these groups. Which should he use?

8.16   Assume that we want to test a null hypothesis about a single mean at $\alpha = .05$, one-tailed. Further assume that all necessary assumptions are met. Could there be a case in which we would be more likely to reject a true H_0 than to reject a false one? (In other words, can power ever be less than α?)

8.17   Let's extend Aronson's study (discussed in Section 8.5) to include women (who, unfortunately, often don't have as strong an investment in their skills in mathematics as men. They probably also are not as tied up in doing better than someone else). For women we expect means of 8.5 and 8.0 for the Control and Threatened condition. Further assume that the estimated standard deviation of 3.10 remains reasonable and that their sample size will be 25. Calculate the power of this experiment to show an effect of stereotyped threat in women.

8.18   Use G*Power or similar software to reproduce the results found in Section 8.5.

8.19   If $\sigma = 15$, $n = 25$, and we are testing $H_0: \mu_0 = 100$ versus $H_1: \mu_0 > 100$, what value of the mean under H_1 would result in power being equal to the probability of a Type II error? (Hint: Try sketching the two distributions; which areas are you trying to equate?)

Discussion Questions

8.20   Create an example in which a difference is just barely statistically significant at $\alpha = .05$. (Hint: Find the critical value for t, invent values for μ_1 and μ_2 and n_1 and n_2, and then solve for the required value of s.) Now calculate the retrospective power of this experiment.

8.21   In the hypothetical study based on Aronson's work on stereotype threat with two independent groups, I could have all male students in a given lab section take the test under the same condition. Then male students in another lab could take the test under the other condition.

  a.   What is wrong with this approach?

  b.   What alternatives could you suggest?

  c.   There are many women in those labs, whom I have ignored. What do you think might happen if I used them as well?

8.22   Prentice and Miller (1992) presented an interesting argument that while most students do their best to increase the effect size of whatever they are studying (e.g., by maximizing the differences between groups), some research focuses on minimizing the effect and still finding a difference. (For example, although it is well known that people favor members of their own group, it has been shown that even if you create groups on the basis of random assignment, the effect is still there.) Prentice and Miller then state "In the studies we have described, investigators have minimized the power of an operationalization and, in so doing, have succeeded in demonstrating the power of the underlying process."

  a.   Does this seem to you to be a fair statement of the situation? In other words, do you agree that experimenters have run experiments with minimal power?

  b.   Does this approach seem reasonable for most studies in psychology?

  c.   Is it always important to find large effects? When would it be important to find even quite small effects?

8.23   Why do you suppose that Exercises 8.21 and 8.24 belong in a statistics text?

8.24   In the modification of Aronson's study to use a matched-sample t test, I always gave the Control condition first, followed by the Threat condition in the next week.

  a.   Why would this be a better approach than randomizing the order of conditions?

  b.   If I give exactly the same test each week, there should be some memory carrying over from the first presentation. How might I get around this problem?

Chapter 9

Correlation and Regression

Objectives

To introduce the concepts of correlation and regression and to begin looking at how relationships between variables can be represented.

Contents

IN CHAPTER 7 WE DEALT WITH TESTING HYPOTHESES concerning differences between sample means. In this chapter we will begin examining questions concerning relationships between variables. Although you should not make too much of the distinction between **relationships** and **differences** (if treatments have *different* means, then means are *related* to treatments), the distinction is useful in terms of the interests of the experimenter and the structure of the experiment. When we are concerned with differences between means, the experiment usually consists of a few quantitative or qualitative levels of the independent variable (e.g., Treatment A and Treatment B) and the experimenter is interested in showing that the dependent variable differs from one treatment to another. When we are concerned with relationships, however, the independent variable (X) usually has many quantitative levels and the experimenter is interested in showing that the dependent variable is some *function* of the independent variable.

relationships

differences

This chapter will deal with two interwoven topics: **correlation** and **regression**. Statisticians commonly make a distinction between these two techniques. Although the distinction is frequently not followed in practice, it is important enough to consider briefly. In problems of simple correlation and regression, the data consist of two observations from each of N subjects, one observation on each of the two variables under consideration. If we were interested in the correlation between the running speed of mice in a maze (Y) and the number of trials to reach some criterion (X) (both common measures of learning), we would obtain a running-speed score and a trials-to-criterion score from each subject. Similarly, if we were interested in the regression of running speed (Y) on the number of food pellets per reinforcement (X), each subject would have scores corresponding to his speed and the number of pellets he received. The difference between these two situations illustrates the statistical distinction between correlation and regression. In both cases, Y (running speed) is a **random variable**, beyond the experimenter's control. We don't know what the mouse's running speed will be until we carry out a trial and measure the speed. In the former case, X is also a random variable, because the number of trials to criterion depends on how fast the animal learns, and this, too, is beyond the control of the experimenter. Put another way, a replication of the experiment would leave us with different values of both Y and X. In the food pellet example, however, X is a **fixed variable.** The number of pellets is determined by the experimenter (for example, 0, 1, 2, or 3 pellets) and would remain constant across replications.

correlation

regression

random variable

fixed variable

To most statisticians, the word *regression* is reserved for those situations in which the value of X is *fixed* or specified by the experimenter before the data are collected. In these situations, no sampling error is involved in X, and repeated replications of the experiment will involve the same set of X values. The word *correlation* is used to describe the situation in which both X and Y are random variables. In this case, the Xs, as well as the Ys, vary from one replication to another and thus sampling error is involved in both variables. This distinction is basically between what are called **linear regression models** and **bivariate normal models**. We will consider the distinction between these two models in more detail in Section 9.9.

linear regression models

bivariate normal models

The distinction between the two models, although appropriate on statistical grounds, tends to break down in practice. We will see instances of situations in which regression (rather than correlation) is the goal even when both variables are random. A more pragmatic distinction relies on the interest of the experimenter. If the purpose of the research is to allow **prediction** of Y on the basis of knowledge about X, we will speak of regression. If, on the other hand, the purpose is merely to obtain a statistic expressing the degree of relationship between the two variables, we will speak of correlation. Although it is possible to raise legitimate objections to this distinction, it has the advantage of describing the different ways in which these two procedures are used in practice.

prediction

But regression is not limited to mere "prediction." In fact, that may be a small part of why behavioral scientists use it. For instance, in an example that we will come to in

Chapter 15, we will look at the relationship between the amount of money that each state spends on education, pupil-teacher ratios, and student performance. We are not particularly interested in taking a specific state, plugging in its expenditures and pupil-teacher ratio, and coming up with a prediction of that state's student achievement. We are much more interested in studying the relationship between those predictor variables and how they work together to explain achievement. The goal of understanding relationships rather than predicting outcomes is a basic goal of regression.

Having differentiated between correlation and regression, we will now proceed to treat the two techniques together, because they are so closely related. The general problem then becomes one of developing an equation to predict one variable from knowledge of the other (regression) and of obtaining a measure of the degree of this relationship (correlation). The only restriction we will impose for the moment is that the relationship between X and Y is linear. Curvilinear relationships will not be considered, although in Chapter 15 we will see how they are handled by closely related procedures.

9.1   Scatterplot

scatterplot

scatter diagram

predictor

criterion

When we collect measures on two variables for the purpose of examining the relationship between these variables, one of the most useful techniques for gaining insight into this relationship is a scatterplot (also called a scatter diagram). In a scatterplot, each experimental subject in the study is represented by a point in two-dimensional space. The coordinates of this point (X_i, Y_i) are the individual's (or object's) scores on variables X and Y, respectively. Examples of three such plots appear in Figure 9.1. These are real data.

In a scatterplot the predictor variable is traditionally represented on the abscissa, or X-axis, and the criterion variable on the ordinate, or Y-axis. If the eventual purpose of the study is to predict or explain one variable from knowledge of the other, the distinction is obvious; the criterion variable is the one to be predicted, whereas the predictor variable is the one from which the prediction is made. If the problem is simply one of obtaining a correlation coefficient, the distinction may be obvious (incidence of cancer would be dependent on amount smoked rather than the reverse, and thus incidence would appear on the ordinate), or it may not (neither running speed nor number of trials to criterion is obviously in a dependent position relative to the other). Where the distinction is not obvious, which variable is labeled X is unimportant.

Consider the three scatter diagrams in Figure 9.1. Figure 9.1a is plotted from data reported by St. Leger, Cochrane, and Moore (1978) on the relationship between infant mortality, adjusted for gross national product, and the number of physicians per 10,000 population.[1] Notice the fascinating result that infant mortality *increases* with the number of physicians. That is certainly an unexpected result, but it is almost certainly not due to chance. As you look at these data and read the rest of the chapter you might think about possible explanations for this surprising result. Justin Fuller at Ohio University offered some interesting suggestions. It is very possible that this is a reporting problem—the more physicians, the better the reporting. It is also possible that physicians increase the rate of live births that then die soon after birth and are counted in the mortality rate but would not have been counted if they had not been born live.

regression lines

The lines superimposed on Figures 9.1a–9.1c represent those straight lines that "best fit the data." How we determine that line will be the subject of much of this chapter. I have included the lines in each of these figures because they help to clarify the relationships. These lines are what we will call the regression lines of Y predicted on X (abbreviated "Y on X"),

---

[1] Negative values for mortality derive from the fact that this is the mortality rate *adjusted for* gross national product. After adjustment the rate can be negative.

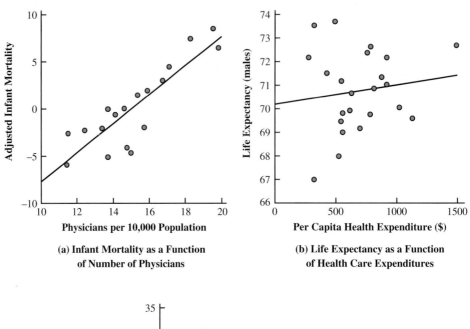

(a) Infant Mortality as a Function
of Number of Physicians

(b) Life Expectancy as a Function
of Health Care Expenditures

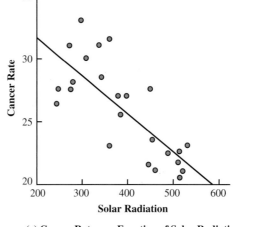

(c) Cancer Rate as a Function of Solar Radiation

Figure 9.1   Three scatter diagrams

© Cengage Learning 2013

and they represent our best prediction of Y_i for a given value of X_i, for the *ith subject or observation*. Given any specified value of X, the corresponding height of the regression line represents our best prediction of Y (designated $\hat{Y}$, and read "Y hat"). In other words, we can draw a vertical line from X_i to the regression line and then move horizontally to the y-axis and read $\hat{Y}_i$. The "hat" over that Y indicates that it is the estimated or predicted Y.

The degree to which the points cluster around the regression line (in other words, the degree to which the actual values of Y agree with the predicted values) is related to the **correlation** (**r**) between X and Y. Correlation coefficients range between 1 and –1. For Figure 9.1a, the points cluster very closely about the line, indicating that there is a strong linear relationship between the two variables. If the points fell exactly on the line, the correlation would be +1.00. As it is, the correlation is actually .81, which represents a high degree of relationship for real variables in the behavioral sciences.

correlation (r)

In Figure 9.1b I have plotted data on the relationship between life expectancy (for males) and per capita expenditure on health care for 23 developed (mostly European) countries. These data are found in Cochrane, St. Leger, and Moore (1978). At a time when there is considerable discussion nationally about the cost of health care, these data give us pause. If we were to measure the health of a nation by life expectancy (admittedly not the only, and certainly far from the best, measure), it would appear that the total amount of money we spend on health care bears no relationship to the resultant quality of health (assuming that different countries apportion their expenditures in similar ways). (Tens of thousands of dollars spent on an organ transplant may increase *an individual's* life expectancy by a few years, but it is not going to make a dent in the *nation's* life expectancy. A similar amount of money spent on prevention efforts with young children, however, may eventually have a very substantial effect—hence the inclusion of this example in a text primarily aimed at psychologists.) The two countries with the longest life expectancy (Iceland and Japan) spend nearly the same amount of money on health care as the country with the shortest life expectancy (Portugal). The United States has the second highest rate of expenditure but ranks near the bottom in life expectancy. Figure 9.1b represents a situation in which there is no apparent relationship between the two variables under consideration. If there were absolutely no relationship between the variables, the correlation would be 0.0. As it is, the correlation is only .14, and even that can be shown not to be reliably different from 0.0.

Finally, Figure 9.1c presents data from an article in *Newsweek* (1991) on the relationship between breast cancer and sunshine. For those of us who love the sun, it is encouraging to find that there may be at least some benefit from additional sunlight. Notice that as the amount of solar radiation increases, the incidence of deaths from breast cancer *decreases*. (There has been considerable research on this topic in recent years, and the reduction in rates of certain kinds of cancer is thought to be related to the body's production of vitamin D, which is increased by sunlight.[2] An excellent article, which portrays the data in a different way, can be found in a study by Gardland and others (2006).) This is a good illustration of a negative relationship, and the correlation here is –.76.

It is important to note that the sign of the correlation coefficient has no meaning other than to denote the direction of the relationship. Correlations of .75 and –.75 signify exactly the same *degree* of relationship. It is only the direction of that relationship that is different. Figures 9.1a and 9.1c illustrate this, because the two correlations are nearly the same except for their signs (.81 versus –.76).

9.2 The Relationship Between Pace of Life and Heart Disease

The examples shown in Figure 9.1 have either been examples of very strong relationships (positive or negative) or of variables that are nearly independent of each other. Now we will turn to an example in which the correlation is not nearly as high, but is still significantly greater than 0. Moreover, it comes even closer to the kinds of studies that behavior scientists do frequently.

There is a common belief that people who lead faster paced lives are more susceptible to heart disease and other forms of fatal illness. (Discussions of "Type A personality" come to mind.) Levine (1990) published data on the "pace of life" and age-adjusted death rates from ischemic heart disease. In his case he collected data from 36 cities, varying in size and

---

[2] A recent study (Lappe, Davies, Travers-Gustafson, and Heaney (2006)) has shown a relationship between Vitamin D levels and lower rates of several types of cancer.

geographical location. He was ingenious when it came to measuring the "pace of life." He surreptitiously used a stopwatch to record the time that it took a bank clerk to make change for a $20 bill, the time it took an average person to walk 60 feet, and the speed at which people spoke. Levine also recorded the age-adjusted death rate from ischemic heart disease for each city. The data follow, where "pace" is taken as the average of the three measures. (The units of measurement are arbitrary. The data on all three pace variables are included in the data set on the web.) Here is an example where we have two dependent measures, but one is clearly the predictor (Pace goes on the X (horizontal) axis and Heart disease goes on the Y (vertical) axis).

The data are plotted in Figure 9.2.

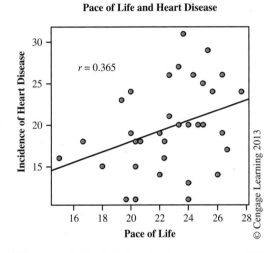

Pace of Life and Heart Disease

$r = 0.365$

Figure 9.2   Relationship between pace of life and age-adjusted rate of heart disease

Table 9.1   Pace of life and death rate due to heart disease in 36 U.S. cities

Pace (X)	27.67	25.33	23.67	26.33	26.33	25.00	26.67	26.33	24.33	25.67
Heart (Y)	24	29	31	26	26	20	17	19	26	24

Pace (X)	22.67	25.00	26.00	24.00	26.33	20.00	24.67	24.00	24.00	20.67
Heart (Y)	26	25	14	11	19	24	20	13	20	18

Pace (X)	22.33	22.00	19.33	19.67	23.33	22.33	20.33	23.33	20.33	22.67
Heart (Y)	16	19	23	11	27	18	15	20	18	21

Pace (X)	20.33	22.00	20.00	18.00	16.67	15.00
Heart (Y)	11	14	19	15	18	16

$\Sigma X = 822.333$ $\Sigma Y = 713$ $\Sigma XY = 16{,}487.67$
$\Sigma X^2 = 19{,}102.33$ $\Sigma Y^2 = 15{,}073$ $N = 36$
$\overline{X} = 22.84$ $\overline{Y} = 19.81$ $\text{cov}_{XY} = 5.74$
$s_X = 3.015$ $s_Y = 5.214$

As you can see from this figure, there is a tendency for the age-adjusted incidence of heart disease to be higher in cities where the pace of life is faster—where people speak more quickly, walk faster, and carry out simple tasks at a faster rate. The pattern is not as clear as it was in previous examples, but it is similar to patterns we find with many psychological variables.

linear relationship

curvilinear relationship

From an inspection of Figure 9.2 you can see a noticeable positive relationship between the pace of life and heart disease—as pace increases, deaths from heart disease also increase, and vice versa. It is a **linear relationship** because the best fitting line is straight. (We say that a relationship is linear if the best (or nearly best) fit to the data comes from a straight line. If the best fitting line were not straight, we would refer to it as a **curvilinear relationship**.) I have drawn in this line to make the relationship clearer. Look at the scatterplot in Figure 9.2. If you just look at the people with the highest pace scores, and those with the lowest scores, you will see that the death rate in nearly twice as high in the former group.

9.3   The Relationship Between Stress and Health

Psychologists have long been interested in the relationship between stress and health, and have accumulated evidence to show that there are real negative effects of stress on both the psychological and physical health of people. The study by Levine (1990) on the pace of life was a good example. We'll take another example and look at it from the point of view of computations and concepts. Wagner, Compas, and Howell (1988) investigated the relationship between stress and mental health in first-year college students. Using a scale they developed to measure the frequency, perceived importance, and desirability of recent life events, they created a measure of negative events weighted by the reported frequency and the respondent's subjective estimate of the impact of each event. This served as their measure of the subject's perceived social and environmental stress. They also asked students to complete the Hopkins Symptom Checklist, assessing the presence or absence of 57 psychological symptoms. The stem-and-leaf displays and Q-Q plots for the stress and symptom measures are shown in Table 9.2.

Before we consider the relationship between these variables, we need to study the variables individually. The stem-and-leaf display for Stress shows that the distribution is unimodal and only slightly positively skewed. Except for a few extreme values, there is nothing about that variable that should disturb us. However, the distribution for Symptoms (not shown) was decidedly skewed. Because Symptoms is on an arbitrary scale anyway, there is nothing to lose by taking a log transformation. The $\log_e$ of Symptoms[3] will pull in the upper end of the scale more than the lower, and will tend to make the distribution more normal. We will label this new variable lnSymptoms because most work in mathematics and statistics uses "ln" to denote $\log_e$. The Q-Q plots in Table 9.2 illustrate that both variables are close to normally distributed. Note that there is a fair amount of variability in each variable. This variability is important; because if we want to show that different stress scores are associated with differences in symptoms, it is important to have these differences in the first place.

---

[3] We can use logs to any base, but work in statistics generally uses the natural logs, which are logs to the base *e*. The choice of base will have no important effect on our results.

Table 9.2   Description of data on the relationship between stress and mental health

lnSymptoms

The decimal point is 1 digit(s) to the left of the |

```
40 | 6
41 | 11334
41 | 67799
42 | 2
42 | 5556899
43 | 0000244
43 | 66677888999
44 | 111222334
44 | 555577888899
45 | 0111223344
45 | 55667
46 | 00001112222224
46 | 567799
47 | 112
47 | 67
48 | 0034
48 | 8
49 | 11
49 | 89
```

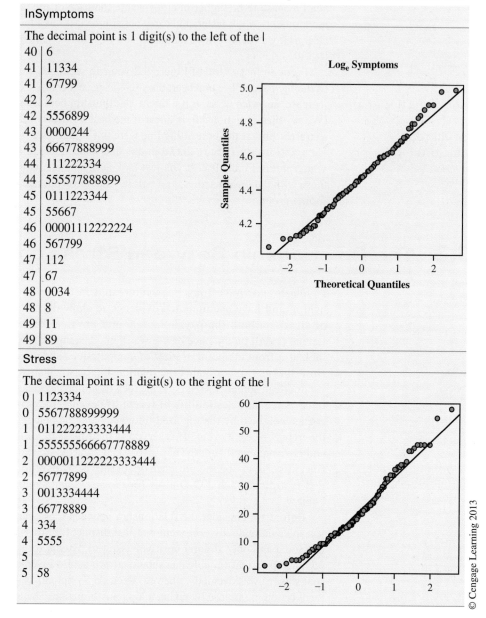

Log_e Symptoms

Stress

The decimal point is 1 digit(s) to the right of the |

```
0 | 1123334
0 | 5567788899999
1 | 011222233333444
1 | 555555566667778889
2 | 0000011222223333444
2 | 56777899
3 | 0013334444
3 | 66778889
4 | 334
4 | 5555
5 |
5 | 58
```

9.4   The Covariance

covariance
(cov_{XY} or s_{XY})

The correlation coefficient we seek to compute on the data[4] in Table 9.3 is itself based on a statistic called the **covariance** (cov_{XY} or s_{XY}). The covariance is basically a number that reflects the degree to which two variables vary together.

To define the covariance mathematically, we can write

$$cov_{XY} = \frac{\sum(X - \overline{X})(Y - \overline{Y})}{N - 1}$$

---

[4] A copy of the complete data set is available on this book's Web site in the file named Table 9-3.dat.

Table 9.3 Data on stress and symptoms for 10 representative participants

Participant	Stress (X)	lnSymptoms (Y)
1	30	4.60
2	27	4.54
3	9	4.38
4	20	4.25
5	3	4.61
6	15	4.69
7	5	4.13
8	10	4.39
9	23	4.30
10	34	4.80
. . .	. . .	. . .

$\Sigma X = 2278$ $\Sigma Y = 479.668$
$\Sigma X^2 = 65{,}038$ $\Sigma Y^2 = 2154.635$
$\overline{X} = 21.290$ $\overline{Y} = 4.483$
$s_X = 12.492$ $s_Y = 0.202$
$\Sigma XY = 10353.66$
$N = 107$

From this equation it is apparent that the covariance is similar in form to the variance. If we changed all the Ys in the equation to Xs, we would have s_X^2; if we changed the Xs to Ys, we would have s_Y^2.

For the data on Stress and lnSymptoms we would expect that high stress scores will be paired with high symptom scores. Thus, for a stressed participant with many problems, both $(X - \overline{X})$ and $(Y - \overline{Y})$ will be positive and their product will be positive. For a participant experiencing little stress and few problems, both $(X - \overline{X})$ and $(Y - \overline{Y})$ will be negative, but their product will again be positive. Thus, the sum of $(X - \overline{X})(Y - \overline{Y})$ will be large and positive, giving us a large positive covariance.

The reverse would be expected in the case of a strong negative relationship. Here, large positive values of $(X - \overline{X})$ most likely will be paired with large negative values of $(Y - \overline{Y})$, and vice versa. Thus, the sum of products of the deviations will be large and negative, indicating a strong negative relationship.

Finally, consider a situation in which there is no relationship between X and Y. In this case, a positive value of $(X - \overline{X})$ will sometimes be paired with a positive value and sometimes with a negative value of $(Y - \overline{Y})$. The result is that the products of the deviations will be positive about half of the time and negative about half of the time, producing a near-zero sum and indicating no relationship between the variables.

For a given set of data, it is possible to show that cov_{XY} will be at its positive maximum whenever X and Y are perfectly positively correlated ($r = 1.00$), and at its negative maximum whenever they are perfectly negatively correlated ($r = -1.00$). When the two variables are perfectly uncorrelated ($r = 0.00$) cov_{XY} will be zero.

For computational purposes a simple expression for the covariance is given by

$$\text{cov}_{XY} = \frac{\Sigma(X - \overline{X})(Y - \overline{Y})}{N - 1} = \frac{\Sigma XY - \dfrac{\Sigma X \Sigma Y}{N}}{N - 1}$$

For the full data set represented in abbreviated form in Table 9.2, the covariance is

$$\text{cov}_{XY} = \frac{10353.66 - \dfrac{(2278)(479.668)}{107}}{106} = \frac{10353.66 - 10211.997}{106} = 1.336$$

9.5 The Pearson Product-Moment Correlation Coefficient (r)

What we said about the covariance might suggest that we could use it as a measure of the degree of relationship between two variables. An immediate difficulty arises, however, because the absolute value of cov_{XY} is also a function of the standard deviations of X and Y. Thus, a value of $\text{cov}_{XY} = 1.336$, for example, might reflect a high degree of correlation when the standard deviations are small, but a low degree of correlation when the standard deviations are high. To resolve this difficulty, we divide the covariance by the size of the standard deviations and make this our estimate of correlation. Thus, we define

$$r = \frac{\text{cov}_{XY}}{s_X s_Y}$$

Because the maximum value of cov_{XY} can be shown to be $\pm s_X s_Y$, it follows that the limits on r are ± 1.00. One interpretation of r, then, is that it is a measure of the degree to which the covariance approaches its maximum.

From Table 9.3 and subsequent calculations, we know that $s_X = 12.492$ and $s_Y = 0.202$, and $\text{cov}_{XY} = 1.336$. Then the correlation between X and Y is given by

$$r = \frac{\text{cov}_{XY}}{s_X s_Y}$$

$$r = \frac{1.336}{(12.492)(0.202)} = .529$$

This coefficient must be interpreted cautiously; do not attribute meaning to it that it does not possess. Specifically, $r = .53$ should *not* be interpreted to mean that there is 53% of a relationship (whatever that might mean) between stress and symptoms. The correlation coefficient is simply a point on the scale between -1 and 1, and the closer it is to either of those limits, the stronger is the relationship between the two variables. For a more specific interpretation, we can speak in terms of r^2, which will be discussed shortly. It is important to emphasize again that the sign of the correlation merely reflects the direction of the relationship and, possibly, the arbitrary nature of the scale. Changing a variable from "number of items correct" to "number of items incorrect" would reverse the sign of a correlation, but it would have no effect on its absolute value.

Adjusted r

correlation coefficient in the population

(ρ) rho

Although the correlation we have just computed is the one we normally report, it is not an unbiased estimate of the **correlation coefficient in the population**, denoted (ρ) rho. To see why this would be the case, imagine two randomly selected pairs of points—for example, (23, 18) and (40, 66). (I pulled those numbers out of the air.) If you plot these points and fit a line to them, the line will fit perfectly, because, as you most likely learned in elementary school, two points determine a straight line. Because the line fits perfectly, the correlation will be 1.00, even though the points were chosen at random. Clearly, that correlation of 1.00 does not mean that the correlation in the population from which those points were drawn is 1.00 or anywhere near it. When the number of observations is small, the sample correlation will be a biased estimate of the population correlation coefficient. To correct for this we can compute what is known as the **adjusted correlation coefficient** (r_{adj}):

adjusted correlation coefficient (r_{adj})

$$r_{adj} = \sqrt{1 - \frac{(1 - r^2)(N - 1)}{N - 2}}$$

This is a relatively unbiased estimate of the population correlation coefficient.

In the example we have been using, the sample size is reasonably large ($N = 107$). Therefore we would not expect a great difference between r and r_{adj}.

$$r_{adj} = \sqrt{1 - \frac{(1 - .529^2)(106)}{105}} = .522$$

which is very close to $r = .529$. This agreement will not be the case, however, for very small samples.

When we discuss multiple regression, which involves multiple predictors of Y, in Chapter 15, we will see that this equation for the adjusted correlation will continue to hold. The only difference will be that the denominator will be $N - p - 1$, where p stands for the number of predictors. (That is where the $N - 2$ came from in this equation.)

We could draw a parallel between the adjusted r and the way we calculate a sample variance. As I explained earlier, in calculating the variance we divide the sum of squared deviations by $N - 1$ to create an unbiased estimate of the population variance. That is comparable to what we do when we compute an adjusted r. The odd thing is that no one would seriously consider reporting anything but the unbiased estimate of the population variance; whereas, we think nothing of reporting a biased estimate of the population correlation coefficient. I don't know why we behave inconsistently like that—we just do. The only reason I even discuss the adjusted value is that most computer software presents both statistics, and students are likely to wonder about the difference and which one they should care about. For all practical purposes it is the unadjusted correlation coefficient that we want.

9.6   The Regression Line

We have just seen that there is a reasonable degree of positive relationship between stress and psychological symptoms ($r = .529$). We can obtain a better idea of what this relationship is by looking at a scatterplot of the two variables and the regression line for predicting symptoms (Y) on the basis of stress (X). The scatterplot is shown in Figure 9.3, where the best-fitting line for predicting Y on the basis of X has been superimposed. We will see shortly where this line came from, but notice first the way in which the log of symptom scores increase linearly with increases in stress scores. Our correlation coefficient told us that such a relationship existed, but it is easier to appreciate just what it means when you see it presented graphically. Notice also that the degree of scatter of points about the regression line remains about the same as you move from low values of stress to high values, although, with a correlation of approximately .50, the scatter is fairly wide. We will discuss scatter in more detail when we consider the assumptions on which our procedures are based.

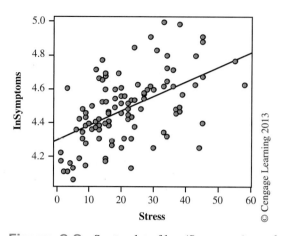

Figure 9.3   Scatterplot of $\log_e$(Symptoms) as a function of Stress

As you may remember from high school, the equation of a straight line is an equation of the form $Y = bX + a$. For our purposes, we will write the equation as

$$\hat{Y} = bX + a$$

Where

$\hat{Y}$ = the predicted value of Y

slope b = the **slope** of the regression line (the amount of difference in $\hat{Y}$ associated with a one-unit difference in X)

intercept a = the **intercept** (the value of $\hat{Y}$ when $X = 0$)

X = the value of the predictor variable

Our task will be to solve for the values of a and b that will produce the best-fitting linear function. In other words, we want to use our existing data to solve for the values of a and b such that the regression line (the values of $\hat{Y}$ for different values of X) will come as close as possible to the actual obtained values of Y. But how are we to define the phrase "best-**errors of**   fitting"? A logical way would be in terms of **errors of prediction**—that is, in terms of the **prediction** $(Y - \hat{Y})$ deviations. Because $\hat{Y}$ is the value of the symptom (lnSymptoms) variable that our equation would *predict* for a given level of stress, and Y is a value that we actually *obtained*, **residual** $(Y - \hat{Y})$ is the error of prediction, usually called the **residual**. We want to find the line (the set of $\hat{Y}$s) that minimizes such errors. We cannot just minimize the *sum* of the errors, however, because for an infinite variety of lines—any line that goes through the point $(\overline{X}, \overline{Y})$—that sum will always be zero. (We will overshoot some and undershoot others.) Instead, we will look for that line that minimizes the sum of the *squared* errors—that minimizes $\sum(Y - \hat{Y})^2$. (Note that I said much the same thing in Chapter 2 when I was discussing the variance. There I was discussing deviations from the mean, and here I am discussing deviations from the regression line—sort of a floating or changing mean. These two concepts—errors of prediction and variance—have much in common, as we shall see.)[5]

The optimal values of a and b are obtained by solving for those values of a and b that minimize $\sum(Y - \hat{Y})^2$. The solution is not difficult, and those who wish can find it in earlier

---

[5] For those who are interested, Rousseeuw and Leroy (1987) present a good discussion of alternative criteria that could be minimized, often to good advantage.

normal equations

editions of this book or in Draper and Smith (1981, p. 13). The solution to the problem yields what are often called the **normal equations**:

$$a = \overline{Y} - b\overline{X}$$

$$b = \frac{\text{cov}_{XY}}{s_X^2}$$

We now have equations for a and b[6] that will minimize $\sum(Y - \hat{Y})^2$. To indicate that our solution was designed to minimize errors in predicting Y from X (rather than the other way around), the constants are sometimes denoted $a_{Y\cdot X}$ and $b_{Y\cdot X}$. When no confusion would arise, the subscripts are usually omitted. [When your purpose is to predict X on the basis of Y (i.e., X on Y), then you can simply reverse X and Y in the previous equations.]

As an example of the calculation of regression coefficients, consider the data in Table 9.3. From that table we know that $\overline{X} = 21.290$, $\overline{Y} = 4.483$, and $s_X = 12.492$. We also know that $\text{cov}_{XY} = 1.336$. Thus,

$$b = \frac{\text{cov}_{XY}}{s_X^2} = \frac{1.336}{12.492^2} = 0.0086$$

$$a = \overline{Y} - b\overline{X} = 4.483 - (0.0086)(21.290) = 4.300$$

$$\hat{Y} = bX + a = 0.0086(X) + 4.300$$

We have already seen the scatter diagram with the regression line for Y on X superimposed in Figure 9.3. This is the equation of that line.[7]

A word about actually plotting the regression line is in order here. To plot the line you can simply take any two values of X (preferably at opposite ends of the scale), calculate $\hat{Y}$ for each, mark these coordinates on the figure, and connect them with a straight line. For our data, we have

$$\hat{Y}_i = (0.0086)(X_i) + 4.300$$

When $X_i = 0$,

$$\hat{Y}_i = (0.0086)(0) + 4.300 = 4.300$$

and when $X_i = 50$,

$$\hat{Y}_i = (0.0086)(50) + 4.300 = 4.730$$

The line then passes through the points ($X = 0$, $Y = 4.300$) and ($X = 50$, $Y = 4.730$), as shown in Figure 9.3. The regression line will also pass through the points $(0, a)$ and $(\overline{X}, \overline{Y})$, which provides a quick check on accuracy.

If you calculate both regression lines (Y on X and X on Y), it will be apparent that the two are not coincident. They do intersect at the point $(\overline{X}, \overline{Y})$, but they have different slopes. The fact that they are different lines reflects the fact that they were designed for different purposes—one minimizes $\sum(Y - \hat{Y})^2$ and the other minimizes $\sum(X - \hat{X})^2$. They both go through the point $(\overline{X}, \overline{Y})$ because a person who is *average* on one variable would be expected to be *average* on the other, but only when the correlation between the two variables is ± 1.00 will the lines be coincident.

---

[6] An interesting alternative formula for b can be written as $b = r(s_y/s_x)$. This shows explicitly the relationship between the correlation coefficient and the slope of the regression line. Note that when $s_y = s_x$, b will equal r. (This will happen when both variables have a standard deviation of 1, which occurs when the variables are standardized.)

[7] An excellent java applet by Gary McClelland that allows you to enter individual data points and see their effect on the regression line is available at http://www.uvm.edu/~dhowell/fundamentals7/SeeingStatisticsApplets/CorrelationPoints.html.

Interpretations of Regression

In certain situations the regression line is useful in its own right. For example, a college admissions officer might be interested in an equation for predicting college performance on the basis of high-school grade point average (although she would most likely want to include multiple predictors in ways to be discussed in Chapter 15). Similarly, a neuropsychologist might be interested in predicting a patient's response rate based on one or more indicator variables. If the actual rate is well below expectation, we might start to worry about the patient's health (see Crawford, Garthwaite, Howell, & Venneri, 2003). But these examples are somewhat unusual. In most applications of regression in psychology, we are not particularly interested in making an actual prediction. Although we might be interested in knowing the relationship between family income and educational achievement, it is unlikely that we would take any particular child's family-income measure and use that to predict his educational achievement. We are usually much more interested in general principles than in individual predictions. A regression equation, however, can in fact tell us something meaningful about these general principles, even though we may never actually use it to form a prediction for a specific case. (You will see a dramatic example of this later in the chapter.)

Intercept

We have defined the intercept as that value of $\hat{Y}$ when X equals zero. As such, it has meaning in some situations and not in others, primarily depending on whether or not $X = 0$ has meaning and is near or within the range of values of X used to derive the estimate of the intercept. If, for example, we took a group of overweight people and looked at the relationship between self-esteem (Y) and weight loss (X) (assuming that it is linear), the intercept would tell us what level of self-esteem to expect for an individual who lost 0 pounds. Often, however, there is no meaningful interpretation of the intercept other than a mathematical one. If we are looking at the relationship between self-esteem (Y) and actual weight (X) for adults, it is obviously foolish to ask what someone's self-esteem would be if he weighed 0 pounds. The intercept would appear to tell us this, but it represents such an extreme extrapolation from available data as to be meaningless. (In this case, a nonzero intercept would suggest a lack of linearity over the wider range of weight from 0 to 300 pounds, but we probably are not interested in nonlinearity in the extremes anyway.)

In many situations it is useful to "center" your data at the mean by subtracting the mean of X from every X value. If you do this, an X value of 0 now represents the mean X and the intercept is now the value predicted for Y when X is at its mean. It is important not to just gloss over this idea. The idea of transforming a variable so that $X = 0$ has a meaningful interpretation has wide applicability in statistics, not just for regression problems. And centering a variable on some point (often, but not exclusively, the mean) has no effect on the slope or the correlation coefficient.

Slope

We have defined the slope as the change in $\hat{Y}$ for a one-unit change in X. As such it is a measure of the predicted *rate of change* in Y. By definition, then, the slope is often a meaningful measure. If we are looking at the regression of income on years of schooling, the slope will tell us how much of a difference in income would be associated with each additional year of school. Similarly, if an engineer knows that the slope relating fuel economy in miles per gallon (mpg) to weight of the automobile is 0.01, and if she can assume a causal relationship between mpg and weight, then she knows that for every pound that she can reduce the weight of the car she will increase its fuel economy by 0.01 mpg. Thus, if the manufacturer replaces a 30-pound spare tire with one of those annoying 20-pound temporary ones, the car will be predicted to gain 0.1 mpg.

Standardized Regression Coefficients

standardized regression coefficient

β (beta)

Although we rarely work with standardized data (data that have been transformed so as to have a mean of zero and a standard deviation of one on each variable), it is worth considering what b would represent if the data for each variable were standardized separately. In that case, a difference of one unit in X or Y would represent a difference of one standard deviation. Thus, if the slope was 0.75, for standardized data, we could say that a one standard deviation increase in X will be reflected in three-quarters of a standard deviation increase in $\hat{Y}$. When speaking of the slope for standardized data, we often refer to the standardized regression coefficient as β (beta) to differentiate it from the coefficient for nonstandardized data (b). We will return to the idea of standardized variables when we discuss multiple regression in Chapter 15. The nice thing is that we can compute standardized coefficients without actually standardizing the data. (What is the intercept if the variables were standardized?)

Correlation and Beta

What we have just seen with respect to the slope for standardized variables is directly applicable to the correlation coefficient. Recall that r is defined as $\text{cov}_{XY}/s_X s_Y$, whereas b is defined as cov_{XY}/s_X^2. If the data are standardized, then $s_X = s_Y = s_X^2 = 1$ and the slope and the correlation coefficient will be equal. Thus, when we have a *single* predictor variable, one interpretation of the correlation coefficient is equal to what the slope would be if the variables were standardized. That suggests that a derivative interpretation of $r = .80$, for example, is that one standard deviation difference in X is associated *on average* with eight-tenths of a standard deviation difference of Y. In some situations such an interpretation can be meaningfully applied.

A Note of Caution

What has just been said about the interpretation of b and r must be tempered with a bit of caution. To say that a one-unit difference in family income is associated with 0.75 units difference in academic achievement is not to be interpreted to mean that raising family income for Mary Smith will automatically raise her academic achievement. In other words, we are not speaking about cause and effect. We can say that people who score higher on the income variable also score higher on the achievement variable without in any way implying causation or suggesting what would happen to a given individual if her family income were to increase. Family income is associated (in a correlational sense) with a host of other variables (e.g., attitudes toward education, number of books in the home, access to a variety of environments) and there is no reason to expect all of these to change merely because income changes. Those who argue that eradicating poverty will lead to a wide variety of changes in people's lives often fall into such a cause-and-effect trap. Eradicating poverty is certainly a worthwhile and important goal, one that I strongly support, but the correlation between income and educational achievement *may* be totally irrelevant to the issue.

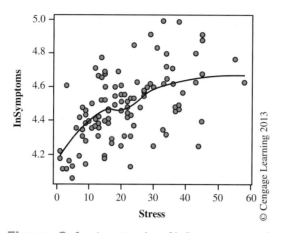

Figure 9.4   A scatterplot of lnSymptoms as a function of Stress with a smoothed regression line superimposed

9.7 Other Ways of Fitting a Line to Data

scatterplot smoothers

splines
loess

While it is common to fit straight lines to data in a scatter plot, and while that is a very useful way to try to understand what is going on, there are other alternatives. Suppose that the relationship is somewhat curvilinear—perhaps it increases nicely for a while and then levels off. In this situation a curved line might best fit the data. There are a number of ways of fitting lines to data and many of them fall under the heading of scatterplot smoothers. The different smoothing techniques are often found under headings like splines and loess, and are discussed in many more specialized texts. In general, smoothing takes place by the averaging of Y values close to the target value of the predictor. In other words we move across the graph computing lines as we go (see Everitt, 2005). An example of a smoothed plot is shown in Figure 9.4. This plot was produced using R, but similar plots can be produced using SPSS and clicking on the Fit panel as you define the scatterplot you want. The advantage of using smoothed lines is that it gives you a better idea about the overall form of the relationship. Given the amount of variability that we see in our data, it is difficult to tell whether the smoothed plot fits significantly better than a straight line, but it is reasonable to assume that symptoms would increase with the level of stress, but that this increase would start to level off at some point.

9.8 The Accuracy of Prediction

The fact that we can fit a regression line to a set of data does not mean that our problems are solved. On the contrary, they have only begun. The important point is not whether a straight line can be drawn through the data (you can always do that) but whether that line represents a reasonable fit to the data—in other words, whether our effort was worthwhile.

In beginning a discussion of errors of prediction, it is instructive to consider the situation in which we wish to predict Y without any knowledge of the value of X.

The Standard Deviation as a Measure of Error

As mentioned earlier, the data plotted in Figure 9.3 represent the log of the number of symptoms shown by students (*Y*) as a function of the number of stressful life events (*X*). Assume that you are now given the task of predicting the number of symptoms that will be shown by a particular individual, but that you have no knowledge of the number of stressful life events he or she has experienced. Your best prediction in this case would be the mean number of lnSymptoms[8] ($\overline{Y}$) (averaged across all subjects), and the error associated with your prediction would be the standard deviation of Y (i.e., s_Y), because your prediction is the mean and s_Y deals with deviations around the mean. We know that s_Y is defined as

$$s_Y = \sqrt{\frac{\sum(Y - \overline{Y})^2}{N - 1}}$$

or, in terms of the variance,

$$s_Y^2 = \frac{\sum(Y - \overline{Y})^2}{N - 1}$$

sum of squares of Y (SS_Y)

The numerator is the sum of squared deviations from $\overline{Y}$ (the point you would have predicted in this example) and is what we will refer to as the **sum of squares of Y (SS_Y)**. The denominator is simply the degrees of freedom. Thus, we can write

$$s_Y^2 = \frac{SS_Y}{df} \quad \text{and} \quad s_Y = \sqrt{\frac{SS_Y}{df}}$$

The Standard Error of Estimate

Now suppose we wish to make a prediction about symptoms for a student who has a specified number of stressful life events. If we had an infinitely large sample of data, our prediction for symptoms would be the mean of those values of symptoms (Y) that were obtained by all students who had that particular value of stress. In other words, it would be a conditional mean—conditioned on that value of X. We do not have an infinite sample, however, so we will use the regression line. (If all of the assumptions that we will discuss shortly are met, the expected value of the Y scores associated with each specific value of X would lie on the regression line.) In our case, we know the relevant value of X and the regression equation, and our best prediction would be $\hat{Y}$. In line with our previous measure of error (the standard deviation), the error associated with the present prediction will again be a function of the deviations of Y about the predicted point, but in this case the predicted point is $\hat{Y}$ rather than Y. Specifically, a measure of error can now be defined as

$$S_{Y \cdot X} = \sqrt{\frac{\sum(Y - \hat{Y})^2}{N - 2}} = \sqrt{\frac{SS_{\text{residual}}}{df}}$$

standard error of estimate

residual variance

error variance

and again the sum of squared deviations is taken about the prediction ($\hat{Y}$). The sum of squared deviations about $\hat{Y}$ is often denoted SS_{residual} because it represents variability that remains *after* we use X to predict Y.[9] The statistic $s_{Y \cdot X}$ is called the **standard error of estimate**. It is denoted as $s_{Y \cdot X}$ to indicate that it is the standard deviation of Y predicted from X. It is the most common (although not always the best) measure of the error of prediction. Its square, $s_{Y \cdot X}^2$, is called the **residual variance** or **error variance**, and it can be shown to be an unbiased estimate of the corresponding parameter ($\sigma_{Y \cdot X}^2$) in the population. We have $N - 2$ df because we lost two degrees of freedom in estimating our regression line. (Both a and b were estimated from sample data.)

---

[8] Rather than constantly repeating "log of symptoms," I will refer to symptoms with the understanding that I am referring to the log transformed values.

[9] It is also frequently denoted SS_{error} because it is a sum of squared errors of prediction.

Table 9.4 Direct calculation of the standard error of estimate

Subject	Stress (X)	lnSymptoms (Y)	$\hat{Y}$	$Y - \hat{Y}$
1	30	4.60	4.557	0.038
2	27	4.54	4.532	0.012
3	9	4.38	4.378	0.004
4	20	4.25	4.472	−0.223
5	3	4.61	4.326	0.279
6	15	4.69	4.429	0.262
7	5	4.13	4.343	−0.216
8	10	4.39	4.386	0.008
9	23	4.30	4.498	−0.193
10	34	4.80	4.592	0.204
. . .	. . .	. . .	. . .	. . .

$$\Sigma(Y - \hat{Y}) = 0$$
$$\Sigma(Y - \hat{Y})^2 = 3.128$$

$$s_{Y \cdot X}^2 = \frac{\Sigma(Y - \hat{Y})^2}{N - 2} = \frac{3.128}{105} = 0.030 \qquad s_{Y \cdot X} = \sqrt{0.030} = 0.173$$

I have suggested that if we had an infinite number of observations, our prediction for a given value of X would be the mean of the Ys associated with that value of X. This idea helps us appreciate what $s_{Y \cdot X}$ is. If we had the infinite sample and calculated the variances for the Ys at each value of X, the average of those variances would be the residual variance, and its square root would be $s_{Y \cdot X}$. The set of Ys corresponding to a specific X is called a **conditional distribution** of Y because it is the distribution of Y scores for those cases that meet a certain condition with respect to X. We say that these standard deviations are conditional on X because we calculate them from Y values corresponding to specific values of X. On the other hand, our usual standard deviation of $Y(s_Y)$ is not conditional on X because we calculate it using all values of Y, regardless of their corresponding X values.

conditional distribution

One way to obtain the standard error of estimate would be to calculate $\hat{Y}$ for each observation and then to find $s_{Y \cdot X}$ directly, as has been done in Table 9.4. Finding the standard error using this technique is laborious and unnecessary. Fortunately, a much simpler procedure exists. It not only provides a way of obtaining the standard error of estimate, but also leads directly into even more important matters.

r^2 and the Standard Error of Estimate

In much of what follows, we will abandon the term *variance* in favor of sums of squares (*SS*). As you should recall, a variance is a sum of squared deviations from the mean (generally known as a sum of squares) divided by the degrees of freedom. The problem with variances is that they are not additive unless they are based on the same *df*. Sums of squares are additive regardless of the degrees of freedom and thus are much easier measures to use.[10]

We earlier defined the residual or error variance as

$$s_{Y \cdot X}^2 = \frac{\Sigma(Y - \hat{Y})^2}{N - 2} = \frac{SS_{\text{residual}}}{N - 2}$$

---

[10] Later in the book when I wish to speak about a variance-type measure but do not want to specify whether it is a variance, a sum of squares, or something similar, I will use the vague, wishy-washy term *variation*.

With considerable algebraic manipulation, it is possible to show

$$s_{Y \cdot X} = s_Y \sqrt{(1 - r^2) \frac{N - 1}{N - 2}}$$

For large samples the fraction $(N-1)/(N-2)$ is essentially 1, and we can thus write the equation as it is often found in statistics texts:

$$s_{Y \cdot X}^2 = s_Y^2 (1 - r^2)$$

or

$$s_{Y \cdot X} = s_Y \sqrt{(1 - r^2)}$$

Keep in mind, however, that for small samples these equations are only an approximation and $s_{Y \cdot X}^2$ will underestimate the error variance by the fraction $(N - 1)/(N - 2)$. For samples of any size, however, $SS_{\text{residual}} = SS_Y(1 - r^2)$. This particular formula is going to play a role throughout the rest of the book, especially in Chapters 15 and 16.

Errors of Prediction as a Function of *r*

Now that we have obtained an expression for the standard error of estimate in terms of r, it is instructive to consider how this error decreases as r increases. In Figure 9.5, we see the amount by which $s_{Y \cdot X}$ is reduced as r increases from .00 to 1.00.

The values in Figure 9.5 are somewhat sobering in their implications. With a correlation of .20, the standard error of our estimate is reduced by only 2% from what it would be if X were unknown. This means that if the correlation is .20, using $\hat{Y}$ as our prediction rather than $\overline{Y}$ (i.e., taking X into account) leaves us with a standard error that is fully 98% of what it would be without knowing X. Even more discouraging is that if r is .50, as it is in our example, the standard error of estimate is still 87% of the standard deviation. To reduce our error to one-half of what it would be without knowledge of X requires a correlation of .866, and even a correlation of .95 reduces the error by only about two-thirds. All of this is not to say that there is nothing to be gained by using a regression equation as the basis of prediction, only that the predictions should be interpreted with a certain degree of caution. All is not lost, however, because it is often the kinds of relationships we see, rather than their absolute magnitudes, that are of interest to us.

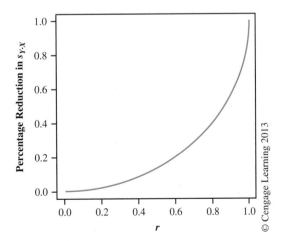

Figure 9.5   The standard error of estimate as a function of *r*

r² as a Measure of Predictable Variability

From the preceding equation expressing residual error in terms of r^2, it is possible to derive an extremely important interpretation of the correlation coefficient. We have already seen that

$$SS_{\text{residual}} = SS_Y \left(1 - r^2\right)$$

Expanding and rearranging, we have

$$SS_{\text{residual}} = SS_Y - SS_Y \left(r^2\right)$$

$$r^2 = \frac{SS_Y - SS_{\text{residual}}}{SS_Y}$$

In this equation, SS_Y, which you know to be equal to $\sum (Y - \overline{Y})^2$, is the sum of squares of Y and represents the totals of

1. The part of the sum of squares of Y that is related to X $\left[\text{i.e. } SS_Y \left(r^2\right)\right]$
2. The part of the sum of squares of Y that is independent of X $\left[\text{i.e. } SS_{\text{residual}}\right]$

In the context of our example, we are talking about that part of the number of symptoms people exhibited that is related to how many stressful life events they had experienced, and that part that is related to other things. The quantity SS_{residual} is the sum of squares of Y that is independent of X and is a measure of the amount of error remaining even after we use X to predict Y. These concepts can be made clearer with a second example.

Suppose we were interested in studying the relationship between the amount of cigarette smoking (X) and age at death (Y). As we watch people die over time, we notice several things. First, we see that not all die at precisely the same age. There is variability in age at death regardless of smoking behavior, and this variability is measured by $SS_Y = \sum (Y - \overline{Y})^2$. We also notice that some people smoke more than others. This variability in smoking regardless of age at death is measured by $SS_X = \sum (X - \overline{X})^2$. We further find that cigarette smokers tend to die earlier than nonsmokers and heavy smokers earlier than light smokers. Thus, we write a regression equation to predict Y from X. Because people differ in their smoking behavior, they will also differ in their *predicted* life expectancy ($\hat{Y}$), and we will label this variability $SS_{\hat{Y}} = \sum (\hat{Y} - \overline{Y})^2$. This last measure is variability in Y that is directly attributable to variability in X, because different values of $\hat{Y}$ arise from different values of X and the same values of $\hat{Y}$ arise from the same value of X—that is, $\hat{Y}$ does not vary unless X varies.

We have one last source of variability: the variability in the life expectancy of those people who smoke exactly the same amount. This is measured by SS_{residual} and is the variability in Y that cannot be explained by the variability in X (because these people do not differ in the amount they smoke). These several sources of variability (sums of squares) are summarized in Table 9.5.

If we considered the absurd extreme that all nonsmokers die at exactly age 72 and all smokers smoke precisely the same amount and die at exactly age 68, then all of the variability in life expectancy is directly predictable from variability in smoking behavior. If you smoke you will die at 68, and if you don't you will die at 72. Here $SS_{\hat{Y}} = SS_Y$, and $SS_{\text{residual}} = 0$.

As a more realistic example, assume smokers tend to die earlier than nonsmokers, but within each group there is a certain amount of variability in life expectancy. This is a situation in which some of SS_Y is attributable to smoking ($SS_{\hat{Y}}$) and some is not (SS_{residual}). What we want to do is specify what *percentage* of the overall variability in life expectancy

Table 9.5   Sources of variance in regression for the study of smoking and life expectancy

SS_X = variability in amount smoked = $\Sigma(X - \overline{X})^2$

SS_Y = variability in life expectancy = $\Sigma(Y - \overline{Y})^2$

$SS_{\hat{Y}}$ = variability in life expectancy directly attributable to variability in smoking behavior = $\Sigma(\hat{Y} - \overline{Y})^2$

SS_{residual} = variability in life expectancy that cannot be attributed to variability in smoking behavior = $\Sigma(Y - \hat{Y})^2 = SS_Y - SS_{\hat{Y}}$

© Cengage Learning 2013

is attributable to variability in smoking behavior. In other words, we want a measure that represents

$$\frac{SS_{\hat{Y}}}{SS_Y} = \frac{SS_Y - SS_{\text{residual}}}{SS_Y}$$

As we have seen, that measure is r^2. In other words,

$$r^2 = \frac{SS_{\hat{Y}}}{SS_Y}$$

This interpretation of r^2 is extremely useful. If, for example, the correlation between amount smoked and life expectancy were an unrealistically high .80, we could say that $.80^2 = 64\%$ of the variability in life expectancy is directly predictable from the variability in smoking behavior. (Obviously, this is an outrageous exaggeration of the real world.) If the correlation were a more likely $r = .10$, we would say that $.10^2 = 1\%$ of the variability in life expectancy is related to smoking behavior, whereas the other 99% is related to other factors.

Phrases such as "accounted for by," "attributable to," "predictable from," and "associated with" are *not* to be interpreted as statements of cause and effect. Thus, you could say, "I can predict 10% of the variability of the weather by paying attention to twinges in the ankle that I broke last year—when it aches we are likely to have rain, and when it feels fine the weather is likely to be clear." This does not imply that sore ankles cause rain, or even that rain itself causes sore ankles. For example, it might be that your ankle hurts when it rains because low barometric pressure, which is often associated with rain, somehow affects ankles.

From this discussion it should be apparent that r^2 is easier to interpret as a measure of correlation than is r, because it represents the degree to which the variability in one measure is attributable to variability in the other measure. I recommend that you always square correlation coefficients to get some idea of whether you are talking about anything important.[11] In our symptoms-and-stress example, $r^2 = .529^2 = .280$. Thus, about one-quarter of the variability in symptoms can be predicted from variability in stress. That strikes me as an impressive level of prediction, given all the other factors that influence psychological symptoms.

There is not universal agreement that r^2 is our best measure of the contribution of one variable to the prediction of another, although that is certainly the most popular measure.

---

[11] Several respected authorities, such as Robert Rosenthal, would argue that if you are using r as a measure of effect size, which it is, you should not square it because that often leads us to perceive the effect as being smaller than it really is. Tradition, however, would have you square it.

proportional reduction in error (PRE)

Judd and McClelland (1989) strongly endorse r^2 because, when we index error in terms of the sum of squared errors, it is the **proportional reduction in error (PRE)**. In other words, when we do not use X to predict Y, our error is SS_Y. When we use X as the predictor, the error is $SS_{residual}$. Because

$$r^2 = \frac{SS_Y - SS_{residual}}{SS_Y}$$

the value of r^2 can be seen to be the percentage by which error is reduced when X is used as the predictor.[12]

proportional improvement in prediction (PIP)

Others, however, have suggested the **proportional improvement in prediction (PIP)** as a better measure.

$$PIP = 1 - \sqrt{(1 - r^2)}$$

For large sample sizes this statistic is the *reduction* in the size of the standard error of estimate. Similarly, as we shall see shortly, it is a measure of the reduction in the width of the confidence interval on our prediction.

The choice between r, r^2, and PIP is really dependent on how you wish to measure error. When we focus on r^2 we are focusing on measuring error in terms of sums of squares. When we focus on PIP we are measuring error in standard deviation units.

I have discussed r^2 as an index of percentage of variation for a particular reason. As we have seen, there is a very strong movement, at least in psychology, toward more frequent reporting of the magnitude of an effect, rather than just a test statistic and a p value. As I mention in Chapter 7, there are two major types of magnitude measures. One type is called effect size, often referred to as the *d*-family of measures, and is represented by Cohen's *d*, which is most appropriate when we have means of two or more groups. The second type of measure, often called the *r*-family, is the "percentage of variation," of which r^2 is the most common representative. We first saw this measure in this chapter, where we found that 25.6% of the variation in psychological symptoms is associated with variation in stress. We will see it again in Chapter 10 when we cover the point-biserial correlation. It will come back again in the analysis of variance chapters (especially Chapters 11 and 13), where it will be disguised as eta-squared and related measures. Finally, it will appear in important ways when we talk about multiple regression. The common thread through all of this is that we want some measure of how much of the variation in a dependent variable is attributable to variation in an independent variable, whether that independent variable is categorical or continuous. I am not as fond of percentage of variation measures as are some people, because I don't think that most of us can take much meaning from such measures. However, they are commonly used, and you need to be familiar with them.

9.9   Assumptions Underlying Regression and Correlation

We have derived the standard error of estimate and other statistics without making any assumptions concerning the population(s) from which the data were drawn. Nor do we need such assumptions to use $s_{Y \cdot X}$ as an unbiased estimator of $\sigma_{Y \cdot X}$. If we are to use $s_{Y \cdot X}$ in any meaningful way, however, we will have to introduce certain parametric assumptions. To

---

[12] It is interesting to note that r^2_{adj} (defined on p. 261) is nearly equivalent to the ratio of the *variance* terms corresponding to the sums of squares in the equation. (Well, it is interesting to *some* people.)

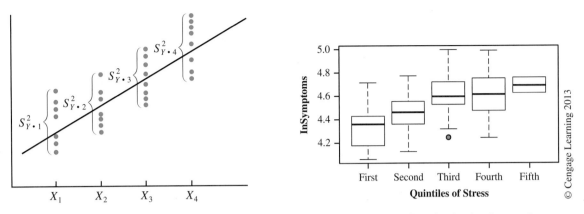

Figure 9.6   a) Scatter diagram illustrating regression assumptions; b) Similar plot for the data on Stress and Symptoms

array

homogeneity of variance in arrays

normality in arrays

conditional array

understand why, consider the data plotted in Figure 9.6a. Notice the four statistics labeled $s_{Y\cdot 1}^2$, $s_{Y\cdot 2}^2$, $s_{Y\cdot 3}^2$, and $s_{Y\cdot 4}^2$. Each represents the variance of the points around the regression line in an **array** of X (the residual variance of Y conditional on a specific X). As mentioned earlier, the average of these variances, weighted by the degrees of freedom for each array, would be $s_{Y\cdot X}^2$, the residual or error variance. If $s_{Y\cdot X}^2$ is to have any practical meaning, it must be representative of the various terms of which it is an average. This leads us to the assumption of **homogeneity of variance in arrays**, which is nothing but the assumption that the variance of Y for each value of X is constant (in the population). This assumption will become important when we apply tests of significance using $s_{Y\cdot X}^2$.

One necessary assumption when we come to testing hypotheses is that of **normality in arrays**. We will assume that in the population the values of Y corresponding to any specified value of X—that is, the **conditional array** of Y for X_i—are normally distributed around $\hat{Y}$. This assumption is directly analogous to the normality assumption we made with the t test—that each treatment population was normally distributed around its own mean—and we make it for similar reasons.

We can examine the reasonableness of these assumptions for our data on stress and symptoms by redefining Stress into five ordered categories, or quintiles. We can then display boxplots of lnSymptoms for each quintile of the Stress variable. This plot is shown in Figure 9.6b. Given the fact that we have only about 20 data points in each quintile, Figure 9.6b reflects the reasonableness of our assumptions quite well.

To anticipate what we will discuss in Chapter 11, note that our assumptions of homogeneity of variance and normality in arrays are equivalent to the assumptions of homogeneity of variance and normality of populations corresponding to different treatments that we will make in discussing the analysis of variance. In Chapter 11 we will assume that the treatment populations from which data were drawn are normally distributed and all have the same variance. If you think of the levels of X in Figure 9.6a and 9.6b as representing different experimental conditions, you can see the relationship between the regression and analysis of variance assumptions.

The assumptions of normality and homogeneity of variance in arrays are associated with the regression model, where we are dealing with fixed values of X. On the other hand, when our interest is centered on the correlation between X and Y, we are dealing with the bivariate model, in which X and Y are both random variables. In this case, we are primarily concerned with using the sample correlation (r) as an estimate of the correlation coefficient in the population (ρ). Here we will replace the regression model assumptions with the assumption that we are sampling from a bivariate normal distribution.

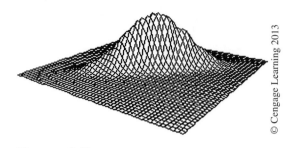

© Cengage Learning 2013

Figure 9.7   Bivariate normal distribution with $r = .90$

The bivariate normal distribution looks roughly like what you see when several dump trucks create piles of dirt where a bridge foundation is being built. The way the dirt pile falls off on all sides resembles a normal distribution. (If there were no correlation between X and Y, the pile would look as though all the dirt were dropped in the center of the pile and spread out symmetrically in all directions. When X and Y are correlated the pile is elongated, as when dirt is dumped along a street and spreads out to the sides and down the ends.) An example of a bivariate normal distribution with $r = .90$ is shown in Figure 9.7. If you were to slice this distribution on a line corresponding to any given value of X, you would see that the cut end is a normal distribution. You would also have a normal distribution if you sliced the pile along a line corresponding to any given value of Y. These are called **conditional distributions** because the first represents the distribution of Y given (conditional on) a specific value of X, whereas the second represents the distribution of X conditional on a specific value of Y. If, instead, we looked at *all* the values of Y regardless of X (or all values of X regardless of Y), we would have what is called the **marginal distribution** of Y (or X). For a bivariate normal distribution, both the conditional and the marginal distributions will be normally distributed. (Recall that for the regression model we assumed only normality of Y in the arrays of X—what we now know as conditional normality of Y. For the regression model, there is no assumption of normality of the conditional distribution of X or of the marginal distributions.)

conditional distributions

marginal distribution

9.10   Confidence Limits on $\hat{Y}$

Before we can create confidence limits on Y we need to decide on the purpose for which we want them. It could be that we want to take some future participant, assess their stress level, and then predict their symptom level. Alternatively, we might wish to set confidence limits on the regression line itself, which is equivalent to setting confidence intervals on the mean symptom score for participants having the same stress score. These look like almost the same question, but they really are not. If we are making predictions about a future individual we will have error associated with the mean of Y for that X, but also variance of the Y values themselves. On the other hand if we use the existing data on stress to predict a mean symptom score conditional on a particular degree of stress, we don't have to worry about that extra source of error. Some people refer to the former interval as the **prediction interval** and the latter as the confidence interval. A prediction interval needs to take into account both the uncertainty of a mean of Y conditional on a fixed value of Y, and the variability of observations around that mean.[13]

prediction interval

---

[13] A nice discussion of this distinction can be found at http://www.ma.utexas.edu/users/mks/statmistakes /CIvsPI.html.

Although the standard error of estimate is useful as an overall measure of error, it is not a good estimate of the error associated with any single prediction. When we wish to predict a value of Y for a given subject whose X score is near the mean, the error in our estimate will be smaller than when X is far from $\overline{X}$. (For an intuitive understanding of this, consider what would happen to the predictions for different values of X if we rotated the regression line slightly around the point $\overline{X}, \overline{Y}$. There would be negligible changes near the means, but there would be substantial changes in the extremes.)

If we wish a prediction interval for Y on the basis of X for a *new* member of the population (someone who was not included in the original sample), the standard error of our prediction is given by

$$s'_{Y \cdot X} = s_{Y \cdot X} \sqrt{1 + \frac{1}{N} + \frac{(X_i - \overline{X})^2}{(N-1)s_X^2}}$$

where $X_i - \overline{X}$ is the deviation of the individual's X score from the mean of X. This leads to the following prediction interval on $\hat{Y}$:

$$CI(Y) = \hat{Y} \pm (t_{\alpha/2})(s'_{Y \cdot X})$$

This equation will lead to elliptical confidence limits around the regression line, which are narrowest for $X = \overline{X}$ and become wider as $|X - \overline{X}|$ increases. (In Figure 9.6 you may need a straightedge to show that the lines are elliptical, but they really are.)

Alternatively, for a confidence interval on the mean Y conditioned on a specific value of X, the standard error is

$$s''_{Y \cdot X} = s_{Y \cdot X} \sqrt{\frac{1}{N} + \frac{(X_i - \overline{X})^2}{(N-1)s_X^2}}$$

and this leads to a confidence interval given by

$$CI(Y) = \hat{Y} \pm (t_{\alpha/2})(s''_{Y \cdot X})$$

To take a specific example, assume that we wanted to set confidence limits on the number of symptoms (Y) experienced by a new participant with a stress score of 10—a fairly low level of stress. We know that

$$s_{Y \cdot X} = 0.173$$

$$s_X^2 = 156.05$$

$$\overline{X} = 21.290$$

$$\hat{Y} = 0.0086(10) + 4.31 = 4.386$$

$$t_{.025} = 1.984$$

$$N = 107$$

Then

$$s'_{Y \cdot X} = s_{Y \cdot X} \sqrt{1 + \frac{1}{N} + \frac{(X_i - \overline{X})^2}{(N-1)s_X^2}}$$

$$s'_{Y \cdot X} = 0.173 \sqrt{1 + \frac{1}{107} + \frac{(10 - 21.290)^2}{(106)156.05}}$$

$$= 0.173 \sqrt{1.017} = 0.174$$

Then

$$CI(Y) = \hat{Y} \pm (t_{\alpha/2})(s'_{Y \cdot X})$$
$$= 4.386 \pm 1.984(0.174)$$
$$= 4.386 \pm .345$$
$$4.041 \leq Y \leq 4.731$$

The prediction interval is 4.041 to 4.731, and the probability is .95 that an interval computed in this way will include the level of symptoms reported by that individual. That interval is wide, but it is not as large as the 95% confidence interval of $3.985 \leq Y \leq 4.787$ that we would have had if we had not used X—that is, if we had just based our confidence interval on the obtained values of Y (and s_Y) rather than making it conditional on X.

If, instead, we wanted to predict the mean value of Y for those with X scores of 10, our estimate of the standard error would be

$$s''_{Y \cdot X} = s_{Y \cdot X} \sqrt{\frac{1}{N} + \frac{(X_i - \overline{X})^2}{(N-1)s_X^2}}$$

$$s''_{Y \cdot X} = 0.173 \sqrt{\frac{1}{107} + \frac{(10 - 21.290)^2}{(106)156.05}}$$

$$= 0.173 \sqrt{.017} = 0.022$$

And the confidence interval would be

$$CI(Y) = \hat{Y} \pm (t_{\alpha/2})(s'_{Y \cdot X})$$
$$= 4.386 \pm 1.984(0.022)$$
$$= 4.386 \pm 0.045$$
$$4.341 \leq Y \leq 4.431$$

In Figure 9.8, which follows, I show the confidence limits around the line itself, labeled as the confidence interval for array means; I also show the prediction interval for future predictions.

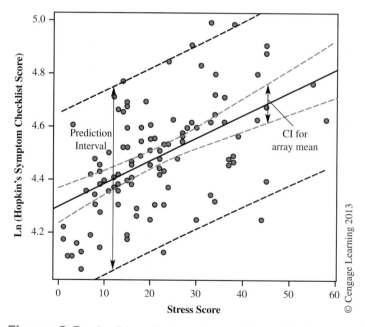

Figure 9.8   Confidence limits on the prediction of log(Symptoms) for new values of Stress

Notice that the latter is very wide. You can produce either the prediction interval or the confidence interval in SPSS by clicking on **Save/Prediction Intervals—Mean and Individual**. This will add the upper and lower limits of each case for each type of interval to your data file.

9.11 A Computer Example Showing the Role of Test-Taking Skills

Most of us can do reasonably well if we study a body of material and then take an exam on that material. But how would we do if we just took the exam without even looking at the material? (Some of you may have had that experience.) Katz, Lautenschlager, Blackburn, and Harris (1990) examined that question by asking some students to read a passage and then answer a series of multiple-choice questions. They also asked other students to answer the questions without even having seen the passage. We will concentrate on the second group. The test items were very much like the items that North American students face when they take the SAT exams for college admission. This led the researchers to suspect that students who did well on the SAT would also do well on this task, because they both involve fundamental test-taking skills such as eliminating unlikely alternatives.

Data with the same sample characteristics as the data obtained by Katz et al., are given in Table 9.6. The variable Score represents the percentage of items answered correctly when the student has not seen the passage, and the variable SATV is the student's verbal SAT score from his or her college application.

Exhibit 9.1 illustrates the analysis using SPSS regression. There are a number of things here to point out. First, we must decide which is the dependent variable and which is the independent variable. This would make no difference if we just wanted to compute the correlation between the variables, but it is important in regression. In this case I have made a relatively arbitrary decision that my interest lies primarily in seeing whether people who do well at making intelligent guesses also do well on the SAT. Therefore, I am using SATV as the dependent variable, even though it was actually taken prior to the experiment. The first two panels of Exhibit 9.1 illustrate the menu selections required for SPSS. The means and standard deviations are found in the middle of the output, and you can see that we are dealing with a group that has high achievement scores (the mean is almost 600, with a standard deviation

Table 9.6   Data based on Katz et al. (1990) for the group that did not read the passage

Score	SATV	Score	SATV
58	590	48	590
48	580	41	490
34	550	43	580
38	550	53	700
41	560	60	690
55	800	44	600
43	650	49	580
47	660	33	590
47	600	40	540
46	610	53	580
40	620	45	600
39	560	47	560
50	570	53	630
46	510	53	620

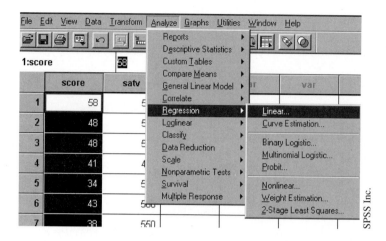

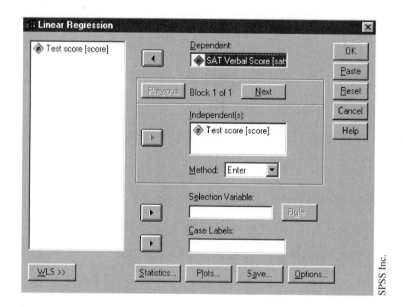

Descriptive Statistics

	Mean	Std. Deviation	N
SAT Verbal Score	598.57	61.57	28
Test Score	46.21	6.73	28

Exhibit 9.1   SPSS output on Katz et al. (1990) study of test-taking behavior

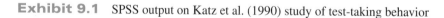

Adapted from output by SPSS, Inc.

Correlations

		SAT Verbal Score	Test score
Pearson Correlation	SAT Verbal Score	1.000	.532
	Test Score	.532	1.000
Sig. (1-tailed)	SAT Verbal Score	.	.002
	Test Score	.002	.
N	SAT Verbal Score	28	28
	Test Score	28	28

Model Summary

Model	R	R Square	Adjusted R Square	Std. Error of the Estimate
1	.532[a]	.283	.255	53.13

[a]Predictors: (Constant), Test score

ANOVA[b]

Model		Sum of Squares	df	Mean Square	F	Sig.
1	Regression	28940.123	1	28940.123	10.251	.004[a]
	Residual	73402.734	26	2823.182		
	Total	102342.9	27			

[a]Predictors: (Constant), Test score
[b]Dependent Variable: SAT Verbal Score

Coefficients[a]

Model		Unstandardized Coefficients		Standardized Coefficients	t	Sig.
		B	Std. Error	Beta		
1	(Constant)	373.736	70.938		5.269	.000
	Test score	4.865	1.520	.532	3.202	.004

[a]Dependent Variable: SAT Verbal Score

Exhibit 9.1   Continued

of about 60). This puts them about 100 points above the average for the SAT. They also do quite well on Katz's test, getting nearly 50% of the items correct. Below these statistics you see the correlation between Score and SATV, which is .532. We will test this correlation for significance in a moment. I might point out that you would not want that correlation to be too high because then the SAT would be heavily dependent on plain old test-taking skills and less a reflection of what the student actually knew about the material being tested.

In the section labeled Model Summary you see both R and R^2. The "R" here is capitalized because if there were multiple predictors it would be a multiple correlation, and we always capitalize that symbol. One thing to note is that here R is calculated as the square root of R^2, and as such it will always be positive, even if the relationship is negative. This is a result of the fact that the procedure is applicable for multiple predictors.

The ANOVA table is a test of the null hypothesis that the correlation is .00 in the population. We will discuss hypothesis testing next, but what is most important here is that the test statistic is F, and that the significance level associated with that F is $p = .004$. Since p is less than .05, we will reject the null hypothesis and conclude that the variables are not linearly independent. In other words, there is a linear relationship between how well students score on a test that reflects test-taking skills, and how well they perform on the SAT. The exact nature of this relationship is shown in the next part of the printout. Here we have a table labeled "Coefficients," and this table gives us the intercept and the slope. The intercept is labeled here as "Constant," because it is the constant that you add to every prediction. In this case it is 373.736. Technically it means that if a student answered 0 questions correctly on Katz's test, we would expect them to have an SAT of approximately 370. Because a score of 0 would be so far from the scores these students actually obtained (and it is hard to imagine anyone earning a 0 even by guessing badly), I would not pay very much attention to that value.

In this table the slope is labeled by the name of the predictor variable. (All software solutions do this, because if there were multiple predictors we would have to know which variable goes with which slope. The easiest way to do this is to use the variable name as the label.) In this case the slope is 4.865, which means that two students who differ by 1 point on Katz's test would be predicted to differ by 4.865 on the SAT. Our regression equation would now be written as $\hat{Y} = 4.865 \times \text{Score} + 373.736$.

The standardized regression coefficient is shown as .532. This means that a one standard deviation difference in test scores is associated with approximately a one-half standard deviation difference in SAT scores. Note that, because we have only one predictor, this standardized coefficient is equal to the correlation coefficient.

To the right of the standardized regression coefficient you will see t and p values for tests on the significance of the slope and intercept. We will discuss the test on the slope shortly. The test on the intercept is rarely of interest, but its interpretation should be evident from what I say about testing the slope.

9.12 Hypothesis Testing

We have seen how to calculate r as an estimate of the relationship between two variables and how to calculate the slope (b) as a measure of the rate of change of Y as a function of X. In addition to estimating r and b, we often wish to perform a significance test on the null hypothesis that the corresponding population parameters equal zero. The fact that a value of r or b calculated from a sample is not zero is not in itself evidence that the corresponding parameters in the population are also nonzero.

Testing the Significance of r

The most common hypothesis that we test for a sample correlation is that the correlation between X and Y in the population, denoted ρ (rho), is zero. This is a meaningful test because the null hypothesis being tested is really the hypothesis that X and Y are linearly independent. Rejection of this hypothesis leads to the conclusion they are not independent and there is some linear relationship between them.

It can be shown that when $\rho = 0$, for large N, r will be approximately normally distributed around zero. (It is not normally distributed around its mean when $\rho \neq 0$.)

A legitimate t test can be formed from the ratio

$$t = \frac{r\sqrt{N-2}}{\sqrt{1-r^2}}$$

which is distributed as t on $N - 2$ df.[14] Returning to the example in Exhibit 9.1, $r = .532$ and $N = 28$. Thus,

$$t = \frac{.532\sqrt{26}}{\sqrt{1 - .532^2}} = \frac{.532\sqrt{26}}{\sqrt{.717}} = 3.202$$

This value of t is significant at $\alpha = .05$ (two-tailed), and we can thus conclude that there is a significant relationship between SAT scores and scores on Katz's test. In other words, we can conclude that differences in SAT are associated with differences in test scores, although this does not necessarily imply a causal association.

In Chapter 7 we saw a brief mention of the F statistic, about which we will have much more to say in Chapters 11–16. You should know that any t statistic on df degrees of freedom can be squared to produce an F statistic on 1 and df degrees of freedom. Many statistical packages use the F statistic instead of t to test hypotheses. In this case you simply take the square root of that F to obtain the t statistics we are discussing here. (From Exhibit 9.1 we find an F of 10.251. The square root of this is 3.202, which agrees with the t we have just computed for this test.)

As a second example, if we go back to our data on stress and psychological symptoms in Table 9.2, and the accompanying text, we find $r = .506$ and $N = 107$. Thus,

$$t = \frac{.529\sqrt{105}}{\sqrt{1 - .529^2}} = \frac{.529\sqrt{105}}{\sqrt{.720}} = 6.39$$

Here again we will reject $H_0: \rho = 0$. We will conclude that there is a significant relationship between stress and symptoms. Differences in stress are associated with differences in reported psychological symptoms.

The fact that we have an hypothesis test for the correlation coefficient does not mean that the test is always wise. There are many situations where statistical significance, while perhaps comforting, is not particularly meaningful. If I have established a scale that purports to predict academic success, but it correlates only $r = .19$ with success, that test is not going to be very useful to me. It matters not whether $r = .19$ is statistically significantly different from .00, it explains so little of the variation that it is unlikely to be of any use. And anyone who is excited because a test-retest reliability coefficient is statistically significant hasn't really thought about what they are doing.

Testing the Significance of *b*

If you think about the problem for a moment, you will realize that a test on b is equivalent to a test on r in the one-predictor case we are discussing in this chapter. If it is true that X and Y are related, then it must also be true that Y varies with X—that is, that the slope is nonzero. This suggests that a test on b will produce the same answer as a test on r, and we could dispense with a test for b altogether. However, because regression coefficients play an important role in multiple regression, and since in multiple regression a significant correlation does not necessarily imply a significant slope for each predictor variable, the exact form of the test will be given here.

We will represent the parametric equivalent of b (the slope we would compute if we had X and Y measures on the whole population) as $b*$.[15]

---

[14] This is the same Student's t that we saw in Chapter 7.
[15] Many textbooks use β instead of $b*$, but that would lead to confusion with the standardized regression coefficient.

It can be shown that b is normally distributed about b^* with a standard error approximated by[16]

$$s_b = \frac{s_{Y\cdot X}}{s_X\sqrt{N-1}}$$

Thus, if we wish to test the hypothesis that the true slope of the regression line in the population is zero $(H_0\colon b^* = 0)$, we can simply form the ratio

$$t = \frac{b - b^*}{s_b} = \frac{b}{\dfrac{s_{Y\cdot X}}{s_X\sqrt{N-1}}} = \frac{(b)(s_X)(\sqrt{N-1})}{s_{Y\cdot X}}$$

which is distributed as t on $N - 2$ df.

For our sample data on SAT performance and test-taking ability, $b = 4.865$, $s_X = 6.73$, and $s_{Y\cdot X} = 53.127$.

Thus

$$t = \frac{(4.865)(6.73)(\sqrt{27})}{53.127} = 3.202$$

which is the same answer we obtained when we tested r. Because $t_{obt} = 3.202$ and $t_{.025}(26) = 2.056$, we will reject H_0 and conclude that our regression line has a nonzero slope. In other words, higher levels of test-taking skills are associated with higher predicted SAT scores.

From what we know about the sampling distribution of b, it is possible to set up confidence limits on b^*,

$$CI(b^*) = b \pm (t_{\alpha/2})\left[\frac{(s_{Y\cdot X})}{s_X\sqrt{N-1}}\right]$$

where $t_{\alpha/2}$ is the two-tailed critical value of t on $N - 2$ df.

For our data the relevant statistics can be obtained from Exhibit 9.1. The 95% confidence limits are

$$CI(b^*) = 4.865 \pm 2.056\left[\frac{53.127}{6.73\sqrt{27}}\right]$$

$$= 4.865 \pm 3.123 = 1.742 \leq b^* \leq 7.988$$

The chances are 95 out of 100 that such limits will encompass the true value of b^*. Note that the confidence limits do not include zero. This is in line with the results of our t test, which rejected $H_0\colon b^* = 0$.

Testing the Difference Between Two Independent *bs*

This test is less common than the test on a single slope, but the question that it is designed to ask is often a very meaningful one. Suppose we have two sets of data on the relationship between the amount that a person smokes and life expectancy. One set is made up of females, and the other of males. We have two separate data sets rather than one large one because we do not want our results to be contaminated by normal

---

[16] There is surprising disagreement concerning the best approximation for the standard error of b. Its denominator is variously given as $s_X\sqrt{N}$, $s_X\sqrt{N-1}$, $s_X\sqrt{N-2}$.

differences in life expectancy between males and females. Suppose further that we obtained the following data:

	Males	Females
b	−0.40	−0.20
$s_{Y \cdot X}$	2.10	2.30
s_X^2	2.50	2.80
N	101	101

It is apparent that for our data the regression line for males is steeper than the regression line for females. If this difference is significant, it means that males decrease their life expectancy more than do females for any given increment in the amount they smoke. If this were true, it would be an important finding, and we are therefore interested in testing the difference between b_1 and b_2.

The t test for differences between two independent regression coefficients is directly analogous to the test of the difference between two independent means. If H_0 is true ($H_0 : b_1^* = b_2^*$), the sampling distribution of $b_1 - b_2$ is normal with a mean of zero and a standard error of

$$s_{b_1 - b_2} = \sqrt{s_{b_1}^2 + s_{b_2}^2}$$

This means that the ratio

$$t = \frac{b_1 - b_2}{\sqrt{s_{b_1}^2 + s_{b_2}^2}}$$

is distributed as t on $N_1 + N_2 - 4 \; df$. We already know that the standard error of b can be estimated by

$$s_b = \frac{s_{Y \cdot X}}{s_X \sqrt{N - 1}}$$

and therefore can write

$$s_{b_1 - b_2} = \sqrt{\frac{s_{Y \cdot X_1}^2}{s_{X_1}^2 (N_1 - 1)} + \frac{s_{Y \cdot X_2}^2}{s_{X_2}^2 (N_2 - 1)}}$$

where $s_{Y \cdot X_1}^2$ and $s_{Y \cdot X_2}^2$ are the error variances for the two samples. As was the case with means, if we assume homogeneity of error variances, we can pool these two estimates, weighting each by its degrees of freedom:

$$s_{Y \cdot X}^2 = \frac{(N_1 - 2)s_{Y \cdot X_1}^2 + (N_2 - 2)s_{Y \cdot X_2}^2}{N_1 + N_2 - 4}$$

For our data,

$$s_{Y \cdot X}^2 = \frac{99(2.10^2) + 99(2.30^2)}{101 + 101 - 4} = 4.85$$

Substituting this pooled estimate into the equation, we obtain

$$s_{b_1 - b_2} = \sqrt{\frac{s_{Y \cdot X_1}^2}{s_{X_1}^2 (N_1 - 1)} + \frac{s_{Y \cdot X_2}^2}{s_{X_2}^2 (N_2 - 1)}}$$

$$= \sqrt{\frac{4.85}{(2.5)(100)} + \frac{4.85}{(2.8)(100)}} = 0.192$$

Given $s_{b_1 - b_2}$, we can now solve for t:

$$t = \frac{b_1 - b_2}{s_{b_1 - b_2}} = \frac{(-0.40) - (-0.20)}{0.192} = -1.04$$

on 198 df. Because $t_{0.025}(198) = 1.97$, we would fail to reject H_0 and would therefore conclude that we have no reason to doubt that life expectancy decreases as a function of smoking at the same rate for males as for females.

It is worth noting that although $H_0: b^* = 0$ is equivalent to $H_0: \rho = 0$, it does not follow that $H_0: b_1^* - b_2^* = 0$ is equivalent to $H_0: \rho_1 - \rho_2 = 0$. If you think about it for a moment, it should be apparent that two scatter diagrams could have the same regression line $(b_1^* = b_2^*)$ but different degrees of scatter around that line (hence $\rho_1 \neq \rho_2$). The reverse also holds—two different regression lines could fit their respective sets of data equally well.

Testing the Difference Between Two Independent *rs*

When we test the difference between two independent *rs*, a minor difficulty arises. When $\rho \neq 0$, the sampling distribution of r is not approximately normal (it becomes more and more skewed as $\rho \Rightarrow \pm 1.00$), and its standard error is not easily estimated. The same holds for the difference $r_1 - r_2$. This raises an obvious problem, because, as you can imagine, we will need to know the standard error of a difference between correlations if we are to create a t test on that difference. Fortunately, the solution was provided by R.A. Fisher.

Fisher (1921) showed that if we transform r to

$$r' = (0.5)log_e \left| \frac{1 + r}{1 - r} \right|$$

then r' is approximately normally distributed around ρ' (the transformed value of ρ) with standard error

$$s_{r'} = \frac{1}{\sqrt{N - 3}}$$

(Fisher labeled his statistic "z," but "r'" is often used to avoid confusion with the standard normal deviate.) Because we know the standard error, we can now test the null hypothesis that $\rho_1 - \rho_2 = 0$ by converting each r to r' and solving for

$$z = \frac{r_1' - r_2'}{\sqrt{\dfrac{1}{N_1 - 3} + \dfrac{1}{N_2 - 3}}}$$

Note that our test statistic is z rather than t, because our standard error does not rely on statistics computed from the sample (other than N) and is therefore a parameter.

Appendix r' tabulates the values of r' for different values of r, which eliminates the need to solve the equation for r'.

Meijs, Cillessen, Scholte, Segers, and Spijkerman (2010) conducted a study on the relationship between academic achievement, social intelligence, and popularity in adolescents. Popularity was further divided into perceived popularity (PP), which reflects social dominance and prestige and is measured by the difference between the number of times a student was nominated as "most popular" and the number of times that student was nominated as "least popular." Sociometric popularity (SP) refers to the degree that a person is liked, and was computed as the difference between nominations for "most *liked*" and "least *liked*." (I would have

Table 9.7   Correlations among main variables by gender

	1	2	3	4
Acad. Achiev.		−.05	−.05	.08
Soc. Intell.	.10		.31*	.19*
Perceived Pop.	−.01	.20*		.57*
Sociometric Pop.	.04	.13	.33*	

(* $p < .05$) Correlations for boys are below the diagonal and for girls are above the diagonal.
$N_{boys} = 225$; $N_{girls} = 287$.

thought that "popular" and "liked" would be the same, but they are not.) The data were broken down by gender because it is reasonable to think that these variables might operate different in boys and girls. The correlations are given below for boys and girls separately.

One interesting finding is that there is apparently no relationship between academic achievement and the other variables, either for boys or girls. The correlations are so low that it is not even worth asking the question. But suppose that we want to compare the correlation between Social Intelligence and Perceived Popularity in boys and girls. For girls this correlation is .31 and for boys it is .20. Then

	Boys	Girls
r	.20	.31
r'	.203	.320
N	225	287

$$z = \frac{.203 - .320}{\sqrt{\dfrac{1}{225 - 3} + \dfrac{1}{287 - 3}}} = \frac{-.117}{\sqrt{.008}} = \frac{-.117}{.089} = -1.32$$

Because $z_{obt} = -1.32$ is less than $z_{.025} = -1.96$, we fail to reject H_0 and conclude, that with a two-tailed test at $\alpha = .05$, we have no reason to doubt that the correlation between Social Intelligence and Perceived Popularity is the same for males as it is for females. However, this is not the case with the relationship between Perceived and Sociometric Popularity, where the correlation is significantly higher for girls.

I should point out that in general it is surprisingly difficult to find a significant difference between two independent rs for any meaningful comparison unless the sample size is quite large. Certainly I can find two correlations that are significantly different, but my experience has been that if I restrict myself to testing relationships that might have theoretical or practical interest, it is usually difficult to obtain a statistically significant difference.

Testing the Hypothesis that ρ Equals any Specified Value

Now that we have discussed the concept of r', we are in a position to test the null hypothesis that ρ is equal to any value, not just to zero. You probably can't think of many situations in which you would like to do that, and neither can I. But the ability to do so allows us to establish confidence limits on ρ, a more useful procedure.

As we have seen, for any value of ρ, the sampling distribution of r' is approximately normally distributed around ρ' (the transformed value of ρ) with a standard error of $\frac{1}{\sqrt{N - 3}}$. From this it follows that

$$z = \frac{r' - \rho'}{\sqrt{\dfrac{1}{N - 3}}}$$

is a standard normal deviate. Thus, if we want to test the null hypothesis that a sample r of .30 (with $N = 103$) came from a population where $\rho = .50$, we proceed as follows

$$r = .30 \qquad r' = .310$$
$$\rho = .50 \qquad \rho' = .549$$
$$N = 103 \qquad s_{r'} = 1/\sqrt{N - 3} = 0.10$$
$$z = \frac{.310 - .549}{0.10} = -0.239/0.10 = -2.39$$

Because $z_{obt} = -2.39$ is more extreme than $z_{.025} = -1.96$, we reject H_0 at $\alpha = .05$ (two-tailed) and conclude that our sample did not come from a population where $\rho = .50$.

Confidence Limits on ρ

We can move from the preceding discussion to easily establish confidence limits on ρ by solving that equation for ρ instead of z. To do this, we first solve for confidence limits on ρ', and then convert ρ' back to ρ.

$$z = \frac{r' - \rho'}{\sqrt{\dfrac{1}{N - 3}}}$$

therefore

$$(\pm z) * \sqrt{\frac{1}{N - 3}} = r' - \rho'$$

and thus

$$CI(\rho') = r' \pm z_{\alpha/2} \sqrt{\frac{1}{N - 3}}$$

For our stress example, $r = .529$ ($r' = .590$) and $N = 107$, so the 95% confidence limits are

$$CI(\rho') = .590 \pm 1.96 \sqrt{\frac{1}{104}}$$
$$= .590 \pm 1.96(0.098) = .590 \pm 0.192$$
$$= .398 \le \rho' \le .782$$

Converting from ρ' back to ρ and rounding,

$$.380 \le \rho \le .654$$

Thus, the limits are $\rho = .380$ and $\rho = .654$. The probability is .95 that limits obtained in this way encompass the true value of ρ. Note that $\rho = 0$ is not included within our limits, thus offering a simultaneous test of $H_0 : \rho = 0$, should we be interested in that information. Note also that the confidence limits are asymmetrically distributed around r because the sampling distribution of r is skewed.

Confidence Limits Versus Tests of Significance

At least in the behavioral sciences, most textbooks, courses, and published research have focused on tests of significance, and paid scant attention to confidence limits. In some cases that is probably appropriate, but in other cases it leaves the reader short.

In this chapter we have repeatedly referred to an example on stress and psychological symptoms. For the first few people who investigated this issue, it really was an important question whether there was a significant relationship between these two variables. But now that everyone believes it, a more appropriate question becomes how large the relationship is. And for that question, a suitable answer is provided by a statement such as the correlation between the two variables was .529, with a 95% confidence interval of $.380 \leq \rho \leq .654$. (A comparable statement from the public opinion polling field would be something like $r = .529$ with a margin of error of $\pm.15$(approx.).)[17]

Testing the Difference Between Two Nonindependent *r*s

Occasionally we come across a situation in which we wish to test the difference between two correlations that are not independent. (In fact, I am probably asked this question a couple of times per year.) One case arises when two correlations share one variable in common. We will see such an example below. Another case arises when we correlate two variables at Time 1 and then again at some later point (Time 2), and we want to ask whether there has been a significant change in the correlation over time. I will not cover that case, but a very good discussion of that particular issue can be found at core.ecu.edu/psyc/wuenschk/StatHelp/ZPF.doc and in a paper by Raghunathan, Rosenthal, and Rubin (1996).

As an example of correlations that share a common variable, Reilly, Drudge, Rosen, Loew, and Fischer (1985) administered two intelligence tests (the WISC-R and the McCarthy) to first-grade children, and then administered the Wide Range Achievement Test (WRAT) to those same children 2 years later. They obtained, among other findings, the following correlations:

	WRAT	WISC-R	McCarthy
WRAT	1.00	.80	.72
WISC-R		1.00	.89
McCarthy			1.00

Note that the WISC-R and the McCarthy are highly correlated but that the WISC-R correlates somewhat more highly with the WRAT (reading) than does the McCarthy. It is of interest to ask whether this difference between the WISC-R–WRAT correlation (.80) and the McCarthy–WRAT correlation (.72) is significant, but to answer that question requires a test on nonindependent correlations because they both have the WRAT in common and are based on the same sample.

When we have two correlations that are not independent—as these are not, because the tests were based on the same 26 children—we must take into account this lack of independence. Specifically, we must incorporate a term representing the degree to which the two tests are themselves correlated. Hotelling (1931) proposed the traditional solution, but a better test was devised by Williams (1959) and endorsed by Steiger (1980). This latter test takes the form

$$t = (r_{12} - r_{13}) \sqrt{\frac{(N-1)(1+r_{23})}{2\left(\frac{N-1}{N-3}\right)|R| + \frac{(r_{12}+r_{13})^2}{4}(1-r_{23})^3}}$$

where

$$|R| = (1 - r_{12}^2 - r_{13}^2 - r_{23}^2) + (2r_{12}r_{13}r_{23})$$

---

[17] I had to insert the label "approx." here because the limits, as we saw above, are not exactly symmetrical around *r*.

This ratio is distributed as t on $N-3$ df. In this equation, r_{12} and r_{13} refer to the correlation coefficients whose difference is to be tested, and r_{23} refers to the correlation between the two predictors. $|R|$ is the determinant of the 3×3 matrix of intercorrelations, but you can calculate it as shown without knowing anything about determinants.

For our example, let

$r_{12} = $ correlation between the WISC-R and the WRAT $= .80$
$r_{13} = $ correlation between the McCarthy and the WRAT $= .72$
$r_{23} = $ correlation between the WISC-R and the McCarthy $= .89$
$N = 26$

then

$$|R| = (1 - .80^2 - .72^2 - .89^2) + (2)(.80)(.72)(.89) = .075$$

$$t = (.80 - .72) \sqrt{\frac{(25)(1 + .89)}{2\left(\frac{25}{23}\right)(.075) + \frac{(.80 + .72)^2}{4}(1 - .89)^3}}$$

$$= 1.36$$

A value of $t_{obt} = 1.36$ on 23 df is not significant. Although this does not prove the argument that the tests are equally effective in predicting third-grade children's performance on the reading scale of the WRAT, because you cannot prove the null hypothesis, it is consistent with that argument and thus supports it.

9.13 One Final Example

I want to introduce one final example because it illustrates several important points about correlation and regression. This example is about as far from psychology as you can get and really belongs to physicists and astronomers, but it is a fascinating example taken from Todman and Dugard (2007) and it makes a very important point. We have known for over one hundred years that the distance from the sun to the planets in our solar system follows a neat pattern. The distances are shown in the following table, which includes Pluto even though it was recently demoted. (The fact that we'll see how neatly it fits the pattern of the other planets might suggest that its demotion to the lowly status of "dwarf planet" may have been rather unfair.)

If we plot these in their original units we find a very neat graph that is woefully far from linear. The plot is shown in Figure 9.9a. I have superimposed the linear regression line on that plot even though the relationship is clearly not linear. In Figure 9.9b you can see the residuals from the previous regression plotted as a function of rank, with a spline superimposed. The residuals show you that there is obviously something going on because they follow a very neat pattern. This pattern would suggest that the data might better be fit with a logarithmic transformation of distance.

In the lower left of Figure 9.9 we see the logarithm of distance plotted against the rank distance, and we should be very impressed with our choice of variable. The relationship

Table 9.8 Distance from the sun in astronomical units

Planet	Mercury	Venus	Earth	Mars	Jupiter	Saturn	Uranus	Neptune	Pluto
Rank	1	2	3	4	5	6	7	8	9
Distance	0.39	0.72	1	1.52	5.20	9.54	19.18	30.06	39.44

© Cengage Learning 2013

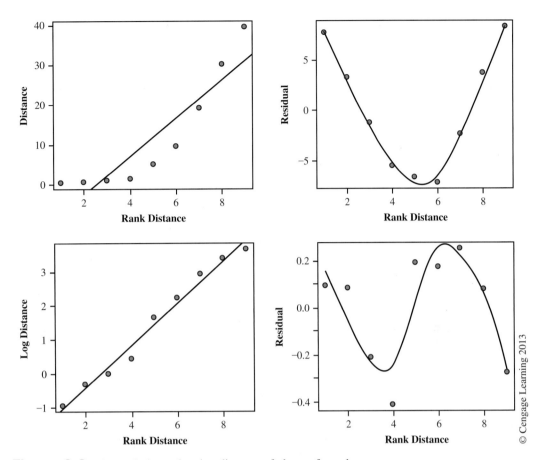

Figure 9.9   Several plots related to distance of planets from the sun

is very nearly linear as you can see by how closely the points stay to the regression line. However, the pattern that you see there should make you a bit nervous about declaring the relationship to be logarithmic, and this is verified by plotting the residuals from this regression against rank distance, as has been done in the lower right. Notice that we still have a clear pattern to the residuals. This indicates that, even though we have done an excellent job of fitting the data, there is still systematic variation in the residuals. I am told that astronomers still do not have an explanation for the second set of residuals, but it is obvious that an explanation is needed.

I have chosen this example for several reasons. First, it illustrates the difference between psychology and physics. I can't imagine any meaningful variable that psychologists study that has the precision of the variables in the physical sciences. In psychology you will never see data fit this well. Second, this example illustrates the importance of looking at residuals—they basically tell you where your model is going wrong. Although it was evident in the first plot in the upper left that there was something very systematic, and nonlinear, going on, that continued to be the case when we plotted log(distance) against rank distance. There the residuals made it clear that more was still to be explained. Finally, this example nicely illustrates the interaction between regression analyses and theory. No one in their right mind would likely be excited about using regression to *predict* the distance of each planet from the sun. We already know those distances. What is important is that by identifying just what that relationship is we can add to or confirm theory. Presumably it is obvious to a physicist what it means to say that the relationship is logarithmic. (I would assume that it relates to the fact that gravitational force varies inversely as the square of the distance, but what do I know.) But even after we explain the logarithmic relationship we can see that there is more that needs explaining. Psychologists use regression for the same purposes, although our variables contain enough random error that it is difficult to make such precise statements. When we come to multiple regression in Chapter 14 you will see again that the role of regression analysis is theory building.

9.14 The Role of Assumptions in Correlation and Regression

There is considerable confusion in the literature concerning the assumptions underlying the use of correlation and regression techniques. Much of the confusion stems from the fact that the correlation and regression models, although they lead to many of the same results, are based on different assumptions. Confusion also arises because statisticians tend to make all their assumptions at the beginning and fail to point out that some of these assumptions are not required for certain purposes.

linearity of regression

curvilinear

The major assumption that underlies both the linear-regression and bivariate-normal models and all our interpretations is that of **linearity of regression**. We assume that whatever the relationship between X and Y, it is a linear one—meaning that the line that best fits the data is a straight one. We just saw an example of a **curvilinear** (nonlinear) relationship, but standard discussions of correlation and regression assume linearity unless otherwise stated. (We do occasionally fit straight lines to curvilinear data, but we do so on the assumption that the line will be sufficiently accurate for our purpose—although the standard error of prediction might be poorly estimated. There are other forms of regression besides linear regression, but we will not discuss them here.)

As mentioned earlier, whether or not we make various assumptions depends on what we wish to do. If our purpose is simply to describe data, no assumptions are necessary. The regression line and r best describe the data at hand, without the necessity of any assumptions about the population from which the data were sampled.

If our purpose is to assess the degree to which variance in Y is linearly attributable to variance in X, we again need make no assumptions. This is true because s_Y^2 and $s_{Y \cdot X}^2$ are both unbiased estimators of their corresponding parameters, independent of any underlying assumptions, and

$$\frac{SS_Y - SS_{\text{residual}}}{SS_Y}$$

is algebraically equivalent to r^2.

If we want to set confidence limits on b or Y, or if we want to test hypotheses about b^*, we will need to make the conditional assumptions of homogeneity of variance and normality in arrays of Y. The assumption of homogeneity of variance is necessary to ensure that $s_{Y \cdot X}^2$ is representative of the variance of each array, and the assumption of normality is necessary because we use the standard normal distribution.

If we want to use r to test the hypothesis that $\rho = 0$, or if we wish to establish confidence limits on ρ, we will have to assume that the (X, Y) pairs are a random sample from a bivariate-normal distribution, but keep in mind that for many studies the significance of r is not particularly an issue, nor do we often want to set confidence limits on r.

9.15 Factors that Affect the Correlation

The correlation coefficient can be substantially affected by characteristics of the sample. Two such characteristics are the restriction of the range (or variance) of X and/or Y and the use of heterogeneous subsamples.

The Effect of Range Restrictions

range restrictions

A common problem concerns restrictions on the range over which X and Y vary. The effect of such **range restrictions** is to alter the correlation between X and Y from what it would have been if the range had not been so restricted. Depending on the nature of the data, the correlation may either rise or fall as a result of such restriction, although most commonly r is reduced.

With the exception of very unusual circumstances, restricting the range of X will increase r only when the restriction results in eliminating some curvilinear relationship. For example, if we correlated reading ability with age, where age ran from 0 to 70 years, the data would be decidedly curvilinear (flat to about age 4, rising to about 17 years of age, and then leveling off) and the correlation, which measures *linear* relationships, would be relatively low. If, however, we restricted the range of ages to 5 to 17 years, the correlation would be quite high, since we would have eliminated those values of Y that were not varying linearly as a function of X.

The more usual effect of restricting the range of X or Y is to reduce the correlation. This problem is especially pertinent in the area of test construction, because here criterion measures (Y) may be available for only the higher values of X. Consider the hypothetical data in Figure 9.10. This figure represents the relation between college GPAs and scores on some standard achievement test (such as the SAT) for a hypothetical sample of students. In the ideal world of the test constructor, all people who took the exam would then be sent on to college and earn a GPA, and the correlation between achievement test scores and GPAs would be computed. As can be seen from Figure 9.10, this correlation would be reasonably high. In the real world, however, not everyone is admitted to college. Colleges take only the more able students, whether this classification is based on achievement test scores, high school performance, or whatever. This means that GPAs are available mainly for students who had relatively high scores on the standardized test. Suppose that this has the effect of allowing us to evaluate the relationship between X and Y for only those values of X that are greater than 400. For the data in Figure 9.10, the correlation will be relatively low, not

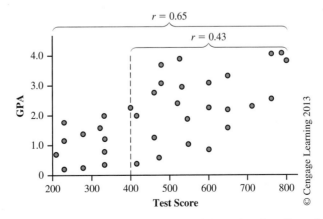

Figure 9.10 Hypothetical data illustrating the effect of restricted range

because the test is worthless, but because the range has been restricted. In other words, when we use the entire sample of points in Figure 9.10, the correlation is .65. However, when we restrict the sample to those students having test scores of at least 400, the correlation drops to only .43. (This is easier to see if you cover up all data points for $X < 400$.)

We must take into account the effect of range restrictions whenever we see a correlation coefficient based on a restricted sample. The coefficient might be inappropriate for the question at hand. Essentially, what we have done is to ask how well a standardized test predicts a person's suitability for college, but we have answered that question by referring only to those people who were actually admitted to college.

Dunning and Friedman (2008), using an example similar to this one, make the point that restricting the range, while it can have severe effects on the value of r, may leave the underlying regression line relatively unaffected. (You can illustrate this by fitting regression lines to the full and then the truncated data shown in Figure 9.10.) However, the effect hinges on the assumption that the data points that we have not collected are related in the same way as points that we have collected.

The Effect of Heterogeneous Subsamples

heterogeneous subsamples

Another important consideration in evaluating the results of correlational analyses deals with **heterogeneous subsamples**. This point can be illustrated with a simple example involving the relationship between height and weight in male and female subjects. These variables may appear to have little to do with psychology, but considering the important role both variables play in the development of people's images of themselves, the example is not as far afield as you might expect. The data plotted in Figure 9.11, using Minitab, come from sample data from the Minitab manual (Ryan et al., 1985). These are actual data from 92 college students who were asked to report height, weight, gender, and several other variables. (Keep in mind that these are self-reported data, and there may be systematic reporting biases.)

When we combine the data from both males and females, the relationship is strikingly good, with a correlation of .78. When you look at the data from the two genders separately, however, the correlations fall to .60 for males and .49 for females. (Males and females have been plotted using different symbols, with data from females primarily in the lower left. The regression equation for males is $\hat{Y}_{male} = 4.36 \times Height_{male} - 149.93$ and for females

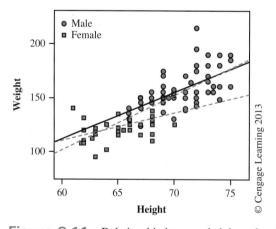

Figure 9.11   Relationship between height and weight for males and females combined. (dashed line = female, solid line = male, dotted line = combined)

is $\hat{Y}_{female} = 2.58 \times Height_{female} - 44.86$.) .) The important point is that the high correlation we found when we combined genders is not due purely to the relation between height and weight. It is also due largely to the fact that men are, on average, taller and heavier than women. In fact, a little doodling on a sheet of paper will show that you could create artificial, and improbable, data where within each gender's weight is negatively related to height, while the relationship is positive when you collapse across gender. The point I am making here is that experimenters must be careful when they combine data from several sources. The relationship between two variables may be obscured or enhanced by the presence of a third variable. Such a finding is important in its own right.

A second example of heterogeneous subsamples that makes a similar point is the relationship between cholesterol level and cardiovascular disease in men and women. If you collapse across both genders, the relationship is not impressive. But when you separate the data by male and female, there is a distinct trend for cardiovascular disease to increase with increased levels of cholesterol. This relationship is obscured in the combined data because men, regardless of cholesterol level, have an elevated level of cardiovascular disease compared to women.

9.16   Power Calculation for Pearson's r

Consider the problem of the individual who wishes to demonstrate a relationship between television violence and aggressive behavior. Assume that he has surmounted all the very real problems associated with designing this study and has devised a way to obtain a correlation between the two variables. He believes that the correlation coefficient in the population (ρ) is approximately .30. (This correlation may seem small, but it is impressive when you consider all the variables involved in aggressive behavior. This value is in line with the correlation obtained in a study by Huesmann, Moise-Titus, Podolski, & Eron (2003), although the strength of the relationship has been disputed by Block & Crain (2007).) Our experimenter wants to conduct a study to find such a correlation but wants to know something about the power of his study before proceeding. Power calculations are easy to make in this situation.

As you should recall, when we calculate power we first define an effect size (d). We then introduce the sample size and compute δ, and finally we use δ to compute the power of our design from Appendix Power.

We begin by defining

$$d = \rho_1 - \rho_0 = \rho_1 - 0 = \rho_1$$

where ρ_1 is the correlation in the population defined by H_1—in this case, .30. We next define

$$\delta = d\sqrt{N-1} = \rho_1\sqrt{N-1}$$

For a sample of size 50,

$$\delta = .30\sqrt{50-1} = 2.1$$

From Appendix Power, for $\delta = 2.1$ and $\alpha = .05$ (two-tailed), power = .56.

A power coefficient of .56 does not please the experimenter, so he casts around for a way to increase power. He wants power = .80. From Appendix Power, we see that this will require $\delta = 2.8$. Therefore,

$$\delta = \rho_1\sqrt{N-1}$$

$$2.8 = .30\sqrt{N-1}$$

Squaring both sides,

$$2.8^2 = .30^2(N - 1)$$
$$\left(\frac{2.8}{.30}\right)^2 + 1 = N = 88$$

Thus, to obtain power $= .80$, the experimenter will have to collect data on nearly 90 participants. (Most studies of the effects of violence on television are based on many more subjects than that.) A short program written in R to calculate power for correlation coefficients is available on the book's Web site and named CorrelationPower.R.

Additional Examples

I have pulled together a few additional examples and useful material on correlation and regression at http://www.uvm.edu/~dhowell/methods8/Supplements/CorrReg.html.

These are more complex examples than we have seen to date, involving several different statistical procedures for each data set. However, you can get a good idea of how correlation is used in practice by looking at these examples, and you can just ignore the other material that you don't recognize. Keep in mind that even with the simple correlational material, there may be more advanced ways of dealing with data that we have not covered here.

Key Terms

Relationships (Introduction)

Differences (Introduction)

Correlation (Introduction)

Regression (Introduction)

Random variable (Introduction)

Fixed variable (Introduction)

Linear-regression models (Introduction)

Bivariate-normal models (Introduction)

Prediction (Introduction)

Scatterplot (9.1)

Scatter diagram (9.1)

Predictor (9.1)

Criterion (9.1)

Regression lines (9.1)

Linear relationship (9.2)

Curvilinear relationship (9.29)

Correlation (r) (9.1)

Covariance (cov_{XY} or s_{XY}) (9.3)

Correlation coefficient in the population ρ (rho) (9.4)

Adjusted correlation coefficient (r_{adj}) (9.4)

Slope (9.5)

Intercept (9.5)

Errors of prediction (9.5)

Residual (9.5)

Normal equations (9.5)

Standardized regression coefficient β (beta) (9.5)

Scatterplot smoothers (9.7)

Splines (9.7)

Loess (9.7)

Sum of squares (SS_Y) (9.8)

Standard error of estimate (9.8)

Residual variance (9.8)

Error variance (9.8)

Conditional distribution (9.8)

Proportional reduction in error (PRE) (9.8)

Proportional improvement in prediction (PIP) (9.8)

Array (9.9)

Homogeneity of variance in arrays (9.9)

Normality in arrays (9.9)

Conditional array (9.9)

Conditional distributions (9.9)

Marginal distribution (9.9)

Prediction interval (9.10)

Linearity of regression (9.13)

Curvilinear (9.13)

Range restrictions (9.15)

Heterogeneous subsamples (9.15)

Exercises

9.1   In Sub-Saharan Africa, more than half of mothers lose at least one child before the child's first birthday. Below are data on 36 countries in the region, giving country, infant mortality, per capita income (in U.S. dollars), percentage of births to mothers under 20, percentage of births to mothers over 40, percentage of births less than 2 years apart, percentage of married women using contraception, and percentage of women with unmet family planning need. (http://www.guttmacher.org/pubs/ib_2-02.html)

Country	InfMort	Income	% mom < 20	% mom > 40	<2 yrs apart	Using contraception	Need family planning
Benin Rep	104	933	16	5	17	3	26
Burkina Faso	109	965	17	5	17	5	26
Cameroon	80	1,573	21	4	25	7	20
Central African Rep	102	1,166	22	5	26	3	16
Chad Rep	110	850	21	3	24	1	missing
Côte d'Ivoire	91	1,654	21	6	16	4	28
Eritrea	76	880	15	7	26	4	28
Ethiopia	113	628	14	6	20	6	23
Gabon	61	6,024	22	4	22	12	28
Ghana	61	1,881	15	5	13	13	23
Guinea	107	1,934	22	5	17	4	24
Kenya	71	1,022	18	3	23	32	24
Madagascar	99	799	21	5	31	10	26
Malawi	113	586	21	6	17	26	30
Mali	134	753	21	4	26	5	26
Mozambique	147	861	24	6	19	5	7
Namibia	62	5,468	15	7	22	26	22
Niger	136	753	23	5	25	5	17
Nigeria	71	853	17	5	27	9	18
Rwanda	90	885	9	7	21	13	36
Senegal	69	1,419	14	7	18	8	35
Tanzania	108	501	19	5	17	17	22
Togo	80	1,410	13	6	14	7	32
Uganda	86	650	23	4	28	8	35
Zambia	108	756	30	4	19	14	27
Zimbabwe	60	2,876	32	4	12	50	13

Source: Guttmacher Institute, Community health centers and family planning, Issues in Brief, New York: Guttmacher, 2002, http://www.guttmacher.org/pubs/ib_2-02.html, accessed May 16, 2011.

a.   Make a scatter diagram of InfMort and income.

b.   Draw (by eye) the line that appears to best fit the data.

c.   What effect do you suppose that the two outliers on income have?

9.2   What are the strongest predictors of infant mortality in Exercise 9.4?

9.3   Using the table in Appendix *t*, how large a correlation would you need for the relationships shown in 9.4 to be significant?

9.4   Calculate the correlations among all numeric variables in Exercise 9.1 using SPSS.

9.5   What can we conclude from the data on infant mortality?

9.6   Down's syndrome is another problem that psychologists deal with. It has been proposed that mothers who give birth at older ages are more likely to have a child with Down's syndrome. Plot the data below relating age to incidence. The data were taken from Geyer (1991).

Age	17.5	18.5	19.5	20.5	21.5	22.5	23.5	24.5	25.5
Births	13,555	13,675	18,752	22,005	23,796	24,667	24,807	23,986	22,860
Downs	16	15	16	22	16	12	17	22	15

Age	26.5	27.5	28.5	29.5	30.5	31.5	32.5	33.5	34.5
Births	21,450	19,202	17,450	15,685	13,954	11,987	10,983	9,825	8,483
Downs	15	27	14	9	12	12	18	13	11

Age	35.5	36.5	37.5	38.5	39.5	40.5	41.5	42.5	43.5
Births	7,448	6,628	5,780	4,834	3,961	2,952	2,276	1,589	1,018
Downs	23	13	17	15	30	31	33	20	16

Age	44.5	45.5	46.5
Births	596	327	249
Downs	22	11	7

Plot a scatter diagram for the percentage of Downs cases (Downs / Births) as a function of age.

9.7   Two predictors of infant mortality seem to be significant. If you could find a way to use both of them as predictors simultaneously, what do you think you would find?

9.8   In Exercise 9.1 the percentage of mothers over 40 does not appear to be important, and yet it is a risk factor in other societies. Why do you think that this might be?

9.9   Infant mortality is a very serious problem to society. Why would psychologists be interested in this problem any more than people in other professions?

9.10   From the previous exercises do you think that we are able to conclude that low income causes infant mortality?

9.11   Why would you not feel comfortable computing a Pearson correlation on the data in Exercise 9.6?

9.12   How many infants would be required for power to be .80 in Exercise 9.13?

9.13   An important developmental question concerns the relationship between severity of cerebral hemorrhage in low-birthweight infants and cognitive deficit in the same children at age 5 years. Suppose we expect a correlation of .20 and are planning to use 25 infants. How much power does this study have?

9.14   One way to get around the problem you see in Exercise 9.11 is to convert the incidence of Down's syndrome to ranked data. Replot the data using ranked incidence and calculate the correlation. This is a Spearman's correlation, as we will see in the next chapter.

9.15   Using the information in Table 9.2 and the computed coefficients, predict the score for log(symptoms) for a stress score of 8.

9.16   You want to demonstrate a relationship between the amount of money school districts spend on education and the performance of students on a standardized test such as the SAT. You are interested in finding such a correlation only if the true correlation is at least .40. What are your chances of finding a significant sample correlation if you have 30 school districts?

9.17   Calculate an equation for the 95% confidence interval in $\hat{Y}$ for predicting psychological symptoms for new cases—you can overlay the confidence limits on Figure 9.2.

9.18 The mean stress score for the data in Table 9.3 was 21.467. What would your prediction for log(symptoms) be for someone who had that stress score? How does this compare to $\bar{Y}$?

9.19 The data file named Galton.dat on this book's Web site contains Galton's actual data on heights of parents and children discussed under the heading of "regression to the mean." In these data Galton multiplied mothers' and daughters' heights by 1.08 to give them the same mean as males' heights, and averaged the heights of both parents to produce the "mid-parent" height. The data are taken from Stigler (1999).

    a. Regress child height against parent height.

    b. Calculate the predicted height for children on the basis of parental height.

    c. The data file contains a variable called Quartile ranging from 1 to 4, with 1 being the lowest quartile. Use SPSS **Analyze/Compare Means/One-way ANOVA** to give child means corresponding to each quartile. (Make Child the dependent variable and Quartile the independent variable.) Do the same for parent means.

    d. Do the children of parents in the highest quartile have a lower mean than their parents, and vice versa for the children of parents in the lowest quartile?

    e. Draw a scatterplot with parent quartile means on the X axis and child quartile means on the Y axis. Also draw a 45 degree line that would represent parents having children with the same mean height.

9.20 In 1886, Sir Francis Galton, an English scientist, spoke about "regression toward mediocrity," which we more charitably refer to today as regression toward the mean. The basic principle is that those people at the ends of any continuum (e.g., height, IQ, or musical ability) tend to have children who are closer to the mean than they are. Use the concept of r as the regression coefficient (slope) with standardized data to explain Galton's idea.

9.21 In Exercise 9.16 how many districts would you need for power $= .80$?

9.22 Katz et al. replicated their experiment using subjects whose SAT Verbal scores showed considerably more within-group variance than those in the first study. In this case the correlation for the group that read the passage was .88 ($N = 52$), whereas for the nonreading group it was .72 ($N = 74$). Were these correlations significantly different?

9.23 In the study by Katz, Lautenschlager, Blackburn, and Harris (1990) used in this chapter and in Exercises 7.13 and 7.29, we saw that students who were answering reading comprehension questions on the SAT without first reading the passages performed at better-than-chance levels. This does not necessarily mean that the SAT is not a useful test. Katz et al. went on to calculate the correlation between the actual SAT Verbal scores on their participants' admissions applications and performance on the 100-item test. For those participants who had read the passage, the correlation was .68 ($N = 17$). For those who had not read the passage, the correlation was .53 ($N = 28$), as we have seen.

    a. Were these correlations significantly different?

    b. What would you conclude from these data?

9.24 Guber (1999) actually assembled the data to address the basic question referred to in Exercises 9.16 and 9.21. She obtained the data for all 50 states on several variables associated with school performance, including expenditures for education, SAT performance, percentage of students taking the SAT, and other variables. We will look more extensively at these data later, but the following table contains the SPSS computer printout for Guber's data.

SPSS

Model Summary[b]

Model	R	R Square	Adjusted R Square	Std. Error of the Estimate
1	.453[a]	.205	.188	65.49

[a]Predictors: (Constant), Current expenditure per pupil—1994–95
[b]Dependent Variable: Average combined SAT 1994–95

ANOVA[b]

Model		Sum of Squares	df	Mean Square	F	Sig.
1	Regression	50920.767	1	50920.767	11.872	.001[a]
	Residual	197303.0	46	4289.197		
	Total	248223.8	47			

[a]Predictors: (Constant), Current expenditure per pupil—1994–95
[b]Dependent Variable: Average combined SAT 1994–95

Coefficients[a]

Model		Unstandardized Coefficients		Standardized Coefficients		
		B	Std. Error	Beta	t	Sig.
1	(Constant)	1112.769	42.341		26.281	.000
	Current expenditure per pupil—1994–95	–23.918	6.942	–.453	–3.446	.001

[a]Dependent Variable: Average combined SAT 1994–1995

Adapted from output by SPSS, Inc.

These data do not reveal the pattern that we would expect. What do they show? (In Chapter 15 we will see that the expected pattern actually is there if we control for other variables. I should point out that testing organizations discourage the use of test scores for this purpose because of so many confounding variables.)

9.25   What conclusions can you draw from the difference between the correlations in Exercises 9.22 and 9.23?

9.26   One of the assumptions lying behind our use of regression is the assumption of homogeneity of variance in arrays. One way to examine the data for violations of this assumption is to calculate predicted values of Y and the corresponding residuals $(Y - \hat{Y})$. If you plot the residuals against the predicted values, you should see a more or less random collection of points. The vertical dispersion should not increase or decrease systematically as you move from right to left, nor should there be any other apparent pattern. Create the scatterplot for the data from Cancer.dat at the Web site for this book. Most computer packages let you request this plot. If not, you can easily generate the appropriate variables by first determining the regression equation and then feeding that equation back into the program in a "compute statement" (e.g., "set Pred = 0.256*GSIT + 4.65," and "set Resid = TotBPT – Pred").

9.27   Moore and McCabe (1989) found some interesting data on the consumption of alcohol and tobacco that illustrate an important statistical concept. Their data, taken from the Family Expenditure Survey of the British Department of Employment, follow. The dependent variables are the average weekly household expenditures for alcohol and tobacco in 11 regions of Great Britain.

Region	Alcohol	Tobacco
North	6.47	4.03
Yorkshire	6.13	3.76
Northeast	6.19	3.77
East Midlands	4.89	3.34
West Midlands	5.63	3.47
East Anglia	4.52	2.92
Southeast	5.89	3.20
Southwest	4.79	2.71

© Cengage Learning 2013

(continued)

Wales	5.27	3.53	
Scotland	6.08	4.51	
Northern Ireland	4.02	4.56	

a.   What is the relationship between these two variables?

b.   Popular stereotypes have the Irish as heavy drinkers. Do the data support that belief?

c.   What effect does the inclusion of Northern Ireland have on our results? (A scatterplot would be helpful.)

9.28   Make up your own example along the lines of the "smoking versus life expectancy" example given on pp. 270–271 to illustrate the relationship between r^2 and accountable variation.

9.29   Using the data referred to in Exercise 9.30,

a.   calculate the correlations among all of the Brief Symptom Inventory subscales. (Hint: Virtually all statistical programs are able to calculate these correlations in one statement. You don't have to calculate each one individually.)

b.   What does the answer to (a) tell us about the relationships among the separate scales?

9.30   Using the data from Mireault and Bond (1992) in the file Mireault.dat, at http://www.uvm.edu/~dhowell/methods8/DataFiles/DataSets.html, is there a relationship between how well a student performs in college (as assessed by GPA) and that student's psychological symptoms (as assessed by GSIT)?

9.31   The following data represent the actual heights and weights referred to earlier for male college students.

Height	Weight	Height	Weight
70	150	73	170
67	140	74	180
72	180	66	135
75	190	71	170
68	145	70	157
69	150	70	130
71.5	164	75	185
71	140	74	190
72	142	71	155
69	136	69	170
67	123	70	155
68	155	72	215
66	140	67	150
72	145	69	145
73.5	160	73	155
73	190	73	155
69	155	71	150
73	165	68	155
72	150	69.5	150
74	190	73	180
72	195	75	160
71	138	66	135

(continued)

74	160	69	160
72	155	66	130
70	153	73	155
67	145	68	150
71	170	74	148
72	175	73.5	155
69	175		

a. Make a scatterplot of the data.

b. Calculate the regression equation of weight predicted from height for these data. Interpret the slope and the intercept.

c. What is the correlation coefficient for these data?

d. Are the correlation coefficient and the slope significantly different from zero?

9.32 The slope (b) used to predict the weights of males from their heights is greater than the slope for females. Is this significant, and what would it mean if it were?

9.33 Using your own height and the appropriate regression equation from Exercise 9.31 and 9.34 predict your own weight. (If you are uncomfortable reporting your own weight, predict mine—I am 5'8" and weigh 146 pounds.)

a. How much is your actual weight greater than or less than your predicted weight? (You have just calculated a residual.)

b. What effect will biased reporting on the part of the students who produced the data play in your prediction of your own weight?

9.34 The following data are the actual heights and weights, referred to in this chapter, of female college students.

a. Make a scatterplot of the data.

b. Calculate the regression coefficients for these data. Interpret the slope and the intercept.

c. What is the correlation coefficient for these data? Is the slope significantly different from zero?

Height	Weight	Height	Weight
61	140	65	135
66	120	66	125
68	130	65	118
68	138	65	122
63	121	65	115
70	125	64	102
68	116	67	115
69	145	69	150
69	150	68	110
67	150	63	116
68	125	62	108
66	130	63	95
65.5	120	64	125
66	130	68	133
62	131	62	110
62	120	61.75	108
63	118	62.75	112
67	125		

9.35   Given a male and a female student who are both 5′6″, how much would they be expected to differ in weight? (*Hint*: Calculate a predicted weight for each of them using the regression equation specific to their gender.)

9.36   Use your scatterplot of the data for students of your own gender and observe the size of the residuals. (*Hint*: You can see the residuals in the vertical distance of points from the line.) What is the largest residual for your scatterplot?

9.37   In Chapter 2 I presented data on the speed of deciding whether a briefly presented digit was part of a comparison set and gave data from trials on which the comparison set had contained one, three, or five digits. Eventually, I would like to compare the three conditions (using only the data from trials on which the stimulus digit had in fact been a part of that set), but I worry that the trials are not independent. If the subject (myself) was improving as the task went along, he would do better on later trials, and how he did would in some way be related to the number of the trial. If so, we would not be able to say that the responses were independent. Using only the data from the trials labeled Y in the condition in which there were five digits in the comparison set, obtain the regression of response on trial number. Was performance improving significantly over trials? Can we assume that there is no systematic linear trend over time?

Discussion Questions

9.38   The distinction between confidence intervals and prediction intervals in regression is often difficult to grasp. Do a Google search to find a clear explanation of the distinction.

9.39   In 2005 an object was discovered out beyond Pluto that was (unofficially) named Xena and now is called Eris. It is larger than Pluto but is not considered a planet—the new title is "plutoid." It is 96.7 astronomical units from the sun. How does such an object fit with the data in Table 9.7?

9.40   In a recent e-mail query, someone asked about how they should compare two air pollution monitors that sit side-by-side and collect data all day. They had the average reading per monitor for each of 50 days and wanted to compare the two monitors; their first thought was to run a t test between the means of the readings of the two monitors. This question would apply equally well to psychologists and other behavioral scientists if we simply substitute two measures of Extraversion for two measures of air pollution and collect data using both measures on the same 50 subjects. How would you go about comparing the monitors (or measures)? What kind of results would lead you to conclude that they are measuring equivalently or differently? This is a much more involved question than it might first appear, so don't just say you would run a t test or obtain a correlation coefficient. Sample data that might have come from such a study are to be found on the Web site in a file named AirQual.dat in case you want to play with data.

9.41   Going back to the example on popularity and academic achievement, run the appropriate test to compare the correlations in males and females between Perceived Popularity and Sociometric Popularity.

9.42   In 1801 a celestial object named Ceres was discovered by Giuseppi Piazzi at 2.767 astronomical units from the sun. It was called a dwarf planet, but those are now plutoids. If it were classed as a planet, how would this fit with the other planets we know as shown in Table 9.7?

Chapter 10

Alternative Correlational Techniques

Objectives

To discuss correlation and regression with regard to dichotomous variables and ranked data, and to present measures of association between categorical variables.

Contents

THE PEARSON PRODUCT-MOMENT CORRELATION COEFFICIENT (r) is only one of many available correlation coefficients. It generally applies to those situations in which the relationship between two variables is basically linear, where both variables are measured on a more or less continuous scale, and where some sort of normality and homogeneity of variance assumptions can be made. As this chapter will point out, r can be meaningfully interpreted in other situations as well, although for those cases it is given a different name and it is often not recognized for what it actually is.

In this chapter we will discuss a variety of coefficients that apply to different kinds of data. For example, the data might represent rankings, one or both of the variables might be dichotomous, or the data might be categorical. Depending on the assumptions we are willing to make about the underlying nature of our data, different coefficients will be appropriate in different situations. Some of these coefficients will turn out to be calculated as if they were Pearson r_S, and some will not. The important point is that they all represent attempts to obtain some measure of the relationship between two variables and fall under the general heading of *correlation* rather than *regression*.

When we speak of relationships between two variables without any restriction on the nature of these variables, we have to distinguish between **correlational measures** and **measures of association**. When at least some sort of order can be assigned to the levels of each variable, such that higher scores represent more (or less) of some quantity, then it makes sense to speak of correlation. We can speak meaningfully of increases in one variable being associated with increases in another variable. In many situations, however, different levels of a variable do not represent an orderly increase or decrease in some quantity. For example, we could sort people on the basis of their membership in different campus organizations, and then on the basis of their views on some issue. We might then find that there is in fact an association between people's views and their membership in organizations, and yet neither of these variables represents an ordered continuum. In cases such as this, the coefficient we will compute is not a correlation coefficient. We will instead speak of it as a measure of association.

There are three basic reasons we might be interested in calculating any type of coefficient of correlation. The most obvious, but not necessarily the most important, reason is to obtain an estimate of ρ, the correlation in the population. Thus, someone interested in the **validity** of a test actually cares about the true correlation between his test and some criterion, and approaches the calculation of a coefficient with this purpose in mind. This use is the one for which the alternative techniques are least satisfactory, although they can serve this purpose.

A second use of correlation coefficients occurs with such techniques as multiple regression and factor analysis. In this situation, the coefficient is not in itself an end product; rather, it enters into the calculation of further statistics. For these purposes, several of the coefficients to be discussed are satisfactory.

The final reason for calculating a correlation coefficient is to use its square as a measure of the variation in one variable accountable for by variation in the other variable. This is a measure of effect size (from the *r*-family of measures), and is often useful as a way of conveying the magnitude of the effect that we found. Here again, the coefficients to be discussed are in many cases satisfactory for this purpose. I will specifically discuss the creation of *r*-family effect size measures in what follows.

correlational measures

measures of association

validity

10.1 Point-Biserial Correlation and Phi: Pearson Correlations by Another Name

In the previous chapter I discussed the standard Pearson product-moment correlation coefficient (r) in terms of variables that are relatively continuous on both measures. However, that same formula also applies to a pair of variables that are dichotomous (having two levels) on one or both measures. We may need to be somewhat cautious in our interpretation, and there are some interesting relationships between those correlations and other statistics that we have discussed, but the same basic procedure is used for these special cases as we used for the more general case.

Point-Biserial Correlation (r_{pb})

dichotomy

Frequently, variables are measured in the form of a **dichotomy**, such as male-female, pass-fail, Experimental group-Control group, and so on. Ignoring for the moment that these variables are seldom measured numerically (a minor problem), it is also quite apparent that they are not measured continuously. There is no way we can assume that a continuous distribution, such as the normal distribution, for example, will represent the obtained scores on the dichotomous variable male-female. If we wish to use r as a measure of relationship between variables, we obviously have a problem, because for r to have certain desirable properties as an estimate of ρ, we need to assume at least an approximation of normality in the joint (bivariate) population of X and Y.

The difficulty over the numerical measurement of X turns out to be trivial for dichotomous variables. If X represents married versus unmarried, for example, then we can legitimately score married as 0 and unmarried as 1, or vice versa. (In fact *any* two values will do. We use 0 and 1, or sometimes 1 and 2, for the simple reason that this makes the arithmetic easier.) Given such a system of quantification, it should be apparent that the sign of the correlation will depend solely on the arbitrary way in which we choose to assign 0 and 1, and is therefore meaningless for most purposes.

point-biserial coefficient (r_{pb})

If we set aside the problem of r as an estimate of ρ until the end of the chapter, things begin to look brighter. For any other purpose, we can proceed as usual to calculate the standard Pearson correlation coefficient (r), although we will label it the **point-biserial coefficient (r_{pb})**. Thus, algebraically, $r_{pb} = r$, where one variable is dichotomous and the other is roughly continuous and more or less normally distributed in arrays.[1] There are special formulae that we could use, but there is nothing to be gained by doing so and it is just something additional to learn and remember.

Calculating r_{pb}

One of the more common questions among statistical discussion groups on the Internet is "Does anyone know of a program that will calculate a point-biserial correlation?" The answer is very simple—any statistical package I know of will calculate the point-biserial correlation, because it is simply Pearson's r applied to a special kind of data.

As an example of the calculation of the point-biserial correlation we will use the data in Table 10.1. These are the first 12 cases of male (Sex = 0) weights and the first 15 cases of female (Sex = 1) weights from Exercises 9.31 and 9.34 in Chapter 9. I have chosen unequal numbers of males and females just to show that it is possible to do so. Keep in mind that these are actual self-report data from real subjects.

The scatterplot for these data is given in Figure 10.1, with the regression line superimposed. There are fewer than 27 data points here simply because some points overlap. Notice that the regression line passes through the mean of each array. Thus, when $X = 0$, $\hat{Y}$ is the intercept and equals the mean weight for males, and when $X = 1$, $\hat{Y}$ is the mean weight for females. These values are shown in Table 10.1, along with the correlation coefficient.

---

[1] When there is a clear criterion variable and when that variable is the one that is dichotomous (for example, success/failure), you might wish to consider logistic regression (see Chapter 15).

Table 10.1   Calculation of point-biserial correlation for weights of males and females

Sex	Weight	Sex	Weight
0	150	1	130
0	140	1	138
0	180	1	121
0	190	1	125
0	145	1	116
0	150	1	145
0	164	1	150
0	140	1	150
0	142	1	125
0	136	1	130
0	123	1	120
0	155	1	130
1	140	1	131
1	120		

$\text{Mean}_{\text{male}} = 151.25$

$s_{\text{male}} = 18.869$

$\text{Mean}_{\text{weight}} = 140.222$

$s_{\text{weight}} = 17.792$

$\text{cov}_{XY} = -5.090$

$\text{Mean}_{\text{female}} = 131.4$

$s_{\text{female}} = 10.979$

$\text{Mean}_{\text{sex}} = 0.556$

$s_{\text{sex}} = 0.506$

$$r = \frac{\text{cov}_{XY}}{s_X s_Y} = \frac{-5.090}{(0.506)(17.792)} = -.565$$

$$b = \frac{\text{cov}_{XY}}{s_X^2} = \frac{-5.090}{(0.506)^2} = -19.85$$

$$a = \overline{Y} - b\overline{X} = 151.25$$

© Cengage Learning 2013

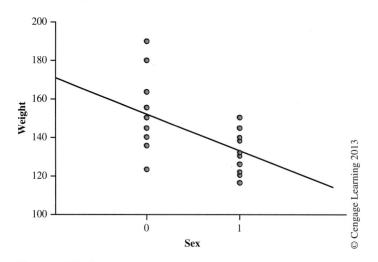

Figure 10.1   Weight as a function of Sex

The slope of the line is negative because we have set "female" = 1 and therefore plotted females to the right of males. If we had reversed the scoring the slope would have been positive.

From Table 10.1 you can see that the correlation between weight and sex is –.565. As noted, we can ignore the sign of this correlation, because the decision about coding sex is arbitrary. A negative coefficient indicates that the mean of the group coded 1 is less than the mean of the group coded 0, whereas a positive correlation indicates the reverse. We can still interpret r^2 as usual, however, and say that $-.565^2 = 32\%$ of the variability in weight can be accounted for by gender. We are not speaking here of cause and effect. One of the more immediate causes of weight is the additional height of males, which is certainly related to gender, but there are a lot of other sex-linked characteristics that enter the picture.

Another interesting fact illustrated in Figure 10.1 concerns the equation for the regression line. Recall that the intercept is the value of $\hat{Y}$ when $X = 0$. In this case, $X = 0$ for males and the predicted weight for males is $\hat{Y} = 151.25$. In other words, the mean weight of the group coded 0 is the intercept. Moreover, the slope of the regression line is defined as the change in $\hat{Y}$ for a one-unit change in X. Because a one-unit change in X corresponds to a change from male to female, and the predicted value ($\hat{Y}$) changes from the mean weight of males to the mean weight of females, the slope (–19.85) will represent the difference in the two means. We will return to this idea in Chapter 16, but it is important to notice it here in a simple context.

The Relationship Between r_{pb} and t

The relationship between r_{pb} and t is very important. It can be shown, although the proof will not be given here, that

$$r_{pb}^2 = \frac{t^2}{t^2 + df}$$

where t is obtained from the t test of the difference of means (for example, between the mean weights of males and females) and df = the degrees of freedom for t, namely $N_1 + N_2 - 2$. For example, if we were to run a t test on the difference in mean weight between male and female subjects, using a t for two independent groups with unequal sample sizes,

$$s_p^2 = \frac{(N_1 - 1)s_1^2 + (N_2 - 1)s_2^2}{N_1 + N_2 - 2}$$

$$= \frac{11(18.869^2) + 14(10.979^2)}{12 + 15 - 2} = 224.159$$

$$t = \frac{\overline{X}_1 - \overline{X}_2}{\sqrt{\dfrac{s_p^2}{N_1} + \dfrac{s_p^2}{N_2}}}$$

$$= \frac{151.25 - 131.4}{\sqrt{\dfrac{224.159}{12} + \dfrac{224.159}{15}}}$$

$$= \frac{19.85}{5.799} = 3.42$$

With 25 df, the difference between the two groups is significant. We now calculate

$$r_{pb}^2 = \frac{t^2}{t^2 + df} = \frac{3.42^2}{3.42^2 + 25} = .319$$

$$r_{pb} = \sqrt{.319} = .565$$

which, with the exception of the arbitrary sign of the coefficient, agrees with the more direct calculation.

Testing the Significance of r_{pb}^2

A test of r_{pb} against the null hypothesis $H_0: \rho = 0$ is simple to construct. Because r_{pb} is a Pearson product-moment coefficient, it can be tested in the same way as any r. Namely,

$$t = \frac{r_{pb}\sqrt{N-2}}{\sqrt{1 - r_{pb}^2}}$$

on $N - 2$ df. Furthermore, because this equation can be derived directly from the definition of r_{pb}^2, the $t = 3.42$ obtained here is the same (except possibly for the sign) as a t test between the two levels of the dichotomous variable. This makes sense when you realize that a statement that males and females differ in weight is the same as the statement that weight varies with sex.

r_{pb}^2 and Effect Size

There is one more important step that we can take. Elsewhere we have considered a measure of effect size put forth by Cohen (1988), who defined

$$d = \frac{\mu_1 - \mu_2}{\sigma}$$

as a measure of the effect of one treatment compared to another. We have to be a bit careful here, because Cohen originally expressed effect size in terms of parameters (i.e., in terms of population means and standard deviations). Others (Glass (1976) and Hedges (1981)) expressed their statistics (g' and g, respectively) in terms of sample statistics, where Hedges used the pooled estimate of the population variance as the denominator (see Chapter 7 for the pooled estimate) and Glass used the standard deviation of one of the groups. The nice thing about any of these effect size measures is that they express the difference between means in terms of the size of a standard deviation. While it is nice to be correct, it is also nice, and sometimes clearer, to be consistent. As I have done elsewhere, I am going to continue to refer to our effect size measure as Cohen's d, with apologies to Hedges and Glass. An excellent discussion of the different measures and their definitions can be found in Kline (2004).

There is a direct relationship between the squared point-biserial correlation coefficient and d.

$$d = \frac{\overline{X}_1 - \overline{X}_2}{s_{pooled}} = \sqrt{\frac{df(n_1 + n_2)r_{pb}^2}{n_1 n_2(1 - r_{pb}^2)}}$$

For our data on weights of males and females, we have

$$d = \frac{\overline{X}_1 - \overline{X}_2}{s_{pooled}} = \sqrt{\frac{df(n_1 + n_2)r_{pb}^2}{n_1 n_2(1 - r_{pb}^2)}}$$

$$= \frac{151.25 - 131.4}{14.972} = 1.33 = \sqrt{\frac{25(12 + 15)(-.565)^2}{12 \times 15(1 - .565^2)}} = \sqrt{1.758} = 1.33$$

We can now conclude that the difference between the average weights of males and females is about 1 1/3 standard deviations. To me, that is more meaningful than saying that sex accounts for about 32% of the variation in weight.

An important point here is to see that these statistics are related in meaningful ways. We can go from r_{pb}^2 to d to t, and vice versa, depending on which seems to be a more meaningful statistic. With the increased emphasis on the reporting of effect sizes and similar measures, it is important to recognize these relationships.

Confidence Limits on *d*

We can go one step further to compute a confidence limit on δ, which is the population parameter corresponding to d. The proper way to construct these limits is to use the noncentral t distribution, and I referred to this approach in Chapter 7, Section 7.5. If we are to settle for an approximation we can use the standard z distribution. Then, using the pooled standard deviation (s_{pooled}), the standard error of standardized mean differences is

$$s_d = \sqrt{\frac{d^2}{2(n_1 - 1)(n_2 - 1)} + \frac{N}{n_1 n_2}}$$

With $z_{.025} = 1.96$, the 95% confidence limits are given by

$$d \pm s_d (z_{.025}) = d \pm s_d \times 1.96$$

For the data on weights of males and females we have

$$d = 1.33$$

$$s_d = \sqrt{\frac{d^2}{2(n_1 - 1)(n_2 - 1)} + \frac{N}{n_1 n_2}}$$

$$= \sqrt{\frac{1.33^2}{2(11)(14)} + \frac{27}{12 \times 15}} = \sqrt{0.0057 + 0.150} = 0.395$$

$$1.33 \pm 0.395 \times 1.96 = 1.33 \pm 0.774$$

$$0.556 \le \delta \le 2.10$$

(More exact limits given by Cumming's ESCI program are $0.4725 \le \delta \le 2.1576$. A program written in R to calculate these limits is available on the book's Web site that gives essentially the same result.)

The Phi Coefficient (*ϕ*)

The point-biserial correlation coefficient deals with the situation in which one of the variables is a dichotomy. When both variables are dichotomies, we will want a different statistic. For example, we might be interested in the relationship between gender and employment, where individuals are scored as either male or female and as employed or unemployed. Similarly, we might be interested in the relationship between employment status (employed-unemployed) and whether an individual has been arrested for drunken driving. As a final example, we might wish to know the correlation between smoking (smokers versus nonsmokers) and death by cancer (versus death by other causes). Unless we are willing

Table 10.2   Calculation of ϕ for Gibson's data

X: 0 = Instruction
       1 = No Instruction
Y: 0 = Sexual Abuse
       1 = No Sexual Abuse

Partial data:

X:	0	0	0	1	0	1	0	0	0	1	0	0	1	0
Y:	0	0	1	0	1	0	0	1	1	0	0	1	0	0

Calculations (based on full data set):

$\overline{X} = 0.3888$ $s_X = 0.4878$ $\text{cov}_{XY} = -0.0169$

$\overline{Y} = 0.8863$ $s_Y = 0.3176$ $N = 818$

$$\phi = r = \frac{\text{cov}_{XY}}{s_X s_Y} = \frac{-0.0169}{(.4878)(.3176)} = -.1094$$

$\phi^2 = .012$

ϕ **(phi) coefficient**

to make special assumptions concerning the underlying continuity of our variables, the most appropriate correlation coefficient is the ϕ **(phi) coefficient**. This is the same ϕ that we considered briefly in Chapter 6.

Calculating ϕ

Table 10.2 contains a small portion of the data from Gibson and Leitenberg (2000) (referred to in Exercise 6.33) on the relationship between sexual abuse training in school (which some of you may remember as "stranger danger" or "good touch-bad touch") and subsequent sexual abuse. Both variables have been scored as 0, 1 variables—an individual received instruction, or she did not, and she was either abused, or she was not.

The appropriate correlation coefficient is the ϕ coefficient, which is equivalent to Pearson's r calculated on these data. Again, special formulae are available but unnecessary.

From Table 10.2 we can see that the correlation between whether a student receives instruction on how to avoid sexual abuse in school, and whether he or she is subsequently abused, is $-.1094$, with a $\phi^2 = .012$. The correlation is in the right direction, but it does not look terribly impressive. But that may be misleading. (I chose to use these data precisely because what looks like a very small effect from one angle, looks like a much larger effect from another angle.) We will come back to this issue shortly.

Significance of ϕ

Having calculated ϕ, we are likely to want to test it for statistical significance. The appropriate test of ϕ against H_0: $\rho = 0$ is a chi-square test, since $N\phi^2$ is distributed as χ^2 on 1 df. For our data,

$$\chi^2 = N\phi^2 = 818(-.1094^2) = 9.79$$

which, on one df, is clearly significant. We would therefore conclude that we have convincing evidence of a relationship between sexual abuse training and subsequent abuse.

Alternatively, we can go from χ^2 to ϕ from the relationship

$$\phi = \sqrt{\frac{\chi^2}{N}}$$

Table 10.3 Calculation of χ^2 for Gibson's data on sexual abuse (χ^2 is shown as "approximate" simply because of the effect of rounding error in the table)

	Training	No Training	
Abused	43 (56.85)	50 (36.15)	93
Not Abused	457 (443.15)	268 (281.85)	725
	500	318	818

$$\chi^2 = \frac{(43 - 56.85)^2}{56.85} + \frac{(50 - 36.15)^2}{36.15} + \frac{(457 - 443.15)^2}{443.15} + \frac{(268 - 281.85)^2}{281.85}$$

$$= 9.79 \,(\text{approx.})$$

For our example,

$$\phi = \sqrt{\frac{9.79}{818}} = \sqrt{0.0120} = .1095$$

(again, with a bit of correction for rounding), which agrees with our previous calculation.

The Relationship Between ϕ and χ^2

The data that form the basis of Table 10.2 could be recast in another form, as shown in Table 10.3. The two tables (10.2 and 10.3) contain the same information; they merely display it differently. You will immediately recognize Table 10.3 as a contingency table. From it, you could compute a value of χ^2 to test the null hypothesis that the variables are independent. In doing so, you would obtain a χ^2 of 9.79—which, on 1 *df*, is significant. It is also the same value for χ^2 that we will compute in the next subsection.

It should be apparent that in calculating ϕ and χ^2, we have been asking the same question in two different ways: Not surprisingly, we have come to the same conclusion. When we calculated ϕ and tested it for significance, we were asking whether there was any correlation (relationship) between *X* and *Y*. When we ran a chi-square test on Table 10.3, we were also asking whether the variables are related (correlated). Because these questions are the same, we would hope that we would come to the same answer, which we did. On the one hand, χ^2 relates to the statistical significance of a relationship. On the other, ϕ measures the degree or magnitude of that relationship.

ϕ^2 as a Measure of the Practical Significance of χ^2

The fact that we can go from χ^2 to ϕ means that we have one way of evaluating the practical significance (importance) of the relationship between two dichotomous variables. We have already seen that for Gibson's data the conversion from χ^2 to ϕ^2 showed that our χ^2 of 9.79 accounted for about 1.2% of the variation. As I said, that does not look very impressive, even if it is significant.

Rosenthal and Rubin (1982) have argued that psychologists and others in the "softer sciences" are too ready to look at a small value of r^2 or ϕ^2, and label an effect as unimportant. They maintain that very small values of r^2 can in fact be associated with important effects. It is easiest to state their case with respect to ϕ, which is why their work is discussed here.

Rosenthal and Rubin pointed to a large-scale evaluation (called a meta-analysis) of over 400 studies of the efficacy of psychotherapy. The authors, Smith and Glass (1977), reported an effect equivalent to a correlation of .32 between presence or absence of psychotherapy and presence or absence of improvement, by whatever measure. A reviewer subsequently squared this correlation ($r^2 = .1024$) and deplored the fact that psychotherapy accounted for only 10% of the variability in outcome. Rosenthal and Rubin were not impressed by the reviewer's perspicacity. They pointed out that if we took 100 people in a control group and 100 people in a treatment group, and dichotomized them as improved or not improved, a correlation of $\phi = .32$ would correspond to $\chi^2 = 20.48$. This can be seen by computing

$$\phi = \sqrt{\chi^2/N}$$

$$\phi^2 = \chi^2/N$$

$$.1024 = \chi^2/200$$

$$\chi^2 = 20.48$$

The interesting fact is that such a χ^2 would result from a contingency table in which 66 of the 100 subjects in the treatment group improved whereas only 34 of the 100 subjects in the control group improved. (You can easily demonstrate this for yourself by computing χ^2 on such a table.) That is a dramatic difference in improvement rates.

But I have more examples. Rosenthal (1990) pointed to a well-known study of (male) physicians who took a daily dose of either aspirin or a placebo to reduce the incidence of heart attacks. (We considered this study briefly in earlier chapters, but for a different purpose.) This study was terminated early because the review panel considered the results so clearly in favor of the aspirin group that it would have been unethical to continue to give the control group a placebo. But, asked Rosenthal, what was the correlation between aspirin and heart attacks that was so dramatic as to cut short such a study? Would you believe $\phi = .034$ ($\phi^2 = .001$)?

Rosenthal also pointed to a study of AZT as a treatment for AIDS. The study was stopped because AZT reduced deaths from 61.5% to 38.5%. Yet r^2 was only .05. There is much to be said for the recommendation by Rosenthal and others that we take as our referent r instead of r^2.

I include Rosenthal's work to make the point that one does not require large values of r^2 (or ϕ^2) to have an important effect. Small values in certain cases can be quite impressive. For further examples, see Rosenthal (1990).

To return to what appears to be a small effect in Gibson's sexual abuse data, we will take an approach adopted in Chapter 6 with odds ratios. In Gibson's data 50 out of 318 children who received no instruction were subsequently abused, which makes the risk of abuse for this group to be $50/318 = 0.157$. On the other hand 43 out of 500 children who received training were subsequently abused, for odds of $43/500 = 0.086$. This gives us risk ratio (the ratio of the two calculated risks) of $0.157/0.086 = 1.83$. A child who does not receive sexual abuse training in school is nearly twice as likely to be subsequently abused as one who does. That looks quite a bit different from a squared correlation of only .012, which illustrates why we must be careful in the statistic we select.

At this point perhaps you are thoroughly confused. I began by showing that you can calculate a correlation between two dichotomous variables. I then showed that this correlation could either be calculated as a Pearson correlation coefficient, or it could be derived directly from a chi-square test on the corresponding contingency table, because there is a nice relationship between ϕ and χ^2. I argued that ϕ or ϕ^2 can be used to provide an r-family effect size measure (a measure of variation accounted for) of the effectiveness of the independent variable. But then I went a step further and said that when you calculate ϕ^2 you may be surprised by how small it is. In that context I pointed to the work of Rosenthal and Rubin, and to Gibson's data, showing in two different ways that accounting for only small amounts of the variation can still be impressive and important. I am mixing different kinds of measures of "importance" (statistical significance, percentage of accountable variation, effect sizes [*d*], and risk ratios), and, while that may be confusing, it is the nature of the problem. Statistical significance is a good thing, but it certainly isn't everything. Percentage of variation is an important kind of measure, but it is not very intuitive and may be small in important situations. The *d*-family measures of effect sizes have the advantage of presenting a difference in more concrete terms (distance between means in terms of standard deviations). Relative risk and odds ratios are very useful when you have a 2×2 table, but less so with more complex or with simpler situations.

10.2   Biserial and Tetrachoric Correlation: Non-Pearson Correlation Coefficients

In considering the point-biserial and phi coefficients, we were looking at data where one or both variables were measured as a dichotomy. We might even call this a "true dichotomy" because we often think of those variables as "either-or" variables. A person is classed as a male or a female, not halfway in between. Those are the coefficients we will almost always calculate with dichotomous data, and nearly all computer software will calculate those coefficients by default.

biserial correlation

tetrachoric correlation

Two other coefficients, to which you are likely to see reference, but are most unlikely to use, are the biserial correlation and the tetrachoric correlation. In earlier editions of this book I showed how to calculate those coefficients, but there does not seem to be much point in doing so anymore. I will simply explain how they differ from the coefficients I have discussed.

As I have said, we usually treat people as male or female, as if they pass or they fail a test, or as if they are abused or not abused. But we know that those dichotomies, especially the last two, are somewhat arbitrary. People fail miserably, or barely fail, or barely pass, and so on. People suffer varying degrees of sexual abuse, and although all abuse is bad, some is worse than others. If we are willing to take this underlying continuity into account, we can make an estimate of what the correlation would have been if the variable (or variables) had been normally distributed instead of dichotomously distributed.

The biserial correlation is the direct analog of the point-biserial correlation, except that the biserial assumes underlying normality in the dichotomous variable. The tetrachoric correlation is the direct analog of ϕ, where we assume underlying normality on both variables. That is all you really need to know about these two coefficients.

10.3   Correlation Coefficients for Ranked Data

In some experiments, the data naturally occur in the form of ranks. For example, we might ask judges to rank objects in order of preference under two different conditions, and wish to know the correlation between the two sets of rankings. Cities are frequently ranked in terms of livability, and we might want to correlate those rankings with rankings given 10 years later. Usually we are most interested in these correlations when we wish to assess the reliability of some ranking procedure, though in the case of the city ranking example, we are interested in the stability of rankings.

A related procedure, which has frequently been recommended in the past, is to rank sets of measurement data when we have serious reservations about the nature of the underlying scale of measurement. In this case, we are substituting ranks for raw scores. Although we could seriously question the necessity of ranking measurement data (for reasons mentioned in the discussion of measurement scales in Section 1.3 of Chapter 1), this is nonetheless a fairly common procedure. It does have the useful effect of down weighting extreme scores, which is sometimes desirable.

Ranking Data

ranking

Students occasionally experience difficulty in **ranking** a set of measurement data, so a short example. Assume we have the following set of data, which have been arranged in increasing order:

[5,   8,   9,   12,   12,   15,   16,   16,   16,   17]

The lowest value (5) is given the rank of 1. The next two values (8 and 9) are then assigned ranks 2 and 3. We then have two tied values (12) that must be ranked. If they were untied, they would be given ranks 4 and 5, so we split the difference and rank them both 4.5. The sixth number (15) is now given rank 6. Three values (16) are tied for ranks 7, 8, and 9; the mean of these ranks is 8. Thus, all are given ranks of 8. The last value is 17, which has rank 10. The data and their corresponding ranks are given below.

X:	5	8	9	12	12	15	16	16	16	17
Ranks:	1	2	3	4.5	4.5	6	8	8	8	10

Spearman's Correlation Coefficient for Ranked Data (r_S)

Spearman's correlation coefficient for ranked data (r_S)

Spearman's rho

Whether data naturally occur in the form of ranks (as, for example, when we are looking at the rankings of 20 cities on two different occasions) or whether ranks have been substituted for raw scores, one appropriate correlation is **Spearman's correlation coefficient for ranked data (r_S)**. (This statistic is sometimes referred to as **Spearman's rho**.)

Calculating r_S

The easiest way to calculate r_S is to apply Pearson's original formula to the ranked data. Alternative formulae do exist, but they have been designed to give exactly the same answer as Pearson's formula as long as there are no ties in the data. When there are ties, the alternative formulae lead to a wrong answer unless a correction factor is applied. Since that correction factor brings you back to where you would have been had you used Pearson's formula to begin with, why bother with alternative formulae?

The Significance of r_S

Recall that in Chapter 9 we imposed normality and homogeneity assumptions to provide a test on the significance of r (or to set confidence limits). With ranks, the data clearly cannot be normally distributed. There is no generally accepted method for calculating the standard error of r_S for small samples. As a result, computing confidence limits on r_S is not practical. Numerous textbooks contain tables of critical values of r_S, but for $N \geq 28$ these tables are themselves based on approximations. Keep in mind in this connection that a typical judge has difficulty ranking a large number of items; therefore, in practice, N is usually small when we are using r_S. There is no really good test of statistical significance for r_S, but most people would fall back on treating it as a normal Pearson correlation and being cautious about borderline cases.

Table 10.4   Alcohol and Tobacco Expenditures in Great Britain

Region	Alcohol	Tobacco	RankA	RankT	Inversions
Northern Ireland	4.02	4.56	1	11	10
East Anglia	4.52	2.92	2	2	1
Southwest	4.79	2.71	3	1	0
East Midlands	4.89	3.34	4	4	1
Wales	5.27	3.53	5	6	2
West Midlands	5.63	3.47	6	5	1
Southeast	5.89	3.20	7	3	0
Scotland	6.08	4.51	8	10	3
Yorkshire	6.13	3.76	9	7	0
Northeast	6.19	3.77	10	8	0
North	6.47	4.03	11	9	0

Kendall's Tau Coefficient (τ)

Kendall's τ

A serious competitor to Spearman's r_S is **Kendall's** τ. Whereas Spearman treated the ranks as scores and calculated the correlation between the two sets of ranks, Kendall based his statistic on the number of *inversions* in the rankings.

We will take as our example a dataset from the Data and Story Library (DASL) Web site, found at http://lib.stat.cmu.edu/DASL/Stories/AlcoholandTobacco.html. These are data on the average weekly spending on alcohol and tobacco in 11 regions of Great Britain. (We saw these data in Exercise 9.27.) The data are shown in Table 10.4 and I have organized the rows to correspond to increasing expenditures on Alcohol. Though it is not apparent from looking at either the Alcohol or Tobacco variable alone, in a bivariate plot it is clear that Northern Ireland is a major outlier. Similarly the distribution of Alcohol expenditures is decidedly nonnormal, whereas the ranked data on alcohol, like all ranks, are rectangularly distributed.

Notice that when the entries are listed in the order of rankings given by Alcohol, there are reversals (or inversions) of the ranks given by Tobacco (rank 11 of tobacco comes before all lower ranks, while rank 10 of tobacco comes before 3 lower ranks). I can count the number of inversions just by going down the Tobacco column and counting the number of times a ranking further down the table is lower than one further up the table. For instance, looking at tobacco expenditures, row 1 has 10 inversions because all 10 values below it are higher. Row 2 has only one inversion because only the rank of "1" is lower than a rank of 2. And so on.[2]

If there were a perfect ordinal relationship between these two sets of ranks, we would not expect to find any inversions. The region that spent the most money on alcohol would spend the most on tobacco, the region with the next highest expenditures on alcohol would be second highest on tobacco, and so on. Inversions of this form are the basis for Kendall's statistic.

Calculating τ

There are $N(N-1)/2 = 11(10)/2 = 55$ pairs of rankings in our data. Eighteen of those rankings are inversions (often referred to as "discordant"). This is found as the sum of the right-most column), and 37 of those pairs are not inversions ("concordant") and this is simply the total number of pairs (55) minus the number of discordant pairs (18).

---

[2] It isn't absolutely necessary to convert the data to ranks; we could simply count the number of raw score observation that are less than each value in an ordered series. But it makes the calculation simpler if we convert to ranks first.

We will let C stand for the number of concordant pairs and D for the number of discordant pairs (inversions).

$$D = \text{Inversions} = 18$$
$$C = 37$$

Kendall defined

$$\tau = 1 - \frac{2(\text{Number of inversions})}{\text{Number of pairs of objects}} \quad \text{or} \quad \frac{2D}{N(N-1)/2}$$

For our data

$$\tau = 1 - \frac{2(\text{Number of inversions})}{\text{Number of pairs of objects}} = 1 - \frac{2(18)}{55} = .345$$

Thus, as a measure of the agreement between rankings on Alcohol and Tobacco, Kendall's $\tau = .345$.

The interpretation of τ is more straightforward than the interpretation of r_S calculated on the same data (0.37). If $\tau = .345$, we can state that if a pair of objects is sampled at random, the probability that the two regions will be ranked in the same order is .345 *higher* than the probability that they will be ranked in the reverse order.

When there are tied rankings, the calculation of τ must be modified. For the appropriate correction for ties, see Hays (1981, p. 602 *ff*) or Google.

Significance of τ

Unlike Spearman's r_S, there is an accepted method for estimation of the standard error of Kendall's τ.

$$s_\tau = \sqrt{\frac{2(2N+5)}{9N(N-1)}}$$

Moreover, τ is approximately normally distributed for $N \geq 10$. This allows us to approximate the sampling distribution of Kendall's τ using the normal approximation.

$$z = \frac{\tau}{s_\tau} = \frac{\tau}{\sqrt{\frac{2(2N+5)}{9N(N-1)}}} = \frac{.345}{\sqrt{\frac{2(27)}{9(11)(10)}}} = \frac{.345}{.2335} = 1.48$$

For a two-tailed test $p = .139$, which is not statistically significant.[3]

With a standard error of 0.2335, the confidence limits on Kendall's τ, assuming normality of τ, would be

$$\text{CI} = \tau \pm 1.96 s_\tau = \tau \pm 1.96\left(\sqrt{\frac{2(2N+5)}{9N(N-1)}}\right) = \tau \pm 1.96(.2335)$$

For our example this would produce confidence limits of $-.11 \leq \tau \leq .80$.

Kendall's τ has generally been given preference of Spearman's r_S because it is a better estimate of the corresponding population parameter, and its standard error is known.

Although there is evidence that Kendall's τ holds up better than Pearson's r on the raw scores to nonnormality in the data, that seems to be true only at quite extreme levels.

---

[3] For small samples there is a more exact test using all possible orderings of the data, but this is rarely necessary. (It is, however, implemented in Kendall.R on the book's Web site.)

In general, Pearson's r on the raw data has been, and remains, the coefficient of choice. (For this data set the Pearson correlation between the original cost values is $r = .22$, $p = .509$.)

10.4 Analysis of Contingency Tables with Ordered Data

In Chapter 6 on chi-square, I referred to the problem that arises when the independent variables are ordinal variables. The traditional chi-square analysis does not take this ordering into account, but it is important for a proper analysis. As I said in Chapter 6, this section was motivated by a question sent to me by Jennifer Mahon at the University of Leicester, England, who has graciously allowed me to use her data for this example. Ms. Mahon was interested in the question of whether the likelihood of dropping out of a study on eating disorders was related to the number of traumatic events the participants had experienced in childhood.

The data from this study are shown below. I have taken the liberty of altering them very slightly so that I don't have to deal with the problem of small expected frequencies at the same time that I am trying to show how to make use of the ordinal nature of the data. The altered data are still a faithful representation of the effects that she found.

| | \multicolumn{6}{c}{**Number of Traumatic Events**} |
	0	**1**	**2**	**3**	**4+**	**Total**
Dropout	25	13	9	10	6	63
Remain	31	21	6	2	3	63
Total	56	34	15	12	9	126

© Cengage Learning 2013

At first glance we might be tempted to apply a standard chi-square test to these data, testing the null hypothesis that dropping out of treatment is independent of the number of traumatic events the person experienced during childhood. If we do that we find a chi-square of 9.459 on 4 df, which has an associated probability of .051. Strictly speaking, this result does not allow us to reject the null hypothesis, and we might conclude that traumatic events are not associated with dropping out of treatment. However, that answer is a bit too simplistic.

Notice that Trauma represents an ordered variable. Four traumatic events are more than 3; 3 traumatic events are more than 2; and so on. If we look at the percentage of participants who dropped out of treatment, as a function of the number of traumatic events they had experienced as children, we see that there is a general, though not a monotonic, increase in dropouts as we increase the number of traumatic events. However, this trend was not allowed to play any role in our calculated chi-square. What we want is a statistic that does take order into account.

A Correlational Approach

There are several ways we can accomplish what we want, but they all come down to assigning some kind of ordered metric to our independent variables. Dropout is not a problem because it is a dichotomy. We could code dropout as 1 and remain as 2, or dropout as 1 and remain as 0, or any other two values we like. The result will not be affected by our choice of values. When it comes to the number of traumatic events, we could simply use the numbers 0, 1, 2, 3, and 4. Alternatively, if we thought that 3 or 4 traumatic events would be much more important than 1 or 2, we might use 0, 1, 2, 4, 6. In practice, as long as we chose numbers that are monotonically increasing, and are not very extreme, the result will not change much as a function of our choice. I will choose to use 0, 1, 2, 3, and 4.

Now that we have established a metric for each independent variable, there are several different ways that we could go. We'll start with one that has good intuitive appeal. We will simply correlate our two variables.[4] Each participant will have a score of 0 or 1 on Dropout, and a score between 0 and 4 on Trauma. The standard Pearson correlation between those two measures is .215, which has an associated probability under the null of .016. This correlation is significant, and we can reject the null hypothesis of independence.

Some people may be concerned about the use of Pearson's r in this situation because the "number of traumatic events" is such a discrete variable. In fact that is not a problem for Pearson's r and no less an authority than Agresti (2002) recommends that approach. Perhaps you are unhappy with the idea of specifying a specific metric for Trauma, although you do agree that it is an ordered variable. If so, you could calculate Kendall's tau instead of Pearson's r. Tau would be the same for any set of values you assign to the levels of Trauma, assuming that they increased across the levels of that variable. For our data tau would be .169, with a probability of .04. So the relationship would still be significant even if we are only confident about the order of the independent variable(s). (The appeal to Kendall's tau as a possible replacement for Pearson's r is the reason why I included this material here rather than in Chapter 9. Agresti, however, has pointed out that if the cell frequencies are very different, there are negative consequences to using either Kendall's tau or Spearman's r_S. I recommend strongly that you simply use r.)

Agresti (2002, p. 87) presents the approach that we have just adopted and shows that we can compute a chi-square statistic from the correlation. He gives

$$M^2 = (N - 1)r^2$$

where M^2 is a chi-square statistic on 1 degree of freedom, r is the Pearson correlation between Dropout and Trauma, and N is the sample size. For our example this becomes

$$M^2 = \chi^2(1) = (N - 1)r^2$$

$$\chi^2(1) = 125(0.215^2) = 5.757$$

which has an associated probability under the null hypothesis of .016.

The probability value was already given by the test on the correlation, so that is nothing new. But we can go one step further. We know that the overall Pearson chi-square on 4 df that we originally computed is 9.459. We also know that we have just calculated a chi-square of 5.757 on 1 *df* that is associated with the *linear* relationship between the two variables. That linear relationship is part of the total chi-square, and if we subtract the linear component from the overall chi-square we obtain

	df	**Chi-square**
Pearson	4	9.459
Linear	1	5.757
Deviation from linear	3	3.702

© Cengage Learning 2013

---

[4] Many articles in the literature refer to Maxwell (1961) as a source for dealing with ordinal data. With one minor exception, Maxwell's approach is the one advocated here, though it is difficult to tell that from his description because his formulae were selected for computational ease.

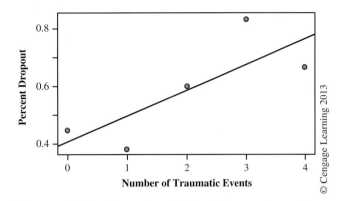

Figure 10.2   Scatterplot of Mahon's data on dropout data

The departure from linearity is itself a chi-square equal to 3.702 on 3 *df*, which has a probability under the null of .295. Thus we do not have any evidence that there is anything other than a linear trend underlying these data. The relationship between Trauma and Dropout is basically linear, as can be seen in Figure 10.2.

Agresti (2002, 2007) has an excellent discussion of the approach taken here, and he makes the interesting point that for small to medium sample sizes, the standard Pearson chi-square is more sensitive to the negative effects of small sample size than is the ordinal chi-square that we calculated. In other words, although some of the cells in the contingency table are small, I am more confident of the ordinal (linear) chi-square value of 5.757 than I am of the Pearson chi-square of 9.459.

You can calculate the chi-square for linearity using SPSS. If you request the chi-square statistic from the statistics dialog box, your output will include the Pearson chi-square, the Likelihood Ratio chi square, and Linear-by-Linear Association. The SPSS printout of the results for Mahon's data is shown below. You will see that the Linear-by-Linear Association measure of 5.757 is the same as the χ^2 that we calculated using $(N - 1)\,r^2$.

Chi-Square Tests

	Value	df	Asymp. Sig. (2-sided)
Pearson Chi-Square	9.459[a]	4	.051
Likelihood Ratio	9.990	4	.041
Linear-by-Linear Association	5.757	1	.016
N of Valid Cases	126		

[a] 2 cells (20.0%) have expected count less than 5. The minimum expected count is 4.50.

© Cengage Learning 2013

There are a number of other ways to approach the problem of ordinal variables in a contingency table. In some cases only one of the variables is ordinal and the other is nominal. (Remember that dichotomous variables can always be treated as ordinal without affecting the analysis.) In other cases one of the variables is clearly an independent variable while the other is a dependent variable. An excellent discussion of some of these methods can be found in Agresti, 2002 and 2007.

10.5 Kendall's Coefficient of Concordance (*W*)

Kendall's coefficient of concordance (*W*)

All of the statistics we have been concerned with in this chapter have dealt with the relationship between two sets of scores (*X* and *Y*). But suppose that instead of having two judges rank a set of objects, we had six judges doing the ranking. What we need is some measure of the degree to which the six judges agree. Such a measure is afforded by **Kendall's coefficient of concordance (*W*)**.

Suppose, as an example, that we asked six judges to rank order the pleasantness of eight colored patches and obtained the data in Table 10.5. If all of the judges had agreed that Patch B was the most pleasant, they would all have assigned it a rank of 1, and the column total for that patch across six judges would have been 6. Similarly, if A had been ranked second by everyone, its total would have been 12. Finally, if every judge assigned the highest rank to Patch H, its total would have been 48. In other words, the column totals would have shown considerable variability.

On the other hand, if the judges showed no agreement, each column would have had some high ranks and some low ranks assigned to it, and the column totals would have been roughly equal. Thus, the variability of the column totals, given disagreement (or random behavior) among judges, would be low.

Kendall used the variability of the column totals in deriving his statistic. He defined *W* as the ratio of the variability among columns to the maximum possible variability.

$$W = \frac{\text{Variance of column totals}}{\text{Maximum possible variance of column totals}}$$

Because we are dealing with ranks, we know what the maximum variance of the totals will be. With a bit of algebra, we can define

$$W = \frac{12 \sum T_j^2}{k^2 N (N^2 - 1)} - \frac{3(N + 1)}{N - 1}$$

where T_j represents the column totals, N = the number of items to be ranked, and k = the number of judges doing the ranking. For the data in Table 10.5,

$$\sum T_j^2 = 11^2 + 9^2 + 18^2 + 30^2 + 28^2 + 36^2 + 45^2 + 39^2 = 7052$$

$$W = \frac{12 \sum T_j^2}{k^2 N (N^2 - 1)} - \frac{3(N + 1)}{N - 1}$$

$$= \frac{12(7052)}{6^2(8)(63)} - \frac{3(9)}{7} = \frac{84624}{18144} - \frac{27}{7}$$

$$= .807$$

As you can see from the definition of *W*, it is not a standard correlation coefficient. It does have an interpretation in terms of a familiar statistic, however: it can be viewed as a function of the average Spearman correlation computed on the rankings of all possible pairs of judges. Specifically,

$$\bar{r}_S = \frac{kW - 1}{k - 1}$$

Table 10.5   Judge's rankings of pleasantness of colored patches

Judges	Colored Patches							
	A	B	C	D	E	F	G	H
1	1	2	3	4	5	6	7	8
2	2	1	5	4	3	8	7	6
3	1	3	2	7	5	6	8	4
4	2	1	3	5	4	7	8	6
5	3	1	2	4	6	5	7	8
6	2	1	3	6	5	4	8	7
Σ	11	9	18	30	28	36	45	39

For our data,

$$\bar{r}_S = \frac{kW - 1}{k - 1} = \frac{6(.807) - 1}{5} = .768$$

Thus, if we took all possible pairs of rankings and computed r_S for each, the average r_S would be .768.

Hays (1981) recommends reporting W but converting to $\bar{r}_S$ for interpretation. Indeed, it is hard to disagree with that recommendation, because no intuitive meaning attaches to W itself. W does have the advantage of being bounded by zero and one, whereas $\bar{r}_S$ does not, but it is difficult to attach much practical meaning to the statement that the variance of column totals is 80.7% of the maximum possible variance. Whatever its faults, $\bar{r}_S$ seems preferable.

A test on the null hypothesis that there is no agreement among judges is possible under certain conditions. If $k \geq 7$, the quantity

$$\chi^2_{(N-1)} = k(N - 1)W$$

is approximately distributed as χ^2 on $N - 1$ degrees of freedom. Such a test is seldom used, however, because W is usually calculated in those situations in which we seek a level of agreement substantially above the minimum level required for significance, and we rarely have seven or more judges.

Key Terms

Correlational measures (Introduction)

Measures of association (Introduction)

Validity (Introduction)

Dichotomy (10.1)

Point-biserial coefficient (r_{pb}) (10.1)

ϕ (phi) coefficient (10.1)

Biserial correlation coefficient (r_b) (10.2)

Tetrachoric correlation (r_t) (10.2)

Spearman's correlation coefficient for ranked data (r_S) (10.3)

Spearman's rho (10.3)

Kendall's τ (10.3)

Kendall's coefficient of concordance (**W**) (10.5)

Exercises

10.1   Some people think that they do their best work in the morning, whereas others claim that they do their best work at night. We have dichotomized 20 office workers into morning or evening people (0 = morning, 1 = evening) and have obtained independent estimates of the quality of work they produced on some specified morning. The ratings were based on a 100-point scale and appear below.

Peak time of day:	0	0	0	0	0	0	0	0	0	0
Performance rating:	65	80	55	60	55	70	60	70	55	70

Peak time of day:	0	0	0	1	1	1	1	1	1	1
Performance rating:	40	70	50	40	60	50	40	50	40	60

a.   Plot these data and fit a regression line.

b.   Calculate r_{pb} and test it for significance.

c.   Interpret the results.

10.2   Why would it not make sense to calculate a biserial correlation on the data in Exercises 10.1 and 10.4?

10.3   Compare the results you obtained in Exercises 10.1 and 10.4. What can you conclude?

10.4   Because of a fortunate change in work schedules, we were able to reevaluate the subjects referred to in Exercise 10.1 for performance on the same tasks in the evening. The data are given below.

Peak time of day:	0	0	0	0	0	0	0	0	0	0
Performance rating:	40	60	40	50	30	40	50	50	20	30

Peak time of day:	0	0	0	1	1	1	1	1	1	1
Performance rating:	40	50	30	30	50	50	40	50	40	60

a.   Plot these data and fit a regression line.

b.   Calculate r_{pb} and test it for significance.

c.   Interpret the results.

10.5   Perform a t test on the data in Exercise 10.1 and show the relationship between this value of t and r_{pb}.

10.6   Visualize the data in Exercise 10.9 as fitting into a contingency table.

a.   Compute the chi-square on this table.

b.   Show the relationship between chi-square and φ.

10.7   Compute the regression equation for the data in Exercise 10.8. Show that the line defined by this equation passes through the means of the two groups.

10.8   A graduate-school admissions committee is concerned about the relationship between an applicant's grade point average in college and whether or not the individual eventually completes the requirements for a doctoral degree. They first looked at the data on 25 randomly selected students who entered the program 7 years ago, assigning a score of 1 to those who completed the PhD program, and of 0 to those who did not. The data follow.

GPA:	2.0	3.5	2.75	3.0	3.5	2.75	2.0	2.5	3.0	2.5	3.5	3.25	3.0
PhD:	0	0	0	0	0	0	0	0	1	1	1	1	1

GPA:	3.0	2.75	3.25	3.0	3.33	2.5	2.75	2.0	4.0	3.0	3.25	2.5
PhD:	1	1	1	1	1	1	1	1	1	1	1	1

a.   Plot these data.

b.   Calculate r_{pb}.

c.   Calculate r_b.

d.   Is it reasonable to look at r_b in this situation? Why or why not?

10.9 Assume that the committee in Exercise 10.8 decided that a GPA-score cutoff of 3.00 would be appropriate. In other words, they classed everyone with a GPA of 3.00 or higher as acceptable and those with a GPA below 3.00 as unacceptable. They then correlated this with completion of the PhD program.

a. Rescore the data in Exercise 10.8 as indicated.

b. Run the correlation.

c. Test this correlation for significance.

10.10 What do the slope and the intercept obtained in Exercise 10.7 represent?

10.11 An investigator is interested in the relationship between alcoholism and a childhood history of attention deficit disorder (ADD). He has collected the following data, where a 1 represents the presence of the relevant problem.

ADD:	0	1	0	0	1	1	0	0	0	1	0	0	1	0	0	1
Alcoholism:	0	1	0	0	0	1	0	0	0	1	1	0	0	0	0	1

ADD:	1	1	0	0	0	0	0	0	0	1	0	0	1	0	0	0
Alcoholism:	0	1	0	0	0	0	0	0	0	1	0	0	1	0	1	0

a. What is the correlation between these two variables?

b. Is the relationship significant?

10.12 In a study of diagnostic processes, entering clinical graduate students are shown a 20-minute videotape of children's behavior and asked to rank order 10 behavioral events on the tape in the order of the importance each has for a behavioral assessment (1 = most important). The data are then averaged to produce an average rank ordering for the entire class. The same thing was then done using experienced clinicians. The data follow.

Events:	1	2	3	4	5	6	7	8	9	10
Experienced clinicians:	1	3	2	7	5	4	8	6	9	10
New students:	2	4	1	6	5	3	10	8	7	9

Use Spearman's r_S to measure the agreement between experienced and novice clinicians.

10.13 For the data in Exercise 10.14,

a. Compute Kendall's τ.

b. Test τ for significance.

10.14 An investigator wants to arrange the 15 items on her scale of language impairment on the basis of the order in which language skills appear in development. Not being entirely confident that she has selected the correct ordering of skills, she asks another professional to rank the items from 1 to 15 in terms of the order in which he thinks they should appear. The data are given below.

Investigator:	1	2	3	4	5	6	7	8	9	10	11	12	13	14	15
Consultant:	1	3	2	4	7	5	6	8	10	9	11	12	15	13	14

a. Use Pearson's formula (r) to calculate Spearman's r_S.

b. Discuss what the results tell you about the ordering process.

10.15 Rerun the analysis on Exercise 10.12 using Kendall's τ.

10.16 Repeat the analysis shown in Exercise 10.19, but this time cross-tabulate ClinCase against Gender.

a. Compare this answer with the results of Exercise 10.20.

b. How does this analysis differ from the one in Exercise 10.20 on roughly the same question?

10.17 On page 312 I noted that Rosenthal and Rubin showed that an r^2 of .1024 actually represented a pretty impressive effect. They demonstrated that this would correspond to a χ^2 of 20.48, and with 100 subjects in each of two groups, the 2×2 contingency table would have a 34:66 split for one row and a 66:34 split for the other row.

    a. Verify this calculation with your own 2×2 table.

    b. What would that 2×2 table look like if there were 100 subjects in each group, but if the r^2 were .0512? (This may require some trial and error in generating 2×2 tables and computing χ^2 on each.)

10.18 Assume in Exercise 10.12 that there were five entering clinical students. They produced the following data:

Student 1:	1	4	2	6	5	3	9	10	7	8
Student 2:	4	3	2	5	7	1	10	8	6	9
Student 3:	1	5	2	6	4	3	8	10	7	9
Student 4:	2	5	1	7	4	3	10	8	6	9
Student 5:	2	5	1	4	6	3	9	7	8	10

Calculate Kendall's W and $\bar{r}_S$ for these data as a measure of agreement. Interpret your results.

10.19 In Exercise 7.50 using Mireault.dat, we compared the responses of students who had lost a parent and students who had not lost a parent in terms of their responses on the Global Symptom Index T score (GSIT), among other variables. An alternative analysis would be to use a clinically meaningful cutoff on the GSIT, classifying anyone over that score as a clinical case (showing a clinically significant level of symptoms) and everyone below that score as a noncase. Derogatis (1983) has suggested a score of 63 as the cutoff (e.g., if GSIT > 63 then ClinCase = 1; else ClinCase = 0).

    a. Use any statistical package to create the variable of ClinCase, as defined by Derogatis. Then cross-tabulate ClinCase against Group. Compute chi-square and Cramér's ϕ_C.

    b. How does the answer to part (a) compare to the answers obtained in Chapter 7?

    c. Why might we prefer this approach (looking at case versus noncase) over the procedure adopted in Chapter 7?

(Hint: SAS will require Proc Freq; and SPSS will use CrossTabs. The appropriate manuals will help you set up the commands.)

10.20 Using Mireault's data on this book's Web site (Mireault.dat), calculate the point-biserial correlation between Gender and the Depression T score. Compare the relevant aspects of this question to the results you obtained in Exercise 7.48. (See "The Relationship Between r_{pb} and t" in Section 10.1.)

Discussion Questions

10.21 Rosenthal and others (cited earlier) have argued that small effects, as indexed by a small r^2, for example, can be important in certain situations. We would probably all agree that small effects could be trivial in other situations.

    a. Can an effect that is not statistically significant ever be important if it has a large enough r^2?

    b. How will the sample size contribute to the question of the importance of an effect?

Chapter *11*

Simple Analysis of Variance

Objectives

To introduce the analysis of variance as a procedure for testing differences among two or more means.

Contents

analysis of
variance
(ANOVA)

THE **ANALYSIS OF VARIANCE (ANOVA)** has long enjoyed the status of being the most used statistical technique in psychological research. The popularity and usefulness of this technique can be attributed to two sources. First, the analysis of variance, like t, deals with differences between or among sample means; unlike t, it imposes no restriction on the number of means. Instead of asking whether two means differ, we can ask whether three, four, five, or k means differ. The analysis of variance also allows us to deal with two or more independent variables simultaneously, asking not only about the individual effects of each variable separately but also about the interacting effects of two or more variables.

This chapter is concerned with the underlying logic of the analysis of variance and the analysis of results of experiments employing only one independent variable. We will also examine a number of related topics that are most easily understood in the context of a **one-way** (one independent variable) **analysis of variance**. Subsequent chapters will deal with comparisons among individual sample means, with the analysis of experiments involving two or more independent variables, and with designs in which repeated measurements are made on each subject.

one-way
analysis of
variance

11.1   An Example

Many features of the analysis of variance are best illustrated by a simple example, so we will begin with a study by Giancola and Corman (2007). They were interested in studying the effects of a distracting task on aggressive behavior of subjects who had consumed a significant amount of alcohol. It is well known that alcohol often leads to aggressive behavior, but why? Giancola and Corman began by assuming that alcohol facilitated aggression by focusing attention on more salient provocative cues rather than on less salient inhibitory ones. They reasoned that if they presented their subjects with a distracting task, attention would be focused on the task rather than on provocative cues, thus limiting aggression. However, they also reasoned that if the task became too complex, its distracting effects would disappear and aggression would take over. (In fact, if the task is too complex that might generate confusion and frustration, which could in turn lead to aggression.)

Giancola and Corman asked their subjects to consume alcohol in an amount that raised their average blood alcohol level to about .10%. (That level would qualify drivers in most, if not all, states as driving while intoxicated.) Subjects then participated in a task that required them to remember the order in which squares in a 3×3 matrix were illuminated. The attentional demands of the task were varied by manipulating the number of squares that subjects had to keep in memory. Subjects played against a fictitious opponent who either delivered mild shocks to the subject or received mild shocks from the subject, dependent on supposed task performance. The dependent variable (aggression) was based on the severity and duration of shocks that subjects delivered to opponents when they had the opportunity. (There was a control condition that did not consume alcohol, but we will ignore that condition. There were no differences due to task difficulty in that condition.)

There were five groups in this study, varying in task difficulty. Subjects had to remember the pattern of either 0, 2, 4, 6, or 8 squares, and the groups were denoted as D0, D2, D4, D6, and D8. There were 12 subjects in each group, and the data, along with the means and standard deviations, are given in Table 11.1. (The data are based on the means and standard deviations reported in the original study.)

Section 11.2   The Underlying Model   327

Table 11.1   Level of shock administered as a function of task difficulty

	D0	D2	D4	D6	D8	Total
	1.28	−1.18	−0.41	−0.85	2.01	
	1.35	0.15	−1.25	0.14	0.40	
	3.31	1.36	−1.33	−1.38	2.34	
	3.06	2.61	−0.47	1.28	−1.80	
	2.59	0.66	−0.60	1.85	5.00	
	3.25	1.32	−1.72	−0.59	2.27	
	2.98	0.73	−1.74	−1.30	6.47	
	1.53	−1.06	−0.77	0.38	2.94	
	−2.68	0.24	−0.41	−0.35	0.47	
	2.64	0.27	−1.20	2.29	3.22	
	1.26	0.72	−0.31	−0.25	0.01	
	1.06	2.28	−0.74	0.51	−0.66	
Mean	1.802	0.675	−0.912	0.544	1.889	0.800
St. Dev.	1.656	1.140	0.515	1.180	2.370	1.800
Var.	2.741	1.299	0.265	1.394	5.616	3.168

© Cengage Learning 2013

11.2   The Underlying Model

The analysis of variance, like all statistical procedures, is built on an underlying model. I am not going to beat the model to death and discuss all of its ramifications, but a general understanding of that model is important for understanding what the analysis of variance is all about and for understanding more complex models that follow in subsequent chapters. Twenty-five years ago we might not even speak of the underlying model. But you will come across this general linear model in discussions of a wide variety of procedures, and this example provides a gentle introduction to the model for the simple one-way analysis of variance.

Suppose that you had to guess a person's score in Giancola and Corman's experiment. One obvious guess would be the grand mean in the population (μ). That wouldn't be a great guess, but it is better than any other that you might make. We can write this (not very satisfactory) model as

$$X_{ij} = \mu$$

But now suppose I told you that the person is in the first group. We will represent the effect of being in Group$_j$ as τ_j. Here τ_j is simply the difference between the mean of group$_j$ and the grand mean (i.e., $\mu_j - \mu$). Now our model would be

$$X_{ij} = \mu + (\mu_j - \mu)$$
$$X_{ij} = \mu + \tau_j$$

This is a better guess because it says that you will predict a person's score as being the grand mean plus or minus how much the relevant group mean differs from the grand mean. What this really means is that you would predict the group's mean, but it is better if we separate the grand mean and the effect of Group$_1$.

But that isn't the final answer. If you are one of the people in $Group_1$, you probably differ from the group's mean in some way. In other words there is a specific component for you, and it is denoted as ε_{ij}, where the ε stands for "error." Now our model is

$$X_{ij} = \mu + (\mu_j - \mu) + (X_{ij} - \mu_j)$$
$$X_{ij} = \mu + \tau_j + \varepsilon_{ij}$$

structural model

This is the **structural model** that underlies the analysis of variance. Mu (μ) represents the grand mean, τ_j represents the specific treatment effect for group j, and ε_{ij} represents the error associated with a specific individual—in other words, how much he or she deviates from the group's mean. In future chapters we will extend the model to more complex situations by adding additional effects beyond τ_j, but the basic idea will remain the same. Of course we do not know the values of the various parameters in this structural model, but that doesn't stop us from positing such a model.

Assumptions

As we know, Giancola and Corman were interested in studying the level of aggression under the five levels of distraction. We can represent these conditions in Figure 11.1, where μ_j and σ_j^2 represent the mean and variance of whole populations of scores that would be obtained under each of these conditions. The analysis of variance is based on certain assumptions about these populations and their parameters. (In this figure the fact that one distribution is to the right of another does not say anything about whether or not its mean is different from others.)

Homogeneity of Variance

A basic assumption underlying the analysis of variance is that each of our populations has the same variance. In other words,

$$\sigma_1^2 = \sigma_2^2 = \sigma_3^2 = \sigma_4^2 = \sigma_5^2 = \sigma_e^2$$

homogeneity of variance
homoscedasticity
error variance

where the notation σ_e^2 or, often, σ_e^2 is used to indicate the common value held by the five population variances. This is called the assumption of **homogeneity of variance**, or, if you like long words, **homoscedasticity**.

The subscript "e" stands for error, and this variance is the **error variance**—the variance unrelated to any treatment differences, which is variability of scores within the same condition. Homogeneity of variance would be expected to occur if the effect of a treatment is to add a constant to everyone's score—if, for example, everyone who was trying to recall the position of eight stimuli scored an extra point above the others on the aggression scale.

As we will see later, under certain conditions the assumption of homogeneity of variance can be relaxed without substantially damaging the test, though it might alter the

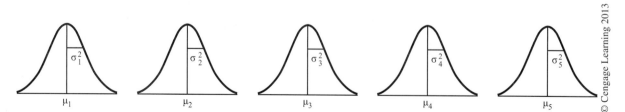

Figure 11.1   Graphical representation of populations of aggression scores

heterogeneity of
variance

heteroscedasticity

meaning of the result. However, there are cases where heterogeneity of variance, or heteroscedasticity (populations having *different* variances), is a problem. We see heterogeneity of variance in the example we are using, but I will ignore that for a moment and come back to it later.

Normality

A second assumption of the analysis of variance is that the scores on aggression for each condition are normally distributed around their mean. In other words, each of the distributions in Figure 11.1 is normal. Because σ_e^2 represents the variability of each person's score around the mean of that condition, a more correct way to write the assumption is to write that *error* is normally distributed within conditions. Thus you will often see the assumption stated in terms of "the normal distribution of error." (You may also see "normally distributed residuals," which means the same thing.) Moderate departures from normality are not usually fatal. We said much the same thing when looking at the *t* test for two independent samples, which is really just a special case of the analysis of variance.

Independence

Our third important assumption is that the observations are independent of one another. (Technically, this assumption really states that the error components (e_{ij}) are independent, but for simple designs like this one that amounts to the same thing.) Thus for any two observations within an experimental treatment, we assume that knowing how one of these observations stands relative to the treatment (or population) mean tells us nothing about the other observation. This is one of the important reasons why subjects are randomly assigned to groups. Violation of the independence assumption can have serious consequences for an analysis (see Kenny and Judd, 1986).

The Null Hypothesis

As we know, Giancola and Corman were interested in testing the *research* hypothesis that the level of aggression varies with the level of distraction afforded by the recall task. Support for such a hypothesis would come from rejection of the standard *null* hypothesis

$$H_0 : \mu_1 = \mu_2 = \mu_3 = \mu_4 = \mu_5$$

The null hypothesis could be false in a number of ways (e.g., all means could be different from each other, the first two could be equal to each other but different from the last three, and so on), but for now we are going to be concerned only with whether the null hypothesis is completely true or is false. This is frequently referred to as the omnibus null hypothesis. In Chapter 12 we will deal with the problem of whether subsets of means are equal or unequal.

11.3   The Logic of the Analysis of Variance

The logic underlying the analysis of variance is really very simple, and once you understand it the rest of the discussion will make considerably more sense. Consider for a moment the effect of our three major assumptions—normality, homogeneity of variance, and the independence of observations (or residuals). By making the first two of these assumptions we have said that the five distributions represented in Figure 11.1 have the same shape and dispersion. As a result, the only way left for them to differ is in terms of their means. (Recall that the normal distribution depends only on two parameters, μ and σ.)

We will begin by making no assumption concerning H_0—it may be true or false. For any one treatment, the variance of the 12 scores in that group would be an estimate of the variance of the population from which the scores were drawn. Because we have assumed that all populations have the same variance, it is also one estimate of the common population variance σ_e^2. If you prefer, you can think of

$$\sigma_1^2 \doteq s_1^2, \qquad \sigma_2^2 \doteq s_2^2, \qquad \cdots, \qquad \sigma_e^2 \doteq s_e^2,$$

where $\doteq$ is read as "is estimated by." Because of our homogeneity assumption, all these are estimates of σ_e^2. For the sake of increased reliability, we can pool the five estimates by taking their mean, if $n_1 = n_2 = \cdots = n_5$, and thus

$$\sigma_e^2 \doteq s_e^2 \doteq \bar{s}_j^2 \doteq \sum s_j^2/k$$

MSerror
MSwithin

where $k =$ the number of treatments (in this case, five).[1] This gives us one estimate of the population variance, which we will later refer to as MS_{error} (read "mean square error"), or, sometimes, MS_{within}. It is important to note that this estimate does not depend on the truth or falsity of H_0, because s_j^2 is calculated on each sample separately. (You could add 30 points to all the observations in Group$_1$ and that would not change its variability in the slightest.) For the data from Giancola and Corman's study, our pooled estimate of σ_e^2 will be

$$\sigma_e^2 \doteq (1.655^2 + 1.140^2 + 0.515^2 + 1.180^2 + 2.370^2)/5 = 11.313/5 = 2.263$$

Now let us assume that H_0 is true. If this is the case, then our five samples of $n = 12$ cases can be thought of as five independent samples from the same population (or, equivalently, from five identical populations), and we can produce another possible estimate of σ_e^2. Recall from Chapter 7 that the central limit theorem states that the variance of means drawn from the same population equals the variance of the population divided by the sample size. If H_0 is true, the sample means have been drawn from the same population (or identical ones, which amounts to the same thing), and therefore the variance of our five sample means estimates σ_e^2/n.

$$\frac{\sigma_e^2}{n} \doteq s_{\bar{X}}^2$$

where n is the size of each sample. We can reverse the usual order of things and calculate the variance of our sample means $\left(s_{\bar{X}}^2\right)$ to obtain the second estimate of σ_e^2:

$$\sigma_e^2 \doteq ns_{\bar{X}}^2$$

MStreatment

This term is referred to as $MS_{treatment}$ often abbreviated as MS_{treat} or MS_{group}; we will return to it shortly.

We now have two estimates of the population variance (σ_e^2). One of these estimates (MS_{error}) is independent of the truth or falsity of H_0. The other ($MS_{treatment}$) is an estimate of σ_e^2 only as long as H_0 is true (only as long as the conditions of the central limit theorem are met; namely, that the means are drawn from one population or several identical populations). Thus, if the two estimates agree, we will have support for the truth of H_0, and if they disagree, we will have support for the falsity of H_0.[2]

---

[1] This is just an extension of the use of a pooled error term with t tests, although for more than two groups. If the sample sizes were not equal, we would still average the five estimates, but in this case we might weight each estimate by the number of degrees of freedom for each sample—just as we did in Chapter 7.

[2] Students often have trouble with the statement that "means are drawn from the same population" when we know in fact that they are often drawn from logically distinct populations. It seems silly to speak of means of males and females as coming from one population when we know that these are really two different populations of people. However, if the population of scores for females is exactly the same as the population of scores for males, then we can legitimately speak of these as being the identical (or the same) population of *scores*, and we can behave accordingly.

From the preceding discussion, we can concisely state the logic of the analysis of variance. To test H_0, we calculate two estimates of the population variance—one that is independent of the truth or falsity of H_0, and another that is dependent on H_0. If the two estimates agree, we have no reason to reject H_0. If they disagree sufficiently, we conclude that underlying treatment differences must have contributed to our second estimate, inflating it and causing it to differ from the first. Therefore, we reject H_0.

Variance Estimation

treatment effect

It might be helpful at this point to state without proof the two values that we are really estimating. We will first define the **treatment effect**, denoted τ_j, as $(\mu_j - \mu)$, the difference between the mean of treatment$_j$ (μ_j) and the grand mean (μ), and we will define θ_τ^2 as the variation of the true populations' means ($\mu_1, \mu_2, \ldots, \mu_5$).[3]

$$\theta_\tau^2 = \frac{\sum (\mu_j - \mu)^2}{k - 1} = \frac{\sum \tau_j^2}{k - 1}$$

expected value

In addition, recall that we defined the **expected value** of a statistic [written $E()$] s its long-range average—the average value that statistic would assume over repeated sampling, and thus our best guess as to its value on any particular trial. With these two concepts we can state

$$E(MS_{\text{error}}) = \sigma_e^2$$

$$E(MS_{\text{treat}}) = \sigma_e^2 + \frac{n \sum \tau_j^2}{k - 1}$$

$$= \sigma_e^2 + n\theta_\tau^2$$

where σ_e^2 is the variance within each population and θ_τ^2 is the variation[4] of the population means (μ_j).

Now, if H_0 is true and $\mu_1 = \mu_2 = \cdots = \mu_5 = \mu$, then the population means don't vary and $\theta_\tau^2 = 0$. If so,

$$E(MS_{\text{error}}) = \sigma_e^2$$

and

$$E(MS_{\text{treat}}) = \sigma_e^2 + n(0) = \sigma_e^2$$

and thus

$$E(MS_{\text{error}}) = E(MS_{\text{treat}})$$

Keep in mind that these are expected values; rarely in practice will the two sample-based mean squares be numerically equal.

If H_0 is false, however, the θ_τ^2 will not be zero, but some positive number. In this case,

$$E(MS_{\text{error}}) < E(MS_{\text{treat}})$$

because MS_{treat} will contain a nonzero term representing the true differences among the μ_j.

---

[3] Technically, θ_τ^2 is not actually a variance, because, having the actual parameter (μ), we should be dividing by k instead of $k - 1$. Nonetheless, we lose very little by thinking of it as a variance, as long as we keep in mind precisely what we have done. Many texts, including previous editions of this one, represent θ_τ^2 as σ_τ^2 to indicate that it is very much like a variance. But in this edition I have decided to be honest and use θ_τ^2.

[4] I use the wishy-washy word "variation" here because I don't really want to call it a "variance," which it isn't, but I want to keep the concept of variance.

11.4   Calculations in the Analysis of Variance

At this point we will use the example from Giancola and Corman to illustrate the calculations used in the analysis of variance. Even though you may think that you will always use computer software to run analyses of variance, it is very important to understand how you would carry out the calculations using a calculator. First of all, it helps you to understand the basic procedure. In addition, it makes it much easier to understand some of the controversies and alternative analyses that are proposed. Finally, no computer program will do everything you want it to do, and you must occasionally resort to direct calculations. So bear with me on the calculations, even if you think that I am wasting my time.

Sum of Squares

sums of squares

In the analysis of variance much of our computation deals with **sums of squares**. As we saw in Chapter 9, a sum of squares is merely the sum of the squared deviations about the mean $[\sum(X - \overline{X})^2]$ or, more often, some multiple of that. When we first defined the sample variance, we saw that

$$s_X^2 = \frac{\sum(X - \overline{X})^2}{n - 1} = \frac{\sum X^2 - (\sum X)^2/n}{n - 1}$$

Here, the numerator is the *sum of squares* of X and the denominator is the degrees of freedom. Sums of squares have the advantage of being additive, whereas mean squares and variances are additive only if they happen to be based on the same number of degrees of freedom.

The Data

The data are reproduced in Table 11.2, along with a plot of the data in Figure 11.2 and the calculations in Table 11.3. (It is important to notice in Figure 11.2 that the "error bars" are labeled as $\pm$ one standard error. Many people who should know better omit this specifica

Table 11.2   Level of shock administered as a function of task difficulty

	D0	D2	D4	D6	D8	Total
	1.28	−1.18	−0.41	−0.45	2.01	
	1.35	0.15	−1.25	0.54	0.40	
	3.31	1.36	−1.33	−0.98	2.34	
	3.06	2.61	−0.47	1.68	−1.80	
	2.59	0.66	−0.60	2.25	5.00	
	3.25	1.32	−1.72	−0.19	2.27	
	2.98	0.73	−1.74	−0.90	6.47	
	1.53	−1.06	−0.77	0.78	2.94	
	−2.68	0.24	−0.41	0.05	0.47	
	2.64	0.27	−1.20	2.69	3.22	
	1.26	0.72	−0.31	0.15	0.01	
	1.06	2.28	−0.74	0.91	−0.66	
Mean	1.802	0.675	−0.912	0.544	1.889	0.800
St. Dev.	1.656	1.140	0.515	1.180	2.370	1.800
Var.	2.741	1.299	0.265	1.394	5.616	3.168

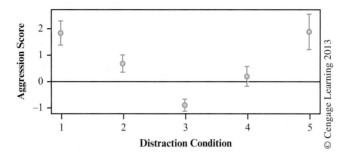

Figure 11.2   Plot of Giancola and Corman's data on aggression as a function of level of distraction. Bars represent ± 1 standard error

Table 11.3   Computations for data in Table 11.2

$$SS_{total} = \Sigma(X_{ij} - \overline{X}_{..})^2 = (1.28 - 0.80)^2 + (1.35 - 0.80)^2 + \cdots + (-0.66 - 0.80)^2$$
$$= 186.918$$

$$SS_{treat} = n\Sigma(\overline{X}_j - \overline{X}_{..})^2 = 12((1.80 - 0.80)^2 + (0.675 - 0.80)^2 + \cdots + (1.889 - 0.80)^2)$$
$$= 12(5.205) = 62.460$$

$$SS_{error} = SS_{total} - SS_{treat} = 186.918 - 62.640 = 124.485$$

Summary Table

Source	df	SS	MS	F
Treatments	4	62.460	15.615	6.90*
Error	55	124.458	2.263	
Total	59	186.918		

* $p < .05$

tion and we don't know whether they are plotting standard deviations or standard errors, or whether they are one or two units long—or perhaps they are confidence limits. Always specify what the bars represent.) We will discuss the calculations and the results in detail. Because these actual data points are fictitious (although the means and variances are not), there is little to be gained by examining the distribution of observations within individual groups—the data were actually drawn from a normally distributed population. With real data, however, it is important to examine these distributions first to make sure that they are not seriously skewed or bimodal and, even more important, that they are not skewed in different directions. Even for this example, it is useful to examine the individual group variances as a check on the assumption of homogeneity of variance. Although the variances are not as similar as we might like (the variance for the most distracting condition is many times the variance for the midlevel condition), we will apply the standard analysis of variance and then come back to the issue of heterogeneity of variance. As we will see later, for the overall analysis looking at all groups simultaneously the analysis of variance is robust against violations of assumptions, especially when we have the same number of observations in each group.

Table 11.3 shows the calculations required to perform a one-way analysis of variance. These calculations require some elaboration.

SS_{total}

SS_{total}

The SS_{total} (read "sum of squares total") represents the sum of squares of all the observations, regardless of which treatment produced them. Letting $\overline{X}_{..}$ represent the grand mean, the definitional formula is

$$SS_{total} = \Sigma(X_{ij} - \overline{X}_{..})^2$$

This is a term we saw much earlier when we were calculating the variance of a set of numbers, and is the numerator for the variance. (The denominator was the degrees of freedom.) This formula, like the ones that follow, is not the formula we would use if we were to do the hand calculations for this problem. However, these are perfectly correct formulae and represent the way we normally think about the analysis. For those who prefer more traditional hand-calculation formulae, they can be found in earlier editions of this book.

SS_{treat}

SS_{treat}

The definitional formula for SS_{treat} is framed in the context of deviations of group means from the grand mean. Here we have

$$SS_{treat} = n\Sigma(\overline{X}_j - \overline{X}_{..})^2$$

You can see that SS_{treat} is just the sum of squared deviations of the treatment means around the grand mean, which is multiplied by n to give us an estimate of the population variance.

SS_{error}

SS_{error}

In practice, SS_{error} is obtained by subtraction. Because it can be easily shown that

$$SS_{total} = SS_{treat} + SS_{error}$$

then it must also be true that

$$SS_{error} = SS_{total} - SS_{treat}$$

This is the procedure presented in Table 11.3, and it makes our calculations easier.

To present SS_{error} in terms of deviations from means, we can write

$$SS_{error} = \Sigma(X_{ij} - \overline{X}_j)^2$$

Here you can see that SS_{error} is simply the sum over groups of the sums of squared deviation of scores around their group's mean. This approach is illustrated below where I have calculated the sum of squares within each of the groups. Notice that for each group there is absolutely no influence of data from other groups, and therefore the truth or falsity of the null hypothesis is irrelevant to the calculations.

$$SS_{within\,D0} = \Sigma((1.28 - 1.802)^2 + (1.35 - 1.802)^2 + \cdots + (1.06 - 1.802)^2) \qquad = 30.148$$
$$SS_{within\,D2} = \Sigma((-1.18 - 0.675)^2 + (0.15 - 1.675)^2 + \cdots + (2.28 - 1.675)^2) \qquad = 14.291$$
$$SS_{within\,D4} = \Sigma((-0.41 - (-0.912))^2 + (-1.25 - (-0.912))^2 + \cdots + (-0.74 - (-0.912))^2) \quad = 2.919$$
$$SS_{within\,D6} = \Sigma((-0.85 - 0.144)^2 + (0.14 - 0.144)^2 + \cdots + (0.51 - 0.144)^2) \qquad = 15.330$$
$$SS_{within\,D8} = \Sigma((2.01 - 1.889)^2 + (0.40 - 1.889)^2 + \cdots + (-0.66 - 1.889)^2) \qquad = \underline{61.771}$$
$$SS_{error} = \qquad\qquad 124.458$$

When we sum these individual terms, we obtain 124.458, which agrees with the answer we obtained in Table 11.3.

The Summary Table

summary table

Table 11.3 also shows the summary table for the analysis of variance. It is called a summary table for the rather obvious reason that it summarizes a series of calculations, making it possible to tell at a glance what the data have to offer. In older journals you will often find the complete summary table displayed. More recently, primarily to save space, usually just the resulting F's (to be defined) and the degrees of freedom are presented.

Sources of Variation

The first column of the summary table contains the sources of variation—the word "variation" being synonymous here with the phrase "sum of squares." As can be seen from the table, there are three sources of variation: the variation due to treatments (variation among treatment means), the variation due to error (variation within the treatments), and the total variation. These sources reflect the fact that we have partitioned the total sum of squares into two portions: one representing variability within the individual groups and the other representing variability among the several group means.

Degrees of Freedom

df_{total}

df_{treat}
df_{error}

The degrees of freedom column in Table 11.3 represents the allocation of the total number of degrees of freedom between the two sources of variation. With 59 df overall (i.e., $N - 1$), four of these are associated with differences among treatment means and the remaining 55 are associated with variability within the treatment groups. The calculation of df is probably the easiest part of our task. The total degrees of freedom (df_{total}) is always $N - 1$, where N is the total number of observations. The number of degrees of freedom between treatments (df_{treat}) is always $k - 1$, where k is the number of treatments. The number of degrees of freedom for error (df_{error}) is most easily thought of as what is left over and is obtained by subtracting df_{treat} from df_{total}. However, df_{error} can be calculated more directly as the sum of the degrees of freedom within each treatment.

To put this in a slightly different form, the total variability is based on N scores and therefore has $N - 1$ df. The variability of treatment means is based on k means and therefore has $k - 1$ df. The variability within any one treatment is based on n scores, and thus has $n - 1$ df, but because we sum k of these within-treatment terms, we will have k times $n - 1$ or $k(n - 1)$ df.

Mean Squares

We will now go to the MS column in Table 11.3. (There is little to be said about the column labeled SS; it simply contains the sums of squares obtained in the section on calculations.) The column of mean squares contains our two estimates of σ_e^2. These values are obtained by dividing the sums of squares by their corresponding df. Thus, $62.460/4 = 15.615$ and $124.458/55 = 2.263$. We typically do not calculate MS_{total}, because we have no need for it. If we were to do so, this term would equal $186.918/59 = 3.168$, which, as you can see from Table 11.3, is the variance of all N observations, regardless of treatment. Although it is true that mean squares are variance estimates, it is important to keep in mind what variances these terms are estimating. Thus, MS_{error} is an estimate of the population variance (σ_e^2), regardless of the truth or falsity of H_0, and is actually the average of the variances within each group when the sample sizes are equal:

$$MS_{error} = (2.741 + 1.299 + 0.265 + 1.394 + 5.616)/5 = 2.263$$

However, MS_{treat} is not the variance of treatment means but rather is the variance of those means multiplied by n to produce a second estimate of the population variance (σ_e^2). Thus

$$s_{treat}^2 = \text{variance}\ (1.802, 0.675, -0.912, 0.144, 1.889)\ =\ 1.301$$
$$MS_{treat} = n(s_{treat}^2) = 12(1.301) = 15.615$$

The *F* Statistic

The last column in Table 11.3, labeled F, is the most important one in terms of testing the null hypothesis. F is obtained by dividing MS_{treat} by MS_{error}. There is a precise way and a sloppy way to explain why this ratio makes sense, and we will start with the latter. As noted earlier, MS_{error} is an estimate of the population variance (σ_e^2). Moreover MS_{treat} is an estimate of the population variance (σ_e^2) *if* H_0 is true, but not if it is false. If H_0 is true, then MS_{error} and MS_{treat} are both estimating the same thing, and as such they should be approximately equal. If this is the case, the ratio of one to the other will be approximately 1, give or take a certain amount for sampling error. Thus, all we have to do is to compute the ratio and determine whether it is close enough to 1 to indicate support for the null hypothesis.

So much for the informal way of looking at F. A more precise approach starts with the *expected mean squares* for error and treatments. From earlier in the chapter, we know

$$E(MS_{error}) = \sigma_e^2$$
$$E(MS_{treat}) = \sigma_e^2 + n\theta_\tau^2$$

We now form the ratio

$$F = \frac{E(MS_{treat})}{E(MS_{error})} = \frac{\sigma_e^2 + n\theta_\tau^2}{\sigma_e^2}$$

The only time this ratio would have an expectation of 1 is when $\theta_\tau^2 = 0$—that is, when H_0 is true and $\mu_1 = \cdots = \mu_5$.[5] When $\theta_\tau^2 > 0$, the expectation will be greater than 1.

The question that remains, however, is, How large a ratio will we accept without rejecting H_0 when we use not *expected* values but *obtained* mean squares, which are computed from data and are therefore subject to sampling error? The answer to this question lies in the fact that we can show that the ratio

$$F = MS_{treat}/MS_{error}$$

is distributed as F on $k - 1$ and $k(n - 1)$ *df*. This is the same F distribution that is sometimes used to test the ratio of two variance estimates (which in fact is what we are doing here).

---

[5] As an aside, note that the expected value of F is not precisely 1 under H_0, although $\frac{E(MS_{treat})}{E(MS_{error})} = 1$ if $\theta_\tau^2 = 0$. To be exact, under H_0, $E(F) = \frac{df_{treat}}{df_{error} - 2}$. For all practical purposes, nothing is sacrificed by thinking of F as having an expectation of 1 under H_0 and greater than 1 under H_1 (the alternative hypothesis).

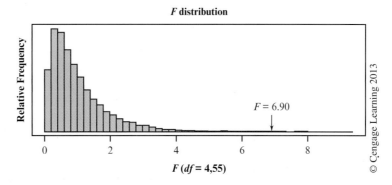

Figure 11.3   Distribution of F with 4 and 55 df

Note that the degrees of freedom represent the df associated with the numerator and de-nominator, respectively.

We will first look at what the F distribution looks like when we have 4 and 55 de-grees of freedom and when the null hypothesis is true. To generate Figure 11.3, I drew 5 samples from a normal population with means all equal to 0.800 (our grand mean in the example) and standard deviations equal to those that Giancola & Corman found. Because all samples were drawn from populations with the same mean, the null hypothesis is, by definition, true. Having drawn my samples I calculated the F statistic and recorded it. I then repeated this process 9,999 more times, so I have 10,000 F values generated under the null hypothesis. (A simple R program to carry out these calculations is available on the book's Web site.) The resulting distribution is shown in Figure 11.3. You can see that the F we calculated from the actual data is very extreme relative to what we would expect with a true H_0, which causes us to reject the null hypothesis. The actual probability of $F(4,55) = 6.90$ under the null hypothesis is 00014.

We certainly don't want to run a sampling study like that in Figure 11.3 every time we want to know if F is significant. Fortunately F is tabled and we simply look up the critical value. For our example, $F = 6.90$. We have 4 df for the numerator and 55 df for the denomi-nator, and can enter the F table (Appendix F) with these values. Appendix F, a portion of which is shown in Table 11.4, gives the critical values for $\alpha = .05$ and $\alpha = .01$. For our particular case we have 4 and 55 df and, with linear interpolation, $F_{.05}(4,55) = 2.54$. Thus, if we have chosen to work at $\alpha = .05$, we would reject H_0 and conclude that there are sig-nificant differences among the treatment means.

Conclusions

On the basis of a significant value of F, we have rejected the null hypothesis that the treat-ment means in the population are equal. Strictly speaking, this conclusion indicates that at least one of the population means is different from at least one other mean, but we don't know exactly which means are different from other means. We will pursue that topic in Chapter 12. It is evident from an examination of the boxplot in Figure 11.2, however, that increasing the level of distraction, *up to a point,* decreases the level of aggressive behavior. But increasing distraction beyond that point is counter-productive. This tells us at least something about the role of alcohol in aggressive behavior.

Table 11.4   Abbreviated version of Appendix F, Critical Values of the F Distribution where $\alpha = .05$

df denom.	Degrees of Freedom for Numerator									
	1	2	3	4	5	6	7	8	9	10
1	161.4	199.5	215.8	224.8	230.0	233.8	236.5	238.6	240.1	242.1
2	18.51	19.00	19.16	19.25	19.30	19.33	19.35	19.37	19.38	19.40
3	10.13	9.55	9.28	9.12	9.01	8.94	8.89	8.85	8.81	8.79
4	7.71	6.94	6.59	6.39	6.26	6.16	6.09	6.04	6.00	5.96
5	6.61	5.79	5.41	5.19	5.05	4.95	4.88	4.82	4.77	4.74
6	5.99	5.14	4.76	4.53	4.39	4.28	4.21	4.15	4.10	4.06
7	5.59	4.74	4.35	4.12	3.97	3.87	3.79	3.73	3.68	3.64
8	5.32	4.46	4.07	3.84	3.69	3.58	3.50	3.44	3.39	3.35
9	5.12	4.26	3.86	3.63	3.48	3.37	3.29	3.23	3.18	3.14
10	4.96	4.10	3.71	3.48	3.33	3.22	3.14	3.07	3.02	2.98
11	4.84	3.98	3.59	3.36	3.20	3.09	3.01	2.95	2.90	2.85
12	4.75	3.89	3.49	3.26	3.11	3.00	2.91	2.85	2.80	2.75
13	4.67	3.81	3.41	3.18	3.03	2.92	2.83	2.77	2.71	2.67
14	4.60	3.74	3.34	3.11	2.96	2.85	2.76	2.70	2.65	2.60
15	4.54	3.68	3.29	3.06	2.90	2.79	2.71	2.64	2.59	2.54
16	4.49	3.63	3.24	3.01	2.85	2.74	2.66	2.59	2.54	2.49
17	4.45	3.59	3.20	2.96	2.81	2.70	2.61	2.55	2.49	2.45
18	4.41	3.55	3.16	2.93	2.77	2.66	2.58	2.51	2.46	2.41
19	4.38	3.52	3.13	2.90	2.74	2.63	2.54	2.48	2.42	2.38
20	4.35	3.49	3.10	2.87	2.71	2.60	2.51	2.45	2.39	2.35
22	4.30	3.44	3.05	2.82	2.66	2.55	2.46	2.40	2.34	2.30
24	4.26	3.40	3.01	2.78	2.62	2.51	2.42	2.36	2.30	2.25
26	4.23	3.37	2.98	2.74	2.59	2.47	2.39	2.32	2.27	2.22
28	4.20	3.34	2.95	2.71	2.56	2.45	2.36	2.29	2.24	2.19
30	4.17	3.32	2.92	2.69	2.53	2.42	2.33	2.27	2.21	2.16
40	4.08	3.23	2.84	2.61	2.45	2.34	2.25	2.18	2.12	2.08
50	4.03	3.18	2.79	2.56	2.40	2.29	2.20	2.13	2.07	2.03
60	4.00	3.15	2.76	2.53	2.37	2.25	2.17	2.10	2.04	1.99
120	3.92	3.07	2.68	2.45	2.29	2.18	2.09	2.02	1.96	1.91
200	3.89	3.04	2.65	2.42	2.26	2.14	2.06	1.98	1.93	1.88
500	3.86	3.01	2.62	2.39	2.23	2.12	2.03	1.96	1.90	1.85
1000	3.85	3.01	2.61	2.38	2.22	2.11	2.02	1.95	1.89	1.84

11.5   Writing Up the Results

Reporting results for an analysis of variance is somewhat more complicated than reporting the results of a t test. This is because we not only want to indicate whether the overall F is significant, but we probably also want to make statements about the differences between individual means. We won't discuss tests on individual means until the next chapter, so this example will be incomplete. We will come back to it in Chapter 12. An abbreviated version of a statement about the results follows.

In a test of the hypothesis that alcohol tends to focus attention on more provocative, rather than less salient inhibitory cues, Giancola and Corman examined the effect of distracting stimuli on aggressive behavior. The groups differed in the level of distraction provided by the competing task. After consuming alcohol, subjects were repeatedly presented with 0, 2, 4, 6, or 8 stimuli appearing in the cells of a 3×3 matrix and were asked to report the order in which the stimuli appeared. They were told that if they responded faster than a fictitious opponent, they would deliver shocks to that opponent. If they were slower, the opponent would deliver shocks to them. When participants were presented with no distracting stimuli, they administered shocks that were higher in intensity and longer in duration than if they experienced low levels of distraction. In addition, as the distraction task increased in complexity beyond a medium level, the decline in shock intensity and duration reversed itself. A one-way analysis of variance revealed that there were significant differences among the means of the five groups ($F(4,55) = 6.90, p < .05$). Visual inspection of the group means revealed that the level of administered shock decreased with increasing distraction but then increased again as the distraction task became more complex, as predicted by the theory. (Note: Further discussion of these differences will have to wait until Chapter 12. The behavior of a control condition that did not consume alcohol showed no significant differences with distraction level, although those data are not reported here.)

11.6 Computer Solutions

Most analyses of variance are now done using standard computer software, and Exhibit 11.1 contains examples of output from SPSS. Other statistical software will produce similar results. (To produce these results in R, see GiancolaExample.R on the book's Web site.) In producing the SPSS printout that follows, I used the **One-Way** selection from the **Compare Means** menu, rather than using the more common **General Linear Model/Univariate**. To obtain this result we need to specify the dependent and independent variables, and then click on **Options** to select "descriptives" and "Means plot."

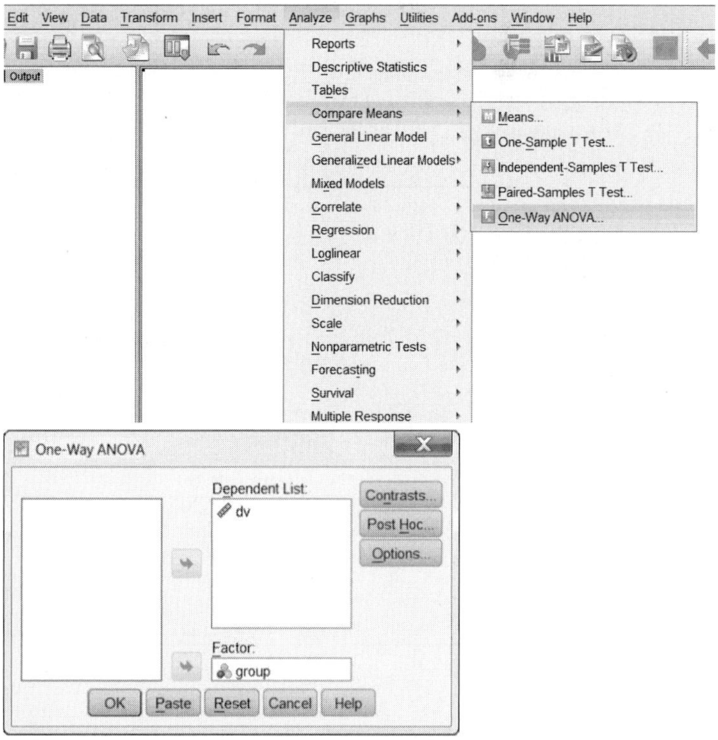

Exhibit 11.1   SPSS Oneway printout

Descriptives

dv

	N	Mean	Std. Deviation	Std. Error	95% Confidence Interval for Mean		Minimum	Maximum
					Lower Bound	Upper Bound		
1	12	1.8025	1.65550	.47790	.7506	2.8544	−2.68	3.31
2	12	.6750	1.13981	.32904	−.0492	1.3992	−1.18	2.61
3	12	−.9125	.51515	.14871	−1.2398	−.5852	−1.74	−.31
4	12	.5442	1.18051	.34078	−.2059	1.2942	−.98	2.69
5	12	1.8892	2.36971	.68408	.3835	3.3948	−1.80	6.47
Total	60	.7997	1.77992	.22979	.3399	1.2595	−2.68	6.47

dv

Levene Statistic	df1	df2	Sig.
3.769	4	55	.009

ANOVA

dv

	Sum of Squares	df	Mean Square	F	Sig.
Between Groups	62.460	4	15.615	6.901	.000
Within Groups	124.458	55	2.263		
Total	186.918	59			

Robust Tests of Equality of Means

dv

	Statistic[a]	df1	df2	Sig.
Welch	14.228	4	25.432	.000
Brown-Forsythe	6.901	4	32.943	.000

[a] Asymptotically F distributed.

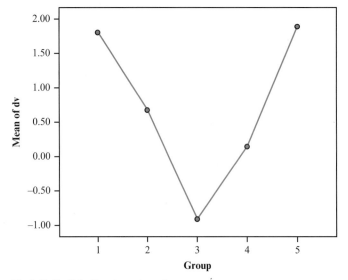

Exhibit 11.1 (*continued*)

The output here looks like the values that we computed. You would get the same general results if you had selected **Analyze/General Linear Model/Univariate** from the menus, although the summary table would contain additional lines of information that I won't discuss until the end of this chapter. You may have noticed that SPSS ran a test of homogeneity of variance (Levene's test, which was discussed in Chapter 7) and that it was significant. That is not a good sign, but we will discuss this further later in the chapter. You will also notice a section entitled "Robust Tests of Equality of Means." We will discuss that shortly.

11.7 Unequal Sample Sizes

balanced designs

Most experiments are originally designed with the idea of collecting the same number of observations in each treatment. (Such designs are generally known as **balanced designs**.) Frequently, however, things do not work out that way. Subjects fail to arrive for testing, or are eliminated because they fail to follow instructions. Animals occasionally become ill during an experiment from causes that have nothing to do with the treatment. I still recall an example first seen in graduate school in which an animal was eliminated from the study for repeatedly biting the experimenter (Sgro and Weinstock, 1963). Moreover, studies conducted on intact groups, such as school classes, have to contend with the fact that such groups nearly always vary in size.

If the sample sizes are not equal, the analysis discussed earlier needs to be modified. For the case of one independent variable, however, this modification is relatively minor. (A much more complete discussion of the treatment of missing data for a variety of analysis of variance and regression designs can be found in Howell (2008), or, in slightly simpler form, at http://www.uvm.edu/~dhowell/StatPages/More_Stuff/Missing_Data/Missing.html.)

Earlier we defined

$$SS_{\text{treat}} = n\Sigma(\overline{X}_j - \overline{X}_{..})^2$$

We were able to multiply the deviations by n because n was common to all treatments. If the sample sizes differ, however, and we define n_j as the number of subjects in the jth treatment ($\sum n_j = N$), we can rewrite the expression as

$$SS_{\text{treat}} = \sum[n_j(\overline{X}_j - \overline{X}_{..})^2]$$

which, when all n_j are equal, reduces to the original equation. This expression shows us that with unequal ns, the deviation of each treatment mean from the grand mean is weighted by the sample size. Thus, the larger the size of one sample relative to the others, the more it will contribute the grand mean ($\overline{X}_{..}$) and to SS_{treat}, all other things being equal.

missing at random

You need to be a bit careful about missing data, even in a simple design such as this. If data are what is called **missing at random**, meaning that people just drop out randomly or some classes in a school that you are studying have a few more or fewer students than others, then there is not much of a problem. All you have done by having missing data is to reduce the power of your experiment. However, if there are systematic reasons why scores are missing, that is a different story. Suppose that you have three different treatments for behavioral problems and one of those treatments is not effective for people with more serious problems. If the ones with serious problems are more likely to drop out because the treatment doesn't help them, the mean for that sample is the mean for people with mild problems, while the other two groups, which do not have this drop out problem, will have means of people with all kinds of problems. It really isn't fair to compare the three means, because they are based on different kinds of people. The problem isn't so much one of unequal sample sizes, though that is what you have, but of groups that cannot fairly be compared.

Effective Therapies for Anorexia

The following example is taken from a study by Everitt that compared the effects of two therapy conditions and a control condition on weight gain in anorexic girls. The data are reported in Hand et al., 1994. Everitt used a control condition that received no intervention, a cognitive-behavioral treatment condition, and a family therapy condition. The dependent variable analyzed here was the gain in weight over a fixed period of time. There was not a dropout problem in this example, so we do not have to worry about the fact that some samples were larger than others, although we do need to take sample sizes into account in performing the analysis. The data are given in Table 11.5 and plotted in Figure 11.4. Although there is some tendency for the Cognitive-Behavior Therapy group to be bimodal,

Table 11.5   Data from Everitt on the treatment of anorexia in young girls

	Control	Cognitive-Behavior Therapy	Family Therapy	Total
	−.5	1.7	11.4	
	−9.3	.7	11.0	
	−5.4	−.1	5.5	
	12.3	−.7	9.4	
	−2.0	−3.5	13.6	
	−10.2	14.9	−2.9	
	−12.2	3.5	−.1	
	11.6	17.1	7.4	
	−7.1	−7.6	21.5	
	6.2	1.6	−5.3	
	−.2	11.7	−3.8	
	−9.2	6.1	13.4	
	8.3	1.1	13.1	
	3.3	−4.0	9.0	
	11.3	20.9	3.9	
	.0	−9.1	5.7	
	−1.0	2.1	10.7	
	−10.6	−1.4		
	−4.6	1.4		
	−6.7	−.3		
	2.8	−3.7		
	.3	−.8		
	1.8	2.4		
	3.7	12.6		
	15.9	1.9		
	−10.2	3.9		
		.1		
		15.4		
		−.7		
Mean	−0.45	3.01	7.26	2.76
St. Dev.	7.989	7.308	7.157	7.984
Variance	63.819	53.414	51.229	63.738
n	26	29	17	72

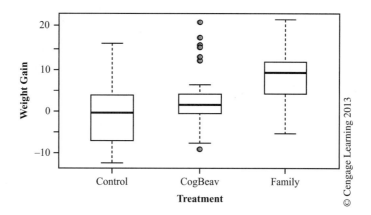

Figure 11.4   Weight gain in Everitt's three groups.

that tendency is probably not sufficient to distort our results. (A nonparametric test (see Chapter 18) that is not influenced by that bimodality produces similar results.)

The computation of the analysis of variance follows, and you can see that the change required by the presence of unequal sample sizes is minor. I should hasten to point out that unequal sample sizes will not be so easily dismissed when we come to more complex designs, but there is no particular difficulty with the one-way design.

$$SS_{total} = \Sigma(X_{ij} - \overline{X}_{..})^2 = [(-0.5 - 2.76)^2 + (-9.3 - 2.76)^2 + \cdots + (10.7 - 2.76)^2]$$
$$= 4525.386$$

$$SS_{treat} = \Sigma n_j(\overline{X}_j - \overline{X}_{..})^2 = 26(-0.45 - 2.76)^2 + 29(3.01 - 2.76)^2 + 17(7.26 - 2.76)^2)$$
$$= 614.644$$

$$SS_{error} = SS_{total} - SS_{treat} = 4525.386 - 614.644$$
$$= 3910.742$$

The summary table for this analysis follows.

Source	df	SS	MS	F
Treatments	2	614.644	307.322	5.422*
Error	69	3910.742	56.677	
Total	71	4525.386		

* $p < .05$

From the summary table you can see that there is a significant effect due to treatment. The presence of this effect is clear in Figure 11.3, where the control group showed no appreciable weight gain, whereas the other two groups showed substantial gain. We do not yet know whether the Cognitive-behavior group and the Family Therapy group were significantly different, nor whether they both differed from the Control group, but we will reserve that problem until the next chapter.

11.8   Violations of Assumptions

As we have seen, the analysis of variance is based on the assumptions of normality and homogeneity of variance. In practice, however, the analysis of variance is a robust statistical procedure, and the assumptions frequently can be violated with relatively minor effects. This is especially true for the normality assumption. For studies dealing with this problem, see Box (1953, 1954a, 1954b), Boneau (1960), Bradley (1964), and Grissom (2000). The latter reference is somewhat more pessimistic than the others, but there is still reason to believe that normality is not a crucial assumption and that the homogeneity of variance assumption can be violated without terrible consequences, especially when we focus on the overall null hypothesis rather than on specific group comparisons.

In general, if the populations can be assumed to be symmetric, or at least similar in shape (e.g., all negatively skewed), and if the largest variance is no more than four times the smallest, the analysis of variance is most likely to be valid. It is important to note, however, that heterogeneity of variance and unequal sample sizes do not mix. If you have reason to anticipate unequal variances, make every effort to keep your sample sizes as equal as possible. This is a serious issue, and people tend to forget that noticeably unequal sample sizes make the test appreciably less robust to heterogeneity of variance.

In Chapter 7 we considered the Levene (1960) test for heterogeneity of variance, and I mentioned similar tests by Brown and Forsythe (1974) and O'Brien (1981). The first two are essentially t tests on the deviations (absolute or squared) of observations from their sample mean or median. If one group has a larger variance than another, then the deviations of scores from the mean or median will also, on average, be larger than for a group with a smaller variance. Thus, a significant t test on the absolute values of the deviations represents a test on group variances. These tests can be readily extended to the case of more than two groups in obvious ways. The only difference is that with multiple groups the t test on the deviations would be replaced by an analysis of variance on those deviations. There is evidence to suggest that the Levene test is the weaker of the two, but it is the one traditionally reported by most statistical software. Wilcox (1987b) reports that this test appears to be conservative.

If you are not willing to ignore the existence of heterogeneity or nonnormality in your data, there are alternative ways of handling the problems that result. We will first consider alternative F tests and then the use of data transformations.

Many years ago Box (1954a) showed that with unequal variances the appropriate F distribution against which to compare F_{obt} is a regular F with altered degrees of freedom. If we define the true critical value of F (adjusted for heterogeneity of variance) as F'_{α}, then Box has proven that

$$F_{\alpha}(1, n - 1) \geq F'_{\alpha} \geq F_{\alpha}[k - 1, k(n - 1)]$$

In other words, the true critical value of F lies somewhere between the critical value of F on 1 and $(n-1)$ df and the critical value of F on $(k - 1)$ and $k(n - 1)$ df. This latter limit is the critical value we would use if we met the assumptions of normality and homogeneity of variance. Box suggested a conservative test by comparing F_{obt} to $F_{\alpha}(1, n - 1)$. If this leads to a significant result, then the means are significantly different regardless of the equality, or inequality, of variances. The only difficulty with Box's approach is that it is extremely conservative. A different approach is one proposed by Welch (1951), which we will consider in the next section, and that is implemented by much of the statistical software that we use.

Wilcox (1987b) has argued that, in practice, variances frequently differ by more than a factor of four, which is often considered a reasonable limit on heterogeneity. He has some strong opinions concerning the consequences of heterogeneity of variance. He recommends Welch's procedure with samples having different variances, especially when the sample sizes are unequal.

The Welch Procedure

Kohr and Games (1974), Keselman, Games, and Rogan (1979), and Tomarken and Serlin (1986) have investigated alternative approaches to the treatment of samples with heterogeneous variances (including the one suggested by Box) and have shown that the procedure proposed by Welch (1951) has considerable advantages in terms of both power and protection against Type I errors, at least when sampling from normal populations. The formulae and calculations are somewhat awkward, but not particularly difficult, and you should use this test whenever you suspect heterogeneity of variance—especially when you have unequal sample sizes. SPSS and SAS offer the Welch test as an option.

Define

$$w_k = \frac{n_k}{s_k^2}$$

$$\overline{X}.' = \frac{\sum w_k \overline{X}_k}{\sum w_k}$$

Then

$$F'' = \frac{\dfrac{\sum w_k (\overline{X}_k - \overline{X}.')^2}{k-1}}{1 + \dfrac{2(k-2)}{k^2-1} \sum \left(\dfrac{1}{n_k-1}\right)\left(1 - \dfrac{w_k}{\sum w_k}\right)^2}$$

This statistic (F'') is approximately distributed as F on $k-1$ and df' degrees of freedom, where

$$df' = \frac{k^2-1}{3 \sum \left(\dfrac{1}{n_k-1}\right)\left(1 - \dfrac{w_k}{\sum w_k}\right)^2}$$

Obviously these formulae are messy, but they are not impossible to use. If you collect all of the terms (such as w_k) first and then work systematically through the problem, you should have no difficulty. (Formulae like this are actually very easy to implement if you use any spreadsheet program.) When you have only two groups, it is probably easier to fall back on a t test with heterogeneous variances, using the approach (also attributable to Welch) taken in Chapter 7. For our example, $F'' = 13.217$ on 4 and 25.43 degrees of freedom. The probability of this result under the null is .000006. A program written in R to make these calculations is available at the book's Web site and is named Welch.R.

BUT!

Having shown how one can deal with heterogeneous variances so as to make an analysis of variance test on group means robust to violations of homogeneity assumptions, I must reiterate a point I made in Chapter 7. The fact that we have tests such as that by Welch does not make the heterogeneous variances go away—it just protects the analysis of variance on the means. Heterogeneity of variance is itself a legitimate finding. In this particular case it would appear that there are a group of people for whom cognitive/behavior therapy is unusually effective, causing the gains in that group to become somewhat bimodal. That is important to notice. But even for the rest of that group, the therapy is at least reasonably effective. If we were to arbitrarily truncate the data for weight gains greater than 10 pounds, thus removing those participants who scored unusually well under cognitive/behavior therapy, the resulting F would still be significant ($F(2, 52) = 4.71, p < .05$). A description of these results would be incomplete without at least some mention of the unusually large variance in the cognitive/behavior therapy condition. Often heterogeneous variances reflect the fact that one treatment is very effective for some and quite ineffective for others, as may be the case here.

11.9   Transformations

In the preceding section we considered one approach to the problem of heterogeneity of variance—calculate F'' on the heterogeneous data and evaluate it against the usual F distribution on an adjusted number of degrees of freedom. This procedure has been shown to work well when samples are drawn from normal populations. But little is known about its behavior with nonnormal populations. An alternative approach is to transform the data to a form that yields homogeneous variances and then run a standard analysis of variance on the transformed values. We did something similar in Chapter 9 with the Symptom score in the study of stress.

Most people find it difficult to accept the idea of transforming data. It somehow seems dishonest to decide that you do not like the data you have and therefore to change them into data you like better or, even worse, to throw out some of them and pretend they were never collected. When you think about it, however, there is really nothing unusual about transforming data. We frequently transform data. We sometimes measure the *time* it takes a rat to run down an alley, but then look for group differences in running *speed*, which is the reciprocal of time (a nonlinear transformation). We measure sound in terms of physical energy, but then report it in terms of decibels, which represents a logarithmic transformation. We ask a subject to adjust the size of a test stimulus to match the size of a comparison stimulus, and then take the radius of the test-patch setting as our dependent variable—but the *radius* is a function of the square root of the *area* of the patch, and we could just as legitimately use area as our dependent variable. On some tests, we calculate the number of items that a student answered correctly, but then report scores in percentiles—a decidedly nonlinear transformation. Who is to say that speed is a "better" measure than time, that decibels are better than energy levels, that radius is better than area, or that a percentile is better than the number correct? Consider a study by Conti and Musty (1984) on the effects of THC (the most psychoactive ingredient in marijuana) on locomotor activity in rats. Conti and Musty measured activity by reading the motion of the cage from a transducer that represented that motion in voltage terms. In what way could their electrically transduced measure of test-chamber vibration be called the "natural" measure of activity? More important, they took postinjection activity as a percentage of preinjection activity as their dependent variable, but would you leap out of your chair and cry "Foul!" because they had used a transformation? Of course you wouldn't—but it was a transformation nonetheless.

We will go back to the study by Giancola and Corman on aggression and alcohol. In that example the variance in the D8 condition was more than 20 times the variance in the D4 condition, although we had relatively small samples. Levene's test statistic was 3.769 on 4 and 55 *df*, which had a probability under the null of .009. This is strong evidence for heterogeneity of variance. We have just seen that the null is rejected even by Welch's test, which takes heterogeneous variances into account. But an alternative approach would be to transform the data so that the variances are no longer heterogeneous. In Giancola and Corman's case, the dependent variable was originally created by transforming both the intensity and duration scores to z scores and then summing them. That seems like a reasonable approach to take, but I think that you would have to agree that there is nothing "natural" about that measure. The log of it, or its square root, would seem just about as natural. Tukey probably had the right idea when he called these calculations "reexpressions" rather than "transformations." You are merely reexpressing what the data have to say in other terms.

As I pointed out earlier in this book, our dependent variables are only convenient and imperfect indicators of the underlying variables we wish to study. No sensible experimenter ever started out with the serious intention of studying, for example, the "number of stressful life events" that a subject reports. The real purpose of such experiments has always been to study *stress*, and the number of reported events is merely a convenient measure of stress. In fact, stress probably does not vary in a linear fashion with number of events. It is quite possible that it varies exponentially—you can take a few stressful events in stride, but once you have a few on your plate, additional ones start having greater and greater effects. If this is true, the number of events raised to some power—for example, $Y = (\text{number of events})^2$—might be a more appropriate variable.

Having said that, it is important to recognize that conclusions you draw on transformed data do not always transfer neatly to the original measurements. Grissom (2000) reports on the fact that the means of transformed variables can occasionally reverse the difference of means of the original variables. This is disturbing, and it is important to think about the meaning of what you are doing, but that is not, in itself, a reason to rule out the use of transformations.

If you are willing to accept that it is permissible to transform one set of measures into another—for example, $Y_i = \log(X_i)$ or $Y_i = \sqrt{X_i}$—then many possibilities become available for modifying our data to fit more closely the underlying assumptions of our statistical tests. The nice thing about most of these transformations is that when we transform the data to meet one assumption, we often come closer to meeting other assumptions as well. Thus, a square root transformation not only may help us equate group variances but, because it compresses the upper end of a distribution more than it compresses the lower end, it may also have the effect of making positively skewed distributions more nearly normal in shape.

A word is in order about reporting transformed data. Although it is legitimate and proper to run a statistical test, such as the analysis of variance, on the transformed values, we often report means in the units of the untransformed scale. This is especially true when the original units are intrinsically meaningful. We would, however, need to inform our reader that the analysis was carried out on transformed data.

One example is the salaries of baseball players from different teams. People who work with salary figures routinely perform their analyses on log(salary). However, log(salary) is not a meaningful measure to most of us. A better approach would be to convert all data to logs (assuming you have chosen to use a logarithmic transformation), find the mean of those log values, and then take the antilog to convert that mean back to the original units. (Alternatively, you could report medians, which are often the measure of choice for variables like salary.) This converted mean almost certainly will not equal the mean of the original values, but it is this converted mean that should be reported. But I would urge you to look at both the converted and unconverted means and make sure that they are telling the same basic story. Do not convert standard deviations—you will do serious injustice if you try that. And be sure to indicate to your readers what you have done.

In this chapter we consider only the most common transformations, because they are the ones that will be most useful to you. Excellent discussions of the whole approach to transformations can be found in Tukey (1977), Hoaglin, Mosteller, and Tukey (1983), and Grissom (2000).

Logarithmic Transformation

The logarithmic transformation is useful whenever the standard deviation is proportional to the mean. It is also useful when the data are markedly positively skewed. The easiest way to appreciate why both of these statements are true is to recall what logarithms do. [Remember that a logarithm is a power—$\log_{10}(25)$ is the power to which 10 must be raised to give 25; therefore, $\log_{10}(25) = 1.39794$ because $10^{1.39794} = 25$. In reverse, the antilogarithm of 1.39794 is $10^{1.39794}$ is 25. In statistics we often use what are called "natural logs," which involve the base $e = 2.71828$, in which case $\log_e(25) = \ln(25) = 3.21887$, $e^{3.21887} = 25$. As long as you are consistent, it doesn't matter what base you use.] If we take the numbers 10, 100, and 1,000, their $\log_{10}$s are 1, 2, and 3. Thus, the distance between 10 and 100, in log units, is now equivalent to the distance between 100 and 1,000. In other words, the right side of the distribution (more positive values) will be compressed more than will the left side by taking logarithms. (This is why the salaries of baseball players offer a good example.) This not only means that positively skewed distributions tend toward symmetry under logarithmic transformations; it also means that if a set of relatively large numbers has a large standard deviation whereas a set of small numbers has a small standard deviation, taking logs will reduce the standard deviation of the sample with large numbers more than it will reduce the standard deviation of the sample with small numbers.

Table 11.6 contains an example from the study by Conti and Musty (1984) on activity levels in rats following administration of THC, the active ingredient in marijuana. (I have

Table 11.6   Original and transformed data from Conti and Musty (1984)

(a) Original Data

	Control	0.1 μg	0.5 μg	1 μg	2 μg
	130	93	510	229	144
	94	444	416	475	111
	225	403	154	348	217
	105	192	636	276	200
	92	67	396	167	84
	190	170	451	151	99
	32	77	376	107	44
	64	353	192	235	84
	69	365	384		284
	93	422			293
Mean	109.40	258.60	390.56	248.50	156.00
					$r = .88$
S.D.	58.50	153.32	147.68	118.74	87.65
Variance	3421.82	23,506.04	21,809.78	14,098.86	7682.22

(b) Log Data

	Control	0.1 μg	0.5 μg	1 μg	2 μg
	2.11	1.97	2.71	2.36	2.16
	1.97	2.65	2.62	2.68	2.04
	2.35	2.60	2.19	2.54	2.34
	2.02	2.28	2.80	2.44	2.30
	1.96	1.83	2.60	2.22	1.92
	2.28	2.23	2.65	2.18	2.00
	1.50	1.89	2.58	2.03	1.64
	1.81	2.55	2.28	2.37	1.92
	1.84	2.56	2.58		2.45
	1.97	2.62			2.47
Mean	1.981	2.318	2.557	2.353	2.124
					$r = -.33$
S.D.	0.241	0.324	0.197	0.208	0.268
Variance	0.058	0.105	0.039	0.043	0.072

reported the activity units (on an arbitrary scale) for each animal over the 10-minute postinjection period, whereas Conti and Musty reported postinjection activity as a percentage of baseline activity.) From the data in Table 11.6a you can see that the variances are unequal: The largest variance is nearly seven times the smallest. This is partly a function of the well-established fact that drugs tend to increase variability as well as means. Not only are the variances unequal, but the standard deviations appear to be proportional to the means. This is easily seen in Figure 11.5a, where I have plotted the standard deviations on the ordinate and the means on the abscissa. There is clearly a linear relationship between these two statistics ($r = .88$). This linearity suggests that a logarithmic transformation might be useful. In Table 11.6b the data have been transformed to logarithms to the base 10. (I could have used any base and still had the same effect. I chose base 10 because of its greater familiarity, though in most statistical work logs to the base e ($\log_e$ or ln) are preferred for technical reasons.) Here the means and the standard deviations are no longer correlated, as can be seen in Figure 11.5b ($r = -.33$: nonsignificant). We have broken up the proportionality between the mean and the standard deviation, and the largest group variance is now less than three times the smallest.

An analysis of variance could now be run on these transformed data. In this case, the Levene test produces an F of 1.557 on 4 and 42 df, which has a probability of .204, which is not significant. This helps to confirm that heterogeneity of variance is no longer a problem. For the analysis of variance, $F(4,42) = 7.2$, which is clearly significant. (The difference is also significant by the Welch test.) Conti and Musty chose to run their analysis of variance on the proportion measures, as I said earlier, both for theoretical reasons and because that is standard practice in their area of research. A case might be made, however, that a logarithmic transformation of the original units might be a more appropriate one for future analyses, especially if problems occur with respect to either the shapes of the distributions or heterogeneity of variance.

As I noted earlier, it makes no difference what base you use for a logarithmic transformation, and most statisticians tend to use $\log_e$. Regardless of the base, however, there are problems when the original values (X_i) are negative or near zero, because logs are only defined for positive numbers. In this case, you should add a constant to make all X values positive before taking the log. In general, when you have near-zero values, you should use $\log(X_i + 1)$ instead of $\log(X_i)$. If the numbers themselves are less than -1, add whatever constant is necessary to make them all greater than zero.

One important use of logarithmic transformations deals with data that are counts. For example, you may be dealing with autistic children in classrooms and your dependent

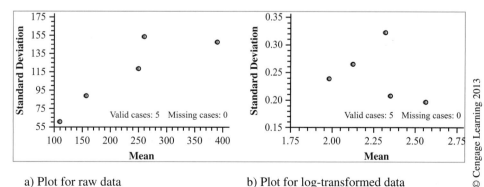

a) Plot for raw data   b) Plot for log-transformed data

Figure 11.5   The relationship between means and standard deviations for original and transformed values of the data in Table 11.6

variable may be the number of inappropriate behaviors that the child exhibits in a 20-minute period. They might be numbers between 0 and 5. You know that these data cannot possibly be normally distributed because no count can be negative. Count data usually follow a Poisson distribution, and the standard approach is to model the log(count) rather than the count itself.

Square-Root Transformation

When the mean is proportional to the *variance* rather than to the standard deviation, we use a square-root transformation. In this case, $Y = \sqrt{X}$ which is useful for stabilizing variances and decreasing skewness. If the values of X are fairly small (i.e., less than 10), then $Y = \sqrt{X + 0.5}$ or $Y = \sqrt{X} + \sqrt{X + 1}$ is often better for stabilizing variances. The problem is that it is usually very difficult for you and me to know if the correlation with the variance is much greater or less than the correlation with the standard deviation. So it's a good idea to try both. For the Conti and Musty data, the mean correlates nearly as well with the variance as it does with the standard deviation. Standard deviations and variances are themselves highly correlated if the range of values is not large (in this case $r_{s \cdot s^2} = .99$).

Reciprocal Transformation

When you have a distribution with very large values in the positive tail, a reciprocal transformation may dramatically reduce the influence of those extreme values even better than a logarithmic transformation. For example, animals in a maze or straight alley often seem to forget their job and stop to sniff at all the photocells and such that they find along the way. Once an animal has been in the apparatus for 30 seconds, it does not matter to us if he takes another 300 seconds to complete the run. One approach was referred to in Chapter 2—if there are several trials per day, you might take the daily median time as your measure. An alternative approach is to use all of the data but to take the reciprocal of time (i.e., speed), because it has the effect of nearly equating long times. Suppose that we collected the following times:

[10, 11, 13, 14, 15, 45, 450]

The reciprocals of these times are

[0.100, 0.091, 0.077, 0.071, 0.067, 0.022, 0.002]

Notice that the differences among the longer times are much reduced from what they were in the original units. (Whereas skew = 0 in normally distributed data, the untransformed data had skew equal to 2.62, whereas for the second set it has been reduced to −0.91.) Moreover, the outliers will have considerably less effect on the size of the standard deviation than they had before the transformation. Similar kinds of effects are found when we apply reciprocal transformations to reaction times, where long reaction times probably indicate less about information-processing speeds than they do about the fact that the subject was momentarily not paying attention or missed the response key that she was supposed to hit.

The Arcsine Transformation

In Chapter 5 we saw that for the binomial distribution, $\mu = Np$ and $\sigma^2 = Npq$. In this case, because both the mean and the variance are dependent on p, the variance will be a direct function of the mean. Suppose that for some experiment our dependent variable was the proportion of items recalled correctly by each subject. Then each item can be thought of as a Bernoulli trial with probability p of being correct (and probability $1 - p$ of being incorrect), and the whole set of items can be thought of as a series of Bernoulli trials. In other words, the results would have a binomial distribution where the variance is dependent on the mean. If this is so, groups with different means would necessarily have different variances, and we would have a problem. For this situation, the arcsine transformation is often helpful. The usual form of this transformation is $Y = 2 \arcsin \sqrt{p}$. In this case p is the proportion correct and Y will be twice the angle whose sine equals the square root of p.[6] The arcsine transformation can be obtained with most calculators (labeled $\sin^{-1}$) if you tell it to work with radians. (It is even easier than that. Do a Google search for "arcsin(.50) =" and you will get 0.523598776. I told you that Google is your friend.)

Both the square-root and arcsine transformations are suitable when the variance is proportional to the mean. There is, however, a difference between them. The square-root transformation compresses the upper tail of the distribution, whereas the arcsine transformation stretches out both tails relative to the middle. Normally the arcsine is more helpful when you are dealing with proportions.

Trimmed Samples

heavy-tailed distributions

Rather than transforming each of your raw scores to achieve homogeneity of variance or normality, an alternative approach with **heavy-tailed distributions** (relatively flat distributions that have an unusual number of observations in the tails) is to use trimmed samples. In Chapter 2 a *trimmed sample* was defined as a sample from which a fixed percentage of the extreme values in each tail have been removed. Thus, with 40 cases, a 5% trimmed sample will be the sample with two of the observations in each tail eliminated. When comparing several groups, as in the analysis of variance, you would trim each sample by the same amount. Although trimmed samples have been around in statistics for a very long time, they have recently received a lot of attention because of their usefulness in dealing with distributions with occasional outliers. You will probably see more of them in the future.

Winsorized samples

Closely related to trimmed samples are **Winsorized samples**, in which the trimmed values are replaced by the most extreme value remaining in each tail. Thus, a 10% Winsorization of

3	7	12	15	17	17	18	19	19	19
20	22	24	26	30	32	32	33	36	50

would replace the two lowest values (3 and 7) by 12s and the two highest values (36 and 50) by 33s, leaving

12	12	12	15	17	17	18	19	19	19
20	22	24	26	30	32	32	33	33	33

[The variance and any test statistics calculated on this sample would be based on $(N - 1 - 4)$ *df*, because we trimmed off four values and replaced them with pseudovalues. It is not really fair to pretend that those pseudovalues are real data.] Experiments with samples containing an unusual number of outliers may profit from trimming and/ or "Winsorizing." When you run an analysis of variance on trimmed data, however, you

---

[6] The arcsine transformation is often referred to as an "angular" transformation because of this property. When p is close to 0 or 1, we often take $2 \arcsin = \sqrt{p \pm \dfrac{1}{2n}}$, where the $+$ is used when p is close to 0, and the minus when p is close to 1.

should base the MS_{error} on the variance of the corresponding Winsorized sample and not on the variance of the trimmed sample. A readable study of the effect of applying t tests (and, by extension, the analysis of variance) to trimmed samples was conducted by Yuen and Dixon (1973); you should read it before running such analyses. You should also look at papers by Wilcox (1993 and 1995). Wilcox has long been an advocate of trimmed samples. A useful reference when we come to multiple comparisons in Chapter 12 is Keselman, Holland, and Cribbie (2005, pp. 1918–1919).

When to Transform and How to Choose a Transformation

You should not get the impression that transformations should be applied routinely to all of your data. As a rule of thumb, "If it's not broken, don't fix it." If your data are reasonably distributed (i.e., are more or less symmetrical and have few if any outliers), and if your variances are reasonably homogeneous, there is probably nothing to be gained by applying a transformation. If you have markedly skewed data or heterogeneous variances, however, some form of transformation may be useful. Furthermore, it is perfectly legitimate to shop around for a transformation that makes the necessary changes to the variance or shape. If a logarithmic transformation does not do what you want (stabilize the variances or improve shape), then consider the square-root (or cubed-root) transformation. If you have near-zero values and $Y = \sqrt{X + 0.5}$ does not work, try $Y = \sqrt{X} + \sqrt{X + 1}$. The only thing that you should *not* do is to try out every transformation, looking for one that gives you a significant result. (You are trying to optimize the *data*, not the resulting F.) Choose your transformation before you run your statistical test. Finally, if you are considering using transformations, it would be a good idea to look at Tukey (1977) or Hoaglin, Mosteller, and Tukey (1983).

Osborne (2008) has an excellent discussion of transformations and their use. He makes the point that, at least with the square-root, logarithmic, and inverse transformations, the effect of the transformation is greatest when the minimum value of the data is 1.0. As a result, he suggests first transforming the data to move the minimum to 1.0, usually by adding or subtracting a constant to the data, before applying one of these transformations. He further points out that these transformations best handle positively skewed data, but they can be applied to negatively skewed data if you first reflect the distribution by multiplying by -1 and then adding or subtracting an appropriate constant.

Resampling

resampling statistics

An old but very valuable approach to statistical hypothesis testing that is beginning to win many more adherents is known as **resampling statistics**. I say a great deal about this approach in Chapter 18, but before leaving methods for dealing with violations of assumptions, I should at least mention that resampling methods offer the opportunity to avoid some of the assumptions required in the analysis of variance. These methods essentially create a population that exactly resembles the combined distribution of obtained data with the same number of observations. Then the computer permutes the data points randomly into groups as if the null hypothesis is true[7] and calculates a test statistic, such as F, for that sample. This process is then repeated a very large number of times, producing a whole distribution of F values that would be expected with a true null hypothesis. It is then simple to calculate how many of these Fs were more extreme than the one from your data, and reject, or fail to reject, depending on the result. Students interested in this approach can jump to Chapter 18, which should not be difficult to understand even without reading the intermediate chapters.

---

[7] Another way to think of this involves shuffling. You could put the individual values on cards, shuffle the full deck, and then assign the first 10 cards to Group 1, the next 10 cards to Group 2, and so on.

11.10   Fixed versus Random Models

We have not said anything about how we choose the levels of our independent variable; we have simply spoken of "treatments." In fact, if you think about it, we could obtain the levels of the treatment variable in at least two different ways: We could, and usually do, deliberately select them or we could sample them at random. The way in which the levels are derived has implications for the generalizations we might draw from our study.

Assume that we have been asked to determine if sixth-grade children in East Aurora, New York read significantly better than the fifth-grade children in that village. East Aurora is not a particularly large village, so we draw 10 children out of each fifth- and sixth-grade classroom and test them. If we were to **replicate** that experiment a number of times, we would always use the same classrooms, though different children, because those are the only fifth- and sixth-grade classrooms in town. So from one replication to another there would be no variability attributable to variability in the classrooms used. We would call "classroom" a fixed variable because we specifically chose the classrooms to use. The important point here is that the levels of classroom are in fact *fixed* in the sense that they do not change randomly from one replication of the study to another. The analysis of such an experiment is referred to as a **fixed-model analysis of variance**.

replicate

fixed-model analysis of variance

But suppose, instead, that the State of New York was asking the same question about schools across the state. We would probably choose a bunch of schools at random, and within those schools we would probably choose classrooms at random. In this case when we think of multiple replications, we know that the results would vary not only by normal sampling error, but also by variability due to the classrooms (and schools) we happened to use. Thus we would call both classrooms and schools random variables. Here the classroom levels are the result of a random process, and the population of interest with respect to classrooms is quite large. Because of the process by which treatment levels are obtained, we speak of treatments as a random variable and of the analysis as a **random-model analysis of variance**.

random-model analysis of variance

We will have much more to say about fixed and random models in Chapters 13 and 14. They are playing an expanded role in the analysis of research in the behavioral sciences, and you need to understand them. The important point at this time is that in a fixed model, the treatment levels are deliberately selected and would remain constant from one replication to another. In a random model, treatment levels are obtained by a random process and would be expected to vary across replications. For a one-way analysis of variance, the distinction is not particularly critical, but it can become quite important when we use more complex designs where we not only have to deal with random variables, but often with what are called "nested variables" as well. In more complex models the independent variable that is a random variable is often not of great importance in its own right. It is often there primarily to increase the generalizability of our study. However, its presence can substantially affect the resulting *F* values.

11.11   The Size of an Experimental Effect

The fact that an analysis of variance has produced a significant *F* simply tells us that there are differences among the means of treatments that cannot be attributed to error. It says nothing about whether these differences are of any practical importance. For this reason, we must look beyond the value of *F* to define an additional measure reflecting the "importance" of the difference. In previous chapters I have made a distinction between the *d*-family of measures, which relate directly to differences among means, and the *r*-family of measures, which are based on correlations between the independent and dependent variables. When we are considering the omnibus F, which looks for any differences among the full set of means, d-family measures may or may not be appropriate, although they do exist and we will discuss them shortly. They will become very appropriate, however, when we discuss individual comparisons in Chapter 12. The r-family of measures is often recommended for the omnibus test of all means, and that is what I will focus on first. I must admit, however, that I don't find r-family measures particularly appealing because it is difficult to know what is a large, or a small, value for that measure. In some situations explaining 5% of the variation may be very important, while in others 5% might be trivial. (But how do we know which kind of situation we are in?)

In this edition I am significantly reducing the attention paid to effect sizes in the *overall* analysis. I do this because I want to focus attention on effect sizes for specific comparisons among the full set of means. Computing effect sizes on specific comparisons draws our attention to those effects and away from the far less useful overall effect.

The set of measures discussed here are often classed as "magnitude of effect" measures and are related to r^2. They represent how much of the overall variability in the dependent variable can be attributed to the treatment effect. At my last count, there were at least six measures of the **magnitude of the experimental effect**—all different and most claiming to be less biased than some other measure. In this section we will focus on only the two most common measures (η^2 and ω^2), because they have the strongest claim to our attention.

magnitude of the experimental effect

Eta-Squared (η^2)

Eta-squared is probably the oldest measure of the strength of an experimental effect, as well as the simplest. If you think of the analysis of variance summary table, SS_{total} is an index of how different the scores in the complete data set are from one another. Furthermore, SS_{treat} is a measure of how much of the differences among observations are attributable to the different treatments. So if we form a ratio of SS_{treat} divided by SS_{total} we will have the percentage of overall variability that can be attributed to treatments. This will give us

$$\eta^2 = \frac{SS_{treat}}{SS_{total}}$$

eta-squared (η^2)

Our statistic is called **eta-squared(η^2)**, though it is sometimes referred to as the **correlation ratio**.

correlation ratio

Applying η^2 to the Giancola and Corman data in Table 11.2 we have

$$\eta^2 = \frac{SS_{treatment}}{SS_{total}} = \frac{62.460}{186.918} = .334$$

An alternative calculation when you don't have access to the two sums of squares is given by

$$\eta^2 = \frac{1}{1 + \dfrac{df_{error}}{F \times df_{treatment}}}$$

For Giancola and Corman's data, 33.4% of the variation in aggression scores can be attributed to differences in the levels of the distractibility task and, therefore, presumably, to the degree to which the task focused subjects' attention away from the provocative stimuli. This is a reasonable amount of explained variation, reflecting the effectiveness of distraction task.

Percent Reduction in Error (PRE)

There is another way to look at η^2 that derives directly from the previous formula and has been recently viewed as a desirable feature of any measure of the magnitude of effect. In the terminology popularized by Judd and McClelland (1989) η^2 is the **Percent Reduction in Error (PRE)**. If we did not take group membership into account, the error associated with our recall scores would be SS_{total}, the variability of all 60 observations. But when we know which group a subject is in, the error associated with our predictions is reduced to SS_{error}, the average variation within groups. But the difference between SS_{total} and SS_{error} is $SS_{treatment}$. Thus $SS_{treatment}$ divided by SS_{total} is the percentage by which the error of our prediction has been *reduced* by considering group membership. In terms of our example, without attending to group membership we had 190.907 units of error. After attending to group membership we only have 124.458 units of error. Thus we have reduced our error by $186.918 - 124.458 = 62.460$ points, or by $62.460/189.918 = 33.4\%$.

It is important to realize that η^2 assumes that the true regression line passes through the individual treatment means. When the data are treated as a population, the assumption is correct. When the data are treated as a sample from some larger population, however, bias is introduced. Because these means are really sample means, they are subject to sampling error, and η^2 will be biased upward—whatever the *true* regression line through the population means, it will probably not pass exactly through each sample mean. Although all measures we discuss will be biased, η^2 is the most biased because of this assumption. Although η^2 has the advantage of simplicity and is intuitively appealing, you may prefer to use a less-biased estimate when our interest is in making general statements about our variables. If we are interested in making statements only about our particular set of data, or if we want a rough idea of the magnitude of the effect, then η^2 is a perfectly good measure. Moreover, η^2 and other, less-biased, measures converge as sample sizes increase.

Omega-Squared (ω^2)

omega-squared (ω^2)

An alternative, and for many purposes better, method of assessing the magnitude of the experimental effect with balanced (equal n's) or nearly balanced designs is **omega-squared (ω^2)**. The derivation of ω^2 is based on the underlying structural model that we discussed earlier, and there are two different formulae for ω^2, depending on whether the independent variable is fixed or random. A random independent variable is rare in one-way designs so we will ignore that version here, though it will become meaningful in the more complex designs in Chapters 13 and 14.

For the fixed-model analysis of variance, a relatively unbiased estimate of the magnitude of experimental effect is given by

$$\omega^2 = \frac{SS_{treat} - (k-1)MS_{error}}{SS_{total} + MS_{error}}$$

Applying this to our data from Table 11.2, we have

$$\omega^2 = \frac{SS_{treat} - (k-1)MS_{error}}{SS_{total} + MS_{error}} = \frac{62.460 - 4(2.26)}{189.918 + 2.26} = \frac{53.42}{187.658} = .285$$

The estimate of ω^2 in this case (.285) is somewhat less than the estimate of $\eta^2 = .334$, reflecting the fact that the latter is more biased.

Lane and Dunlap (1978) raise some important reservations about the routine reporting of magnitude measures and their interpretation in light of the fact that journals mainly publish studies with significant results. Cohen (1973) outlines some important considerations in the calculation and interpretation of magnitude measures. Although Cohen is primarily concerned with factorial designs (to be discussed in Chapter 13), the philosophy behind his comments is relevant even here. All the papers cited are clear and readable, and I recommend them.

d-Family Measures of Effect Size

root-mean-square standardized effect (RMSSE)

I will have much more to say about *d*-family measures of effect size in the next chapter, but here I want to briefly discuss a measure favored by Steiger (2004) called the **root-mean-square standardized effect (RMSSE)**. It is based on a logical measure of group differences and applies to the case of multiple groups. Moreover, it is nearly equivalent to the effect size that we will use in calculating power.

One measure of how much a particular group mean deviated from the overall grand mean would be

$$d_j = \frac{(\mu_j - \mu)}{\sigma}$$

Notice that this is simply a standardized difference between a specific mean and the grand mean, and is similar to, though not quite the same as, the *d* that we saw in Chapter 7. It is logical to average these measures over all groups, but we will need to square them first or the average would come out to be zero. This gives us a measure that can be written as

$$d = \sqrt{\left(\frac{1}{k-1}\right)\Sigma\left(\frac{\mu_j - \mu}{\sigma}\right)^2}$$

We divide by $(k - 1)$ instead of k to get the average because with a fixed variable the sum of the deviations from the grand mean must be 0. We have only $(k - 1)$ *df* from groups, and that is our divisor. The name for this statistic seems a bit awkward, but it is in fact a very accurate description. For each group we take the difference between its mean and the grand mean, and divided by the standard deviation. Therefore we have a standardized effect. We then square them and average them over all groups, so we have a mean squared standardized effect. Then we take the square root of the result to give us a root mean squared standardized effect. (I don't know why we have to say "root mean squared" when we really mean the square root of the mean, but I guess it sounds more impressive.)

The RMSSE is a logical measure of the effect size because it is a direct measure of the differences of the group means that has been standardized by dividing by the standard deviation.

For the Giancola and Corman study of alcohol and aggression, the means were

D0	D2	D4	D6	D8	Grand Mean
1.802	0.675	−0.912	0.544	1.889	0.800

The sum of the squared deviations from the grand mean is 5.5345 and the square root of MS_{error} is 2.26. Thus

$$d = \sqrt{\left(\frac{1}{k-1}\right)\Sigma\left(\frac{\mu_j - \mu}{\sigma}\right)^2} = \sqrt{\left(\frac{1}{k-1}\right)\frac{\Sigma(\mu_j - \mu)^2}{\sigma^2}} = \sqrt{\frac{1}{k-1}\left(\frac{\Sigma(\overline{X}_j - \overline{X}_{..})^2}{MS_{error}}\right)}$$

$$= \sqrt{\frac{5.205}{4(2.26)}} = \sqrt{.5758} = .759$$

Thus the group means differ, on average, by approximately 3/4 of a standard deviation from the grand mean, which is a considerable difference. (If you use the G*Power software, to be introduced in the next section, you will obtain almost exactly the same effect size, indicating that the authors of that software compute RMSSE.)

Steiger (2004) discusses setting confidence limits on this measure and provides free software (see his paper). Kelley (2008) provides similar software written as functions for R that do even more. (See the Web site for an example named CIonRMSSE.R.) Using such software we can show that the confidence limits on RMSSE for the Giancola and Corman experiment are $.378 \leq \delta \leq 1.038$. (I used δ in this expression because we are estimating a parameter.) The important thing about this result is that the lower limit on our 95% confidence interval is still approximately .40, meaning that we have a lower limit of about one half of a standard deviation as the average group difference. This suggests that we are talking about a substantial difference among groups. We will have more to say about such measures in the next chapter, but in that case we will focus on *pairs* of means rather than the complete set of means. In this chapter I have focused on measures that relate to differences among many groups simultaneously. I think that you will find in your research that it is specific group differences that are most important, and in that situation *d*-family measures have a distinct advantage.

11.12 Power

Estimating power in the analysis of variance is a straightforward extension of the power analysis for *t*, although the notation is different, as are the tables. Just as with *t*, we will define a statistic, phi prime (ϕ'), based on the expected differences among the μ_j, then derive a second statistic, phi (ϕ), which is a function of n and ϕ', and finally calculate power from tables of the **noncentral *F* distribution**. A more complete treatment of power can be found in Cohen (1988) and Koele (1982).

noncentral
F distribution

Discussions in the past have almost always calculated power from tables of the noncentral *F* distribution, but with a great deal of software currently available, we can largely ignore those tables and compute power directly. But to do so we still need to understand noncentrality parameters and related statistics. In what follows I have dropped the computations involving tables and focused on two different statistical programs (SPSS and G*Power) and a resampling technique.

Resampling for Power

One of the easiest ways to understand power for the one-way analysis of variance is to run a simple resampling study. It may seem strange to use the word "simple" for a process that draws samples perhaps 10,000 times, but that actually is simple. You can do it with SPSS or SAS, or you can use R.[8] The reason I discuss this approach, in addition to the fact that it makes clear what power represents, is that I am finding more and more research articles that use resampling in some way. And as time goes on that usage will only increase.

An Example

Earlier we considered a study by Conti and Musty (1984) on the effect of THC on behavior in rats. In Table 11.6 we used the data in the original units because that made for a good

---

[8] The necessary R code to solve this problem can be found at the book's Web site named ResamplingPower.R.

example of transformations. But Conti and Musty actually used the level of activity after a THC injection as a percentage of pre-injection activity. We will use these data here. The data file for Table 11.6 on the Web also contains a variable labeled "DV" and that is what we will use as our dependent variable.

The means for each condition follow.

Control	0.1μg	0.5μg	1μg	2μg	GM
34.00	50.80	60.33	48.50	38.10	46.346

The average sample variance (MS_{error}) was 240.345, which gives us an estimate of each group standard deviation as $\sqrt{240.345} = 15.503$.

We can set up a simple resampling study in which we draw random data for 5 groups from populations with means corresponding to our group means and standard deviation $= \sqrt{MS_{error}} = 15.503$. In other words we are taking sample statistics as if they are exact estimates of the corresponding parameters. We know that the critical value for F is 2.579. We repeat this process 10,000 times, each time recording the resulting F. The power of this experiment is now the percentage of times, out of 10,000, that the obtained F exceeds 2.579. That is virtually the definition of power. In our case the sampling took 1 minute and 12 seconds and the resulting probability was .9074. That is the power of our new study *if* the populations means and standard deviations are exactly equal to the ones that Conti and Musty found. That value for power is remarkably close to values we find by other means. (If we modify the study to have exactly 10 subjects in every group, the estimated power is .9206.)

We have just seen one way to calculate, and think about, power. There are others. An R package by Stéphane Champely called "pwr" can be downloaded from the cran.r-project.org Web site and computes power for the analysis of variance assuming equal sample sizes. For this example with 10 subjects per group, this program estimates power at .92065. You can't get much closer than that. Another way to calculate power is to use an add-on package for SPSS, which your university may have available, though mine does not, or to take the Conti and Musty data, run an analysis of variance in SPSS, and click on the "observed power" option. I think that it is a misnomer to call it "observed" power, but it is the power of the next experiment if the means and standard deviations have been exactly estimated. We will see how to use G*Power for this purpose shortly.

A Little Bit of Theory

Even though you can run the calculations just knowing the means, standard deviations, and sample sizes, you need to know about effect sizes and noncentrality parameters.

We already know that

$$\frac{E(MS_{treat})}{E(MS_{error})} = \frac{\sigma_e^2 + n\sum \tau_j^2/(k-1)}{\sigma_e^2}$$

If H_0 is true, $\sum \tau_j^2 = 0$ and the ratio becomes $F = MS_{treat}/MS_{error}$. It will be distributed as the usual (central) F distribution. The mean of this distribution is $df_{error}/(df_{error} - 2)$, which is very close to 1.00 for reasonable sample sizes. (See footnote, p. 336.) If H_0 is false, this ratio becomes

$$\frac{E(MS_{treat})}{E(MS_{error})} = 1 + \frac{n\sum \tau_j^2/(k-1)}{\sigma_e^2} = 1 + \frac{\lambda}{(k-1)}$$

where

$$\lambda = \frac{n \sum \tau_j^2}{\sigma_e^2}$$

lambda (λ)
noncentrality
parameter (ncp)

is called **lambda** (λ) or the **noncentrality parameter** (*ncp*).

You can see that the noncentrality parameter simply displaces the F distribution in a positive direction away from one, with the amount of displacement depending on the true differences among the population means. The noncentrality parameter tells us how much the F distribution has been displaced and is used by most computer software to generate power estimates. If we are expecting to replicate this experiment with 10 animals in each group, the noncentrality parameter would be

$$\lambda = \frac{n \Sigma \alpha_j^2}{MS_{\text{error}}} = \frac{10[(34.00 - 46.346)^2 + \cdots + (38.10 - 43.346)^2]}{240.345} = 18.329$$

Effect Size

For calculating power, most approaches begin with an effect size measure (denoted as ϕ' or f, depending on who is writing). This measure is simply the standard deviation of the expected population means divided by the expected within-cell variance, which we will estimate with MS_{error}. But we are treating Conti and Musty's sample variances as if they are population variances for the purpose of computing power, so we divide by the number of means, not the df for groups, in calculating their standard deviation. This leaves us with

$$\phi' = f = \sqrt{\frac{\Sigma \alpha_j^2 / k}{MS_{\text{error}}}} = \sqrt{\frac{[(34.00 - 46.346)^2 \cdots (38.10 - 43.346)^2]/5}{240.345}} = \sqrt{\frac{440.534/5}{240.345}}$$

$$= \sqrt{0.3666} = .605$$

Calculating Power Using G*Power

By far the best power calculator that I have come across is available free over the Internet at http://www.psycho.uni-duesseldorf.de/aap/projects/gpower/. It will do just about everything that you want and is being continually updated. Version 3.0, though much more powerful than version 2, does take some getting used to. Just play until you get the right answer. (Or start by downloading version 2.) We saw the use of G*Power in Chapter 8, but will expand on that here.

I have used G*Power to produce the following printout. Although the software makes it easy for me to deal with unequal sample sizes, I have used samples of size 10 for consistency. (In addition, I am predicting what will happen in a future experiment, and I would assume that I would at least try to have 10 subjects for each group.) G*Power bases its calculations on the average sample size anyway. The screen on the right in Exhibit 11.2 shows the results of calculating the effect size. I have specified that I want power for an analysis of variance and have entered the means and sample sizes for the five groups. The program automatically computes the effect size when I click on the "Calculate and transfer" button. In this case it is 0.6054, which is the same answer that we calculated earlier and labeled f or ϕ'. When we come to factorial analyses of variance in Chapter 13 we will need to calculate f directly. (The effect size is independent of the number of observations, so it is immaterial whether we take our unequal sample sizes into account at this point.) I then clicked on the "Calculate" button in the left window to calculate power. I requested that it calculate post-hoc power because I am using the actual sample means and error term from the Conti and Musty data.[9]

You will notice that the calculated power is .92066, which is exactly what we calculated earlier.

Koele (1982) presents methods for calculating the power of random models. Random models, while not particularly common in a one-way layout, are more common in higher-order designs and present particular problems because they generally have a low level of power. For these models, two random processes are involved—random sampling of participants and random sampling of treatment levels. As Koele phrased it, "Not only should there be many observations per level, but also many levels per treatment (independent variable). Experiments that have random factors with only two or three levels must be considered as absurd as *t* tests on samples with two or three observations" (p. 516). This is important advice to keep in mind when you are considering random models. We will say more about this in Chapter 13.

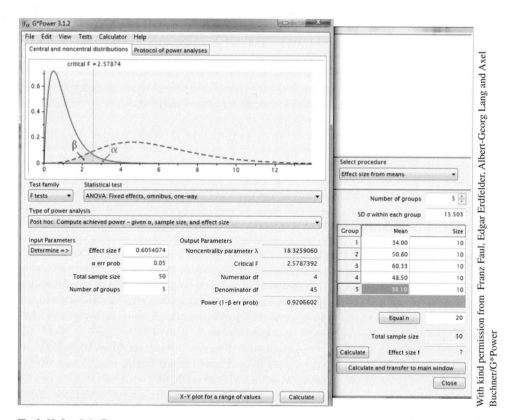

Exhibit 11.2   G*Power estimation of power for Conti and Musty experiment

With kind permission from Franz Faul, Edgar Erdfelder, Albert-Georg Lang and Axel Buchner/G*Power

---

[9] If I had been writing this software I would not have used the phrase "post-hoc power" here because it conveys different meanings to different people. What I am really doing is making parameter estimates from a previous study and using those estimates to calculate power. That is a very valid approach even among those, like me, who decry what is often labeled post-hoc power.

One final point should be made about power and design considerations. McClelland (1997) has argued persuasively that with fixed variables we often use far more levels of our independent variable than we need. For example, if McClelland were running the Giancola and Corman (2007) experiment on alcohol and aggression, I suspect that he would run only three groups (D0, D4, and D8). He would argue that to use five groups dilutes the effect across four degrees of freedom. Similarly, he would probably use only the 0, 0.5 μg, and 2 μg groups in the Conti and Musty (1984) study, putting the same number of subjects in the 0.5 μg group as in the other two conditions combined. I recommend this paper to those who are concerned about maximizing power and good experimental design. It is important and very readable.

11.13   Computer Analyses

Exhibit 11.3 contains printout for the SPSS analysis of Everitt's data on the treatment of anorexic girls. Instead of choosing the one-way procedures from Analyze/Compare Means/One-Way Anova, I have used the Analyze/General Linear Model/Univariate Procedure. (Menu selections are not shown, but they should be evident.) This is the procedure we will use in Chapters 13 and 14, and it produces the same answers as the oneway procedure. It also produces some output that will not be familiar to you, which is explained below.

Descriptive Statistics

Dependent Variable: WTGAIN

Treatment Group	Mean	Std. Deviation	N
Control	−.450000	7.988705	26
CogBehav	3.006897	7.308504	29
Family	7.264706	7.157421	17
Total	2.763889	7.983598	72

Tests of Between-Subjects Effects

Dependent Variable: WTGAIN

Source	Type III Sum of Squares	df	Mean Square	F	Sig.	Eta Squared	Noncent. Parameter	Observed Power[a]
Corrected Model	614.644[b]	2	307.322	5.422	.006	.136	10.845	.830
Intercept	732.075	1	732.075	12.917	.001	.158	12.917	.943
GROUP	614.644	2	307.322	5.422	.006	.136	10.845	.830
Error	3910.742	69	56.677					
Total	5075.400	72						
Corrected Total	4525.386	71						

[a] Computed using alpha =.05
[b] R Squared = .136 (Adjusted R Squared = .111)

Exhibit 11.3   SPSS general linear model analysis of Everitt's data on treatment of anorexia

Notice in the summary table that the first line is labeled "Corrected Model." If there were two or more independent variables (e.g., Group and Gender), then this line would represent the combined effects of those variables. Because there is only one independent variable, the Model and the Group effects will be exactly the same.

The line labeled "Intercept" refers to a test on the null hypothesis that the grand mean is equal to 0 in the population. We very rarely care about this test, although in this case it is a test of a meaningful question about whether the girls in this study, averaged across groups, gained any weight.

The lines labeled "Group", "Error", and "Corrected total" are the same as the results we saw in Exhibit 11.1.

Notice that the entry of eta-squared for the Group effect is the same as the "R-squared" given at the bottom of the table. This tells us that 14% of the variation in weight gain could be attributable to differences between treatments.

SPSS then calculates "observed power" (a misnomer), treating the obtained means as parameters, and the obtained MS_{error} as an accurate estimate of the population variance. Because there are unequal sample sizes in this example, you will have difficulty reproducing these values exactly.

Key Terms

Analysis of variance (ANOVA) (Introduction)

One-way analysis of variance (Introduction)

Structural model (11.2)

Homogeneity of variance (11.2)

Homoscedasticity (11.2)

Error variance (11.2)

Heterogeneity of variance (11.2)

Heteroscedasticity (11.2)

MS_{error} (11.3)

MS_{within} (11.3)

$MS_{treatment}$ (11.3)

Treatment effect (11.3)

Expected value (11.3)

Sums of squares (11.4)

SS_{total} (11.4)

SS_{treat} (11.4)

SS_{error} (11.4)

Summary table (11.4)

df_{total} (11.4)

df_{treat} (11.4)

df_{error} (11.4)

Balanced designs (11.7)

Missing at random (11.7)

Heavy-tailed distributions (11.9)

Winsorized samples (11.9)

Resampling Statistics (11.9)

Replicate (11.10)

Fixed-model analysis of variance (11.10)

Random-model analysis of variance (11.10)

Magnitude of the experimental effect (11.11)

Eta-squared (η^2) (11.11)

Correlation ratio (11.11)

Percent reduction in error (PRE) (11.11)

Omega-squared (ω^2) (11.11)

Root-mean-squared standardized effect (RMSSE) (11.11)

Noncentral F distribution (11.12)

Lambda (λ) (11.12)

Noncentrality Parameter (ncp) (11.12)

Exercises

11.1   Eysenck (1974) ran a study in which participants were required to recall a list of words. The conditions varied in terms of whether subjects simply counted the number of letters in a word, thought of a rhyming word, thought of an appropriate adjective, created images of the word, or was told to study the words for later recall. The dependent variable was the number of words recalled on a test trial. These data are shown below.

	Counting	Rhyming	Adjective	Imagery	Intentional	Total
	9	7	11	12	10	
	8	9	13	11	19	
	6	6	8	16	14	
	8	6	6	11	5	
	10	6	14	9	10	
	4	11	11	23	11	
	6	6	13	12	14	
	5	3	13	10	15	
	7	8	10	19	11	
	7	7	11	11	11	
Mean	7.00	6.90	11.00	13.40	12.00	10.06
St. Dev.	1.83	2.13	2.49	4.50	3.74	4.01
Variance	3.33	4.54	6.22	20.27	14.00	16.058

© Cengage Learning 2013

Run a one-way analysis of variance on these data.

11.2   Refer to Exercise 11.3. Now run an analysis of variance on treatments 1 and 2 combined compared with treatments 3 and 4 combined. What hypothesis are we testing?

11.3   Another way of looking at the data from Eysenck's (1974) study is to compare four groups of subjects. One group consisted of Younger subjects who were presented the words to be recalled in a condition that elicited a Low level of processing. A second group involved Younger subjects who were given a task requiring the Highest level of processing (as in Exercise 11.4). The two other groups were Older subjects who were given tasks requiring either Low or High levels of processing. The data follow.

Younger/Low:	8	6	4	6	7	6	5	7	9	7
Younger/High:	21	19	17	15	22	16	22	22	18	21
Older/Low:	9	8	6	8	10	4	6	5	7	7
Older/High:	10	19	14	5	10	11	14	15	11	11

a.   Run a one-way analysis of variance on these data.

b.   Now run a one-way analysis of variance on treatments 1 and 3 combined ($n = 20$) versus treatments 2 and 4 combined. What question are you answering?

c.   Why might your answer to part (b) be difficult to interpret?

11.4   Another aspect of the study by Eysenck (1974), referred to in Exercise 11.1, compared Younger and Older subjects on their ability to recall material in the face of instructions telling them that they would be asked to memorize the material for later recall—the Intentional group. (Presumably this task required a high level of processing.) The data follow, where the dependent variable is the number of items recalled.

Younger:	21	19	17	15	22	16	22	22	18	21
Older:	10	19	14	5	10	11	14	15	11	11

a.   Run the analysis of variance comparing the means of these two groups.

b.   Run an independent group's t test on the data and compare the results to those you obtained in part (a).

11.5 Refer to Exercise 11.4. Suppose that we collected additional data and had two more subjects in the Younger group, with scores of 13 and 15.

    a.   Rerun the analysis of variance.

    b.   Run an independent groups t test without pooling the variances.

    c.   Run an independent groups t test after pooling the variances.

    d.   For (b) and (c), which of these values of t corresponds (after squaring) to the F in (a)?

11.6 What would happen if the sample sizes in Exercise 11.10a were twice as large as they actually were, but all other statistics remained the same?

11.7 Calculate η^2 and ω^2 for the data in Exercise 11.3.

11.8 Calculate η^2 and ω^2 for the data in Exercise 11.4. Would you assume a fixed or a random model?

11.9 Calculate η^2 and ω^2 for the data in Exercise 11.10 and interpret the results.

11.10 Foa, Rothbaum, Riggs, and Murdock (1991) conducted a study evaluating four different types of therapy for rape victims. The Stress inoculation therapy (SIT) group received instructions on coping with stress. The Prolonged exposure (PE) group went over the events in their minds repeatedly. The Supportive counseling (SC) group was taught a general problem-solving technique. Finally, the Waiting list (WL) control group received no therapy. The data follow, where the dependent variable was the severity rating of a series of symptoms.

Group	n	Mean	S.D.
SIT	14	11.07	3.95
PE	10	15.40	11.12
SC	11	18.09	7.13
WL	10	19.50	7.11

    a.   Run the analysis of variance, ignoring any problems with heterogeneity of variance, and draw whatever conclusions are warranted.

    b.   Apply Welch's procedure for heterogeneous variances. Does this affect your conclusions?

    c.   Draw a graph showing the means of the four groups.

    d.   What does rejection of H_0 mean in this case?

11.11 Reanalyze the data in Table 11.1 for the Giancola study using a logarithmic transformation. What effect does that transformation have?

11.12 Write an appropriate statistical model for Exercise 11.4.

11.13 Write an appropriate statistical model for Exercise 11.1.

11.14 The data for Exercise 11.10 can be found on the Web site at Ex11.12.dat. Run that analysis using SPSS or other software, and include tests for heterogeneity of variance and Welch's modification to allow for heterogeneity of variance. How does this result compare to your answer to Exercise 11.10b?

11.15 Write an appropriate statistical model for Exercise 11.3. Save it for later use in Chapter 13.

11.16 Run the analysis of variance for the transformed data you obtained in Exercise 11.19.

11.17 Howell and Huessy (1981) classified children as exhibiting (or not exhibiting) attention deficit disorder (ADD)-related behaviors in second, fourth, and fifth grade. The subjects were then sorted on the basis of the year(s) in which the individuals were classed as exhibiting such behavior. They then looked at GPA for these children when the latter were in high school. The data are given in terms of mean GPA per group.

	Never ADD	Second Only	Fourth Only	Second and Fourth
Mean	2.6774	1.6123	1.9975	2.0287
S.D.	0.9721	1.0097	0.7642	0.5461
n	201	13	12	8

	Fifth Only	Second and Fifth	Fourth and Fifth	Second, Fourth, and Fifth
Mean	1.7000	1.9000	1.8986	1.4225
S.D.	0.8788	1.0318	0.3045	0.5884
n	14	9	7	8

© Cengage Learning 2013

Run the analysis of variance and draw the appropriate conclusion.

11.18 When F is less than 1, we usually write "<1" rather than the actual value. What meaning can be attached to an F appreciably less than 1? Can we speak intelligently about an F "significantly" less than 1? Include $E(MS)$ in your answer.

11.19 Apply a square-root transformation to the data in Table 11.6.

11.20 Rerun the analysis of Exercise 11.17, leaving out the Never ADD group. In what way does this analysis clarify the interpretation of the data?

11.21 Calculate η^2 and ω^2 for the data in Exercise 11.17.

11.22 Would a transformation of the data in Table 11.2 be useful in terms of equalizing the variances? What transformation would you suggest applying, if any?

11.23 In Exercise 11.24 the data were transformed from their original units, which were in seconds. What effect would this have on the shape of the distributions?

11.24 Darley and Latané (1968) recorded the speed with which subjects summoned help for a person in trouble. Subjects thought either that they were the only one listening to the person (Group 1, $n = 13$), that one other person was listening (Group 2, $n = 26$), or that four other people were listening (Group 3, $n = 13$). The dependent variable was the speed with which the person summoned help ($= 1/\text{time} \times 100$). The mean speed scores for the three groups were 0.87, 0.72, and 0.51, respectively. The MS_{error} was 0.053. Reconstruct the analysis of variance summary table. What can you conclude?

11.25 Suppose that we wanted to run a study comparing recall of nouns and verbs. We present each subject with 25 nouns or 25 verbs and later ask for recall of the list. We look at both differences between parts of speech and between different words within the category of "noun." What variable is a fixed variable and what is probably a random variable?

11.26 Use the data in Epinuneq.dat to run three separate one-way analyses of variance, one at each retention interval. In each case, test the null hypothesis that the three dosage means are equal. Have your statistical package print out the means and standard deviations of the three dosage groups for each analysis. Now run a separate analysis testing the hypotheses that the three Interval means are equal. In this case you will simply ignore Dosage.

11.27 Davey, Startup, Zara, MacDonald, and Field (2003) were interested in the role of mood on the degree of compulsive checking in which a person engaged. (Compulsive checking is involved in a number of psychopathologies.) Three groups of 10 participants each listened to music designed to induce positive, negative, or neutral mood. They were then asked to "list as many things around your home that you should check for safety or security reasons before you go away for three weeks." The dependent variable was the number of things listed. The actual data follow.

Induced Mood

Negative	Positive	None
7	9	8
5	12	5
16	7	11
13	3	9
13	10	11
24	4	10
20	5	11
10	4	10
11	7	7
7	9	5

© Cengage Learning 2013

a. Run the appropriate analysis of variance and draw you own conclusion.

b. Which column means would you be interested in comparing for theoretical reasons when we to discussing multiple comparisons in the next chapter?

11.28 Give an example of a study in which the main independent variable would be a random variable.

11.29 On the reasonable assumption that there are no important differences from one interval to the next, combine the data by ignoring the Interval variable and run the analysis of variance on Dosage. Use the data in Epinuneq.dat. (You will have 42 observations for the 0.0 and 0.3 mg/kg doses and 37 subjects for the 1.0 mg/kg dose.)

11.30 In Exercise 7.48 you had data on students who had lost a parent through death, who came from a divorced household, or who grew up with two parents. You then ran three separate *t* tests comparing those groups.

a. Now reanalyze those data using an analysis of variance with GSIT as the dependent variable.

b. How does your answer to this question differ from your answer in Chapter 7?
Use the following material to answer Exercises 11.26, 11.29 and 11.31.

Introini-Collison and McGaugh (1986) examined the hypothesis that hormones normally produced in the body can play a role in memory. Specifically, they looked at the effect of post-training injections of epinephrine on retention of a previously learned discrimination. To oversimplify the experiment, they first trained mice to escape mild shock by choosing the left arm of a Y maze. Immediately after training they injected the mice with either 0.0, 0.3, or 1.0 mg/kg of epinephrine. (The first group was actually injected with saline.) They predicted that low doses of epinephrine would facilitate retention, whereas high doses would inhibit it.

Either 1 day, 1 week, or 1 month after original training, each mouse was again placed in the Y maze, but this time was required to run to the right arm of the maze to escape shock. Presumably the stronger the memory of the original training, the more it would interfere with the learning of this new task and the more errors the subject would make.

There are two data sets for this experiment, and they are described in Appendix Computer Data Sets. The original study used 18 animals in the three dosage groups tested after 1 day, and 12 animals in each group tested after intervals of 1 week and 1 month. Hypothetical data that closely reproduce the original results are contained in Epinuneq.dat, although for our purposes there are data for only 7 subjects in the 1.0 mg/kg dose at the 1-month test. A second data set was created with 12 observations in each of the 9 cells, and is called Epineq. dat. In both cases the need to create data that were integers led to results that are slightly conservative relative to the actual data, but the conclusions with respect to H_0 are the same.

11.31 Rerun Exercise 11.29, this time using Epineq.dat. (The results will differ somewhat because the data are different.) Calculate the average of the three error terms (MS_{error}) and show that this is equal to the average of the variances within each of the nine groups in the experiment. Save this value to use in Chapter 13.

11.32 Strayer, Drews, & Couch (2006) ran a study in which they compared the driving behavior of a control group, a group that was at the legal limit for alcohol, and a group that was talking on a cell phone. I have modified their study slightly to make it suitable for this chapter, but the results are consistent with theirs. The three groups are given below (the data are available on the Web site for this book at Ex11-32.dat).

Control:

808 757 773 937 726 788 806 792 751 765 853 655 626 721 630 722 683 709

718 812 703 791 586 864 737 701 799 844 639 705 822 935 842 827 784 838

795 823 791 819

Alcohol:

631 656 621 706 937 538 947 855 661 887 750 945 663 880 873 830 751 855

815 593 666 730 1021 906 821 956 606 660 802 961 629 603 826 531 828 959

743 745 922 829

Cell Phone:

909 712 805 852 859 781 841 822 740 910 900 912 863 785 863 809 927 847 918 810 788
929 798 863 981 842 1021 827 876 736 640 851 787 703 942 758 843 781 969 872

From these data is there evidence that cell phones lead to longer reaction times than baseline conditions? How does the cell phone condition differ from the alcohol-impaired condition?

11.33 Gouzoulis-Mayfrank et al. (2000) examined task performance of users of the drug Ecstacy and compared that with a group of Cannibis users and a control group of Nonusers. There were 28 participants in each group, and the Ecstacy users were almost all users of Cannibis as well. Performance was evaluated on several different tasks, but we will focus on a test of abstract thinking. The data given below were created to have the same means and variances as in the original study, and higher scores represent better performance. The data are available on the Web site as Ex11-33.dat.

Ecstacy: 25 25 23 32 21 28 34 26 23 22 26 21 29 28

23 24 29 23 30 18 25 25 25 25 32 23 29 32

Control: 29 31 31 25 33 21 18 40 35 32 29 31 25 32

33 34 28 28 25 22 27 34 38 31 30 31 26 30

Cannibis: 28 28 28 29 37 34 27 25 34 28 25 27 30 29 31 32

30 29 32 25 32 31 32 22 31 25 28 34

a. Run an analysis of variance comparing the means of the three groups.

b. Calculate Cohen's d to examine the pairwise effect sizes—in other words, calculate d on the comparison of each group with each of the other groups.

c. What is a reasonable set of conclusions from this study?

Discussion Questions

11.34 With four groups you could have the means equally spaced along some continuum, or you could have three means approximately equal to each other and a fourth one different, or you could have two means approximately equal but different from two other approximately equal means, or some other pattern. Using very simple data that you create yourself (holding within-groups variance constant), how does the F statistic vary as a function of the pattern of means?

11.35 In the study by Conti and Musty (1984) on the effects of THC on activity, the means clearly do not increase linearly with dosage. What effect, if any, should this have on any magnitude-of-effect measure?

11.36 Some experimenters have a guilty conscience whenever they transform data. Construct a reasoned argument why transformations are generally perfectly acceptable.

11.37 Linda Teri and her colleagues (Teri, 1997) examined nonpharmacological treatments of patients with Alzheimer's disease suffering from depression. They had two behavioral treatments, one emphasizing pleasant events (BT-PE) and the other emphasizing caregiver problem solving (BT-PS). They also had a typical care group (TCC) and a waiting-list control group (WLC). The dependent variable was the change in depression, as measured by the Hamilton Depression Rating Scale, from the beginning of treatment to the end (higher numbers represent more improvement.) The data are available on the Web site at www.uvm.edu/~dhowell/methods8/DataFiles/Teri.dat. They were generated to have approximately the same means and variances as the original, with a reasonable estimate of the correlation between pre- and post-test scores. We will return to these data in Chapter 14. What conclusions can you draw from these data?

Chapter 12

Multiple Comparisons Among Treatment Means

Objectives

To extend the analysis of variance by examining ways of making comparisons within a set of means.

Contents

A SIGNIFICANT F IN AN ANALYSIS OF VARIANCE is simply an indication that not all the population means are equal. It does not tell us which means are different from other means. As a result, the overall analysis of variance often raises more questions than it answers. We now face the problem of examining differences among individual means, or sets of means, for the purpose of isolating significant differences or testing specific hypotheses. We want to make statements of the form $\mu_1 = \mu_2 = \mu_3$, and $\mu_4 = \mu_5$, but the first three means are different from the last two, and all of them are different from μ_6.

Many different techniques for making comparisons among means are available, and the list grows each year. Here we will limit coverage to only the most common and useful ones. A thorough discussion of this topic can be found in Hochberg and Tamhane (1987) and Toothaker (1991). Keselman, Holland, and Cribbie (2005) offer an excellent review of some of the newer methods. The papers by Games (1978a, 1978b) are also helpful, as is the paper by Games and Howell (1976) on the treatment of unequal sample sizes.

It may be helpful to the reader to understand how this chapter has changed through various editions. The changes largely reflect the way people look at experimental results and focus on the most useful procedures. Originally this chapter covered a few of the most common test procedures and left it at that. Then as time went on I kept adding to the number of procedures and focused at length on ways to make many individual comparisons among means. But in this edition I am returning to covering only a few test procedures, which are the ones that almost everyone now uses. I am also emphasizing the fact that we should direct our attention to those differences we really care about and not fill our results section with all of the other differences that we can test but don't actually care about. This philosophy carries over to calculating effect sizes and selecting appropriate error terms. If you are interested in a few specific comparisons, then taking a standard multiple comparison test such as Tukey's (which is an excellent test for the purpose for which it was designed) and testing every conceivable pairwise null hypothesis is a very poor idea. It wastes power, it often leads to the use of inappropriate error terms, it gives poor measures of effect size, and generally confuses what is often a clear and simple set of results. The fact that you are able to do something is rarely a sufficient reason for actually doing it. I will cover Tukey's test because it is such a commonly used approach, but I think that it is more in line with Tukey's general approach to statistics to lay the main emphasis elsewhere.

12.1   Error Rates

The major issue in any discussion of multiple-comparison procedures is the question of the probability of Type I errors. Most differences among alternative techniques result from different approaches to the question of how to control these errors. The problem is in part technical, but it is really much more a subjective question of how you want to define the error rate and how large you are willing to let the maximum possible error rate be.

Here we will distinguish two basic ways of specifying error rates, or the probability of Type I errors.[1] (Later we will discuss an alternative view of error rates called the False Discovery Rate, which has received a lot of attention in the last few years.) In doing so, we shall use the terminology that has become more or less standard since an extremely important unpublished paper by Tukey in 1953. (See also Ryan, 1959; O'Neil and Wetherill, 1971.)

---

[1] There is another error rate called the error rate per experiment (*PE*), which is the expected *number* of Type I errors in a set of comparisons. The error rate per experiment is not a probability, and we typically do not attempt to control it directly. We can easily calculate it, however, as $PE = c\alpha$, where c is the number of comparisons and α is the per comparison error rate.

Error Rate Per Comparison (*PC*)

error rate per
comparison (*PC*)

We have used the **error rate per comparison** (*PC*) in the past and it requires little elaboration. It is the probability of making a Type I error on any given comparison. If, for example, we make a comparison by running a *t* test between two groups and we reject the null hypothesis because our *t* exceeds $t_{.05}$, then we are working at a per comparison error rate of .05.

Familywise Error Rate (*FW*)

When we have completed running a set of comparisons among our group means, we will arrive at a set (often called a *family*) of conclusions. For example, the family might consist of the statements

$\mu_1 < \mu_2$

$\mu_3 < \mu_4$

$\mu_1 < (\mu_3 + \mu_4)/2$

familywise error
rate (*FW*)

The probability that this family of conclusions will contain *at least* one Type I error is called the **familywise error rate** (*FW*).[2] Many of the procedures we will examine are specifically directed at controlling the *FW* error rate, and even those procedures that are not intended to control *FW* are still evaluated with respect to what the level of *FW* is likely to be.

In an experiment in which only one comparison is made, both error rates will be the same. As the number of comparisons increases, however, the two rates diverge. If we let α' represent the error rate for any one comparison and c represent the number of comparisons, then

Error rate per comparison (*PC*): $\alpha = \alpha'$

Familywise error rate (*FW*): $\alpha = 1 - (1 - \alpha')^c$
(if comparisons are independent)

If the comparisons are not independent, the per comparison error rate remains unchanged, but the familywise rate is affected. In most situations, however, $1 - (1 - \alpha')^c$ still represents a reasonable approximation to *FW*. It is worth noting that the limits on *FW* are $PC \leq FW \leq c\alpha$; in most reasonable cases *FW* is in the general vicinity of $c\alpha$. This fact becomes important when we consider the Bonferroni tests.

The Null Hypothesis and Error Rates

Until now we have been speaking as if the null hypothesis in question is what is usually called the *complete, or omnibus, null hypothesis* ($\mu_1 = \mu_2 = \mu_3 = \cdots = \mu_k$). This is the null hypothesis tested by the overall analysis of variance. In many, if not most, experiments, however, nobody is seriously interested in the complete null hypothesis; rather, people are concerned about a few more restricted null hypotheses, such as ($\mu_1 = \mu_2 = \mu_3$, $\mu_4 = \mu_5$, $\mu_6 = \mu_7$), with differences among the various subsets. If this is the case, the problem becomes more complex, and it is not always possible to specify *FW* without knowing the pattern of population means. We will need to take this into account in designating the error rates for the different tests we shall discuss.

---

[2] This error rate is frequently referred to, especially in older sources, as the "experimentwise" error rate. However, Tukey's term "familywise" has become more common. In more complex analyses of variance, the experiment often may be thought of as comprising several different families of comparisons.

A Priori versus Post Hoc Comparisons

**a priori
comparisons**

**post hoc
comparisons**

In the earlier editions of this book I carefully followed tradition and distinguished between **a priori comparisons**, which are chosen before the data are collected, and **post hoc comparisons**, which are planned after the experimenter has collected the data, looked at the means, and noted which of the latter are far apart and which are close together. This is a traditional distinction, but one that seems to be less and less important to people who run such comparisons. In practice the real distinction seems to come down to the difference between deliberately making a few comparisons that are chosen because of their theoretical or practical nature (and not just because the means looked different) and making comparisons among all possible pairs of means. I am going to continue to make the a priori/post hoc distinction because it organizes the material nicely and is referred to frequently, but keep in mind that the distinction is a rather fuzzy one.

To take an example that you have already seen, we will return to the study by Foa, Rothbaum, Riggs, and Murdock (1991), which formed Exercise 11.10 in the preceding chapter. Foa et al. (1991) conducted a study evaluating four different types of therapy for rape victims. The Stress Inoculation Therapy (SIT) group received instructions on coping with stress. The Prolonged Exposure (PE) group went over the events in their minds repeatedly. The Supportive Counseling (SC) group was taught a general problem-solving technique. Finally, the Waiting List (WL) control group received no therapy.

Suppose you ran that study and your real goal was to compare Stress Inoculation Therapy (SIT) with Prolonged Exposure (PE), and you also wanted to check that these two therapies considered as a set were more effective than the two control conditions (SC and WL). But then suppose that you looked at your results and found that SC, which you expected to be quite ineffective, appeared to do much better than the Waiting List control. That is a comparison that you never planned to make, but it looks as if you should. So what do you do? That is no longer a simple question. The first two comparisons are clearly a priori—that's why you ran the study. But the third comparison is post hoc—you weren't intending to make it until you saw the results. The traditional answer is to use a post hoc test to make all pairwise comparisons. Otherwise you risk making a Type I error just because of the unusual difference between the control groups. An alternative approach, not as well grounded in theory, would be to treat this last comparison as a priori as well but to be a bit cautious if it comes out to be significant, especially if the probability is near your critical cutoff. We will consider both approaches in what follows.

It is important to realize that when we speak of a priori tests, we commonly mean a relatively small set of comparisons. If you are making *all* possible pairwise comparisons among several means, for example, it won't make any difference whether that was planned in advance or not. (I would wonder, however, if you really wanted to make all possible comparisons.)

Significance of the Overall *F*

Some controversy surrounds the question of whether one should insist that the overall *F* on treatments be significant before conducting multiple comparisons between individual group means. In the past, the general advice was that without a significant group effect, individual comparisons were inappropriate. In fact, the rationale underlying the error rates for Fisher's least significant different test, to be discussed in Section 12.4, required overall significance.

However, this is a case where the general advice is wrong. The logic behind most of our multiple comparison procedures does not require overall significance before making specific comparisons. First of all, the hypotheses tested by the overall test and a multiple-comparison test are quite different, with quite different levels of power. For example, the overall F actually distributes differences among groups across the number of degrees of freedom for groups. This has the effect of diluting the overall F in the situation where several group means are equal to each other but different from some other mean. Second, requiring overall significance will actually change the FW, making the multiple comparison tests conservative. The tests were designed, and their significance levels established, without regard to the overall F.

Wilcox (1987a) has considered this issue and suggested that "there seems to be little reason for applying the (overall) F test at all" (p. 36). Wilcox would jump straight to multiple-comparisons without even computing the F. Others have said much the same thing. That position may have seemed a bit extreme in the past, though it does emphasize the point. However, it does not seem as extreme today as it did 20 years ago. If you recognize that typical multiple-comparison procedures do not require a significant overall F, you will examine group differences regardless of the value of that F. Why, then, do we even need that F except to provide a sense of closure? The only reason I can think of is "tradition," and that is a powerful force. You would need to go as far as calculating MS_{error} anyway, so you might as well take the extra step and calculate the omnibus F.

12.2   Multiple Comparisons in a Simple Experiment on Morphine Tolerance

In discussing the various procedures, it will be helpful to have a data set to which each of the approaches can be applied. We will take as an example a study similar to an important experiment on morphine tolerance by Siegel (1975). Although the data are fictitious and a good deal of liberty has been taken in describing the conditions, the means (and the significance of the differences among the means) are the same as those in Siegel's paper. It will be necessary to describe this study in some detail, but the example is worth the space required. It will be to your advantage to take the time to understand the hypotheses and the treatment labels.

Morphine is a drug that is frequently used to alleviate pain. Repeated administrations of morphine, however, lead to morphine tolerance, in which morphine has less and less of an effect (pain reduction) over time. (You may have experienced the same thing if you eat spicy food very often. You will find that the more you eat it, the hotter you have to make it to taste the way it did when you started.) A common experimental task that demonstrates morphine tolerance involves placing a rat on an uncomfortably warm surface. When the heat becomes too uncomfortable, the rat will lick its paws, and the latency of the paw-lick is used as a measure of the rat's sensitivity to pain. A rat that has received a single morphine injection typically shows a longer paw-lick latency, indicating a reduced pain sensitivity. The development of morphine tolerance is indicated by a progressive shortening of paw-lick latencies (indicating increased sensitivity, or decreased insensitivity) with repeated morphine injections.

Siegel noted that there are a number of situations involving drugs other than morphine in which *conditioned* (learned) drug responses are opposite in direction to the unconditioned (natural) effects of the drug. For example, an animal injected with atropine will usually show a marked decrease in salivation. However if physiological saline (which should have no effect whatsoever) is suddenly injected (*in the same physical setting*) after repeated injections of atropine, the animal will show an *increase* in salivation. It is as if the animal were compensating for the anticipated effect of atropine. In such studies, it appears that a learned compensatory mechanism develops over trials and counterbalances the effect of the drug. (You experience the same thing if you leave the seasoning out of food that you normally add seasoning to. It will taste unusually bland, though the Grape Nuts you eat for breakfast does not taste bland—and I hope that you don't put seasoning on Grape Nuts.)

Siegel theorized that such a process might help to explain morphine tolerance. He reasoned that if you administered a series of pretrials in which the animal was injected with morphine and placed on a warm surface, morphine tolerance would develop. Thus, if you again injected the subject with morphine on a subsequent test trial, the animal would be only as sensitive to pain as would a naive animal (one who had never received morphine) because of the tolerance that has fully developed. Siegel further reasoned that if on the test trial you instead injected the animal with physiological saline *in the same test setting as the normal morphine injections*, the conditioned hypersensitivity that results from the repeated administration of morphine would not be counterbalanced by the presence of morphine, and the animal would show very short paw-lick latencies and heighten sensitivity. Siegel also reasoned that if you gave the animal repeated morphine injections in one setting but then tested it with morphine in a *new* setting, the new setting would not elicit the conditioned compensatory hypersensitivity to counterbalance the morphine. As a result, the animal would respond as would an animal that was being injected for the first time. Heroin is a morphine derivative. Imagine a heroin addict who is taking large doses of heroin because he has built up tolerance to it. If his response to this now large dose were suddenly that of a first-time (instead of a tolerant) user, because of a change of setting, the result could be, and often is, lethal. We're talking about a serious issue here, and drug overdoses often occur in novel settings.

You may think that an experiment conducted 30 years ago, which is before most of the readers of this book were born, is too old to be interesting. But a quick search of Google will reveal a great many recent studies that have derived directly from Siegel's early work. A particularly interesting one by Mann-Jones, Ettinger, Baisden, and Baisden has shown that a drug named Dextromethorphan can counteract morphine tolerance. That becomes interesting when you learn that Dextromethorphan is an important ingredient in cough syrup. This suggests that heroin addicts don't want to take cough syrup any more than they want to administer heroin in novel environments. The study can be found at www.eou.edu/psych /re/morphinetolerance.doc.

Our version of Siegel's experiment is based on the predictions just outlined. The experiment involved five groups of rats. Each group received four trials, but the data for the analysis come from only the critical fourth (test) trial. The groups are designated by indicating the treatment on the first three trials and then the treatment on the fourth trial. Group M-M received morphine on the first three trials in the test setting and then again on the fourth trial in the same test setting. This is the standard morphine-tolerant group, and, because morphine tolerance develops very quickly, we would expect to see normal, or at least near-normal, levels of pain sensitivity by that fourth trial. Group M-S received morphine on the first three trials but then received saline on the fourth trial (in the same test setting). These animals would be expected to be hypersensitive to the pain stimulus because the conditioned hypersensitivity would not be balanced by any compensating effects of morphine. Group M(cage)-M (abbreviated Mc-M) received morphine on the first three trials in their home cage but then received morphine on the fourth trial in the standard test setting, which was new to them. For this group, cues originally associated with morphine injection were not present on the test trial, and therefore, according to Siegel's model, the animals should not exhibit morphine tolerance on that trial. The fourth group (group S-M) received saline on the first three trials (in the test setting) and morphine on the fourth trial. These animals would be expected to show the least sensitivity to pain because there has been no opportunity for morphine tolerance to develop. Finally, group S-S received saline on all four trials.

Table 12.1   Data and analysis on morphine tolerance

(a) Data

	M-S	M-M	S-S	S-M	Mc-M
	3	2	14	29	24
	5	12	6	20	26
	1	13	12	36	40
	8	6	4	21	32
	1	10	19	25	20
	1	7	3	18	33
	4	11	9	26	27
	9	19	21	17	30
Mean	4.00	10.00	11.00	24.00	29.00
St. Dev	3.16	5.13	6.72	6.37	6.16

(b) Summary Table

Source	df	SS	MS	F
Treatment	4	3497.60	874.40	27.33*
Error	35	1120.00	32.00	
Total	39	4617.60		

*$P < .05$

© Cengage Learning 2013

If Siegel's model is correct, group S-M should show the longest latencies (indicating least sensitivity), whereas group M-S should show the shortest latency (most sensitivity). Group Mc-M should resemble group S-M, because cues associated with group Mc-M's first three trials would not be present on the test trial. Groups M-M and S-S should be intermediate. Whether group M-M will be equal to group S-S will depend on the rate at which morphine tolerance develops. The pattern of anticipated results is

$$S\text{-}M = Mc\text{-}M > M\text{-}M \ ? \ S\text{-}S > M\text{-}S$$

The "?" indicates no prediction. The dependent variable is the latency (in seconds) of paw-licking.

The results of this experiment, which closely follow Siegel's results, are presented in Table 12.1a, and the overall analysis of variance is presented in Table 12.1b. Notice that the within-group variances are more or less equal (a test for heterogeneity of variance was not significant), and there are no obvious outliers. The overall analysis of variance is clearly significant, indicating differences among the five treatment groups.

Magnitude of Effect

We can calculate η^2 for these data as $SS_{\text{treat}} / SS_{\text{total}} = 3497.60/4617.60 = .76$, indicating that treatment differences account for 76% of the variation in the study. A nearly unbiased estimate would be ω^2, which would be

$$\omega^2 = \frac{SS_{\text{treat}} - (k-1)MS_{\text{error}}}{SS_{\text{total}} + MS_{\text{error}}} = \frac{3497.60 - 4(32)}{4617.60 + 32} = \frac{3369.6}{4649.6} = 0.72$$

Both estimates indicate that group treatment differences account for a very substantial proportion of the variation in this study.

12.3 A Priori Comparisons

There are two reasons for starting our discussion with a priori comparisons and *t* tests. In the first place, standard *t* tests between pairs of means can be a perfectly legitimate method of comparison. Second, the basic formula for *t*, and minor modifications on it, are applicable to a large number of procedures (a priori and post hoc), and a review at this time is useful.

contrasts

As we have seen, a priori comparisons (also called **contrasts**) are planned before the data have been collected. There are several different kinds of a priori comparison procedures, and we will discuss them in turn.

Multiple *t* Tests

One of the simplest methods of running preplanned comparisons is to use individual *t* tests between pairs of groups. In running individual *t* tests, if the assumption of homogeneity of variance is tenable, we usually replace the individual variances, or the pooled variance estimate, with MS_{error} from the overall analysis of variance and evaluate the *t* on df_{error} degrees of freedom. When the variances are heterogeneous but the sample sizes are equal, we do not use MS_{error}, but instead use the individual sample variances and evaluate *t* on $2(n - 1)$ degrees of freedom. Finally, when we have heterogeneity of variance and unequal sample sizes, we use the individual variances and correct the degrees of freedom using the Welch–Satterthwaite approach (see Chapter 7). (In Chapter 7 we saw that Hayes and Cai (2007) argued against the basic idea of pooling variances when running *t* tests on independent means. However, when we have an analysis of variance with several groups, we lose a considerable amount of power by using the variance estimates from only the groups in question. If the sample variances appear to be homogeneous I would use the overall MS_{error}, and its degrees of freedom, in computing my *t* values, but there is room for disagreement on this.)

The indiscriminate use of multiple *t* tests is typically brought up as an example of a terrible approach to multiple comparisons. In some ways, this is an unfair criticism. It *is* a terrible thing to jump into a set of data and lay waste all around you with *t* tests on each and every pair of means that looks as if it might be interesting. The familywise error rate will be outrageously high. However, if you have only one or two comparisons to make and if those comparisons were truly planned in advance (you cannot cheat and say, "Oh well, I would have planned to make them if I had thought about it"), the *t*-test approach has much to recommend it. With only two comparisons, for example, the maximum *FW* would be approximately 0.10 if each comparison were run at $\alpha = .05$, and would be approximately 0.02 if each comparison were run at $\alpha = .01$. For a discussion of the important role that individual contrasts can play in an analysis, see Howell (2008c).

In the study on morphine tolerance described previously, we would probably not use multiple *t* tests simply because too many important comparisons should be considered. (In fact, we would probably use one of the post hoc procedures for making all pairwise comparisons unless we can restrict ourselves to relatively few comparisons.) For the sake of an example, however, consider two fundamental comparisons that were clearly predicted by the theory and that can be tested easily with a *t* test. The theory predicted that a rat that had received three previous morphine trials and was then tested in the same environment using a saline injection would show greater pain sensitivity than would an animal that had always been tested using saline. This involves a comparison of group M-S with group S-S. Furthermore, the theory predicted that group Mc-M would show less sensitivity to pain than would group M-M, because the former would be tested in an environment different from the one in which it had previously received morphine. Because the sample variances are similar and the sample sizes are equal, we will use MS_{error} as the pooled variance estimate and will evaluate the result on df_{error} degrees of freedom.

Our general formula for t, replacing individual variances with MS_{error}, will then be

$$t = \frac{\overline{X}_i - \overline{X}_j}{\sqrt{\dfrac{MS_{error}}{n} + \dfrac{MS_{error}}{n}}} = \frac{\overline{X}_i - \overline{X}_j}{\sqrt{\dfrac{2MS_{error}}{n}}}$$

Substituting the data from our example, the contrast of group M-S with group S-S yields

$$\overline{X}_{M\text{-}S} = 4.00 \qquad \overline{X}_{S\text{-}S} = 11.00 \qquad MS_{error} = 32.00$$

$$t = \frac{\overline{X}_{M\text{-}S} - \overline{X}_{S\text{-}S}}{\sqrt{\dfrac{2MS_{error}}{n}}} = \frac{4.00 - 11.00}{\sqrt{\dfrac{2(32.00)}{8}}} = \frac{-7}{\sqrt{8}} = -2.47$$

And group Mc-M versus group M-M yields

$$\overline{X}_{Mc\text{-}M} = 29.00 \qquad \overline{X}_{M\text{-}M} = 10.00 \qquad MS_{error} = 32.00$$

$$t = \frac{\overline{X}_{Mc\text{-}M} - \overline{X}_{M\text{-}M}}{\sqrt{\dfrac{2MS_{error}}{n}}} = \frac{29.00 - 10.00}{\sqrt{\dfrac{2(32.00)}{8}}} = \frac{19}{\sqrt{8}} = 6.72$$

Both of these obtained values of t would be evaluated against $t_{.025}(35) = 2.03$, and both would lead to rejection of the corresponding null hypothesis. We can conclude that with two groups of animals tested with saline, the group that had previously received morphine in the same situation will show a heightened sensitivity to pain. We can also conclude that changing the setting in which morphine is given significantly reduces, if it does not eliminate, the conditioned morphine-tolerance effect. Because we have tested two null hypotheses, each with $\alpha = .05$ per comparison, the *FW* will approach .10 *if both null hypotheses are true*, which seems quite unlikely. In fact, given the position of Jones and Tukey (2000) that it is highly unlikely that either null hypothesis would be true, or that we can only incorrectly find a significant difference in the wrong direction, the probability of an error in this situation is at most .05. That is important to keep in mind when we speak of the advantages and disadvantages of individual contrasts on pairs of means.

The basic t test that we have just used is the basis for almost everything to follow. I may tweak the formula here or there, and I will certainly use a number of different tables and decision rules, but it remains your basic t test—even when I change the formula and call it q.

Linear Contrasts

The use of individual t tests is a special case of a much more general technique involving what are known as linear contrasts.[3] In particular, t tests allow us to compare one group with another group, whereas linear contrasts allow us to compare one group *or set of groups* with another group or set of groups. Although we can use the calculational procedures of linear contrasts with post hoc tests as well as with a priori tests, they are discussed here

---

[3] The words "contrast" and "comparison" are used pretty much interchangeably in this context.

linear combination

under a priori tests because that is where they are most commonly used. Keep in mind that tests on contrasts are just an extension of standard t tests.

To define linear contrasts, we must first define a **linear combination**. A linear combination of means takes the form

$$L = a_1\overline{X}_1 + a_2\overline{X}_2 + \cdots + a_k\overline{X}_k = \sum a_j\overline{X}_j$$

This equation simply states that a linear combination is a weighted sum of treatment means. If, for example, the a_j were all equal to 1, L would just be the sum of the means. If, on the other hand, the a_j were all equal to $1/k$, then L would be the mean of the means.

When we impose the restriction that $\sum a_j = 0$, a linear combination becomes what is called a **linear contrast**. By convention we designate the fact that it is a linear contrast by replacing "L" with the Greek psi (ψ). With the proper selection of the a_j, a linear contrast is very useful. It can be used, for example, to compare one mean with another mean, giving the same result as a t test, or the mean of one condition with the combined mean of several conditions. As an example, consider three means ($\overline{X}_1$, $\overline{X}_2$, and $\overline{X}_3$). Letting $a_1 = 1$, $a_2 = -1$, and $a_3 = 0$, $\sum a_j = 0$,

linear contrast

$$\psi = (1)\overline{X}_1 + (-1)\overline{X}_2 + (0)\overline{X}_3 = \overline{X}_1 - \overline{X}_2$$

In this case, ψ is simply the difference between the means of group 1 and group 2, with the third group left out. If, on the other hand, we let $a_1 = 1/2$, $a_2 = 1/2$, and $a_3 = -1$, then

$$\psi = (1/2)\overline{X}_1 + (1/2)\overline{X}_2 + (-1)\overline{X}_3 = \frac{\overline{X}_1 + \overline{X}_2}{2} - \overline{X}_3$$

in which case ψ represents the difference between the mean of the third treatment and the average of the means of the first two treatments.

Sum of Squares for Contrasts

One of the advantages of linear contrasts is that they can be converted to sums of squares very easily and can represent the sum of squared differences between the means of sets of treatments. If we write

$$\psi = a_1\overline{X}_1 + a_2\overline{X}_2 + \cdots + a_k\overline{X}_k = \sum a_j\overline{X}_j$$

it can be shown that

$$SS_{contrast} = \frac{n\psi^2}{\sum a_j^2} = \frac{n(\sum a_j\overline{X}_j)^2}{\sum a_j^2}$$

is a component of the overall SS_{treat} on 1 df, where n represents the number of scores per treatment.[4]

Suppose we have three treatments such that

$$n = 10 \quad \overline{X}_1 = 1.5 \quad \overline{X}_2 = 2.0 \quad \overline{X}_3 = 3.0$$

---

[4] For unequal sample sizes, $SS_{contrast} = \dfrac{\psi^2}{\sum(a_j^2/n_j)}$

For the overall analysis of variance,

$$SS_{\text{treat}} = n\sum(\overline{X}_j - \overline{X}_{..})^2 = 10[(1.5 - 2.167)^2 + (2 - 2.167)^2 + (3 - 2.167)^2]$$

$$= 10[0.4449 + 0.0278 + 0.6939] = 11.667$$

Suppose we wanted to compare the average of treatments 1 and 2 with treatment 3. Let $a_1 = 1/2$, $a_2 = 1/2$, $a_3 = -1$. Then

$$\psi = \sum a_j\overline{X}_j = (\tfrac{1}{2})(1.5) + (\tfrac{1}{2})(2.0) + (-1)(3.0) = -1.25$$

$$SS_{\text{contrast}} = \frac{n\psi^2}{\sum a_j^2} = \frac{10(-1.25)^2}{1.5} = \frac{15.625}{1.5} = 10.417$$

This sum of squares is a component of the overall SS_{treat} on 1 df. We have 1 df because we are really comparing two quantities (the mean of the first two treatments with the mean of the third treatment).

Now suppose we obtain an additional linear contrast comparing treatment 1 with treatment 2. Let $a_1 = 1$, $a_2 = -1$, and $a_3 = 0$. Then

$$\psi = \sum a_j\overline{X}_j = (1)(1.5) + (-1)(2.0) + (0)(3.0) = -0.5$$

$$SS_{\text{contrast}} = \frac{n\psi^2}{\sum a_j^2} = \frac{10(-0.5)^2}{2} = \frac{2.5}{2} = 1.25$$

This SS_{treat} is also a component of SS_{treat} on 1 df. In addition, because of the particular contrasts that we chose to run,

$$SS_{\text{treat}} = SS_{\text{contrast}_1} + SS_{\text{contrast}_2}$$

$$11.667 = 10.417 + 1.25$$

the two contrasts account for all of the SS_{treat} and all of the df attributable to treatments. We say that we have *completely* **partitioned** SS_{treat}.

partitioned

The Choice of Coefficients

In the previous example, it should be reasonably clear why we chose the coefficients we did. They weight the treatment means in what seems to be a logical way to perform the contrast in question. Suppose, however, that we have five groups of equal size and wish to compare the first three with the last two. We need a set of coefficients (a_j) that will accomplish this task and for which $\sum a_j = 0$. The simplest rule is to form the two sets of treatments and to assign as weights to each set the reciprocal of the number of treatment groups in that set. One arbitrary set of coefficients is then given a minus sign. For example, take the means

$$\overline{X}_1 \quad \overline{X}_2 \quad \overline{X}_3 \quad \overline{X}_4 \quad \overline{X}_5$$

We want to compare $\overline{X}_1$, $\overline{X}_2$, and $\overline{X}_3$ combined with $\overline{X}_4$ and $\overline{X}_5$ combined. The first set contains three means, so for $\overline{X}_1$, $\overline{X}_2$, and $\overline{X}_3$ the $a_j = 1/3$. The second set contains two means, so for $\overline{X}_4$ and $\overline{X}_5$ the $a_j = 1/2$. We will let the 1/2s be negative. Then we have

Means:	$\overline{X}_1$	$\overline{X}_2$	$\overline{X}_3$	$\overline{X}_4$	$\overline{X}_5$	
a$_j$:	1/3	1/3	1/3	−1/2	−1/2	$\sum a_j = 0$

Then $\sum a_j \overline{X}_j$ reduces to $\frac{1}{3}(\overline{X}_1 + \overline{X}_2 + \overline{X}_3) - \frac{1}{2}(\overline{X}_4 + \overline{X}_5)$, which you can see is the mean of the first three conditions minus the mean of the last two conditions, which is what we want.

(If you go back to Siegel's experiment on morphine, lump the first three groups together and the last two groups together, and look at the means of the combined treatments, you will get an idea of why this system makes sense.) [5]

There are other ways of setting up the coefficients using whole numbers, and for many purposes you will arrive at the same result. I used to like alternative approaches because I find fractions messy, but using fractional values as I did here, where the sum of the *absolute values* of all coefficients is equal to 2, has some important implications when it comes to estimating effect sizes. The set of coefficients whose sum of absolute values equals 2 is often referred to as a standard set.

standard set

The Test of Significance

We have seen that linear contrasts can be easily converted to sums of squares on 1 degree of freedom. These sums of squares can be treated exactly like any other sums of squares. They happen also to be mean squares because they always have 1 degree of freedom (you are always comparing two quantities), and can thus be divided by MS_{error} to produce an F. Because *all* contrasts have 1 degree of freedom

$$F = \frac{MS_{contrast}}{MS_{error}} = \frac{n\psi^2 / \sum a_j^2}{MS_{error}} = \frac{n\psi^2}{\sum a_j^2 MS_{error}}$$

This F will have one and df_{error} degrees of freedom. And if you feel more comfortable with t, you can take the square root of F and have a t on df_{error} degrees of freedom.

For our example, suppose we had planned (a priori) to compare the mean of the two groups for whom the morphine should be maximally effective, either because they had never had morphine (Condition S-M) or because they had received morphine in a different context (Mc-M), with the mean of the other three groups (M-M, S-S, and M-S). We also planned to compare group Mc-M with group M-M, and group M-S with group S-S, for the same reasons given in the discussion of individual t tests. Finally, we planned to compare group M-M with group S-S to see whether morphine tolerance developed to such an extent that animals that always received morphine were no different after only four trials from animals that always received saline. (As we will see shortly, these four contrasts are not independent, but they answer substantive questions.) The analysis is shown in Table 12.2.

Each of these F values can be evaluated against $F_{.05}(1,35) = 4.12$. As expected, the first three contrasts are significant. The fourth contrast, comparing M-M with S-S, is not significant, indicating that complete morphine tolerance seems to develop in as few as four trials. (Be careful here, as I am acting as if I can prove the null hypothesis, when we know that is not possible.) Note that contrasts 2 and 3 test the same hypotheses that we tested using individual t tests. If you take the square root of the Fs for these two contrasts, they will equal 6.72 and 2.47, which are precisely the values we obtained for t earlier. This simply illustrates the fact that t tests are a special case of linear contrasts.

---

[5] If we have different numbers of subjects in the several groups, we *may* need to obtain our coefficients somewhat differently. If the sample sizes differ in non-essential ways, such as when a few subjects are missing at random, the approach above will be the appropriate one. It will not weight one group mean more than another just because the group happens to have a few more subjects. However, if the sample sizes are systematically different, not just different at random, and *if* we want to give more weight to the means from the larger groups, then we need to do something different. Because there really are very few cases where I can imagine wanting the different sample sizes to play an important role, I have dropped that approach from this edition of the book. However, you can find it in earlier editions and on the Web pages referred to earlier.

Table 12.2   A set of a priori comparisons on morphine data

Groups:	M-S	M-M	S-S	S-M	Mc-M	$\sum a_j^2$	$\psi = \sum a_j \overline{X}_j$
Means:	4.00	10.00	11.00	24.00	29.00		
Coefficient							
a_j	$-1/3$	$-1/3$	$-1/3$	$1/2$	$1/2$	0.833	18.167
b_j	0	-1	0	0	1	2	19
c_j	-1	0	1	0	0	2	7
d_j	0	1	-1	0	0	2	-1

$$SS_{contrast_1} = \frac{n(\sum a_j \overline{X}_j)^2}{\sum a_j^2} = \frac{8(18.17)^2}{0.8333} = \frac{2641.19}{0.8333} = 3169.42$$

$$F = \frac{MS_{contrast}}{MS_{error}} = \frac{3169.42}{32.00} = 99.04$$

$$SS_{contrast_2} = \frac{n(\sum b_j \overline{X}_j)^2}{\sum b_j^2} = \frac{8(19)^2}{2} = \frac{2888}{2} = 1444.00$$

$$F = \frac{MS_{contrast}}{MS_{error}} = \frac{1444.00}{32.00} = 45.125$$

$$SS_{contrast_3} = \frac{n(\sum c_j \overline{X}_j)^2}{\sum c_j^2} = \frac{8(7)^2}{2} = \frac{392}{2} = 196.00$$

$$F = \frac{MS_{contrast}}{MS_{error}} = \frac{196.00}{32.00} = 6.125$$

$$SS_{contrast_4} = \frac{n(\sum d_j \overline{X}_j)^2}{\sum d_j^2} = \frac{8(-1)^2}{2} = \frac{8}{2} = 4.00$$

$$F = \frac{MS_{contrast}}{MS_{error}} = \frac{4.00}{32.00} = 0.125$$

With four contrasts, we have an *FW* approaching .20 if all null hypotheses are true, which seems highly unlikely.[6] This error rate is uncomfortably high, although some experimenters would accept it, especially for a priori contrasts. One way of reducing the error rate would be to run each comparison at a more stringent level of α; for example, $\alpha = .01$. Another alternative would be to use a different a priori procedure, the Bonferroni procedure, which amounts to almost the same thing as the first alternative but is conducted in a more precise manner. We will consider this procedure after we briefly discuss a special type of linear contrast, called orthogonal contrasts. Yet a third way to control *FW* is to run fewer contrasts. For example, the comparison of M-M with S-S is probably not very important. Whether

---

[6] I should elaborate on that statement. We *know* that morphine tolerance is a well-established fact. So, for example, does it seem likely that rats receiving morphine for the first time behave like rats receiving it for the fourth time? I don't think so. So right off the bat there weren't four true null hypotheses that could be falsely rejected, so a probability as high as .20 is unreasonable. Without knowing anything more about the study I would be surprised if there are more than two true null hypotheses, in which case the actual *FW* error rate should not be above .10.

complete tolerance develops on the fourth trial or on the sixth or seventh trial is of no great theoretical interest. By eliminating that contrast, we could reduce the maximum FW to .15. You should never choose to run contrasts the way you eat peanuts or climb mountains—just because they are there. In general, if a contrast is not important, do not run it.

Orthogonal Contrasts

orthogonal
contrasts

Linear contrasts as they have been defined allow us to test a series of hypotheses about treatment differences. Sometimes contrasts are independent of one another, and sometimes they are not. For example, knowing that $\overline{X}_1$ is greater than the average of $\overline{X}_2$ and $\overline{X}_3$ tells you nothing about whether $\overline{X}_3$ is greater than $\overline{X}_2$ nor whether $\overline{X}_4$ is likely to be greater than $\overline{X}_5$. These contrasts are independent. However, knowing that $\overline{X}_1$ is greater than the average of $\overline{X}_2$ and $\overline{X}_3$ suggests that there is a better than 50:50 chance that $\overline{X}_1$ is greater than $\overline{X}_2$. These two contrasts are not independent. When members of a set of contrasts are independent of one another, they are called orthogonal contrasts, and the sums of squares of a complete set of orthogonal contrasts sum to SS_{treat}. (If the contrasts are not orthogonal, they contain overlapping amounts of information and do not have this additivity property.) From a calculational point of view, what sets orthogonal contrasts apart from other types of contrasts we might choose is the relationship between the coefficients for one contrast and the coefficients for other contrasts in the set. Other than that, the computations are exactly the same.

Orthogonal Coefficients

Given that sample sizes are equal, for contrasts to be orthogonal the coefficients must meet the following three criteria:

1. $\Sigma a_j = 0$
2. $\Sigma a_j b_j = 0$

where a_j and b_j are the sets of coefficients for different contrasts. Furthermore, for the $SS_{contrast}$ to sum to SS_{treat}, we need to add a third criterion:

3. Number of comparisons = number of df for treatments

The first restriction has been discussed already; it results in the contrast's being a sum of squares. The second restriction ensures that the contrasts are independent of (or orthogonal to) one another, and thus that we are summing nonoverlapping components. The third restriction says nothing more than that if you want the parts to sum to the whole, you need to have all the parts.

At first glance, it would appear that finding sets of coefficients satisfying the requirement $\Sigma a_j b_j = 0$ would require that we either undertake a frustrating process of trial and error or else solve a set of simultaneous equations. In fact, a simple rule exists for finding orthogonal sets of coefficients; although the rule will not find all possible sets, it will lead to most of them. The rule for forming the coefficients visualizes the process of breaking down SS_{treat} in terms of a tree diagram. The overall F for five treatments deals with all five treatment means simultaneously. That is the trunk of the tree. If we then compare the combination of treatments 1 and 2 with the combination of treatments 3, 4, and 5, we have formed two branches of our tree, one representing treatments 1 and 2 and the other representing treatments 3, 4, and 5. As discussed earlier, the value of a_j for the treatment means on the left will be equal to the reciprocal of the number of treatments in that set, and vice versa, with one of the sets being negative. In this case the coefficients are (½ , ½, $-\frac{1}{3}$, $-\frac{1}{3}$, $-\frac{1}{3}$) for the five treatments, respectively.

Now that we have formed two limbs or branches of our tree, we can never compare treatments on one limb with treatments on another limb, although we can compare treatments on the same limb. Thus, comparing treatment 3 with the combination of treatments 4 and 5 is an example of a legitimate comparison. The coefficients in this case would be $(0, 0, 1, -\frac{1}{2}, -\frac{1}{2})$. Treatments 1 and 2 have coefficients of 0 because they are not part of this comparison. Treatment 3 has a coefficient of 1 because it contains one treatment. Treatments 4 and 5 received coefficients of $-\frac{1}{2}$ because there are two treatments in that set. The negative signs can be arbitrarily assigned to either side of the comparison.

The previous procedure could be carried on until we have exhausted all possible sets of comparisons. This will occur when we have made as many comparisons as there are *df* for treatments. As a result of this procedure, we might arrive at the comparisons and coefficients shown in Figure 12.1. To show that these coefficients are orthogonal, we need to show only that all *pairwise* products of the coefficients sum to zero. For example,

$$\sum a_j b_j = \left(\tfrac{1}{2}\right)(1) + \left(\tfrac{1}{2}\right)(-1) + \left(-\tfrac{1}{3}\right)(0) + \left(-\tfrac{1}{3}\right)(0) + \left(-\tfrac{1}{3}\right)(0) = 0$$

and

$$\sum a_j c_j = \left(\tfrac{1}{2}\right)(0) + \left(\tfrac{1}{2}\right)(0) + \left(-\tfrac{1}{3}\right)(2) + \left(-\tfrac{1}{3}\right)(-1) + \left(-\tfrac{1}{3}\right)(-1) = 0$$

Thus, we see that the first and second and the first and third contrasts are both independent. Similar calculations will show that all the other contrasts are also independent of one another.

These coefficients will lead to only one of many possible sets of orthogonal contrasts. If we had begun by comparing treatment 1 with the combination of treatments 2, 3, 4, and 5, the resulting set of contrasts would have been entirely different. It is important for the experimenter to decide which contrasts she considers important and to plan accordingly. Keep in mind that just because you can arrange coefficients to yield a legitimate contrast doesn't mean that you actually have to carry out that contrast.

The actual computation of F or t with orthogonal contrasts is the same as when we are using nonorthogonal contrasts. Because of this, there is little to be gained by working through an example here. It would be good practice, however, for you to create a complete set of orthogonal contrasts and to carry out the arithmetic. You can check your answers by showing that the sum of the sums of squares equals SS_{treat}.

When I first started teaching and writing about statistics, orthogonal contrasts were a big deal, just as was the distinction between a priori and post hoc tests. Authors went out of their way to impress on you the importance of orthogonality, and the need to feel guilty if you ran comparisons that were not orthogonal. That attitude has changed over the years. Although it is nice to have a set of orthogonal comparisons, in part because they sum to SS_{treat}, people are far more willing to run nonorthogonal contrasts. I would certainly not suggest that you pass up an important contrast just because it is not orthogonal to others that you ran. In fact, the contrasts that I ran earlier are not orthogonal to each other, and that does not worry me much. They address important questions (well, possibly not S-S versus M-M, as I said). Nor should you use a contrast in which you have no interest, just because

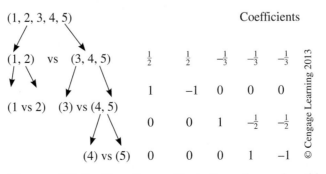

Figure 12.1   Tree diagram illustrating orthogonal partition of SS_{treat}

it is part of an orthogonal set. But keep in mind that being nonorthogonal means that these contrasts are not independent of each other.

Bonferroni *t* (Dunn's test)

Dunn's test

Bonferroni *t*

Bonferroni inequality

I suggested earlier that one way to control the familywise error rate when using linear contrasts is to use a more conservative level of α for each comparison. The proposal that you might want to use $\alpha = .01$ instead of $\alpha - .05$ was based on the fact that our statistical tables are set up that way. (Tables do not usually have many critical values of t for α between .05 and .01, although statistical software to compute and print them is widely available.) A formal way of controlling *FW* more precisely by manipulating the per comparison error rate can be found in a test proposed by Dunn (1961), which is particularly appropriate when you want to make only a few of all possible comparisons. Although this test had been known for a long time, Dunn was the first person to formalize it and to present the necessary tables, and it is sometimes referred to as **Dunn's test**. It now more commonly goes under the name **Bonferroni *t***. The Bonferroni *t* test is based on what is known as the **Bonferroni inequality**, which states that the probability of occurrence of one *or more* events can never exceed the sum of their individual probabilities. This means that when we make three comparisons, each with a probability of $\alpha' = .05$ of a Type I error, the probability of *at least* one Type I error can never exceed $3 \times .05 = .15$. In more formal terms, if c represents the number of comparisons and α' represents the probability of a Type I error for each comparison, then *FW* is less than or equal to $c\alpha'$. From this it follows that if we set $\alpha' = \alpha/c$ for each comparison, where $\alpha = $ the desired maximum *FW*, then $FW \leq c\alpha' = c(\alpha/c) = \alpha$. Dunn (1961) used this inequality to design her test in which each comparison is run at $\alpha' = \alpha/c$, leaving the $FW \leq \alpha$ for the set of comparisons. This can be accomplished by using the standard t test procedure but referring the result to modified t tables.

The problem that you immediately encounter when you attempt to run each comparison at $\alpha' = \alpha/c$ is that standard tables of Student's t do not provide critical values for the necessary levels of α. If you want to run each of three comparisons at $\alpha' = \alpha/c = .05/3 = .0167$, you would need tables of critical values of t at $\alpha = .0167$, or software[7] that will easily compute it. Dunn's major contribution was to provide such tables. However, we no longer need those tables because all software solutions produce the actual p value, and if we do the calculations by hand, we can use readily available probability calculators. I will omit them from this edition.

For the Bonferroni test on pairwise comparisons (i.e., comparing one mean with one other mean), define

$$t' = \frac{\overline{X}_i - \overline{X}_j}{\sqrt{\dfrac{MS_{\text{error}}}{n} + \dfrac{MS_{\text{error}}}{n}}} = \frac{\overline{X}_i - \overline{X}_j}{\sqrt{\dfrac{2MS_{\text{error}}}{n}}} \quad \text{or} \quad F' = \frac{\psi^2}{\dfrac{\Sigma a_j^2 MS_{\text{error}}}{n}}$$

and evaluate t' against the critical value of t' at α/c, which is $(t_{\alpha/c,\, df})$. Notice that we still use the standard formula for t. The only difference between t' and a standard t is the tables used in their α/c evaluation. With unequal sample sizes but homogeneous variances, replace the ns in the leftmost equation with n_i and n_j. With heterogeneity of variance, see the solution by Games and Howell later in this chapter.

To write a general expression that allows us to test any comparison of means, pairwise or not, we can express t' in terms of linear contrasts.

$$\psi = \sum a_j \overline{X}_j \quad \text{and} \quad t' = \frac{\psi}{\sqrt{\dfrac{\sum a_j^2 MS_{\text{error}}}{n}}}$$

---

[7] Free probability calculators can be found at http://www.danielsoper.com/statcalc/. This book's Web site contains code in R to instantly produce the critical value (tProb.R, FProb.R, and chisqProb.R).

This represents the most general form for the Bonferroni t, and it can be shown that if ψ is *any* linear combination (not necessarily even a linear contrast, requiring $\sum a_j = 0$), the *FW* with c comparisons is at most α (Dunn, 1961). To put it most simply, the Bonferroni t runs a regular t test but evaluates the result against a modified critical value of t that has been chosen so as to limit *FW*.

I would offer one word of caution when it comes to the Bonferroni test and variations on it. These tests are appropriate when you have a limited number of planned contrasts, whether they are pairwise or complex. However SPSS and SAS offer the Bonferroni test only with pairwise post hoc tests, for which it is usually inappropriate. Under that system you automatically set c equal to the number of *possible* pairwise comparisons whether you care about all of them or not. If you want to apply such a correction to a planned set of contrasts, you need to specify those contrasts and then evaluate significance on your own in relation to α/c. And to specify those contrast coefficients you will need to use **Compare Means/One-way ANOVA** and not the **univariate** procedure. In SAS you will need to use a contrast statement with Proc GLM.

A variation on the Bonferroni procedure was proposed by Šidák (1967). His test is based on the multiplicative inequality $p(FW) \leq 1 - (1 - \alpha)^c$ and evaluates t' at $\alpha' = 1 - (1 - \alpha)^{1/c}$. (This is often called the **Dunn-Šidák test**.) A comparison of the power of the two tests shows only very minor differences in favor of the Šidák approach, and we will stick with the Bonferroni test because of its much wider use. Many computer software programs, however, provide Šidák's test.

When we considered linear contrasts earlier in this section, we ran four comparisons, which had a maximum *FW* of nearly .20. (Our test of each of those contrasts involved an F statistic but, because each contrast involves 1 df, we can go from t to F and vice versa by means of the relationship $t = \sqrt{F}$.) If we wish to run those same comparisons but to keep *FW* at a maximum of .05 instead of $4 \times (.05) = .20$, we can use the Bonferroni t test. In each case, we will solve for t' and evaluate t' against the standard t at $\alpha' = \alpha/4$. Taking the pairwise tests first, the calculations follow. For four contrasts the critical value of t', adjusted for the number of contrasts, will be that value of t that cuts off $5/4 = .0125 = 1.25\%$ of the t distribution, which, when you have a two-tailed test is .00625 in each tail. If you are using standard software, which prints out p values, you simple change your rejection level to .0125. Or, using the software mentioned in footnote 6, you will find that the cutoff value of $df = 35$ is $t_{.00625, 35} = 2.63$.[8]

The calculations for these tests are shown below. We want to identify contrasts with $t \geq \pm 2.63$.

Mc-M versus M-M:

$$t' = \frac{\overline{X}_i - \overline{X}_j}{\sqrt{\dfrac{2MS_{\text{error}}}{n}}} = \frac{29.00 - 10.00}{\sqrt{\dfrac{(2)(32.00)}{8}}} = \frac{19}{\sqrt{8}} = 6.72$$

S-S versus M-S:

$$t' = \frac{\overline{X}_i - \overline{X}_j}{\sqrt{\dfrac{2MS_{\text{error}}}{n}}} = \frac{11.00 - 4.00}{\sqrt{\dfrac{(2)(32.00)}{8}}} = \frac{7}{\sqrt{8}} = 2.47$$

M-M versus S-S:

$$t' = \frac{\overline{X}_i - \overline{X}_j}{\sqrt{\dfrac{2MS_{\text{error}}}{n}}} = \frac{10.00 - 11.00}{\sqrt{\dfrac{(2)(32.00)}{8}}} = \frac{-1}{\sqrt{8}} = -0.35$$

---

[8] To use Daniel Soper's excellent probability calculators, choose the link to Student's t distribution and click on Student's t calculator.

Dunn-Šidák test

The calculations for the more complex contrast, letting the $a_j = 1/3, 1/3, 1/3, -1/2, -1/2$ as before, follow.

S-M and Mc-M versus M-M, S-S and M-S:

$$t' = \frac{\sum a_j \bar{X}_j}{\sqrt{\dfrac{\sum a_j^2 MS_{error}}{n}}} = \frac{(\frac{1}{2})(24) + \cdots + (-\frac{1}{3})(4)}{\sqrt{\dfrac{(0.833)(32.00)}{8}}} = \frac{18.167}{\sqrt{3.3333}} = 9.95$$

In this case, the first and last contrasts exceed 2.63 and are significant, but the other two are not.[9] Whereas we earlier rejected the hypothesis that groups S-S and M-S were sampled from populations with the same mean, using the more conservative Bonferroni t test we are no longer able to reject that hypothesis. Here we cannot conclude that prior morphine injections lead to hypersensitivity to pain. The difference in conclusions between the two procedures is a direct result of our use of the more conservative familywise error rate. If we wish to concentrate on per comparison error rates, ignoring FW, then we evaluate each t (or F) against the critical value at $\alpha = .05$. On the other hand, if we are primarily concerned with controlling FW, then we evaluate each t, or F, at a more stringent level. The difference is not in the arithmetic of the test; it is in the critical value we choose to use. The choice is up to the experimenter.

Multistage Bonferroni Procedures

The Bonferroni multiple-comparison procedure has a number of variations. Although these are mentioned here in the context of the analysis of variance, they can be applied equally well whenever we have multiple hypothesis tests for which we wish to control the familywise error rate. These procedures have the advantage of setting a limit on the FW error rate at α against any set of possible null hypotheses, as does the Tukey HSD (to be discussed shortly), while at the same time being less conservative than Tukey's test *when our interest is in a specific subset of contrasts*. In general, however, Bonferroni procedures would not be used as a substitute when making all pairwise comparisons among a set of means, though the multistage procedures, which change the critical value as null hypotheses are rejected, can be used for that purpose.

As you saw, the Bonferroni test is based on the principle of dividing up FW for a family of contrasts among each of the individual contrasts. Thus, if we want FW to be .05 and we want to test four contrasts, we test each one at $\alpha = .05/4 = .0125$. The multistage tests follow a similar principle, the major difference being in the way they choose to partition α. They basically test the largest difference (or correlation coefficient). If that is significant they move to the next largest contrast but reduce the "number of tests" by 1. This continues until the first nonsignificant difference. The logic behind this approach hinges on the fact that the familywise error rate is the probability of making *at least* one Type I error. Suppose that we have four contrasts to test. If you make an error on the first contrast, you already have your one error, and making more won't hurt. (Well, any error hurts, but making more than one won't affect the familywise error rate.) If you did not make a Type I error on that test, there are at most three possible true null hypotheses to reject, so we can set $\alpha' = \alpha/3$.

Rather than elaborate here on these procedures, I have moved that discussion to this book's Web site to save space. These are powerful procedures when you organize your tests in steps, and I recommend reading those pages.

---

[9] The actual probabilities would be .000, .018, .726, and .000.

Trimmed Means

I want to include one more approach that is very general and can be shown to be more powerful than standard procedures when the data come from long-tailed distributions. This is the use of trimmed means. The nice thing about this approach is that it can be adapted to carry out any of the procedures in this chapter, simply by substituting the appropriate trimmed means and squared standard errors.

I will assume that you have reasonably large sample sizes because we will trim those samples from each end. Wilcox recommends 20% trimming, which results in a sizable drop in the effective sample size, but with a corresponding gain in power. For convenience, assume that we have 40 observations in each of several groups and that we will go along with Wilcox's suggestion of 20% trimming. That means that we will omit the lowest $(.20)(40) = 8$ observations and the highest 8 observations, leaving us with a sample of 24 observations for each condition. The trimmed means will be the means of those 24 observations in each group. To calculate the variance, we will use Winsorized samples, in which the lowest 8 scores are replaced with the 9th lowest score and the highest 8 scores are replaced with the 9th highest score. This leaves us with samples of $n_i = 40$ scores, but only $h_i = 24$ of those are independent observations from the ith sample. If we let $s^2_{W_i}$ represent the variance of the Winsorized sample of 40 scores, then the squared standard error of the mean for that sample would be

$$s^2_{W_{\bar{X}_i}} = \frac{(n_j - 1)s^2_{W_i}}{h_j(h_j - 1)}$$

and the robust pairwise t test on the difference between two means can be written as

$$t_W = \frac{\bar{Y}_{ti} - \bar{Y}_{tj}}{\sqrt{s^2_{W_{\bar{X}_i}} + s^2_{W_{\bar{X}_j}}}}$$

Notice that we are not doing anything very surprising here. We are replacing means with trimmed means and variances with variances that are based on Winsorized samples, but using h_j (the size of the trimmed sample) to adjust n_i to account for the trimming. Other than that, we have a standard t test, and it can be used as a replacement for the t in any of the procedures we have discussed, or will discuss, in this chapter. There is one complication, however, and that refers to the estimated degrees of freedom. The degrees of freedom are estimated as

$$df_W = \frac{(s^2_{W_{\bar{X}_i}} + s^2_{W_{\bar{X}_j}})^2}{s^2_{W_{\bar{X}_i}}(h_i - 1) + s^2_{W_{\bar{X}_j}}(h_j - 1)}$$

That is a messy formula, but not very difficult to work out. As Keselman et al. (2005) noted, "When researchers feel they are dealing with nonnormal data, they can replace the usual least squares estimators of central tendency and variability with robust estimators and apply these estimators in any of the previously recommended" multiple comparison procedures.

NOTE

I want to emphasize one more time that the Bonferroni test and its variants are completely general. They are not the property of the analysis of variance or of any other statistical procedure. If you have several tests that were carried by any statistical procedure (and perhaps by different procedures), you can use the Bonferroni approach to control FW. For example, I recently received an e-mail message in which someone asked how they might go about applying the Bonferroni to logistic regression. He would do it the same way he would do it for the analysis of variance. Take the set of statistical tests that came from his logistic regression, divide α by the number of tests he ran, and declare a test to be significant only if its resulting probability was less than α / c. You don't even need to know anything about logistic regression to do that.

12.4 Confidence Intervals and Effect Sizes for Contrasts

Having run a statistical significance test on the data from an experiment, and looked at individual comparisons, often called "individual contrasts," we will generally want to look at some measure of the amount of difference between group means. In Chapter 11 we saw that when we have the omnibus F, which compares all means together, the most commonly used measure is a member of the r-family measures, such as η^2 or ω^2. However, when we are looking at comparisons of individual means, or sets of means, it generally makes more sense to calculate confidence limits on our differences and/or to use a d-family measure of the effect size.

There are several ways that we could approach d-family measures. One very simple way is to go back to Chapter 7, which discussed t tests, and apply the measures that were discussed there. We will come out at the same place, however, if we approach the problem through linear contrasts. Remember that when you are looking at two groups, it makes no difference whether you run a t test between those groups, or compute a linear contrast and then an F, and take the square root of that F. The advantage of going with linear contrasts is that they are more general, allowing us to compare means of sets of groups rather than just two individual groups.

We will take an example from our morphine study by Siegel. One contrast that really interests me is the contrast between Group M-M and Group Mc-M. If their means are statistically significantly different, then that tells us that there is something important about changing the physical context in which the morphine is given. The group statistics are given below.

Condition	M-M	Mc-M
Mean	10.00	29.00
St. Dev	5.13	6.06
Variance	26.32	37.95
MS_{error}	32.00	

© Cengage Learning 2013

The coefficients for the linear contrast of these two groups would be "-1" for M-M, "$+1$" for Mc-M, and "0" for the other three conditions.

Confidence Interval

Let us first compute a confidence interval on the difference between conditions. The general formula for a confidence interval on a contrast of two means is

$$CI_{.95} = (\overline{X}_i - \overline{X}_j) \pm t_{.025}s_{\overline{X}_i - \overline{X}_j}$$

or, if we let "ψ_j" represent the value of the contrast, where $\psi_j = \Sigma a_i\overline{X}_i$, then

$$CI_{.95} = (\psi_j) \pm t_{.025}s_{error}$$

The standard error of the contrast (s_{error}), is

$$\sqrt{\frac{2MS_{error}}{n}}$$

For our confidence interval on the difference between the two conditions of interest I have

$$CI_{.95} = (-1(10) + 1(29)) \pm 2.03\sqrt{8.00}$$
$$= 19 \pm 2.03(2.828) = 19 \pm 5.74$$
$$13.26 \le \mu_{M\text{-}M} - \mu_{Mc\text{-}M} \le 24.74$$

The probability is .95 that the interval will include the true difference between the population means.

When it comes time to form our effect size measure, we have a choice of what we will use as the error term—the standard deviation in the equation. I could choose to use the square root of MS_{error} from the overall analysis, because that represents the square root of the average variance within each of the five groups. Kline (2004) recommends this approach. I have two other perfectly reasonable alternatives, however. First I could take the square root of the average sample variance of the two groups in question (perhaps weighted if the sample sizes were unequal). In this case it would be $(26.32 + 37.95)/2 = 32.135$ and $\sqrt{32.135} = 5.669$. This would make sense if I were worried about heterogeneity of variance among the full set of five groups. Alternatively, I could consider one of the groups to be a control group and use its standard deviation as my error term. Here I might argue that M-M is like a control group because the conditions don't change on trial 4. In this case I would let $s_{error} = 5.13$. I think that my preference in general would be to base my estimate on the average of the variances of the groups in question. If the variances are homogeneous across all five groups, then the average of the groups in question won't deviate much from the average of the variances of all five groups, so I haven't lost much. Others might take a different view.

Effect Size

We have just seen that the confidence interval on the difference between Mc-M and M-M is $13.26 \leq (\mu_{Mc\text{-}M} - \mu_{m\text{-}m}) \leq 24.74$. Both limits are on the same side of 0, reflecting the fact that the difference was statistically significant. However, the dependent variable here is the length of time before the animal starts to lick its paws, and I don't suppose that any of us has a strong intuitive understanding of what a long or short interval is for this case. A difference of at least thirteen seconds seems pretty long, but I would like some better understanding of what is happening. One way to compute that would be to calculate an effect size on the difference between these means.

Our effect size measure will be essentially the same as it was in the case for t tests for independent samples. However, I will write it slightly differently because doing so will generalize to more complex comparisons. We have just seen that ψ represents a contrast between two means or sets of means, so it is really just a difference in means. We will take this difference and standardize it, which simply says that we want to represent the difference in group means in standard deviation units. (That is what we did in Chapter 7 as well.)

In Chapter 7 we defined

$$\hat{d} = \frac{\overline{X}_i - \overline{X}_j}{s_p}$$

where s_p is the square root of our pooled variance estimate and is a measure of the average standard deviation within the groups. We are going to calculate essentially the same thing here, but I will write its expression as

$$\hat{d} = \frac{\psi}{s_e} = \frac{\sum (a_i \overline{X}_i)}{s_e}$$

The numerator is a simple linear contrast, while the denominator is some estimate of the within groups standard deviation.

The preceding formula raises two points. In the first place, the coefficients must form what we have called a "standard set." This simply means that the absolute values of the coefficients must sum to 2. For example, if we want to compare the mean of two groups with the mean of a third, we could use coefficients of (½, ½, –1) to form our contrast. We would

Table 12.3   Means of conditions in our morphine example

Groups:	M-S	M-M	S-S	S-M	Mc-M	Σa_j^2	$\psi = \sum a_j \overline{X}_j$
Means:	4.00	10.00	11.00	24.00	29.00		
			Coefficient				
a_j	$-1/2$	$1/3$	$-1/2$	$1/3$	$1/3$	0.833	18.167
b_j	0	-1	0	0	1	2	19
c_j	-1	0	1	0	0	2	7
d_j	0	1	-1	0	0	2	-1

M-M, S-M, Mc-M versus M-S, S-S

$$\hat{d}_1 = \frac{\Sigma a_i \overline{X}_i}{s_{\text{error}}} = \frac{(-\frac{1}{3})\overline{X}_{\text{M-S}} + (-\frac{1}{3})\overline{X}_{\text{M-M}} + (-\frac{1}{3})\overline{X}_{\text{S-S}} + (\frac{1}{2})\overline{X}_{\text{S-M}} + (\frac{1}{2})\overline{X}_{\text{Mc-M}}}{\sqrt{MS_{\text{error}}}}$$

$$= \frac{(-\frac{1}{3})4.00 + (-\frac{1}{3})10.00 + (-\frac{1}{3})11.00 + (\frac{1}{2})24.00 + (\frac{1}{2})29}{\sqrt{32}}$$

$$= \frac{-\dfrac{4.00 + 10.00 + 11.00}{3} + \dfrac{24.00 + 29.00}{2}}{\sqrt{32}} = \frac{-8.333 + 26.5}{5.657} = \frac{18.167}{5.657} = 3.21$$

M-M versus Mc-M

$$\hat{d}_2 = \frac{\Sigma b_i \overline{X}_i}{s_{\text{error}}} = \frac{(-1)\overline{X}_{\text{M-M}} + (1)\overline{X}_{\text{Mc-M}}}{\sqrt{MS_{\text{error}}}}$$

$$= \frac{(-1)10.00 + (1)29.00}{\sqrt{32}}$$

$$= \frac{-10.00 + 29.00}{32} = \frac{19}{5.657} = 3.36$$

get to the same place as far as our test of significance is concerned by using $(1, 1, -2)$ or $(3, 3, -6)$; the resulting F would be the same. But only the first would give us a numerical answer for the contrast that is the difference between the mean of the first two groups and the mean of the third. This is easily seen when you write

$$\psi = (\tfrac{1}{2})\overline{X}_1 + (\tfrac{1}{2})\overline{X}_2 + (-1)\overline{X}_3$$

$$= \frac{\overline{X}_1 + \overline{X}_2}{2} - \overline{X}_3$$

You can see clearly that we are taking the difference between the means of sets of groups.

The second issue raised by our equation for $\hat{d}$ is the choice of the denominator. As I mentioned a few paragraphs back, there are at least three possible estimates. We could use the square root of MS_{error}, or the square root of the average of the variances in the groups being contrasted, or we could conceive of one of the groups as a control group, and use its standard deviation as our estimate. The most common approach is to use the square root of MS_{error}, and that is what I will do here because the variances in our example are quite similar.

Earlier we looked at four contrasts that seemed to be of interest for theoretical reasons. The traditional Bonferroni procedure showed that two of the contrasts were statistically significant, while the other two were not. Computation of the effect sizes for significant contrasts are shown in Table 12.3. In these calculations I have used the square root of MS_{error} as my denominator for consistency.

Because our tests showed that the last two contrasts were not nearly statistically significant, our best approach would probably be to treat these effect sizes as 0.00. There are no differences between groups. An interesting question arises as to what we would do if the test statistic had been nearly large enough to be significant. In that case I would present my effect size measure but caution that the corresponding hypothesis test was not significant.

You can see that the other effect sizes are substantial, all showing a difference of at least three standard deviations. I will speak about these effects in the following section.

12.5   Reporting Results

We have run several different tests on these data, and the following is a report based on the Bonferroni procedure.

> This experiment examined the phenomenon of morphine tolerance in rats placed on a warm surface. The underlying hypothesis was that with repeated injections of morphine animals develop a hypersensitivity to pain, which reduces the effect of the drug. When animals are then tested without the drug, or with the drug in a different context, this hypersensitivity will be expressed in a shorter paw-lick latency.

> The omnibus F from the overall analysis was statistically significant ($F(4,35) = 27.33$, $p < .05$). Subsequent contrasts on important comparisons using the Bonferroni test revealed that morphine's effects were as predicted. The groups receiving morphine on the test trial after having received either saline or morphine in the same of different context on trials 1–3 showed longer reaction times than the average of groups who received saline on the test trial ($t(35) = 9.95$, $t_{.006, 35} = 2.64$). The standardized effect size was 3.21, indicating a difference of nearly 3¼ standard deviations between the means of the two sets of groups.

> The effect of context is seen in a statistically longer mean paw-lick latency in the Mc-M ($\overline{X} = 29$) condition than in the M-M condition ($\overline{X} = 10$) ($t(35) = 6.72$, $t_{\alpha/3} = t_{.0167} = \pm 2.52$). The standardized effect size here was 3.36.

12.6   Post Hoc Comparisons

There is much to recommend the use of linear contrasts and the Bonferroni t test when a relatively small number of comparisons can be specified a priori. In fact, my strong preference would be to ask a few very pointed questions, which would best be approached by setting up linear contrasts. The use of broader post hoc comparisons may lose power by asking questions that you don't care about, but that approach does have advantages in experiments involving many hypotheses[10] and/or hypotheses that are clearly arrived at only after the data have been examined. In this situation, a number of a posteriori or post hoc techniques are available.

---

[10] If there are many hypotheses to be tested, regardless of whether they were planned in advance, the procedures discussed here are usually more powerful than is the Bonferroni t test.

Fisher's Least Significant Difference (LSD) Procedure

Fisher's Least Significant Difference (LSD)

Fisher's protected *t*

One of the oldest methods for making post hoc comparisons is known as **Fisher's Least Significant Difference (LSD)** test (also known as **Fisher's protected *t***). People sometimes (rightfully) complain about the use of this procedure when there are many means, but when we only have a few means to compare (particularly when we only have three), this is a very legitimate and useful procedure. The procedure consists of simply running pairwise comparisons among the means using a standard Student's *t* test. The only difference between the post hoc LSD procedure and the a priori multiple *t* test procedure discussed earlier is that the LSD requires a significant *F* for the overall analysis of variance. When the complete null hypothesis is true (all population means are equal), the requirement of a significant overall *F* ensures that the familywise error rate will equal α. Unfortunately, if the complete null hypothesis is *not* true but some other more limited null hypotheses involving subsets of means are true, which is most likely to be the case, the overall *F* may no longer affords protection for *FW*. For this reason, some recommend that you not use this test, although Carmer and Swanson (1973) have shown it to be the most powerful of the common post hoc multiple-comparison procedures. If your experiment involves three means, the LSD procedure is an excellent one because *FW* will stay at α, and you will gain the added power of using standard *t* tests. (The *FW* error rate will be α with three means because if the complete null hypothesis is true, you have a probability equal to α of making a Type I error with your overall *F*, and any subsequent Type I errors you might commit with a *t* test will not affect *FW*. If the complete null is not true but a more limited one is, with three means there can be at most one null difference among the means and, therefore, only one chance of making a Type I error, again with a probability equal to α.) You should generally be reluctant to use the LSD for more than three means unless you have good reason to believe that there is at most one true null hypothesis hidden in the means.

The Studentized Range Statistic (*q*)

Studentized range statistic (*q*)

Because many of the post hoc are based on the Studentized Range Statistic or special variants of it, we will consider this statistic before proceeding. The **Studentized range statistic (*q*)** is defined as

$$q_r = \frac{\overline{X}_l - \overline{X}_s}{\sqrt{\dfrac{MS_{\text{error}}}{n}}}$$

where $\overline{X}_l$ and $\overline{X}_s$ represent the largest and smallest of a set of treatment means and *r* is the number of treatments in the set. You probably have noticed that the formula for *q* is very similar to the formula for *t*. In fact

$$q_r = \frac{\overline{X}_l - \overline{X}_s}{\sqrt{\dfrac{MS_{\text{error}}}{n}}}$$

$$t = \frac{\overline{X}_i - \overline{X}_j}{\sqrt{\dfrac{2(MS_{\text{error}})}{n}}}$$

and the only difference is that the formula for *t* has a "$\sqrt{2}$" in the denominator. Thus, *q* is a linear function of *t* and we can always go from *t* to *q* by the relation $q = t\sqrt{2}$. The real difference between *q* and *t* tests comes from the fact that the tables of *q* (Appendix *q*) are set up to allow us to adjust the critical value of q for the number of means involved, as will become apparent shortly. When there are only two treatments, whether we solve for t or q is irrelevant as long as we use the corresponding table.

When we have only two means or when we wish to compare two means chosen *at random* from the set of available means, t is an appropriate test.[11] Suppose, however, that we looked at a set of means and deliberately selected the largest and smallest means for testing. It is apparent that we have drastically altered the probability of a Type I error. Given that H_0 is true, the largest and smallest means certainly have a greater chance of being called "significantly different" than do means that are adjacent in an ordered series of means. This is the point at which the Studentized range statistic becomes useful. It was designed for just this purpose.

To use q, we first order the means from smallest to largest. We then take into account the number of steps between the means to be compared. For adjacent means $r = 2$ and no change is made. Thus $q_{.05} = t_{.05}\sqrt{2}$. For means that are not adjacent, however, the critical value of q increases, growing in magnitude as the number of intervening steps between means increases.

As an example of the use of q, consider the data on morphine tolerance. The means are

$\overline{X}_1$	$\overline{X}_2$	$\overline{X}_3$	$\overline{X}_4$	$\overline{X}_5$
4	10	11	24	29

with $n = 8$, $df_{error} = 35$, and $MS_{error} = 32.00$. The largest mean is 29 and the smallest is 4, and there are a total (r) of 5 means in the set (in the terminology of most tables, we say that these means are $r = 5$ steps apart).

$$q_5 = \frac{\overline{X}_1 - \overline{X}_s}{\sqrt{\dfrac{MS_{error}}{n}}} = \frac{29 - 4}{\sqrt{\dfrac{32.00}{8}}} = \frac{25}{\sqrt{4}} = 12.5$$

Notice that r is not involved in the calculation. It is involved, however, when we go to the tables. From Appendix q, for $r = 5$ and $df_{error} = 35$, $q_{.05}(5,35) = 4.07$. Because $12.5 > 4.07$, we will reject H_0 and conclude that there is a significant difference between the largest and smallest means.

An alternative to solving for q_{obt} and referring q_{obt} to the sampling distribution of q would be to solve for the smallest difference that would be significant and then to compare our actual difference with the minimum significant difference. This seems like an unnecessary test, but that approach is frequently taken by computer based post hoc procedures, such as those used by SPSS. That explains the way some of your computer printout is displayed. Either way leads to the same results.

12.7 Tukey's Test

Tukey's test

Tukey's HSD (Honestly Significant Difference) test

WSD (Wholly Significant Difference) test

Much of the work on multiple comparisons has been based on the original work of John Tukey, and an important test bears his name. The **Tukey test**, also called the **Tukey's HSD (Honestly Significant Difference) test** or the **WSD (Wholly Significant Difference) test**, uses the Studentized q statistic for its comparisons, except that q_{HSD} is always taken as the maximum value of q_r. In other words, if there are five means, *all* differences are tested as if they were five steps apart. The effect is to fix the familywise error rate at α against all possible null hypotheses, not

---

[11] With only two means we obtain all of the information we need from the F in the analysis of variance table and would have no need to run any contrast.

just the complete null hypothesis, although with some loss of power. The Tukey HSD is the favorite pairwise test for many people because of the control it exercises over α.

If we apply the Tukey HSD to the data on morphine tolerance, we first arrange the means in the order of increasing magnitude, as follows.

M-S	M-M	S-S	S-M	Mc-M
4	10	11	24	29

From Appendix q we find that with 35 df for MS_{error} and r set at 5, the critical value of q equals 4.07. We will use that critical value for all contrasts.

We could run the necessary q test between each pair of means, but that is not the way that most software goes about it. We know MS_{error}, df, q, and the critical value of q (4.07) will be the same for all contrasts. In that case it is easiest to decide what minimal difference between means will be significant.

$$q = \frac{\overline{X}_I - \overline{X}_J}{\sqrt{\dfrac{MS_{error}}{n}}} \quad \text{therefore} \quad q\sqrt{\frac{MS_{error}}{n}} = \overline{X}_I - \overline{X}_J$$

$$= 4.07\sqrt{\frac{32.00}{8}} = 8.14$$

This result means that if the difference between two means is greater than 8.14, a q test would be significant, otherwise it would not. From our means given above, we can see that the following differences are significant because they are all greater than 8.14.

M-S versus S-M $= 4.00 - 24.00 = -20$
M-S versus Mc-M $= 4.00 - 29.00 = -25$
M-M versus S-M $= 10.00 - 24.00 = -14$
M-M versus Mc-M $= 10.00 - 29.00 = -19$
S-S versus S-M $= 11.00 - 24.00 = -13$
S-S versus Mc-M $= 11.00 - 29.00 = -18$

Thus we can write

(M-S = M-M = S-S) $\neq$ (S-M = Mc-M)

The equal signs indicate simply that we could not reject the null hypothesis of equality, not that we have proven the means to be equal.

Unequal Sample Sizes and Heterogeneity of Variance

The Tukey procedure was designed primarily for the case of equal sample sizes ($n_1 = n_2 = \cdots = n_k = n$). Frequently, however, experiments do not work out as planned, and we find ourselves with unequal numbers of observations and still want to carry out a comparison of means. A good bit of work has been done on this problem with respect to the Tukey HSD test (see particularly Games and Howell, 1976; Keselman and Rogan, 1977; Games, Keselman, and Rogan, 1981).

One solution, known as the Tukey–Kramer approach, is to replace $\sqrt{MS_{error}/n}$ with

$$\sqrt{\frac{\dfrac{MS_{error}}{n_i} + \dfrac{MS_{error}}{n_j}}{2}}$$

and otherwise conduct the test the same way you would if the sample sizes were equal. This is the default solution with SPSS.

An alternative, and generally preferable, test was proposed by Games and Howell (1976). The Games and Howell procedure uses what was referred to as the Behrens–Fisher approach to t tests in Chapter 7. The authors suggest that a critical difference between means (i.e., W_r) be calculated separately for every pair of means using

$$W_r = \overline{X}_i - \overline{X}_j = q_{.05}(r, df')\sqrt{\frac{\frac{s_i^2}{n_i} + \frac{s_j^2}{n_j}}{2}}$$

where $q_{.05}(r, df')$ is taken from the tables of the Studentized range statistic on

$$df' = \frac{\left(\frac{s_i^2}{n_i} + \frac{s_j^2}{n_j}\right)^2}{\frac{\left(\frac{s_i^2}{n_i}\right)^2}{n_i - 1} + \frac{\left(\frac{s_j^2}{n_j}\right)^2}{n_j - 1}}$$

degrees of freedom. This is basically the solution referred to earlier in the discussion of multiple t tests, although here we are using the Studentized range statistic instead of t, and it is an optional solution in SPSS. This solution is laborious, but the effort involved is still small compared to that of designing the study and collecting the data. The need for special procedures arises from the fact that the analysis of variance and its attendant contrasts are especially vulnerable to violations of the assumption of homogeneity of variance when the sample sizes are unequal. Moreover, regardless of the sample sizes, if the sample variances are nearly equal you may replace s_i^2 and s_j^2 in the formula for W_r with MS_{error} from the overall analysis of variance. And regardless of the sample size, if the variances are heterogeneous you should probably use the Games and Howell procedure.

Other Range-Based Tests

There are many other tests that have been developed on the basis of the Studentized Range Statistic, and they can be found on the Web site for this book. I just want to mention what they are and how they differ.

Newman–Keuls Test

The Newman–Keuls test has long been controversial, but it is still in use and can be obtained from SPSS. The basic difference between the Newman–Keuls test and Tukey's test is that the latter fixes r at the number of levels of the independent variable, whereas the former continually adjusts r to equal the number of ordered means of from which we are testing the largest and smallest. (In many ways the logic here is similar to the logic for the adjusted Bonferroni test discussed a few pages back.) For example, if we tested M-S versus S-S, they are the largest and smallest of three means, so $r = 3$. The advantage of doing this is that we have a more powerful test. The disadvantage is that we lose some control over α.

The Ryan Procedure

The Ryan procedure (now known as the REGWQ test) is a modification of the Tukey in the direction of the Newman–Keuls. This test adjusts r as we go along, but it does so in a way that keeps the maximum FEW at α. I prefer this test over the Tukey, but it is rarely used.

The Scheffé Test

Scheffé test

The Scheffé test is one of our oldest tests and was based on Tukey's procedure. But this test allows us to hold α at .05 against any and all comparisons, not just pairwise comparisons. Scheffé acknowledged that the test lacked power when applied to pairwise comparisons, and he recommended that it *not* be used to make pairwise comparisons. Unfortunately SPSS and others do not take his advice and, when they use this test, are robbing themselves of power. (Don't blame Scheffé, he told them not to do that.) See Howell (2010) for more information.

Dunnett's Test

Dunnett's test

Dunnett's test is a test designed to compare one treatment (usually a control treatment) with each of the other treatment means. It is more powerful for this purpose, though it lacks the flexibility of other tests. It uses its own tables, which can also be found on the Web site.

Benjamini–Hochberg Test

I have given only a brief sketch of some competing tests for pairwise comparisons. But I feel the need to bring in one more approach, in part because statisticians like it and it will likely play a more important role in the behavioral sciences over time. Each of the post hoc tests that we have discussed has focused on controlling the familywise error rate (FW), and several of them have been sequential tests, which change the critical value as you move through a series on comparisons. Benjamini and Hochberg (1995, 2000) have developed tests that are becoming more popular, are sequential, and are not based on the *FW*. They advocate using what they

False Discovery Rate (FDR)

call the False Discovery Rate (FDR) instead of the familywise error rate. When Tukey began advocating *FW* in the early 1950s he, perhaps unintentionally, oriented our thinking almost exclusively toward controlling the probability of even one Type I error. When you compute a familywise rate, you are dealing with the probability of *one or more* Type I errors. In effect you are saying that your whole set of conclusions are erroneous when you make even one Type I error. (Curiously we don't consider our conclusions to be erroneous if we make Type II errors.) Hochberg and Benjamini have looked at the problem somewhat differently and asked "What percentage of the significant results ("discoveries") that we have found are false discoveries?" Suppose that we carry out nine comparisons (either simple contrasts, complex contrasts, tests on a single mean, or any other test). We find that there are four significant effects but, unknown to us, one of those significant effects is really a Type I error. The FDR is then defined as

$$\text{FDR} = \frac{\text{Number of False Rejections}}{\text{Number of Total Rejections}} = \frac{1}{4} = .25$$

I will take an example of a simple "thought experiment" from Maxwell and Delaney (2004), who have an excellent discussion of the FDR. Imagine that we have a situation in which we test 10 null hypotheses, three of which are known to be false and the others true. Suppose that we mentally run our experiment 100 times, testing all 10 hypotheses for each run. Further suppose that we have very considerable power to reject false null hypotheses, so that we nearly always reject the three false null hypotheses. Finally assume that we have chosen a critical value so as to set the *familywise* error rate at .20. (You probably think that .20 is too high, but bear with me.) Then out of our 100 hypothetical experiments, 80% of the time (1 – 20%) we will make no Type I errors (we will nearly always reject the three truly significant null hypotheses and retain the other seven). Furthermore 20% of the time we will make one Type I error (assuming that we don't make two type I errors in any experiment) because we set the familywise error rate at .20. Because we have a great deal of power, we will almost always reject the three false null hypotheses. Here our FW is .20, which perhaps made you wince. But what about the FDR? Given the description above, we will make no errors in 80% of the experiments. In the other 20 experiments we will make one Type I error and three correct rejections, for an FDR of ¼ = .25 for those 20 experiments and an FDR of 0 for the other 80 experiments. Over the long haul of 100 experiments, the average FDR will be .05, while the FWE will be .20. Thus the critical value that sets the familywise FWE at .20 leaves the FDR at only .05. The problem is how we choose that critical value. Unfortunately, that choice is quite complicated in the general case, but fortunately it is fairly simple in the case of either independent contrasts or pairwise contrasts. See Keselman, Cribbie, and Holland (1999). In this chapter I have been a strong advocate of pairwise contrasts, so restricting ourselves to that case is not particularly onerous.

Benjamini and Hochberg's Linear Step Up (LSU) procedure

The procedure we will follow is called the **Benjamini and Hochberg's Linear Step Up (LSU) procedure.**[12] I will not take the space to develop the logic of this test, but the paper by Benjamini and Hochberg (1995) and the chapter by Maxwell and Delaney (2004) are reasonably clear. Thissen, Steinberg, and Kuang (2002) present a simple method to carry out the Benjamini Hochberg test using spreadsheets. I will frame this discussion in terms of the steps needed to perform the test.

Assume that we have performed 10 pairwise contrasts on Siegel's morphine data. The results are shown in Table 12.4 ordered by p value. The column labeled "i" is the index of the comparison and simply ranks the p values from highest to lowest. The critical part of the table is labeled p_{crit}, the critical value for our test. We define

$$p_{crit} = \left(\frac{i}{k}\right)\alpha$$

where "i" is the index, "k" is the number of tests (here $k = 10$), and α is the desired FDR (here $\alpha = .05$). To carry out the test we work our way down the table. If $p > p_{crit}$ we retain the null hypothesis and move on to the next row. As soon as $p < p_{crit}$ we reject that null hypothesis and all subsequent ones.

Using the Benjamini-Hochberg test we would declare that M-M vs. S-S, S-M vs. Mc-M, and M-S vs. M-M are not different from each other pairwise. All other contrasts are judged statistically significant. With Tukey's test we only rejected six null hypotheses, retaining M-S vs. S-S, which was rejected by Benjamin-Hochberg. That is a contrast that we would like to find significant, because it says that if you get saline in the same condition in which you had received morphine your sensitivity will increase.

Table 12.4   Benjamini-Hochberg test on Siegel's data

Group	t	p	i	p_{crit}	Significance
M-M vs. S-S	−.354	.726	10	.05	No
S-M vs. Mc-M	−1.768	.086	9	.045	No
M-S vs. M-M	−2.121	.041	8	.040	No
M-S vs. S-S	−2.475	.018	7	.035	Yes
S-S vs. S-M	−4.596	.00007	6	.030	Yes
M-M vs. S-M	−4.950	.00003	5	.025	Yes
S-S vs. Mc-M	−6.364	.00000	4	.020	Yes
M-M vs. Mc-M	−6.717	.00000	3	.015	Yes
M-S vs. S-M	−7.071	.00000	2	.010	Yes
M-S vs. Mc-M	−8.839	.00000	1	.005	Yes

© Cengage Learning 2013

[12] Benjamini and Hochberg (2000) recommended a variation on the test given here, sometimes called their "adaptive" test. It is more powerful than the LSU test, but somewhat more cumbersome. Both of these tests are different from the Hochberg GT2 test produced by SPSS. A program in R (BenjaminiHochbergLSU.R) is available at the book's Web site.

12.8 Which Test?

Choosing the most appropriate multiple-comparison procedure for your specific situation is not easy. Many tests are available, and they differ in a number of ways. The choice is a bit easier if we consider the two extremes first.

If you have planned your test in advance and you want to run only one comparison, I would suggest that you run a standard *t* test (correcting for heterogeneity of variance if necessary), or, if you have a complex comparison, a linear contrast. If you have several a priori contrasts to run, not necessarily pairwise, the multistage Bonferroni *t* does a good job of controlling *FW* while at the same time maximizing power.

If you have a large number of groups and wish to make many comparisons, whether or not you are interested in all of the possible pairwise comparisons, you would probably be well advised to use Tukey's test (or the REGWQ if possible). I can't think of a situation where I would personally recommend the Scheffé, but I presented it here because it is a common test and real hard-liners like it.

What about the Benjamini-Hochberg test? This is a difficult test to place in a table because it controls an entirely different error rate. It is not fair to say that one test is more powerful than another when they are working on different error rates. I have considerable fondness for the Benjamini-Hochberg test just because it is not based on the idea that one false rejection invalidates a family of conclusions. If you are willing to accept an occasional Type I error to gain power for other contrasts, there is much to recommend this test.

12.9 Computer Solutions

Most software packages will perform multiple comparison procedures, but not all packages have all procedures available. Exhibit 12.1 contains the results of an analysis of the morphine data using SAS. I chose SAS because it has a broad choice of procedures and is one of the major packages. It also has more information in its printout than does SPSS and is thus somewhat more useful for our purpose. I have included the Scheffé test for comparison even though I have already said that it is totally inappropriate for simple pairwise comparisons.

Exhibit 12.1 begins with the SAS program commands and the overall analysis of variance. This analysis agrees with the summary table shown in Table 12.1. The $R^2 = .757$ is simply η^2. You can see that our experimental manipulation accounts for a substantial portion of the variance. The remainder of the exhibit includes the results of the Newman–Keuls, Ryan, Tukey, and Scheffé tests, some of which I have mentioned only briefly.

The Newman–Keuls, as the least conservative test, reports the most differences between conditions. If you look first at the means and "SNK Grouping" at the end of that portion of the printout, you will see a column consisting of the letters A, B, and C. Conditions that share the same letter are judged to not differ from one another. Thus the means of Conditions Mc-M and S-M are not significantly different from one another, but, because they don't have a letter in common with other conditions, they are different from the means of S-S, M-M, and M-S. Similarly, Conditions S-S and M-M share the letter B and their means are thus not significantly different from each other, but are different from the means of the other three conditions. Finally, the mean of Condition M-S is different from the means of all other conditions.

```
Data Siegel;
     Infile 'Siegel.dat';
     Input Subject Condition latency;
Run;

Proc GLM Data = Siegel;
     Class Condition;
     Model Latency = Condition/SS3;
     Means Condition/ SNK Tukey REGWQ Scheffe;
Run;
```

The SAS System   11:15 Wednesday
                                              August 18, 2010

The GLM Procedure

Dependent Variable: LATENCY

Source	DF	Sum of Squares	Mean Square	F Value	Pr > F
Model	4	3497.600000	874.400000	27.33	< .0001
Error	35	1120.000000	32.000000		
Corrected Total	39	4617.600000			

$\eta^2 \longrightarrow$

R-Square	Coeff Var	Root MSE	LATENCY Mean
0.757450	36.26189	5.656854	15.60000

Source	DF	Type III SS	Mean Square	F Value	Pr > F
CONDITION	4	3497.600000	874.400000	27.33	<.0001

F for Condition

Student-Newman-Keuls Test for LATENCY

NOTE: This test controls the Type I experimentwise error rate under the
complete null hypothesis but not under partial null hypotheses.

Alpha = 0.05   Error Degrees of Freedom = 35   Error Mean Square = 32

Number of Means	2	3	4	5
Critical Range	5.7420599	6.9219411	7.6279954	8.1319062

$w_5 = q_5$

Means with the same letter are not significantly different.

SNK Grouping	Mean	N	Condition
A	29.000	8	Mc-M
A	24.000	8	S-M
B	10.000	8	S-S
B	10.000	8	M-M
C	4.000	8	M-S

Exhibit 12-1   *(Continues)*

Ryan-Einot-Gabriel-Welsch Multiple Range Test for LATENCY

NOTE: This test controls the Type I experimentwise error rate.

Alpha = 0.05   Error Degrees of Freedom = 35   Error Mean Square = 32

	Number of Means	2	3		4	5
Larger than for SNK →	Critical Range	(6.8765475	7.5391919)		(7.6279954	8.1319062)

Means with the same letter are not significantly different.

→ Same as SNK

REGWQ Grouping		Mean	N	CONDITION
	A	29.000	8	Mc-M
	A	24.000	8	S-M
	B	11.000	8	S-S
	B	10.000	8	M-M
	B	4.000	8	M-S

Tukey's Studentized Range (HSD) Test for LATENCY

NOTE: This test controls the Type I experimentwise error rate, but it generally has a higher Type II error rate than REGWQ.

Alpha = 0.05   Error Degrees of Freedom = 35   Error Mean Square = 32

Critical Value of Studentized Range = 4.06595

Minimum Significant Difference = (8.1319)   ← Critical range for all differences

Means with the same letter are not significantly different.

Tukey Grouping		Mean	N	CONDITION
	A	29.000	8	Mc-M
	A	24.000	8	S-M
	B	11.000	8	S-S
	B	10.000	8	M-M
	B	4.000	8	M-S

Scheffe's Test for LATENCY

NOTE: This test controls the Type I experimentwise error rate.

Alpha = 0.05   Error Degrees of Freedom = 35   Error Mean Square = 32

Critical Value of F = 2.64147

Minimum Significant Difference = (9.1939)   ← Critical range for all differences

Means with the same letter are not significantly different.

Scheffe Grouping		Mean	N	CONDITION
	A	29.000	8	Mc-M
	A	24.000	8	S-M
	B	11.000	8	S-S
	B	10.000	8	M-M
	B	4.000	8	M-S

Exhibit 12-1   *(Continued)*

If you look a bit higher in the table you will see a statement about how this test deals with the familywise (here called "experimentwise") error rate. As I said earlier, the Newman-Keuls holds the familywise error rate at α against the complete null hypothesis, but allows it to rise in the case where a subset of null hypotheses is true. You next see a statement saying that the test is being run at $\alpha = .05$, that we have 35 df for the error term, and that $MS_{error} = 32.00$. Following this information you see the critical ranges. These are the minimum differences between means that would be significant for different values of r. The critical ranges are equal to

$$W_r = q_{.05}(r, df_e)\sqrt{\frac{MS_{error}}{n}}$$

For example, when $r = 3$ (a difference between the largest and smallest of three means)

$$W_3 = q_{.05}(3, df_e)\sqrt{\frac{MS_{error}}{n}} = 3.46\sqrt{\frac{32}{8}} = 3.46(2) = 6.92$$

Because all three step differences (e.g., $29 - 11 = 18$; $24 - 10 = 14$; $11 - 4 = 7$) are greater than 6.92, they will all be declared significant.

The next section of Exhibit 12.1 shows the results of the Ryan (REGWQ) test. Notice that the critical ranges for $r = 2$ and $r = 3$ are larger than they were for the Newman–Keuls (though smaller than they will be for the Tukey). As a result, for $r = 3$ we need to exceed a difference of 7.54, whereas the difference between 11 and 4 is only 7. Thus this test will not find Group 1 (M-S) to be different from Group 3 (S-S), whereas it was different for the more liberal Newman–Keuls. However, the maximum familywise error rate for this set of comparisons is $\alpha = .05$, whereas it would be nearly $\alpha = .10$ for the Newman–Keuls.

The Tukey test is presented slightly differently, but you can see that Tukey requires all differences between means to exceed a critical range of 8.1319 to be declared significant, regardless of where they lie in an ordered series. For this specific set of data our conclusions are the same as they were for the Ryan test, although that will certainly not always be the case.

Although the Scheffé test is run quite differently from the others, it is possible to compute a critical range for all pairwise comparisons. From Exhibit 12.1 we can see that this range is 9.1939, almost a full point larger than the critical range for Tukey. This reflects the extreme conservatism of the Scheffé procedure, especially with just pairwise contrasts, and illustrates my major objection to the use of this test for this purpose.

SAS will also produce a number of other multiple comparison tests, including the Bonferroni and the Dunn-Šidák. I do not show those here because it is generally foolish to use either of those tests when you want to make *all possible* pairwise comparisons among means. The Ryan or Tukey test is almost always more powerful and still controls the family wise error rate. I suppose that if I had a limited number of pairwise contrasts that I was interested in, I could use the Bonferroni procedure in SAS (BON) and promise not to look at the contrasts that were not of interest.

12.10   Trend Analysis

The analyses we have been discussing are concerned with identifying differences among group means, whether these comparisons represent complex contrasts among groups or simple pairwise contrasts. Suppose, however, that the groups defined by the independent variable are ordered along some continuum. An example might be a study of the beneficial effects of aspirin in preventing heart disease. We could ask subjects to take daily doses of 1, 2, 3, 4, or 5 of 81mg aspirin, often referred to as "baby aspirin." In this study we would not be concerned so much with whether a 4-pill dose was better than a 2-pill dose, for example, as with whether the beneficial effects of aspirin increase with increasing the dosage of the drug. In other words, we are concerned with the **trend** in effectiveness rather than multiple comparisons among specific means.

To continue with the aspirin example, consider two possible outcomes. In one outcome we might find that the effectiveness increases linearly with dosage. In this case the more aspirin you take, the greater the effect, at least within the range of dosages tested. A second, alternative, finding might be that effectiveness increases with dosage up to some point, but then the curve relating effectiveness to dosage levels off and perhaps even decreases. This would be either a "quadratic" relationship or a relationship with both linear and quadratic components. It would be important to discover such relationships because they would suggest that there is some optimal dose, with lower doses being less effective and higher doses adding little, if anything, to the effect.

linear

quadratic functions

Typical **linear** and **quadratic functions** are illustrated in Figure 12.2. It is difficult to characterize quadratic functions neatly because the shape of the function depends both on the sign of the coefficient of X^2 and on the sign of X (the curve changes direction when X passes from negative to positive, and for positive values of X the curve rises if the coefficient is positive and falls if it is negative). Also included in Figure 12.2 is a function with both linear and quadratic components. Here you can see that the curvature imposed by a quadratic function is superimposed on a rising linear trend.

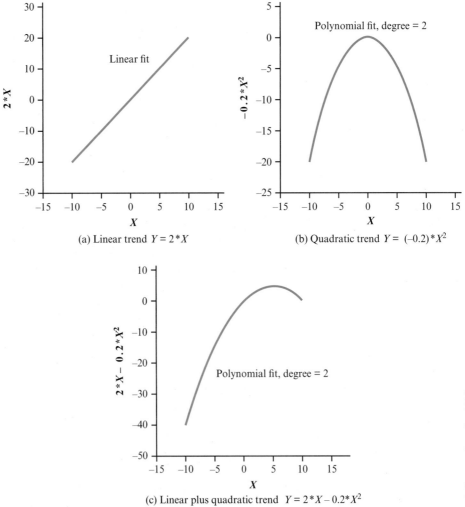

(a) Linear trend $Y = 2*X$ (b) Quadratic trend $Y = (-0.2)*X^2$

(c) Linear plus quadratic trend $Y = 2*X - 0.2*X^2$

Figure 12.2   Typical linear and quadratic functions

Tests of trend differ in an important way from the comparison procedures we have been discussing. In all of the previous examples, the independent variable was generally qualitative. Thus, for example, we could have written down the groups in the morphine-tolerance example in any order we chose. Moreover, the F or t values for the contrasts depended only on the numerical value of the means, not on which particular groups went with which particular means. In the analysis we are now considering, F or t values will depend on both the group means and the particular ordering of those means. To put this slightly differently using the aspirin example, a test between the largest and the smallest means will not be affected by which group happens to have which mean. However, in trend analysis the results would be quite different if the 1-grain and 5-grain groups had the smallest and largest means than if the 4- and 2-grain groups had the smallest and largest means, respectively. (A similar point was made in Section 6.7 in discussing the nondirectionality of the chi-square test.)

Alcohol and Aggression

We will take the example of the study by Giancola and Corman (2007) on the relationship between alcohol and aggression in the presence of a distracting task. This is the study that began Chapter 11, and the data and summary tables are presented in Table 12.5. The levels of the independent variable (D0, D2, D4, D6, and D8) refer to the number of illuminated squares that participants had to report in the distracting task. Notice that they increase linearly from 0 to 8. Obvious questions are whether aggression decreases linearly with distraction, whether it decreases to some level and then holds steady, or whether it decreases and then starts to increase again. A glance at the means would suggest the latter, but we want to test that.

A standard one-way analysis of variance produced the following summary table.

Summary Table

Source	df	SS	MS	F
Treatments	4	62.460	15.615	6.90*
Error	55	124.458	2.263	
Total	59	189.918		

* $p < .05$

Table 12.5   Level of shock administered as a function of task difficulty

	D0	D2	D4	D6	D8	Total
	1.28	−1.18	−0.41	−0.85	2.01	
	1.35	0.15	−1.25	0.14	0.40	
	3.31	1.36	−1.33	−1.38	2.34	
	3.06	2.61	−0.47	1.28	−1.80	
	2.59	0.66	−0.60	1.85	5.00	
	3.25	1.32	−1.72	−0.59	2.27	
	2.98	0.73	−1.74	−1.30	6.47	
	1.53	−1.06	−0.77	0.38	2.94	
	−2.68	0.24	−0.41	−0.35	0.47	
	2.64	0.27	−1.20	2.29	3.22	
	1.26	0.72	−0.31	−0.25	0.01	
	1.06	2.28	−0.74	0.51	−0.66	
MeanMean	1.802	0.675	−0.912	0.544	1.889	0.800
St. Dev.	1.656	1.140	0.515	1.180	2.370	1.800
Var.	2.741	1.299	0.265	1.394	5.616	3.168

From the summary table it is apparent that there are significant differences among the five groups. One way to examine these differences would be to plot the group means as a function of the number of illuminated squares. This is shown in Figure 12.3, and it is apparent that the effectiveness of distraction in reducing aggression increases up to a point but with higher levels of distraction aggression returns to base levels.

The overall analysis of variance really asked if a horizontal straight line through Y = 0.800 (the grand mean) would fit the data adequately. The *F* led to rejection of that null hypothesis because sample means were as high as 1.9 and as low as −.9. Our next question asks whether a nonhorizontal straight line provides a good fit to the data. A glance at Figure 12.3 would suggest that this probably is not the case, or at least the fit would be poor. We will then follow that question by asking whether systematic residual (nonerror) variance remains in the data after fitting a linear function, and, if so, whether this residual variance can be explained by a quadratic function.

To run a trend analysis, we will return to the material we discussed under the headings of linear and orthogonal contrasts. (Don't be confused by the use of the word *linear* in the last sentence. We will use the same approach when it comes to fitting a quadratic function. Linear in this sense simply means that we will form a linear combination of coefficients and means, where nothing is raised to a power.)

In Section 12.3 we defined a linear contrast as

$$\psi = a_1\overline{X}_1 + a_2\overline{X}_2 + a_3\overline{X}_3 + \cdots + a_k\overline{X}_k = \sum a_j\overline{X}_j$$

The only difference between what we are doing here and what we did earlier will be in the coefficients we use. In the case in which there are equal numbers of subjects in the groups and the values on the abscissa are equally spaced, the coefficients for linear, quadratic, and higher-order functions (**polynomial trend coefficients**) are easily tabled and are found in Appendix Polynomial. From Appendix Polynomial we find that for five groups the linear and quadratic coefficients are

polynomial trend coefficients

Linear:	−2	−1	0	1	2
Quadratic:	2	−1	−2	−1	2

We will not be using the cubic and quartic coefficients, but their use will be evident from what follows. Notice that like any set of orthogonal linear coefficients, the requirements that $\Sigma a_j = 0$ and $\Sigma a_i b_j = 0$ are met. The coefficients do not form a "standard set," because the sum of the absolute values of the coefficients does not equal 2. That is not a problem here.

As you should recall from Section 12.3, we calculate a sum of squares for the contrast as

$$SS_{\text{contrast}} = \frac{n\psi^2}{\Sigma a_j^2}$$

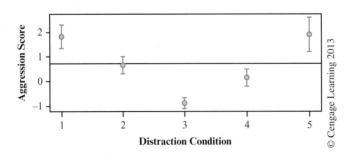

Figure 12.3   Aggression as a function of distraction

In our case,

$$\psi_{\text{linear}} = (-2)1.802 + (-1)0.675 + (0)-1.912 + (1)0.544 + (2)1.889$$

$$= 0.0425$$

$$SS_{\text{linear}} = \frac{n\psi^2}{\sum a_j^2} = \frac{12(0.0425^2)}{10} = .002$$

Like all contrasts, this contrast has a single degree of freedom, and therefore $SS_{\text{linear}} = MS_{\text{linear}}$. As you probably suspect from what you already know, we can convert this mean square for the contrast to an F by dividing by MS_{error}:

$$F = \frac{MS_{\text{linear}}}{MS_{\text{error}}}$$

$$= \frac{.002}{2.263} = 0.0009$$

This is an F on 1 and 55 degrees of freedom; from Appendix F we find that $F_{.05}(1,55) = 4.015$. Because the F for the linear component (0.0009) is far less than 4.015, we will retain H_0 and conclude that there is no significant linear trend in our means. In other words, we will conclude that aggressiveness does not vary linearly with increasing levels of distraction. Notice here that a nonsignificant F means that the trend component we are testing is not significantly different from 0.[13]

Although our data do not show a linear trend, it would appear that they do show a quadratic one—the line goes down and then up. It is also common to find data with both a linear and a quadratic trend, which would look like the plot in Figure 12.2c.

The next step is to ask whether the residual variance remaining after we fit the linear component is significantly greater than the error variance that we already know is present. If SS_{linear} accounted for virtually all of $SS_{\text{treatment}}$, there would be little or nothing left over for higher-order terms to explain. On the other hand, if SS_{linear} were a relatively small part of $SS_{\text{treatment}}$, then it would make sense to look for higher-order components. From our previous calculations we obtain

$$SS_{\text{residual}} = SS_{\text{Treatment}} - SS_{\text{linear}}$$

$$= 62.460 - 0.002$$

$$= 62.458$$

$$df_{\text{residual}} = df_{\text{Treatment}} - df_{\text{linear}}$$

$$= 4 - 1$$

$$= 3$$

$$MS_{\text{residual}} = \frac{SS_{\text{residual}}}{df_{\text{residual}}}$$

$$= \frac{62.458}{3}$$

$$= 20.819$$

---

[13] I recently received a message from someone with similar data. He was studying the experimental hypothesis that drug effects increased with dosage. He had obtained a nonsignificant overall F, but when he computed a test on linear trend, the result was "highly significant." He wanted to know what to do. Because the linear trend tested his hypothesis directly, whereas the overall F did not, my recommendation was to rely solely on the test for trend.

$$F_{\text{residual}} = \frac{MS_{\text{residual}}}{MS_{\text{error}}}$$
$$= \frac{20.819}{2.263}$$
$$= 9.20$$

Because F for the residual is greater than $F_{.(05, 3, 55)}$, we will reject the null hypothesis and conclude that there is significant variability left to be explained over and above that accounted for by the linear component. The calculations for the quadratic component are essentially the same as above with the exception that quadratic coefficients take the place of linear ones.

$$\psi_{\text{quadratic}} = (2)1.802 + (-1)0.675 + (-2)(-0.912) + (-1)0.544 + (2)1.889$$
$$= 7.989$$

$$SS_{\text{quadratic}} = \frac{n\psi^2}{\sum b_j^2}$$
$$= \frac{12(7.989^2)}{14}$$
$$= 54.706$$

$$F = \frac{MS_{\text{quadratic}}}{MS_{\text{error}}}$$
$$= \frac{54.706}{2.263}$$
$$= 24.17$$

This test is clearly significant, showing that there is a quadratic trend to our data. That should not come as any surprise because it is obvious from the plot.

A word of caution is in order at this point. You might be tempted to go ahead and apply the cubic and quartic coefficients that you find in Appendix Polynomial. You might also observe that having done this, the four sums of squares ($SS_{\text{linear}}, \ldots, SS_{\text{quartic}}$) will sum to $SS_{\text{treatment}}$ and be impressed that you have accounted for all of the sums of squares between groups. Before you get too impressed, think about how proud you would be if you showed that you could draw a straight line that exactly fit two points. The same idea applies here. Regardless of the data, you know before you begin that a polynomial of order $k - 1$ will exactly fit k points. That is one reason why I was not eager to go much beyond fitting the quadratic components to the data at hand. Moreover, if you were to fit a fourth-order polynomial and find that the quartic component was significant, what would you have to say about the results? A linear or quadratic component would make some sense, but a quartic component could not be explained by any theory I know.

Unequal Intervals

In the preceding section we assumed that the levels of the independent variable are equally spaced along some continuum. It is possible to run a trend analysis when we do not have equal intervals, and the arithmetic is the same. The only problem comes when we try to obtain the trend coefficients, because we cannot take our coefficients from Appendix Polynomial unless the intervals are equal.

Calculating quadratic coefficients is not too difficult and a good explanation can be found in Keppel (1973). For higher-order polynomials the calculations are more laborious, but a description of the process can be found in Robson (1959). For most people, their analyses will be carried out with standard statistical software, and that software will often handle the problem of unequal spacing. Without diving deeply into the manuals, it is often difficult to determine how your software handles the spacing problem.

An example containing both a quadratic and a cubic component can be found in Exercise 12.25. Working through that exercise can teach you a lot about trend analysis.

Key Terms

Error rate per comparison (*PC*) (12.1)

Familywise error rate (*FW*) (12.1)

Omnibus null hypothesis (12.1)

A priori comparisons (12.1)

Post hoc comparisons (12.1)

Contrasts (12.3)

Linear combination (12.3)

Linear contrast (12.3)

Partition (12.3)

Orthogonal contrasts (12.3)

Dunn's test (12.3)

Bonferroni *t* (12.3)

Bonferroni inequality (12.3)

Dunn-Šidák test (12.3)

Fisher's least significance difference (LSD) (12.6)

Studentized range statistic (*q*) (12.6)

Tukey test (12.6)

Tukey HSD (honestly significant difference) test (12.6)

Newman–Keuls test (12.6)

Ryan procedure (REGWQ) (12.6)

Scheffé test (12.6)

Dunnett's test (12.6)

False Discovery Rate (FDR) (12.6)

Benjamini and Hochberg's Linear Step Up (LSU) procedure (12.6)

Trend (12.9)

Quadratic function (12.9)

Polynomial trend coefficients (12.9)

Exercises

12.1 Assume that the data that follow represent the effects of food and/or water deprivation on behavior in a learning task. Treatments 1 and 2 represent control conditions in which the animal received ad lib food and water (1) or else food and water twice per day (2). In treatment 3 animals were food deprived, in treatment 4 they were water deprived, and in treatment 5 they were deprived of both food and water. The dependent variable is the number of trials to reach a predetermined criterion. Assume that before running our experiment we decided that we wanted to compare the combined control groups (treatments 1 and 2) with the combined experimental groups, the control groups with each other, the singly deprived treatments with the doubly deprived treatment, and the singly deprived treatments with each other.

Ad Lib Control	Two per Day Control	Food Deprived	Water Deprived	Food and Water Deprived
18	20	6	15	12
20	25	9	10	11
21	23	8	9	8
16	27	6	12	13
15	25	11	14	11
90	120	40	60	55

© Cengage Learning 2013

a. Analyze the data using linear contrastsb.

b. Show that the contrasts are orthogonal.

c. Show that the sums of squares for the contrasts sum to SS_{treat}.

12.2 Compute F for the linear contrast on the two groups in Exercise 11.4. Is this a waste of time? Why or why not?

12.3 What would be the per comparison and familywise error rates in Exercise 12.4? (*Hint*: Are the contrasts orthogonal?)

12.4 Using the data from the first exercise in Chapter 11, compute the linear contrasts for Counting and Rhyming versus Adjective and Imagery, and then compare the Adjective versus Imagery conditions. Use $\alpha = .05$ for each contrast. (*Note that this and subsequent exercises refer to exercises in Chapter 11, not this chapter.*)

12.5 Compute the Studentized range statistic for the two groups in Exercise 11.4 and show that it is equal to $t\sqrt{2}$ (where t is taken from Exercise 11.4b).

12.6 Run the Games and Howell (1976) approach to Tukey's HSD procedure for unequal sample sizes on the following data.

Group	1	2	3	4	5
$\overline{X}_j$	10	18	19	21	29
n_j	8	5	8	7	9
s_j^2	7.4	8.9	8.6	7.2	9.3

© Cengage Learning 2013

12.7 Run the Bonferroni t test on the data for Exercise 11.1, using the contrasts supplied in Exercise 12.4. Set the maximum FW at .05.

12.8 Compute the Fs for the following linear contrasts in Exercise 11.3. Save the results for use in Chapter 13.

   a. 1 and 2 versus 3 and 4

   b. 1 and 3 versus 2 and 4

   c. 1 and 4 versus 2 and 3

   d. What questions do the contrasts in (a), (b), and (c) address?

12.9 Why might you be more interested in running specific contrasts on the data referred to in Exercises 12.10?

12.10 Run a Tukey test on the example given in Table 11.2 (page 332) and interpret the results.

12.11 Use the Scheffé test on the data in Exercise 12.06 to compare groups 1, 2, and 3 (combined) with groups 4 and 5 (combined). Then compare group 1 with groups 2, 3, and 4 (combined).

12.12 How could a statistical package that did not have a Bonferroni command be used to run the Bonferroni t test on the data in Exercise 12.7?

12.13 Using SPSS to apply Dunnett's test to the log transformed data in Table 11.6.

12.14 Apply the Tukey procedure to the log transformed THC data from Table 11.6 (page 348). What is the maximum FW for this procedure?

12.15 The Bonferroni multistage test is sometimes referred to as a modified sequentially rejective procedure. Why?

12.16 Using the data in Epineq.dat, compute both the linear and quadratic trend tests on the three drug dosages. Do this separately for each of the three intervals. (*Hint*: The linear coefficients are [−0.597110, −0.183726, 0.780836], and the quadratic coefficients are [0.556890, −0.795557, 0.238667].)

12.17 Write a brief report of the results computed for Exercise 12.17.

12.18 Fit linear and quadratic trend components to the Conti and Musty (1984) log transformed data in Table 11.6. The control condition received 0 μg of THC. For purposes of this example, assume that there were 10 subjects in all groups. (You could add a 2.56 to the 0.5 μg group and a 2.35 and 2.36 to the 1 μg group without altering the results appreciably.) The linear coefficients (calculated with unequal spacing on the independent variable) are $[-0.72, -0.62, -0.22, 0.28, 1.28]$. The quadratic coefficients are $[0.389, 0.199, -0.362, -0.612, 0.387]$. Verify your answers using SPSS ONEWAY if you have it available.

12.19 In Exercise 12.20 it would not have made much of a difference whether we combined the data across the three intervals or not. Under what conditions would you expect that it would make a big difference?

12.20 Use any statistical package to apply the Tukey and Scheffé procedures to the data from Introini-Collison and McGaugh (1986), described in the exercises for Chapter 11 (page 366). Do these analyses for both Epineq.dat and Epinuneq.dat, which are on the book's Web site. Do not combine across the levels of the interval variable.

12.21 Interpret the results in Exercise 12.16.

12.22 In Exercise 11.10 we considered a study by Foa et al. concerning therapy for victims of rape. The raw data can be found on the Web site at Ex12.26.dats. Apply the Benjamini & Hochberg LSU procedure to these data.

12.23 Using the data from Exercise 12.1, compute confidence interval for the first comparison (contrast) described in that question. Interpret your answer. (If you use SPSS, use the Compare Means/One-Way ANOVA procedure, which allows you to specify coefficients.)

12.24 Stone, Rudd, Ragozzino, and Gold (1992) investigated the role that glucose plays in memory. Mice were raised with a 12-hour light-on/light-off cycle, starting at 6:00 A.M. During training mice were placed in the lighted half of an experimental box and given foot shock when they moved into the dark half. The mice quickly learned to stay in the lighted half. The day/night cycle was then advanced by 4 hours for all mice, which is known to interfere with memory of the original training. Three days later mice were retested 30 minutes after being injected with 0, 1, 10, 100, 250, or 500 mg/kg of sucrose. The purpose was to see whether sucrose would reduce the disruptive effects of changing the diurnal cycle, and whether different doses would have different effects. Data that have been generated to loosely mimic the results of Stone et al., are given below, where the dependent variable is the latency to enter the dark chamber.

Glucose Level in mg/kg					
0	1	10	100	250	500
295	129	393	653	379	521
287	248	484	732	530	241
91	350	308	570	364	162
260	278	112	434	385	197
193	150	132	690	355	156
52	195	414	679	558	384

© Cengage Learning 2013

a. Plot these data using both the actual dosage, and the values 1, 2, 3, 4, 5, 6 as the values of X.

b. Run a trend analysis using SPSS One-way, if available, with the actual dosage as the independent variable.

c. Repeat part (b) using the 1, 2, 3, 4, 5, 6 coding as the independent variable.

d. Interpret your results. How might these results have something to say to students who stay up all night studying for an exam?

e. Why might you, or Stone et al., prefer one coding system over another?

12.25 Using the data from Exercise 11.27, perform the appropriate test(s) to draw meaningful conclusions from the study by Davey et al. (2003).

12.26 Using the data from Exercise 12.1, compute effect sizes on all of the contrasts that you ran with that question. How would you interpret these effect sizes? Why are these called standardized effect sizes, and what would an unstandardized effect size be?

Discussion Questions

12.27 Students often have difficulty seeing why a priori and post hoc tests have different family-wise error rates. Make up an example (not necessarily from statistics) that would help to explain the difference to others.

12.28 Find an example in the research literature of a study that used at least five different conditions and create a data set that might have come from this experiment. Apply several of the techniques we have discussed, justifying their use and interpreting the results. (You would never apply several different techniques to a set of data except for an example such as this. *Hint*: You can generate data with a given mean and variance by taking any set of numbers [make them at least unimodal and symmetrical], standardizing them, multiplying the standard scores by the desired standard deviation, and then adding the desired mean to the result. Do this *for each group separately* and you will have your data.)

Of this total, we know how much can be attributed to A, C, and AC. What is left over represents unaccountable variation or error. Thus

$$SS_{error} = SS_{total} - (SS_A + SS_C + SS_{AC})$$

However, since $SS_A + SS_C + SS_{AC} = SS_{cells}$, it is simpler to write

$$SS_{error} = SS_{total} - SS_{cells}$$

This provides us with our sum of squares for error, and we now have all of the necessary sums of squares for our analysis.

A more direct, but tiresome, way to calculate SS_{error} exists, and it makes explicit just what the error sum of squares is measuring. SS_{error} represents the variation within each cell, and as such can be calculated by obtaining the sum of squares for each cell separately. For example,

$$SS_{cell_{11}} = (9-7)^2 + (8-7)^2 + \cdots + (7-7)^2 = 30$$

We could perform a similar operation on each of the remaining cells, obtaining

$$
\begin{aligned}
SS_{cell_{11}} &= 30.0 \\
SS_{cell_{12}} &= 40.9 \\
\cdots &\quad \cdots \\
\frac{SS_{cell_{25}}}{SS_{error}} &= \frac{64.1}{722.30}
\end{aligned}
$$

The sum of squares within each cell is then summed over the 10 cells to produce SS_{error}. Although this is the hard way of computing an error term, it demonstrates that SS_{error} is in fact the sum of within-cell variation. When we come to mean squares, MS_{error} will turn out to be just the average of the variances within each of the $2 \times 5 = 10$ cells.

Table 13.2c shows the summary table for the analysis of variance. The source column and the sum of squares column are fairly obvious from what you already know. Next look at the degrees of freedom. The calculation of df is straightforward. The total number of degrees of freedom (df_{total}) is always equal to $N - 1$. The degrees of freedom for Age and Condition are the number of levels of the variable minus 1. Thus, $df_A = a - 1 = 1$ and $df_C = c - 1 = 4$. The number of degrees of freedom for any interaction is simply the product of the degrees of freedom for the components of that interaction. Thus, $df_{AC} = df_A \times df_C = (a-1)(c-1) = 1 \times 4 = 4$. These three rules apply to *any* analysis of variance, no matter how complex. The degrees of freedom for error can be obtained either by subtraction ($df_{error} = df_{total} - df_A - df_C - df_{AC}$), or by realizing that the error term represents variability within each cell. Because each cell has $n - 1$ df, and since there are ac cells, $df_{error} = ac(n-1) = 2 \times 5 \times 9 = 90$.

Just as with the one-way analysis of variance, the mean squares are again obtained by dividing the sums of squares by the corresponding degrees of freedom. This same procedure is used in any analysis of variance.

Finally, to calculate F, we divide each MS by MS_{error}. Thus for Age, $F_A = MS_A/MS_{error}$; for Condition, $F_C = MS_C/MS_{error}$; and for AC, $F_{AC} = MS_{AC}/MS_{error}$. To appreciate why MS_{error} is the appropriate divisor in each case, we will digress briefly in a moment and consider the underlying structural model and the expected mean squares. First, however, we need to consider what the results of this analysis tell us.

Interpretation

From the summary table in Table 13.2c, you can see that there were significant effects for Age, Condition, and their interaction. In conjunction with the means, it is clear that younger participants recall more items overall than do older participants. It is also clear that those tasks that involve greater depth of processing lead to better recall overall than do tasks involving less processing. This is in line with the differences we found in Chapter 11. The significant interaction tells us that the effect of one variable depends on the level of the other variable. For example, differences between older and younger participants on the easier tasks such as counting and rhyming are much less than age differences on tasks, such as imagery and intentional, that involve greater depths of processing. Another view is that differences among the five conditions are less extreme for the older participants than they are for the younger ones.

These results support Eysenck's hypothesis that older participants do not perform as well as younger participants on tasks that involve a greater depth of processing of information, but perform about equally with younger participants when the task does not involve much processing. These results do not mean that older participants are not *capable* of processing information as deeply. Older participants simply may not make the effort that younger participants do. Whatever the reason, however, they do not perform as well on those tasks.

13.2   Structural Models and Expected Mean Squares

Recall that in discussing a one-way analysis of variance, we employed the structural model

$$X_{ij} = \mu + \tau_j + e_{ij}$$

where $\tau_j = \mu_j - \mu$ represented the effect of the jth treatment. In a two-way design we have two "treatment" variables (call them A and B) and their interaction. These can be represented in the model by α, β, and $\alpha\beta$, producing a slightly more complex model. This model can be written as

$$X_{ijk} = \mu + \alpha_i + \beta_j + \alpha\beta_{ij} + e_{ijk}$$

where

$$\begin{aligned}
X_{ijk} &= \text{any observation} \\
\mu &= \text{the grand mean} \\
\alpha_i &= \text{the effect of Factor } A_i = \mu_{A_i} - \mu \\
\beta_j &= \text{the effect of Factor } B_j = \mu_{B_j} - \mu \\
\alpha\beta_{ij} &= \text{the interaction effect of Factor } A_i \text{ and Factor } B_j \\
&= \mu - \mu_{A_i} - \mu_{B_j} + \mu_{ij}; \sum_i \alpha\beta_{ij} = \sum_j \alpha\beta_{ij} = 0 \\
e_{ijk} &= \text{the unit of error associated with observation } X_{ijk} \\
&= N(0, \sigma_e^2)
\end{aligned}$$

From this model it can be shown that with fixed variables the expected mean squares are those given in Table 13.3. It is apparent that the error term is the proper denominator for each F ratio, because the $E(MS)$ for any effect contains only one term other than σ_e^2.

Table 13.3   Expected mean squares for two-way analysis of variance (fixed)

Source	$E(MS)$
A	$\sigma_e^2 + nb\theta_\alpha^2$
B	$\sigma_e^2 + na\theta_\beta^2$
AB	$\sigma_e^2 + n\theta_{\alpha\beta}^2$
Error	σ_e^2

© Cengage Learning 2013

where $\theta_\alpha^2 = \dfrac{\Sigma\alpha_j^2}{a-1} = \dfrac{\Sigma(\mu_i - \mu)^2}{a-1}$

Consider for a moment the test of the effect of Factor A:

$$\frac{E(MS_A)}{E(MS_{\text{error}})} = \frac{\sigma_e^2 + nb\theta_\alpha^2}{\sigma_e^2}$$

If H_0 is true, then $\mu_{A_1} = \mu_{A_2} = \mu$ and θ_α^2, and thus $nb\theta_\alpha^2$, will be 0. In this case, F will be the ratio of two different estimates of error, and its expectation is approximately 1 and will be distributed as the standard (central) F distribution. If H_0 is false, however, θ_α^2 will not be 0 and F will have an expectation greater than 1 and will not follow the central F distribution. The same logic applies to tests on the effects of B and AB. We will return to structural models and expected mean squares in Section 13.8 when we discuss alternative designs that we might use. There we will see that the expected mean squares can become much more complicated, but the decision on the error term for a particular effect will reflect the logic of what we have seen here.

13.3 Interactions

One of the major benefits of factorial designs is that they allow us to examine the interaction of variables. Indeed, in many cases, the interaction term may well be of greater interest than are the main effects (the effects of factors taken individually). Consider, for example, the study by Eysenck. The means are plotted in Figure 13.1 for each age group separately. Here you can see clearly what I referred to in the interpretation of the results when I said that the differences due to Conditions were greater for younger participants than for older ones. The fact that the two lines are not parallel is what we mean when we speak of an interaction. If Condition differences were the same for the two Age groups, then the lines would be parallel—whatever differences between Conditions existed for younger participants would be equally present for older participants. This would be true regardless of whether younger participants were generally superior to older participants or whether the two groups were comparable. Raising or lowering the entire line for younger participants

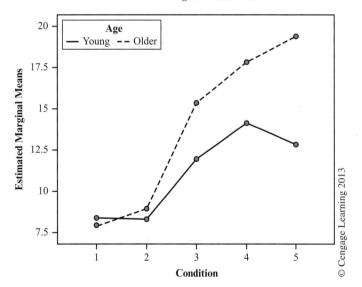

Figure 13.1   Cell means for data in Table 13.2

© Cengage Learning 2013

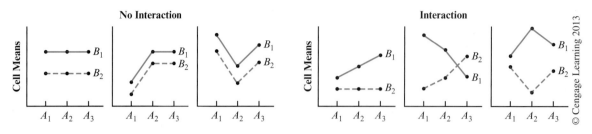

Figure 13.2   Illustration of possible noninteractions and interactions

would change the main effect of Age, but it would have no effect on the interaction because it would not affect the degree of parallelism between the lines.

It may make the situation clearer if you consider several plots of cell means that represent the presence or absence of an interaction. In Figure 13.2 the first three plots represent the case in which there is no interaction. In all three cases the lines are parallel, even when they are not straight. Another way of looking at this is to say that the simple effect of Factor B at A_1 is the same as it is at A_2 and at A_3. In the second set of three plots, the lines clearly are not parallel. In the first, one line is flat and the other rises. In the second, the lines actually cross. In the third, the lines do not cross, but they move in opposite directions. In every case, the simple effect of B is *not* the same at the different levels of A. Whenever the lines are (significantly) nonparallel, we say that we have an interaction.

Many people will argue that if you find a significant interaction, the main effects should be ignored. I have come to accept this view, in part because of comments on the Web by Gary McClelland. (McClelland, 2008, downloaded on 2/3/2011 from http://finzi.psych.upenn .edu/Rhelp10/2008-February/153837.html.) He argues that with a balanced design (equal cell frequencies), what we call the main effect of A is actually the average of the simple effects of A. But if we have a significant interaction that is telling us that the simple effects are different from each other, and an average of them has little or no meaning. Moreover, when I see an interaction my first thought is to look specifically at simple effects of one variable at specific levels of the other, which is far more informative than worrying about main effects.

This discussion of the interaction effects has focused on examining cell means. I have taken that approach because it is the easiest to see and has the most to say about the results of the experiment. Rosnow and Rosenthal (1989) have pointed out that a more accurate way to look at an interaction is first to remove any row and column effects from the data. They raise an interesting point, but most interactions are probably better understood in terms of the explanation above.

13.4 Simple Effects

I earlier defined a simple effect as the effect of one factor (independent variable) at one level of the other factor—for example, the differences among Conditions for the younger participants. The analysis of simple effects can be an important technique for analyzing data that contain significant interactions. In a very real sense, it allows us to "tease apart" interactions.

I will use the Eysenck data to illustrate how to calculate and interpret simple effects. Table 13.4 shows the cell means and the summary table reproduced from Table 13.2. The table also contains the calculations involved in obtaining all the simple effects.

The first summary table in Table 13.4c reveals significant effects due to Age, Condition, and their interaction. We already discussed these results earlier in conjunction with the original analysis. As I said there, the presence of an interaction means that there are

Table 13.4   Illustration of calculation of simple effects (data taken from Table 13.2)

(a) Cell means ($n = 10$)

	Counting	Rhyming	Adjective	Imagery	Intention	Mean
Older	7.0	6.9	11.0	13.4	12.0	10.06
Younger	6.5	7.6	14.8	17.6	19.3	13.16
Mean	6.75	7.25	12.90	15.50	15.65	11.61

(b) Calculations

Conditions at Each Age

$$SS_{C \text{ at Old}} = 10 \times [(7.0 - 10.06)^2 + (6.9 - 10.06)^2 + \cdots + (12 - 10.06)^2] = 351.52$$

$$SS_{C \text{ at Young}} = 10 \times [(6.5 - 13.16)^2 + (7.6 - 13.16)^2 + \cdots + (19.3 - 13.16)^2] = 1353.72$$

Age at Each Condition

$$SS_{A \text{ at Counting}} = 10 \times [(7.0 - 6.75)^2 + (6.5 - 6.75)^2] = 1.25$$

$$SS_{A \text{ at Rhyming}} = 10 \times [(6.9 - 7.25)^2 + (7.6 - 7.25)^2] = 2.45$$

$$SS_{A \text{ at Adjective}} = 10 \times [(11.0 - 12.9)^2 + (14.8 - 12.9)^2] = 72.2$$

$$SS_{A \text{ at Imagery}} = 10 \times [(13.4 - 15.5)^2 + (17.6 - 15.5)^2] = 88.20$$

$$SS_{A \text{ at Intentional}} = 10 \times [(12.0 - 15.65)^2 + (19.3 - 15.65)^2] = 266.45$$

(c) Summary Tables

Overall Analysis

Source	df	SS	MS	F
A (Age)	1	240.25	240.25	29.94*
C (Condition	4	1514.94	378.735	47.19*
AC	4	190.30	47.575	5.93*
Error	90	722.30	8.026	
Total	99	2667.79		

* $p < .05$

Simple Effects

Source	df	SS	MS	F
Conditions				
C at Old	4	351.52	87.88	10.95*
C at Young	4	1353.72	338.43	42.15*
Age				
A at Counting	1	1.25	1.25	<1
A at Rhyming	1	2.45	2.45	<1
A at Adjective	1	72.20	72.20	9.00*
A at Imagery	1	88.20	88.20	10.99*
A at Intentional	1	266.45	266.45	33.20*
Error	90	722.30	8.03	

* $p < .05$

different Condition effects for the two Ages, and there are different Age effects for the five Conditions. It thus becomes important to ask whether our general Condition effect really applies for older as well as younger participants, and whether there really are Age differences under all Conditions. The analysis of these simple effects is found in Table 13.4b and the second half of Table 13.4c. I have shown all possible simple effects for the sake of completeness of the example, but in general you should calculate only those effects in which you are interested. When you test many simple effects you either raise the familywise error rate to unacceptable levels or else you control the familywise error rate at some reasonable level and lose power for each simple effect test. One rule of thumb is "Don't calculate a contrast or simple effect unless it is relevant to your discussion when you write up the results." The more effects you test, the higher the familywise error rate will be.

Calculation of Simple Effects

In Table 13.4b you can see that $SS_{C\text{ at Old}}$ is calculated in the same way as any sum of squares. We simply calculate SS_C *using only the data for the older participants*. If we consider only those data, the five Condition means are 7.0, 6.9, 11.0, 13.4, and 12.0. Thus, the sum of squares will be

$$SS_{C\text{ at Old}} = n \sum (\overline{X}_{1j} - \overline{X}_{1.})^2$$
$$= 10 \times [(7 - 10.06)^2 + (6.9 - 10.06)^2 + \cdots + (12 - 10.06)^2] = 351.52$$

The other simple effects are calculated in the same way—by ignoring all data in which you are not at the moment interested. The sum of squares for the simple effect of Condition for older participants (351.52) is the same value as you would have obtained in Exercise 11.1 when you ran a one-way analysis of variance on only the data from older participants.

The degrees of freedom for the simple effects are calculated in the same way as for the corresponding main effects. This makes sense because the number of means we are comparing remains the same. Whether we use all of the participants or only some of them, we are still comparing five conditions and have $5 - 1 = 4$ *df* for Conditions.

To test the simple effects, we generally use the error term from the overall analysis (MS_{error}). The expected mean squares are presented in Table 13.5, and they make it clear why this is the appropriate error term. The expected mean square for each simple effect contains only one effect other than error (e.g., $n\sigma^2_{\alpha\text{ at }\beta_j}$), whereas MS_{error} is an estimate of error variance (σ^2_e). In fact, the only difference between what I have done in Table 13.4 and what I would do if I ran a standard one-way analysis of variance on the Old participants' data (which is the way I usually calculate sums of squares for simple effects when I use

Table 13.5 Expected mean squares for simple effects

Source	E(MS)
Simple Effects of *A*	
A at B_1	$\sigma^2_e + n\theta^2_{\alpha\text{ at }\beta_1}$
A at B_2	$\sigma^2_e + n\theta^2_{\alpha\text{ at }\beta_2}$
A at B_3	$\sigma^2_e + n\theta^2_{\alpha\text{ at }\beta_3}$
Simple Effect of *B*	
B at A_1	$\sigma^2_e + n\theta^2_{\beta\text{ at }\alpha_1}$
B at A_2	$\sigma^2_e + n\theta^2_{\beta\text{ at }\alpha_2}$
Error	σ^2_e

© Cengage Learning 2013

computer software) is the error term. MS_{error} is normally based on all the data because it is a better estimate with more degrees of freedom.

Interpretation

From the column labeled F in the bottom table in Table 13.4c, it is evident that differences due to Conditions occur for both ages although the sum of squares for the older participants is only about one-quarter of what it is for the younger ones. With regard to the Age effects, however, no differences occur on the lower-level tasks of counting and rhyming, but differences do occur on the higher-level tasks. In other words, differences between age groups show up on only those tasks involving higher levels of processing. This is basically what Eysenck set out to demonstrate.

In general, we seldom look at simple effects unless a significant interaction is present. However, it is not difficult to imagine data for which an analysis of simple effects would be warranted even in the face of a nonsignificant interaction, or to imagine studies in which the simple effects are the prime reason for conducting the experiment.

Additivity of Simple Effects

All sums of squares in the analysis of variance (other than SS_{total}) represent a partitioning of some larger sum of squares, and the simple effects are no exception. The simple effect of Condition at each level of Age represents a partitioning of SS_C and $SS_{A \times C}$, whereas the effects of Age at each level of Condition represent a partitioning of SS_A and $SS_{A \times C}$. Thus

$$\sum SS_{C \text{ at } A} = 351.52 + 1353.72 = 1705.24$$

$$SS_C + SS_{A \times C} = 1514.94 + 190.30 = 1705.24$$

and

$$\sum SS_{A \text{ at } C} = 1.25 + 2.45 + 72.20 + 88.20 + 266.45 = 430.55$$

$$SS_A + SS_{A \times C} = 240.25 + 190.30 = 430.55$$

A similar additive relationship holds for the degrees of freedom. The fact that the sums of squares for simple effects sum to the combined sums of squares for the corresponding main effect and interaction affords us a quick and simple check on our calculations.

13.5   Analysis of Variance Applied to the Effects of Smoking

This next example is based on a study by Spilich, June, and Renner (1992), who investigated the effects of smoking on performance. They used three tasks that differed in the level of cognitive processing that was required to perform them, with different participants serving in each task. The first task was a Pattern recognition task in which the participants had to locate a target on a screen. The second was a Cognitive task in which the participants were required to read a passage and then recall it at a later time. The third task was a Driving simulation video game. In each case the dependent variable was the number of errors that the participant committed. (This wasn't really true for all tasks in the original study, but it allows me to treat Task as an independent variable. I am not seriously distorting the results that Spilich et al. obtained.)

Participants were further divided into three Smoking groups. Group AS was composed of people who actively smoked during or just before carrying out the task. Group DS participants were regular smokers who had not smoked for 3 hours before the task (D stands for delay). Group NS were nonsmokers.

The data follow, but before you look at those data you should make some predictions about the kinds of effects that you might find for Task, Smoking, and their interaction.

Pattern Recognition															
NS:	9	8	12	10	7	10	9	11	8	10	8	10	8	11	10
DS:	12	7	14	4	8	11	16	17	5	6	9	6	6	7	16
AS:	8	8	9	1	9	7	16	19	1	1	22	12	18	8	10

Cognitive Task															
NS:	27	34	19	20	56	35	23	37	4	30	4	42	34	19	49
DS:	48	29	34	6	18	63	9	54	28	71	60	54	51	25	49
AS:	34	65	55	33	42	54	21	44	61	38	75	61	51	32	47

Driving Simulation															
NS:	3	2	0	0	6	2	0	6	4	1	0	0	6	2	3
DS:	7	0	6	0	12	17	1	11	4	4	3	5	16	5	11
AS:	15	2	2	14	5	0	16	14	9	17	15	9	3	15	13

I will omit hand calculations here on the assumption that you can carry them out yourself. In fact, it would be good practice to do so. In Exhibit 13.1 you will find the analysis of these data using SPSS.

(a) Descriptive Statistics

Dependent Variable: Errors

Smoke Grp	Task	Mean	Std. Deviation	N
Nonsmokers	Pattern Recognition	9.40	1.404	15
	Cognitive Task	28.87	14.687	15
	Driving Simulation	2.33	2.289	15
	Total	13.53	14.130	45
Delayed Smokers	Pattern Recognition	9.60	4.405	15
	Cognitive Task	39.93	20.133	15
	Driving Simulation	6.80	5.441	15
	Total	18.78	19.359	45
Active Smokers	Pattern Recognition	9.93	6.519	15
	Cognitive Task	47.53	14.652	15
	Driving Simulation	9.93	6.006	15
	Total	22.47	20.362	45
Total	Pattern Recognition	9.64	4.513	45
	Cognitive Task	38.78	18.055	45
	Driving Simulation	6.36	5.701	45
	Total	18.26	18.393	135

Exhibit 13.1 Analysis of Spilich et al. data

(b) Summary table

Tests of Between-Subjects Effects

Dependent Variable: Errors

Source	Type III Sum of Squares	df	Mean Square	F	Sig.	Partial Eta Squared	Noncent. Parameter	Observed Power[b]
Corrected Model	31744.726[a]	8	3968.091	36.798	.000	.700	294.383	1.000
Intercept	45009.074	1	45009.074	417.389	.000	.768	417.389	1.000
Task	28661.526	2	14330.763	132.895	.000	.678	265.791	1.000
SmokeGrp	1813.748	2	906.874	8.410	.000	.118	16.820	.961
Task* SmokeGrp	1269.452	4	317.363	2.943	.023	.085	11.772	.776
Error	13587.200	126	107.835					
Total	90341.000	135						
Corrected Total	45331.926	134						

[a] R Squared = .700 (Adjusted R Squared = .681)
[b] Computed using alpha = .05

(c) Interaction plot

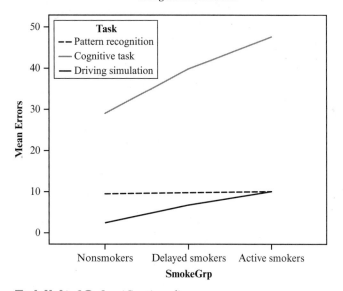

Marginal Mean Errors

Exhibit 13.1   *(Continued)*

An SPSS summary table for a factorial design differs somewhat from others you have seen in that it contains additional information. The line labeled "Corrected model" is the sum of the main effects and the interaction. As such its sum of squares is what we earlier called SS_{cells}. The line labeled "Intercept" is a test on the grand mean, here showing that the grand mean is significantly different from 0.00, which is hardly a surprise. Near the bottom the line labeled "Corrected total" is what we normally label "Total," and the line that they label "Total" is $(\sum X^2/N)$. These extra lines rarely add anything of interest.

The summary table reveals that there are significant effects due to Task and to the interaction of Task and SmokeGrp, but there is no significant effect due to the SmokeGrp variable.

The Task effect is of no interest, because it simply says that people make more errors on some kinds of tasks than others. This is like saying that your basketball team scored more points in yesterday's game than did your soccer team. You can see the effects graphically in the interaction plot, which is self-explanatory. Notice in the table of descriptive statistics that the standard deviations, and thus the variances, are very much higher on the Cognitive task than on the other two tasks. We will want to keep this in mind when we carry out further analyses.

13.6   Comparisons Among Means

All of the procedures discussed in Chapter 12 are applicable to the analysis of factorial designs. Thus we can test the differences among the five Condition means in the Eysenck example, or the three SmokeGrp means in the Spilich example using standard linear contrasts, the Bonferroni t test, the Tukey test, or any other procedure. Keep in mind, however, that we must interpret the "n" that appears in the formulae in Chapter 12 to be the number of observations on which each treatment mean was based. Because the Condition means are based on $(a \times n)$ observations that is the value that you would enter into the formula, not n. Because the interaction of Task with SmokeGrp is significant, I would be unlikely to want to examine the main effects further. However, an examination of simple effects will be very useful.

In the Spilich smoking example, there is no significant effect due to SmokeGrp, so you would probably not wish to run contrasts among the three levels of that variable. Because the dependent variable (errors) is not directly comparable across tasks, it makes no sense to look for specific Task group differences there. We could do so, but no one would be likely to care. (Remember the basketball and soccer teams referred to above.) However, I would expect that smoking might have its major impact on cognitive tasks, and you might wish to run either a single contrast (active smokers versus nonsmokers) or multiple comparisons on that simple effect. Assume that we want to take the simple effect of SmokeGrp at the Cognitive Task and compute the contrast on the nonsmokers versus the active smokers. You could run this test in SPSS by restricting yourself just to the data from the Cognitive task by choosing Data/Select Cases and specifying the data from the Cognitive task. The Compare Means/One-Way ANOVA procedure will allow you to specify contrasts, whereas the General Linear Model/Univariate procedure won't, so we will use that.

From SPSS we have

ANOVA
Errors

	Sum of Squares	df	Mean Square	F	Sig.
Between Groups	2643.378	2	1321.689	4.744	.014
Within Groups	11700.400	42	278.581		
Total	14343.778	44			

Robust Tests of Equality of Means
Errors

	Statistic[a]	df1	df2	Sig.
Welch	5.970	2	27.527	.007
Brown-Forsythe	4.744	2	38.059	.014

[a] Asymptotically F distributed.

Adapted from output by SPSS, Inc.

Notice that the error term for testing the simple effect (278.581) is much larger than it was for the overall analysis (107.835). This reflects the heterogeneity of variance referred to earlier. Whether we use the error term in the standard analysis or the Welch (or Brown-Forsythe) correction for heterogeneity of variance, the result is clearly significant.

When we break down that simple effect by comparing people who are actively smoking with those who don't smoke at all, our test would be

Contrast Coefficients

Contrast	SmokeGrp		
	Nonsmokers	Delayed Smokers	Active Smokers
1	1	0	−1

Contrast Tests

		Contrast	Value of Contrast	Std. Error	t	df	Sig. (2-tailed)
Errors	Assume equal variances	1	−18.67	6.095	−3.063	42	.004
	Does not assume equal variances	1	−18.67	5.357	−3.485	28.000	.002

And again we see a significant difference of whether or not we pool variances. While visual inspection suggests that smoking does not have an important effect in the Pattern Recognition or Driving condition, it certainly appears to have an effect in when it comes to the performance of cognitive tasks.

If, instead of comparing the two extreme groups on the smoking variable, we use a standard post hoc multiple comparison analysis such as Tukey's test, we get a frequent, but unwelcome, result. You will find that the Nonsmoking group performs significantly better than the Active group, but not significantly better than the Delayed group. The Delayed group is also not significantly different from the Active group. Representing this graphically by underlining groups that are not significantly different from one another we have

Nonsmoking   Delayed   Active
_____

_____

If you just came from your class in Logic 132, you know that it does not make sense to say $A = B, B = C$, but $A \neq C$. But, don't confuse Logic, which is in some sense exact, with Statistics, which is probabilistic. Don't forget that a failure to reject H_0 does not mean that the means are equal. It just means that they are not sufficiently different for us to know which one is larger. Here we don't have enough evidence to conclude that Delayed is different from Nonsmoking, but we *do* have enough evidence (i.e., power) to conclude that there is a significant difference between Active and Nonsmoking. This kind of result occurs frequently with multiple-comparison procedures, and we just have to learn to live with a bit of uncertainty.

13.7   Power Analysis for Factorial Experiments

Calculating power for fixed-variable factorial designs is basically the same as it was for one-way designs. In the one-way design we defined

$$\phi' = \sqrt{\frac{\sum \tau_j^2}{k\sigma_e^2}}$$

and

$$\phi = \phi'\sqrt{n}$$

where $\sum \tau_j^2 = \sum(\mu_j - \mu)^2$, k = the number of treatments, and n = the number of observations in each treatment. And, as with the one-way, ϕ' is often denoted as f, which is the way G*Power names it. In the two-way and higher-order designs we have more than one "treatment," but this does not alter the procedure in any important way. If we let $\alpha_i = \mu_{i.} - \mu$, and $\beta_j = \mu_{.j} - \mu$, where $\mu_{i.}$ represents the parametric mean of Treatment A_i (across all levels of B) and $\mu_{.j}$ represents the parametric mean of Treatment B_j (across all levels of A), then we can define the following terms:

$$\phi'_\alpha = \sqrt{\frac{\sum \alpha_j^2}{a\sigma_e^2}}$$

$$\phi_\alpha = \phi'_\alpha \sqrt{nb}$$

and

$$\phi'_\beta = \sqrt{\frac{\sum \beta_j^2}{b\sigma_e^2}}$$

$$\phi_\beta = \phi'_\beta \sqrt{na}$$

Examination of these formulae reveals that to calculate the power against a null hypothesis concerning A, we act as if variable B did not exist. To calculate the power of the test against a null hypothesis concerning B, we similarly act as if variable A did not exist.

Calculating the power against the null hypothesis concerning the interaction follows the same logic. We define

$$\phi'_{\alpha\beta} = \sqrt{\frac{\sum \alpha\beta_{ij}^2}{ab\sigma_e^2}}$$

$$\phi_{\alpha\beta} = \phi'_{\alpha\beta}\sqrt{n}$$

where $\alpha\beta_{ij}$ is defined as for the underlying structural model $(\alpha\beta_{ij} = \mu - \mu_{i.} - \mu_{.j} + \mu_{ij})$. Given $\phi_{\alpha\beta}$, we can simply obtain the power of the test just as we did for the one-way design.

To illustrate the calculation of power for an interaction, we will use the cell and marginal means for the Spilich et al. study. These means are

	Pattern	**Cognitive**	**Driving**	**Mean**
Nonsmoker	9.400	28.867	2.333	13.533
Delayed	9.600	39.933	6.800	18.778
Active	9.933	47.533	9.933	22.467
Mean	9.644	38.778	6.356	18.259

© Cengage Learning 2013

$$\phi' = \sqrt{\frac{\sum \alpha\beta_{ij}^2}{ab\sigma_e^2}}$$

$$= \sqrt{\frac{(9.40 - 13.533 - 9.644 + 18.259)^2 + \cdots + (9.933 - 22.467 - 6.356 + 18.259)^2}{3 \times 3 \times 107.835}}$$

$$= \sqrt{\frac{20.088 + \cdots + 0.398}{970.515}} = \sqrt{\frac{84.626}{970.515}} = \sqrt{0.087} = .295$$

Assume that we want to calculate the expected level of power in an exact replication of Spilich's experiment assuming that Spilich has exactly estimated the corresponding population parameters. (He almost certainly has not, but those estimates are the best guess we have of the parameters.) Using 0.295 as the effect size (which G*Power calls *f*) we have the following result.

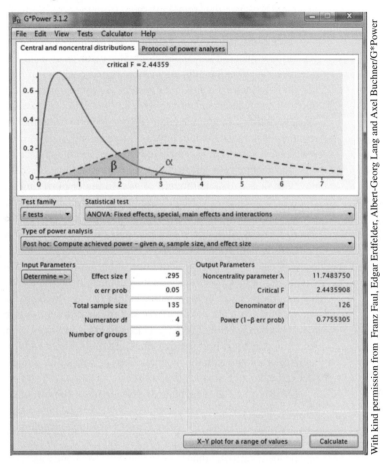

Therefore, if the means and variances that Spilich obtained accurately reflect the corresponding population parameters, the probability of obtaining a significant interaction in a replication of that study is .776, which agrees exactly with the results obtained by SPSS.

To remind you what the graph at the top is all about, the solid distribution represents the distribution of F under the null hypothesis. The dashed distribution represents the (noncentral) distribution of F given the population means we expect. The vertical line shows the critical value of F under the null hypothesis. The shaded area labeled β represents those values of F that we will obtain, if estimated parameters are correct, that are less than the critical value of F and will not lead to rejection of the null hypothesis. Power is then $1 - \beta$.

In certain situations a two-way factorial is more powerful than are two separate one-way designs, in addition to the other advantages that accrue to factorial designs. Consider two hypothetical studies, where the number of participants per treatment is held constant across both designs.

In Experiment 1 an investigator wishes to examine the efficacy of four different treatments for post-traumatic stress disorder (PTSD) in rape victims. She has chosen to use both male and female therapists. Our experimenter is faced with two choices. She can run a one-way analysis on the four treatments, ignoring the sex of the therapist (SexTher) variable entirely, or she can run a 4×2 factorial analysis on the four treatments and two sexes. In this case the two-way has more power than the one-way. In the one-way design we would ignore any differences due to SexTher and the interaction of Treatment with SexTher, and these would go toward increasing the error term. In the two-way we would take into account differences that can be attributed to SexTher and to the interaction between Treatment and SexTher, thus removing them from the error term. The error term for the two-way would thus be smaller than for the one-way, giving us greater power.

For Experiment 2, consider the experimenter who had originally planned to use only female therapists in her experiment. Her error term would not be inflated by differences among SexTher and by the interaction, because neither of those exist. If she now *expanded* her study to include male therapists, SS_{total} would increase to account for additional effects due to the new independent variable, but the error term would remain constant because the extra variation would be accounted for by the extra terms. Because the error term would remain constant, she would have no increase in power in this situation over the power she would have had in her original study, except for an increase in n.

As a general rule, a factorial design is more powerful than a one-way design only when the extra factors can be thought of as refining or purifying the error term. In other words, when extra factors or variables account for variance that would normally be incorporated into the error term, the factorial design is more powerful. Otherwise, all other things being equal, it is not, although it still possesses the advantage of allowing you to examine the interactions and simple effects.

You need to be careful about one thing, however. When you add a factor that is a random factor (e.g., Classroom) you may actually decrease the power of your test. As you will see in a moment, in models with random factors the fixed factor, which may well be the one in which you are most interested, will probably have to be tested using $MS_{interaction}$ as the error term instead of MS_{error}. This is likely to cost you a considerable amount of power. And you can't just pretend that the Classroom factor didn't exist, because then you will run into problems with the independence of errors. For a discussion of this issue, see Judd, McClelland, and Culhane (1995).

There is one additional consideration in terms of power that we need to discuss. McClelland and Judd (1993) have shown that power can be increased substantially using what they call "optimal" designs. These are designs in which sample sizes are apportioned to the cells unequally to maximize power. McClelland has argued that we often use more levels of the independent variables than we need, and we frequently assign equal numbers of participants to each cell when in fact we would be better off with fewer (or no) participants in some cells (especially the central levels of ordinal independent variables). For example, imagine two independent variables that can take up to five levels, denoted as A_1, A_2, A_3, A_4, and A_5 for Factor A, and B_1, B_2, B_3, B_4, and B_5 for Factor B. McClelland and Judd (1993) show that a 5×5 design using all five levels of each variable is only 25% as efficient as a design using only A_1 and A_5, and B_1 and B_5. A 3×3 design using A_1, A_3, and A_5, and B_1, B_3, and B_5 is 44% as efficient. I recommend a close reading of their paper.

13.8 Alternative Experimental Designs

For traditional experimental research in psychology, fixed models with crossed independent variables have long been the dominant approach and will most likely continue to be. In such designs the experimenter chooses a few fixed levels of each independent variable, which are the levels that are of primary interest and would be the same levels he or she would expect to use in a replication. In a factorial design each level of each independent variable is paired (**crossed**) with each level of all other independent variables.

crossed

However, there are many situations in psychology and education where this traditional design is not appropriate, just as there are a few cases in traditional experimental work. In many situations the levels of one or more independent variables are sampled at random (e.g., we might sample 10 classrooms in a given school and treat Classroom as a factor), giving us a **random factor**. In other situations one independent variable is nested within another independent variable. An example of the latter is when we sample 10 classrooms from school district A and another 10 classrooms from school district B. In this situation the district A classrooms will not be found in district B and vice versa, and we call this a **nested design**. Random factors and nested designs often go together, which is why they are discussed together here, though they do not have to.

When we have **random** and/or **nested designs**, the usual analyses of variance that we have been discussing are not appropriate without some modification. The primary problem is that the error terms that we usually think of are not correct for one or more of the Fs that we want to compute. In this section I will work through three possible designs, starting with the traditional fixed model with crossed factors and ending with a random model with nested factors. I certainly cannot cover all aspects of all possible designs, but the generalization from what I discuss to other designs should be reasonably apparent. I am doing this for two different reasons. In the first place, modified traditional analyses of variance, as described below, are quite appropriate in many of these situations. In addition, there has been a general trend toward incorporating what are called **hierarchical models** or **mixed models** in our analyses, and an understanding of those models hinges crucially on the concepts discussed here.

In each of the following sections I will work with the same set of data but with different assumptions about how those data were collected, and with different names for the independent variables. The raw data that I will use for all examples are the same data that we saw in Table 13.2 on Eysenck's study of age and recall under conditions of varying levels of processing of the material. I will change, however, the variable names to fit with my example.

One important thing to keep firmly in mind is that virtually all statistical tests operate within the idea of the results of an infinite number of replications of the experiment. Thus the Fs that we have for the two main effects and the interaction address the question of "If the null hypothesis was true and we replicated this experiment 10,000 times, how often would we obtain an F statistic as extreme as the one we obtained in this specific study?" If that probability is small, we reject the null hypothesis. There is nothing new there. But we need to think for a moment about what would produce different F values in our 10,000 replications of the same basic study. Given the design that Eysenck used, every time we repeated the study we would use one group of older subjects and one group of younger subjects. There is no variability in that independent variable. Similarly, every time we repeat the study we will have the same five Recall Conditions (Counting, Rhyming, Adjective, Imagery, Intention). So again there is no variability in that independent variable. This is why we refer to this experiment as a fixed effect design—the levels of the independent variable are fixed and will be the same from one replication to another. The only reason why we would obtain different F values from one replication to another is sampling error, which comes from the fact that each replication uses different subjects. (You will shortly see that this conclusion does not apply with random factors.)

To review the basic structural model behind the fixed-model analyses that we have been running up to now, recall that the model was

$$X_{ijk} = \mu + \alpha_i + \beta_j + \alpha\beta_{ij} + e_{ijk}$$

Over replications the only variability comes from the last term (e_{ijk}), which explains why MS_{error} can be used as the denominator for all three F tests. That will be important as we go on.

random factor

nested design

random

nested designs

hierarchical models

mixed models

Table 13.6   Analysis of variance of Eysenck's basic fixed variable design

Source	df	SS	MS	F
A (Age)	1	240.25	240.250	29.94*
C (Condition)	4	1514.94	378.735	47.19*
AC	4	190.30	47.575	5.93*
Error	90	722.30	8.026	
Total	99	2667.79		

© Cengage Learning 2013

* $p < .05$

A Crossed Experimental Design with Fixed Variables

crossed experimental design

The original example is what we will class as a **crossed experimental design** with fixed factors. In a crossed design each level of one independent variable (factor) is paired with each level of any other independent variable. For example, both older and younger participants are tested under each of the five recall conditions. In addition, the levels of the factors are fixed because these are the levels that we actually want to study—they are not, for example, a random sample of ages or of possible methods of processing information.

Simply as a frame of reference, the results of the analysis of this study are repeated in Table 13.6. We see that MS_{error} was used as the test term for each effect, that it was based on 90 df, and that each effect is significant at $p < .05$.

A Crossed Experimental Design with a Random Variable

Now we will move from the study we just analyzed to another in which one of the factors is random but crossed with the other (fixed) factor. I will take an example based on one used by Judd and McClelland (1989). Suppose that we want to test whether subjects are quicker to identify capital letters than they are lower case letters. We will refer to this variable as "Case." Case here is a fixed factor. We want to use several different letters, so we randomly sample five of them (e.g., A, G, D, K, W) and present them as either upper or lower case. Here Letter is crossed with Case (i.e., each letter appears in each case), so we have a crossed design, but we have randomly sampled Letters, giving us a random factor. Each subject will see only one letter and the dependent variable will be the response time to identify that letter.

In this example Case takes the place of Age in Eysenck's study and Letter takes the place of Condition. If you think about many replications of this experiment, you would expect to use the same levels of Case (there are only two cases after all), but you would probably think of taking a different random sample of Letters for each experiment. This means that the F values that we calculate will vary not only on the basis of sampling error, but also as a result of the letters that we happened to sample. What this is going to mean is that any interaction between Case and Letter will show up in the expected mean squares for the fixed effect (Case), though I won't take the space here to prove that algebraically. This will affect the expected mean squares for the effect of Case, and we need to take that into account when we form our F ratios. (Maxwell & Delaney, 2004, p. 475, do an excellent job of illustrating this phenomenon.)

expected mean squares

To see the effect of random factors we need to consider **expected mean squares**, which we discussed only briefly in Section 11.4. Expected mean squares tell us what is being estimated by the numerator and denominator in an F statistic. Rather than providing a derivation of expected mean squares, as I have in the past (see Howell, 2007 for that development), I will simply present a table showing the expected mean squares for fixed, random, and mixed models. Here a random model is one in which both factors are random and is not often found in the behavioral sciences. A mixed model is one with both a random and a fixed factor, as

Table 13.7   Expected mean squares for fixed, random, and mixed models and crossed designs

Source	Fixed A fixed B fixed	Random A random B random	Mixed A fixed B random
A	$\sigma_e^2 + nb\theta_\alpha^2$	$\sigma_e^2 + n\sigma_{\alpha\beta}^2 + nb\sigma_\alpha^2$	$\sigma_e^2 + n\sigma_{\alpha\beta}^2 + nb\theta_\alpha^2$
B	$\sigma_e^2 + na\theta_\beta^2$	$\sigma_e^2 + n\sigma_{\alpha\beta}^2 + na\sigma_\beta^2$	$\sigma_e^2 + na\sigma_\beta^2$
AB	$\sigma_e^2 + n\theta_{\alpha\beta}^2$	$\sigma_e^2 + n\sigma_{\alpha\beta}^2$	$\sigma_e^2 + n\sigma_{\alpha\beta}^2$
Error	σ_e^2	σ_e^2	σ_e^2

we are dealing with here, and they are much more common. (I present the expected mean squares of random models only to be complete.) Notice that for fixed factors the "variance" for that term is shown as θ^2 rather than as σ^2. The reason for this is that the term is formed by dividing the sum of squared deviations by the degrees of freedom. For example,

$$\theta_\alpha^2 = \frac{\Sigma\alpha_j^2}{a-1}$$

But because in a fixed model we are treating the levels of the factor that we actually used as the entire population of that factor in which we are interested, it is not actually a variance because, as the parameter, it would have to be divided by the number of levels of A, not the *df* for A. This is not going to make any difference in what you do, but the distinction needs to be made for accuracy. The variance terms for the random factors are represented as σ^2. Thus the variance of Letter means is σ_β^2 and the error variance, which is the variance due to subjects, which is always considered a random term, is σ_e^2.

If you look at the column for a completely fixed model you will see that the expected mean squares for the main effects and interaction contain a component due to error and a single component reflecting differences among the means for the main effect or interaction. The error term, on the other hand, contains only an error component. So if you form a ratio of the mean squares for A, B, or AB divided by MS_{error} the only reason that the expected value of F will depart much from 1 will be if there is an effect for the term in question. (We saw something like this when we first developed the F statistic in section 11.4.) This means that for all factors in fixed models MS_{error} is the appropriate error term.

Look now at the column representing the mixed model, which is the one that applies to our current example. Leaving aside the test on our fixed effect (A) for a moment, we will focus on the other two effects. If we form the ratio

$$E(F) = E\left(\frac{MS_B}{MS_{\text{error}}}\right) = \frac{\sigma_e^2 + nb\sigma_\beta^2}{\sigma_e^2}$$

that ratio will be significantly different from 1 only if the component for the (random) B effect ($nb\sigma_b^2$) is non-zero. Thus MS_{error} is an appropriate denominator for the F test on B. In this case we can divide MS_{Letter} by MS_{error} and have a legitimate test.

The same kind of argument holds for our test on the interaction, because

$$E(F) = E\left(\frac{MS_{AB}}{MS_{\text{error}}}\right) = \frac{\sigma_e^2 + n\sigma_{\alpha\beta}^2}{\sigma_e^2}$$

and the result will be significant only if the interaction component is significant.[1]

---

[1] If an interaction is the product of both a fixed and a random factor, the interaction is treated as random.

But now look at the test on A, the fixed effect. If we form our usual F ratio

$$E(F) = E\left(\frac{\sigma_e^2 + n\sigma_{\alpha\beta}^2 + nb\sigma_a^2}{\sigma_e^2}\right)$$

we no longer have a legitimate test on A. The ratio could be large if *either* the interaction is significant or the effect of A is significant, and we can't tell which is causing a result. This creates a problem, and the only way we can form a legitimate F for A is to divide MS_A by MS_{AB}, giving us

$$E(F) = \frac{MS_A}{MS_{AB}} = E\left(\frac{\sigma_e^2 + n\sigma_{\alpha\beta}^2 + nb\sigma_a^2}{\sigma_e^2 + n\sigma_{\alpha\beta}^2}\right)$$

I know from experience that people are going to tell me that I made an error here because I have altered the test on the fixed effect rather than on the random effect, which is the effect that is causing all of the problems. I wish I were wrong, but I'm not. Having a random effect alters the test for the fixed effect. For a very nice explanation of why this happens I strongly recommend looking at Maxwell & Delaney (2004, p. 475).

For our example we can create our F tests as

$$F_{\text{Case}} = \frac{MS_{\text{Case}}}{MS_{\text{C}\times\text{L}}} = \frac{240.25}{47.575} = 5.05$$

$$F_{\text{Letter}} = \frac{MS_{\text{Letter}}}{MS_{\text{error}}} = \frac{378.735}{8.026} = 47.19$$

$$F_{\text{L}\times\text{C}} = \frac{MS_{\text{L}\times\text{C}}}{MS_{\text{error}}} = \frac{47.575}{8.026} = 5.93$$

The results of this analysis are presented in Table 13.8.[2]

Nested Designs

Now let's modify our basic study again while retaining the same values of the dependent variable so that we can compare results. Suppose that your clinical psychology program is genuinely interested in whether female students are better therapists than male students. To run the study the department will randomly sample 10 graduate students, split them

Table 13.8   Analysis of variance with one fixed and one random variable

Source	df	SS	MS	F
Case	1	240.25	240.250	5.05*
Letter	4	1514.94	378.735	47.19*
C × L	4	190.30	47.575	5.93*
Error	90	722.30	8.026	
Total	99	2667.79		

*$p < .05$
Adapted from output by SPSS, Inc.

---

[2] These results differ from those produced by some software packages, which treat the mixed model as a random model when it comes to the denominator for F. But they are consistent with the expected mean squares given above and with the results obtained by other texts. You can reproduce these results in SPSS by using the following syntax:
Manova dv by Case(1,2) Letter(1,5)
    /design = Case vs 1
        Case by Letter = 1 vs within
        Letter vs within.

into two groups based on Gender, and have each of them work with 10 clients and produce a measure of treatment effectiveness. In this case Gender is certainly a fixed variable because every replication would involve Male and Female therapists. However, Therapist is best studied as a random factor because therapists were sampled at random and we would want to generalize to male and female therapists in general, not just to the particular therapists we studied. Therapist is also a *nested* factor because you can't cross Gender with Therapist—Mary will never serve as a male therapist and Bob will never serve as a female therapist. Over many replications of the study the variability in F will depend on random error (MS_{error}) and also on the therapists who happen to be used. This variability must be taken into account when we compute our F statistics.[3]

The study as I have described it looks like our earlier example with Letter and Case, but it really is not. In this study therapists are *nested* within gender. (Remember that in the first example each Condition (Letter, etc.) was paired with each Case, but that is not the situation here.) The fact that we have a nested design is going to turn out to be very important in how we analyze the data. For one thing we cannot compute an interaction. We obviously cannot ask if the differences between Barbara, Lynda, Stephanie, Susan, and Joan look different when they are males than when they are females. There are going to be differences among the five females, and there are going to be differences among the five males, but this will not represent an interaction.

In running this analysis we can still compute a difference due to Gender, and for these data this will be the same as the effect of Case in the previous example. However, when we come to Therapist we can only compute differences due to therapists *within females*, and differences due to therapist *within males*. These are really just the simple effects of Therapist at each Gender. We will denote this as "Therapist within Gender" and write it as Therapist(Gender). As I noted earlier, we cannot compute an interaction term for this design, so that will not appear in the summary table. Finally, we are still going to have the same source of random error as in our previous example, which, in this case, is a measure of variability of client scores within each of the Gender/Therapist cells.

For a nested design our model will be written as

$$X_{ijk} = \mu + \alpha_i + \beta_{j(i)} + e_{ijk}$$

Notice that this model has a term for the grand mean (μ), a term for differences between genders (α_i), and a term for differences among therapists, but with subscripts indicating that Therapist was nested within Gender ($\beta_{j(i)}$). There is no interaction because none can be computed, and there is a traditional error term (e_{ijk}).

Calculation for Nested Designs

The calculations for nested designs are straightforward, though they differ a bit from what you are used to seeing. We calculate the sum of squares for Gender the same way we always would—sum the squared deviations for each gender and multiply by the number of observations for each gender. For the nested effect we simply calculate the simple effect of therapist for each gender and then sum the simple effects. For the error term we just calculate the sum of squares error for each Therapist/Gender cell and sum those. The calculations are shown in Table 13.9. However, before we can calculate the F values for this design, we need to look at the expected mean squares when we have a random variable that is nested within a fixed variable. These expected mean squares are shown in Table 13.10, where I have broken them down by fixed and random models, even though I am only discussing a nested design with one random factor here.

---

[3] It is possible to design a study in which a nested variable is a fixed variable, but that rarely happens in the behavioral sciences and I will not discuss that design except to show the expected mean squares in a table.

Table 13.9 Nested design with a random effect

$$SS_{total} = \sum(X - \overline{X}..)^2$$
$$= (9 - 11.61)^2 + (8 - 11.61)^2 + \cdots + (21 - 11.61)^2$$
$$= 2667.79$$
$$SS_G = nc\sum(\overline{X}_{i.} - \overline{X}..)^2$$
$$= 5 \times 4[(10.06 - 11.61)^2 + (13.16 - 11.61)^2]$$
$$= 240.25$$
$$SS_{T(Male)} = n\sum(\overline{X}_j - \overline{X}..)^2$$
$$= 10[(7.0 - 10.06)^2 + (6.9 - 10.06)^2 + \cdots + (12.0 - 10.06)^2]$$
$$= 10(35.152) = 351.52$$
$$SS_{T(Female)} = n\sum(\overline{X}_j - \overline{X}..)^2$$
$$= 10[(6.5 - 13.16)^2 + (7.6 - 13.16)^2 + \cdots + (19.3 - 13.16)^2]$$
$$= 10(135.372) = 1353.72$$
$$SS_{Therapist(Gender)} = SS_{Therapist(Male)} + SS_{Therapist(Female)} = 351.52 + 1353.72 = 1705.24$$
$$SS_{error} = SS_{total} - SS_G - SS_{T(G)} = 2667.79 - 240.25 - 1705.24 = 722.30$$

I don't usually include syntax for SPSS and SAS, but nested designs cannot be run directly from menus in SPSS, so I am including the syntax for the analysis of these data.

SPSS Code
```
UNIANOVA
    dv BY Gender Therapist
    /RANDOM = Therapist
    /METHOD = SSTYPE(3)
    /INTERCEPT = INCLUDE
    /CRITERIA = ALPHA(.05)
    /DESIGN = Gender Therapist(Gender).
```

SAS Code
```
data GenderTherapist;
    infile 'C:\Documents and Settings\David Howell\
    My Documents\Methods8\Chapters\Chapter13\GenderTherapist.dat';
input Gender Therapist dv;

Proc GLM data = GenderTherapist;
    Class Gender Therapist;
    Model dv = Gender Therapist(Gender);
    Random Therapist(Gender)/test ;
    Test H = Gender E = Therapist(Gender);
run;
```

Table 13.10 Expected mean squares for nested designs

Source	Fixed A fixed B fixed	Random A random B random	Mixed A fixed B random
A	$\sigma_e^2 + nb\theta_\alpha^2$	$\sigma_e^2 + n\sigma_\beta^2 + nb\sigma_\alpha^2$	$\sigma_e^2 + n\sigma_\beta^2 + nb\theta_\alpha^2$
B(A)	$\sigma_e^2 + na\theta_\beta^2$	$\sigma_e^2 + n\sigma_\beta^2$	$\sigma_e^2 + n\sigma_\beta^2$
Error	σ_e^2	σ_e^2	σ_e^2

Table 13.11   Tests for a nested design with a random nested factor

Source	df	SS	MS	F
Gender	1	240.25	240.250	1.127
Error$_1$	8	1705.24	213.155	26.56*
Therapist(Gender)	8	1705.24	213.155	
Error$_2$	90	722.30	8.026	
Total	99	2667.79		

*$p < .05$

© Cengage Learning 2013

Notice in Table 13.10 that when we have a nested design with a random variable nested within a fixed variable our F statistic is going to be computed differently. We can test the effect of Therapist(Gender) by dividing $MS_{T(G)}$ by MS_{error}, but when we want to test Gender we must divide MS_G by $MS_{T(G)}$. The resulting Fs are shown in Table 13.11, where I have subscripted the error terms to indicate how the Fs were constructed.

Notice that the Gender effect has the same sum of squares that it had in the original study, but the F is quite different because Therapist(Gender) served as the error term and there was considerable variability among therapists. Notice also that $SS_{Therapist(Gender)}$ is equal to the sum of $SS_{Condition}$ and $SS_{Age \times Condition}$ in the first example, although I prefer to think of it as the sum of the two simple effects.

Having a random factor such as Therapist often creates a problem. We really set out to study Gender differences, and that is what we most care about. We don't really care much about therapist differences because we know that they will be there. But the fact that Therapist is a random effect, which it should be, dramatically altered our test on Gender. The F went from nearly 30 to nearly 1.0. This is a clear case where the design of the study has a dramatic effect on power, even with the same values for the data. Maxwell and Delaney (2004) make the point that in designs with random factors, power depends on both the number of subjects (here, clients) and the number of levels of the random variable (here, therapists). Generally the number of levels of the random variable is far more important.

Summary

I have presented three experimental designs. The crossed design with fixed factors is the workhorse for most traditional experimental studies. The nested design with a random factor is an important design in much research in education and more applied areas of psychology. The crossed design with a random factor occurs occasionally but is not as common. In general when you have crossed effects they are most often fixed, and when you have nested effects the nested factor is most often random. This helps to explain why when you go to other sources to look up nested (or random) designs you will often find the two discussed together. A final point to keep in mind is that in all of the between-subjects designs in this book, subjects are nested within other factors and are considered to be a random factor. All of our F statistics are computed taking that into account.

13.9   Measures of Association and Effect Size

We can look at the magnitude of an effect in two different ways, just as we did with the one-way analysis. We can either calculate an r-family measure, such as η^2, or we can calculate a d-family measure such as d. Normally when we are examining an omnibus F, we use an r-family measure. However, when we are looking at a contrast between means, it is usually more meaningful to calculate an effect size estimate (d). We have seen both types of measures in previous chapters.

r-Family Measures

As with the one-way design, it is possible to calculate the magnitude of effect associated with each independent variable. The easiest, but also the most biased, way to do this is to calculate η^2. Here we would simply take the relevant sum of squares and divide by SS_{total}. Thus, the magnitude of effect for variable A is $\eta_\alpha^2 = SS_A/SS_{\text{total}}$ and for variable B is $\eta_\beta^2 = SS_B/SS_{\text{total}}$, whereas the magnitude of effect for the interaction is $\eta_{\alpha\beta}^2 = SS_{AB}/SS_{\text{total}}$.

There are two difficulties with the measure that we have just computed. In the first place η^2 is a biased estimate of the true magnitude of effect in the population. To put this somewhat differently, η^2 is a very good descriptive statistic, but a poor inferential statistic. Second, η^2, as we calculated it here, may not measure what we want to measure. We will speak about that shortly when we discuss **partial η^2**.

partial η^2

Although ω^2 is also biased, the bias is much less than for η^2. In addition, the statistical theory underlying ω^2 allows us to differentiate between fixed, random, and mixed models and to act accordingly.

To develop ω^2 for two-way and higher-order designs, we begin with the set of expected mean squares given in Table 13.8, derive estimates of σ_α^2, σ_β^2, $\sigma_{\alpha\beta}^2$, and σ_e^2, and then form ratios of each of these components relative to the total variance. Rather than derive the formulae for calculating ω^2 for the three different models, as I have done in previous editions of this book, I will present the results in a simple table. I strongly suspect that no student remembered the derivation five minutes after he or she read it, and that many students were so numb by the end of the derivation that they missed the final result.

For a factorial analysis of variance the basic formula to estimate ω^2 remains the same whether we are looking at fixed or random variables. The only difference is in how we calculate the components of that formula. We will start by letting $\hat{\sigma}_{\text{effect}}^2$ refer to the estimate of the variance of the independent variable we care about at the moment, such as A, B, or AB, and by letting $\hat{\sigma}_{\text{total}}^2$ refer to the sum of all sources of variance. (If an effect is fixed, replace σ^2 by θ^2.) Then if we know the value of these terms we can estimate ω_{effect}^2 as

$$\hat{\omega}_{\text{effect}}^2 = \frac{\hat{\sigma}_{\text{effect}}^2}{\hat{\sigma}_{\text{total}}^2}$$

For the main effect of A, for example, this becomes

$$\omega_\alpha^2 = \frac{\hat{\sigma}_\alpha^2}{\hat{\sigma}_{\text{total}}^2} = \frac{\hat{\sigma}_\alpha^2}{\hat{\sigma}_\alpha^2 + \hat{\sigma}_\beta^2 + \hat{\sigma}_{\alpha\beta}^2 + \hat{\sigma}_e^2}$$

All we have to know is how to calculate the variance components $(\hat{\sigma}_{\text{effect}}^2)$.

Table 13.12 contains the variance components for fixed and random variables for two-way factorial designs, where the subscripts in the leftmost column stand for fixed (*f*) or random (*r*) variables.[4] You simply calculate each of these terms as given, and then form the appropriate ratio. This procedure is illustrated using the summary table from the design in Table 13.8, where subjects were asked to identify an upper- or lower case letter and the Letters used were random.[5]

If we let α represent the fixed effect of Case and β represent the random effect of Letter, then we have (using the formulae in Table 13.9)

$$\hat{\sigma}_\alpha^2 = (a - 1)(MS_A - MS_{AB})/nab$$
$$= (2 - 1)(240.25 - 47.575)/(10 \times 2 \times 5) = 1.927$$

---

[4] If you need such a table for higher-order designs, you can find one at www.uvm.edu/~dhowell/StatPages/More_Stuff/Effect_size_components.html

[5] Some authors do as I do and use ω^2 for effects of both random and fixed factors. Others use ω^2 to refer to effects of fixed factors and ρ^2 (the squared intraclass correlation coefficient) to refer to effects of random factors.

Table 13.12   Estimates of variance components in two-way factorial designs

Model	Variance Component
$A_f B_f$	$\hat{\theta}_\alpha^2 = (a - 1)(MS_A - MS_e)/nab$
	$\hat{\theta}_\beta^2 = (b - 1)(MS_B - MS_e)/nab$
	$\hat{\theta}_{\alpha\beta}^2 = (a - 1)(b - 1)(MS_{AB} - MS_e)/nab$
	$\sigma_e^2 = MS_e$
$A_f B_r$	$\hat{\theta}_a^2 = (a - 1)(MS_A - MS_{AB})/nab$
	$\sigma_b^2 = (MS_B - MS_e)/na$
	$\hat{\theta}_{\alpha\beta}^2 = (a - 1)(MS_{AB} - MS_e)/na$
	$\sigma_e^2 = MS_e$
$A_r B_r$	$\sigma_\alpha^2 = (MS_A - MS_{AB})/nb$
	$\sigma_\beta^2 = (MS_B - MS_{AB})/na$
	$\sigma_{\alpha\beta}^2 = (MS_{AB} - MS_e)/n$
	$\sigma_e^2 = MS_e$

The summary table for Eysenck's data using the appropriate variable names is reproduced below for convenience.

Source	df	SS	MS	F
C (Case)	1	240.25	240.250	29.94*
L (Letter)	4	1514.94	378.735	47.19*
CL	4	190.30	47.575	5.93*
Error	90	722.30	8.026	
Total	99	2667.79		

*$p < .05$

$$\hat{\sigma}_\beta^2 = (MS_\beta - MS_{\text{error}})/na$$
$$= (378.735 - 8.026)/10 \times 5 = 7.414$$

$$\hat{\sigma}_{\alpha\beta}^2 = (a - 1)(MS_{AB} - MS_{\text{error}})/na$$
$$= (2 - 1)(47.575 - 8.026)/(10 \times 2) = 1.977$$

$$\hat{\sigma}_e^2 = MS_{\text{error}} = 8.026$$

Thus

$$\hat{\sigma}_{\text{total}}^2 = \hat{\sigma}_\alpha^2 + \hat{\sigma}_\beta^2 + \hat{\sigma}_{\alpha\beta}^2 + \hat{\sigma}_e^2$$
$$= 1.927 + 7.414 + 1.977 + 8.026 = 19.344$$

We can now estimate ω^2 for each effect:

$$\hat{\omega}_{\text{Case}}^2 = \frac{\hat{\sigma}_\alpha^2}{\hat{\sigma}_{\text{total}}^2} = \frac{1.927}{19.344} = 0.10$$

$$\hat{\omega}_{\text{Letter}}^2 = \frac{\hat{\sigma}_\beta^2}{\hat{\sigma}_{\text{total}}^2} = \frac{7.414}{19.344} = 0.38$$

$$\hat{\omega}_{\text{Case} \times \text{Letter}}^2 = \frac{\hat{\sigma}_{\alpha\beta}^2}{\hat{\sigma}_{\text{total}}^2} = \frac{1.977}{19.344} = 0.10$$

Partial Effects

Both η^2 and ω^2 represent the size of an effect (SS_{effect}) relative to the total variability in the experiment (SS_{total}). Often it makes more sense just to consider one factor separately from the others. For example, in the Spilich et al. (1992) study of the effects of smoking under different kinds of tasks, the task differences were huge and of limited interest in themselves. If we want a measure of the effect of smoking, we probably don't want to dilute that measure with irrelevant variance. Thus we might want to estimate the effect of smoking relative to a total variability based only on smoking and error. This can be written

$$\text{partial } \omega^2 = \frac{\hat{\sigma}^2_{\text{effect}}}{\hat{\sigma}^2_{\text{effect}} + \hat{\sigma}^2_e}$$

partial effect

We then simply calculate the necessary terms and divide. For example, in the case of the **partial effect** of the smoking by task interaction, treating both variables as fixed, we would have

$$\hat{\sigma}^2_{S \times T} = (s - 1)(t - 1)(MS_{ST} - MS_e)/nst$$

$$= (3 - 1)(3 - 1)(682 - 108)/(15)(3)(3) = \frac{5166}{135} = 38.26$$

$$\hat{\sigma}_e = MS_{\text{error}} = 108$$

$$\omega^2_{ST(\text{partial})} = \frac{\hat{\sigma}_{ST}}{\hat{\sigma}_{ST} + \hat{\sigma}_{\text{error}}} = \frac{38.26}{38.26 + 108} = 0.26$$

This is a reasonable sized effect.

d-Family Measures

The *r*-family measures (η^2 and ω^2) make some sense when we are speaking about an omnibus *F* test involving several levels of one of the independent variables, but when we are looking closely at differences among individual groups or sets of groups, the *d*-family of measures often is more useful and interpretable. Effect sizes (*d*) are a bit more complicated when it comes to factorial experiments, primarily because you have to decide what to consider "error." They also become more complicated when we have unequal sample **unbalanced** sizes (called an **unbalanced design**). In this chapter we will deal only with estimation with **design** balanced, or nearly balanced, designs. The reader is referred to Kline (2004) for a more thorough discussion of these issues.

As was the case with *t* tests and the one-way analysis of variance, we will define our effect size as

$$\hat{d} = \frac{\hat{\psi}}{\hat{s}}$$

where the "hats" indicate that we are using estimates based on sample data. There is no real difficulty in estimating Ψ because it is just a linear contrast. You will see an example in a minute in case you have forgotten what that is, but it is really just a difference between means of two groups or sets of groups. On the other hand, our estimate of the appropriate standard deviation will depend on our variables. Some variables normally vary in the population (e.g., amount of caffeine a person drinks in a day) and are, at least potentially, what Glass, McGraw, and Smith (1981) call a "variable of theoretical interest." Gender, extraversion, metabolic rate, and hours of sleep are other examples. On the other hand, many experimental variables, such as the number of presentations of a stimulus, area of cranial stimulation, size of a test stimulus, and presence or absence of a cue during recall do not normally vary in the population, and are of less theoretical interest. I am very aware that the distinction is a slippery one, and if a manipulated variable is not of theoretical interest, why are we manipulating it?

It might make more sense if we look at the problem slightly differently. Suppose that I ran a study to investigate differences among three kinds of psychotherapy. If I just ran that as a one-way design, my error term would include variability due to all sorts of things, one of which would be variability between men and women in how they respond to different kinds of therapy. Now suppose that I ran the same study but included gender as an independent variable. In effect I am controlling for gender, and MS_{error} would not include gender differences because I have "pulled them out" in my analysis. So MS_{error} would be smaller here than in the one-way. That's a good thing in terms of power, but it may not be a good thing if I use the square root of MS_{error} in calculating the effect size. If I did, I would have a different sized effect due to psychotherapy in the one-way experiment than I have in the factorial experiment. That doesn't seem right. The effect of therapy ought to be pretty much the same in the two cases. So what I will do instead is to put that gender variability, and the interaction of gender with therapy, back into error when it comes to computing an effect size.

But suppose that I ran a slightly different study where I examined the same three different therapies, but also included, as a second independent variable, whether or not the patient sat in a tub of cold water during therapy. Now patients don't normally sit in a cold tub of water, but it would certainly be likely to add variability to the results. That variability would not be there in the one-way design because we can't imagine some patients bringing in their own tub of water and sitting in it. And it is variability that I wouldn't want to add back into the error term, because it is in some way artificial. The point is that I would like the effect size for types of therapy to be the same whether I used a one-way or a factorial design. To accomplish that I would add effects due to Gender and the Gender X Therapy interaction back into the error term in the first study, and withhold the effects of Water and its interaction with Therapy in the second example. What follows is an attempt to do that. The interested reader is referred to Glass et al. (1981) for further discussion.

We will return to working with the example from Eysenck's (1974) study. The means and the analysis of variance summary table are presented below for easy reference.

	Counting	Rhyming	Adjective	Imagery	Intention	Mean
Older	7.0	6.9	11.0	13.4	12.0	10.06
Younger	6.5	7.6	14.8	17.6	19.3	13.16
Mean	6.75	7.25	12.90	15.50	15.65	11.61

Source	df	SS	MS	F
A (Age)	1	240.25	240.25	29.94*
C (Condition)	4	1514.94	378.735	47.19*
AC	4	190.30	47.575	5.93*
Error	90	722.30	8.026	
Total	99	2667.79		

*$p < .05$

© Cengage Learning 2013

One of the questions that would interest me is the contrast between the two lower levels of processing (Counting and Rhyming) and the two higher levels (Adjective and Imagery).

I don't have any particular thoughts about the Intentional group, so we will ignore that. My coefficients for a standard linear contrast, then, are

Counting	Rhyming	Adjective	Imagery	Intention
$-\frac{1}{2}$	$-\frac{1}{2}$	$\frac{1}{2}$	$\frac{1}{2}$	0

$$\hat{\psi} = \left(-\frac{1}{2}\right)(6.75) + \left(-\frac{1}{2}\right)(7.25) + \left(\frac{1}{2}\right)(12.90) + \left(\frac{1}{2}\right)(15.50) + (0)(11.61) = 7.20$$

The test on this contrast is

$$t = \frac{\hat{\psi}}{\sqrt{\dfrac{(\Sigma a_i^2)MS_{\text{error}}}{n}}} = \frac{7.20}{\sqrt{\dfrac{(1)(8.026)}{10}}} = \frac{7.20}{0.896} = 8.04$$

This t is clearly significant, showing that higher levels of processing lead to greater levels of recall. But I want an effect size for this difference.

I am looking for an effect size on a difference between two sets of conditions, but I need to consider the error term. Age is a normal variable in our world, and it leads to variability in people's responses. (If I had just designed this experiment as a one-way on Conditions, and ignored the age of my participants, that age variability would have been a normal part of MS_{error}). I need to have any Age effects contributing to error when it comes to calculating an effect size. So I will add SS_{Age} and $SS_{A \times C}$ back into the error.

$$s_{\text{error}} = \sqrt{\frac{SS_{\text{error}} + SS_{\text{Age}} + SS_{A \times C}}{df_{\text{error}} + df_{\text{Age}} + df_{A \times C}}} = \sqrt{\frac{722.30 + 240.25 + 190.30}{90 + 1 + 4}}$$

$$= \sqrt{\frac{1152.85}{95}} = \sqrt{12.135} = 3.48$$

Having computed our error term for this effect, we find

$$\hat{d} = \frac{\hat{\psi}}{\hat{s}} = \frac{7.20}{3.48} = 2.07$$

The difference between recall with high levels of processing and recall with low levels of processing is about two standard deviations, which is a considerable difference. Thinking about the material you are studying certainly helps you to recall it. Who would have thought?

Now suppose that you wanted to look at the effects of Age. Because we can guess that people vary in the levels of processing that they normally bring to a memory task, then we should add the main effect of Condition and its interaction with Age to the error term in calculating the effect size. Thus

$$s_{\text{error}} = \sqrt{\frac{SS_{\text{error}} + SS_{\text{Condition}} + SS_{A \times C}}{df_{\text{error}} + df_{\text{Condition}} + df_{A \times C}}} = \sqrt{\frac{722.30 + 1514.94 + 190.30}{90 + 4 + 4}}$$

$$= \sqrt{\frac{2427.54}{98}} = \sqrt{24.77} = 4.98$$

Because we only have two ages, the contrast (Ψ) is just the difference between the two means, which is $(13.16 - 10.06) = 3.10$.

$$\hat{d} = \frac{\hat{\psi}}{\hat{s}} = \frac{3.10}{4.98} = 0.62$$

In this case younger subjects differ from older participants by nearly two-thirds of a standard deviation.

Simple Effects

The effect sizes for simple effects are calculated in ways directly derived from the way we calculate main effects. The error term in these calculations is the same error term as that used for the corresponding main effect. Thus for the simple effect of Age for highest level of processing (Imagery) is

$$\hat{d} = \frac{\hat{\psi}}{\hat{s}} = \frac{(17.6 - 13.4)}{4.98} = \frac{4.20}{4.98} = 0.84$$

Similarly, for the contrast of low levels of processing versus high levels among young participants we would have

$$\psi = \left(-\frac{1}{2}\right)(6.5) + \left(-\frac{1}{2}\right)(7.6) + \left(\frac{1}{2}\right)(14.8) + \left(\frac{1}{2}\right)(17.6) + (0)(19.3) = 9.15$$

and the effect size is

$$\hat{d} = \frac{\hat{\psi}}{\hat{s}} = \frac{9.15}{3.48} = 2.63$$

which means that for younger participants there is nearly a $2\frac{2}{3}$ standard deviation difference in recall between the high and low levels of processing.

13.10   Reporting the Results

We have carried out a number of calculations to make various points, and I would certainly not report all of them when writing up the results. What follows is the basic information that I think needs to be presented.

In an investigation of the effects of different levels of information processing on the retention of verbal material, participants were instructed to process verbal material in one of four ways, ranging from the simple counting of letters in words to forming a visual image of each word. Participants in a fifth condition were not given any instructions about what to do with the items other than to study them for later recall. A second dimension of the experiment compared Younger and Older participants in terms of recall, thus forming a 2×5 factorial design.

The dependent variable was the number of items recalled after three presentations of the material. There was a significant Age effect ($F(1,90) = 29.94, p < .05, \omega^2 = .087$), with younger participants recalling more items than older ones. There was also a significant effect due to Condition ($F(4,90) = 47.19, p < .05, \omega^2 = .554$), and visual inspection of the means shows that there was greater recall for conditions in which there was a greater degree of processing. Finally the Age by Condition interaction was significant ($F(4,90) = 5.93, p < .05, \omega^2 = .059$), with a stronger effect of Condition for the younger participants.

A contrast of lower levels of processing (Counting and Rhyming) with higher levels of processing (Adjective and Imagery) produced a clearly statistically significant effect in favor of higher levels of processing ($t(90) = 8.04, p < .05$). This corresponds to an effect size of $\hat{d} = 2.07$, indicating that participants with higher levels of processing outperform those with lower levels of processing by over two standard deviations. This effect is even greater if we look only at the younger participants, where $\hat{d} = 2.63$.

13.11   Unequal Sample Sizes

Although many (but certainly not all) experiments are designed with the intention of having equal numbers of observations in each cell, the cruel hand of fate frequently intervenes to upset even the most carefully laid plans. Participants fail to arrive for testing, animals die, data are lost, apparatus fails, patients drop out of treatment, and so on. When such problems arise, we are faced with several alternative solutions, with the choice depending on the nature of the data and the reasons why data are missing.

When we have a plain one-way analysis of variance, the solution is simple and we have already seen how to carry that out. When we have more complex designs, the solution is not simple. With unequal sample sizes in factorial designs, the row, column, and interaction effects are no longer independent. This lack of independence produces difficulties in interpretation, and deciding on the best approach depends both on why the data are missing and how we conceive of our model.

There has been a great deal written about the treatment of unequal sample sizes, and we won't see any true resolution of this issue for a long time. (That is in part because there is no single answer to the complex questions that arise.) However, there are some approaches that seem more reasonable than others for the general case. Unfortunately, the most reasonable and the most common approach is available only using standard computer packages, and a discussion of that will have to wait until Chapter 15. I will, however, describe a pencil-and-paper solution to illustrate how we might think of the analysis. (I don't expect that you would actually use this approach in calculation, but it nicely illustrates some of the issues and helps to understand what SPSS are most other programs are doing.) This approach is commonly referred to as an **unweighted means** solution or an **equally weighted means** solution because we weight the cell means equally, regardless of the number of observations in those cells. My primary purpose in discussing this approach is not to make you get out your pencil and a calculator, but to help provide an understanding of what SPSS and SAS do if you take the default options. Although I will not work out an example, such an example can be found in Exercise 13.18. And, if you have difficulty with that, the solution can be found online in the Student Manual (www.uvm.edu/~dhowell/methods8/StudentManual/StudentManual.html).

unweighted means

equally weighted means

The Problem

You can see what our problem is if we take a very simple 2×2 factorial where we know what is happening. Suppose that we propose to test vigilance on a simple driving task when participants are either sober or are under the influence of alcohol. The task involves using a driving simulator and having participants respond when cars suddenly come out of driveways and when pedestrians suddenly step into the street. We would probably expect that sober drivers would make many fewer errors on this task than drivers who had been plied with alcohol. We will have two investigators working together on this problem, one from Michigan and one from Arizona, and each of them will run about half of the participants in their own facilities. We have absolutely no reason to believe that participants in Michigan are any different from participants in Arizona, nor do we have any reason to believe that there would be a significant interaction between State and Alcohol condition, though a plot of the data would be unlikely to show lines that are exactly parallel. I constructed the data with those expectations in mind.

Suppose that we obtained the quite extreme data shown in Table 13.13 with unequal numbers of participants in the four cells. The dependent variable is the number of errors each driver made in one half-hour session. From the cell means in this table you can see

Table 13.13   Illustration of the contaminating effects of unequal sample sizes

	Non-Drinking	Drinking	Row Means
Michigan	13 15 16 12	18 20 22 19 21	
		23 17 18 22 20	$\overline{X}_{1.} = 18.30$
	$\overline{X}_{11} = 14$	$\overline{X}_{12} = 20$	
Arizona	9 11 14 10 6	28 29 21 20 22	
	8 12 13 11 6 10		$\overline{X}_{2.} = 14.38$
	$\overline{X}_{21} = 10$	$\overline{X}_{22} = 24$	
Col Means	$\overline{X}_{.1} = 11.07$	$\overline{X}_{.2} = 21.33$	

© Cengage Learning 2013

that the data came out as expected. The Drinking participants made, on average, about 10 more errors than the participants in the Non-Drinking condition, and they did so whether they came from Michigan or Arizona. Unexpectedly there were more errors in Michigan than in Arizona, though this might not be significant. So what's wrong with this picture?

Well, if you look at the column means you see what you expect, but if you look at the row means you find that the mean for Michigan is 18.3, whereas the mean for Arizona is only 14.38. It looks as if we have a difference between States, even after we went to such pains to make sure there wasn't one here. What you are seeing is really a Drinking effect disguised as a State effect. And that is allowed to happen only because you have unequal numbers of participants in the cells. Michigan's mean is relatively high because they have more Drinking participants, and Arizona's mean is relatively low because they have more Non-Drinking participants. Now I suppose that if we had used actual people off the street, and Michigan had more drunks, perhaps a higher mean for Michigan would make some sort of sense. But that isn't what we did, and we don't usually want State effects contaminated by Drinking effects. So what do we do?

The most obvious thing to do would be to calculate row and column means *ignoring* the differing cell sizes. We could simply average cell means, paying no attention to how many participants are in each cell. If we did this, the means for both Michigan and Arizona would be $(14 + 20)/2 = 17$ and $(10 + 24)/2 = 17$, and there would be no difference due to States. You could then substitute those means in standard formulae for a factorial analysis of variance, but what are you going to use for the sample size? Your first thought might be that you would just use the average sample size, and that is actually quite close. Instead you will use the harmonic mean of the sample sizes. The harmonic mean is defined as

$$\overline{X}_h = \frac{k}{\dfrac{1}{X_1} + \dfrac{1}{X_2} + \dfrac{1}{X_3} + \cdots + \dfrac{1}{X_k}}$$

where the subscript "h" stands for "harmonic" and k represents the number of observations whose mean we are calculating. You can now use the formulae shown in Table 13.2 by replacing n with n_h and the row and column means with the means of the cells in those rows and columns. For the current example the row means would be 17 and 17, the column means would be 12 and 22, and the grand mean would be the mean of the cell means. The one difference is that the error term (SS_{error}) is not obtained by subtraction; instead, we calculate $SS_{\text{within cell}}$ for each cell of the design and then sum these terms to obtain the sum of squares due to error.

I am not recommending that you solve your problem with unbalanced designs this way. The answer would be very close to the answer given by the solution that I will recommend in Chapter 15, although with designs larger than 2×2 the F values are not exactly distributed as Fisher's F distribution. I present this approach here because I think that it helps to clarify what most software programs do when you have unequal sample sizes and select the default option (Type III sum of squares). I think that it also makes it easier to understand how a column effect can actually show up as a row effect even when the unweighted column means do not differ.

13.12 Higher-Order Factorial Designs

All of the principles concerning a two-way factorial design apply equally well to a three-way or higher-order design. With one additional piece of information, you should have no difficulty running an analysis of variance on any factorial design imaginable, although the arithmetic becomes increasingly more tedious as variables are added. We will take a simple three-way factorial as an example, because it is the easiest to use.

The only major way in which the three-way differs from the two-way is in the presence of more than one interaction term. To see this, we must first look at the underlying structural model for a factorial design with three variables:

$$X_{ijkl} = \mu + \alpha_i + \beta_j + \gamma_k + \alpha\beta_{ij} + \alpha\gamma_{ik} + \beta\gamma_{jk} + \alpha\beta\gamma_{ijk} + e_{ijkl}$$

**first-order
interactions**

**second-order
interaction**

In this model we have not only main effects, symbolized by α_i, β_j, and γ_k, but also two kinds of interaction terms. The two-variable or **first-order interactions** are $\alpha\beta_{ij}$, $\alpha\gamma_{ik}$, and $\beta\gamma_{jk}$, which refer to the interaction of variables A and B, A and C, and B and C, respectively. We also have a **second-order interaction** term, $\alpha\beta\gamma_{ijk}$, which refers to the joint effect of all three variables. We have already examined the first-order interactions in discussing the two-way. The second-order interaction can be viewed in several ways. The easiest way to view the ABC interaction is to think of the AB interaction itself interacting with variable C. Suppose that we had two levels of each variable and plotted the AB interaction separately for each level of C. We might have the result shown in Figure 13.3. Notice that for C_1 we have one AB interaction, whereas for C_2 we have a different one. Thus, AB depends on C, producing an ABC interaction. This same kind of reasoning could be invoked using the AC interaction at different levels of B, or the BC interaction at different levels of A. The result would be the same.

As I have said, the three-way factorial is merely an extension of the two-way, with a slight twist. The twist comes about in obtaining the interaction sums of squares. In the two-way, we took an $A \times B$ table of cell means, calculated SS_{cells}, subtracted the main effects, and were left with SS_{AB}. In the three-way, we have several interactions, but we will calculate them using techniques analogous to those employed earlier. Thus, to obtain SS_{BC} we will take a $B \times C$ table of cell means (averaging over A), obtain $SS_{cells\ BC}$, subtract the main effects of B and C, and end up with SS_{BC}. The same applies to SS_{AB} and SS_{AC}. We also follow the same procedure to obtain SS_{ABC}, but here we need to begin with an $A \times B \times C$ table of cell means, obtain $SS_{cells\ ABC}$, and then subtract the main effects *and* the lower-order interactions to arrive at SS_{ABC}. In other words, for each interaction we start with a different

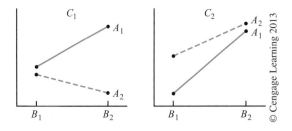

Figure 13.3   Plot of second-order interaction

table of cell means, collapsing over the variable(s) in which we are not at the moment interested. We then obtain an SS_{cells} for that table and subtract from it any main effects and lower-order interactions that involve terms included in that interaction.

Variables Affecting Driving Performance

For an example, consider a hypothetical experiment concerning the driving ability of two different types of drivers—inexperienced (A_1) and experienced (A_2). These people will drive on one of three types of roads—first class (B_1), second class (B_2), or dirt (B_3), under one of two different driving conditions—day (C_1) and night (C_2). Thus we have a $2 \times 3 \times 2$ factorial. The experiment will include four participants per condition (for a total of 48 participants), and the dependent variable will be the number of steering corrections in a one-mile section of roadway. The raw data are presented in Table 13.14a.

Table 13.14   Illustration of calculations for $2 \times 3 \times 2$ factorial design

(a) Data

	C_1			C_2		
	B_1	B_2	B_3	B_1	B_2	B_3
A_1	4	23	16	21	25	32
	18	15	27	14	33	42
	8	21	23	19	30	46
	10	13	14	26	20	40
A_2	6	2	20	11	23	17
	4	6	15	7	14	16
	13	8	8	6	13	25
	7	12	17	16	12	12

Cell Means

	C_1			C_2			
	B_1	B_2	B_3	B_1	B_2	B_3	Means
A_1	10.000	18.000	20.000	20.000	27.000	40.000	22.500
A_2	7.500	7.000	15.000	10.000	15.500	17.500	12.083
Means	8.750	12.500	17.500	15.000	21.250	28.750	17.292

More Cell Means

	AB Cells					AC Cells		
	B_1	B_2	B_3	Means		C_1	C_2	Means
A_1	15.000	22.500	30.000	22.500	A_1	16.000	29.000	22.500
A_2	8.750	11.250	16.250	12.083	A_2	9.833	14.333	12.083
Means	11.875	16.875	23.125	17.292	Means	12.917	21.667	17.292

	BC Cells			
	B_1	B_2	B_3	Means
C_1	8.750	12.500	17.500	12.917
C_2	15.000	21.250	28.750	21.667
Means	11.875	16.875	23.125	17.292

Table 13.14   *(continued)*

(b) Calculations

$$SS_{total} = \sum(X - \overline{X}...)^2 = (4 - 17.292)^2 + \cdots + (12 - 17.292)^2 = 4727.92$$

$$SS_A = nbc\sum(\overline{X}_{i..} - \overline{X}...)^2 = 4 \times 3 \times 2[(22.50 - 17.292)^2 + (12.083 - 17.292)^2]$$
$$= 1302.08$$

$$SS_B = nac\sum(\overline{X}_{.j.} - \overline{X}...)^2 = 4 \times 2 \times 2[(11.875 - 17.292)^2 + \cdots$$
$$+ (23.125 - 17.292)^2] = 1016.67$$

$$SS_C = nab\sum(\overline{X}_{..k} - \overline{X}...)^2 = 4 \times 2 \times 3[(12.917 - 17.292)^2 + (21.667 - 17.292)^2]$$
$$= 918.75$$

$$SS_{Cell\,AB} = nc\sum(\overline{X}_{ij.} - \overline{X}...)^2 = 4 \times 2[(15.00 - 17.292)^2 + \cdots + (16.25 - 17.292)^2]$$
$$= 2435.42$$

$$SS_{AB} = SS_{Cell\,AB} - SS_A - SS_B = 2435.42 - 1302.08 - 1016.67$$
$$= 116.67$$

$$SS_{Cell\,AC} = nb\sum(\overline{X}_{i.k} - \overline{X}...)^2 = 4 \times 3[(16.00 - 17.292)^2 + \cdots + (14.333 - 17.292)^2]$$
$$= 2437.58$$

$$SS_{AC} = SS_{Cell\,AC} - SS_A - SS_C = 2437.58 - 1302.08 - 918.75$$
$$= 216.75$$

$$SS_{Cell\,BC} = na\sum(\overline{X}_{.jk} - \overline{X}...)^2 = 4 \times 2[(8.75 - 17.292)^2 + \cdots + (28.75 - 17.292)^2]$$
$$= 1985.42$$

$$SS_{BC} = SS_{Cell\,BC} - SS_B - SS_C = 1985.42 - 1016.67 - 918.75$$
$$= 50.00$$

$$SS_{Cell\,ABC} = n\sum(\overline{X}_{ijk} - \overline{X}...)^2 = 4[(10.00 - 17.292)^2 + \cdots + (17.50 - 17.292)^2]$$
$$= 3766.92$$

$$SS_{ABC} = SS_{Cell\,ABC} - SS_A - SS_B - SS_C - SS_{AB} - SS_{AC} - SS_{BC}$$
$$= 3766.92 - 1302.08 - 1016.67 - 918.75 - 116.67 - 216.75 - 50.00$$
$$= 146.00$$

$$SS_{error} = SS_{total} - SS_{Cell\,ABC} = 4727.92 - 3766.92 = 961.00$$

(c) Summary table

Source	df	SS	MS	F
A (Experience)	1	1302.08	1302.08	48.78*
B (Road)	2	1016.67	508.33	19.04*
C (Conditions)	1	918.75	918.75	34.42*
AB	2	116.67	58.33	2.19
AC	1	216.75	216.75	8.12*
BC	2	50.00	25.00	<1
ABC	2	146.00	73.00	2.73
Error	36	961.00	26.69	
Total	47	4727.92		

*$p < .05$

The lower part of Table 13.14a contains all the necessary matrices of cell means for the subsequent calculation of the interaction sums of squares. These matrices are obtained simply by averaging across the levels of the irrelevant variable. Thus, the upper left-hand cell of the AB summary table contains the sum of all scores obtained under the treatment combination AB_{11}, regardless of the level of C (i.e., $ABC_{111} + ABC_{112}$). (*Note: You should be aware that I have rounded everything to two decimals for the tables, but the computations were based on more decimals. Beware of rounding error.*[6])

Table 13.14b shows the calculations of the sums of squares. For the main effects, the sums of squares are obtained exactly as they would be for a one-way. For the first-order interactions, the calculations are just as they would be for a two-way, taking two variables at a time. The only new calculation is for the second-order interaction, and the difference is only a matter of degree. Here we first obtain the SS_{cells} for the three-dimensional matrix. This sum of squares represents all of the variation among the cell means in the full-factorial design. From this, we must subtract all of the variation that can be accounted for by the main effects *and* by the first-order interactions. What remains is the variation that can be accounted for by only the joint effect of all three variables, namely SS_{ABC}.

The final sum of squares is SS_{error}. This is most easily obtained by subtracting $SS_{cells\,ABC}$ from SS_{total}. Since $SS_{cells\,ABC}$ represents all of the variation that can be attributable to differences among cells ($SS_{cells\,ABC} = SS_A + SS_B + SS_C + SS_{AB} + SS_{AC} + SS_{BC} + SS_{ABC}$), subtracting it from SS_{total} will leave us with only that variation within the cells themselves.

The summary table for the analysis of variance is presented in Table 13.14c. From this we can see that the three main effects and the $A \times C$ interaction are significant. None of the other interactions is significant.[7]

Simple Effects

Because we have a significant interaction, the main effects of A and C should be interpreted with caution, if at all. To this end, the AC interaction has been plotted in Figure 13.4. When plotted, the data show that for the inexperienced driver, night conditions produce considerably more steering corrections than do day conditions, whereas for the experienced driver the difference in the number of corrections made under the two conditions is relatively slight. Although the data might give us some confidence in reporting a significant effect for A (the difference between experienced and inexperienced drivers), they should leave us a bit suspicious about differences due to variable C. At a quick glance, it would appear that there is a significant C effect for the inexperienced drivers, but possibly not for the experienced drivers. To examine this question more closely, we must consider the simple effects of C under A_1 and A_2 separately. This analysis is presented in Table 13.15, from which we can see that there is a significant effect between day and night condition, not only for the inexperienced drivers, but also for the experienced drivers. (Note that we can again check the accuracy of our calculations; the simple effects should sum to $SS_C + SS_{AC}$.)

---

[6] The fact that substantial rounding error accumulates when you work with means is one major reason why formulae for use with calculators worked with totals. I am using the definitional formulae in these chapters because they are clearer, but that means that we need to put up with occasional rounding errors. Good computing software uses very sophisticated algorithms optimized to minimize rounding error.

[7] You will notice that this analysis of variance included seven F values and thus seven hypothesis tests. With so many hypothesis tests, the experimentwise error rate would be quite high. (That may be one of the reasons why Tukey moved to the name "familywise," because each set of contrasts on an effect can be thought of as a family.) Most people ignore the problem and simply test each F at a per-comparison error rate of $\alpha = .05$. However, if you are concerned about error rates, it would be appropriate to employ the equivalent of either the Bonferroni or multistage Bonferroni t procedure. This is generally practical only when you have the probability associated with each F, and can compare this probability against the probability required by the Bonferroni (or multistage Bonferroni) procedure. An interesting example of this kind of approach is found in Rosenthal and Rubin (1984). I suspect that most people will continue to evaluate each F on its own, and not worry about familywise error rates.

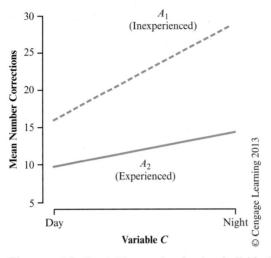

Figure 13.4 AC interaction for data in Table 13.14

From this hypothetical experiment, we would conclude that there are significant differences among the three types of roadway, and between experienced and inexperienced drivers. We would also conclude that there is a significant difference between day and night conditions, for both experienced and inexperienced drivers.

Table 13.15 Simple effects for data in Table 13.14

(a) Data

	C_1	C_2	Mean
A_1	16.000	29.000	22.500
A_2	9.833	14.333	12.083

(b) Computations

$$SS_{C\ at\ A_1} = nb \sum (\overline{X}_{1.k} - \overline{X}_{1..})^2$$
$$= 4 \times 3[(16.000 - 22.500)^2 + (29.000 - 22.500)^2] = 1014.00$$

$$SS_{C\ at\ A_2} = nb \sum (\overline{X}_{2.k} - \overline{X}_{2..})^2$$
$$= 4 \times 3[(9.833 - 12.083)^2 + (14.333 - 12.083)^2] = 121.50$$

(c) Summary table

Source	df	SS	MS	F
C at A_1	1	1014.00	1014.00	37.99*
C at A_2	1	121.50	121.50	4.55*
Error	36	961.00	26.69	

*$p < .05$

(d) Decomposition of sums of squares

$$SS_{C\ at\ A_1} + SS_{C\ at\ A_2} = SS_C + SS_{AC}$$

$$1014.00 + 121.50 = 918.75 + 216.75$$

$$1135.50 = 1135.50$$

Simple Interaction Effects

simple main effects

simple interaction effect

With higher-order factorials, not only can we look at the effects of one variable at individual levels of some other variable (what we have called simple effects but what should more accurately be called **simple main effects**), but we can also look at the interaction of two variables at individual levels of some third variable. This we will refer to as a **simple interaction effect**.

Basically simple interaction effects are obtained in the same we that we obtain simple main effects. We just use the data for one level of a variable at a time. Thus if we wanted to look at the simple AB interactions in our example, we would take the data separately for C_1 and C_2 and treat those as two two-way analyses. I won't work an example because it should be apparent what you will do.

Although there is nothing to prevent someone from examining simple interaction effects in the absence of a significant higher-order interaction, cases for which this would make any logical sense are rare. If, however, the experimenter has a particular reason for looking at, for example, the AB interaction at each level of C, he is perfectly free to do so. On the other hand, if a higher-order interaction is significant, the experimenter should cast a wary eye on all lower-order effects and consider testing the important simple effects. However, to steal a line from Winer (1971, p. 442), "Statistical elegance does not necessarily imply scientifically meaningful inferences." Common sense is at least as important as statistical manipulations.

13.13   A Computer Example

The following example illustrates the analysis of a three-way factorial design with unequal numbers of participants in the different cells. It is roughly based on a study by Seligman, Nolen-Hoeksema, Thornton, and Thornton (1990), although the data are contrived and one of the independent variables (Event) is fictitious. The main conclusions of the example are in line with the results reported. Note that we will not discuss how SPSS and other programs handle unequal sample sizes in this example until we come to Chapter 15.

The study involved collegiate swimming teams. At a team practice, all participants were asked to swim their best event as fast as possible, but in each case the time that was reported was falsified to indicate poorer than expected performance. Thus each swimmer was disappointed at receiving a poor result. Half an hour later, each swimmer was asked to perform the same event, and their times were again recorded. The authors predicted that on the second trial more pessimistic swimmers would do worse than on their first trial, whereas optimists would do better.

Participants were classified by their explanatory Style (optimism vs. pessimism), Sex, and the preferred Event. The dependent variable was the ratio of $Time_1/Time_2$, so a value greater than 1.00 means that the swimmer did better on the second trial. The data and results are given in Table 13.16. The results were obtained using SPSS. In examining the results remember that SPSS prints several lines of output that we rarely care about, and they can just be ignored.

From the SPSS computer output you can see that there is a significant effect due to the attributional style, with Optimists showing slightly improved performance after a perceived failure, and pessimists doing worse. The difference in means may appear to be small, but when you consider how close a race of this type usually is, even a tiny difference is important. You can also see that there is a Optim $\times$ Sex interaction. Looking at the means we see that there is almost no difference between Optimistic males and females, but this is not true of pessimists. Pessimistic males appear in these data to be much more affected by a perceived loss than are females. This Optim $\times$ Sex interaction is plotted as a bar chart following the summary table. This plot has collapsed across Event, because that variable had no effect.[8]

---

[8] To be fair to Seligman et al. (1990), I should say that this is not a result they appeared to have analyzed for, and therefore not one they found. I built it in to illustrate a point.

Table 13.16   Analysis of variance on responses to failure by optimists and pessimists

(a) Data

	Optimists						Pessimists					
	Male			Female			Male			Female		
	Free	Breast	Back	Free	Breast	Back	Free	Breast	Back	Free	Breast	Back
	0.986	1.026	1.009	1.108	1.048	1.004	0.983	0.962	0.936	0.997	1.045	1.045
	1.108	1.045	1.065	0.985	1.027	0.936	0.947	0.944	0.995	0.983	1.095	0.864
	1.080	0.996	1.053	1.001		1.040	0.932	0.941	0.872	1.105	0.944	0.982
	0.952	0.923		0.924			1.078	0.831		1.116	1.039	0.915
	0.998	1.000		0.968			0.914			0.997	0.927	1.047
	1.017	1.003					0.955			0.960	0.988	
	1.080	0.934									1.015	
$\overline{X}$	1.032	0.990	1.042	0.997	1.038	0.993	0.968	0.920	0.934	1.026	1.008	0.971

(b) Summary Table from SPSS

Tests of Between-Subjects Effects

Dependent Variable: PERFORM

Source	Type III Sum of Squares	df	Mean Square	F	Sig.
Corrected Model	6.804E-02[a]	11	6.186E-03	1.742	.094
Corrected Model	48.779	1	48.779	13738.573	.000
OPTIM	2.412E-02	1	2.412E-02	6.793	.012
SEX	7.427E-03	1	7.427E-03	2.092	.155
STROKE	4.697E-03	2	2.348E-03	.661	.521
OPTIM * SEX	1.631E-02	1	1.631E-02	4.594	.037
OPTIM * STROKE	5.612E-03	2	2.806E-03	.790	.460
SEX * STROKE	1.142E-02	2	5.708E-03	1.608	.211
OPTIM * SEX * STROKE	1.716E-03	2	8.578E-04	.242	.786
Error	.163	46	3.550E-03		
Total	57.573	58			
Corrected Total	.231	57			

[a] R Squared = .294 (Adjusted R Squared = .125)

(c) Plot of Sex × Optim Interaction

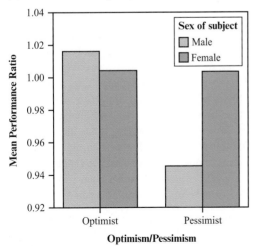

Key Terms

Factors (Introduction)	SS$_{cells}$ (13.1)	Partial effect (13.9)
Two-way factorial design (Introduction)	Crossed (13.8)	Unbalanced design (13.9)
Factorial design (Introduction)	Random factor (13.8)	Unweighted means (13.11)
Repeated-measures design (Introduction)	Nested design (13.8)	Equally weighted means (13.11)
Interaction (Introduction)	Random design (13.8)	First-order interactions (13.12)
2 × 5 factorial (Introduction)	Hierarchical models (13.8)	Second-order interaction (13.12)
Cell (Introduction)	Mixed models (13.8)	Simple main effects (13.12)
Main effect (13.1)	Crossed experimental design (13.8)	Simple interaction effect (13.12)
Simple effect (13.1)	Expected mean squares (13.8)	
Conditional effect (13.1)	partial η^2 (13.9)	

Exercises

The following problems can all be solved by hand, but any of the standard computer software packages will produce the same results.

13.1 In a study of mother–infant interaction, mothers are rated by trained observers on the quality of their interactions with their infants. Mothers are classified on the basis of whether or not this was their first child (primiparous versus multiparous) and on the basis of whether this was a low-birthweight (LBW) infant or normal-birthweight (NBW) infant. Mothers of LBW infants were further classified on the basis of whether or not they were under 18 years old. The data represent a score on a 12-point scale; a higher score represents better mother–infant interaction. Run and interpret the appropriate analysis of variance.

Primiparous			Multiparous			Primiparous			Multiparous		
LBW <18	LBW >18	NBW	LBW <18	LBW >18	NBW	LBW <18	LBW >18	NBW	LBW <18	LBW >18	NBW
4	6	8	3	7	9	7	6	2	7	2	10
6	5	7	4	8	8	4	2	5	1	1	9
5	5	7	3	8	9	5	6	8	4	9	8
3	4	6	3	9	9	4	5	7	4	9	7
3	9	7	6	8	3	4	5	7	4	8	10

13.2 Use simple effects to compare the three groups of multiparous mothers in Exercise 13.1.

13.3 Refer to Exercise 13.1. It seems obvious that the sample sizes do not reflect the relative frequency of age and parity characteristics in the population. Under what conditions would this be a relevant consideration, and under what conditions would it not be?

13.4 In Exercise 13.1 the design may have a major weakness from a practical point of view. Notice the group of multiparous mothers less than 18 years of age. Without regard to the data, would you expect this group to lie on the same continuum as the others?

13.5 In a study of memory processes, animals were tested in a one-trial avoidance-learning task. The animals were presented with a fear-producing stimulus on the learning trial as soon as they stepped across a line in the test chamber. The dependent variable was the time it took them to step across the line on the test trial. Three groups of animals differed in terms of the area in which they had electrodes implanted in their cortex (Neutral site, Area A, or Area B). Each group was further divided and given electrical stimulation 50, 100, or 150 milliseconds after crossing the line and being presented with the fear-inducing stimulus. If the brain area that was stimulated is involved in memory, stimulation would be expected to interfere with memory consolidation and retard learning of the avoidance response, and the animal should not show any hesitancy in recrossing the line. The data on latency to recross the line are as follows:

Stimulation Area

Neutral Site			Area A			Area B		
50	100	150	50	100	150	50	100	150
25	30	28	11	31	23	23	18	28
30	25	31	18	20	28	30	24	21
28	27	26	26	22	35	18	9	30
40	35	20	15	23	27	28	16	30
20	23	35	14	19	21	23	13	23

© Cengage Learning 2013

Run the analysis of variance.

13.6 Use simple effects to examine the effect of delay of stimulation in area A for the data in Exercise 13.5.

13.7 For the study in Exercise 13.5, to what would α_1 refer (if A were used to represent Area)?

13.8 Plot the cell means in Exercise 13.5.

13.9 Use the Bonferroni test to compare the neutral site to each of the other areas in Exercise 13.5, ignoring the length of stimulation. (*Hint:* Follow the procedures outlined in Chapters 11 and 12, but be sure that you take n as the number of scores on which the mean is based.)

13.10 Use simple effects to clarify the results for the Area factor in Exercise 13.5. Show that these simple effects sum to the correct figure.

13.11 Refer to Exercise 11.3a in Chapter 11. You will see that it forms a 2×2 factorial. Run the factorial analysis and interpret the results.

13.12 Make up a set of data for a 2×2 design that has no main effects but does have an interaction.

13.13 Make up a set of data for a 2×2 design that has two main effects but no interaction.

13.14 In Exercise 11.3 you ran a test between Groups 1 and 3 combined versus Groups 2 and 4 combined. How does that compare to testing the main effect of Level of processing in Exercise 13.11? Is there any difference?

13.15 Describe a reasonable experiment for which the primary interest would be in the interaction effect.

13.16 Calculate $\hat{d}$ for the data in Exercise 13.5.

13.17 Calculate η^2 and $\hat{\omega}^2$ for Exercise 13.1.

13.18 Klemchuk, Bond, & Howell (1990) examined role-taking ability in younger and older children depending on whether or not they attended daycare. The dependent variable was a scaled role-taking score. The sample sizes were distinctly unequal. The data follow

	Younger					Older			
No Daycare	−0.139	−2.002	−1.631	−2.173	0.179	−0.167	−0.285	0.851	−0.397
	−0.829	−1.503	0.009	−1.934	−1.448	0.351	−0.240	0.160	−0.535
	−1.470	−1.545	−0.137	−2.302		−0.102	0.273	0.277	0.714
Daycare	−1.412	−0.681	0.638	−0.222	0.668	0.859	0.782	0.851	−0.158
	−0.896	−0.464	−1.659	−2.096	0.493				

© Cengage Learning 2013

Use SPSS to run the analysis of variance and draw the appropriate conclusions.

13.19 Calculate η^2 and $\hat{\omega}^2$ for Exercise 13.5.

13.20 Calculate $\hat{d}$ for the data in Exercise 13.1.

13.21 To study the effects of early experience on conditioning, an experimenter raised four groups of rats in the presence of (1) no special stimuli, (2) a tone stimulus, (3) a vibratory stimulus, and (4) both a tone and a vibratory stimulus. The rats were later classically conditioned using either a tone or a vibratory stimulus as the conditioned stimulus and one of three levels of foot shock as the unconditioned stimulus. This is a $4 \times 2 \times 3$ factorial design. The cell means, rather than the raw data, follow. The $SS_{total} = 41,151.00$ and $n_{ijk} = 5$. The dependent variable was the number of trials to a predetermined criterion.

| | Conditioned Stimulus | | | | | |
| | Tone | | | Vibration | | |
	High	Med	Low	High	Med	Low
Control	11	16	21	19	24	29
Tone	25	28	34	21	26	31
Vibration	6	13	20	40	41	52
Tone and Vibration	22	30	30	35	38	48

© Cengage Learning 2013

Analyze the data and interpret the results.

13.22 In Exercise 11.26 you calculated the average of the nine cell variances. How does that answer compare to the MS_{error} from Exercise 13.23?

13.23 Use any statistical package to run the two-way analysis of variance on Interval and Dosage for the data in Epineq.dat on the Web site. Compare the results you obtain here with the results you obtained in Chapter 11, Exercises 11.26, 11.29 and 11.30.

13.24 In Chapter 2 we considered Sternberg's experiment on the time it takes to report whether a test stimulus was part of a prior stimulus display. The independent variables were the number of stimuli in the display (1, 3, or 5) and whether the test stimulus had been included in the display (Yes or No). The data are found in RxTime.dat on the website (www.uvm.edu/~dhowell /methods8/DataFiles/Tab13-22.dat). This is a two-way analysis of variance. Run the analysis and interpret the results, including mention and interpretation of effect sizes.

13.25 Obtain the Tukey test for Dosage from the analysis of variance in Exercise 13.23. Interpret the results.

13.26 Rerun the analysis in Exercise 13.29 but treat both variables as fixed and crossed. Show that the $SS_{school(code)}$ in Ex13-31 is the sum of SS_{school} and $SS_{school*code}$ in this analysis. (*Hint:* If you run this using SPSS you will have to have both sets of schools numbered 1–7.)

13.27 Using the data from Exercise 13.28, reproduce the simple effects shown in Table 13.14.

13.28 The data for the three-way analysis of variance given in Table 13.14 are found on the Web. They are named Tab13–14.dat. The first three entries in each record represent the coding for A (Experience), B (Road), and C (Conditions). The fourth entry is the dependent variable. Use any analysis of variance package to reproduce the summary table found in Table 13.14c.

13.29 An educational researcher wanted to test the hypothesis that schools that implemented strict dress codes produced students with higher academic performance. She randomly selected 7 schools in the state with dress codes and 7 schools that had no dress code. She then randomly selected 10 students within each school and noted their performance on a standardized test. The results follow.

| | Dress Code | | | | | | | No Dress Code | | | | | | |
School	1	2	3	4	5	6	7	8	9	10	11	12	13	14
	91	75	80	84	59	62	87	69	72	78	66	67	52	63
	78	73	77	92	67	93	78	74	56	77	55	82	71	65
	86	65	70	78	68	83	83	67	71	75	58	76	73	75
	70	68	68	78	64	78	79	64	92	56	73	78	68	82
	78	70	70	77	75	65	53	61	88	84	55	87	65	77
	48	60	69	76	74	71	66	76	64	83	70	87	69	81
	89	72	64	74	67	65	76	74	79	67	64	63	79	67
	90	77	73	81	56	85	67	71	73	70	52	68	67	73
	85	75	70	75	61	74	74	62	72	31	64	86	66	72
	82	80	74	81	67	83	72	67	70	70	79	84	64	56

© Cengage Learning 2013

13.30 A psychologist interested in esthetics wanted to compare composers from the classical period to composers from the romantic period. He randomly selected four composers from each period, played one work from each of them, and had 5 subjects rate each of them. Different subjects were used for each composer. The data are given below. (Note that this is a nested design.) Run the appropriate analysis of variance.

Composer	Classical Period				Romantic Period			
	A	B	C	D	E	F	G	H
	12	10	15	21	10	9	8	12
	14	9	18	17	11	12	7	14
	15	10	16	16	9	7	11	9
	11	12	18	18	8	15	12	7
	16	13	17	17	13	8	8	8

© Cengage Learning 2013

13.31 Gartlett & Bos (2010) presented data on the outcomes of male and female children raised by same-sex (lesbian) parents and those raised by opposite-sex parents. In a longitudinal study following 78 children of same-sex parents for 17 years, she collected data on Achenbach's Child Behavior Checklist when the children were 17. She used an equal sample of raw data from normative data collected by Achenbach on a random sample of children. For convenience we will assume that each cell contained 43 children. The data are shown below.

Group	Same-Sex Males	Same-Sex Females	Opposite-Sex Males	Opposite-Sex Females
Mean	25.8	26.3	23.0	20.3
sd	3.6	5.0	4.0	4.5
n	43	43	43	43

© Cengage Learning 2013

Compute an analysis of variance on these data and interpret the results. (Higher scores reflect greater competence.) (The F values differ somewhat from hers because she analyzed the data with a multivariate analysis of variance, but the means agree with hers. An SPSS version of data with these means and variances is available on the Web as Ex13-31.sav.)

Discussion Questions

13.32 In the analysis of Seligman et al. (1990) data on explanatory style (Table 13.15), you will note that there are somewhat more males than females in the Optimist group and more females than males in the Pessimist group. Under what conditions might this affect the way you would want to deal with unequal sample sizes, and when might you wish to ignore it?

13.33 Find an example of a three-way factorial in the research literature in which at least one of the interactions is significant and meaningful. Then create a data set that mirrors those results.

Chapter 14

Repeated-Measures Designs

Objectives

To discuss the analysis of variance by considering experimental designs in which the same subject is measured under all levels of one or more independent variables.

Contents

IN OUR DISCUSSION OF THE ANALYSIS OF VARIANCE, we have concerned ourselves with experimental designs that have different subjects in the different cells. More precisely, we have been concerned with designs in which the cells are independent, or uncorrelated. (Under the assumptions of the analysis of variance, *independent* and *uncorrelated* are synonymous in this context.) In this chapter we are going to be concerned with the problem of analyzing data where some or all of the cells are not independent. Such designs are somewhat more complicated to analyze, and the formulae become more complex. Most, or perhaps even all, readers will approach the problem using computer software such as SPSS or SAS. However, to understand what you are seeing, you need to know something about how you would approach the problem by hand; and that leads to lots and lots of formulae. I urge you to treat the formulae lightly, and not feel that you have to memorize any of them. This chapter needs to be complete, and that means we have to go into the analysis at some depth, but remember that you can always come back to the formulae when you need them, and don't worry about the calculations too much until you do need them.

If you think of a typical one-way analysis of variance with different subjects serving under the different treatments, you would probably be willing to concede that the correlations between treatments 1 and 2, 1 and 3, and 2 and 3 have an expectation of zero.

Treatment 1	Treatment 2	Treatment 3
X_{11}	X_{21}	X_{31}
X_{12}	X_{22}	X_{32}
$\ldots$	$\ldots$	$\ldots$
X_{1n}	X_{2n}	X_{3n}

However, suppose that in the design diagrammed here the same subjects were used in all three treatments. Thus, instead of $3n$ subjects measured once, we have n subjects measured three times. In this case, we would be hard put to believe that the intercorrelations of the three treatments would have expectancies of zero. On the contrary, the better subjects under treatment 1 would probably also perform well under treatments 2 and 3, and the poorer subjects under treatment 1 would probably perform poorly under the other conditions, leading to significant correlations among treatments.

partition

partialling out

repeated-measures designs

This lack of independence among the treatments would cause a serious problem if it were not for the fact that we can separate out, or **partition**, and remove the dependence imposed by repeated measurements on the same subjects. (To use a term that will become much more familiar in Chapter 15, we can say that we are **partialling out** effects that cause the dependence.) In fact, one of the main advantages of **repeated-measures designs** is that they allow us to reduce overall variability by using a common subject pool for all treatments, and at the same time allow us to remove subject differences from our error term, leaving the error components independent from treatment to treatment or cell to cell.

As an illustration, consider the highly exaggerated set of data on four subjects over three treatments presented in Table 14.1. Here the dependent variable is the number of trials to criterion on some task. If you look first at the treatment means, you will see some slight differences, but nothing to get too excited about. There is so much variability within each treatment that it would at first appear that the means differ only by chance. But look at the subject means. It is apparent that subject 1 learns quickly under all conditions, and that subjects 3 and 4 learn remarkably slowly. These differences among the subjects are producing most of the differences *within* treatments, and yet they have nothing to do with the treatment effect. If we could remove these subject differences we would have a better

Table 14.1   Hypothetical data for simple repeated-measures designs

	Treatment			
Subject	1	2	3	Mean
1	2	4	7	4.33
2	10	12	13	11.67
3	22	29	30	27.00
4	30	31	34	31.67
Mean	16	19	21	18.67

© Cengage Learning 2013

(and smaller) estimate of error. At the same time, it is the subject differences that are creating the high positive intercorrelations among the treatments, and these too we will partial out by forming a separate term for subjects.

One laborious way to do this would be to put all the subjects' contributions on a common footing by equating subject means without altering the relationships among the scores obtained by that particular subject. Thus, we could set $X'_{ij} = X_{ij} - \overline{X}_i$, where $\overline{X}_i$ is the mean of the ith subject. Now subjects would all have the same means ($\overline{X}'_i = 0$), and any remaining differences among the scores could be attributable only to error or to treatments. Although this approach would work, it is not practical. An alternative, and easier, approach is to calculate a sum of squares between subjects (denoted as either $SS_{\text{between subj}}$ or SS_S) and remove this from SS_{total} before we begin. This can be shown to be algebraically equivalent to the first procedure and is essentially the approach we will adopt.

$SS_{\text{between subj}}$

The solution is represented diagrammatically in Figure 14.1. Here we partition the overall variation into variation between subjects and variation within subjects. We do the same with the degrees of freedom. Some of the variation within a subject is attributable to the fact that his scores come from different treatments, and some is attributable to error; this further partitioning of variation is shown in the third line of the figure. We will always think of a repeated-measures analysis as *first* partitioning the SS_{total} into $SS_{\text{between subj}}$ and $SS_{\text{within subj}}$. Depending on the complexity of the design, one or both of these partitions may then be further partitioned.

The following discussion of repeated-measures designs can only begin to explore the area. For historical reasons, the statistical literature has underemphasized the importance of these designs. As a result, they have been developed mostly by behavioral scientists, particularly psychologists. By far the most complete coverage of these designs is found in Winer, Brown, and Michels (1991). Their treatment of repeated-measures designs is excellent and extensive, and much of this chapter reflects the influence of Winer's work.

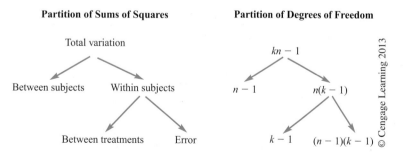

Figure 14.1   Partition of sums of squares and degrees of freedom

14.1 The Structural Model

First, some theory to keep me happy. Two structural models could underlie the analysis of data like those shown in Table 14.1. The simpler model is

$$X_{ij} = \mu + \pi_i + \tau_j + e_{ij}$$

where

μ = the grand mean

π_i = a constant associated with the ith person or subject, representing how much that person differs from the average person

τ_j = a constant associated with the jth treatment, representing how much that treatment mean differs from the average treatment mean

e_{ij} = the experimental error associated with the ith subject under the jth treatment

The variables π_i and e_{ij} are assumed to be independently and normally distributed around zero within each treatment. Their variances, σ_π^2 and σ_e^2, are assumed to be homogeneous across treatments. With these assumptions it is possible to derive the expected mean squares shown in Model I of Table 14.2. (In presenting expected means square, I am using the notation developed in the preceding chapters. The error term and subject factor are considered to be random, so those variances are presented as σ_π^2 and σ_e^2. [Subjects are always treated as random.] However, the treatment factor is generally a fixed factor, so its variation is denoted as θ_τ^2.)

An alternative and probably more realistic model is given by

$$X_{ij} = \mu + \pi_i + \tau_j + \pi\tau_{ij} + e_{ij}$$

Here we have added a Subject × Treatment interaction term to the model, which allows different subjects to change differently over treatments. The assumptions of the first model will continue to hold, and we will also assume the $\pi\tau_{ij}$ to be distributed around zero independently of the other elements of the model. This second model gives rise to the expected mean squares shown in Model II of Table 14.2.

The discussion of these two models and their expected mean squares may look as if it is designed to bury the solution to a practical problem (comparing a set of means) under a mountain of statistical theory. However, it is important to an explanation of how we will run our analyses and where our tests come from. You'll need to bear with me only a little longer.

14.2 F Ratios

The expected mean squares in Table 14.2 indicate that the model we adopt influences the F ratios we employ. If we are willing to assume that there is no Subject × Treatment interaction, we can form the following ratios:

$$\frac{E(MS_{\text{between subj}})}{E(MS_{\text{error}})} = \frac{\sigma_e^2 + k\sigma_\pi^2}{\sigma_e^2}$$

Table 14.2 Expected mean squares for simple repeated-measures designs

Model I		Model II	
$X_{ij} = \mu + \pi_i + \tau_j + e_{ij}$		$X_{ij} = \mu + \pi_i + \tau_j + \pi\tau_{ij} + e_{ij}$	
Source	E(MS)	Source	E(MS)
Subjects	$\sigma_e^2 + k\sigma_\pi^2$	Subjects	$\sigma_e^2 + k\sigma_\pi^2$
Treatments	$\sigma_e^2 + n\theta_\tau^2$	Treatments	$\sigma_e^2 + \sigma_{\pi\tau}^2 + n\theta_\tau^2$
Error	σ_e^2	Error	$\sigma_e^2 + \sigma_{\pi\tau}^2$

and

$$\frac{E(MS_{\text{treat}})}{E(MS_{\text{error}})} = \frac{\sigma_e^2 + n\theta_\tau^2}{\sigma_e^2}$$

Given an additional assumption about sphericity, which we will discuss in the next section, both of these lead to respectable F ratios that can be used to test the relevant null hypotheses.

Usually, however, we are cautious about assuming that there is no Subject $\times$ Treatment interaction. In much of our research it seems more reasonable to assume that different subjects will respond differently to different treatments, especially when those "treatments" correspond to phases of an ongoing experiment. As a result we usually prefer to work with the more complete model.

The full model (which includes the interaction term) leads to the following ratios:

$$\frac{E(MS_{\text{between subj}})}{E(MS_{\text{error}})} = \frac{\sigma_e^2 + k\sigma_\pi^2}{\sigma_e^2 + \sigma_{\pi\tau}^2}$$

and

$$\frac{E(MS_{\text{treat}})}{E(MS_{\text{error}})} = \frac{\sigma_e^2 + \sigma_{\pi\tau}^2 + n\theta_\tau^2}{\sigma_e^2 + \sigma_{\pi\tau}^2}$$

Although the resulting F for treatments is appropriate (the numerator contains only one term that is not found in the denominator), the F for subjects is biased. If we did form this latter ratio and obtained a significant F, we would be fairly confident that subject differences really did exist. However, if the F were not significant, the interpretation would be ambiguous. A nonsignificant F could mean either that $k\sigma_\pi^2 = 0$ or that $k\sigma_\pi^2 > 0$ but $\leq \sigma_{\pi\tau}^2$. Because we usually prefer this second model, and hate ambiguity, we seldom test the effect due to Subjects. This represents no great loss, however, since we have little to gain by testing the Subject effect. The main reason for obtaining $SS_{\text{between subj}}$ in the first place is to absorb the correlations between treatments and thereby remove subject differences from the error term. A test on the Subject effect, if it were significant, would merely indicate that people are different—hardly a momentous finding. The important thing is that both underlying models show that we can use MS_{error} as the denominator to test the effect of treatments.

14.3   The Covariance Matrix

An important assumption that is required for any F ratio in a repeated-measures design to be distributed as the central (tabled) F is that of compound symmetry of the covariance matrix.[1] To understand what this means, consider a matrix $(\hat{\Sigma})$ representing the covariances among the three treatments for the data given in Table 14.1.

$$\hat{\Sigma} = \begin{array}{c|ccc} & A_1 & A_2 & A_3 \\ \hline A_1 & 154.67 & 160.00 & 160.00 \\ A_2 & 160.00 & 176.67 & 170.67 \\ A_3 & 160.00 & 170.67 & 170.00 \end{array}$$

---

[1] This assumption is overly stringent and will shortly be relaxed somewhat. It is nonetheless a sufficient assumption, and it is made often.

main diagonal

off-diagonal elements

compound symmetry

covariance matrix (Σ)

sphericity

On the **main diagonal** of this matrix are the variances within each treatment $(\hat{\theta}^2_{A_j})$. Notice that they are all more or less equal, indicating that we have met the assumption of homogeneity of variance. The **off-diagonal elements** represent the covariances among the treatments (cov_{12}, cov_{13}, and cov_{23}). Notice that these are also more or less equal. (The fact that they are also of the same magnitude as the variances is irrelevant, reflecting merely the very high intercorrelations among treatments.) A pattern of constant variances on the diagonal and constant covariances off the diagonal is referred to as **compound symmetry**. (Again, the relationship between the variances and covariances is irrelevant.) The assumption of compound symmetry of the (*population*) **covariance matrix** (Σ) of which $\hat{\Sigma}$ is an estimate, represents a sufficient condition underlying a repeated-measures analysis of variance. The more general condition is known as **sphericity**, and you will often see references to that broader assumption. If we have compound symmetry we will meet the sphericity assumption, but it is possible, though not likely in practice, to have sphericity without compound symmetry. (Older textbooks generally make reference to compound symmetry, even though that is too strict an assumption. In recent years the trend has been toward reference to "sphericity," and that is how we will generally refer to it here, though we will return to compound symmetry when we consider mixed models at the end of this chapter.) Without this sphericity assumption, the F ratios may not have a distribution given by the distribution of F in the tables. Although this assumption applies to any analysis of variance design, when the cells are independent the covariances are always zero, and there is no problem—we merely need to assume homogeneity of variance. With repeated-measures designs, however, the covariances will not be zero and we need to assume that they are all equal. This has led some people (e.g., Hays, 1981) to omit serious consideration of repeated-measures designs. However, when we do have sphericity, the Fs are valid; and when we do not, we can use either very good approximation procedures (to be discussed later in this chapter) or alternative methods that do not depend on assumptions about Σ. One alternative procedure that does not require any assumptions about the covariance matrix is **multivariate analysis of variance (MANOVA)**. This is a **multivariate procedure**, which is essentially one that deals with multiple dependent variables simultaneously. This procedure, however, requires complete data and is now commonly being replaced by analyses of mixed models, which are introduced in Section 14.12.

multivariate analysis of variance (MANOVA)

multivariate procedure

Many people have trouble thinking in terms of covariances because they don't have a simple intuitive meaning. There is little to be lost by thinking in terms of correlations. If we truly have homogeneity of variance, compound symmetry reduces to constant correlations between trials.

14.4 Analysis of Variance Applied to Relaxation Therapy

As an example of a simple repeated-measures design, we will consider a study of the effectiveness of relaxation techniques in controlling migraine headaches. The data described here are fictitious, but they are in general agreement with data collected by Blanchard, Theobald, Williamson, Silver, and Brown (1978), who ran a similar, although more complex, study.

In this experiment we have recruited nine migraine sufferers and have asked them to record the frequency and duration of their migraine headaches. After 4 weeks of baseline recording during which no training was given, we had a 6-week period of relaxation training. (Each experimental subject participated in the program at a different time, so such things as changes in climate and holiday events should not systematically influence the data.) For our example we will analyze the data for the last 2 weeks of baseline and the last 3 weeks of training. The dependent variable is the duration (hours/week) of headaches

Table 14.3   Analysis of data on migraine headaches

(a) Data

Subject	Baseline Week 1	Baseline Week 2	Training Week 3	Training Week 4	Training Week 5	Subject Means
1	21	22	8	6	6	12.6
2	20	19	10	4	4	11.4
3	17	15	5	4	5	9.2
4	25	30	13	12	17	19.4
5	30	27	13	8	6	16.8
6	19	27	8	7	4	13.0
7	26	16	5	2	5	10.8
8	17	18	8	1	5	9.8
9	26	24	14	8	9	16.2
Week Means	22.333	22.000	9.333	5.778	6.778	13.244

(b) Calculations

$$SS_{total} = \sum(X - \overline{X}_{..})^2 = (21 - 13.244)^2 + \cdots + (9 - 13.244)^2 = 3166.31$$

$$SS_{subjects} = w\sum(\overline{X}_S - \overline{X}_{..})^2 = 5[(12.6 - 13.244)^2 + \cdots + (16.2 - 13.244)^2] = 486.71$$

$$SS_{weeks} = n\sum(\overline{X}_W - \overline{X}_{..})^2 = 9[(22.333 - 13.244)^2 + \cdots + (6.778 - 13.244)^2] = 2449.20$$

$$SS_{error} = SS_{total} - SS_{subjects} - SS_{weeks} = 3166.31 - 486.71 - 2449.20 = 230.40$$

(c) Summary table

Source	df	SS	MS	F
Between subjects	8	486.71		
Within subjects	36	2679.60		
Weeks	4	2449.20	612.30	85.04*
Error	32	230.40	7.20	
Total	44	3166.31		

*$p < .05$

in each of those 5 weeks. The data and the calculations are shown in Table 14.3.[2] It is important to note that I have identified the means with a subscript naming the variable. Thus instead of using the standard "dot notation" (e.g., $\overline{X}_{i.}$ for the Week means), I have used the letter indicating the variable name as the subscript (e.g., the means for Weeks are denoted $\overline{X}_W$ and the means for Subjects are denoted $\overline{X}_S$). As usual, the grand mean is denoted $\overline{X}_{..}$, and X represents the individual observations.

Look first at the data in Table 14.3a. Notice that there is a great deal of variability, but much of that variability comes from the fact that some people have more and/or longer-duration headaches than do others, which really has very little to do with the intervention program. As I have said, what we are able to do with a repeated-measures design but were not able to do with between-subjects designs is to remove this variability from SS_{error}, producing a smaller MS_{error} than we would otherwise have.

---

[2] Because I have rounded the means to three decimal places, there is rounding error in the answers. The answers given here have been based on more decimal places.

From Table 14.3b you can see that SS_{total} is calculated in the usual manner. Similarly, $SS_{subjects}$ and SS_{weeks} are calculated just as main effects always are (take the sum of the squared deviations from the grand mean and multiply by the appropriate constant [i.e., the number of observations contributing to each mean]). Finally, the error term is obtained by subtracting $SS_{subjects}$ and SS_{weeks} from SS_{total}.

The summary table is shown in Table 14.3c and looks a bit different from ones you have seen before. In this table I have made a deliberate split into Between Subject factors and Within Subject factors. The terms for Weeks and Error are parts of the Within Subject term, and so are indented under it. (In this design the Between Subject factor is not further broken down, which is why nothing is indented under it. But wait a few pages and you will see that happen too.) Notice that I have computed an F for Weeks but not for subjects, for the reasons given earlier. The F value for Weeks is based on 4 and 32 degrees of freedom, and $F_{.05}(4,32) = 2.68$. We can therefore reject $H_0: \mu_1 = \mu_2 = \cdots = \mu_5$ and conclude that the relaxation program led to a reduction in the duration per week of headaches reported by subjects. Examination of the means in Table 14.3 reveals that during the last three weeks of training, the amount of time per week involving headaches was about one-third of what it was during baseline.

You may have noticed that no Subject $\times$ Weeks interaction is shown in the summary table. With only one score per cell, the interaction term *is* the error term, and in fact some people prefer to label it $S \times W$ instead of error. To put this differently, in the design discussed here it is impossible to separate error from any possible Subject $\times$ Weeks interaction, because they are completely confounded. As we saw in the discussion of structural models, both of these effects, if present, are combined in the expected mean square for error.

I spoke earlier of the assumption of sphericity, or compound symmetry. For the data in the example, the variance–covariance matrix follows, represented by the notation $\hat{\Sigma}$, where the ^ is used to indicate that this is an estimate of the population variance–covariance matrix Σ.

$$
\hat{\Sigma} = \begin{matrix}
21.000 & 11.750 & 9.250 & 7.833 & 7.333 \\
11.750 & 28.500 & 13.750 & 16.375 & 13.375 \\
9.250 & 13.750 & 11.500 & 8.583 & 8.208 \\
7.833 & 16.375 & 8.583 & 11.694 & 10.819 \\
7.333 & 13.375 & 8.208 & 10.819 & 16.945
\end{matrix}
$$

Visual inspection of this matrix suggests that the assumption of sphericity is reasonable. The variances on the diagonal range from 11.5 to 28.5, whereas the covariances off the diagonal range from 7.333 to 16.375. Considering that we have only nine subjects, these values represent an acceptable level of constancy. (Keep in mind that the variances do not need to be equal to the covariances; in fact, they seldom are.) A statistical test of this assumption of sphericity was developed by Mauchly (1940) and is given in Winer (1971, p. 596). It would in fact show that we have no basis for rejecting the sphericity hypothesis. Although it is not a popular test—most statisticians point to its dependence on normality assumptions and it has low power when we most need it—most statistical software routinely print the results of that test. I would suggest ignoring Mauchly's test and opting for alternatives discussed in Section 14.7.

As already mentioned, one of the major advantages of the repeated-measures design is that it allows us to reduce the error term by using the same subject for all treatments. Suppose for a moment that the data illustrated in Table 14.3 had actually been produced by five independent groups of subjects. For such an analysis, SS_{error} would equal 717.11. In this case, we would not be able to pull out a subject term because $SS_{between\ subj}$ would be synonymous with SS_{total}. (A subject total and an individual score are identical.) As a result, differences among subjects would be inseparable from error, and in fact SS_{error}

would be the sum of what, for the repeated-measures design, are SS_{error} and $SS_{between subj}$ ($= 230.4 + 486.71 = 717.11$ on $32 + 8 = 40$ df). This would lead to

$$F = \frac{MS_{weeks}}{MS_{error}} = \frac{612.30}{17.93} = 34.15$$

which, although still significant, is less than one-half of what it was in Table 14.3.

To put it succinctly, subjects differ. When subjects are observed only once, these subject differences contribute to the error term. When subjects are observed repeatedly, we can obtain an estimate of the degree of subject differences and partial these differences out of the error term. In general, the greater the differences among subjects, the higher the correlations between pairs of treatments. The higher the correlations among treatments, the greater the relative power of repeated-measures designs.

14.5 Contrasts and Effect Sizes in Repeated Measures Designs

As we did in the case of one-way and factorial designs, we need to consider how to run contrasts among means of repeated measures variables. Fortunately there is not really much that is new here. We will again be comparing the mean of a condition or set of conditions against the mean of another condition or set of conditions, and we will be using the same kinds of coefficients that we have used all along.

In our example the first two weeks were Baseline measures, and the last three weeks were Training measures. Our omnibus F told us that there were statistically significant differences among the five Weeks, but not where those differences lie. Now I would like to contrast the means of the set of Baseline weeks with the mean of the set of Training weeks. The coefficients that will do this are shown below, along with the means.

	Week 1	Week 2	Week 3	Week 4	Week 5
Coefficient	1/2	1/2	$-1/3$	$-1/3$	-1.3
Mean	22.333	22.000	9.333	5.778	6.778

© Cengage Learning 2013

Just as we have been doing, we will define our contrast as

$$\hat{\psi} = \Sigma a_i \bar{X}_i$$

$$= \left(\frac{1}{2}\right)(22.333) + \left(\frac{1}{2}\right)(22.000) + \left(-\frac{1}{3}\right)(9.333) + \left(-\frac{1}{3}\right)(5.778) + \left(-\frac{1}{3}\right)(6.778)$$

$$= \frac{22.333 + 22.000}{2} - \frac{9.333 + 5.778 + 6.778}{3} = \frac{44.333}{2} - \frac{21.889}{3}$$

$$= 22.166 - 7.296$$

$$= 14.870$$

We can test this contrast with either a t or an F, but I will use t here. (F is just the square of t.)

$$t = \frac{\hat{\psi}}{\sqrt{\frac{(\Sigma a_i^2)MS_{error}}{n}}} = \frac{14.870}{\sqrt{\frac{0.833(7.20)}{9}}} = \frac{14.870}{\sqrt{0.667}} = \frac{14.870}{0.816} = 18.21$$

This is a t on $df_{error} = 32$ df, and is clearly statistically significant.

Notice that in calculating my t I used the MS_{error} from the overall analysis. And this was the same error term that was used to test the Weeks effect. I point that out only because when we come to more complex analyses we will have multiple error terms, and the one to use for a specific contrast is the one that was used to test the main effect of that independent variable.

Effect Sizes

Although there was a direct translation from one-way designs to repeated measures designs in terms of testing contrasts among means, the situation is a bit more complicated when it comes to estimating effect sizes. We will continue to define our effect size as

$$\hat{d} = \frac{\hat{\psi}}{s_{\text{error}}}$$

There should be no problem with $\hat{\psi}$, because it is the same contrast that we computed above—the difference between the mean of the baseline weeks and the mean of the training weeks. But there are several choices for s_{error}. Kline (2004) gives three possible choices for our denominator, but points out that two of these may be unsatisfactory either because they ignore the correlation between weeks or because they standardize $\hat{\psi}$ by a standard deviation that is not particularly meaningful.

What we will actually do is create an error term that is unique to the particular contrast. Imagine that instead of two baseline and three treatment measures we had one of each. The appropriate test here would be a repeated measures t test, and the denominator for our effect size measure would most likely be the standard deviation of the baseline scores. With our ANOVA a reasonable standardizing measure for this contrast would be the standard deviation of the means of the two baseline scores. For this example those means would be

21.5   19.5   16.0   27.5   28.5   23.0   21.0   17.5   25.0

And their standard deviation would be 4.272. Then a meaningful effect size measure would be

$$\hat{d} = \frac{\hat{\psi}}{s_{\text{error}}} = \frac{14.87}{4.272} = 4.95$$

This indicates that headaches during treatment were about 5 standard deviations less severe than they were during baseline. That is a very substantial reduction. See Kline (2004) and Olejnik & Algina (2000) for a discussion of alternative ways of computing an effect size.

14.6   Writing Up the Results

In writing up the results of this experiment we could simply say:

> To investigate the effects of relaxation therapy on the severity of migraine headaches, nine participants rated the severity of headaches on each of two weeks before receiving relaxation therapy and for three weeks while receiving therapy. An overall analysis of variance for repeated measures showed a significant difference between weeks ($F(4,32) = 85.04$, $p < .05$). The mean severity rating during baseline weeks was 22.166, which dropped to a mean of 7.296 during training, for a difference of 14.87. A contrast on this difference was significant ($t(32) = 18.21$, $p < .05$). Using the standard deviation of baseline measures as our standardizing measure produced an effect size measure of $d = 4.95$, documenting the importance of relaxation therapy in treating migraine headaches.

14.7   One Between-Subjects Variable and One Within-Subjects Variable

We have been speaking of the simple case in which we have one independent variable (other than subjects) and test each subject on every level of that variable. In actual practice, there are many different ways that we could design a study using repeated measures. For example, we could set up an experiment using two independent variables and test each subject under all combinations of both variables. Alternatively, each subject might serve under only one level of one of the variables, but under all levels of the other. If we had three variables, the possibilities are even greater. In this chapter we will discuss only a few of the possible designs. If you understand the designs discussed here, you should have no difficulty generalizing to even the most complex problems.

Consider the data presented in Table 14.4. These are actual data from a study by King (1986). This study in some ways resembles the one on morphine tolerance by Siegel (1975) that we examined in Chapter 12. King investigated motor activity in rats following injection of the drug midazolam. The first time that this drug is injected, it typically leads to a distinct decrease in motor activity. Like morphine, however, a tolerance for midazolam develops rapidly. King wished to know whether that acquired tolerance could be explained on the basis of a *conditioned* tolerance related to the physical context in which the drug was administered, as in Siegel's work. He used three groups, collecting the crucial data (presented in Table 14.4) on only the last day, which was the test day. During pretesting, two groups of animals were repeatedly injected with midazolam over several days, whereas the Control group was injected with physiological saline. On the test day, one group—the "Same" group—was injected with midazolam in the *same* environment in which it had earlier been injected. The "Different" group was also injected with midazolam, but in a *different* environment. Finally, the Control group was injected with midazolam for the first time. This Control group should thus show the typical initial response to the drug (decreased ambulatory behavior), whereas the Same group should show the normal tolerance effect—that is, they should decrease their activity little or not at all in response to the drug on the last trial. If King is correct, however, the Different group should respond similarly to the Control group, because although they have had several exposures to the drug, they are receiving it in a novel context and any conditioned tolerance that might have developed will not have the necessary cues required for its elicitation. The dependent variable in Table 14.4 is a measure of ambulatory behavior, in arbitrary units. Again, the first letter of the name of a variable is used as a subscript to indicate what set of means we are referring to.

Because the drug is known to be metabolized over a period of approximately 1 hour, King recorded his data in 5-minute blocks, or Intervals. We would expect to see the effect of the drug increase for the first few intervals and then slowly taper off. Our analysis uses the first six blocks of data. The design of this study can then be represented diagrammatically as

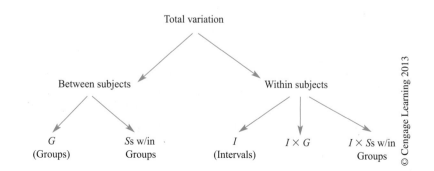

Table 14.4 Ambulatory behavior by Group and Trial

(a) Data

		Interval						Mean
		1	2	3	4	5	6	
Control		150	44	71	59	132	74	88.333
		335	270	156	160	118	230	211.500
		149	52	91	115	43	154	100.667
		159	31	127	212	71	224	137.333
		159	0	35	75	71	34	62.333
		292	125	184	246	225	170	207.000
		297	187	66	96	209	74	154.833
		170	37	42	66	114	81	85.000
	Mean	213.875	93.250	96.500	128.625	122.875	130.125	130.875
Same		346	175	177	192	239	140	211.500
		426	329	236	76	102	232	233.500
		359	238	183	123	183	30	186.000
		272	60	82	85	101	98	116.333
		200	271	263	216	241	227	236.333
		366	291	263	144	220	180	244.000
		371	364	270	308	219	267	299.833
		497	402	294	216	284	255	324.667
	Mean	354.625	266.250	221.000	170.000	198.625	178.625	231.521
Different		282	186	225	134	189	169	197.500
		317	31	85	120	131	205	148.167
		362	104	144	114	115	127	161.000
		338	132	91	77	108	169	152.500
		263	94	141	142	120	195	159.167
		138	38	16	95	39	55	63.500
		329	62	62	6	93	67	103.167
		292	139	104	184	193	122	172.333
	Mean	290.125	98.250	108.500	109.000	123.500	138.625	144.667
	Interval mean	286.208	152.583	142.000	135.875	148.333	149.125	169.021

(b) Calculations

$$SS_{\text{total}} = \sum (X - \overline{X}_{...})^2 = (150 - 169.021)^2 + \cdots + (122 - 169.021)^2 = 1{,}432{,}292.9$$

$$SS_{\text{subj}} = i \sum (\overline{X}_S - \overline{X}_{...})^2 = 6[(88.333 - 169.021)^2 + \cdots + (172.333 - 169.021)^2] = 670{,}537.1$$

$$SS_{\text{groups}} = ni \sum (\overline{X}_G - \overline{X}_{...})^2 = 8 \times 6[(130.875 - 169.021)^2 + \cdots + (144.667 - 169.021)^2] = 285{,}815.0$$

$$SS_{\text{intervals}} = ng \sum (\overline{X}_I - \overline{X}_{...})^2 = 8 \times 3[(286.208 - 169.021)^2 + \cdots + (149.125 - 169.021)^2] = 399{,}736.5$$

$$SS_{\text{cells}} = n \sum (\overline{X}_{GI} - \overline{X}_{...})^2 = 8[(213.875 - 169.021)^2 + \cdots + (138.625 - 169.021)^2] = 766{,}371.5$$

$$SS_{I \times G} = SS_{\text{cells}} - SS_{\text{interval}} - SS_{\text{groups}} = 766{,}371.5 - 285{,}815.0 - 399.736.5 = 80{,}820.0$$

(*continues*)

Table 14.4   (*continued*)

(c) Summary Table

Source	df	SS	MS	F
Between subjects	23	670,537.1		
Groups	2	285,815.0	142,907.5	7.80*
Ss w/in groups**	21	384,722.0	18,320.1	
Within subjects**	120	761,755.8		
Intervals	5	399,736.5	79,947.3	29.85*
$I \times G$	10	80,820.0	8,082.0	3.02*
$I \times Ss$ w/in groups**	105	281,199.3	2,678.1	
Total	143	1,432,292.9		

* $p < .05$;

** Calculated by subtraction

Here we have distinguished those effects that represent differences between subjects from those that represent differences within subjects. When we consider the between-subjects term, we can partition it into differences between groups of subjects (G) and differences between subjects in the same group (Ss w/in groups). The within-subject term can similarly be subdivided into three components—the main effect of Intervals (the repeated measure) and its interactions with the two partitions of the between-subject variation. You will see this partitioning represented in the summary table when we come to it.

Partitioning the Between-Subjects Effects

Let us first consider the partition of the between-subjects term in more detail. From the design of the experiment, we know that this term can be partitioned into two parts. One of these parts is the main effect of Groups (G), because the treatments (Control, Same, and Different) involve different groups of subjects. This is not the only source of differences among subjects, however. We have eight different subjects within the control group, and differences among them are certainly between-subjects differences. The same holds for the subjects within the other groups. Here we are speaking of differences among subjects in the same group—that is, Ss within groups.

If we temporarily ignore intervals entirely (e.g., we simply collect our data over the entire session rather than breaking it down into 5-minute intervals), we can think of the study as producing the following data:

Control	Same	Different
88.333	211.500	197.500
211.500	233.500	148.167
100.667	186.000	161.000
137.333	116.333	152.500
62.333	236.333	159.167
207.000	244.000	63.500
154.833	299.833	103.167
85.000	324.667	172.333
130.875	231.521	144.667

where the "raw scores" in this table are the subject means from Table 14.4. Because each subject is represented only once in these totals, the analysis we will apply here is the same as a one-way analysis of variance on independent groups. Indeed, except for a constant representing the number of scores per subject (which cancels out in the end), the sums of squares for the simple one-way on these data would be the same as those in the actual analysis. The F that tests the main effect of Groups if this were a simple one-way on subject totals would be equal to the one that we will obtain from the full analysis. Thus, the between-subjects partition of the total variation can be seen as essentially a separate analysis of variance, with its own error term (sometimes referred to as $\text{error}_{\text{between}}$) independent of the within-subjects effects.

error_{between}

Partitioning the Within-Subjects Effects

Next consider the within-subjects element of the partition of SS_{total}. As we have already seen, this is itself partitioned into three terms. A comparison of the six intervals involves comparisons of scores from the same subject, and thus Intervals is a within-subjects term—it depends on differences within each subject. Because Intervals is a within-subjects term, the interaction of Intervals with Groups is also a within-subjects effect. The third term (Intervals × Ss within groups) is sometimes referred to as $\text{error}_{\text{within}}$ because it is the error term for the within-subjects effects. The $SS_{\text{Intervals} \times Ss \text{ w/in groups}}$ term is actually the sum of the sums of squares for the $I \times S$ interactions calculated separately for each group. Thus, it can be seen as logically equivalent to the error term used in the previous design.

error_{within}

The Analysis

Before considering the analysis in detail, it is instructive to look at the general pattern of results. Although there are not enough observations in each cell to examine the distributions in any serious way, it is apparent that on any given interval there is substantial variability within groups. For example, for the second interval in the control group, scores range from 0 to 270. There do not appear to be any extreme outliers, however, as often happens in this kind of research, and the variances within cells, although large, are approximately equal. You can also see that there are large individual differences, with some of the animals consistently showing relatively little ambulatory behavior and some showing a great deal. These are the kinds of differences that will be partialled out by our analysis. Looking at the Interval means, you will see that, as expected, behavior decreased substantially after the first 5-minute interval and then increased slightly during the rest of the session. Finally, looking at the difference between the means for the Control and Same groups, you will see the anticipated tolerance effect, and looking at the Different group, you see that it is much more like the Control group than it is like the Same group. This is the result that King predicted.

Very little needs to be said about the actual calculations in Table 14.4b because they are really no different from the usual calculations of main and interaction effects. Whether a factor is a between-subjects or within-subjects factor has no bearing on the calculation of its sum of squares, although it does affect its placement in the summary table and the ultimate calculation of the corresponding F.

In the summary table in Table 14.4c, the source column reflects the design of the experiment, with SS_{total} first partitioned into $SS_{\text{between subj}}$ and $SS_{\text{w/in subj}}$. Each of these sums of squares is further subdivided. The double asterisks next to the three terms show we calculate these by subtraction ($SS_{\text{w/in subj}}$, $SS_{Ss \text{ w/in groups}}$, and $SS_{I \times Ss \text{ w/in groups}}$), based on the fact that sums of squares are additive and the whole must be equal to the sum of its parts. This simplifies our work considerably. Thus

$$SS_{\text{w/in subj}} = SS_{\text{total}} - SS_{\text{between subj}}$$

$$SS_{Ss\text{ w/in groups}} = SS_{\text{between subj}} - SS_{\text{groups}}$$

$$SS_{I \times Ss\text{ w/in groups}} = SS_{\text{w/in subj}} - SS_{\text{intervals}} - SS_{IG}$$

These last two terms will become error terms for the analysis.

The degrees of freedom are obtained in a relatively straightforward manner. For each of the main effects, the number of degrees of freedom is equal to the number of levels of the variable minus 1. Thus, for Subjects there are $24 - 1 = 23$ df, for Groups there are $3 - 1 = 2$ df, and for Intervals there are $6 - 1 = 5$ df. As for all interactions, the df for $I \times G$ is equal to the product of the df for the component terms. Thus, $df_{IG} = (6 - 1)(3 - 1) = 10$. The easiest way to obtain the remaining degrees of freedom is by subtraction, just as we did with the corresponding sums of squares.

$$df_{\text{w/in subj}} = df_{\text{total}} - df_{\text{between subj}}$$

$$df_{Ss\text{ w/in groups}} = df_{\text{between subj}} - df_{\text{groups}}$$

$$df_{I \times Ss\text{ w/in groups}} = df_{\text{w/in subj}} - df_{\text{intervals}} - df_{IG}$$

These df can also be obtained directly by considering what these terms represent. Within each subject, we have $6 - 1 = 5$ df. With 24 subjects, this amounts to $(5)(24) = 120$ $df_{\text{w/in subj}}$. Within each level of the Groups factor, we have $8 - 1 = 7$ df between subjects, and with three Groups we have $(7)(3) = 21$ $df_{\text{w/in groups}}$. $I \times Ss$ w/in groups is really an interaction term, and as such its df is simply the product of df_I and $df_{Ss\text{ w/in groups}} = (5)(21) = 105$.

Skipping over the mean squares, which are merely the sums of squares divided by their degrees of freedom, we come to F. From the column of F it is apparent that, as we anticipated, Groups and Intervals are significant. The interaction is also significant, reflecting, in part, the fact that the Different group was at first intermediate between the Same and the Control group, but that by the second 5-minute interval it had come down to be equal to the Control group. This finding can be explained by a theory of conditioned tolerance. The really interesting finding is that, at least for the later intervals, simply injecting an animal in an environment different from the one in which it had been receiving the drug was sufficient to overcome the tolerance that had developed. These animals respond almost exactly as do animals that had never experienced midazolam. We will return to the comparison of Groups at individual Intervals later.

Assumptions

For the F ratios actually to follow the F distribution, we must invoke the usual assumptions of normality, homogeneity of variance, and sphericity of $\hat{\Sigma}$. For the *between-subjects* term(s), this means that we must assume that the variance of subject means within any one level of *Group* is the same as the variance of subject means within every other level of *Group*. If necessary, this assumption can be tested by one of the tests proposed by Levene (1960), Brown & Forsythe (1974), and O'Brien (1981), which were referred to in Chapter 7. In practice, however, the analysis of variance is relatively robust against reasonable violations of this assumption (see Collier, Baker, and Mandeville, 1967; and Collier, Baker, Mandeville, and Hayes, 1967). Because the groups are independent, compound symmetry, and thus sphericity, of the covariance matrix is assured if we have homogeneity of variance, because all off-diagonal entries will be zero.

For the *within-subjects* terms we must also consider the usual assumptions of homogeneity of variance and normality, along with the assumption of sphericity. The homogeneity of variance assumption in this case is that the $I \times S$ interactions are constant across the Groups.

There are two assumptions on the covariance matrix (or matrices) in addition to homogeneity of variance. Again, we will let $\hat{\Sigma}$ represent the matrix of variances and covariances among the levels of I (Intervals). Thus with six intervals,

$$
\hat{\Sigma} =
\begin{array}{cccccc}
I_1 & I_2 & I_3 & I_4 & I_5 & I_6 \\
\hline
\hat{\sigma}_{11} & \hat{\sigma}_{12} & \hat{\sigma}_{13} & \hat{\sigma}_{14} & \hat{\sigma}_{15} & \hat{\sigma}_{16} \\
\hat{\sigma}_{21} & \hat{\sigma}_{22} & \hat{\sigma}_{23} & \hat{\sigma}_{24} & \hat{\sigma}_{25} & \hat{\sigma}_{26} \\
\hat{\sigma}_{31} & \hat{\sigma}_{32} & \hat{\sigma}_{33} & \hat{\sigma}_{34} & \hat{\sigma}_{35} & \hat{\sigma}_{36} \\
\hat{\sigma}_{41} & \hat{\sigma}_{42} & \hat{\sigma}_{43} & \hat{\sigma}_{44} & \hat{\sigma}_{45} & \hat{\sigma}_{46} \\
\hat{\sigma}_{51} & \hat{\sigma}_{52} & \hat{\sigma}_{53} & \hat{\sigma}_{54} & \hat{\sigma}_{55} & \hat{\sigma}_{56} \\
\hat{\sigma}_{61} & \hat{\sigma}_{62} & \hat{\sigma}_{63} & \hat{\sigma}_{64} & \hat{\sigma}_{65} & \hat{\sigma}_{66} \\
\end{array}
$$

© Cengage Learning 2013

For each Group we would have a separate population variance–covariance matrix Σ_{G_i}. (Σ and Σ_{G_i} are estimated by $\hat{\Sigma}$ and $\hat{\Sigma}_{G_i}$, respectively.) For $MS_{I \times Ss\ w/in\ groups}$ to be an appropriate error term, we will first assume that the individual variance–covariance matrices (Σ_{G_i}) are the same for all levels of G. This can be thought of as an extension (to covariances) of the common assumption of homogeneity of variance.

The second assumption concerning covariances deals with the overall matrix Σ, where Σ is the pooled average of the Σ_{G_i}. (For equal sample sizes in each group, an entry in Σ will be the average of the corresponding entries in the individual Σ_{G_i} matrices.) A common and sufficient, but not necessary, assumption is that the matrix exhibits compound symmetry—meaning, as I said earlier, that all the variances on the main diagonal are equal, and all the covariances off the main diagonal are equal. Again, the variances do not have to equal the covariances, and usually will not. This assumption is in fact more stringent than necessary. All that we really need to assume is that the standard errors of the differences between pairs of Interval means are constant—in other words, that $\sigma^2_{\bar{I}_i - \bar{I}_j}$ is constant for all i and j ($j \neq i$). This sphericity requirement is met automatically if Σ exhibits compound symmetry, but other patterns of Σ will also have this property. Sphericity can be tested using the Mauchley test, discussed, and discouraged, above. However rather than using Mauchley's test, you are probably further ahead not worrying about sphericity but using corrections provided by Greenhouse and Geisser (1959) and/or Huynh and Feldt (1976), discussed below, which correct for a lack of sphericity if it exists.

For a more extensive discussion of the covariance assumptions, see Huynh and Feldt (1970) and Huynh and Mandeville (1979); a particularly good discussion can be found in Edwards (1985, pp. 327–329, 336–339).

Adjusting the Degrees of Freedom

Greenhouse and Geisser (1959) considered the effects of departure from the sphericity assumption on Σ. They showed that regardless of the form of Σ, the F ratio from the within-subjects portion of the analysis of variance will be approximately distributed as F on

$$(i - 1)\varepsilon, \ g(n - 1)(i - 1)\varepsilon$$

df for the Interval effect and

$$(g - 1)(i - 1)\varepsilon, \ g(n - 1)(i - 1)\varepsilon$$

df for the $I \times G$ interaction, where $i =$ the number of intervals and ε is estimated by

$$\hat{\varepsilon} = \frac{i^2(\overline{s}_{jj} - \overline{s})^2}{(i-1)(\sum s_{jk}^2 - 2i\sum \overline{s}_j^2 + i^2\overline{s}^2)}$$

Here,

$\overline{s}_{jj} =$ the mean of the entries on the main diagonal of $\hat{\Sigma}$

$\overline{s} =$ the mean of all entries in $\hat{\Sigma}$

$s_{jk} =$ the jkth entry in $\hat{\Sigma}$

$\overline{s}_j =$ the mean of all entries in the jth row of $\hat{\Sigma}$

The effect of using $\hat{\varepsilon}$ is to decrease both df_{effect} and df_{error} from what they would normally be. Thus $\hat{\varepsilon}$ is simply the proportion by which we adjust them. Greenhouse and Geisser recommended that we adjust our degrees of freedom using $\hat{\varepsilon}$. They further showed that when the sphericity assumptions are met, $\varepsilon = 1$, and as we depart more and more from sphericity, ε approaches $1/(i-1)$ as a minimum.

There is some suggestion that for large values of ε, even using $\hat{\varepsilon}$ to adjust the degrees of freedom can lead to a conservative test. Huynh and Feldt (1976) investigated this correction and recommended a modification of $\hat{\varepsilon}$ when there is reason to believe that the true value of ε lies near or above 0.75. Huynh and Feldt, as later corrected by Lecoutre (1991),[3] defined

$$\tilde{\varepsilon} = \frac{(N - g + 1)(i - 1)\hat{\varepsilon} - 2}{(i - 1)[N - g - (i - 1)\hat{\varepsilon}]}$$

where $N = n \times g$. We then use $\hat{\varepsilon}$ or $\tilde{\varepsilon}$, depending on our estimate of the true value of ε. (Under certain circumstances, $\tilde{\varepsilon}$ will exceed 1, at which point it is set to 1.)

Because tests of sphericity, such as Mauchley's, are likely to have serious problems when we need them the most, it has been suggested that we *always* use the correction to our degrees of freedom afforded by $\hat{\varepsilon}$ or $\tilde{\varepsilon}$, whichever is appropriate, or use a multivariate procedure to be discussed later. (I suggested a similar strategy for a t test of two independent means based on results of Hayes and Cai (2007). They recommend using the Welch-Satterthwaite approach in all situations without bothering with a test on homogeneity of variance.)

We can calculate $\hat{\varepsilon}$ and $\tilde{\varepsilon}$ and evaluate F on the appropriate df. The pooled variance–covariance matrix (averaged across the separate matrices) is presented in Table 14.5. (I have not presented the variance–covariance matrices for the several groups because they are roughly equivalent and because each of the elements of the matrix is based on only eight observations.)

From Table 14.5 we can see that our values of $\hat{\varepsilon}$ and $\tilde{\varepsilon}$ are .6569 and .8674, respectively. Because these are in the neighborhood of .75, we will follow Huynh and Feldt's suggestion and use $\tilde{\varepsilon}$. In this case, the degrees of freedom for the interaction are

$$(g - 1)(i - 1)(0.7508) = 7.508$$

and

$$g(n - 1)(i - 1)(0.7508) = 78.834$$

The exact critical value of $F_{.05}(7.508, 78.834)$ is 2.09, which means that we will reject the null hypothesis for the interaction. Thus, regardless of any problems with sphericity, all the effects in this analysis are significant. (They would also be significant if we used $\hat{\varepsilon}$ instead of $\tilde{\varepsilon}$.)

---

[3] Chen and Dunlap (1994) later confirmed Lecoutre's correction to the original Huynh and Feldt formula. However both SPSS and SAS continue to calculate the wrong value for the Huynh and Feldt epsilon.

Table 14.5 Variance-covariance matrix and calculation of $\hat{\varepsilon}$ and $\tilde{\varepsilon}$

			Interval			
1	2	3	4	5	6	Mean
6388.173	4696.226	2240.143	681.649	2017.726	1924.066	2991.330
4696.226	7863.644	4181.476	2461.702	2891.524	3531.869	4271.074
2240.143	4181.476	3912.380	2696.690	2161.690	3297.762	3081.690
681.649	2461.702	2696.690	4601.327	2248.600	3084.589	2629.093
2017.726	2891.524	2161.690	2248.600	3717.369	989.310	2337.703
1924.066	3531.869	3297.762	3084.589	989.310	5227.649	3009.208

$$\bar{s}_{jj} = \frac{6388.173 + 7863.644 + \cdots + 5227.649}{6} = 5285.090$$

$$\bar{s} = \frac{6388.173 + 4696.226 + \cdots + 989.310 + 5227.649}{36} = 3053.350$$

$$\sum s_{jk}^2 = 6388.173^2 + 4696.226^2 + \cdots + 5227.649^2 = 416{,}392{,}330$$

$$\sum \bar{s}_j^2 = 2991.330^2 + \cdots + 3009.208^2 = 58{,}119{,}260$$

$$\hat{\varepsilon} = \frac{i^2(\bar{s}_{jj} - \bar{s})^2}{(i-1)(\sum s_{jk}^2 - 2i\sum \bar{s}_j^2 + i^2\bar{s}^2)}$$

$$= \frac{36(5285.090 - 3053.350)^2}{(6-1)[416{,}392{,}330 - (2)(6)(58{,}119{,}260) + (36)(3053.350^2)]}$$

$$= \frac{179{,}303{,}883}{5[416{,}392{,}330 - 697{,}431{,}120 + 335{,}626{,}064]} = 0.6569$$

$$\tilde{\varepsilon} = \frac{(N - g + 1)(i - 1)\hat{\varepsilon} - 2}{(i-1)[N - g - (i-1)\hat{\varepsilon}]}$$

$$= \frac{(24 - 3 + 1)(5)(0.6569) - 2}{5[25 - 3 - 5(0.6569)]} = \frac{70.259}{5[22 - 5(0.6569)]} = 0.7508$$

Simple Effects

The Interval $\times$ Group interaction is plotted in Figure 14.2; the interpretation of the data is relatively clear. It is apparent that the Same group consistently performs above the level of the other two groups—that is, the conditioned tolerance to midazolam leads to greater activity in that group than in the other groups. It is also clear that activity decreases noticeably after the first 5-minute interval (during which the drug is having its greatest effect). The interaction appears to be produced by the fact that the Different group is intermediate between the other two groups during the first interval, but it is virtually indistinguishable from the Control group thereafter. In addition, the Same group continues declining until at least the fourth interval, whereas the other two groups drop precipitously and then level off. Simple effects will prove useful in interpreting these results, especially in terms of examining group differences during the first and the last intervals. Simple effects will also be used to test for differences between intervals within the Control group, but only for purposes of illustration—it should be clear that Interval differences exist within each group.

Marginal Means of Activity

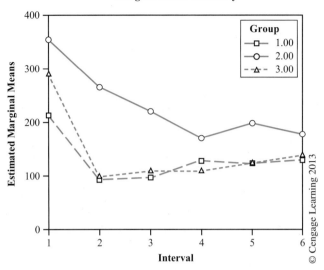

Figure 14.2   Interval $\times$ Group interaction for data from Table 14.4

As I have suggested earlier, the Greenhouse and Geisser and the Huynh and Feldt adjustments to degrees of freedom appear to do an adequate job of correcting for problems with the sphericity assumption when testing for overall main effects or interactions. However, a serious question about the adequacy of the adjustment arises when we consider within-subjects simple effects (Boik, 1981; Harris, 1985). The traditional approach to testing simple effects involves testing individual within-subjects contrasts against a pooled error term ($MS_{I \times Ss \text{ w/in groups}}$). If there are problems with the underlying assumption, this error term will sometimes underestimate and sometimes overestimate what would be the proper denominator for F, playing havoc with the probability of a Type I error. For that reason we are going to adopt a different, and in some ways simpler, approach.

The approach we will take follows the advice of Boik that a separate error term be derived for each tested effect. Thus, when we look at the simple effect of Intervals for the Control condition, for example, the error term will speak specifically to that effect and will not pool other error terms that apply to other simple effects. In other words, it will be based solely on the Control group. We can test the Interval simple effects quite easily by running separate repeated-measures analyses of variance for each of the groups. For example, we can run a one-way repeated-measures analysis on Intervals for the Control group, as discussed in Section 14.4. We can then turn around and perform similar analyses on Intervals for the Same and Different groups separately. These results are shown in Table 14.6. In each case the Interval differences are significant, even after we correct the degrees of freedom using $\hat{\varepsilon}$ or $\tilde{\varepsilon}$, whichever is appropriate.

If you look at the within-subject analyses in Table 14.6, you will see that the average MS_{error} is $(2685.669 + 3477.571 + 1871.026)/3 = 2678.089$, which is $MS_{I \times Ss \text{ w/in groups}}$ from the overall analysis found on page 469. Here these denominators for the F ratios are noticeably different from what they would have been had we used the pooled term, which is the traditional approach. You can also verify with a little work that the MS_{Interval} terms for each analysis are the same as those that we would compute if we followed the usual procedures for obtaining simple effects mean squares.

For the between-subjects simple effects (e.g., Groups at Interval 1) the procedure is more complicated. Although we could follow the within-subject example and perform

Table 14.6   Calculation of within-subjects simple effects for data from King (1986)

(a) Interval at Control

Source	df	SS	MS	F
Between subjects	7	134,615.58		
Interval	5	76,447.25	15,289.45	5.69*
Error	35	93,998.42	2685.67	
Total	47	305,061.25		

*$p < .05$; $\hat{\varepsilon} = .404$; $\widetilde{\varepsilon} = .570$

(b) Interval at Same

Source	df	SS	MS	F
Between subjects	7	175,600.15		
Interval	5	193,090.85	38,618.17	11.10*
Error	35	121,714.98	3477.57	
Total	47	490,405.98		

*$p < .05$; $\hat{\varepsilon} = .578$; $\widetilde{\varepsilon} = 1.00$

(c) Interval at Different

Source	df	SS	MS	F
Between subjects	7	74,506.33		
Interval	5	211,018.42	42,203.68	22.56*
Error	35	65,485.92	1871.03	
Total	47	351,010.67		

*$p < .05$; $\hat{\varepsilon} = .598$; $\widetilde{\varepsilon} = 1.00$

separate analyses at each Interval, we would lose considerable degrees of freedom unnecessarily. Here it is usually legitimate to pool error terms, and it is generally wise to do so.

For this example we will examine the simple effects of Group at Interval 1 and Group at Interval 6. The original data can be found in Table 14.4 on page 468. The sums of squares for these effects are

$$SS_{G \text{ at Int. 1}} = 8[(213.875 - 286.208)^2 + (354.625 - 286.208)^2$$
$$+ (290.125 - 286.208)^2]$$
$$= 79,426.33$$
$$SS_{G \text{ at Int. 6}} = 8[(130.125 - 149.125)^2 + (178.625 - 149.125)^2$$
$$+ (138.625 - 149.125)^2]$$
$$= 10,732.00$$

Testing the simple effects of between-subjects terms is a little trickier. Consider for a moment the simple effect of Group at Interval 1. This is essentially a one-way analysis of variance with no repeated measures, because the Group means now represent the average of single—rather than repeated—observations on subjects. Thus, subject differences are confounded with experimental error. In this case, the appropriate error sum of squares is $SS_{\text{w/in cell}}$, where, from Table 14.4,

$$SS_{\text{w/in cell}} = SS_{Ss \text{ w/in group}} + SS_{I \times Ss \text{ w/in groups}}$$
$$= 384,722.03 + 281,199.34 = 665,921.37$$

and

$$MS_{\text{w/in cell}} = \frac{SS_{\text{w/in cell}}}{df_{Ss \text{ w/in group}} + df_{I \times Ss \text{ w/in group}}}$$

$$= \frac{665,921.37}{21 + 105} = 5285.09$$

It may be easier to understand why we need this special $MS_{\text{w/in cell}}$ error term if you think about what it really represents. If you were presented with only the data for Interval 1 in Table 14.4 and wished to test the differences among the three groups, you would run a standard one-way analysis of variance, and the MS_{error} would be the average of the variances within each of the three groups. Similarly, if you had only the data from Interval 2, Interval 3, and so on, you would again average the variances within the three treatment groups. The $MS_{\text{w/in cell}}$ that we have just finished calculating is in reality the average of the error terms for these six different sets (Intervals) of data. As such, it is the average of the variance within each of the 18 cells.

We can now proceed to form our F ratios.

$$F_{G \text{ at Int. 1}} = \frac{MS_{G \text{ at Int. 1}}}{MS_{\text{w/in cell}}} = \frac{79,426.33/2}{5285.09} = 7.51$$

$$F_{G \text{ at Int. 6}} = \frac{MS_{G \text{ at Int. 6}}}{MS_{\text{w/in cell}}} = \frac{10,732/2}{5285.09} = 1.02$$

A further difficulty arises in the evaluation of F. Because $MS_{\text{w/in cell}}$ also represents the sum of two *heterogeneous* sources of error [as can be seen by examination of the $E(MS)$ for Ss w/in groups and $I \times Ss$ w/in groups], our F will not be distributed on 2 and 126 df. We will get ourselves out of this difficulty in the same way we did when we faced a similar problem concerning t in Chapter 7. We will simply calculate the relevant df against which to evaluate F—more precisely; we will calculate a statistic denoted as f' and evaluate F_{obt} against $F_{.05}(a - 1, f')$. In this case, the value of f' is given by Welch (1938) and Satterthwaite (1946) as

$$f' = \frac{(u + v)^2}{\dfrac{u^2}{df_u} + \dfrac{v^2}{df_v}}$$

where

$$u = SS_{Ss \text{ w/in groups}}$$

$$v = SS_{I \times Ss \text{ w/in groups}}$$

and df_u and df_v are the corresponding degrees of freedom. For our example,

$$u = 384,722.03 \quad df_u = 21$$

$$v = 281,199.34 \quad df_v = 105$$

$$f' = \frac{(384,722.03 + 281,199.34)^2}{\dfrac{384,722.03^2}{21} + \dfrac{281,199.34^2}{105}} = 56.84$$

Rounding to the nearest integer gives $f' = 57$. Thus, our F is distributed on $(g - 1, f') = (2, 57)$ df under H_0. For 2 and 57 df, $F_{.05} = 3.16$. Only the difference at Interval 1 is significant. By the end of 30 minutes, the three groups were performing at equivalent levels. It is logical to conclude that somewhere between the first and the sixth interval the three groups become nonsignificantly different, and many people test at each interval to find that point. However, I strongly recommend against this practice as a general rule. We have already run a number of significance tests, and running more of them serves only to increase the error rate. Unless there is an important theoretical reason to determine the point at which the group differences become nonsignificant—and I suspect that there are very few such cases—then there is nothing to be gained by testing each interval. Tests should be carried out to answer important questions, not to address idle curiosity or to make the analysis look "complete."

Multiple Comparisons

Several studies have investigated the robustness of multiple-comparison procedures for testing differences among means on the within-subjects variable. Maxwell (1980) studied a simple repeated-measures design with no between-subject component and advised adopting multiple-comparison procedures that do not use a pooled error term. We discussed such a procedure (the Games–Howell procedure) in Chapter 12. (I did use a pooled error term in the analysis of the migraine study, but there it was reasonable to assume homogeneity of variance and I was using all of the weeks. If I had only been running a contrast involving three of the weeks, I would seriously consider calculating an error term based on just the data from those weeks.)

Keselman and Keselman (1988) extended Maxwell's work to designs having one between-subject component and made a similar recommendation. In fact, they showed that when the Groups are of different sizes and sphericity is violated, familywise error rates can become very badly distorted. In the simple effects procedures that we have just considered, I recommended using separate error terms by running one-way repeated-measures analyses for each of the groups. For subsequent multiple-comparison procedures exploring those simple effects, especially with unequal sample sizes, it would probably be wise to employ the Games–Howell procedure using those separate covariance matrices. In other words, to compare Intervals 3 and 4 for the Control group, you would generate your error term using only the Intervals 3 and 4 data from just the Control group.

Myers (1979) has suggested making post hoc tests on a repeated measure using paired t-tests and a Bonferroni correction. (This is essentially what I did for the migraine example, though a Bonferroni correction was not necessary because I ran only one contrast.) Maxwell (1980) showed that this approach does a good job of controlling the familywise error rate, and Baker and Lew (1987) showed that it generally compared well against Tukey's test in terms of power. Baker proposed a simple modification of the Bonferroni that had even greater power.

14.8 Two Between-Subjects Variables and One Within-Subjects Variable

The basic theory of repeated-measures analysis of variance has already been described in the discussion of the previous designs. However, experimenters commonly plan experiments with three or more variables, some or all of which represent repeated measures on the same subjects. We will briefly discuss the analysis of these designs. The calculations are straightforward, because the sums of squares for main effects and interactions are obtained in the usual way and the error terms are obtained by subtraction.

We will not consider the theory behind these designs at any length. Essentially, it amounts to the extrapolation of what has already been said about the two-variable case. For an excellent discussion of the underlying statistical theory see Maxwell and Delaney (2004).

I will take as an example a study by St. Lawrence, Brasfield, Shirley, Jefferson, Alleyne, and O'Bannon (1995) on an intervention program to reduce the risk of HIV infection among African-American adolescents. The study involved a comparison of two approaches, one of which was a standard 2-hour educational program used as a control condition (EC) and the other was an 8-week behavioral skills training program (BST). Subjects were Male and Female adolescents, and measures were taken at Pretest, Posttest, and 6 and 12 months follow-up (FU6 and FU12). There were multiple dependent variables in the study, but the one that we will consider is log(freq + 1), where freq is the frequency of condom-protected intercourse.[4] This is a $2 \times 2 \times 4$ repeated-measures design, with Intervention and Sex as between-subjects factors and Time as the within-subjects factor. This design may be diagrammed as follows, where G_i represents the ith group of subjects.

	Behavioral Skills Training				Educational Control			
	Pretest	Posttest	FU6	FU12	Pretest	Posttest	FU6	FU12
Male	G_1	G_1	G_1	G_1	G_1	G_2	G_2	G_2
Female	G_3	G_3	G_3	G_3	G_4	G_4	G_4	G_4

© Cengage Learning 2013

The raw data and the necessary summary tables of cell totals are presented in Table 14.7a. (These data have been generated to closely mimic the data reported by St. Lawrence et al., though they had many more subjects. Decimal points have been omitted.) In Table 14.7b are the calculations for the main effects and interactions. Here, as elsewhere, the calculations are carried out exactly as they are for any main effects and interactions. This is a place where you would probably do just as well to skip the calculations until you need them and focus on the layout of the design and the results.

Table 14.7   Data and analysis of study by St. Lawrence et al. (1995)

(a) Data

	Male				Female			
	Pretest	Posttest	FU6	FU12	Pretest	Posttest	FU6	FU12
Behavioral Skill Training	7	22	13	14	0	6	22	26
	25	10	17	24	0	16	12	15
	50	36	49	23	0	8	0	0
	16	38	34	24	15	14	22	8
	33	25	24	25	27	18	24	37
	10	7	23	26	0	0	0	0
	13	33	27	24	4	27	21	3
	22	20	21	11	26	9	9	12
	4	0	12	0	0	0	14	1
	17	16	20	10	0	0	12	0
Educational Control	0	0	0	0	15	28	26	15
	69	56	14	36	0	0	0	0
	5	0	0	5	6	0	23	0
	4	24	0	0	0	0	0	0
	35	8	0	0	25	28	0	16
	7	0	9	37	36	22	14	48
	51	53	8	26	19	22	29	2
	25	0	0	15	0	0	5	14
	59	45	11	16	0	0	0	0
	40	2	33	16	0	0	0	0

© Cengage Learning 2013

(*continues*)

---

[4] The authors used a logarithmic transformation here because the original data, being count data, were very positively skewed. They took the log of $(X + 1)$ instead of X because log(0) is not defined.

Table 14.7 (*continued*)

Group × Sex × Time means

		Pretest	Posttest	FU6	FU12	Mean
BST	Male	19.7	20.7	24.0	18.1	20.625
BST	Female	7.2	9.8	13.6	10.2	10.200
EC	Male	29.5	18.8	7.5	15.1	17.725
EC	Female	10.1	10.0	9.7	9.5	9.825
Mean		16.625	14.825	13.700	13.225	14.594

Group × Sex means

	Male	Female	Mean
BST	20.625	10.200	15.412
EC	17.725	9.825	13.775
Mean	19.175	10.012	14.594

(b) Calculations

$$SS_{total} = \sum (X - \overline{X})^2 = (7 - 14.594)^2 + \cdots + (0 - 14.594)^2 = 35404.594$$

$$SS_{subj} = t \sum (\overline{X}_{Subj} - \overline{X})^2 = 4[(14 - 14.594)^2 + \cdots + (0 - 14.594)^2] = 21490.344$$

$$SS_{group} = nts \sum (\overline{X}_G - \overline{X})^2 = 10 \times 4 \times 2[(15.412 - 14.594)^2 + (13.775 - 14.594)^2] = 107.256$$

$$SS_{Sex} = ntg \sum (\overline{X}_{Sex} - \overline{X})^2 = 10 \times 4 \times 2[(19.175 - 14.594)^2 + (10.012 - 14.594)^2] = 3358.056$$

$$SS_{cells\ GS} = nt \sum (\overline{X}_{cells\ GS} - \overline{X})^2 = 10 \times 4[(20.625 - 14.594)^2 + \cdots + (9.825 - 14.594)^2] = 3529.069$$

$$SS_{GS} = SS_{cells\ GS} - SS_G - SS_S = 3529.069 - 107.256 - 3358.056 = 63.757$$

$$SS_{time} = ngs \sum (\overline{X}_T - \overline{X})^2 = 10 \times 2 \times 2[(16.625 - 14.594)^2 + \cdots + (13.225 - 14.594)^2] = 274.069$$

$$SS_{cells\ TG} = ns \sum (\overline{X}_{cells\ TG} - \overline{X})^2 = 10 \times 2[(13.45 - 14.594)^2 + \cdots + (12.300 - 14.594)^2] = 1759.144$$

$$SS_{TG} = SS_{cells\ TG} - SS_T - SS_G = 1759.144 - 274.069 - 107.256 = 1377.819$$

$$SS_{cells\ TS} = ng \sum (\overline{X}_{cells\ TS} - \overline{X})^2 = 10 \times 2[(24.60 - 14.594)^2 + \cdots + (9.85 - 14.594)^2] = 4412.044$$

$$SS_{TS} = SS_{cells\ TS} - SS_T - SS_S = 4412.044 - 274.069 - 3358.056 = 779.919$$

$$SS_{cells\ GTS} = n \sum (\overline{X}_{cells\ GTS} - \overline{X})^2 = 10[(19.7 - 14.594)^2 + \cdots + (9.50 - 14.594)^2] = 6437.294$$

$$SS_{GTS} = SS_{cells\ GTS} - SS_G - SS_T - SS_S - SS_{GT} - SS_{GS} - SS_{TS}$$
$$= 6437.294 - 107.256 - 274.069 - 3358.056 - 1377.819 - 63.757 - 779.919 = 476.419$$

(c) Summary Table

Source	df	SS	MS	F
Between subjects	39	21,490.344		
Group (Condition)	1	107.256	107.256	0.21
Sex	1	3358.056	3358.056	6.73*
$G \times S$	1	63.757	63.757	0.13
Ss w/in groups**	36	17,961.275	498.924	
Within subjects**	120	13,914.250		
Time	3	274.069	91.356	0.90
$T \times G$	3	1377.819	459.273	4.51*
$T \times S$	3	779.919	259.973	2.55
$T \times G \times S$	3	476.419	158.806	1.56
$T \times Ss$ w/in groups**	108	11,006.025	101.908	
Total	159	35,404.594		

*$p < .05$

** Obtained by subtraction

Table 14.8   Expected mean squares with *A*, *B*, and *C* fixed

Source	df	E(MS)
Between subjects	$abn - 1$	
A	$a - 1$	$\sigma_e^2 + c\sigma_\pi^2 + nbc\theta_\alpha^2$
B	$b - 1$	$\sigma_e^2 + c\sigma_\pi^2 + nac\theta_\beta^2$
AB	$(a - 1)(b - 1)$	$\sigma_e^2 + c\sigma_\pi^2 + nc\theta_{\alpha\beta}^2$
Ss w/in groups	$ab(n - 1)$	$\sigma_e^2 + c\sigma_\pi^2$
Within subjects	$abn(c - 1)$	
C	$c - 1$	$\sigma_e^2 + \sigma_{\gamma\pi}^2 + nab\theta_\gamma^2$
AC	$(a - 1)(c - 1)$	$\sigma_e^2 + \sigma_{\gamma\pi}^2 + nb\theta_{\alpha\gamma}^2$
BC	$(b - 1)(c - 1)$	$\sigma_e^2 + \sigma_{\gamma\pi}^2 + na\theta_{\beta\gamma}^2$
ABC	$(a - 1)(b - 1)(c - 1)$	$\sigma_e^2 + \sigma_{\gamma\pi}^2 + n\theta_{\alpha\beta\gamma}^2$
$C \times Ss$ w/in groups	$ab(n - 1)(c - 1)$	$\sigma_e^2 + \sigma_{\gamma\pi}^2$
Total	$N - 1$	

The summary table for the analysis of variance is presented in Table 14.7c. In this table, the ** indicate terms that were obtained by subtraction. Specifically,

$$SS_{\text{w/in subj}} = SS_{\text{total}} - SS_{\text{between subj}}$$

$$SS_{Ss \text{ w/in groups}} = SS_{\text{between subj}} - SS_G - SS_S - SS_{GS}$$

$$SS_{T \times Ss \text{ w/in groups}} = SS_{\text{w/in subj}} - SS_T - SS_{TG} - SS_{TS} - SS_{TGS}$$

These last two terms are the error terms for between-subjects and within-subjects effects, respectively. That these error terms are appropriate is shown by examining the expected mean squares presented in Table 14.8.[5] For the expected mean squares of random and mixed models, see Kirk (1968) or Winer (1971).

From the column of *F* in the summary table of Table 14.7c, we see that the main effect of Sex is significant, as is the Time × Group interaction. Both of these results are meaningful. As you will recall, the dependent variable is a measure of the frequency of use of condoms (log(freq + 1)). Examination of the means reveals adolescent girls report a lower frequency of use than adolescent boys. That could mean either that they have a lower frequency of intercourse, or that they use condoms a lower percentage of the time. Supplementary data supplied by St. Lawrence et al. show that females do report using condoms a lower percentage of the time than males, but not enough to account for the difference that we see here. Apparently what we are seeing is a reflection of the reported frequency of intercourse.

The most important result in this summary table is the Time × Group interaction. This is precisely what we would be looking for. We don't really care about a Group effect, because we would like the groups to be equal at pretest, and that equality would dilute any overall group difference. Nor do we particularly care about a main effect of Time, because we expect the Control group not to show appreciable change over time, and that would dilute any Time effect. What we really want to see is that the BST group increases their use over time, whereas the EC group remains constant. That is an interaction, and that is what we found.

---

[5] As in earlier tables of expected mean squares, we use the σ^2 to refer to the variance of random terms and θ^2 to refer to the variability of fixed terms. Subjects are always treated as random, whereas in this study the two main independent variables are fixed.

Simple Effects for Complex Repeated-Measures Designs

In the previous example we saw that tests on within-subjects effects were occasionally disrupted by violations of the sphericity assumption, and we took steps to work around this problem. We will have much the same problem with this example.

The cell means plotted in Figure 14.3 reveal the way in which frequency of condom use changes over time for the two treatment conditions and for males and females separately. It is clear from this figure that the data do not tell a simple story.

We are again going to have to distinguish between simple effects on between-subject factors and simple effects on within-subject factors. We will start with between-subject simple effects. We have three different between-subjects simple effects that we could examine—namely: the simple main effects of Condition and Sex at each Time, and the Sex × Condition simple interaction effect at each Time. For example, we might wish to check that the two Conditions (BST and EC) do not differ at pretest. Again, we might also want to test that they do differ at FU6 and/or at FU12. Here we are really dissecting the Condition × Time interaction effect, which we know from Table 14.7 to be significant.

By far the easiest way to test these between-subjects effects is to run separate two-way (Condition × Sex) analyses at each level of the Time variable. These four analyses will give you all three simple effects at each Time with only minor effort. You can then accept the *F* values from these analyses, as I have done here for convenience, or you can pool the error terms from the four separate analyses and use that pooled error term in testing the mean square for the relevant effect. If these terms are heterogeneous, you would be wise not to pool them. On the other hand, if they represent homogeneous sources of variance, they may be pooled, giving you more degrees of freedom for error. For these effects you don't need to worry about sphericity because each simple effect is calculated on only one level of the repeated-measures variable. (A word of caution here. Just because you *can* look at the Condition × Sex interaction at each time is not a reason that you *should*. The more tests that you run, they higher the probability of a Type I error. Only test those effects that are important to the overall questions that you are asking.)

The within-subjects simple effects are handled in much the same way. For example, there is some reason to look at the simple effects of Time for each Condition separately to see whether the EC condition shows changes over time in the absence of a complete intervention. Similarly, we would like to see how the BST condition changes with time. However, we want to include Sex as an effect in both of these analyses so as not to inflate

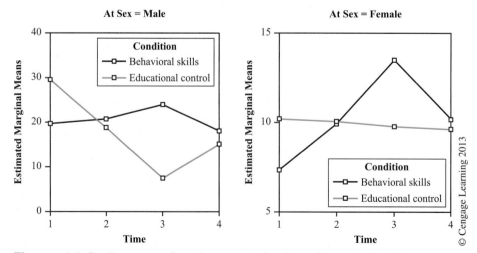

Figure 14.3 Frequency of condom use as a function of Sex and Condition

Table 14.9   Analysis of simple effects

(a) Between-subjects effects (Condition, Sex, and Condition × Sex) at Pretest

Source	df	SS	MS	F
Condition	1	403.225	403.225	1.45
Sex	1	2544.025	2544.025	9.13*
Condition × Sex	1	119.025	119.025	0.43
Error	36	10027.100	278.530	
Total	39	13093.375		

(b) Within-subjects effects (Sex, Time, Time × Sex) at BST

Source	df	SS	MS	F
Between subjects	19	7849.13		
Sex	1	2173.61	2173.61	6.89*
Error (between)	18	5675.52	315.30	
Within subjects	60	3646.26		
Time	3	338.94	112.98	1.88
$T \times S$	3	54.54	18.18	0.30
Error (within)	54	3252.78	60.24	
Total	79	11495.39		

*$p < .05$

© Cengage Learning 2013

the error term unnecessarily. We also want to use a separate error term for each analysis, rather than pooling these across Conditions.

The relevant analyses are presented in Table 14.9 for simple effects at one level of the other variable. Tests at the other levels would be carried out in the same way, but have been omitted to save space. Although this table has more simple effects than we care about, they are presented to illustrate the way in which tests were constructed. You would probably be foolish to consider all of the tests that result from this approach, because you would seriously inflate the familywise error rate. Decide what you want to look at before you run the analyses, and then stick to that decision. If you really want to look at a large number of simple effects, consider adopting one of the Bonferroni approaches discussed in Chapter 12.

From the between-subjects analysis in Table 14.9a we see that at Time 1 (Pretest) there was a significant difference between males and females (females show a lower frequency of use). But there were no Condition effects nor was there a Condition × Sex interaction. Males exceed females by just about the same amount in each Condition. The fact that there is no Condition effect is reassuring, because it would not be comforting to find that subjects in our two conditions differed before we had applied any treatment.

From the results in Table 14.9b we see that for the BST condition there is again a significant difference due to Sex, but there is no Time effect, nor a Time × Sex interaction. This is discouraging: It tells us that when we average across Sex there is no change in frequency of condom use as a result of our intervention. This runs counter to the conclusion that we might have drawn from the overall analysis where we saw a significant Condition by Time interaction, and it speaks to the value of examining simple effects. The fact that an effect we seek is significant does not necessarily mean that it is significant in the direction we desire.

14.9 Two Within-Subjects Variables and One Between-Subjects Variable

The design we just considered can be seen as a straightforward extension of the case of one between- and one within-subjects variable. All that we needed to add to the summary table was another main effect and the corresponding interactions. However, when we examine a design with two within-subjects main effects, the problem becomes slightly more complicated because of the presence of additional error terms. To use a more generic notation, we will label the independent variables as A, B, and C.

Suppose that as a variation on the previous study we continued to use different subjects for the two levels of variable A *(Gender)*, but we ran each subject under all combinations of variables B (Condition) and C (Trials). This design can be diagrammed as

	A_1			A_2		
	C_1	C_2	C_3	C_1	C_2	C_3
B_1	G_1	G_1	G_1	G_2	G_2	G_2
B_2	G_1	G_1	G_1	G_2	G_2	G_2
B_3	G_1	G_1	G_1	G_2	G_2	G_2

© Cengage Learning 2013

Before we consider an example, we will examine the expected mean squares for this design. These are presented in Table 14.10 for the case of the model in which all factors other than subjects are fixed (subjects are treated as a random factor). From the expected mean squares it is evident that we will have four error terms for this design. As before, the $MS_{Ss\ w/in\ groups}$ is used to test the between-subjects effect. When it comes to the within-subjects terms, however, B and the interaction of B with A are tested by $B \times Ss$ within groups; C and its interaction with A are tested by $C \times Ss$ within groups; and BC and its interaction with A are tested by $BC \times Ss$ within groups. Why this is necessary is apparent from the expected mean squares.

Table 14.10 Expected mean squares

Source	df	E(MS)
Between subjects	$an - 1$	
A (groups)	$a - 1$	$\sigma_e^2 + bc\sigma_\pi^2 + nbc\theta_\alpha^2$
Ss w/in groups	$a(n - 1)$	$\sigma_e^2 + bc\sigma_\pi^2$
Within subjects	$na(bc - 1)$	
B	$b - 1$	$\sigma_e^2 + c\sigma_{\beta\pi}^2 + nac\theta_\beta^2$
AB	$(a - 1)(b - 1)$	$\sigma_e^2 + c\sigma_{\beta\pi}^2 + nc\theta_{\alpha\beta}^2$
$B \times Ss$ w/in groups	$a(b - 1)(n - 1)$	$\sigma_e^2 + c\sigma_{\beta\pi}^2$
C	$c - 1$	$\sigma_e^2 + b\sigma_{\gamma\pi}^2 + nab\theta_\gamma^2$
AC	$(a - 1)(c - 1)$	$\sigma_e^2 + b\sigma_{\gamma\pi}^2 + nb\theta_{\alpha\gamma}^2$
$C \times Ss$ w/in groups	$a(c - 1)(n - 1)$	$\sigma_e^2 + b\sigma_{\gamma\pi}^2$
BC	$(b - 1)(c - 1)$	$\sigma_e^2 + n\sigma_{\beta\gamma\pi}^2 + na\theta_{\beta\gamma}^2$
ABC	$(a - 1)(b - 1)(c - 1)$	$\sigma_e^2 + n\sigma_{\beta\gamma\pi}^2 + n\sigma_{\alpha\beta\gamma}^2$
$BC \times Ss$ w/in groups	$a(b - 1)(c - 1)(n - 1)$	$\sigma_e^2 + n\sigma_{\beta\gamma\pi}^2$
Total	$N - 1$	

© Cengage Learning 2013

An Analysis of Data on Conditioned Suppression

Assume that a tiny "click" on your clock radio always slightly precedes your loud and intrusive alarm going off. Over time that click (psychologists would call it a "CS") could come to elicit the responses normally produced by the alarm (the "US"). (I had a college roommate who never set his alarm because it always clicked anyway and that got him up.) Moreover, it is possible that simply presenting the click might lead to the suppression of an ongoing behavior, even if that click is not accompanied by the alarm. (If you were lying there reading, you might pause in your reading.) In a laboratory investigation of how the click affects (suppresses) ongoing behavior, Bouton and Swartzentruber (1985) investigated the degree to which a tone, which had previously been paired with shock, would suppress the rate of an ongoing bar-pressing response in rats. Suppression was measured by taking the ratio of the number of bar presses during a 1-minute test period following the tone to the total number of bar presses during both a baseline period and the test period. For all groups, behavior was assessed in two Phases—a Shock phase (shock accompanied the tone) and a No-shock phase (shock did not accompany the tone) repeated over a series of four Cycles of the experiment.

It may be easier to understand the design of the study if you first glance at the layout of Table 14.11. During Phase I, Group *A-B* was placed in Box *A*. After a 1-minute baseline interval, during which the animal bar-pressed for food, a tone was presented for 1 minute and was followed by a mild shock. The degree of suppression of the bar-pressing response when the tone was present (a normal fear response) was recorded. The animal was then placed in Box *B* for Phase II of the cycle, where, after 1 minute of baseline bar-pressing, only the tone stimulus was presented. Because the tone was previously paired with shock, it should suppress bar-pressing behavior to some extent. Over a series of *A-B* cycles, however, the subject should learn that shock is never administered in Phase II and that Box *B* is therefore a "safe" box. Thus, for later cycles there should be less suppression on the no-shock trials.

Group *L-A-B* was treated in the same way as Group *A-B* except that these animals previously had had experience with a situation in which a light, rather than a tone, had been paired with shock. Because of this previous experience, the authors expected the animals to perform slightly better (less suppression during Phase II) than did the other group, especially on the first cycle or two.

Group *A-A* was also treated in the same way as Group *A-B* except that both Phases were carried out in the same box—Box *A*. Because there were no differences in the test boxes to serve as cues (i.e., animals had no way to distinguish the no-shock from the shock phases), this group would be expected to show the most suppression during the No-shock phases.

Bouton and Swartzentruber predicted that overall there would be a main effect due to Phase (i.e., a difference between shock and no-shock Phases), a main effect due to Groups (*A-B* and *L-A-B* showing less suppression than *A-A*), and a main effect due to Cycles (animals tested in Box *B* would learn over time that it was a safe location). They also predicted that each of the interactions would be significant. (One reason I chose to use this example, even though it is difficult to describe concisely, is that it is one of those rare studies in which all effects are predicted to be significant and meaningful.)

The data and analysis of variance for this study are presented in Table 14.11. The analysis has not been elaborated in detail because it mainly involves steps that you already know how to do. The results are presented graphically in Figure 14.4 for convenience, and for the most part they are clear-cut and in the predicted direction. Keep in mind that for these data a lower score represents more suppression—that is, the animals are responding more slowly.

Table 14.11   Analysis of conditioned suppression (Lower scores represent greater suppression.)

(a₁) Data

Group	Cycle 1 Phase I	Cycle 1 Phase II	Cycle 2 Phase I	Cycle 2 Phase II	Cycle 3 Phase I	Cycle 3 Phase II	Cycle 4 Phase I	Cycle 4 Phase II	Subject Mean
A-B	1*	28	22	48	22	50	14	48	29.125
	21	21	16	40	15	39	11	56	27.375
	15	17	13	35	22	45	1	43	23.875
	30	34	55	54	37	57	57	68	49.000
	11	23	12	33	10	50	8	53	25.000
	16	11	18	34	11	40	5	40	21.875
	7	26	29	40	25	50	14	56	30.875
	0	22	23	45	18	38	15	50	26.375
Mean$_{AB}$	12.625	22.750	23.500	41.125	20.000	46.125	15.625	51.750	29.188
A-A	1	6	16	8	9	14	11	33	12.250
	37	59	28	36	34	32	26	37	36.125
	18	43	38	50	39	15	29	18	31.250
	1	2	9	8	6	5	5	15	6.375
	44	25	28	42	47	46	33	35	37.500
	15	14	22	32	16	23	32	26	22.500
	0	3	7	17	6	9	10	15	8.375
	26	15	31	32	28	22	16	15	23.125
Mean$_{AA}$	17.750	20.875	22.375	28.125	23.125	20.750	20.250	24.250	22.188
L-A-B	33	43	40	52	39	52	38	48	43.125
	4	35	9	42	4	46	23	51	26.750
	32	39	38	47	24	44	16	40	35.000
	17	34	21	41	27	50	13	40	30.375
	44	52	37	48	33	53	33	43	42.875
	12	16	9	39	9	59	13	45	25.250
	18	42	3	62	45	49	60	57	42.000
	13	29	14	44	9	50	15	48	27.750
Mean$_{LAB}$	21.625	36.250	21.375	46.875	23.750	50.375	26.375	46.500	34.141
Total	17.333	26.625	22.417	38.708	22.292	39.083	20.750	40.833	28.505

*Decimal points have been omitted in the table, but included in the calculations.

Rather than present literally three pages of tables and calculations, which few people would have the patience to work through, I have chosen to carry out the analysis using SPSS.[6] The data would be entered just as they appear in Table 14.11, with a column for Groups on the left. You would select **Analyze, General Linear Model, Repeated Measures** from the drop-down menus and specify that there were two repeated measures (Cycles with 4 levels and Phases with 2 levels). Then click on **Define** and specify the variables that are associated with each of the cells and the variable(s) that define the Between-Subject Factor(s). This dialogue box follows, where C1P1 – C4P2 would be moved to the Within-Subjects Variables box and Group would be moved to the Between-Subjects Factor(s) box.

---

[6] For those who want to see the calculations, the corresponding pages from previous editions can be found at www.uvm.edu/~dhowell/methods8/Supplements/.

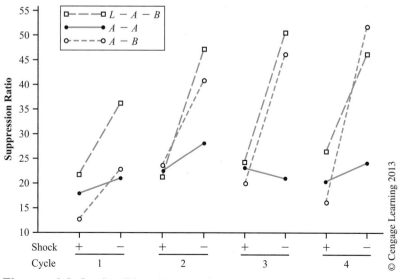

From the bottom row of that dialogue box you can specify what plots you would like to see, what contrasts you would like to run, and any descriptive statistics you want printed out. Then click on OK to run the analysis.

An abbreviated summary table appears on the next page. Notice that SPSS presents separate tables for Within-Subjects factors and Between-Subjects factors, though I would prefer to have them combined into one table with appropriate indentations.

Notice that there are multiple error terms in the table. The Group effect is tested by the Error term in the Between-Subjects table. Then Cycle and Cycle $\times$ Group are tested by Error(Cycle), Phase and Phase $\times$ Group are tested by Error(Phase), and Cycle $\times$ Phase and Cycle $\times$ Phase $\times$ Group are tested by Error(Cycle $\times$ Phase).

From the summary table in Table 14.12, it is clear that nearly all the predictions were supported. The only effect that was not significant was the main effect of Groups, but that

Figure 14.4   Conditioned suppression data

Table 14.12   SPSS output of the analysis of conditioned suppression data

Tests of Between-Subjects Effects

Measure: MEASURE_1
Transformed Variable: Average

Source	Type III Sum of Squares	df	Mean Square	F	Sig.	Partial Eta Squared
Intercept	156009.005	1	156009.005	208.364	.000	.908
Group	4616.760	2	2308.380	3.083	.067	.227
Error	15723.359	21	748.731			

Tests of Within-Subjects Effects

Measure: MEASURE_1

Source		Type III Sum of Squares	df	Mean Square	F	Sig.	Partial Eta Squared
Cycle	Sphericity Assumed	2726.974	3	908.991	12.027	.000	.364
	Greenhouse-Geisser	2726.974	2.362	1154.735	12.027	.000	.364
	Huynh-Feldt	2726.974	2.934	929.571	12.027	.000	.364
	Lower-bound	2726.974	1.000	2726.974	12.027	.002	.364
Cycle*Group	Sphericity Assumed	1047.073	6	174.512	2.309	.044	.180
	Greenhouse-Geisser	1047.073	4.723	221.691	2.309	.061	.180
	Huynh-Feldt	1047.073	5.867	178.463	2.309	.046	.180
	Lower-bound	1047.073	2.000	523.536	2.309	.124	.180
Error(Cycle)	Sphericity Assumed	4761.328	63	75.577			
	Greenhouse-Geisser	4761.328	49.593	96.009			
	Huynh-Feldt	4761.328	61.605	77.288			
	Lower-bound	4761.328	21.000	226.730			
Phase	Sphericity Assumed	11703.130	1	11703.130	129.855	.000	.861
	Greenhouse-Geisser	11703.130	1.000	11703.130	129.855	.000	.861
	Huynh-Feldt	11703.130	1.000	11703.130	129.855	.000	.861
	Lower-bound	11703.130	1.000	11703.130	129.855	.000	.861
Phase*Group	Sphericity Assumed	4054.385	2	2027.193	22.493	.000	.682
	Greenhouse-Geisser	4054.385	2.000	2027.193	22.493	.000	.682
	Huynh-Feldt	4054.385	2.000	2027.193	22.493	.000	.682
	Lower-bound	4054.385	2.000	2027.193	22.493	.000	.682
Error(Phase)	Sphericity Assumed	1892.609	21	90.124			
	Greenhouse-Geisser	1892.609	21.000	90.124			
	Huynh-Feldt	1892.609	21.000	90.124			
	Lower-bound	1892.609	21.000	90.124			
Cycle*Phase	Sphericity Assumed	741.516	3	247.172	4.035	.011	.161
	Greenhouse-Geisser	741.516	2.137	346.969	4.035	.022	.161
	Huynh-Feldt	741.516	2.613	283.767	4.035	.015	.161
	Lower-bound	741.516	1.000	741.516	4.035	.058	.161
Cycle*Phase* Group	Sphericity Assumed	1273.781	6	212.297	3.466	.005	.248
	Greenhouse-Geisser	1273.781	4.274	298.013	3.466	.013	.248
	Huynh-Feldt	1273.781	5.226	243.728	3.466	.008	.248
	Lower-bound	1273.781	2.000	636.891	3.466	.050	.248
Error(Cycle* Phase)	Sphericity Assumed	3859.078	63	61.255			
	Greenhouse-Geisser	3859.078	44.880	85.987			
	Huynh-Feldt	3859.078	54.875	70.324			
	Lower-bound	3859.078	21.000	183.766			

effect is not crucial because it represents an average across the shock and the no-shock phases, and the experimenters had predicted little or no group differences in the shock phase. In this context, the Phase $\times$ Group interaction is of more interest, and it is clearly significant.

14.10 Intraclass Correlation

We will leave the calculation-filled complex designs and return to something a bit more manageable. One of the important issues in designing experiments in any field is the question of the reliability of the measurements. Most of you would probably expect that the *last* place to look for anything about reliability is in a discussion of the analysis of variance, but that is exactly where you will find it. (For additional material on the intraclass correlation, go to http://www.uvm.edu/~dhowell/StatPages/More_Stuff/icc/icc.html)

Suppose that we are interested in measuring the reliability with which judges rate the degree of prosocial behavior in young children. We might investigate this reliability by having two or more judges each rate a behavior sample of a number of children, assigning a number from 1 to 10 to reflect the amount of prosocial behavior in each behavior sample. I will demonstrate the procedure with some extreme data that were created to make a point. Look at the data in Table 14.13.

In Table 14.13a the judges are in almost perfect agreement. They all see wide differences among children, they all agree on which children show high levels of prosocial behavior and which show low levels, *and* they are nearly in agreement on how high or low those levels are. In this case nearly all of the variability in the data involves differences among children—there is almost no variability among judges and almost no random error.

In Table 14.13b we see much the same pattern, but with a difference. The judges do see overall differences among the children, and they do agree on which children show the highest (and lowest) levels of the behavior. But the judges disagree in terms of the amount of prosocial behavior they see. Judge II sees slightly less behavior than Judge I (his mean is 1 point lower), and Judge III sees relatively more behavior than do the others. In other words, while the judges agree on *ordering* children, they disagree on *level*. Here the data involve both variability among children and variability among judges. However, the random error component is still very small. This is often the most realistic model of how people rate behavior because each of us has a different understanding of how much behavior is required to earn a rating of "7," for example. Our assessment of the reliability of a rating system must normally take variability among judges into account.

Finally, Table 14.13c shows a pattern where not only do the judges disagree in level, they also disagree in ordering children. A large percentage of the variability in these data is error variance.

So what do we do when we want to talk about reliability? One way to measure reliability when judges use only a few levels or categories is to calculate the percentage of

Table 14.13   Data for intraclass correlation examples

Child	(a) Judge I	II	III	(b) Judge I	II	III	(c) Judge I	II	III
1	1	1	2	1	0	3	1	3	7
2	3	3	3	3	2	5	3	1	5
3	5	5	5	5	4	7	5	7	4
4	5	6	6	5	4	7	5	5	5
5	7	7	7	7	6	8	7	6	7

times that two judges agree on their rating, but this measure is biased because of high levels of chance agreement whenever one or two categories predominate. (But see the discussion earlier of Cohen's kappa.) Another common approach is to correlate the ratings of two judges, and perhaps average pairwise correlations if you have multiple judges. But this approach will not take differences between judges into account. (If one judge always rates five points higher than another judge the correlation will be 1.00, but the judges are saying different things about the subjects.) A third way is to calculate what is called the **intraclass correlation**, taking differences due to judges into account. That is what we will do here.

You can calculate an intraclass correlation coefficient in a number of different ways, depending on whether you treat judges as a fixed or random variable and whether judges evaluate the same or different subjects. The classic reference for intraclass correlation is Shrout and Fleiss (1979), who discuss several alternative approaches. I am going to discuss only the most common approach here, one in which we consider our judges to be a random sample of all judges we could have used and in which each judge rates the same set of subjects once. (In what follows I am assuming that judges are rating "subjects," but they could be rating pictures, cars, or the livability of cities. Take the word "subject" as a generic term for whatever is being rated.)

We will start by assuming that the data in Table 14.13 can be represented by the following model:

$$X_{ij} = \mu + \alpha_i + \pi_j + \alpha\pi_{ij} + e_{ij}$$

In this model α_i stands for the effect of the ith judge, π_j stands for the effect of the jth subject (person), $\alpha\pi_{ij}$ is the interaction between the ith judge and the jth subject (the degree to which the judge changes his or her rating system when confronted with that particular subject), and e_{ij} stands for the error associated with that specific rating. Because each judge rates each subject only once, it is not possible in this model to estimate $\alpha\pi_{ij}$ and e_{ij} separately, but it is necessary to keep them separate in the model.

If you look back to the previous chapter you will see that when we calculated a magnitude-of-effect measure (which was essentially an r^2-family measure), we took the variance estimate for the effect in question (in this case differences among subjects) relative to the sum of the estimates of the several sources of variance. That is precisely what we are going to do here. We will let

Intraclass correlation $= \sigma_\pi^2/(\sigma_\alpha^2 + \sigma_\pi^2 + \sigma_{\alpha\pi}^2 + \sigma_e^2)$

If most of the variability in the data is due to differences between subjects, with only a small amount due to differences between judges, the interaction of judges and subjects, and error, then this ratio will be close to 1.00. If judges differ from one another in how high or low they rate people in general, or if there is a judge by subject interaction (different judges rate different people differently), or if there is a lot of error in the ratings, the denominator will be substantially larger than the numerator and the ratio will be much less than 1.00.

To compute the intraclass correlation we are first going to run a Subjects $\times$ Judges analysis of variance with Judges as a repeated measure. Because each judge rates each subject only once, there will not be an independent estimate of error, and we will have to use the Judge $\times$ Subject interaction as the error term. From the summary table that results, we will compute our estimate of the intraclass correlation as

$$\text{Intraclass correlation} = \frac{MS_{\text{Subjects}} - MS_{J \times S}}{MS_{\text{Subjects}} + (j-1)MS_{J \times S} + j(MS_{\text{Judge}} - MS_{J \times S})/n}$$

where j represents the number of judges and n represents the number of subjects.

To illustrate this, I have run the analysis of variance on the data in Table 14.13b, which is the data set where I have deliberately built in some differences due to subjects and judges. The summary table for this analysis follows.

Source	df	SS	MS	F
Between subjects	4	57.067	14.267	
Within subjects	10	20.666	2.067	
Judge	2	20.133	10.067	150.25
Judge × Subjects	8	0.533	0.067	
Total	14	77.733		

© Cengage Learning 2013

We can now calculate the intraclass correlation as

$$\text{Intraclass correlation} = \frac{14.267 - 0.067}{14.267 + (3-1)0.067 + 3(10.067 - 0.067)/5}$$

$$= \frac{14.200}{14.267 + 0.134 + 6} = \frac{14.2}{20.401} = .70$$

Thus, our measure of reliability is .70, which is probably not as good as we would like to see it. But we can tell from the calculation that the main thing that contributed to low reliability was not error, but differences among judges. This would suggest that we need to have our judges work together to decide on a consistent scale where a "7" means the same thing to each judge.

14.11   Other Considerations with Repeated Measures Analyses

Sequence Effects

sequence effects

carryover effects

Repeated-measures designs are notoriously susceptible to **sequence effects** and **carryover** (practice) **effects**. Whenever the possibility exists that exposure to one treatment will influence the response to another treatment, the experimenter should consider very seriously before deciding to use a repeated-measures design. In certain studies, carryover effects are desirable. In learning studies, for example, the basic data represent what is carried over from one trial to another. In other situations, however, carryover effects (and especially differential carryover effects) are considered a nuisance—something to be avoided.

Unequal Group Sizes

One of the pleasant features of repeated-measures designs is that when a subject fails to arrive for an experiment, it often means that that subject is missing from every cell in which he was to serve. This has the effect of keeping the cell sizes proportional, even if unequal. If you are so unlucky as to have a subject for whom you have partial data, the common procedure is to eliminate that subject from the analysis. If, however, only one or two scores are missing, it is possible to replace them with estimates, and in many cases this is a satisfactory approach. For a discussion of this topic, see Federer (1955, pp. 125–126, 133ff), and especially Little and Rubin (1987), and Howell (2008) and the discussion in Section 14.12.

Matched Samples and Related Problems

In discussing repeated-measures designs, we have spoken in terms of repeated measurements on the same subject. Although this represents the most common instance of the use of these designs, it is not the only one. The specific fact that a subject is tested several times really has nothing to do with the matter. Technically, what distinguishes repeated-measures designs (or, more generally, randomized blocks designs, of which repeated-measures designs are a special case) from the common factorial designs with equal ns is the fact that for repeated-measures designs, the off-diagonal elements of Σ do not have an expectation of zero—that is, the treatments are correlated. Repeated use of the same subject leads to such correlations, but so does use of matched samples of subjects. Thus, for example, if we formed 10 sets of three subjects each, with the subjects matched on driving experience, and then set up an experiment in which the first subject under each treatment came from the same matched triad, we would have correlations among treatments and would thus have a repeated-measures design. Any other data-collection procedure leading to nonzero correlations (or covariances) could also be treated as a repeated-measures design.

14.12 Mixed Models for Repeated-Measures Designs

Earlier in the chapter I said that the standard repeated-measures analysis of variance requires an assumption about the variance–covariance matrix known as *sphericity*, a specific form of which is known as *compound symmetry*. When we discussed $\hat{\varepsilon}$ and $\tilde{\varepsilon}$ we were concerned with correction factors that we could apply to the degrees of freedom to circumvent some of the problems associated with a failure of the sphericity assumption.

There is a considerable literature on repeated-measures analyses and their robustness in the face of violations of the underlying assumptions. Although there is not universal agreement that the adjustments proposed by Greenhouse and Geisser and by Huynh and Feldt are successful, the adjustments work reasonably well as long as we focus on overall main or interaction effects, or as long as we use only data that relate to specific simple effects (rather than using overall error terms). Where we encounter serious trouble is when we try to run individual contrasts or simple effects analyses using pooled error terms. Boik (1981) has shown that in these cases the repeated-measures analysis is remarkably sensitive to violations of the sphericity assumption unless we adopt separate error terms for each contrast. However, there is another way of dealing with assumptions about the covariance matrix, and that is to not make such assumptions. But to do that we need to take a different approach to the analysis itself.

Standard repeated measures analysis of variance has two problems that we have lived with for many years and will probably continue to live with for some time to come. (That is why I have spent so much time on such analyses and then say "but there may be a better way.") It assumes both compound symmetry (or sphericity) and complete data. If a participant does not appear for one testing session, even if he appears for all of the others, he must be eliminated from the analysis. There is an alternative approach to the analysis of repeated measures designs that does not hinge on either sphericity assumptions or complete data. This analysis is often referred to as mixed models, multilevel modeling, or hierarchical modeling. There is a bit of confusion here because we have already used the phrase "mixed models" to refer to any experimental design that involves both fixed and random factors. That is a perfectly legitimate usage. But when we are speaking of a method of analysis, such as we are here, the phrase "mixed models" refers more to a particular type of solution, involving both fixed and random factors, using a different approach to the arithmetic. More

maximum
likelihood
restricted
maximum
likelihood (REML)

specifically, when someone claims to have done their analysis using mixed models, they are referring to a solution that employs maximum likelihood or, more likely, restricted maximum likelihood (REML) in place of the least squares approaches that we have focused on up to now and will focus on again in the next two chapters.[7] (When we have missing data our analysis often hinges on why the data are missing. Ideally, they are missing at random.)

In this section I will discuss a small part of the broader topic of hierarchical or multilevel models. For these models the repeated measure (e.g., Time or Trials) is a fixed factor while Subjects is a random factor. The between-subjects factor is also usually a fixed factor. By approaching the problem using restricted maximum likelihood (REML) as the method of parameter estimation, the solution can take cognizance from the very beginning of the analysis that one or more factors are fixed and one or more factors are random. Least squares solutions of standard analysis of variance treats all factors as fixed until it comes to determining error terms for F statistics.

No one would seriously attempt to do a mixed model analysis by hand. You must use computer software to perform the analysis. However, there are many software programs available, some of them even free. The ones that you will have most access to are probably SPSS Mixed and SAS Proc Mixed. I will use SPSS for our example, though SAS Proc Mixed is probably more flexible. A more complete discussion of the analysis of alternative designs can be found at http://www.uvm.edu/~dhowell/StatPages/More_Stuff/Missing_Data/Mixed Models for Repeated Measures.pdf For an example I have chosen a design with one between subject variable and one within subject variable. The example has missing data because that will illustrate an analysis that you cannot do with standard analysis of variance.

The Data

I created data to have a number of characteristics. There are two groups—a Control group and a Treatment group, measured at 4 times. These times are labeled as 0 (pretest), 1 (one month posttest), 3 (three months follow-up), and 6 (six months follow-up). I had a study of treatment of depression in mind, so I created the treatment group to show a sharp drop in depression at post-test and then sustain that drop (with slight regression) at 3 and 6 months. The Control group declines slowly over the 4 intervals but does not reach the low level of the Treatment group.

The data are shown in Table 14.14. An ellipses is used to indicate missing values.

One difference between data files for mixed models and others is that we use what is often called a "long form." Instead of putting each subject's data on one line, we have a separate line for every value of the dependent variable. Thus our data file will be structured like the one in Table 14.15

Instead of showing you how to use the graphical interface in SPSS, which would take quite a bit of space, I am simply giving you the syntax for the commands.[8] After you have entered your data, open a new Syntax window, paste in the following commands, and select

---

[7] In previous editions I used the MANOVA approach under SPSS/Univariate/Repeated measures as a way of avoiding assumptions of compound symmetry. This approach does not require compound symmetry, but it does require balanced designs. I have dropped it in favor of the mixed model precisely because the mixed model will handle missing data much better.

[8] The following is quick description of using the menu selections. Select analysis/mixed/linear, specify Subj for the Subjects box and Time for the Repeated box. Click continue and move to the next screen. Specify the dependent variable (dv) and the factors (Group and Time). Select fixed from the bottom of the box, highlight both Group and Time and click the add button, click continue. Now click on the random button and add Subj to the bottom box. Then click paste to make sure that you have syntax similar to what I gave.

Table 14.14 Data for mixed model analysis

Group	Subj	Time0	Time1	Time3	Time6
1	1	296	175	187	242
1	2	376	329	236	126
1	3	309	238	150	173
1	4	222	60	82	135
1	5	150	...	250	266
1	6	316	291	238	194
1	7	321	364	270	358
1	8	447	402	...	266
1	9	220	70	95	137
1	10	375	335	334	129
1	11	310	300	253	...
1	12	310	245	200	170
2	13	282	186	225	134
2	14	317	31	85	120
2	15	362	104	...	...
2	16	338	132	91	77
2	17	263	94	141	142
2	18	138	38	16	95
2	19	329	...	...	6
2	20	292	139	104	.
2	21	275	94	135	137
2	22	150	48	20	85
2	23	319	68	67	...
2	24	300	138	114	174

© Cengage Learning 2013

Table 14.15 Data restructured into a long form

Subj	Time	Group	dv
1	0	1	296
1	1	1	175
1	3	1	187
1	6	1	242
...	...	...	...
24	3	2	114
24	6	2	174

© Cengage Learning 2013

Run from the toolbar. I have left out a number of commands that do fine tuning, but what I have will run your analysis nicely.

```
MIXED
dv BY Group Time
/FIXED = Group Time Group*Time | SSTYPE(3)
/METHOD = REML
/PRINT = DESCRIPTIVES SOLUTION
/REPEATED = Time | SUBJECT(Subj) COVTYPE(CS)
/EMMEANS = TABLES(Group)
/EMMEANS = TABLES(Time)
/EMMEANS = TABLES(Group*Time)
```

I am only presenting the most important parts of the printout, but you can see the rest by running the analysis yourself. (The data are available on the book's Web site as WicksellLongMiss.dat.)

Information Criteria[a]

−2 Restricted Log Likelihood	905.398
Akaike's Information Criterion (AIC)	909.398
Hurvich and Tsai's Criterion (AICC)	909.555
Bozdogan's Criterion (CAIC)	916.136
Schwarz's Bayesian Criterion (BIC)	914.136

The information criteria are displayed in smaller-is-better forms.
[a] Dependent Variable: dv.

Fixed Effects
Type III Tests of Fixed Effects[a]

Source	Numerator df	Denominator df	F	Sig.
Intercept	1	22.327	269.632	.000
Group	1	22.327	16.524	.001
Time	3	58.646	32.453	.000
Group *Time	3	58.646	6.089	.001

[a] Dependent Variable: dv.

Covariance Parameters
Estimates of Covariance Parameters[a]

Parameter		Estimate	Std. Error
Repeated Measures	CS diagonal offset	2954.544	551.1034
	CS covariance	2558.656	1026.581

[a] Dependent Variable: dv.

Adapted from output by SPSS, Inc.

I will not discuss the section labeled "Information criteria" here, but I will come back to it when we compare the fit of different models. The fixed effects part of the table looks just like one that you would see in most analyses of variance except that it does not include sums of squares and mean squares. That is because of the way that maximum likelihood solutions go about solving the problem. In some software it is possible to force them into the printout. Notice the test on the Intercept. That is simply a test that the grand mean is 0, which is of no interest to us here. The other three effects are all significant. We don't really care very much about the two main effects. The groups started off equal on pre-test, and those null differences would influence any overall main effect of groups. Similarly, we don't care a great deal about the Time effect because we expect different behavior over time from the two groups. What we do care about, however, is the interaction. This tells us that the two groups perform differently over Time, which is what we hoped to see. You can see this effect in Figure 14.5.

There are two additional results in the printout that need to be considered. The section headed "Covariance Parameters" is the random part of the model. The term labeled "CS diagonal offset" represents the residual variance and, with balanced designs, would be the error term for the within-subject tests. The term labeled "CS covariance" is the variance of the intercepts, meaning that if you plot the dependent variable against time for each

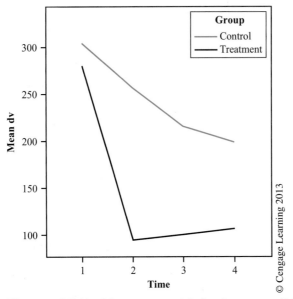

© Cengage Learning 2013

Figure 14.5   Means across trials for the two conditions

Table 14.16   Correlations among trials

Estimated *R* Correlation Matrix for Subject 1

Row	Col1	Col2	Col3	Col4
1	1.0000	0.5121	0.4163	−0.08840
2	0.5121	1.0000	0.8510	0.3628
3	0.4163	0.8510	1.0000	0.3827
4	−0.0884	0.3628	0.3827	1.0000

© Cengage Learning 2013

subject, the differences in intercepts of those lines would represent differences due to subjects (some lines are higher than others) and it is this variance that we have here. For most of us that variance is not particularly important, but there are studies in which it is.

As I said earlier, mixed model analyses do not require an assumption of compound symmetry. In fact, that assumption is often incorrect. In Table 14.16 you can see the pattern of correlations among trials. These are averaged over the separate groups, but give you a clear picture that the structure is not one of compound symmetry.

There are a number of things that we could do to alter the model that we just ran, which specifically requested a solution based on compound symmetry. We could tell SPSS to solve the problem without assuming anything about the correlations or covariances. (That is essentially what the MANOVA approach does to repeated measures.) The problem with this approach is that the solution has to derive estimates of those correlations and that will take away degrees of freedom, perhaps needlessly. There is no point in declaring that you are totally ignorant when you are really only partially ignorant. Another approach would be to assume a specific (but different) form of the covariance matrix. For example, we could use what is called an autoregressive solution. Such a solution assumes that correlations between observations decrease as the observations move further apart in time. It further assumes that each correlation depends only on the preceding correlation plus some (perhaps much) error. If the average correlation between adjacent trials is, for example, 0.5121 (as it is in the study we are discussing), then times that are two steps apart are assumed to correlate $.5121^2 = .2622$ and times three steps apart are assumed to correlate $.5121^3 = .1343$. This leads to a matrix of correlations that decrease regularly the more removed the observations are from each other. That sounds like a logical expectation for what we would find when we measure depression over time. For now we are going to consider the autoregressive covariance structure.

Having decided on a correlational (or covariance) structure we simply need to tell SPSS to use that structure and solve the problem as before. The only change we will make is to the **repeated** command, where we will replace covtype(cs) with covtype(AR1).

```
MIXED
dv BY Group Time
/FIXED = Group Time Group*Time | SSTYPE(3)
/METHOD = REML
/PRINT = DESCRIPTIVES SOLUTION
/REPEATED = Time | SUBJECT(Subj) COVTYPE(AR1)
/EMMEANS = TABLES(Group)
/EMMEANS = TABLES(Time)
/EMMEANS = TABLES(Group*Time) .
```

Information Criteria[a]

–2 Restricted Log Likelihood	895.066
Akaike's Information Criterion (AIC)	899.066
Hurvich and Tsai's Criterion (AICC)	899.224
Bozdogan's Criterion (CAIC)	905.805
Schwarz's Bayesian Criterion (BIC)	903.805

The information criteria are displayed in smaller-is-better forms.
[a] Dependent Variable: *dv*.

Fixed Effects
Type III Tests of Fixed Effects[a]

Source	Numerator *df*	Denominator *df*	*F*	Sig.
Intercept	1	26.462	270.516	.000
Group	1	26.462	17.324	.001
Time	3	57.499	30.821	.000
Group *Time	3	57.499	7.721	.001

[a] Dependent Variable: *dv*.

Covariance Parameters
Estimates of Covariance Parameters[a]

Parameter		Estimate	Std. Error
Repeated Measures	AR1 diagonal	5349.879	1060.035
	AR1 rho	.618198	.084130

[a] Dependent Variable: *dv*.

Adapted from output by SPSS, Inc.

Here we see that all effects are still significant, which is encouraging. But which of these two models (one assuming a compound symmetry structure to the covariance matrix and the other assuming a first order autoregressive structure) is the better choice. We are going to come to the same conclusion with either model in this case, but that is often not true, and we still want to know which model is better. One way of doing that is to compare the sections labeled "Information Criteria" for each analysis. These are reproduced below for the two models.

Compound Symmetry

Information Criteria[a]

−2 Restricted Log Likelihood	905.398
Akaike's Information Criterion (AIC)	909.398
Hurvich and Tsai's Criterion (AICC)	909.555
Bozdogan's Criterion (CAIC)	916.136
Schwarz's Bayesian Criterion (BIC)	914.136

The information criteria are displayed in smaller-is-better forms.

[a] Dependent Variable: *dv*.

Autoregressive (1)

Information Criteria[a]

−2 Restricted Log Likelihood	895.066
Akaike's Information Criterion (AIC)	899.066
Hurvich and Tsai's Criterion (AICC)	899.224
Bozdogan's Criterion (CAIC)	905.805
Schwarz's Bayesian Criterion (BIC)	903.805

The information criteria are displayed in smaller-is-better forms.

[a] Dependent Variable: *dv*.

© Cengage Learning 2013

A good way to compare models is to compare either the Akaike's Information Criterion (AIC) or the Bayesian Information Criterion (BIC). In general a model with a smaller value is better. For our examples the two AIC criteria are 909.398 and 899.066. It would appear that the Autoregressive (1) model is to be preferred, which is in line with what our eyes told us about the covariance structures. (If we had rerun the analysis using an unstructured covariance matrix (COVTYPE(UN)), AIC would be 903.691 and BIC would be 927.385, so we would still choose the autoregressive model.)

Mixed models have a great deal to offer in terms of fitting data to models and allow us to compare underlying models to best interpret our data. They also can be very valuable in both the presence and absence of missing data. However, they are more difficult to work with and the software, while certainly improving, is far from intuitive in some cases. Nevertheless, I think that this is the direction that more and more analyses will take over the next decade, and it is important to understand them.

Papers by Overall, Tonidandel, and others illustrate the problems with mixed models. The major problem is the fact that it is very difficult to know how to correctly specify your model, and different specifications can lead to different results and sometimes rather low power. An excellent paper in this regard is by Overall and Shivakumar (1999) and another by Overall and Tonidandel (2007). I recommend that you look at those papers when considering the use of mixed models, although those authors used SAS **Proc Mixed** for their analyses and it is not entirely clear how those models relate to models you would have using SPSS. What seems to be critically important is the case where missing data depend on the participant's initial response at baseline and attempts to use this measure as a covariate.

Key Terms

Partition (Introduction)

Partialling out (Introduction)

Repeated-measures designs (Introduction)

$SS_{\text{between subj}}$ (SS_S) (Introduction)

$SS_{\text{within subj}}$ (Introduction)

Main diagonal (14.3)

Off-diagonal elements (14.3)

Compound symmetry (14.3)

Covariance matrix (Σ) (14.3)

Sphericity (14.3)

Multivariate analysis of variance (MANOVA) (14.3)

Multivariate procedure (14.3)

$Error_{\text{between}}$ (14.7)

$Error_{\text{within}}$ (14.7)

Intraclass correlation (14.10)

Sequence effects (14.11)

Carryover effects (14.11)

Randomized blocks designs (14.11)

Matched samples (14.11)

Exercises

14.1 It is at least part of the folklore that repeated experience with any standardized test leads to better scores, even without any intervening study. Suppose that we obtain eight subjects and give them a standardized admissions exam every Saturday morning for 3 weeks. The data follow:

S	First	Second	Third
1	550	570	580
2	440	440	470
3	610	630	610
4	650	670	670
5	400	460	450
6	700	680	710
7	490	510	510
8	580	550	590

© Cengage Learning 2013

a. Write the statistical model for these data.

b. Run the analysis of variance.

c. What, if anything, would you conclude about practice effects on the GRE?

14.2 An experimenter with only a modicum of statistical training took the data in Exercise 14.3 and ran an independent-groups t test instead, using the difference scores (training minus baseline) as the raw data.

a. Run that analysis.

b. Square the value of t and compare it to the Fs you obtained in Exercise 14.3.

c. Explain why t^2 is not equal to F for Groups.

14.3 To demonstrate the practical uses of basic learning principles, a psychologist with an interest in behavior modification collected data on a study designed to teach self-care skills to severely developmentally handicapped children. An experimental group received reinforcement for activities related to self-care. A second group received an equivalent amount of attention, but no reinforcement. The children were scored (blind) by a rater on a 10-point scale of self-sufficiency. The ratings were done in a baseline session and at the end of training. The data follow:

Reinforcement		No Reinforcement	
Baseline	Training	Baseline	Training
8	9	3	5
5	7	5	5
3	2	8	10
5	7	2	5
2	9	5	3
6	7	6	10
5	8	6	9
6	5	4	5
4	7	3	7
4	9	5	5

© Cengage Learning 2013

Run the appropriate analysis and state your conclusions.

14.4 Using the data from Exercise 14.1,

a. Delete the data for the third session and run a (matched-sample) *t* test between Sessions 1 and 2.

b. Now run a repeated-measures analysis of variance on the two columns you used in part (a) and compare this *F* with the preceding *t*.

14.5 To understand just what happened in the experiment involving the training of severely developmentally handicapped children (Exercise 14.3), our original experimenter evaluated a third group at the same times as he did the first two groups, but otherwise provided no special treatment. In other words, these children did not receive reinforcement, or even the extra attention that the control group did. Their data follow:

Baseline:	3	5	8	5	5	6	6	6	3	4
Training:	4	5	6	6	4	7	7	3	2	2

a. Add these data to those in Exercise 14.3 and rerun the analysis.

b. Plot the results.

c. What can you conclude from the results you obtained in parts (a) and (b)?

d. Within the context of this three group experiment, run the contrast of the two conditions that you have imported from Exercise 14.3.

e. Compute the effect size for the contrast in part (d).

14.6 In an investigation of cigarette smoking, an experimenter decided to compare three different procedures for quitting smoking (tapering off, immediate stopping, and aversion therapy). She took five subjects in each group and asked them to rate (on a 10-point scale) their desire to smoke "right now" in two different environments (home versus work) both before and after quitting. Thus, we have one between-subjects variable (Treatment group) and two within-subjects variables (Environment and Pre/Post).

	Pre		Post	
	Home	Work	Home	Work
Taper	7	6	6	4
	5	4	5	2
	8	7	7	4
	8	8	6	5
	6	5	5	3
Immediate	8	7	7	6
	5	5	5	4
	7	6	6	5
	8	7	6	5
	7	6	5	4
Aversion	9	8	5	4
	4	4	3	2
	7	7	5	3
	7	5	5	0
	8	7	6	3

© Cengage Learning 2013

a. Run the appropriate analysis of variance.

b. Interpret the results.

14.7 Refer to Exercise 14.8.

a. Calculate the simple effect of reading ability for children.

b. Calculate the simple effect of items for adult good readers.

14.8 In a study of the way children and adults summarize stories, we selected 10 fifth-graders and 10 adults. These were further subdivided into equal groups of good and poor readers (on the hypothesis that good and poor readers may store or retrieve story information differently). All subjects read 10 short stories and were asked to summarize the story in their own words immediately after reading it. All summaries were content analyzed, and the numbers of statements related to Settings, Goals, and inferred Dispositions were recorded. The data are collapsed across the 10 stories:

Age Items	Adults			Children		
	Setting	Goal	Disp.	Setting	Goal	Disp.
Good readers	8	7	6	5	5	2
	5	6	4	7	8	4
	5	5	5	7	7	4
	7	8	6	6	4	3
	6	4	4	4	4	2
Poor readers	7	6	3	2	2	2
	5	3	1	2	0	1
	6	6	2	5	4	1
	4	4	1	4	4	2
	5	5	3	2	2	0

© Cengage Learning 2013

Run the appropriate analysis.

14.9 Suppose we had instructed our subjects to limit their summaries to 10 words. What effect might that have on the data in Exercise 14.8?

14.10 Calculate the within-groups covariance matrices for the data in Exercise 14.8.

14.11 Plot the results you obtained in Exercise 14.6.

14.12 The SPSS printout in Exhibit 14.1 was obtained by treating the data in Exercise 14.8 as though all variables were between-subjects variables (i.e., as though the data represented a standard three-way factorial). Show that the error terms for the correct analysis represent a partition of the error term for the factorial analysis.

Tests of Between-Subjects Effects

Dependent Variable: DV

Source	Type III Sum of Squares	df	Mean Square	F	Sig.
Corrected Model	170.800[a]	11	15.527	9.001	.000
Intercept	1058.400	1	1058.400	613.565	.000
AGE	68.267	1	68.267	39.575	.000
READTYPE	29.400	1	29.400	17.043	.000
PART	60.400	2	30.200	17.507	.000
AGE * READTYPE	3.267	1	3.267	1.894	.175
AGE * PART	.933	2	.467	.271	.764
READTYPE * PART	.000	2	.000	.000	1.000
AGE * READTYPE * PART	8.533	2	4.267	2.473	.095
Error	82.800	48	1.725		
Total	1312.000	60			
Corrected Total	253.600	59			

[a] R Squared = .674 (Adjusted R Squared = .599)

Adapted from output by SPSS, Inc.

Exhibit 14.1

14.13 The abbreviated printout in Exhibit 14.2 represents the analysis of the data in Exercise 14.5.

    a.   Compare this printout with the results you obtained in Exercise 14.5.

    b.   What does a significant F for "MEAN" tell us?

    c.   Relate $MS_{w/in\ cell}$ to the table of cell standard deviations.

```
BMDP2V – ANALYSIS OF VARIANCE AND COVARIANCES
WITH REPEATED MEASURES.

PROGRAM CONTROL INFORMATION
/PROBLEM        TITLE IS 'BMDP2V ANALYSIS OF EXERCISE 14.5'.
/INPUT          VARIABLES ARE 3.
                FORMAT IS '(3F2.0)'.
                CASES ARE 30.

/VARIABLE       NAMES ARE GROUP, PRE, POST.
/DESIGN         DEPENDENT ARE 2, 3.
                LEVELS ARE 2.
                NAME IS TIME.
                GROUP = 1.
/END
```

CELL MEANS FOR 1-ST DEPENDENT VARIABLE

					MARGINAL
GROUP	=	* 1.0000	* 2.0000	*3.0000	
	TIME				
PRE	1	4.80000	4.70000	5.10000	4.86667
POST	2	7.00000	6.40000	4.60000	6.00000
MARGINAL		5.90000	5.55000	4.85000	5.43333
COUNT		10	10	10	30

STANDARD DEVIATIONS FOR 1-ST DEPENDENT VARIABLE

GROUP	=	* 1.0000	* 2.000	*3.0000
	TIME			
PRE	1	1.68655	1.76698	1.52388
POST	2	2.16025	2.45855	1.89737

SOURCE	SUM OF SQUARES	DEGREES OF FREEDOM	MEAN SQUARE	F	TAIL PROBABILITY
MEAN	1771.26667	1	1771.26667	322.48	0.0000
GROUP	11.43333	2	5.71667	1.04	0.3669
1 ERROR	148.30000	27	5.49259		
TIME	19.26667	1	19.26667	9.44	0.0048
TG	20.63333	2	10.31667	5.06	0.0137
2 ERROR	55.10000	272.04074			

Adapted from output by SPSS, Inc.

Exhibit 14.2

14.14 Run simple effects on the data in Exercise 14.6 to clarify the results.

14.15 Outline the summary table for an $A \times B \times C \times D$ design with repeated measures on A and B and independent measures on C and D.

14.16 In the data file Stress.dat, available on the Web site, are data on the stress level reported by cancer patients and their spouses at two different times—shortly after the diagnosis and 3 months later. The data are also distinguished by the gender of the respondent. As usual, a "." indicates each missing data point. See description in Appendix: Computer Data Sets, p. 686.

a. Use any statistical package to run a repeated-measures analysis of variance with Gender and Role (patient versus spouse) as between-subject variables and Time as the repeated measure. (You may have to instruct the program on the symbol for missing data or else change that symbol in the data.)

b. Have the program print out cell means, and plot these means as an aid in interpretation.

c. There is a significant three-way interaction in this analysis. Interpret it along with the main effects.

14.17 Using the data from Exercise 14.18 use SPSS to run a mixed models analysis of variance, specifying an appropriate form for the covariance matrix, and compare the results with those you obtained in Exercise 14.18.

14.18 Foa, Rothbaum, Riggs, and Murdock (1991) ran a study comparing different treatments for posttraumatic stress disorder (PTSD). They used three groups (plus a waiting list control). One group received Stress Inoculation Therapy (SIT), another received a Prolonged Exposure (PE) treatment, and a third received standard Supportive Counseling (SC). All clients were measured at Pretreatment, Posttreatment, and a 3.5-month Follow-up. The data below closely approximate the data that they collected, and the dependent variable is a measure of PTSD.

SIT			PE			SC		
Pre	Post	Followup	Pre	Post	Followup	Pre	Post	Followup
19	6	1	20	5	0	12	14	18
28	14	16	21	18	21	27	18	9
18	6	8	36	26	17	24	19	13
23	6	11	25	11	9	32	21	11
21	6	13	26	2	7	26	20	18
24	10	8	30	31	10	18	20	26
26	10	7	19	6	11	38	35	34
15	6	13	19	7	5	26	22	22
18	8	6	22	4	4	23	10	8
34	13	8	22	17	20	22	19	19
20	10	16	24	19	1	34	27	23
34	10	1	28	22	16	22	15	12
29	16	23	29	23	20	27	18	13
33	19	39	27	15	20	23	21	19
22	7	16	27	7	3	26	18	13

© Cengage Learning 2013

a. Run a repeated measures analysis of variance on these data.

b. Draw the appropriate conclusions.

14.19 Now analyze the data in Exercise 14.20 using a mixed models approach withan appropriate form for the covariance matrix. How do those results differ from the results you found in Exercise 14.20?

14.20 The following data come from Exercise 14.18 with some observations deleted. (An entry of "999" represents a missing observation.)

SIT			PE			SC		
Pre	Post	Followup	Pre	Post	Followup	Pre	Post	Followup
19	6	1	20	5	0	12	14	18
28	14	16	999	999	21	27	18	9
18	6	8	36	26	17	24	999	13
999	6	11	25	11	9	32	21	11
21	6	13	26	999	7	26	20	18
24	10	8	30	31	10	18	20	26
26	10	999	19	6	11	38	35	34
15	6	13	19	7	999	26	22	999
18	8	6	22	4	999	23	10	8
34	13	8	22	17	20	22	19	19
20	999	999	24	19	1	34	999	999
34	10	1	28	22	16	22	15	12
29	16	23	29	23	20	27	18	13
33	19	39	27	15	20	23	21	19
22	7	16	27	7	3	26	18	13

a. Analyze these data using a standard repeated measures analysis of variance.

b. How do your results differ from the results you found in Exercise 14.16?

14.21 Everitt reported data on a study of three treatments for anorexia in young girls. One treatment was cognitive behavior therapy, a second was a control condition with no therapy, and a third was a family therapy condition. The data follow:

a. Run an analysis of variance on group differences in Gain scores.

b. Repeat the analysis, but this time use a repeated measures design where the repeated measures are Pretest and Posttest.

c. How does the answer to part (b) relate to the answer to part (a)?

d. Plot scatterplots of the relationship between Pretest and Posttest separately for each group. What do these plots show?

e. Run a test on the null hypothesis that the Gain for the Control is 0.00. What does this analysis tell you? Are you surprised?

f. Why would significant gains in the two experimental groups not be interpretable without the control group?

Group	Pretest	Posttest	Gain	Group	Pretest	Posttest	Gain
1	80.5	82.2	1.7	1	70.0	90.9	20.9
1	84.9	85.6	.7	1	80.4	71.3	−9.1
1	81.5	81.4	−.1	1	83.3	85.4	2.1
1	82.6	81.9	−.7	1	83.0	81.6	−1.4
1	79.9	76.4	−3.5	1	87.7	89.1	1.4
1	88.7	103.6	14.9	1	84.2	83.9	−.3
1	94.9	98.4	3.5	1	86.4	82.7	−3.7
1	76.3	93.4	17.1	1	76.5	75.7	−.8
1	81.0	73.4	−7.6	1	80.2	82.6	2.4
1	80.5	82.1	1.6	1	87.8	100.4	12.6
1	85.0	96.7	11.7	1	83.3	85.2	1.9
1	89.2	95.3	6.1	1	79.7	83.6	3.9
1	81.3	82.4	1.1	1	84.5	84.6	.1
1	76.5	72.5	−4.0	1	80.8	96.2	15.4

Group	Pretest	Posttest	Gain	Group	Pretest	Posttest	Gain
1	87.4	86.7	−.7	2	84.4	84.7	0.3
2	80.7	80.2	−.5	2	79.6	81.4	1.8
2	89.4	80.1	−9.3	2	77.5	81.2	3.7
2	91.8	86.4	−5.4	2	72.3	88.2	15.9
2	74.0	86.3	12.3	2	89.0	78.8	−10.2
2	78.1	76.1	−2.0	3	83.8	95.2	11.4
2	88.3	78.1	−10.2	3	83.3	94.3	11.0
2	87.3	75.1	−12.2	3	86.0	91.5	5.5
2	75.1	86.7	11.6	3	82.5	91.9	9.4
2	80.6	73.5	−7.1	3	86.7	100.3	13.6
2	78.4	84.6	6.2	3	79.6	76.7	−2.9
2	77.6	77.4	−0.2	3	76.9	76.8	−0.1
2	88.7	79.5	−9.2	3	94.2	101.6	7.4
2	81.3	89.6	8.3	3	73.4	94.9	21.5
2	78.1	81.4	3.3	3	80.5	75.2	−5.3
2	70.5	81.8	11.3	3	81.6	77.8	−3.8
2	77.3	77.3	0.0	3	82.1	95.5	13.4
2	85.2	84.2	−1.0	3	77.6	90.7	13.1
2	86.0	75.4	−10.6	3	83.5	92.5	9.0
2	84.1	79.5	−4.6	3	89.9	93.8	3.9
2	79.7	73.0	−6.7	3	86.0	91.7	5.7
2	85.5	88.3	2.8	3	87.3	98.0	10.7

Discussion Questions

14.22 What do you think is the importance of the fact that the "parent" who supplies the parent rating changes from child to child?

14.23 In Exercise 14.16 you probably noticed that many observations at Time 2 are missing. (This is partly because for many patients it had not yet been 3 months since the diagnosis.)

a. Compare the means at Time 1 for those subjects who did, and who did not, have data at Time 2.

b. If there are differences in (a), what would this suggest to you about the data?

In a study of behavior problems in children we asked 3 "judges" to rate each of 20 children on the level of aggressive behavior. These judges were the child's Parent, the child's Teacher, and the child him/herself (Self). The data follow.

Child	1	2	3	4	5	6	7	8	9	10	11	12	13	14	15	16	17	18	19	20
Parent	10	12	14	8	16	21	10	15	18	6	22	14	19	22	11	14	18	25	22	7
Teacher	8	13	17	10	18	24	9	16	18	8	24	19	15	20	10	18	19	30	20	10
Self	12	17	16	15	24	24	13	17	21	13	29	23	16	20	15	17	21	25	25	14

These data are somewhat different from the data we saw in Section 14.10 because in that case the same people judged each child, whereas here the Parent and Self obviously change from child to child. We will ignore that for the moment and simply act as if we could somehow have the same parent and the same "self" do all the ratings.

14.24 In Exercise 14.16 we ignored the fact that we have pairs of subjects from the same family.

a. What is wrong with doing this?

b. Under what conditions would it be acceptable to ignore this problem?

c. What alternative analyses would you suggest?

14.25 What do your calculations tell you about the sources of variability in this data set?

14.26 What is the reliability of this data set in terms of the intraclass correlation coefficient?

14.27 Under what conditions might you not be interested in differences among judges?

14.28 Suppose that you had no concern about the fact that one source systematically rates children higher or lower than another source. How might you evaluate reliability differently?

14.29 Strayer, Drews, and Crouch (2006) (which we saw set up as a between-subjects design in Exercise 11.32) examined the effects of cell phone use on driving ability. They had 40 drivers drive while speaking on a cell phone, drive while at the legal limit for alcohol (0.08%), and drive under normal conditions. (The conditions were counterbalanced across drivers.) The data for this study are found at www.uvm.edu/~dhowell/methods8/DataFiles/Ex14-29. dat. (I assumed interitem correlations of approximately .45.) Their hypothesis, based on the research of others, was that driving while speaking on a cell phone would have as much of an effect as driving while intoxicated. The dependent variable in this example is "braking reaction time." The data have exactly the same means and standard deviations as they found.

a. Run the analysis of variance for a repeated measures design.

b. Use the appropriate contrasts to compare the three conditions. Did the results support the experimenters' predictions?

14.30 In Exercise 11.37 we saw a study by Teri (1997) examining nonpharmacological treatments of patients with Alzheimer's disease. There I only gave the change scores for each group. The data including the pre- and post-test scores can be found at www.uvm.edu/~dhowell/ methods8/DataFiles/Teri.dat. Run a repeated measures analysis of variance and compare your results to the summary table you created in Chapter 11.

Chapter 15

Multiple Regression

Objectives

To show how we can predict a criterion variable on the basis of several predictor variables simultaneously and to point out the problems inherent in this procedure.

Contents

IN CHAPTER 9 WE CONSIDERED the situation in which we have one criterion variable (Y) and one predictor variable (X) and wish to predict Y on the basis of X. In this chapter we will consider the case in which we still have only one criterion (Y) but have multiple predictors ($X_1, X_2, X_3, \ldots, X_p$), and want to predict Y on the basis of *simultaneous* knowledge of all p predictors. The situation we examined in Chapter 9 can be viewed as a special case of the one discussed in this chapter. We will continue to use many familiar concepts such as the correlation coefficient, the slope, the standard error of estimate, and $SS_{\text{regression}}$.

This chapter will focus on software solutions. There is very little to be gained, and much to be lost, by focusing on the calculations. By freeing ourselves from computation we are able to concentrate on the really important issues that lie behind choosing an appropriate regression solution. Generally, there can be little argument over formulae. On the other hand, questions about the optimal number of predictors, the use of regression diagnostics, the relative importance of various predictors, and the selection of predictors do not have universally accepted answers. Be forewarned that the opinions expressed in this chapter are only opinions, and are open to dispute—but then that is part of what makes statistics interesting. Excellent and readable advanced sources for the study of multiple regression are Cohen, Cohen, West, and Aiken (2003) and Stevens (1992), and the best coverage I know of testing model assumptions is Fox (2002), though that discussion is built around R.

15.1 Multiple Linear Regression

The problem of multiple regression is that of finding a regression equation to predict Y (sometimes denoted X_0) on the basis of p predictors ($X_1, X_2, X_3, \ldots, X_p$). Thus, we might wish to predict success in graduate school (Y) on the basis of undergraduate grade point average (X_1), Graduate Record Exam scores (X_2), number of courses taken in the major discipline (X_3), and some rating of "favorableness" of letters of recommendation (X_4). Similarly, we might wish to predict the time it takes to go from one point in a city to another on the basis of number of traffic lights (X_1), posted speed limit (X_2), presence or absence of "right turn on red" (X_3), and traffic density (X_4). These examples are both analyzed in the same way, although in the first we presumably care about predictions for individual applicants, whereas in the second we might be less interested in the prediction itself and more interested in the role played by each of the predictors. In fact, the most common use of multiple regression is to understand the relationship between variables rather than to actually make a prediction from the equation we derive.

The Regression Equation

In Chapter 9 we started with the equation of a straight line ($\hat{Y} = bX + a$) and solved for the two unknowns (a and b) subject to the constraint that $\sum(Y - \hat{Y})^2$ is a minimum. In multiple regression we are going to do the same thing, although in this case we will solve the equation $\hat{Y} = b_0 + b_1X_1 + b_2X_2 + \cdots + b_pX_p$ where b_0 represents the intercept and $b_1, b_2, \ldots, b_p$ are the **regression coefficients** for the predictors $X_1, X_2, \ldots, X_p$, respectively. We will retain the least squares restriction that $\sum(Y - \hat{Y})^2$ is to be minimized, because it still makes sense to find predicted values that come as close as possible to the obtained values of Y.[1] The calculations required to estimate the b_i become more cumbersome as the number of predictors increases, but we are not concerned with these calculations

regression coefficients

---

[1] There are alternatives to the standard least squares criteria that often produce estimates that are in some ways superior to the estimates obtained by least squares. These procedures, often referred to as Robust Regression, are less common, but many of them can be found in Rousseeuw and Leroy (1987).

here. Instead, we will begin with an example and assume that the solution was obtained by any available computer program, such as SPSS, Minitab, or SAS. The main data file used here can be imported from this book's Web site and is named Table 15-1.dat.

This example that we will use originated in a paper by Guber (1999), but I have added variables to carry the analysis further in the exercises at the end of this chapter. There has been an ongoing debate in this country about what we can do to improve the quality of primary and secondary education. It is generally assumed that spending more money on education will lead to better prepared students, but that is just an assumption. Guber addressed that question by collecting data for each of the 50 (U.S.) states. She recorded the amount spent on education, the pupil/teacher ratio, average teacher's salary, the percentage of students in that state taking the SAT exams, and the combined SAT score. I have dropped the separate Verbal and Math scores (though they are contained in the file on the Web site). I have added the percentage of students in each state taking the ACT and the mean ACT score for that state. The data are shown in Table 15.1. An abstract, and a complete copy, of Guber's paper are available at http://www.amstat.org/publications/jse/v7n2_abstracts.html.

Table 15.1   Data on performance versus expenditures on education

State	Expend	PTratio	Salary	PctSAT	SAT	PctACT	ACT
Alabama	4.405	17.2	31.144	8	1029	61	20.2
Alaska	8.963	17.6	47.951	47	934	32	21.0
Arizona	4.778	19.3	32.175	27	944	27	21.1
Arkansas	4.459	7.1	28.934	6	1005	66	20.3
California	4.992	24.0	41.078	45	902	11	21.0
Colorado	5.443	18.4	34.571	29	980	62	21.5
Connecticut	8.817	14.4	50.045	81	908	3	21.4
Delaware	7.030	16.6	39.076	68	897	3	21.0
Florida	5.718	19.1	32.588	48	889	36	20.4
Georgia	5.193	16.3	32.291	65	854	16	20.2
Hawaii	6.078	17.9	38.518	57	889	17	21.6
Idaho	4.210	19.1	29.783	15	979	62	21.4
Illinois	6.136	17.3	39.431	13	1048	69	21.2
Indiana	5.826	17.5	36.785	58	882	19	21.2
Iowa	5.483	15.8	31.511	5	1099	64	22.1
Kansas	5.817	15.1	34.652	9	1060	74	21.7
Kentucky	5.217	17.0	32.257	11	999	65	20.1
Louisiana	4.761	16.8	26.461	9	1021	80	19.4
Maine	6.428	13.8	31.972	68	896	2	21.5
Maryland	7.245	17.0	40.661	64	909	11	20.7
Massachusetts	7.287	14.8	40.795	80	907	6	21.6
Michigan	6.994	20.1	41.895	11	1033	68	21.3
Minnesota	6.000	17.5	35.948	9	1085	60	22.1
Mississippi	4.080	17.5	26.818	4	1036	79	18.7
Missouri	5.383	15.5	31.189	9	1045	64	21.5

(continues)

Table 15.1 (*Continued*)

State	Expend	PTratio	Salary	PctSAT	SAT	PctACT	ACT
Montana	5.692	16.3	28.785	21	1009	55	21.9
Nebraska	5.935	14.5	30.922	9	1050	73	21.7
Nevada	5.160	18.7	34.836	30	917	39	21.3
New Hampshire	5.859	15.6	34.720	70	935	4	22.3
New Jersey	9.774	13.8	46.087	70	898	3	20.8
New Mexico	4.586	17.2	28.493	11	1015	59	20.3
New York	9.623	15.2	47.612	74	892	16	21.9
North Carolina	5.077	16.2	30.793	60	865	11	19.3
North Dakota	4.775	15.3	26.327	5	1107	78	21.4
Ohio	6.162	16.6	36.802	23	975	60	21.3
Oklahoma	4.845	15.5	28.172	9	1027	66	20.6
Oregon	6.436	19.9	38.555	51	947	12	22.3
Pennsylvania	7.109	17.1	44.510	70	880	8	21.0
Rhode Island	7.469	14.7	40.729	70	888	2	21.4
South Carolina	4.797	16.4	30.279	58	844	13	18.9
South Dakota	4.775	14.4	25.994	5	1068	68	21.3
Tennessee	4.388	18.6	32.477	12	1040	83	19.7
Texas	5.222	15.7	31.223	47	893	30	20.2
Utah	3.656	24.3	29.082	4	1076	69	21.5
Vermont	6.750	13.8	35.406	68	901	7	21.9
Virginia	5.327	14.6	33.987	65	896	6	20.7
Washington	5.906	20.2	36.151	48	937	16	22.4
West Virginia	6.107	14.8	31.944	17	932	57	20.0
Wisconsin	6.930	15.9	37.746	9	1073	64	22.3
Wyoming	6.160	14.9	31.285	10	1001	70	21.4

I have chosen to work with this particular data set because it illustrates several things. In the first place, it is a real data set that pertains to a topic of current interest. That also means that the variables are not as beautifully distributed as they would be had I generated them using appropriate random number generators. In fact, they are a bit messy. In addition, the data set illustrates what is, at first, a very puzzling result, and then allows us to explore that result and make sense of it. The difference between what we see with one predictor and what we see with two predictors is quite dramatic and illustrates some of the utility of multiple regression. Finally, these data illustrate well the need to think carefully about your measures and not simply assume that they measure what you think they measure.

This book is used by many people outside of the United States and Canada, and a word is necessary about the variables. The SAT and the ACT are two separate standardized tests that are used for university admissions. The SAT scores range from 200 to 800, while the ACT scores range from 1 to 36. The SAT has been characterized as mainly a test of ability, while the ACT has been characterized as more of a test of material covered in school. The standard deviation is considerably smaller for the ACT even after we account for the fact that its mean is also very much smaller. (The coefficients of variation are 0.077 and 0.042, respectively.) Most importantly, the SAT tends to be used by universities in the northeast and the west and by the more prestigious schools (though that seems to be slowly changing). Students living elsewhere are probably more likely to take the ACT unless they are applying to schools on either coast, such as Harvard, Princeton, Berkeley, or Stanford. This is certainly an overly sweeping generalization, but it will become important shortly.

Before we consider the regression solution itself, we need to look at the distribution of each variable. These are shown for several variables as histograms, qqplots, and scatterplots in Figure 15.1. It is clear from these plots that our variables are not normally distributed. From these displays it is apparent that the criterion variable and three of the predictors are fairly well distributed. The distribution of the percentage of students taking the SAT is definitely bimodal, reflecting the fact that each test is taken either by most students in that state or by few. In addition the relationship between PctSAT and SAT score is curvilinear, in part reflecting that bimodality. The distribution becomes slightly better when we take a $\log_e$ transformation of PctSAT, and its relationship with SAT is more linear. The scatterplot against the SAT is shown in the lower right. We will make use of this log-transformed variable instead of PctSAT itself because it makes an important point, though its distribution is still decidedly bimodal. The combined SAT score shows a wide distribution.

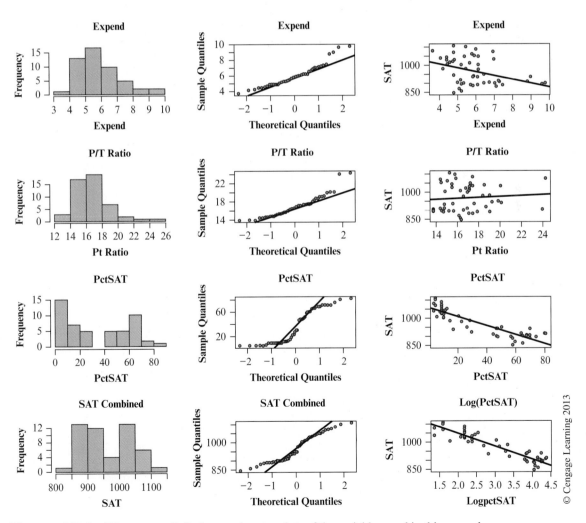

Figure 15.1   Histograms, Q-Q plots, and scatterplots of the variables used in this example

Two Variable Relationships

The most obvious thing to do with these data is to ask about the relationship between expenditure and outcome. We will ignore the ACT data for now and concentrate on the relationship between performance on the SAT and expenditures for education. While we are doing that we will also look at the correlations between other possible predictors of test performance. We would presumably like to see that the more money we spend on education, the better our students do. In addition, it would be of interest to ask whether the pupil/teacher ratio is related to outcome, as many people have argued, and whether higher salaries for teachers play a role. Keep in mind that the SAT score is our measure of educational performance, and it is a good measure for our purposes in this example, though it is not a good general measure of school performance, *nor was it ever intended as such.*

The graphic in the upper right corner of Figure 15.1 is a scatterplot of SAT scores against expenditures. In addition Table 15.2 shows the Pearson correlations between some of our variables, the most interesting being the negative correlation of SAT and Expend. The relationship is somewhat surprising, because it would suggest that the more money we spend on educating our children the worse they do. The regression line is clearly decreasing and the correlation is −.381. Although that correlation is not terribly large, it is statistically significant ($p = .006$) and cannot just be ignored. Those students who come from wealthier schools tend to do worse. Why should this be? The other interesting thing that we see from the table of correlations is that there appears to be no relationship between pupil/teach ratio and performance. What are we to make of this?

An answer to our puzzle comes from what I said previously about the SAT test itself. Not all colleges and universities require that students take the SAT, and there is a tendency

Table 15.2 Correlations between selected variables

Correlations

		Expend	PTratio	Salary	PctSAT	SAT	LogPctSAT
Expend	Pearson Correlation	1	−.371**	.870**	.593**	−.381**	.561**
	Sig. (2-tailed)		.008	.000	.000	.006	.000
	N	50	50	50	50	50	50
PTratio	Pearson Correlation	−.371**	1	−.001	−.213	.081	−.132
	Sig. (2-tailed)	.008		.994	.137	.575	.361
	N	50	50	50	50	50	50
Salary	Pearson Correlation	.870**	−.001	1	.617**	−.440**	.613**
	Sig. (2-tailed)	.000	.994		.000	.001	.000
	N	50	50	50	50	50	50
PctSAT	Pearson Correlation	.593**	−.213	.617**	1	−.887**	.961**
	Sig. (2-tailed)	.000	.137	.000		.000	.000
	N	50	50	50	50	50	50
SAT	Pearson Correlation	−381**	.081	−.440**	−.887**	1	−.926**
	Sig. (2-tailed)	.006	.575	.001	.000		.000
	N	50	50	50	50	50	50
LogPctSAT	Pearson Correlation	.561**	−.132	.613**	.961**	−.926**	1
	Sig. (2-tailed)	.000	.361	.000	.000	.000	
	N	50	50	50	50	50	50

** Correlation is significant at the 0.01 level (2-tailed).

for those that do require it to be the more prestigious universities that take only the top students. In addition, the percentage of students taking the SAT varies drastically from state to state, with 81% of the students in Connecticut and only 4 % of the students in Utah. The states with the lowest percentages tend to be in the Midwest, with the highest in the Northeast. In those states where a small percentage of the students are taking the exam, the students are most likely to be those who are focused on being admitted to the best schools. These are students who are likely to do well. In Massachusetts and Connecticut, where most of the students take the SAT—the less able as well as the more able—the poorer students are going to lower the state average relative to states whose best students are mainly the ones being tested. If this were true, we would expect to see a negative relationship between the percentage of students taking the exam and the state's mean score. This is what we see when we look at the correlation between the SAT and LogPctSAT and at the scatterplot in the lower right of Figure 15.1.

Looking at One Predictor While Controlling for Another

The question that now arises is what would happen if we used both variables (Expend and LogPctSAT) simultaneously as predictors of the SAT score. What this really means, though it may not be immediately obvious, is that we will look at the relationship between Expend and SAT *controlling for LogPctSAT*. (We will also look at the relationship between LogPctSAT and SAT controlling for Expend.) When I say that we are controlling for LogPctSAT, I mean that we are looking at the relationship while holding LogPctSAT constant. Imagine that we had many thousands of states instead of only 50. Imagine also that we could pull out a collection of states that had exactly the same percentage of students taking the SAT—for example, 60%. Then we could look at only the students from those states and compute the correlation and regression coefficient for predicting SAT from Expend. Then we could draw another sample of states, perhaps those with 40% of their students taking the exam. Again we could correlate Expect and SAT for only those states and compute a regression coefficient. Notice that I have calculated two correlations and two regression coefficients here, each with PctSAT held constant at a specific value (40% or 60%). Because we are only imagining that we had thousands of states, we can go further and imagine that we repeated this process many times, with PctSAT held at a different specific value each time. For each of those analyses we would obtain a regression coefficient for the relationship between Expend and SAT, and an average of those many regression coefficients will be very close to the overall regression coefficient that we will shortly examine. Though we often refer to these as "regression coefficients," they are more accurately called partial regression coefficients because they refer to the relationship between the dependent variable and one of the predictors, partialling out, or controlling for, other predictors. The same is true if we averaged the correlations coefficients to get partial correlations. (Without introducing a more complex model we are assuming that whatever the relationship between SAT and Expend, it is the same for each level of Log PctSAT.)

Obviously we don't have thousands of states—we have only 50 and that is not likely to get much larger. However, that does not stop us from mathematically estimating what we would obtain if we could carry out the imaginary exercise that I just explained. And that is exactly what multiple regression is all about.

The Multiple Regression Equation

There are ways to think about multiple regression other than fixing the level of one or more variables, but before I discuss those I will go ahead and run a multiple regression on these data. I used SPSS to do so, and the results are shown in Exhibit 15.1. I specifically asked

SPSS to first produce the regression using just Expend as the predictor and then to add LogPctSAT and run the regression again with both variables. I normally would not do that (I would just run the one regression with both predictors), but it makes it easier for us to see what is happening. I have left out some of the printout to save space.

Notice that each table has two parts—one where Expend is the sole predictor and another where both Expend and LogPctSAT are the predictors. The first table that I want to discuss is labeled Model Summary. From the summary you can see that when Expend is the sole predictor the correlation between Expend and SAT is –.381, just as we saw before. But when we add LogPctSAT the correlation jumps to .941, which is a very long way from the correlation of –.381 that we obtained with Expend alone.

Several things need to be said here. In multiple regression the correlations are always going to be positive, whereas in simple Pearson correlation they can be either positive or

Model Summary

Model	R	R Square	Adjusted R Square	Std. Error of the Estimate
1	.381[a]	.145	.127	69.909
2	.941[b]	.886	.881	25.781

[a] Predictors: (Constant), Expend
[b] Predictors: (Constant), Expend, LogPctSAT

ANOVA[c]

Model		Sum of Squares	df	Mean Square	F	Sig.
1	Regression	39722.059	1	39722.059	8.128	.006[a]
	Residual	234585.621	48	4887.200		
	Total	274307.680	49			
2	Regression	243065.908	2	121532.954	182.834	.000[b]
	Residual	31241.772	47	664.719		
	Total	274307.680	49			

[a] Predictors: (Constant), Expend
[b] Predictors: (Constant), Expend, Log Percent taking SAT
[c] Dependent Variable: SAT Combined

Coefficients[a]

Model		Unstandardized Coefficients B	Unstandardized Coefficients Std. Error	Standardized Coefficients Beta	t	Sig.	95.0% Confidence Interval for B Lower Bound	95.0% Confidence Interval for B Upper Bound
1	(Constant)	1089.294	44.390		24.539	.000	1000.042	1178.546
	expend	–20.892	7.328	–.381	–2.851	.006	–35.627	–6.158
2	(Constant)	1147.100	16.701		68.684	.000	1113.501	1180.698
	expend	11.129	3.264	.203	3.409	.001	4.562	17.696
	Log Percent taking SAT	–78.203	4.471	–1.040	–17.490	.000	–87.198	–69.208

[a] Dependent Variable: SAT Combined

Adapted from output by SPSS, Inc.

Exhibit 15.1   Multiple regression predicting SAT from Expend and LogPctSAT

negative. There is a good reason for this, but I don't want to elaborate on that now. (If the correlations are always positive, how do we know when the relationship is negative? We look at the sign of the regression coefficient, and I'll come to that in a minute.) You might recall that in Table 15.2 we saw that the simple correlation between SAT and LogPctSAT was −.93, whereas the correlation between SAT and Expend was −.38. While LogPctSAT adds a great deal to the regression that only used Expend, adding Expend after using only LogPctSAT adds much less. We will also look at this more closely in a minute.

In the subtable named Model Summary you will also see the squared correlations. The squared correlation in multiple regression has the same meaning that it had in simple regression. Using Expend alone we were able to explain $(-.381)^2 = .145 = 14.5\%$ of the variation in SAT scores. Using both Expend and LogPctSAT we can explain $.941^2 = .886 = 88.6\%$ of the variability in the SAT score. To the right of these values you will see a column labeled Adj. R square. You can largely ignore that column. The adjusted R squared is actually a less-biased estimate of the true squared correlation in the population, but we rarely report it, even though we preferred unbiased estimates in other procedures. Simply use R and not adjusted R.

The third subtable in Exhibit 15.1 is labeled ANOVA, which is an analysis of variance testing the significance of the regression. The F is a test on whether the multiple correlation coefficient in question is significantly different from 0. This is the same kind of test that we saw in Chapters 9 and 10, though it uses an F statistic instead of t. When we have only one predictor (Expend) the correlation is −.38, as we saw in Table 15.2, and the probability of getting a correlation that high if the null hypothesis is true was .006. This is well less than .05 and we can declare that correlation to be significantly different from 0. When we move to multiple regression and include the predictor LogPctSAT along with Expend, we have two questions to ask. The first is whether the multiple correlation using both predictors together is significantly different from 0.00, and the second is whether each of the predictor variables is contributing at greater than chance levels to that relationship. From the ANOVA table we see an $F = 182.856$, with an associated probability of .000 to three decimal places. This tells us that using both predictors our correlation is significantly greater than 0. I will ask about the significance of the individual predictors in the next section.

Now we come to the most interesting part of the output. In the subtable labeled "Coefficients" we see the full set of **regression coefficients** when using both predictors at the same time. Just as a simple regression was of the form

$$\hat{Y} = bX + a,$$

a multiple regression is written as

$$\hat{Y} = b_1X_1 + b_2X_2 + b_0$$

where X_1 and X_2 are the predictors and b_0 is the intercept. From the table we can see that, with both predictors, the coefficient for Expend (call it b_1) is 11.129, and for LogPctSAT the coefficient is −78.203. From the sign of these coefficients we can tell whether the relationship is positive or negative. These values, plus the intercept, give us our regression equation.

$$\hat{Y} = 1147.100 + 11.129(\text{Expend}) - 78.203(\text{LogPctSAT})$$

The value of 1147.100 is the intercept, often denoted b_0 and here denoted simply as "(constant)." This is the predicted value of SAT if both Expend and LogPctSAT were 0.00, which they will never be. We need the intercept because it forces the average of our predictions to equal the average of the obtained values, but we rarely pay any real attention to it. We can use this regression equation in exactly the same way we used the simple regression

regression
coefficients

equation in Chapter 9. Simply substitute the values of Expend and LogPctSAT for a given state and you can predict that state's mean SAT score. To take the state of Colorado as an example, our predicted mean SAT score would be

$$\hat{Y} = 1147.100 + 11.129(\text{Expend}) - 78.203(\text{LogPctSAT})$$
$$= 1147.100 + 11.129(5.443) - 78.203(\text{Log}(29))$$
$$= 1147.100 + 11.129(5.443) - 78.203(3.367) = 944.366$$

residual error

Because the actual mean for Colorado was 980, we have somewhat underestimated the mean and our **residual error** is $980 - 944.352 = 35.648$. That is a small residual given the relative magnitude of SAT scores. On the other hand, the residual for West Virginia is -61.510.

The positive coefficient for Expend tells us that *now that we have controlled LogPct-SAT* the relationship between expenditures and performance is positive—the more the state spends, the higher their (adjusted) SAT score. That should make us feel much better. We can also see that when we control Expend, the relationship between LogPctSAT and SAT is negative, which makes sense. I explained earlier why increasing the percentage of a state's students taking the SAT would be expected to lower the overall mean for that state.

But you may have noticed that LogPctSAT itself had a correlation of $-.93$ with SAT, and perhaps Expend wasn't adding anything important to the relationship—after all, the correlation only increased to .941. If you look at the table of coefficients, you will see two columns to the right labeled t and sig. These relate to significance tests on the regression coefficients. You saw similar t tests in Chapter 9. From the "sig." column we can tell that all three coefficients are significant at $p < .05$. The intercept has no meaning because it would refer to a case in which a state spent absolutely nothing on education and had no students taking the SAT. The coefficient for Expend is meaningful because it shows that increased spending does correlate with higher scores *after we control for* the percentage of students taking the exam. Similarly, after we control for expenditures, SAT scores are higher for those states who have few (presumably their best) students taking the test. So although adding Expend to LogPctSAT as predictors didn't raise the correlation very much, it was a statistically significant contributor.

I discussed above one of the ways of interpreting what a multiple regression means— for any predictor variable the slope is the relationship between that variable and the criterion variable if we could hold all other variables constant. And by "hold constant" we mean having a collection of participants who had all the same scores on each of the other variables. But there are two other ways of thinking about regression that are useful.

Another Interpretation of Multiple Regression

When we just correlate Expend with SAT and completely ignore LogPctSAT, there is a certain amount of variability in the SAT scores that is directly related to variability in Log-PctSAT, and that was what was giving us that peculiar negative result. What we would really like to do is to examine the correlation between Expend and the SAT score when both are adjusted to be free from the influences of LogPctSAT. To put it another way, some of the differences in SAT are due to differences in Expend and some are due to differences in LogPctSAT. We want to eliminate those differences in both SAT and Expend that can be attributed to LogPctSAT and then correlate the adjusted variables. That is actually a lot simpler than it sounds. I can't imagine anyone intentionally running a multiple regression the way that I am about to, but it illustrates what is going on.

We know that if we ran the simple regression predicting SAT from LogPctSAT alone, the resulting set of predicted scores would represent that part of SAT that is predictable

residuals

from LogPctSAT. If we subtract the predicted scores from the actual scores, the resulting **residuals**, call them ResidSAT, will be that part of SAT that is *not* predictable from (is independent of) LogPctSAT. We can now do the same thing predicting Expend from LogPctSAT. We will get the predicted scores, subtract them from the obtained scores, and have a new set of residuals, call them ResidExpend, that is also independent of LogPctSAT. So we now have two sets of residual scores—ResidSAT and ResidExpend that are both independent of LogPctSAT. So LogPctSAT can play no role in their relationship.[2]

If I now run the regression to predict the adjusted SAT score from the adjusted Expend score (i.e., ResidSAT with ResidExpend), I will have

Coefficients[a]

Model		Unstandardized Coefficients		Standardized Coefficients	t	Sig.
		B	Std. Error	Beta		
1	(Constant)	$-3.1\text{E-}015$	3.608		.000	1.000
	Unstandardized Residual	11.130	3.230	.445	3.446	.001

[a]Dependent Variable: Unstandardized Residual
Adapted from output by SPSS, Inc.

Notice that the regression coefficient predicting the adjusted SAT score from the adjusted expend score is 11.130, which is the same value (within rounding error) that we had for Expend doing things the normal way. Notice also that the following table shows us that the correlation between these two corrected variables is .445, which is the correlation between Expend and SAT after we have removed any effects attributable to LogPctSAT. (Also notice that it is now positive.)

Model Summary[b]

Model	R	R Square	Adjusted R Square	Std. Error of the Estimate
1	.445[a]	.198	.182	25.51077434

[a]Predictors: (Constant), Unstandardized Residual
[b]Dependent Variable: Unstandardized Residual
Adapted from output by SPSS, Inc.

I hope that no one thinks that they should actually do their regression this way. The reason I went through the exercise was to make the point that when we have multiple predictor variables we are adjusting each predictor for all other predictors in the equation. And the phrases "adjusted for," "controlling," "partialling out," and "holding constant" all are ways of saying the same thing.

A Final Way to Think of Multiple Regression

There is a third way to think of multiple regression, and in some ways I find it the most useful. We know that in multiple regression we solve for an equation of the form

$$\hat{Y} = b_1X_1 + b_2X_2 + b_0$$

---

[2] In SPSS it is very easy to obtain these residuals. From the main regression window just click on the "Save" button and select "Unstandardized residuals." They will appear in your data file after you run the regression.

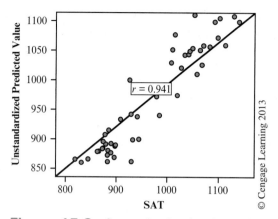

Figure 15.2   Scatterplot showing the relationship between SAT and the best linear combination of the predictors

or, in terms of the variables we have been using,

$$\widehat{SAT} = b_1 \text{Expend} + b_2 \text{LogPctSAT} + b_0$$

I obtained the predicted scores from $\widehat{SAT} = 11.129 \times \text{Expend} - 78.203 \times \text{LogPctSAT} + 1147.100$ and stored the predicted scores as PredSAT. Now if I correlate actual SAT with PredSAT the resulting correlation will be .941, which is our multiple correlation. A scatterplot of this relationship is shown in Figure 15.2.

The point of this last approach is to show that you can think of a multiple correlation coefficient as the simple Pearson correlation between the criterion (SAT) and the best linear combination of the predictors. When I say "best linear combination" I mean that there is no set of weights (partial regression coefficients) that will do a better job of predicting the state's mean SAT score from those predictors. This is actually a very important point. There are a number of advanced techniques in statistics, which we are not going to cover in this book, that really come down to creating a new variable that is some optimally weighted sum of other variables, and then using that variable in the main part of the analysis. This approach also explains why multiple correlations are always positive, even if the relationship between two variables is negative. You would certainly expect the predicted values to be positively correlated with the criterion.

Review

We now have several ways of thinking of multiple regression, and each of them gives us a somewhat different view of what is going on. If one of them makes more sense to you than the others, you can focus on that approach.

- We can treat a regression coefficient as the coefficient we would get if we had a whole group of states that did not differ on any of the predictors except the one under consideration. In other words all predictors but one are held constant, and we look at what varying that one predictor does.

- We can think of a regression coefficient in multiple regression as the same thing we would have in simple regression if we adjusted our two variables for any of the variables we want to control. In this example it meant adjusting both SAT and Expend for LogPctSAT (by computing the difference between the obtained score for that variable and the score predicted from the "nuisance variable" (or the "to be controlled variable")). The coefficient (slope) that we obtain is the same coefficient we find in the multiple regression solution.

- We can think of the multiple correlation as the simple Pearson correlation between the criterion (call it Y) and another variable (call it $\hat{Y}$) that is the best linear combination of the predictor variables.

> **NOTE**
>
> The Educational Testing Service, which produces the SAT, tries to have everyone put a disclaimer on results broken down by states that says the SAT is not a fair way to compare the performance of different states. Having gone through this example you can see that one reason they say this is because different states have different cohorts of students taking the exam, and this makes the test inappropriate as a way of judging a state's performance, even if it is a good way of judging the performance of individuals. We could create a new variable that is the SAT score adjusted for LogPctSAT, but I would be wary of using that measure to compare states. It is possible that it would be fair, but it is also possible that there are a number of other variables that I have not taken into account.

15.2 Using Additional Predictors

Before we look at other characteristics of multiple regression we should ask what would happen if we used additional variables to predict SAT. We have two potential variables in our data that we have not used—the pupil/teacher ratio and teachers' salaries. We could add both of them to what we already have, but I am only going to add PTratio. Folklore would have it that a lower ratio would be associated with better performance. At the same time, lower pupil/teacher ratios cost money, so PTratio should overlap with Expend and might not contribute significant new information.

Table 15.3 shows the results of using Expend, LogPctSAT, and PTratio to predict SAT. There are several things to say about this table.

The regression equation that results from this analysis is now

$$\hat{Y} = 1132.033 + 11.665\text{Expend} - 78.393\text{LogPctSAT} - 0.742\text{PTratio}$$

Notice that Expend and LogPctSAT are still significant ($t = 3.302$ and -17.293, respectively, but PTratio is far from significant ($t = 0.418$). This shows us that adding PTratio to our model did not improve our ability to predict. (Even the simple correlation

Table 15.3   Adding PTratio to the prediction equation

Coefficients[a]

Model		Unstandardized Coefficients		Standardized Coefficients			Collinearity Statistics	
		B	Std. Error	Beta	t	Sig.	Tolerance	VIF
1	(Constant)	1132.033	39.787		28.452	.000		
	Expend	11.665	3.533	.212	3.302	.002	.596	1.679
	LogPctSAT	−78.393	4.533	−1.042	−17.293	.000	.679	1.473
	PTratio	.742	1.774	.022	.418	.678	.854	1.171

[a] Dependent Variable: SAT

Adapted from output by SPSS, Inc.

between PTratio and SAT was not significant ($r = .081$).) You will see two new columns in Table 15.3, label **Tolerance** and **VIF (Variance Inflation Factor)**. When predictor variables are correlated among themselves we have what is called **collinearity** or **multicollinearity**. Collinearity has the effect of increasing the standard error of a regression coefficient, which increases the width of the confidence interval and decreases the t value for that coefficient. This is what is measured by the VIF. Moreover, when two predictors are highly correlated one has little to add over and above the other and only serves to increase the instability of the regression equation.

Tolerance is the reciprocal of the VIF and can be computed as $1 - R_j^2$, where R_j is the multiple correlation between variable$_j$ and all other *predictor* variables. So we want a low value of VIF and a high value of Tolerance. Tolerance tells us two things. First, it tells us the degree of overlap among the predictors, helping us to see which predictors have information in common and which are relatively independent. (The higher the tolerance, the lower the overlap.) Just because two variables substantially overlap in their information is not reason enough to eliminate one of them, but it does alert us to the possibility that their joint contribution might be less than we would like.

Second, the tolerance statistic alerts us to the potential problems of instability in our model. With very low levels of tolerance, the stability of the model and sometimes even the accuracy of the arithmetic can be in danger. In the extreme case where one predictor can be perfectly predicted from the others, we will have what is called a **singular** covariance (or correlation) matrix and most programs will stop without generating a model. If you see a statement in your printout that says the matrix is singular or "not positive-definite," the most likely explanation is that one predictor has a tolerance of 0.00 and is perfectly correlated with others. In this case you will have to drop at least one predictor to break up that relationship. Such a relationship most frequently occurs when one predictor is the simple sum or average of the others, or where all p predictors sum to a constant.

One common mistake is to treat the relative magnitudes of the b_i as an index of the relative importance of the individual predictors. By this (mistaken) logic, we might be tempted to conclude that Expend is a less important predictor than is LogPctSAT, because its coefficient (11.129) is appreciably smaller than the coefficient for LogPctSAT (-78.203). Although it might actually be the case that Expend is a less important predictor, we cannot draw such a conclusion based on the regression coefficients. The relative magnitudes of the coefficients are in part a function of the standard deviations of the corresponding variables. Because the standard deviation of LogPctSAT is (slightly) smaller than the standard deviation of Expend, its regression coefficient (b_2) will have a tendency to be larger than that of Expend regardless of the importance of that variable.

It may be easier for you to appreciate this last point if you look at the problem somewhat differently. (For this example we will act as if our predictor was PctSAT instead of LogPctSAT just because that makes the example easier to see.) For one state to have an Expend rating one point higher than another state would be a noticeable accomplishment (the range of expenditures is only about 6 points), whereas having a difference of one percentage point in PctSAT is a trivial matter (the range of PctSAT is 77 points). We hardly expect on a priori grounds that these two one-point differences will lead to equal differences in the predicted SAT, regardless of the relative importance of the two predictors.

Standardized Regression Coefficients

As we shall see later, the question of the relative importance of variables has several different answers depending on what we mean by **importance**. One measure of importance should be mentioned here, however, because it is a legitimate statistic in its own right.

Suppose that before we obtained our multiple regression equation, we had standardized each of our variables. As you will recall, standardizing a variable sets its mean at 0 and its standard deviation at 1. It also expresses the result in standard deviation units. (You should recall that we standardize many of our effect size measures by dividing by the standard deviation.) Now all of our variables would have equal standard deviations (1) and a one-unit difference between two states on one variable would be comparable to a one-unit difference between those states on any other variable. If we now solved for our regression coefficients using the standardized variables, we would obtain

$$\hat{Y}_z = 0.203 Z_{\text{Expend}} - 1.040 Z_{\text{LogPctSAT}}$$

where Z is used to denote standardized variables. In this case, the regression coefficients are called **standardized regression coefficients**, labeled "Beta" by SPSS and denoted β_i. Thus

standardized regression coefficients

$$\beta_1 = 0.203$$
$$\beta_2 = -1.040$$

When variables have been standardized, the intercept (β_0) is equal to 0 and is not shown.

From the preceding values of β_i we can conclude that a one-unit difference (i.e., a difference of one standard deviation) between states in Z_1 (the standardized Expend variable) with LogPctSAT held constant will be associated with a difference in $\hat{Y}_Z$ of 0.203 units and therefore a difference in $\hat{Y}$ of 0.203 standard deviations. A one unit differences in Z_2 will be associated with differences in $\hat{Y}$ of -1.040. It begins to look as if LogPctSAT may be a more important predictor than Expend. Although the relative magnitudes of the β_i are not necessarily the best indicators of "importance," they have a simple interpretation, are printed by most regression computer programs, and generally give at least a rough estimate of the relative contributions of the variables in the equation. Standardized regression coefficients can be obtained from nearly all statistical software that will run a regression analysis.

15.3   Standard Errors and Tests of Regression Coefficients

Once we have a regression coefficient, standardized or not, we normally test it for statistical significance. If the coefficient relating Expend to SAT is not statistically significantly different from 0, then Expend will serve no useful purpose in the prediction of SAT. As you might suspect, it doesn't matter whether we test the raw score regression coefficients (b_i) or the standardized coefficients (β_i). They are simply linear transformations of one another, and we would obtain the same test statistic in either case.

To test a regression coefficient (or most other statistics for that matter), we need to know the standard error of that statistic. The standard errors for the b_is are given in Exhibit 15.1 and labeled "Std. Error." For example, the standard error of b_0, the intercept, is 16.700, and the standard error for b_1 is 3.264. As with other standard errors, the standard error of the regression coefficient refers to the variability of the statistic over repeated sampling. Suppose we repeated the study many times on different independent samples of students. (I know that we can't do that, but we can at least pretend that we can.) Each replication would be expected to give us a slightly different value of b_1, although each of these would be an unbiased estimate of the true coefficient in the population, which we will denote as b_1^*. The many b_1s would be normally distributed about b_1^* with a standard deviation estimated to be 3.264, the standard error of b_1.

We can use these standard errors to form a t test on the regression coefficients. Specifically,

$$t = \frac{b_j - b_j^*}{s_{b_j}}$$

on $N - p - 1$ degrees of freedom.[3]

Then to test $H_0: b_j^* = 0$,

$$t = \frac{b_j}{s_{b_j}}$$

For a test on the regression coefficient of Expend, we have

$$t = \frac{11.129}{3.264} = 3.410$$

This is a standard Student's t on $N - p - 1 = 50 - 2 - 1 = 47$ df, and the critical value is found in Appendix t to be 2.01. Thus, we can reject H_0 and conclude that the regression coefficient in the population is not equal to 0. We don't actually need tables of t, because our printout gives not only t, but also its (two-tailed) significance level. Thus a b as large as 11.130 (for Expend) has a two-tailed probability of .001 under H_0. In other words, the predicted value of Y increases with increasing scores on Expend, and Expend thus makes a significant contribution to the prediction of SAT.

A corresponding test on the coefficient for LogPctSAT would produce

$$t = \frac{-78.203}{4.471} = -17.491$$

This result is also significant ($p = .000$), meaning that LogPctSAT contributes significantly to the prediction of SAT *over and above* what Expend contributes. When we added the PTratio to the model, the resulting t was 0.481, which was not significant. We might consider dropping this predictor from our model, but there will be more on this issue later. It is important to recognize that a test on a variable is done in the context of all other variables in the equation. A variable might have a high individual correlation with the criterion, as does Salary with a significant Pearson r with SAT $= -.440$ ($p = .001$), but have nothing useful to contribute once several other variables are included. That is the situation here. (Salary correlates .87 with Expend, so once we take Expend into account there is little left over for Salary to explain.)

Some computer programs prefer to print standard errors for, and test, standardized regression coefficients (β_j). It makes no difference which you do. Similarly, some programs provide an F test (on 1 and $N - p - 1$ df) instead of t. This F is simply the square of our t, so again it makes no difference which approach you take.

15.4 A Resampling Approach

In several places in this book we have discussed traditional hypothesis testing procedures, such as Student's t test or the chi-square test, and then looked at resampling approaches as another way to test the same, or similar, hypotheses. I have done so because such procedures are beginning to replace the traditional tests, which were themselves developed at a time when we had no reasonable way of doing the necessary resampling in any reasonable

---

[3] A number of authors (e.g., Draper and Smith, 1981; Huberty, 1989) have pointed out that in general this is not exactly distributed as Student's t. However, it is generally treated as if it were, but one should not take the associated probability too literally.

time. Resampling procedures certainly have not taken over yet, which is why it is important to cover the traditional techniques, but they are moving in that direction.

Suppose that we consider our data set for the 50 states as a population. (After all, they do exhaust the possible states, but we could treat them as a population even if that were not the case.) We can create bootstrap samples by sampling *with replacement* from that population. We will draw a sample in which some states will probably be represented more than once and other states will not be included. We will then fit a regression equation to the data and record the regression coefficients. We will then replicate this procedure another 9,999 times, storing away the coefficients. We then plot the resulting coefficients and calculate percentile confidence limits on them. Percentile limits are formed by taking the values that cut off the lowest 2.5% of our sample and the highest 2.5%, assuming that we want a 95% interval. These limits are very likely to not be symmetrically distributed about the mean b_i. If the limits do not include 0, we can conclude that the regression coefficient is significantly different from 0.

I have performed this resampling for two different cases. For the first case I have used Expend and LogPctSAT to predict the combined SAT score. We have already found that those are both significant predictors. I then repeated the process using Expend and PTratio because I wanted an example where one of the predictors was not significant. These results can be seen in Figure 15.3.

In the top row we have the regression using two significant predictors. Notice that the re-sampled b_i values for the Expenditure variable are all positive, while those for LogPctSAT are all well below 0. This is what we would expect. For this model, the 95% confidence interval for Expend is $5.70 \le b^* \le 18.56$. For LogPctSAT the interval is $-86.88 \le b^* \le -68.65$.

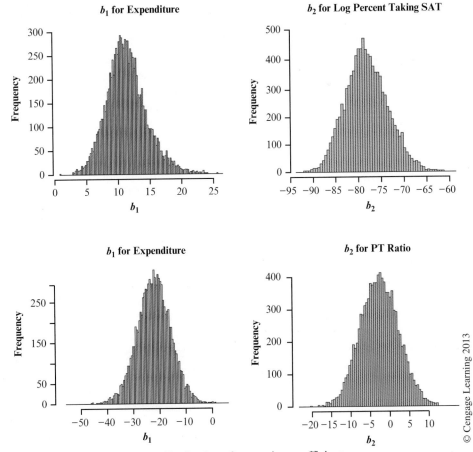

Figure 15.3   Sampling distribution of regression coefficients

But, when we use PTratio as a predictor, along with Expend, Expend has a very few coefficients that are positive, while PTratio has a great many that are positive and a great many that are negative. This latter interval includes 0, leading us to retain the null hypothesis. For this model the 95% confidence for Expend is $-35.34 \le b^* \le -9.76$, while for PTratio the interval is $-12.04 \le b^* \le 7.29$. These intervals are in line with what we would have from the traditional approach.

NOTE

It is important to note that we do not use this bootstrapping approach to get a better estimate of b_j. We use it to get an estimate of the sampling variability (the standard error) of the b_j. Over the 10,000 resamples, the average of our regression coefficients should come out to be nearly the regression coefficients in the original sample; not the population regression coefficients. But the variability of those estimates allows us to calculate confidence limits on our estimates.

15.5 Residual Variance

We have earlier considered the standard error of the regression coefficient, recognizing that sampling error is involved in the estimation of the corresponding population regression coefficient, whether we approach the problem by traditional procedures or by resampling. A somewhat different kind of error is involved in the estimation of the predicted Ys. In terms of the SAT data, we would hope that the SAT score is, at least in part, a function of such variables as Expend, LogPctSAT, and so on. (If we didn't think that, we would not have collected data on those variables in the first place.) At the same time, we probably do not expect that the two or three variables we have chosen will predict Y perfectly, even if they could be measured, and the coefficients estimated, without error. Error will still be involved in the prediction of Y after we have taken all of our predictors into account. This error is called **residual variance** or **residual error** and is defined as

residual variance
residual error

$$\frac{\sum (Y - \hat{Y})^2}{N - p - 1}$$

and is denoted as $MS_{residual}$ or MS_{error} or $s^2_{0.12345}$. In Exhibit 15.1 it is given as the error term in the analysis of variance summary table as 664.646.

The concept of residual error is important because it is exactly the thing we hope to minimize in our study. We want our estimates of Y to be as accurate as possible. We will return to this concept later in the chapter.

The square root of $MS_{residual}$ is called the *standard error of estimate* and has the same meaning as the standard error of estimate in Chapter 9. It is the standard deviation of the column of residual scores $(Y - \hat{Y})$. In Exhibit 15.1 it is given in the section labeled "Model Summary" before the analysis of variance summary table and denoted "Std. Error of the Estimate." In this example that value is 25.781.

15.6 Distribution Assumptions

So far we have made no assumptions about the nature of the distributions of our variables. The statistics b_i, β_i, and R (the multiple correlation coefficient) are legitimate measures independent of any distribution assumptions. Having said that, however, it is necessary to point out that certain assumptions will be necessary if we are to use these measures in several important ways. (It may be helpful to go back to Chapter 9 and quickly reread the brief discussions in the introduction [p. 525] and in Sections 9.7 and 9.14 [p. 266 and p. 290]. Those sections explained the distinction between linear-regression models and bivariate-normal models and discussed the assumptions involved.)

multivariate normal

To provide tests on the statistics we have been discussing, we will need to make one of two different kinds of assumptions, depending on the nature of our variables. If $X_1, X_2, \ldots, X_p$ are thought of as random variables, as they are in this example because we measure the predictors as we find them rather than fixing them in advance, we will make the general assumption that the joint distribution of $Y, X_1, X_2, \ldots, X_p$ is **multivariate normal**. (This is the extension to multiple variables of the bivariate-normal distribution described in Section 9.12.) Although in theory this assumption is necessary for many of our tests, rather substantial departures from a multivariate-normal distribution are likely to be tolerable. (This is fortunate for us, because we can see from Figure 15.1 that our data do not look like they are going to be multivariate normal.) First, our tests are reasonably robust. Second, in actual practice we are concerned not so much about whether R is significantly different from 0 as about whether R is large or small. In other words, with X_i random, we are not as interested in hypothesis testing with respect to R as we were in the analysis of variance problems. Whether $R = .10$ is statistically significant or not when it comes to prediction may be largely irrelevant, because it accounts for only 1% of the variation.

If the variables $X_1, X_2, \ldots, X_p$ are fixed variables, we will simply make the assumption that the conditional distributions of Y (i.e., the distribution of Y for specific levels of X_i) are normally and independently distributed. Here again moderate departures from normality are tolerable. We will expand on this discussion in Section 15.9, where we will cover regression diagnostics, which will help us evaluate how well or badly we meet the underlying assumptions.

The fixed model and the corresponding assumption of normality in Y will be considered in Chapter 16. In this chapter we generally will be concerned with random variables. The multivariate-normal assumption is more stringent than is necessary for much of what follows, but it is sufficient. For example, calculation of the standard error of b_j does not require an assumption of multivariate normality. However, a person seldom wishes to find the standard error of b_j unless he or she wishes to test (or form confidence limits on) b_j, and this test requires the normality assumption. We will therefore impose this assumption on our data.

15.7   The Multiple Correlation Coefficient

multiple correlation coefficient
$R_{0,123 \ldots p}$

Exhibit 15.1 shows that the multiple correlation between SAT and two predictors (Expend and LogPctSAT) is equal to .941. The **multiple correlation coefficient** is often denoted $R_{0,123 \ldots p}$. The notation denotes the fact that the criterion (Y or X_0) is predicted from predictors 1, 2, 3... p simultaneously. When there is no confusion as to which predictors are involved, we generally drop the subscripts and use plain old R.

As we have seen, R is defined as the correlation between the criterion (Y) and the best linear combination of the predictors. As such, R is really nothing but $r_{Y\hat{Y}}$, where

$$\hat{Y} = b_0 + b_1 X_1 + b_2 X_2 + \cdots + b_p X_p$$

Thus, if we wished, we could use the regression equation to generate $\hat{Y}$, and then correlate Y and $\hat{Y}$, as we did in Figure 15.2. Although no one would seriously propose calculating R in this way, it is helpful to realize that this is what the multiple correlation actually represents. In practice, R (or R^2) is printed out by every multiple regression computer program.

For our data, the multiple correlation between SAT and Expend and LogPctSAT taken simultaneously is .886.

The coefficient R is a regular correlation coefficient and can be treated just like any other Pearson product-moment correlation. (This is obviously true, because $R = r_{Y\hat{Y}}$.) However, in multiple correlation (as is often the case with simple correlation) we are more interested in R^2 than in R, because it can be directly interpreted in terms of percentage of accountable variation. Thus $R^2 = .941^2 = .886$, and we can say that 88.6% of the variation in the overall test performance can be predicted on the basis of the two predictors. This is nearly 75 percentage points more than could be predicted on the basis of Expend alone, where we explained 14.5% of the variation.

Unfortunately, R^2 is not an unbiased estimate of the corresponding parameter in the population ($R^{*2}_{.123...p}$). The extent of this bias depends on the relative size of N and p. When $N = p + 1$, prediction is perfect and $R = 1$, regardless of the true relationship between Y and $X_1, X_2, \ldots, X_p$ in the population. (A straight line will perfectly fit any two points; a plane, like the three legs of a milking stool, will perfectly fit any three points; and so on.) A relatively unbiased estimate of R^{*2} is given by

$$\text{est } R^{*2} = 1 - \frac{(1 - R^2)(N - 1)}{N - p - 1}$$

For our data,

$$\text{est } R^{*2} = 1 - \frac{(1 - .886)(49)}{47} = .881$$

This value agrees with the "Adjusted R Square" printed by the SPSS procedure in Exhibit 15.1.

It should be apparent from the definition of R that it can take on values only between 0 and 1. This follows both from the fact that it is defined as the positive square root of R^2, and from the fact that it can be viewed as $r_{Y\hat{Y}}$—we would hardly expect $\hat{Y}$ to be negatively correlated with Y. This is an important point, because if we were to predict SAT just from Expend, the multiple correlation will be .381, whereas we know that the simple correlation was −.381. As long as you understand what is happening here, there should not be any confusion.

Because R^2_{adj} is a less biased estimate of the squared population coefficient than R^2, you might expect that people would routinely report R^2_{adj}. In fact, R^2_{adj} is seldom seen except on computer printout. I don't know why that should be, but R or R^2 is what you would normally report.

Testing the Significance of R^2

We have seen how to ask whether each of the variables is making a significant contribution to the prediction of Y by testing its regression coefficient (b_j). But perhaps a question that should be asked first is, "Does the set of variables taken together predict Y at better-than-chance levels?" I suggest that this question has priority because there is little point in looking at individual variables if no overall relationship exists.

The easiest way to test the overall relationship between Y and $X_1, X_2, \ldots, X_p$ is to test the multiple correlation coefficient for statistical significance. This amounts to testing $H_0: R^* = 0$, where R^* represents the correlation coefficient in the population. By the nature of our test, it is actually easier to test R^2 than R, but that amounts to the same thing. The test on R^2 is recognizable as a simple extension of the test given in Chapter 9 when we had only one predictor. In this case we have p predictors and

$$F = \frac{(N - p - 1)R^2}{p(1 - R^2)}$$

is distributed as the standard F distribution on p and $N - p - 1$ degrees of freedom. [With only one predictor this F statistic reduces to the familiar $(N - 2)(r^2)/(1 - r^2)$.] For our data, $N = 50$, $p = 5$, and $R^2 = .886$. Then

$$F = \frac{(50 - 2 - 1)(.886)}{2(.114)} = \frac{47(.886)}{.228} = 182.64 \text{ }^{4}$$

This is the same F as that given in the summary table in Exhibit 15.1. An F of 182.64 on 2 and 47 df is obviously significant beyond $p = .05$, and we can therefore reject $H_0: R^* = 0$ and conclude that we can predict at better-than-chance levels. (The printout shows the probability associated with this F under H_0 to three decimal places as .000.)

Sample Sizes

As you can tell from the formula for an adjusted R square and from the preceding formula for F, our estimate of the correlation depends on both the size of the sample (N) and the number of predictors (p). People often assume that if there is no relation between the criterion and the predictors, R should come out near 0. In fact, the expected value of R *for random data* is $p/(N - 1)$.

Thus, with 2 predictors, 50 cases, and no true relationship between the predictors and the criterion, an $R = .04$ would be the expected value, not 0. So it is important that we have a relatively large sample size. A rule of thumb that has been kicking around for years is that we should have *at least* 10 observations for every predictor. Harris (1985) points out, however, that he knows of no empirical evidence supporting this rule. It certainly fails in the extreme, because no one would be satisfied with 10 observations and 1 predictor. Harris advocates an alternative rule dealing not with the ratio of p to N, but with their difference. His rule is that N should exceed p by at least 50. Others have suggested the slightly more liberal $N \geq p + 40$. Whereas these two rules relate directly to the reliability of a correlation coefficient, Cohen, Cohen, West, and Aiken (2003) approach the problem from the direction of statistical power. They show that in the one-predictor case, to have power = .80 for a population correlation of .30 would require $N = 124$. With 5 predictors, a population correlation of .30 would require 187 subjects for the same degree of power. As you can see, a reasonable amount of power requires fairly large samples. Perhaps Darlington's (1990) rule of thumb is the best—"more is better."

15.8 Partial and Semipartial Correlation

Two closely related correlation coefficients involve partialling out, or controlling for, the effects of one or more other variables. These correlations are the partial and semipartial correlation coefficients.

---

[4] Here, as elsewhere, what you might calculate with a calculator will differ from the answers I give because of rounding error. Computer software uses far more significant digits than it prints out, and the answers are themselves more accurate. In this particular equation, using 3-digit numbers would yield an answer of 27.118 when the correct answer is 27.184—quite a difference. I give the answer that agrees with the printout.

Partial Correlation

partial correlation
$r_{01.2}$

We have seen that a **partial correlation** $r_{01.2}$ is the correlation between two variables with one or more variables partialled out of *both X and Y*. More specifically, it is the correlation between the two sets of residuals formed from the prediction of the original variables by one or more other variables.

Consider an experimenter who wanted to investigate the relationship between earned income and success in college. He obtained measures for each variable and ran his correlation, which turned out to be significant. Elated with the results, he harangued his students with the admonition that if they did not do well in college they were not likely to earn large salaries. In the back of the class, however, was a bright student who realized that both variables were (presumably) related to IQ. She argued that people with high IQs tend to do well in college and also earn good salaries, and that the correlation between income and college success is an artifact of this relationship.

The simplest way to settle this argument is to calculate the partial correlation between Income and college Success with IQ partialled out of both variables. Thus, we regress Income on IQ and obtain the residuals. These residuals represent the variation in Income that cannot be attributed to IQ. You might think of this as a "purified" income measure—purified of the influence of IQ. We next regress Success on IQ and again obtain the residuals, which here represent the portion of Success that is not attributable to IQ. We can now answer the important question: Can the variation in Income not explained by (independent of) IQ be predicted by the variation in Success that is also independent of IQ? The correlation between these two variables is the partial correlation of Income and Success, partialling out IQ.

The partial correlation coefficient is represented by $r_{01.23\ldots p}$. The two subscripts to the left of the dot represent the variables being correlated, and the subscripts to the right of the dot represent those variables being partialled out of both.

Semipartial Correlation

**semipartial r
correlation** $r_{0(1.2)}$

A type of correlation that will prove exceedingly useful both here and in Chapter 16 is the **semipartial correlation** $r_{0(1.2)}$ sometimes called the *part*[5] correlation. As the name suggests, a semipartial correlation is the correlation between the criterion and a partialled predictor variable. In other words, whereas the partial correlation ($r_{01.2}$) has variable 2 partialled out of both the criterion and predictor 1, the semipartial correlation $r_{0(1.2)}$ has variable 2 partialled out of only predictor 1. In this case, the semipartial correlation is simply the correlation between Y and the residual ($X_1 - \hat{X}_1 = X_{1r}$) of X_1 predicted on X_2. As such, it is the correlation of Y with that part of X_1 that is independent of X_2. A different way to view the semi-partial correlation is in terms of the difference between two models, one of which contains fewer predictors than the other. It can be shown that

$$r_{0(1.2)}^2 = R_{0.12}^2 - r_{02}^2$$

We can use our example of expenditures for education to calculate the semipartial correlation between SAT and Expend with LogPctSAT partialed out of SAT. For those data,

$$R_{\text{SAT.Expend, Log PctSAT}}^2 = .886, \text{ and } R_{\text{SAT.LogPctSAT}}^2 = .857$$

---

[5] The only text that I have seen using "part correlation" was McNemar (1969) when I was just out of graduate school. But the name seems to have stuck with someone, and you will find SPSS employing that term.

Thus

$$r^2_{\text{SAT(Expend.LogPctSAT)}} = R^2_{\text{SAT.Expend,LogPctSAT}} - R^2_{\text{SAT.LogPctSAT}}$$

$$= .886 - .857 = .029$$

$$r_{\text{SAT(Expend.LogPctSAT)}} = \sqrt{.029} = .170$$

The preceding formula for $r_{0(1.2)}$ affords an opportunity to explore further just what multiple regression equations and correlations represent. Rearranging the formula we have

$$R^2_{0.12} = r^2_{02} + r^2_{0(1.2)}$$

This formula illustrates that the squared multiple correlation is the sum of the squared correlation between the criterion and one of the variables plus the squared correlation between the criterion and the part of the other variable that is independent of the first. Thus, we can think of R and R^2 as being based on as much information as possible from one variable, any *additional, nonredundant* information from a second, and so on. In general

$$R^2_{0.123\ldots p} = r^2_{01} + r^2_{0(2.1)} + r^2_{0(3.12)} + \cdots + r^2_{0(p.123\ldots p-1)}$$

where $r^2_{0(3.12)}$ is the squared correlation between the criterion and variable 3, with variables 1 and 2 partialled out of 3. This way of looking at multiple regression will be particularly helpful when we consider the role of individual variables in predicting the criterion, and when we consider the least squares approach to the analysis of variance in Chapter 16. As an aside, it should be mentioned that when the predictors are independent of one another, the preceding formula reduces to

$$R^2_{0.123\ldots p} = r^2_{01} + r^2_{02} + r^2_{03} + \cdots + r^2_{0p}$$

because, if the variables are independent, there is no variance in common to be partialled out.

The squared *partial* correlation between SAT and Expend, partialling the LogPctSAT from both SAT and Expend, by the method discussed next is .198, showing that 20% of the variation in SAT *that could not be explained by LogPctSAT* can be accounted for by that portion of Expend *that could not be explained by LogPctSAT*. To put that in perhaps clearer terms, 20% of the variation is SAT independent of LogPctSAT can be accounted for by that portion of Expend independent of LogPctSAT. This point will be elaborated in the next section.

We do not need a separate significance test for semipartial or partial correlations, because we already have such a test in the test on the regression coefficients. If that test is significant, then the corresponding β, partial, and semipartial coefficients are also significant.[6] Therefore, from Exhibit 15.1 we also know that these coefficients for Expend are all significant. Keep in mind, however, that when we speak about the significance of a coefficient we are speaking of it within the context of the other variables in the model. For example, we saw earlier that when Salary is included in the model it does not make a significant contribution. That does not mean that it would not contribute to any other model predicting SAT. (In fact, when used as the only predictor, it predicts SAT at better-than-chance levels. $R = -.440, p = .001$.) It only means that once we have the other predictors in our model, Salary does not have any independent (or unique) contribution to make.

Alternative Interpretation of Partial and Semipartial Correlation

There is an alternative way of viewing the meaning of partial and semipartial correlations that can be very instructive. This method is best presented in terms of what are called

---

[6] You will note that we consider both partial and semipartial correlation but only mentioned the *partial* regression coefficient (b_j). This coefficient could equally well be called the *semipartial* regression coefficient.

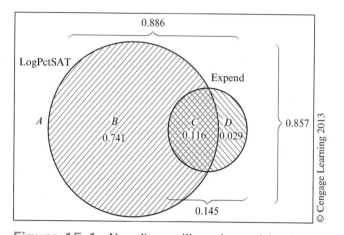

Figure 15.4 Venn diagram illustrating partial and semipartial correlation

Venn diagrams

Venn diagrams. The Venn diagram shown in Figure 15.4 is definitely not drawn to scale, but it does illustrate various aspects of the relationship between SAT and the two predictors.

Suppose that the box in Figure 15.4 is taken to represent all the variability in the criterion (SAT). We will set the area of the box equal to 1.00—the proportion of the variation in SAT to be explained. The circle labeled LogPctSAT is taken to represent the proportion of the variation in SAT that is explained by LogPctSAT. In other words, the area of the circle is equal to $r^2_{01} = .857$. Similarly, the area of the circle labeled Expend is the percentage of the variation in SAT explained by Expend and is equal to $r^2_{02} = .145$. Finally, the overlap between the two circles represents the portion of SAT that both LogPctSAT and Expend have in common, and equals .116. The area outside of either circle but within the box is the portion of SAT that cannot be explained by either variable and is the residual variation = .059.

The areas labeled *B*, *C*, and *D* in Figure 15.4 represent portions of the variation in SAT that can be accounted for by LogPctSAT *and/or* Expend. (Area *A* represents the portion that cannot be explained by either variable or their combination, the residual variation.) Thus, the two predictors in our example account for 88.6% of the variation of *Y*: $B + C + D = .741 + .116 + .029 = 0.886$. The *squared semipartial correlation* between LogPctSAT and SAT, with Expend partialled out of LogPctSAT, is the portion of the variation of SAT that LogPctSAT accounts for *over and above* the portion accounted for by Expend. As such, it is .741 and is labeled as B

$$r^2_{0(1.2)} = R^2_{0.12} - r^2_{01} = .886 - .145 = .741$$

The semipartial correlation is the square root of this quantity.

$$r_{0(1.2)} = \sqrt{.741} = .861$$

The *squared partial correlation* has a similar interpretation. Instead of being the additional percentage of SAT that LocPctSAT explains but that Expend does not, which is the squared *semi-partial correlation*, it is the additional amount that LogPctSAT explains *relative to* the amount that Expend left to be explained. For example, $r^2_{02} = -.381^2 = .145$ and $1 - r^2_{02} = .855$,

$$r^2_{01.2} = \frac{r^2_{0(1.2)}}{1 - r^2_{02}}$$

$$= \frac{.741}{.855} = .866$$

$$r_{01.2} = \sqrt{.866}$$

$$= .931$$

Schematically, squared multiple, partial, and semipartial correlations can be represented as

$$r^2_{0(1.2)} = B = \text{the squared semipartial correlation}$$

$$r^2_{01.2} = \frac{B}{A + B} = \text{the squared partial correlation}$$

$$= \frac{r^2_{0(1.2)}}{1 - r^2_{02}}$$

In addition,
$$A = 1 - R^2_{0.12} = \text{the residual (unexplained) variation in } Y \text{ (SAT)}$$
$$D = r^2_{0(2.1)} = \text{the other squared semipartial correlation}$$
$$B + C + D = R^2_{0.12} = \text{the squared multiple correlation}$$
$$B + C = r^2_{01} = \text{the squared correlation between } Y \text{ (SAT) and } X_1 \text{ (Expend)}$$
$$C + D = r^2_{02} = \text{the squared correlation between } Y \text{ (Sat) and } X_2 \text{ (LogPctSAT)}$$

Why Do We Care About Partial and Semipartial Correlations?

You might ask why we bother to worry about partial and semipartial correlations. What do they add to what we already know? The answer is that they add a great deal. They allow us to control for variables that we might perceive as "nuisance" variables, and in so doing allow us to make statements of the form "The correlation between Y and A is .65, *after we control for the influence of B*." To take an example from a study that we will discuss later in the chapter, Leerkes and Crockenberg (1999) were interested in the relationship between the maternal care a woman received when she was a child and the level of self-confidence or self-efficacy she feels toward her own mothering skills. Leerkes and Crockenberg asked whether this relationship was influenced by the fact that those who received high quality maternal care also showed high levels of self-esteem. Perhaps if we controlled for differences in self-esteem, the maternal care → self-efficacy relationship would disappear. This is a case where they are partialling out the influence of self-esteem to look at the relationship that remains. Partial and semipartial correlations are a tool to "get our hands around" a number of confusing relationships.

15.9   Suppressor Variables

suppressor variable

Suppose we have a multiple regression problem in which all variables are scored so as to correlate positively with the criterion. Because the scoring of variables is often arbitrary, this presents no difficulty (if X is negatively related to Y, $C - X$ will be positively related to Y, where C is any constant). In such a situation, we would expect all the regression coefficients (β_i or b_i) to be positive. Occasionally, however, a regression coefficient in this situation will be *significantly* negative. Such a variable, if significant, is called a **suppressor variable**.[7]

Suppressor variables seem, at first glance, to be unreasonable. We know that the simple correlation between the criterion and the variable is positive (by our definition), yet in the resulting regression equation an increment on this variable produces a decrement in $\hat{Y}$. Moreover, it can be shown that $R^2 = \sum \beta_i r_{0i}$. If r_{0i} is positive and β_i is negative, the product $\beta_i r_{0i}$ will be negative. Thus, by assigning β_i a negative value, the regression solution (which has the task of minimizing error) would *appear* to be reducing R^2. This does not fit

---

[7] Cohen and Cohen (1983) discuss two additional types of suppression, and their discussion is helpful when faced with results that seem contrary to intuition. That discussion has been omitted in the more recent Cohen, Cohen, West, and Aiken (2003), so you need to go back to the earlier edition.

with our preconceived ideas of what should be happening, and yet obviously there must be some logical explanation.

Space considerations do not allow an extensive discussion of the theory of suppressor variables, but it is important to illustrate one intuitively sensible explanation. For a more extensive discussion of suppressor variables, see Cohen and Cohen (1983) and Darlington (1968). (The discussion in Cohen and Cohen is particularly helpful.) Here we will take an example from Darlington (1990). Suppose a speeded history examination (a long exam with a short time in which to complete it) is used as a measure of some external criterion of knowledge of history. Although knowledge of history is presumably independent of reading speed, performance on the speeded test will not be. Thus, some of the variance in test scores will reflect differences in the reading speed of the students rather than differences in their actual knowledge. What we would really like to do is penalize students who did well *only* because they read quickly, and help students who did poorly *only* because they read slowly. This is precisely what is accomplished when reading speed serves as a suppressor variable. It is suppressing some of the error in the exam scores.

As Darlington points out, a variable will serve as a suppressor variable when it correlates more highly with Y_r than with Y (where Y_r represents the residual when predicting history knowledge from history score), and will not serve as a suppressor variable when it correlates more highly with Y than Y_r. Cohen, Cohen, West, and Aiken (2003) point out that suppressor relationships are hard to find in psychology (at least statistically significant ones), though they are easily found in biology and economics. In those fields they relate to homeostatic mechanisms, where an increase in X leads to an increase in Y, which in turn causes an increase in Z which leads back to a decrease in Y. Although these mechanisms are not as common in psychology, I am frequently asked about suppression effects—most of which turn out to be statistically nonsignificant.

15.10   Regression Diagnostics

In predicting state SAT performance from variables that described educational expenditures and characteristics of test taking, we skipped an important step because of the need to first lay out some of the important concepts in multiple regression. It is now time to go back and fill that gap. Before throwing all of the observations and predictors into the model and asking computer software to produce an answer to be written up and interpreted, we need to look more closely at the data. We can do this by using a variety of tools supplied by nearly all multiple regression computer programs. Once we are satisfied with the data, we can then go on and use other available tools to help us decide which variables to include in the model. A much more complete and readable treatment of the problem of regression diagnostics can be Cohen et al. (2003) and Fox (2002).

The first step in examining the data has already been carried out in Figure 15.1 with graphical presentations of important variables. At that point we noted that most of the variables were fairly messy with the percentage of students taking the SAT being decidedly bimodal. SAT scores were also somewhat bimodal, and much of that can probably be related to the bimodal nature of PctSAT. For reasons that will become clear shortly we used the log of PctSAT rather than PctSAT itself. This at least had the effect of reducing the curvilinear relationship between the SAT scores and the percentage of students in each state taking the SAT. None of our variables had extreme outliers, especially after we used a log transformation of PctSAT.

The fact that we don't have more outliers when we look at the variables individually does not necessarily mean that all is well. There is still the possibility of having **multivariate outliers**. A case might seem to have reasonable scores on each of the variables taken

multivariate outliers

separately but have an unusual *combination* of scores on two or more variables. For example, it is not uncommon to be 6 feet tall, nor is it uncommon to weigh 125 pounds. But it clearly would be unusual to be 6 feet tall *and* weigh 125 pounds.

Having temporarily satisfied ourselves that the data set does not contain unreasonable data points and that the distributions are not seriously distorted, a useful second step is to conduct a preliminary regression analysis using all the variables, as we have done. I say "preliminary" because the point here is to use that analysis to examine the data rather than as an end in itself.

Instead of jumping directly into the educational expenditure data set, we will first investigate diagnostic tools with a smaller data set created to illustrate the use of those tools. These data are shown below and are plotted in Figure 15.5.

X:	1	1	3	3	3	4	5	5	7	6	10	13
Y:	1	2	3	5	7	6	8	10	10	5	4	14

The three primary classes of diagnostic statistics, each of which is represented in Figure 15.5, are

Distance

1. **Distance**, which is useful in identifying potential outliers in the dependent variable (Y).

Leverage

2. **Leverage** (h_i), which is useful in identifying potential outliers in the independent variables ($X_1, X_2, \ldots, X_p$).

Influence

3. **Influence**, which combines distance and leverage to identify unusually influential observations. An observation is influential if the location of the regression surface would change markedly depending on the presence or absence of that observation.

Our most common measure of distance is the residual ($Y_i - \hat{Y}_i$). It measures the vertical distance between any point and the regression line. Points A and C in Figure 15.5 have large residuals (they lie far from the regression line). Such points may represent random error, they may be data that are incorrectly recorded, or they may reflect unusual cases that don't really belong in this data set. (An example of this last point would arise if we were trying to predict physical reaction time as a function of cognitive processing features of a task, and our subjects included one individual who suffered from a neuromuscular disorder that seriously slowed his reaction time.) Residuals are a standard feature of all regression analyses, and you should routinely request and examine them in running your analyses.

Leverage (often denoted h_i, or "hat diag") measures the degree to which a case is unusual with respect to the predictor variables X_j. In the case of one predictor, leverage is simply a function of the deviation of the score on that predictor from the predictor mean. Point B in Figure 15.5 is an example of a point with high leverage because the X score for that point (13) is far from $\overline{X}$. Most programs for multiple regression compute and print the leverage of each observation if requested. Possible values on leverage range from a low of

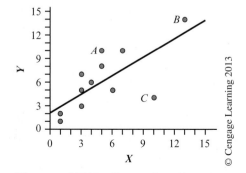

© Cengage Learning 2013

Figure 15.5 Scatterplot of Y on X

$1/N$ to a high of 1.0, with a mean of $(p + 1)/N$, where p = the number of predictors. Stevens (1992) recommends looking particularly closely at those leverage values that exceed $3(p + 1)/n$.

Points that are high on either distance or leverage do not necessarily have an important influence on the regression, but they have the potential for it. In order for a point to be high on influence, it must have relatively high values on both distance and leverage. In Figure 15.5, Point B is very high on leverage, but it has a relatively small residual (distance). Point A, on the other hand, has a large residual but, because it is near the mean on X, has low leverage. Point C is high on leverage and has a large residual, suggesting that it is high on influence. The most common measure of influence is known as Cook's D. It is a function of the sum of the squared *changes* in b_j that would occur if the ith observation were removed from the data and the analysis rerun.

Cook's D

Exhibit 15.2 contains various diagnostic statistics for the data shown in Figure 15.5. These diagnostics were produced by an SAS, but similar statistics would be produced by almost any other program.

To take the diagnostic statistics in order, consider first the column headed Resid., which is a measure of distance. This column reflects what we can already see in Figure 15.5—that the 8th and 11th observations have the largest residuals. Considering that the Y values range only from 1 to 14, a residual of -5.89 seems substantial.

If the data met the underlying assumptions, we would expect the values of Y to be normally distributed about the regression line. In other words, with a very large data set all of the Y values corresponding to a specific value of X would have a normal distribution. Five percent of these values would lie more than 1.96 adjusted standard errors from the regression line. (I use the word "adjusted" because the size of the standard error will depend in part on the degree to which X departs from the mean of X, as measured by its leverage value h_i.) Within this context, it may be meaningful to ask if a point lies significantly far from the regression line. If so, we should be concerned about it. A t test on the magnitude of the residuals is given by the statistic RStudent, sometimes called the **Studentized residual**. This can be interpreted as a standard t statistic on $(N - p - 1)$ degrees of freedom. Here we see that for case 11 RStudent = -3.54. This should give us pause because that is a substantial, and significant, deviation. It is often useful to think of RStudent less as

	OBS	X	Y	PRED	RES1D	RSTUDENT	HAT DIAG H	MSE	COOK'S D
	1	1	1	3.23	−2.23	−0.87	0.20	8.22	0.10
	2	1	2	3.23	−1.22	−0.47	0.20	8.71	0.03
	3	3	3	4.71	−1.71	−0.62	0.11	8.55	0.03
	4	3	5	4.71	0.29	0.10	0.11	8.91	0.00
	5	3	7	4.71	2.29	0.85	0.11	8.26	0.05
	6	4	6	5.45	0.55	0.19	0.09	8.88	0.00
	7	5	8	6.19	1.81	0.65	0.08	8.52	0.02
"A"->	8	5	10	6.19	3.81	1.49	0.08	7.16	0.09
	9	6	5	6.93	−1.93	−0.69	0.09	8.46	0.02
	10	7	10	7.77	2.33	0.86	0.1 1	8.24	0.05
"C"->	11	10	4	9.89	−5.89	−3.54	0.26	3.73	1.01
"B"->	12	13	14	12 .11	1.89	0.98	0.54	8.06	0.55

Exhibit 15.2   Diagnostic statistics for data in Figure 15.5

a hypothesis-testing statistic and more as just an indicator of the magnitude of the residual. (Remember that here we are computing N t-tests, with a resulting very large increase in the familywise error rate.) But significant or not, something that is 3.54 standard errors from the line is unusual and therefore noteworthy. We are not predicting that case well.

We now turn to leverage (h_i), shown in the column headed Hat Diag. Here we see that most observations have leverage values that fall between about 0.00 and 0.20. The mean leverage is $(p + 1)/N = 2/12 = 0.167$, and that is about what we would expect. Notice, however, that two cases have larger leverage; namely, cases 11 and 12, which exceeds Stevens rule of thumb of $3(p + 1)/n = 3(2)/12 = .50$. We have already seen that 11 has a large residual, so its modest leverage may make it an influential point. Case 12 has a leverage value nearly twice as large. However, it falls quite close to the regression line with a fairly small residual, and it is likely to be less influential.

Cook's D, which is a measure of influence, varies as a function of distance (residual), leverage (h_i), and $MS_{residual}$. Most of the values in the last column are quite small, but cases 11 and 12 are exceptions. In particular, observation 11 has a D exceeding 1.00. The sampling distribution of Cook's D is in dispute, and there is no general rule for what constitutes a large value, but values over 1.00 are unusual.

We can summarize the results shown in Exhibit 15.2 by stating that each of the three points labeled in Figure 15.5 is reflected in that table. Point A has a fairly, though not significantly, large residual but has small values for both leverage and influence. Point B has a large leverage, but Cook's D is not high and its removal would not substantially reduce $MS_{residual}$. Point C has a large residual, a fairly large leverage, and a substantial Cook's D; its removal would provide a substantial reduction in $MS_{residual}$. This is the kind of observation that we should consider seriously. Although data should not be deleted merely because they are inconvenient and their removal would make the results look better, it is important to pay attention to observations such as case 11. There may be legitimate reasons to set that case aside and to treat it differently. Or it may in fact be erroneous. Because this is not a real data set, we cannot do anything further with it.

It may seem like overkill to compute regression diagnostics simply to confirm what anyone can see simply by looking at a plot of the data. However, we have looked only at a situation with one predictor variable. With multiple predictors there is no reasonable way to plot the data and visually identify influential points. In that situation you should at least create univariate displays, perhaps bivariate plots of each predictor against the criterion looking for peculiar distributions of points, and compute diagnostic statistics. From those statistics you can then target particular cases for closer study.

Returning briefly to the data on school expenditures and SAT scores, we can illustrate some additional points concerning diagnostic statistics. Exhibit 15.3 contains additional statistics that were not shown in Exhibit 15.1, but came from that SPSS analysis.[8] These values are obtained by choosing the "Save" option in the regression dialog box and then selecting the appropriate statistics.

If we look at these cases in the diagnostic statistics above, we can see that some of them have large residuals and studentized residuals. The only studentized residual that is particularly noteworthy is for State 48, which is West Virginia. But when we look at Cook's D we see that no state comes even close to having unusual values. The highest Cook's D for this data set is 0.1230. From these results we are safe in concluding that no one state is having a disproportionate influence on our results.

---

[8] SPSS calculates leverage, and hence the Studentized Range Statistic, slightly differently than do SAS, JMP, SYSTAT, BMDP, and others. The leverage values are lower by a factor of $1/N$, but this makes no substantive difference in the interpretation (except that the mean leverage will now be p/N instead of $(p + 1)/N$).

Observation	Residual	Rstudent	Cook's D	Hat Diag (h_i)
1	−4.5159	−.1798	.0006	.0312
2	−11.7667	.4899	.0122	.1121
3	1.4609	.0580	.0000	.0248
4	−51.6151	−2.0661	.0924	.0410
5	−2.9717	−.1189	.0003	.0407
…	…	…	…	…
29	54.9324	2.1943	.0972	.0371
30	−25.6401	−1.1063	.0968	.1718
…	…	…	…	…
48	−61.5098	−2.4168	.0508	.0054
49	20.5930	.8368	.0227	.0688
50	−34.5975	−1.3757	.0321	.0284

Adapted from output by SPSS, Inc.

Exhibit 15.3   Diagnostic statistics

Diagnostic Plots

Just because no one state or collection of states does not appear to have a disproportionate influence on our regression equation does not mean that we have nothing to worry about. It is possible that there are other problems with the data. In fact, there was a problem that I passed over by using the log of PctSAT.

Our tests on the regression coefficients assume that the residuals are homoscedastic, meaning that the variance of the residuals is constant conditional on the level of each of the predictor variables and on the overall $\hat{Y}$ from the final regression equation. Two important things that we should always look at are a plot of the residuals against the predicted values and a Q-Q plot of the residuals to check for normality. In the top of Figure 15.6 you will see these two plots when I used PctSAT instead of LogPctSAT in the regression equation along with Expend.

The line drawn through the plot in the upper left is a smoothed regression line fitting the data. Notice that it is distinctly curved. There should be no pattern to the residuals, but clearly there is. Crawley (2007) suggests that this plot should look like the sky at night, with points scattered all over the place. That is not the case here. In the lower left you see a similar plot but with LogPctSAT and Expend used as the predictors. Here there is much less of a pattern to the display, which is why I chose to use LogPctSAT as my predictor. On the right of Figure 15.6 you can see that both sets of residuals were reasonably normal, which is important. Cohen et al. (2003) describe a test of heterogeneity of residuals devised by Levene. It is basically the same Levene test that we discussed in Chapter 7 when considering heterogeneity of variance for a *t* test on independent samples and focuses on residuals that increase or decrease with increasing values along the *X* axis. Cai and Hayes (2008) have proposed a test of the regression coefficients that is much more robust against heterogeneity of regression. Applying their test to our data confirms that the coefficients for both Expend and LogPctSAT are significant.[9]

Comparing Models

nested models

hierarchical

Often we have what are called **nested models** or **hierarchical** models in which the variables in one model represent a subset of the variables in a second model. For example, we might wonder if we do better predicting SAT from Expend, LogPctSAT, PTratio, and

---

[9] Cai and Hayes (2008) provide a SAS macro to perform these tests. Although their paper is complex, their macro is reasonably simple to implement. You simply include it in your SAS program and call it as shown in their paper.

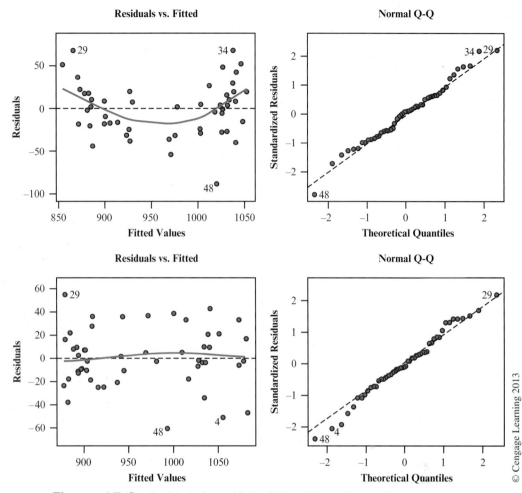

Figure 15.6   Residual plots with PctSAT and Expend as predictors (top row) and with LogPctSAT and Expend as predictors (bottom row)

Salary than we do with a model that does not include either PTratio or Salary but does include the other two predictors. In the case of nested models, it is relatively easy to test whether one is significantly better than another. We can just compare their R^2 values or the sums of squares for regression.

For example, suppose that we start with a model that contains Expend, LogPctSAT, PTratio, and Salary. (I chose this model because it has two more predictors than the simpler one that we have looked at.) The multiple R^2 is .888 and the analysis of variance summary table is

ANOVA[b]

Model		Sum of Squares	df	Mean Square	F	Sig.
1	Regression	243689.5	4	60922.385	89.539	.000[a]
	Residual	30618.141	45	680.403		
	Total	274307.7	49			

[a]Predictors: (Constant), Salary, PTratio, LogPctSAT, Expend
[b]Dependent Variable: SAT
Adapted from output by SPSS, Inc.

© Cengage Learning 2013

Next we drop PTratio and Salary and just use Expend and LogPctSAT. Now the R^2 is .886 and the analysis of variance summary table is

ANOVA[b]

Model		Sum of Squares	df	Mean Square	F	Sig.
1	Regression	243069.3	2	121534.649	182.856	.000[a]
	Residual	31238.381	47	664.646		
	Total	274307.7	49			

[a]Predictors: (Constant), LogPctSAT, Expend
[b]Dependent Variable: SAT
Adapted from output by SPSS, Inc.

Notice that the first model explained slightly more variation than the second. If we compute the difference in $SS_{\text{regression}}$ we have $243{,}689.5 - 243{,}069.3 = 620.2 = SS_{\text{difference}}$. This difference in the sum of squares can be converted to a mean square by dividing by the degrees of freedom, but what are the degrees of freedom? They are simply the difference in the number of predictors, which is 2. Therefore $MS_{\text{difference}} = SS_{\text{difference}}/df = 620.2/2 = 310.1$. Moreover, this mean square can be tested by dividing by the residual mean square from the fuller model. So

$$F = \frac{\dfrac{SS_{\text{reg(full)}} - SS_{\text{reg(reduced)}}}{df_{\text{reg(full)}} - df_{\text{reg(reduced)}}}}{MS_{\text{residual(full)}}} = \frac{\dfrac{(243{,}689.5 - 243{,}069.3)}{2}}{664.646} = \frac{310.1}{664.646} = 0.467$$

This is an F on 2 and 45 degrees of freedom and is clearly not significant. We do not do a better job of predicting SAT scores with the additional two predictors.

If we take the model with Expend, LogPctSAT, and PTratio as our full model and compare it against the model without PTratio, our resulting F would be 0.175, and its square root would be 0.418, which is exactly the t for the test of PTratio in the fuller model. In other words if we only want to drop one predictor we know whether that drop will be significant simply by looking at the t-test on the predictor in the fuller model.

But what do we do if we do not have nested models? That question arises in this example when we ask if I made a wise choice to use LogPctSAT rather than PctSAT as my predictor. Because the models using LogPctSAT as the predictor and the one using PctSAT as the predictor are not nested, we cannot simply test the difference in $SS_{\text{regression}}$ for the two models. Instead we are going to use **Akaike's Information Criterion (AIC)**, which is based on a likelihood ratio statistic that we will not explore. To compute Akaike's AIC statistic using SPSS you need to resort to tampering with the syntax, but that is fairly simple. You simply set up the regression as you normally would, being sure to ask for at least one statistic (e.g., coefficients). Then instead of submitting the analysis directly, choose the **Paste** option and edit the resulting syntax by adding "selection" to the statistics subcommand. You will have the following:

Akaike's Information Criterion (AIC)

```
REGRESSION
    /MISSING LISTWISE
    /STATISTICS COEFF OUTS SELECTION
    /CRITERIA=PIN(.05) POUT(.10)
    /NOORIGIN/DEPENDENT CombinedSAT
    /METHOD=ENTER expend PctSat.
```

If you do this for the two models, the model using PctSAT will give you the following summary.

Model Summary

					Selection Criteria			
Model	R	R Square	Adjusted R Square	Std. Error of the Estimate	Akaike Information Criterion	Amemiya Prediction Criterion	Mallows' Prediction Criterion	Schwarz Bayesian Criterion
1	.905[a]	.819	.812	32.459	350.906	.204	3.000	356.642

[a]Predictors: (Constant), PctSAT, Expend
Adapted from output by SPSS, Inc.

The model using LogPctSAT will next give you the following summary.

Model Summary

					Selection Criteria			
Model	R	R Square	Adjusted R Square	Std. Error of the Estimate	Akaike Information Criterion	Amemiya Prediction Criterion	Mallows' Prediction Criterion	Schwarz Bayesian Criterion
1	.941[a]	.886	.881	25.781	327.869	.128	3.000	333.605

[a]Predictors: (Constant), LogPctSAT, Expend
Adapted from output by SPSS, Inc.

With Akaike's AIC, smaller is better. Notice that you have a noticeably smaller AIC when LogPctSAT is the predictor. Unfortunately, there is no statistical test to tell us whether 327.869 is significantly smaller than 350.906. You will just have to take my word for it that using the log of the percentage of students taking the SAT is preferable.

15.11   Constructing a Regression Equation

A major problem for anyone who has ever attempted to write a regression equation to predict some criterion or to understand a set of relationships among variables concerns choosing the variables to be included in the model. We often suffer from having too many potential variables rather than too few. Although it would be possible to toss in all of the variables to see what would happen, this solution is neither practical nor wise. We have already seen that tolerance and the variance inflation factor can be useful in helping us to identify variables that are highly correlated with each other and thus redundant when it comes to predicting Y. But we also have other ways of optimizing our equation.

Selection Methods

There are many ways to construct some sort of "optimal" regression equation from a large set of variables. This section will briefly describe several of these approaches. But first we must raise the issue of whether this whole approach is generally appropriate. In many cases it is not.

If we assume that you have a large set of variables and a large number of data points, and are truly interested in a question of prediction (you want to predict who will do well at some job and have no particular theoretical axe to grind), then one of these methods may be for you. However, if you are trying to test some theoretical model by looking to see if certain variables are related to some outcome (e.g., can you predict adolescents' psychological symptoms on the basis of major stressful events, daily hassles, and parental stress), then choosing a model on the basis of some criterion such as the maximum R^2 or the minimum $MS_{residual}$ is not likely to be particularly helpful. In fact, it may be particularly harmful by causing you to focus on statistically derived models that fit only slightly, and perhaps nonsignificantly, better than some other more logically appropriate model. Conducting a stepwise analysis, for example, so as to report which of two competing psychological variables is second to enter the equation often adds a spurious form of statistical elegance to a poor theory. Solid arguments against the use of stepwise regression for the purpose of ordering variables by importance have been given by Huberty (1989). Henderson and Denison (1989), in an excellent article that summarizes many of the important issues, suggest that "stepwise regression" should be called "unwise regression."

On the assumption that you still want to construct a regression model using some form of variable-selection process, we will consider three alternative approaches: all subsets regression, backward elimination, and stepwise regression. A readable and much more thorough discussion of this topic can be found in Draper and Smith (1981, Chapter 6).

All Subsets Regression

all subsets regression

The simplest of these methods at a conceptual level is called all subsets regression for the rather obvious reason that it looks at all possible subsets of the predictor variables and chooses the set that is optimal in some way (such as maximizing R^2 or minimizing the mean square error). With three or four predictors and some patience you could conduct such an analysis by using any standard computer package to calculate multiple analyses. However, with a large number of variables the only way to go about this is to use a specialized program, such as SAS PROC RSQUARE, which allows you to specify the largest and smallest number of predictors to appear in each subset and the number of subsets of each size. (For example, you can say, "Give me the eight models with the highest R^2s using five predictors.")

You can define "best" in several different ways; these ways do not always lead to the same models. You can select models on the basis of (1) the magnitude of R^2, (2) the magnitude of $MS_{residual}$, (3) a statistic called Mallow's C_p, and (4) a statistic called PRESS. The magnitudes of R^2 and $MS_{residual}$ have already been discussed. We search for that combination of predictors with the highest R^2 (or better yet, adjusted R^2) or that set that minimizes error. Mallow's C_p statistic compares the relative magnitudes of the error term in any particular model with the error term in the complete model with all predictors present (see Draper & Smith, 1981, p. 299). As such it only applies to nested models, as does the PRESS statistic to follow. Because the error term in the reduced model must be greater than (or equal to) the error term in the full model, we want to minimize that ratio.

PRESS (Predicted RESidual Sum of Squares) is a statistic similar to $MS_{residual}$ in that it looks at $\sum(Y_i - \hat{Y}_i)^2$, but in the case of PRESS the predictions are made from a data set that includes all cases *except* the one to be predicted. Ordering models on the basis of PRESS would generally, though not always, be similar to ordering them on the basis of $MS_{residual}$. The advantage of PRESS is that it is more likely to focus on influential data points (see Draper & Smith, 1981, p. 325).

The major disadvantage of all subsets regression, aside from the enormous amount of computer time it can involve, is the fact that it has a substantial potential for capitalizing on chance. By fitting all possible models to the data, or at least the best of all possible models, you run the serious risk of selecting those models that best fit the peculiar data points that are unique to your data set. The final R^2 cannot reasonably be thought of as an unbiased estimate of the corresponding population parameter.

Backward Elimination

backward
elimination

The backward elimination procedure, as well as the stepwise regression procedure to fol-low, are generally lumped under the term *stepwise procedures* because they go about their task in a logical stepwise fashion. They both have the advantage of being easy to carry out interactively using standard regression procedures, although programs to carry them out automatically are readily available.

In the backward elimination procedure, we begin with a model that includes all of the predictors. Having computed that model, we examine the tests on the individual regression coefficients, or look at the partial or semipartial correlations and remove the variable that contributes the least to the model (assuming that its contribution is statistically nonsignifi-cant). We then rerun the regression without that predictor, again looking for the variable with the smallest contribution, remove that, and continue. Normally we continue until we come to a model in which all of the remaining predictors are statistically significant, although al-ternative stopping points are possible. For example, we could plot R^2 or $MS_{residual}$ against the number of predictors in the model and stop when that curve shows a break in direction.

Most computer programs that run backward elimination or stepwise regression use some combination of terms called "F to enter," "F to remove," "p to enter," and "p to remove." To take just one of these, consider "p to remove." If we plan to remove predic-tors from the model if they fail to reach significance at $\alpha = .05$, then we set "p to remove" at .05. The "F to remove" would simply be the critical value of F corresponding to that level of p.[10] (Those programs that calculate t statistics instead of F would simply make the appropriate change.) The situation is actually more complicated than I have made it seem (see Draper & Smith, 1981, p. 311), but for practical purposes it is as I have described.

An important disadvantage of backward elimination is that it too capitalizes on chance. Because it begins with many predictors, it has the opportunity to identify and account for any suppressor relations among variables that can be found in the data. For example, if variables 7 and 8 have some sort of suppressor relationship between them, this method has a good chance of finding it and making those variables a part of the model. If that is a true relationship, then backward elimination has done what we want it to. On the other hand, if the relationship is spurious, we have just wasted extra variables explaining something that does not deserve explanation. Darlington (1990, p. 166) made this point about both backward elimination and all subsets regression. True suppressor relationships are fairly rare, but apparent ones are fairly common. Therefore, methods that systematically look for them, especially without accompanying hypothesis tests, may be misleading more often than simpler methods that ignore them.

Stepwise Regression

stepwise
regression

The stepwise regression method is more or less the reverse of the backward elimination method.[11] However, because at each stage we do not have all of the other variables in the model and therefore immediately available to test, as we did with backward elimination, we will go about it in a slightly different way.

---

[10] As Draper and Smith (1981) point out, when we are testing *optimal* models the F statistics are not normal Fs and their probability values should not be interpreted as if they were. Thus, although both F and p form the basis of a le-gitimate ordering of potential variables, do not put too much faith in the actual probabilities. McIntyre, Montgomery, Srinivason, and Weitz (1983) address this problem directly and illustrate the liberal nature of the test. They also pro-vide guidelines on more appropriate tests on stepwise correlation coefficients, should you wish to follow this route.

[11] The terminology here is terrible, but you'll just have to bear with me. Backward elimination is *a* stepwise pro-cedure, as is forward elimination, but when we refer to *the* stepwise approach we normally mean the procedure that I'm about to discuss.

Stepwise regression relies on the fact that

$$R_{0.123\ldots p}^2 = r_{01}^2 + r_{0(2.1)}^2 + r_{p(3.12)}^2 + \cdots$$

If we define variable 1 as that variable with the highest validity (correlation with the criterion), then the first step in the process involves only variable 1. We then calculate all semipartials of the form $r_{0(i.1)}$, $i = 2 \ldots p$. The variable (assume that it is X_2) with the highest (first-order) semipartial correlation with the criterion is the one that will produce the greatest increment in R^2. This variable is then entered and we obtain the regression of Y on X_1 and X_2. We now test to see whether that variable contributes significantly to the model containing two variables. We could either test the regression coefficient or the semipartial correlation directly, or test to see if there was a significant increment in R^2. The result would be the same. Because the test on the increment in R^2 will prove useful later, we will do it that way here. A test on the difference between an R^2 based on f predictors and an R^2 based on r predictors (where the r predictors are a subset of the f predictors) is given by

$$F_{(f-r, \, N-f-1)} = \frac{(N - f - 1)(R_f^2 - R_r^2)}{(f - r)(1 - R_f^2)}$$

where R_f^2 is the R^2 for the full model $= R_{0.12}^2$, R_r^2 is the R^2 for the reduced model $= R_{0.1}^2$, f is the number of predictors in the full model, and r is the number of predictors in the reduced model.

This process is repeated until the addition of further variables produces no significant (by whatever criterion we wish to use) improvement. At each step in the process, before we add a new variable we first ask whether a variable that was added on an earlier step should now be removed on the grounds that it is no longer making a significant contribution. If the test on a variable falls below "F to remove" (or above "p to remove") that variable is removed before another variable is added. Procedures that do not include this step are often referred to as **forward selection** procedures.

forward selection

Of the three variable selection methods discussed here, the stepwise regression method is probably the best. Both Draper and Smith (1981) and Darlington (1990) recommend it as the best compromise between finding an "optimal" equation for predicting future randomly selected data sets from the same population and finding an equation that predicts the maximum variance for the specific data set under consideration. I would phrase things somewhat differently. Instead of saying that it is the best compromise, I would say that it is the best of a set of poor choices. I recommend against any mechanistic way of arriving at a final solution. You need to make use of what you know about your variables and what you see in separate regressions. You probably have at least some theoretical reasons for choosing certain variables.

Cross-Validation

cross-validation

The stumbling block for most multiple regression studies is the concept of **cross-validation** of the regression equation against an independent data set. For example we might break our data into two or more data sets and derive a regression equation for the first set. We then apply the regression coefficients obtained from that sample against the data in the other sample to obtain predicted values of Y on a cross-validation sample ($\hat{Y}_{cv}$). Our interest then focuses on the question of the relationship between Y and $\hat{Y}_{cv}$ in the new subsample. If the regression equations have any reasonable level of validity, then the cross-validation correlation (R_{cv}—the correlation between Y and $\hat{Y}_{cv}$ predicted on the *other* sample's regression equation) should be high. If they do not, our solution does not amount to much. R_{cv}^2 will in almost all cases be less than R^2, because R^2 depends on a regression equation tailored for that set of data. Essentially, we have an equation that does its best to account for every bump and wiggle (including sampling error) in the data. We should not be surprised when it does not do as well in accounting for different bumps and wiggles in a different set of data. However, substantial differences between R^2 and R_{cv}^2 are an indication that our solution lacks appreciable validity.

Missing Observations

imputing deletion

casewise deletion

pairwise deletion

Missing data are often a problem in regression analyses, and a number of alternative methods have been devised to deal with them. The most common approach is simply to delete all cases not having complete data on the variables being investigated. This is called **listwise** (or **casewise**) **deletion**, because when an observation is missing we delete the whole case.

A second approach, which is available in SPSS but is deliberately not available in many programs, is called **pairwise deletion**. Here we use whatever data are at hand. If the 13th subject has data on both X and Y, then that subject is included in the calculation of r_{XY}. But if subject 13 does not have a score on Z, that subject is not included in the calculation of r_{XZ} or r_{YZ}. Once the complete intercorrelation matrix has been computed using pairwise deletion, the rest of the regression solution follows directly from that matrix.

Both of these solutions have their problems. Listwise deletion may result in relatively low sample sizes, and, if the data are not missing completely at random, in samples that are not a fair reflection of the population from which they were presumably sampled. Pairwise deletion, on the other hand, can result in an intercorrelation matrix that does not resemble the matrix that we would have if we had complete data on all cases. In fact, pairwise deletion can result in an "impossible" intercorrelation matrix. It is well known that given r_{XY} and r_{XZ}, the correlation between Y and Z *must* fall within certain limits. But if we keep changing the data that go into the correlations, we could obtain an r_{YZ} that is inconsistent with the other two correlations. When we then try to use such an inconsistent matrix, we find ourselves in serious trouble.

imputing

In recent years considerable attention has focused on **imputing** additional values to take the place of missing values. Basically we replace missing values by some optimal guess as to what they would be if we had them. There are a large number of ways that this can be done, but perhaps the easiest to see, but certainly not the best, is regression imputation. In regression imputation you run a regression, using the observations you have, to predict one independent variable from values of the other variables, perhaps using listwise deletion. When you have created your regression equation you then plug in the subject's scores on existing variables and predict that person's score on the missing variable. In this way you can systematically replace all of the missing data. You can then run your analysis on the complete data set. I want to stress that I do not recommend this particular approach, but I present it because it gives you a sense of the approaches that I do recommend. The important point is to see that the data that we have are used to make intelligent estimates of the observations that we don't have. A much more complete treatment of missing data is available in Howell (2008b) and at http://www.uvm.edu/~dhowell/StatPages/More_Stuff /Missing_Data/Missing.html.

15.12 The "Importance" of Individual Variables

When an investigator derives a regression equation to predict some criterion on the basis of several variables, it is logical for her to want to know which of the variables is most important in predicting Y. Unfortunately, that question has no simple answer, except in the unusual case in which the predictors are mutually independent. As we have seen, β_j (or β_j^2) is sometimes taken as a measure of importance. This is done on the grounds that β^2 can be interpreted as the *unique* contribution of each variable to the prediction of Y. Thus, X_1 has some variance in common with Y that is not shared by any of the other variables, and this variance is represented by β_1^2. The difficulty with this measure is that it has nothing to say about the portion of the variance of Y that X_1 *does* share with the other variables but that is in some sense part of the contribution of X_1 to the prediction of Y. Moreover, what does it mean to speak of the independent contribution of variables that are not independent?

Darlington (1990) has argued against using β_j as a measure of importance. β_j does represent the difference, in standard deviation units, between two cases that are equal on all other predictor variables but differ by one unit on X_j. However, this does not take into account the fact that when variables are highly correlated such cases will rarely, if ever, exist.

Basing a measure of importance on the β weights has the further serious drawback that when variables are highly correlated (a condition known as multicollinearity), the values of β are very unstable from sample to sample, although R^2 may change very little. Given two sets of data, it would not be particularly unusual to find

$$\hat{Y} = 0.50Z_1 + 0.25Z_2$$

in one case and

$$\hat{Y} = 0.25Z_1 + 0.50Z_2$$

in the other, with nearly equal values of R^2 associated with the two equations. If we now seek a measure of the contribution of each of the predictors in accounting for Y (as opposed to using regression to simply predict Y for a given set of data), we could come to quite different conclusions for the two data sets. Darlington (1968) presents an interesting discussion of this issue and concludes that β_i has only limited utility as a measure of "importance." An even stronger stand is taken by Cooley and Lohnes (1971), who point out that our estimate of β ultimately relies on our estimates of the elements of the intercorrelation matrix. Because this matrix contains $p + p(p - 1)/2$ intercorrelations that are all subject to sampling error, Cooley and Lohnes suggested that we must be exceedingly careful about attaching practical significance to the regression coefficients.

It is easy to illustrate the problem we have here. In earlier editions of this book I used an example in which 50 university courses were rated on several variables and a regression equation was computed to predict the overall rating from the ratings of other variables, such as how good a teacher the instructor was, how fair the exams were, and so on. The regression equation that was derived from that data set, using standardized regression coefficients, was

$$Z_{\hat{Y}} = 0.662\,\text{Teach} + 0.106\,\text{Exam} + 0.325\,\text{Knowledge} - 0.105\,\text{Grade} + 0.124\,\text{Enroll}$$

The multiple R^2 was .755. I then took a second set of 50 courses sampled from the same source as the original data. In this case, R^2 was more or less the same as it had been for the first example ($R^2 = .710$), but the regression equation looked quite different. In terms of standardized variables the equation was,

$$Z_{\hat{Y}} = 0.371\,\text{Teach} + 0.113\,\text{Exam} + 0.567\,\text{Knowledge} - 0.27\,\text{Grade} + 0.184\,\text{Enroll}$$

If you compare these two equations, it is clear that there are substantial differences in some of the values of β_i.

Another measure of importance, which has much to recommend it, is the squared semipartial correlation between predictor j and the criterion (with all other predictors partialled out of predictor j)—that is, $r_{0(i.123...p)}^2$. Darlington (1968) refers to this measure as the "usefulness" of a predictor. As we have already seen, this squared semipartial correlation represents the decrement in R^2 that would result from the elimination of the ith predictor from the model (or the increment that would result from its addition). When the main goal is prediction rather than explanation, this is probably the best measure of "importance." Fortunately, it is easy to obtain from most computer printouts, because

$$r_{0(i.123...p)}^2 = \frac{F_i(1 - R_{0.123...p}^2)}{N - p - 1}$$

where F_i is the F test on the individual β_i (or b_i) coefficients. (If your program uses t tests on the coefficient, $F = t^2$.) Because all terms but F_i are constant for $i = 1 \ldots p$, the F_is order the variables in the same way as do the squared semipartials, and thus can be used to rank order the variables in terms of their usefulness.

Darlington (1990) has made a strong case for not squaring the semipartial correlation when speaking about the importance of variables. His case is an interesting one. However, whether or not the correlations are squared will not affect the ordering of variables. (If you wish to argue persuasively about the absolute importance of a variable, you should read Darlington's argument.)

One common, but unacceptable, method of ordering the importance of variables is to rank them by the order of their inclusion in a stepwise regression solution. The problem with this approach is that it ignores the interrelationships among the variables. Thus, the first variable to be entered is entered solely on the strength of its correlation with the criterion. The second variable entered is chosen on the basis of its correlation with the criterion after partialling the first variable but ignoring all others. The third is chosen on the basis of how it correlates with the criterion after partialling the first two variables, and so on. In other words, each variable is chosen on a different basis, and it makes little sense to rank them according to order of entry. To take a simple example, assume that variables 1, 2, and 3 correlate .79, .78, and .32 with the criterion. Assume further that variables 1 and 2 are correlated .95, whereas 1 and 3 are correlated .20. They will then enter the equation in the order 1, 3, and 2, with the last entry being nonsignificant. But in what sense do we mean to say that variable 3 ranks above variable 2 in importance? I would hate to defend such a statement to a reviewer—in fact, I would be hard pressed even to say what I meant by importance in this situation. A similar point has been made well by Huberty (1989). For an excellent discussion of measures of importance, see Harris (1985, 79ff).

15.13 Using Approximate Regression Coefficients

I have pointed out that regression coefficients frequently show substantial fluctuations from sample to sample without producing drastic changes in R. This might lead someone to suggest that we might use rather crude approximations of these coefficients as a substitute for the more precise estimates obtained from the data. For example, suppose that a five-predictor problem produced the following regression equation:

$$\hat{Y} = 9.2 + 0.85X_1 + 2.1X_2 - 0.74X_3 + 3.6X_4 - 2.4X_5$$

We might ask how much loss we would suffer if we rounded these values to

$$\hat{Y} = 10 + 1X_1 + 2X_2 - 1X_3 + 4X_4 - 2X_5$$

The answer is that we would probably lose very little. Excellent discussions of this problem are given by Cohen et al. (2003), Dawes and Corrigan (1974), and Wainer (1976, 1978).

This method of rounding off regression coefficients is more common than you might suppose. For example, the college admissions officer who quantifies the various predictors he has available and then weights the grade point average twice as highly as the letter of recommendation is really using crude estimates of what he thinks would be the actual regression coefficients. Similarly, many scoring systems for the Minnesota Multiphasic Personality Inventory (MMPI) are in fact based on the reduction of coefficients to convenient integers. Whether the use of these *diagnostic signs* produces results that are better than, worse than, or equivalent to the use of the usual linear regression equations is still a matter of debate. A dated but very comprehensive study of this question is presented in Goldberg (1965). Rather than undermining our confidence in multiple regression, I think the fact that rounded-off coefficients do nearly as well (sometimes better if we are applying them to new data) speaks to the robustness of regression. It also suggests that you not put too much faith in small differences in coefficients.

15.14   Mediating and Moderating Relationships

One of the most frequently cited papers the psychological literature related to multiple regression in the past 25 years has been a paper by Baron and Kenny (1986) on what they called the moderator-mediator distinction. The important point for both moderating and mediating relationships is that a third variable plays an important role in governing the relationship between two other variables. I will spend more than the usual amount of space on this issue because it directly addresses some of the things that psychologists really care about. It is one attempt to explain relationships that we see in data by looking closely at the underlying mechanism behind such a relationship.

Mediation
mediating relationship

A **mediating relationship** is what it sounds like—some variable mediates the relationship between two other variables. For example, take a situation I referred to earlier, in which high levels of care from your parents leads to feelings of competence and self-esteem on your part, which, in turn, leads to high confidence in your abilities (efficacy) when you become a mother. Here we would say that your feelings of competence and self-esteem *mediate* the relationship between how you were parented and how you feel about mothering your own children.

Baron and Kenny (1986) wrote a very influential paper in which they examined the whole issue of mediation. Their approach laid out several requirements that they felt must be met before we can speak of a mediating relationship. Although the necessity of these rules is controversial, we will start with them and then move on. Consider the diagram below as being representative of a mediating relationship that we want to explain.

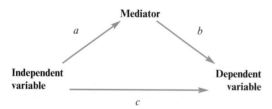

© Cengage Learning 2013

The predominant relationship that we want to explain is labeled "*c*," and is the direct path from the independent to the dependent variable. The mediating path has two parts, comprised of "*a*," the path connecting the independent variable to the potential mediator, and "*b*," the path connecting that mediator to the dependent variable.

Baron and Kenny argued that for us to claim a mediating relationship, we need to first show that there is a significant relationship between the independent variable and the mediator. That may seem obvious, but it is in fact controversial. The next step is to show that there is a significant relationship between the mediator and the dependent variable, for reasons similar to those for the first requirement, and between the independent and dependent variable. (Although these requirements sound perfectly logical, a good case can be made that none of them is necessary (see Hayes, 2009).) MacKinnon, Lockwood, Hoffman, West, and Sheets (2002) have also shown that basing mediation on such requirements results in very low statistical power.

These three conditions require that the three paths (a, b, and c) are all individually significant. Baron and Kenny's final step consists of demonstrating that when the mediator and the independent variable are used simultaneously to predict the dependent variable, the previously significant path between the independent and dependent variables (c) is now greatly reduced, if not nonsignificant. In other words, when we partial the mediator out of the relationship, the relationship between the independent and dependent variable is noticeably reduced. Maximum evidence for mediation would occur if c drops to 0. In my experience I have never seen a path go away completely. Most likely to happen is that c becomes a weaker, though perhaps still significant, path.

Leerkes and Crockenberg (1999) were interested in studying the relationship between how children were raised by their own mothers, and their later feelings of maternal self-efficacy when they, in turn, became mothers. Their sample consisted of 92 mothers of five-month-old infants. They expected to find that high levels of maternal care when the mother was a child translated to high levels of self-efficacy when that child later became a mother. But Leerkes and Crockenberg went further, postulating that the mediating variable in this relationship is self-esteem. They argued that high levels of maternal care lead to high levels of self-esteem in the child, and that this high self-esteem later translates into high levels of self-efficacy as a mother. Similarly, low levels of maternal care are expected to lead to low levels of self-esteem, and thus to low levels of self-efficacy. This relationship is diagrammed below.

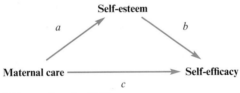

© Cengage Learning 2013

If we want to require Baron and Kenny's initial conditions, they can be tested by looking at the simple correlations among the variables. These are shown below as produced by SPSS.

		Correlations		
		MatCare	Esteem	Efficacy
MatCare	Pearson Correlation	1	.403**	.267*
	Sig. (2-tailed)		.000	.010
	N	92	92	92
Esteem	Pearson Correlation	.403**	1	.377**
	Sig. (2-tailed)	.000		.000
	N	92	92	92
Efficacy	Pearson Correlation	.267*	.377**	1
	Sig. (2-tailed)	.010	.000	
	N	92	92	92

Adapted from output by SPSS, Inc.

**Correlation is significant at the 0.01 level (2-tailed).
*Correlation is significant at the 0.05 level (2-tailed).

Here we can see that maternal care is correlated with self-esteem and with self-efficacy, and that self-esteem is also correlated with self-efficacy. These relationships satisfy Baron and Kenny's basic prerequisites. The next step is to use both self-esteem and maternal care as predictors of self-efficacy. This is shown in the following output, where the dependent variable is self-efficacy.

Coefficients[a]

Model		Unstandardized Coefficients		Standardized Coefficients			Correlations		
		B	Std. Error	Beta	t	Sig.	Zero-order	Partial	Part
1	(Constant)	3.266	.140		23.243	.000			
	MatCare	.110	.042	.267	2.631	.010	.267	.267	.267
2	(Constant)	2.936	.173		16.954	.000			
	MatCare	.057	.044	.138	1.297	.198	.267	136	.126
	Esteem	.146	.048	.321	3.022	.003	.377	.305	.294

[a]Dependent Variable: Efficacy

Adapted from output by SPSS, Inc.

The first model in this table uses maternal care as the sole predictor. The second model has added self-esteem as a predictor. Here you can see that when we add self-esteem to maternal care, which was clearly significant when used alone to predict self-efficacy, maternal care is no longer significant ($t = 1.297$, $p = 0.198$). This is evidence that self-esteem is serving a mediating role between maternal care and self-efficacy. The output also shows what SPSS calls the "part correlation," but which the rest of us call the semipartial correlation. The semipartial correlation between maternal care and self-efficacy, partialling out self-esteem, is 0.126, whereas the simple correlation (zero-order) between maternal care and self-efficacy was 0.287.

These results support Leerkes and Crockenberg's hypothesis that self-esteem played a mediating role between maternal care and self-efficacy. Caring parents seem to produce children with higher levels of self-esteem, and this higher self-esteem translates into positive feelings of self-efficacy when the child, in turn, becomes a mother.

In this situation Leerkes and Crockenberg were fortunate to have a situation in which the direct path from maternal care to self-efficacy dropped to nonsignificance when self-esteem was added, thus meeting Baron and Kenny's second requirement. Unfortunately, that does not always happen. (In fact, it seems to happen relatively infrequently.) The more common result is that the direct path becomes less important, though it remains significant. There has been considerable discussion about what to do in this situation. We will look at two quite different approaches. Sobel (1982) proposed a relatively simple test that was advocated by Baron and Kenny. That test is given below, but it has several problems. In the first place, no one seems to agree on the standard error that is needed to form the t ratio. Moreover, it assumes that the sampling distribution of the indirect effect (Maternal care $\rightarrow$ Self Esteem $\rightarrow$ Self-Efficacy) is normally distributed, when we know that it usually is not. We will see that shortly.

When we have a situation in which the direct path remains significant, though at a lower value, one way to test for a mediating relationship is to ask whether the complete mediating path from independent variable to mediator to dependent variable is significant. That is what the Sobel test does. To do this we need to know the regression coefficients and their standard errors for the two paths in the mediating chain.

The important statistics from the two regressions are shown in Table 15.4. Because SPSS does not report the standard error of beta, we need to calculate it. The t statistic given in these tables can be computed as either the unstandardized regression coefficient

Table 15.4   Regression coefficients and standard errors for two parts of mediating path

Path *a*		Path *b* (partialling MatCare)	
Maternal Care →	Self-Esteem	Self-Esteem →	Self-Efficacy
b	0.364	*b*	0.146
β	0.403	β	0.321
$S_{\beta a}$	0.096	$S_{\beta b}$	.106
t	4.178*	*t*	3.033*

© Cengage Learning 2013

(*b*) divided by its standard error, or the standardized regression coefficient divided by its standard error. Thus we can solve

$$t = \frac{\beta}{s_\beta}; \quad s_\beta = \frac{\beta}{t} = \frac{0.403}{4.178} = 0.096$$

Similarly for the path from Self-esteem to Self-efficacy, partialling Maternal care, we have

$$t = \frac{\beta}{s_\beta}; \quad s_\beta = \frac{\beta}{t} = \frac{0.323}{3.041} = 0.106$$

These results yield the following Table 15-4.

Then the regression coefficient for the path from Maternal care → Self-esteem → Self-efficacy is equal to $\beta_a \times \beta_b = 0.403 \times 0.321 = 0.129$, where *a* and *b* refer to the relevant paths. Notice that this is also equal to the semipartial correlation between maternal care and self-efficacy, partialling out self-esteem. (Path *c* is the direct path from Maternal care to Self-efficacy.) In addition, we know that the standard error of this two-part path is given by

$$s_{\beta_a \beta_b} = \sqrt{\beta_a^2 s_b^2 + \beta_b^2 s_a^2 - s_a^2 s_b^2}$$

where β_a and β_b are the paths, and s_a^2 and s_b^2 are the corresponding squared standard errors of the standardized regression coefficients for those paths.[12] We can calculate the standard error of the combined path as:

$$s_{\beta_a \beta_b} = \sqrt{\beta_a^2 s_b^2 + \beta_b^2 s_a^2 - s_a^2 s_b^2} = \sqrt{.403^2(.106^2) + .321^2(.096^2) - (.106^2)(.096^2)}$$
$$= \sqrt{0.0027}$$
$$= 0.052$$

We now know the path coefficient ($0.403 \times 0.321 = 0.129$) and its standard error (0.052), and we can form a *t* ratio as

$$t = \frac{\beta_a \beta_b}{s_{\beta_a \beta_b}} = \frac{.129}{.052} = 2.48$$

Sobel (1982) stated that this ratio is asymptotically normally distributed, which, for large samples, would lead to rejection of the null hypothesis at $\alpha = 0.05$ when the ratio exceeds ± 1.96. It would presumably have a *t* distribution on $N - 3$ *df* for small samples. In our case the path is clearly significant, as we would expect from the previous results. Therefore we can conclude that we have convincing evidence of a strong mediating pathway from maternal care through self-esteem to self-efficacy. Because the regression coefficient

---

[12] As I mentioned earlier, there is disagreement over the exact form of these equations, but the one given here is recommended by Baron and Kenny.

(and semipartial correlation) for the direct path from maternal care to self-efficacy is not significant, the main influence of maternal care is through its mediating relationship with self-esteem.

An Alternative Approach Using Bootstrapping

The original paper by Baron and Kenny, while extremely influential in helping us to understand mediation, has been challenged on several grounds. (See MacKinnon, Lockwood, Hoffman, West, and Sheets (2002).) Preacher and Hayes (2009) have made a persuasive case that the rules set forth by Baron and Kenny and the test put forth by Sobel should be ignored and replaced with a bootstrapping approach testing only the statistical significance of the indirect path. For an explanation of why Baron and Kenny's rules are not necessary, even though they seem quite reasonable on the surface, see the Preacher and Hayes's paper.

We will begin with the model that Leerkes and Crockenberg derived, as shown below.

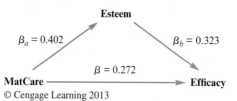

© Cengage Learning 2013

The indirect path from MatCare to Efficacy via Esteem can be defined as $\beta_a \times \beta_b = 0.402 \times 0.323 = 0.130$. The question is whether this path is statistically significantly different from 0.00. One approach to asking this question is to create a bootstrap sample by making 10,000 draws with replacement of 92 observations, each from the original data. For each draw we will calculate the standardized regression coefficients and compute $\beta_a\beta_b$. The distribution of these 10,000 values will be the sampling distribution of $\beta_a\beta_b$, and its standard deviation will be the standard error of $\beta_a\beta_b$. We can then take the values that cut off the 2.5 and 97.5 percentiles as our confidence limits on the indirect path. If those limits do not include 0.00, we can conclude that the indirect path is significant. (A program written in R to perform this resampling can be found on this book's Web site.)

This result is shown on the left in Figure 15.7 below. You can see that the sampling distribution is somewhat positively skewed. The confidence limits are shown on the figure

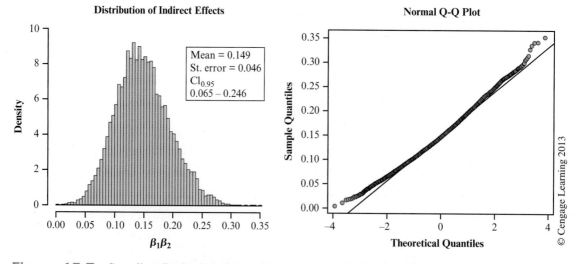

Figure 15.7   Sampling distribution of the indirect path from MatCare to Efficacy

as $0.065 \leq \beta_a\beta_b \leq 0.246$, and these do not include 0.00, leading us to declare the indirect path to be significant. On the right of that figure you see the Q-Q plot illustrating again that the sampling distribution is skewed, as Hayes has pointed out that it should be, although with 92 observations in each sample the skew is not too extreme.

There has been considerable discussion in the literature about the best approach to testing mediation. For an online t-test approach using three alternative estimations of the standard error, go to http://people.ku.edu/~preacher/sobel/sobel.htm Preacher and Hayes (2004) (available at that Web site) present SPSS and SAS macros that allow you to use bootstrapping methods to address this question. A very well-written description of mediation has been put on the Web by Paul Jose, at the University of Wellington. It can be found at http://www.victoria.ac.nz/psyc/paul-jose-files/helpcentre/help7 _mediation_example.php. In addition, Jose offers a free mediation calculator, which runs under Excel, at http://www.victoria.ac.nz/psyc/paul-jose-files/medgraph/medgraph. php I have found that very useful. Finally, an extensive comparison of alternative approaches can be found in MacKinnon, Lockwood, Hoffman, West, and Sheets (2002). A good discussion of the whole issue of mediating and moderating relationships can be found in Beaujian (2008).

Moderating Relationships

moderating
relationships

Whereas a mediating relationship attempts to identify a variable or variables through which the independent variable acts to influence the dependent variable, **moderating relationships** refer to situations in which the relationship between the independent and dependent variables changes as a function of the level of a third variable (the moderator).

Wagner, Compas, and Howell (1988) hypothesized that individuals who experience more stress, as assessed by a measure of daily hassles, will exhibit higher levels of symptoms than those who experience little stress. That is what, in analysis of variance terms, would be the main effect of hassles. However, they also expected that if a person had a high level of social support to help deal with his or her stress, symptoms would increase only slowly with increases in hassles. For those who had relatively little social support, symptoms were expected to rise more quickly as hassles increased.

Wagner et al. (1988) studied students who were attending an orientation before starting their first year of college. Students were asked to report on the number of minor stressful events (labeled hassles) that they had recently experienced, and also to report on their perceived level of social support. They then completed a symptom checklist on the number of symptoms they had experienced in the past month. For this part of the study there were complete data on 56 participants. These data are available on the Web in a file named hassles.dat.

Our first step is to look at the relationships between these variables. The correlation matrix is shown below.

Correlations

Pearson Correlation

	Hassles	Support	Symptoms
Hassles	1.000	−.167	.577**
Support	−.167	1.000	−.134
Symptoms	.577**	−.134	1.000

** Correlation is significant at the 0.01 level

© Cengage Learning 2013

As expected, there is a significant relationship between Hassles and Symptoms ($r = .577$), though Support is not related to Symptoms, or to Hassles. This does not, however, answer the question that they really wanted to ask, which is whether the relationship between Hassles and Symptoms depends on the degree of social support.[13]

If you think about this question it starts to sound very much like the question behind an interaction in the analysis of variance. In fact, it is an interaction, and the way that we will test for that interaction is to create a variable that is the product of Hassles and Support. (This is also similar to what we will do in the general linear model approach to the analysis of variance in the next chapter.) However, if we just multiply Hassles and Support together, there will be two problems with what results. In the first place, either Hassles or Support or both will be highly correlated with their product, which will make for multicollinearity in the data. This will seriously affect the magnitude, and tests of significance, of the coefficients for the main effect of Hassles and Support. The second problem is that any effect of Hassles or Support in the regression analysis will be evaluated at a value of 0 for the other variable. In other words the test on Hassles will be a test on whether Hassles is related to Symptoms if a participant had exactly no social support. Similarly the test on Support would be evaluated for those participants who have exactly no hassles. Both the problem of multicollinearity and the problem of evaluating one main effect at an extreme value of the other main effect are unwelcome.

center

To circumvent these two problems we are going to **center** our data. This means that we are going to create deviation scores by subtracting each variable's mean from the individual observations. After doing so a score of 0 for (centered) Hassles represents someone who has the mean level of Hassles, which seems an appropriate place to examine any effects of support, and anyone with a 0 on (centered) support represents someone with a mean level of support. This has solved one of our problems, because we are now evaluating the main effects at a reasonable level of the other main effect. It has also helped to solve our other problem, because if you look at the resulting correlations, multicollinearity will have been significantly reduced.

Having centered our variables we will then form a product of our centered variables, and this will represent our interaction term. The means for hassles, support, and symptoms are 170.1964, 28.9643, and 90.4286, respectively, and the equations for creating centered variables and their interaction follow. The letter "c" at the beginning of the variable name indicates that it is centered.

chassles = hassles − 170.1964

csupport = support − 28.9643

chassupp = chassles × csupport

The correlations among the centered (and uncentered) variables are shown in the following table. I have included the product of the uncentered variables simply to show how high the correlation between hassles and hassupp is, but we are not going to use this variable. You can see that by centering the variables we have substantially reduced the correlation between the main effects and the interactions. That was our goal. Notice that centering the variables did not change their correlations with each other—only with the interaction.

We can now examine the interaction of the two predictor variables by including the interaction term in the regression with the other centered predictors. The dependent variable is Symptoms. This regression is shown in Table 15.5. (As long as we use the product

Correlations

Pearson Correlation

	Hassles	Support	Symptoms	hassupp	chassles	csupport	chassupp
Hassles	1.000	−.167	.577**	.910**	1.000**	−.167	−.297*
Support	−.167	1.000	−.134	−.510**	−.167	1.000**	.402**
Symptoms	.577**	−.134	1.000	.585**	.577**	−.134	−.391**
hassupp	.910**	−.510**	.585**	1.000	.910**	−.510**	−.576**
chassles	1.000**	−.167	.577**	.910**	1.000	−.167	−.297*
csupport	−.167	1.000**	−.134	−.510**	−.167	1.000	.402**
chassupp	−.297*	.402**	−.391**	−.576**	−.297*	.402**	1.000

© Cengage Learning 2013

** Correlation is significant at the 0.01 level (2-tailed).
* Correlation is significant at the 0.05 level (2-tailed).

Table 15.5 Regression solution for moderated relationship between hassles and symptoms

Model Summary

Model	R	R Square	Adjusted R Square	Std. Error of the Estimate
1	.623[a]	.388	.353	16.8932

[a]Predictors: (Constant), CHASSUPP, CHASSLES, CSUPPORT

ANOVA[b]

Model		Sum of Squares	df	Mean Square	F	Sig.
1	Regression	9427.898	3	3142.633	11.012	.000[a]
	Residual	14839.816	52	285.381		
	Total	24267.714	55			

[a]Predictors: (Constant), chassupp, chassles, csupport
[b]Dependent Variable: Symptoms

Coefficients[a]

Model		Unstandardized Coefficients		Standardized Coefficients	t	Sig.
		B	Std. Error	Beta		
1	(Constant)	89.585	2.292		39.094	.000
	chassles	8.594E-02	.019	.509	4.473	.000
	csupport	.146	.305	.057	.479	.634
	chassupp	−5.06E-03	.002	−.262	−2.144	.037

[a] Dependent Variable: Symptoms
Adapted from output by SPSS, Inc.

of centered variables, it doesn't matter [except for the intercept] if we use the centered or uncentered main effects. I have used the centered ones here.)

From the printout you can see that $R^2 = .388$, which is significant. (Without the interaction term, R^2 would have been .334 (not shown).) From the table of regression coefficients you see that both the centered hassles and the interaction terms are significant ($p = .000$ and .037, respectively), but the social support variable is not significant. By convention we leave social support in our regression solution, because it is involved in the interaction, even though the associated t value shows that deleting that variable would not lead to a significant decrease in R^2.

Our regression equation now becomes

$$\hat{Y} = .086 \text{ chassles} + 0.146 \text{ csupport} - .005 \text{chassupp} + 89.585.$$

We have answered our initial questions (social support does moderate the relationship between hassles and symptoms), but it would be helpful if we could view this graphically to interpret the meaning of the interactive effect. Excellent discussions of this approach can be found in Finney, Mitchell, Cronkite, and Moos (1984), Jaccard, Turrisi, and Wan (1990), and Aiken and West (1991). The latter is the authoritative work on moderation. Normand Péladeau has a free program called Italassi,[14] available on the web at http://www.provalis-research.com/. This program will plot the interaction on your screen and provides a slider so that you can vary the level of the support variable.

The simplest solution is to look at the relationship between chassles and csymptoms for fixed levels of social support. Examination of the distribution of csupport scores shows that they range from about -21 to $+19$. Thus scores of $-15, 0$, and $+15$ would represent low, neutral, and high scores on csupport. (You don't have to be satisfied with these particular values, you can use any that you like. I have picked extremes to better illustrate what is going on.)

First I will rewrite the regression equation, substituting generic labels for the regression coefficients. I will also substitute chassles $\times$ csupport for chassupp, because that is the way that I calculated chssupp. Finally, I will also reorder the terms a bit just to make life easier.

$$\hat{Y} = b_1 \text{chassles} + b_2 \text{csupport} - b_3 \text{chassupp} + b_0$$
$$\hat{Y} = b_0 + b_2 \text{csupport} + b_3 (\text{chassles} \times \text{csupport}) + b_1 \text{chassles}$$

Collecting terms I have

$$\hat{Y} = b_0 + b_2 \text{csupport} + \text{chassles}(b_3 \text{csupport} + b_1)$$

Next I will substitute the actual regression coefficients to get

$$\hat{Y} = [89.585 + 0.146 \text{csupport}] + \text{chassles}(-.005 \text{csupport} + .086)$$

Notice the first term in square brackets. For any specific level of csupport (e.g., 15) this is a constant. Similarly, for the terms in parentheses after chassles, that is also a constant for a fixed level of support. To see this most easily, we can solve for $\hat{Y}$ when csupport is at 15, which is a high level of support. This gives us

$$\hat{Y} = [89.585 + 0.146 \times 15] + \text{chassles}(-.005 \times 15 + .086)$$
$$= 91.755 + 0.011 \times \text{chassles}$$

which is just a plain old linear equation. This is the equation that represents the relationship between $\hat{Y}$ and chassles when social support is high (i.e., 15).

Now we can derive two more simple linear equations, one by substituting 0 for csupport and one by substituting -15.

---

[14] Although there is a charge for the Peladeau's SimStat program, the Italassi program is free.

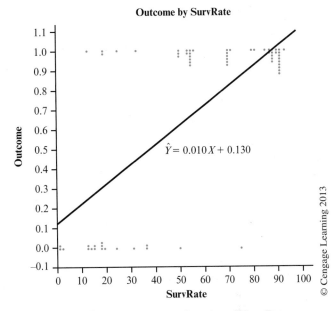

Figure 15.9   Outcome as a function of SurvRate

One way to look at the relationship between SurvRate and Outcome would be to simply create a scatterplot of the two variables, with Outcome on the *Y* axis. Such a plot is given in Figure 15.9. (In this figure I have offset overlapping points slightly so that you could see them pile up. That explains why there seems to be string of points at SurvRate = 91 and Outcome = 1, for example.) From this plot it is apparent that the proportion of people who improve is much higher when the survival rating is high, as we would expect. Assume for the moment that we had a great many subjects and could calculate the mean Outcome score (the mean of 0s and 1s) associated with each value of SurvRate. (These are **conditional means** because they are conditional on the value of SurvRate.) The conditional means would be the proportion of people with that value of SurvRate who improved. If we fit a standard regression line to these data, this would be the regression line that fits the *probability* of improvement as a function of SurvRate. But as you can imagine, for many values of SurvRate the *predicted* probability would be outside the bounds 0 and 1, which is impossible. That alone would make standard linear regression a poor choice. There is a second problem. If you were to calculate the *variances* of Outcome for different values of SurvRate, you would see that they are quite small for both large and small values of SurvRate (because almost everyone with low values of SurvRate has a 0 and almost everyone with high values of SurvRate has a 1). But for people with mid-level SurvRate values there is nearly an even mix of 0s and 1s, which will produce a relatively larger variance. This will clearly violate our assumption of homogeneity of variance in arrays, to say nothing of normality. Because of these problems, standard linear regression is not a wise choice with a dichotomous dependent variable, though it would provide a pretty good estimate if the percentage of improvement scores didn't fall below 20% or above 80% across all values of Survrate. Another problem is that the true relationship is not likely to be linear. Differences in SurvRate near the center of the scale will lead to noticeably larger differences in Outcome than will comparable differences at the ends of the scale.

While a straight line won't fit the data in Figure 15.9 well, an S-shaped, or **sigmoidal** curve will. This line changes little as we move across low values of SurvRate, then changes rapidly as we move across middle values, and finally changes slowly again across high values. In no case does it fall below 0 or above 1. This line is shown in Figure 15.10. Notice

conditional means

sigmoidal

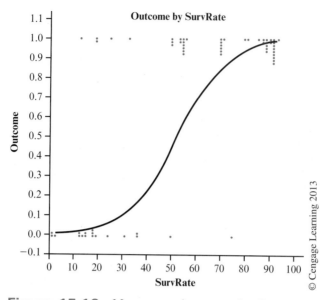

Figure 15.10   More appropriate regression line for predicting outcome

that it is quite close to the whole cluster of points in the lower left, rises rapidly for those values of SurvRate that have a roughly equal number of patients who improve and don't improve, and then comes close to the cluster of points in the upper right. When you think about how you might expect the probability of improvement to change with SurvRate, this curve makes sense.

There is another way to view what is happening that provides a tie to standard linear regression. If you think back to what we have said in the past about regression, you will recall that, at least with large samples, there is a whole collection of *Y* values corresponding to each value of *X*. You saw this diagrammatically in Figure 9.5, when I spoke about the assumptions of normality and homogeneity of variance in arrays. Rather than classifying people as improved or not improved, suppose that we could somehow measure their disease outcomes more precisely. (For example, we could rate their condition on a 100-point scale.) Then for a rating of SurvRate = 20, for example, we would have a whole distribution of disease outcome scores; similarly for people with SurvRate = 30, SurvRate = 40, and so on. These distributions are shown schematically in Figure 15.11.

When we class someone as improved, we are simply saying that their disease outcome score is sufficiently high for us to say that they fall in that category. They may be completely cured, they may be doing quite a bit better, or they may be only slightly improved,

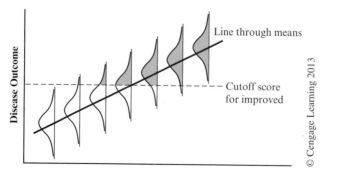

Figure 15.11   Disease outcome as a function of SurvRate

but they at least meet our criterion of "improved." Similarly, someone else may have remained constant, gotten slightly worse, or died, but in any event their outcome was below our decision point.

censored data

What we have here are called **censored data**. When I speak of censoring I'm not talking about some nasty little man with a big black marker who blocks out things he doesn't want others to see. We are talking about a situation where something that is above a cutoff is classed as a success, and something below the cutoff is classed as a failure. It could be performance on a test, obtaining a qualifying time for the Boston Marathon, or classifying an airline flight as "on time" or "late." From this point of view, logistic regression can be thought of as applying linear regression to censored data. Because the data are censored to provide only success or failure, we have to fit our model somewhat differently.

The horizontal line across the plot in Figure 15.11 represents a critical value. Anyone scoring above that line would be classed as improved, and anyone below it would be classed as not improved. As you can see, the proportion improving, as given by the shaded area of each curve, changes slowly at first, then much more rapidly, and then slowly again as we move from left to right. This should remind you of the sigmoidal curve we saw in Figure 15.10, because this is what gives rise to that curve. The regression line that you see in Figure 15.11 is the linear regression of the *continuous* measure of outcome against SurvRate, and it goes through the mean of each distribution. If we had the continuous measure, we could solve for this line. But we have censored data, containing only the dichotomous values, and for that we are much better off solving for the sigmoidal function in Figure 15.10.

We have seen that although our hypothetical continuous variable is a linear function of SurvRate, our censored dichotomous variable (or the probability of improvement) is not. But a simple transformation from p(improvement) to odds(improvement) to log odds(improvement) will give us a variable that *is* a linear function of SurvRate. Therefore we can convert p(improvement) to log odds(improvement) and get back to a linear function. An excellent discussion of what we are doing here can be found in Allison (1999). Although that manual was written for people using SAS, it is one of the nicest descriptions that I know and is useful whether you use SAS or not.

Before continuing, it will be helpful to remind people of odds and log odds. We have not seen them since Chapter 6. Dabbs and Morris (1990) ran an interesting study in which they classified male military personnel as High or Normal in testosterone, and as either having, or not having, a history of delinquency. The results follow:

		Delinquent		
		Yes	No	Total
Testosterone	Normal	402	3614	4016
	High	101	345	446
		503	3959	4462

For these data, the odds of being delinquent if you are in the Normal group are (frequency delinquent)/(frequency not delinquent). (Using probabilities instead of frequencies, this comes down to $p_{delinquent}/p_{not\ delinquent} = p$(delinquent)/(1 − p(delinquent)).) For the Normal testosterone group the odds of being delinquent are 402/3614 = .1001 The odds of being not delinquent if you are in the Normal group is the reciprocal of this, which is 3614/402 = 8.990. This last statistic can be read as meaning that if you are a male with normal testosterone levels you are nearly 9 times more likely to be not delinquent than delinquent (or, if you prefer, 9 times *less likely* to be delinquent than not delinquent). If we look at the High testosterone group, however, the odds of being delinquent are $101/345 = 0.293$, and the odds of being not delinquent are $345/101 = 3.416$. Both groups of males are more likely to be not delinquent than delinquent, but that isn't saying much, because we would hope that most people are not delinquent. But notice that as you move from the Normal to the High group, your odds of being delinquent nearly triple, going from 0.111 to 0.293. If we form the ratio of these odds we get $0.293/0.111 = 2.64$, which is the odds ratio. For these data you are 2.64 more likely to be delinquent if you have high testosterone levels than if you have normal levels. That is a pretty impressive statistic.

We will set aside the odds ratio for a moment and just look at odds. With our cancer data we will focus on the odds of survival. (We can return to odds ratios any time we wish simply by forming the ratio of the odds of survival and non-survival for each of two different levels of SurvRate.)

For what we are doing here (predicting the odds of surviving breast cancer), we will work with the *natural logarithm*[17] of the odds, the result is called the log odds of survival. For our delinquency example the log odds of being delinquent for a male with high testosterone,

$$\text{log odds} = \log_e(\text{odds}) = \ln(\text{odds}) = \ln(0.293) = -0.228$$

The log odds will be positive for odds greater than 1 and negative for odds less than 1. (They are undefined for odds $= 0$.) You will sometimes see log odds referred to as the **logit** and the transformation to log odds referred to as the **logit transformation**.

logit

logit transformation

Returning to the cancer study, we will start with the simple prediction of Outcome on the basis of SurvRate. Letting $p =$ the probability of improvement and $1 - p =$ the probability of nonimprovement, we will solve for an equation of the form:

$$\log(p/1 - p) = \text{log odds} = b_0 + b_1 \text{SurvRate}$$

Here b_1 will be the amount of increase in the *log odds* for a one unit increase in SurvRate. It is important to keep in mind how the data were coded. For the Outcome variable, $1 =$ improvement and $2 =$ no change or worse. For SurvRate, a higher score represents a better prognosis. So you might expect to see that SurvRate would have a positive coefficient, being associated with a better outcome. But with SPSS that will not be the case. SPSS will transform Outcome $= 1$ and 2 to 0 and 1, and then try to predict a 0 (better). Thus its coefficient will be negative. (SAS would try to predict a 1, and its coefficient would be positive, though of exactly the same magnitude.)

In simple linear regression we had formulae for b_0 and b_1 and could use methods of least squares to solve the equations with pencil and paper. Things are not quite so simple in logistic regression, in part because our data consist of 0 and 1 for SurvRate, not the conditional proportions of improvement. For logistic regression we are going to have to use maximum likelihood methods and solve for our regression coefficients **iteratively**. Our computer program will begin with some starting values for b_0 and b_1, see how well the estimated log odds fit the data, adjust the coefficients, again examine the fit, and so on until no further adjustments in the coefficients will lead to a better fit. This is not something you would attempt by hand.

iteratively

In simple linear regression you also had standard F and t statistics testing the significance of the relationship and the contribution of each predictor variable. We are going to have something similar in logistic regression, although here we will use χ^2 tests instead of F or t.

---

[17] The natural logarithm of X is the logarithm to the base e of X. In other words, it is the power to which e must be raised to produce X, where e is the base of the natural number system $= 2.71828$.

In Exhibit 15.4 you will see SPSS results of using SurvRate as our only predictor of Outcome. I am beginning with only one predictor just to keep the example simple. We will shortly move to the multiple predictor case, where nothing will really change except that we have more predictors to discuss. The fundamental issues are the same regardless of the number of predictors.

I will not discuss all of the statistics in Exhibit 15.4, because to do so would take us away from the fundamental issues. For more extensive discussion of the various statistics see Darlington (1990), Hosmer and Lemeshow (1989), and Lunneborg (1994). My purpose here is to explain the basic problem and approach.

The first part of the printout is analogous to the first part of a multiple regression print-out, where we have a test on whether the model (all predictors taken together) predicts the dependent variable at greater than chance levels. For multiple regression we have an F test, whereas here we have (several) χ^2 tests.

Start with the line indicating Beginning Block Number 0, and the row labeled "-2 log *Likelihood*." At this point there is no predictor in the model and -2 log likelihood $=$ 77.345746. This is a measure of the overall variability in the data. You might think of it

Number of selected cases:	66
Number rejected because of missing data:	0
Number of cases included in the analysis:	66

Dependent Variable Encoding:

Original Value	Internal Value
1.00	0
2.00	1

Dependent Variable.   OUTCOME   Cancer Outcome

Beginning Block Number 0. Initial Log Likelihood Function

-2 Log Likelihood 77.345746

* Constant is included in the model.

Beginning Block Number 1. Method: Enter

Variable(s) Entered on Step Number
1.   SURVRATE   Survival Rating by Physician

-2 Log Likelihood	37.323
Goodness of Fit	57.235
Cox & Snell $- R^2$	.455
Nagelkerke $- R^2$	.659

	Chi-Square	df	Significance
Model	40.022	1	.0000
Block	40.022	1	.0000
Step	40.022	1	.0000

--------------------------------------- Variables in the Equation ---------------------------------------

Variable	B	S.E.	Wald	df	Sig	R	Exp(B)
SURVRATE	$-.0812$	.0193	17.7558	1	.0000	$-.4513$	.9220
Constant	2.6836	.8113	10.9408	1	.0009		

Exhibit 15.4   Logistic analysis of cancer survival

as being analogous to SS_{total} in the analysis of variance. The quantity $-2 \log L$ can be interpreted as a χ^2 test on how well a model with *no* predictors would fit the data. That χ^2 is 77.3457, which is a significant departure from a good fit, as we would expect with no predictors. (χ^2 would be 0.00 if the fit were perfect.)

For the next block SPSS adds SurvRate as the (only) predictor and produces another value of $-2 \log$ likelihood $= 37.323$. This is the amount of variability that remains after Survrate is taken into account, and the difference ($77.345 - 37.323 = 40.022$) represents a reduction in χ^2 that can be attributed to adding the predictor. Because we have added one predictor, this is itself a χ^2 on 1 *df*, and can be evaluated as such. You can see that the significance level is given as .0000, meaning that SurvRate added significantly to our ability to predict. (You will note that there are lines labeled Model, Block, and Step, and they are all the same because we have added all of our predictors (1) at the same time.)

The next section of the table contains, and tests, the individual predictors. (Here there is only one predictor—SurvRate.) From this section we can see that the optimal logistic regression equation is

$$\text{Log odds} = -0.0812 \text{ SurvRate} + 2.6836$$

The negative coefficient here for SurvRate indicates that the log odds go down as the physician's rating of survival increases. This reflects the fact that SPSS is trying to predict whether a patient will get worse, or even die, and we would expect that the likelihood of getting worse will decrease as the physician's rating increases.

We can also see that SurvRate is a significant predictor, as tested by Wald's $\chi^2 = 17.7558$ on 1 *df*, which is significant at $p = .0001$. You will notice that the χ^2 test, that is, $-2 \log L$, on the whole model and the Wald χ^2 test on SurvRate disagree. Because SurvRate *is* the whole model, you might think that they should say the same thing. This is certainly the case in standard linear regression, where our F on regression is, with one predictor, just the square of our t on the regression coefficient. This disagreement stems from the fact that they are based on different estimates of χ^2. Questions have been raised about the behavior of the Wald criterion, and Hosmer and Lemeshow (1989) suggest relying on the likelihood ratio test ($-2 \log L$) instead.

Looking at the logistic regression equation we see that the coefficient for SurvRate is -0.0812, which can be interpreted to mean that a one-point increase in SurvRate will decrease the log odds of getting worse by 0.0812. But you and I probably don't care about things like log odds. We probably want to at least work with odds. But that's easy—we simply exponentiate the coefficient. Don't get excited! "exponentiate" is just an important sounding word that means "raise e to that power." If you have a calculator that cost you more than \$9.99, it probably has a button labeled e^x. Just enter –0.0812, press that button, and you'll have 0.9220. This means that if you increase SurvRate by one point you *multiply* the odds of deterioration by 0.9220. A simple example will show what this means.

Suppose we take someone with a SurvRate score of 40. That person will have a log odds of

$$\text{Log odds} = -0.0812(40) + 2.6837 = -0.5643$$

If we calculate $e^{-0.5643}$ we will get 0.569. This means that the person's odds of deteriorating are 0.569, which means that she is 0.569 times more likely to deteriorate than improve.[18] Now suppose we take someone with SurvRate = 41, one point higher. That person would have predicted log odds of

---

[18] (If you don't like odds, you can even turn this into a probability. Because odds $= p/(1 - p)$, then $p = $ odds/$(1 + $odds$)$.)

Log odds $= -0.0812(41) + 2.6837 = -0.6455$

And $e^{-0.6455} = .524$. So this person's log odds are $-0.6455 - (-0.5643) = -.0812$ lower than the first person's, and her odds are $e^{-0.0812} = 0.9220$ times larger $(0.569 \times 0.922 = .524)$. Now 0.922 may not look like a very large number, but if you have cancer a one-point higher survival rating gives you about a 7.8% lower chance of deterioration, and that's certainly not something to sneer at.

I told you that if you wanted to see the effect of SurvRate expressed in terms of odds rather than log odds you needed to take out your calculator and exponentiate. In fact that isn't strictly true here, because SPSS does it for you. The last column in this section is labeled "Exp (B)" and contains the exponentiated value of b $(e^{-0.0812} = .9220)$.

Although SurvRate is a meaningful and significant predictor of survivability of cancer, it does not explain everything. Epping-Jordan, Compas, and Howell (1994) were interested in determining whether certain behavioral variables also contribute to how a person copes with cancer. They were interested in whether people who experience a high rate of intrusive thoughts (Intrus) have a poorer prognosis. (People who experience intrusive thoughts are people who keep finding themselves thinking about their cancer and related events. They can't seem to put it out of their minds.) These authors were also interested in the effect of avoidant behavior (Avoid), which is exhibited by people who just don't want to think about cancer and who try to avoid dealing with the problem. [Intrus and Avoid are variables computed from the Impact of Events Scale (Horowitz, Wilner, and Alvarez, 1979).]

Exhibit 15.5 presents the results of using SurvRate, Intrus, and Avoid as predictors of Outcome. Here you can again see that the overall model fits at better-than-chance levels. With no predictors, -2 log likelihood $= 77.346$. Adding the three predictors to the model reduces -2 log likelihood to 31.650, for an improvement of $77.346 - 31.650 = 45.696$. This difference is a χ^2 on 3 df, because we have three predictors, and it is clearly significant. We would have expected a significant model because we knew that SurvRate alone was a significant predictor. From the bottom section of the table we see that the Wald chi-square is significant for both SurvRate and for Avoid, but not for Intrus. This tells us that people who exhibit a high level of avoidance behavior do not do as well as those who do less avoiding (Wald chi-square $= 4.3310$, $p = .0374$).[19] More specifically, the regression coefficient for Avoid is 0.1618. This can be interpreted to mean that a one-point increase in Avoid, holding the other two variables constant, increases the log odds of deterioration by 0.1618 points. Exponentiating this we obtain $e^{0.1618} = 1.1756$. Thus a one-point increase in Avoid multiplies the odds of deterioration by 1.1756, which would increase them.

The Wald chi-square test on Intrus produced a χ^2 of 0.5281, which was not even close to being significant ($p = .4674$). Thus this variable is not contributing to our prediction. If Intrus is not making a significant contribution of predicting Outcome, perhaps it should be dropped from the model. There is in fact a very good reason to do just that. Recall that when we had only one predictor our overall χ^2, as given by -2 log L, was 40.022. We have now added two more predictors, and our overall χ^2 has become 45.696. The nice thing about χ^2 is that a difference between two chi-squares is itself distributed as χ^2 on df equal to the difference between the df for the two models. This means that we can compare the fit of the two models by subtracting $45.696 - 40.022 = 5.674$ and testing this as a χ^2 on $3 - 1 = 2$ df. But the critical value of $\chi^2_{.05}(2) = 5.99$, which means that the degree of improvement between the two models is not significant. It is no greater than we would expect if we just

---

[19] In line with Hosmer and Lemeshow's (1989) concern with the validity of the Wald chi-square, we might treat this test with some caution. However Wald's test tends to be conservative, so confidence in this effect is probably not misplaced. You will see some confirmation of that statement shortly.

Dependent Variable Encoding:

Original   Internal
Value   Value
  1.00   0
  2.00   1

Dependent Variable.   OUTCOME   Cancer Outcome

Beginning Block Number 0. Initial Log Likelihood Function

−2 Log Likelihood 77.345746

* Constant is included in the model.

Beginning Block Number 1. Method: Enter

Variable(s) Entered on Step Number
1.   SURVRATE   Survival Rating by Physician
                INTRUS
                AVOID

−2 Log Likelihood   31.650
Goodness of Fit   35.350
Cox & Snell – R^2   .500
Nagelkerke – R^2   .724

	Chi-Square	df	Significance
Model	45.696	3	.0000
Block	45.696	3	.0000
Step	45.696	3	.0000

------------------------------------ Variables in the Equation ------------------------------------

Variable	B	S.E.	Wald	df	Sig	R	Exp(B)
SURVRATE	−.0817	.0211	14.9502	1	.0001	−.4092	.9215
INTRUS	−.0589	.0811	.5281	1	.4674	.0000	.9428
AVOID	.1618	.0777	4.3310	1	.0374	.1736	1.1756
Constant	1.6109	1.1780	1.8700	1	.1715		

Exhibit 15.5   Outcome as a function of Survival Rate, Intrusive thoughts, and Avoidance

added a couple of useless predictors. But we know that Avoid was significant, as well as SurvRate, so what went wrong?

Well, what went wrong is that we have taken the improvement that we gained by adding Avoid, and spread it out over the nonimprovement that we gained by adding Intrus, and their average is not enough to be considered significant. In other words, we have diluted the added contribution of Avoid with Intrus. If our goal had been to predict Outcome, rather than to test a model that includes Intrus, we would have been much better off if we had just stayed with Avoid. So I would suggest noting that Intrus does not contribute significantly and then dropping back to the two-predictor model with SurvRate and Avoid, giving us

$$\text{Log odds} = -0.0823 \text{ SurvRate} + 0.1325 \text{ Avoid} + 1.1961$$

Both of these predictors are significant, as is the degree of improvement over the one-predictor case. The fact that adding Avoid leads to a significant improvement in the model over the one-predictor case is welcome confirmation of the significant Wald chi-square for this effect.

The example that was used here included only continuous predictors because that was the nature of the data set. However, there is nothing to preclude dichotomous predictors, and in fact they are often used. The nice thing about a dichotomous predictor is that a one unit change in that predictor represents a shift from one category to another. For example, if we used Sex as a predictor and coded Male = 1, Female = 2, then a one unit increase in Sex would move us from Male to Female. The exponentiated coefficient for Sex would then represent the difference in the odds between males and females. Suppose that Sex had been a predictor in the cancer study and that the coefficient was 0.40.[20] Exponentiating this we would have 1.49. This would mean that, holding all other variables constant, the odds of a female improving are about 1.5 times greater than the odds of a male improving. You will often see statements in the press of the form "Researchers have concluded that people who exercise regularly have a 44% lower chance of developing heart problems than those who do not." Such statements are often based on the kind of reasoning that we are discussing here.

There is much more to logistic regression than I can cover in this short introduction, but perhaps the biggest stumbling block that people experience is the movement to odds and log odds when they are used to thinking about 0 and 1 or about probabilities. My major purpose in this section was to get you past that barrier (and to supply you with arguments why you should consider logistic regression over linear regression or discriminant analysis when you have a dichotomous dependent variable). Everything else that could be said about logistic regression is mainly about the technicalities, and you can find those in a number of texts, particularly the ones by Allison (1999), Hosmer and Lemeshow (1989), and Kleinbaum and Klein (2002).

Key Terms

Regression coefficients (15.1)

Residuals (15.1)

Tolerance (15.2)

Variance inflation factor (VIF) (15.2)

Collinearity (15.2)

Multicollinearity (15.2)

Singular (15.2)

Standardized regression coefficients (15.2)

Residual variance (15.5)

Residual error (15.5)

Multivariate normal (15.6)

Multiple correlation coefficient ($R_{0.123\ldots p}$) (15.7)

Partial correlation ($r_{0.12}$) (15.8)

Semipartial correlation ($r_{0.12}$) (15.8)

Venn diagrams (15.8)

Suppressor variable (15.9)

Multivariate outliers (15.10)

Distance (15.10)

Leverage (h_i) (15.10)

Influence (15.10)

Cook's D (15.10)

Studentized residual (15.10)

Tolerance (15.10)

Cross-correlation (15.10)

Singular (15.10)

Nested models (15.10)

Hierarchical models (15.10)

Akaike's Information Criterion (AIC), (15.10)

All subsets regression (15.11)

Backward elimination (15.11)

Stepwise regression (15.11)

Forward selection (15.11)

Cross-validation (15.11)

Listwise deletion (15.11)

Casewise deletion (15.11)

Pairwise deletion (15.11)

Imputing (15.11)

Mediating relationships (15.14)

Moderating relationships (15.14)

Center (15.14)

Logistic regression (15.15)

Discriminant analysis (15.15)

Conditional means (15.15)

Sigmoidal (15.15)

Censored data (15.15)

Logit (15.15)

Logit transformation (15.15)

Iteratively (15.15)

---

[20] Because this was a study of breast cancer, sex is not a reasonable predictor here, but it would be a reasonable predictor if we were studying lung cancer, for example.

Exercises

Note: Many of these exercises are based on a very small data set for reasons of economy of space and computational convenience. For actual applications of multiple regression, sample sizes should be appreciably larger than those used here.

15.1 A psychologist studying perceived "quality of life" in a large number of cities ($N = 150$) came up with the following equation using mean temperature (Temp), median income in $1000 (Income), per capita expenditure on social services (Socser), and population density (Popul) as predictors.

$$[\hat{Y} = 5.37 - 0.01\,\text{Temp} + 0.05\,\text{Income} + 0.003\,\text{Socser} - 0.01\,\text{Popul}]$$

a. Interpret the regression equation in terms of the coefficients.

b. Assume there is a city that has a mean temperature of 55 degrees, a median income of $12,000, spends $500 per capita on social services, and has a population density of 200 people per block. What is its predicted quality of life score?

c. What would we predict in a different city that was identical in every way except that it spent $100 per capita on social services?

15.2 A large corporation is interested in predicting a measure of job satisfaction among its employees. They have collected data on 15 employees who each supplied information on job satisfaction, level of responsibility, number of people supervised, rating of working environment, and years of service. The data follow:

Satisfaction:	2	2	3	3	5	5	6	6	6	7	8	8	8	9	9
Responsibility:	4	2	3	6	2	8	4	5	8	8	9	6	3	7	9
No. Supervised:	5	3	4	7	4	8	6	5	9	8	9	3	6	9	9
Environment:	1	1	7	3	5	8	5	5	6	4	7	2	8	7	9
Years of Service:	5	7	5	3	3	6	3	2	7	3	5	5	8	8	1

Exhibit 15.6 is an abbreviated form of the printout.

a. Write out the regression equation using all five predictors.

b. What are the β_i s?

15.3 For the values of β in Exercise 15.4, the corresponding standard errors are

[0.397   0.252   0.052   0.025]

Which, if any, predictor would you be most likely to drop if you wanted to refine your regression equation?

15.4 Refer to Exercise 15.1. Assume that

$$\beta = [-0.438 \quad 0.762 \quad 0.081 \quad -0.132]$$

Interpret the results.

15.5 Refer to Exercise 15.2.

a. Which variable has the largest semipartial correlation with the criterion, partialling out the other variables?

b. The overall F in Exercise 15.2 is not significant, yet Environment correlates significantly ($r = .58$) with Y. How is this possible?

15.6 Using the data in Exercise 15.2, generate $\hat{Y}$ and show that $R_{0.1234} = r_{Y\hat{Y}}$.

15.7 All other things being equal, the ability of two variables to predict a third will increase as the correlation between them decreases. Explain this fact in terms of semipartial correlation.

15.8 Calculate the adjusted R^2 for the data in Exercise 15.2.

15.9 What does the Tolerance column in Exhibit 15.8 contribute to the answers in Exercises 15.7 and 15.10?

15.10 All other things being equal, the stability of any given regression coefficient across different samples of data is partly a function of how that variable correlates with other predictors. Explain this fact.

DEPENDENT VARIABLE . . . .   1 SATIF
TOLERANCE 0.0100

ALL DATA CONSIDERED AS A SINGLE GROUP

MULTIPLE R	0.6974	STD. ERROR OF EST.	2.0572
MULTIPLE R-SQUARE	0.4864		

ANALYSIS OF VARIANCE

	SUM OF SQUARES	DF	MEAN SQUARE	F RATIO	P(TAIL)
REGRESSION	40.078	4	10.020	2.367	0.12267
RESIDUAL	42.322	10	4.232		

VARIABLE		COEFFICIENT	STD. ERROR	STD. REG COEFF	T	P(2 TAIL)	TOLERANCE
INTERCEPT		1.66926					
RESPON	2	0.60516	0.428	0.624	1.414	0.188	0.263940
NUMSUP	3	−0.33399	0.537	−0.311	−0.622	0.548	0.205947
ENVIR	4	0.48552	0.276	0.514	1.758	0.109	0.600837
YRS	5	0.07023	0.262	0.063	0.268	0.794	0.919492

Exhibit 15.6   Printout for regression analysis of data in Exercise 15.2

15.11 Use Y and $\hat{Y}$ from Exercise 15.6 to show that MS_{residual} is $\sum (Y - \hat{Y})^2/(N - p - 1)$.

15.12 Refer to the first three variables from Exercise 15.2.

   a.   Use any computer program to calculate the squared semipartial correlation and the squared partial correlation for Satisfaction as the criterion and No. Supervised as the predictor, partialling out Responsibility.

   b.   Draw a Venn diagram to illustrate these two coefficients.

15.13 Calculate the adjusted R^2 for the 15 cases in Exercise 15.14.

15.14 Using the following (random) data, demonstrate what happens to the multiple correlation when you drop cases from the data set (e.g., use 15 cases, then 10, 6, 5, 4).

Y	5	0	5	9	4	8	3	7	0	4	7	1	4	7	9
X_1	3	8	1	5	8	2	4	7	9	1	3	5	6	8	9
X_2	7	6	4	3	1	9	7	5	3	1	8	6	0	3	7
X_3	1	7	4	1	8	8	6	8	3	6	1	9	7	7	7
X_4	3	6	0	5	1	3	5	9	1	1	7	4	2	0	9

15.15 Refer to the first three variables in Exercise 15.2.

   a.   Draw a figure comparable to Figure 15.1.

   b.   Obtain the regression solution for these data and relate the solution to the figure.

15.16 For the data in Exercise 15.18, compute $\hat{Y} = 1X_2 + 1X_4 - 3X_5$. How well does this equation fit compared with the optimal equation? Why should this be the case?

15.17 In Exercise 15.18 what meaning attaches to R^* as far as the Vermont Department of Health is concerned?

15.18 The State of Vermont is divided into 10 Health Planning Districts—they correspond roughly to counties. The following data represent the percentage of live births of babies weighing

under 2500 grams (Y), the fertility rate for females 17 years of age or younger (X_1), total high-risk fertility rate for females younger than 17 or older than 35 years of age (X_2),
percentage of mothers with fewer than 12 years of education (X_3), percentage of births to
unmarried mothers (X_4), and percentage of mothers not seeking medical care until the third
trimester (X_5).

Y	X_1	X_2	X_3	X_4	X_5
6.1	22.8	43.0	23.8	9.2	6
7.1	28.7	55.3	24.8	12.0	10
7.4	29.7	48.5	23.9	10.4	5
6.3	18.3	38.8	16.6	9.8	4
6.5	21.1	46.2	19.6	9.8	5
5.7	21.2	39.9	21.4	7.7	6
6.6	22.2	43.1	20.7	10.9	7
8.1	22.3	48.5	21.8	9.5	5
6.3	21.8	40.0	20.6	11.6	7
6.9	31.2	56.7	25.2	11.6	9

© Cengage Learning 2013

A stepwise regression is shown in Exhibit 15.7. (Only the first three steps are shown to conserve space. For purposes of this exercise, we will not let the lack of statistical significance
worry us.)

a. What are the values of R for the successive steps?

b. From the definition of a partial correlation (in terms of Venn diagrams), show that
the R^2 at step 2 is a function of R^2 at step 1 and the partial correlation listed under
step 1—"VARIABLES NOT IN EQUATION."

```
STEP NO. 1
VARIABLE ENTERED     3  X2
MULTIPLE R              0.6215
MULTIPLE R-SQUARE       0.3862
ADJUSTED R-SQUARE       0.3095
STD. ERROR OF EST.      0.5797

ANALYSIS OF VARIANCE
```

	SUM OF SQUARES	DF	MEAN SQUARE	F RATIO
REGRESSION	1.6917006	1	1.691701	5.03
RESIDUAL	2.6882995	8	0.3360374	

			VARIABLES IN EQUATION					VARIABLES NOT IN EQUATION			
VARIABLE	COEFFICIENT	STD. ERROR OF COEFF	STD. REG COEFF	TOLERANCE	F TO REMOVE	LEVEL	VARIABLE	PARTIAL CORR.	TOLERANCE	F TO ENTER	LEVEL
(Y-INTERCEPT	3.529)										
X2 3	0.069	0.031	0.621	1.00000	5.03	1	. X1 2	−0.19730	0.25831	0.28	1
							. X3 4	−0.25039	0.43280	0.47	1
							. X4 5	0.00688	0.69838	0.00	1
							. X5 6	−0.59063	0.58000	3.75	1

```
STEP NO. 2
VARIABLE ENTERED     6  X5
MULTIPLE R              0.7748
MULTIPLE R-SQUARE       0.6003
ADJUSTED R-SQUARE       0.4862
STD. ERROR OF EST.      0.5001
```

Adapted from output by SPSS, Inc.

(continued)

Exhibit 15.7   Stepwise regression of data on low birthweight

ANALYSIS OF VARIANCE

	SUM OF SQUARES	DF	MEAN SQUARE	F RATIO
REGRESSION	2.6294919	2	1.314746	5.26
RESIDUAL	1.7505082	7	0.2500726	

		VARIABLES IN EQUATION					.	VARIABLES NOT IN EQUATION				
VARIABLE	COEFFICIENT	STD. ERROR OF COEFF	STD. REG COEFF	TOLERANCE	F TO REMOVE	LEVEL	. VARIABLE		PARTIAL CORR.	TOLERANCE	F TO ENTER	LEVEL
(Y-INTERCEPT	2.949)						.					
X2 3	0.113	0.035	1.015	0.58000	10.47	1	. X1	2	−0.09613	0.24739	0.06	1
X5 6	−0.223	0.115	−0.608	0.58000	3.75	1	. X3	4	−0.05399	0.37826	0.02	1
							. X4	5	0.41559	0.53416	1.25	1

STEP NO. 3
VARIABLE ENTERED   5 X4
MULTIPLE R   0.8181
MULTIPLE R-SQUARE   0.6694
ADJUSTED R-SQUARE   0.5041
STD. ERROR OF EST.   0.4913

ANALYSIS OF VARIANCE

	SUM OF SQUARES	DF	MEAN SQUARE	F RATIO
REGRESSION	2.9318295	3	0.9772765	4.05
RESIDUAL	1.4481706	6	0.2413618	

		VARIABLES IN EQUATION					.	VARIABLES NOT IN EQUATION				
VARIABLE	COEFFICIENT	STD. ERROR OF COEFF	STD. REG COEFF	TOLERANCE	F TO REMOVE	LEVEL	. VARIABLE		PARTIAL CORR.	TOLERANCE	F TO ENTER	LEVEL
(Y-INTERCEPT	1.830)						.					
X2 3	0.104	0.035	0.942	0.55484	8.93	1	. X1	2	−0.14937	0.24520	0.11	1
X4 5	0.190	0.170	0.359	0.53416	1.25	1	. X3	4	0.14753	0.31072	0.11	1
X5 6	−0.294	0.130	−0.799	0.44362	5.14	1	.					

Exhibit 15.7   *(continued)*

15.19 In Exercise 15.18 the fifth predictor has a very low correlation with the criterion ($r = .05$) and yet plays a significant role in the regression. Why?

15.20 In Exercise 15.4 the adjusted R^2 would actually be lower for five predictors than for three predictors. Why?

15.21 For the data in Exercise 15.18 would it be safe to conclude that decreasing the number of mothers who fail to seek medical care before the third trimester is a good way to decrease the incidence of low-birthweight infants?

15.22 Create a set of data on 10 cases that illustrates leverage, distance, and influence. Use any standard regression program to produce statistics measuring these attributes.

15.23 Produce a set of data where the variance of Y values associated with large values of X is greater than the variance of Y values associated with small values of X. Then run the regression and plot the residuals on the ordinate against X on the abscissa. What pattern emerges?

15.24 Notice that in the diagram in Exercise 15.27 SuppTotl has both a direct and an indirect effect on Depression. Its direct effect is the arrow that goes from SuppTotl to DepressT. The indirect effect (which here is not significant) comes from the fact that SuppTotl influences PVLoss, which in turn affects DepressT. Explain these direct and indirect effects in terms of semipartial regression coefficients.

Computer Exercises

15.25 A compulsive researcher who wants to cover all possibilities might throw in the total score on perceived vulnerability (PVTotal) as well as PVLoss. (The total includes vulnerability to accidents, illness, and life-style related problems.)

 a. Run this analysis adding PVTotal to the variables used in Exercise 15.26.

 b. What effect did the inclusion of PVTotal have on R^2? What effect did it have on the standard error of the regression coefficient for PVLoss? If your program will also give you tolerance and VIF, what effect does the inclusion of PVTotal have on them?

 c. What would you conclude about the addition of PVTotal to our model?

15.26 Use the data set Mireault.dat from Mireault (1990), described in the Appendix and found on the Web site for this book, to examine the relationship between current levels of depression and other variables. A reasonable model might propose that depression (DepressT) is a function of (1) the person's current perceived level of vulnerability to additional loss (PVLoss), (2) the person's level of social support (SuppTotl), and (3) the age at which the person lost a parent during childhood (AgeAtLos). Use any statistical package to evaluate the model outlined here. (Because only subjects in Group 1 lost a parent to death during childhood, your analysis will be restricted to that group.)

15.27 Draw one diagram to illustrate the relationships examined in Exercises 15.26 and 15.28. Use arrows to show predicted relationships, and write the standardized regression coefficients next to the arrows. (You have just run a simple path analysis.)

15.28 In Exercise 15.26 we posited a model in which depression was a function of perceived vulnerability, social support, and age at loss. An alternative, or additional, view might be that vulnerability itself is a function of social support and age at loss. (If you lost a parent when you were very young and you have little social support, then you might feel particularly vulnerable to future loss.)

 a. Set up the regression problem for this question and run the appropriate analysis. (Use PVLoss, SuppTotl, and AgeAtLos.)

 b. Interpret your results.

15.29 Repeat the analysis of Exercise 15.26, requesting statistics on regression diagnostics.

 a. What, if anything, do these statistics tell you about the data set?

 b. Delete the subject with the largest measure of influence (usually indexed by Cook's D). What effect does that have for this particular data set?

15.30 Repeat Exercise 15.31 but this time use just the dichotomous predictor Marital Status. Create a contingency table of Married/Unmarried by Report/No Report, calculate odds ratios, and compare those ratios to the results of the logistic regression. (The result will not be significant, but that is not important.)

15.31 The data set Harass.dat contains slightly modified data on 343 cases created to replicate the results of a study of sexual harassment by Brooks and Perot (1991). The dependent variable is whether or not the subjects reported incidents of sexual harassment, and the independent variables are, in order, Age, Marital Status (1 = married, 2 = single), Feminist Ideology, Frequency of the behavior, Offensiveness of the behavior, and whether or not it was reported (0 = no, 1 = yes). (For each variable, higher numbers represent more of the property. Using any logistic regression program, examine the likelihood that a subject will report sexual harassment on the basis of the independent variables.

15.32 It is useful to examine the effects of measurement reliability on the outcome of a regression problem. In Exercise 15.26 the variable PVLoss was actually a reasonably reliable variable. However, for purposes of illustration we can manufacture a new, and less reliable, measure from it by adding a bit of random error to PVLoss.

 a. Create a new variable called UnrelLos with a statement *of the form* UnrelLos = PVLoss + 7.5 × random" [Here "random" is a random-number function available with most statistical programs. You will need to check the manual to determine the exact form of the statement. I used a multiplier of 7.5 on the assumption that the random-number function will sample from an $N(0, 1)$ population. Multiplying by 7.5 will increase the standard deviation of UnrelLos by 50% (see the variance sum law). You may want to play with other constants.]

b. Now repeat Exercise 15.26 using UnrelLos in place of PVLoss.

c. What effect does this new variable have on the contribution of the perceived vulnerability of loss to the prediction of DepressT? How has the regression coefficient changed? How has its standard error changed? How does a test on its statistical significance change? What changes occurred for the other variables in the equation?

15.33 I was surprised to see that frequency of the behavior was not related to the likelihood of reporting. Can you suggest reasons why this might be so?

15.34 Using the data you created in Exercise 15.37, demonstrate the effect of "centering" your predictor variables.

15.35 In Exercise 15.36 we had a data set where BlamBeh was related to later distress at time 2. When it is included as a predictor along with Stress1 and BlamPer it is no longer a significant predictor. Why would this be likely to happen?

15.36 Malcarne, Compas, Epping, and Howell (1995) examined 126 cancer patients soon after they were diagnosed with cancer and at a four-month follow-up. At the initial interviews (Time 1) they collected data on the patients' current levels of distress (Distress1), the degree to which they attributed the blame for the cancer to the type of person they are (BlamPer), and the degree to which they attributed the cancer to the kind of behaviors in which they had engaged, such as smoking or high fat diets (BlamBeh). At the four-month follow-up (Time 2) the authors again collected data on the levels of psychological distress that the patients reported (Distress2). (They also collected data on a number of other variables, which do not concern us here.) The data are available on the Web site for this course and named Malcarne.dat.

a. What would you conclude if you attempt to predict Distress2 from Distress1 and BlamPer?

b. Why would I want to include Distress1 in the analysis for part a?

15.37 Make up a very simple example with very simple variables to illustrate how one could see the effect of an interaction between two predictors.

15.38 What are some of the reasons why stepwise regression (broadly defined) would not find favor with most statisticians?

15.39 As you know, the regression coefficient gives the effect of one variable holding all other variables constant. How would you view this interpretation when you have an interaction term in your model?

15.40 In this chapter we spent a lot of time with Guber's study of educational expenditures and found that when we controlled for the percentage of students taking the SAT exam, Expend was not a significant predictor. However, the SAT is not a good dependent variable in discussing the quality of education in a state. Perhaps the ACT, which tests something somewhat different, is a better predictor. Use SPSS and the data set, which is available on the book's Web site and named Tab15-1.dat, to answer that question. Be complete in your answer, examining the individual variables and the residuals.

15.41 Feinberg & Willer (2011) studied the effect of just-world beliefs on people's willingness to accept the concept of global warming. They presented participants with material designed to prime them toward or away from just-world beliefs, and then had them fill out a questionnaire concerning their skepticism toward global warming and their willingness to reduce their carbon footprint. They found the following path diagram for the model. (Note: The coefficients for the path from Skepticism to Willingness has also partialled out the effect of Just-World beliefs.)

When the authors used both the Just-World Prime and Global Warming Skepticism as predictors, the standardized regression coefficients between Just-World Prime and Willingness to Reduce Carbon Footprint dropped to -0.16, with a standard error of 0.13. Those who were primed with statements that the world is just reported higher levels of skepticism than those primed with statements suggesting that the world was unjust. The authors suggest that fear-based appeals can actually undercut the effectiveness of the message. Test the decline in the regression coefficients as you did in exercise 15.42 and draw the appropriate conclusions.

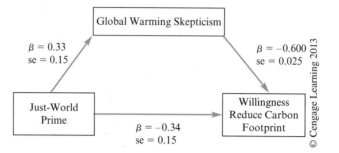

15.42 Paul Jose has a Web site referred to in the section on mediation. He discusses a problem in which he believes that stress leads to depression through a mediating path via rumination. (In other words, some stressed people ruminate, and as a consequence they become depressed.) The path diagram derived from his analysis of actual data are shown below. The beta given for the path from stress to depression is from the multiple regression of depression on stress and rumination. Predicting depression only from stress had a beta of 0.471. Test the decline in the coefficient for the direct path from stress to depression using Sobel's test. (You can check your work at Jose's website at http://www.victoria.ac.nz/psyc /paul-jose-files/helpcentre/help7_mediation_example.php, though the answers will not be exactly equal.)

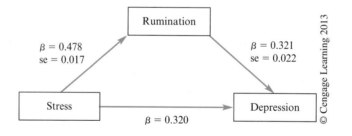

Chapter *16*

Analyses of Variance and Covariance as General Linear Models

Objectives

To show how the analysis of variance can be viewed as a special case of multiple regression; to present procedures for the treatment of unequal sample sizes; to present the analysis of covariance.

Contents

MOST PEOPLE THINK OF MULTIPLE regression and the analysis of variance as two totally separate statistical techniques that answer two entirely different sets of questions. In fact, this is not at all the case. In the first place they ask the same kind of questions, and in the second place they return the same kind of answers, although the answers may be phrased somewhat differently. The analysis of variance tells us that three treatments (T_1, T_2, and T_3) have different means ($\overline{X}_i$). Multiple regression tells us that means ($\overline{Y}_i$) are related to treatments (T_1, T_2, and T_3), which amounts to the same thing. Furthermore, the analysis of variance produces a statistic (F) on the differences among means. The analysis of regression produces a statistic (F) on the significance of R. As we shall see shortly, these Fs are equivalent.

16.1   The General Linear Model

general linear model

Just as multiple regression and the analysis of variance are concerned with the same general type of question, so are they basically the same technique. In fact, the analysis of variance is a special case of multiple linear regression, which in turn is a special case of what is commonly referred to as the **general linear model**. The fact that the analysis of variance has its own formal set of equations can be attributed primarily to good fortune. It happens that when certain conditions are met (as they are in the analysis of variance), the somewhat cumbersome multiple-regression calculations are reduced to a few relatively simple equations. If it were not for this, there probably would not be a separate set of procedures called the analysis of variance.

For the student interested solely in the application of statistical techniques, a word is in order in defense of even including a chapter on this topic. Why, you may ask, should you study what amounts to a cumbersome way of doing what you already know how to do in a simple way? Aside from the cry of "intellectual curiosity," there are several practical (applied) answers to such a question. First, this approach represents a relatively straightforward way of handling particular cases of unequal sample sizes, and understanding this approach helps you make intelligent decisions about various options in statistical software. Second, it provides us with a simple and intuitively appealing way of running, and especially of understanding, an analysis of covariance—which is a very clumsy technique when viewed from the more traditional approach. Last, and most important, it represents a glimpse at the direction in which statistical techniques are moving. With the greatly extended use of powerful and fast computers, many of the traditional statistical techniques are giving way to what were previously impractical procedures. We saw an example when we considered the mixed models approach to repeated measures analysis of variance. Other examples are such techniques as structural equation modeling and that old and much-abused standby, factor analysis. Unless you understand the relationship between the analysis of variance and the general linear model (as represented by multiple linear regression), and unless you understand how the data for simple analysis of variance problems can be cast in a multiple-regression framework, you will find yourself in the near future using more and more techniques about which you know less and less. This is not to say that t, χ^2, F, and so on are likely to disappear, but only that other techniques will be added, opening up entirely new ways of looking at data. The recent rise in the use of Structural Equation Modeling is a case in point, because much of what that entails builds on what you already know about regression, and what you will learn about underlying models of processes.

In the past 25 years, several excellent and very readable papers on this general topic have been written. The clearest presentation is still Cohen (1968). A paper by Overall and Spiegel (1969) is also worth reviewing. Both of these papers appeared in the *Psychological*

Bulletin and are therefore readily available. Other good discussions can be found in Overall (1972), Judd and McClelland (1989), and Cohen, Cohen, West, and Aiken (2003). Also, Cramer and Appelbaum (1980) and Howell and McConaughy (1982) provide contrasting views on the choice of the underlying model and the procedures to be followed.

There are two different ways to read this chapter, both legitimate. The first is to look for general concepts and to go lightly over the actual techniques of calculation. That is the approach I often tell my students to follow. I want them to understand where the reasoning leads, and I want them to feel that they could carry out all of the steps if they had to (with the book in front of them), but I don't ask them to commit very much of the technical material to memory. On the other hand, some instructors may want their students to grasp the material at a deeper level. There are good reasons for doing so. But I would still suggest that the first time you read the chapter, you look for general understanding. To develop greater expertise, sit down with both a computer and a calculator and work lots and lots of problems.

The Linear Model

Consider first the traditional multiple-regression problem with a criterion (Y) and three predictors (X_1, X_2, and X_3). We can write the usual model

$$Y_i = b_0 + b_1 X_{1i} + b_2 X_{2i} + b_3 X_{3i} + e_i$$

or, in terms of *vector* notation

$$\mathbf{y} = \mathbf{b}_0 + b_1 \mathbf{x}_1 + b_2 \mathbf{x}_2 + b_3 \mathbf{x}_3 + \mathbf{e}$$

where $\mathbf{y}$, $\mathbf{x}_1$, $\mathbf{x}_2$, and $\mathbf{x}_3$ are ($n \times 1$) vectors (columns) of data, $\mathbf{e}$ is a ($n \times 1$) vector of errors, and $\boldsymbol{b_0}$ is a ($n \times 1$) vector whose elements are the intercept. This equation can be further reduced to

$$\mathbf{y} + \mathbf{Xb} + \mathbf{e}$$

where $\mathbf{X}$ is a $n \times (p + 1)$ matrix of predictors, the first column of which is 1s, and $\mathbf{b}$ is a $(p + 1) \times 1$ vector of regression coefficients[1]. This called a linear model because Y is the sum of a linear combination of predictor variables—nothing is raised to a power other than 1.

Now consider the traditional model for a one-way analysis of variance:

$$Y_{ij} = \mu + \tau_j + e_{ij}$$

Here the symbol τ_j is simply a shorthand way of writing $\tau_1, \tau_2, \tau_3, \ldots \tau_p$, where for any given subject we are interested in only that value of τ_j that pertains to the particular treatment in question. To see the relationship between this model and the traditional regression model, it is necessary to introduce the concept of a design matrix. Design matrices are used in a wide variety of situations, not simply the analysis of variance, so it is important to understand them.

Design Matrices

design matrix

A **design matrix** is a matrix of *coded*, or *dummy*, or *counter* variables representing group membership. The *complete* form of the design matrix (X) will have $p + 1$ columns, representing the mean (μ) and the p treatment effects. A subject is always scored 1 for μ, since

---

[1] Although a few equations in this chapter are laid out in matrix format, you do not need to know the rules of matrix algebra to understand the material.

μ is part of all observations. In all other columns, she is scored 1 if she is a member of the treatment associated with that column, and 0 otherwise. Thus, for three treatments with two subjects per treatment, the complete design matrix would be

$$\Sigma = \begin{array}{c} \\ 1 \\ 2 \\ 3 \\ 4 \\ 5 \\ 6 \end{array} \begin{array}{cccc} S & \mu & A_1 & A_2 & A_3 \\ \left[\begin{array}{cccc} 1 & 1 & 0 & 0 \\ 1 & 1 & 0 & 0 \\ 1 & 0 & 1 & 0 \\ 1 & 0 & 1 & 0 \\ 1 & 0 & 0 & 1 \\ 1 & 0 & 0 & 1 \end{array}\right] \end{array}$$

Notice that subjects 1 and 2 (who received Treatment A_1) are scored 1 on μ and A_1, and 0 on A_2 and A_3, since they did not receive those treatments. Similarly, subjects 3 and 4 are scored 1 on μ and A_2, and 0 on A_1 and A_3.

We will now define the vector τ of treatment effects as $[\mu \ \ \tau_1 \ \ \tau_2 \ \ \tau_3]$. Taking $\mathbf{X}$ as the design matrix, the analysis of variance model can be written in matrix terms as

$$\mathbf{y} = \mathbf{X}\tau + \mathbf{e}$$

which can be seen as being of the same form as the traditional regression equation. The elements of τ are the effects of each dummy treatment variable, just as the elements of b in the regression equation are the effects of each independent variable. Expanding, we obtain

$$\mathbf{y} = \begin{bmatrix} 1 & 1 & 0 & 0 \\ 1 & 1 & 0 & 0 \\ 1 & 0 & 1 & 0 \\ 1 & 0 & 1 & 0 \\ 1 & 0 & 0 & 1 \\ 1 & 0 & 0 & 1 \end{bmatrix} \times \begin{bmatrix} \mu \\ \tau_1 \\ \tau_2 \\ \tau_3 \end{bmatrix} + \begin{bmatrix} e_{11} \\ e_{21} \\ e_{12} \\ e_{22} \\ e_{13} \\ e_{23} \end{bmatrix}$$

$$\mathbf{y} = \qquad \mathbf{X} \qquad \times \ \tau \ + \ \mathbf{e}$$

which, following the rules of matrix multiplication, produces

$$Y_{11} = \mu + \tau_1 + e_{11}$$
$$Y_{21} = \mu + \tau_1 + e_{21}$$
$$Y_{12} = \mu + \tau_2 + e_{12}$$
$$Y_{22} = \mu + \tau_2 + e_{22}$$
$$Y_{13} = \mu + \tau_3 + e_{13}$$
$$Y_{23} = \mu + \tau_3 + e_{23}$$

For each subject we now have the model associated with her response. Thus, for the second subject in Treatment 2, $Y_{22} = \mu + \tau_2 + e_{22}$, and for the ith subject in Treatment j, we have $Y_{ij} = \mu + \tau_j + e_{ij}$, which is the usual analysis of variance model.

The point is that the design matrix allows us to view the analysis of variance in a multiple-regression framework, in that it permits us to go from

$$Y_{ij} = \mu + \tau_j + e_{ij} \qquad \text{to} \qquad \mathbf{y} = \mathbf{Xb} + \mathbf{e}$$

Moreover, the elements of **b** are the values of μ, τ_1, τ_2, ..., τ_k. In other words, these are the actual treatment effects in which we are interested.

The design matrix we have been using has certain technical limitations that must be circumvented. We are going to turn it into something that looks quite different but actually carries all of the same information. First, the matrix is redundant in the sense that if we are told that a subject is not in A_1 or A_2, we know without being told that she must be in A_3. This is another way of saying that there are only 2 *df* for treatments. For this reason we will eliminate the column headed A_3, leaving only $a - 1$ columns for the treatment effects. (We could eliminate any one of the three columns, but we usually drop the last one.) A second change is necessary if we want to use any computer program that obtains a multiple-regression equation by way of first calculating the intercorrelation matrix. The column headed μ has no variance, and therefore cannot enter into a standard multiple-regression program—it would cause us to attempt division by 0. Thus, it too must be eliminated. This is no real loss, since our ultimate solution will not be affected. In fact, the software will sneak it back in.

One further change will be made simply for the sake of allowing us to test the desired null hypotheses using the method to be later advocated for factorial designs. Because we have omitted a column dealing with the third (or *a*th) level of treatments, solutions given our modified design matrix would produce estimates of treatment effects in relation to $\overline{X}_3$ rather than in relation to $\overline{X}$. In other words, b_1 would turn out to be $(\overline{X}_1 - \overline{X}_3)$ rather than $(\overline{X}_1 - \overline{X})$. This is fine if that's what you want, but I would much rather see treatment effects as deviations from the grand mean. It just seems tidier. So we will modify the design matrix to make the mean $(\overline{X}_i)$ of each column of **X** equal to 0. Under this new system, a subject is scored 1 in column A_i if she is a member of Treatment A_i; she is scored -1 if she is a member of the *a*th (last) treatment; and she is scored 0 if neither of these conditions apply. (This restriction corresponds to the fixed-model analysis of variance requirement that $\sum \tau_i = 0$.)

These modifications have led us from

$$
\mathbf{X} = \begin{bmatrix} 1 & 1 & 0 & 0 \\ 1 & 1 & 0 & 0 \\ 1 & 0 & 1 & 0 \\ 1 & 0 & 1 & 0 \\ 1 & 0 & 0 & 1 \\ 1 & 0 & 0 & 1 \end{bmatrix} \text{ to } \begin{bmatrix} 1 & 1 & 0 \\ 1 & 1 & 0 \\ 1 & 0 & 1 \\ 1 & 0 & 1 \\ 1 & 0 & 0 \\ 1 & 0 & 0 \end{bmatrix} \text{ to } \begin{bmatrix} 1 & 1 \\ 1 & 0 \\ 0 & 1 \\ 0 & 1 \\ 0 & 0 \\ 0 & 0 \end{bmatrix} \text{ to } \begin{bmatrix} 1 & 0 \\ 1 & 0 \\ 0 & 1 \\ 0 & 1 \\ -1 & -1 \\ -1 & -1 \end{bmatrix}
$$

Although these look like major changes in that the last form of **X** appears to be far removed from where we started, it actually carries all the necessary information. We have merely eliminated redundant information, removed a constant term, and then caused the treatment effects to be given as deviations from $\overline{X}$.

16.2 One-Way Analysis of Variance

At this point a simple example is in order. Table 16.1 contains data for three subjects in each of four treatments. Table 16.1b shows the summary table for the corresponding analysis of variance, along with the value of η^2 (discussed in Chapter 11). Table 16.1c contains the estimated treatment effects $(\hat{\tau}_i)$ where $\hat{\tau}_i = \hat{\mu}_i - \hat{\mu}$. Because the fixed-model analysis of variance imposes the restriction that $\sum \tau_i = 0$, τ_4 is automatically defined by τ_1, τ_2, and τ_3 $(\tau_4 = 0 - \sum \tau_j)$.

Table 16.1 Illustrative calculations for simple one-way design with equal ns

(a) Data

Treatment 1	Treatment 2	Treatment 3	Treatment 4
8	5	3	6
9	7	4	4
7	3	1	9
8	5	2.667	6.333
			$\overline{X}_{..} = 5.500$

(b) Summary Table

Source	df	SS	MS	F	η^2
Treatments	3	45.667	15.222	4.46	.626
Error	8	27.333	3.417		
Total	11	73.000			

(c) Estimated Treatment Effects

$$\hat{\tau}_1 = \overline{X}_1 - \overline{X}_{..} = 8.0 - 5.5 = 2.5$$

$$\hat{\tau}_2 = \overline{X}_2 - \overline{X}_{..} = 5.0 - 5.5 = -0.5$$

$$\hat{\tau}_3 = \overline{X}_3 - \overline{X}_{..} = 2.67 - 5.5 = -2.83$$

Now let us approach the statistical treatment of these data by means of least-squares multiple linear regression. We will take as our criterion (Y) the raw data in Table 16.1. For the predictors we will use a design matrix *of the form*

$$X = \begin{array}{c} \text{Treatment 1} \\ \text{Treatment 1} \\ \text{Treatment 1} \\ \text{Treatment 1} \end{array} \begin{array}{ccc} A_1 & A_2 & A_3 \\ \left[\begin{array}{ccc} 1 & 0 & 0 \\ 0 & 1 & 0 \\ 0 & 0 & 1 \\ -1 & -1 & -1 \end{array}\right] \end{array}$$

Here the elements of any one row of the design matrix are taken to apply to *all the subjects in the treatment*. The multiple-regression solution using the design matrix **X** as the matrix of predictors is presented in Exhibit 16.1. Here the dependent variable (**Y**) is the first column of the data matrix. The next three columns together form the matrix **X**. SPSS was used to generate this solution, but any standard program would be suitable. (I have made some very minor changes in the output to simplify the discussion.)

Notice the patterns of intercorrelations among the **X** variables in Exhibit 16.1. This type of pattern with constant off-diagonal correlations will occur whenever there are equal numbers of subjects in the various groups. (The fact that we don't have constant off-diagonal correlations with unequal-n factorial designs is what makes our life more difficult in those situations.)

Notice that the regression coefficients are written in a column. This column can be called a *vector*, and is the vector **b**, or, in analysis of variance terms, the vector τ. Notice that $b_1 = 2.50$, which is the same as the estimated treatment effect of Treatment 1 shown in Table 16.1. In other words, $b_1 = \tau_1$. This also happens for b_2 and b_3. This fact necessarily follows from our definition of **X** and τ. Moreover, if we were to

	Y	X1	X2	X3
1	8.00	1.00	.00	.00
2	9.00	1.00	.00	.00
3	7.00	1.00	.00	.00
4	5.00	.00	1.00	.00
5	7.00	.00	1.00	.00
6	3.00	.00	1.00	.00
7	3.00	.00	.00	1.00
8	4.00	.00	.00	1.00
9	1.00	.00	.00	1.00
10	6.00	-1.00	-1.00	-1.00
11	4.00	-1.00	-1.00	-1.00
12	9.00	-1.00	-1.00	-1.00

Correlations

		Y	X1	X2	X3
Pearson Correlation	Y	1.000	.239	−.191	−.526
	X1	.239	1.000	.500	.500
	X2	−.191	.500	1.000	.500
	X3	−.526	.500	.500	1.000

Model Summary

Model	R	R Square	Adjusted R Square	Std.Error of the Estimate
1	.791(a)	.626	.485	1.848

[a] Predictors: (Constant), X3, X2, X1

Coefficients[a]

Model		Unstandardized Coefficients		Standardized Coefficients	t	Sig.
		B	Std. Error	Beta		
1	(Constant)	5.500	.534		10.307	.000
	X1	2.500	.924	.717	2.705	.027
	X2	−.500	.924	−.143	−.541	.603
	X3	−2.833	.924	−.812	−3.066	.015

[a] Dependent Variable:Y

ANOVA[b]

Model		Sum of Squares	df	Mean Square	F	Sig.
1	Regression	45.667	3	15.222	4.455	.040[a]
	Residual	27.333	8	3.417		
	Total	73.000	11			

[a]Predictors: (Constant), X3, X2, X1
[b]Dependent Variable:Y

Exhibit 16.1 SPSS regression analysis of data in Table 16.1

examine the significance of the b_i, given as the column of t-ratios, we would simultaneously have tests on the hypothesis ($H_0 : \tau_j = \mu_i - \mu = 0$). Notice further that the intercept (b_0) is equal to the grand mean ($\overline{Y}$). This follows directly from the fact that we scored the ath treatment as -1 on all coded variables. Using the (-1) coding, the mean of every column of $\mathbf{X}$ ($\overline{X}_j$) is equal to 0 and, as a result, $\sum b_1 \overline{X}_j = 0$ and therefore $b_0 = \overline{Y} - \sum b_1 \overline{X}_j = \overline{Y} - 0 = \overline{Y}$. This situation holds only in the case of equal ns, because otherwise $\overline{X}_i$ would not be 0 for all i. However, in all cases, b_0 is our best estimate of μ in a least squares sense.

The value of $R^2 = .626$ is equivalent to η^2, because they both estimate the percentage of variation in the dependent variable accounted for by variation among treatments.

If we test R^2 for significance, we have $F = 4.46, p = .040$. This is the F value we obtained in the analysis of variance, although this F can be found by the formula that we saw for testing R^2 in Chapter 15.

$$F(p, N - p - 1) = \frac{R^2(N - p - 1)}{(1 - R^2)p}$$

$$F(3,8) = \frac{.626(8)}{.374(3)} = 4.46$$

Notice that the sums of squares for Regression, Error, and Total in Exhibit 16.1 are exactly equivalent to the sums of squares for Between, Error, and Total in Table 16.1. This equality makes clear that there is complete correspondence between sums of squares in regression and the analysis of variance.

The foregoing analysis has shown the marked similarity between the analysis of variance and multiple regression. This is primarily an illustration of the fact that there is no important difference between asking whether different treatments produce different means, and asking whether means are a function of treatments. We are simply looking at two sides of the same coin.

We have discussed only the most common way of forming a design matrix. This matrix could take a number of other useful forms, but we won't go into that here. For a good discussion of these, see Cohen (1968).

16.3 Factorial Designs

We can readily extend the analysis of regression to two-way and higher-order factorial designs, and doing so illustrates some important features of both the analysis of variance and the analysis of regression. (A good discussion of this approach, and the decisions that need to be made, can be found in Harris (2005).) We will consider first a two-way analysis of variance with equal ns.

The Full Model

The most common model for a two-way analysis of variance is

$$Y_{ijk} = \mu + \alpha_i + \beta_j + \alpha\beta_{ij} + e_{ijk}$$

As we did before, we can expand the α_i and β_j terms by using a design matrix. But then how should the interaction term be handled? The answer to this question relies on the fact that an interaction represents a multiplicative effect of the component variables. Suppose we consider the simplest case of a 2×2 factorial design. *Letting the entries in each row represent the coefficients for all subjects in the corresponding cell* of the design, we can write our design matrix as

$$\mathbf{X} = \begin{array}{c} \\ a_1b_1 \\ a_1b_2 \\ a_2b_1 \\ a_2b_2 \end{array} \begin{array}{ccc} A_1 & B_1 & AB_{11} \\ \left[\begin{array}{ccc} 1 & 1 & 1 \\ 1 & -1 & -1 \\ -1 & 1 & -1 \\ -1 & -1 & 1 \end{array}\right] \end{array}$$

The first column represents the main effect of A, and distinguishes between those subjects who received A_1 and those who received A_2. The next column represents the main effect of B, separating B_1 subjects from B_2 subjects. The third column is the interaction of A and B. Its elements are obtained by multiplying the corresponding elements of columns 1 and 2. Thus, $1 = 1 \times 1$, $-1 = 1 \times -1$, $-1 = -1 \times 1$, and $1 = -1 \times -1$. Once again, we have as many columns per effect as we have degrees of freedom for that effect. We have no entries of 0 simply because with only two levels of each variable a subject must either be in the first or last level.

Now consider the case of a 2×3 factorial. With two levels of A and three levels of B, we will have $df_A = 1$, $df_B = 2$, and $df_{AB} = 2$. This means that our design matrix will require one column for A and two columns each for B and AB. This leads to the following matrix:

$$\mathbf{X} = \begin{array}{c} \\ a_1b_1 \\ a_1b_2 \\ a_1b_3 \\ a_2b_1 \\ a_2b_2 \\ a_2b_3 \end{array} \begin{array}{ccccc} A_1 & B_1 & B_2 & AB_{11} & AB_{13} \\ \left[\begin{array}{ccccc} 1 & 1 & 0 & 1 & 0 \\ 1 & 0 & 1 & 0 & 1 \\ 1 & -1 & -1 & -1 & -1 \\ -1 & 1 & 0 & -1 & 0 \\ -1 & 0 & 1 & 0 & -1 \\ -1 & -1 & -1 & 1 & 1 \end{array}\right] \end{array}$$

Column A_1 distinguishes between those subjects who are in treatment level A_1 and those in treatment level A_2. Column 2 distinguishes level B_1 subjects from those who are not in B_1, and Column 3 does the same for level B_2. Once again, subjects in the first $a-1$ and first $b-1$ treatment levels are scored 1 or 0, depending on whether or not they served in the treatment level in question. Subjects in the ath or bth treatment level are scored -1 for each column related to that treatment effect. The column labeled AB_{11} is simply the product of columns A_1 and B_1, and AB_{12} is the product of A_1 and B_2.

The analysis for a factorial design is more cumbersome than the one for a simple one-way design, since we wish to test two or more main effects and one or more interaction effects. If we consider the relatively simple case of a two-way factorial, however, you should have no difficulty generalizing it to more complex factorial designs. The basic principles are the same—only the arithmetic is messier.

As an illustration, we will consider a case of a 2×4 factorial with four subjects per cell. Such a design is analyzed by the conventional analysis of variance in Table 16.2, which also includes means, estimated effects, and values of η^2. From the summary

Table 16.2   Sample data and summary table for 2×4 factorial design

(a) Data

	B_1	B_2	B_3	B_4	Means
A_1	5	2	8	11	
	7	5	11	15	
	9	7	12	16	
	8	3	14	10	
	7.25	4.25	11.25	13.00	8.92750
A_2	7	3	9	11	
	9	8	12	14	
	10	9	14	10	
	9	11	8	12	
	8.75	7.75	10.75	11.75	9.75000
Means	8.000	6.000	11.000	12.375	9.34375

(b) Summary Table

Source	df	SS	MS	F	$\eta2$
A	1	5.282	5.282	<1	.014
B	3	199.344	66.448	11.452*	.537
AB	3	27.344	9.115	1.571	.074
Error	24	139.250	5.802		
Total	31	371.220			

*$p < .05$

(c) Estimated Treatment Effects

$\hat{\mu} = 9.34375$

$\hat{\alpha}_1 = A_1 - \overline{X}_{..} = 8.9375 - 9.34375 = -0.40625$

$\hat{\beta}_1 = \overline{B}_1 - \overline{X}_{..} = 8.0000 - 9.34375 = -1.34375$

$\hat{\beta}_2 = \overline{B}_2 - \overline{X}_{..} = 6.0000 - 9.34375 = -3.34375$

$\hat{\beta}_3 = \overline{B}_3 - \overline{X}_{..} = 11.0000 - 9.34375 = 1.65625$

$\widehat{\alpha\beta} = \overline{AB}_{11} - \overline{A}_1 - \overline{B}_1 + \overline{X}_{..} = 7.2500 - 8.9375 - 8.0000 + 9.34375 = -.34375$

$\widehat{\alpha\beta}_{12} = \overline{AB}_{12} - \overline{A}_1 - \overline{B}_2 + \overline{X}_{..} = 4.2500 - 8.9375 - 6.0000 + 9.34375 = -1.34375$

$\widehat{\alpha\beta}_{13} = \overline{AB}_{13} - \overline{A}_1 - \overline{B}_3 + \overline{X}_{..} = 11.2500 - 8.9375 - 11.0000 + 9.34375 = 0.65625$

table, it is apparent that the main effect of B is significant but that the effects of A and AB are not.

To analyze these data from the point of view of multiple regression, we begin with the following design matrix. Once again, the elements of each row apply to all subjects in the corresponding treatment combination.

$$\mathbf{X} = \begin{array}{c} \\ a_1b_1 \\ a_1b_2 \\ a_1b_3 \\ a_1b_4 \\ a_2b_1 \\ a_2b_2 \\ a_2b_3 \\ a_2b_4 \end{array} \begin{array}{ccccccc} A_1 & B_1 & B_2 & B_3 & AB_{11} & Ab_{12} & AB_{13} \\ \left[\begin{array}{ccccccc} 1 & 1 & 0 & 0 & 1 & 0 & 0 \\ 1 & 0 & 1 & 0 & 0 & 1 & 0 \\ 1 & 0 & 0 & 0 & 0 & 0 & 1 \\ 1 & -1 & -1 & -1 & -1 & -1 & -1 \\ -1 & 1 & 0 & 0 & -1 & 0 & 0 \\ -1 & 0 & 1 & 0 & 0 & -1 & 0 \\ -1 & 0 & 0 & 1 & 0 & 0 & -1 \\ -1 & -1 & -1 & -1 & 1 & 1 & 1 \end{array}\right] \end{array}$$

The first step in a multiple-regression analysis is presented in Exhibit 16.2 using all seven predictors (A_1 to AB_{13}). The results were obtained using SAS PROC CORR and PROC REG, although every software package should give the same answers. A program for doing this in R is presented on the Web site.

Exhibit 16.2 has several important features. First, consider the matrix of correlations among variables, often symbolized as **R**. Suppose that we simplify this matrix by defining the following sets of predictors: $A' = [A_1]$, $B' = [B_1, B_2, B_3]$, and $AB' = [AB_{11}, AB_{12}, AB_{13}]$. If we then rewrite the intercorrelation matrix, we have

$$\begin{array}{c} A' \\ B' \\ AB' \end{array} \begin{array}{ccc} A' & B' & AB' \\ \left[\begin{array}{ccc} 1.00 & 0.00 & 0.00 \\ 0.00 & 1.00 & 0.00 \\ 0.00 & 0.00 & 1.00 \end{array}\right] \end{array}$$

Notice that each of the effects is independent of the others (the intercorrelations are 0.00). Such a pattern occurs only if there are equal (or proportional) numbers of subjects in each cell; this pattern is also what makes simplified formulae for the analysis of variance possible. The fact that this structure disappears in the case of unequal ns is what makes our life more difficult when we have missing subjects.

Next notice the vector **b**, labeled as the Parameter Estimate. The first entry (b_0) is labeled Intercep and is the grand mean of all of the observations. The subsequent entries ($b_1 \ldots b_7$) are the estimates of the corresponding treatment effects. Thus $b_1 = \alpha_1$, $b_2 = \beta_1$, $b_5 = \alpha\beta_{11}$, and so on. Tests on these regression coefficients represent tests on the corresponding treatment effects. The fact that we have only the $(a-1)(b-1) = 3$ interaction effects presents no problem, due to the restrictions that these effects must sum to 0 across rows and down columns. Thus if $\alpha\beta_{12} = -1.34$, then $\alpha\beta_{22}$ must be $+1.34$. Similarly, $\alpha\beta_{14} = 0 - \Sigma\alpha\beta_{1j} = -\Sigma\alpha\beta_{1j} = 1.03$.

The value of $R^2 = .625$ represents the percentage of variation that can be accounted for by all the variables simultaneously. With equal ns, and therefore independent effects, it is equivalent to $\eta_A^2 + \eta_B^2 + \eta_{AB}^2 = .014 + .537 + .074 = .625$. The test on R^2 produces an F of 5.711 on 7 and 24 df, which, because it is significant ($p = .0006$), shows that there is a nonchance relationship between the treatment variables, considered together, and the dependent variable (Y).

Two more parallels can be drawn between Table 16.2, the analysis of variance, and Exhibit 16.2, the regression analysis. First, notice that $SS_{\text{regression}} = SS_{\text{Model}} = SS_Y(1 - R^2) = 231.969$. This is the variation that can be predicted by a linear combination of the predictors. This value is equal to $SS_A + SS_B + SS_{AB}$, although from Exhibit 16.2 we cannot yet partition the variation among the separate sources. Finally, notice that $SS_{\text{residual}} = SS_{\text{error}} = SS_Y(1 - R^2) = 139.250$, which is the error sum of squares in the analysis of variance. This makes sense when you recall that error is the variation that cannot be attributed to the separate or joint effects of the treatment variables.

```
Data Anova;
     infile 'Ex162.dat';
     input A1 B1 B2 B3 dv;
     AB11 = A1*B1;
     AB12 = A1*B2;
     AB13 = A1*B3;

Run;

Proc Corr Data = Anova;
     Var A1 B1 B2 B3 AB11 AB12 AB13;
Run;
Proc Reg Data = Anova;
     Model dv = A1 B1 B2 B3 AB11 AB12 AB13;
Run;
```

Pearson Correlation Coefficients, N = 32
Prob > |r| under H0: Rho=0

	A1	B1	B2	B3	AB11	AB12	AB13
A1	1.00000	0.00000	0.00000	0.00000	0.00000	0.00000	0.00000
		1.0000	1.0000	1.0000	1.0000	1.0000	1.0000
B1	0.00000	1.00000	0.50000	0.50000	0.00000	0.00000	0.00000
	1.0000		0.0036	0.0036	1.0000	1.0000	1.0000
B2	0.00000	0.50000	1.00000	0.50000	0.00000	0.00000	0.00000
	1.0000	0.0036		0.0036	1.0000	1.0000	1.0000
B3	0.00000	0.50000	0.50000	1.00000	0.00000	0.00000	0.00000
	1.0000	0.0036	0.0036		1.0000	1.0000	1.0000
AB11	0.00000	0.00000	0.00000	0.00000	1.00000	0.50000	0.50000
	1.0000	1.0000	1.0000	1.0000		0.0036	0.0036
AB12	0.00000	0.00000	0.00000	0.00000	0.50000	1.00000	0.50000
	1.0000	1.0000	1.0000	1.0000	0.0036		0.0036
AB13	0.00000	0.00000	0.00000	0.00000	0.50000	0.50000	1.00000
	1.0000	1.0000	1.0000	1.0000	0.0036	0.0036	

The REG Procedure
Dependent Variable: dv

Analysis of Variance

Source	DF	Sum of Squares	Mean Square	F Value	Pr > F
Model	7	231.96875	33.13839	5.71	0.0006
Error	24	139.25000	5.80208		
Corrected Total	31	371.21875			

Root MSE	2.40875	R-Square	0.6249
Dependent Mean	9.34375	Adj R-Sq	0.5155
Coeff Var	25.77928		

(continued)

Adapted from output by SAS Institute Inc.

Exhibit 16.2   Regression solutions using all predictors for data in Table 16.2

Parameter Estimates

Variable	DF	Parameter Estimate	Standard Error	t Value	Pr > |t|
Intercep	1	9.34375	0.42581	21.94	<.0001
A1	1	−0.40625	0.42581	−0.95	0.3496
B1	1	−1.34375	0.73753	−1.82	0.0809
B2	1	−3.34375	0.73753	−4.53	0.0001
B3	1	1.65625	0.73753	2.25	0.0342
AB11	1	−0.34375	0.73753	−0.47	0.6454
AB12	1	−1.34375	0.73753	−1.82	0.0809
AB13	1	0.65625	0.73753	0.89	0.3824

Exhibit 16.2   *(continued)*

Reduced Models

At this point we know only the amount of variation that can be accounted for by all of the predictors simultaneously. What we wish to know is how this variation can be partitioned among *A*, *B*, and *AB*. This information can be readily obtained by computing several reduced regression equations.

Because in the subsequent course of the analysis we must compute several multiple regression sums of squares relating to the different effects, we will change our notation and use the effect labels (α, β, and $\alpha\beta$) as subscripts. For the multiple regression just computed, the model contained variables to account for α, β, and $\alpha\beta$. Thus, we will designate the sum of squares regression in that solution as $SS_{\text{regression}_{\alpha,\beta,\alpha\beta}}$. $SS_{\text{regression}}$. If we dropped the last three predictors (AB_{11}, AB_{12}, and AB_{13}) we would be deleting those predictors carrying information concerning the interaction but would retain those predictors concerned with α and β. Thus, we would use the designation $SS_{\text{regression}_{\alpha,\beta}}$. If we used only *A*, AB_{11}, AB_{12}, and AB_{13} as predictors, the model would account for only α and $\alpha\beta$, and the result would be denoted $SS_{\text{regression}_{\alpha,\alpha\beta}}$.

I have run the individual regression solutions for our example, and the results are

$$SS_{\text{regression}_{\alpha,\beta,\alpha\beta}} = 231.969$$
$$SS_{\text{regression}_{\alpha,\beta}} = 204.625$$
$$SS_{\text{regression}_{\beta,\alpha\beta}} = 226.687$$
$$SS_{\text{regression}_{\alpha,\alpha\beta}} = 32.635$$

Now this is the important part. If the interaction term accounts for any of the variation in *Y*, then removing the interaction predictors from the model should lead to a decrease in accountable variation. This decrease will be equal to the variation that can be attributable to the interaction. By this and similar reasoning,

$$SS_{AB} = SS_{\text{regression}_{\alpha,\beta,\alpha\beta}} - SS_{\text{regression}_{\alpha,\beta}}$$
$$SS_{A} = SS_{\text{regression}_{\alpha,\beta,\alpha\beta}} - SS_{\text{regression}_{\beta,\alpha\beta}}$$
$$SS_{B} = SS_{\text{regression}_{\alpha,\beta,\alpha\beta}} - SS_{\text{regression}_{\alpha,\alpha\beta}}$$

Table 16.3   Regression solution for the data in Table 16.2

$$SS_{\text{regression}_{\alpha,\beta,\alpha\beta}} = 231.969 \qquad R^2 = .625$$

$$SS_{\text{residual}_{\alpha,\beta,\alpha\beta}} = 139.250$$

$$SS_{\text{regression}_{\alpha,\beta}} = 204.6245 \qquad R^2 = .551$$

$$SS_{\text{regression}_{\beta,\alpha\beta}} = 226.687 \qquad R^2 = .611$$

$$SS_{\text{regression}_{\alpha,\alpha\beta}} = 32.625 \qquad R^2 = .088$$

$$SS_{AB} = SS_{\text{regression}_{\alpha,\beta,ab}} - SS_{\text{regression}_{\alpha,\beta}} = 231.969 - 204.625 = 27.344$$

$$SS_A = SS_{\text{regression}_{\alpha,\beta,ab}} - SS_{\text{regreesion}_{\beta,\alpha\beta}} = 231.969 - 226.687 = 5.282$$

$$SS_B = SS_{\text{regression}_{\alpha,\beta,ab}} - SS_{\text{regression}_{\alpha,\alpha\beta}} = 231.969 - 32.625 = 199.344$$

$$SS_{\text{error}} = SS_{\text{residual}_{\alpha,\beta,ab}} = 139.250$$

Summary Table

Source	df	SS	MS	F
A	1	5.282	5.282	<1
B	3	199.344	66.448	11.452*
AB	3	27.344	9.115	1.571
Error	24	139.250	5.802	
	31	371.220		

*$p < .05$

The relevant calculations are presented in Table 16.3. (I leave it to you to verify that these are the sums of squares for regression that result when we use the relevant predictors.)

Looking first at the AB interactions, we see from Exhibit 16.2 that when the interaction terms were deleted from the model, the sum of squares that could be accounted for by the model decreased by

$$SS_{AB} = SS_{\text{regression}_{\alpha,\beta,\alpha\beta}} - SS_{\text{regression}_{\alpha,\beta}} = 231.969 - 204.625 = 27.344$$

This decrement can only be attributable to the predictive value of the interaction terms, and therefore

$$SS_{AB} = 27.344$$

By a similar line of reasoning, we can find the other sums of squares.[2]

Notice that these values agree exactly with those obtained by the more traditional procedures. Notice also that the corresponding decrements in R^2 agree with the computed values of η^2.

As Overall and Spiegel (1969) pointed out, the approach we have taken in testing the effects of A, B, and AB is not the only one we could have chosen. They presented two

---

[2] A number of authors (e.g. Judd & McClelland) prefer to use the increase in the error term (rather than the decrease in $SS_{\text{regression}}$) when an effect is deleted. The result will be the same.

alternative models that might have been considered in place of this one. Fortunately, however, the different models all lead to the same conclusions in the case of equal sample sizes, since in this situation effects are independent of one another and therefore are additive. When we consider the case of unequal sample sizes, however, the choice of an underlying model will require careful consideration.

16.4 Analysis of Variance with Unequal Sample Sizes

The least-squares approach to the analysis of variance is particularly useful for the case of factorial experiments with unequal sample sizes. However, special care must be used in selecting the particular restricted models that are employed in generating the various sums of squares.

Several different models could underlie an analysis of variance. Although in the case of equal sample sizes these models all lead to the same results, in the unequal n case they do not. This is because with unequal ns, the row, column, and interaction effects are no longer orthogonal and thus account for overlapping portions of the variance. [I would strongly recommend quickly reviewing the example given in Chapter 13, Section 13.11 (pp. 444–446).] Consider the Venn diagram in Figure 16.1. The gray area enclosed by the surrounding square will be taken to represent SS_{total}. Each circle represents the variation attributable to (or accounted for by) one of the effects. The area outside the circles but within the square represents SS_{error}. Finally, the total area enclosed by the circles represents $SS_{\text{regression}_{\alpha,\beta,\alpha\beta}}$, which is the sum of squares for regression when all the terms are included in the model. If we had equal sample sizes, none of the circles would overlap, and each effect would be accounting for a separate, independent, portion of the variation. In that case, the decrease in $SS_{\text{regression}}$ resulting from deleting of an effect from the model would have a clear interpretation—it would be the area enclosed by the omitted circle and thus would be the sum of squares for the corresponding effect.

But what do we do when the circles overlap? If we were to take a model that included terms for A, B, and AB and compared it to a model containing only A and B terms, the decrement would not represent the area of the AB circle, because some of that area still would be accounted for by A and/or B. Thus, SS_{AB}, which we calculate as $SS_{\text{regression}_{\alpha,\beta,\alpha\beta}} - SS_{\text{regression}_{\alpha,\beta}}$, represents only the portion of the enclosed area that is *unique* to AB—the area labeled with a "3." So far, all the models that have been seriously proposed are in agreement. SS_{AB} is that portion of the AB circle remaining after adjusting for A and B.

But now things begin to get a little sticky. Different and meaningful approaches have been put forth that differ in the way the remainder of the pie is allotted to

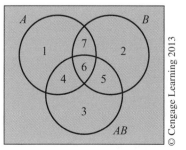

Figure 16.1   Venn diagram representing portions of overall variation

A and *B*. Overall and Spiegel (1969) put forth three models for the analysis of variance, and these models continue to generate a voluminous literature debating their proper use and interpretation, even though the discussion began 30 years ago. We will refer to these models as Type I, Type II, and Type III, from the terminology used by SPSS and SAS. (Overall and Spiegel numbered them in the reverse order, just to make things more confusing.) Basically, the choice between the three models hinges on how we see the relationship between the sample size and the treatments themselves, or, more specifically, how we want to weight the various cell means to produce row and column means. Before exploring that issue, however, we must first examine the competing methods.

Method III

Type III Sum of squares

Method III, (or **Type III Sum of squares**) is the method we used in the preceding section. In this case, each effect is adjusted for all other effects. Thus we obtain SS_{AB} as $SS_{\text{regression}_{\alpha,\beta,\alpha\beta}} - SS_{\text{regression}_{\alpha,\beta}}$, SS_A as $SS_{\text{regression}_{\alpha,\beta,\alpha\beta}} - SS_{\text{regression}_{\beta,\alpha\beta}}$, and SS_B as $SS_{\text{regression}_{\alpha,\beta,\alpha\beta}} - SS_{\text{regression}_{\alpha,\alpha\beta}}$. In terms of Figure 16.1, each effect is defined as the part of the area that is unique to that effect. Thus, SS_A is represented by area "1," SS_B by area "2," and SS_{AB} by area "3."

Method II

Type II SS

Method II (or **Type II SS**) breaks up the pie differently. We continue to define SS_{AB} as area "3." But now that we have taken care of the interaction, we still have areas "1," "2," "4," "5," "6," and "7," which can be accounted for by the effects of *A* and/or *B*. Method II essentially redefines the full model as $SS_{\text{regression}_{\alpha,\beta}}$ and obtains $SS_A = SS_{\text{regression}_{\alpha,\beta}} - SS_{\text{regression}_{\beta}}$, and SS_B as $SS_{\text{regression}_{\alpha,\beta}} - SS_{\text{regression}_{\alpha}}$. Thus, *A* is allotted areas "1" and "4," whereas *B* is allotted areas "2" and "5." Methods II and III are summarized in Table 16.4.

Table 16.4 Alternative models for solution of nonorthogonal designs

Method III
$$Y_{ijk} = \mu + \alpha_i + \beta_j + \alpha\beta_{ij} + e_{ijk}$$

Source	df	SS	Portion of Diagram
A	$a-1$	$SS_{\text{regression}_{\alpha,\beta,\alpha\beta}} - SS_{\text{regression}_{\beta,\alpha\beta}}$	1
B	$b-1$	$SS_{\text{regression}_{\alpha,\beta,\alpha\beta}} - SS_{\text{regression}_{\alpha,\alpha\beta}}$	2
AB	$(a-1)(b-1)$	$SS_{\text{regression}_{\alpha,\beta,\alpha\beta}} - SS_{\text{regression}_{\alpha,\beta}}$	3
Error	$N-ab$	$SS_{\text{residual}_{\alpha,\beta,\alpha\beta}}$	
Total	$N-1$	SS_Y	

Method II
$$Y_{ijk} = \mu + \alpha_i + \beta_j + \alpha\beta_{ij} + e_{ijk}$$
and
$$Y_{ijk} = \mu + \alpha_i + \beta_j + e_{ijk}$$

Source	df	SS	Portion of Diagram
A	$a-1$	$SS_{\text{regression}_{\alpha,\beta}} - SS_{\text{regression}_{\beta}}$	1 + 4
B	$b-1$	$SS_{\text{regression}_{\alpha,\beta}} - SS_{\text{regression}_{\alpha}}$	2 + 5
AB	$(a-1)(b-1)$	$SS_{\text{regression}_{\alpha,\beta,\alpha\beta}} - SS_{\text{regression}_{\alpha,\beta}}$	3
Error	$N-ab$	$SS_{\text{residual}_{\alpha,\beta,\alpha\beta}}$	
Total	$N-1$	SS_Y	

Both of these methods make a certain amount of sense when looked at from the point of view of the Venn diagram in Figure 16.1. However, the diagram is only a crude approximation and we have pushed it about as far as we can go.[3]

As Carlson and Timm (1974) argued, a more appropriate way to compare the models is to examine the hypotheses they test. These authors point out that Method III represents an estimation of treatment effects when cell means are weighted equally and is particularly appropriate whenever we consider sample size to be independent of treatment conditions. A convincing demonstration of this is presented in Overall, Spiegel, and Cohen (1975).[4] Carlson and Timm also showed that Method II produces estimates of treatment effects when row and column means are weighted by the sample size, but only when no interaction is present. When an interaction is present, simple estimates of row and column effects cannot be made, and, in fact, the null hypotheses actually tested are very bizarre indeed [see Carlson and Timm (1974) for a statement of the null hypotheses for Method II]. SPSS, which once relied on a method similar to Method II, finally saw the light some years ago and came around to using Method III as the default. They labeled this method "Unique SS" because each effect is assigned only that portion of the variation that it uniquely explains. SAS has always tested Type III sums of squares as the default. An excellent discussion of the hypotheses tested by different approaches is presented in Blair and Higgins (1978) and Blair (1978). Hector, von Felten, and Schmid (2010) provide an excellent discussion of the alternative analyses. As Cochran and Cox suggested, "the only complete solution of the 'missing data' problem is not to have them" (p. 82).

There is a third method of computing sums of squares that at first seems particularly bizarre. Just to make matters even more confusing than they need to be, this is the method that SPSS and SAS refer to as "**Type I SS**," or **Method I**, but which I will refer to as **hierarchical sums of squares**, though it is sometimes referred to as **sequential sums of squares**, which is the term that SPSS uses. The peculiar thing about this approach is that it is dependent on the order in which you name your variables. Thus if you tell SAS or SPSS to model (predict or account for) the dependent variable on the basis of A, B, and AB, the program will first assign $SS_A = SS_{\text{regression}_\alpha}$. Then $SS_B = SS_{\text{regression}_{\alpha,\beta}} - SS_{\text{regression}_\alpha}$, and finally $SS_{AB} = SS_{\text{regression}_{\alpha,\beta,\alpha\beta}} - SS_{\text{regression}_{\alpha,\beta}}$. In this situation the first effect is assigned all of the sums of squares it can possibly account for. The next effect is assigned all that it can account for *over and above* what was accounted for by the first one. Finally, the interaction effect is assigned only what it accounts for over and above the two main effects. But, if you ask the software to model the dependent variable on the basis of B, A, and AB, then SS_B will equal $SS_{\text{regression}_\beta}$, which is quite a different thing from $SS_{\text{regression}_{\alpha,\beta}} - SS_{\text{regression}_\alpha}$. The only time I could recommend using this approach is if you have a strong reason to want to control the variables in a particular order.[5] If you can defend the argument that Variable A is so important that it should be looked at first without controlling for any other variables, then perhaps this is a method you can use. But I have never seen a case where I would want to do that, with the possible exception of dealing

Type I SS

Method I

hierarchical sums
of squares

sequential sums
of squares

---

[3] From this discussion you could easily get the impression that Method II will always account for more of the variation than Method III. This is not necessarily the case, because the degree of overlap represents the correlation between effects, and suppressor relationships might appear as "black holes," canceling out accountable variation.

[4] If you go back to this older literature, it is important to note that when those papers were written, what we call Method III was then called Method 1 and vice versa.

[5] There is a good and honorable tradition of prioritizing variables in this way for theoretical studies using standard multiple regression with continuous variables. I have never seen a similar application in an analysis of variance framework, though I have seen a number of people talk about hypothetical examples.

with a variable as a covariate, which we will discuss shortly. The only reason that I bring the issue up here at all is to explain some of the choices you will have to make in using computer software.

Many people writing in the R community have very strong and vocal opinions about the model to be tested, and they hold strongly to the Model I solution. That is the solution provided by the "anova" command in the base version of R. Fox (2002) supports the Type II solution and his library of functions in R (called "car") can produce either Type II or Type III solutions assuming that you specify the proper contrasts. (Fox's main function is called Anova, with a capital A, whereas the base system uses a lower case "a" and solves for Type I sums of squares.) I prefer the Type III approach because most cases of unequal sample size in the behavioral have no reason to wish to weight some cells more than others. However, keep in mind that if there is a significant interaction you will probably not care to look at the main effects (simple effects would be more revealing), and in that case Methods II and III will bring you to the same place. However, if there is a noticeable, but nonsignificant interaction, the two models will lead you to different results. The battle over Type II and Type III sums of squares has gone on for a very long time, and there is no resolution in sight. I prefer Type III sums of squares but would not have a fit if I sat on a dissertation committee where the candidate used Type II sums of squares. Howell and McConaughy (1982) argued that there are very few instances in which one would want to test the peculiar null hypotheses tested by Method II when an interaction is present, but it is not worth falling on a sword in defense of either position. However, the conclusion to be drawn from the literature at present is that for the most common situations Method III is appropriate, because we usually want to test unweighted means. (This is the default method employed by SPSS. Method III sum of squares are the values labeled as Type III SS in SAS, and now by more recent versions of SPSS.) It is also the method that is approximated by the *unweighted means solution* discussed in Chapter 13. (You may recall that in Chapter 13 we saw that the traditional label "unweighted means solution" really should be the " **equally weighted means** solution," if that name hadn't been appropriated in the past for a different procedure, because, using it, we are treating all means equally, regardless of the sample sizes.) Method III essentially assumes that observations are missing completely at random, so there is no reason that a cell with more observations should carry any more weight than one with fewer observations. If this is not the case you should consider a different method.

equally weighted means

As an illustration of Method III, we will take the data used in the previous example but add six additional observations to produce unequal cell sizes. The data are given in Table 16.5, with the unweighted and weighted row and column means and the values resulting from the various regression solutions. The unweighted means are the mean of means (therefore, the mean of row_1 is the mean of the four cell means in that row). The weighted mean of row_1, for example, is just the sum of the scores in row_1 divided by the number of scores in row_1.

From Table 16.5 we see that $R^2_{\alpha,\beta,\alpha\beta} = .541$, indicating that approximately 54% of the variation can be accounted for by a linear combination of the predictor variables. We do not know, however, how this variation is to be distributed among A, B, and AB. For that we need to form and calculate the reduced models.

Testing the Interaction Effects

First, we delete the predictors associated with the interaction term and calculate $R^2_{\alpha,\beta}$. For these data, $R^2_{\alpha,\beta} = .483$, representing a drop in R^2 of about .05. If we examine the predictable

Table 16.5   Illustrative calculations for nonorthogonal factorial design

	B_1	B_2	B_3	B_4	Unweighted Mean	Weighted Mean
A_1	5	2	8	11		
	7	5	11	15		
	9	7	12	16	8.975	8.944
	8	3	14	10		
		9		9		
A_2	7	3	9	11		
	9	8	12	14		
	10	9	14	10		
	9	11	8	12	9.590	9.950
			7	13		
				11		
				12		
Unweighted Mean	8.000	6.475	10.625	12.029	9.282	
Weighted Mean	8.000	6.333	10.556	12.00		9.474

Full Model

$$R^2_{\alpha,\beta,\alpha\beta} = .541$$
$$SS_{\text{regression}_{\alpha,\beta,\alpha\beta}} = 216.017$$
$$SS_{\text{residual}} = 183.457$$

Reduced Models

$$R^2_{\alpha,\beta} = .490$$
$$SS_{\text{regression}_{\alpha,\beta}} = 195.805$$
$$R^2_{\beta,\alpha\beta} = .532$$
$$SS_{\text{regression}_{\beta,\alpha\beta}} = 212.552$$
$$R_{\alpha,\alpha\beta} = 0.77$$
$$SS_{\text{regression}_{\alpha,\alpha\beta}} = 30.845$$

sum of squares ($SS_{\text{regression}}$), we see that eliminating the interaction terms has produced a decrement in $SS_{\text{regression}}$ of

$$SS_{\text{regression}_{\alpha,\beta,\alpha\beta}} = 216.017$$
$$SS_{\text{regression}_{\alpha,\beta}} = \underline{195.805}$$
$$SS_{AB} = 20.212$$

This decrement is the sum of squares attributable to the AB interaction (SS_{AB}).

In the case of unequal ns, it is particularly important to understand what this term represents. You should recall that $SS_{\text{regression}_{\alpha,\beta,\alpha\beta}}$, for example, equals $SS_Y(R^2_{\alpha,\beta,\alpha\beta})$. Then

$$SS_{AB} = SS_Y(R^2_{\alpha,\beta,\alpha\beta}) - SS_Y(R^2_{\alpha,\beta})$$
$$= SS_Y(R^2_{\alpha,\beta,\alpha\beta} - R^2_{\alpha,\beta})$$
$$= SS_Y(R^2_{0(\alpha\beta.\alpha,\beta)})$$

The final term in parentheses is the squared semipartial correlation between the criterion and the interaction effects, partialling out (adjusting for) the effects of A and B. In other words, it is the squared correlation between the criterion and the part of the AB interaction that is orthogonal to A and B. Thus, we can think of SS_{AB} as really being $SS_{AB(adj)}$, where the adjustment is for the effects of A and B. (In the equal-n case, the issue does not arise because A, B, and AB are independent, and therefore there is no overlapping variation to partial out.)[6]

Testing the Main Effects

Because we are calculating Method III SS, we will calculate the main effects of A and B in a way that is directly comparable to our estimation of the interaction effect. Here, each main effect represents the sum of squares attributable to that variable after partialling out the other main effect and the interaction.

To obtain SS_A, we will delete the predictor associated with the main effect of A and calculate $SS_{\text{regression}_{\beta,\alpha\beta}}$. For these data, $R^2_{\beta,\alpha\beta} = .523$, producing a drop in R^2 of $.532 - .523 = .009$. In terms of the predictable sum of squares ($SS_{\text{regression}}$), the elimination of α from the model produces a decrement in $SS_{\text{regression}}$ of

$$SS_{\text{regression}_{\alpha,\beta,\alpha\beta}} = 216.017$$
$$SS_{\text{regression}_{\beta,\alpha\beta}} = \underline{212.552}$$
$$SS_{AB} = 3.465$$

This decrement is the sum of squares attributable to the main effect of A.

By the same reasoning, we can obtain SS_B by comparing $SS_{\text{regression}}$ for the full model and for a model omitting β.

$$SS_{\text{regression}_{\alpha,\beta,\alpha\beta}} = 216.017$$
$$SS_{\text{regression}_{\alpha,\alpha\beta}} = \underline{30.845}$$
$$SS_B = 185.172$$

These results are summarized in Table 16.6, with the method by which they were obtained. Notice that the sums of squares do not sum to SS_{total}. This is as it should be, because the overlapping portions of accountable variation (segments "4," "5," "6," and "7" of Figure 16.1) are not represented anywhere. Also notice that SS_{error} is taken as the SS_{residual} from the full model, just as in the case of equal sample sizes. Here again we define SS_{error} as the portion of the total variation that cannot be explained by any one or more of the independent variables.

---

[6] Some people have trouble understanding the concept of nonindependent treatment effects. As an aid, perhaps an extreme example will help point out how a row effect could cause an *apparent* column effect, or vice versa. Consider the following two-way table. When we look at differences among means, are we looking at a difference due to A, B, or AB? There is no way to tell.

	B_1	B_2	Means
A_1	$\bar{X} = 10$		10
	$n = 20$	$n = 0$	
A_2		$\bar{X} = 30$	30
	$n = 0$	$n = 20$	
Means	10	30	

Table 16.6   Calculation of sums of squares using Method III—the unweighted means solution

Method III (Unweighted Means)

Source	df	SS
A	$a-1$	$SS_Y(R^2_{\alpha,\beta,\alpha\beta} - R^2_{\beta,\alpha\beta})$
B	$b-1$	$SS_Y(R^2_{\alpha,\beta,\alpha\beta} - R^2_{\alpha,\alpha\beta})$
AB	$(a-1)(b-1)$	$SS_Y(R^2_{\alpha,\beta,\alpha\beta} - R^2_{\alpha,\beta})$
Error	$N-ab$	$SS_Y(1 - R^2_{\alpha,\beta,\alpha\beta})$
Total	$N-1$	SS_Y

Summary Table for Analysis of Variance

Source	df	SS	MS	F
A	1	3.465	3.465	<1
B	3	185.172	61.724	10.094
AB	3	20.212	6.737	<1
Error	30	183.457	6.115	
Total	37	(399.474)		

© Cengage Learning 2013

As I mentioned earlier, the unweighted-means solution presented in Chapter 13 is an approximation of the solution (Method III) given here. The main reason for discussing that solution in this chapter is so that you will understand what the computer program is giving you and how it is treating the unequal sample sizes.

A computer-based solution using SPSS is shown in Exhibit 16.3. It illustrates that the Type III sums of squares from SPSS do, in fact, produce the appropriate analysis of the data in Table 16.5.

Tests of Between-Subjects Effects

Dependent Variable: DV

Source	Type III Sum of Squares	df	Mean Square	F	Sig.
Corrected Model	216.017[a]	7	30.860	5.046	.001
Intercept	3163.341	1	3163.841	517.370	.000
Rows	3.464	1	3.464	.566	.458
Columns	185.172	3	61.724	10.093	.000
Rows* Columns	20.212	3	6.737	1.102	.364
Error	183.457	30	6.115		
Total	3810.000	38			
Corrected Total	399.474	37			

[a]R Squared = .541 (Adjusted R Squared = .434)

Adapted from output by SPSS, Inc.

Exhibit 16.3   SPSS analysis of the data in Table 16.7

16.5 The One-Way Analysis of Covariance

analysis of covariance

An extremely useful tool for analyzing experimental data is the **analysis of covariance**. As presented within the context of the analysis of variance, the analysis of covariance appears to be unpleasantly cumbersome, especially so when there is more than one covariate. Within the framework of multiple regression, however, it is remarkably simple, requiring little, if any, more work than does the analysis of variance. I will present the approach using coded dummy variables and multiple regression. However, once you understand the basic logic, you will understand the results from using SPSS or SAS without having to set up the design matrix yourself.

Suppose we wish to compare driving proficiency on three different sizes of cars to test the experimental hypothesis that small cars are easier to handle. We have available three different groups of drivers, but we are not able to match individual subjects on driving experience, which varies considerably within each group. Let us make the simplifying assumption, which will be discussed in more detail later, that the mean level of driving experience is equal across groups. Suppose further that using the number of steering errors as our dependent variable, we obtain the somewhat exaggerated data plotted in Figure 16.2. In this figure the data have been plotted separately for each group (size of car), as a function of driving experience (the **covariate**), and the separate regression lines have been superimposed.

covariate

One of the most striking things about Figure 16.2 is the large variability in both performance and experience within each treatment. This variability is so great that an analysis of variance on performance scores would almost certainly fail to produce a significant effect. Most of the variability in performance, however, is directly attributable to differences in driving experience, which has nothing to do with what we wish to study. If we could somehow remove (partial out) the variance that can be attributed to experience (the covariate), we would have a clearer test of our original hypothesis. This is exactly what the analysis of covariance is designed to do, and this is precisely the situation in which it does its job best—its job in this case being to reduce the error term.

A more controversial use of the analysis of covariance concerns situations in which the treatment groups have different covariate (driving experience) means. Such a situation (using the same hypothetical experiment) is depicted in Figure 16.3, in which two of the treatments

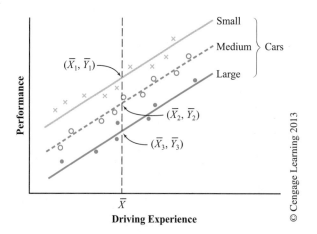

Figure 16.2 Hypothetical data illustrating error-reduction in the analysis of covariance

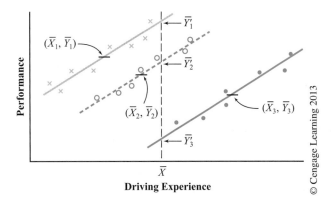

Figure 16.3 Hypothetical data illustrating mean adjustment in the analysis of covariance

adjusted Y
means

have been displaced along the X axis. At the point at which the three regression lines intersect the vertical line $X = \overline{X}$, you can see the values Y_1', Y_2', and Y_3'. These are the **adjusted Y means** and represent our best guess as to what the Y means would have been *if the treatments had not differed on the covariate*. The analysis of covariance then tests whether these *adjusted* means differ significantly, again using an error term from which the variance attributable to the covariate has been partialled out. Notice that the adjusted performance means are quite different from the unadjusted means. The adjustment has increased $\overline{Y}_1$ and decreased $\overline{Y}_3$.

Although the structure and procedures of the analysis of covariance are the same regardless of whether the treatment groups differ on the covariate means, the different ways of visualizing the problem as represented in Figures 16.2 and 16.3 are instructive. In the first case, we are simply reducing the error term. In the second case, we are both reducing the error term *and* adjusting the means on the dependent variable. We will have more to say about this distinction later in the chapter.

Assumptions of the Analysis of Covariance

homogeneity of
regression

Aside from the usual analysis of variance assumptions of normality and homogeneity of variance, we must add two more assumptions. First, we will assume that whatever the relationship between Y and the covariate (C), this relationship is linear.[7] Second, we will assume **homogeneity of regression**—that the regression coefficients are equal across treatments—$b_1^* = b_2^* = b_3^* = \cdots = b^*$. This is merely the assumption that the three lines in Figures 16.2 or 16.3 are parallel, and it is necessary to justify our substitution of one regression line (the pooled within-groups regression line) for the separate regression lines. As we shall see shortly, this assumption is testable. Note that no assumption has been made about the nature of the covariate; it may be either a fixed or a random variable. (It can even be a categorical variable if we create dummy variables to represent the different levels of the variable, as we did in the earlier parts of this chapter.)

Calculating the Analysis of Covariance

When viewed within the framework of multiple regression, the analysis of covariance is basically no different from the analysis of variance, except that we wish to partial out the

---

[7] Methods for handling nonlinear relationships are available but will not be discussed here.

effects of the covariate. As Cohen (1968) put it, "A covariate is, after all, nothing but an independent variable which, because of the logic dictated by the substantive issues of the research, assumes priority among the set of independent variables as a basis for accounting for *Y* variance." (p. 439).

If we want to ask about the variation in *Y* after the covariate (*C*) has been partialled out, and if the variation in *Y* can be associated with only *C*, the treatment effect (α), and error, then $SS_{\text{regression}_{C,\alpha}}$ represents the total amount of accountable variation. If we now compare $SS_{\text{regression}_{C,\alpha}}$ with $SS_{\text{regression}_C}$, the difference will be the variation attributable to treatment effects *over and above* that attributable to the covariate.

We will take as an example a variation on the study by Conti and Musty (1984) presented in Chapter 11. As you may recall, in that study the authors were interested in examining the effects of different amounts of THC, the major active ingredient in marijuana, injected directly into the brains of rats. The dependent variable was locomotor activity, which normally increases with the administration of THC by more traditional routes. Because of the nature of the experimental setting (all animals were observed under baseline conditions and then again after the administration of THC), activity should decrease in all animals as they become familiar and more comfortable with the apparatus. If THC has its effect through the nucleus accumbens, however, the effects of moderate doses of THC should partially compensate for this anticipated decrease, leading to relatively greater activity levels in the moderate-dose groups as compared to the low- or high-dose groups.

Conti and Musty (1984) actually analyzed postinjection activity as a percentage of preinjection activity, because that is the way such data are routinely analyzed in their field. An alternative procedure would have been to run an analysis of covariance on the postinjection scores, partialling out preinjection differences. Such a procedure would adjust for the fact that much of the variability in postinjection activity could be accounted for by variability in preinjection activity. It would also control for the fact that, by chance, there were group differences in the level of preinjection activity that could contaminate postinjection scores.

As will become clear later, it is important to note here that all animals were assigned at random to groups. Therefore, we would *expect* the group means on the preinjection phase to be equal. Any differences that do appear on the preinjection phase, then, are due to chance, and, *in the absence of any treatment effect*, we would expect that postinjection means, adjusted for chance preinjection differences, would be equal. The fact that subjects were assigned at random to treatments is what allows us to expect equal adjusted group means at postinjection (if H_0 is true), and this in turn allows us to interpret group differences at postinjection to be a result of real treatment differences rather than of some artifact of subject assignment.

The data and the design matrix for the Conti and Musty (1984) study are presented in Table 16.7. The raw data have been divided by 100 simply to make the resulting sums of squares manageable.[8] In the design matrix that follows the data, only the first and last subject in each group are represented. Columns 6 through 9 of *X* represent the interaction of the covariate and the group variables. These columns are used to test the hypothesis of homogeneity of regression coefficients across groups:

$$H_0: b_1^* = b_2^* = b_3^* = b_4^* = b_5^*$$

---

[8] If the data had not been divided by 100, the resulting sums of squares and mean squares would be $100^2 = 10,000$ times their present size. The *F* and *t* values would be unaffected.

Table 16.7   Pre- and postinjection data from Conti and Musty (1984)

	Control		0.1 μ g		0.5 μ g		1 μ g		2 μ g	
	Pre	Post	Pre	Post	Pre	Post	Pre	Post	Pre	Post
	4.34	1.30	1.55	0.93	7.18	5.10	6.94	2.29	4.00	1.44
	3.50	0.94	10.56	4.44	8.33	4.16	6.10	4.75	4.10	1.11
	4.33	2.25	8.39	4.03	4.05	1.54	4.90	3.48	3.62	2.17
	2.76	1.05	3.70	1.92	10.78	6.36	3.69	2.76	3.92	2.00
	4.62	0.92	2.40	0.67	6.09	3.96	4.76	1.67	2.90	0.84
	5.40	1.90	1.83	1.70	7.78	4.51	4.30	1.51	2.90	0.99
	3.95	0.32	2.40	0.77	5.08	3.76	2.32	1.07	1.82	0.44
	1.55	0.64	7.67	3.53	2.86	1.92	7.35	2.35	4.94	0.84
	1.42	0.69	5.79	3.65	6.30	3.84			5.69	2.84
	1.90	0.93	9.58	4.22					5.54	2.93
Mean	3.377	1.094	5.387	2.586	6.494	3.906	5.045	2.485	3.943	1.560

		Design Matrix									
	Cov	T_1	T_2	T_3	T_4	CT_1	CT_2	CT_3	CT_4		
	4.34	1	0	0	0	4.34	0	0	0		1.30
	...	...	...	...	...	...	...	...	...		...
	1.90	1	0	0	0	1.90	0	0	0		0.93
	1.55	0	1	0	0	0	1.55	0	0		0.93
	...	...	...	...	...	...	...	...	...		...
	9.58	0	1	0	0	0	9.58	0	0		4.22
	7.18	0	0	1	0	0	0	7.18	0		5.10
$X =$	...	...	...	...	...	...	...	...	...	$Y =$	...
(47×9)	6.30	0	0	1	0	0	0	6.30	0	(47×1)	3.84
	3.94	0	0	0	1	0	0	0	3.94		2.29
	...	...	...	...	...	...	...	...	...		...
	7.35	0	0	0	1	0	0	0	7.35		2.35
	4.00	−1	−1	−1	−1	−4.00	−4.00	−4.00	−4.00		1.44
	...	...	...	...	...	...	...	...	...		...
	5.54	−1	−1	−1	−1	−5.54	−5.54	−5.54	−5.54		2.93

The full model (including the interaction predictors) states that

$$Y_{ij} = \tau_j + c + c\tau_j + e_{ij}$$

where τ_j represents the treatment effect for the jth treatment, c represents the covariate, $c\tau_j$ represents our term testing homogeneity of regression, and e_{ij} represents the error associated with the ith subject in treatment j.

We can compare two models either on the basis of the change in $SS_{\text{regression}}$ between the two models (using the residual from the more complete model for our error term), or on the basis of the decrease in R^2. In this case the latter is somewhat simpler.

The regression analysis of this model would produce

$$R^2_{\tau,c,c\tau} = .8238$$

If there is no significant difference in within-treatment regressions—that is, if the regression lines are parallel and thus the slopes of the regression lines that could be calculated for each group separately are homogeneous—called homogeneity of regression—the deletion of the interaction term should produce only a trivial decrement in the percentage of accountable variation. When we delete the CT terms, we have

$$R^2_{\tau,c} = .8042$$

The F test on this decrement is the usual F test on the difference between two models:

$$F(f - r, N - f - 1) = \frac{(N - f - 1)(R^2_{\tau,c,c\tau} - R^2_{\tau,c})}{(f - r)(1 - R^2_{\tau,c,c\tau})}$$

$$= \frac{(47 - 9 - 1)(.8238 - .8042)}{(4)(.1762)} = 1.03$$

Given an F of 1.03 on 4 and 37 degrees of freedom, we have no basis to reject the assumption of homogeneity of regression (common regression coefficients) within the five treatments. Thus, we can proceed with the analysis on the basis of the revised full model that does not include the covariate by treatment interaction:

$$Y_{ij} = \mu + \tau_j + c + e_{ij}$$

This model will serve as the basis against which we compare reduced models.

The three sets of results of the multiple-regression solutions using (1) the covariate and dummy treatment variables, (2) just the treatment variables, and then (3) just the covariates are presented in Table 16.8.

From Table 16.8 you can see that using both the covariate (Pre) and the group membership dummy variates ($T_1 \ldots T_4$), the sum of squares for regression ($SS_{\text{regression}_{\tau,c}}$) is equal to 82.6435, which is the portion of the total variation that can be accounted for by these two sets of predictors. You can also see that the residual sum of squares (SS_{residual}) is 20.1254, which is the variability that cannot be predicted. In our analysis of covariance summary table, this will become the sum of squares for error.

When we remove the dummy group membership variates from the equation and use only the covariate (Pre) as a predictor, $SS_{\text{regression}}$ drops from 82.6435 to 73.4196. The difference between $SS_{\text{regression}}$ with and without the group membership predictors must be the amount of the sum of squares that can be attributable to treatment *over and above* the amount that can be explained by the covariate. For our data, this is

$$SS_{\text{treat(adj)}} = SS_{\text{regression}_{\tau,c}} - SS_{\text{regression}_c}$$

$$= 82.6435 - 73.4196$$

$$= 9.2239$$

This last value is called the *adjusted* treatment sum of squares for the analysis of covariance, because it has been adjusted for any effects of the covariate. In this case, it has been adjusted for the fact that the five groups differed on the pretest measure.

We need one additional term to form our analysis of covariance summary table, and that is the sum of squares to be attributed to the covariate. There are a number of different ways to define this term, but the most common is to define it analogously to the way the adjusted treatment effect was defined. We will attribute to the covariate that portion of the variation that cannot be defined by the treatment effect. In other words, we will take the model with both the covariate and treatment predictors and compare it to a model with only the treatment predictors. The difference in the two sums of squares due to regression will

Table 16.8   Regression analysis

(a) Full Model

$$\hat{Y}_{ij} = 0.4347(\text{Pre}) - 0.5922(T1) + 0.0262(T2) + 0.8644(T3)$$
$$+ 0.0738(T4) + 0.2183$$
$$R^2_{\tau,c} = .8042$$

Analysis of Variance Summary Table for Regression

Source	df	SS	MS	F
Regression	5	82.6435	16.5287	33.6726
Residual	41	20.1254	0.4909	
Total	46	102.7689		

(b) Reduced Model—Omitting Treatment Predictors

$$\hat{Y}_{ij} = 0.5311(\text{Pre}) - 0.26667$$
$$R^2_c = .7144$$

Analysis of Variance Summary Table for Regression

Source	df	SS	MS	F
Regression	1	73.4196	73.4196	112.5711
Residual	45	29.3493	0.6522	
Total	46	102.7689		

(c) Reduced Model—Omitting Covariate (Pre)

$$\hat{Y}_{ij} = -1.2321(T1) + 0.2599(T2) + 1.5794(T3) + 0.1589(T4) + 2.3261$$
$$R^2_\tau = .4311$$

Analysis of Variance Summary Table for Regression

Source	df	SS	MS	F
Regression	4	44.3028	11.0757	7.9564
Residual	42	58.4661	1.3921	
Total	46	102.7689		

be the sum of squares that the covariate accounts for *over and above* what is accounted for by treatment effects.[9] For our data, this is

$$SS_{\text{covariate}} = SS_{\text{regression}_{\tau,c}} - SS_{\text{regression}_\tau}$$
$$= 82.6435 - 44.3028$$
$$= 9.2239$$

We now have all the information necessary to construct the analysis of covariance summary table. This is presented in Table 16.9. Notice that in this table the error term is SS_{residual} from the full model and the other sums of squares are as calculated before.

---

[9] Not all software arranges things this way, so do not be surprised if you find printout with a different $SS_{\text{covariate}}$.

Table 16.9   Summary tables for analysis of covariance

General Summary Table for One-Way Analysis of Covariance

Source	df	SS
Covariate	c	$SS_{\text{regression}_{(r,c)}} - SS_{\text{regression}_{(r)}}$
Treat (adj)	$k - 1$	$SS_{\text{regression}_{(r,c)}} - SS_{\text{regression}_{(c)}}$
Error	$N - k - 1$	$SS_{\text{residual}_{(r,c)}}$
Total	$N - 1$	

Summary Table for Data in Table 16.7

Source	df	SS	MS	F
Covariate	1	38.3407	38.3407	78.108*
Treat (adj)	4	9.2239	2.3060	4.698*
Residual	41	20.1254	0.4909	
Total	46	102.7689		

Full Model:

$$\hat{Y}ij = 0.4347(Pre) - 0.5922(T_1) + 0.0262(T_2) + 0.8644(T_3)$$
$$+ 0.0738(T_4) + 0.2183$$

*$p < .05$

© Cengage Learning 2013

Notice also that there is one degree of freedom for the covariate, because there is one covariate; there are $(k - 1) = (5 - 1) = 4$ *df* for the adjusted treatment effect; and there are $N - k - c = 41$ *df* for error (where k represents the number of groups and c represents the number of covariates).

From the summary table we see that $SS_{\text{treat(adj)}} = 9.2239$. On 4 *df* this gives us $MS_{\text{treat(adj)}} = 2.3060$. Dividing that term by $MS_{\text{error}} = 0.4909$ we have $F = 4.698$ on (4,41) *df*, which is significant at $p < .05$. Thus, we can conclude that after we control for individual preinjection differences in activity, the treatment groups do differ on postinjection activity.

Adjusted Means

Because $F_{.05}(4,41) = 2.61 < F_{\text{obt}} = 4.698$, we have rejected $H_0: \mu_1(\text{adj}) = \mu_2(\text{adj}) = \mu_3(\text{adj}) = \mu_4(\text{adj}) = \mu_5(\text{adj})$ and conclude that there were significant differences among the treatment means after the effect of the covariate has been partialled out of the analysis. To interpret these differences, it would be useful, if not essential, to obtain the treatment means adjusted for the effects of the covariate. We are basically asking for an estimate of what the postinjection treatment means would have been had the groups not differed on the preinjection means. The adjusted means are readily obtained from the regression solution using the covariate and treatments as predictors.

From the analysis of the revised full model, we obtained (see Table 16.8)

$$\hat{Y}_{ij} = 0.4347(\text{Pre}) - 0.5922(T1) + 0.0262(T2) + 0.8644(T3)$$
$$+ 0.0738(T4) + 0.2183$$

Writing this in terms of means and representing adjusted means as $\overline{Y}'_j$, we have

$$\overline{Y}'_j = 0.4347(\overline{Pre}) - 0.5922(T1) + 0.0262(T2) + 0.8644(T3)$$
$$+ 0.0738(T4) + 0.2183$$

where $\overline{Pre} = 4.8060$ (the mean preinjection score) and T_1, T_2, T_3, and T_4 are $(0, 1, -1)$ variables. (We substitute the mean Pre score for the individual Pre score because we are interested in the adjusted means for Y if all subjects had received the mean score on the covariate.) For our data, the adjusted means of the treatments are:

$$\overline{Y}'_1 = 0.4347(4.8060) - 0.5922(1) + 0.0262(0) + 0.8644(0)$$
$$+ 0.0738(0) + 0.2183$$
$$= 1.7153$$

$$\overline{Y}'_2 = 0.4347(4.8060) - 0.5922(0) + 0.0262(1) + 0.8644(0)$$
$$+ 0.0738(0) + 0.2183$$
$$= 2.3336$$

$$\overline{Y}'_3 = 0.4347(4.8060) - 0.5922(0) + 0.0262(0) + 0.8644(1)$$
$$+ 0.0738(0) + 0.2183$$
$$= 3.1719$$

$$\overline{Y}'_4 = 0.4347(4.8060) - 0.5922(0) + 0.0262(0) + 0.8644(0)$$
$$+ 0.0738(1) + 0.2183$$
$$= 2.3813$$

$$\overline{Y}'_5 = 0.4347(4.8060) - 0.5922(-1) + 0.0262(-1) + 0.8644(-1)$$
$$+ 0.0738(-1) + 0.2183$$
$$= 1.9353$$

The adjusted means are plotted in Figure 16.4.

The grand mean is

$$\overline{Y}'_. = 0.4347(4.8060) - 0.5922(0) + 0.0262(0) + 0.8644(0)$$
$$+ 0.0738(0) + 0.2183$$
$$= 2.3075$$

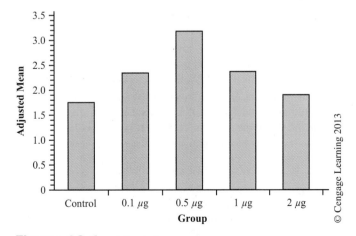

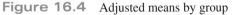

Figure 16.4   Adjusted means by group

which is the mean of the adjusted means. (In a case in which we have equal sample sizes, the adjusted grand mean will equal the unadjusted grand mean.)[10]

Now we are about to go into deep water in terms of formulae, and I expect eyes to start glazing over. I can't imagine that anyone is going to expect you to memorize these formulae. Just try to understand what is happening and remember where to find them when you need them. Don't expect to find them printed out by most statistical software.

Any individual comparisons among treatments would now be made using these adjusted means. In this case, however, we must modify our error term from that of the overall analysis of covariance. If we let $SS_{e(c)}$ represent the error sum of squares from an analysis of variance on the *covariate*, then Huitema (1980), in an excellent and readable book on the analysis of covariance, gives as a test of the difference between two adjusted means

$$F(1, N - a - 1) = \frac{(\overline{Y}_j' - \overline{Y}_k')^2}{MS_{error}'\left[\left(\frac{1}{n_j} + \frac{1}{n_k}\right) + \frac{(C_j - C_k)^2}{SS_{e(c)}}\right]}$$

MS_{error}'

where MS_{error}' is the error term from the analysis of covariance. For an excellent discussion of effective error terms and comparisons among means, see Winer (1971, pp. 771ff) and, especially, Huitema (1980). Huitema has a new edition due out soon.

As an example, suppose we wish to compare $\overline{Y}_1'$ and $\overline{Y}_3'$, which theory had predicted would show the greatest difference. From the preceding analysis, we either know or can compute

$$MS_{error}' = 0.4909$$

$$SS_{e(c)} = 202.938 \qquad \text{[calculation not shown]}$$

$$\overline{C}_1 = 3.3770 \qquad \overline{C}_3 = 6.4944$$

$$\overline{Y}_1' = 1.7153 \qquad \overline{Y}_3' = 3.1719$$

$$F(1, 41) = \frac{(1.7153 - 3.1719)^2}{0.4909\left[\left(\frac{1}{10} + \frac{1}{9}\right) + \frac{(3.3770 - 6.4944)^2}{202.938}\right]}$$

$$= \frac{2.1217}{0.1271} = 16.69$$

The critical value $F_{.05}(1,41) = 4.08$. We would thus reject the null hypothesis that the adjusted means of these two conditions are equal in the population. Even after adjusting for the fact that the groups differed by chance on the pretest, we find significant postinjection differences.

Exhibit 16.4 contains SPSS output for the analysis of variance. (The pretest and posttest means were computed using the **Compare means** procedure.) Notice that I requested a "spread versus level" plot from the options menu. This plots the group means against the group variances. If the variances are homogeneous and independent of the means, this plot should look random. The plot reveals that there is a correlation between the size of the mean and the size of the variance. Notice, however, that the relationship appears very much reduced when we plotted the relationship between the adjusted means and their standard errors.

---

[10] An alternative approach to calculating adjusted means is to define

$$\overline{Y}_j' = \overline{Y}_j - b_w(\overline{C}_j - \overline{C})$$

where $\overline{C}_j$ is the covariate mean for Group j, $\overline{C}$ is the covariate grand mean, and b_w is the regression coefficient for the covariate from the complete model (here $b_w = 0.4347$). This more traditional way of calculating adjusted means makes it clear that the adjusted mean is some function of how deviant that group was on the covariate. The same values for the adjusted means will result from using either approach.

Report

Treatment Group		PRETEST	POSTTEST
Control	Mean	3.3770	1.0940
	N	10	10
	Std. Deviation	1.3963	.5850
0.1 μg	Mean	5.3870	2.5860
	N	10	10
	Std. Deviation	3.4448	1.5332
0.5 μg	Mean	6.4944	3.9056
	N	9	9
	Std. Deviation	2.3781	1.4768
1 μg	Mean	5.0450	2.4850
	N	8	8
	Std. Deviation	1.6876	1.1874
2 μg	Mean	3.9430	1.5600
	N	10	10
	Std. Deviation	1.2207	.8765
Total	Mean	4.8060	2.2857
	N	47	47
	Std. Deviation	2.3788	1.4947

Tests of Between-Subjects Effects

Dependent Variable: POSTTEST

Source	Type III Sum of Squares	df	Mean Square	F	Sig.	Eta Squared
Corrected Model	82.644[a]	5	16.529	33.673	.000	.804
Intercept	.347	1	.347	.707	.405	.017
PRETEST	38.341	1	38.341	78.108	.000	.656
GROUP	9.224	4	2.306	4.698	.003	.314
Error	20.125	41	.491			
Total	348.327	47				
Corrected Total	102.769	46				

[a] R Squared = .804 (Adjusted R Squared = .780)

Estimated Marginal Means

Treatment Group

Dependent Variable: POSTTEST

Treatment Group	Mean	Std. Error	95% Confidence Interval Lower Bound	95% Confidence Interval Upper Bound
Control	1.715[a]	.232	1.246	2.185
0.1 μg	2.333[a]	.223	1.882	2.785
0.5 μg	3.172[a]	.248	2.671	3.672
1 μg	2.381[a]	.248	1.880	2.882
2 μg	1.935[a]	.226	1.480	2.391

Exhibit 16.4   SPSS output for analysis of Conti and Musty data

(continued)

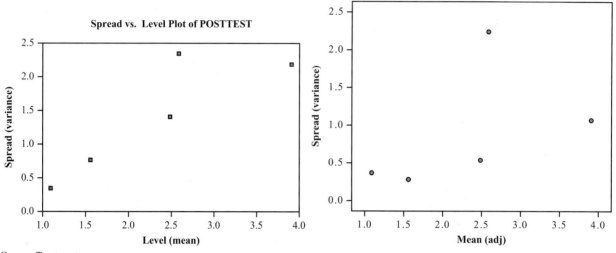

Groups: Treatment group

Exhibit 16.4   *(continued)*

16.6   Computing Effect Sizes in an Analysis of Covariance

As you might expect, computing effect sizes is a bit more complicated in analysis of covariance than it was in the analysis of variance. That is because we have choices to make in terms of the means we compare and the error term we use. You may recall that with factorial designs and repeated measures designs we had a similar problem concerning the choice of the error term for the effect size.

As before, we can look at effect size in terms of *r*-family and *d*-family measures. Normally I would suggest *r*-family measures when looking at an omnibus *F* test, and a *d*-family measure when looking at specific contrasts. We will start with an *r*-family example, and then move to the *d*-family. The example we have been using based on the study by Conti and Musty produced a significant *F* on the omnibus null hypothesis. Probably the most appropriate way to talk about this particular example would make use of the fact that Group (or Dose) was a metric variable, increasing from 0 to 2μg.[11] However, I am going to take a "second-best" approach here because the majority of the studies we run do not have the independent variable distributed as such an ordered variable.

r-Family Measure

As our *r*-family measure of association we will use η^2, acknowledging that it is positively biased. You should recall that η^2 is defined as the treatment *SS* divided by the total *SS*. But which sums of squares for treatments should we use—the ones from an analysis of variance on the dependent variable, or the ones from the analysis of covariance? Kline (2004) offers both of those alternatives, though he uses an adjusted SS_{total} in the second,[12] without

---

[11] SPSS will test polynomial contrasts on the adjusted means. Just click on the CONTRAST button and ask for polynomial contrasts. For this example there is a significant quadratic component.
[12] SPSS uses this same adjustment if you request effect sizes, and it is simply $SS_{\text{treat}} + SS_{\text{error}}$.

suggesting a choice. If the covariate naturally varies in the population (as it does in this case, where we expect different animals to vary in their pretest score, then it makes the most sense to divide the SS_{treat} from the analysis of covariance by the SS_{total} (unadjusted) from that analysis. This will produce a value of η^2, which is the percentage of "normal variation" accounted for by the independent variable.[13] Then

$$\eta^2 = \frac{SS_{treat(adj)}}{SS_{total}} = \frac{9.2239}{102.7689} = .09$$

An alternative approach, which will produce the same answer, is to take η^2 as the difference between the R^2 from a model predicting the dependent variable from only the covariate (the pretest) and one predicting the dependent variable from both the covariate and the treatment. The increase in explained variation from the first of these models to the second represents what the treatment contributes after controlling for the covariate. For our example R^2 using just the covariate is .714. (You can obtain this by an analysis of variance using the covariate as the independent variable, or by a regression of the independent variable on the covariate.) When you add in the treatment effect the R^2 is .804. These values are shown in the following table.

Step	Predictors	R^2	Change in R^2	F for change
1	Pretest	.714		
2	Pretest, Treatment	.804	.090	4.689

η^2 is the difference between these two values of R^2, which is the contribution to explained variation of the treatment after controlling for the covariate. This is the same value we obtained by the first approach.

d-Family Measure

Measures from the *d*-family often are more interpretable, and they are most often used for specific contrasts between two means. The example we have been using is not a very good one for a contrast of two means because the independent variable is a continuum. But I will use the contrast between the control group and the 0.5 μg group as an example, because these are the two conditions that Conti and Musty's theory would have expected to show the greatest mean difference. Because we are working with an analysis of covariance, the appropriate means to compare are the adjusted means $(\overline{Y}_i)$ from that analysis. In this case they are 3.1719 for the .5 μg condition and 1.7153 for the control condition. (You may recall that we performed a test on the difference between these adjusted means in the previous section, and it was significant.)

We have generally used

$$d = \frac{\hat{\psi}}{\hat{\sigma}}$$

as our effect size estimate. When we are comparing two group means, $\hat{\psi}$ is simply the difference between the two means because the coefficients are $[-1\ 0\ 1\ 0\ 0]$. For our example, $\hat{\psi}$ is $3.1719 - 1.7153 = 1.4566$. But the question of most importance is what we will use for the estimate of the standard deviation. One of several choices would be the square root of MS_{error} from an analysis of variance, because this would be an estimate of the average variability within each group, and would thus standardize the mean difference in the

---

[13] If you were interested in the η^2 for the quadratic relationship between dose and the activity level, controlling for the pretest activity level, you could just divide the $SS_{quadratic}$ by SS_{total}.

metric of the original measurements. (Recall that we used SS_{total} from the analysis of variance when we calculated η^2.) An alternative would be the square root of MS_{error} from the analysis of covariance, which would standardize the mean difference in the metric of the adjusted scores, which is a bit more difficult to understand. Cortina and Nouri (2000) have made the sensible suggestion that when the covariate normally varies in the population, as ours does, we want to include that variability in our estimate of error. This means that we would use the square root of MS_{error} from the analysis of variance on the posttest scores. In that analysis MS_{error} is 1.392, which is simply the weighted mean of the group variances. Then

$$d = \frac{\hat{\psi}}{\hat{\sigma}} = \frac{\overline{X}_3 - \overline{X}_1}{\sqrt{MS_{\text{error}}}} = \frac{3.1719 - 1.7153}{\sqrt{1.392}} = \frac{1.4566}{1.1798} = 1.23$$

Injection of the optimal dose of THC (0.5 μg) leads to an increase of postinjection activity by nearly 1 and a quarter standard deviations relative to the control group.

16.7 Interpreting an Analysis of Covariance

Interpreting an analysis of covariance can present certain problems, depending on the nature of the data and, more important, the design of the experiment. A thorough and readable discussion of most of these problems is presented by Huitema (1980). Other important sources for consideration of these problems are Anderson (1963), Evans and Anastasio (1968), Huitema (2005), Lord (1967, 1969), Maxwell and Cramer (1975), Reichardt (1979), Smith (1957), and Weisberg (1979).

The ideal application for an analysis of covariance is an experiment in which participants are randomly assigned to treatments (or cells of a factorial design). In that situation, the *expected value* of the covariate mean for each group or cell is the same, and any differences can be attributed only to chance, assuming that the covariate was measured before the treatments were applied. In this situation, the analysis of covariance will primarily reduce the error term, but it will also, properly, remove any bias in the dependent variable means caused by chance group differences on the covariate. This was the situation in the Conti and Musty (1984) study that we have been discussing.

In a randomized experiment in which the covariate is measured *after* the treatment has been applied and has affected the covariate, interpreting the results of an analysis of covariance is difficult at best. In this situation the expected values of the group covariate means are not equal, even though the subjects were assigned randomly. It is difficult to interpret the results of the analysis because you are asking what the groups would have been like had they not differed on the covariate, when in fact the covariate differences may be an integral part of the treatment effect. This problem is particularly severe if the covariate was measured with error (i.e., if it is not perfectly reliable). In this case an alternative analysis, called the **true-score analysis of covariance**, may be appropriate if the other interpretive problems can be overcome. Such an analysis is discussed in Huitema (1980, Chapter 14).

true-score analysis of covariance

nonequivalent groups design

When subjects are not assigned to the treatment groups at random, interpreting the analysis of covariance can be even more troublesome. The most common example of this problem is what is called the **nonequivalent groups design**. In this design, two (or more) intact groups are chosen (e.g., schools or classrooms of children), a pretest measure is obtained from subjects in both groups, the treatment is applied to one of the groups, and the two groups are then compared on some posttest measure. Since participants are not assigned to the groups at random, we have no basis for assuming that any differences that exist on the pretest are to be attributed to chance. Similarly, we have no basis for expecting the two groups to have the same mean on the posttest in the absence of a real treatment effect. Huitema (1980, pp. 149ff) gives an excellent demonstration that when the groups differ at the beginning of the experiment, the phenomenon of regression to the mean could lead to posttest differences even in the absence of a treatment effect. For alternative analyses that are useful under certain conditions, see Huitema (1980). Maris (1998) takes a different view of the issue.

The problems of interpreting results of designs in which subjects are not randomly assigned to the treatment groups are not easily overcome. This is one of the reasons why random assignment is even more important than random selection of subjects. It is difficult to overestimate the virtues of random assignment, both for interpreting data and for making causal statements about the relationship between variables. In what is probably only a slight overstatement of the issue, Lord (1967) remarked, "In the writer's opinion, the explanation is that with the data usually available for such studies, there is simply no logical or statistical procedure that can be counted on to make proper allowances for uncontrolled pre-existing differences between groups" (p. 305). (Lord was *not* referring to differences that arise by chance through random assignment.) Anderson (1963) made a similar point by stating, "One may well wonder exactly what it means to ask what the data would be like if they were not what they are" (p. 170). All of this is not to say that the analysis of covariance has no place in the analysis of data in which the treatments differ on the covariate. Anyone using covariance analysis, however, must think carefully about her data and the practical validity of the conclusions she draws.

16.8   Reporting the Results of an Analysis of Covariance

The only difference between describing the results of an analysis of covariance and an analysis of variance is that we must refer to the covariate and to adjusted means. For the experiment by Conti and Musty we could write

> Conti and Musty (1984) examined the effect of THC on locomotor activity in rats. They predicted that moderate doses of THC should show the greatest increase in activity (or the least decrease due to adaptation). After a pretesting session five different groups of rats were randomly assigned to receive 0, 0.1 μg, 0.5 μg, 1 μg, or 2 μg of THC. Activity level was measured in a 10-minute postinjection interval. Because there was considerable variability in pretest activity, the pretest measure was used as a covariate in the analysis.

> The analysis of covariance was significant ($F(4,41) = 4.694$, $p = .003$), with intermediate doses showing greater effect. Eta-squared was .09 using a SS_{total} that has not been adjusted for the covariate. A contrast of the means of the control group and the 0.5 μg group revealed a significant difference ($F(1,41) = 16.69$, $p < .05$), with a standardized effect size (d) of 1.23.

16.9   The Factorial Analysis of Covariance

The analysis of covariance applies to factorial designs just as well as it does to single-variable designs. Once again, the covariate may be treated as a variable that, because of methodological considerations, assumes priority in the analysis. In this section we will deal only with the case of equal cell sizes, but the generalization to unequal ns is immediate.

The logic of the analysis is straightforward and follows that used in the previous examples. $SS_{\text{regression}_{c,\alpha,\beta,\alpha\beta}}$ is the variation attributable to a linear combination of the covariate, the main effects of A and B, and the AB interaction. Similarly, $SS_{\text{regression}_{c,\alpha,\beta}}$ is the variation attributable to the linear combination of the covariate and the main effects of A and B. The difference

$$SS_{\text{regression}_{c,\alpha,\beta,\alpha\beta}} - SS_{\text{regression}_{c,\alpha,\beta}}$$

is the variation attributable to the AB interaction, with the covariate and the main effects partialled out. Since, with equal sample sizes, the two main effects and the interaction are orthogonal, all that is *actually* partialled out in equal n designs is the covariate.

By the same line of reasoning

$$SS_{\text{regression}_{c,\alpha,\beta,\alpha\beta}} - SS_{\text{regression}_{c,\alpha,\alpha\beta}}$$

represents the variation attributable to B, partialling out the covariate, and

$$SS_{\text{regression}_{c,\alpha,\beta,\alpha\beta}} - SS_{\text{regression}_{c,\beta,\alpha\beta}}$$

represents the variation attributable to the main effect of A, again partialling out the covariate.

The error term represents the variation remaining after controlling for A, B, and AB, and the covariate. As such it is given by

$$SS_{\text{residual}_{c,\alpha,\beta,\alpha\beta}}$$

The general structure of the analysis is presented in Table 16.10. Notice that once again the error term loses a degree of freedom for each covariate. Because the independent variable and the covariate account for overlapping portions of the variation, their sums of squares will not equal SS_{total}.

As an example, consider the study by Spilich et al. (1992) that we examined in Chapter 13 on performance as a function of cigarette smoking. In that study subjects performed either a Pattern Recognition task, a Cognitive task, or a Driving Simulation task. The subjects were divided into three groups. One group (Active Smoking) smoked during or just before the task. A second group (Delayed Smoking) were smokers who had not smoked for three hours, and a third group (NonSmoking) was composed of NonSmokers. The dependent variable was the number of errors on the task. To make this suitable for an analysis of covariance I have added an additional (hypothetical) variable, which is the subject's measured level of distractibility. (Higher distractibility scores indicate a greater ease at being distracted.)

The data are presented in Table 16.11 and represent a 3×3 factorial design with one covariate (Distract).

Table 16.12 contains an abbreviated form of the design matrix, showing only the entries for the first and last subject in each cell. Notice that the matrix contains a column for

Table 16.10 Structure of the analysis of covariance for factorial designs

Source	df	SS
A(adj)	$a-1$	$SS_{\text{regression}_{c,\alpha,\beta,ab}} - SS_{\text{regression}_{c,\beta,ab}}$
B(adj)	$b-1$	$SS_{\text{regression}_{c,\alpha,\beta,ab}} - SS_{\text{regression}_{c,\alpha,ab}}$
AB (adj)	$(a-1)(b-1)$	$SS_{\text{regression}_{c,\alpha,\beta,ab}} - SS_{\text{regression}_{c,\alpha,\beta}}$
Error	$N-ab-c$	$SS_{\text{residual}_{c,\alpha,\beta,ab}}$
Covariate	c	$SS_{\text{regression}_{c,\alpha,\beta,ab}} - SS_{\text{regression}_{\alpha,\beta,ab}}$
Total	$N-1$	

© Cengage Learning 2013

Table 16.11   Hypothetical data on smoking and performance (modeled on Spilich et al., 1992)

							Pattern Recognition									
NS: Errors	9	8	12	10	7	10	9	11	8	10	8	10	8	11	10
Distract	107	133	123	94	83	86	112	117	130	111	102	120	118	134	97
DS: Errors	12	7	14	4	8	11	16	17	5	6	9	6	6	7	16
Distract	101	75	138	94	138	127	126	124	100	103	120	91	138	88	118
AS: Errors	8	8	9	1	9	7	16	19	1	1	22	12	18	8	10
Distract	64	135	130	106	123	117	124	141	95	98	95	103	134	119	123
							Cognitive Task									
NS: Errors	27	34	19	20	56	35	23	37	4	30	4	42	34	19	49
Distract	126	154	113	87	125	130	103	139	85	131	98	107	107	96	143
DS: Errors	48	29	34	6	18	63	9	54	28	71	60	54	51	25	49
Distract	113	100	114	74	76	162	80	118	99	146	132	135	111	106	96
AS: Errors	34	65	55	33	42	54	21	44	61	38	75	61	51	32	47
Distract	108	191	112	98	128	145	76	107	128	128	142	144	131	110	132
							Driving Simulation									
NS: Errors	3	2	0	0	6	2	0	6	4	1	0	0	6	2	3
Distract	130	83	91	92	109	106	99	109	136	102	119	84	68	67	114
DS: Errors	7	0	6	0	12	17	1	11	4	4	3	5	16	5	11
Distract	93	102	108	100	123	131	99	116	81	103	78	103	139	101	102
AS: Errors	15	2	2	14	5	0	16	14	9	17	15	9	3	15	13
Distract	110	96	112	114	137	125	168	102	109	111	137	106	117	101	116

the covariate (denoted C), the usual design matrix elements for the main effects of Task (T) and Group (G), and the Task $\times$ Group interaction. I have also added columns representing the interaction of the covariate with the Task $\times$ Group interaction. The latter will be used to test the hypothesis $H_0 : b_i^* = b_j^*$ for all values of i and j, because the assumption of homogeneity of regression applies to any analysis of covariance.

It is important to consider just what the interactions involving the covariate represent. If I had included the terms CT_1 and CT_2 I could have used them to test the null hypothesis that the regression lines of Errors as a function of Distract have equivalent slopes in the three tasks. Similarly, if I had included CG_1 and CG_2, I could have tested homogeneity of regression in each of the three smoking groups. Because I am most interested in testing the hypothesis of homogeneity of regression in each of the nine cells, I have included only the CTG_{ij} terms.

The first regression is based on all predictors in X. From this analysis we obtain

$$SS_{\text{regression}_{c, \alpha, \beta, \alpha\beta, c\alpha\beta}} = 36724.771$$

$$MS_{\text{residual}_{c, \alpha, \beta, \alpha\beta, c\alpha\beta}} = 71.134$$

If we drop the interaction terms representing the interaction of the covariate (Distract) with the Task $\times$ Group interaction, we have

$$SS_{\text{regression}_{c, \alpha, \beta, \alpha\beta}} = 36389.60175$$

The difference between these two sums of squares = 335.16925. The most complete model had 13 degrees of freedom, while the second had 9 df, meaning that the above sum of squares is based on $13 - 9 = 4$ df. Converting to mean squares we have

$$MS_{\text{difference}} = 335.16925/4 = 83.79231$$

Table 16.12 Design matrix for the analysis of covariance for smoking data

	C	T_1	T_2	G_1	G_2	TG_{11}	TG_{12}	TG_{21}	TG_{22}	cTG_{11}	cTG_{12}	cTG_{21}	cTG_{22}		
	107	1	0	1	0	1	0	0	0	107	0	0	0		9
	...	...	...	...	...	...	...	...	...	...	...	...	...		...
	97	1	0	1	0	1	0	0	0	97	0	0	0		10
	101	1	0	0	1	0	1	0	0	0	101	0	0		12
	...	...	...	...	...	...	...	...	...	...	...	...	...		...
	118	1	0	0	1	0	1	0	0	0	118	0	0		16
	64	1	0	−1	−1	−1	−1	0	0	−64	−64	0	0		8
	...	...	...	...	...	...	...	...	...	...	...	...	...		...
	123	1	0	−1	−1	−1	−1	0	0	−123	−123	0	0		10
	126	0	1	1	0	0	0	1	0	0	0	126	0		27
	...	...	...	...	...	...	...	...	...	...	...	...	...		...
	143	0	1	1	0	0	0	1	0	0	0	143	0		49
	113	0	1	0	1	0	0	0	1	0	0	0	113	**Y**	48
	...	...	...	...	...	...	...	...	...	...	...	...	...	=	...
X	96	0	1	0	1	0	0	0	1	0	0	0	96		49
=	108	0	1	−1	−1	0	0	−1	−1	0	0	−108	−108		34
	...	...	...	...	...	...	...	...	...	...	...	...	...		...
	132	0	1	−1	−1	0	0	−1	−1	0	0	−132	−132		47
	130	−1	−1	1	0	−1	0	1	0	−130	0	−130	0		3
	...	...	...	...	...	...	...	...	...	...	...	...	...		...
	114	−1	−1	1	0	−1	0	1	0	−114	0	−114	0		3
	93	−1	−1	0	1	0	−1	0	−1	0	−93	0	−93		7
	...	...	...	...	...	...	...	...	...	...	...	...	...		...
	102	−1	−1	0	1	0	−1	0	−1	0	−102	0	−102		11
	110	−1	−1	−1	−1	1	1	1	1	110	110	110	110		15
	...	...	...	...	...	...	...	...	...	...	...	...	...		...
	116	−1	−1	−1	−1	1	1	1	1	116	116	116	116		13

We can test the difference between these two models by using MS_{residual} from the more complete model and computing

$$F = \frac{MS_{\text{difference}}}{MS_{\text{residual}}} = \frac{83.792}{71.134} = 1.18$$

This is an F on $[(f - r), (N - f - 1)] = 4$ and 121 df. The critical value is $F_{.05}(4,121) = 2.45$, so we will not reject the null hypothesis of homogeneity of regression. We will conclude that we have no reason to doubt that the regression lines relating Errors to Distract have the same slope in the nine cells. This will allow us to adopt a much simpler full model against which to compare subsequent reduced models. Our revised full model is

$$\hat{Y} = b_0 + b_1C + b_2T_1 + b_3T_2 + b_4G_1 + b_5G_2 + b_6TG_{11} + b_7TG_{12} + b_8TG_{21} + b_9TG_{22}$$

or, in more traditional analysis of variance terms,

$$Y_{ijk} = \mu + C_k + \alpha_i + \beta_j + \alpha\beta_{ij} + \varepsilon_{ijk}$$

The results of the several multiple regression solutions needed for the analysis of covariance are shown in Table 16.13. By calculating and testing the differences between full and reduced models, you will be able to compute the complete analysis of covariance.

Exhibit 16.5 contains the results of an SPSS analysis of these data. You should compare your results with the results in that exhibit.

Table 16.13   Regression results for various models for data in Table 16.11

Model	$SS_{regression}$	$MS_{residual}$	R^2
C, T, G, TG	36,389.602	71.539	.803
C, T, G	35,154.816		.775
C, G, TG	12,519.117		.276
C, T, TG	35,416.789		.781
T, G, TG	31,744.726		.700

© Cengage Learning 2013

Tests of Between-Subjects Effects

Dependent Variable: ERRORS

Source	Type III Sum of Squares	df	Mean Square	F	Sig.	Eta Squared	Noncent. Parameter	Observed Power[a]
Corrected Model	36389.602[b]	9	4043.289	56.519	.000	.803	508.671	1.000
Intercept	892.395	1	892.395	12.474	.001	.091	12.474	.939
DISTRACT	4644.876	1	4644.876	64.928	.000	.342	64.928	1.000
TASK	23870.485	2	11935.243	166.836	.000	.727	333.673	1.000
SMKGRP	563.257	2	281.629	3.937	.022	.059	7.873	.699
TASK * SMKGRP	1626.511	4	406.628	5.684	.000	.154	22.736	.977
Error	8942.324	125	71.539					
Total	90341.000	135						
Corrected Total	45331.926	134						

[a] Computed using alpha = .05
[b] R Squared = .803 (Adjusted R Squared = .789)

1. Task * Smoking Group

Dependent Variable: ERRORS

				95% Confidence Interval	
Task	Smoking Group	Mean	Std. Error	Lower Bound	Upper Bound
Patrecog	NonSmokers	9.805[a]	2.184	5.482	14.128
	Delayed smokers	9.732[a]	2.184	5.410	14.054
	Active Smokers	9.558[a]	2.184	5.235	13.882
Cognitive	NonSmokers	27.770[a]	2.188	23.440	32.101
	Delayed smokers	40.436[a]	2.185	36.112	44.760
	Active Smokers	43.785[a]	2.233	39.366	48.204
Driving	NonSmokers	8.505[a]	2.191	4.169	12.842
	Delayed smokers	8.921[a]	2.200	4.568	13.275
	Active Smokers	5.820[a]	2.226	1.414	10.226

[a] Evaluated at covariates appeared in the model:DISTRACT = 112.52.

Exhibit 16.5   SPSS analysis of covariance of Spilich data

Adapted from output by SPSS, Inc.

(continued)

2. Task

Dependent Variable: ERRORS

Task	Mean	Std. Error	95% Confidence Interval	
			Lower Bound	Upper Bound
Patrecog	9.699[a]	1.261	7.203	12.194
Cognitive	37.330[a]	1.274	34.810	39.851
Driving	7.749[a]	1.273	5.230	10.268

[a] Evaluated at covariates appeared in the model: DISTRACT = 112.52.

3. Smoking Group

Dependent Variable: ERRORS

Smoking Group	Mean	Std. Error	95% Confidence Interval	
			Lower Bound	Upper Bound
NonSmokers	15.360[a]	1.264	12.859	17.862
Delayed smoker	19.696[a]	1.266	17.191	22.202
Active Smokers	19.721[a]	1.261	17.225	22.217

[a] Evaluated at covariates appeared in the model: DISTRACT = 112.52.

Exhibit 16.5   *(continued)*

For purposes of comparison I have presented the analysis of variance from Exhibit 13.1. This is the analysis on the same data, but without the covariate.

Source	df	SS	MS	F
Task	2	28,661.526	14,330.763	132.895*
Group	2	1813.748	906.874	8.410*
Task × Group	4	1269.452	317.363	2.943*
Error	126	13,587.200	107.835	
Total	134	45,331.926		

© Cengage Learning 2013

$p < .05$

Notice that in this analysis we have a significant effect due to Task, which is uninteresting because the tasks were quite different and we would expect that some tasks would lead to more errors than others. We have a significant effect due to Group, but the interaction better addresses our interests. We have a Task × Group interaction, which was what we were seeking because it tells us that smoking makes a difference in certain kinds of situations (which require a lot of cognitive processing) but not in others. Notice also that our MS_{error} was 107.835, whereas in the analysis of covariance it was 71.539.

When we look at our analysis of covariance, one of the first things we see is that MS_{error} (71.539) is about one-third smaller than it was in the analysis of variance. This is due to the fact that the covariate (Distract) was able to explain much of the variability in Errors that had been left unexplained in the analysis of variance.

Notice that Exhibit 16.5 presents *partial* eta-squared for the effects. These effect-size measures can be calculated as the difference between two R^2 values, divided by $(1 - R^2_{\text{reduced}})$. For example, the model without the dummy variables for Task has an $R^2 = .276$. This leaves $1 - .276 = 72.4\%$ of the variation unexplained. When we add in the Task variables (going to the full model) we have $R^2 = .803$. This is an increase of $.803 - .276 = .527$, which accounts for $.527/.724 = 72.8\%$ of the variation *that had been left unexplained*. This is the value given in Exhibit 16.5 for Task, although SPSS doesn't mention that this is a partial η^2. Similar calculations will reproduce the other values.

Adjusted Means

The method of obtaining adjusted means is simply an extension of the method employed in the Conti and Musty example. We want to know what the cell means would have been if the treatment combinations had not differed on the covariate.

From the full model we have

$$\hat{Y} = b_0 + b_1 C + b_2 T_1 + b_3 T_2 + b_4 G_1 + b_5 G_2 + b_6 TG_{11} + b_7 TG_{12} + b_8 TG_{21} + b_9 TG_{22}$$

which equals

$$\hat{Y} = -14.654 - 8.561 T_1 + 19.071 T_2 - 3.794 G_1 + 1.437 G_2 + 3.901 TG_{11} - 1.404 TG_{12}$$
$$- 5.766 TG_{21} + 1.668 TG_{22} + 0.293 \text{Distract}$$

Because we want to know what the Y means would be if the treatments did not differ on the covariate, we will set $C = \overline{C} = 112.518$ for all treatments.

For all observations in Cell$_{11}$ the appropriate row of the design matrix, with C replaced by $\overline{C}$, is

$$1 \quad 0 \quad 1 \quad 0 \quad 1 \quad 0 \quad 0 \quad 0 \qquad 112.518$$

Applying the regression coefficients and taking the intercept into account, we have

$$\hat{Y} = -14.654 - 8.561(1) + 19.071(0) - 3.794(1) + 1.437(0) + 3.901(1)$$
$$- 1.404(0) - 5.766(0) + 1.668(0) + 0.293(112.518)$$
$$= 5.860$$

Applying this procedure to all cells we obtain the following adjusted cell means

	Pattern Rec	Cognitive	Driving	Row Means
NonSmokers	9.805	27.770	5.820	14.465
Delayed	9.732	40.436	8.921	19.696
Active	9.558	43.785	8.505	20.616
Column Means	9.699	37.330	7.749	18.259

© Cengage Learning 2013

These are the cell means given in Exhibit 16.5, and the row and column means can be found as the mean of the cells in that row or column.

Testing Adjusted Means

The adjusted means are plotted in Figure 16.5. They illustrate the interaction and also the meaning that may be attached to the main effects. Further analyses of these data are probably unnecessary because differences due to smoking seemed to be confined to the condition that requires high levels of cognitive processing. However, for the sake of completeness we will assume that you wish to make a comparison between the mean of the NonSmoking group and the combined means of the Active and Delayed groups. In this case you want to compare $\overline{X}'_{1.}$ with $\overline{X}'_{2.}$ and $\overline{X}'_{3.}$ combined. This comparison requires some modification of the error term, to account for differences in the covariate. This adjustment is given by Winer (1971) as

$$MS''_{\text{error}} = MS'_{\text{error}} \left[1 + \frac{\dfrac{SS_{g(c)}}{g-1}}{SS_{e(c)}} \right]$$

where $SS_{g(c)}$ and $SS_{e(c)}$ represent the sum of squares attributable to Groups and Error (respectively) in an analysis of variance on the *covariate*, and MS'_{error} is the error term from the overall analysis of covariance. This is not a very memorable formula, and it is one that I can see no reason to remember.

$$MS'_{\text{error}} = 71.538$$

$$SS_{g(c)} = 2701.215$$

$$SS_{e(c)} = 54285.867$$

Thus

$$MS''_{\text{error}} = 71.538 \left[1 + \frac{\dfrac{2701.215}{2-1}}{54285.867} \right] = 75.098$$

To compare the adjusted means we have

$$\psi = 2(14.465) - 1(19.696) - 1(20.616) = -11.382$$

$$F(1,125) = \frac{n\psi^2}{\sum a_i^2 \, MS''_{\text{error}}} = \frac{45(-11.382)^2}{6(75.098)} = 12.938$$

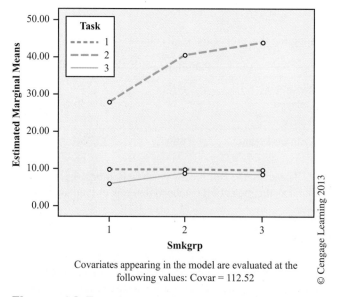

Estimated Marginal Means of Predicted Value for Score

Covariates appearing in the model are evaluated at the following values: Covar = 112.52

© Cengage Learning 2013

Figure 16.5   Adjusted cell means as a function of Group and Task

Because $F_{.05}(1,125) = 3.92$, we can reject H_0 and conclude that the Active Smoking group performs more poorly (overall) than the average of the other two groups.

Another experimenter might be interested in examining the effects of Group only for the Cognitive task. If we want to examine these simple effects, we will again need to modify our error term in some way. This is necessary because we will be looking at Groups for only some of the data, and the covariate mean of the Cognitive task subjects may differ from the covariate mean for all subjects. Probably the safest route here would be to run a separate analysis of covariance for only those subjects performing the cognitive task. Although this method has the disadvantage of costing us degrees of freedom for error, it has the advantage of simplicity and eliminates the need to make discomforting assumptions in the adjustment of our error term.

To complete our discussion of the tests we might wish to conduct, consider the experimenter who wants to compare two particular adjusted cell means (whether or not they are in the same row or column). The adjusted error term for this comparison was given by Winer (1971) as

$$MS''_{error} = \frac{2MS'_{error}}{n}\left[1 + \frac{\dfrac{SS_{cells(c)}}{tg-1}}{SS_{e(c)}}\right]$$

where $SS_{cells(c)}$ is the sum of squares from an analysis of variance on the covariate.

You may wonder why we continually worry about adjusting the error term in making comparisons. The general nature of the answer is apparent when you recall what the confidence limits around the regression line looked like in Chapter 9. (They were curved—in fact, they were elliptical.) For $X_i = \overline{X}$, we were relatively confident about $\hat{Y}$. However, as X_i departed more and more from $\overline{X}$ we became less and less confident of our prediction, and consequently the confidence limits widened. If you now go back to Figure 16.3, you will see that the problem applies directly to the case of adjusted means. In that figure, $\overline{Y}'_1$ is a long way from $\overline{Y}_1$, and we would probably have relatively little confidence that we have estimated it correctly. On the other hand, we can probably have a reasonable degree of confidence in our estimate of $\overline{Y}'_2$. It is just this type of consideration that causes us constantly to adjust our error term.

The example we have used points up an important feature of the analysis of covariance—the fact that the covariate is just another variable that happens to receive priority. In designing the study, we were concerned primarily with evaluating the effects of smoking. However, we had two variables that we considered it necessary to control: type of task and distractibility. The first one (Task) we controlled by incorporating it into our design as an independent variable. The second (Distractibility) we controlled by measuring it and treating it as a covariate. In many respects, these are two ways of treating the same problem. Although there are obvious differences in the way these two variables are treated, there are also important similarities. In obtaining SS_{group}, we are actually partialling out *both* Task and the covariate. It is true that in the case of equal ns Task is orthogonal to Group, leaving nothing to partial out; but that is merely a technicality. In the case of unequal ns, the partialling out of both variables is a very real procedure. Although it is important not to lose sight of the fact that the analysis of covariance is a unique technique with its own additional assumptions, it is equally important to keep in mind that a covariate is just another variable.

16.10 Using Multiple Covariates

We have been concerned with the use of a single covariate. There is no theoretical or practical reason, however, why we must restrict ourselves in this way. For example, a study on the effectiveness of several different teaching methods might wish to treat IQ, Age, and

Type of School (progressive or conservative) as covariates. When viewed from the point of view of multiple regression, this presents no particular problem, whereas when viewed within the traditional framework of the analysis of variance, the computational complexities for only a very few covariates would be overwhelming.

In the expression $R^2_{c, \alpha, \beta, \alpha\beta}$, β is really only a shorthand way of representing a set of predictors (e.g., $B_1, B_2, ..., B_b$). By the same token, c can be used to stand for a set of covariates $(C_1, C_2, ..., C_k)$. Thus, in terms of the more specific notation, $R^2_{c, \alpha, \beta, \alpha\beta}$ might really represent

$$R^2_{0.IQ, Age, School, A_1, B_1, B_2, AB_{11}, AB_{12}}$$

When seen in this light, the use of multiple covariates is no different from that of single covariates. If C represents the covariates IQ, Age, and School, then $SS_{AB(adj)}$ remains

$$SS_{AB(adj)} = SS_{regression(IQ, Age, School, A_1, B_1, B_2, AB_{11}, AB_{12})} - SS_{regression(IQ, Age, School, A_1, B_1, B_2)}$$

It should be apparent from the previous example that no restriction is placed on the nature of the covariate, other than that it is assumed to be linearly related to the criterion. It can be a continuous variable, as in the case of IQ and Age, or a discrete variable, as in the dichotomous classification of Schools as progressive and conservative.

A word of warning: Just because it is possible (and in fact easy) to use multiple covariates is not a good reason for adopting this procedure. Interpreting an analysis of covariance may be difficult enough (if not impossible) with only one covariate. The problems increase rapidly with the addition of multiple covariates. Thus, it might be easy to *say*, in evaluating several methods of teaching English, that such and such a method is better if groups are equated for age, IQ, type of school, parents' occupation, and so on. But the experimenter must then ask himself if such equated groups actually exist in the population. If they do not, he has just answered a question about what would happen in groups that could never exist, and it is unlikely that he will receive much applause for his efforts. Moreover, even if it is possible to form such groups, will they behave in the expected manner? The very fact that the students are now in homogeneous classes may itself have an effect on the dependent variable that could not have been predicted.

16.11 Alternative Experimental Designs

stratification

The analysis of covariance is not the only way to handle data in which a covariate is important. Two common alternative procedures are also available: **stratification** (matched samples) and difference scores.

If we have available measures on the covariate and are free to assign subjects to treatment groups, then we can form subsets of subjects who are homogeneous with respect to the covariate, and then assign one member of each subset to a different treatment group. In the resulting analysis of variance, we can then pull out an effect due to blocks (subsets) from the error term.

The use of matched samples and the analysis of covariance are almost equally effective when the regression of Y on C is linear. If ρ equals the correlation in the population between Y and C, and σ^2_e represents the error variance in a straight analysis of variance on Y, then the use of matched samples reduces the error variance to

$$\sigma^2_e(1 - \rho^2)$$

The reduction due to the analysis of covariance in this situation is given by

$$\sigma^2_e(1 - \rho^2)\frac{(f_e)}{(f_e - 1)}$$

where f_e is the degrees of freedom for the error variance. Obviously, for any reasonable value of f_e, the two procedures are almost equally effective, assuming linearity of regression. If the relationship between Y and C is not linear, however, matching will be more effective than covariance analysis.

difference scores   A second alternative to the analysis of covariance concerns the use of **difference scores**. If the covariate (C) represents a test score before the treatment is administered and Y a score on the same test after the administration of the treatment, the variable $C - Y$ is sometimes used as the dependent variable in an analysis of variance to control for initial differences on C. Obviously, this approach will work only if C and Y are comparable measures. We could hardly justify subtracting a driving test score (Y) from an IQ score (C). If the relationship between C and Y is linear and *if $b_{CY} = 1.00$*, which is rarely true, the analysis of difference scores and the analysis of covariance will give the same estimates of the treatment effects. When b_{CY} is not equal to 1, the two methods will produce different results, and in this case it is difficult to justify the use of difference scores. In fact, for the Conti and Musty (1984) data on THC, if we took the *difference* between the Pre and Post scores as our dependent variable, the results would be decidedly altered ($F_{4,42} = 0.197$). In this case, the analysis of covariance was clearly a more powerful procedure. Exercise 16.20 at the end of the chapter illustrates this view of the analysis of covariance. For a more complete treatment of this entire problem, see Harris (1963) and Huitema (1980, 2005).

The thing to keep in mind here is that a slope of 1.0 on the relationship between pre- and post-test scores implies that the intervention led to a similar increase in scores, regardless of where people started. But it might be that the change is *proportional* to where people started out. Someone who is very poor in math may have much more to gain by an intervention program than someone who was doing well, and thus the gain score will be directly (and negatively) related to the pretest score. In the example from Conti and Musty (1984), more active animals were likely to change more than less active animals, which may be why they took as their dependent variable the posttest score as a percentage of the pretest score, rather than just the difference between their two scores.

Key Terms

General linear model (16.1)

Design matrix (16.1)

Method III (16.4)

Type III SS (16.4)

Method II (16.4)

Type II SS (16.4)

Method I (16.4)

Type I SS (16.4)

Hierarchical sums of squares (16.4)

Sequential sums of squres (16.4)

Equally weighted means (16.4)

Analysis of covariance (16.5)

Covariate (16.5)

Adjusted Y means (16.5)

Homogeneity of regression (16.5)

MS'_{error} (16.5)

True-score analysis of covariance (16.6)

Nonequivalent groups design (16.6)

Stratification (16.11)

Difference scores (16.11)

Exercises

16.1 The following hypothetical data were obtained from poor, average, and good readers on the number of eye fixations per line of text.

Poor	Average	Good
10	5	3
7	8	5
8	4	2
11	6	3
5	5	4

© Cengage Learning 2013

    a. Construct the design matrix for these data.

    b. Use any standard regression program to calculate a least-squares analysis of variance.

    c. Run the analysis of variance in the traditional manner and compare your answers.

16.2 Rerun the analysis of Exercise 16.4 for the amended data from Exercise 16.3.

16.3 Taking the data from Exercise 16.1, add the scores 5 and 8 to the Average group and the scores 2, 3, 3, and 5 to the Good group. Rerun the analysis for Exercise 16.1 using the more complete data.

16.4 For the data in Exercise 16.1,

    a. Calculate treatment effects and show that the regression model reproduces these treatment effects.

    b. Demonstrate that R^2 for the regression model is equal to η^2 for the analysis of variance.

16.5 A psychologist was concerned with the relationship between Gender, Socioeconomic Status (SES), and perceived Locus of Control. She took eight adults (age = 25 to 30 years) in each Gender–SES combination and administered a scale dealing with Locus of Control (a high score indicates that the individual feels in control of his or her everyday life).

	SES		
	Low	Average	High
Male	10	16	18
	12	12	14
	8	19	17
	14	17	13
	10	15	19
	16	11	15
	15	14	22
	13	10	20
Female	8	14	12
	10	10	18
	7	13	14
	9	9	21
	12	17	19
	5	15	17
	8	12	13
	7	8	16

© Cengage Learning 2013

    a. Run a traditional analysis of variance on these data.

    b. The following sums of squares have been computed on the data using the appropriate design matrix (α = Gender, β = SES).

$$SS_Y = 777.6667 \quad SS_{reg(\alpha, \beta, \alpha\beta)} = 422.6667$$

$$SS_{reg(\alpha, \beta)} = 404.0000 \quad SS_{reg(\beta, \alpha\beta)} = 357.333$$

$$SS_{reg(\alpha, \alpha\beta)} = 84.000$$

Compute the summary table for the analysis of variance using these sums of squares.

16.6 For the data in Exercise 16.7, the complete model is

$$1.2306A_1 - 3.7167B_1 - 0.3500B_2 + 0.4778AB_{11} - 0.5444AB_{12} + 13.6750$$

    a. Show that this model reproduces the treatment and interaction effects as calculated in Table 16.3.

16.7 When we take the data in Exercise 16.5 and delete the last two low-SES males, the last three average-SES males, and the last two high-SES females, we obtain the following sums of squares:

$$SS_Y = 750.1951 \quad SS_{reg(\alpha,\beta,\alpha\beta)} = 458.7285$$

$$SS_{reg(\alpha,\beta)} = 437.6338 \quad SS_{reg(\beta,\alpha\beta)} = 398.7135$$

$$SS_{reg(\alpha,\alpha\beta)} = 112.3392 \quad SS_{reg(\alpha)} = 95.4511$$

$$SS_{reg(\beta)} = 379.3325$$

$$SS_{reg(\alpha\beta)} = 15.8132$$

Compute the analysis of variance using these sums of squares.

16.8 Using the SES portion of the design matrix as our predictor, we find that $SS_{reg(\beta)} = 338.6667$.

a. Why is this value the same as SS_{SES} in the answer to Exercise 16.5?

b. Will this be the case in all analyses of variance?

16.9 For the data in Exercise 16.5, the complete model is
$$1.1667A_1 - 3.1667B_1 - 0.1667B_2 + 0.8333AB_{11} - 0.1667AB_{12} + 13.4167$$

a. Show that this model reproduces the treatment and interaction effects as calculated by the method shown in Table 16.2.

16.10 Using only the SES predictors for the data in Exercise 16.7, we find $SS_{reg(\beta)} = 379.3325$. Why is this not the same as SS_{SES} in Exercise 16.7?

16.11 Using the following data, demonstrate that Method III (the method advocated in this chapter) really deals with unweighted means.

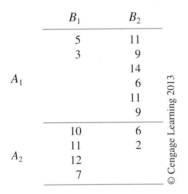

	B_1	B_2
	5	11
	3	9
		14
A_1		6
		11
		9
	10	6
	11	2
A_2	12	
	7	

© Cengage Learning 2013

16.12 If you have access to SAS, use that program to analyze the data in Exercise 16.7. Add /SS1 SS2 SS3 SS4 to the end of your Model command and show that

a. Type I sums of squares adjust each term in the model only for those that come earlier in the model statement.

b. Type II sums of squares adjust main effects only for other main effect variables, while adjusting the interaction for each of the main effects.

c. Type III sums of squares adjust each term for all other terms in the model.

d. Type IV sums of squares in this case are equal to the Type II sums of squares.

16.13 Draw a Venn diagram representing the sums of squares in Exercise 16.7.

16.14 Draw a Venn diagram representing the sums of squares in Exercise 16.5.

16.15 In studying the energy consumption of families, we have broken them into three groups. Group 1 consists of those who have enrolled in a time-of-day electrical-rate system (the charge per kilowatt-hour of electricity is higher during peak demand times of the day). Group 2 is made up of those who inquired into such a system but did not use it. Group 3 represents those who have shown no interest in the system. We record the amount of the electrical bill per month for each household as our dependent variable (Y). As a covariate, we take the electrical bill for that household for the same month last year (C). The data follow:

Group 1		Group 2		Group 3	
Y	C	Y	C	Y	C
58	75	60	70	75	80
25	40	30	25	60	55
50	68	55	65	70	73
40	62	50	50	65	61
55	67	45	55	55	65

© Cengage Learning 2013

   a.   Set up the design matrix.

   b.   Run the analysis of covariance.

16.16 Compute the energy savings per household for the data in Exercise 16.18 by subtracting this year's bill from last year's bill. Then run an analysis of variance on the savings scores and compare that to the analysis of covariance.

16.17 Compute the adjusted means for the data in Exercise 16.18.

16.18 To refine the experiment described in Exercise 16.15, a psychologist added an additional set of households to each group. This group had a special meter installed to show them exactly how fast their electric bill was increasing. (The amount-to-date was displayed on the meter.) The data follow; the nonmetered data are the same as those in Exercise 16.15.

	Y	C	Y	C	Y	C
Nonmetered	58	75	60	70	75	80
	25	40	30	25	60	55
	50	68	55	65	70	73
	40	62	50	50	65	61
	55	67	45	55	55	65
Metered	25	42	40	55	55	56
	38	64	47	52	62	74
	46	70	56	68	57	60
	50	67	28	30	50	68
	55	75	55	72	70	76

© Cengage Learning 2013

   a.   Run the analysis of covariance on these data—after first checking the assumption of homogeneity of regression.

   b.   Draw the appropriate conclusions.

16.19 Klemchuk, Bond, and Howell (1990) examined role taking in children. Children were administered a battery of role-taking tasks. They were classified as being in daycare or not being in daycare, and as ages 2–3 or ages 4–5. The hypothesis was that children with daycare experience would perform better on role-taking tasks. The data are available at the book's Web site as Ex16-19.dat. Run the appropriate analysis.

Computer Exercises

16.20 Everitt reported data on a study of three treatments for anorexia in young girls. One treatment was cognitive behavior therapy, a second was a control condition with no therapy, and a third was a family therapy condition. These are the same data we examined in Chapter 14. The data follow and are available on the Web site.

Group	Pretest	Posttest	Gain	Group	Pretest	Posttest	Gain
1	80.5	82.2	1.7	2	75.1	86.7	11.6
1	84.9	85.6	.7	2	80.6	73.5	−7.1
1	81.5	81.4	−.1	2	78.4	84.6	6.2
1	82.6	81.9	−.7	2	77.6	77.4	−0.2
1	79.9	76.4	−3.5	2	88.7	79.5	−9.2
1	88.7	103.6	14.9	2	81.3	89.6	8.3
1	94.9	98.4	3.5	2	78.1	81.4	3.3
1	76.3	93.4	17.1	2	70.5	81.8	11.3
1	81.0	73.4	−7.6	2	77.3	77.3	0.0
1	80.5	82.1	1.6	2	85.2	84.2	−1.0
1	85.0	96.7	11.7	2	86.0	75.4	−10.6
1	89.2	95.3	6.1	2	84.1	79.5	−4.6
1	81.3	82.4	1.1	2	79.7	73.0	−6.7
1	76.5	72.5	−4.0	2	85.5	88.3	2.8
1	70.0	90.9	20.9	2	84.4	84.7	0.3
1	80.4	71.3	−9.1	2	79.6	81.4	1.8
1	83.3	85.4	2.1	2	77.5	81.2	3.7
1	83.0	81.6	−1.4	2	72.3	88.2	15.9
1	87.7	89.1	1.4	2	89.0	78.8	−10.2
1	84.2	83.9	−.3	3	83.8	95.2	11.4
1	86.4	82.7	−3.7	3	83.3	94.3	11.0
1	76.5	75.7	−.8	3	86.0	91.5	5.5
1	80.2	82.6	2.4	3	82.5	91.9	9.4
1	87.8	100.4	12.6	3	86.7	100.3	13.6
1	83.3	85.2	1.9	3	79.6	76.7	−2.9
1	79.7	83.6	3.9	3	76.9	76.8	−0.1
1	84.5	84.6	.1	3	94.2	101.6	7.4
1	80.8	96.2	15.4	3	73.4	94.9	21.5
1	87.4	86.7	−.7	3	80.5	75.2	−5.3
2	80.7	80.2	−.5	3	81.6	77.8	−3.8
2	89.4	80.1	−9.3	3	82.1	95.5	13.4
2	91.8	86.4	−5.4	3	77.6	90.7	13.1
2	74.0	86.3	12.3	3	83.5	92.5	9.0
2	78.1	76.1	−2.0	3	89.9	93.8	3.9
2	88.3	78.1	−10.2	3	86.0	91.7	5.7
2	87.3	75.1	−12.2	3	87.3	98.0	10.7

a. Run an analysis of variance on group differences in Gain scores. (You may have already done this in Chapter 14.)

b. Now run the analysis on Posttest scores, ignoring Pretest scores.

c. Finally, run the analysis on Posttest scores using Pretest as the covariate.

d. How do these three answers relate to one another, and what do they show about the differences and similarities between analysis of covariance and the treatment of gain (or change) scores?

e. Calculate η^2 on Groups for the analysis of covariance.

f. Calculate d for the contrast on the two therapy groups (ignoring the control group) using adjusted means.

16.21 Use the data from Mireault and Bond (1992) in the file named Mireault.dat referred to in Exercise 7.8 to run a two-way analysis of variance on the Global Symptom Index T score (GSIT) using Gender and Group as independent variables. Plot out the cell means and interpret the results.

16.22 Use the data set named in Epinuneq.dat on the Web site to examine the results of the study by Introini-Collison and McGaugh (1986) described prior to Exercises 11.29, 11.31 and 11.32. Using any statistical package, run a two-way analysis of variance with unequal sample sizes. What would you conclude from this analysis?

16.23 In Exercise 16.24 we used YearColl as the covariate. Run an analysis of variance on YearColl, using Gender and Group as the independent variables. What does this tell us that is relevant to the preceding analysis of covariance?

16.24 Using the same data as in Exercise 16.21, run an analysis of covariance instead, using year in college (YearColl) as the covariate.

a. Why would we want to consider YearColl as a covariate?

b. How would you interpret the results?

16.25 Write up the results of Everitt's experiment, including effect sizes.

Discussion Questions

16.26 Make up or find an example with respect to Exercise 16.25 where the slope is not nearly 1.0. Analyze it using both the analysis of covariance and a t test on difference scores. Do either of these analyses make sense?

16.27 I said that in any experiment where we have pretest and posttest scores we could either look at the difference scores (compared across groups) or use the pretest as a covariate. These two analyses will be equivalent only when the slope relating posttest to pretest scores is 1.00. How likely do you think it is that such a condition would be met (or at least approximated)? What does $b = 1.00$ actually imply?

16.28 I initially thought of creating an analysis of variance example from the example in Chapter 14, Section 14.7. I could have used Sex and Group as the independent variables, posttest scores as the dependent variable, and pretest scores as the covariate (ignoring FU6 and FU12 entirely). This would have made a very bad example for the analysis of covariance. Why would that be? Is there any way in which we might be able to salvage the study as an analysis of covariance example?

Chapter 17

Meta-Analysis and Single-Case Designs

Objectives

To present meta-analysis as a way of making sense out of a collection of separate studies, and to follow up by showing how we can use the techniques associated with meta-analysis to handle single-case designs.

Contents

In the previous sixteen chapters we focused on individual studies, comparing group means, looking at correlation and regression models, analyzing contingency tables, and so on. Most of the time that is the bulk of what researchers in the behavioral sciences do. However, after we have a collection of similar studies on the same research question, we should ask how we can put these studies together and draw some general conclusions. One researcher may have studied avoidance behavior in mice following the administration of shock and found that avoidance increases with shock intensity. Another may have run a similar study and found no significant effect with, for example, a *p* value of 0.17. What are we to make of this? Does shock level really affect avoidance, does it not, does it affect avoidance under only limited conditions, or is this second study perfectly consistent with the first? Those are the kinds of questions we will look at in this chapter, though we will consider more than two studies at once.

A related question that will come up in the second half of this chapter concerns the researcher who implements a behavioral intervention on single cases or subjects. How can we best consolidate those cases? It may seem strange to put together what seem like two disparate topics, but, in fact, one leads nicely into the other and there is a need to address both of these issues.

META-ANALYSIS

An excellent book on meta-analysis by Borenstein, Hedges, Higgins, and Rothstein (2009) begins by pointing to the fact that for many years Dr. Benjamin Spock, along with other pediatricians, counseled parents to lay their baby to sleep on its stomach. (If you don't know about Dr. Spock, and, no, he wasn't in *Star Trek*, your mother certainly does. He probably had more effect on child rearing in this country during the last half of the 20th century than any other single person.) Also during those years more than 100,000 babies died of Sudden Infant Death Syndrome (SIDS)—many while sleeping on their stomach. During that time, evidence was accumulating about the dangers of this practice, but people never put all of the studies together until it was too late. When they finally did, SIDS deaths decreased dramatically when parents were instructed to place their infant on its back. I use this as a simple but dramatic example of the need to confront all of the existing literature in a field and combine it into sensible conclusions. **Meta-analysis** is designed to do this. Meta-analysis has been a core feature of what is called Evidence Based Medicine, and the Cochrane Coalition has published literally thousands of such analyses in just about every area of medicine, much of it of direct relevance to behavioral scientists. We will use data from their collection in this chapter.

Meta-analysis

Early attempts at consolidating evidence were based on what are called narrative studies. Here a researcher would read a large amount of literature on a topic, make some subjective judgments about the studies he or she read, and then issue a conclusion. Such conclusions were highly subjective, weighting different studies in whatever way the researcher chose. Moreover, the approach was primarily limited to published literature, which, almost by its nature, focuses on statistically significant results. It ignored what Rosenthal called the "**file drawer problem**," where negative results remained unpublished in someone's files.

file drawer problem

Put in its simplest terms, meta-analysis averages the results of many studies on a single topic. It is a very sophisticated averaging, beginning with effect sizes and weighting studies according to the precision of their results, but it is averaging nonetheless. I am going to begin with an example that deals with studies comparing treatment and control groups of children suffering from adolescent depression. But the important point to keep in mind is that once you have your measure of effect size, whether it is *d*, or a risk ratio, or a correlation, the equations for combining and testing effect sizes are all the same. So when you see d in an equation, you could substitute Fisher's transformation of r, or $\log(RR)$, or some other effect size measure and simply carry on the calculations using those numbers.

17.1 A Brief Review of Effect Size Measures

Before continuing, I want to digress and briefly review effect sizes measures. We have seen these in separate chapters, and it makes sense to bring them all together. The following section is not exhaustive, but it does cover the most important measures.

Measures on Means

I will consider several measures on means. They are all a form of Cohen's d, although Hedges' correction known as g applies to all of them.

- **Two Independent Groups—Treatment and Control**
    - Pooling variances

    $$d = \frac{\overline{X}_1 - \overline{X}_2}{s_{\text{pooled}}}$$

    $$s_d = \sqrt{\frac{n_1 + n_2}{n_1 \times n_2} + \frac{d^2}{2(n_1 + n_2)}}$$

    - Standardizing on standard deviation of Control group

    $$d = \frac{\overline{X}_1 - \overline{X}_2}{s_C}$$

    $$s_d = \sqrt{\frac{n_1 + n_2}{n_1 \times n_2} + \frac{d^2}{2n_1}}$$

- **Paired Measurements**
    - Standardizing on average standard deviation

    $$d = \frac{\overline{X}_{\text{post}} - \overline{X}_{\text{pre}}}{s_p} = \frac{\overline{X}_{\text{post}} - \overline{X}_{\text{pre}}}{s_{\text{diff}}/\sqrt{2(1 - r)}}$$

    $$s_d = \sqrt{\left(\frac{1}{n} + \frac{d^2}{2n}\right) \times 2(1 - r)}$$

    where r is the correlation between pre- and post-treatment scores.
    - Standardizing on s_{diff}—rarely recommended

    $$d = \frac{\overline{X}_{\text{post}} - \overline{X}_{\text{pre}}}{s_{\text{diff}}}$$

- **Multiple Independent Groups**
  It generally makes sense to calculate treatment effects on two groups or sets of groups, so I will skip formulae for effects of several groups.

- **Hedges' g**

  To this point we have used d as our standardized mean difference, and for this chapter we will continue to do so. This is essentially Cohen's d, although the idea of dividing by the standard deviation of the control group rather than a pooled standard deviation was first proposed by Glass. We'll keep on crediting Cohen. The problem with d is that it is slightly biased and tends to overestimate δ when the sample size is small.

  Hedges (1981) proposed a minor modification that involves solving for a correction factor

  $$J = 1 = \frac{3}{4df - 1}$$

  and multiplying both d and s_d by J.

  $$g = d \times J$$
  $$s_g = s_d \times J$$

  This would give us Hedges' g, and we then could continue to work with g in exactly the same way we will work with d. I'll stick with d for this example, but the point is important. Once we have our effect sizes it doesn't matter if they are d, g, or some other effect size such as a log(risk ratio). The mathematics from then on are the same.

Effect Sizes Based on Contingency Tables

Assume the following summary table

Condition	Events	Non-Events	N
Treated	A	B	A + B
Control	C	D	C + D

© Cengage Learning 2013

- Relative Risk = Risk Ratio

  $$RR = \frac{A}{A + B} \bigg/ \frac{C}{C + D} = \frac{A(C + D)}{B(A + B)}$$

  However, we generally deal with risk ratios on a logarithmic scale. Then

  $$\text{LogRiskRatio} = \ln(RR)$$

  $$Var_{\text{LogRiskRatio}} = \frac{1}{A} - \frac{1}{A + B} + \frac{1}{C} - \frac{1}{C + D}$$

  $$S_{\text{LogRiskRatio}} = \sqrt{Var_{\text{LogRiskRatio}}}$$

  $$CI_{\ln(RR)} = \text{LogRiskRatio} \pm 1.96 \times s_{\text{LogOddsRatio}}$$

  We carry out our calculations of effect sizes and their confidence intervals using these statistics, but then convert the mean and confidence limits back to the original metric by

  $$\text{Mean} = e^{\ln(RR)}$$
  $$\text{Lower} = e^{\text{lower}_{\text{LogRiskRatio}}}$$
  $$\text{Upper} = e^{\text{upper}_{\text{LogRiskRatio}}}$$

  Where e is the base of the natural number system, which is 2.71828.

- Odds ratios

  $$OR = \frac{A/B}{C/D} = \frac{A \times D}{B \times C}$$

Here again we normally work with the log of odds ratios, in which case

$$\text{LogOddsRatio} = \ln(OR)$$

$$Var_{\text{LogOddsRatio}} = \frac{1}{A} - \frac{1}{B} + \frac{1}{C} - \frac{1}{D}$$

$$s_{\text{LogOddsRatio}} = \sqrt{Var_{\text{LogOddsRatio}}}$$

$$CI_{\ln(OR)} = \text{LogOddsRatio} \pm 1.96 \times s_{\text{LogOddsRatio}}$$

As with risk ratios, we carry out all of our calculations with the log values, but then convert the final result back to odds ratios by

$$\text{Mean} = e^{\ln(OR)}$$
$$\text{Lower} = e^{\text{lower}_{\text{LogOddsRatio}}}$$
$$\text{Upper} = e^{\text{upper}_{\text{LogOddsRatio}}}$$

You might ask why we operate on a logarithmic scale for both RR and OR. One reason is that the distribution of each is bound by 0 at the lower end but is unbounded at the upper end, thus having a positively skewed distribution. By taking the log of either ratio we have a statistic that is nearly normally distributed. A second reason is that with risk ratios there is no simple relationship between the risk ratio of a good outcome and the risk ratio of a bad outcome, although with odds ratios one is simply the inverse of the other.

Effect Sizes with Correlations

Correlation coefficients are often used as measures of effect size, but, as we have seen earlier, their distribution is skewed unless the population parameter is 0. For this reason we use Fisher's transformation, which I have called r'.

$$r' = 0.5 \times \ln\left(\frac{1 + r}{1 - r}\right)$$

$$s_{r'}^2 = \frac{1}{n - 3}$$

$$s_{r'} = \sqrt{\frac{1}{n - 3}}$$

Here again we base our calculations in the meta-analysis on the transformed values, but then transform the result back to the original uses.

$$r = \frac{e^{2r'} - 1}{e^{2r'} + 1}$$

Converting Among Measures of Effect Size

Suppose that you and I and some other people all run studies that are roughly equivalent. They don't need to be exact replications, but they need to address the same general question. Your study may end up with an odds ratio, mine might involve a t test between two group means, and another study might calculate a correlation coefficient in some way. In an ideal world we might all come to a statistically significant result, and we could happily say that when examined from a variety of directions the results are consistent and support the phenomenon under study. But we don't live in an ideal world, and we need to confront inconsistent, and often statistically nonsignificant, results. But how do we add together

Table 17.1 Converting among effect size measures

LogOddsRatio to d

$$d = \text{LogOddsRatio} \times \frac{\sqrt{3}}{\pi}$$

$$\text{var}(d) = \text{var}(\text{LogOddsRatio}) \times \frac{3}{\pi^2}$$

r to d

$$d = \frac{2 \times r}{\sqrt{1 - r^2}}$$

$$\text{var}(d) = \frac{4 \times \text{var}(r)}{(1 - r^2)^3}$$

LogRiskRatio to d

$$d = \ln\left(\frac{RR}{1 - RR}\right) \times \frac{\sqrt{3}}{\pi}$$

$$\text{var}(d) = \text{var}(\text{LogOddsRatio}) \times \frac{3}{\pi^2}$$

a t statistic, a χ^2, and a correlation coefficient and then divide by 3? The simple answer is that we can't. We need some common metric to put the studies on the same scale. It turns out that the effect size measures that we have seen throughout this book are ideally suited to this task. A major reason for that is that we know how to convert from one effect size to another.

It is relatively easy to go from one effect size measure to another. Table 17.1 shows how to make several of these conversions. If there is a conversion that you need that is not included in this table, a quick search on the Internet will provide one. (A nice online calculator is available from P. D Ellis. (2009), "Effect size equations," Web site: http://www.polyu.edu.hk/mm/effectsizefaqs/calculator/calculator.html accessed on 1/23/2011.)

17.2 An Example—Child and Adolescent Depression

Depression in children and adolescents has long been a concern in our society, and there have been many efforts to institute prevention programs to lower its incidence. Some of these are "universal" programs that are administered to all members of some target population. For example, a school district may introduce lectures or other changes in curriculum to affect all students in the district. A few of these programs are "selective," that is, aimed at smaller groups of students who are deemed to be at risk for depression. And a third category of programs, classed as "indicated" interventions, are aimed at children who are already displaying subclinical symptoms. Horowitz and Garber (2006) conducted a meta-analysis of such intervention programs, asking whether intervention in general was effective and whether effectiveness varied across classes of programs. They first searched the PsychINFO database using "depression" and "prevention" as search terms. This search included dissertations so as to minimize publication bias. They then manually searched 15 journals over a 30-year span, looking for any additional studies. The point of this intensive journal search was to catch as many studies as possible so as to minimize bias. They found 30 studies that they could use. Each of these studies contained a treatment and a control condition. Although I will not focus on the data collection phase, there is a large literature on the mechanics, as opposed to the statistics, of meta-analysis and anyone planning to conduct such a study needs to examine that literature. (Cooper, 2009 provides a thorough coverage of the process, as opposed to the statistics, of meta-analysis, and anyone planning a meta-analysis should consult that reference or a similar one before beginning. Other references that are helpful are Borenstein et al. (2009) and Cooper, Hedges, & Valentine (2009).)

Having collected all available studies, the authors categorized them by author, target (Universal, Selective, and Indicated), sample size, mean age, percent female, length, effect size at post-intervention and follow-up periods, and a summary of the intervention. Such classification is routine in most meta-analyses. For our purposes we will focus on the effect sizes. I discussed effect size measures for studies with two groups in Chapter 7 and considered alternative ways of defining the standardizing measure (the standard deviation). Horowitz and Garber chose to calculate the effect size as the difference between the treatment and control mean depression scores at post-test divided by the standard deviation of the control group.

$$d = \frac{\overline{X}_{\text{Control}} - \overline{X}_{\text{Treatment}}}{s_{\text{Control}}}$$

This measure is what we earlier called Cohen's *d,* with apologies to Glass who actually proposed it. The results of the analysis are given in Table 17.2. Each study contained

Table 17.2   Results from Horowitz and Garber (2006)

Author	Target	N	d_1	d_2	d_3
Clarke1	U	662	0.06	−.06	−.06
Clarke2	U	380	0.09	0.14	0.14
Kellam	U	575	−.01	NA	NA
HainsEllman	U	21	0.36	−.04	−.04
Cecchini	U	100	0.11	−.15	−.15
Petersen	U	335	−.12	NA	NA
Pattison	U	66	−.01	0.40	0.40
Lowry-Web	U	594	0.17	NA	NA
Shochet	U	260	0.39	0.25	0.25
Spence	U	1500	0.29	0.03	0.03
Merry	U	364	0.02	−.13	0.05
Gwynn-	S	60	1.37	NA	NA
Roosa	S	81	0.41	NA	NA
Sandler	S	72	0.24	NA	NA
Wolchik	S	94	−.06	NA	NA
Beardslee	S	52	0.20	0.42	0.42
Seligman	S	235	0.32	0.12	0.25
Quayle	S	47	−.62	0.62	0.62
Cardemil1	S	49	0.99	1.24	1.24
Cardemil2	S	106	0.16	0.31	0.31
Jaycox	I	143	0.18	0.32	0.20
Clarke3	I	150	0.31	0.07	0.01
Reivich	I	152	0.12	0.40	0.22
Lamb	I	41	0.70	NA	NA
Forsyth	I	59	1.51	1.95	1.95
Clarke4	I	94	0.41	0.47	0.04
Yu-Selig	I	220	0.23	0.30	0.30
Freres1	I	268	−.06	0.16	0.03
Freres2	I	74	0.07	0.56	0.56

a treatment and a control group. (One study is omitted from that table because it was not possible to compute an effect size measure.) They did not give the sample sizes for each group, so I am acting as if the cases were evenly split between the two conditions. (Data in that file that are entered as NA are missing values, and you may need to use a different notation depending on your software.) The first effect size measure (d_1) was taken at the end of intervention. The second measurement (d_2) was taken as close to 6 months after the end of the intervention as possible. The last column is the effect size at last follow-up, which may also be the 6 month follow-up score. Eight studies were missing an effect size at the 6-month follow-up (d_3).

I am interested in performance at the 6-month follow-up because I want to know if a program is going to have some long term effect. Therefore, we will analyze the results for the 21 studies with data on that dependent variable (d_2).

From Table 17.1 you can see that most of the effect sizes at 6 months are positive, but some are very small. The table does not show a significance test, but we will have that in a moment when we compute confidence limits on effect sizes. The fact that so many are positive would lead me to suspect that intervention has a positive effect overall, though we will have to wait to see if it is more effective in some type of interventions than in others.

Forest Plots

forest plot

A very simple way to examine these results is in terms of what is called a forest plot. This plots each study on a separate line, indicating its effect size and the confidence interval on that effect size. You can see this plot in Figure 17.1. The dashed vertical line represents an effect size of 0, so we want to see our effect sizes to its right. The values on the far right are the effect size and confidence limits on that effect size for each study.[1] The plot was created using the metafor library in R, but any software for meta-analysis will give similar plots. (The code to present the forest plot is available on the Web as part of Horowitz.R.)

The square boxes represent the point estimate from the study in question. You will notice that each box has confidence limits associated with it. It should be obvious that the narrower the interval the more confident we are in our estimates. In general the width of the interval is also associated with the size of the sample, so that large samples lead to more precision. You will also note that the boxes vary in size. That variability is also directly related to the precision of the estimate.

Fixed and Random Models

Before continuing we need to distinguish between fixed and random effects models. In a fixed effect model we assume that there is one true effect size and we are trying to estimate that effect size by looking at the results of multiple experiments.[2] If you were an astronomer attempting to measure the luminosity of a particular star, it is reasonable to think that it does have one true luminosity and the difference between the measurements of you and

---

[1] I will comment on the calculation of these confidence limits later in the chapter.
[2] Viechtbauer (2010) argued that if we intend to restrict all inferences to only the studies under discussion, we do not actually need to assume that all effect sizes are equal in the population, and we can take our mean as simply an estimate of the average of population effect sizes. However, such a situation is probably quite rare—we almost always want to project to a broader population of effects.

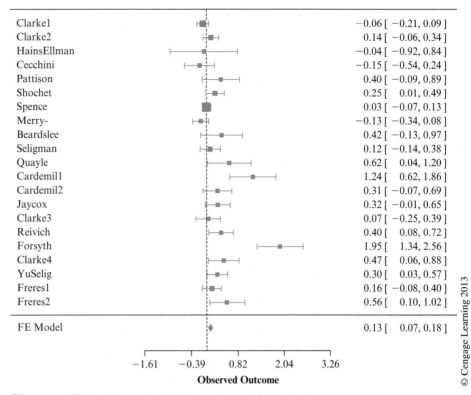

Figure 17.1   Forest plot for Horowitz and Gabler's data

your colleagues is just error variance, perhaps due to variability in instruments, the density of the night sky, and other factors. The important point about a fixed effect model is that we assume that the only reason for variability in measurements is random sampling error. If each of our studies had an infinite number of participants, all studies would come to the same result because they are all measuring the same thing.

In the behavioral sciences most of the things that we measure are not so simple. Depression, for example, probably depends on gender, age, family settings, and a host of other variables. Therefore when you and I go out to measure depression in our two different samples, we may, in fact, be measuring something more than depression. If your sample has more female subjects than mine the true effect size that you are estimating may be different from the true effect size that I am estimating. That means that our measurements differ by more than random sampling error. For random effects models we will assume that the true effects are randomly and normally distributed around some value.

With a random model we assume that the measurement we take has two parts. One is the fact that our measurement involves random error. The other is the fact that the true effects we are aiming for may well differ from study to study and are not all equal to some overall mean effect. This gives us a model very much like that in the analysis of variance with

$$Y_i = \mu + \tau_j + \varepsilon_{ij}$$

Where Y_i represents the effect size in experiment $_i$, μ represents the overall mean effect, τ_j represents the difference between the true effect that we are measuring in this study and the overall mean true effect, and ε_{ij} represents sampling error. This means that we need to consider both the variance of τ_j and the variance of ε. In the fixed model we can simply ignore τ because it would not have any meaning—all studies are estimating the same quantity.

Now that I have distinguished between fixed and random models, which one should we use? You might think that the decision is clear. If there are lots of variables that affect the level of depression, and if you and I conduct different studies with different kinds of participants, then we should probably think there are many true effects, depending on the characteristics of our sample and intervention. That would suggest we obviously have a random design. However, Hedges (2009) has argued that the decision is not really that clear. If I ran an analysis of variance on a design comparing three specific types of psychotherapy, we might argue that it has to be treated as a fixed design because I did not sample therapies at random. However, whether the design is fixed or not, I will probably generalize my results to other quite similar therapies and no one would likely object very loudly even though I am doing so from a fixed model. We have a similar kind of problem with a random model because that model allows me to generalize to the universe of conditions from which my independent variable was sampled. But what is that universe? What levels are close enough to think that they made up part of the sampled universe? With the studies in Table 17.2 it might be reasonable to treat the subset of studies within each Target as fixed but with difference between the Targets. I will start there. When we have relatively few studies, we are almost forced to treat the design as fixed because we don't have sufficient power to accurately estimate true differences.

Calculating the Overall Effect

The results in Table 17.3 are the summary statistics that can be computed from the data in Table 17.2. Each of the columns directly refers to quantities in our formulae that follow. In column 6 you see the weights, which are defined as $W_i = 1/s_{d_i}^2$. We want these weights because we want to weight each effect size in proportion to its precision, which is basically the inverse of the variance estimate. We will begin by treating the analysis as a fixed model. For the moment ignore the fact that the table actually has three sections, corresponding to the targets of the intervention. We will begin by examining the full set of 21 studies.

We have defined d as

$$d = \frac{\overline{X}_{\text{Control}} - \overline{X}_{\text{Treatment}}}{s_{\text{Control}}}$$

We will further define the variance of d and its standard error as

$$s_d^2 = \frac{n_1 + n_2}{n_1 n_2} + \frac{d^2}{2(n_1)}$$

$$s_d = \sqrt{s_d^2}$$

The statistics s_d and s_d^2 are estimates of the standard error and variance of d. (The variance terms are shown in Column 5 of Table 17.3.) Each study has one value of d, but we estimate what the variability of that statistic would be over an infinite number of replications of that specific study, although this is the only replication of that study we will ever do. This is directly analogous to computing the standard error of the mean on the basis of one study.

Next we compute confidence limits on the d estimates separately for each study. Here

$$CI_{.95} = d \pm 1.96 s_d$$

Table 17.3   Summary statistics for data in Table 17.2

Study	Target	$n_1 = n_2$	d_i	sd^2	W_i	$W_i * d$	$W_i d^2$	W_i^2
Clarke1	U	331	−0.06	0.006	165.426	−9.9255	0.5955	27365.6154
Clarke2	U	190	0.14	0.010	94.7678	13.2675	1.8574	8980.9395
HainsEllm	U	10	−0.04	0.200	4.9990	−0.2000	0.0080	24.9900
Cecchini	U	50	−0.15	0.040	24.9299	−3.7395	0.5609	621.4992
Pattison	U	33	0.40	0.061	16.1765	6.4706	2.5882	261.6782
Shochet	U	130	0.25	0.015	64.4961	16.1240	4.0310	4159.7500
Spence	U	750	0.03	0.002	374.958	11.2487	0.3375	140593.3647
Merry-	U	182	−0.13	0.011	90.8082	11.8051	1.5347	8246.1233
SUM					836.561	21.4408	11.5133	190253.9603
Beardsl	S	26	0.42	0.078	12.7195	5.3422	2.2437	161.7866
Seligma	S	118	0.12	0.017	58.8940	7.0673	0.8481	3468.5022
Quayle	S	24	0.62	0.087	11.4498	7.0989	4.4013	131.0987
Cardem	S	24	1.24	0.099	10.0654	12.4811	15.4766	101.3128
Cardem	S	53	0.31	0.038	26.1854	8.1175	2.5164	685.6777
SUM					119.314	40.1070	25.4861	4548.3779
Jaycox	I	72	0.32	0.028	35.5450	11.3744	3.6398	1263.4487
Clarke3	I	75	0.07	0.026	37.4770	2.6234	0.1836	1404.5289
Reivich	I	76	0.40	0.026	37.2549	14.9020	5.9608	1387.9277
Forsyth	I	30	1.95	0.098	10.1673	19.8263	38.6613	103.3748
Clarke4	I	47	0.47	0.043	22.8685	10.7482	5.0517	522.9702
YuSelig	I	110	0.30	0.018	54.3881	16.3164	4.8949	2958.0691
Freresl	I	134	0.16	0.015	66.7863	10.6858	1.7097	4460.4077
Freres2	I	37	0.56	0.056	17.8022	9.9692	5.5828	316.9167
SUM					282.239	96.4457	65.6846	12417.6439
OVERALL SUM					1238.164	157.9935	102.6840	207219.9982

You may recall that earlier in this book we computed confidence limits on effect sizes using the noncentral t distribution. That is the most accurate way to do it. However, in meta-analysis the standard approach seems to be to compute the confidence interval using $\bar{d} \pm s_d \times (z_{\alpha/2})$. Given the number of studies we usually combine, this approximation for the confidence intervals on the overall effect is probably sufficiently accurate. However, using the approach to calculate confidence limits on d for the individual studies with small sample sizes might be questioned (Hedges and Olkin (1985), but see Hedges (2009)).

Horowitz and Gabler computed d and its standard error for each study. Having these statistics, we will now weight each effect size by the inverse of its variance, which will give greater weight to effects having greater precision. We will then compute the mean treatment effect ($\bar{d}_i$), and its standard error ($s_{\bar{d}}$) across all 21 studies. Using the totals in the bottom row of the table we have

$$W_i = \frac{1}{s_{d_i}^2} = \frac{1}{0.0006}, \frac{1}{0.010}, \cdots, \frac{1}{0.056}$$

$$\bar{d} = \frac{\sum W_i d_i}{\sum W_i} = \frac{157.9935}{1238.164} = 0.128$$

$$s_{\bar{d}} = \sqrt{\frac{1}{\sum W_i}} = \sqrt{\frac{1}{1238.164}} = 0.028$$

$$CI = \bar{d} \pm 1.96(s_{\bar{d}})$$

$$CI_{lower} = 0.128 - 1.96(0.028) = 0.073$$

$$CI_{upper} = 0.128 + 1.96(0.028) = 0.183$$

$$0.073 \le \delta \le 0.183$$

Notice that the confidence interval does not include 0, so the overall effect is significant. If you look back at Figure 17.1 you will notice that near the bottom of that figure is a diamond-shaped figure. The center of that diamond is the estimated overall effect size, and its width is the confidence interval that we just discussed. It is labeled FE because it was computed for the fixed-effect model.

Heterogeneity of Effect Sizes

Now that we have the mean and confidence limits of d across all studies, we want to look more closely at the data to determine if the effect size estimates are heterogeneous, suggesting that not all studies are estimating the same true effect. The data could be heterogeneous for two different reasons. It could be that the three target audiences respond differently to the intervention, so that study differences are really Target differences. Alternatively there may be differences in the estimated parameters even among studies within the same set of targets. Or perhaps it is a mixture of both.

We will take as our measure of heterogeneity the statistic Q. It is defined as

$$Q = \sum_{i=1}^{k} W_i(d_i - \bar{d})^2 = \sum W_i d_i^2 - \frac{(\sum W_i d_i)^2}{\sum W_i}$$

Like many of the formulae that we will see in this chapter, this one looks unpleasantly messy, which results mostly from the fact that we want to give greater weight to more precise estimates of d. Q is simply a weighted sum of squared deviations of effect sizes for each study from the mean effect size. The more variable the effect sizes, the greater the value of Q. It is analogous to SS_{Between} in the analysis of variance. Because of the weights we used (the inverse of the variances) it is also a standardized measure. Although Q is calculated using d in this example, we could substitute other effect size measures and use the same formulae. For our example

$$Q = \sum W_i d_i^2 - \frac{(\sum W_i d_i)^2}{\sum W_i}$$

$$= 102.6840 - \frac{157.9935^2}{1238.164} = 82.5235$$

The nice thing about Q is that under the null hypothesis of no differences in effect sizes it is distributed as χ^2 on $k - 1$ df where k is the number of studies. With 21 studies, $\chi^2(20) = 31.41$. Because $82.52 > 31.41$ we can reject the null hypothesis and conclude that the studies are not all estimating the same true effect. I should point out that the general opinion in meta-analysis is that we don't base our decision on fixed versus random models on the results of such a test—that decision should be based on substantive information about the studies themselves—but an overall test is still worthwhile. You might think of it as being analogous to the overall F in a one-way analysis of variance.

If we have a random model underlying our results, even if we don't explicitly identify it as random, we can calculate the variance of the true effects (σ_τ^2). In a fixed model there is only one true effect, but for a random model the variance of true effects is a meaningful statistic. To estimate (σ_τ^2) we will use what is known as the DerSimonian and Laird method. While it is not the optimal measure, it is very close and is easy to compute. If we let τ represent the deviation of a study's true effect from the average true effect, which is exactly analogous to what we did in the analysis of variance, then the estimate of the variance of τ is defined as

$$T^2 = \frac{Q - df}{C}$$

where

$$C = \sum W_i - \frac{\sum W_i^2}{\sum W_i}$$

For our example,

$$Q = 82.5235$$

$$C = \sum W_i - \frac{\sum W_i^2}{\sum W_i} = 1238.164 - \frac{207219.9982}{1238.164} = 1070.8033$$

$$T^2 = \frac{Q - df}{C} = \frac{82.5235 - 20}{1070.8033} = 0.0584$$

$$T = \sqrt{T^2} = \sqrt{0.0584} = 0.2416$$

The definition if T^2 is not as odd as it may seem. Q measures the differences among effect size measures, while *df* is the expected variability if the null hypothesis is true. So the numerator is the excess variability that cannot be attributed to random differences among studies. You can think of C as a term analogous to the within groups term in the analysis of variance, but you can also think of it as standardizing the result much as dividing $\overline{X} - \mu$ by the standard deviation standardizes d. As Borenstein et al. (2009) have phrased it, we start with Q, which is a measure of a weighted sum of squares between studies, subtract the *df*, which adjusts for the number of studies in our meta-analysis, and divide by C, which puts everything back in the original metric and standardizes it.

Subgroup Differences

We have concluded that we have good reason to believe that different studies are estimating different true effect sizes, and it is reasonable to ask if the Target audience is associated with those different effects. We will continue to hold with a fixed model for effect sizes within target audience, but not between audiences. To investigate this issue we will compute Q separately for each level of Target, and then ask if those Q values are themselves significantly different.

The information necessary to compute Q within each audience type can be found in the summary rows within Table 17.2. These calculations are shown below, where the subscript on Q refers to Target.

$$Q = \sum W_i d_i^2 - \frac{(\sum W_i d_i)^2}{\sum W_i}$$

$$Q_1 = 11.5133 - \frac{21.4408^2}{836.561} = 10.9638$$

$$Q_2 = 25.4861 - \frac{40.1070^2}{119.314} = 12.0043$$

$$Q_3 = 65.6846 - \frac{96.4457^2}{282.289} = 32.7334$$

We will now let Q_{within} represent the sum of Q_i within each of the audience types, so

$$Q_{within} = Q_1 + Q_2 + Q_3 = 10.9638 + 12.0043 + 32.7334$$
$$= 55.7015$$

From earlier calculations we have Q for the 21 studies as $Q_{total} = 82.5235$. Then

$$Q_{between} = Q_{total} - Q_{within}$$
$$= 82.5235 - 55.7015$$
$$= 26.822$$

This should all seem somewhat familiar because it is directly analogous to what we do with the analysis of variance. Under the null hypothesis that the effect size is the same for all *groups*, $Q_{between}$ is distributed as chi-square on $g - 1$ df, where g represents the number of groups. For our example, $\chi^2(2) = 5.99$, so we can reject the null hypothesis and conclude that target audience is a factor in the effectiveness of treatments. Moreover, the separate values of Q_i are themselves chi-squares on degrees of freedom equal to one less that the number of studies in a set. The critical values then are $\chi^2(7) = 14.07$ and $\chi^2(4) = 9.49$, and we can reject the assumption of homogeneity in both the Selective and the Indicated condition. Apparently the effects of the intervention depend on more than simply the difference in the way the recipients of the interaction are identified.

Random Model

I am going to say only a bit more about the random model and refer the interested reader to Borenstein et al. (2009). As we know, the major difference in a random model is that the variability in our results is attributed to two sources. As with the fixed model, there is variability due to the participants who happen to have been used. But there is also variability due to the fact that different studies are assumed to be estimating a different true effect. What we will do is to include both of these variances in computing the weights that we will use for each study. The rest of the calculations are the same.

For the fixed model we assumed that the only source of variability was error variance. Using d_i to represent our effect size measure, although it could be some other effect size such as $\log(RR)$, we had

$$W_i = \frac{1}{s_d^2}$$

$$\bar{d} = \frac{W_j d_i}{\sum W_i}$$

For the random model the variability is made up of error variance, as estimated by s_d^2 and true variability in the effects estimated by each study (T^2). We will therefore weight the studies somewhat differently and use

$$W_i^* = \frac{1}{s_d^2 + T^2}$$

The asterisk on "$W*$" is used to distinguish this from the weights in the fixed model. We now define the weighted mean and standard error of the effect size estimates as

$$\overline{d} = \frac{\sum W_i^* d_i}{\sum W_i^*}$$

$$s_{\overline{d}} = \sqrt{\frac{1}{\sum W_i^*}}$$

We use these values, instead of the ones we computed for a fixed model, in all subsequent calculations. Calculating our confidence limits on $\overline{d}$ using z as an approximation rather than a noncentral t, we would have

$$\overline{d} \pm 1.96(s_{\overline{d}})$$

Rather than repeat the calculations, which are the same as we have just done except that we use different weights, the results are shown in Figure 17.2. The only difference between this figure and Figure 17.1 is at the bottom of the table where we see the confidence limits

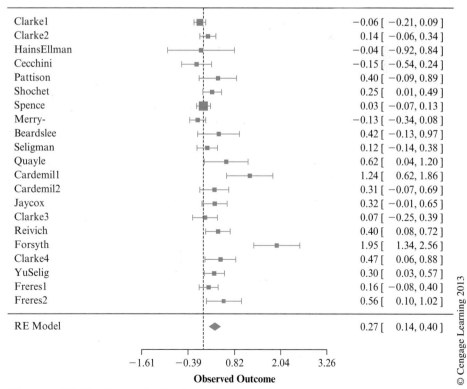

Figure 17.2   Forest plot for the random model

assuming a random model. Notice that the estimated summary effect is now 0.27 instead of 0.13, but the confidence interval is noticeably wider (0.14, 0.40), reflecting the added source of uncertainty.

17.3 A Second Example—Nicotine Gum and Smoking Cessation

Psychologists have long been interested in helping people to quit smoking, and in the last 20 years we have seen the widespread use of nicotine gum and patches for this purpose. A very large meta-analysis of the effectiveness of such aids was published in the Cochrane database, referred to earlier, by Stead, Perera, Bullen, Mant, and Lancaster T. (2008). They examined 132 different studies, 53 of which compared nicotine gum to a control condition. We are going to use about half of those studies just to save space, but our results will be essentially the same as theirs. (Stead et al. used what is known as the Mantel-Haenzsel method of weighting studies, so our results will differ somewhat from theirs, but not in any important way.) The data for 26 studies comparing gum with a control are shown in Table 17.4.

Table 17.4   Data on nicotine gum as an aid in stopping smoking

(SuccessT and TotalT stand for number of success and the total number of cases in the treatment condition.)

Study	Year	SuccessT	TotalT	SuccessC	TotalC	RR	Log$_{RR}$
Ahluwalia	2006	53	378	42	377	1.23	0.20
Areechon	1988	56	99	37	101	1.35	0.33
Blondal	1989	30	92	22	90	1.25	0.22
BrThorSociety	1983	39	410	111	1208	1.03	0.03
Campbell	1987	13	424	9	412	1.39	0.33
Campbell	1991	21	107	21	105	0.98	−.02
Clavel	1985	24	205	6	222	3.98	1.38
Clavel-Chapelon	1992	47	481	42	515	1.18	0.17
Cooper	2005	17	146	15	147	1.13	0.12
Fagerstrom	1982	30	50	23	50	1.19	0.17
Fagerstrom	1984	28	96	5	49	2.44	0.89
Fee1982	1982	23	180	15	172	1.41	0.35
Fortmann	1995	110	552	84	522	1.20	0.18
Garcia	1989	21	68	5	38	2.03	0.71
Garvey	2000	75	405	17	203	2.02	0.70
Gilbert	1989	11	112	9	111	1.19	0.18
Gross95	1995	37	131	6	46	1.91	0.65
Hall85	1985	18	41	10	36	1.40	0.34
Hall87	1987	30	71	14	68	1.74	0.55
Hall96	1996	24	98	28	103	0.92	−.08
Harackiewicz	1988	12	99	7	52	0.91	−.09
Herrera	1995	30	76	13	78	1.98	0.68
Hjalmarson	1984	31	106	16	100	1.64	0.50
Huber88	1988	13	54	11	60	1.25	0.23
Hughes	1989	23	210	6	105	1.83	0.60
Hughes	1990	15	59	5	19	0.97	−.03

The forest plot for the data above is shown below. (Notice that the effect sizes given on the right are the log risk ratios rather than the risk ratios themselves.) You will note that almost every study had an effect size that was great than 1.0 (for the risk ratio) or greater than 0 (for the log risk ratio). This strongly suggests that nicotine gum is effective in helping people to quit smoking and not to relapse.

Although we are working with risk ratios rather than standardized mean differences, there are only minor changes in our calculations. In the first place we immediately convert the risk ratios to log risk ratios. We will then work with the logarithmic values until the end, when we will convert back to the standard metric.

The risk ratio is defined as

$$\text{RiskRatio} = \frac{\text{SuccessT/TotalT}}{\text{SuccessC/TotalC}}$$

$$\text{LogRiskRatio} = \ln(\text{RiskRatio})$$

The variance and standard error, to a close approximation, are given by

$$\text{Var}_{\text{LogRiskRatio}} = \frac{1}{\text{SuccessT}} - \frac{1}{\text{TotalT}} + \frac{1}{\text{SuccessC}} - \frac{1}{\text{TotalC}}$$

$$s_{\text{LogRiskRatio}} = \sqrt{\text{Var}_{\text{LogRiskRatio}}}$$

We do not bother to calculate the variance and standard error of the risk ratio itself because we will never need them.

We still need to calculate summary statistics for the mean risk ratio and its confidence limits. To do so we work with the logarithmic values. We use the same basic formulae that we did before, except that we substitute the log risk ratio for d.

$$\text{Mean}_{\text{LogRR}} = \frac{\sum W_i \text{LogRR}_i}{\sum W_i} = \frac{73.766}{267.416} = 0.278$$

$$\text{Var}_{\text{LogRR}} = \frac{1}{\sum W_i} = \frac{1}{267.416} = .0037$$

$$SE_{\text{LogRR}} = \sqrt{\text{Var}_{\text{LogRR}}} = \sqrt{.0037} = .06$$

$$CI = \text{mean}_{\text{LogRR}} \pm 1.96(SE_{\text{LogRR}}) = .276 \pm 1.96(.06) = .276 \pm 0.118$$

$$CI_{\text{lower}} = 0.158$$

$$CI_{\text{upper}} = 0.394$$

$$\exp(\text{mean}) = \exp(.276) = 1.32$$

$$\exp(CI_{\text{lower}}) = \exp(0.158) = 1.17$$

$$\exp(CI_{\text{upper}}) = \exp(0.394) = 1.48$$

The last step above converted the6 logarithmic values back to the original metric of the risk ratio. Therefore we can write the confidence interval on the risk ratio as

$$1.17 \le \text{RiskRatio} \le 1.48$$

Our risk ratio is significantly greater than 1, indicating that the likelihood of a successful outcome is greater in the group that used nicotine gum, and the lower bound of the interval reflects about a 25% higher chance of success for that group. We are not quite done yet because we want a test for heterogeneity of study effects. All of the studies were sufficiently similar so that it is reasonable to assume that we are dealing with a fixed model. As we did in the earlier example we will calculate Q and evaluate it against χ^2 on $k - 1 = 25$ *df*.

$$Q = \sum W_i (\log RR)_i^2 - \frac{\left(\sum W_i \log RR_i \right)^2}{\sum W_i} = 39.570 - \frac{5441.402}{276.4161} = 19.22$$

$$\chi^2_{(25,.05)} = 37.65$$

We will not reject the assumption of homogeneity of effect sizes. That pretty much confirms the visual impression of Figure 17.3.

There is far more that we could cover on meta-analysis, but what we have here should be sufficient to make you feel comfortable going to the literature. You know the basic differences between random and fixed models, you can calculate a mean effect size and its standard error, and you can set confidence limits on that effect size. Collecting all of the data to do a meta-analysis is the really hard part. You have a good handle on the rest. There are certainly a lot of formulae, but if you work through them systematically

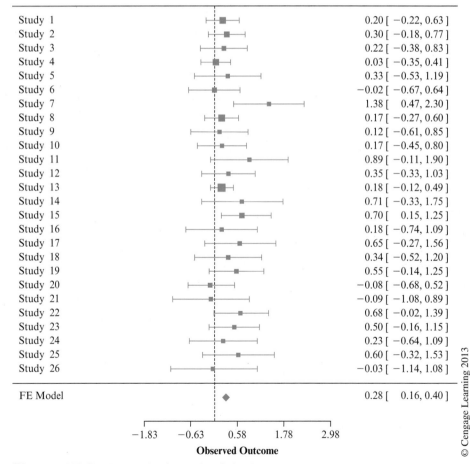

Figure 17.3   Forest plot for study of nicotine gum

they are not complicated, and no one would expect you to remember them all. Each of the sources cited above is excellent and provides the information you need. There are also software programs that will not only carry out the calculations, but will allow you to organize the data about each study and examine the question of whether effect sizes are dependent on other variables such as gender or age. One of the best packages is the Comprehensive Meta-Analysis (CMA) package, developed by Borenstein, Hedges, Higgins, and Rothstein. It is not freeware, but you can hope that your university has a license for it. In addition, the Cochrane Collaboration has developed software named RevMan, which is free, and will do just about everything you would want and more. William Shadish keeps a list of available meta-analysis software at http://faculty.ucmerced.edu/wshadish/Meta-Analysis Software.htm. It contains links to many programs. Finally, R has at least three packages for meta-analysis, of which "metafor" is my favorite. Programs that will run the two analyses that were used as examples are available from this book's Web site.

SINGLE-CASE DESIGNS

17.4 Analyses that Examine Standardized Mean Differences

In some areas of the behavioral sciences research designs called "single-subject designs" or "single-case designs" are common. For example, in studies of behavioral problems, or learning disorders, or attention disorders, it is common to take a single case, measure some behavior (e.g., distraction) over a baseline period, introduce some intervention such as reinforcement of an alternative desired behavior, and continue to measure the unwanted behavior over subsequent intervention trials. It might well be that we have several individuals who show behavior problems, but the problems might not be exactly the same. One child gazes off into space, another pokes his neighbor, and a third doodles on his desk. Because of this we can't simply combine the different behaviors and average over children—we must treat each child as his own case. In one sense the label "single-case design" is misleading because most studies deal with several different cases. But we deal with each child on his or her own. The issue then becomes how we go about analyzing the data from several different cases to come to a single conclusion. This has been an area of disagreement for years and will probably go on being so, but there are some things that we know that allow us to pull the literature together and make some reasonable recommendations. Some of the issues that are raised could also be raised about traditional between-group designs, but in that case there has come to be some general agreement among researchers on how to go about the analysis. For example, if we were investigating anorexia we could randomly assign cases to a treatment or control condition, introduce some intervention, and then weigh each of our participants at the end of treatment. A *t* test between the means of the two groups would seem like a reasonable approach and there would not be much disagreement among researchers on that analysis. But in single-case studies the analysis is not so clear-cut.

A-B designs   In this chapter I will focus on what are called **A-B designs** because they are the easiest to lay out and form the basis for analyses of results for more complex designs.

An A-B design is one in which data are collected for a number of trials at baseline (A), and then an intervention is introduced and data are collected over the remaining trials (B). An A-B-A design would be one in which there is a third phase during which the intervention is withheld and we expect to see performance return to near baseline levels. This is sometimes called a withdrawal design. An A-B-A-B design then reintroduces the intervention in the fourth phase. The analyses that I will discuss in this section can be extended to these more complex designs. The advantage of such designs is that they offer protection against premature conclusions that the intervention is effective. Excellent coverage of all single-case research designs can be found in Franklin, Allison, and Gorman (1996).

One of the biggest issues in single case studies is the choice of a statistic to measure performance changes. For example, we could compare the mean performance under each phase of the study. But we could also compare the slopes of the lines relating the dependent variable to trials, the percentage of trials during the intervention phase that exceed the median of trials during the baseline phase, or any of several other statistics. The choice is important for how we handle the data. In this chapter I am going to demonstrate two quite different approaches. The first will deal with mean differences and the second with changes in slope and intercept. You will find that the two analyses look quite different. The choice between them depends largely on how you expect performance to change over time, and that is a separate decision for each experimenter.

17.5 A Case Study of Depression

We will begin with an example of a psychiatrist who is interested in examining the effects of a new drug on patients with depression. Being a believer in controlled experiments, he collects pre-intervention data on depression levels from each client for six or more weeks prior to the intervention. He then starts the client on the drug in question and records data for at least another six trials. Because the drug takes some time to build up in the body, and therefore its effects should increase with time at first, no data are collected for the first three weeks after beginning the drug. As we know, people vary over time in how they feel, so we do not expect that all of the baseline measures will be the same, nor will all of the post-intervention measures. There will be within-phase variance. However, by separating the measures by a week, we do not expect that there will be serious autocorrelation of scores. In other words, there is no trend in the within-phase data and adjacent observations are at least largely independent. I will explain shortly why we want the autocorrelations to be near zero. Our psychiatrist has four clients who agree to participate, but each one will start at a different time and have a different number of baseline measures and perhaps even a different drug dose, depending on responsiveness. This is an A-B design, where phase A is the baseline phase and phase B is the intervention phase. The data from this hypothetical study are shown in Figure 17.4.

One of the most common ways of approaching data like these is to calculate a standardized mean difference (d) between pre- and post-intervention trials for each case. A standardized mean difference (d) has an advantage over a raw mean difference because it will put each client on a common scale. Overall differences in depression levels among clients will not affect the analysis. Although this approach is very commonly, and appropriately, used, I will later return to this issue and briefly discuss why it may not be the best approach in many studies.

Our dependent variable in this study is the weekly depression score, and our resulting statistic for each patient is the effect size (d) between baseline and intervention phases. We

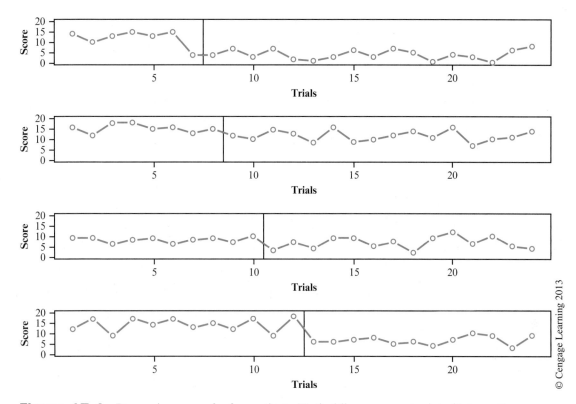

© Cengage Learning 2013

Figure 17.4   Depression scores for four patients. Vertical lines represent point of intervention

have a choice of standard deviation to be used in computing d. We could take the standard deviation at baseline, the separate non-pooled standard deviations for the two phases, or the pooled standard deviation over phases. We will use the latter, but a good case can be made for using the baseline standard deviation if we expect noticeably greater variability during intervention. Finally, we will treat each patient as a separate case and only combine over cases at the end.

In Table 17.5 you will see d for each client alone. As I said before, I used the pooled standard deviation to calculate d for each client. I also calculated the standard error of d and confidence limits. The formulae for these calculations are

$$d = \frac{\overline{X}_{\text{Post}} - \overline{X}_{\text{Pre}}}{s_{\text{pooled}}}$$

$$s_d = \sqrt{\frac{1}{n_{\text{Pre}}} + \frac{1}{n_{\text{Post}}} + \frac{d^2}{2(n_{\text{Pre}} + n_{\text{Post}})}}$$

(If I had used the standard deviation of the control group to compute d, the denominator on the right would be $2(n_{\text{Pre}})$. See Gleser and Olkin (2009).)

From the confidence interval on d you can see that clients 1, 2, and 4 showed significant increases in performance while patient 3 did not—the confidence limits on d for that patient include 0. Notice that most confidence intervals are quite wide.

We can now go on to compute a mean of d over the four patients. In this case, just as in the meta-analyses we have just examined, we do not just average the four d values. Instead

Table 17.5 Depression scores for baseline and intervention phases
(P_i represents Phase$_i$, and Y_i represents the score$_i$ for the ith case)

	P_1	Y_1	P_2	Y_2	P_3	Y_3	P_4	Y_4
	A	14	A	16	A	9	A	12
	A	10	A	12	A	9	A	17
	A	13	A	18	A	6	A	9
	A	15	A	18	A	8	A	17
	A	13	A	15	A	9	A	14
	A	15	A	16	A	6	A	17
	B	4	A	13	A	8	A	13
	B	4	A	15	A	9	A	15
	B	7	B	12	A	7	A	12
	B	3	B	10	A	10	A	17
	B	7	B	15	B	3	A	9
	B	2	B	13	B	7	A	18
	B	1	B	9	B	4	B	6
	B	3	B	16	B	9	B	6
	B	6	B	9	B	9	B	7
	B	3	B	10	B	5	B	8
	B	7	B	12	B	7	B	5
	B	5	B	14	B	2	B	6
	B	0	B	11	B	9	B	4
	B	4	B	16	B	12	B	7
	B	3	B	7	B	6	B	10
	B	0	B	10	B	10	B	9
	B	6	B	11	B	5	B	3
	B	8	B	14	B	4	B	9
Mean (A)		13.333		15.375		8.100		14.167
SD (A)		1.862		2.134		1.370		3.186
Mean( )B		4.056		11.812		6.571		6.667
SD (B)		2.437		2.664		2.928		2.103
s_{pooled}		2.319		2.507		2.415		2.700
d		4.001		1.421		0.633		2.778
s_d		1.248		0.560		0.438		0.699
CI_{lower}		1.556		0.323		−0.225		1.408
CI_{upper}		6.447		2.519		1.490		4.147
Weight		0.642		3.188		5.223		2.048

we will again use a weighted average that will give more weight to those values of d that have small standard errors. For our purposes

$$W_i = \frac{1}{s_{d_i}^2} = \frac{1}{1.248^2} ; \frac{1}{0.560^2} ; \frac{1}{0.438^2} ; \frac{1}{0.669^2}$$

$$\bar{d} = \frac{\sum W_i d_i}{\sum W_i} = 1.450$$

$$s_{\overline{d}} = \sqrt{\frac{1}{\sum W_i}} = 0.300$$

$$CI(\overline{d}) = \overline{d} \pm 1.96 s_{\overline{d}}$$

$$= 1.450 \pm 1.96 \times 0.300$$

$$0.861 \le \delta \le 2.038$$

Notice that our summary statistic for the combined set of data is $\overline{d} = 1.450$ with a confidence interval of $0.861 \le \delta \le 2.038$. In other words our average effect size is a drop in depression scores of nearly 1.5 standard deviations. Even the bottom of the interval is over 8/10ths of a standard deviation. We can be quite confident in concluding that the drug in question can reduce depression noticeably.

Although we could continue along the lines of the first half of the chapter and discuss fixed versus random models, compute an estimate of τ, and so on, we won't do that here. Usually single-case designs have relatively few cases and there is little to be gained from performing the more refined analysis that you would perform in a typical meta-analysis.

Points to Consider

I am confident that for these data this meta-analysis does what we want it to do and accurately reflects the results of the individual case studies. I created this example so that this would be the case. However, while it represents a perfectly good study, other perfectly good studies might not be suitable for this particular analysis.

First of all, there are often problems with autocorrelation. For this study we assumed that responses within phases were independent. That seems a reasonable assumption here. But in many A-B designs the person's performance on trial$_i$ is related to that person's performance on trial $_{i-1}$. In other words we need to worry about the autocorrelation (within phases) of observations. If, for example, the person is showing a general upward or downward trend over trials, the autocorrelation is likely to be large. But even concern about autocorrelation is in dispute. Manolov and Solanas (2008) conducted a simulation study and concluded that the type of analysis used here is at least as good as alternative analyses that are designed to address autocorrelation. Huitema has argued in several papers (e.g., Huitema and McKean (1991)) that autocorrelation is not the problem we think it to be. What we are worried about is really autocorrelation of *residuals* after we have conducted our analysis. If we can include terms in our analysis to absorb or account for the correlations, the residuals will be reasonably independent. For example, if the autocorrelation is caused by a general upward trend in the data over trials, and if we can include trials as a variable in our analysis, that will adjust the autocorrelation conditional on trial. However I need to point out that this is not the universal view of the matter.

A second issue to be considered is the fact that alternative ways of examining single-subject data have been proposed and are taken seriously. In the next example we will look at a proposal by Center, Skiba, and Casey (1985–1986), and a refinement of that approach by Huitema and McKean (2000), that takes a regression approach to the problem. Van den Noortgate and Onghena (2003a & b) have proposed the use of hierarchical linear models, which we will not cover. They, too, do an excellent job of modeling behavior. Finally, Bulté and Onghena (2008) have developed powerful resampling procedures that can handle autocorrelation, but focus primarily on significance testing of mean differences.

17.6 A Second Approach to a Single-Case Design—Using Piecewise Regression

We will take an example from Zeigler (1994) that illustrates some of the complexities in analyzing single-case designs and differs considerably from the previous example. Zeigler was concerned with training soccer players to respond quickly to appropriate environmental cues. She selected four players whose performance was poor and observed their ability to hit a target with the ball over a series of trials. The number of baseline trials was different for each player. She then introduced an attentional shift-training intervention and continued to record the accuracy of performance. The data are plotted in Figure 17.5 and the individual scores are given in Table 17.6.

From Figure 17.5 it looks as if the intervention was effective. Performance for three players improved after the baseline period, although one might wonder about Subject #3. With a little imagination you might suspect that his performance had been improving all along and simply continued to improve at roughly the same rate after the intervention. In other words a regression line fitted to those data might fit very nicely and suggest that the post-intervention performance was simply a continuation of the baseline trend.

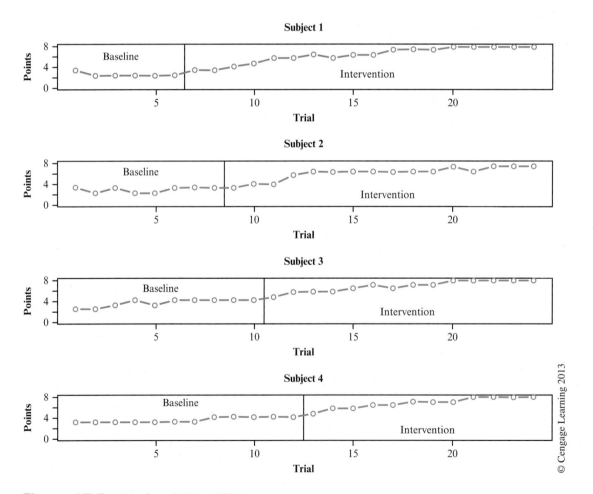

Figure 17.5   Data from Zeigler (1994)

© Cengage Learning 2013

Table 17.6   Performance on a soccer test for four players

(P_i represents treatment phase and Y_i represents the dependent variable for player$_i$)

P_1	Y_1	P_2	Y_2	P_3	Y_3	P_4	Y_4
A	4	A	4	A	3	A	4
A	3	A	3	A	3	A	4
A	3	A	4	A	4	A	4
A	3	A	3	A	5	A	4
A	3	A	3	A	4	A	4
A	3	A	4	A	5	A	4
B	4	A	4	A	5	A	4
B	4	A	4	A	5	A	5
B	5	B	4	A	5	A	5
B	6	B	5	A	5	A	5
B	7	B	5	B	6	A	5
B	7	B	7	B	7	A	5
B	8	B	8	B	7	B	6
B	7	B	8	B	7	B	7
B	8	B	8	B	8	B	7
B	8	B	8	B	9	B	8
B	9	B	8	B	8	B	8
B	9	B	8	B	9	B	9
B	9	B	8	B	9	B	9
B	10	B	9	B	10	B	9
B	10	B	8	B	10	B	10
B	10	B	9	B	10	B	10
B	10	B	9	B	10	B	10
B	10	B	9	B	10	B	10

As I mentioned earlier, we have a choice of the statistic that we use to measure performance. In the previous example we used the standardized mean difference. However, a number of other statistics have been proposed that have strong advocates. Some have proposed regression approaches in which we condition on trends in the data and look at what remains after we have accounted for trends. There have also been suggestions to measure the percentage of nonoverlapping data, which means that we count the number of observations during the intervention phase that are above (or below) the highest (or lowest) observation at baseline. Others have suggested counting the observations during intervention that exceed the baseline median. Unfortunately these measures often do not correlate well with each other (Owens, Farmer, Ferron, & Allsopp, 2010).

Work by Center, Skiba, and Casey (1985–1986) and Huitema and McKean (1998 & 2000), offer at least one way forward that needs to be considered. It involves more work than simply looking as the standardized mean difference, but it provides us with more information and is often more relevant to the data at hand. The approach is known as **piecewise regression** and works by fitting regression lines using time, phase, and their interaction as predictors. (There are slight differences between the proposals by Center et al. (1985–1986) and Huitema and McKean (2000), and I recommend the latter approach.)

Consider for a moment just the fourth soccer player in our data. I chose this player because there is a clear change in slope. We can code Trials as simply the numbers 1 to 24. We can then create another variable called Phase, which will be 0 for those observations at

piecewise regression

Table 17.7   Data for fourth case in Zeigler's study

Y	4	4	4	4	4	4	4	5	5	5	5	5	6	7	7
P	0	0	0	0	0	0	0	0	0	0	0	0	1	1	1
T	1	2	3	4	5	6	7	8	9	10	11	12	13	14	15
PT	0	0	0	0	0	0	0	0	0	0	0	0	0	1	2

Y	8	8	9	9	9	10	10	10	10
P	1	1	1	1	1	1	1	1	1
T	16	17	18	19	20	21	22	23	24
PT	3	4	5	6	7	8	9	10	11

© Cengage Learning 2013

baseline and 1 for those observations at intervention. Finally, we can multiply Phase times (Trial − (*nb*-1)), where *nb* represents the number of baseline trials. This will code the interaction of Time and Phase. The effect of this last coding is to code all the baseline trials as 0 and to code the intervention trials as 0, 1, 2, 3, … The data for the fourth case is shown in Table 17.7. I have chosen to illustrate that case because visually there is a clear difference in both slope and level from baseline to intervention.

For demonstration purposes only we will examine the regression of Y_i on $Trial_i$ for the data in the baseline phase of the fourth case. I will then do the same thing for the data from the intervention phase. Finally, I will use each equation to predict that case's score on $Trial_{13}$, the first intervention trial. The results are given below.

<u>Regression on baseline data</u>

$$\hat{Y}_i = 3.6212 + .1224 \times Trial_i$$

<u>Regression on intervention data</u>

$$\hat{Y}_i = 1.7914 + .3671 \times Trial_i$$

<u>Prediction for Trial$_{13}$</u>

$$\hat{Y}_i = 3.6212 + .1224 \times 13 = 5.2124 \qquad \hat{Y}_i = 1.7914 + .3671 \times 13 = 6.5637$$

We can see that the effect of the intervention is to move the predicted value for $Trial_{13}$ from 5.2124 to 6.5637, for a difference of 1.3513.

It is important to realize what we have here—or, more importantly, what we do not have. Using the piecewise regression approach a change in "level" is a change in the predicted score on the first intervention trial. It is not calculated as a change in the mean from baseline to intervention. If you look at Player 3 in Figure 17.5 and draw imaginary regression lines, I suspect you will see that whether we base our prediction for the first intervention trial on the baseline data or the intervention phase data, the predictions will be pretty much the same. And this in spite of the fact that the means for the two phases look very much different. (The predictions will differ by about 0.85, which is not significant. The means, on the other hand, will differ by 4.17.)

Finally, we can use the three predictors (Trial, Phase, and TP) to predict Y_i, the score on $Trial_i$. This result follows for case number 4.

Model = $Y = b_0 + b_1(\text{Trial}) + b_2(\text{Phase}) + b_3(\text{T} \times \text{P})$

	b_i	s_b	t	p	r_{sp}
Intercept	3.6212	0.2140	16.924	.000*	
Phase	1.3519	0.2853	4.738	.000*	.146
Trial	0.1224	0.0291	4.209	.000*	.129
P × T	0.2448	0.0411	5.953	.000*	.183

© Cengage Learning 2013

If you look at the regression coefficients for this result, you will see some interesting values. The intercept in the full model is 3.6212, which is the intercept computed on the baseline data. The coefficient for Trials (0.1224) is the regression coefficient for Trials in the baseline data. More interestingly, the difference between the two predictions for $Trial_{13}$, based on baseline and on intervention data, is 1.3519, which is the regression coefficient for Phase in the full model. If we look at the difference between the two slopes (for baseline and intervention data separately) it is $0.3671 - 0.1224 = .2448$, which is the coefficient for the interaction in the full model. In other words when the data are structured as I have structured them here, the full model gives us coefficients for the change in level and the change in slope, both of which we want. But be careful. The change in level refers to predicted performance on the first intervention trial. It is not the mean difference between the two phases. In addition, remember that the effect for Trial is only the slope of the baseline data, which is probably not of much interest. The fact that it happens to be significant here relates to an important point made by Huitema (in press). When we are dealing with single-case studies, it is common to have little within-phase variance, especially for baseline, and so tests of significance and effect sizes are likely to be greater than we would normally expect in a between-subjects design.

The advantage of a system that drops one predictor at a time is that we only have to look at the full model to have a t test of each predictor's effect. It is the t test on the coefficients. For the fourth player there was a significant difference in both change in level and change in slope, as well as the difference due to Trials.

But what we really want is to get back to an effect size measure so that we can combine data over cases. That turns out to be a lot easier than you might guess. As Center et al. (1985–1986) point out, we can convert from the t values for the test on each coefficient to d by

$$d = \frac{2|t|}{\sqrt{df_{error}}}$$

(Notice that we use the absolute value of t for this calculation.) It may seem strange to compute a measure that we normally associate with a standardized mean difference in conjunction with a regression model, particularly of changes in slope. Center et al. argue that "effect sizes derived from a regression approach can best be interpreted as indices of the amount of variance accounted for as a function of the treatment, expressed in units of standard error of estimate" (p. 398). They also make the important point, as does Huitema, that it is not clear that effect sizes from single-case studies are the same as effect sizes from group studies. In fact they probably are a substantial overestimate, at least in part because the standard errors will be much smaller than we expect from group studies, as we will see.

If we repeat the t to d conversion for each player we will have the following result

Player	d_{Phase}	d_{Trial}	$d_{T \times P}$
1	1.88*	0.46	1.61*
2	0.97*	0.22	0.76
3	0.86	1.94*	0.62
4	1.74*	1.88*	2.66*

* Significant t in full model.
© Cengage Learning 2013

Notice that there is considerable variability in these results. All four cases showed a change in level of at least nearly one standard deviation. (Three of those changes were statistically significant.) Two cases showed a significant change in slope, also with strong effects. (I earlier commented that the data for Case 3 might represent a general continuation of increasing performance that started at baseline. This result would support that

Table 17.8 Effect sizes and the calculation of the mean and standard error of d

Case	d_{phase}	s_{bphase}	W_{phase}	d_{time}	s_{btime}	W_{time}	d_{int}	s_{bint}	W_{int}
1	1.88*	.60	2.78	0.46	.14	51.02	1.61*	.14	51.02
2	0.97*	.71	1.98	0.22	.12	69.44	0.76	.13	59.17
3	0.86	.41	5.95	1.94*	.05	400.00	0.62	.06	277.78
4	1.74*	.29	11.89	1.88*	.03	1111.11	2.66*	.04	625.00
$\bar{d}$	1.46			1.78			1.94		
$s_{\bar{d}}$	0.044			0.001			0.001		

suggestion.) But notice that in this paragraph I am examining changes on an individual basis. The point of a meta-analysis is to look across cases (or studies). Assume that we had a study with an overall power of .70. That means that 70% of our differences are expected to be significant, but that 30% are not. It makes little sense to focus on those nonsignificant differences as if they "prove" the null hypothesis. A bunch of nonsignificant differences is expected to occur whenever the power of a study is less than 1.00. So a nonsignificant difference in the right direction can even be seen as representing support for the experimental hypothesis, and a fair test requires that we combine across results.

Having computed d values for each case, we can combine them over cases just as we did earlier. A question arises concerning the choice of weights for combining cases. In the past we used the reciprocal of the within-subject variances as our estimate of precision and thus as the metric for weights. In this case we are using the semi-partial regression coefficients, and their t values for effect sizes, so it makes sense to use reciprocals of the squares of the standard errors of the regression coefficients as our weights. The effect of this, however, will be to produce quite small standard errors for d that may look dubious.

The calculations for the meta-analysis across the four cases are shown below. To calculate the mean d we first need the weights, which are defined as

$$W_i = \frac{1}{s_d^2}$$

which, for the level difference in phases for first case is

$$W_{dphase} = \frac{1}{.60^2} = 2.78$$

Similar calculations give us the remaining values, which are shown in Table 17.8, along with the standard errors of the semi-partial regression coefficients.

We further define the mean effect of d for each result as the weighted sum of the d values divided by the sum of the weights. For the Phase effect this becomes

$$\bar{d} = \frac{\sum W_i d_i}{\sum W_i} = \frac{2.78 \times 1.88 + 1.98 \times 0.97 + 5.95 \times 0.86 + 11.89 \times 1.74}{2.78 + 1.98 + 5.95 + 11.89}$$

$$= \frac{32.9526}{22.62} = 1.46$$

$$s_{\bar{d}} = \sqrt{\frac{1}{\sum W_i}} = \sqrt{\frac{1}{22.62}} = .044$$

The remainder of the calculations are shown in the bottom half of Table 17.8. Notice how small the standard errors are, reflecting the precision that we can obtain in single-case designs.

Key Terms

Meta-analysis (Introduction)

File drawer problem, (Introduction)

Forest plot (17.2)

A-B Design (17.4)

Piecewise regression (17.5)

Exercises

Mazzucchelli, Kane, and Rees (2010) examined studies of behavioral activation as a way to improve feelings of subjective well-being. (They defined behavioral activation as "intentional behavioral, cognitive, or volitional activity . . . intended to cultivate positive feelings, behaviors, and/or cognitions." They report data on 11 studies comparing treatment and control groups. These data are shown below broken down by those who showed minimal symptoms of depression and those who showed elevated symptoms. The results follow.

Author	Subgroup	n_E (est.)	n_C (est.)	Hedges' g	Standard error
Barlow86a	Elevated	12	12	−.134	0.523
Besyner79	Elevated	14	16	0.675	0.423
Lovett88	Elevated	33	27	0.204	0.305
Stark	Elevated	10	9	0.043	0.439
Van den Hout	Elevated	15	14	0.644	0.371
Weinberg	Elevated	10	9	0.976	0.467
Wilson	Elevated	9	11	1.466	0.524
Barlow86b	Minimal	12	13	0.133	0.352
Fordyce77	Minimal	50	60	0.609	0.195
Fordyce83	Minimal	40	13	1.410	0.483
Reich81	Minimal	49	49	0.378	0.179

© Cengage Learning 2013

17.1 Create a forest plot of these data.

17.2 Test the hypothesis that there are no differences between the two subgroups in this table.

17.3 Calculate confidence limits on the mean effect size computed in the previous exercise.

17.4 Assuming a random model, calculate a mean effect size and its standard error.

17.5 Recompute the mean effect size and its confidence limits assuming that the underlying model is fixed.

Bloch et al (2009) conducted a meta-analysis on the treatment of Attention-deficit/hyperactivity disorder. There have been reports that psychostimulant medications given to children with ADHD who have a history of Tourette's syndrome can increase the severity of tics. The authors found (among other studies) four studies that compared methylphenidate derivatives against placebo-controlled condition by rating scales for tic and ADHD severity. The results of these four studies for presence and frequency of tics are shown below. (The standard errors of d were estimated from the published results.)

Study	n	d	CI		s_d
Gadow92	11	0.11	−0.55	−0.77	0.336
Castellanos	20	0.29	−0.18	−0.76	0.240
TSSG	103	0.64	0.27	−1.00	0.184
Gadow07	71	0.06	−0.17	−0.29	0.117

© Cengage Learning 2013

17.6 Three of the studies referred to in the previous exercises also looked at ratings of ADHD severity. These results are shown below.

Study	n	d	CI	s_d
Gadow92	11	1.11	0.44 – 1.77	0.341
TSSG	103	0.56	0.19 – 0.92	0.189
Gadow07	71	0.76	0.53 – 0.99	0.117

© Cengage Learning 2013

a. Compute the mean effect size from these studies.

b. Compute confidence limits on the mean effect size.

17.7 Why would it not make sense to try to treat this meta-analysis as a random model?

17.8 Calculate the mean effect size estimate and its confidence limits for the data in this table.

17.9 For the Bloch et al. study what would you conclude about the risk of increasing tic behavior using methylphenidate?

17.10 Create a forest plot for the data in Bloch's study.

17.11 Create a forest plot for these results.

17.12 Compute a mean effect size and its confidence limits.

Kapoor, Rajkumar, et al. (2011) collected data on the treatment of myeloma, which is a cancer of the blood. (You may think that this has little to do with psychology, but I have myeloma, so I have a particular interest in the results.) Kapoor, Rajkumar, et al. found four studies since 2007 that compared a standard chemotherapy treatment for myeloma with the same treatment that also included thalidomide. (Thalidomide was a drug prescribed as a sedative to pregnant women in the 1950s and was then found to create horrible problems with birth defects and was immediately withdrawn, but not until after causing 10,000–20,000 birth defects worldwide. It has recently been found to be an excellent treatment for some forms of cancer, though it is used with a great deal of caution.) The following table presents the results of the four studies.

Study	Success Thalidomide	Total Thalidomide	Success Control	Total Control
Palumbo	21	129	5	126
Facon	16	125	4	198
Hulin	8	113	1	116
Hovon	3	165	1	108

© Cengage Learning 2013

17.13 Create a forest plot for these results.

17.14 Why does it make little sense to look for heterogeneity of effect sizes in this example?

Bauer and Döpfmer (1999) examined the efficacy of lithium as a augmentation to conventional antidepressants. They found 9 placebo-controlled studies testing lithium for those cases that did not respond to other antidepressants. The data, as estimated from their paper, follow:

Study	n	d	s_d	CI	
Stein	34	−0.30	0.82	−1.10	−0.50
Zusky	16	0.19	0.86	−0.65	−1.03
Katona	61	0.50	0.51	0.02	−1.02
Schopf	27	1.36	1.39	0.05	−2.77

(continued)

Study	n	d	s_d	CI	
Baumann	24	0.97	0.99	0.09	-1.85
Browne	17	0.51	0.87	-0.34	-1.36
Kantor	7	0.51	1.55	-1.01	-2.03
Heninger	15	1.33	1.38	-0.02	-2.68
Joffe	33	0.76	0.70	-0.02	-1.36

© Cengage Learning 2013

17.15 Compute risk ratios for each study as well as log risk ratios.

17.16 Apply a meta-analysis to these data and draw the appropriate conclusions.

Social stories have been used in education to help children with autism spectrum learn appropriate social skills to reduce unwanted behavior that might otherwise appear. Eckelberry (2007) examined the use of social stories to help three children with attention and hyperactivity disorders. She used an A-B design with one week of baseline observation and two weeks of intervention. The dependent variable was the number of disruptive behaviors recorded each day. The following table presents her results.

Student	Baseline	Intervention
A	13 12 12 15 16	14 12 08 10 06 03 03 02 00 00
B	10 12 13 08 12	11 10 07 06 02 05 00 06 00 03
C	22 20 25 20 25	20 18 22 20 17 24 19 22 20 20

© Cengage Learning 2013

17.17 Compute confidence limits on the mean risk ratio and draw the appropriate conclusions.

17.18 Compute the weighted mean risk ratio across the four studies.

17.19 Why might it not make much sense to examine the results for heterogeneity of effects?

Bisson and Andrew (2007) conducted a meta-analysis of cognitive behavior therapy (CBT) as a treatment for post-traumatic stress disorder (PTSD). The found 14 studies for which they had clinician's ratings of PTSD symptoms in both a CBT focused condition and a wait list/usual care condition. The results are presented below.

	CBT			Control		
Study	N	Mean	St. Dev	N	Mean	St. Dev
Kubany1	45	15.80	14.40	40	71.90	23.80
Foa1	45	12.60	8.37	15	26.93	8.47
Kubany2	18	10.10	19.30	14	76.10	25.20
Resick	81	23.00	19.92	40	69.73	19.19
Cloitre	22	31.00	25.20	24	62.00	22.70
Foa2	10	15.40	11.09	10	19.50	7.18
Keane	11	28.80	10.05	13	31.90	31.90
Ehlers	14	21.58	28.56	14	74.55	19.12
Vaughan	13	23.00	10.20	17	28.50	8.90
Brom	27	56.20	24.10	23	66.40	24.30
Blanchard	27	23.70	26.20	24	54.00	25.90
Fecteau	10	37.50	30.40	10	74.60	24.70
Gersons	22	3.00	10.00	20	9.00	13.00
Rothbaum	20	21.25	22.50	20	64.55	19.87

© Cengage Learning 2013

17.20 Can we conclude that thalidomide is beginning to redeem its awful reputation?

17.21 Plot the data above on in a way similar to Figure 17.4.

17.22 Draw the appropriate conclusions from this study.

Howard and Kendall (1996) tested cognitive-behavioral family therapy with six anxiety-disordered children. Each child received 2, 4, or 6 baseline measures before family therapy was begun. Over the next several weeks there were 18 family therapy sessions. Among other things, children rated themselves each week on coping skills. The results, as transcribed from graphical displays are shown below. An asterisk next to the value indicates a baseline measurement. (The data are available on the Web site as Ex17-25.dat.)

Week	Child 1	Child 2	Child 3	Child 4	Child 5	Child 6
1	2.0*	6.0*	6.3*	4.0*	4.4*	2.3*
2	2.5*	6.7*	3.4*	3.9*	3.8*	2.3*
3	2.5*	6.7*	3.2*	4.0	3.4*	2.0*
4	2.8*	6.3*	3.4*	2.6	4.0*	1.9*
5	2.3*	6.7*	3.2*	3.8	4.5	2.6
6	2.3*	6.9*	2.8*	3.9	4.9	3.1
7	2.6	6.2	7.1	2.3	3.9	3.0
8	2.2	6.6	2.9	4.0	4.0	3.3
9	1.7	6.6	3.2	3.2	4.3	4.2
10	3.0	6.9	3.4	4.0	4.2	3.3
11	3.0	6.9	2.9	3.7	4.2	5.4
12	5.1	6.8	3.8	7.1	4.2	4.9
13	3.0	6.3	2.6	4.0	4.2	6.2
14	3.6	6.9	3.4	6.9	4.2	6.7
15	2.7	6.9	3.2	7.0	4.3	6.2
16	2.7	6.9	7.1	7.0	4.0	6.7
17	4.0	6.9	4.1	7.0	4.7	6.7
18	3.0	6.9	3.0	7.1	4.9	6.5
19	4.9	6.9	3.3	7.1	4.9	6.8
20	4.0	6.6	3.6	7.1	4.9	6.8
21	6.0	6.9	3.7	7.1	4.8	6.8
22	5.4	6.9	6.7	7.1	4.9	6.2
23	5.1	6.9	3.3	6.3	4.8	6.6
24	5.3	6.1	4.7	5.9	5.1	6.6
25	5.3	6.9	4.8	6.5	5.7	6.9
26	5.0	6.9	4.1	6.9	5.3	6.9
27	5.6	7.0	4.1	6.6	5.9	6.9
28	5.6	6.9	4.8	5.6	5.1	6.2
29	5.3	6.9	4.1	6.6	5.7	6.2
30	5.6	7.0	5.2	5.9	5.3	6.2
31	5.1	7.0	4.7	5.9	5.4	5.9
32	4.9	6.9	4.7	6.6	5.4	6.7
33	6.9	6.9	4.7	5.5	5.4	5.8
34	5.3	6.9	5.0	5.5	5.4	6.4
35	5.0	7.0	5.1	5.6	5.5	6.3
36	4.1	7.0	5.0	5.7	5.5	5.6

17.23 Compute a summary statistic (mean(d)) and its confidence interval.

17.24 For each student compute d as a standardized mean difference and find its standard error.

that the assumptions normally cited as being required of parametric tests are overly restrictive in practice and that the parametric tests are remarkably unaffected by violations of distribution assumptions. See Rasmussen (1987) for an example where parametric tests win out even with their assumptions violated.

The major disadvantage generally attributed to nonparametric tests is their (reputed) lower power relative to the corresponding parametric test. In general, when the assumptions of the parametric test are met, the nonparametric test requires somewhat more observations than does the comparable parametric test for the same level of power. Thus, for a given set of data, the parametric test is more likely to lead to rejection of a false null hypothesis than is the corresponding nonparametric test. Moreover, even when the distribution assumptions are violated to a moderate degree, the parametric tests are thought to maintain their advantage. A number of studies, however, have shown that for perfectly reasonable data sets nonparametric tests may have greater power than the corresponding parametric test. The problem is that we generally do not know when the nonparametric test will be more powerful.

Some nonparametric tests have an additional advantage. Because many of them rank the raw scores and operate on those ranks, they offer a test of differences in central tendency that are not affected by one or a few very extreme scores (outliers). An extreme score in a set of data actually can make the parametric test less powerful, because it inflates the variance, and hence the error term, as well as biasing the mean by shifting it toward the outlier (the latter may increase or decrease the mean difference).

The next section will be an introduction to bootstrapping. These procedures are particularly important in those situations where we are interested in statistics, such as the median, whose sampling distribution and standard error cannot be derived analytically.[2] Although **bootstrapping procedures** can, and will, allow us to test null hypotheses, their most frequent use, and the main reason for their development, falls in the area of parameter estimation, especially of variation. Bootstrapping is distinguished by the fact that it deals with resampling data *with replacement* from some population. (**Permutation tests**, on the other hand, sample *without replacement* and are most often directed at hypothesis testing.) This presentation is not intended as an exhaustive discussion of bootstrapping, but as a demonstration of what bootstrapping is all about. There are important refinements available to reduce bias, but we don't need to discuss those to understand the general nature of bootstrapping.

We will look at two examples of the use of bootstrapping, one involving a median and another involving correlation coefficients. We will then move on to permutation tests, which rely on looking at all permutations of the data (usually an unwieldy task) or on sampling without replacement to simulate what we would have if we could reasonably examine all possible permutations. Whereas bootstrapping involves sampling with replacement, permutation tests involve **sampling without replacement**.

bootstrapping procedures

Permutation tests

sampling without replacement

18.1   Bootstrapping as a General Approach

In previous chapters we have seen bootstrapping techniques used to illustrate the sampling distribution of a statistic when the population distribution is not normal or is unknown. In fact, bootstrapping is most often used to estimate population parameters rather than to test hypotheses. However, as we will see, it also has an important role to play in hypothesis testing. Think for a moment about the situation in which we wish to set confidence limits on the mean of some population. If the population is normally distributed we know that we can use the sample mean and standard deviation as estimators of the population mean and standard deviation. We then calculate the standard error of the mean by dividing the standard deviation by n and then use z or $t_{(.025, df)}$ to calculate the confidence limits. But this works only if your sampling

---

[2] If the population is normally distributed, the standard error of the median is approximately 1.25 times the standard error of the mean. If the distribution is skewed, however, the standard error of the median cannot easily be calculated.

distribution is normally distributed, which is often not the case with extremely nonnormal populations and small sample sizes. But what about the situation in which the population is noticeably nonnormal and the sample size is small? Or suppose that we want a confidence interval on some parameter other than the mean? That is where bootstrapping comes in.

If I asked you to calculate a confidence interval on a mean, and I told you that the population from which the data came was normal, you could solve the problem. In particular, you know that the standard error of the mean is equal to the population standard deviation (perhaps estimated by the sample standard deviation) divided by the square root of *n*. You could then measure off the appropriate number of standard errors from the mean using the normal (or *t*) distribution, and you would have your answer. But suppose that I asked you for the confidence limit on the median instead of the mean. Now you are stuck, because you don't have a nice simple formula to calculate the standard error of the median. What's a body to do? You use the bootstrap.

Macauley (1999, personal communication) collected mental status information on older adults. One of her dependent variables was a memory score on the Neurobehavioral Cognitive Status Examination for the 20 participants who were 80–84 years old. As you might expect, these data were negatively skewed, because some, but certainly not all, of her participants had lost some cognitive functioning. Her actual data are shown in Figure 18.1. Macauley wanted to establish confidence limits on the population median for this age group. Here she was faced with both problems outlined above. It does not seem reasonable to base that confidence interval on the assumption that the population is normally distributed (it most clearly is not), and we want confidence limits on a median, but don't have a convenient formula for the standard error of the median.

What we will do is to assume that the population is distributed *exactly as our sample*. In other words, we will assume that the shape of the parent population is *exactly* as shown in Figure 18.1.

It might seem like a substantial undertaking to create an infinitely large population of numbers such as that seen in Figure 18.1, but, in fact, it is trivially easy, and we have done it several times before. All that we have to do is to take the sample on which it is based, as represented in Figure 18.1, and draw as many observations as we need, *with replacement*, from that sample. Because we are sampling with replacement, it is as if we were sampling

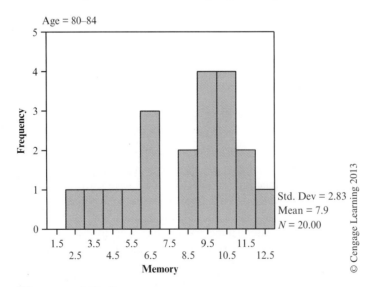

Figure 18.1   Sample distribution of memory scores for participants 80–84 years of age

from an infinitely large population. This is the way that all bootstrapping programs work. In other words, 20 individual observations from an infinite population shaped as in Figure 18.1 is exactly the same as 20 individual observations drawn *with replacement* from the sample distribution. In the future when I speak of a population created to exactly mirror the shape of the sample data, I will refer to this as a pseudo-population.

18.2 Bootstrapping with One Sample

Macauley was interested in defining a 95% confidence interval on the median of memory scores of older participants. As I said above, she had reason to doubt that the population of scores was normally distributed, and there is no general formula defining the standard error of the median. But neither of those considerations interferes with computing the confidence interval she sought. All that she had to do was to assume that the shape of the population was accurately reflected in the distribution of her sample, then draw a large number of new samples (each of $n = 20$) from that population. For each of these samples she computed the median, and when she was through she examined the distribution of these medians. She could then empirically determine those values that encompassed 95% of the sample medians.

It is quite easy to solve Macauley's problem using a simple computer program. One such program written in R can be found on the book's Web site. A "giftware[3]" program that works very well can be found at www.statistics101.net, and I recommend trying that. We will see another downloadable program shortly. The program that I used first reads in the data and calculates the sample median. It then sets up a variable to hold the medians of 10,000 resamples. Next the program draws 20 observations, with replacement, from the raw data file and calculates and stores the median for that sample. It then repeats this process 9,999 more times. When it is done it draws a histogram of the resampled medians and computes a 95% confidence interval by sorting the medians and finding the values that cut off the lowest and highest 2.5% of the outcomes. The results of this process are shown in Figure 18.2. The horizontal line across the figure represents the 95% confidence interval, which is 6 ≤ median ≤ 10. (The minimum and maximum of the sample medians were 5 and 11.)

The distribution in Figure 18.2 is quite discrete because the median is going to be the middle value in a limited set of numbers. You couldn't get a median of 9.63, for example, no matter how many samples you drew. For this particular population the medians must be an integer (or the average of two integers in the ordered array) between 2 and 12. There are no other possibilities.

Ideally, to calculate a 95% confidence interval we would like to find those outcomes that cut off 2.5% of the observations at each end of the distribution.[4] With the very discrete distribution we have with medians, there is no point that cuts off the lowest 2.5% of the distribution. At the extreme, 4/10,000 = .04% lie at or below a median of 5, and (496 + 4)/10,000 = 5.00% lie at or below a median of 6. At the other end of the distribution, 4006/10,000 = 40.6% lie at or below 9, and 9997/10,000 = 99.97% lie at or below 10. To obtain the results above I took the .025 × 10,000 = 250th and .975 × 10,000 = 9750th observation from the sorted series. An examination of the sampling distribution gives us a more complete understanding of the performance of this age cohort. The fact that there are a number of individuals whose scores are well below 10, often taken as a lower limit for "normal behavior," might lead us to seek a different confidence interval, that being limits on the *proportion* of people in that age group who fall below 10. While that would be a perfectly legitimate use of bootstrapping for these data, we will not pursue that question here.

---

[3] Giftware is software that you can download for free. If you like it, send the author something—at least a nice note.
[4] This is the simplest approach to obtaining confidence limits, and relies on the 2.5 and 97.5 percentiles of the sampling distribution of the median. There are a number of more sophisticated estimators, but the one given here best illustrates the approach.

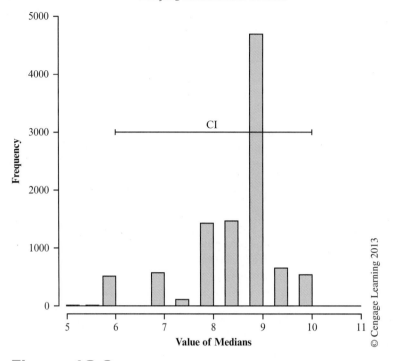

Figure 18.2   Results of bootstrapping the sample median 10,000 times

This may not seem like the most inspiring example of bootstrapping, because it makes bootstrapping look rather imprecise. It is a good example, nonetheless, because it reflects the sometimes awkward nature of real data. As we will see, however, not all data lead to such discrete distributions. In addition, the discreteness of the result is inherent in the data, not in the process itself. If we drew 10,000 samples from this population and calculated t values, the resulting t distribution would be almost as discrete. The problem comes from drawing samples from a distribution with a limited number of different values, instead of modeling the results of drawing from continuous (e.g., normal) distributions. If it is not reasonable to assume normality, it is not reasonable to draw from normal distributions just to get a prettier graph.

18.3   Bootstrapping Confidence Limits on a Correlation Coefficient

The standard approach to correlation problems is to calculate a correlation coefficient and then to apply a hypothesis test with the hope of showing that the correlation is significantly different from 0.00. However, there are a lot of significant correlations that are so low that they are not particularly important, even if they are significantly different from 0.00. Along with the recent emphasis on effect size measures comes an increase in the use of confidence limits.

As we saw in Chapter 9, Fisher's arcsine transformation

$$r' = (0.5) \log_e \left| \frac{1 + r}{1 - r} \right|$$

provides one way to adjust for the skewed sampling distribution of r when $\rho \neq 0$. An attractive alternative is to draw bootstrapped samples on the assumption that the bivariate data reflect the relationship in the population, and then to obtain confidence limits simply by taking the cutoffs for the $\alpha/2$ percent of each end of the distribution.

As an example, we can look at the data from Macauley on the mental status scores of older adults. Macauley's data included 123 adults between the ages of 60 and 97, and we can look at the relationship between memory performance and age. We would probably expect to see a negative correlation between the two variables, but the significance of the correlation is not as useful as confidence limits on this correlation, which give us a better sense of how strong the relationship really is.

The bootstrap approach to obtaining these confidence limits would involve sampling 123 cases, with replacement, from the *XY* pairs in the sample, computing the correlation between the variables, and repeating this process a large number of times. We then find the 2.5 and 97.5 percentile of the sampling distribution, and that gives us our 95% confidence limits.

I have written a Windows program, which is available at http://www.uvm.edu/~dhowell /StatPages/Resampling/ResamplingPackage.zip that will carry out this procedure. (It will also calculate a number of other resampling procedures.) There is also an R program available at the book's Web site. The results of drawing 1000 resamples with replacement from the pseudo-population of pairs of scores are shown in Figure 18.3.

In the center of this figure you can see the sampling distribution of *r*. To the left is the obtained correlation ($-.268$) and upper and lower confidence limits. These are $-.43$ and $-.11$.

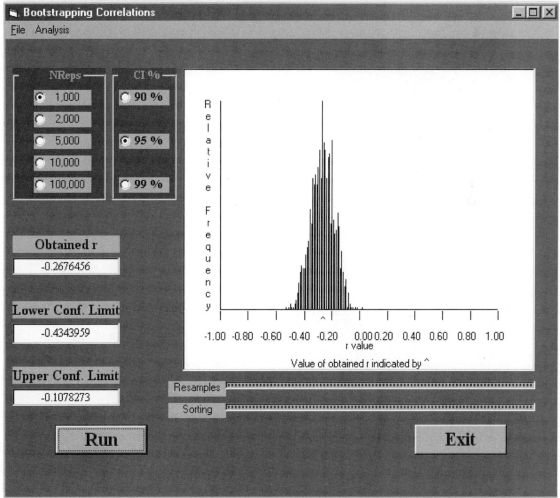

Figure 18.3   Sampling distribution and confidence limits on correlation between age and memory performance in older adults

Because they are both on the same side of 0.00, we also know that our correlation is significant. The confidence interval may strike you as surprisingly wide, but confidence intervals on correlation coefficients often are. A correlation coefficient at the upper end of that interval might be meaningful, but I doubt that one at the lower end would be.

The example from Macauley involved a fairly low correlation coefficient that, because it was only $-.268$, was nearly symmetrically distributed around 0.00. Hoaglin, Mosteller, and Tukey (1983) looked at the role of beta-endorphins in response to stress. They were interested in testing whether beta-endorphin levels rose in stressful situations. They recorded beta-endorphin levels in 19 patients 12 hours before surgery and again, for the same patients, 10 minutes before surgery. If we run the same analysis on the beta-endorphin data we can easily see the skewed nature of the sampling distribution for large correlations. This result is shown in Figure 18.4.

Figure 18.4 presents two interesting results. In the first place, notice that, because the correlation is fairly large ($r = .699$), the sampling distribution is very negatively skewed. In addition, notice how asymmetrical the confidence limits are. The upper limit is .91, which is a bit more than 20 points higher than r. However, the lower limit is .11, which is nearly 60 points lower. Whenever we have large correlations the sampling distribution will be skewed and our confidence limits will be asymmetrical.

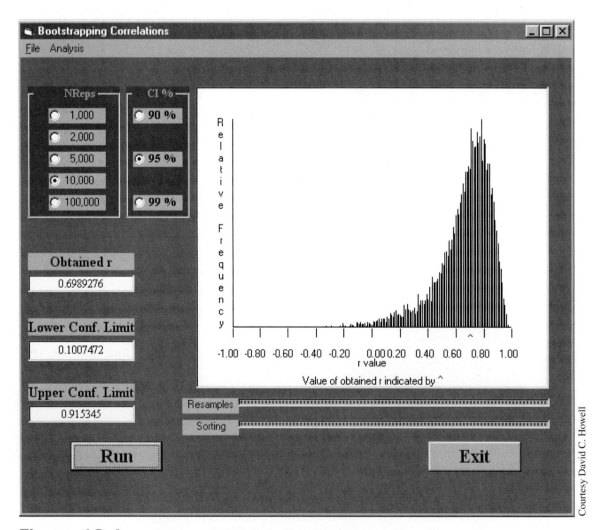

Figure 18.4   Sampling distribution of r for beta-endorphin data for 10,000 resamples

Courtesy David C. Howell

An excellent discussion of bootstrapped estimates of confidence limits can be found in Mooney and Duval (1993). They discuss corrections for bias that are relatively easy to apply. Excellent sources on both bootstrapping and randomization tests can be found in Edgington (1995), Manly (1997), and Efron and Tibshirani (1993). Efron has undoubtedly been the most influential developer of the bootstrap approach, and his book with Tibshirani is an important source. Good (2000) has a presentation of permutation tests, and Lunnenborg (2000) addresses resampling methods at a sophisticated, but very readable, level.

Additional information on bootstrapping and resampling is available from the Web site that I maintain at http://www.uvm.edu/~dhowell/StatPages/Resampling/Resampling .html. These particular pages cover the whole philosophy behind resampling procedures, including bootstrapping, and the ways in which they differ from parametric procedures. This is a rapidly expanding field, and a wealth of new results are being published on a regular basis.

Although I happen to like my own programs best, for obvious personal reasons, the R programming environment, which is free and can be downloaded at www.r-project .org, and its commercial application S-Plus, do an excellent job of handling resampling procedures because of their flexibility and the way they implement repetitive sampling. Example programs written in R for the examples in this chapter are available on the book's Web site.

18.4   Resampling Tests with Two Paired Samples

We will now move from the bootstrap, where we drew large numbers of samples from a pseudo-population using sampling with replacement, to randomization, or permutation test procedures that involve taking the full set of observations and randomly shuffling them and assigning them to conditions randomly. We will return to bootstrapping shortly.

The data from Hoaglin, Mosteller, and Tukey (1983) on the role of beta-endorphins in response to stress follow in Table 18.1 in fmol/ml.[5]

Because these are paired scores, we are primarily interested in the difference scores. We want to test the null hypothesis that the average difference score was 0.0, which would indicate that there was no change in endorphin levels on average. The difference scores are shown in the bottom line of the table, where it is clear that most differences are positive, and those that are negative are relatively small. If you were to plot the differences in this example, you would find that they are very positively skewed, which might discourage us from using a standard parametric t test. Moreover, if we were particularly interested in the median of the differences, a t test would not be appropriate. We will solve our problem by drawing on resampling statistics.

Table 18.1   Endorphine levels 12 hours and 10 minutes before surgery

12 hours	10.0	6.5	8.0	12.0	5.0	11.5	5.0	3.5	7.5	5.8	4.7
10 min.	20.0	14.0	13.5	18.0	14.5	9.0	18.0	6.5	7.4	6.0	25.0
Difference	10.0	7.5	5.5	6.0	9.5	−2.5	13.0	3.0	−0.1	0.2	20.3

12 hours	8.0	7.0	17.0	8.8	17.0	15.0	4.4	2.0
10 min.	12.0	15.0	42.0	16.0	52.0	11.5	2.5	2.1
Difference	4.0	8.0	25.0	7.2	3.50	−3.5	−1.9	0.1

© Cengage Learning 2013

---

[5] I have made two very trivial changes to avoid difference scores of 0.0, just to make the explanation easier. With differences of zero, we normally simply remove those cases from the data.

Our resampling procedure, often called a permutation test, is based on the idea that if the null hypothesis is true and stress does not affect beta-endorphin levels, a patient's 10-minute score was just as likely to be larger than his 12-hour score as it was to be smaller. If a patient has scores of 8.0 and 13.5, and if the null hypothesis is true, the 13.5 could just as likely come from the 12-hour measurement as from the 10-minute measurement. The test is called a "permutation test" because we are permuting the order of the 8.0 and the 13.5. Under H_0 each difference had an equal chance of being positive or negative. This tells us how to model what the data would look like under H_0. We will simply draw a very large number of samples of the 19 difference scores and assign positive and negative signs to the differences at random. For each sample we will calculate the median of the differences, and then plot the sampling distribution of these differences. Remember, this is the sampling distribution of the differences when H_0 is true. We can compare our obtained median difference against this distribution to test H_0.

The results of this process are shown in Figure 18.5.

Figure 18.5 is reassuring because it shows us that when the null is true, the resampled medians are distributed symmetrically about 0, which is what we would expect. From the raw data we can see that the obtained median difference score was 6. From that figure we can also see that our obtained median of 6 is extreme under H_0. Although it is not shown here, a simple calculation showed that only 10 medians were 6.0 or greater and 8 medians less than or equal to -6, for a two-tailed probability of $18/10000 = .0018$. These results, thus, tell us that if we were sampling from a model where H_0 is true, the probability is very small that we would obtain a sample median as extreme as the one we obtained. Therefore we will reject the null hypothesis and conclude that beta-endorphin levels do increase as the time for surgery approaches. This is really a very good thing, because endorphins act as the body's pain pills.

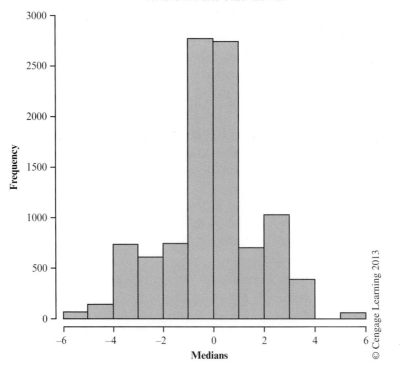

Figure 18.5   Histogram of resampled medians for endorphin study

18.5 Resampling Tests with Two Independent Samples

Now we will move on to the resampling equivalent of the *t* test for two independent samples. The example we will use involves data collected by Epping-Jordan, Compas, and Howell (1994) on the effect of avoidance on women's recovery from breast cancer. Epping-Jordan was interested in examining the question of whether people who try to actively avoid thinking about their cancer, constantly refusing to think about it, have a poorer prognosis over a one-year period than those who do not report high levels of avoidance behavior. She collected data on the incidence of avoidance shortly after patients had been diagnosed with breast cancer. At the end of one year she sorted patients into those who were in remission (49 cases) and those who were no better or who had died (28 cases). These groups were labeled Success and Fail, respectively. The data are shown in Table 18.2. Epping-Jordan then compared the earlier reported level of avoidance for the two groups.

For this example we will compare the medians of the two groups, although we could just as easily compare their means.

If the null hypothesis is true in Epping-Jordan's case, the two samples (Success and Fail) can be thought of as having been drawn from one population. Any particular Avoidance score would be as likely to belong to the Success group as to belong to the Fail group. We could model this null situation by assigning a random sample of 49 of the scores to the Success group and the remaining 18 scores to the Fail group. (Notice here that we are sampling without replacement. All of the scores are assigned to one or the other of the two groups.) The difference between those two groups' medians would be an example of a median difference that we might reasonably obtain under H_0. We can repeat this procedure (randomly assigning 49 scores to the Success group and 18 scores to the Fail group) many times, and look at the median differences we obtain. Finally, we can compare the difference we actually found with those we obtained when we modeled the null hypothesis.

The above procedure is quite easy to do, because we simply shuffle the complete data set. You can think of this as tossing all 67 scores in a hat, blindly pulling out 49 of them and assigning those to the first group, and assigning the remaining 18 scores to the second group. We then compute and record the medians and the median differences, shuffle the data again, and repeat this process 10,000 times. The result of such a procedure is shown in Figure 18.6. The program to do the resampling is available on the book's Web site.

Table 18.2   Data on avoidance from Epping-Jordan et al. (1994)

	Success				Fail		
19	14	17	10	18	17	17	21
23	12	10	14	17	15	8	12
20	21	8	12	16	11	27	18
8	11	13	23	13	22	18	18
11	9	8	20	22	16		
13	15	18	15				
13	8	16	15				
16	14	11	19				
10	12	12	15				
8	12	12	17				
20	18	25	12				
9	23	11	21				
13							

	Success	Fail
Median	13	17
n	49	18

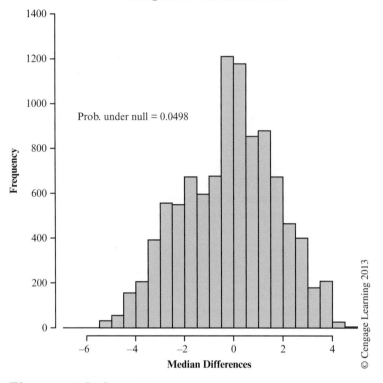

Figure 18.6 Summary results of resampling from Epping-Jordan et al. data

From Table 18.2 we can see that the median Avoidance score for the Success group was 13, and the median for the Fail group was 17. The group who failed to improve exhibited more avoidance behavior early in treatment. The difference in median avoidance is −4. From the plot you can see that a median difference of ±4 is not a very likely occurrence, and the notation in the plot gives its probability under the null of .0498, which would allow us to reject the null hypothesis. We can conclude that those in the Fail group experienced significantly more avoidance behavior early in treatment than those who later were classed as successes.[6]

18.6 Wilcoxon's Rank-Sum Test

Wilcoxon rank-sum test

We will now move away from bootstrapping and randomization to the more traditional non-parametric tests. Although we don't usually think of things this way, the traditional tests are in fact permutation tests, but the things to be permuted are ranks. I will discuss this point at some length shortly. One of the most common and best-known of these tests is the **Wilcoxon rank-sum test** for two independent samples. This test is often thought of as the nonparametric analogue of the *t* test for two independent samples, although it tests a slightly different, and broader, null hypothesis. Its null hypothesis is the hypothesis that the two samples were drawn at random from identical populations (not just populations with the same mean), but it is especially sensitive to population differences in central tendency. Thus, rejection of H_0 is generally interpreted to mean that the two distributions had

---

[6] If we had run a standard *t* test on the means of these data, that probability would have been .0397.

different central tendencies, but it is possible that rejection actually resulted from some other difference between the populations. Notice that when we gain one thing (freedom from assumptions) we pay for it with something else (loss of specificity).

The logical basis of Wilcoxon's rank-sum test is particularly easy to understand. Assume that we have two independent treatment groups, with n_1 observations in group 1 and n_2 observations in group 2. Further assume that the null hypothesis is *false* to a very substantial degree and that the population from which group 1 scores have been sampled contains values generally lower than the population from which group 2 scores were drawn. Then, if we were to rank all $n_1 + n_2 = N$ scores from lowest to highest without regard to group membership, we would expect that the lower ranks would fall primarily to group 1 scores and the higher ranks to group 2 scores. Going one step further, if we were to sum the ranks assigned to each group, the sum of the ranks in group 1 would be expected to be appreciably smaller than the sum of the ranks in group 2.

Now consider the opposite case, in which the null hypothesis is *true* and the scores for the two groups were sampled from identical populations. In this situation if we were to rank all N scores without regard to group membership, we would expect some low ranks and some high ranks in each group, and the sum of the ranks assigned to group 1 would be roughly equal to the sum of the ranks assigned to group 2. These situations are illustrated in Table 18.3.

Wilcoxon based his test on the logic just described, using the sum of the ranks in one of the groups as his test statistic. If that sum is too small relative to the other sum, we will reject the null hypothesis. More specifically, we will take as our test statistic the sum of the ranks assigned to the *smaller* group, or, if $n_1 = n_2$, the *smaller* of the two sums.[7] Given this value, we can use tables of the Wilcoxon statistic (W_S) to test the null hypothesis.

To take a specific example, consider the following hypothetical data on the number of recent stressful life events reported by a group of Cardiac Patients in a local hospital and a control group of Orthopedic Patients in the same hospital. It is well known that stressful life events (marriage, new job, death of spouse, and so on) are associated with illness, and it is reasonable to expect that, on average, many cardiac patients would have experienced more recent stressful events than would orthopedic patients (who just happened to break an ankle while tearing down a building or a leg while playing touch football). It would appear from the data that this expectation is borne out. Because we have some reason to suspect that life stress scores probably are not symmetrically distributed in the population (especially for cardiac patients, if our research hypothesis is true), we will choose to use a nonparametric test. In this case, we will use the Wilcoxon rank-sum test because we have two independent groups.

Table 18.3   Illustration of typical results to be expected under H_0 false and H_0 true

						H_0 False						
Raw Data	10	12	17	13	19	20	30	26	25	33	18	27
Ranks (R_i)	1	2	4	3	6	7	11	9	8	12	5	10
$\Sigma(R_t)$				23						55		

						H_0 True						
Raw Data	22	28	32	19	24	33	18	25	29	20	23	34
Ranks (R_i)	4	8	10	2	6	11	1	7	9	3	5	12
$\Sigma(R_t)$				41						37		

© Cengage Learning 2013

---

[7] Because the sum of the ranks in the smaller group plus the sum of the ranks in the larger group sum to a constant, we only need to use one of those sums.

	Cardiac Patients						Orthopedic Patients				
Raw Data	32	8	7	29	5	0	1	2	2	3	6
Ranks	11	9	8	10	6	1	2	3.5	3.5	5	7

To apply Wilcoxon's test we first rank all 11 scores from lowest to highest, assigning tied ranks to tied scores (see the discussion on ranking in Chapter 10). The orthopedic group is the smaller of the two and, if those patients generally have had fewer recent stressful life events, then the sum of the ranks assigned to that group should be relatively low. Letting W_S stand for the sum of the ranks in the smaller group (the orthopedic group), we find

$$W_S = 2 + 3.5 + 3.5 + 5 + 7 = 21$$

We can evaluate the obtained value of W_S by using Wilcoxon's table (Appendix W_S), which gives the *smallest* value of W_S that we would expect to obtain by chance if the null hypothesis were true. From Appendix W_S we find that for $n_1 = 5$ subjects in the smaller group and $n_2 = 6$ subjects in the larger group (n_1 is *always* the number of subjects in the smaller group if group sizes are unequal), the entry for $\alpha = .025$ (one-tailed) is 18. This means that for a difference between groups to be significant at the one-tailed .025 level, or the two-tailed .05 level, W_S must be less than or equal to 18. Because we found W_S to be equal to 21, we cannot reject H_0. The actual probability under the null is .1198. (By way of comparison, if we ran a *t* test on these data, ignoring the fact that one sample variance is almost 50 times the other and that the data suggest that our prediction of the shape of the distribution of cardiac scores may be correct, *t* would be 1.92 on 9 *df*, a nonsignificant result with $p = .110$. Using a resampling program on the means of the raw data, the probability of an outcome this extreme would be .059. A similar test on medians would yield $p = .059$. A resampling test on the ranks produced $p = .11$.)

The entries in Appendix W_s are for a one-tailed test and will lead to rejection of the null hypothesis only if the sum of the ranks for the smaller group is sufficiently *small*. It is possible, however, that the larger ranks could be congregated in the smaller group, in which case if H_0 is false, the sum of the ranks would be larger than chance expectation rather than smaller. One rather awkward way around this problem would be to rank the data all over again, this time ranking from high to low. If we did this, then the smaller ranks would now appear in the smaller group and we could proceed as before. We do not have to go through the process of reranking data, however. We can accomplish the same thing by using the symmetric properties of the distribution of the rank sum by calculating a statistic called W_S'. The statistic W_S' is the sum of the ranks for the smaller group that we would have found if we had reversed our ranking and ranked from highest to lowest:

$$W_S' = 2\overline{W} - W_S$$

where $2\overline{W} = n_1(n_1 + n_2 + 1)$ and is shown in the table in Appendix W_S. We can then evaluate W_S' against the tabled value and have a one-tailed test on the *upper* tail of the distribution. For a two-tailed test of H_0 (which is what we normally want), we calculate W_S and W_S', enter the table with whichever is smaller, and double the listed value of α.

To illustrate W_S and W_S', consider the two sets of data in Table 18.4. Notice that the two data sets exhibit the same degree of *extremeness*, in the sense that for the first set four of the five lowest ranks are in group 1, and in the second set four of the five highest ranks are in group 1. Moreover, W_S for set 1 is equal to W_S' for set 2, and vice versa. Thus, if we establish the rule that we will calculate both W_S and W_S' for the *smaller* group and refer the *smaller* of W_S and W_S' to the tables, we will come to the same conclusion with respect to the two data sets.

Table 18.4   Sample data for Wilcoxon's rank-sum test

Set 1		Group 1				Group 2			
X	2	15	16	19	18	23	25	37	82
Ranks	1	2	3	5	4	6	7	8	9
$W_S = 11$									
$W_S' = 29$									

Set 2		Group 1				Group 2			
X	60	40	24	21	23	18	15	14	4
Ranks	9	8	7	5	6	4	3	2	1
$W_S = 29$									
$W_S' = 11$									

© Cengage Learning 2013

The Normal Approximation

Appendix W_S is suitable for all cases in which n_1 and n_2 are less than or equal to 25. For larger values of n_1 and/or n_2, we can make use of the fact that the distribution of W_S approaches a normal distribution as sample sizes increase. This distribution has

$$\text{Mean} = \frac{n_1(n_1 + n_2 + 1)}{2}$$

and

$$\text{Standard error} = \sqrt{\frac{n_1 n_2(n_1 + n_2 + 1)}{12}}$$

Because the distribution is normal and we know its mean and standard deviation (the standard error), we can calculate

$$z = \frac{\text{Statistic} - \text{Mean}}{\text{Standard deviation}} = \frac{W_S - \dfrac{n_1(n_1 + n_2 + 1)}{2}}{\sqrt{\dfrac{n_1 n_2(n_1 + n_2 + 1)}{12}}}$$

and obtain from the tables of the normal distribution an approximation of the true probability of a value of W_S at least as low as the one obtained. (It is immaterial whether we use W_S or W_S' in this situation, since they will produce equal values of z, differing only in sign.)

To illustrate the computations for the case in which the larger ranks fall in the smaller groups and to illustrate the use of the normal approximation (although we do not really need to use an approximation for such small sample sizes), consider the data in Table 18.5. These data are hypothetical (but not particularly unreasonable) data on the birthweight (in grams) of children born to mothers who did not seek prenatal care until the third trimester and those born to mothers who received prenatal care starting in the first trimester.

For the data in Table 18.5 the sum of the ranks in the smaller group equals 100. From Appendix W_S we find $2\overline{W} = 152$, and thus $W_S' = 2\overline{W} - W_S = 52$. Because 52 is smaller than 100, we enter Appendix W_S with $W_S' = 52$, $n_1 = 8$, and $n_2 = 10$. (n_1 is defined as the smaller sample size.) Because we want a two-tailed test, we will double the tabled value of α. The critical value of W_S (or W_S') for a two-tailed test at $\alpha = .05$ is 53, meaning that only 5% of the time would we expect a value of W_S or W_S' less than or equal to 53 if H_0 is true. Our obtained value of W_S is 52, which thus falls in the rejection region, and we will reject H_0. We will conclude that mothers who do not receive prenatal care until the third trimester tend to give birth to smaller babies. This probably does not mean that not seeking care until the third

Table 18.5 Hypothetical data on birthweight of infants born to mothers with different levels of prenatal care

Beginning of Care			
Third Trimester		First Trimester	
Birthweight	Rank	Birthweight	Rank
1680	2	2940	10
3830	17	3380	16
3110	14	4900	18
2760	5	2810	9
1700	3	2800	8
2790	7	3210	15
3050	12	3080	13
2660	4	2950	11
1400	1		
2775	6		

$$W_S = \sum(\text{Ranks in Group 2}) = 100$$
$$W_S' = 2\overline{W} - W_S = 152 - 100 = 52$$

$$= \frac{W_S - \dfrac{n_1(n_1 + n_2 + 1)}{2}}{\sqrt{\dfrac{n_1 n_2(n_1 + n_2 + 1)}{12}}}$$

$$= \frac{100 - \dfrac{8(8 + 10 + 1)}{2}}{\sqrt{\dfrac{8(10)(8 + 10 + 1)}{12}}}$$

$$= \frac{100 - 76}{\sqrt{126.6667}} = 2.13$$

© Cengage Learning 2013

trimester *causes* smaller babies, but only that variables associated with delayed care (e.g., young mothers, poor nutrition, or poverty) are also associated with lower birthweight.

The use of the normal approximation for evaluating W_S is illustrated in the bottom part of Table 18.5. Here we find that $z = 2.13$. From Appendix z we find that the probability of W_S as large as 100 or as small as 52 (a z as extreme as ± 2.13) is 2(.0166) = .033. (The exact probability calculated using an R function is .03428, which is quite close to .033.) Because this value is smaller than our traditional cutoff of $\alpha = .05$, we will reject H_0 and again conclude that there is sufficient evidence to say that failing to seek early prenatal care is related to lower birthweight. Note that both the exact solution and the normal approximation lead to the same conclusion with respect to H_0. However, a resampling test on the means using randomization would yield $p = .059$ (two-tailed). (It would be instructive for you to calculate t for the same set of data.)

The Treatment of Ties

When the data contain tied scores, any test that relies on ranks is likely to be somewhat distorted. Ties can be dealt with in several different ways. You can assign tied ranks to tied scores (as we have been doing), you can flip a coin and assign consecutive ranks to tied scores, or you can assign untied ranks in whatever way will make it hardest to reject H_0. In actual practice, most people simply assign tied ranks. Although that may not be the best way to proceed statistically, it is clearly the most common and is the method that we will use here.

The Null Hypothesis

Wilcoxon's rank-sum test evaluates the null hypothesis that the two sets of scores were sampled from identical populations. This is broader than the null hypothesis tested by the corresponding t test, which dealt specifically with means (primarily as a result of the underlying assumptions that ruled out other sources of difference). If the two populations are assumed to have the same shape and dispersion, then the null hypothesis tested by the rank-sum test will actually deal with the central tendency (in this case the medians) of the two populations, and if the populations are also symmetric, the test will be a test of means. In any event, the rank-sum test is particularly sensitive to differences in central tendency.

Wilcoxon's Test and Resampling Procedures

rank-randomiza-
tion tests

An interesting feature of Wilcoxon's test is that it is actually not anything you haven't seen before. Wilcoxon derived his test as a permutation test on ranked data, and such tests are often referred to as **rank-randomization tests**. In other words, if you took the data we had earlier, converted them to ranks, and ran a standard permutation test (which is really a randomization test where we draw every possible permutation once and only once), you would obtain the same result that Wilcoxon's test produces. The reason that Wilcoxon was able to derive his test many years before computers could reasonably do the calculations, and why he could create tables for it, is that the test uses ranks. We know a good many things about ranks, such as their sum and mean, without having to do the calculations. If we have five numbers, we know that their ranks will be the numbers 1 to 5, and the sum of the ranks will be 15, regardless of what the individual raw scores are. This allowed Wilcoxon to derive the resulting sampling distributions once, and only once, and thus create his tables.

The Mann–Whitney U Statistic

Mann–Whitney U
test

A common competitor to the Wilcoxon rank-sum test is the **Mann–Whitney U test**. We do not need to discuss the Mann-Whitney test at any length, however, because the two are equivalent tests, and there is a perfect linear relationship between W_s and U. The only reason for its inclusion here is that you may run across a reference to U, and therefore you should know what it is. Very simply,

$$U = \frac{n_1(n_1 + 2n_2 + 1)}{2} - W_S$$

where n_1 is the smaller of the two sample sizes. From this formula we can see that for any given set of sample sizes, U and W_S differ by only a constant (as do their critical values). Because we have this relationship between the two statistics, we can always convert U to W_S and evaluate W_S using Appendix W_S.

18.7   Wilcoxon's Matched-Pairs Signed-Ranks Test

Wilcoxon is credited with developing not only the most popular nonparametric test for independent groups, but also the most popular test for matched groups (or paired scores). This test is the nonparametric analogue of the t test for related samples, and it tests the null hypothesis that two related (matched) samples were drawn either from identical populations or from symmetric populations with the same mean. More specifically, it tests the null hypothesis that the distribution of difference scores (in the population) is symmetric about zero. This is the same hypothesis tested by the corresponding t test when that test's normality assumption is met.

Wilcoxon matched-pairs signed-ranks test

The development of the logic behind the Wilcoxon matched-pairs signed-ranks test is as straightforward as it was for his rank-sum test and can be illustrated with a simple example. Assume that we want to test the often-stated hypothesis that a long-range program of running will reduce blood pressure. To test this hypothesis, we measure the blood pressure of a number of participants, ask them to engage in a systematic program of running for 6 months, and again test their blood pressure at the end of that period. Our dependent variable will be the change in blood pressure over the 6-month interval. If running does reduce blood pressure, we would expect most of the participants to show a lower reading the second time, and thus a positive pre–post difference. We also would expect that those whose blood pressure actually went up (and thus have a negative pre–post difference) would be only *slightly* higher. On the other hand, if running is ineffective as a method of controlling blood pressure, then about one-half of the difference scores will be positive and one-half will be negative, and the positive differences will be about as large as the negative ones. In other words, if H_0 is really true, we would no longer expect most changes to be in the predicted direction with only small changes in the unpredicted direction. Notice that we have two expectations here: (1) Most of the changes will be in the same direction; (2) those that are in the opposite direction will be small ones. We will relax that second expectation when we shortly come to the Sign test, but with a concomitant loss in power.

As is illustrated in the following numerical example, in carrying out the Wilcoxon matched-pairs signed ranks test we first calculate the difference score for each pair of measurements. We then rank all difference scores *without* regard to the sign of the difference, then assign the algebraic sign of the differences to the ranks themselves, and finally sum the positive and negative ranks separately. The test statistic (T) is taken as the smaller of the absolute values (i.e., ignoring the sign) of the two sums, and is evaluated against the tabled entries in Appendix T. (It is important to note that in calculating T we attach algebraic signs to the ranks only for convenience. We could just as easily, for example, circle those ranks that went with improvement and underline those that went with deterioration. We are merely trying to differentiate between the two cases.)

Assume that the study previously described produced the following data on systolic blood pressure before and after the 6-month training session:

Before:	130	170	125	170	130	130	125	160
After:	120	163	120	135	143	136	124	120
Difference ($B - A$):	10	7	5	35	−13	−6	1	40
Rank of Difference:	5	4	2	7	6	3	1	8
Signed Rank:	5	4	2	7	−6	−3	1	8

$$T_+ = \sum (\text{positive ranks}) = 27$$
$$T_- = \sum (\text{negative ranks}) = -9$$

The first two rows contain the participants' blood pressures as measured before and after a 6-month program of running. The third row contains the difference scores, obtained by subtracting the "after" score from the "before." Notice that only two participants showed a negative change—increased blood pressure. Because these difference scores do not appear to reflect a population distribution that is anywhere near normal, we have chosen to use a nonparametric test. In the fourth row, all the difference scores have been ranked without regard to the direction of the change; in the fifth row, the appropriate sign has been appended to the ranks to discriminate those participants whose blood pressure decreased from those whose blood pressure increased. At the bottom of the table we see the sum of the positive and negative ranks $(T_+ \text{ and } T_-)$. Because T is defined as the smaller absolute value of T_+ and T_-, $T = 9$.

To evaluate T we refer to Appendix T, a portion of which is shown in Table 18.6. This table has a format that is quite different from that of the other tables we have seen. The easiest way to understand what the entries in the table represent is by way of an analogy. Suppose that to test the fairness of a coin you were going to flip it eight times and reject the null hypothesis, at $\alpha = .05$ (one-tailed), if there were too few heads. Out of eight flips of a coin there is no set of outcomes that has a probability of *exactly* .05 under H_0. The probability of one or fewer heads is .0352, and the probability of two or fewer heads is .1445. Thus, if we want to work at $\alpha = .05$, we can either reject for one or fewer heads, in which case the probability of a Type I error is actually .0352 (less than .05), or we can reject for two or fewer heads, in which case the probability of a Type I error is actually .1445 (very much greater than .05). The same kind of problem arises with T because it, like the binomial distribution that gave us the probabilities of heads and tails, is a discrete distribution.[8]

In Appendix T we find that for a one-tailed test at $\alpha = .025$ (or a two-tailed test at $\alpha = .05$) with $n = 8$, the entries are 3 (0.0195) and 4 (0.0273). This tells us that if we want to work at a (one-tailed) $\alpha = .025$, which is the equivalent of a two-tailed test at $\alpha = .05$, we can either reject H_0 for $T \leq 3$ (in which case α actually equals .0195) or we can reject for $T \leq 4$ (in which case the true value of α is .0273). Because we want a two-tailed test, the probabilities should be doubled to 3 (0.0390) and 4 (0.0546). Because we obtained a T value of 9, we would not reject H_0, whichever cutoff we chose. We will conclude therefore that we have no reason to doubt that blood pressure is unaffected by a short (6-month)

Table 18.6   Critical lower-tail values of T and their associated probabilities (abbreviated version of Appendix T)

					Nominal α (One-Tailed)							
	.05			.025			.01			.005		
N	T	α		T	α		T	α		T	α	
5	0	.0313										
	1	.0625										
6	2	.0469		0	.0156							
	3	.0781		1	.0313							
7	3	.0391		2	.0234		0	.0078				
	4	.0547		3	.0391		1	.0156				
8	5	.0391		3	.0195		1	.0078		0	.0039	
	6	.0547		4	.0273		2	.0117		1	.0078	
9	8	.0488		5	.0195		3	.0098		1	.0039	
	9	.0645		6	.0273		4	.0137		2	.0059	
10	10	.0420		8	.0244		5	.0098		3	.0049	
	11	.0527		9	.0322		6	.0137		4	.0068	
11	13	.0415		10	.0210		7	.0093		5	.0049	
	14	.0508		11	.0269		8	.0122		6	.0068	
...	...	...		...	...		...	...		...	...	

© Cengage Learning 2013

[8] A similar situation arises for the Wilcoxon rank-sum test, but the standard tables for that test give only the conservative cutoff.

period of daily running. It is going to take a lot more than 6 months to make up for a lifetime of dissipated habits.

Ties

Ties can occur in the data in two different ways. One way would be for a participant to have the same before and after scores, leading to a difference score of 0, which has no sign. In this case, we normally eliminate that participant from consideration and reduce the sample size accordingly, although this leads to some bias in the data.

In addition, we could have tied difference scores that lead to tied rankings. If both the tied scores are of the same sign, we can break the ties in any way we wish (or assign tied ranks) without affecting the final outcome. If the scores are of opposite signs, we normally assign tied ranks and proceed as usual.

The Normal Approximation

When the sample size is larger than 50, which is the limit for Appendix T, a normal approximation is available to evaluate T. For larger sample sizes, we know that the sampling distribution of T is approximately normally distributed with

$$\text{Mean} = \frac{n(n + 1)}{4} \quad \text{and} \quad \text{Standard error} = \sqrt{\frac{n(n + 1)(2n + 1)}{24}}$$

Thus we can calculate

$$z = \frac{T - \dfrac{n(n + 1)}{4}}{\sqrt{\dfrac{n(n + 1)(2n + 1)}{24}}}$$

and evaluate z using Appendix z. The procedure is directly analogous to that used with the rank-sum test and will not be repeated here.

Another interesting example of the use of Wilcoxon's signed-ranks matched-pairs test is found in a study by Manning, Hall, and Gold (1990). These investigators were interested in studying the role of glucose in memory, in particular its effects on performance of memory tasks for elderly people. There has been considerable suggestion in the literature that participants with poor glucose regulation show poor memory and decreased performance on other kinds of neuropsychological tests.

Manning et al. asked 17 elderly volunteers to perform a battery of tests early in the morning after having drunk an 8-ounce lemon-flavored drink sweetened with either glucose or saccharin. Saccharin would taste as sweet but would not elevate blood glucose levels. Participants performed these tasks under both conditions, so we have matched sets of data. On one of these tasks, for which they had data on only 16 people, participants were read a narrative passage and were asked for recall of that passage 5 minutes later. The dependent variable was not explicitly defined, but we will assume that it was the number of specific propositions recalled from the passage.

The data given in Table 18.7 were generated to produce roughly the same means, standard deviations, and test results as the data found by Manning et al. From Appendix T with $N = 16$ and a two-tailed test at $\alpha = .05$, we find that the critical value of T is 35 or 36, depending on whether you prefer to err on the liberal or conservative side. Our value of $T_{\text{obt}} = 14.5$ is less than either and is therefore significant. This is the same conclusion that Manning et al. came to when they reported improved recall in the Glucose condition.

Table 18.7   Recall scores for elderly participants after drinking a glucose or saccharin solution

Participant	1	2	3	4	5	6	7	8	9	10	11	12	13	14	15	16
Glucose	0	10	9	4	8	6	9	3	12	10	15	9	5	6	10	6
Saccharin	1	9	6	2	5	5	7	2	8	8	11	3	6	8	8	4
Difference	−1	1	3	2	3	1	2	1	4	2	4	6	−1	−2	2	2
Positive ranks		3	12.5	8.5	12.5	3	8.5	3	14.5	8.5	14.5	16			8.5	8.5
Negative ranks	−3												−3	−8.5		

$$T_+ = \Sigma \text{ (positive ranks)} = 121.5$$
$$T_- = \Sigma \text{ (negative ranks)} = 14.5$$

As an example of using the normal approximation, we can solve for the normal variate (z score) associated with a T of 14.5 for $N = 16$. In this case,

$$z = \frac{T - \dfrac{n(n+1)}{4}}{\sqrt{\dfrac{n(n+1)(2n+1)}{24}}} = \frac{14.5 - \dfrac{(16)(17)}{4}}{\sqrt{\dfrac{(16)(17)(33)}{24}}} = -2.77$$

which has a two-tailed probability under H_0 of .0056. A resampling procedure on the means would produce $p = .002$ (two-tailed).

18.8   The Sign Test

The Wilcoxon matched-pairs signed-ranks test is an excellent distribution-free test for differences with matched samples. However, unlike Student's t test, it makes less than maximum use of the data, in that it substitutes ranks for raw score differences, thus losing some of the subtle differences among the data points. When the assumptions of Student's t hold, it also has somewhat less power. When those assumptions do not hold, however, it may have greater power. A test that goes even further in the direction of gaining freedom from assumptions at the cost of power is the **sign test**. This test loses even more information by ignoring the values altogether and looking only at the sign of the differences. As a result, it loses even more power. We discussed the test briefly in Chapter 6, but I will give a second example here for completeness.

sign test

We can use the example from Manning et al. (1990) in the preceding section. It might be argued that this is a good candidate for such a test because the Wilcoxon test was forced to rely on a large number of tied ranks. This argument is not all that persuasive because the results would have been the same no matter how you had broken the tied ranks, but it would be comforting to know that Manning et al.'s results are sufficiently solid that a sign test would also reveal their statistical significance.

The data from Manning et al. are repeated in Table 18.8. From these data you can see that 13 out of 16 participants showed higher recall under the Glucose condition, whereas only 3 of the 16 showed higher recall under the Saccharin condition. The sign test consists

Table 18.8   Data from Manning et al. (1990)

Participant	1	2	3	4	5	6	7	8	9	10	11	12	13	14	15	16
Glucose	0	10	9	4	8	6	9	3	12	10	15	9	5	6	10	6
Saccharin	1	9	6	2	5	5	7	2	8	8	11	3	6	8	8	4
Difference	−1	1	3	2	3	1	2	1	4	2	4	6	−1	−2	2	2
Sign	−	+	+	+	+	+	+	+	+	+	+	+	−	−	+	+

simply of asking the question of whether a 3-to-13 split would be likely to occur if recall under the two conditions were equally good.

This test could be set up in several ways. We could solve for the binomial probability of 13 or more successes out of 16 trials given $p = .50$. From standard tables, or the binomial formula, we would find

$$p(13) = .0085$$
$$p(14) = .0018$$
$$p(15) = .0002$$
$$p(16) = \underline{.0000}$$
$$\text{Sum}\quad .0105$$

Because the binomial distribution is symmetric for $p = .50$, we would then double this probability to obtain the two-tailed probability, which in this case is .021. Because this probability is less than .05, we would reject the null hypothesis and conclude that recall is greater in the Glucose condition.

We could also solve for this probability by using the normal approximation given in Chapter 5. We would again come to essentially the same result, differing only by the accuracy of the approximation.

Yet a third possibility, which is logically equivalent to the others, is to use a goodness of fit χ^2 test. In this case we would take 8 as our expected frequency for each cell, because if the two conditions lead to equal recall we would expect half of our 16 participants to do better by chance under each condition. We would then set up the table

	Glucose	Saccharin
Observed	13	3
Expected	8	8

$$\chi^2 = \sum \frac{(O - E)^2}{E} = \frac{(13 - 8)^2}{8} + \frac{(3 - 8)^2}{8} = 6.25$$

The critical value of χ^2 on 1 df is 3.84, so we can reject H_0 and again conclude that the difference is significant. (The probability of $\chi^2 \geq 6.25$ is .0124, which agrees well enough, given the small sample size, with the exact binomial probability.) All three of these tests are more or less equivalent, and you can use whichever is most convenient.

18.9   Kruskal–Wallis One-Way Analysis of Variance

Kruskal–Wallis one-way analysis of variance

The **Kruskal–Wallis one-way analysis of variance** is a direct generalization of the Wilcoxon rank-sum test to the case in which we have three or more independent groups. As such, it is the nonparametric analogue of the one-way analysis of variance discussed in Chapter 11. It tests the hypothesis that all samples were drawn from identical populations and is particularly sensitive to differences in central tendency.

To perform the Kruskal–Wallis test, we simply rank all scores without regard to group membership and then compute the sum of the ranks for each group. The sums are denoted by R_i. If the null hypothesis is true, we would expect the R_is to be more or less equal (aside from difference due to the size of the samples). A measure of the degree to which the R_i differ from one another is provided by

$$H = \frac{12}{N(N + 1)} \sum_{i=1}^{k} \frac{R_i^2}{n_i} - 3(N + 1)$$

Table 18.9   Kruskal-Wallis test applied to data on problem solving

Depressant		Stimulant		Placebo	
Score	Rank	Score	Rank	Score	Rank
55	9	73	15	61	11
0	1.5	85	18	54	8
1	3	51	7	80	16
0	1.5	63	12	47	5
50	6	85	18		
60	10	85	18		
44	4	66	13		
		69	14		
R_i	35		115		40

$$H = \frac{12}{N(N+1)} \sum_{i=1}^{k} \frac{R_i^2}{n_i} - 3(N+1)$$

$$= \frac{12}{19(20)} \left(\frac{35^2}{7} + \frac{115^2}{8} + \frac{40^2}{4} \right) - 3(19+1)$$

$$= \frac{12}{380}(2228.15) - 60$$

$$= 70.36 - 60$$

$$= 10.36$$

$$\chi_{.05}^2(2) = 5.99$$

where

k = the number of groups
n_i = the number of observations in group$_i$
R_i = the sum of the ranks in group$_i$
$N = \sum n_i$ = total sample size

H is then evaluated against the χ^2 distribution $k - 1$ *df*.

As an example, assume that the data in Table 18.9 represent the number of simple arithmetic problems (out of 85) solved (correctly or incorrectly) in 1 hour by participants given a depressant drug, a stimulant drug, or a placebo. Notice that in the Depressant group three of the participants were too depressed to do much of anything, and in the Stimulant group three of the participants ran up against the limit of 85 available problems. These data are decidedly nonnormal, and we will use the Kruskal–Wallis test. The calculations are shown in the lower part of the table. The obtained value of H is 10.36, which can be treated as χ^2 on $3 - 1 = 2$ *df*. The critical value of $\chi_{.05}^2(2)$ is found in Appendix χ^2 to be 5.99. Because $10.36 > 5.99$, we can reject H_0 and conclude that the three drugs lead to different rates of performance.

18.10   Friedman's Rank Test for *k* Correlated Samples

Friedman's rank test for *k* correlated samples

The last test to be discussed in this chapter is the nonparametric analogue of the one-way repeated-measures analysis of variance, **Friedman's rank test for *k* correlated samples**. It was developed by the well-known economist Milton Friedman—in the days before he was a well-known economist. This test is closely related to a standard repeated-measures analysis of variance applied to ranks instead of raw scores. It is a test on the null hypothesis that the scores for each treatment were drawn from identical populations, and it is especially sensitive to population differences in central tendency.

Assume that we want to test the hypothesis that the judged quality of a lecture is related to the number of visual aids used. The experimenter obtains 17 people who frequently give lectures to local business groups on a variety of topics. Each lecturer delivers the same lecture to three different, but equivalent, audiences—once with no visual aids, once with a few transparencies to illustrate major points, and once with transparencies and flip charts to illustrate every point made. At the end of each lecture, the audience is asked to rate the lecture on a 75-point scale, and the mean rating across all members of the audience is taken as the dependent variable. Because the same lecturers serve under all three conditions, we would expect the data to be correlated. Terrible lecturers are terrible no matter how many visual aids they use. Hypothetical data are presented in Table 18.10, in which a higher score represents a more favorable rating. The ranking of the raw scores *within each participant* are shown in parentheses.

If the null hypothesis is true, we would expect the rankings to be randomly distributed within each lecturer. Thus, one lecturer might do best with no visual aids, another might do best with many aids, and so on. If this were the case, the sum of the rankings in each

Table 18.10   Hypothetical data on rated quality of lectures

	Number of Visual Aids		
Lecturer	None	Few	Many
1	50 (1)	58 (3)	54 (2)
2	32 (2)	37 (3)	25 (1)
3	60 (1)	70 (3)	63 (2)
4	58 (2)	60 (3)	55 (1)
5	41 (1)	66 (3)	59 (2)
6	36 (2)	40 (3)	28 (1)
7	26 (3)	25 (2)	20 (1)
8	49 (1)	60 (3)	50 (2)
9	72 91)	73 92)	75 (3)
10	49 (2)	54 (3)	42 (1)
11	52 (2)	57 (3)	47 (1)
12	36 (2)	42 (3)	29 (1)
13	37 (3)	34 (2)	31 (1)
14	58 (3)	50 (1)	56 (2)
15	39 (1)	48 (3)	44 (2)
16	25 (2)	29 (3)	18 (1)
17	51 (1)	63 (2)	68 (3)
	30	45	27

$$\chi_F^2 = \frac{12}{Nk(k+1)}\sum_{i=1}^{k}R_i^2 - 3N(K+1)$$

$$= \frac{12}{17(3)(4)}(30^2 + 45^2 + 27^2) - 3(17)(4)$$

$$= \frac{12}{204}(3654) - 204$$

$$= 10.94$$

condition (column) would be approximately equal. On the other hand, if a few visual aids were to lead to the most popular lecture, then most lecturers would have their highest rating under that condition, and the sum of the rankings for the three conditions would be decidedly unequal.

To apply Friedman's test, we rank the raw scores for each lecturer separately and then sum the rankings for each condition. We then evaluate the variability of the sums by computing

$$\chi_F^2 = \frac{12}{Nk(k+1)}\sum_{i=1}^{k} R_i^2 - 3N(k+1)$$

where

R_i = the sum of the ranks for the ith condition
N = the number of subjects (lecturers)
k = the number of conditions

This value of χ_F^2 can be evaluated with respect to the standard χ^2 distribution on $k-1$ df. For the data in Table 18.9, $\chi_F^2 = 10.94$ on 2 df. Because $\chi_{.05}^2(2) = 5.99$, we will reject H_0 and conclude that the judged quality of a lecture differs as a function of the degree to which visual aids are included. The data suggest that some visual aids are helpful, but that too many of them can detract from what the lecturer is saying. (*Note:* The null hypothesis we have just tested says nothing about differences among participants [lecturers], and in fact participant differences are completely eliminated by the ranking procedure.)

Key Terms

Parametric tests (Introduction)

Nonparametric tests (Introduction)

Distribution-free tests (Introduction)

Resampling tests (Introduction)

Sampling with replacement (Introduction)

Bootstrapping procedures (Introduction)

Permutation tests (Introduction)

Randomization tests (Introduction)

Sampling without replacement (Introduction)

Wilcoxon rank-sum test (18.6)

Rank-randomization tests (18.6)

Mann–Whitney U test (18.6)

Wilcoxon matched-pairs signed-ranks test (18.7)

Sign test (18.8)

Kruskal–Wallis one-way analysis of variance (18.9)

Friedman's rank test for k correlated samples (18.10)

Exercises

18.1 McConaughy (1980) has argued that younger children organize stories in terms of simple descriptive ("and then...") models, whereas older children incorporate causal statements and social inferences. Suppose that we asked two groups of children differing in age to summarize a story they just read. We then counted the number of statements in the summary that can be classed as inferences. The data follow:

Younger Children:	0	1	0	3	2	5	2
Older Children:	4	7	6	4	8	7	

© Cengage Learning 2013

a. Analyze these data using the two-tailed rank-sum test.

b. What can you conclude?

c. How would you go about analyzing these data if you had access to a program that would do resampling for you?

18.2 Repeat the analysis in Exercise 18.4 using the appropriate one-tailed test.

18.3 Repeat the analysis in Exercise 18.4 using the normal approximation.

18.4 Kapp, Frysinger, Gallagher, and Hazelton (1979) have demonstrated that lesions in the amygdala can reduce certain responses commonly associated with fear (e.g., decreases in heart rate). If fear is really reduced, then it should be more difficult to train an avoidance response in lesioned animals because the aversiveness of the stimulus will be reduced. Assume two groups of rabbits: One group has lesions in the amygdala, and the other is an untreated control group. The following data represent the number of trials to learn an avoidance response for each animal:

Group with Lesions:	15	14	15	8	7	22	36	19	14	18	17
Control Group:	9	4	9	10	6	6	4	5	9		

© Cengage Learning 2013

a. Analyze the data using the Wilcoxon rank-sum test (two-tailed).

b. What can you conclude?

18.5 Nurcombe and Fitzhenry-Coor (1979) have argued that training in diagnostic techniques should lead a clinician to generate (and test) more hypotheses in coming to a decision about a case. Suppose we take 10 psychiatric residents who are just beginning their residency and ask them to watch a videotape of an interview and to record their thoughts on the case every few minutes. We then count the number of hypotheses each resident includes in his or her written remarks. The experiment is repeated at the end of the residency with a comparable videotape. The data follow:

Subject:	1	2	3	4	5	6	7	8	9	10
Before:	8	4	2	2	4	8	3	1	3	9
After:	7	9	3	6	3	10	6	7	8	7

© Cengage Learning 2013

a. Analyze the data using Wilcoxon's matched-pairs signed-ranks test.

b. What can you conclude?

18.6 How would we run a standard resampling test for the data in Exercise 18.10?

18.7 How would you go about applying a resampling procedure to test the difference between Before and After scores in Exercise 18.8?

18.8 Refer to Exercise 18.5.

a. Repeat the analysis using the normal approximation.

b. How well do the two answers (18.5a and 18.8a) agree? Why do they not agree exactly?

18.9 Rerun the analysis in Exercise 18.10 using the normal approximation.

18.10 It has been argued that first-born children tend to be more independent than later-born children. Suppose we develop a 25-point scale of independence and rate each of 20 first-born children and their second-born siblings using our scale. We do this when both siblings are adults, thus eliminating obvious age effects. The data on independence are as follows (a higher score means that the person is more independent):

Sibling Pair:	1	2	3	4	5	6	7	8	9	10
	11	12	13	14	15	16	17	18	19	20
First Born:	12	18	13	17	8	15	16	5	8	12
	13	5	14	20	19	17	2	5	15	18
Second Born:	10	12	15	13	9	12	13	8	10	8
	8	9	8	10	14	11	7	7	13	12

© Cengage Learning 2013

a. Analyze the data using Wilcoxon's matched-pairs signed-ranks test.

b. What can you conclude?

18.11 The results in Exercise 18.10 are not quite as clear-cut as we might like. Plot the differences as a function of the first-born's score. What does this figure suggest?

18.12 One of the arguments put forth in favor of nonparametric tests is that they are more appropriate for ordinal-scale data. This issue was addressed earlier in the book in a different context. Give a reason why this argument is not a good one.

18.13 What is the difference between the null hypothesis tested by Wilcoxon's matched-pairs signed-ranks test and the corresponding t test?

18.14 What is the difference between the null hypothesis tested by Wilcoxon's rank-sum test and the corresponding t test?

18.15 Why is rejection of the null hypothesis using a t test a more specific statement than rejection of the null hypothesis using the appropriate nonparametric test?

18.16 The test referred to in Exercise 18.19 is available on in the Window's program on the book's Web site. Run that program on the data for Exercise 18.20 and report the results. (There is a "read-me" file on the disk that will tell you how to run the resampling program.)

18.17 A psychologist operating a group home for delinquent adolescents needs to show that it is successful at reducing delinquency. He samples nine adolescents living in their parents' home that the police have identified as having problems, nine similar adolescents living in foster homes, and nine adolescents living in the group home. As an indicator variable, he uses truancy (number of days truant in the past semester), which is readily obtained from school records. On the basis of the following data, draw the appropriate conclusions.

Natural Home:	15	18	19	14	5	8	12	13	7
Foster Home:	16	14	20	22	19	5	17	18	12
Group Home:	10	13	14	11	7	3	4	18	2

© Cengage Learning 2013

18.18 Three rival professors teaching English I all claim the honor of having the best students. To settle the issue, eight students are randomly drawn from each class and are given the same exam, which is graded by a neutral professor who does not know from which class the students came. The data follow:

Professor A:	82	71	56	58	63	64	62	53
Professor B:	55	88	85	83	71	70	68	72
Professor C:	65	54	66	68	72	78	65	73

© Cengage Learning 2013

Run the appropriate test and draw the appropriate conclusions.

18.19 I did not discuss randomization tests on the evaluation of data that are laid out like a one-way analysis of variance (as in Exercise 18.17), but you should be able to suggest an analysis that would be appropriate if we had the software to carry out the calculations. How would you outline that test?

18.20 As an alternative method of evaluating a group home, suppose that we take 12 adolescents who have been declared delinquent. We take the number of days truant (1) during the month before they are placed in the home, (2) during the month they live in the home, and (3) during the month after they leave the home. The data follow:

Adolescent:	1	2	3	4	5	6	7	8	9	10	11	12
Before:	10	12	12	19	5	13	20	8	12	10	8	18
During:	5	8	13	10	10	8	16	4	14	3	3	16
After:	8	7	10	12	8	7	12	5	9	5	3	2

© Cengage Learning 2013

Apply Friedman's test. What do you conclude?

18.21 What advantage does the study described in Exercise 18.20 have over the study described in Exercise 18.17?

18.22 The history of statistical hypothesis testing really began with a tea-tasting experiment (Fisher, 1935), so it seems fitting for this book to end with one. The owner of a small tea-room does not think that people really can tell the difference between the first cup made with a given tea bag and the second and third cups made with the same bag (perhaps that is why it is still a small tearoom). He chooses eight different brands of tea bags, makes three cups of tea with each, reusing the same tea bag, and then has a group of customers rate each cup on a 20-point scale (without knowing which cup is which). The data are shown here, with higher ratings indicating better tea.

Tea Brands	First Cup	Second Cup	Third Cup
1	8	3	2
2	15	14	4
3	16	17	12
4	7	5	4
5	9	3	6
6	8	9	4
7	10	3	4
8	12	10	2

© Cengage Learning 2013

Using Friedman's test, draw the appropriate conclusions.

18.23 For the data in Exercise 18.5, we could say that 3 out of 10 residents used fewer hypotheses the second time and 7 used more. We could test this with χ^2. How would this differ from Friedman's test applied to those data?

18.24 It would be possible to apply Friedman's test to the data in Exercise 18.5. What would we lose if we did?

Appendices

Appendix: Data Set

Howell and Huessy (1985) reported on a study of 386 children who had, and had not, exhibited symptoms of attention deficit disorder (ADD)—previously known as hyperkinesis or minimal brain dysfunction—during childhood. In 1965, teachers of all second-grade school children in a number of schools in northwestern Vermont were asked to complete a questionnaire for each of their students dealing with behaviors commonly associated with ADD. Questionnaires on these same children were again completed when the children were in the fourth and fifth grades and, for purposes of this data set only, those three scores were averaged to produce a score labeled ADDSC. The higher the score, the more ADD-like behaviors the child exhibited. At the end of ninth grade and again at the end of twelfth grade, information on the performances of these children was obtained from school records. These data offer the opportunity to examine questions about whether later behavior can be predicted from earlier behavior and to examine academically related variables and their interrelationships. The data are referred to in many of the exercises at the end of each chapter. A description of each variable follows.

ADDSC	Average of the three ADD-like behavior scores obtained in elementary school
GENDER	1 = male; 2 = female
REPEAT	1 = repeated at least one grade; 0 = did not repeat a grade
IQ	IQ obtained from a group-administered IQ test
ENGL	Level of English in ninth grade: 1 = college prep; 2 = general; 3 = remedial
ENGG	Grade in English in ninth grade: 4 = A; 3 = B; and so on
GPA	Grade point average in ninth grade
SOCPROB	Social problems in ninth grade: 1 = yes; 0 = no
DROPOUT	1 = dropped out before completing high school; 0 = did not drop out

Appendix: Computer Data Sets

The Web site (www.uvm.edu/~dhowell/methods8/) contains many data sets. The data sets represent a combination of data from actual studies, data that have been created to mimic the data from actual studies, data from all examples and exercises at the end of each chapter. It also contains two sets of random numbers that have been generated to illustrate certain points.

All of these data sets are standard ASCII files, meaning that they can be read by virtually all computer programs and can be edited if necessary with standard editors available on any computer system (for example, Microsoft Wordpad). In addition, they can be edited by any word processor that can produce an ASCII file (sometimes referred to as a text file or a DOS file). Each file has the variables listed on the first line.

The following, unusually complex, data sets are the focus of a number of homework exercises in many different chapters. The descriptions that follow are intended to explain the study from which the data were drawn and to describe how the data are arranged in the data set. You should refer to these descriptions when working with these data sets. The data sets drawn directly from tables and exercises are much simpler, and their structure can be inferred from the text.

In addition, this Web site contains copies of data from most of the examples and exercises in the book. Those data sets are described in a file on the Web site, and will not be described further here.

Add.dat

The data in this file come from a study by Howell and Huessy (1985). The data are described above.

Variable Name	Columns	Description
ID	1–3	Subject identification number
ADDSC	5–6	ADD score averaged over 3 years
GENDER	8	1 = male; 2 = female
REPEAT	10	1 = repeated a grade, 0 = did not repeat
IQ	12–14	IQ obtained from group-administered IQ test
ENGL	16	Level of English: 1 = college prep; 2 = general; 3 = remedial
ENGG	18	Grade in English: 4 = A, 3 = B, and so on
GPA	20–23	Grade point average in ninth grade
SOCPROB	25	Social problems: 0 = no, 1 = yes
DROPOUT	27	1 = Dropped out of school before finishing 0 = Did not drop out

Data from a study by Compas (1990, personal communication)

The first four lines of data are shown here:

```
1   45   1   0   111   2   3   2.60   0   0
2   50   1   0   102   2   3   2.75   0   0
3   49   1   0   108   2   4   4.00   0   0
4   55   1   0   109   2   2   2.25   0   0
```

Badcancr.dat

For a description of both the study behind these data and the data set, see the following section on Cancer.dat. The data in this file differ from those in Cancer.dat only by the inclusion of deliberate errors.

These data have been deliberately changed for purposes of an assignment. Errors have been added, and at least one variable has been distorted. The correct data are in Cancer.dat, which should be used for all *future* analyses. Virtually any program is likely to fail at first until errors are found and corrected, and even when it runs, impossible values will remain. The quickest way to find many of the errors is to print out the file and scan the columns.

Cancer.dat

The data in this file come from a study by Compas (1990, personal communication) on the effects of stress in cancer patients and their families. Only a small portion of the data that were collected are shown here, primarily data related to behavior problems in children and psychological symptoms in the patient and her or his spouse. The file contains data on 89 families, and many of the data points are missing because of the time in the study at which these data were selected. This example does, however, offer a good opportunity to see preliminary data on important psychological variables.

The codebook (the listing of variables, descriptions, location, and legitimate values) for the data in Cancer.dat is shown following the sample data.

Missing observations are represented with a period. The first four lines of data are shown here as an example.

```
101   2   62   50   52   39   52   1   42   44   41   40   42   .   .   .   .   .   .   .
104   1   56   65   55   40   57   2   53   73   68   67   71   1   11   12   28   58   57   60
105   1   56   57   67   65   61   2   41   67   63   66   65   2   7    7   15   47   48   45
106   2   41   61   64   53   57   1   60   60   59   67   62   1   6   10   15   49   52   48
```

Variable	Description	Columns	Legal Values
FamNum	Family ID number	1–3	100–400
	GSI Variables		
	Patient Variables		
SexP	Gender of patient	5	1 = male; 2 = female
SomTP	Somaticism T score	8–9	41–80
DepTP	Depression T score	12–13	42–80
AnxTP	Anxiety T score	16–17	38–80
HosTP	Hostility T score	20–21	39–80
GSITP	Global Symptom Index T score	24–25	33–80
	Spouse Variables		
SexS	Gender of spouse	27	1 = male; 2 = female
SomTS	Somaticism T score	30–31	41–80
DepTS	Depression T score	34–35	42–80
AnxTS	Anxiety T score	38–39	38–80
HosTS	Hostility T score	42–43	39–80
GSITS	GSI T score	46–47	33–80
	Child Behavior Checklist Variables		
SexChild	Gender of child	49	1 = male; 2 = female
Intern	Internalizing subscale	51–52	0–98
Extern	Externalizing subscale	54–55	0–102
TotBP	Total behavior problems	57–58	0–240
InternT	Internalizing T score	60–61	33–100
ExternT	Externalizing T score	63–64	30–100
TotBPT	Total behavior problem T score	66–67	30–100

Data from a study by Compas (1990, personal communication)

Epineq.dat, Epinuneq.dat

Introini-Collison and McGaugh (1986) examined the hypothesis that hormones normally produced in the body can play a role in memory. Specifically, they looked at the effect of posttraining injections of epinephrine on retention of a previously learned discrimination. They first trained mice to escape mild shock by choosing the left arm of a Y-maze. Immediately after training, the researchers injected the mice with either 0.0, 0.3, or 1.0 mg/kg of epinephrine. They predicted that low doses of epinephrine would facilitate retention, whereas high doses would inhibit it.

Either 1 day, 1 week, or 1 month after original training, each mouse was again placed in the Y-maze. But this time, running to the right arm of the maze led to escape from shock. Presumably, the stronger the memory of the original training, the more it would interfere with the learning of this new task and the more errors the subjects would make.

This experiment has two data sets, named Epineq.dat and Epinuneq.dat. The original study used 18 animals in the three dosage groups tested after 1 day, and 12 animals in each group tested after intervals of 1 week and 1 month. Hypothetical data that closely reproduce the original results are contained in Epinuneq.dat, although five subjects having a 1-month recall interval have been deleted from the 1.0 mg/kg condition. A second data set was created with 12 observations in each of the 9 cells, and is called Epineq.dat. In both cases, the need to create data that were integers led to results that are slightly conservative relative to the actual data. But the conclusions with respect to H_0 are the same.

For both data sets, there is a three-digit ID; dosage is coded (1, 2, or 3) in column 5; the retention interval is coded (1, 2, or 3) in column 7; and the number of errors in learning the second discrimination is coded in column 9. The first four lines of data follow:

001	1	1	0
002	1	1	3
003	1	1	4
004	1	1	2

Mireault.dat

Mireault (1990) collected data from 381 college students, some of whom had lost a parent by death during their childhood. She had three groups of students. Group 1 was composed of subjects who had lost a parent. Group 2 was composed of subjects whose parents were still alive and married to each other. Group 3 consisted of students whose parents were divorced.

Mireault was interested in observing the effects of parental loss on the person's current level of symptomatology (as measured by the Brief Symptom Inventory, Derogatis, 1983) and on the individual's self-perceived vulnerability to future loss. In the interest of space, the data set includes only the total vulnerability measure, and not the subscales. There is also a single measure for social support. For all measures, a higher score represents more of the concept being measured.

The variables, and their location in the file, are listed following the sample data.

Missing data are represented by a period. The first three lines of data are shown below as an example.

```
002 2 1 1 4 2 .  . 42 53 59 57 49 57 47 51 46 51 112 24 66
007 1 2 1 2 . 1 18 65 80 64 71 72 73 63 67 67 72 100 23 73
008 2 2 1 1 4 .  . 52 67 60 62 65 78 60 65 58 65 118 28 64
```

Variable Name	Columns	Description
ID	1–3	Subject identification number
Group	5	1 = loss; 2 = married; 3 = divorced
Gender	7	1 = male; 2 = female
YearColl	9	1 = first year; 2 = sophomore; and so on
College	11	1 = arts and sciences; 2 = health; 3 = engineering; 4 = business; 5 = agriculture
GPA	13	4 = A; 3 = B; 2 = C; 1 = D; 0 = F
LostPGen	15	Gender of lost parent
AgeAtLos	17–18	Age at parent's death
SomT	20–21	Somatization T score
ObsessT	23–24	Obsessive-compulsive T score
SensitT	26–27	Interpersonal sensitivity T score
DepressT	29–30	Depression T score
AnxT	32–33	Anxiety T score

(*continued*)

Variable Name	Columns	Description
HostT	35–36	Hostility T score
PhobT	38–39	Phobic anxiety T score
ParT	41–42	Paranoid ideation T score
PsyT	44–45	Psychoticism T score
GSIT	47–48	Global symptom index T score
PVTotal	50–52	Perceived vulnerability total score
PVLoss	54–56	Perceived vulnerability to loss
SuppTotl	58–60	Social support score

Data from Mireault and Bond (1992)

Stress.dat

The data in this file are a subset of data being collected by Compas and his colleagues on stress and coping in cancer patients. The file contains the family number, the gender of the respondent (1 = Male; 2 = Female), the role of the respondent (1 = Patient; 2 = Spouse), and two stress measures (one obtained shortly after diagnosis and one 3 months later). The variables are in the following order: FamNum, Gender, Role, Time1, Time2. The first six cases follow:

```
101   2   1   2   .
101   1   2   2   .
104   1   1   4   .
104   2   2   5   .
105   1   1   3   4
105   2   2   5   4
```

Appendix χ^2: Upper Percentage Points of the χ^2 Distribution

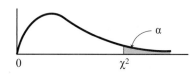

df	0.995	0.990	0.975	0.950	0.900	0.750	0.500	0.250	0.100	0.050	0.025	0.010	0.005
1	0.00	0.00	0.00	0.00	0.02	0.10	0.45	1.32	2.71	3.84	5.02	6.63	7.88
2	0.01	0.02	0.05	0.10	0.21	0.58	1.39	2.77	4.61	5.99	7.38	9.21	10.60
3	0.07	0.11	0.22	0.35	0.58	1.21	2.37	4.11	6.25	7.82	9.35	11.35	12.84
4	0.21	0.30	0.48	0.71	1.06	1.92	3.36	5.39	7.78	9.49	11.14	13.28	14.86
5	0.41	0.55	0.83	1.15	1.61	2.67	4.35	6.63	9.24	11.07	12.83	15.09	16.75
6	0.68	0.87	1.24	1.64	2.20	3.45	5.35	7.84	10.64	12.59	14.45	16.81	18.55
7	0.99	1.24	1.69	2.17	2.83	4.25	6.35	9.04	12.02	14.07	16.01	18.48	20.28
8	1.34	1.65	2.18	2.73	3.49	5.07	7.34	10.22	13.36	15.51	17.54	20.09	21.96
9	1.73	2.09	2.70	3.33	4.17	5.90	8.34	11.39	14.68	16.92	19.02	21.66	23.59
10	2.15	2.56	3.25	3.94	4.87	6.74	9.34	12.55	15.99	18.31	20.48	23.21	25.19
11	2.60	3.05	3.82	4.57	5.58	7.58	10.34	13.70	17.28	19.68	21.92	24.72	26.75
12	3.07	3.57	4.40	5.23	6.30	8.44	11.34	14.85	18.55	21.03	23.34	26.21	28.30
13	3.56	4.11	5.01	5.89	7.04	9.30	12.34	15.98	19.81	22.36	24.74	27.69	29.82
14	4.07	4.66	5.63	6.57	7.79	10.17	13.34	17.12	21.06	23.69	26.12	29.14	31.31
15	4.60	5.23	6.26	7.26	8.55	11.04	14.34	18.25	22.31	25.00	27.49	30.58	32.80
16	5.14	5.81	6.91	7.96	9.31	11.91	15.34	19.37	23.54	26.30	28.85	32.00	34.27
17	5.70	6.41	7.56	8.67	10.09	12.79	16.34	20.49	24.77	27.59	30.19	33.41	35.72
18	6.26	7.01	8.23	9.39	10.86	13.68	17.34	21.60	25.99	28.87	31.53	34.81	37.15
19	6.84	7.63	8.91	10.12	11.65	14.56	18.34	22.72	27.20	30.14	32.85	36.19	38.58
20	7.43	8.26	9.59	10.85	12.44	15.45	19.34	23.83	28.41	31.41	34.17	37.56	40.00
21	8.03	8.90	10.28	11.59	13.24	16.34	20.34	24.93	29.62	32.67	35.48	38.93	41.40
22	8.64	9.54	10.98	12.34	14.04	17.24	21.34	26.04	30.81	33.93	36.78	40.29	42.80
23	9.26	10.19	11.69	13.09	14.85	18.14	22.34	27.14	32.01	35.17	38.08	41.64	44.18
24	9.88	10.86	12.40	13.85	15.66	19.04	23.34	28.24	33.20	36.42	39.37	42.98	45.56
25	10.52	11.52	13.12	14.61	16.47	19.94	24.34	29.34	34.38	37.65	40.65	44.32	46.93
26	11.16	12.20	13.84	15.38	17.29	20.84	25.34	30.43	35.56	38.89	41.92	45.64	48.29
27	11.80	12.88	14.57	16.15	18.11	21.75	26.34	31.53	36.74	40.11	43.20	46.96	49.64
28	12.46	13.56	15.31	16.93	18.94	22.66	27.34	32.62	37.92	41.34	44.46	48.28	50.99
29	13.12	14.26	16.05	17.71	19.77	23.57	28.34	33.71	39.09	42.56	45.72	49.59	52.34
30	13.78	14.95	16.79	18.49	20.60	24.48	29.34	34.80	40.26	43.77	46.98	50.89	53.67
40	20.67	22.14	24.42	26.51	29.06	33.67	39.34	45.61	51.80	55.75	59.34	63.71	66.80
50	27.96	29.68	32.35	34.76	37.69	42.95	49.34	56.33	63.16	67.50	71.42	76.17	79.52
60	35.50	37.46	40.47	43.19	46.46	52.30	59.34	66.98	74.39	79.08	83.30	88.40	91.98
70	43.25	45.42	48.75	51.74	55.33	61.70	69.34	77.57	85.52	90.53	95.03	100.44	104.24
80	51.14	53.52	57.15	60.39	64.28	71.15	79.34	88.13	96.57	101.88	106.63	112.34	116.35
90	59.17	61.74	65.64	69.13	73.29	80.63	89.33	98.65	107.56	113.14	118.14	124.13	128.32
100	67.30	70.05	74.22	77.93	82.36	90.14	99.33	109.14	118.49	124.34	129.56	135.82	140.19

Source: The entries in this table were computed by the author.

Appendix *F*: Critical Values of the *F* Distribution

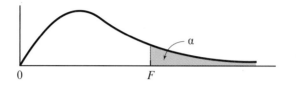

Table 1 $\alpha = 0.05$

Degrees of Freedom for Numerator

	1	2	3	4	5	6	7	8	9	10	15	20	25	30	40	50
1	161.4	199.5	215.8	224.8	230.0	233.8	236.5	238.6	240.1	242.1	245.2	248.4	248.9	250.5	250.8	252.6
2	18.51	19.00	19.16	19.25	19.30	19.33	19.35	19.37	19.38	19.40	19.43	19.44	19.46	19.47	19.48	19.48
3	10.13	9.55	9.28	9.12	9.01	8.94	8.89	8.85	8.81	8.79	8.70	8.66	8.63	8.62	8.59	8.58
4	7.71	6.94	6.59	6.39	6.26	6.16	6.09	6.04	6.00	5.96	5.86	5.80	5.77	5.75	5.72	5.70
5	6.61	5.79	5.41	5.19	5.05	4.95	4.88	4.82	4.77	4.74	4.62	4.56	4.52	4.50	4.46	4.44
6	5.99	5.14	4.76	4.53	4.39	4.28	4.21	4.15	4.10	4.06	3.94	3.87	3.83	3.81	3.77	3.75
7	5.59	4.74	4.35	4.12	3.97	3.87	3.79	3.73	3.68	3.64	3.51	3.44	3.40	3.38	3.34	3.32
8	5.32	4.46	4.07	3.84	3.69	3.58	3.50	3.44	3.39	3.35	3.22	3.15	3.11	3.08	3.04	3.02
9	5.12	4.26	3.86	3.63	3.48	3.37	3.29	3.23	3.18	3.14	3.01	2.94	2.89	2.86	2.83	2.80
10	4.96	4.10	3.71	3.48	3.33	3.22	3.14	3.07	3.02	2.98	2.85	2.77	2.73	2.70	2.66	2.64
11	4.84	3.98	3.59	3.36	3.20	3.09	3.01	2.95	2.90	2.85	2.72	2.65	2.60	2.57	2.53	2.51
12	4.75	3.89	3.49	3.26	3.11	3.00	2.91	2.85	2.80	2.75	2.62	2.54	2.50	2.47	2.43	2.40
13	4.67	3.81	3.41	3.18	3.03	2.92	2.83	2.77	2.71	2.67	2.53	2.46	2.41	2.38	2.34	2.31
14	4.60	3.74	3.34	3.11	2.96	2.85	2.76	2.70	2.65	2.60	2.46	2.39	2.34	2.31	2.27	2.24
15	4.54	3.68	3.29	3.06	2.90	2.79	2.71	2.64	2.59	2.54	2.40	2.33	2.28	2.25	2.20	2.18
16	4.49	3.63	3.24	3.01	2.85	2.74	2.66	2.59	2.54	2.49	2.35	2.28	2.23	2.19	2.15	2.12
17	4.45	3.59	3.20	2.96	2.81	2.70	2.61	2.55	2.49	2.45	2.31	2.23	2.18	2.15	2.10	2.08
18	4.41	3.55	3.16	2.93	2.77	2.66	2.58	2.51	2.46	2.41	2.27	2.19	2.14	2.11	2.06	2.04
19	4.38	3.52	3.13	2.90	2.74	2.63	2.54	2.48	2.42	2.38	2.23	2.16	2.11	2.07	2.03	2.00
20	4.35	3.49	3.10	2.87	2.71	2.60	2.51	2.45	2.39	2.35	2.20	2.12	2.07	2.04	1.99	1.97
22	4.30	3.44	3.05	2.82	2.66	2.55	2.46	2.40	2.34	2.30	2.15	2.07	2.02	1.98	1.94	1.91
24	4.26	3.40	3.01	2.78	2.62	2.51	2.42	2.36	2.30	2.25	2.11	2.03	1.97	1.94	1.89	1.86
26	4.23	3.37	2.98	2.74	2.59	2.47	2.39	2.32	2.27	2.22	2.07	1.99	1.94	1.90	1.85	1.82
28	4.20	3.34	2.95	2.71	2.56	2.45	2.36	2.29	2.24	2.19	2.04	1.96	1.91	1.87	1.82	1.79
30	4.17	3.32	2.92	2.69	2.53	2.42	2.33	2.27	2.21	2.16	2.01	1.93	1.88	1.84	1.79	1.76
40	4.08	3.23	2.84	2.61	2.45	2.34	2.25	2.18	2.12	2.08	1.92	1.84	1.78	1.74	1.69	1.66
50	4.03	3.18	2.79	2.56	2.40	2.29	2.20	2.13	2.07	2.03	1.87	1.78	1.73	1.69	1.63	1.60
60	4.00	3.15	2.76	2.53	2.37	2.25	2.17	2.10	2.04	1.99	1.84	1.75	1.69	1.65	1.59	1.56
120	3.92	3.07	2.68	2.45	2.29	2.18	2.09	2.02	1.96	1.91	1.75	1.66	1.60	1.55	1.50	1.46
200	3.89	3.04	2.65	2.42	2.26	2.14	2.06	1.98	1.93	1.88	1.72	1.62	1.56	1.52	1.46	1.41
500	3.86	3.01	2.62	2.39	2.23	2.12	2.03	1.96	1.90	1.85	1.69	1.59	1.53	1.48	1.42	1.38
1000	3.85	3.01	2.61	2.38	2.22	2.11	2.02	1.95	1.89	1.84	1.68	1.58	1.52	1.47	1.41	1.36

Degrees of Freedom for Denominator

Source: The entries in this table were computed by the author.

Table 2 $\alpha = 0.025$

Degrees of Freedom for Numerator

	1	2	3	4	5	6	7	8	9	10	15	20	25	30	40	50
1	647.8	799.5	864.2	899.6	921.8	937.1	948.2	956.7	963.3	968.6	984.9	993.1	998.1	1001	1006	1008
2	38.51	39.00	39.17	39.25	39.30	39.33	39.36	39.37	39.39	39.40	39.43	39.45	39.46	39.46	39.47	39.48
3	17.44	16.04	15.44	15.10	14.89	14.73	14.62	14.54	14.47	14.42	14.25	14.17	14.12	14.08	14.04	14.01
4	12.22	10.65	9.98	9.60	9.36	9.20	9.07	8.98	8.90	8.84	8.66	8.56	8.50	8.46	8.41	8.38
5	10.01	8.43	7.76	7.39	7.15	6.98	6.85	6.76	6.68	6.62	6.43	6.33	6.27	6.23	6.18	6.14
6	8.81	7.26	6.60	6.23	5.99	5.82	5.70	5.60	5.52	5.46	5.27	5.17	5.11	5.07	5.01	4.98
7	8.07	6.54	5.89	5.52	5.29	5.12	4.99	4.90	4.82	4.76	4.57	4.47	4.40	4.36	4.31	4.28
8	7.57	6.06	5.42	5.05	4.82	4.65	4.53	4.43	4.36	4.30	4.10	4.00	3.94	3.89	3.84	3.81
9	7.21	5.71	5.08	4.72	4.48	4.32	4.20	4.10	4.03	3.96	3.77	3.67	3.60	3.56	3.51	3.47
10	6.94	5.46	4.83	4.47	4.24	4.07	3.95	3.85	3.78	3.72	3.52	3.42	3.35	3.31	3.26	3.22
11	6.72	5.26	4.63	4.28	4.04	3.88	3.76	3.66	3.59	3.53	3.33	3.23	3.16	3.12	3.06	3.03
12	6.55	5.10	4.47	4.12	3.89	3.73	3.61	3.51	3.44	3.37	3.18	3.07	3.01	2.96	2.91	2.87
13	6.41	4.97	4.35	4.00	3.77	3.60	3.48	3.39	3.31	3.25	3.05	2.95	2.88	2.84	2.78	2.74
14	6.30	4.86	4.24	3.89	3.66	3.50	3.38	3.29	3.21	3.15	2.95	2.84	2.78	2.73	2.67	2.64
15	6.20	4.77	4.15	3.80	3.58	3.41	3.29	3.20	3.12	3.06	2.86	2.76	2.69	2.64	2.59	2.55
16	6.12	4.69	4.08	3.73	3.50	3.34	3.22	3.12	3.05	2.99	2.79	2.68	2.61	2.57	2.51	2.47
17	6.04	4.62	4.01	3.66	3.44	3.28	3.16	3.06	2.98	2.92	2.72	2.62	2.55	2.50	2.44	2.41
18	5.98	4.56	3.95	3.61	3.38	3.22	3.10	3.01	2.93	2.87	2.67	2.56	2.49	2.44	2.38	2.35
19	5.92	4.51	3.90	3.56	3.33	3.17	3.05	2.96	2.88	2.82	2.62	2.51	2.44	2.39	2.33	2.30
20	5.87	4.46	3.86	3.51	3.29	3.13	3.01	2.91	2.84	2.77	2.57	2.46	2.40	2.35	2.29	2.25
22	5.79	4.38	3.78	3.44	3.22	3.05	2.93	2.84	2.76	2.70	2.50	2.39	2.32	2.27	2.21	2.17
24	5.72	4.32	3.72	3.38	3.15	2.99	2.87	2.78	2.70	2.64	2.44	2.33	2.26	2.21	2.15	2.11
26	5.66	4.27	3.67	3.33	3.10	2.94	2.82	2.73	2.65	2.59	2.39	2.28	2.21	2.16	2.09	2.05
28	5.61	4.22	3.63	3.29	3.06	2.90	2.78	2.69	2.61	2.55	2.34	2.23	2.16	2.11	2.05	2.01
30	5.57	4.18	3.59	3.25	3.03	2.87	2.75	2.65	2.57	2.51	2.31	2.20	2.12	2.07	2.01	1.97
40	5.42	4.05	3.46	3.13	2.90	2.74	2.62	2.53	2.45	2.39	2.18	2.07	1.99	1.94	1.88	1.83
50	5.34	3.97	3.39	3.05	2.83	2.67	2.55	2.46	2.38	2.32	2.11	1.99	1.92	1.87	1.80	1.75
60	5.29	3.93	3.34	3.01	2.79	2.63	2.51	2.41	2.33	2.27	2.06	1.94	1.87	1.82	1.74	1.70
120	5.15	3.80	3.23	2.89	2.67	2.52	2.39	2.30	2.22	2.16	1.94	1.82	1.75	1.69	1.61	1.56
200	5.10	3.76	3.18	2.85	2.63	2.47	2.35	2.26	2.18	2.11	1.90	1.78	1.70	1.64	1.56	1.51
500	5.05	3.72	3.14	2.81	2.59	2.43	2.31	2.22	2.14	2.07	1.86	1.74	1.65	1.60	1.52	1.46
1000	5.04	3.70	3.13	2.80	2.58	2.42	2.30	2.20	2.13	2.06	1.85	1.72	1.64	1.58	1.50	1.45

Degrees of Freedom for Denominator (row labels)

Source: The entries in this table were computed by the author.

Table 3 $\alpha = 0.01$

Degrees of Freedom for Numerator

	1	2	3	4	5	6	7	8	9	10	15	20	25	30	40	50
1	4048	4993	5377	5577	5668	5924	5992	6096	6132	6168	6079	6168	6214	6355	6168	6213
2	98.50	99.01	99.15	99.23	99.30	99.33	99.35	99.39	99.40	99.43	99.38	99.48	99.43	99.37	99.44	99.59
3	34.12	30.82	29.46	28.71	28.24	27.91	27.67	27.49	27.34	27.23	26.87	26.69	26.58	26.51	26.41	26.36
4	21.20	18.00	16.69	15.98	15.52	15.21	14.98	14.80	14.66	14.55	14.20	14.02	13.91	13.84	13.75	13.69
5	16.26	13.27	12.06	11.39	10.97	10.67	10.46	10.29	10.16	10.05	9.72	9.55	9.45	9.38	9.29	9.24
6	13.75	10.92	9.78	9.15	8.75	8.47	8.26	8.10	7.98	7.87	7.56	7.40	7.30	7.23	7.14	7.09
7	12.25	9.55	8.45	7.85	7.46	7.19	6.99	6.84	6.72	6.62	6.31	6.16	6.06	5.99	5.91	5.86
8	11.26	8.65	7.59	7.01	6.63	6.37	6.18	6.03	5.91	5.81	5.52	5.36	5.26	5.20	5.12	5.07
9	10.56	8.02	6.99	6.42	6.06	5.80	5.61	5.47	5.35	5.26	4.96	4.81	4.71	4.65	4.57	4.52
10	10.04	7.56	6.55	5.99	5.64	5.39	5.20	5.06	4.94	4.85	4.56	4.41	4.31	4.25	4.17	4.12
11	9.65	7.21	6.22	5.67	5.32	5.07	4.89	4.74	4.63	4.54	4.25	4.10	4.01	3.94	3.86	3.81
12	9.33	6.93	5.95	5.41	5.06	4.82	4.64	4.50	4.39	4.30	4.01	3.86	3.76	3.70	3.62	3.57
13	9.07	6.70	5.74	5.21	4.86	4.62	4.44	4.30	4.19	4.10	3.82	3.66	3.57	3.51	3.43	3.38
14	8.86	6.51	5.56	5.04	4.69	4.46	4.28	4.14	4.03	3.94	3.66	3.51	3.41	3.35	3.27	3.22
15	8.68	6.36	5.42	4.89	4.56	4.32	4.14	4.00	3.89	3.80	3.52	3.37	3.28	3.21	3.13	3.08
16	8.53	6.23	5.29	4.77	4.44	4.20	4.03	3.89	3.78	3.69	3.41	3.26	3.16	3.10	3.02	2.97
17	8.40	6.11	5.18	4.67	4.34	4.10	3.93	3.79	3.68	3.59	3.31	3.16	3.07	3.00	2.92	2.87
18	8.29	6.01	5.09	4.58	4.25	4.01	3.84	3.71	3.60	3.51	3.23	3.08	2.98	2.92	2.84	2.78
19	8.18	5.93	5.01	4.50	4.17	3.94	3.77	3.63	3.52	3.43	3.15	3.00	2.91	2.84	2.76	2.71
20	8.10	5.85	4.94	4.43	4.10	3.87	3.70	3.56	3.46	3.37	3.09	2.94	2.84	2.78	2.69	2.64
22	7.95	5.72	4.82	4.31	3.99	3.76	3.59	3.45	3.35	3.26	2.98	2.83	2.73	2.67	2.58	2.53
24	7.82	5.61	4.72	4.22	3.90	3.67	3.50	3.36	3.26	3.17	2.89	2.74	2.64	2.58	2.49	2.44
26	7.72	5.53	4.64	4.14	3.82	3.59	3.42	3.29	3.18	3.09	2.81	2.66	2.57	2.50	2.42	2.36
28	7.64	5.45	4.57	4.07	3.75	3.53	3.36	3.23	3.12	3.03	2.75	2.60	2.51	2.44	2.35	2.30
30	7.56	5.39	4.51	4.02	3.70	3.47	3.30	3.17	3.07	2.98	2.70	2.55	2.45	2.39	2.30	2.25
40	7.31	5.18	4.31	3.83	3.51	3.29	3.12	2.99	2.89	2.80	2.52	2.37	2.27	2.20	2.11	2.06
50	7.17	5.06	4.20	3.72	3.41	3.19	3.02	2.89	2.78	2.70	2.42	2.27	2.17	2.10	2.01	1.95
60	7.08	4.98	4.13	3.65	3.34	3.12	2.95	2.82	2.72	2.63	2.35	2.20	2.10	2.03	1.94	1.88
120	6.85	4.79	3.95	3.48	3.17	2.96	2.79	2.66	2.56	2.47	2.19	2.03	1.93	1.86	1.76	1.70
200	6.76	4.71	3.88	3.41	3.11	2.89	2.73	2.60	2.50	2.41	2.13	1.97	1.87	1.79	1.69	1.63
500	6.69	4.65	3.82	3.36	3.05	2.84	2.68	2.55	2.44	2.36	2.07	1.92	1.81	1.74	1.63	1.57
1000	6.67	4.63	3.80	3.34	3.04	2.82	2.66	2.53	2.43	2.34	2.06	1.90	1.79	1.72	1.61	1.54

Degrees of Freedom for Denominator

Source: The entries in this table were computed by the author.

Appendix *ncF*: Critical Values of the Noncentral *F* Distribution

Power = 1 − (Table Entry)

df_e	α	0.50	1.0	1.2	1.4	1.6	1.8	2.0	2.2	2.6	3.0
						$df_t = 1$					
2	0.05	0.93	0.86	0.83	0.78	0.74	0.69	0.64	0.59	0.49	0.40
	0.01	0.99	0.97	0.96	0.95	0.94	0.93	0.91	0.90	0.87	0.83
4	0.05	0.91	0.80	0.74	0.67	0.59	0.51	0.43	0.35	0.22	0.12
	0.01	0.98	0.95	0.93	0.90	0.87	0.83	0.78	0.73	0.62	0.50
6	0.05	0.91	0.78	0.70	0.62	0.52	0.43	0.34	0.26	0.14	0.06
	0.01	0.98	0.93	0.90	0.86	0.81	0.75	0.69	0.61	0.46	0.31
8	0.05	0.90	0.76	0.68	0.59	0.49	0.39	0.30	0.22	0.11	0.04
	0.01	0.98	0.92	0.89	0.84	0.78	0.70	0.62	0.54	0.37	0.22
10	0.05	0.90	0.75	0.66	0.57	0.47	0.37	0.28	0.20	0.09	0.03
	0.01	0.98	0.92	0.87	0.82	0.75	0.67	0.58	0.49	0.31	0.17
12	0.05	0.90	0.74	0.65	0.56	0.45	0.35	0.26	0.19	0.08	0.03
	0.01	0.97	0.91	0.87	0.81	0.73	0.65	0.55	0.46	0.28	0.14
16	0.05	0.90	0.74	0.64	0.54	0.43	0.33	0.24	0.17	0.07	0.02
	0.01	0.97	0.90	0.85	0.79	0.71	0.61	0.52	0.42	0.24	0.11
20	0.05	0.90	0.73	0.63	0.53	0.42	0.32	0.23	0.16	0.06	0.02
	0.01	0.97	0.90	0.85	0.78	0.69	0.59	0.49	0.39	0.21	0.10
30	0.05	0.89	0.72	0.62	0.52	0.40	0.31	0.22	0.15	0.06	0.02
	0.01	0.97	0.89	0.83	0.76	0.67	0.57	0.46	0.36	0.19	0.08
∞	0.05	0.89	0.71	0.60	0.49	0.38	0.28	0.19	0.12	0.04	0.01
	0.01	0.97	0.88	0.81	0.72	0.62	0.51	0.40	0.30	0.14	0.05
df_e	α					$df_t = 2$					
2	0.05	0.93	0.88	0.85	0.82	0.78	0.75	0.70	0.66	0.56	0.48
	0.01	0.99	0.98	0.97	0.96	0.95	0.94	0.93	0.92	0.89	0.86
4	0.05	0.92	0.82	0.77	0.70	0.62	0.54	0.46	0.38	0.24	0.14
	0.01	0.98	0.96	0.94	0.92	0.89	0.85	0.81	0.76	0.66	0.54
6	0.05	0.91	0.79	0.71	0.63	0.53	0.43	0.34	0.26	0.13	0.05
	0.01	0.98	0.94	0.91	0.87	0.82	0.76	0.70	0.62	0.46	0.31
8	0.05	0.91	0.77	0.68	0.58	0.48	0.37	0.28	0.20	0.08	0.03
	0.01	0.98	0.93	0.89	0.84	0.78	0.70	0.61	0.52	0.34	0.19
10	0.05	0.91	0.75	0.66	0.55	0.44	0.34	0.24	0.16	0.06	0.02
	0.01	0.98	0.92	0.88	0.82	0.74	0.65	0.55	0.45	0.26	0.13
12	0.05	0.90	0.74	0.64	0.53	0.42	0.31	0.22	0.14	0.05	0.01
	0.01	0.98	0.91	0.86	0.80	0.71	0.61	0.51	0.40	0.22	0.09
16	0.05	0.90	0.73	0.62	0.51	0.39	0.28	0.19	0.12	0.04	0.01
	0.01	0.97	0.90	0.84	0.77	0.67	0.57	0.45	0.34	0.16	0.06
20	0.05	0.90	0.72	0.61	0.49	0.36	0.26	0.17	0.11	0.03	0.01
	0.01	0.97	0.90	0.83	0.75	0.65	0.53	0.42	0.31	0.14	0.04
30	0.05	0.90	0.71	0.59	0.47	0.35	0.24	0.15	0.09	0.02	0.00
	0.01	0.97	0.88	0.82	0.72	0.61	0.49	0.37	0.26	0.10	0.03
∞	0.05	0.89	0.68	0.56	0.43	0.30	0.20	0.12	0.06	0.01	0.00
	0.01	0.97	0.86	0.77	0.66	0.53	0.40	0.28	0.18	0.05	0.01

(continued)

Appendix *ncF*   (*continued*)

		ϕ									
		0.50	1.0	1.2	1.4	1.6	1.8	2.0	2.2	2.6	3.0
df_e	α	$df_t = 3$									
2	0.05	0.93	0.89	0.86	0.83	0.80	0.76	0.73	0.69	0.60	0.52
	0.01	0.99	0.98	0.97	0.96	0.96	0.95	0.94	0.93	0.90	0.88
4	0.05	0.92	0.83	0.77	0.71	0.63	0.55	0.47	0.39	0.25	0.14
	0.01	0.98	0.96	0.94	0.92	0.89	0.86	0.82	0.77	0.67	0.55
6	0.05	0.91	0.79	0.71	0.62	0.52	0.42	0.33	0.24	0.11	0.04
	0.01	0.98	0.94	0.91	0.87	0.82	0.76	0.69	0.61	0.44	0.29
8	0.05	0.91	0.76	0.67	0.57	0.46	0.35	0.25	0.17	0.06	0.02
	0.01	0.98	0.93	0.89	0.84	0.77	0.68	0.59	0.49	0.30	0.16
10	0.05	0.91	0.75	0.65	0.53	0.41	0.30	0.21	0.13	0.04	0.01
	0.01	0.98	0.92	0.87	0.80	0.72	0.62	0.52	0.41	0.22	0.09
12	0.05	0.90	0.73	0.62	0.50	0.38	0.27	0.18	0.11	0.03	0.01
	0.01	0.98	0.91	0.85	0.78	0.69	0.58	0.46	0.35	0.17	0.06
16	0.05	0.90	0.71	0.60	0.47	0.34	0.23	0.14	0.08	0.02	0.00
	0.01	0.97	0.90	0.83	0.74	0.64	0.51	0.39	0.28	0.11	0.03
20	0.05	0.90	0.70	0.58	0.45	0.32	0.21	0.13	0.07	0.01	0.00
	0.01	0.97	0.89	0.82	0.72	0.60	0.47	0.35	0.24	0.08	0.02
30	0.05	0.89	0.68	0.55	0.42	0.29	0.18	0.10	0.05	0.01	0.00
	0.01	0.97	0.87	0.79	0.68	0.55	0.42	0.29	0.18	0.05	0.01
∞	0.05	0.88	0.64	0.50	0.36	0.23	0.13	0.07	0.03	0.00	0.00
	0.01	0.97	0.84	0.73	0.59	0.44	0.30	0.18	0.10	0.02	0.00
df_e	α	$df_t = 4$									
2	0.05	0.94	0.89	0.87	0.84	0.81	0.77	0.74	0.70	0.62	0.54
	0.01	0.99	0.98	0.97	0.97	0.96	0.95	0.94	0.93	0.91	0.88
4	0.05	0.92	0.83	0.78	0.71	0.64	0.55	0.47	0.39	0.25	0.14
	0.01	0.98	0.96	0.94	0.92	0.89	0.86	0.82	0.78	0.67	0.56
6	0.05	0.92	0.79	0.71	0.62	0.52	0.41	0.31	0.23	0.10	0.04
	0.01	0.98	0.94	0.91	0.87	0.82	0.76	0.68	0.60	0.43	0.28
8	0.05	0.91	0.76	0.66	0.55	0.44	0.33	0.23	0.15	0.05	0.01
	0.01	0.98	0.93	0.89	0.83	0.76	0.67	0.57	0.47	0.28	0.14
10	0.05	0.91	0.74	0.63	0.51	0.39	0.27	0.18	0.11	0.03	0.01
	0.01	0.98	0.92	0.86	0.79	0.70	0.60	0.49	0.37	0.19	0.07
12	0.05	0.90	0.72	0.61	0.48	0.35	0.24	0.15	0.08	0.02	0.00
	0.01	0.98	0.91	0.85	0.76	0.66	0.55	0.42	0.31	0.13	0.04
16	0.05	0.90	0.70	0.57	0.44	0.31	0.19	0.11	0.06	0.01	0.00
	0.01	0.97	0.89	0.82	0.72	0.60	0.47	0.34	0.23	0.08	0.02
20	0.05	0.89	0.68	0.55	0.41	0.28	0.17	0.09	0.04	0.01	0.00
	0.01	0.97	0.88	0.80	0.69	0.56	0.42	0.29	0.18	0.05	0.01
30	0.05	0.89	0.66	0.52	0.37	0.24	0.14	0.07	0.03	0.00	0.00
	0.01	0.97	0.86	0.77	0.64	0.50	0.35	0.22	0.13	0.03	0.00
∞	0.05	0.88	0.60	0.45	0.29	0.17	0.08	0.04	0.01	0.00	0.00
	0.01	0.96	0.81	0.68	0.53	0.36	0.22	0.11	0.05	0.01	0.00

Source: Abridged from M. L. Tiku (1967), Tables of the power of the *F* test, *Journal of the American Statistical Association, 62,* 525–539, with the permission of the author and the editors.

Appendix Polynomial: Orthogonal Polynomial Coefficients

k	Polynomial	X = 1	2	3	4	5	6	7	8	9	10	Σa_i^2
3	Linear	−1	0	1								2
	Quadratic	1	−2	1								6
4	Linear	−3	−1	1	3							20
	Quadratic	1	−1	−1	1							4
	Cubic	−1	3	−3	1							20
5	Linear	−2	−1	0	1	2						10
	Quadratic	2	−1	−2	−1	2						14
	Cubic	−1	2	0	−2	1						10
	Quartic	1	−4	6	−4	1						70
6	Linear	−5	−3	−1	1	3	5					70
	Quadratic	5	−1	−4	−4	−1	5					84
	Cubic	−5	7	4	−4	−7	5					180
	Quartic	1	−3	2	2	−3	1					28
7	Linear	−3	−2	−1	0	−1	2	3				28
	Quadratic	5	0	−3	−4	−3	0	5				84
	Cubic	−1	1	1	0	1	−1	1				6
	Quartic	3	−7	1	6	1	−7	3				154
8	Linear	−7	−5	−3	−1	1	3	5	7			168
	Quadratic	7	1	−3	−5	−5	−3	1	7			168
	Cubic	−7	5	7	3	−3	−7	−5	7			264
	Quartic	7	−13	−3	9	9	−3	−13	7			616
	Quintic	−7	23	−17	−15	15	17	−23	7			2184
9	Linear	−4	−3	−2	−1	0	1	2	3	4		60
	Quadratic	28	7	−8	−17	−20	−17	−8	7	28		2772
	Cubic	−14	7	13	9	0	−9	−13	−7	14		990
	Quartic	14	−21	−11	9	18	9	−11	−21	14		2002
	Quintic	−4	11	−4	−9	0	9	4	−11	4		468
10	Linear	−9	−7	−5	−3	−1	1	3	5	7	9	330
	Quadratic	6	2	−1	−3	−4	−4	−3	−1	2	6	132
	Cubic	−42	14	35	31	12	−12	−31	−35	−14	42	8580
	Quartic	18	−22	−17	3	18	18	3	−17	−22	18	2860
	Quintic	−6	14	−1	−11	−6	6	11	1	−14	6	780

Source: The entries in this table were computed by the author.

Appendix Power: Power as a Function of δ and Significance Level (α)

	α for Two-Tailed Test			
δ	0.10	0.05	0.02	0.01
1.00	0.26	0.17	0.09	0.06
1.10	0.29	0.20	0.11	0.07
1.20	0.33	0.22	0.13	0.08
1.30	0.37	0.26	0.15	0.10
1.40	0.40	0.29	0.18	0.12
1.50	0.44	0.32	0.20	0.14
1.60	0.48	0.36	0.23	0.17
1.70	0.52	0.40	0.27	0.19
1.80	0.56	0.44	0.30	0.22
1.90	0.60	0.48	0.34	0.25
2.00	0.64	0.52	0.37	0.28
2.10	0.68	0.56	0.41	0.32
2.20	0.71	0.60	0.45	0.35
2.30	0.74	0.63	0.49	0.39
2.40	0.78	0.67	0.53	0.43
2.50	0.80	0.71	0.57	0.47
2.60	0.83	0.74	0.61	0.51
2.70	0.85	0.77	0.65	0.55
2.80	0.88	0.80	0.68	0.59
2.90	0.90	0.83	0.72	0.63
3.00	0.91	0.85	0.75	0.66
3.10	0.93	0.87	0.78	0.70
3.20	0.94	0.89	0.81	0.73
3.30	0.95	0.91	0.84	0.77
3.40	0.96	0.93	0.86	0.80
3.50	0.97	0.94	0.88	0.82
3.60	0.98	0.95	0.90	0.85
3.70	0.98	0.96	0.92	0.87
3.80	0.98	0.97	0.93	0.89
3.90	0.99	0.97	0.94	0.91
4.00	0.99	0.98	0.95	0.92
4.10	0.99	0.98	0.96	0.94
4.20	—	0.99	0.97	0.95
4.30	—	0.99	0.98	0.96
4.40	—	0.99	0.98	0.97
4.50	—	0.99	0.99	0.97
4.60	—	—	0.99	0.98
4.70	—	—	0.99	0.98
4.80	—	—	0.99	0.99
4.90	—	—	—	0.99
5.00	—	—	—	0.99

Source: The entries in this table were computed by the author.

Appendix q: Critical Values of the Studentized Range Statistic (q)

Table 1 $\alpha = 0.05$

r = Number of Steps Between Ordered Means

Error df	2	3	4	5	6	7	8	9	10	11	12	13	14	15
1	17.97	26.98	32.82	37.08	40.41	43.12	45.40	47.36	49.07	50.59	51.96	53.20	54.33	55.36
2	6.08	8.33	9.80	10.88	11.74	12.44	13.03	13.54	13.99	14.39	14.75	15.08	15.38	15.65
3	4.50	5.91	6.82	7.50	8.04	8.48	8.85	9.18	9.46	9.72	9.95	10.15	10.35	10.53
4	3.93	5.04	5.76	6.29	6.71	7.05	7.35	7.60	7.83	8.03	8.21	8.37	8.52	8.66
5	3.64	4.60	5.22	5.67	6.03	6.33	6.58	6.80	7.00	7.17	7.32	7.47	7.60	7.72
6	3.46	4.34	4.90	5.31	5.63	5.90	6.12	6.32	6.49	6.65	6.79	6.92	7.03	7.14
7	3.34	4.16	4.68	5.06	5.36	5.61	5.82	6.00	6.16	6.30	6.43	6.55	6.66	6.76
8	3.26	4.04	4.53	4.89	5.17	5.40	5.60	5.77	5.92	6.05	6.18	6.29	6.39	6.48
9	3.20	3.95	4.42	4.76	5.02	5.24	5.43	5.60	5.74	5.87	5.98	6.09	6.19	6.28
10	3.15	3.88	4.33	4.65	4.91	5.12	5.30	5.46	5.60	5.72	5.83	5.94	6.03	6.11
11	3.11	3.82	4.26	4.57	4.82	5.03	5.20	5.35	5.49	5.60	5.71	5.81	5.90	5.98
12	3.08	3.77	4.20	4.51	4.75	4.95	5.12	5.26	5.40	5.51	5.62	5.71	5.79	5.88
13	3.06	3.74	4.15	4.45	4.69	4.88	5.05	5.19	5.32	5.43	5.53	5.63	5.71	5.79
14	3.03	3.70	4.11	4.41	4.64	4.83	4.99	5.13	5.25	5.36	5.46	5.55	5.64	5.71
15	3.01	3.67	4.08	4.37	4.60	4.78	4.94	5.08	5.20	5.31	5.40	5.49	5.57	5.65
16	3.00	3.65	4.05	4.33	4.56	4.74	4.90	5.03	5.15	5.26	5.35	5.44	5.52	5.59
17	2.98	3.63	4.02	4.30	4.52	4.70	4.86	4.99	5.11	5.21	5.31	5.39	5.47	5.54
18	2.97	3.61	4.00	4.28	4.50	4.67	4.82	4.96	5.07	5.17	5.27	5.35	5.43	5.50
19	2.96	3.59	3.98	4.25	4.47	4.64	4.79	4.92	5.04	5.14	5.23	5.32	5.39	5.46
20	2.95	3.58	3.96	4.23	4.45	4.62	4.77	4.90	5.01	5.11	5.20	5.28	5.36	5.43
24	2.92	3.53	3.90	4.17	4.37	4.54	4.68	4.81	4.92	5.01	5.10	5.18	5.25	5.32
30	2.89	3.49	3.84	4.10	4.30	4.46	4.60	4.72	4.82	4.92	5.00	5.08	5.15	5.21
40	2.86	3.44	3.79	4.04	4.23	4.39	4.52	4.64	4.74	4.82	4.90	4.98	5.04	5.11
60	2.83	3.40	3.74	3.98	4.16	4.31	4.44	4.55	4.65	4.73	4.81	4.88	4.94	5.00
120	2.80	3.36	3.69	3.92	4.10	4.24	4.36	4.47	4.56	4.64	4.71	4.78	4.84	4.90
∞	2.77	3.31	3.63	3.86	4.03	4.17	4.29	4.39	4.47	4.55	4.62	4.68	4.74	4.80

Source: Abridged from H. L. Harter (1960), Tables of range and Studentized range, *Annals of Mathematical Statistics, 31*, 1122–1147, with permission of the author and the publisher.

Table 2 $\alpha = 0.01$

r = Number of Steps Between Ordered Means

Error df	2	3	4	5	6	7	8	9	10	11	12	13	14	15
1	90.03	135.0	164.3	185.6	202.2	215.8	227.2	237.0	245.6	253.2	260.0	266.2	271.8	277.0
2	14.04	19.02	22.29	24.72	26.63	28.20	29.53	30.68	31.69	32.59	33.40	34.13	34.81	35.43
3	8.26	10.62	12.17	13.33	14.24	15.00	15.64	16.20	16.69	17.13	17.53	17.89	18.22	18.52
4	6.51	8.12	9.17	9.96	10.58	11.10	11.55	11.93	12.27	12.57	12.84	13.09	13.32	13.53
5	5.70	6.98	7.80	8.42	8.91	9.32	9.67	9.97	10.24	10.48	10.70	10.89	11.08	11.24
6	5.24	6.33	7.03	7.56	7.97	8.32	8.62	8.87	9.10	9.30	9.48	9.65	9.81	9.95
7	4.95	5.92	6.54	7.00	7.37	7.68	7.94	8.17	8.37	8.55	8.71	8.86	9.00	9.12
8	4.75	5.64	6.20	6.62	6.96	7.24	7.47	7.68	7.86	8.03	8.18	8.31	8.44	8.55
9	4.60	5.43	5.96	6.35	6.66	6.92	7.13	7.32	7.50	7.65	7.78	7.91	8.02	8.13
10	4.48	5.27	5.77	6.14	6.43	6.67	6.88	7.06	7.21	7.36	7.48	7.60	7.71	7.81
11	4.39	5.15	5.62	5.97	6.25	6.48	6.67	6.84	6.99	7.13	7.25	7.36	7.46	7.56
12	4.32	5.05	5.50	5.84	6.10	6.32	6.51	6.67	6.81	6.94	7.06	7.17	7.26	7.36
13	4.26	4.96	5.40	5.73	5.98	6.19	6.37	6.53	6.67	6.79	6.90	7.01	7.10	7.19
14	4.21	4.90	5.32	5.63	5.88	6.08	6.26	6.41	6.54	6.66	6.77	6.87	6.96	7.05
15	4.17	4.84	5.25	5.56	5.80	5.99	6.16	6.31	6.44	6.56	6.66	6.76	6.84	6.93
16	4.13	4.79	5.19	5.49	5.72	5.92	6.08	6.22	6.35	6.46	6.56	6.66	6.74	6.82
17	4.10	4.74	5.14	5.43	5.66	5.85	6.01	6.15	6.27	6.38	6.48	6.57	6.66	6.73
18	4.07	4.70	5.09	5.38	5.60	5.79	5.94	6.08	6.20	6.31	6.41	6.50	6.58	6.66
19	4.05	4.67	5.05	5.33	5.55	5.74	5.89	6.02	6.14	6.25	6.34	6.43	6.51	6.58
20	4.02	4.64	5.02	5.29	5.51	5.69	5.84	5.97	6.09	6.19	6.28	6.37	6.45	6.52
24	3.96	4.55	4.91	5.17	5.37	5.54	5.69	5.81	5.92	6.02	6.11	6.19	6.26	6.33
30	3.89	4.46	4.80	5.05	5.24	5.40	5.54	5.65	5.76	5.85	5.93	6.01	6.08	6.14
40	3.82	4.37	4.70	4.93	5.11	5.26	5.39	5.50	5.60	5.69	5.76	5.84	5.90	5.96
60	3.76	4.28	4.60	4.82	4.99	5.13	5.25	5.36	5.45	5.53	5.60	5.67	5.73	5.78
120	3.70	4.20	4.50	4.71	4.87	5.01	5.12	5.21	5.30	5.38	5.44	5.51	5.56	5.61
∞	3.64	4.12	4.40	4.60	4.76	4.88	4.99	5.08	5.16	5.23	5.29	5.35	5.40	5.45

Source: Abridged from H. L. Harter (1960), Tables of range and Studentized range, *Annals of Mathematical Statistics, 31,* 1122–1147, with permission of the author and the publisher.

Appendix *r'*: Table of Fisher's Transformation of *r* to *r'*

r	*r'*	*r*	*r'*	*r*	*r'*	*r*	*r'*	*r*	*r'*
0.000	0.000	0.200	0.203	0.400	0.424	0.600	0.693	0.800	1.099
0.005	0.005	0.205	0.208	0.405	0.430	0.605	0.701	0.805	1.113
0.010	0.010	0.210	0.213	0.410	0.436	0.610	0.709	0.810	1.127
0.015	0.015	0.215	0.218	0.415	0.442	0.615	0.717	0.815	1.142
0.020	0.020	0.220	0.224	0.420	0.448	0.620	0.725	0.820	1.157
0.025	0.025	0.225	0.229	0.425	0.454	0.625	0.733	0.825	1.172
0.030	0.030	0.230	0.234	0.430	0.460	0.630	0.741	0.830	1.188
0.035	0.035	0.235	0.239	0.435	0.466	0.635	0.750	0.835	1.204
0.040	0.040	0.240	0.245	0.440	0.472	0.640	0.758	0.840	1.221
0.045	0.045	0.245	0.250	0.445	0.478	0.645	0.767	0.845	1.238
0.050	0.050	0.250	0.255	0.450	0.485	0.650	0.775	0.850	1.256
0.055	0.055	0.255	0.261	0.455	0.491	0.655	0.784	0.855	1.274
0.060	0.060	0.260	0.266	0.460	0.497	0.660	0.793	0.860	1.293
0.065	0.065	0.265	0.271	0.465	0.504	0.665	0.802	0.865	1.313
0.070	0.070	0.270	0.277	0.470	0.510	0.670	0.811	0.870	1.333
0.075	0.075	0.275	0.282	0.475	0.517	0.675	0.820	0.875	1.354
0.080	0.080	0.280	0.288	0.480	0.523	0.680	0.829	0.880	1.376
0.085	0.085	0.285	0.293	0.485	0.530	0.685	0.838	0.885	1.398
0.090	0.090	0.290	0.299	0.490	0.536	0.690	0.848	0.890	1.422
0.095	0.095	0.295	0.304	0.495	0.543	0.695	0.858	0.895	1.447
0.100	0.100	0.300	0.310	0.500	0.549	0.700	0.867	0.900	1.472
0.105	0.105	0.305	0.315	0.505	0.556	0.705	0.877	0.905	1.499
0.110	0.110	0.310	0.321	0.510	0.563	0.710	0.887	0.910	1.528
0.115	0.116	0.315	0.326	0.515	0.570	0.715	0.897	0.915	1.557
0.120	0.121	0.320	0.332	0.520	0.576	0.720	0.908	0.920	1.589
0.125	0.126	0.325	0.337	0.525	0.583	0.725	0.918	0.925	1.623
0.130	0.131	0.330	0.343	0.530	0.590	0.730	0.929	0.930	1.658
0.135	0.136	0.335	0.348	0.535	0.597	0.735	0.940	0.935	1.697
0.140	0.141	0.340	0.354	0.540	0.604	0.740	0.950	0.940	1.738
0.145	0.146	0.345	0.360	0.545	0.611	0.745	0.962	0.945	1.783
0.150	0.151	0.350	0.365	0.550	0.618	0.750	0.973	0.950	1.832
0.155	0.156	0.355	0.371	0.555	0.626	0.755	0.984	0.955	1.886
0.160	0.161	0.360	0.377	0.560	0.633	0.760	0.996	0.960	1.946
0.165	0.167	0.365	0.383	0.565	0.640	0.765	1.008	0.965	2.014
0.170	0.172	0.370	0.388	0.570	0.648	0.770	1.020	0.970	2.092
0.175	0.177	0.375	0.394	0.575	0.655	0.775	1.033	0.975	2.185
0.180	0.182	0.380	0.400	0.580	0.662	0.780	1.045	0.980	2.298
0.185	0.187	0.385	0.406	0.585	0.670	0.785	1.058	0.985	2.443
0.190	0.192	0.390	0.412	0.590	0.678	0.790	1.071	0.990	2.647
0.195	0.198	0.395	0.418	0.595	0.685	0.795	1.085	0.995	2.994

Source: The entries in this table were computed by the author.

Appendix *t*: Percentage Points of the *t* Distribution

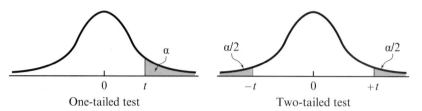

	One-tailed test				Two-tailed test			

Level of Significance for One-Tailed Test

	0.25	0.20	0.15	0.10	0.05	0.025	0.01	0.005	0.0005

Level of Significance for Two-Tailed Test

df	0.50	0.40	0.30	0.20	0.10	0.05	0.02	0.01	0.001
1	1.000	1.376	1.963	3.078	6.314	12.706	31.821	63.657	636.620
2	0.816	1.061	1.386	1.886	2.920	4.303	6.965	9.925	31.599
3	0.765	0.978	1.250	1.638	2.353	3.182	4.541	5.841	12.924
4	0.741	0.941	1.190	1.533	2.132	2.776	3.747	4.604	8.610
5	0.727	0.920	1.156	1.476	2.015	2.571	3.365	4.032	6.869
6	0.718	0.906	1.134	1.440	1.943	2.447	3.143	3.707	5.959
7	0.711	0.896	1.119	1.415	1.895	2.365	2.998	3.499	5.408
8	0.706	0.889	1.108	1.397	1.860	2.306	2.896	3.355	5.041
9	0.703	0.883	1.100	1.383	1.833	2.262	2.821	3.250	4.781
10	0.700	0.879	1.093	1.372	1.812	2.228	2.764	3.169	4.587
11	0.697	0.876	1.088	1.363	1.796	2.201	2.718	3.106	4.437
12	0.695	0.873	1.083	1.356	1.782	2.179	2.681	3.055	4.318
13	0.694	0.870	1.079	1.350	1.771	2.160	2.650	3.012	4.221
14	0.692	0.868	1.076	1.345	1.761	2.145	2.624	2.977	4.140
15	0.691	0.866	1.074	1.341	1.753	2.131	2.602	2.947	4.073
16	0.690	0.865	1.071	1.337	1.746	2.120	2.583	2.921	4.015
17	0.689	0.863	1.069	1.333	1.740	2.110	2.567	2.898	3.965
18	0.688	0.862	1.067	1.330	1.734	2.101	2.552	2.878	3.922
19	0.688	0.861	1.066	1.328	1.729	2.093	2.539	2.861	3.883
20	0.687	0.860	1.064	1.325	1.725	2.086	2.528	2.845	3.850
21	0.686	0.859	1.063	1.323	1.721	2.080	2.518	2.831	3.819
22	0.686	0.858	1.061	1.321	1.717	2.074	2.508	2.819	3.792
23	0.685	0.858	1.060	1.319	1.714	2.069	2.500	2.807	3.768
24	0.685	0.857	1.059	1.318	1.711	2.064	2.492	2.797	3.745
25	0.684	0.856	1.058	1.316	1.708	2.060	2.485	2.787	3.725
26	0.684	0.856	1.058	1.315	1.706	2.056	2.479	2.779	3.707
27	0.684	0.855	1.057	1.314	1.703	2.052	2.473	2.771	3.690
28	0.683	0.855	1.056	1.313	1.701	2.048	2.467	2.763	3.674
29	0.683	0.854	1.055	1.311	1.699	2.045	2.462	2.756	3.659
30	0.683	0.854	1.055	1.310	1.697	2.042	2.457	2.750	3.646
40	0.681	0.851	1.050	1.303	1.684	2.021	2.423	2.704	3.551
50	0.679	0.849	1.047	1.299	1.676	2.009	2.403	2.678	3.496
100	0.677	0.845	1.042	1.290	1.660	1.984	2.364	2.626	3.390
∞	0.674	0.842	1.036	1.282	1.645	1.960	2.326	2.576	3.291

Source: The entries in this table were computed by the author.

Appendix *T*: Critical Lower-Tail Values of *T* (and Their Associated Probabilities) for Wilcoxon's Matched-Pairs Signed-Ranks Test

Nominal α (One-Tailed)

	0.05		0.025		0.01		0.005	
N	*T*	α	*T*	α	*T*	α	*T*	α
5	0	0.0313						
	1	0.0625						
6	2	0.0469	0	0.0156				
	3	0.0781	1	0.0313				
7	3	0.0391	2	0.0234	0	0.0078		
	4	0.0547	3	0.0391	1	0.0156		
8	5	0.0391	3	0.0195	1	0.0078	0	0.0039
	6	0.0547	4	0.0273	2	0.0117	1	0.0078
9	8	0.0488	5	0.0195	3	0.0098	1	0.0039
	9	0.0645	6	0.0273	4	0.0137	2	0.0059
10	10	0.0420	8	0.0244	5	0.0098	3	0.0049
	11	0.0527	9	0.0322	6	0.0137	4	0.0068
11	13	0.0415	10	0.0210	7	0.0093	5	0.0049
	14	0.0508	11	0.0269	8	0.0122	6	0.0068
12	17	0.0461	13	0.0212	9	0.0081	7	0.0046
	18	0.0549	14	0.0261	10	0.0105	8	0.0061
13	21	0.0471	17	0.0239	12	0.0085	9	0.0040
	22	0.0549	18	0.0287	13	0.0107	10	0.0052
14	25	0.0453	21	0.0247	15	0.0083	12	0.0043
	26	0.0520	22	0.0290	16	0.0101	13	0.0054
15	30	0.0473	25	0.0240	19	0.0090	15	0.0042
	31	0.0535	26	0.0277	20	0.0108	16	0.0051
16	35	0.0467	29	0.0222	23	0.0091	19	0.0046
	36	0.0523	30	0.0253	24	0.0107	20	0.0055
17	41	0.0492	34	0.0224	27	0.0087	23	0.0047
	42	0.0544	35	0.0253	28	0.0101	24	0.0055
18	47	0.0494	40	0.0241	32	0.0091	27	0.0045
	48	0.0542	41	0.0269	33	0.0104	28	0.0052
19	53	0.0478	46	0.0247	37	0.0090	32	0.0047
	54	0.0521	47	0.0273	38	0.0102	33	0.0054
20	60	0.0487	52	0.0242	43	0.0096	37	0.0047
	61	0.0527	53	0.0266	44	0.0107	38	0.0053
21	67	0.0479	58	0.0230	49	0.0097	42	0.0045
	68	0.0516	59	0.0251	50	0.0108	43	0.0051

(continued)

Appendix *T*   *(continued)*

Nominal α (One-Tailed)

N	0.05		0.025		0.01		0.005	
	T	α	T	α	T	α	T	α
22	75	0.0492	65	0.0231	55	0.0095	48	0.0046
	76	0.0527	66	0.0250	56	0.0104	49	0.0052
23	83	0.0490	73	0.0242	62	0.0098	54	0.0046
	84	0.0523	74	0.0261	63	0.0107	55	0.0051
24	91	0.0475	81	0.0245	69	0.0097	61	0.0048
	92	0.0505	82	0.0263	70	0.0106	62	0.0053
25	100	0.0479	89	0.0241	76	0.0094	68	0.0048
	101	0.0507	90	0.0258	77	0.0101	69	0.0053
26	110	0.0497	98	0.0247	84	0.0095	75	0.0047
	111	0.0524	99	0.0263	85	0.0102	76	0.0051
27	119	0.0477	107	0.0246	92	0.0093	83	0.0048
	120	0.0502	108	0.0260	93	0.0100	84	0.0052
28	130	0.0496	116	0.0239	101	0.0096	91	0.0048
	131	0.0521	117	0.0252	102	0.0102	92	0.0051
29	140	0.0482	126	0.0240	110	0.0095	100	0.0049
	141	0.0504	127	0.0253	111	0.0101	101	0.0053
30	151	0.0481	137	0.0249	120	0.0098	109	0.0050
	152	0.0502	138	0.0261	121	0.0104	110	0.0053
31	163	0.0491	147	0.0239	130	0.0099	118	0.0049
	164	0.0512	148	0.0251	131	0.0105	119	0.0052
32	175	0.0492	159	0.0249	140	0.0097	128	0.0050
	176	0.0512	160	0.0260	141	0.0103	129	0.0053
33	187	0.0485	170	0.0242	151	0.0099	138	0.0049
	188	0.0503	171	0.0253	152	0.0104	139	0.0052
34	200	0.0488	182	0.0242	162	0.0098	148	0.0048
	201	0.0506	183	0.0252	163	0.0103	149	0.0051
35	213	0.0484	195	0.0247	173	0.0096	159	0.0048
	214	0.0501	196	0.0257	174	0.0100	160	0.0051
36	227	0.0489	208	0.0248	185	0.0096	171	0.0050
	228	0.0505	209	0.0258	186	0.0100	172	0.0052
37	241	0.0487	221	0.0245	198	0.0099	182	0.0048
	242	0.0503	222	0.0254	199	0.0103	183	0.0050

Source: The entries in this table were computed by the author.

Appendix *T* *(continued)*

Nominal α (One-Tailed)

N	0.05		0.025		0.01		0.005	
	T	α	T	α	T	α	T	α
38	256	0.0493	235	0.0247	211	0.0099	194	0.0048
	257	0.0509	236	0.0256	212	0.0104	195	0.0050
39	271	0.0492	249	0.0246	224	0.0099	207	0.0049
	272	0.0507	250	0.0254	225	0.0103	208	0.0051
40	286	0.0486	264	0.0249	238	0.0100	220	0.0049
	287	0.0500	265	0.0257	239	0.0104	221	0.0051
41	302	0.0488	279	0.0248	252	0.0100	233	0.0048
	303	0.0501	280	0.0256	253	0.0103	234	0.0050
42	319	0.0496	294	0.0245	266	0.0098	247	0.0049
	320	0.0509	295	0.0252	267	0.0102	248	0.0051
43	336	0.0498	310	0.0245	281	0.0098	261	0.0048
	337	0.0511	311	0.0252	282	0.0102	262	0.0050
44	353	0.0495	327	0.0250	296	0.0097	276	0.0049
	354	0.0507	328	0.0257	297	0.0101	277	0.0051
45	371	0.0498	343	0.0244	312	0.0098	291	0.0049
	372	0.0510	344	0.0251	313	0.0101	292	0.0051
46	389	0.0497	361	0.0249	328	0.0098	307	0.0050
	390	0.0508	362	0.0256	329	0.0101	308	0.0052
47	407	0.0490	378	0.0245	345	0.0099	322	0.0048
	408	0.0501	379	0.0251	346	0.0102	323	0.0050
48	426	0.0490	396	0.0244	362	0.0099	339	0.0050
	427	0.0500	397	0.0251	363	0.0102	340	0.0051
49	446	0.0495	415	0.0247	379	0.0098	355	0.0049
	447	0.0505	416	0.0253	380	0.0100	356	0.0050
50	466	0.0495	434	0.0247	397	0.0098	373	0.0050
	467	0.0506	435	0.0253	398	0.0101	374	0.0051

Source: The entries in this table were computed by the author.

Appendix t': Critical Values of Bonferroni Multiple Comparison Test

Table 1 $\alpha = 0.05$

Number of Comparisons

df	2	3	4	5	6	7	8	9	10	15	20	25	30	35	40	45	50	55
5	3.16	3.53	3.81	4.03	4.22	4.38	4.53	4.66	4.77	5.25	5.60	5.89	6.14	6.35	6.54	6.71	6.87	7.01
6	2.97	3.29	3.52	3.71	3.86	4.00	4.12	4.22	4.32	4.70	4.98	5.21	5.40	5.56	5.71	5.84	5.96	6.07
7	2.84	3.13	3.34	3.50	3.64	3.75	3.86	3.95	4.03	4.36	4.59	4.79	4.94	5.08	5.20	5.31	5.41	5.50
8	2.75	3.02	3.21	3.36	3.48	3.58	3.68	3.76	3.83	4.12	4.33	4.50	4.64	4.76	4.86	4.96	5.04	5.12
9	2.69	2.93	3.11	3.25	3.36	3.46	3.55	3.62	3.69	3.95	4.15	4.30	4.42	4.53	4.62	4.71	4.78	4.85
10	2.63	2.87	3.04	3.17	3.28	3.37	3.45	3.52	3.58	3.83	4.00	4.14	4.26	4.36	4.44	4.52	4.59	4.65
11	2.59	2.82	2.98	3.11	3.21	3.29	3.37	3.44	3.50	3.73	3.89	4.02	4.13	4.22	4.30	4.37	4.44	4.49
12	2.56	2.78	2.93	3.05	3.15	3.24	3.31	3.37	3.43	3.65	3.81	3.93	4.03	4.12	4.19	4.26	4.32	4.37
13	2.53	2.75	2.90	3.01	3.11	3.19	3.26	3.32	3.37	3.58	3.73	3.85	3.95	4.03	4.10	4.16	4.22	4.27
14	2.51	2.72	2.86	2.98	3.07	3.15	3.21	3.27	3.33	3.53	3.67	3.79	3.88	3.96	4.03	4.09	4.14	4.19
15	2.49	2.69	2.84	2.95	3.04	3.11	3.18	3.23	3.29	3.48	3.62	3.73	3.82	3.90	3.96	4.02	4.07	4.12
16	2.47	2.67	2.81	2.92	3.01	3.08	3.15	3.20	3.25	3.44	3.58	3.69	3.77	3.85	3.91	3.96	4.01	4.06
17	2.46	2.65	2.79	2.90	2.98	3.06	3.12	3.17	3.22	3.41	3.54	3.65	3.73	3.80	3.86	3.92	3.97	4.01
18	2.45	2.64	2.77	2.88	2.96	3.03	3.09	3.15	3.20	3.38	3.51	3.61	3.69	3.76	3.82	3.87	3.92	3.96
19	2.43	2.63	2.76	2.86	2.94	3.01	3.07	3.13	3.17	3.35	3.48	3.58	3.66	3.73	3.79	3.84	3.88	3.93
20	2.42	2.61	2.74	2.85	2.93	3.00	3.06	3.11	3.15	3.33	3.46	3.55	3.63	3.70	3.75	3.80	3.85	3.89
21	2.41	2.60	2.73	2.83	2.91	2.98	3.04	3.09	3.14	3.31	3.43	3.53	3.60	3.67	3.73	3.78	3.82	3.86
22	2.41	2.59	2.72	2.82	2.90	2.97	3.02	3.07	3.12	3.29	3.41	3.50	3.58	3.64	3.70	3.75	3.79	3.83
23	2.40	2.58	2.71	2.81	2.89	2.95	3.01	3.06	3.10	3.27	3.39	3.48	3.56	3.62	3.68	3.72	3.77	3.81
24	2.39	2.57	2.70	2.80	2.88	2.94	3.00	3.05	3.09	3.26	3.38	3.47	3.54	3.60	3.66	3.70	3.75	3.78
25	2.38	2.57	2.69	2.79	2.86	2.93	2.99	3.03	3.08	3.24	3.36	3.45	3.52	3.58	3.64	3.68	3.73	3.76
30	2.36	2.54	2.66	2.75	2.82	2.89	2.94	2.99	3.03	3.19	3.30	3.39	3.45	3.51	3.56	3.61	3.65	3.68
40	2.33	2.50	2.62	2.70	2.78	2.84	2.89	2.93	2.97	3.12	3.23	3.31	3.37	3.43	3.47	3.51	3.55	3.58
50	2.31	2.48	2.59	2.68	2.75	2.81	2.85	2.90	2.94	3.08	3.18	3.26	3.32	3.38	3.42	3.46	3.50	3.53
75	2.29	2.45	2.56	2.64	2.71	2.77	2.81	2.86	2.89	3.03	3.13	3.20	3.26	3.31	3.35	3.39	3.43	3.45
100	2.28	2.43	2.54	2.63	2.69	2.75	2.79	2.83	2.87	3.01	3.10	3.17	3.23	3.28	3.32	3.36	3.39	3.42
∞	2.24	2.39	2.50	2.58	2.64	2.69	2.73	2.77	2.81	2.94	3.02	3.09	3.14	3.19	3.23	3.26	3.29	3.32

Source: The entries in this table were computed by the author.

Table 2 $\alpha = 0.01$

Number of Comparisons

df	2	3	4	5	6	7	8	9	10	15	20	25	30	35	40	45	50	55
5	4.77	5.25	5.60	5.89	6.14	6.35	6.54	6.71	6.87	7.50	7.98	8.36	8.69	8.98	9.24	9.47		
6	4.32	4.70	4.98	5.21	5.40	5.56	5.71	5.84	5.96	6.43	6.79	7.07	7.31	7.52	7.71	7.87	8.02	8.16
7	4.03	4.36	4.59	4.79	4.94	5.08	5.20	5.31	5.41	5.80	6.08	6.31	6.50	6.67	6.81	6.94	7.06	7.17
8	3.83	4.12	4.33	4.50	4.64	4.76	4.86	4.96	5.04	5.37	5.62	5.81	5.97	6.11	6.23	6.34	6.44	6.53
9	3.69	3.95	4.15	4.30	4.42	4.53	4.62	4.71	4.78	5.08	5.29	5.46	5.60	5.72	5.83	5.92	6.01	6.09
10	3.58	3.83	4.00	4.14	4.26	4.36	4.44	4.52	4.59	4.85	5.05	5.20	5.33	5.44	5.53	5.62	5.69	5.76
11	3.50	3.73	3.89	4.02	4.13	4.22	4.30	4.37	4.44	4.68	4.86	5.00	5.12	5.22	5.31	5.38	5.45	5.52
12	3.43	3.65	3.81	3.93	4.03	4.12	4.19	4.26	4.32	4.55	4.72	4.85	4.96	5.05	5.13	5.20	5.26	5.32
13	3.37	3.58	3.73	3.85	3.95	4.03	4.10	4.16	4.22	4.44	4.60	4.72	4.82	4.91	4.98	5.05	5.11	5.17
14	3.33	3.53	3.67	3.79	3.88	3.96	4.03	4.09	4.14	4.35	4.50	4.62	4.71	4.79	4.87	4.93	4.99	5.04
15	3.29	3.48	3.62	3.73	3.82	3.90	3.96	4.02	4.07	4.27	4.42	4.53	4.62	4.70	4.77	4.83	4.88	4.93
16	3.25	3.44	3.58	3.69	3.77	3.85	3.91	3.96	4.01	4.21	4.35	4.45	4.54	4.62	4.68	4.74	4.79	4.84
17	3.22	3.41	3.54	3.65	3.73	3.80	3.86	3.92	3.97	4.15	4.29	4.39	4.47	4.55	4.61	4.66	4.71	4.76
18	3.20	3.38	3.51	3.61	3.69	3.76	3.82	3.87	3.92	4.10	4.23	4.33	4.42	4.49	4.55	4.60	4.65	4.69
19	3.17	3.35	3.48	3.58	3.66	3.73	3.79	3.84	3.88	4.06	4.19	4.28	4.36	4.43	4.49	4.54	4.59	4.63
20	3.15	3.33	3.46	3.55	3.63	3.70	3.75	3.80	3.85	4.02	4.15	4.24	4.32	4.39	4.44	4.49	4.54	4.58
21	3.14	3.31	3.43	3.53	3.60	3.67	3.73	3.78	3.82	3.99	4.11	4.20	4.28	4.34	4.40	4.45	4.49	4.53
22	3.12	3.29	3.41	3.50	3.58	3.64	3.70	3.75	3.79	3.96	4.08	4.17	4.24	4.31	4.36	4.41	4.45	4.49
23	3.10	3.27	3.39	3.48	3.56	3.62	3.68	3.72	3.77	3.93	4.05	4.14	4.21	4.27	4.33	4.37	4.42	4.45
24	3.09	3.26	3.38	3.47	3.54	3.60	3.66	3.70	3.75	3.91	4.02	4.11	4.18	4.24	4.29	4.34	4.38	4.42
25	3.08	3.24	3.36	3.45	3.52	3.58	3.64	3.68	3.73	3.88	4.00	4.08	4.15	4.21	4.27	4.31	4.35	4.39
30	3.03	3.19	3.30	3.39	3.45	3.51	3.56	3.61	3.65	3.80	3.90	3.98	4.05	4.11	4.15	4.20	4.23	4.27
40	2.97	3.12	3.23	3.31	3.37	3.43	3.47	3.51	3.55	3.69	3.79	3.86	3.92	3.98	4.02	4.06	4.09	4.13
50	2.94	3.08	3.18	3.26	3.32	3.38	3.42	3.46	3.50	3.63	3.72	3.79	3.85	3.90	3.94	3.98	4.01	4.04
75	2.89	3.03	3.13	3.20	3.26	3.31	3.35	3.39	3.43	3.55	3.64	3.71	3.76	3.81	3.85	3.88	3.91	3.94
100	2.87	3.01	3.10	3.17	3.23	3.28	3.32	3.36	3.39	3.51	3.60	3.66	3.72	3.76	3.80	3.83	3.86	3.89
∞	2.81	2.94	3.02	3.09	3.14	3.19	3.23	3.26	3.29	3.40	3.48	3.54	3.59	3.63	3.66	3.69	3.72	3.74

Source: The entries in this table were computed by the author.

Appendix t_d: Critical Values of Dunnett's t Statistic (t_d)

Error df	α	**Two-Tailed Comparisons** k = Number of Treatment Means, Including Control								
		2	3	4	5	6	7	8	9	10
5	0.05	2.57	3.03	3.29	3.48	3.62	3.73	3.82	3.90	3.97
	0.01	4.03	4.63	4.98	5.22	5.41	5.56	5.69	5.80	5.89
6	0.05	2.45	2.86	3.10	3.26	3.39	3.49	3.57	3.64	3.71
	0.01	3.71	4.21	4.51	4.71	4.87	5.00	5.10	5.20	5.28
7	0.05	2.36	2.75	2.97	3.12	3.24	3.33	3.41	3.47	3.53
	0.01	3.50	3.95	4.21	4.39	4.53	4.64	4.74	4.82	4.89
8	0.05	2.31	2.67	2.88	3.02	3.13	3.22	3.29	3.35	3.41
	0.01	3.36	3.77	4.00	4.17	4.29	4.40	4.48	4.56	4.62
9	0.05	2.26	2.61	2.81	2.95	3.05	3.14	3.20	3.26	3.32
	0.01	3.25	3.63	3.85	4.01	4.12	4.22	4.30	4.37	4.43
10	0.05	2.23	2.57	2.76	2.89	2.99	3.07	3.14	3.19	3.24
	0.01	3.17	3.53	3.74	3.88	3.99	4.08	4.16	4.22	4.28
11	0.05	2.20	2.53	2.72	2.84	2.94	3.02	3.08	3.14	3.19
	0.01	3.11	3.45	3.65	3.79	3.89	3.98	4.05	4.11	4.16
12	0.05	2.18	2.50	2.68	2.81	2.90	2.98	3.04	3.09	3.14
	0.01	3.05	3.39	3.58	3.71	3.81	3.89	3.96	4.02	4.07
13	0.05	2.16	2.48	2.65	2.78	2.87	2.94	3.00	3.06	3.10
	0.01	3.01	3.33	3.52	3.65	3.74	3.82	3.89	3.94	3.99
14	0.05	2.14	2.46	2.63	2.75	2.84	2.91	2.97	3.02	3.07
	0.01	2.98	3.29	3.47	3.59	3.69	3.76	3.83	3.88	3.93
15	0.05	2.13	2.44	2.61	2.73	2.82	2.89	2.95	3.00	3.04
	0.01	2.95	3.25	3.43	3.55	3.64	3.71	3.78	3.83	3.88
16	0.05	2.12	2.42	2.59	2.71	2.80	2.87	2.92	2.97	3.02
	0.01	2.92	3.22	3.39	3.51	3.60	3.67	3.73	3.78	3.83
17	0.05	2.11	2.41	2.58	2.69	2.78	2.85	2.90	2.95	3.00
	0.01	2.90	3.19	3.36	3.47	3.56	3.63	3.69	3.74	3.79
18	0.05	2.10	2.40	2.56	2.68	2.76	2.83	2.89	2.94	2.98
	0.01	2.88	3.17	3.33	3.44	3.53	3.60	3.66	3.71	3.75
19	0.05	2.09	2.39	2.55	2.66	2.75	2.81	2.87	2.92	2.96
	0.01	2.86	3.15	3.31	3.42	3.50	3.57	3.63	3.68	3.72
20	0.05	2.09	2.38	2.54	2.65	2.73	2.80	2.86	2.90	2.95
	0.01	2.85	3.13	3.29	3.40	3.48	3.55	3.60	3.65	3.69
24	0.05	2.06	2.35	2.51	2.61	2.70	2.76	2.81	2.86	2.90
	0.01	2.80	3.07	3.22	3.32	3.40	3.47	3.52	3.57	3.61
30	0.05	2.04	2.32	2.47	2.58	2.66	2.72	2.77	2.82	2.86
	0.01	2.75	3.01	3.15	3.25	3.33	3.39	3.44	3.49	3.52
40	0.05	2.02	2.29	2.44	2.54	2.62	2.68	2.73	2.77	2.81
	0.01	2.70	2.95	3.09	3.19	3.26	3.32	3.37	3.41	3.44
60	0.05	2.00	2.27	2.41	2.51	2.58	2.64	2.69	2.73	2.77
	0.01	2.66	2.90	3.03	3.12	3.19	3.25	3.29	3.33	3.37
120	0.05	1.98	2.24	2.38	2.47	2.55	2.60	2.65	2.69	2.73
	0.01	2.62	2.85	2.97	3.06	3.12	3.18	3.22	3.26	3.29
∞	0.05	1.96	2.21	2.35	2.44	2.51	2.57	2.61	2.65	2.69
	0.01	2.58	2.79	2.92	3.00	3.06	3.11	3.15	3.19	3.22

Source: Reproduced from C. W. Dunnett (1964), New tables for multiple comparisons with a control, *Biometrics 20*, 482–491. With permission of The Biometric Society.

Appendix W_S: Critical Lower-Tail Values of W_S for Rank-Sum Test for Two Independent Samples ($N_1 \leq N_2$)

	$N_1 = 1$							$N_1 = 2$							
N_2	0.001	0.005	0.010	0.025	0.05	0.10	$2\overline{W}$	0.001	0.005	0.010	0.025	0.05	0.10	$2\overline{W}$	N_2
2							4						—	10	2
3							5						3	12	3
4							6					—	3	14	4
5							7					3	4	16	5
6							8					3	4	18	6
7							9				—	3	4	20	7
8						—	10				3	4	5	22	8
9						1	11				3	4	5	24	9
10						1	12				3	4	6	26	10
11						1	13				3	4	6	28	11
12						1	14			—	4	5	7	30	12
13						1	15			3	4	5	7	32	13
14						1	16			3	4	6	8	34	14
15						1	17			3	4	6	8	36	15
16						1	18			3	4	6	8	38	16
17						1	19			3	5	6	9	40	17
18					—	1	20		—	3	5	7	9	42	18
19					1	2	21		3	4	5	7	10	44	19
20					1	2	22		3	4	5	7	10	46	20
21					1	2	23		3	4	6	8	11	48	21
22					1	2	24		3	4	6	8	11	50	22
23					1	2	25		3	4	6	8	12	52	23
24					1	2	26		3	4	6	9	12	54	24
25	—	—	—	—	1	2	27	—	3	4	6	9	12	56	25

	$N_1 = 3$							$N_1 = 4$							
N_2	0.001	0.005	0.010	0.025	0.05	0.10	$2\overline{W}$	0.001	0.005	0.010	0.025	0.05	0.10	$2\overline{W}$	N_2
3					6	7	21								
4				—	6	7	24			—	10	11	13	36	4
5				6	7	8	27		—	10	11	12	14	40	5
6			—	7	8	9	30		10	11	12	13	15	44	6
7			6	7	8	10	33		10	11	13	14	16	48	7
8		—	6	8	9	11	36		11	12	14	15	17	52	8
9		6	7	8	10	11	39	—	11	13	14	16	19	56	9
10		6	7	9	10	12	42	10	12	13	15	17	20	60	10
11		6	7	9	11	13	45	10	12	14	16	18	21	64	11
12		7	8	10	11	14	48	10	13	15	17	19	22	68	12
13		7	8	10	12	15	51	11	13	15	18	20	23	72	13
14		7	8	11	13	16	54	11	14	16	19	21	25	76	14
15		8	9	11	13	16	57	11	15	17	20	22	26	80	15

(continued)

Appendix W_S *(continued)*

N_2	$N_1 = 3$							$N_1 = 4$							N_2
	0.001	0.005	0.010	0.025	0.05	0.10	$2\overline{W}$	0.001	0.005	0.010	0.025	0.05	0.10	$2\overline{W}$	
16	—	8	9	12	14	17	60	12	15	17	21	24	27	84	16
17	6	8	10	12	15	18	63	12	16	18	21	25	28	88	17
18	6	8	10	13	15	19	66	13	16	19	22	26	30	92	18
19	6	9	10	13	16	20	69	13	17	19	23	27	31	96	19
20	6	9	11	14	17	21	72	13	18	20	24	28	32	100	20
21	7	9	11	14	17	21	75	14	18	21	25	29	33	104	21
22	7	10	12	15	18	22	78	14	19	21	26	30	35	108	22
23	7	10	12	15	19	23	81	14	19	22	27	31	36	112	23
24	7	10	12	16	19	24	84	15	20	23	27	32	38	116	24
25	7	11	13	16	20	25	87	15	20	23	28	33	38	120	25

N_2	$N_1 = 5$							$N_1 = 6$							N_2
	0.001	0.005	0.010	0.025	0.05	0.10	$2\overline{W}$	0.001	0.005	0.010	0.025	0.05	0.10	$2\overline{W}$	
5		15	16	17	19	20	55								
6		16	17	18	20	22	60	—	23	24	26	28	30	78	6
7	—	16	18	20	21	23	65	21	24	25	27	29	32	84	7
8	15	17	19	21	23	25	70	22	25	27	29	31	34	90	8
9	16	18	20	22	24	27	75	23	26	28	31	33	36	96	9
10	16	19	21	23	26	28	80	24	27	29	32	35	38	102	10
11	17	20	22	24	27	30	85	25	28	30	34	37	40	108	11
12	17	21	23	26	28	32	90	25	30	32	35	38	42	114	12
13	18	22	24	27	30	33	95	26	31	33	37	40	44	120	13
14	18	22	25	28	31	35	100	27	32	34	38	42	46	126	14
15	19	23	26	29	33	37	105	28	33	36	40	44	48	132	15
16	20	24	27	30	34	38	110	29	34	37	42	46	50	138	16
17	20	25	28	32	35	40	115	30	36	39	43	47	52	144	17
18	21	26	29	33	37	42	120	31	37	40	45	49	55	150	18
19	22	27	30	34	38	43	125	32	38	41	46	51	57	156	19
20	22	28	31	35	40	45	130	33	39	43	48	53	59	162	20
21	23	29	32	37	41	47	135	33	40	44	50	55	61	168	21
22	23	29	33	38	43	48	140	34	42	45	51	57	63	174	22
23	24	30	34	39	44	50	145	35	43	47	53	58	65	180	23
24	25	31	35	40	45	51	150	36	44	48	54	60	67	186	24
25	25	32	36	42	47	53	155	37	45	50	56	62	69	192	25

Appendix W_S *(continued)*

	$N_1 = 7$								$N_1 = 8$							
N_2	0.001	0.005	0.010	0.025	0.05	0.10	$2\overline{W}$	0.001	0.005	0.010	0.025	0.05	0.10	$2\overline{W}$	N_2
7	29	32	34	36	39	41	105								
8	30	34	35	38	41	44	112	40	43	45	49	51	55	136	8
9	31	35	37	40	43	46	119	41	45	47	51	54	58	144	9
10	33	37	39	42	45	49	126	42	47	49	53	56	60	152	10
11	34	38	40	44	47	51	133	44	49	51	55	59	63	160	11
12	35	40	42	46	49	54	140	45	51	53	58	62	66	168	12
13	36	41	44	48	52	56	147	47	53	56	60	64	69	176	13
14	37	43	45	50	54	59	154	48	54	58	62	67	72	184	14
15	38	44	47	52	56	61	161	50	56	60	65	69	75	192	15
16	39	46	49	54	58	64	168	51	58	62	67	72	78	200	16
17	41	47	51	56	61	66	175	53	60	64	70	75	81	208	17
18	42	49	52	58	63	69	182	54	62	66	72	77	84	216	18
19	43	50	54	60	65	71	189	56	64	68	74	80	87	224	19
20	44	52	56	62	67	74	196	57	66	70	77	83	90	232	20
21	46	53	58	64	69	76	203	59	68	72	79	85	92	240	21
22	47	55	59	66	72	79	210	60	70	74	81	88	95	248	22
23	48	57	61	68	74	81	217	62	71	76	84	90	98	256	23
24	49	58	63	70	76	84	224	64	73	78	86	93	101	264	24
25	50	60	64	72	78	86	231	65	75	81	89	96	104	272	25

	$N_1 = 9$								$N_1 = 10$							
N_2	0.001	0.005	0.010	0.025	0.05	0.10	$2\overline{W}$	0.001	0.005	0.010	0.025	0.05	0.10	$2\overline{W}$	N_2
9	52	56	59	62	66	70	171								
10	53	58	61	65	69	73	180	65	71	74	78	82	87	210	10
11	55	61	63	68	72	76	189	67	73	77	81	86	91	220	11
12	57	63	66	71	75	80	198	69	76	79	84	89	94	230	12
13	59	65	68	73	78	83	207	72	79	82	88	92	98	240	13
14	60	67	71	76	81	86	216	74	81	85	91	96	102	250	14
15	62	69	73	79	84	90	225	76	84	88	94	99	106	260	15
16	64	72	76	82	87	93	234	78	86	91	97	103	109	270	16
17	66	74	78	84	90	97	243	80	89	93	100	106	113	280	17
18	68	76	81	87	93	100	252	82	92	96	103	110	117	290	18
19	70	78	83	90	96	103	261	84	94	99	107	113	121	300	19
20	71	81	85	93	99	107	270	87	97	102	110	117	125	310	20
21	73	83	88	95	102	110	279	89	99	105	113	120	128	320	21
22	75	85	90	98	105	113	288	91	102	108	116	123	132	330	22
23	77	88	93	101	108	117	297	93	105	110	119	127	136	340	23
24	79	90	95	104	111	120	306	95	107	113	122	130	140	350	24
25	81	92	98	107	114	123	315	98	110	116	126	134	144	360	25

(continued)

Appendix W_S *(continued)*

$N_1 = 11$ / $N_1 = 12$

N_2	0.001	0.005	0.010	0.025	0.05	0.10	$2\overline{W}$	0.001	0.005	0.010	0.025	0.05	0.10	$2\overline{W}$	N_2
11	81	87	91	96	100	106	253								
12	83	90	94	99	104	110	264	98	105	109	115	120	127	300	12
13	86	93	97	103	108	114	275	101	109	113	119	125	131	312	13
14	88	96	100	106	112	118	286	103	112	116	123	129	136	324	14
15	90	99	103	110	116	123	297	106	115	120	127	133	141	336	15
16	93	102	107	113	120	127	308	109	119	124	131	138	145	348	16
17	95	105	110	117	123	131	319	112	122	127	135	142	150	360	17
18	98	108	113	121	127	135	330	115	125	131	139	146	155	372	18
19	100	111	116	124	131	139	341	118	129	134	143	150	159	384	19
20	103	114	119	128	135	144	352	120	132	138	147	155	164	396	20
21	106	117	123	131	139	148	363	123	136	142	151	159	169	408	21
22	108	120	126	135	143	152	374	126	139	145	155	163	173	420	22
23	111	123	129	139	147	156	385	129	142	149	159	168	178	432	23
24	113	126	132	142	151	161	396	132	146	153	163	172	183	444	24
25	116	129	136	146	155	165	407	135	149	156	167	176	187	456	25

$N_1 = 13$ / $N_1 = 14$

N_2	0.001	0.005	0.010	0.025	0.05	0.10	$2\overline{W}$	0.001	0.005	0.010	0.025	0.05	0.10	$2\overline{W}$	N_2
13	117	125	130	136	142	149	351								
14	120	129	134	141	147	154	364	137	147	152	160	166	174	406	14
15	123	133	138	145	152	159	377	141	151	156	164	171	179	420	15
16	126	136	142	150	156	165	390	144	155	161	169	176	185	434	16
17	129	140	146	154	161	170	403	148	159	165	174	182	190	448	17
18	133	144	150	158	166	175	416	151	163	170	179	187	196	462	18
19	136	148	154	163	171	180	429	155	168	174	183	192	202	476	19
20	139	151	158	167	175	185	442	159	172	178	188	197	207	490	20
21	142	155	162	171	180	190	455	162	176	183	193	202	213	504	21
22	145	159	166	176	185	195	468	166	180	187	198	207	218	518	22
23	149	163	170	180	189	200	481	169	184	192	203	212	224	532	23
24	152	166	174	185	194	205	494	173	188	196	207	218	229	546	24
25	155	170	178	189	199	211	507	177	192	200	212	223	235	560	25

$N_1 = 15$ / $N_1 = 16$

N_2	0.001	0.005	0.010	0.025	0.05	0.10	$2\overline{W}$	0.001	0.005	0.010	0.025	0.05	0.10	$2\overline{W}$	N_2
15	160	171	176	184	192	200	465								
16	163	175	181	190	197	206	480	184	196	202	211	219	229	528	16
17	167	180	186	195	203	212	495	188	201	207	217	225	235	544	17
18	171	184	190	200	208	218	510	192	206	212	222	231	242	560	18
19	175	189	195	205	214	224	525	196	210	218	228	237	248	576	19
20	179	193	200	210	220	230	540	201	215	223	234	243	255	592	20
21	183	198	205	216	225	236	555	205	220	228	239	249	261	608	21
22	187	202	210	221	231	242	570	209	225	233	245	255	267	624	22
23	191	207	214	226	236	248	585	214	230	238	251	261	274	640	23
24	195	211	219	231	242	254	600	218	235	244	256	267	280	656	24
25	199	216	224	237	248	260	615	222	240	249	262	273	287	672	25

Appendix W_S *(continued)*

	$N_1 = 17$							$N_1 = 18$							
N_2	*0.001*	*0.005*	*0.010*	*0.025*	*0.05*	*0.10*	$2\overline{W}$	*0.001*	*0.005*	*0.010*	*0.025*	*0.05*	*0.10*	$2\overline{W}$	N_2
17	210	223	230	240	249	259	595								
18	214	228	235	246	255	266	612	237	252	259	270	280	291	666	18
19	219	234	241	252	262	273	629	242	258	265	277	287	299	684	19
20	223	239	246	258	268	280	646	247	263	271	283	294	306	702	20
21	228	244	252	264	274	287	663	252	269	277	290	301	313	720	21
22	233	249	258	270	281	294	680	257	275	283	296	307	321	738	22
23	238	255	263	276	287	300	697	262	280	289	303	314	328	756	23
24	242	260	269	282	294	307	714	267	286	295	309	321	335	774	24
25	247	265	275	288	300	314	731	273	292	301	316	328	343	792	25

	$N_1 = 19$							$N_1 = 20$							
N_2	*0.001*	*0.005*	*0.010*	*0.025*	*0.05*	*0.10*	$2\overline{W}$	*0.001*	*0.005*	*0.010*	*0.025*	*0.05*	*0.10*	$2\overline{W}$	N_2
19	267	283	291	303	313	325	741								
20	272	289	297	309	320	333	760	298	315	324	337	348	361	820	20
21	277	295	303	316	328	341	779	304	322	331	344	356	370	840	21
22	283	301	310	323	335	349	798	309	328	337	351	364	378	860	22
23	288	307	316	330	342	357	817	315	335	344	359	371	386	880	23
24	294	313	323	337	350	364	836	321	341	351	366	379	394	900	24
25	299	319	329	344	357	372	855	327	348	358	373	387	403	920	25

	$N_1 = 21$							$N_1 = 22$							
N_2	*0.001*	*0.005*	*0.010*	*0.025*	*0.05*	*0.10*	$2\overline{W}$	*0.001*	*0.005*	*0.010*	*0.025*	*0.05*	*0.10*	$2\overline{W}$	N_2
21	331	349	359	373	385	399	903								
22	337	356	366	381	393	408	924	365	386	396	411	424	439	990	22
23	343	363	373	388	401	417	945	372	393	403	419	432	448	1012	23
24	349	370	381	396	410	425	966	379	400	411	427	441	457	1034	24
25	356	377	388	404	418	434	987	385	408	419	435	450	467	1056	25

	$N_1 = 23$							$N_1 = 24$							
N_2	*0.001*	*0.005*	*0.010*	*0.025*	*0.05*	*0.10*	$2\overline{W}$	*0.001*	*0.005*	*0.010*	*0.025*	*0.05*	*0.10*	$2\overline{W}$	N_2
23	402	424	434	451	465	481	1081								
24	409	431	443	459	474	491	1104	440	464	475	492	507	525	1176	24
25	416	439	451	468	483	500	1127	448	472	484	501	517	535	1200	25

	$N_1 = \mathbf{25}$						
N_2	*0.001*	*0.005*	*0.010*	*0.025*	*0.05*	*0.10*	$2\overline{W}$
25	480	505	517	536	552	570	1275

Source: Table 1 in L. R. Verdooren (1963), Extended tables of critical values for Wilcoxon's test statistic, *Biometrika, 50,* 177–186, with permission of the author and the editor.

Appendix z: The Normal Distribution (z)

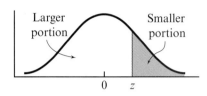

z	Mean to z	Larger Portion	Smaller Portion	y	z	Mean to z	Larger Portion	Smaller Portion	y
0.00	0.0000	0.5000	0.5000	0.3989	0.36	0.1406	0.6406	0.3594	0.3739
0.01	0.0040	0.5040	0.4960	0.3989	0.37	0.1443	0.6443	0.3557	0.3725
0.02	0.0080	0.5080	0.4920	0.3989	0.38	0.1480	0.6480	0.3520	0.3712
0.03	0.0120	0.5120	0.4880	0.3988	0.39	0.1517	0.6517	0.3483	0.3697
0.04	0.0160	0.5160	0.4840	0.3986	0.40	0.1554	0.6554	0.3446	0.3683
0.05	0.0199	0.5199	0.4801	0.3984	0.41	0.1591	0.6591	0.3409	0.3668
0.06	0.0239	0.5239	0.4761	0.3982	0.42	0.1628	0.6628	0.3372	0.3653
0.07	0.0279	0.5279	0.4721	0.3980	0.43	0.1664	0.6664	0.3336	0.3637
0.08	0.0319	0.5319	0.4681	0.3977	0.44	0.1700	0.6700	0.3300	0.3621
0.09	0.0359	0.5359	0.4641	0.3973	0.45	0.1736	0.6736	0.3264	0.3605
0.10	0.0398	0.5398	0.4602	0.3970	0.46	0.1772	0.6772	0.3228	0.3589
0.11	0.0438	0.5438	0.4562	0.3965	0.47	0.1808	0.6808	0.3192	0.3572
0.12	0.0478	0.5478	0.4522	0.3961	0.48	0.1844	0.6844	0.3156	0.3555
0.13	0.0517	0.5517	0.4483	0.3956	0.49	0.1879	0.6879	0.3121	0.3538
0.14	0.0557	0.5557	0.4443	0.3951	0.50	0.1915	0.6915	0.3085	0.3521
0.15	0.0596	0.5596	0.4404	0.3945	0.51	0.1950	0.6950	0.3050	0.3503
0.16	0.0636	0.5636	0.4364	0.3939	0.52	0.1985	0.6985	0.3015	0.3485
0.17	0.0675	0.5675	0.4325	0.3932	0.53	0.2019	0.7019	0.2981	0.3467
0.18	0.0714	0.5714	0.4286	0.3925	0.54	0.2054	0.7054	0.2946	0.3448
0.19	0.0753	0.5753	0.4247	0.3918	0.55	0.2088	0.7088	0.2912	0.3429
0.20	0.0793	0.5793	0.4207	0.3910	0.56	0.2123	0.7123	0.2877	0.3410
0.21	0.0832	0.5832	0.4168	0.3902	0.57	0.2157	0.7157	0.2843	0.3391
0.22	0.0871	0.5871	0.4129	0.3894	0.58	0.2190	0.7190	0.2810	0.3372
0.23	0.0910	0.5910	0.4090	0.3885	0.59	0.2224	0.7224	0.2776	0.3352
0.24	0.0948	0.5948	0.4052	0.3876	0.60	0.2257	0.7257	0.2743	0.3332
0.25	0.0987	0.5987	0.4013	0.3867	0.61	0.2291	0.7291	0.2709	0.3312
0.26	0.1026	0.6026	0.3974	0.3857	0.62	0.2324	0.7324	0.2676	0.3292
0.27	0.1064	0.6064	0.3936	0.3847	0.63	0.2357	0.7357	0.2643	0.3271
0.28	0.1103	0.6103	0.3897	0.3836	0.64	0.2389	0.7389	0.2611	0.3251
0.29	0.1141	0.6141	0.3859	0.3825	0.65	0.2422	0.7422	0.2578	0.3230
0.30	0.1179	0.6179	0.3821	0.3814	0.66	0.2454	0.7454	0.2546	0.3209
0.31	0.1217	0.6217	0.3783	0.3802	0.67	0.2486	0.7486	0.2514	0.3187
0.32	0.1255	0.6255	0.3745	0.3790	0.68	0.2517	0.7517	0.2483	0.3166
0.33	0.1293	0.6293	0.3707	0.3778	0.69	0.2549	0.7549	0.2451	0.3144
0.34	0.1331	0.6331	0.3669	0.3765	0.70	0.2580	0.7580	0.2420	0.3123
0.35	0.1368	0.6368	0.3632	0.3752	0.71	0.2611	0.7611	0.2389	0.3101

Appendix z *(continued)*

z	Mean to z	Larger Portion	Smaller Portion	y	z	Mean to z	Larger Portion	Smaller Portion	y
0.72	0.2642	0.7642	0.2358	0.3079	1.14	0.3729	0.8729	0.1271	0.2083
0.73	0.2673	0.7673	0.2327	0.3056	1.15	0.3749	0.8749	0.1251	0.2059
0.74	0.2704	0.7704	0.2296	0.3034	1.16	0.3770	0.8770	0.1230	0.2036
0.75	0.2734	0.7734	0.2266	0.3011	1.17	0.3790	0.8790	0.1210	0.2012
0.76	0.2764	0.7764	0.2236	0.2989	1.18	0.3810	0.8810	0.1190	0.1989
0.77	0.2794	0.7794	0.2206	0.2966	1.19	0.3830	0.8830	0.1170	0.1965
0.78	0.2823	0.7823	0.2177	0.2943	1.20	0.3849	0.8849	0.1151	0.1942
0.79	0.2852	0.7852	0.2148	0.2920	1.21	0.3869	0.8869	0.1131	0.1919
0.80	0.2881	0.7881	0.2119	0.2897	1.22	0.3888	0.8888	0.1112	0.1895
0.81	0.2910	0.7910	0.2090	0.2874	1.23	0.3907	0.8907	0.1093	0.1872
0.82	0.2939	0.7939	0.2061	0.2850	1.24	0.3925	0.8925	0.1075	0.1849
0.83	0.2967	0.7967	0.2033	0.2827	1.25	0.3944	0.8944	0.1056	0.1826
0.84	0.2995	0.7995	0.2005	0.2803	1.26	0.3962	0.8962	0.1038	0.1804
0.85	0.3023	0.8023	0.1977	0.2780	1.27	0.3980	0.8980	0.1020	0.1781
0.86	0.3051	0.8051	0.1949	0.2756	1.28	0.3997	0.8997	0.1003	0.1758
0.87	0.3078	0.8078	0.1922	0.2732	1.29	0.4015	0.9015	0.0985	0.1736
0.88	0.3106	0.8106	0.1894	0.2709	1.30	0.4032	0.9032	0.0968	0.1714
0.89	0.3133	0.8133	0.1867	0.2685	1.31	0.4049	0.9049	0.0951	0.1691
0.90	0.3159	0.8159	0.1841	0.2661	1.32	0.4066	0.9066	0.0934	0.1669
0.91	0.3186	0.8186	0.1814	0.2637	1.33	0.4082	0.9082	0.0918	0.1647
0.92	0.3212	0.8212	0.1788	0.2613	1.34	0.4099	0.9099	0.0901	0.1626
0.93	0.3238	0.8238	0.1762	0.2589	1.35	0.4115	0.9115	0.0885	0.1604
0.94	0.3264	0.8264	0.1736	0.2565	1.36	0.4131	0.9131	0.0869	0.1582
0.95	0.3289	0.8289	0.1711	0.2541	1.37	0.4147	0.9147	0.0853	0.1561
0.96	0.3315	0.8315	0.1685	0.2516	1.38	0.4162	0.9162	0.0838	0.1539
0.97	0.3340	0.8340	0.1660	0.2492	1.39	0.4177	0.9177	0.0823	0.1518
0.98	0.3365	0.8365	0.1635	0.2468	1.40	0.4192	0.9192	0.0808	0.1497
0.99	0.3389	0.8389	0.1611	0.2444	1.41	0.4207	0.9207	0.0793	0.1476
1.00	0.3413	0.8413	0.1587	0.2420	1.42	0.4222	0.9222	0.0778	0.1456
1.01	0.3438	0.8438	0.1562	0.2396	1.43	0.4236	0.9236	0.0764	0.1435
1.02	0.3461	0.8461	0.1539	0.2371	1.44	0.4251	0.9251	0.0749	0.1415
1.03	0.3485	0.8485	0.1515	0.2347	1.45	0.4265	0.9265	0.0735	0.1394
1.04	0.3508	0.8508	0.1492	0.2323	1.46	0.4279	0.9279	0.0721	0.1374
1.05	0.3531	0.8531	0.1469	0.2299	1.47	0.4292	0.9292	0.0708	0.1354
1.06	0.3554	0.8554	0.1446	0.2275	1.48	0.4306	0.9306	0.0694	0.1334
1.07	0.3577	0.8577	0.1423	0.2251	1.49	0.4319	0.9319	0.0681	0.1315
1.08	0.3599	0.8599	0.1401	0.2227	1.50	0.4332	0.9332	0.0668	0.1295
1.09	0.3621	0.8621	0.1379	0.2203	1.51	0.4345	0.9345	0.0655	0.1276
1.10	0.3643	0.8643	0.1357	0.2179	1.52	0.4357	0.9357	0.0643	0.1257
1.11	0.3665	0.8665	0.1335	0.2155	1.53	0.4370	0.9370	0.0630	0.1238
1.12	0.3686	0.8686	0.1314	0.2131	1.54	0.4382	0.9382	0.0618	0.1219
1.13	0.3708	0.8708	0.1292	0.2107	1.55	0.4394	0.9394	0.0606	0.1200

(continued)

Appendix z *(continued)*

z	Mean to z	Larger Portion	Smaller Portion	y	z	Mean to z	Larger Portion	Smaller Portion	y
1.56	0.4406	0.9406	0.0594	0.1182	1.98	0.4761	0.9761	0.0239	0.0562
1.57	0.4418	0.9418	0.0582	0.1163	1.99	0.4767	0.9767	0.0233	0.0551
1.58	0.4429	0.9429	0.0571	0.1145	2.00	0.4772	0.9772	0.0228	0.0540
1.59	0.4441	0.9441	0.0559	0.1127	2.01	0.4778	0.9778	0.0222	0.0529
1.60	0.4452	0.9452	0.0548	0.1109	2.02	0.4783	0.9783	0.0217	0.0519
1.61	0.4463	0.9463	0.0537	0.1092	2.03	0.4788	0.9788	0.0212	0.0508
1.62	0.4474	0.9474	0.0526	0.1074	2.04	0.4793	0.9793	0.0207	0.0498
1.63	0.4484	0.9484	0.0516	0.1057	2.05	0.4798	0.9798	0.0202	0.0488
1.64	0.4495	0.9495	0.0505	0.1040	2.06	0.4803	0.9803	0.0197	0.0478
1.65	0.4505	0.9505	0.0495	0.1023	2.07	0.4808	0.9808	0.0192	0.0468
1.66	0.4515	0.9515	0.0485	0.1006	2.08	0.4812	0.9812	0.0188	0.0459
1.67	0.4525	0.9525	0.0475	0.0989	2.09	0.4817	0.9817	0.0183	0.0449
1.68	0.4535	0.9535	0.0465	0.0973	2.10	0.4821	0.9821	0.0179	0.0440
1.69	0.4545	0.9545	0.0455	0.0957	2.11	0.4826	0.9826	0.0174	0.0431
1.70	0.4554	0.9554	0.0446	0.0940	2.12	0.4830	0.9830	0.0170	0.0422
1.71	0.4564	0.9564	0.0436	0.0925	2.13	0.4834	0.9834	0.0166	0.0413
1.72	0.4573	0.9573	0.0427	0.0909	2.14	0.4838	0.9838	0.0162	0.0404
1.73	0.4582	0.9582	0.0418	0.0893	2.15	0.4842	0.9842	0.0158	0.0396
1.74	0.4591	0.9591	0.0409	0.0878	2.16	0.4846	0.9846	0.0154	0.0387
1.75	0.4599	0.9599	0.0401	0.0863	2.17	0.4850	0.9850	0.0150	0.0379
1.76	0.4608	0.9608	0.0392	0.0848	2.18	0.4854	0.9854	0.0146	0.0371
1.77	0.4616	0.9616	0.0384	0.0833	2.19	0.4857	0.9857	0.0143	0.0363
1.78	0.4625	0.9625	0.0375	0.0818	2.20	0.4861	0.9861	0.0139	0.0355
1.79	0.4633	0.9633	0.0367	0.0804	2.21	0.4864	0.9864	0.0136	0.0347
1.80	0.4641	0.9641	0.0359	0.0790	2.22	0.4868	0.9868	0.0132	0.0339
1.81	0.4649	0.9649	0.0351	0.0775	2.23	0.4871	0.9871	0.0129	0.0332
1.82	0.4656	0.9656	0.0344	0.0761	2.24	0.4875	0.9875	0.0125	0.0325
1.83	0.4664	0.9664	0.0336	0.0748	2.25	0.4878	0.9878	0.0122	0.0317
1.84	0.4671	0.9671	0.0329	0.0734	2.26	0.4881	0.9881	0.0119	0.0310
1.85	0.4678	0.9678	0.0322	0.0721	2.27	0.4884	0.9884	0.0116	0.0303
1.86	0.4686	0.9686	0.0314	0.0707	2.28	0.4887	0.9887	0.0113	0.0297
1.87	0.4693	0.9693	0.0307	0.0694	2.29	0.4890	0.9890	0.0110	0.0290
1.88	0.4699	0.9699	0.0301	0.0681	2.30	0.4893	0.9893	0.0107	0.0283
1.89	0.4706	0.9706	0.0294	0.0669	2.31	0.4896	0.9896	0.0104	0.0277
1.90	0.4713	0.9713	0.0287	0.0656	2.32	0.4898	0.9898	0.0102	0.0270
1.91	0.4719	0.9719	0.0281	0.0644	2.33	0.4901	0.9901	0.0099	0.0264
1.92	0.4726	0.9726	0.0274	0.0632	2.34	0.4904	0.9904	0.0096	0.0258
1.93	0.4732	0.9732	0.0268	0.0620	2.35	0.4906	0.9906	0.0094	0.0252
1.94	0.4738	0.9738	0.0262	0.0608	2.36	0.4909	0.9909	0.0091	0.0246
1.95	0.4744	0.9744	0.0256	0.0596	2.37	0.4911	0.9911	0.0089	0.0241
1.96	0.4750	0.9750	0.0250	0.0584	2.38	0.4913	0.9913	0.0087	0.0235
1.97	0.4756	0.9756	0.0244	0.0573	2.39	0.4916	0.9916	0.0084	0.0229

Appendix z *(continued)*

z	Mean to z	Larger Portion	Smaller Portion	y	z	Mean to z	Larger Portion	Smaller Portion	y
2.40	0.4918	0.9918	0.0082	0.0224	2.75	0.4970	0.9970	0.0030	0.0091
2.41	0.4920	0.9920	0.0080	0.0219	2.76	0.4971	0.9971	0.0029	0.0088
2.42	0.4922	0.9922	0.0078	0.0213	2.77	0.4972	0.9972	0.0028	0.0086
2.43	0.4925	0.9925	0.0075	0.0208	2.78	0.4973	0.9973	0.0027	0.0084
2.44	0.4927	0.9927	0.0073	0.0203	2.79	0.4974	0.9974	0.0026	0.0081
2.45	0.4929	0.9929	0.0071	0.0198	2.80	0.4974	0.9974	0.0026	0.0079
2.46	0.4931	0.9931	0.0069	0.0194	2.81	0.4975	0.9975	0.0025	0.0077
2.47	0.4932	0.9932	0.0068	0.0189	2.82	0.4976	0.9976	0.0024	0.0075
2.48	0.4934	0.9934	0.0066	0.0184	2.83	0.4977	0.9977	0.0023	0.0073
2.49	0.4936	0.9936	0.0064	0.0180	2.84	0.4977	0.9977	0.0023	0.0071
2.50	0.4938	0.9938	0.0062	0.0175	2.85	0.4978	0.9978	0.0022	0.0069
2.51	0.4940	0.9940	0.0060	0.0171	2.86	0.4979	0.9979	0.0021	0.0067
2.52	0.4941	0.9941	0.0059	0.0167	2.87	0.4979	0.9979	0.0021	0.0065
2.53	0.4943	0.9943	0.0057	0.0163	2.88	0.4980	0.9980	0.0020	0.0063
2.54	0.4945	0.9945	0.0055	0.0158	2.89	0.4981	0.9981	0.0019	0.0061
2.55	0.4946	0.9946	0.0054	0.0154	2.90	0.4981	0.9981	0.0019	0.0060
2.56	0.4948	0.9948	0.0052	0.0151	2.91	0.4982	0.9982	0.0018	0.0058
2.57	0.4949	0.9949	0.0051	0.0147	2.92	0.4982	0.9982	0.0018	0.0056
2.58	0.4951	0.9951	0.0049	0.0143	2.93	0.4983	0.9983	0.0017	0.0055
2.59	0.4952	0.9952	0.0048	0.0139	2.94	0.4984	0.9984	0.0016	0.0053
2.60	0.4953	0.9953	0.0047	0.0136	2.95	0.4984	0.9984	0.0016	0.0051
2.61	0.4955	0.9955	0.0045	0.0132	2.96	0.4985	0.9985	0.0015	0.0050
2.62	0.4956	0.9956	0.0044	0.0129	2.97	0.4985	0.9985	0.0015	0.0048
2.63	0.4957	0.9957	0.0043	0.0126	2.98	0.4986	0.9986	0.0014	0.0047
2.64	0.4959	0.9959	0.0041	0.0122	2.99	0.4986	0.9986	0.0014	0.0046
2.65	0.4960	0.9960	0.0040	0.0119	3.00	0.4987	0.9987	0.0013	0.0044
2.66	0.4961	0.9961	0.0039	0.0116	. . .	. . .	. . .	. . .	. . .
2.67	0.4962	0.9962	0.0038	0.0113	3.25	0.4994	0.9994	0.0006	0.0020
2.68	0.4963	0.9963	0.0037	0.0110	. . .	. . .	. . .	. . .	. . .
2.69	0.4964	0.9964	0.0036	0.0107	3.50	0.4998	0.9998	0.0002	0.0009
2.70	0.4965	0.9965	0.0035	0.0104	. . .	. . .	. . .	. . .	. . .
2.71	0.4966	0.9966	0.0034	0.0101	3.75	0.4999	0.9999	0.0001	0.0004
2.72	0.4967	0.9967	0.0033	0.0099	. . .	. . .	. . .	. . .	. . .
2.73	0.4968	0.9968	0.0032	0.0096	4.00	0.5000	1.0000	0.0000	0.0001
2.74	0.4969	0.9969	0.0031	0.0093	. . .	. . .	. . .	. . .	. . .

Source: The entries in this table were computed by the author.

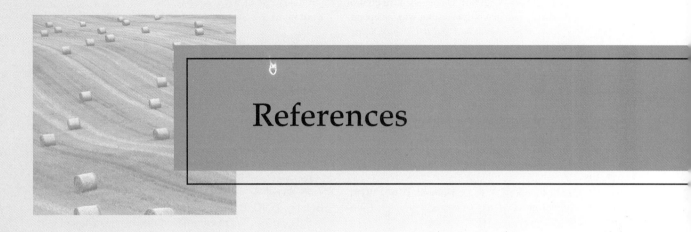

References

Achenbach, T. M. (1991a). *Manual for the Child Behavior Checklist/4–18 and 1991 profile.* Burlington, VT: University of Vermont Department of Psychiatry.

Achenbach, T. M. (1991b). *Manual for the Youth Self-Report and 1991 profile.* Burlington. VT: University of Vermont Department of Psychiatry.

Achenbach, T. M., Howell, C. T., Aoki, M. F., & Rauh, V. A. (1993). Nine-year outcome of the Vermont Intervention Program for low-birthweight infants. *Pediatrics, 91,* 45–55.

Adams, H. E., Wright, L. W. (Jr.), & Lohr, B. A. (1996). Is homophobia associated with homosexual arousal? *Journal of Abnormal Psychology, 105,* 440–445.

Agresti, A. (1984). *Analysis of ordinal categorical data.* New York: Wiley.

Agresti, A. (2002). *Categorical data analysis* (2nd ed.). New York: Wiley.

Agresti, A. (2007). *An introduction to categorical data analysis* (2nd ed.). New York: Wiley.

Aiken, L. S., & West, S. G. (1991). *Multiple regression: Testing and interpreting interactions.* Newbury Park, CA: Sage.

Algina, J., Keselman, H. J., & Penfield, R. D. (2005). An alternative to Cohen's standardized mean difference effect size: A robust parameter and confidence interval in the two independent groups case. *Psychological Methods, 10,* 317–328.

Allison, P. D. (1999). *Logistic regression using the SAS® System: Theory and Application.* Cary, NC: SAS Institute, Inc.

Anderson, N. H. (1963). Comparison of different populations: Resistance to extinction and transfer. *Psychological Review, 70,* 162–179.

Appelbaum, M. I., & Cramer, E. M. (1974). Some problems in the nonorthogonal analysis of variance. *Psychological Bulletin, 81,* 335–343.

Appleton, D. R., French, J. M., & Vanderpump, M. P. J. (1996). Ignoring a covariate: An example of Simpson's paradox. *The American Statistician, 50,* 340–341.

Arnholt, A. T. (2007). Resampling with R. *Teaching Statistics, 29*(1), 21–26.

Aronson, J., Lustina, M. J., Good, C., Keough, K., Steele, C. M., & Brown, J. (1998). When white men can't do math: Necessary and sufficient factors in stereotype threat. *Journal of Experimental Social Psychology, 35,* 29–46.

Baker, S. P., & Lew, R. (1987). A Monte Carlo comparison of Tukey's and Bonferroni's methods with an optimized Bonferroni multiple comparison procedure in repeated measures experiments. Paper presented at the annual meeting of the American Statistical Association. San Francisco. CA.

Baron, R. M., & Kenny, D. A. (1986). The moderator-mediator variable distinction in social psychological research: Conceptual, strategic, and statistical considerations. *Journal of Personality and Social Psychology, 51,* 1173–1182.

Bauer, M., & Dopfmer, S. (1999). Lithium augmentation in treatment-resistant depression, meta-analysis of placebo-controlled studies. *Journal of Clinical Psychopharmacology,* 19, 427–434.

Beaujean, A. A. (2008) Mediation, moderation, and the study of individual differences. In J. Osborne (Ed.), *Best practices in quantitative methods* (pp. 341–357). Thousand Oaks, CA, Sage, 2008.

Bell, R. A., Buerkel-Rothfuss, N. L., & Gore, K. E. (1987). "Did you bring the yarmulke for the Cabbage Patch kid?": The idiomatic communication among young lovers. *Human Communication Research, 14,* 47–67.

Benjamini, Y., & Hochberg, Y. (1995). Controlling the false discovery rate: A practical and powerful approach to multiple testing. *Journal of the Royal Statistical Society, Series B, 57,* 289–300.

Benjamini, Y., & Hochberg, Y. (2000). On the adaptive control of the false discovery rate in multiple testing with independent statistics. *Journal of Educational and Behavioral Statistics, 25,* 60–83.

Berger, V. I. (2005). Mid-p values. In B. S. Everitt & D. C Howell, *Encyclopedia of Statistics in Behavioral Sciences.* Chichester, England: Wiley.

Bhoj, D. S. (1978). Testing equality of means of correlated variates with missing data on both responses. *Biometrika* 65, 225–228.

Bickel, P. J., Hammel, E. A., & O'Connell, J. W. (1975). Sex bias in graduate admissions: Data from Berkeley, *Science, 187,* 398–403.

Bishop, Y. M. M., Fienberg, S. E., & Holland, P. W. (1975). *Discrete multivariate analysis: Theory and practice.* Cambridge. MA: MIT Press.

Bisson J., & Andrew, M. (2007). Psychological treatment of post-traumatic stress disorder (PTSD). *Cochrane Database of Systematic Reviews* 2007, Issue 3. Art. No.: CD003388. DOI: 10.1002/14651858.CD003388.pub3.m

Blair, R. C. (1978). I've been testing some statistical hypotheses. . . . Can you guess what they are? *Journal of Educational Research, 72,* 116–118.

Blair, R. C., & Higgins, J. J. (1978). Tests of hypotheses for unbalanced factorial designs under various regression/coding method combinations. *Educational and Psychological Measurement, 38,* 621–631.

Blair, R. C., & Higgins, J. J. (1980). A comparison of the power of Wilcoxon's rank-sum statistic to that of Student's *t* statistic under various nonnormal distributions. *Journal of Educational Statistics, 5,* 309–335.

Blair, R. C., & Higgins, J. J. (1985). Comparison of the power of the paired samples *t* test to that of Wilcoxon's signed-ranks test under various population shapes. *Psychological Bulletin, 97,* 119–128.

Blanchard, E. B., Theobald, D. E., Williamson, D. A., Silver, B. V., & Brown, D. A. (1978). Temperature biofeedback in the treatment of migraine headaches. *Archives of General Psychiatry, 35,* 581–588.

Bloch, M. H., Panza, K. E., Landeros-Weisenberger, A., & Leckman, J. F. (2009). Meta-analysis: treatment of attention-deficit/hyperactivity disorder in children with comorbid tic disorders. *Journal of the American Academy of Child & Adolescent Psychiatry, 48,* 884.

Block J. J., & Crain B. R. (2007). Omissions and errors in "media violence and the American public." *The American Psychologist, 62,* 252–253.

Boik, R. J. (1981). A priori tests in repeated measures designs: Effects of nonsphericity. *Psychometrika, 46,* 241–255.

Boneau, C. A. (1960). The effects of violations of assumptions underlying the *t* test. *Psychological Bulletin, 57,* 49–64.

Borenstein, M., & Cohen, J. (1988). *Statistical power analysis: A computer program.* Hillsdale, NJ: Lawrence Erlbaum.

Borenstein, M., Hedges, L. V., Higgins, J. P. T., & Rothstein, H. R. (2009). *Introduction to meta-analysis.* Chichester, England: John Wiley & Sons, Ltd.

Bouton, M., & Swartzentruber, D. (1985). Unpublished raw data, University of Vermont.

Box, G. E. P. (1953). Non-normality and tests on variance. *Biometrika, 40,* 318–335.

Box, G. E. P. (1954a). Some theorems on quadratic forms applied in the study of analysis of variance problems: I. Effect of inequality of variance in the one-way classification. *Annals of Mathematical Statistics, 25,* 290–302.

Box, G. E. P. (1954b). Some theorems on quadratic forms applied in the study of analysis of variance problems: II. Effect of inequality of variance and of correlation of errors in the two-way classification. *Annals of Mathematical Statistics, 25,* 484–498.

Bradley, D. R., Bradley, T. D., McGrath, S. G., & Cutcomb, S. D. (1979). Type I error rate of the chi-square test of independence in $R \times C$ tables that have small expected frequencies. *Psychological Bulletin, 86,* 1290–1297.

Bradley, D. R. (1988). *DATASIM.* Lewiston ME: Desktop Press.

Bradley, D. R., Russell, R. L., & Reeve, C. P. (1996). Statistical power in complex experimental designs. *Behavioral Research Methods, Instruments, and Computers, 28,* 319–326.

Bradley, J. V. (1963). *Studies in research methodology: IV A sampling study of the central limit theorem and the robustness of one sample parametric tests* (AMRL Tech. Rep. No. 63–29). Aerospace Medical Research Laboratories, Wright-Patterson Air Force Base, OH.

Bradley, J. V. (1964). *Studies in research methodology: VI. The central limit effect for a variety of populations and the robustness of z, t, and F* (AMRL Tech. Rep. No. 64–123). Aerospace Medical Research Laboratories, Wright-Patterson Air Force Base, OH.

Bradley, J. V. (1968). *Distribution free statistical tests.* Englewood Cliffs, NJ: Prentice-Hall.

Brand, A., Bradley, M. T., Best, L. A., & Stoica, G. (2008). Accuracy of effect size estimates from published psychological research. *Perceptual Motor Skills, 106,* 645–649.

Brooks, L., & Perot, A. R. (1991). Reporting sexual harassment. *Psychology of Women Quarterly, 15,* 31–47.

Brown, M. B. (1976). Screening effects in multidimensional contingency tables. *Applied Statistics, 25,* 37.

Brown, M. B., & Forsythe, A. B. (1974). The ANOVA and multiple comparisons for data with heterogeneous variances. *Biometrics, 30,* 719–724.

Bulté, I., & Onghena, P. (2008). An R package for single-case randomization tests. *Behavior Research Methods, 40,* 467–478.

Cai, L., & Hayes, A. F. (2008). A new test of linear hypotheses in OLS regression under heteroscedasticity of unknown form. *Journal of Educational and Behavioral Statistics, 33,* 21–40.

Camilli, G., & Hopkins, K. D. (1978). Applicability of chi-square to 2 × 2 contingency tables with small expected cell frequencies. *Psychological Bulletin, 85,* 163–167.

Camilli, G., & Hopkins, K. D. (1979). Testing for association in 2 × 2 contingency tables with very small sample sizes. *Psychological Bulletin, 86,* 1011–1014.

Campbell, A., Converse, P. E., & Rogers, W. L. (1976). *The quality of American life.* New York: Russell Sage Foundation.

Campbell, I. (2007). Chi-squared and Fisher-Irwin tests of two-by-two tables with small sample recommendations. *Statistics in Medicine, 26,* 3661–3675.

Carmer, S. G., & Swanson, M. R. (1973). An evaluation of ten multiple comparison procedures by Monte Carlo methods. *Journal of the American Statistical Association, 68,* 66–74.

Center, B., Skiba, R., & Casey, A. (1985–1986). Quantitative synthesis of intra-subject design literature. *The Journal of Special Education, 19,* 387–400.

Chen, R., & Dunlap, W. P. (1994). A Monte Carlo study of the performance of a corrected formula for $\tilde{\varepsilon}$ suggested by Lecoutre. *Journal of Educational Statistics, 19,* 119–126.

Christensen, R. (1997). *Log-linear models and logistic regression.* New York: Springer-Verlag.

Clark, H. H. (1973). The language-as-fixed-effect fallacy: A critique of language statistics in psychological research. *Journal of Verbal Learning and Verbal Behavior, 12,* 335–359.

Clark, K. B., & Clark, M. K. (1939). The development of consciousness of self in the emergence of racial identification in Negro pre-school children. *Journal of Social Psychology, 10,* 591–599.

Cochran, W. G. (1954). Some methods of strengthening the common chi-square test. *Biometrics, 10,* 417–451.

Cochran, W. G., & Cox, G. M. (1957). *Experimental designs* (2nd ed.). New York: Wiley.

Cochrane, A. I., St. Leger, A. S., & Moore, F. (1978). Health service "input" and mortality "output" in developed countries. *Journal of Epidemiology and Community Health, 32,* 200–205.

Cohen, J. (1960). A coefficient of agreement for nominal scales. *Educational and Psychological Measurement, 20,* 37–46.

Cohen, J. (1962). The statistical power of abnormal-social psychological research: A review. *Journal of Abnormal and Social Psychology, 65,* 145–153.

Cohen, J. (1965). Some statistical issues in psychological research. In B. B. Wolman (Ed.), *Handbook of clinical psychology.* New York: McGraw-Hill.

Cohen, J. (1968). Multiple regression as a general data-analytic system. *Psychological Bulletin, 70,* 426–443.

Cohen, J. (1969). *Statistical power analysis for the behavioral sciences* (1st ed.). Hillsdale, NJ: Erlbaum.

Cohen, J. (1973). Eta-squared and partial eta-squared in fixed factor ANOVA designs. *Educational and Psychological Measurement, 33,* 107–112.

Cohen, J. (1988). *Statistical power analysis for the behavioral sciences* (2nd ed.). New York: Academic Press.

Cohen, J. (1992a). A power primer. *Psychological Bulletin, 112,* 155–159.

Cohen, J. (1992b). Statistical power analysis. *Current Directions in Psychological Science, 1,* 98–101.

Cohen, J., & Cohen, P. (1983). *Applied multiple regression/correlation analysis for the behavioral sciences.* Hillsdale, NJ: Erlbaum.

Cohen, J., Cohen, P., West, S. G., & Aiken, L. S. (2003). *Applied multiple regression/correlation analysis for the behavioral sciences* (3rd ed.). Mahwah, N.J.: Lawrence Erlbaum Associates.

Cohen, S., Kaplan, J. R., Cunnick, J. E., Manuck, S. B., & Rabin, B. S. (1992). Chronic social stress, affiliation, and cellular immune response in nonhuman primates. *Psychological Science, 3,* 301–304.

Collier, R. O., Jr., Baker, F. B., & Mandeville, G. K. (1967). Tests of hypotheses in a repeated measures design from a permutation viewpoint. *Psychometrika, 32,* 15–24.

Collier, R. O., Jr., Baker, F. B., Mandeville, G. K., & Hayes, T. F. (1967). Estimates of test size for several test procedures based on conventional variance ratios in the repeated measures design. *Psychometrika, 32,* 339–353.

Compas, B. E., Howell, D. C., Phares, V., Williams, R. A., & Giunta, C. (1989). Risk factors for emotional/behavioral problems in young adolescents: A prospective analysis of adolescent and parental stress symptoms. *Journal of Consulting and Clinical Psychology, 57,* 732–740.

Compas, B. E., Worsham, N. S., Grant, K., Mireault, G., Howell, D. C., & Malcarne, V. L. (1994). When mom or dad has cancer: I. Symptoms of depression and anxiety in cancer patients, spouses, and children. *Health Psychology, 13,* 507–515.

Conti, L., & Musty, R. E. (1984). The effects of delta-9tetrahydrocannabinol injections to the nucleus accumbens on the locomotor activity of rats. In S. Aquell et al. (Eds.), *The cannabinoids: Chemical, pharmacologic, and therapeutic Aspects.* New York: Academic Press.

Cooley, W. W., & Lohnes, P. R. (1971). *Multivariate data analysis.* New York: Wiley.

Cooper, H. (2009). *Research synthesis and meta-analysis* (4th ed.). Los Angeles, Sage.

Cooper, H. M., Hedges, L. V., & Valentine J. (Eds.). (2009). *The Handbook of Research Synthesis and Meta-Analysis, 2nd Edition.* New York: The Russell Sage Foundation.

Cortina, J. M., & Nouri, H. (2000). *Effect size for ANOVA designs.* Thousand Oaks, CA: Sage.

Craik, F. I. M., & Lockhart, R. S. (1972). Levels of processing: A framework for memory research, *Journal of Verbal Learning and Verbal Behavior, 11,* 671–684.

Cramer, E. M., & Appelbaum, M. I. (1980). Nonorthogonal analysis of variance—Once again. *Psychological Bulletin, 87,* 51–57.

Cramér, H. (1946). *Mathematical methods of statistics.* Princeton, NJ: Princeton University Press.

Crawford, J. R., Garthwaite, P. H., & Howell, D. C. (2009). On comparing a single case with a control sample: An alternative perspective. *Neuropsychologica, 47,* 2690–2695.

Crawford, J. R., Garthwaite, P. H., Howell, D. C., & Venneri, A. (2003). Intra–individual measures of association in neuropsychology: Inferential methods for comparing a single case with a control or normative sample. *Journal of the International Neuropsychological Society, 9*, 989–1000.

Crawford, J. R., & Howell, D. C. (1998). Comparing an individual's test score against norms derived from small samples. *The Clinical Neuropsychologist, 12,* 482–486.

Crawley, M. J. (2007). *The R book.* Chichester, England: Wiley.

Cumming, G. (2008). Replication and *p* intervals. *Perspectives on Psychological Science,* 3, 286–300.

Cumming, G., & Finch, S. (2001). A primer on the understanding, use, and calculation of confidence intervals that are based on central and noncentral distributions. *Educational and Psychological Measurement, 61*, 532–574.

Czitrom, V. (1999). One-factor-at-a-time versus designed experiments, *American Statistician, 53*, 126–131.

Dabbs, J. M., Jr., & Morris, R. (1990). Testosterone, social class, and antisocial behavior in a sample of 4462 men. *Psychological Science, 1*, 209–211.

D'Agostino, R. B., & Stephens, M. A. (1986). *Goodness-of-fit techniques.* New York: Marcel Dekker.

Darley, J. M., & Latané B. (1968). Bystander intervention in emergencies: Diffusion of responsibility. *Journal of Personality and Social Psychology, 8*, 377–383.

Darlington, R. B. (1968). Multiple regression in psychological research and practice. *Psychological Bulletin, 69*, 161–182.

Darlington, R. B. (1990). *Regression and linear models.* New York: McGraw-Hill.

Davey, G. C. L., Startup, H. M., Zara, A., MacDonald, C. B., & Field, A. P. (2003). The perseveration of checking thoughts and mood-as-input hypothesis. *Journal of Behavior Therapy & Experimental Psychiatry, 34*, 141–160.

Dawes, R. M., & Corrigan, B. (1974). Linear models in decision making. *Psychological Bulletin, 81*, 95–106.

Delucchi, K. L. (1983). The use and misuse of chi-square: Lewis and Burke revisited. *Psychological Bulletin, 94*, 166–176.

Derogatis, L. R. (1983). *SCL90-R: Administration, scoring, and procedures manual* (vol. 1.). Towson, MD: Clinical Psychometric Research.

Dodd, D. H., & Schultz, R. F., Jr. (1973). Computational procedures for estimating magnitude of effect for some analysis of variance designs. *Psychological Bulletin, 79*, 391–395.

Doob, A. N., & Gross, A. E. (1968). Status of frustrator as an inhibitor of horn-honking responses. *Journal of Social Psychology, 76*, 213–218.

Dracup, C. (2005). Confidence intervals. In B. S. Everitt & D. C. Howell (Eds,), *Encyclopedia of statistics in behavioral sciences.* Chichester, England: Wiley.

Draper, N. R., & Smith, H. (1981). *Applied regression analysis* (2nd ed.). New York: Wiley.

Dunlap, G., & Fox, L. (1999). A demonstration of *behavioral support* for young children with *autism. Journal of Positive Behavioral Intervention, 1*, 77–87.

Dunn, O. J. (1961). Multiple comparisons among means. *Journal of the American Statistical Association, 56*, 52–64.

Dunnett, C. W. (1955). A multiple comparison procedure for comparing several treatments with a control. *Journal of the American Statistical Association, 50*, 1096–1121.

Dunnett, C. W. (1964). New tables for multiple comparisons with a control. *Biometrics, 20*, 482–491.

Dunning, T., & Freedman, D. A. (2008). Modeling selection effects. In W. Outhwaite & S. P. Turner (Eds.), *The Sage handbook of social science methodology* (pp 225–231). London, Sage.

Eckelberry, E. (2009). *Using social stories with children with autism, learning disabilities, and ADHA.* Unpublished Master's Thesis. Ohio University.

Edgington, E. S. (1995). *Randomization tests.* New York: Marcel Dekker.

Edwards, A. L. (1985). *Experimental design in psychological research* (5th ed.). New York: Harper & Row.

Efron, B., & Tibshirani, R. (1993). *An Introduction to the bootstrap.* New York: Chapman and Hall.

Einot, I., & Gabriel, K. R. (1975). A study of the powers of several methods of multiple comparisons. *Journal of the American Statistical Association, 70*, 574–583.

Epping-Jordan, J. E., Compas, B. E., & Howell, D. C. (1994). Predictors of cancer progression in young adult men and women: Avoidance, intrusive thoughts, and psychological symptoms. *Health Psychology, 13*, 539–547.

Evans, S. H., & Anastasio, E. J. (1968). Misuse of analysis of covariance when treatment effect and covariate are confounded. Ps*ychological Bulletin, 69*, 225–234.

Everitt, B. (1994). Cited in Hand et al. (1994), p. 229.

Everitt, B. S. (2005). *An R and S-PLUS companion to multivariate analysis.* London: Springer-Verlag

Everitt, B., & Hothorn, T. (2006). *A handbook of statistical analyses using R.* London: Chapman & Hall/CRC.

Eysenck, M. W. (1974). Age differences in incidental learning. *Developmental Psychology, 10*, 936–941.

Faul, F., Erdfelder, E., Lang, A. -G., & Buchner, A. (2007). G*Power 3: A flexible statistical power analysis program for the social, behavioral, and biomedical sciences. *Behavior Research Methods, 39*, 175–191.

Federer, W. T. (1955). *Experimental design: Theory and application.* New York: Macmillan.

Feinberg, M., & Willer, R. (2011). Apocalypse soon? Dire messages reduce belief in global warming by contradicting just-world beliefs. *Psychological Science, 22,* 34–38.

Fidalgo, A. M. (2005). Mantel-Haenszel methods. In B. S. Everitt & D. C. Howell (Eds.), *Encyclopedia of statistics in behavioral science.* Chichester, England: Wiley.

Finney, J. W., Mitchell, R. E., Cronkite, R. C., & Moos, R. H. (1984). Methodological issues in estimating main and interactive effects: Examples from coping/social support and stress field. *Journal of Health and Social Behavior, 25*, 85–98.

Fisher, R. A. (1921). On the probable error of a coefficient of correlation deduced from a small sample. *Metron, 1,* 3–32.

Fisher, R. A. (1935). *The design of experiments.* Edinburgh: Oliver & Boyd.

Fisher, R. A., & Yates, F. (1953). *Statistical tables for biological, agricultural, and medical research* (4th ed.). Edinburgh: Oliver & Boyd.

Fleiss, J. L. (1969). Estimating the magnitude of experimental effects. *Psychological Bulletin, 72,* 273–276.

Fleiss, J. L., Nee, J. C. M., & Landis, J. R. (1979). Large sample variance of kappa in the case of different sets of raters. *Psychological Bulletin, 86,* 974–977.

Foa, E. B., Rothbaum, B. O., Riggs, D. S., & Murdock, T. B. (1991). Treatment of posttraumatic stress disorder in rape victims: A comparison between cognitive-behavioral procedures and counseling. *Journal of Consulting and Clinical Psychology, 59,* 715–723.

Fowler, R. L. (1985). Point estimates and confidence intervals in measures of association. *Psychological Bulletin, 98,* 160–165.

Fox, J. (2002). *An R and S-PLUS companion to applied regression.* Thousand Oaks, CA: Sage Publications.

Franklin, R. D., Allison, D. B., & Gorman, B. S. (Eds.). (1996). *Design and analysis of single-case Research.* Mahwah, NJ: Lawrence Erlbaum.

Frigge, M., Hoaglin, D. C., & Iglewicz B. (1989). Some implementations of the boxplot. *American Statistician, 43,* 50–54.

Galton, F. (1886). Regression towards mediocrity in hereditary stature. *Journal of the Anthropological Institute, 15,* 246–263.

Games, P. A. (1978a). A three-factor model encompassing many possible statistical tests on independent groups. *Psychological Bulletin, 85,* 168–182.

Games, P. A. (1978b). A four-factor structure for parametric tests on independent groups. *Psychological Bulletin, 85,* 661–672.

Games, P. A., & Howell, J. F. (1976). Pairwise multiple comparison procedures with unequal *n's* and/or variances: A Monte Carlo study. *Journal of Educational Statistics, 1,* 113–125.

Games, P. A., Keselman, H. J., & Rogan, J. C. (1981). Simultaneous pairwise multiple comparison procedures for means when sample sizes are unequal. *Psychological Bulletin, 90,* 594–598.

Garland, C. F., Garland, F. C., Gorham, E. D., Lipkin, M., Newmark, H., Mohr, S. B., & Holick, M. F. (2006). The role of vitamin D in cancer prevention. *American Journal of Public Health, 96,* 252–261.

Gartrell, N., & Bos, H. (2010). U.S. National Longitudinal Lesbian Family Study: Psychological adjustment of 17-year-old adolescents. *Pediatrics, 126,* 28–36.

Geffen, G., Moar, K. J., O'Hanlon, A. P., Clark, C. R., & Geffen, L. B. (1990). Performance measure of 16- to 86-year-old males and females on the Auditory Verbal Learning Test. *The Clinical Neuropsychologist, 4,* 45–63.

Geller, E. S., Witmer, J. F., & Orebaugh, A. L. (1976). Instructions as a determinant of paper disposal behaviors. *Environment and Behavior, 8,* 417–439.

Geyer, C. J. (1991). Constrained maximum likelihood exemplified by isotonic convex logistic regression. *Journal of the American Statistical Association, 86,* 717–724.

Giancola, P. R., & Corman, M. D. (2007). Alcohol and aggression: A test of the attention-allocation model. *Psychological Science, 18,* 649–655.

Gibson, L., & Leitenberg, H. (2000). Child sexual abuse prevention programs: Do they decrease the occurrence of child sexual abuse? *Child Abuse & Neglect, 24,* 1115–1125.

Gigerenzer, G., Swijtink, Z., Porter, T., Daston, L., Beatty, J., & Krüger, L. (1989). *The empire of chance.* Cambridge: Cambridge University Press.

Glass, G. V. (1976). Primary, secondary, and meta-analysis of research. *Educational Researcher, 5,* 3–8.

Glass, G. V., McGraw, B., & Smith, M. L. (1981). *Meta-analysis in social research.* Beverly Hills: Sage Publications.

Gleser, L. J., & Olkin, I. (2009). Stochastically dependent effect sizes. In H. Cooper, L. V. Hedges, & J. C. Valentine (Eds.), *The handbook of research synthesis and meta-analysis.* New York: Russell Sage Foundation.

Goldberg, L. R. (1965). Diagnosticians versus diagnostic signs: The diagnosis of psychosis versus neurosis from the MMPI. *Psychological Monographs, 79* (9, Whole No. 602).

Goldstein, R. (1989). Power and sample size via MS/PC-DOS computers. *American Statistician, 43,* 253–260.

Good, P. I. (1999). Resampling methods: A practical guide to data analysis. Boston: Birkhäuser.

Good, P. (2000). *Permutation tests: A practical guide to resampling methods for testing hypotheses* (2nd ed.). New York: Springer-Verlag.

Gouzoulis-Mayfrank, E., Daumann, J., Tuchtenhagen, F., Pelz, S., Becker, S., Kunert, H. -J., Fimm, B., & Sasa, H. (2000). Impaired cognitive performance in drug free users of recreational ecstasy (MDMA). *Journal of Neurology, Neurosurgery, and Psychiatry, 68,* 719–725.

Green, J. A. (1988). Loglinear analysis of cross-classified ordinal data: Applications in developmental research. *Child Development, 59,* 1–25.

Green, S. B., Marquis, J. G., Hershberger, S. L., Thompson, M. S., & McCollam, K. M. (1999). The overparameterized analysis of variance model. *Psychological Methods, 4,* 214–233.

Greenhouse, S. W., & Geisser, S. (1959). On methods in the analysis of profile data. *Psychometrika, 24,* 95–112.

Grissom, R. J. (2000). Heterogeneity of variance in clinical data. *Journal of Consulting and Clinical Psychology, 68,* 155–165.

Gross, J. S. (1985). Weight modification and eating disorders in adolescent boys and girls. Unpublished doctoral dissertation, University of Vermont.

Guber, D. L. (1999) Getting what you pay for: The debate over equity in public school expenditures. *Journal of Statistics Education, 7*, No. 2.

Hand, D. J., Daly, F., Lunn, A. D., McConway, K. J., & Ostrowski, E. (1994). *Handbook of small data sets.* London: Chapman & Hall.

Hansen, J. C., & Swanson, J. L. (1983). Stability of interests and the predictive and concurrent validity of the 1981 Strong-Campbell Interest Inventory for college majors. *Journal of Counseling Psychology, 30*, 194–201.

Harris, C. W. (Ed.). (1963). *Problems in measuring change.* Madison, WI: University of Wisconsin Press.

Harris, R. J. (1985). *A primer of multivariate statistics* (2nd ed.). New York: Academic Press.

Harris, R. J. (2005) Classical statistical inference: Practice versus presentation. In B. E. Everitt & D. C. Howell (Eds.), *Encyclopedia of Statistics in Behavioral Science* (pp. 268–278). London: Wiley.

Harter, H. L. (1960). Tables of range and Studentized range. *Annals of Mathematical Statistics, 31*, 1122–1147.

Hays, W. L. (1981). *Statistics* (3rd ed.). New York: Holt, Rinehart & Winston.

Hays, W. L. (1994). *Statistics* (5th ed.). New York: Harcourt, Brace.

Hayes, A. F., & Cai, L. (2007). Further evaluating the conditional decision rule for comparing two independent means. *British Journal of Mathematical and Statistical Psychology, 60*, 217–244.

Hector, A., von Felten, S., & Schmid, B. (2010). Analysis of variance with unbalanced data: An update for ecology and evolution. *Journal of Animal Ecology, 9*, 308–316.

Hedges, L. V. (1981). Distribution theory for Glass's estimator of effect size and related estimators. *Journal of Educational Statistics, 6*, 107–128.

Hedges, L. V. (1982). Estimation of effect size from a series of independent experiments. *Psychological Bulletin, 92*, 490–499.

Hedges, L. V. (2009). Statistical considerations. In H. Cooper, L. V. Hedges, & J. C. Valentine (Eds.), *The handbook of research synthesis and meta-analysis.* New York: Russell Sage Foundation.

Hedges, L. V., & Olkin, I. (1985) *Statistical methods for meta-analysis* Orlando: Academic Press.

Henderson, D. A., & Denison, D. R. (1989). Stepwise regression in social and psychological research. *Psychological Reports, 64*, 251–257.

Hindley, C. B., Filliozat, A. M., Klackenberg, G., Nicolet-Meister, D., & Sand, E. A. (1966). Differences in age of walking for five European longitudinal samples. *Human Biology, 38*, 364–379.

Hoaglin, D. C., Mosteller, F., & Tukey, J. W. (1983). *Understanding robust and exploratory data analysis.* New York: Wiley.

Hochberg, Y., & Tamhane, A. C. (1987). *Multiple comparison procedures.* New York: Wiley.

Hoenig, J. M., & Heisey, D. M. (2001). The abuse of power: The pervasive fallacy of power calculations for data analysis. *American Statistician, 55*, 19–24.

Holm, S. (1979). A simple sequentially rejective multiple test procedure. *Scandinavian Journal of Statistics, 6*, 65–70.

Holmes, T. H., & Rahe, R. H. (1967). The social readjustment rating scale. *Journal of Psychosomatic Research, 11*, 213.

Holway, A. H., & Boring, E. G. (1940). The moon illusion and the angle of regard. *American Journal of Psychology, 53*, 509–516.

Horowitz, J., & Garber, J. (2006). The prevention of depressive symptoms in children and adolescents: A meta-analytic review. *Journal of Consulting and Clinical Psychology, 74*, 401–415.

Horowitz, M. J., Wilner, N., & Alvarez, W. (1979). Impact of event scale: A measure of subjective stress. *Psychosomatic Medicine, 41*, 209–218.

Hosmer, D. W., & Lemeshow, S. (1989). *Applied logistic regression.* New York: Wiley.

Hotelling, H. (1931). The generalization of Student's ratio. *Annals of Mathematical Statistics, 2*, 360–378.

Hout, M., Duncan, O. D., & Sobel, M. E. (1987). Association and heterogeneity: Structural models of similarities and differences. In C. C. Clegg (Ed.), *Sociological methodology, 17*, 145ff.

Howard, B. L., & Kendall, P. C. (1996). Cognitive-behavioral family therapy for anxiety-disordered children: A multiple-baseline evaluation. *Cognitive Therapy and Research, 5*, 423–443.

Howell, D. C. (1987). *Statistical methods for psychology* (2nd ed.). Boston: PWS-KENT.

Howell, D. C. (1997). *Statistical methods for psychology* (4th ed.). Pacific Grove, CA: Duxbury.

Howell, D. C. (2007). *Statistical methods for psychology* (6th ed.). Belmont, CA: Wadsworth Cengage Learning.

Howell, D. C. (2008a). *Fundamental statistics for the behavioral sciences* (6th ed.). Pacific Grove, CA: Duxbury.

Howell, D. C. (2008b). The treatment of missing data, Chapter 1. In W. Outhwaite & S. P. Turner (Eds.), *The Sage handbook of social science methodology* (pp. 208–224). London: Sage.

Howell, D. C. (2008c). Best practices in the analysis of variance. In J. Osborne (Ed.), *Best practices in quantitative methods* (pp. 341–357). Thousand Oaks, CA: Sage.

Howell, D. C. (2010). Scheffé test. In N. J. Salkind, D. M. Dougherty, & B. Frey (Eds.), *Encyclopedia of research design.* Thousand Oaks, CA: Sage.

Howell, D. C., & Gordon, L. R. (1976). Computing the exact probability of an R by C contingency table with fixed marginal totals. *Behavior Research Methods and Instrumentation, 8*, 317.

Howell, D. C., & Huessy, H. R. (1981). Hyperkinetic behavior followed from 7 to 21 years of age. In M. Gittelman (Ed.), *Intervention strategies with hyperactive children* (pp. 201–214). White Plains, NY: M. E. Sharpe.

Howell, D. C., & Huessy, H. R. (1985). A fifteen-year follow-up of a behavioral history of Attention Deficit Disorder (ADD). *Pediatrics, 76,* 185–190.

Howell, D. C., & McConaughy, S. H. (1982). Nonorthogonal analysis of variance: Putting the question before the answer. *Educational and Psychological Measurement, 42,* 9–24.

Hraba, J., & Grant, G. (1970). Black is beautiful: A reexamination of racial preference and identification. *Journal of Personality and Social Psychology, 16,* 398–402.

Huberty, C. J. (1989). Problems with stepwise methods—better alternatives. In B. Thompson (Ed.), *Advances in social science methodology* (Vol. 1) (pp. 43–70). Greenwich, CT: JAI Press.

Huesmann, L. R., Moise-Titus, J., Podolski, C., & Eron, L. D. (2003). Longitudinal relations between children's exposure to TV violence and their aggressive and violent behavior in young adulthood: 1977–1992. *Developmental Psychology, 39,* 201–221.

Huitema, B. E. (1980). *The analysis of covariance and alternatives.* New York: Wiley.

Huitema, B. E. (in press). *The analysis of covariance and alternatives* (2nd ed.). New York: Wiley.

Huitema, B. E. (2005). Analysis of covariance. In B. S. Everitt & D. C. Howell (Eds.), *Encyclopedia of Statistics in Behavioral Sciences.* Chichester, England: Wiley.

Huitema, B. E., & McKean, J. W. (1991). Autocorrelation estimation and inference with small samples. *Psychological Bulletin, 110,* 291–304.

Huitema, B. E., & McKean, J. W. (1998). Irrelevant autocorrelation in least-squares intervention models. *Psychological Bulletin, 3,* 104–116.

Huitema, B. E., & McKean, J. W. (2000). Design specification issues in time-series intervention models. *Educational and Psychological Measurement, 60,* 38–58.

Hunter, J. E. (1997). Needed: a ban on the significance test. *Psychological Science, 8,* 3–7.

Huynh, H., & Feldt, L. S. (1970). Conditions under which mean square ratios in repeated measurement designs have exact *F* distributions. *Journal of the American Statistical Association, 65,* 1582–1589.

Huynh, H., & Feldt, L. S. (1976). Estimation of the Box correction for degrees of freedom from sample data in the randomized block and split plot designs. *Journal of Educational Statistics, 1,* 69–82.

Huynh, H., & Mandeville, G. K. (1979). Validity conditions in repeated measures designs. *Psychological Bulletin, 86,* 964–973.

Introini-Collison, I., & McGaugh, J. L. (1986). Epinephrine modulates long-term retention of an aversively-motivated discrimination task. *Behavioral and Neural Biology, 45,* 358–365.

Jaccard, J., Turrisi, R., & Wan, C. K. (1990). *Interaction effects in multiple regression.* Newbury Park, CA: Sage.

Jankowski, M. K., Leitenberg, H., Henning, K., & Coffey, P. (2002). Parental caring as a possible buffer against sexual revictimization in young adult survivors of child sexual abuse. *Journal of Traumatic Stress, 15,* 235–244.

Jones, L.V., & Tukey, J. W. (2000). A sensible formulation of the significance test. *Psychological Methods, 5,* 411–414.

Judd, C. M., & McClelland, G. H. (1989). *Data analysis: a model comparison approach.* San Diego, CA: Harcourt Brace Jovanovich.

Judd, C. M., McClelland, G. H., & Culhane, S. E. (1995). Data analysis: Continuing issues in the everyday analysis of psychological data. *Annual Review of Psychology, 46,* 433–455.

Kapoor, P., Rajkumar, S. V., Dispenzieri, A., Gertz, M. A., Lacy, M. Q., Dingli, D., Mikhael, J. R., Roy, V., Kyle, R. A., Greipp, P. R., Kumar, S., & Mandrekar, S. (2011). Melphalan and prednisone versus melphalan, prednisone and thalidomide for elderly and/or transplant ineligible patients with multiple myeloma: a meta-analysis. *Leukemia 25(4),* 689–696.

Kapp, B., Frysinger, R., Gallagher, M., & Hazelton, J. (1979). Amygdala central nucleus lesions: Effects on heart rate conditioning in the rabbit. *Physiology and Behavior, 23,* 1109–1117.

Katz, S., Lautenschlager, G. J., Blackburn, A. B., & Harris, F. H. (1990). Answering reading comprehension items without passages on the SAT. *Psychological Science, 1,* 122–127.

Kaufman, L., & Rock, I. (1962). The moon illusion, I. *Science, 136,* 953–961.

Kaufman, L., & Kaufman, J. (2000). Explaining the Moon illusion. *Proceedings of the National Academy of Sciences, 97,* 500–504.

Keen, K. J. (2010). *Graphics for Statistics and Data Analysis with R.* New York: Chapman and Hall.

Kelley, K. (2008). Methods for the behavioral, educational, and social sciences: An R package. *Behavioral Research Methods, 39,* 979–984.

Kendall, M. G. (1948). *Rank correlation methods.* London: Griffin.

Kennedy, J. J. (1983). *Analyzing qualitative data: Introductory loglinear analysis for behavioral research.* New York: Praeger.

Kenny, D. A., & Judd, C. M. (1986). Consequences of violating the independence assumption in analysis of variance. *Psychological Bulletin, 99,* 422–431.

Keppel, G. (1973). *Design and analysis: A researcher's handbook.* Englewood Cliffs, NJ: Prentice-Hall.

Keselman, H. J., Cribbie, R., & Holland, B. (1999). The pairwise multiple comparison multiplicity problem: An alternative approach to familywise and comparisonwise Type I error control. *Psychological Methods, 4,* 58–69.

Keselman, H. J., Games, P. A., & Rogan, J. C. (1979). Protecting the overall rate of Type I errors of pairwise comparisons with an omnibus test statistic. *Psychological Bulletin, 86,* 884–888.

Keselman, H. J., Holland, B., & Cribbie, R. A. (2005). Multiple comparison procedures. In Everitt, B. S. and Howell, D. C. *Encyclopedia of Statistics in Behavioral Sciences.* Chichester, England: Wiley.

Keselman, H. J., & Keselman, J. C. (1988). Repeated measures multiple comparison procedures: Effects of violating multisample sphericity in unbalanced designs. *Journal of Educational Statistics, 13*, 215–226.

Keselman, H. J., & Rogan, J. C. (1977). The Tukey multiple comparison test: 1953–1976. *Psychological Bulletin, 84*, 1050–1056.

Keselman, H. J., Rogan, J. C., Mendoza, J. L., & Breen, L. J. (1980). Testing the validity conditions of repeated measures *F* tests. *Psychological Bulletin, 87*, 479–481.

King, D. A. (1986). Associative control of tolerance to the sedative effects of a short-acting benzodiazepine. Unpublished doctoral dissertation, University of Vermont.

Kirk, R. E. (1968). *Experimental design: Procedures for the behavioral sciences.* Belmont, CA: Brooks/Cole.

Kleinbaum, D. G., & Klein, M. (2002). *Logistic Regression: A self-learning text.* New York: Springer.

Klemchuk, H. P., Bond, L. A., & Howell, D. C. (1990). Coherence and correlates of level 1 perspective taking in young children. *Merrill-Palmer Quarterly, 36*, 369–387.

Kline, R. B. (2004). *Beyond significance testing.* Washington, D. C.: American Psychological Association.

Koele, P. (1982). Calculating power in analysis of variance. *Psychological Bulletin, 92*, 513–516.

Kohr, R. L., & Games, P. A. (1974). Robustness of the analysis of variance, the Welch procedure, and a Box procedure to heterogeneous variances. *The Journal of Experimental Education, 43*, 61–69.

Kruger, J., & Dunning, D. (1999). Unskilled and Unaware of it: How difficulties in recognizing one's own incompetence lead to inflated self-assessments. *Journal of Personality and Social Psychology, 77*, 1121–1134.

Landwehr, J. M., & Watkins, A. E. (1987). *Exploring data.* Palo Alto, CA: Dale Seymour Publications.

Lane, D. M., & Dunlap, W. P. (1978). Estimating effect size: Bias resulting from the significance criterion in editorial decisions. *British Journal of Mathematical and Statistical Psychology, 31*, 107–112.

Langlois, J. H., & Roggman, L. A. (1990). Attractive faces are only average. *Psychological Science, 1*, 115–121.

Lappe, J. M., Davies, K. M., Travers-Gustafson, D., & Heaney, R. P. (2006). Vitamin D status in a rural postmenopausal female population. *Journal of the American College of Nutrition, 25*, 395–402.

Larzelere, R. E., & Mulaik, S. A. (1977). Single-sample tests for many correlations. *Psychological Bulletin, 84*, 557–569.

Latané, B., & Dabbs, J. M., Jr. (1975). Sex, group size, and helping in three cities. *Sociometry, 38*, 180–194.

Lecoutre, B. (1991). A correction for the $\tilde{\varepsilon}$ approximate test in repeated measures designs with two or more independent groups. *Journal of Educational Statistics, 16*, 371–372.

Leerkes, E., & Crockenberg, S. (1999). The development of maternal self-efficacy and its impact on maternal behavior. Poster presentation at the Biennial Meetings of the Society for Research in Child Development, Albuquerque, NM, April.

Lehman, E. L. (1993). The Fisher, Neyman-Pearson theories of testing hypotheses: One theory or two? *Journal of the American Statistical Association, 88*, 1242–1249.

Lenth, R. V. (2001) Some practical guidelines for effective sample size determination. *American Statistician, 55*, 187–193.

Levene, H. (1960). Robust tests for the equality of variance. In I. Olkin (Ed.), *Contributions to probability and statistics.* Palo Alto, CA: Stanford University Press.

Levine, R. (1990). The pace of life and coronary heart disease. *American Scientist, 78*, 450–459.

Lewis, C., & Keren, G. (1977). You can't have your cake and eat it too: Some considerations of the error term. *Psychological Bulletin, 84*, 1150–1154.

Lewis, D., & Burke, C. J. (1949). The use and misuse of the chi square test. *Psychological Bulletin, 46*, 433–489.

Little, R. J. A., & Rubin, D. B. (1987). *Statistical analysis with missing data.* New York, Wiley.

Lock, J., Le Grange, D., Agras, S., Moye, A., Bryson, S., & Jo, B. (2010). Randomized clinical trial comparing family-based treatment with adolescent-focused individual therapy for adolescents with anorexia nervosa. *Archives of General Psychiatry, 67*, 1025–1032.

Lord, F. M. (1953). On the statistical treatment of football numbers. *American Psychologist, 8*, 750–751.

Lord, F. M. (1967). A paradox in the interpretation of group comparisons. *Psychological Bulletin, 68*, 304–305.

Lord, F. M. (1969). Statistical adjustments when comparing preexisting groups. *Psychological Bulletin, 72*, 336–337.

Lunneborg, C. E. (1994). *Modeling experimental and observational data.* Belmont, CA: Duxbury.

Lunneborg, C. E. (2000). *Data analysis by resampling: Concepts and applications.* Pacific Grove, CA: Duxbury.

MacKinnon, D. P., Lockwood, C. M., Hoffman, J. M., West, S. G., & Sheets, V. (2002). A comparison of methods to test mediation and other intervening variable effects. *Psychological Methods, 7*, 83–104.

Macnaughton, D. B. (1998). Which sums of squares are best in unbalanced analysis of variance. Unpublished paper available at http://www.matstat.com/ss/.

Maimaris, C., Summer, C. L., Browning, C., & Palmer, C. R. (1994). Injury patterns in cyclists attending an accident and emergency department: A comparison of helmet wearers and non-wearers. *British Medical Journal, 308*, 1537–1540.

Maindonald, J., & Braun, J. (2007). *Data analysis and graphics using R: An example-based approach* (2nd ed.). Cambridge, England: Cambridge University Press.

Malcarne, V. L., Compas, B. E., Epping-Jordan, J. E., & Howell, D. C. (1995). Cognitive factors in adjustment to cancer: Attributions of self-blame and perceptions of control. *Journal of Behavioral Medicine, 18*, 401–417.

Manly, B. F. J. (1997). *Randomization, Bootstrap, and Monte Carlo Methods in Biology* (2nd ed.). London: Chapman & Hall.

Mann-Jones, J. M., Ettinger, R. H., Baisden, J., & Baisden, K. (Unpublished). Dextromethorphan modulation of context-dependent morphine tolerance. Retrieved December 12, 2007 at www.eou.edu/psych/re/morphine-tolerance.doc.

Manning, C. A., Hall, J. L., & Gold, P. E. (1990). Glucose effects on memory and other neuropsychological tests in elderly humans. *Psychological Science, 1,* 307–311.

Manolov, R., & Solanas, A. (2008). Comparing $N = 1$ effect size indices in presence of autocorrelation. *Behavior Modification, 32,* 860–875.

Mantel, N., & Haenszel, W. (1959). Statistical aspects of the analysis of data from retrospective studies of disease. *Journal of the American Statistical Association, 22,* 719–748.

Marascuilo, L. A., & Busk, P. L. (1987) Log-linear models: A way to study main effects and interactions for multidimensional contingency tables with categorical data. *Journal of Counseling Psychology, 34,* 443–455.

Marascuilo, L. A., & Serlin, R. C. (1979). Tests and contrasts for comparing change parameters for a multiple sample McNemar data model. *British Journal of Mathematical and Statistical Psychology, 32,* 105–112.

Marascuilo, L. A., & Serlin, R. C. (1990). *Statistical methods for the social and behavioral sciences.* New York: Freeman.

Maris, E. (1998). Covariance adjustment versus gain scores—revisited. *Psychological Methods, 3,* 309–327.

Masson, M. E. J., & Loftus, G. R. (2003). Using confidence intervals for graphically based data interpretation. *Canadian Journal of Experimental Psychology, 57,* 203–220.

Mauchly, J. W. (1940). Significance test for sphericity of a normal n-variate distribution. *Annals of Mathematical Statistics, 11,* 204–209.

Maxwell, A. E. (1961). *Analyzing Quantitative Data.* London, Methuen.

Maxwell, S. E. (1980). Pairwise multiple comparisons in repeated measures designs. *Journal of Educational Statistics, 5,* 269–287.

Maxwell, S. E., & Cramer, E. M. (1975). A note on analysis of covariance. *Psychological Bulletin, 82,* 187–190.

Maxwell, S. E., & Delaney, H. D. (2004). *Designing experiments and analyzing data: A model comparison approach* (2nd ed.). Belmont, CA: Wadsworth.

Maxwell, S. E., Delaney, H. D., & Mannheimer, J. M. (1985). ANOVA of residuals and ANCOVA: Correcting an illusion by using model comparisons and graphs. *Journal of Educational Statistics, 10,* 197–209.

Mazzucchelli, T., Kane, R. T., & Rees, C. S. (2010). Behavioral activation interventions for well-being: A meta-analysis. *Journal of Positive Psychology, 5, 105–121.*

McClelland, G. H. (1997). Optimal design in psychological research. *Psychological Methods, 2,* 3–19.

McClelland, G. H., & Judd, C. M. (1993). Statistical difficulties of detecting interactions and moderator effects. *Psychological Bulletin, 114,* 376–390.

McConaughy, S. H. (1980). Cognitive structures for reading comprehension: Judging the relative importance of ideas in short stories. Unpublished doctoral dissertation, University of Vermont.

McGrath, R. E., & Meyer, G. J. (2006). When effect sizes disagree: The case of r and d. *Psychological Methods, 11,* 386–401.

McIntyre, S. H., Montgomery, D. B., Srinivasan, V., & Weitz, B. A. (1983). "Evaluating the statistical significance of models developed by stepwise regression," *Journal of Marketing Research, 20,* 1–11.

McNemar, Q. (1947). Note on the sampling error of the difference between correlated proportions or percentages. *Psychometrika, 12,* 153–157.

McNemar, Q. (1969). *Psychological statistics* (4th ed.). New York: Wiley.

Meijs, N., Cillessen, A. H. N., Scholte, R. H. J., Segers, E., & Spijkerman, R. (2010). Social intelligence and academic achievement as predictors of adolescent popularity. *Journal of Youth and Adolescence, 39,* 9373 –9379.

Miller, R. G., Jr. (1981). *Simultaneous statistical inference* (2nd ed.). New York: McGraw-Hill.

Mireault, G. C., & Bond, L. A. (1992). Parent death in childhood, perceived vulnerability, and adult depression and anxiety. *American Journal of Orthopsychiatry, 62,* 517–524.

Mood, A. M. (1950). *Introduction to the theory of statistics.* New York: McGraw-Hill.

Mood, A. M., & Graybill, F. A. (1963). *Introduction to the theory of statistics* (2nd ed.). New York: McGraw-Hill.

Mooney, C. Z., & Duval, R. D. (1993). *Bootstrapping: A nonparametric approach to statistical inference.* Newbury Park, CA: Sage.

Moore, D. S., & McCabe, G. P. (1989). *Introduction to the practice of statistics.* New York: Freeman.

Murphy, K. R., & Myors, B. (1998). *Statistical power analysis: A simple and general model for traditional and modern hypothesis tests.* Mahwah, NJ: Lawrence Erlbaum.

Myers, J. L. (1979). *Fundamentals of experimental design* (3rd ed.). Boston: Allyn & Bacon.

Neter, J., & Wasserman, W. (1974). *Applied linear statistical models.* Homewood, IL: Richard D. Irwin.

Neyman, J., & Pearson, E. S. (1933). On the problem of the most efficient tests of statistical hypotheses. *Philosophic Transactions of the Royal Society of London (Series A), 231,* 289–337.

Nickerson, R. S. (2000). Null hypothesis significance testing: A review of an old and continuing controversy. *Psychological Methods, 5,* 241–301.

Nie, N. H., Hull, C. H., Jenkins, J. G., Steinbrenner, K., & Bent, D. H. (1975). *SPSS: Statistical package for the social sciences* (2nd ed.). New York: McGraw-Hill.

Norton, D. W. (1953). Study reported in E. F. Lindquist, *Design and analysis of experiments in psychology and education.* New York: Houghton Mifflin.

Norusis, M. J. (1985). SPSS[X] *advanced statistics guide.* New York: McGraw-Hill.

Nurcombe, B., & Fitzhenry-Coor, I. (1979). Decision making in the mental health interview: I. An introduction to an education and research problem. Paper delivered at the Conference on Problem Solving in Medicine, Smuggler's Notch, Vermont.

Nurcombe, B., Howell, D. C., Rauh, V. A., Teti, D. M., Ruoff, P., & Brennan, J. (1984). An intervention program for mothers of low birthweight infants: Preliminary results. *Journal of the American Academy of Child Psychiatry, 23,* 319–325.

Oakes, M. (1990) *Statistical inference.* Chestnut Hill, MA: Epidemiology Resources, Inc.

O'Brien, R. G. (1976). Comment on "Some problems in the nonorthogonal analysis of variance." *Psychological Bulletin, 83,* 72–74.

O'Brien, R. G. (1981). A simple test for variance effects in experimental designs. *Psychological Bulletin, 89,* 570–574.

O'Grady, K. E. (1982). Measures of explained variation: Cautions and limitations. *Psychological Bulletin, 92,* 766–777.

Olejnik, S., & Algina, J. (2000). Measures of effect size for comparative studies: Applications, interpretations, and limitations. *Contemporary Educational Psychology, 25,* 241–286.

O'Neil, R., & Wetherill, G. B. (1971). The present state of multiple comparison methods. *Journal of the Royal Statistical Society (Series B), 33,* 218–250.

Osbourne, J. W. (2008). *Best practices in quantitative methods.* Thousand Oaks, CA: Sage.

Overall, J. E. (1972). Computers in behavioral science: Multiple covariance analysis by the general least squares regression method. *Behavioral Science, 17,* 313–320.

Overall, J. E. (1980). Power of chi-square tests for 2×2 contingency tables with small expected frequencies. *Psychological Bulletin, 87,* 132–135.

Overall, J. E., & Klett, C. J. (1972). *Applied multivariate analysis.* New York: McGraw-Hill.

Overall, J. E., & Shivakumar, C. (1999). Testing differences in response trends across a normalized time domain. *Journal of Clinical Psychology, 55,* 857–867.

Overall, J. E., & Spiegel, D. K. (1969). Concerning least squares analysis of experimental data. *Psychological Bulletin, 72,* 311–322.

Overall, J. E., Spiegel, D. K., & Cohen, J. (1975). Equivalence of orthogonal and nonorthogonal analysis of variance. *Psychological Bulletin, 82,* 182–186.

Overall, J. E., & Tonidandel, S. (2007). Analysis of data from a controlled repeated measurements design with baseline-dependent dropouts. *Methodology, 3,* 58–66.

Owens, C. M., Farmer, J. L., Ferron, J. M., & Allsopp, D. H. (2010). The correspondence among alternative approaches to summarizing effects in single-case studies. Paper presented conference of the American Educational Research Association, Denver, CO.

Ozer, D. J. (1985). Correlation and the coefficient of determination. *Psychological Bulletin, 97,* 307–315.

Pearson, K. (1900). On a criterion that a given system of deviations from the probable in the case of a correlated system of variables is such that it can reasonably be supposed to have arisen in random sampling. *Philosophical Magazine, 50,* 157–175.

Peterson, W. P. (2001). Topics for discussion from current newspapers and journals. *Journal of Statistics Education, 9* (pages not numbered).

Preacher, K. J., & Hayes, A. F. (2004). SPSS and SAS procedures for estimating indirect effects in simple mediation models. *Behavior Research Methods, Instruments, and Computers, 36,* 717–737.

Preacher, K. J., & Hayes, A. F. (2009). Asymptotic and resampling strategies for assessing and comparing indirect effects in multiple mediation models. *Behavior Research Methods, 40,* 871–891.

Preacher, K. J., & Leonardelli, G. J. (2001, March). Calculation for the Sobel test: An interactive calculation tool for mediation tests [Computer software]. Available from http://www.people.ku.edu/~preacher/sobel/sobel.htm.

Prentice, D. A., & Miller, D. T. (1992). When small effects are impressive. *Psychological Bulletin, 112,* 160–164.

Pugh, M. D. (1983). Contributory fault and rape convictions: Loglinear models for blaming the victim. *Social Psychology Quarterly, 46,* 233–242.

Raghunathan, T. E., Rosenthal, R., & Rubin, D. B. (1996). Comparing correlated but non-overlapping correlations, *Psychological Methods, 1,* 178–183.

Ramsey, F. L., & Schafer, D. W. (1997). *The statistical sleuth: A course in methods of data analysis.* Belmont, CA: Duxbury Press.

Rasmussen, J. L. (1987). Estimating correlation coefficients: Bootstrap and parametric approaches. *Psychological Bulletin, 101,* 136–139.

Reichardt, C. S. (1979). The statistical analysis of data from nonequivalent control group designs. In T. D. Cook & D. T. Campbell (Eds.), *Quasi-experimentation: Design and analysis issues for field settings* (pp. 147–205). Boston: Houghton Mifflin.

Reilly, T. P., Drudge, O. W., Rosen, J. C., Loew, D. E., & Fischer, M. (1985). Concurrent and predictive validity of the WISC-R, McCarthy Scales, Woodcock-Johnson, and academic achievement. *Psychology in the Schools, 22,* 380–382.

Reynolds, C. R., & Richmond, B. O. (1978). What I think and feel: A revised measure of children's manifest anxiety. *Journal of Abnormal Child Psychology, 6,* 271–280.

Robson, D. S. (1959). A simple method for constructing orthogonal polynomials when the independent variable is unequally spaced. *Biometrics, 15,* 187–191.

Rogers, R. W., & Prentice-Dunn, S. (1981). Deindividuation and anger-mediated aggression: Unmasking regressive racism. *Journal of Personality and Social Psychology, 41,* 63–73.

Rosa, L., Rosa, E., Sarner, L., & Barrett, S. (1998) A close look at Therapeutic Touch. *Journal of the American Medical Association, 279,* 1005–1010.

Rosenthal, R. (1994). Parametric measures of effect size. In H. Cooper & L. V. Hedges (Eds.), *The handbook of research synthesis.* New York: Russell Sage Foundation.

Rosenthal, R. (1979). The "file drawer problem" and tolerance for null results. *Psychologocal Bulletin, 86,* 638–641.

Rosenthal, R. (1990). How are we doing in soft psychology? Comment in *American Psychologist, 45,* 775–777.

Rosenthal, R., & Rubin, D. B. (1982). A simple, general purpose display of magnitude of experimental effect. *Journal of Educational Psychology, 74,* 166–169.

Rosenthal, R., & Rubin, D. B. (1984). Multiple contrasts and ordered Bonferroni procedures. *Journal of Educational Psychology, 76,* 1028–1034.

Rosnow, R. L., & Rosenthal, R. (1989). Definition and interpretation of interaction effects. *Psychological Bulletin, 105,* 143–146.

Rousseeuw, P. J., & Leroy, A. M. (1987). *Robust regression and outlier detection.* New York: Wiley.

Ruback, R. B., & Juieng, D. (1997). Territorial defense in parking lots: Retaliation against waiting drivers. *Journal of Applied Social Psychology, 27,* 821–834.

Ryan, B. F., Joiner, B. L., & Ryan, T. A. (1985). *Minitab handbook* (2nd ed.). Boston: Duxbury Press.

Ryan, T. A. (1959). Multiple comparisons in psychological research. *Psychological Bulletin, 56,* 26–47.

Ryan, T. A. (1960). Significance tests for multiple comparisons of proportions, variances, and other statistics. *Psychological Bulletin, 57,* 318–328.

Sackett, D. L., Deeks, J. J., & Altman, D. G. (1996). Down with odds ratios! *Evidence-Based Medicine, 1,* 164–166.

Saint-Exupery, A. de. (1943). *The little prince.* Tr. by K. Woods. New York: Harcourt Brace Jovanovich.

Satterthwaite, F. E. (1946). An approximate distribution of estimates of variance components. *Biometrics Bulletin, 2,* 110–114.

Sauerland, S., Lefering, R., Bayer-Sandow, T., & Neugebauer, F. A. M. (2003). Fingers, hands, or patients? The concept of independent observations. *The Journal of Hand Surgery: Journal of the British Society of Surgery of the Hand, 28,* 102–105.

Scheffé, H. A. (1953). A method for judging all possible contrasts in the analysis of variance. *Biometrika, 40,* 87–104.

Scheffé, H. A. (1959). *The analysis of variance.* New York: Wiley.

Sedlmeier, P., & Gigerenzer, G. (1989). Do studies of statistical power have an effect on the power of studies? *Psychological Bulletin, 105,* 309–316.

Seligman, M. E. P., Nolen-Hoeksema, S., Thornton, N., & Thornton, K. M. (1990). Explanatory style as a mechanism of disappointing athletic performance. *Psychological Science, 1,* 143–146.

Sgro, J. A., & Weinstock, S. (1963). Effects of delay on subsequent running under immediate reinforcement. *Journal of Experimental Psychology, 66,* 260–263.

Shrout, P. E., & Fleiss, J. L. (1979). Intraclass correlations: Uses in assessing rater reliability. *Psychological Bulletin, 86,* 420–428.

Sĭdák, Z. (1967). Rectangular confidence regions for the means of multivariate normal distributions. *Journal of the American Statistical Association, 62,* 623–633.

Siegel, S. (1975). Evidence from rats that morphine tolerance is a learned response. *Journal of Comparative and Physiological Psychology, 80,* 498–506.

Simon, J. L., & Bruce, P. *Resampling Stats.* Software available at http://www.resample.com.

Smith, H. F. (1957). Interpretation of adjusted treatment means and regression in analysis of covariance. *Biometrics, 13,* 282–308.

Smith, M. L., & Glass, G. V. (1977). Meta-analysis of psychotherapy outcome studies. *American Psychologist, 32,* 752–760.

Sobel, M. E. (1982). Asymptotic confidence intervals for indirect effects in structural equation models. In S. Leinhart (Ed.), *Sociological methodology* (pp. 290–312). San Francisco: Jossey-Bass.

Spilich, G. J., June, L., & Renner, J. (1992). Cigarette smoking and cognitive performance. *British Journal of Addiction 87,* 1313–1326.

St. Lawrence, J. S., Brasfield, T. L., Shirley, A., Jefferson, K. W., Alleyne, E., & O'Bannon, R. E. III. (1995). Cognitive-behavioral intervention to reduce African American adolescents' risk for HIV infection. *Journal of Consulting and Clinical Psychology, 63,* 221–237.

Stead, L. F., Perera, R., Bullen, C., Mant, D., & Lancaster, T. (2008). Nicotine replacement therapy for smoking cessation. *Cochrane Database of Systematic Reviews* 2008, Issue 1. Art. No.: CD000146. DOI: 10.1002/14651858.CD000146.pub3.

St. Leger, A. S., Cochrane, A. L., & Moore, F. (1978). The anomaly that wouldn't go away. *Lancet, ii,* 1153.

Steiger, J. H. (1980). Tests for comparing elements of a correlation matrix. *Psychological Bulletin, 87,* 245–251.

Steiger, J. H. (2004). Beyond the *F* test: Effect size confidence intervals and tests of close fit in the analysis of variance and contrast analysis. *Psychological Methods, 9,* 164–182.

Sterling, T. D. (1959). Publication decisions and their possible effects on inferences drawn from tests of significance or vice versa. *Journal of the American Statistical Association, 54,* 30–34.

Sternberg, S. (1966). High speed scanning in human memory. *Science, 153,* 652–654.

Stevens, J. (1992). *Applied multivariate statistics for the social sciences.* Hillsdale, NJ: Erlbaum.

Stevens, S. S. (1951). Mathematics, measurement, and psychophysics. In S. S. Stevens (Ed.), *Handbook of experimental psychology* (pp. 1–49). New York: Wiley.

Stigler, S. M. (1999). *Statistics on the table: A history of statistical concepts and methods.* Harvard University Press: Cambridge, MA.

Stone, W. S., Rudd, R. J., Ragozzino, M. E., & Gold, P. E. (1992). Glucose attenuation of deficits in memory retrieval in altered light/dark cycles. *Psychobiology, 20,* 47–50.

Strayer, D. L., Drews, F. A., & Crouch, D. J. (2006). A comparison of the cell phone driver and the drunk driver. *Human Factors, 48,* 381–391.

Stuetzle, W. (2005). Cross-validation. In B. S. Everitt & D. C. Howell, *Encyclopedia of statistics in behavioral sciences.* Chichester, England: Wiley.

Sullivan, C. M., & Bybee, D. I. (1999). Reducing violence using community-based advocacy for women with abusive partners. *Journal of Consulting and Clinical Psychology, 67,* 43–53.

Tabachnick, B. G., & Fidell, L. S. (2007). *Using multivariate statistics* (5th ed.). New York: Harper & Row.

Teri, L., Logdon, R. G., Uomoto, J., & McCurry, S. M. (1997). Behavioral treatment of depression in dementia patients: A controlled clinical trial. *Journals of Gerontology, 52B,* 159–166.

Thissen, D., Steinberg, L., & Kuang, D. (2002). Quick and easy implementation of the Benjamini-Hochberg procedure for controlling the false positive rate in multiple comparisons. *Journal of Educational and Behavioral Statistics, 27,* 77–83.

Thompson, B. (2000). A suggested revision to the forthcoming 5th edition of the APA *Publication Manual.* Retrieved from http://people.cehd.tamu.edu/~bthompson/apaeffec.htm accessed on 6/1/2011.

Tiku, M. L. (1967). Tables of the power of the *F* test. *Journal of the American Statistical Association, 62,* 525–539.

Todman, J., & Dugard, P. (2007). *Approaching multivariate analysis: An introduction for psychology.* Psychology Press.

Tolman, E. C., Ritchie, B. F., & Kalish, D. (1946). Studies in spatial learning: I. Orientation and the short cut. *Journal of Experimental Psychology, 36,* 13–24.

Tomarken, A. J., & Serlin, R. C. (1986). Comparison of ANOVA alternatives under variance heterogeneity and specific noncentrality structures. *Psychological Bulletin, 99,* 90–99.

Toothaker, L. (1991). *Multiple comparisons for researchers.* Newbury Park, CA: Sage.

Tufte, E. R. (1983). *The visual display of quantitative information.* Cheshire, CT: Graphics Press.

Tukey, J. W. (1949). One degree of freedom for nonadditivity. *Biometrics, 5,* 232–242.

Tukey, J. W. (1953). The problem of multiple comparisons. Unpublished manuscript, Princeton University.

Tukey, J. W. (1977). *Exploratory data analysis.* Reading, MA: Addison-Wesley.

Tversky, A., & Kahneman, C. (1980) Causal schemata in judgments under uncertainty. In M. Fishbein (Ed.), *Progress in social psychology, Vol. 1.* Hillsdale, NJ: Lawrence Erlbaum Associates.

Unah, I., & Boger, J. (2001). Race and the death penalty in North Carolina: An empirical analysis: 1993–1997. Available online at http://www.deathpenaltyinfo.org/article.php?did=246&scid=.

U.S. Department of Commerce. (1977). *Social indicators, 1976.* (Document #C3.2: S01/2/976). Washington, DC: U.S. Government Printing Office.

U.S. Department of Justice, Bureau of Justice Statistics. (1983). *Prisoners in 1982,* Bulletin NCJ-87933. Washington, DC: U.S. Government Printing Office.

Van den Noortgate, W., & Onghena, P. (2003a). Combining single-case experimental data using hierarchical linear models. *School Psychology Quarterly, 18,* 325–346.

Van den Noortgate, W., & Onghena, P. (2003b). Hierarchical linear models for the quantitative integration of effect sizes in single-case research. *Behavioral Research Methods, Instruments, and Computers, 35,* 1–10.

Vaughan, G. M., & Corballis, M. C. (1969). Beyond tests of significance: Estimating strength of effects in selected ANOVA designs. *Psychological Bulletin, 72,* 204–223.

Venables, W. N. (2000). Exegeses on Linear Models. Paper presented to the S-PLUS User's Conference. Washington, DC, 8–9th October, 1998. Available at http://www.stats.ox.ac.uk/pub/MASS3/Exegeses.pdf.

Verdooren, L. R. (1963). Extended tables of critical values for Wilcoxon's test statistic. *Biometrika, 50,* 177–186.

Vermont Department of Health. (1982). *1981 annual report of vital statistics in Vermont.* Burlington, VT.

Viechtbauer, W. (2010). Conducting meta-analyses in R with the metaphor package. *Journal of Statistical Software, 36,* 1–48. <URL: http://www.jstatsoft.org/v36/i03/>.

Visintainer, M. A., Volpicelli, J. R., & Seligman, M. E. P. (1982). Tumor rejection in rats after inescapable or escapable shock. *Science, 216,* 437–439.

Wagner, B. M., Compas, B. E., & Howell, D. C. (1988). Daily and major life events: A test of an integrative model of psychosocial stress. *American Journal of Community Psychology, 61,* 189–205.

Wainer, H. (1976). Estimating coefficients in linear models: It don't make no nevermind. *Psychological Bulletin, 83,* 213–217.

Wainer, H. (1978). On the sensitivity of regression and regressors. *Psychological Bulletin, 85,* 267–273.

Wainer, H. (1984). How to display data badly. *American Statistician, 38,* 137–147.

Walsh, T. B., Kaplan, A. S., Attia, E., Olmsted, M., Parides, M., Carter, J. C., Pike, K. M., Devlin, M. J., Woodside, B., Roberto, C. A., & Rockert, W. (2006). Fluoxetine after weight restoration in anorexia nervosa. *Journal of the American Medical Association, 295,* 2605–2612.

Watkins, A. E. (1995). The law of averages. *Chance, 8,* 28–32.

Weaver, K. A. (1999). The statistically marvelous medical growth chart: A tool for teaching variability. *Teaching of Psychology, 26,* 284–286.

Weinberg, C. R., & Gladen, B. C. (1986). The beta-geometric distribution applied to comparative fecundability studies. *Biometrics, 42,* 547–560.

Weisberg, H. I. (1979). Statistical adjustments and uncontrolled studies. *Psychological Bulletin, 86,* 1149–1164.

Welch, B. L. (1938). The significance of the difference between two means when the population variances are unequal. *Biometrika, 29,* 350–362.

Welch, B. L. (1947). The generalization of Student's problem when several difference population variances are involved. *Biometrika, 34,* 29–35.

Welch, B. L. (1951). On the comparison of several mean values: An alternative approach. *Biometrika, 38,* 330–336.

Welkowitz, J., Ewen, R. B., & Cohen, J. (2000). *Introductory statistics for the behavioral sciences* (5th ed.). New York: Harcourt/Academic Press.

Welsch, R. E. (1977). Stepwise multiple comparison procedures. *Journal of the American Statistical Association, 72,* 566–575.

Werner, M., Stabenau, J. B., & Pollin, W. (1970). TAT methods for the differentiation of families of schizophrenics, delinquents, and normals. *Journal of Abnormal Psychology, 75,* 139–145.

Wickens, T. D. (1989). *Multiway contingency table analysis for the social sciences.* Hillsdale, NJ: Erlbaum.

Wilcox, R. R. (1986). Critical values for the correlated *t*-test when there are missing observations. *Communications in Statistics, Simulation and Computation, 15,* 709–714.

Wilcox, R. R. (1987a). New designs in analysis of variance. *Annual Review of Psychology, 38,* 29–60.

Wilcox, R. R. (1987b). *New statistical procedures for the social sciences.* Hillsdale, NJ: Erlbaum.

Wilcox, R. R. (1992). Why can methods for comparing means have relatively low power, and what can you do to correct the problem? *Current Directions in Psychological Science, 1,* 101–105.

Wilcox, R. R. (1993). Analyzing repeated measures or randomized block designs using trimmed means. *British Journal of Mathematical and Statistical Psychology, 46,* 63–76.

Wilcox, R. R. (1995). ANOVA: The practical importance of heteroscedastic methods, using trimmed means versus means, and designing simulation studies. *British Journal of Mathematical and Statistical Psychology, 48,* 99–114.

Wilcox, R. R. (2005). Trimmed means. In Everitt, B. E. & Howell, D. C. *Encyclopedia of statistics in behavioral science.* Chichester, England: Wiley.

Wilcox, R. R. (2008). Robust methods for detecting and describing associations. In Osborne, J. R. *Best practices in quantitative methods.* Thousand Oaks, CA, Sage.

Williams, E. J. (1959). The comparison of regression variables. *Journal of the Royal Statistical Society (Series B), 21,* 396–399.

Wilkinson, L. (1994). Less is more: Two and three dimensional graphics for data display. *Behavior Research Methods, Instrumentation, and Computers, 26,* 172–176.

Wilkinson, L. (1999). Statistical methods in psychology journals: Guidelines and explanations. *American Psychologist, 54,* 594–604.

Willer, R. (2005). "Overdoing Gender: A Test of the Masculine Overcompensation Thesis." Paper presented at the Annual Meeting of the American Sociological Association. Philadelphia, PA.

Williamson, J. A. (2008). Correlates of Coping Styles in Children of Depressed Parents: Observations of Positive and Negative Emotions in Parent-Child Interactions. Honors Thesis, Vanderbilt University.

Winer, B. J. (1962). *Statistical principles in experimental design.* New York: McGraw-Hill.

Winer, B. J. (1971). *Statistical principles in experimental design* (2nd ed.). New York: McGraw-Hill.

Winer, B. J., Brown, D. R., & Michels, K. M. (1991). *Statistical Principles in Experimental Design* (3rd ed.). New York: McGraw-Hill.

Yates, F. (1934). Contingency tables involving small numbers and the χ^2 test. Supplement. *Journal of the Royal Statistical Society (Series B),1,* 217–235.

Yuen, K. K., & Dixon, W. J. (1973). The approximate behavior and performance of the two-sample trimmed *t. Biometrika, 60,* 369–374.

Ziegler, S. G. (1994). The effects of attentional shift training on the execution of soccer skills: A preliminary investigation. *Journal of Applied Behavior Analysis, 27,* 545–552.

Zuckerman, M., Hodgins, H. S., Zuckerman, A., & Rosenthal, R. (1993). Contemporary issues in the analysis of data. *Psychological Science, 4,* 49–53.

Zumbo, B. D., & Zimmerman, D. W. (2000). Scales of measurement and the relation between parametric and nonparametric statistical tests. In B. Thompson (Ed.), *Advances in social science methodology, Vol. 6.* Greenwich, CT: JAI Press.

Answers to Exercises

I am supplying the answers to most of the odd-numbered exercises. (Answers to even-numbered items are not given because many instructors want at least some questions without answers.) More complete answers, especially for later chapters, can be found at this book's Web site (www.uvm.edu/~dhowell/methods8/). Some odd-numbered answers have been omitted because the question asks that you draw a figure or compare computer output to the results of hand calculation. Others have been omitted when the question simply asks you to apply computer software to a set of data. Either you will be able to do so—and almost certainly get the correct answer—or you won't be able to set up the problem in the first place (in which case the numerical answer is of no help). You will sometimes be frustrated because I have often omitted any answers to the Discussion Questions. Very often there is no simple answer to these questions. On other occasions there is a straightforward answer, but I want you to think about the problem a while and see what you come up with. Frequently you will find much more of interest than the simple answer that I might give. I recognize that it is frustrating when you cannot figure out what the exercise is getting at; I, too, hate those situations. But that's the nature of discussion questions.

Chapter 1

1.1 The entire student body of your college or university would be considered a population under any circumstances in which you want to generalize *only* to the student body of your school.

1.3 The students of your college or university are a non-random sample of U.S. students, for example, because not all U.S. students have an equal chance of being included in the sample.

1.5 Independent variables: first-grade students who attended kindergarten versus those who did not; seniors, masters, submasters, and juniors as categories of marathon runners. Dependent variables: social-adjustment scores assigned by first-grade teachers; time to run 26.2 miles.

1.7 Continuous variables: length of gestation; typing speed in words/minute; number of books in the library collection.

1.9 The planners of a marathon race would like to know the average times of senior, master, submaster, and junior runners so they can plan accordingly.

1.11 (a) The number of Brown University students in an October 1984, referendum voting for and the number voting against the university's stockpiling suicide pills in case of nuclear disaster.

   (b) The number of students in a small Midwestern college who are white, African American, Hispanic American, Asian, or other.

   (c) One year after an experimental program to treat alcoholism, the number of participants who are "still on the wagon," "drinking without having sought treatment," or "again under treatment."

1.13 Children's scores in an elementary school could be reported numerically (a measurement variable), or the students could be categorized as Bluebirds (Rating > 90), Robins (Rating = 70–90), or Cardinals (Rating < 70).

1.15 For adults of a given height and gender, weight is a ratio scale of body weight, but it is at best an ordinal scale of strength.

1.17 Speed is probably a much better index of motivation than of learning.

1.19 (a) The final grade-point average for low-achieving students taking courses that interest them could be compared with the averages of low-achieving students taking courses that do not interest them. (b) The frequency of sexual intercourse could be compared for happily versus unhappily married couples.

1.21 An interesting study of the health effects of smoking in China can be found at http://berkeley.edu/news/media/releases/2005/09/04_smoking.shtml.

Chapter 2

2.1 (b) Unimodal and positively skewed.

2.3 The problem with making a stem-and-leaf display of the data in Exercise 2.1 is that most of the values fall on only two leaves if we use the usual tens' digits for stems. And things are not much better even if we double the number of stems.

2.5 There is no specific answer.

2.7 There is no specific answer.

2.9 The first quartile for males is approximately 77, whereas for females it is about 80. The third quartiles are nearly equal for males and females, with a value of 87.

2.11 The shape of the distribution of the number of movies attended per month for the next 200 people you meet would be positively skewed with a peak at 0 movies per month and a sharp dropoff to essentially the baseline by about 5 movies per month.

2.13 This is a stem-and-leaf display.

2.15 (a) $Y_1 = 9$, $Y_{10} = 2$ (b) $\Sigma Y = 9 + 9 + \ldots + 2 = 57$
   $(\Sigma Y)^2 = (9 + 9 + \cdots + 2)^2 = 3249$

2.17 (a) $\Sigma Y^2 = 9^2 + 9^2 \cdots 2^2 = 377$

   (b) $\dfrac{\Sigma Y^2 - \dfrac{(\Sigma Y)^2}{N}}{N - 1} = \dfrac{377 - \dfrac{3249}{10}}{9} = 5.789$

   (c) $\sqrt{5.789} = 2.406$

   (d) The units of measurement were squared musicality scores in part (b) and musicality scores in part (c).

2.19 (a) $\Sigma(X + Y) = (10 + 9) + (8 + 9)$
   $+ \cdots + (7 + 2) = 134$
   $\Sigma X + \Sigma Y = 77 + 57 = 134$

   (b) $\Sigma XY = 10(9) + 3(8) + \cdots + 3(7) = 460$
   $\Sigma X \Sigma Y = (77)(57) = 4389$

   (c) $\Sigma CX = \Sigma 3X = 3(10) + 3(8) + \cdots + 3(7)$
   $= 231$
   $C\Sigma X = 3(77) = 231$

   (d) $\Sigma X^2 = 10^2 + 8^2 + \cdots 7^2 = 657$
   $(\Sigma X)^2 = 77^2 = 5929$

2.21 The results in Exercise 2.20 support the sequential-processing hypothesis.

2.23 The data are not likely to be independent observations because the subject is probably learning the task over the early trials and later getting tired as the task progresses. Thus responses closer in time are more likely to be similar than responses further away in time.

2.25 The amount of shock that a subject delivers to a white participant does not depend on whether or not that subject has been insulted by the experimenter. On the other hand, black participants do suffer when the experimenter insults the subject.

2.27 This question asks for a graphic.

2.29 There is a strong increase in age at marriage, although the difference between males and females remains about the same. It is likely that what we are seeing is an increase in the percentage of couples initially living together without marrying.

2.31 The mean falls above the median.

2.33 mean = 21.33; median = 21

2.35 If you multiple by 3, for example, the mean will go from 4.83 to 14.5, the median and the mode will go from 5 to 15.

2.37 These fit nicely with what the earlier exercises led me to expect.

2.39 This is a computer question.

2.41 Range = 16; variance = 11.592; standard deviation = 3.405.

2.43 The interval = 9.908 to 27.892

2.45 Simply divide the original data by 2.1, which is the original standard deviation.

2.47 This is a graphical display.

2.49 CV = 0.351.

2.51 10% trimmed mean = 32.675.

2.53 This is a graphical display.

2.55 This is an Internet search.

CHAPTER 3

3.1 (b) $-3, -2, -2, -1, -1, -1, 0, 0, 0, 0, 1, 1, 1, 2, 2, 3$

(c) $-1.84, -1.23, -1.23, -0.61, -0.61, -0.61, 0, 0, 0, 0, 0.61, 0.61, 0.61, 1.23, 1.23, 1.84$

3.3 (a) 68% (b) 50% (c) 84%

3.5 $z = (950 - 975)/15 = -1.67$; only 4.75% of the time would we expect a count as low as 950, given what we know about the distribution. The two-tailed probability would be .095.

3.7 The answers to parts (b) and (c) of Exercise 3.6 will be equal when the two distributions have the same standard deviation.

3.9 (a) $2,512.68 (b) $1,342.00

3.11 Divide the raw scores by 7/10 to raise the standard deviation to 10, and then add 11.43 points to each new score to bring the mean up to 80.

3.13 $z = (600 - 489)/126 = 0.88$. Therefore 81% of the scores fall below this, so 600 represents the 81st percentile.

3.15 $z = 0.79, p = .7852; X = 586.591$

For seniors and nonenrolled college graduates, a GRE score of 600 is at the 79th percentile, and a score of 587 would correspond to the 75th percentile.

3.17 The 75th percentile for GPA is 3.04.

3.19 There is no meaningful discrimination to be made among those scoring below the mean, and therefore all people who score in that range are given a T score of 50.

3.21 The post-intervention weights are reasonably normal, but the weight gain and percentage gain are far from normal. However we have a very small sample.

3.23 I would first draw 16 scores from a normally distributed population with $\mu = 0$ and $\sigma = 1$. Call this variable z1. The sample (z1) would almost certainly have a sample mean and standard deviation that are not 0 and 1. Then I would create a new variable z2 = z1–mean(z1). This would have a mean of 0.00. Then I would divide z2 by sd(z1) to get a new distribution (z3) with mean = 0 and sd = 1. Then make that variable have a st. dev. of 4.25 by multiplying it by 4.25. Finally, add 16.3 (the new mean). Now the mean is exactly 16.3 and the standard deviation is exactly 4.25.

3.25 The combined data are bimodal, but the adjusted data are much closer to a normal distribution, although with such a small data set it is hard to be very definite.

CHAPTER 4

4.1 (a) I set up the null hypothesis that last night's game was actually an NHL hockey game.

(b) On the basis of that hypothesis, I expected that each team would earn somewhere between 0 and 6 points. I then looked at the actual points and concluded that they were way out of line with what I would expect if this were an NHL hockey game. I therefore rejected the null hypothesis.

4.3 Concluding that I had been shortchanged when in fact I had not.

4.5 The critical value would be that amount of change below which I would decide that I had been shortchanged. The rejection region would be all amounts of change less than the critical value—that is, all amounts that would lead to rejection of H_0.

4.7 $z = (490 - 650)/50 = -3.2$. The probability that a student drawn at random from those properly admitted would have a GRE score as low as 490 is .0007. I suspect that the fact that his mother was a member of the board of trustees played a role in his admission.

4.9 The distribution would drop away smoothly to the right for the same reason that it always does—there are few high-scoring people. It would drop away steeply to the left because fewer of the borderline students would be admitted (no matter how high the borderline is set).

4.11 M is called a test statistic.

4.13 The alternative hypothesis is that this student was sampled from a population of students whose mean is not equal to 650.

4.15   The word "distribution" refers to the set of values obtained for any set of observations. The phrase "sampling distribution" is reserved for the distribution of outcomes (either theoretical or empirical) of a sample statistic.

4.17   (a) *Research hypothesis*—Children who attend kindergarten adjust to 1st grade faster than those who do not. *Null hypothesis*—1st grade adjustment rates are equal for children who did and did not attend kindergarten.

(b) *Research hypothesis*—Sex education in junior high school decreases the rate of pregnancies among unmarried mothers in high school. *Null hypothesis*—The rate of pregnancies among unmarried mothers in high school is the same regardless of the presence or absence of sex education in junior high school.

4.19   For $\alpha = .01$, z must be -2.327. The cutoff score is therefore approximately 53.46. The corresponding value for z when a cutoff score of 53.46 is applied to the curve for H_1, is $z = -1.33$. From Appendix Z we find $\beta = .9082$.

4.21   To determine whether there is a true relationship between grades and course evaluations, I would find a statistic that reflected the degree of relationship between two variables. (You will see such a statistic (r) in Chapter 9.) I would then calculate the sampling distribution of that statistic in a situation in which there is no relationship between two variables. Finally, I would calculate the statistic for a representative set of students and classes, and compare my sample value with the sampling distribution of that statistic.

4.23   (a) You could draw a large sample of boys and a large sample of girls in the class and calculate the mean allowance for each group. The null hypothesis would be the hypothesis that the mean allowance, in the population, for boys is the same as the mean allowance, in the population, for girls.

(b) I would use a two-tailed test because I want to reject the null hypothesis whether girls receive significantly more allowance or significantly less allowance than boys.

(c) I would reject the null hypothesis if the difference between the two sample means were greater than I could expect to find due to chance. Otherwise I would not reject the null.

(d) The most important thing to do would be to have some outside corroboration for the amount of allowance reported by the children.

4.25   In the parking lot example the traditional approach to hypothesis testing would test the null hypothesis that the mean time to leave a space is the same whether someone is waiting or not. If their test failed to reject the null hypothesis they would simply fail to reject the null hypothesis and would do so at a two-tailed level of $\alpha = .05$. Jones and Tukey on the other hand would not consider

that the null hypothesis of equal population means could possibly be true. They would focus on making a conclusion about which population mean is higher. A "nonsignificant result" would only mean that they didn't have enough data to draw any conclusion. Jones and Tukey would also be likely to work with a one-tailed $\alpha = .025$, but actually making a two-tailed test because they would not have to specify a hypothesized direction of difference.

4.27   Proportion seeking help who are women

(a) It is quite unlikely that we would have 61% of our sample being women if $p = .50$. In my particular sampling distribution as score of 61 or higher was obtained on $16/1000 = 1.6\%$ of the time.

(b) I would repeat the same procedure again except that I would draw from a binomial distribution where $p = .75$.

CHAPTER 5

5.1   (a) Analytic: If two tennis players are exactly evenly skillful—so that the outcome of their match is random, the probability is .50 that Player A will win their upcoming match.

(b) Relative frequency: If in past matches Player A has beaten Player B on 13 of the 17 occasions they played, then Player A has a probability of $13/17 = .76$ of winning their upcoming match.

(c) Subjective: Player A's coach feels that he has a probability of .90 of winning his upcoming match against Player B.

5.3   (a) $p = 1/9 = .111$ that you will win second prize given that you do not win first prize.

(b) $p = (2/10)(1/9) = (.20)(.111) = .022$ that he will win first and you second.

(c) $p = (1/10)(2/9) = (.111)(.20) = .022$ that you will win first and he second.

(d) p (you are first and he is second [$= .022$]) $+ p$(he is the first and you second [$= .022$]) $= p$(you and he will be first and second) $= .044$.

5.5   Conditional probabilities were involved in Exercise 5.3a.

5.7   Conditional probabilities: What is the probability that skiing conditions will be good on Wednesday, *given* that they are good today?

5.9 $p = (2/13)(3/13) = (.154)(.231) = .036$.

5.11   A continuous distribution for which we care about the probability of an observation's falling within some specified interval is exemplified by the probability that your baby will be born on its due date.

5.13   Two examples of discrete variables: Variety of meat served at dinner tonight; Brand of desktop computer owned.

5.15   (a) 20%, or 60 applicants, will fall at or above the 80th percentile and 10 of these will be chosen. Therefore p(that an applicant with the highest rating will be admitted) $= 10/60 = .167$.

(b) No one below the 80th percentile will be admitted, therefore p(that an applicant with the lowest rating will be admitted) = .00.

5.17   (a) $z = -.33$; p(larger portion) = .6293

(b) 29/55 = 53% > 50; 32/55 = 58% $\geq$ 50.

5.19   Compare the probability of dropping out of school, ignoring the ADDSC score, with the conditional probability of dropping out given that ADDSC in elementary school exceeded some value (e.g., 66).

5.21   Probabilities of correct choices on trial 1 of a 5-choice task:

$p(0) = .1074$	$p(6) = .0055$
$p(1) = .2684$	$p(7) = .0008$
$p(2) = .3020$	$p(8) = .0001$
$p(3) = .2013$	$p(9) = .0000$
$p(4) = .0881$	$p(10) = .0000$
$p(5) = .0264$	

5.23   At $\alpha = .05$, up to 4 correct choices indicate chance performance, but 5 or more correct choices would lead me to conclude that they are no longer performing at chance levels.

5.25   If there is no housing discrimination, then a person's race and whether or not they are offered a particular unit of housing are independent events. We could calculate the probability that a particular unit (or a unit in a particular section of the city) will be offered to anyone in a specific income group. We can also calculate the probability that the customer is a member of an ethnic minority. We can then calculate the probability of that person being shown the unit *assuming independence,* and compare that answer against the actual proportion of times a member of an ethnic minority was offered such a unit.

5.27   The number of subjects needed in Exercise 5.26's verbal learning experiment if each subject can see only two of the four classes of words is the number of permutations of 4 things taken 2 at a time = 4!/2! = 12.

5.29   The total number of ways of making ice cream cones = 63. (You can't have an ice cream cone without ice cream, so exclude the combination of 6 things taken 0 at a time.)

5.31   Because the probability of 11 correct by chance is .16, the probability of 11 *or more* correct must be greater than .16. Therefore we cannot reject the hypothesis that $p = .50$ (the student is guessing) at $\alpha = .05$.

5.33   Driving test passed by 22 out of 30 drivers when 60% expected to pass:

$$z = \frac{22 - 30(.60)}{\sqrt{30(.60)(.40)}} = 1.49;$$ we cannot reject H_0

at $\alpha = .05$.

5.35   Students should come to understand that nature does not have a responsibility to make things come out even in

the end, and that it has a terrible memory of what has happened in the past. Any "law of averages" refers to the results of a long term series of events, and it describes what we would expect to see. It does not have any self-correcting mechanism built into it.

5.37   It is low because the probability of breast cancer is itself very low. But don't be too discouraged. Having collected some data (a positive mammography) the probability is 7.8 times higher than it would otherwise have been. (And if you are a woman, please don't stop having mammographies.)

CHAPTER 6

6.1 $\chi^2 = 11.33$ on 2 df; reject H_0 and conclude that students do not enroll at random.

6.3 $\chi^2 = 29.35$ on 1 df; reject H_0 and conclude that the children did not choose dolls at random (at least with respect to color).

6.5 $\chi^2 = 34.184$ on 1 df; reject H_0 and conclude that the distribution of choices between black and white dolls was different in the two studies. Choice is *not* independent of Study. We are no longer asking whether one color of doll is preferred over the other color, but whether the *pattern* of preference is constant across studies.

6.7   (a)   Take a group of subjects at random and sort them by gender and by life style (categorized across *3* levels).

(b) Deliberately take an equal number of males and females and ask them to specify a preference among 3 types of life styles.

(c) Deliberately take 10 males and 10 females and have them divide themselves into two teams of 10 players each.

6.9   (a) $\chi^2 = 10.306$

(b) This demonstration shows that the obtained value of χ^2 is exactly doubled, while the critical value remains the same. Thus the sample size plays a very important role, with larger samples being more likely to produce significant results—as is also true with other tests.

6.11 $\chi^2 = 5.50$. Reject H_0 and conclude that women voted differently from men. Women were much more likely to vote for Civil Unions—the odds ratio is (35/9)/(60/41) = 3.89/1.46 = 2.66, meaning that women had 2.66 times the odds of voting for civil unions than men. That is a substantial difference, and likely reflects fundamental differences in attitude.

6.13   (a) $\chi^2 = 37.141$ on 2 df; reject H_0 and conclude that adolescent girls' preferred weight varies with race.

(b) The number of girls desiring to lose weight was far in excess of the number of girls who were really overweight.

6.15   Likelihood ratio $\chi^2 = 12.753$ on 7 df; do not reject H_0.

6.17   (a) $\chi^2 = 9.0$
        (b)   If watching Monday Night Football really changes people's opinions (in a negative direction), then of those people who change, more should change from positive to negative than vice versa, which is what happened.
        (c)   The analysis does not take into account all of those people who did not change. It only reflects direction of change if a person changes.

6.19   (b)   Row percents take entries as a percentage of row totals, while column percents take entries as a percentage of column totals.
        (c)   These are the probabilities (to four decimal places) of a $\chi^2 \geq \chi^2_{obs}$, under H_0.
        (d)   The correlation between the variables is approximately .25.

6.21   (a)   Cramér's $\phi_C = \sqrt{26.903/22,071} = .0349$.
        (b)   Odds Fatal | Placebo $= 18/10,845 = .00166$. Odds Fatal | Aspirin $= 5/10,933 = .000453$. Odds Ratio $= .00166/.000453 = 3.66$. The odds that you will die from a myocardial infarction if you do not take aspirin are 3.66 greater than if you do.

6.23   For Table 6.4 the odds ratio for a death sentence as a function of race is $(33/251)/(33/508) = 2.017$. A person is about twice as likely to be sentenced to death if they are nonwhite than if they are white.

6.25   For the Dabbs and Morris (1990) study, $\chi^2 = 64.08$ on 1 df. We can reject H_0 and conclude that antisocial behavior in males is linked to testosterone levels.

6.27   (a) $\chi^2 = 15.57$ on 1 df. Reject H_0.
        (b)   There is a significant relationship between high levels of testosterone in adult men and a history of delinquent behaviors during childhood.
        (c)   This result shows that we can tie the two variables (delinquency and testosterone) together historically.

6.29   (a) $\chi^2 = 9.79$. Reject H_0.
        (b)   Odds ratio $= (43/457)/(50/268) = 0.094/.186 = .505$ Those who receive the program have about half the odds of subsequently suffering abuse.

6.31   (a) $\chi^2 = 0.232, p = .630$.
        (b)   There is no relationship between the gender of the parent and the gender of the child.
        (c)   We would be unable to separate effects due to parent's gender from effects due to the child's gender. They would be completely confounded.

6.33   We could ask a series of similar questions, evenly split between "right" and "wrong" answers. We could then sort the replies into positive and negative categories and ask whether faculty were more likely than students to give negative responses.

6.35   If the scale points mean different things to men and women, it is possible that the relationship could be distorted by the closed-end nature of the scales.

6.37   Fidalgo's study of bullying in the work force.
        (a)   Collapsing over job categories $\chi^2 = 4.20, p = .05$
        (b)   **OR** $= .70$.
        (c)   and
        (d)   The Mantel-Haenszel statistic is 2.285. When we condition on job category there is no relationship between bullying and gender and the odds ratio drops to 1.36.
        (e)   For males $\chi^2 = 6.609$. For females $\chi^2 = 0.510$. For males bullying declines as job categories increase, but this is not the case for women.

6.39   Appleton, French, & Vanderpump (1996) study.

        There is a tendency for more younger people to smoke than older people. Because younger people generally have a longer life expectancy than older people that would make the smokers appear as if they had a lower risk of death. What looks like a smoking effect is an age effect.

CHAPTER 7

7.1   This is a graphic example.

7.3   The mean and standard deviation of the sample are 4.46 and 2.69. The mean and standard deviation are very close to the other parameters of the population from which the sample was drawn (4.5 and 2.7, respectively.) The mean of the distribution of means is 4.45, which is close to the population mean, and the standard deviation is 1.20.
        (a)   The Central Limit Theorem would predict a sampling distribution of the mean with a mean of 4.5 and a standard deviation of $2.69\sqrt{5} = 1.20$.
        (b)   These values are very close to what we would expect.

7.5   If you had drawn 50 samples of size 15, the mean of the sampling distribution should still approximate the mean of the population, but the standard error of that distribution would now be only $2.69\sqrt{15} = 0.69$.

7.7   I used a two-tailed test in the last problem, but a one-tailed test could be justified on the grounds that we had no interest in showing that these students thought that they were below average, but only in showing that they thought they were above average.

7.9   Although the group that was near the bottom certainly had less room to underestimate their performance than to overestimate it, and the fact that they overestimated by so much is significant. (If they were in the bottom quartile the best that they could have scored as at the 25th percentile, yet their mean estimate was at the 68th percentile.)

7.11   Mean gain $= 3.01$, standard deviation $= 7.3$. $t = 2.22$. With 28 df the critical value $= 2.048$, so we will reject the null hypothesis and conclude that the girls gained at better than chance levels. The effect size was $3.01/7.31 = 0.41$.

7.13 (a) $t = 20.70$ on 27 df. We can reject the null hypothesis.

(b) This does not mean that the SAT is not a valid measure, but it does show that people who do well at guessing at answers also do well on the SAT. This is not very surprising.

7.15 $CI_{.95} = 3.51 \leq \mu \leq 5.27$. An interval formed as this one was has a probability of .95 of encompassing the mean of the population. Because this interval includes the hypothesized population mean, it is consistent with the results in Exercise 7.14.

7.17 Confidence limits on beta-endorphine changes $2.906 \leq \mu \leq 12.494$

7.19 The means for males and females were 2.73 and 2.79 respectively, producing a $t = -0.485$ on 90 df. We cannot reject the null hypothesis that males and females are equally satisfied. A matched-sample t is appropriate because it would not seem reasonable to assume that the sexual satisfaction of a husband is independent of that of his wife.

7.21 The correlation between the scores of husbands and wives was .334, which is significant and confirms the assumption that the scores would be related.

7.23 The important question is what would the sampling distribution of the mean (or differences between means) look like, and with 91 pairs of scores that sampling distribution would be substantially continuous with a normal distribution of means.

7.25 $t = 2.545$, $p < .05$, which tells us that the quality of life was better for the intervention group.

7.27 $CI_{.95} = 0.24 \leq \mu \leq 5.80$

7.29 (a) Null hypothesis—there is not a significant difference in test scores between those who have read the passage and those who have not.

(b) Alternative hypothesis—there is a significant difference between the two conditions.

(c) $t = 8.89$ on 43 df if we pool the variances. This difference is significant.

(d) We can conclude that students do better on this test if they read the passage on which they are going to answer questions.

7.31 Girls in the Control group lost an average of 0.45 pounds, while girls in the Cognitive Behavior Therapy group gained 3.01 pounds. A t on two independent groups $= -1.68$ on 53 df, which is not significant. Cognitive Behavior Therapy did not lead to significantly greater weight gain. (Variances were homogeneous.)

7.33 If those means had actually come from independent samples, we could not remove differences due to couples, and the resulting t would have been somewhat smaller.

7.35 The correlation was fairly low.

7.37 (a) I would assume that the experimenters expected that there would be more stories exhibiting positive parent-child relationships among the mothers or children in the Normal group.

(b) The means were 3.55 and 2.10 for the normal and schizophrenic groups, respectively, with $t = 2.66$ on 38 df, which is significant. The experimental hypothesis in (a) was supported.

7.39 It is just as likely that having a schizophrenic child might lead to deterioration in parent-child relationships. Because we can't assign children to groups at random, we cannot speak confidently about causation.

7.41 Confidence limits on Exercise 7.40: $CI_{.95} = 1.153 \pm (2.131)(1.965) = -3.04 \leq \mu \leq 5.34$. Because the confidence limits include 0, these results are in agreement with the previous non-significant result.

7.43 $t = 2.134$. Because the variances are very dissimilar, we could run a conservative test by using the smaller of $n_1 - 1$ and $n_2 - 1$ df, which would produce a nonsignificant result. We would have a nonsignificant result even if we used the full $n_1 + n_2 - 2$ df.

7.45 If you take the absolute differences between the observations and their group means and run a t test comparing the two groups on the absolute differences, you obtain $t = 0.625$. Squaring this you have $F = 0.391$, which makes it clear that Levene's test in SPSS is operating on the absolute differences. (The t for squared differences would equal 0.213, which would give an F of 0.045.)

7.47 Computer exercise

7.49 The effect size (d) was 0.62 using the standard deviation of weights before therapy. This indicates a gain of roughly 2/3 of a standard deviation over the course of therapy.

7.51 (a) The scale of measurement is important because if we rescaled the categories as 1, 2, 4, and 6, for example, we would have quite different answers.

(b) The first exercise asks if there is a relationship between the satisfaction of husbands and wives. The second simply asks if males (husbands) are more satisfied, on average, than females (wives).

(c) You could adapt the suggestion made in the text about combining the t on independent groups and the t on matched groups.

(d) I'm really not very comfortable with the t test because I am not pleased with the scale of measurement. An alternative would be a ranked test, but the number of ties is huge, and that probably worries me even more.

CHAPTER 8

8.1 (a) 0.250 (b) 2.50 (c) 0.71

8.3 $n = 99$, 126, and 169 (I have rounded up since N is always an integer.)

8.5 This is a graphic.

8.7 (a) For power $= .50$, $\delta = 1.95$ and $n = 15.21 \approx 16$

(b) For power $= .80$, $\delta = 2.80$ and $n = 31.36 \approx 32$

8.9 $(d) = .50$, $\delta = 1.46$, power $= .31$

8.11 $t (= -1.98)$ is numerically equal to δ, although t is calculated from statistics and δ is calculated from parameters. In other words, δ equals the t that you would get if the data exactly match what you think are the values of the parameters.

8.13 This is a graphic.

8.15 He should use the Dropout group. Assuming equal standard deviations, the H.S. dropout group of 25 would result in a higher value of δ and therefore higher power. (You can let σ be any value as long as it is the same for both calculations. Then calculate δ for each situation.)

8.17 Power $= .49$.

8.19 When $\mu = 104.935$, power will equal β.

8.21 (a) I would not be assigning subjects to groups at random, and there might be differences between labs that would confound the results. (b) I should pool my subjects and randomly assign them to conditions. (c) Sex differences, if they exist, would confound the results. We would need to use a procedure (see Chapter 13) that separates any sex differences and looks for different patterns of results in males and females.

8.23 Both of these questions point to the need to design studies carefully so that the results are clear and interpretable.

CHAPTER 9

9.1 This is a graphic.

9.3 With $n = 25$ we would need a population correlation of .396.

9.5 Family income is a strong predictor of infant mortality, followed by the percentage of women using family planning.

9.7 This variable has very little variance, and without differences between cases the correlation cannot be very high.

9.9 Psychologists are very much interested in ways to change behavior, and being able to decrease infant mortality is an important goal.

9.11 Pearson's r deals with linear relationships, and this one is definitely curvilinear.

9.13 Power $= .17$.

9.15 The predicted value for ln(symptoms) $= 4.37$.

9.17
$$s'_{Y.X} = 0.1726\sqrt{1 + \frac{1}{107} + \frac{(X_i - \overline{X})^2}{(N-1)s_X^2}}$$
$$t_{\alpha/2} = 1.984$$
$$CI(Y) = \hat{Y} \pm (t_{\alpha/2})s'_{Y.X}$$

You can calculate $\hat{Y}$ and s'_{YX} for several different values of X, and then plot the results.

9.19 Galton's results:
(a) $r = .459$
(b) Child $= 0.646 \times$ midparent $+ 23.942$
(c) Children 67.12 68.02 68.71 70.18; Parents 66.66 68.50 69.50 71.18
(d) Parents in the highest quartile are, on average, taller than their children. The reverse holds for the lowest quartile.

9.21 For power $= .80$, $\delta = 2.80$. Therefore $N = 50$.

9.23 (a) $z = 0.797$. The correlations are not significantly different. (b) We do not have reason to argue that the relationship between performance and prior test scores is affected by whether or not the student read the passage.

9.25 It is difficult to tell whether the significant difference is to be attributable to the larger sample sizes or the higher (and thus more different) values of r'. It is likely to be the former.

9.27 (a) $r = .224$, $p = .509$. Do not reject H_0. (b) The Irish are heavy smokers, but they certainly are not heavy drinkers compared to other regions. (c) The inclusion of Northern Ireland distorts the data. If we leave them out, $r = .784$, $p = .007$, and there is a strong relationship between smoking and drinking.

9.29 (a) See table below.
(b) All of these correlations are significant, showing that the symptoms are correlated with one another.

9.31 (b) For a one inch gain in height, we would expect a 4.356 pound gain in weight. Someone who is 0 inches tall would be expected to weight -149.934 pounds. The unreasonable answer reflects curvilinearity of the relationship at the extremes. The correlation

	SomT	ObsessT	SensitT	DepressT	AnxT	HostT	PhobT	ParT	PsyT
ObsessT	0.482								
SensitT	0.377	0.539							
DepressT	0.400	0.599	0.654						
AnxT	0.569	0.621	0.550	0.590					
HostT	0.420	0.470	0.451	0.508	0.475				
PhobT	0.466	0.509	0.613	0.568	0.528	0.411			
ParT	0.400	0.524	0.677	0.621	0.547	0.494	0.540		
PsyT	0.334	0.503	0.625	0.725	0.509	0.404	0.529	0.651	
GSIT	0.646	0.791	0.770	0.820	0.786	0.633	0.679	0.766	0.741

is .904, and both the slope and the correlation are significant.

9.33 As a 5'8" male, my predicted weight is $\hat{Y} = 4.356(\text{Height}) - 149.934 = 4.356 \times 68 - 149.934 = 146.27$ pounds.

(a) I weigh 146 pounds. (Well, I did a few years ago.) Therefore the residual in the prediction is $Y - \hat{Y} = 146 - 146.27 = -0.27$.

(b) If the students on which this equation is based under- or overestimated their own height or weight, the prediction for my weight will be based on invalid data and will be systematically in error.

9.35 The male would be predicted to weigh 137.562 pounds, while the female would be predicted to weigh 125.354 pounds. The predicted difference between them would be 12.712 pounds.

9.37. Although the regression line has a slight positive slope, the slope is not significantly different from zero. The equation for the regression line is $\hat{Y} = 0.429X + 221.843$.

9.39 Eris doesn't fit the plot as well as I would have liked. It is a bit too far away.

9.41 $z = 3.30$. The difference between the two correlations is significant.

CHAPTER 10

10.1 (b) $r_{pb} = -.540$; $t = -2.72$ (c) Performance in the morning is significantly related to people's perception of their peak periods.

10.3 It looks as though morning people vary their performance across time, but evening people are uniformly poor performers.

10.5 $t = 2.725$. This is equal to the t test on r_{pb}.

10.7 $\hat{Y} = 0.202X + 0.093$; when $X = \overline{X} = 2.903$, $\hat{Y} = 0.68 = \overline{Y}$.

10.9 (b) $\phi = .256$ (c) $t = 1.27$, not significant.

10.11 (a) $\phi = .628$ (b) $\chi^2 = 12.62, p < .05$

10.13 (a) $\tau = .886$ (b) $z = 4.60, p < .05$.

10.15 $\tau = .733$

10.17 An $r^2 = .0512$ would correspond to $\chi^2 = 10.24$. The closest you can come to this result is if the subjects were split 61/39 in the first condition and 39/61 in the second (rounding to integers).

10.19 (a) $\chi^2 = 2.815 \, [p = .245] \, \phi_C = .087$ (c) This approach would be preferred over the approach used in Chapter 7 if you had reason to believe that differences in depression scores below the clinical cutoff were of no importance and should be ignored.

10.21 (b) If a statistic is not significant that means we have no reason to believe that it is reliably different from 0

(or whatever the parameter under H_0). Here we have no reason to believe that there is a relationship between the variables. Therefore, it we have no reason to believe it to be important. (c) With the exception of issues of power, sample size will not make an effect more important than it is. It will simply increase the level of significance.

CHAPTER 11

11.1 Summary Table

Source	df	SS	MS	F
Treatments	4	351.52	87.88	9.08
Error	45	435.30	9.67	
Total	49	786.82		

11.3 (a)

ANOVA

RECALL

	Sum of Squares	df	Mean Square	F	Sig.
Between Groups	1059.800	3	353.267	53.301	.000
Within Groups	238.600	36	6.628		
Total	1298.400	39			

(b)

Source	df	SS	MS	F
Group	1	792.10	792.10	59.451*
Error	38	506.30	13.324	
Total	39	1,298.40		

*p < .05 [$F_{.05}(1,38) = 4.10$]

(c) The results are difficult to interpret because the error term now includes variance between younger and older participants, Moreover, we don't know if the levels of processing effect applies to both age groups.

11.5 (a)

Source	df	SS	MS	F
Group	1	224.583	224.583	18.8*
Error	20	238.917	11.946	
Total	21	463.500		

*p < .05 [$F_{.05}(1,20) = 4.35$]

(b) t without pooled variance $= 4.27$ $t^2 = 18.2$

(c) t with pooled variance $= 4.34$ $t^2 = 18.8$.

(d) The t with pooled variances is equivalent to the F in (a).

11.7 $\eta^2 = .816$; $\omega^2 = .796$

11.9 $\eta^2 = .182$; $\omega^2 = .120$.

Eta-squared tells us that approximately 18% of the variability in the severity of symptoms can be accounted for by differences in treatment, whereas omega-squared tells us that a less-biased estimate would be 12%. Because the F was significant, both of these estimates are at better than chance levels.

11.11

ANOVA

RECALL

	Sum of Squares	df	Mean Square	F	Sig.
Between Groups	4.280	4	1.070	4.117	.005
Within Groups	14.294	55	.260		
Total	18.574	59			

11.13 $X_{ij} = \mu + \tau_j + e_{ij}$ where μ is the grand mean, τ_j is the effect for the jth treatment, and e_{ij} is the unit of error for the ith subject in treatment j.

11.15 $X_{ij} = \mu + \tau_j + e_{ij}$ where μ is the grand mean, τ_j is the effect for the jth treatment, and e_{ij} is the unit of error for the ith subject in treatment j.

11.17

Source	df	SS	MS	F
Group	7	44.557	6.365	7.27*
Error	264	231.282	0.876	
Total	271	275.839		

*p < .05 [$F_{.05}(7,264) = 2.06$]

11.19 There is nothing that I can write out here.

11.21 $\eta^2 = .16$; $\omega^2 = .14$

11.23 Transforming time to speed involves a reciprocal transformation. The effect of the transformation is to decrease the relative distance between large values.

11.25 Parts of speech are a fixed variable, because we deliberately chose which parts of speech to use. Words within the noun category are most likely random, because we would probably choose our nouns at random (within certain constraints, such as the number of letters in the word). We would choose nouns at random because we care how people respond to nouns in general, not specifically to "house," "car," "tree," etc.

11.27 The $F = 4.88$, and we can reject the null hypothesis. This question addresses differences among all three groups, rather than simply pairwise differences.

11.29 Analysis of Epinuneq.dat ignoring Interval

ANOVA

ERRORS

	Sum of Squares	df	Mean Square	F	Sig.
Between Groups	147.970	2	73.985	36.197	.000
Within Groups	241.187	118	2.044		
Total	389.157	120			

11.31 The three error terms are 2.40, 1.83, and 2.26, for an average of 2.162, which is, within rounding error, the average of the 9 cell variances.

11.33 Gouzoulis-Mayfrank et al. (2000) study

(a)

ANOVA

PERFORMANCE

	Sum of Squares	df	Mean Square	F	Sig.
Between Groups	238.738	2	119.369	7.082	.001
Within Groups	1365.214	81	16.854		
Total	1603.952	83			

(b) The pairwise differences are 3.678, 3.464, and 0.214, and the square root of MS_{error} is 4.105. This gives d values of 0.896, 0.844, and 0.05.

(c) It is reasonable to tentatively conclude that Ecstacy produces lower scores than either the Control condition or the Cannibis condition, which don't differ.

11.35 There should be no effect on the magnitude of the data because η^2 is not dependent on the underlying metric of the independent variable.

11.37

CHANGE

	Sum of Squares	df	Mean Square	F	Sig.
Between Groups	391.391	3	130.464	12.922	.000
Within Groups	686.570	68	10.097		
Total	1077.961	71			

Chapter 12

12.1 (a)

Source	df	SS	MS	F
Treatments	4	816.00	204.00	36.43*
1,2 vs. 3,4,5	1	682.67	682.67	121.90*
1 vs. 2	1	90.00	90.00	16.07*
3,4 vs. 5	1	3.33	3.33	<1
3 vs. 4	1	40.00	40.00	7.14*
Error	20	112.00	5.60	
Total	24	928.00		

*$p < .05$ [$F_{.05}(1, 20) = 4.35$; $F_{.05}(4, 20) = 2.87$]
*$p < .01$ [$F_{.01}(1, 20) = 8.10$; $F_{.01}(4, 20) = 4.43$]

(b) Orthogonality of contrasts:
Cross-products of coefficients:

$\sum a_j b_j = (.5)(1) + (.5)(-1) + (.333)(0)$
$+ (.333)(0) + (.333)(0) = 0$

$\sum a_j c_j = (.5)(0) + (.5)(0) + (.333)(.5)$
$+ (.333)(.5) + (.333)(-1) = 0$

$\sum a_j d_j = (.5)(0) + (.5)(0) + (.333)(1)$
$+ (.333)(-1) + (.333)(0) = 0$

$\sum b_j c_j = (1)(0) + (-1)(0) + (0)(.5)$
$+ (0)(.5) + (0)(-1) = 0$

$c_j d_j = (0)(0) + (0)(0) + (.5)(1)$
$+ (.5)(-1) + (1)(0) = 0$

(c) $682.67 + 90.00 + 3.33 + 40.00 = 816.00$

12.3 for $\alpha = .05$; PC $= \alpha$; FW $= 1 - (1-\alpha)^2 = .0975$

12.5 $q = 7.101$; $t\sqrt{2} = 7.101$

12.7 $t'_1 = -5.34$ reject H_0. $t'_2 = -1.72$; do not reject H_0

12.9 A post hoc test like the Tukey or the REGWQ often does not get at the specific questions we have in mind, and, at the same time, often answers questions in which we have no interest.

12.11 $F_{\text{contrast #1}} = 113.26$; $F_{\text{contrast #2}} = 61.57$; $F_{\text{crit}} = 4(2.69) = 10.76$ Therefore both contrasts are significant.

12.13 Group 1 (the Control) is different from Groups 2, 3, and 4.

12.15 They are sequentially modified because you change the critical value each time you reject another null hypothesis.

12.17 Conti and Musty (1984) recorded locomotive behavior in rats in response to injection of THC in the active brain region. The raw data showed a clear linear relationship between group means and standard deviations, but a logarithmic transformation of the data largely removed this relationship. Mean locomotive behavior increased with dosage up to 0.5 mg, but further dose increases resulting in decreased behavior. Polynomial trend analysis revealed no linear trend but a significant quadratic trend.

12.19 If there were significant differences due to Interval and we combined across intervals, those differences would be incorporated into the error term, decreasing power.

12.21 At all three intervals there was a significant linear and quadratic trend, indicating that the effect of epinephrine on memory increases with a moderate dose but then declines with a greater dose. The linear trend reflects the fact that in the high dose condition the animals do even worse than with no epinephrine.

12.23 Confidence interval:

$CI_{.95} = (\psi) \pm t_{.05} s_{\text{error}}$
$= (10.67) \pm (2.086)(2.366)$
$= (10.67) \pm 4.935$
$= 5.735 \leq \mu_1 - \mu_2 \leq 15.605$

12.25 Davey et al. (2003) study: The contrast between the Positive and Negative mood conditions was significant ($t(27) = 3.045$, $p < .05$). This leads to an effect size of $d = \Psi/\sqrt{MS_{\text{error}}} = 5.6/\sqrt{16.907} = 5.6/4.11 = 1.36$. The two groups differ by over 1 1/3 standard deviations.

12.27 This requires students to make up their own example.

Chapter 13

13.1

Source	df	SS	MS	F
Parity	1	13.067	13.067	3.354
Size/Age	2	97.733	48.867	12.541*
$P \times S$	2	17.733	8.867	2.276
Error	54	210.400	3.896	
Total	59	338.933		

*$p < .05$ $F_{.05(2,54)} = 3.17$

13.3 The mean for these primiparous mothers would not be expected to be a good estimate of the mean for the population of all primiparous mothers because the sample is not representative of the population. For example, 50% of the population of primiparous mothers would not be expected to give birth to LBW infants.

13.5 Exercise 11.3 as a factorial

Source	df	SS	MS	F
Delay	2	188.578	94.289	3.22
Area	2	356.044	178.022	6.07*
$D \times A$	4	371.956	92.989	3.17*
Error	36	1055.200	29.311	
Total	44	1971.778		

*$p < .05$ $F_{.05(2,36)} = 3.27$; $F_{.05(4,36)}$ 2.64

13.7 In Exercise 13.5, if A refers to Area:

$\hat{\alpha}_1 =$ the treatment effect for the Neutral site

$\overline{X}_{.1} - \overline{X}_{..} = 24.222 - 28.2 = 3.978$

13.9 Group N vs. Group A: $t = 3.03$. Group N vs. Group B: $t = 3.00$. With two t tests, each on 36 df (for MS_{error}) with $\alpha = .05/2 = .025$ (two-tailed), the critical value is ± 2.339. We would reject H_0 in each case.

13.11 Exercise 11.3 as factorial

Source	df	SS	MS	F
Age	1	115.60	115.60	17.44*
Level	1	792.10	792.10	119.51*
Age × Level	1	152.10	152.10	22.95*
Error	36	238.60	6.6278	
Total	39	1298.40		

*$p < .05$ $F_{.05\,(1,36)} = 4.12$

13.13 Made-up data with main effects but no interaction:

Cell means:	8	12
	4	6

13.15 The interaction was of primary interest in an experiment by Nisbett in which he showed that obese people varied the amount of food they consumed depending on whether a lot or a little food was visible, while normal weight subjects ate approximately the same amount under the two conditions.

13.17 $\eta_P^2 = \dfrac{SS_{parity}}{SS_{total}} = \dfrac{13.067}{338.933} = .04$

$\eta_S^2 = \dfrac{SS_{size}}{SS_{total}} = \dfrac{97.733}{338.933} = .29$

$\eta_{PS}^2 = \dfrac{SS_{PS}}{SS_{total}} = \dfrac{17.733}{338.933} = .05$

$\omega_P^2 = \dfrac{SS_{parity} - (p - 1)MS_{error}}{SS_{total} + MS_{error}}$

$= \dfrac{13.067 - (1)(3.896)}{338.933 + 3.896} = .03$

$\omega_S^2 = \dfrac{SS_{size} - (S - 1)MS_{error}}{SS_{total} + MS_{error}}$

$= \dfrac{97.733 - (2)(3.896)}{338.933 + 3.896} = .26$

$\omega_{PS}^2 = \dfrac{SS_{PS} - (p - 1)(s - 1)MS_{error}}{SS_{total} + MS_{error}}$

$= \dfrac{17.733 - (1)(2)(3.896)}{338.933 + 3.896} = .03$

13.19 Magnitude of effect for avoidance learning data in Exercise 13.5:

$\eta_{DA}^2 = \dfrac{SS_{delay}}{SS_{total}} = \dfrac{188.578}{1971.778} = .10$

$\eta_A^2 = \dfrac{SS_{Area}}{SS_{total}} = \dfrac{356.044}{1971.778} = .18$

$\eta_{DA}^2 = \dfrac{SS_{DA}}{SS_{total}} = \dfrac{371.956}{1971.778} = .19$

$\omega_D^2 = \dfrac{SS_{delay} - (d - 1)MS_{error}}{SS_{total} + MS_{error}}$

$= \dfrac{188.578 - (2)(29.311)}{1971.778 + 29.311} = .06$

$\omega_A^2 = \dfrac{SS_{area} - (a - 1)MS_{error}}{SS_{total} + MS_{error}}$

$= \dfrac{356.044 - (2)(29.311)}{1971.778 + 29.311} = .15$

$\omega_{DA}^2 = \dfrac{SS_{DA} - (d - 1)(a - 1)MS_{error}}{SS_{total} + MS_{error}}$

$= \dfrac{371.956 - (2)(2)(29.311)}{1971.778 + 29.311} = .13$

13.21 Three-way on early experience:

Source	df	SS	MS	F
Experience	3	2931.667	977.222	3.544*
Intensity	2	2326.250	1163.125	4.218*
Cond Stim	1	4563.333	4563.333	16.550*
E × I	6	67.083	11.181	<1
E × C	3	4615.000	1538.333	5.579*
I × C	2	55.417	27.708	<1
E × I × C	6	121.250	20.208	<1
Error	96	26,471.000	275.740	
Total	119	41,151.000		

*$p < .05$ $F_{.05(1,96)} = 3.94$; $F_{.05(2,96)} = 3.09$; $F_{.05(3,96)} = 2.70$; $F_{.05(6,96)} = 2.19$

There are significant main effects for all variables with a significant Experience × Conditioned Stimulus interaction.

13.23 Analysis of Epineq.dat:

Tests of Between-Subjects Effects

Dependent Variable: Trials to reversal

Source	Type III Sum of Squares	df	Mean Square	F	Sig.
Corrected Model	141.130[a]	8	17.641	8.158	.000
Intercept	1153.787	1	1153.787	533.554	.000
DOSE	133.130	2	66.565	30.782	.000
DELAY	2.296	2	1.148	.531	.590
DOSE * DELAY	5.704	4	1.426	.659	.622
Error	214.083	99	2.162		
Total	1509.000	108			
Corrected Total	355.213	107			

[a] R Squared = .397 (Adjusted R Squared = .349)

13.25 Tukey on Dosage data from Exercise 13.25

Multiple Comparisons

Dependent Variable: Trials to reversal Tukey HSD

(I) dosage of epinephrine	(J) dosage of epinephrine	Mean Difference (I−J)	Std. Error	Sig.
0.0 mg/kg	0.3 mg/kg	−1.67*	.35	.000
	1.0 mg/kg	1.03*	.35	.010
0.3 mg/kg	0.0 mg/kg	1.67*	.35	.000
	1.0 mg/kg	2.69*	.35	.000
1.0 mg/kg	0.0 mg/kg	−1.03*	.35	.010
	0.3 mg/kg	−2.69*	.35	.000

Based on observed means.
*. The mean difference is significant at the .05 level.

All of these groups differed from each other at $p \leq .05$.

13.27 Simple effects on data in Exercise 13.28

Source	df	SS	MS	F
Condition	1	918.750	918.75	34.42*
Cond @ Inexp.	1	1014.00	1014.00	37.99*
Cond @ Exp.	1	121.50	121.50	4.55*
Cond × Exper	1	216.750	216.75	8.12*
Other Effects	9	2631.417		
Error	36	961.000	26.694	
Total	47	4727.917		

*$p < .05$ $F_{.05(1,36)} = 4.12$

13.29 Dress codes and performance:

Source	df	SS	MS	F
Code	1	494.290	494.290	2.166
Error$_1$	12	2737.280	228.107	
School(Code)	12	2737.280	288.107	2.784*
Error$_2$	126	10,323.080	81.931	
Total	139	13,554.650		

*$p < .05$

The F for Code is not significant but the F for the nested effect of School is. But notice that the two F values are not all that far apart, but their p values are very different. The reason for this is that we only have 12 df for error to test Code, but 126 df for error to test School(Code).

13.31 Analysis of Gartlett & Bos (2010)

Source	df	SS	MS	F
Parents	1	832.38	832.38	44.87*
Gender	1	52.03	52.03	2.80
P × G	1	110.08	110.08	5.93*
Error$_2$	168		18.55	
Total	171			

*$p < .05$

13.35 This question does not have a fixed answer.

CHAPTER 14

14.1 (a)

$$X_{ij} = \mu + \pi_j + \tau_j + \pi\tau_{ij} + e_{ij} \text{ or}$$
$$X_{ij} = \mu + \pi_j + \tau_j + e'_{ij}$$

(b)

Source	df	SS	MS	F
Subjects	7	189,666.66		
Within subj	16	5266.67		
Test session	2	1808.33	904.17	3.66 ns
Error	14	3458.33	247.02	
Total	23	194,933.33		

(c) There is no significant difference among the session means—scores don't increase as a function of experience.

14.3

Source	df	SS	MS	F
Between Subj	19	106.475		
Groups	1	1.125	1.125	0.19
Ss w/in Grps	18	105.250	5.847	
Within Subj	20	83.500		
Phase	1	38.025	38.025	15.26*
P × G	1	0.625	0.625	0.25
P × Ss w/in Grps	18	44.850	2.492	
Total	39	189.975		

*$p < .05$ [$F_{.05(1,18)} = 4.41$]

There is a significant change from baseline to training, but it does not occur differentially between the two groups, and there are no overall differences between the groups.

14.5

Source	df	SS	MS	F
Between subj	29	159.7333		
Groups	2	11.4333	5.7166	1.04
Ss w/ Grps	27	148.300	5.4926	
Within subj	30	95.0000		
Phase	1	19.2667	19.2667	9.44*
$P \times G$	2	20.6333	10.3165	5.06*
$P \times Ss$ w/ Grps	27	55.1000	2.0407	
Total	59	254.733		

(b) $SS_{\text{items at adult good}} = 4.133$; $F = 3.52*$

14.7   For the data in Exercise 14.6:

(a)   Because we are using only the data from Children, it would be wise not to use a pooled error term. The following is the relevant printout from SPSS for the Between-subject effect of Reader.

Tests of Between-Subjects Effects[a]

Measure: MEASURE_1

Transformed Variable: Average

Source	Type III Sum of Squares	df	Mean Square	F	Sig.
Intercept	367.500	1	367.500	84.483	.000
READERS	50.700	1	50.700	11.655	.009
Error	34.800	8	4.350		

[a]AGE = Children

(b)   Again, we do not want to pool error terms. The following is the relevant printout from SPSS for Adult Good readers. The difference is not significant, nor would it be for any decrease in the df if we used a correction factor.

Tests of Within-Subjects Effects

Measure: MEASURE_1

Sphericity Assumed

Source	Type III Sum of Squares	df	Mean Square	F	Sig.
ITEMS	4.133	2	2.067	3.647	.075
Error(ITEMS)	4.533	8	.567		

14.9   It would certainly affect the covariances because we would force a high level of covariance among items. As the number of responses classified at one level of Item went up, another item would have to go down.

14.11 Plot of results in Exercise 14.10:

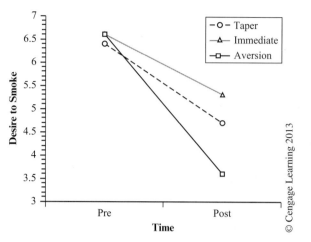

14.13 Analysis of data in Exercise 14.5

(b)   The F for Mean is a test on $H_0: \mu = 0$.

(c) $MS_{\text{w/in Cell}}$ is the average of the cell variances.

14.15 Source column of summary table for four-way ANOVA with repeated measures on A and B and independent measures on C and D.

Source
Between Ss
C
D
CD
Ss w/in groups
Within Ss
A
AC
AD
ACD
$A \times Ss$ w/in groups
B
BC
BD
BCD
$B \times Ss$ w/in groups
AB
ABC
ABD
ABCD
$AB \times Ss$ w/in groups
Total

14.17 Using the mixed models procedure.

The covariance matrix shows a decreasing pattern in covariances as you move to the right. Therefore I requested that the solution include a covariance matrix that was AR1. The results follow.

Fixed Effects

Type III Tests of Fixed Effects[a]

Source	Numerator df	Denominator df	F	Sig.
Intercept	1	43.256	422.680	.000
Group	2	43.256	3.521	.038
Time	2	81.710	71.356	.000
Group × Tirne	4	81.710	5.578	.001

[a]DependentVariable: dv.

14.19 Mixed model analysis with unequal size example:

Fixed Effects

Type III Tests of Fixed Effects[a]

Source	Numerator df	Denominator df	F	Sig.
Intercept	1	41.724	393.118	.000
Group	2	41.724	2.877	.068
Time	2	70.480	64.760	.000
Group × Time	4	70.459	5.266	.001

[a]DependentVariable: dv.

14.21 SPSS printout on gain scores:

Tests of Between-Subjects Effects

Dependent Variable: GAIN

Source	Type III Sum of Squares	df	Mean Square	F	Sig.
Corrected Model	614.644[a]	2	307.322	5.422	.006
Intercept	732.075	1	732.075	12.917	.001
TREAT	614.644	2	307.322	5.422	.006
Error	3910.742	69	56.677		
Total	5075.400	72			
Corrected Total	4525.386	71			

[a] R Squared = .136 (Adjusted R Squared = .111)

(b)　SPSS printout using pretest and posttest:

Tests of Within-Subjects Effects

Measure: MEASURE_1

Sphericity Assumed

Source	Type III Sum of Squares	df	Mean Square	F	Sig.
TIME	366.037	1	366.037	12.917	.001
TIME × TREAT	307.322	2	153.661	5.422	.006
Error(TIME)	1955.371	69	28.339		

(c)　The F comparing groups on gain scores is exactly the same as the F for the interaction in the repeated measures design.

(e)　$t = -0.287$. This group did not gain significantly over the course of the study. This suggests that any gain we see in the other groups can not be attributed to normal gains seen as a function of age.

(f)　Without the control group we could not separate gains due to therapy from gains due to maturation.

14.23 (a)　$t = -0.555$. There is no difference in Time 1 scores between those who did, and did not, have a score at Time 2.

(b)　If there had been differences, I would worry that people did not drop out at random.

14.25 Differences due to judges play an important role.

14.27 If I was particularly interested in differences between subjects, and recognized that judges probably didn't have a good anchoring point, and if this lack was not meaningful, I would not be interested in considering it.

14.29 Strayer et al. (2006)

$t_{1-2} = 0.07$; $t_{1-3} = 2.52*$; $t_{2-3} = 2.45*$

Both Baseline and Alcohol conditions show poorer performance than the cell phone condition, but they do not differ from each other.

Tests of Within-Subjects Effects

Measure: MEASURE 1

Source		Type III Sum of Squares	df	Mean Squares	F	Sig.
Condition	Sphericity Assumed	134696.067	2	67348.033	4.131	.020
	Greenhouse-Geisser	134696.067	1.992	67619.134	4.131	.020
	Huynh-Feldt	134696.067	2.000	67348.033	4.131	.020
	Lower-bound	134696.067	1.000	134696.067	4.131	.049
Error(Condition)	Sphericity Assumed	1271689.267	78	16303.709		
	Greenhouse-Geisser	1271689.267	77.687	16369.337		
	Huynh-Feldt	1271689.267	78.000	16303.709		
	Lower-bound	1271689.267	39.000	32607.417		

CHAPTER 15

15.1 Predicting Quality of Life:

(a) All other variables held constant, a difference of $+1$ degree in Temperature is associated with a difference of $-.01$ in perceived Quality of Life. A difference of $1,000$ in median Income, again all other variables held constant, is associated with a $+.05$ difference in perceived Quality of Life. A similar interpretation applies to b_3 and b_4. Because values of 0.00 cannot reasonably occur for all predictors, the intercept has no meaningful interpretation.

(b) $\hat{Y} = 5.37 - .01(55) + .05(12) + .003(500) - .01(200) = 4.92$

(c) $\hat{Y} = 5.37 - .01(55) + .05(12) + .003(100) - .01(200) = 3.72$

15.3 I would thus delete Temperature, because it has the smallest t ($t = -1.104$), and therefore the smallest semi-partial correlation with the dependent variable.

15.5 (a) Environment has the largest semi-partial correlation with the criterion, because it has the largest value of t.

(b) The gain in prediction (from $r = .58$ to $R = .697$), which we obtain by using all the predictors, is more than offset by the loss of power we sustain as p became large relative to N.

15.7 As the correlation between two variables decreases, the amount of variance in a third variable that they share decreases. Thus, the higher will be the possible squared semi-partial correlation of each variable with the criterion. They each can account for more previously unexplained variation.

15.9 Numsup and Respon are fairly well correlated with the other predictors, whereas YRS is nearly independent of them.

15.11 $MS_{residual} = 4.232$.

15.13 $R^2_{adj} = est\ R^{2*} = -.158$. Because a squared value cannot be negative, we will declare it undefined. This is all the more reasonable in light of the fact that we cannot reject $H_0 : R^* = 0$.

15.15 $\hat{Y} = 0.4067Respon + 0.1845NumSup + 2.3542$.

15.17 It has no meaning in that we have the data for the population of interest (the 10 districts).

15.19 It plays an important role through its correlation with the residual components of the other variables.

15.21 Within the context of a multiple-regression equation, we cannot look at one variable alone. The slope for one variable is only the slope for that variable when all other variables are held constant.

15.23 There is no fixed answer to this question.

15.25 (b) The value of R^2 was virtually unaffected. However, the standard error of the regression coefficient for PVLoss increased from 0.105 to 0.178. Tolerance for PVLoss decreased from .981 to .345, whereas VIF increased from 1.019 to 2.900. (c) PVTotal should not be included in the model because it is redundant with the other variables.

15.27

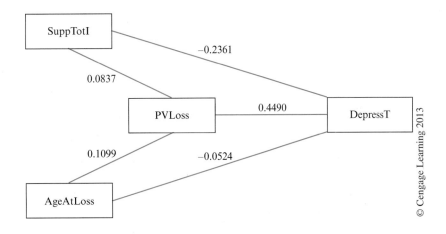

© Cengage Learning 2013

15.29 Case #104 has the largest value of Cook's D (.137) but not a very large Studentized residual ($t = -1.88$). When we delete this case the squared multiple correlation is increased slightly. More importantly, the standard error of regression and the standard error of one of the predictors (PVLoss) also decrease slightly. This case is not sufficiently extreme to have a major impact on the data.

15.31 Logistic regression on Harass.dat

The only predictor that contributes significantly is the Offensiveness of the behavior, which has a Wald χ^2 of 26.43. The exponentiation of the regression coefficient yields 1.649. This means that a 1-point increase in Offensiveness multiplies the odds of reporting by 1.65.

15.33 It may well be that the frequency of the behavior is tied in with its offensiveness, which is related to the likelihood of reporting. In fact, the correlation between those two variables is .20, which is significant at $p < .000$. (I think my explanation would be more convincing if Frequency were a significant predictor when used on its own.)

15.35 BlamPer and BlamBeh are correlated at a moderate level ($r = .52$), and once we condition on BlamPer by including it in the equation, there is little left for BlamBeh to explain.

15.37 This problem required you to make up an example.

15.39 It is impossible to change one of the variables without changing the interaction in which that variable plays a role. I can't think of a sensible interpretation of "holding all other variables constant" in this situation.

15.41 Analysis of results from Feinberg and Willer (2011).

The following comes from using the program by Preacher and Leonardelli referred to in the chapter. I calculated the t values from the regression coefficients and their standard errors and then inserted those t values in the program. You can see that the mediated path is statistically significant regardless of which standard error you use for that path.

t on path a $= 2.27$ t on path b $= -4.90$

Test	Sobel	Aroian	Goodman
Statistic	2.059	2.025	2.10
p	.039	.043	.036

CHAPTER 16

16.1

Source	df	SS	MS	F
Group	2	57.733	28.867	9.312*
Error	12	37.200	3.100	
Total	14	94.933		

$* p < .05$ $[F_{.05(2,12)} = 3.89]$

16.3 (a)

Source	df	SS	MS	F
Group	2	79.0095	39.5048	14.92*
Error	18	47.6571	2.6476	
Total	20	126.6666		

$* p < .05$ $[F_{.05(2,18)} = 3.55]$

16.5

Source	df	SS	MS	F
Gender	1	65.333	65.333	7.730*
SES	2	338.667	169.333	20.034*
$G \times S$	2	18.667	9.333	1.104
Error	42	355.000	8.452	
Total	47	777.667		

16.7

Source	df	SS	MS	F
Gender	1	60.015	60.015	7.21*
SES	2	346.389	173.195	20.80*
$G \times S$	2	21.095	10.547	1.27
Error	35	291.467	8.328	
Total	40			

* $p < .05$ [$F_{.05(1,35)} = 4.12$; $F_{.05(2,35)} = 3.27$]

16.9 $\hat{\mu} = 13.4167$; $\alpha_1 = 1.167$; $\beta_1 = -3.167$
$\beta_2 = -0.167$; $\alpha\beta_{11} = 0.833$; $\alpha\beta_{12} = -0.167$

16.11 If we are actually dealing with unweighted means, SS_A and SS_B will be 0 because means of means are 7 for all rows and columns.

16.13   SS(total)

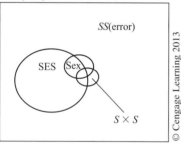

© Cengage Learning 2013

16.15 (a)   Design matrix using only the first entry in each group for illustration purposes:

$$X = \begin{bmatrix} 1 & 0 & 58 & 75 \\ \cdots & \cdots & \cdots & \cdots \\ 0 & 1 & 60 & 70 \\ \cdots & \cdots & \cdots & \cdots \\ -1 & -1 & 75 & 80 \end{bmatrix}$$

(b)

Source	df	SS	MS	F
Covariate	1	1250.6779	1250.6779	55.81*
A (Group)	2	652.9228	326.4614	14.57*
Error	11	246.5221	22.4111	
Total	14	2615.7333		

* $p < .05$ [$F_{.05(1, 11)} = 4.84$; $F_{.05(2, 11)} = 3.98$]

16.17 $\hat{Y} = -7.9099A_1 + 0.8786A_2 - 2.4022B + 0.5667AB_{11} + 0.1311AB_{21} + 0.7260C + 6.3740$

The adjusted means are 41.1556, 44.8276, 49.5095, 54.0517, 54.8333, and 61.0333

16.19 Klemchuk, Bond, & Howell (1990) (on bottom of this page).

16.21 Analysis of GSIT in Mireault.dat (on next page).

16.23 (a)   These data reveal a significant difference between males and females in terms of Year Coll. Females are slightly ahead of males. If the first year of college is in fact more stressful than later years, this could account for some of the difference we found in Exercise 16.21.

16.25 Everitt compared two therapy groups and a control group treatment for anorexia. The groups differed significantly in posttest weight when controlling for pretest weight ($F = 8.71$, $p < .0001$, with the Control group weighing

Results for Exercise 16.19

Tests of Between-Subjects Effects

Dependent Variable: DV

Source	Type III Sum of Squares	df	Mean Square	F	Sig.
Corrected Model	15.7283	3	5.243	8.966	.000
Intercept	2.456	1	2.456	4.201	.048
Daycare	2.640	1	2.640	4.515	.041
Age	11.703	1	11.703	20.016	.000
Daycare* Age	.037	1	.037	.064	.802
Error	21.050	36	.585		
Total	46.111	40			
Corrected Total	36.778	39			

[a]R Squared = .428 (Adjusted R Squared = .380)

Results for Exercise 16.21

Tests of Between-Subjects Effects

Dependent Variable: GSIT

Source	Type III Sum of Squares	df	Mean Square	F	Sig.
Corrected Model	1216.924[a]	5	243.385	2.923	.013
Intercept	1094707.516	1	1094707.516	13146.193	.000
GENDER	652.727	1	652.727	7.839	.005
GROUP	98.343	2	49.172	.590	.555
GENDER × GROUP	419.722	2	209.861	2.520	.082
Error	30727.305	369	83.272		
Total	1475553.000	375			
Corrected Total	31944.229	374			

[a]R Squared = .038 (Adjusted R Squared = .025)

the least at posttest. When we examine the difference between just the two treatment groups at posttest, the F does not reach significant, $F = 3.745$, $p = .060$, though the effect size for the difference between means (again controlling for pretest weights) is 0.62 with the Family Therapy group weighing about six pounds more than the Cognitive/Behavior Therapy group. It is difficult to know just how to interpret that result given the nonsignificant F.

16.27 A slope of 1.0 would mean that the treatment added a constant to people's pretest scores, which seems somewhat unlikely. Students might try taking any of the data in the book with a pretest and posttest score and plotting the relationship.

This relationship between difference scores and the analysis of covariance would suggest that in general an analysis of covariance might be the preferred approach. The only time I might think otherwise is when the difference score is really the measure of interest.

CHAPTER 17

17.1 – 5 Mazzucchelli et al. (2010) study

Author	Gro	nl	n2	£	sg^2	weight	Wg	$W \times g^2$	W^2	$V(gi\text{-}gbar)^2$
Barlow86a	E	12.00	12.00	−0.134	0.2740	3.6496	−0.4891	0.0655	13.3198359	1.4609
Besyner79	E	14.00	16.00	0.675	0.1790	5.5866	3.7709	2.5454	31.21001217	0.1737
Lovett88	E	33.00	27.00	0.204	0.0930	10.7527	2.1935	0.4475	115.6203029	0.9338
Stark	E	10.00	9.00	0.043	0.1930	5.1813	0.2228	0.0096	26.84635829	1.0759
VanDenHa	E	15.00	14.00	0.644	0.1380	7.2464	4.6667	3.0053	52.5099769	0.1530
Weinberg	E	10.00	9.00	0.976	0.2180	4.5872	4.4771	4.3696	21.04199983	1.0451
Wilson	E	9.00	11.00	1.466	0.2750	3.6364	5.3309	7.8151	13.2231405	3.4025
SUM		103.00	98.00			40.6402	20.1729	18.2580	273.7716	
Barlow86a	M	12.00	13.00	0.133	0.1240	8.0645	1.0726	0.1427	65.0364204	1.0784
Fordyce77	M	50.00	60.00	0.609	0.0380	26.3158	16.0263	9.7600	692.5207756	0.3202
Fordyce83	M	40.00	13.00	1.41	0.2330	4.2918	6.0515	8.5326	18.41993774	3.5644
Reich81	M	49.00	49.00	0.378	0.0320	31.2500	11.8125	4.4651	976.5625	0.4552
SUM		151.00	135.00			69.9222	34.9629	22.9004	1752.5396	
GrandSum		254.00	233.00			110.5623	55.1358		2026.3113	13.6631

Mean g =	0.4987	Q =	13.6631
se(Mean)	0.0951		
CI-lower	0.3123	C =	92.2350
CI-upper	0.6851		
		Tau =	0.1993

Fixed-Effects Model (k = 11)

   Test for Heterogeneity:
   Q(df = 10) = 13.6678, p-val = 0.1887

   Model Results:

estimate	se	zval	pval	ci.lb	ci.ub	
0.4987	0.0951	5.2428	<.0001	0.3122	0.6851	***

Signif. codes: 0 '***' 0.001 '**' 0.01 '*' 0.05 '.' 0.1 ' ' 1

17.6 – 17.12 Bloch et al. (2009) study:

Fixed-Effects Model (k = 4)

   Test for Heterogeneity:
   Q(df = 3) = 7.2655, p-val = 0.0639

   Model Results:

estimate	se	zval	pval	ci.lb	ci.ub	
0.2274	0.0881	2.5813	0.0098	0.0547	0.4001	**

Signif. codes: 0 '***' 0.001 '**' 0.01 '*' 0.05 '.' 0.1 ' ' 1

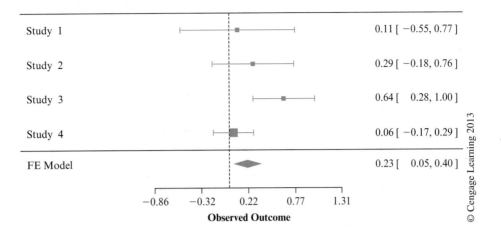

It doesn't make sense to try to fit a random model because we have so few studies that we could not reasonably test for randomness.

The confidence interval does not include 0, and we can safely reject the null hypothesis and conclude that methylphenidate does increase the severity of tics in these children.

Fixed-Effects Model (k = 3)

Test for Heterogeneity:
Q(df = 2) = 2.1121, p-val = 0.3478

Model Results:

estimate	se	zval	pval	ci.lb	ci.ub	
0.7364	0.0955	7.7109	<.0001	0.5492	0.9236	***

Signif. codes: 0 '***' 0.001 '**' 0.01 '*' 0.05 '.' 0.1 ' ' 1

17.13 – 17.14

Forest Plot Omitted

Fixed-Effects Model (k = 9)

Test for Heterogeneity:
Q(df = 8) = 2.1826, p-val = 0.9749

Model Results:

estimate	se	zval	pval	ci.lb	ci.ub	
0.5239	0.2826	1.8542	0.0637	–0.0299	1.0777	.

Signif. codes: 0 '***' 0.001 '**' 0.01 '*' 0.05 '.' 0.1 ' ' 1

17.15 – 17.19 Rajkumar (2010)

The risk ratios and log risk ratios are

Risk Ratio
4.102326 6.336000 8.212389 1.963636

Log Risk Ratio
1.411554 1.846248 2.105644 0.674798

Mean Risk Ratio and confidence limits

Log Risk Ratio

Estimate	se	zval	pval	ci.lb	ci.ub
1.5747	0.3277	4.8055	<.0001	0.9324	2.2170

Risk Ratio	**CIlower**	**CIupper**
4.8293	2.5406	9.1798

Even at the low end of the confidence interval the addition of thalidomide increases the chances of success to 2.5 times the chance of success in the control group.

17.20 – 17.24 Bisson & Martin (2007)

Random-Effects Model (k = 14; tau^2 estimator: REML)

tau ^ 2 (estimate of total amount of heterogeneity): 438.6370 (SE = 189.2833)
tau (sqrt of the estimate of total heterogeneity): 20.9437
I ^ 2 (% of total variability due to heterogeneity): 94.80%
H ^ 2 (total variability / within-study variance): 19.24

Test for Heterogeneity:
Q(df = 13) = 236.1772, p-val < .0001

Model Results:

estimate	se	zval	pval	ci.lb	ci.ub	
–28.6212	5.8774	–4.8697	<.0001	–40.1407	–17.1017	***

Plots omitted

Note that we can reject the null hypothesis in our test for heterogeneity, though we have no specific variable that might explain that variability. We can also conclude that VBT is a more effective treatment than the Control treatment.

Mean(A)	13.6	11	22.4	
SD(A)	1.817	2	2.51	
Mean(B)	5.8	5	20.2	
SD(B)	5.007	3.8	2.044	
s(pooled)	4.286260671	3.350774882	2.197933015	
d	1.819767998	1.790630589	1.000940422	
s(d)	0.640613133	0.637870361	0.577404587	
CIlower	0.564166258	0.540404682	−0.130772569	
Ciupper	3.075369738	3.040856496	2.132653414	
Weight	2.436735134	2.457735569	2.999435588	7.893906291
Widi	4.434292616	4.40089649	3.002256323	11.83744543
dbar	1.499567514			
s(dbar)	0.355921331			
CIlow(dbar)	0.801961705			
CIup(dbar)	2.197173322			

Two of the three subjects showed significant improvement (their confidence intervals did not include 0, and the overall confidence interval also did not include 0, indicating significant overall improvement).

17.25 – 17.28 Howard & Kendall (1996)

Graphics omitted

$$\bar{d} = -1.0435$$
$$s_{\bar{d}} = 0.2114$$
$$-1.458 \le \bar{d} \le -0.629$$

17.29 – 17.31 Dunlap & Fox (1999)

Individual regressions—shown only for subject number 1

Subject 1
Coefficients:

	Estimate	Std. Error	t value	Pr(>|t|)	d	Wt
(Intercept)	5.000e+01	2.182e+01	2.291	0.0342*		
Phase	−2.482e+01	2.272e+01	−1.092	0.2891	0.515	0.002
trial	−7.106e−15	1.010e+01	0.000	1.0000	0.000	0.010
int1	−1.447e+00	1.012e+01	−0.143	0.8879	0.943	0.010

Residual standard error: 14.29 on 18 degrees of freedom
Multiple R-squared: 0.5717, Adjusted R-squared: 0.5003
F-statistic: 8.008 on 3 and 18 DF, p-value: 0.000

From the columns for t and d we see that taken individually, the only significant difference was for the change of slope for Subject 3, although many of the d values were reasonably large.

We can compute the mean of d and its standard error from the above.

Phase

$$\bar{d}_{\text{Phase}} = \frac{\Sigma W_i d_1}{\Sigma W_i} = 0.467$$

$$s_{\bar{d}} = \sqrt{\frac{1}{\Sigma W_i}} = \sqrt{\frac{1}{0.015}} = 8.165$$

Trial

$$\bar{d}_{\text{Trial}} = \frac{0.068}{.149} = 0.046$$

$$s_{\bar{d}} = \sqrt{\frac{1}{0.149}} = 2.59$$

Interaction

$$\bar{d}_{\text{int}} = \frac{0.070}{0.147} = 0.476$$

$$s_{\bar{d}} = \sqrt{\frac{1}{0.147}} = 2.608$$

It is apparent from the above results that the mean of d is not significant for any effect. Contrary to the example in the text, the standard errors were very large.

CHAPTER 18

18.1 (a) $W_S = 23$; $W_{.025} = 27$.

   (b) Reject H_0 and conclude that older children include more inferences in their summaries.

18.3 $z = -3.15$; reject H_0.

18.5 (a) $T = 8.5$; $T_{.025} = 8$; do not reject H_0.

   (b) We cannot conclude that we have evidence supporting the hypothesis that there is a reliable increase in hypothesis generation and testing over time. (Here is a case in which alternative methods of breaking ties could lead to different conclusions.)

18.7 I would randomly assign the order within each pair of Before and After scores, and for each set of assignments I would calculate a statistic. (That statistic could be the mean of the difference scores, or a t test on the difference scores.) I would then calculate the number of times I came out with a result as extreme as the one I actually obtained, and that, divided by the number of resamples, would give me the probability under the null.

18.9 $z = -2.20$ $p(z \geq \pm 2.20) = .0278$. Again reject H_0, which agrees with our earlier conclusion.

18.11 The scatter plot shows that the difference between the pairs is heavily dependent upon the score for the first born.

18.13 The Wilcoxon matched-pairs signed-ranks test tests the null hypothesis that paired scores were drawn from identical populations or from symmetric populations with the same mean (and median). The corresponding t test tests the null hypothesis that the paired scores were drawn from populations with the same mean and assumes normality.

18.15 Rejection of the H_0 by a t test is a more specific statement than rejection using the appropriate distribution free test because, by making assumptions about normality and homogeneity of variance, the t test refers specifically to population means.

18.17 $H = 6.757$; reject H_0.

18.19 Take the data for all N subjects and shuffle them to random order. Then take the first n_1 observations and assign them to Treatment 1, the next n_2 observations and assign them to Treatment 2, and so on. Then calculate an F statistic on that set of resampled data and record the F. Repeat this a large number of times (e.g., 1,000) and look at the sampling distribution of F. The proportion of F values that are equal to, or greater than the F obtained on the original data will give you the probability under the null.

18.21 The study in Exercise 18.18 has an advantage over the one in Exercise 18.17 in that it eliminates the influence of individual differences (differences in overall level of truancy from one person to another).

18.23 These are equivalent tests in this case.

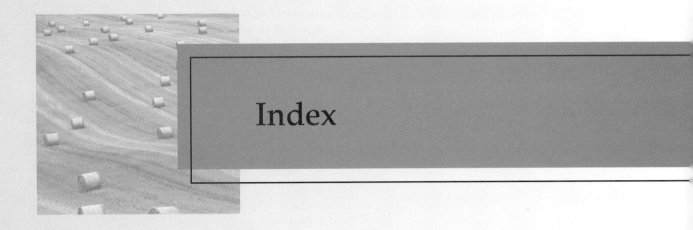

Index

Glossary of Symbols

Greek Letter Symbols

α	Alpha: level of significance, probability of a Type I error
α_i	Treatment effect for the ith level of A
β	Beta: probability of a Type II error
β_i	Standardized regression coefficient; treatment effect for the ith level of B
Γ	Gamma function (related to factorial)
δ	Delta: noncentrality parameter; population effect size
$\hat{\varepsilon}, \tilde{\varepsilon}$	Epsilon: symbols for correction factors for degrees of freedom in repeated-measures analysis of variance
η^2	Eta squared: squared correlation ratio
μ, μ_X	Mu: population mean
$\mu_{\overline{X}}$	Mean of the sampling distribution of means
ρ	Rho: population correlation coefficient
σ, σ_X	Sigma (lower case): population standard deviation
σ^2, σ_X^2	Population variance
σ_e^2	Error variance
Σ	Sigma (upper case): summation notation; variance-covariance matrix
τ	Kendall's tau: a nonparametric measure of correlation
τ_j	Treatment effect for the jth treatment
ϕ	Phi coefficient: a correlation coefficient computed for a 2×2 contingency table
ϕ_C	Cramér's phi: an extension of phi to contingency tables larger than 2×2
χ^2	Chi-square statistic: most commonly used as test of contingency table
χ_F^2	Friedman's χ^2
ψ	Psi: linear contrast
ω^2	Omega-squared: most often an r-family measure of effect size

English Letter Symbols

a	Intercept; number of levels of variable A
b, b_i	Regression coefficient—slope; number of levels of variable B
b_0	Intercept in multiple regression
d	Effect size estimate
df	Degrees of freedom
e_{ij}	Unit of error associated with subject i in treatment j
$E(MS)$	Expected mean square

F	F statistic
FW	Familywise error rate
GM	Grand mean
H	Kruskal–Wallis statistic
$H_0; H_1$	Null hypothesis; alternative hypothesis
$\ln$	Natural logarithm
MS	Mean square
n, n_i, N_i	Number of cases in a sample
N	Total sample size
$N(0, 1)$	Read "normally distributed with $\mu = 0$ and $\sigma^2 = 1$"
p	General symbol for probability; in binomial, probability of success
q	Studentized range statistic; probability of failure
r, r_{XY}	Correlation coefficient
r'	Fisher's transformation of r
$r_b; r_{pb}; r_t$	Biserial, point-biserial, and tetrachoric correlation coefficient
r_S	Spearman's correlation coefficient
$R, R_{0.1234}$	Multiple correlation coefficient
$r_{01.234}$	Partial correlation coefficient
$r_{0(1.234)}$	Semipartial correlation coefficient
$R^*, R^*_{0.123}$	Population correlation coefficient
$R_{\alpha, \beta, \alpha\beta}$	R using predictors associated with variables A, B, and the AB interaction
s, s_X	Standard deviation
s_D	Standard deviation of difference scores
s_p^2	Pooled sample variance
$s_{\overline{X}}; s_{\overline{X} - \overline{X}}$	Standard error of mean; standard error of mean differences
$s_{Y \cdot X}$	Standard error of estimate
s_X^2	Variance of X
SS_A	Sum of squares of variable A
SS_{AB}	Interaction sum of squares
SS_{error}	Error sum of squares
$SS_{\text{regression}}$	Sum of squares due to regression
SS_{residual}	Sum of squares residual (not accounted for by regression)
t	Student's t statistic
t'	t statistic with heterogeneous variances
t_d	Dunnett's t statistic
T	Wilcoxon's matched-pairs signed-ranks statistic
W	Kendall's coefficient of concordance
W_r	Critical width for range tests
W_S	Wilcoxon's rank-sum statistic
$\overline{X}, \overline{X}_1$	Sample mean
$\overline{X}_h$	Harmonic mean
$\hat{Y}, \hat{Y}_i$	Predicted value of Y
z	Normal deviate (also called a standard score)